The Handbook of
Education and Human Development

THE HANDBOOK OF

Education and Human Development

New Models of Learning, Teaching and Schooling

Edited by

DAVID R. OLSON

and

NANCY TORRANCE

First published 1996
First published in paperback 1998

2 4 6 8 10 9 7 5 3 1

Blackwell Publishers Inc.
350 Main Street
Malden , Massachusetts 02148
USA

Blackwell Publishers Ltd
108 Cowley Road
Oxford OX4 1JF
 UK

Library of Congress Cataloging-in-Publication Data is available.

ISBN 1-55786-460-8 (hbk)
     0-631-21186-1 (pbk)

British Library Cataloguing in Publication Data

A CIP catalogue record for this book is available from the British Library.

Typeset in 10.5pt on 12.5pt Photina
by Graphicraft Typesetters Ltd, Hong Kong
Printed in Great Britain by T J International, Padstow, Cornwall

This book is printed on acid-free paper

Contents

Preface   viii

List of contributors   x

1. Introduction: Rethinking the Role of Psychology in Education   1
   DAVID R. OLSON AND NANCY TORRANCE

**Section I. Setting the Stage: How Theories of Human Development   7
Relate to Education**

Part A. Psychological Foundations of Child-centered Pedagogy   9

2. Folk Psychology and Folk Pedagogy   9
   DAVID R. OLSON AND JEROME S. BRUNER

3. The Age of Innocence Reconsidered: Preserving the Best of the   28
   Progressive Traditions in Psychology and Education
   HOWARD GARDNER, BRUCE TORFF, AND THOMAS HATCH

4. A Rereading of Dewey's *Art as Experience*: Pointers Toward a   56
   Theory of Learning
   MAXINE GREENE

5. Changing Views of Knowledge and Their Impact on Educational   75
   Research and Practice
   ROBBIE CASE

6. Rethinking the Historical Role of Psychology in Educational Reform   100
   BARBARA BEATTY

Part B. Pedagogical Perspectives on Human Development   117

7. Rethinking the Concept of Learning Disabilities: The Demise of   117
   Aptitude/Achievement Discrepancy
   KEITH E. STANOVICH AND PAULA J. STANOVICH

8. Rethinking Readiness for Learning   148
   RITA WATSON

9. Language and Literacy Development: Discontinuities and Differences   173
   LOWRY HEMPHILL AND CATHERINE SNOW

10. Accommodating Diversity in Early Literacy Learning   202
    MARIE M. CLAY

11. Writing and Learning to Write   225
    GUNTHER KRESS

12. Rethinking the Role of Emotions in Education   257
    KEITH OATLEY AND SEEMA NUNDY

Section II. Biological and Cultural Foundations of Pedagogy   275

Part A. The Very Possibility of Education   277

13. Pedagogy and Imitation in Monkeys: Yes, No, or Maybe?   277
    ELISABETTA VISALBERGHI AND DOROTHY M. FRAGASZY

14. Why Animals Lack Pedagogy and Some Cultures Have   302
    More of it Than Others
    DAVID PREMACK AND ANN JAMES PREMACK

15. Humanly Possible: Education and the Scope of the Mind   324
    MARGARET DONALDSON

16. Acceptable Ignorance, Negotiable Disagreement: Alternative   345
    Views of Learning
    JACQUELINE J. GOODNOW

Part B. Cultural Context of Human Development and Education   369

17. Cultural Learning and Learning Culture   369
    ANN C. KRUGER AND MICHAEL TOMASELLO

18. Models of Teaching and Learning: Participation in a Community   388
    of Learners
    BARBARA ROGOFF, EUGENE MATUSOV, AND CYNTHIA WHITE

19. The Individual-Society Antinomy Revisited: Productive Tensions in   415
    Theories of Human Development, Communication, and Education
    JAMES V. WERTSCH AND WILLIAM R. PENUEL

20. Some Educational Implications of Genre-based Mental Models: 434
    The Interpretive Cognition of Text Understanding
    CAROL FLEISHER FELDMAN AND DAVID A. KALMAR

21. Habits of Mind for a Learning Society: Educating for Human   461
    Development
    DANIEL KEATING

Section III. Schooling Minds   483

Part A. The Language and Culture of Schooling   485

22. Rethinking Learning   485
    CARL BEREITER AND MARLENE SCARDAMALIA

23. The Development of Understanding 514
KIERAN EGAN

24. The Learner's Experience of Learning 534
FERENCE MARTON AND SHIRLEY BOOTH

25. Understanding and Empowering the Child as a Learner 565
INGRID PRAMLING

26. The Language of Mind: Its Role in Teaching and Learning 593
JANET WILDE ASTINGTON AND JANETTE PELLETIER

Part B. Coping with Content 621

27. Schooling and the Acquisition of Theoretical Knowledge 621
FRANK C. KEIL AND CHANA S. SILBERSTEIN

28. From Folk Biology to Scientific Biology 646
SCOTT ATRAN

29. Cognitive and Cultural Factors in the Acquisition of Intuitive Biology 683
GIYOO HATANO AND KAYOKO INAGAKI

30. What Do "Just Plain Folk" Know About Physics?
ANDREA A. DISESSA

31. Agreeing to Disagree: Developing Sociable Mathematical Discourse 731
MAGDALENE LAMPERT, PEGGY RITTENHOUSE, AND CAROL CRUMBAUGH

32. Conceptualizing the Growth of Historical Understanding 765
PETER SEIXAS

Author Index 785

Subject Index 799

Preface

The idea of this handbook was planted by Philip Taylor, then Commissioning Editor at Falmer Press, who asked if I would be interested in editing a major volume on education and human development. For some time I had believed that the impact of the "cognitive revolution" with its concern with knowledge and knowing viewed from the perspective of the knower had yet to make its place felt in educational psychological research and theory and it seemed plausible that a handbook would be the very sort of vehicle for exploring this issue. I invited Jerry Bruner, Carol Feldman and Michael Tomasello, to join Carl Bereiter, Marlene Scardamalia, Janet Astington, Keith Oatley, Keith Stanovich and myself for a meeting at the Ontario Institute for Studies in Education in April of 1992. Our discussions focused on the relations between conceptions of knowledge, learning, and thinking and their relations to the particular forms of pedagogy that were practiced. It was Tomasello who stated the question most succinctly: "Why would you attempt to teach someone something unless you assumed that they did not know something?" That is, teaching of whatever form occurs only because of some assumptions about a learner. He used this to explain why chimps did not teach and why they did not invent a culture—they lacked a theory of mind. But why do we teach, talk, demonstrate, argue, exemplify? Because of the assumption we make about learners' knowledge and beliefs—in a word, about their minds.

We were off. Nancy Torrance kept careful notes of the topics and names of prospective authors that would be critical to addressing the mind-pedagogy issues, letters were mailed, pleading telephone calls followed, papers came in, were read, rewritten, and compiled into a volume that I find, now that it is complete, absolutely breathtaking.

Why would all of these wonderful authors make a contribution to our book? We will never know, but we do wish to express our utter gratitude to them for persevering with us and for the extraordinary efforts they manifest in their writing. These are authors who must be heard if our theories and practices of education are to be both productive and informed.

We also wish to express our sincere gratitude to Susan Milmoe of Blackwell and to Alison Mudditt her successor who took up the volume on the untimely retirement of Philip Taylor from Falmer and who both aided and encouraged us through to completion. Denese Coulbeck assisted us with many technical details in the preparation of the manuscript.

Finally, we wish to express our gratitude to the Spencer Foundation for its continuing support. The contributions to this volume importantly inform our long-term research program on "Belief in Education" and in fact go far beyond what we could achieve on our own.

DRO

Contributors

Janet Wilde Astington, Institute for Child Study, University of Toronto, 45 Walmer Road, Toronto, ON M5R 2X2, Canada

Scott Atran, CNRS-CREA, École Polytechnique, 1 Rue Descartes, 75005 Paris, and Institute for Social Research, University of Michigan, PO Box 1248, Ann Arbor, MI 48109–1382, USA

Barbara Beatty, Department of Education, Wellesley College, 106 Central Street, Wellesley, MA 02181–8256, USA

Carl Bereiter, Centre for Applied Cognitive Science, Ontario Institute for Studies in Education, 252 Bloor Street West, Toronto, ON M5S 1V6, Canada

Shirley Booth, Department of Education and Educational Research, Göteborg University, Box 1010, S-43126 Mölndal, Sweden

Jerome S. Bruner, Faculty of Law, New York University, 6 Washington Place, New York, NY 10003, USA

Robbie Case, Institute for Child Study, University of Toronto, and School of Education, Stanford University. Correspondence to: Institute for Child Study, 45 Walmer Road, Toronto, ON M5R 2X2, Canada

Marie M. Clay, University of Auckland, New Zealand. Correspondence to: Flat 4, 153 Bassett Road, Remuera, Auckland 5, New Zealand

Carol Crumbaugh, Department of Teacher Education, Michigan State University, Erickson Hall, East Lansing, MI 48824, USA

Andrea A. diSessa, Graduate School of Education, EMST Division, University of California at Berkeley, 4533 Tolman Hall, Berkeley, CA 94720–1670, USA

Margaret Donaldson, Department of Developmental Psychology, University of Edinburgh. Correspondence to: 27 Blackford Road, Edinburgh EH9 2DT, Scotland, UK

Kieran Egan, Faculty of Education, Simon Fraser University, Burnaby, BC V5A 1S6, Canada

Carol F. Feldman, Department of Psychology, New York University, 6 Washington Place, New York, NY 10003, USA

Dorothy M. Fragaszy, Department of Psychology, University of Georgia, Athens, GA 30602–3013, USA

Howard Gardner, Harvard Project Zero, Harvard Graduate School of Education, 323 Longfellow Hall, Appian Way, Cambridge, MA 02138, USA

Jacqueline J. Goodnow, School of Behavioral Sciences, Macquarie University, North Ryde 2113, Sydney, NSW 2109, Australia

Maxine Greene, Philosophy, Social Sciences, and Education, Teachers College, Columbia University, New York, NY 10027, USA

Giyoo Hatano, Dokkyo University. Correspondence to: 6–7–12 Honkomagome, Bunkyo-ku, Tokyo 113, Japan

Thomas Hatch, Harvard Project Zero, 323 Longfellow Hall, Appian Way, Harvard University, Cambridge, MA 02138, USA

Lowry Hemphill, Human Development and Psychology, Graduate School of Education, Harvard University, Roy E. Larsen Hall, Appian Way, Cambridge, MA 02138, USA

Kayoko Inagaki, Chiba University. Correspondence to: 1–20–8 Togoshi, Shinagawa-ku, Tokyo 142, Japan

David A. Kalmar, Department of Psychology, New York University, 6 Washington Place, New York, NY 10003, USA

Daniel Keating, Centre for Applied Cognitive Science, Ontario Institute for Studies in Education, and Canadian Institute for Advanced Research. Correspondence to: Centre for Applied Cognitive Science, Ontario Institute for Studies in Education, 252 Bloor Street West, Toronto, ON M5S 1V6, Canada

Frank C. Keil, Department of Psychology, 228 Uris Hall, Cornell University, Ithaca, NY 14853, USA

Gunther Kress, Institute of Education, University of London, 20 Bedford Way, London WC1H 0AL, UK

Ann C. Kruger, Department of Educational Foundations, Georgia State University, Atlanta, GA 30303, USA

Magdalene Lampert, School of Education, University of Michigan, 610 E. University, Ann Arbor, MI 48109–1259, USA

Ference Marton, Department of Education and Educational Research, Göteborg University, Box 1010, S-43126 Mölndal, Sweden

Eugene Matusov, Department of Psychology, University of California at Santa Cruz, Kerr Hall, Santa Cruz, CA 95064, USA

Seema Nundy, Centre for Applied Cognitive Science, Ontario Institute for Studies in Education, 252 Bloor Street West, Toronto, ON M5S 1V6, Canada

Keith Oatley, Centre for Applied Cognitive Science, Ontario Institute for Studies in Education, 252 Bloor Street West, Toronto, ON M5S 1V6, Canada

David R. Olson, Centre for Applied Cognitive Science, Ontario Institute for Studies in Education, 252 Bloor Street West, Toronto, ON M5S 1V6, Canada

Janette Pelletier, Institute for Child Study, University of Toronto, 45 Walmer Road, Toronto, ON M5R 2X2, Canada

William R. Penuel, School Social Work Division, Metropolitan Nashville Public Schools, Nashville, TN, USA

Ingrid Pramling, Department of Methodology in Teachers' Education, Göteborg University, Box 1010, S-43126 Mölndal, Sweden

Ann James Premack, Laboratoire de Psycho-Biologie du Développement, EPHE-CNRS (U.R.A. 315), 41, Rue Gay-Lussac, F-75005 Paris, France

David Premack, Laboratoire de Psycho-Biologie du Développement, EPHE-CNRS (U.R.A. 315), 41, Rue Gay-Lussac, F-75005 Paris, France

Peggy Rittenhouse, Department of Teacher Education, Michigan State University, Erickson Hall, East Lansing, MI 48824, USA

Barbara Rogoff, Department of Psychology, University of California at Santa Cruz, Kerr Hall, Santa Cruz, CA 95064, USA

Marlene Scardamalia, Centre for Applied Cognitive Science, Ontario Institute for Studies in Education, 252 Bloor Street West, Toronto, ON M5S 1V6, Canada

Peter Seixas, Department of Curriculum Studies, Faculty of Education, University of British Columbia, Vancouver BC, V6T 1Z4, Canada

Chana S. Silberstein, Department of Psychology, Cornell University, 228 Uris Hall, Ithaca, NY 14853, USA

Catherine Snow, Human Development and Psychology, Graduate School of Education, Harvard University, Larsen Hall, Appian Way, Cambridge, MA 02138–3752, USA

Keith E. Stanovich, Department of Curriculum, and Centre for Applied Cognitive Science. Correspondence to: Department of Curriculum, Ontario Institute for Studies in Education, 252 Bloor Street West, Toronto, ON M5S 1V6, Canada

Paula J. Stanovich, Faculty of Education, University of Toronto, 371 Bloor Street West, Toronto, ON M5S 2R7, Canada

Michael Tomasello, Department of Psychology, Emory University, Atlanta, GA 30322, USA

Bruce Torff, Harvard Project Zero, and Boston College. Correspondence to: Harvard Project Zero, Harvard University, 323 Longfellow Hall, Appian Way, Cambridge, MA 02138, USA

Nancy Torrance, Centre for Applied Cognitive Science, Ontario Institute for Studies in Education, 252 Bloor Street West, Toronto, ON M5S 1V6, Canada

Elisabetta Visalberghi, Istituto di Psicologia, Consiglio Nazionale delle Ricerche, Via Aldrovandi 16 B, 00197 Rome, Italy

Rita Watson, Faculty of Education, University of British Columbia, and Department of Education, Hebrew School of Jerusalem, Mt. Scopus, Jerusalem, 91905 Israel

James V. Wertsch, Department of Education, Washington University, St. Louis, MO 63130–4899, USA

Cynthia White, Department of Psychology, University of California at Santa Cruz, Kerr Hall, Santa Cruz, CA 95064, USA

1

Introduction: Rethinking the Role of Psychology in Education

DAVID R. OLSON
NANCY TORRANCE

We are not the first generation of scholars to concern ourselves with the implications of a new understanding of human development for educational theory and practice. Progressivism with its concern for child-centered education became a dominant theme early in the twentieth century and has fueled a passion for developmental psychology as well as a deep respect for the role of the school in promoting that development, a development that continues into the present (Lagemann, 1989). Dewey's influential books—including *The child and the curriculum* (1902/1956), *Experience and education* (1938/1972), and *Art as experience* (1934/1958)—while both reporting and fostering educational reforms (Cremin, 1964), encouraged us to see knowledge and experience from the child's point of view. More recent writings in that tradition—including Bruner's *The process of education* (1960), Donaldson's *Children's minds* (1978), and Gardner's *The unschooled mind* (1991)—all called for and demonstrated the possibility of a new, more humane education based on a respect for children's knowledge, interest, ability and integrity—in a word, for their conscious experience.

But perhaps we are the first generation of scholars to recognize the limitations and excesses that good beginnings sometimes leave in their wake (Gillham, 1980). Child-centered education never made an easy peace with the knowledge and skills that adults assumed to be the end product of educational experience. Furthermore, while most would agree that schools are operated in the interests of children, parents and the larger culture have an investment as well and it was never clear how to adjudicate those interests. Indeed, a newly emerging understanding of cultural diversity has made it increasingly difficult to see education as a means for achieving a single common cultural goal. Finally, it has become clear that the sciences designed to assist children in their development have become means of classifying children into categories that are then used to justify and legitimize poor performance rather than improve it. We have become increasingly self-conscious about the uses and implications of our theories and to recognize that poor theories are not merely false but harmful.

It is therefore inappropriate to merely chart "advances" in the study of human development with the assumption that further discoveries along the same lines will be helpful to all the variety of interests served by the school. Rather it is time to reassess the very nature of schooling and the role that the study of human development has played, and may profitably play, in the education of children. While we recognize that education alone cannot address the more fundamental social problems of poverty, justice, violence, cultural dislocation, and identity, education can play a direct role in the advancement of understanding of the world, of others, and of oneself, and those understandings at least play an indirect part in solving the larger social problems. The contributions to this volume are all directed to the enterprise of rethinking the relations between the study of human development and the nature and improvement of that institution designed explicitly to further it—namely, the school.

This volume sets out three, potentially revolutionary, changes in our understanding of education and human development; these three perspectives make up the three sections of the volume.

Section I   This section presents a new understanding of how psychology relates to pedagogy. Psychology's early promise was that of classifying students on the basis of traits so that appropriate social roles could be assigned to them and to a lesser extent so that instruction could be designed to meet their needs. The first function was an overwhelming success, the last a major disappointment. The classification of children on the basis of traits became a self-fulfilling prediction. The second function, of greater appeal to the child-centered movement, was that initiated by Piaget, who showed that cognitive stages rather than enduring traits determine what can be learned, and to a lesser extent by Vygotsky, who showed that neither trait nor stage determined what could be learned but rather what was appropriately taught. The promise of those views is far from exhausted. However, in their place we have tried to set out new ways of examining the relation between psychological theory and educational practice.

In the first part of Section I we examine the ways in which pedagogical practices of teachers are premised on the assumptions about the mind, knowledge, and consciousness of the learner. Forms of pedagogy are built upon certain understandings or assumptions about the psychology of the learner; conversely, psychological assumptions about mind, knowledge, and ability play into and recruit certain forms of pedagogy. David Olson and Jerome Bruner spell out the relations between the implicit "folk psychology" of a culture or a subculture and the educational practices, the "folk pedagogy" adopted by that culture. Howard Gardner, Bruce Torff, and Thomas Hatch reexamine the assumptions of progressivism in the light of current knowledge of human development. Maxine Greene examines the nature of experience and learning by means of a rereading of Dewey's classic *Art as Experience*. Robbie Case examines how shifting perspectives in the theory of human development have brought with them important alterations in pedagogy. Barbara Beatty examines the historical relations between psychological theory and the educational practice of the progressive movement.

The second part of Section I is concerned with how psychological theory has misguided educational theory and practice and suggests more appropriate forms of analysis. Keith and Paula Stanovich show the conceptual poverty and counter-productive effects of the concept of "learning disabilities." Rita Watson reexamines the uses and misuses of the concept of "readiness" in early education. Lowry Hemphill and Catherine Snow argue that the child-centered approach to literacy exemplified by "whole-language" theory fails to account for the distinctive properties of written language. Marie Clay sets out ways to accommodate diversity in early literacy learning without simply perpetuating it. Gunther Kress examines the nature of writing and the transformation from sequential to hierarchical organization of ideas in learning to write. Keith Oatley and Seema Nundy examine the role of emotions in educational theory and practice.

Section II   This section examines the insight that education is what in fact makes culture possible. Schooling is just one of the means by which cultures are created and transmitted. To understand human development and education, we must examine the cognitive and social conditions that allow the formation, transformation, and transmission of culture. Elisabetta Visalberghi and Dorothy Fragaszy examine the biological roots of social imitation and the importance of the recognition of intention for any growth of culture. David and Ann Premack trace the origins of culture to the peculiarly human ability to understand inability and ignorance in others. That recognition invites pedagogical initiatives and, in some cultures, those initiatives take the form of such institutions as schools. Margaret Donaldson shows how child-centered notions can lead us to overlook the importance of adult perspectives on experience, especially in the area of the development of emotions and values. Jacqueline Goodnow examines alternative views of learning, learning not just what to know but what may be systematically ignored.

In the second part of Section II the critical relation between culture and education is examined. Ann Kruger and Michael Tomasello extend their important work on the relations between models of mind and models of teaching, focusing primarily on "instructed learning." Barbara Rogoff, Eugene Matusov, and Cynthia White show how models of pedagogy and learning shift when classrooms are thought of not as adult-centered or child-centered institutions but rather as communities of learners. James Wertsch and William Penuel extend this argument by examining the relations between models of communication and models of pedagogy. Carol Feldman and David Kalmar consider how the genres of literature provide models for the interpretive cognitions of readers. And Daniel Keating considers the development of habits of mind that are called for by a "learning society."

Section III   This section explores a new conception of just what it is to know, to learn, and to understand, and the role of traditional subject matter disciplines in the advancement of human understanding. Current conceptions make greater allowance for the role of beliefs, hypotheses, intuitions, and preconceptions as well as for the role of particular forms of discourse and particular subject matters in growth and development. Forms of knowledge are not all the same and special efforts are required if children's understandings in such domains as physics, mathematics, biology, and history are to be advanced. Carl Bereiter and Marlene Scardamalia offer a new perspective on knowledge and its acquisition—a new epistemology for a new education. Kieran Egan advances a new account of the growth of understanding across four historical and developmental stages that he describes as mythic, heroic, romantic, and ironic. Ference Marton and Shirley Booth bring a phenomenological analysis to the learner's experience of learning. Ingrid Pramling shows that young children's understanding of their own learning is quite sophisticated but frequently at odds with that assumed by their teachers— a discrepancy that severely limits the impact of teaching. Janet Astington and Jan Pelletier show how teachers' assumptions about the minds of their learners influence both the kind of pedagogical moves they make and the extent to which they employ a metacognitive language, a language for talking about the mind.

The second part of Section III addresses the theme that development is as much a product of education as a precondition for it. In particular it addresses the relation between the implicit theories held by children and the explicit content of various disciplined forms of knowledge. Frank Keil and Chana Silberstein examine how schooling alters the implicit theoretical knowledge that children bring to the classroom. Scott Atran examines the biological knowledge of ordinary "folk" and the impact of scientific theory on that knowledge. Giyoo Hatano and Kayoko Inagaki examine the effects of different cultures on the understanding of biology. Andrea diSessa examines recent research and theory in the learning and teaching of physics. Magdalene Lampert, Peggy Rittenhouse, and Carol Crumbaugh examine the role of children's discourse in the advance of their mathematical understandings. And Peter Seixas sets out the major considerations involved in developing a mature understanding of history.

Four more general perspectives run through the volume as a whole. First, the study of human development has recently taken a turn toward a more "first-person" point of view, how the world appears to children themselves, a view that allows us to recognize that children, too, have an understanding of the physical, biological, and social worlds as well as some epistemological understandings of what it is to know, think, believe, desire, and intend as well as what it is to learn, remember, forget, and understand. Older psychologies of "abilities," "potentials," "skills," and "knowledge" are now seen as providing too restricted access to the actual beliefs and intentions, understandings and misunderstandings of the child. The latter have become the central concern of the new pedagogies.

Second, there is currently a recognition that a new approach to children's knowledge and beliefs implies, indeed requires, not only a new pedagogy but also a new conception of the classroom. Classrooms can no longer be seen merely as locations where information is transferred from adult to child but rather as sites for "collaborative discourse" or as "communities of learners" in which genuine social discourse can take place—beliefs can be expressed, criticized, revised and shared— rather than merely replaced by the authoritative teacher. This theme is explicitly developed in Section B of Part II, but appears as well in papers by Case, Kress, Marton and Booth, Pramling, Astington and Pelletier, and Lampert, Rittenhouse, and Crumbaugh.

Third, a new understanding of mind as composed of intersubjectively held beliefs and intentions allows a new level of mutuality between the explanations offered for success and failure by the teacher and those offered or accepted by the learner. Far from alienating children, this new psychology allows children and teachers to share an understanding of learning and thinking, to hold the same theories, and to share the same language. The teacher's epistemologies are directly linked to children's metacognitions. No longer are children to be treated as an entomologist treats a colony of ants, regarding them as an alien species to be studied from the outside, but as members of a mutually comprehensible culture.

Fourth, that psychology, when mastered by the learner, may provide just the tools children need to manage their own learning in a self-conscious, deliberate and reflective way. Children's understanding of their own thoughts, beliefs, and theories as well as the grounds for adopting, holding, or rejecting them, and the means for sharing them, is just the understanding they need for conducting the kind of systematic, scientific thinking so valued by the larger culture. This is a genuinely new and promising role for a psychology of teaching and learning.

This book thus reflects what we take to be the central problems of our discipline, including the nature of knowledge, of knowing, of learning, of thinking, and above all of the ways in which culture is accumulated and transmitted to the young. Consequently, many of the traditional issues that have dominated theory in psychology and education have either been abandoned or reconstrued. These include such topics as the relation between heredity and environment, theories of mental abilities, theories of learning and transfer, theories of readiness, trait theories that distinguish so-called "types" of children and their "learning styles," and theories that attempt to specify variables that predict the outcomes of schooling. Even the more objective "cognitive processes" have yielded pride of place to a concern with children's beliefs, goals, plans, and values and the ways in which educators can understand, address, and ultimately, share them.

If we were to simplify our enterprise as a whole we would emphasize two principles: an internalist perspective on learning and a social perspective on theory formation. By the first, we mean that the theories of human development considered herein have taken on an increasingly internalist or insider's view of thinking, learning, and knowing. Whereas externalist theories focus on what an adult can do to foster learning, thereby making up the bulk of traditional educational psychology, internalist theories focus on what the child can do, what the child thinks he or she is doing, and how learning and teaching can be premised on those intentional states.

The second, the social perspective, is that a new degree of common understanding or intersubjectivity may be found not only between children but also between theorist, whether psychologist or pedagogue, and child subject. Externalist theorists, as mentioned, regard children as an entomologist would regard a colony of ants; there is no assumption that the subjects see themselves in the same terms that the theorist does. The psychologist who tests a child and files a confidential report unavailable to either the child or parent is, we suggest, to be set aside in favor of the psychologist who applies to children the same theories and understanding that children will come to apply to themselves. Hence this new psychology creates the genuine possibility of constructing psychological theories that are as useful for children themselves in organizing their learning and managing their lives as they are for the adults that work with them. Rethinking the role of developmental psychology in educational practices will require new conceptions not only of the child as an intentional being but of knowledge as "manmade," the product of the elaboration of shared beliefs and shared frameworks for understanding.

This new perspective on the development of mind, then, may offer an improved vantage point from which to reexamine our classical assumptions about education and human development and to advance some principles to guide research and practice in the psychology of education for the next century. That is our purpose here.

References

Bruner, J. S. (1960). *The process of education.* Cambridge: Harvard University Press.

Cremin, L. A. (1964). *The transformation of the school: Progressivism in American education 1876–1957,* New York: Vintage Books, Random House.

Donaldson, M. (1978). *Children's minds.* New York: Norton.

Dewey, J. (1902/1956). *The child and the curriculum.* Chicago: University of Chicago Press.

Dewey, J. (1934/1958). *Art as experience.* New York: Capricorn Books.

Dewey, J. (1938/1972). *Experience and education.* New York: Collier Books.

Gardner, H. (1991). *The unschooled mind.* New York: Basic Books.

Gillham, B. (1980). *Reconstructing educational psychology.* London: Billing.

Lagemann, E. (1989). The plural worlds of educational research. *History of Education Quarterly, 29,* 185–213.

Setting the Stage:
How Theories of Human Development Relate to Education

2

Folk Psychology and Folk Pedagogy

DAVID R. OLSON
JEROME S. BRUNER

It is never easy to apply theoretical knowledge to practical problems. On the practical art of being a physician, Aristotle wrote in his *Nichomachean Ethics*: "It is an easy matter to know the effects of honey, wine, hellebore, cautery, and cutting. But to know how, for whom, and when we should apply these as remedies is no less an undertaking than being a physician." Scientific advances increasingly inform us of the effects of various treatments but the art of knowing "how, for whom, and when" to apply them remains as difficult as ever.

This is exactly the problem we face in relating theoretical knowledge to practical contexts of education. Theoretical knowledge of how children develop continues to grow but just how to relate this knowledge to the practical contexts in which adults intentionally and systematically intervene to foster this development, in a word, to educate, remains almost as mysterious as when such efforts first began.

Attempts to specify the route from what teachers can or should do—teach, mentor, monitor, and criticize—to what children do—think and learn, remember, generalize—make up a long and less than satisfactory story. We need not recite the unpromising history of attempts to formulate general laws of learning whether of rats in mazes or undergraduates in psychology laboratories nor even the attempt to construct theories of abilities that would predict what and how quickly skills would be acquired, in order to recognize the absence from such theories of those features most critical to pedagogy—namely, the goals, purposes, beliefs, and intentions of both the teachers and the learners. It is that absence which creates the gap between theory and practice.

Thus a new kind of theory is required. Learning theories that tend to ignore what is being learned and by whom and for what purpose must give way to theories that tie learning to the prior understanding as well as the goals and intentions of the learner. And ability theories that attempt to predict learning without regard to the goals and intentions of the actor must give way to those indicating how actors exploit what they know in the course of attempting to achieve understood goals. Teaching and learning are no longer to be seen as two activities, causally linked—one knows X because one was taught X—but rather as one special form of sharing or coming to share beliefs, goals, and intentions—in a word, as a culture.

But how do human beings achieve such meetings of mind, especially across the age and experience gaps that separate teachers from children? More particularly, as expressed by teachers, "How do we reach the children?" or as expressed by children, "What are they trying to get at?" This is the classic problem of Other Minds, as it was originally called in philosophy, and its relevance to education has mostly been overlooked until very recently. In the last decade, it has become a topic of passionate interest and intense research among psychologists, particularly those interested in development. It is what the present chapter is about—the application of this new understanding of minds to the process of education.

To a degree almost entirely overlooked by the antisubjective behaviorists, including the aforementioned learning and ability theorists, our interactions with others are deeply affected by our everyday intuitive theories about how our own minds and the minds of others work. These theories, rarely made explicit, are omnipresent in practical and educational decisions. Such lay theories are now referred to professionally by the rather condescending name of "folk psychology." Folk psychologies reflect not only certain wired in human tendencies (like seeing people normally as operating under their own control) but they also reflect certain deeply ingrained cultural beliefs about the mind. Hence Wundt (1916), who introduced the notion, argued that each distinctive culture in each historical period had a distinctive folk psychology which it was the duty of anthropologically minded psychologists to uncover. But whereas Wundt's experimental psychology was picked up so that Wundt came to be called the father of such psychology, his folk psychology has lain dormant for much of this century. The revival of folk psychology that accompanied "the cognitive revolution" with its interest in concepts, consciousness and intentionality revived folk psychology as the study of mind without due attention to culture and cultural transmission, that is, our pedagogy. Not only are we steered in ordinary interaction by our folk psychology, but we are steered in the activity of helping children learn about the world by a body of assumptions that make up what we may call a "folk pedagogy." Folk pedagogy is visible in many contexts: Watch any mother, any teacher, even any baby-sitter with a child and you will be struck at how much of what they do is guided by notions of what children's minds are like and how one may help them learn, even though they may not be able to verbalize their pedagogical principles. Furthermore, as we shall see, the differences between mothers, like those between teachers, arise from their different assumptions about the minds of these children. Their folk pedagogy, we shall argue, reflects their folk psychology.

A consideration of the relations between "folk psychology" and "folk pedagogy" has given rise to a new, perhaps even a revolutionary, insight. In theorizing about the practice of education in the classroom (or any other setting, for that matter), we must take into account the folk pedagogical theories that those engaged in teaching and learning already have, because any innovations will have to compete with, replace, or otherwise modify the folk theories that *already* guide both teachers and pupils. For example, a theorist convinced that children construct their own knowledge will have to confront the established view that knowledge is imparted; the theorist convinced that aptitude for learning is a matter of prior knowledge will have to confront the entrenched view that readiness is a matter of fixed abilities. So the introduction of any innovation will necessarily involve changing the folk psychological and folk pedagogical theories of teachers—and to a surprising extent, of pupils as well.

Teaching, then, is inevitably based on teachers' notions about the nature of the learner's mind. Beliefs and assumptions about teaching, whether in a school or in any other context, are a direct reflection of the beliefs and assumptions the teacher holds about the learner. Later, we will consider the other side of this coin: how learning is affected by the child's notion of the teacher's mind, as when girls come to believe that teachers expect them not to come up with unconventional answers (see Goodnow, this volume, chap. 16). Of course, like most deep truths, this one is already "well known." Teachers have always tried to adjust their teaching to the backgrounds, abilities, styles, and interests of the children they teach. That is important, but it is not quite what we are after. Our purpose, rather, is to explore more general ways in which learners' minds are conventionally thought about, and the pedagogic practices that follow from these ways of thinking about mind. Nor will we stop there, for we also want to offer some reflections on "consciousness raising" in this setting: what can be accomplished by getting teachers (and students) to think *explicitly* about their folk psychological assumptions and to bring them more clearly out of the shadows of tacit knowledge so that children can use them deliberately in the management of their own thinking and learning (see also Marton and Booth, this volume, chap. 24; Pramling, this volume, chap. 25).

To see most clearly the affinities between folk psychology and folk pedagogy, we may begin by contrasting our own human species with nonhuman primates. In our species, children show an astonishingly strong "predisposition to culture," a sensitivity to and an eagerness to adopt the folkways of those they see around them. They show a striking interest in the activity of their parents and peers and with no prompting at all try to imitate what they observe. On the adult side, as Premack and Premack (this volume, chap. 14) point out, there is a uniquely human "pedagogic disposition" to exploit this tendency, for adults to demonstrate correct performance for the benefit of the learner. One finds these matching tendencies in all human societies (Rogoff, Matusov, and White, this volume, chap. 18).

This is one of the ways in which humans differ most from other species; contrary to widely held beliefs, these imitative and demonstrational dispositions seem scarcely to exist at all in monkeys (Visalberghi and Fragaszy, this volume, chap. 13) nor in our nearest primate kin, the chimpanzee. Not only do adult chimpanzees not "teach" their young by demonstrating correct performance, the young for their part seem not to imitate the actions of adults either, at least if we use a sufficiently stringent definition of imitation. If by imitation we mean the ability not only to observe the goal achieved but also the means to that achievement, there is little evidence of imitation in chimpanzees raised in the wild (Tomasello, Kruger, and Ratner, 1993; Kruger and Tomasello, this volume, chap. 17) and, even more conspicuously, little attempt at teaching. The differences between human and chimpanzee although dramatic may not be absolute. For example, when a young chimpanzee is raised "as if" it were a human child and exposed to the ways of humans, it begins to show more imitative dispositions (Savage-Rumbaugh et al., 1993). Rudimentary dispositions to provide demonstrations may be found in adult chimpanzees but evidence on this point is equivocal (Fouts, Fouts, and Schoenfeld, 1984; Goodall, 1986).

Instruction and imitation fail to occur, Tomasello, Kruger, and Ratner (1993) were the first to suggest, because nonhuman primates do not naturally attribute beliefs and knowledge to others nor recognize the presence of such states in themselves. We humans show, tell, or teach someone something only because we first recognize that they do not know, or that what they believe they know is false. The failure of nonhuman primates to ascribe ignorance or false beliefs to their young may, therefore, explain the absence of pedagogic efforts, for it is only when these states are recognized that one may try to correct the deficiency by demonstration, explanation, or discussion. Even the most humanly "enculturated" chimpanzee shows little, if any, of the attribution that leads to instructional activity (Savage-Rumbaugh et al., 1993).

Research on lesser primates shows the same picture but more starkly. On the basis of their observations of the behavior of vervet monkeys in the wild, Cheney and Seyfarth (1990) were led to conclude: "While monkeys may use abstract concepts and have motives, beliefs, and desires, they. . .seem unable to attribute mental states to others: they lack a 'theory of mind.'" Work on other species of monkeys reveals the same picture (Visalberghi and Fragaszy, 1990, and in this volume, chap. 13). The general point is clear: assumptions about the mind of the learner underlie attempts at teaching. No ascription of ignorance, no effort to teach.

To say only that all humans display some understanding of other minds along with a matching disposition to teach the incompetent is to fail to take account of the variety of ways in which these matters express themselves in different cultures. The variety is stunning (Rogoff, Mistry, Goncu, and Mosier, 1993), and we need to know much more about cultural diversity in this sphere; we need an anthropology of pedagogy. Or to put it in terms already familiar, we need much more knowledge about the relation between folk psychology and folk pedagogy in different cultural settings and in different historical periods.

The understanding of this relationship takes on some urgency, we believe, in evaluating current debates on educational reform. For once we recognize that a teacher's conception of the learner has a direct bearing on the form of instruction he or she employs, then the first step in "equipping" teachers (or parents) for their task is to provide them access to the best available understanding of the mind of the child, and to provide teachers as well with insight into what they assume or believe about children's minds and how those beliefs and assumptions are manifest in their own teaching.

Folk pedagogies, for example, reflect a variety of assumptions about children: children may be thought of as willful and in need of correction; as innocent and in need of protection from a vulgar society; as lacking in skills and abilities that can be developed through demonstration and practice; as ignorant, lacking knowledge that only adults can provide; as holding personal private egocentric beliefs that have to be socialized; as already having implicit "intuitions" that can be more explicitly represented in the subject-matter disciplines of the school. Conversely, children may be conceived of as undisciplined, lacking in ability, ignorant, possessed by a desire for quick gratification and so on. The impact on teaching activities needs to be examined in more detail (see Astington and Pelletier, this volume, chap. 26).

A more culturally oriented cognitive psychology has less of a tendency to disparage and dismiss folk psychology as mere superstition to be ignored save by the anthropologist-connoisseur of quaint folkways. Bruner (1990), for example, has argued that explaining what children *do* is not enough; the new agenda is to determine what they *think* they are doing and what their reasons are for doing it, a view very much in keeping with new work on children's theories of mind (Astington, Harris, and Olson, 1988). The brunt of that work emphasizes the importance of understanding that children only gradually come to appreciate that they are acting not directly *on* the world but in terms of the beliefs they hold *about* that world. This crucial shift from naive realism to an understanding of beliefs takes place in the late preschool and early school years. Once it occurs, there can be a corresponding shift in what teachers can do to help children. The shift marks the point, for example, at which children can understand the possibilities of changing their beliefs and the point at which they can be given more responsibility for their own learning and thinking (Bereiter and Scardamalia, 1993, and in this volume, chap. 22), an opportunity not always seized upon by teachers. Gardner (1991) in *The Unschooled Mind*, summarizes his views on early education thus: "I have proposed that we must place ourselves inside the heads of our students and try to understand as far as possible the sources and strengths of their conceptions" (p. 253). In some ways this recent work may be seen as an extension of Dewey's idea that educational reform would result from seeing how a child's "experience already contains within itself elements—facts and truths—of just the same sort as those entering into [systematic] study" (1902/1966, p. 11).

Stated boldly, the emerging thesis is that educational practices are premised on a set of beliefs about learners' minds. Some of these earlier assumptions may have worked against the child's own welfare and need to be reexamined. Different approaches to learning and different forms of instruction—from imitation, to instruction, to discovery, to collaboration—reflect differing beliefs and assumptions about the learner—from actor, to knower, to private experiencer, to collaborative thinker (Tomasello, Kruger, and Ratner, 1993). What higher primates lack and humans continue to evolve is a set of beliefs about the mind. These beliefs, in turn, alter beliefs about the sources of and communicability of thought and action. Thus advances in understanding children's minds are fundamental to an improved pedagogy.

Conceptions of learners, of course, involve much more than just their minds; learners are persons, living in families and communities, who are struggling to reconcile their desires, beliefs, and goals with the world around them. Although our concern is primarily cognitive, with knowledge and its uses, we do not mean to focus exclusively on the so-called "rational" mind. Egan (1988, p. 45) reminds us that "Apollo without Dionysus may indeed by a well-informed, good citizen, but he's a dull fellow. He may even be 'cultured,' in the sense one often gets from traditionalist writings in education. . . . But without Dionysus he will never make and remake a culture." While we have focused our discussion of folk psychology and folk pedagogy on "teaching and learning," we could as easily have emphasized other aspects of the human spirit as well, aspects that are equally important for educational practice: conceptions of meaning, intention, and even desire and other emotions (Oatley and Nundy, this volume, chap. 12). But even the notion of "knowledge" is not as peacefully Apollonian as all that.

Take for example the issue of what "knowledge" is, where it comes from, in what form we have it. To begin with, there is the distinction between knowing something concretely and in particular, and knowing it as an exemplar of some general rule. Take arithmetic—addition and multiplication. Suppose that some students have just learned the former. What does it mean to grasp the idea that multiplication is simply repeated addition, something they already "know"? Well, for one thing, it means that they can *derive* the unknown from the known. That is a pretty heady notion about knowledge, one that might even delight the action-minded Dionysus.

In some much deeper sense, it is also a start toward appreciating the fact that seemingly complicated knowledge can often be derivationally reduced to simpler forms of knowledge that one already possesses. The Ellery Queen mystery stories used to include a note inserted on a crucial page in the text telling readers that they now had all the knowledge necessary to solve the crime. Suppose that after the children had learned multiplication the teacher announced that they now had enough knowledge to understand something called "logarithms," special kinds of numbers that simply bore the names "1," "2," "3," "4," and "5" and that they ought to be able to figure it all out from three examples because each number in each series also bore those names: the first series 2, 4, 8, 16, 32; the second series 3, 9, 27, 81, 243, and the third series 10, 100, 1000, 10,000, 100,000. Why is it that 8 can be called "3" or "the third" but so too can 27 and 1000? Not only do children (and, dear reader, you too) "discover" (or invent) the idea of an *exponent* or *power*, but also the idea of exponents to some *base*: that 2 to the third power is 8, that 3 to the third power is 27, and that 10 to the third power is 1000. Once children (say around age ten) have gone through that experience, their conception of mathematical knowledge as "derivational" will be forever altered: once they know addition and know that addition can be repeated different numbers of times to make multiplication, they already, in a sense, know what logarithms are (see Lampert, Rittenhouse, and Crumbaugh, this volume, chap. 31).

Or if that is too "mathematical," you can try getting children to act out Little Red Riding Hood, respectively, as a class ritual with everybody having a part, then by actors chosen to represent the main characters to an audience, then as a story to be told or read by a storyteller to a group. How do they differ? The moment some child informs you that in the first instance there are only actors and no audience, but in the second there are both, etc., the class will be off and running into a discussion of "drama" to match Victor Turner (1982) for excitement. As with the previous example, you will have led children to recognize that they know far more than they ever thought they knew, but that they have to "think about it" to know what they know. And that, in effect, was what the Renaissance and the Age of Reason were all about! But to teach and learn that way means that you have adopted a new theory of mind.

Or take the issue of *where* you *get* knowledge, an equally profound matter. Children usually begin by assuming that the teacher has the knowledge and passes it on to the class. Under appropriate conditions, they soon learn that others in the class might have knowledge too, and that it can be *shared*. (Of course they know this from the start, but only about things like where things are to be found, etc.) In this second phase, knowledge exists in the group. But inertly in the group. What about *group discussion* as a way of *creating* knowledge rather than merely finding who has what knowledge (Brown and Campione, 1990)?

And there is even one step beyond that, one of the most profound aspects of human knowledge. If nobody in the group knows the answer, there are still ways of finding out! Where do we go to find things out? This is the true leap into culture. There are things known by each individual (more than each one realizes), more still is known by the group or discoverable by discussion within the group, and much more still is stored somewhere else—in the "culture," say, not only in the heads of more knowledgeable people, but also in the cultural archive, in directories, books, maps, and CD-ROMs. Virtually by definition, nobody in a culture knows all there is to know about a topic or all that "is known." So what do we do when we get stuck? And what are the problems we run into in getting the knowledge we need? When we start answering that question, we are on the high road toward understanding what a culture is. In no time at all, we can be certain that some kid will begin to recognize that knowledge is power, or that it is a form of wealth, or that it is a safety net.

We could argue just as persuasively that the same approach can be taken to matters like desire, hope, belief, or whatever other aspects of mental life we want to subject to inquiry by a class. But again, such an approach is premised, as always, upon a theory of mind and a folk pedagogy that goes with it.

So let us consider, then, some alternative conceptions of the learner that are held, or may be held, by theorists, educators, and ultimately the children themselves, and how they may determine the forms that educational practice takes in different cultural contexts.

Linking Conceptions of Mind to Models of Learning and Teaching

Building on the lead of Tomasello et al. (1993), we can distinguish four models of learners' minds that are held by theorists, educators, and children, each with varying degrees of appropriateness to different educational goals. These models represent not only conceptions of mind and beliefs about teaching and education but also conceptions of the culture, as well as the relations between minds and cultures. Rethinking educational psychology is a matter of examining the implications of these alternative conceptions of human development and their implications for learning and teaching.

Seeing Children as Doers: The Acquisition of "Know-How"

When an adult deliberately provides a demonstration or a model of a successful or a skillful action, that demonstration is premised on the adult's belief that the learner does not know how to do x, and on the further assumption that children can learn how to do x by being *shown*. Even more fundamentally, it assumes that the learner wants to do x and may, in fact, be trying to do x. To learn by imitation, children must recognize the compatibility of their own goals with the goals pursued by adults, the means used to achieve those goals, and that the demonstrated action will successfully lead to the goal. By the time they are two years of age, children, unlike chimpanzees raised in the wild, are capable of just such imitation. Adults, recognizing children's proclivity for imitation, tend to turn their own teaching actions into performances, to demonstrate more clearly just what is involved in doing it "right." Adults typically provide what Bruner (1961) described as "noiseless exemplars," clear cases of the desired actions (see also Bruner and Olson, 1973).

Turned into demonstrations, modeling provides the basis of apprenticeship, the progressive induction of a novice into the skilled ways of the expert. The expert possesses a skill or ability acquired through repeated practice, which may be demonstrated but which, for success, must be repeatedly practiced by the novice. Little distinction is drawn between procedural knowledge—knowing how—and propositional knowledge—knowing that, a distinction made famous by Ryle (1949). The underlying assumption is that others can learn by being shown how, and conversely, that the ability to learn through imitation permits the accumulation of culturally relevant knowledge, even the growth of culture (Tomasello et al., 1993) and its transmission from one generation to the next.

But using imitation as the vehicle for teaching also entails some additional assumptions about human competence: that it consists of talents, skills, and abilities rather than knowledge and understanding. Competence on the imitative view comes only through practice. It is a view that precludes teaching about logarithms or drama in the way earlier described. Usually, imitative practices "just grow up as habits" and are linked neither to an explicit theory nor subjected to argument. Indeed, we even label cultures that rely heavily upon such folk psychology and folk pedagogy as "traditional."

We now recognize that more technically advanced cultures also rely heavily upon such implicit imitative theories—e.g., on apprenticeships for transmitting sophisticated skills. Becoming a scientist or a poet requires more than "knowing the theory" (Latour and Woolgar, 1986) or knowing the rules of iambic pentameter. It is also a matter of being socialized into a cultural way of doing. It is Aristotle and the physician all over again.

So what do we know about demonstration and apprenticeship? Not much, but more than we might suspect. For example, simply demonstrating "how to" and providing practice at doing so is known not to be enough. Studies of expertise demonstrate that just knowing how to perform skillfully does not get a learner to the same level of real skill as learning to perform skillfully while knowing in some conceptual, reasoned way why one performs as one does—much as really skillful pianists need more than clever hands; they need to know as well something about the theory of harmony, about scales, about melodic structure (see Gardner, Torff, and Hatch, this volume, chap. 3). So if a simple theory of imitative learning suits a "traditional" society (and it usually turns out on close inspection that there is more to it than that [see Gladwin, 1970]) or even a medieval "guild" society, it certainly does not suit a more specialized or technically advanced one. Which leads us to the next set of assumptions about human minds.

Seeing Children as Knowers: The Acquisition of Propositional Knowledge

The folk pedagogy exemplified in didactic teaching is based on the notion that pupils should be presented with facts, principles, and rules of action that are to be learned, remembered, and then applied. This pedagogy, too, assumes a certain theory of mind—namely, that the learner "does not know that *p*," that he or she is ignorant or innocent of certain facts, rules or principles that can be conveyed by telling. What is to be learned by the pupil is conceived of as "in" the minds of teachers as well as in books, maps, art, computer databases, or wherever. Knowledge is simply to be "looked up" or "listened to." Knowledge is the explicit canon or corpus—a representation of what is known. Procedural knowledge, knowing how to, is assumed to follow rather automatically from knowing certain propositions expressed as facts, theories, and the like: "the square of the hypotenuse of a right triangle is equal to the sum of the squares of the other two sides." So, if a baseball diamond is 90 feet square, what is the distance from second base to home plate? Problem solving is seen as applied theory. Again, Aristotle's quandary.

In this teaching scenario, abilities are no longer conceived of as knowing how to *do* something skillfully but rather as the ability to acquire new knowledge by the aid of certain "mental abilities": verbal, spatial, numerical, interpersonal, or whatever. This is probably the most widely adhered to line of "folk pedagogy" in practice today—whether in history, in social studies, in literature, in geography, even in science and mathematics. Its principal appeal is that by virtue of its clear conception of what is known it purports to offer a clear specification of just what is to be taught, and equally, it purports to offer standards for assessing its achievement. And it accommodates the learner by acknowledging differences in "mental ability."

More than any other theory of folk pedagogy, it has spawned the testing movement whether for prognosis in the form of ability testing or for achievement. To determine whether students have "learned" the capital of Albania, all we need do is offer them a multiple choice of Tirana, Milano, Smyrna, Samarkand (and Edmonton!).

But damning the didactic assumption is a common pastime with resonances to Whitehead's "inert" knowledge, Dewey's "dead weight" of facts (1902/1966, p. 25), or Friere's "banking" model of education. We would emphasize rather that the didactic pedagogy rests on one psychology, on one folk conception of mind. Indeed, there are contexts in which knowledge can usefully be treated as "objective" and given—like knowing the different writs under which a case can be brought under English common law or knowing that the Fugitive Slave Law became an American statute in 1793 or that the Lisbon earthquake destroyed that city in 1755, or that Newton's three laws can exhaustively characterize motion. The world is indeed full of facts. But facts are not of much use when offered by the hatful—either by teacher to student in class, or in the reverse direction as name dropping in an "objective" exam. Nor are facts merely learned and remembered; they are interpreted or misinterpreted, remembered or forgotten on the basis of an often implicit conceptual framework. In any case, we shall return to this point in considering our fourth perspective later.

For now let us look again at the conception of the child's mind that the didactic view offers and the perspectives it imposes on teaching—its folk pedagogy. The learner's mind is conceived as a tabula rasa, a blank slate lacking knowledge but equipped with the ability to learn. At best, knowledge put into the mind is seen as cumulative, later knowledge building upon existing knowledge. More important is its assumption that the child's mind is passive, a receptacle waiting to be filled. Interpretation and construal do not come into this picture of mind. The didactic view manages the child from the outside, from a third-person perspective, rather than attempting to "enter the child's thoughts" and to cultivate understanding. It is, moreover, blankly one-way: teaching is not a natural dialogue but a telling by one to the other. If children fail to perform adequately, finally, the educational establishment can always fall back on their inattention, or their lack of "mental abilities," the other plank of this folk pedagogy.

It is the effort to achieve a first-person perspective, to reconstruct the child's point of view, that marks the third folk pedagogy, to which we turn now.

Seeing Children as Thinkers: The Development of Intersubjective Interchange

The new wave of research on understanding other minds is part of a general effort to recover the child's perspective. The teacher, according to this view, is concerned with understanding what children think and how they arrived at what they believe. Children, like adults, are seen as engaged in constructing a *model* of the world to aid them in construing what they experience. Pedagogy is thought of as helping children understand better, more powerfully, more relevantly with respect to their other interests, and so on. Their understanding is fostered through discussion and collaboration, with each child encouraged to present her own way of construing the subject at hand better to achieve some meeting of minds with peers and teachers.

Such a pedagogy of discussion and collaboration is based on the assumption that the human mind is the repository of privately held beliefs and ideas which, by means of discussion and interaction, may be brought into a shared frame of reference. Children no less than adults are thought of and treated as having a point of view, and they are encouraged to recognize that point of view and to recognize that others have points of view that may not always agree with their own, though differing views may all be based on recognizable reasons. These reasons in turn may be appealed to in adjudicating rival beliefs. Sometimes you are "wrong," sometimes someone else is—the process depending on how well reasoned out the views are. Sometimes opposing views are both right—or both wrong. Children are not seen merely as ignorant or as empty vessels, but as individuals able to understand, to reason, to make sense, both on their own and through discourse with others. Moreover, children no less than adults are seen as capable of thinking about their own thinking, and taken as capable of correcting their ideas and notions by virtue of such reflection—"going meta," as it is sometimes called. In a word, children are seen as epistemologists as well as learners. Piaget took the first step in seeing children as epistemologists; we propose to add a second—children seeing themselves as epistemologists too.

According to this view, the child, no less than the adult, is thought of as holding more or less coherent "theories" about the world, but also as holding theories about the mind and how it works. These naive theories are brought into congruence with those of parents and teachers not through imitation, and not through didactic instruction, but through discourse, collaboration, negotiation. Knowledge is what is shared within discourse (Feldman, 1991), within a "textual" community (Stock, 1983), or within a paradigm (Kuhn, 1962). Truths are the product of evidence, argument, and construction rather than holding by dint of authority, whether textual or pedagogic. The model of education is dialectical, more concerned with interpretation and understanding, than in the achievement of factual knowledge or skilled performance.

It is not simply that this view is "child-centered" (a not very meaningful term at best), but that it is much less patronizing toward the child's mind. It attempts to build an exchange of understanding between the teacher and the child: to find in the intuitions of the child the roots of systematic knowledge, as Dewey urged.

Four lines of recent research have enriched this perspective on teaching and learning. While they are all closely related, they are worth distinguishing. The first has to do with how children develop their ability to "read other minds," to get to know what others are thinking or feeling. It usually gets labeled as research on *intersubjectivity*. It begins with studies of infant and mother's pleasure in eye to eye contact in the opening weeks of life, moves quickly into the two of them sharing joint attention on common objects, and culminates with the child and a caretaker achieving a meeting of minds by an early exchange of words—an achievement that is never finished (see Bruner, 1995).

The second line of research is on the child's grasp of another's "intentional states"—their beliefs, promises, intentions, and desires, which researchers often refer to as their *theories of mind* (Astington, Harris, and Olson, 1988; Perner, 1991; Wellman, 1990). It is a program of inquiry into how children come to their understanding of how they themselves or others come to hold or relinquish various mental states. Only in the late preschool years do children come to understand, for example, the possibility that they may act on a false belief, that they could lie, or that "hide and seek" depends upon another's not knowing. Importantly it highlights the fact that such understanding is both learned and applied to the self no less than to others. Only when children recognize false beliefs in others do they also come to acknowledge that possibility in themselves. It is particularly concerned, as well, with the child's sorting of people's beliefs and opinions as being correct or incorrect and in so doing it opens them up to the possibilities of factual and hypothetical discourse.

The third line of research is the study of *metacognition*—what children think about learning, remembering and thinking (especially their own), and how thinking about their own cognitive operations affects their mental procedures. At the forefront of this work was a study by Ann Brown (1975) that illustrated how remembering strategies could be profoundly changed by children turning their inner eye on how they themselves proceeded in attempting to commit something to memory. To think of this as introspection oversimplifies the issue somewhat; rather, it is a matter of acquiring a model of mind and cognition and seeing one's thoughts in terms of that model.

Studies in *collaborative learning* and problem solving comprise the fourth line of new research, which focuses on how children explicate and revise their beliefs in the context of discourse (Brown and Campione, 1990; Bereiter and Scardamalia, 1993; Pea, 1994; Scardamalia et al., 1992). This research has flourished not only in America but also in Sweden, where much recent pedagogical research (Marton, Hounsell, and Entwistle, 1984; Pramling, this volume, chap. 25) has been given over to studying how children understand and how they manage their own learning.

What all this research has in common is an effort to understand how children themselves organize their own learning, remembering, guessing, thinking. Unlike older psychological theories, bent on imposing "scientific" models on children's cognitive activities, this work explores children's own frameworks to understand better how they come to the views that finally prove most useful to them. The child's *own* folk psychology (and its growth) becomes the object of study. And, of course, such research provides teachers with a far deeper and less condescending sense of what they will encounter in the teaching-learning situation. Equally important, it allows the formation of a theory that may be shared equally by teacher and student, expert and client.

Some say that the weakness of this approach is that it tolerates an unacceptable degree of relativity in what is taken as knowledge. More is required to justify beliefs than merely to share them with others. That "more" is the machinery of justification for one's beliefs, the canons of scientific and philosophical reasoning. Knowledge, after all, is *justified* belief. We are both sufficiently pragmatist in our views of the nature of knowledge to recognize the importance of such criticism. Neither of us is post-modernist enough to accept the view that all claims to knowledge are justified by finding or forming an "interpretive community" that agrees. Nor are we so old guard as to insist that knowledge is only knowledge when it is "true" in a way that invalidates all other competing claims. "True history," without regard to the perspective from which it was written, is plainly a mockery (see Seixas, this volume, chap. 32) and can just as plainly be a political mischief. But regardless of perspective, beliefs must be justified.

So how are they justified? By appeal to reasons for believing or, in the logician's stricter sense, by the ability of a belief to resist disproof. Reasons for believing (or for doubting) obviously include a test by appeal to evidence, the test of falsifiability. But falsifiability is rarely a "yes-no" proposition, and there are often variant interpretations that are compatible with existing evidence—if not all of the evidence, then enough of it to be convincing. There is no reason a priori why the third approach to teaching and learning should not be compatible with this more pragmatic epistemology. It is a very different conception of knowledge than what was discussed in the second perspective where knowledge was seen as fixed and independent of the knower's perspective. The very nature of the knowledge enterprise has changed. Hacking (1975) points out, for example, that prior to the seventeenth century there was thought to be an unbridgeable gap between knowledge and opinion—the former objective, the latter subjective. What modernism sponsors, we believe, is a healthy skepticism about the absoluteness of the gap. An opinion, conjecture or guess can be raised to become a claim to knowledge by the simple expedients of clarifying definitions and amassing evidence.

Thus, we suggest that it is possible to go one step further in considering folk pedagogy. It is a step that, like the others we have considered, rests on notions about epistemology. At issue is how subjectively held beliefs are turned into theories and/or facts. We begin with beliefs; the task is to turn them into hypotheses that stand not on the faith we place in them but on how they stand up in the public marketplace of evidence, interpretation, and agreement with other useful knowledge. Hypotheses are not privately "sponsored" but openly tested. "Today is Tuesday" turns into a conventional fact, not only by virtue of its being "true" but also by being in conformity with conventions for naming the days of the week. It comes to be held intersubjectively, agreed to by all. It takes on the status of "fact" and is seen as independent of the beliefs of the individuals who initiated it. This is the point made by Popper (1972) in his defense of "objective knowledge" and by Nagel (1986) in his discussion of what he calls "the view from nowhere."

It is precisely issues of this sort that are most admirably and directly dealt with from the third perspective that we have been discussing. Now let us turn to the fourth and last of the perspectives.

Children as Knowledgeable: The Management of "Objective" Knowledge

If we focus too exclusively on beliefs and subjective states and on their expression and interpretation in discourse, we risk overestimating the importance of social exchange in constructing knowledge. Somehow, that emphasis leads us to underestimate the accumulated knowledge achieved by past human effort. For a culture preserves a tradition of reliable knowledge much as the common law preserves a record of how past communal conflicts were adjudicated. In each example, there is an effort to achieve consistency, to shun abitrariness, to find general principles. This does not mean that either culture or law is not open to reconstrual. But in both cases, reconstrual is always undertaken (to use the legal expression) with "restraint." We do not take the achievement of past knowledge and successful practice lightly. This is as true in science as it is in other pursuits of knowledge: we do not stampede into "scientific revolutions," profligately throwing our old "paradigms" away (Kuhn, 1962). A people that does not know its history. . . .

Early on, children come into contact with the hoary distinction between what is known by "us" (friends, parents, teachers, etc.) and what in some larger sense is simply "known." In these post-positivist, "post-modern" times, we recognize all too well that the "known" is neither God-given truth nor, as it were, written irrevocably in the Book of Nature. Knowledge in this dispensation is always putatively revisable. But revisability is not to be confused with free-for-all relativism, the view that since *no* theory is the ultimate truth, *all* theories, like all people, are equal. We surely recognize the distinction between Popper's "World Two," the world of our personally held beliefs, hunches and opinions, and his "World Three," the world of justified knowledge (Popper, 1972). But what makes the latter "objective" is not that it comprises some positivisit's free-standing aboriginal reality but rather that it has stood up to sustained scrutiny and has been tested by the best available evidence. All knowledge has a history, not only a personal one.

What this fourth perspective offers is a way for learners to grasp the distinction between personal knowledge, on the one side, and "what is taken to be known" by the culture on the other. Not only to grasp the distinction but to understand its basis, as it were, in the history of knowledge. How is this distinction to be captured by children and how is it to be incorporated into our pedagogy? Stated another way, what have children gained when they begin to distinguish what is known canonically from what they know personally and idiosyncratically?

One suggestion is that it opens the door to considerations of how we know— that is, a consideration of evidence and reasons for holding particular beliefs and the distinctive ways in which beliefs can be held—as assumptions, as hypotheses, as warranted beliefs and the like. Astington (personal communication, April 1994) offers an interesting twist on this classic problem. She finds that when children begin to understand how evidence is used to check beliefs, they often see the process as a kind of a belief about a belief, "I now have reason to believe that this belief is true (or false)." "Reasons for believing" a hypothesis are not of the same order as the belief embodied in the hypothesis itself, and if the former work out well, then the latter, as it were, graduates from being a belief (or hypothesis) to becoming something more robust—a proven theory or even a fact. In a similar way, the "facts" of arithmetic, multiplication, logarithms, decimals, or whatever, can graduate into a set of generative principles, literally, a tiny core of theoretical ideas from which we can generate endless facts.

In a similar way, we can come to see our personal ideas or beliefs as relating to "what is known," the personal conjecture viewed against the background of what is generally believed to have stood the test of time. Those presently engaged become participants in discourse with those long dead. But in addition we can ask how that conjecture got settled into something more solid over the years—what are the reasons for that belief? You can share Newton with see-saw partners on the playground and know how he came to hold his view. But what about your interpretation of *Taming of the Shrew* as being like the class tomboy? Could that be what Shakespeare had in mind? There is something appealing and, indeed, enspiriting, about facing off with the "knowledge" and foibles of the archivally famous in our past.

The fourth perspective holds that there is something special about "talking" to authors, dead but alive through their ancient texts. So long as the objective of the encounter is not worship but discourse, interpretation, or "going meta" on what's involved, the efforts are justified. For example, we may encourage several trios of teenagers, each staging a play on the astonishingly brief account in Genesis of God's instruction to Abraham to take Isaac, his only son, for sacrifice on Mount Moriah. In fact, there is a famous set of "versions" of the Abraham story that Kierkegaard set out in *Fear and Trembling*. So too with works of art: we may try any easily gathered collection of reproductions of Annunciation paintings, paintings in which the Angel announces to the Virgin that she is to be Queen of Heaven. Some 15-year-olds were asked what they thought might be going through Mary's mind—in one painting she was depicted as a haughty Renaissance princess, in another as a humble Martha, in yet another as a worldly-wise strumpet. What happens in these examples goes beyond collaboration, beyond intersubjectivity, beyond both by leaping across the gulf that separates Popper's subjective World Two from the "objective" World Three. The teacher reaches beyond what the learner knows in pursuit of goals more remote than a child as knower is capable of envisioning alone (Donaldson, 1992, this volume, chap. 15).

Again, note the relation between the assumption regarding mind and knowledge—the folk psychology—and the processes required to advance knowledge and understanding in the learner—the folk pedagogy. The child is seen as possessing beliefs and theories that are formed and revised on the basis of evidence; pedagogy is a matter of assisting them in evaluating their beliefs and theories reflectively, collaboratively, and finally, archivally. The product is not just the preservation of the past, but more importantly, the beliefs and theories acquired will be those held for good reasons.

We may summarize our four ways of thinking about minds and the forms of pedagogy each implies in a table (see Table 2.1). As we noted, each form of pedagogy implies a conception of learners that may in time be adopted by them as the appropriate way of thinking about themselves, their learning, indeed, their ability to learn. The choice of pedagogy inevitably communicates a conception of the learner. Pedagogy is never innocent. Hacking (1990) has described how what was at first offered as a neutral characterization of an action can take on a normative force and serve as an explicit guide to action of those so described. In this way mere descriptions can have a "looping" effect—the effect of creating what they

Table 2.1 *A comparison of folk psychology and folk pedagogy*

	Folk psychology		Folk pedagogy		
Concept of person[a]	What is acquired	What makes learning possible	Role of teacher[a]	Role of learner	Concept of teacher
Doer	Skill/ability	Ability to do	Demonstration	Imitation	Craftsperson
Knower	Knowledge	Ability to learn	Expositor	Comprehension	Authority
Thinker	Beliefs	Ability to think	Collaborator	Interpreter	Colleague
Expert	"Objective" knowledge and expertise	Ability to contribute to cultural store	Information manager	Knowledge constructor	Consultant

[a] Based in part on Tomasello, Kruger, and Ratner (1993), who linked the concept of the person to the cultural learning processes.

first merely purported to describe. This, presumably, is the way children come to think of themselves as skilled and knowledgeable on the one hand or as untalented and ignorant on the other. Conceptions of self and mind may be the product of pedagogy just as well as the reverse (Strauss and Shilony, 1994).

Summary: Rethinking Minds, Cultures, and Education

We conclude with two ways of summarizing across these alternative models of mind and pedagogy. What changes as we move from the simplest pedagogies to the most sophisticated, is the development of an increasingly internalist or insider's view of thinking, learning, and knowing. Externalist theories focus on what an adult can do to foster learning—a view that makes up the bulk of traditional educational psychology. Internalist theories, on the other hand, focus on what children can do, or what they think they are doing, and how learning can be premised on those intentional states.

The second way of summarizing across these folk psychologies and folk pedagogies is to note the increasing degree of common understanding or inter-subjectivity to be found between theorist and subject. Externalist theorists regard children as an elephant-trainer regards an elephant; there is no assumption that the subjects see themselves in the same terms that the theorist does, nor is there even the belief that such an understanding is possible or desirable. They aspire to the objective, detached view of the scientist. Internalist theories, on the other hand, apply the same theories to themselves as they do to their clients. Further, they aspire to apply the same theories to children as children come to apply to themselves. Hence, they create the genuine possibility of constructing psychological theories that are as useful for children in organizing their learning and managing their lives as they are for the adults who organize their experience for them. Rethinking the role of developmental psychology in educational practices will require new conceptions not only of the child as an intentional being but of knowledge as "man-made," the product of the elaboration of shared beliefs and shared frameworks for understanding, frameworks that may be shared with the learners themselves. Such rethinking would provide a foundation for a new psychology of education with new models of thinking, learning, and teaching suited to the twenty-first century.

References

Astington, J., Harris, P., and Olson, D. (Eds.). (1988). *Developing theories of mind.* Cambridge, England: Cambridge University Press.

Bereiter, C. and Scardamalia, M. (1993). *Surpassing ourselves: An inquiry into the nature and implications of expertise.* Chicago: Open Court.

Brown, A. (1975). The development of memory: Knowing, knowing about knowing, and knowing how to know. In H. W. Reese (Ed.), *Advances in child development and behavior* (Vol. 10). New York: Academic Press.

Brown, A. L. and Campione, J. C. (1990). Communities of learning and thinking, or a context by any other name. *Contributions to Human Development, 21,* 108–126.

Bruner, J. (1961). *The process of education.* Cambridge: Harvard University Press.

Bruner, J. (1990). *Acts of meaning.* Cambridge: Harvard University Press.

Bruner, J. (1995). From joint attention to the meeting of minds. In C. Moore and F. Dunham (Eds.), *Joint attention.* New York: Academic Press.

Bruner, J. S. and Olson, D. R. (1973). Learning through experience and learning through media. In G. Gerbner, L. P. Gross, and W. Melody (Eds.), *Communications technology and social policy: Understanding the new "cultural revolution."* New York: Wiley.

Cheney, D. L. and Seyfarth, R. M. (1990). *How monkeys see the world.* Chicago: University of Chicago Press.

Dewey, J. (1902/1966). *The child and the curriculum.* Chicago: University of Chicago Press.

Egan, K. (1988). *Primary understanding.* New York: Routledge.

Donaldson, M. (1992). *Human minds: An exploration.* London: Allen Lane, Penguin Press.

Feldman, C. F. (1991). Oral metalanguage. In D. R. Olson and N. Torrance (Eds.), *Literacy and orality* (pp. 47–65). Cambridge, England: Cambridge University Press.

Fouts, R. S., Fouts, D. H., and Schoenfeld, D. (1984). Sign language conversational interaction between chimpanzees. *Sign Language Studies, 42,* 1–12.

Gardner, H. (1991). *The unschooled mind.* New York: Basic Books.

Gladwin, T. (1970). *East is a big bird.* Cambridge: Harvard University Press.

Goodall, J. (1986). *The chimpanzees of Gombe: Patterns of behavior.* Cambridge: Harvard University Press.

Hacking, I. (1975). *The emergence of probability: A philosophical study of early ideas about probability, induction and statistical inference.* Cambridge, England: Cambridge University Press.

Hacking, I. (1990). *The taming of chance.* Cambridge, England: Cambridge University Press.

Kuhn, T. (1962). *The structure of scientific revolution.* Chicago: University of Chicago Press.

Latour, B. and Woolgar, S. (1986). *Laboratory life: The social construction of scientific facts.* Princeton: Princeton University Press.

Marton, F., Hounsell, D., and Entwistle, N. (Eds.). (1984). *The experience of learning.* Edinburgh: Scottish Academic Press.

Nagel, T. (1986). *The view from nowhere.* New York: Oxford University Press.

Pea, R. D. (1994). Seeing what we build together: Distributed multimedia learning environments for transformative communications. *The Journal of the Learning Sciences, 3* (3), 219–225.

Perner, J. (1991). *Understanding the representational mind.* Cambridge: Bradford Books/MIT Press.

Popper, K. (1972). *Objective knowledge: An evolutionary approach.* Oxford, England: Clarendon.

Rogoff, B., Mistry, J., Goncu, A., and Mosier, C. (1993). Guided participation in cultural activity by toddlers and caregivers. *Monographs of the Society for Research in Child Development, 58* (8, serial no. 236).

Ryle, G. (1949). *The concept of mind.* London: Hutchinson.

Savage-Rumbaugh, E. S., Murphy, J., Sevcik, R. A., Brakke, K. E., Williams, S. L., and Rumbaugh, D. L. (1993). Language comprehension in ape and child. *Monographs of the Society for Research in Child Development, 58* (3–4, serial no. 233).

Scardamalia, M., Bereiter, C., Brett, C., Burtis, P. J., Calhoun, C., and Smith Lea, N. (1992). Educational applications of a networked communal database. *Interactive Learning Environments, 2* (1), 45–71.

Stock, B. (1983). *The implications of literacy*. Princeton: Princeton University Press.

Strauss, S. and Shilony, T. (1994). Teachers' models of children's minds and learning. In L. A. Hirschfeld and S. A. Gelman (Eds.), *Mapping the mind: Domain specificity in cognition and culture* (pp. 455–473). Cambridge, England: Cambridge University Press.

Tomasello, M., Kruger, A. C., and Ratner, H. (1993). Cultural learning. *Behavioral and Brain Sciences, 16* (3), 495–511.

Turner, V. (1982). *From ritual to theater: The human seriousness of play*, New York: Performing Arts Journal Publications.

Visalberghi, E. and Fragaszy, D. M. (1990). Do monkeys ape? In S. T. Parker and K. R. Gibson (Eds.), *"Language" and intelligence in monkeys and apes: Comparative developmental perspectives* (pp. 247–273). Cambridge, England: Cambridge University Press.

Wellman, H. M. (1990). *The child's theory of mind*. Cambridge: Bradford Books/MIT Press.

Wundt, W. (1916). *Elements of folk psychology* (E. L. Schaub, Trans.). New York: Macmillan.

3

The Age of Innocence Reconsidered: Preserving the Best of the Progressive Traditions in Psychology and Education

HOWARD GARDNER
BRUCE TORFF
THOMAS HATCH

A Canonical View in Psychology and Education at Midcentury

Both the passage of time and the exigencies of argument can conspire to yield a past that appears appealingly simple. Succumbing to those pressures, we can readily compose views of the child and of education that are optimistic in tone and in harmony with one another. While scarcely going unchallenged, such views associated with an earlier time have done much to frame current discussions of the nature of childhood and the preferred course of education.

From the discipline of developmental psychology, which arose in significant measure out of a Rousseauian tradition, there emerged a view of the child as a relatively freestanding spirit, one destined to pass in the fullness of time through a series of preordained stages. Assuming only a nonabusive environment, the Piagetian child (Piaget, 1983) would first learn about the world directly through spontaneous and natural actions upon the physical world; then, acquiring a set of more complex cognitive structures in a preordained fashion, that child could perform "mental operations" of increasing abstraction and power on the representations of the world that she had constructed. Moving along parallel lines, the Eriksonian child (1963) would confront in turn a set of psychosexual and psychosocial tensions; and again, assuming a relatively supportive environment, the child would emerge as trustworthy, autonomous, competent, and a viable member of the community. While putting forth less totalistic schemes, other developmentalists subscribed to this basic linear and progressive view (Bruner, 1965; Kohlberg, 1969; Werner, 1948); and some added a distinctly social dimension to the developing child (Mead, 1934; Vygotsky, 1978).

A related intellectual tradition underlay that view of education that has been particularly celebrated among those with a deep interest in childhood. Dewey (1916, 1899/1967) and, perhaps even more, his "progressivist" successors saw the child as the centerpiece of the educational firmament. Children learned best through their explorations of the world around them; the opportunity to pursue their own interests at their own pace was a crucial ingredient. In a manner that recalled the developmental tradition, Dewey asserted that youngsters must construct their own meanings out of daily school and community experiences.

Armed with a more determinedly social vision than that of the prototypical developmentalist, Dewey emphasized the importance of the support of other human beings, especially well-trained teachers, and the desirability of learning about the roles and practices featured in the community. Yet, he did not fundamentally question the need to educate youngsters in the major disciplines; he assumed that there would be a natural and typically unproblematic progression from more project-centered activities in the community to the more scholastic regimen of academic disciplines.

Though these developmental and educational traditions evolved in relative independence of one another, it is important to underscore their essential compatibility. Both focused on children's interests and personally initiated activities; both expected relatively smooth progress toward scholastic mastery and toward full citizenship in the community. While each perspective acknowledged that children differed from one another, in terms of both their interests and their native intellectual potential, neither dwelled on these differences: "the child" was a more natural way of speaking than "the children." And perhaps not surprisingly, both of these traditions reflected the environments in which they were wrought: environments that from today's perspective can be seen as comfortably middle-class, and ensconced in a democratic society, be it a Swiss canton or a New England village.

Since we shall here assume a somewhat critical stance toward this canonical view, it is important to indicate the kinds of conceptions against which these progressive views were reacting. Within child study, scholars like Piaget and Erikson were critiquing strong forms of environmentalism, on the one hand, and biological determinism on the other. Against the "blank slate" empiricists of a Lockean or Skinnerian persuasion, they were acknowledging organismic constraints on the ways in which human beings develop. Against committed hereditarians, they were underscoring the need for interactions with a specific environment, as well as the possibility that development might not proceed properly or might even be derailed. More positively, they saw the child as passing through a set of ordered but qualitatively different stages, each with its own organization and integrity. Children were not merely shorter or less intelligent adults; they embodied particular views of reality and engaged cognitive and emotional problems in ways that were appropriate for their life situation. Indeed, it was important to see the various facets of the child—cognitive, emotional, social—as working together to yield an integrated person.

"Child-centered" educators were analogously engaged in characteristic responses to previously prevalent perspectives. They opposed the view of faculty psychologists, who saw the child as a collection of separate mental abilities, each to be independently fostered. They equally rejected the atomistic views of pedants, who sought to present curricula as a set of isolated facts or of disparate skills.

Particularly problematic from their point of view was a factory model of education, where children were marched through their paces so that they could ultimately be sorted into their proper roles in an increasingly industrialized society. Progressivists rejected the classroom in which an adult, her head filled with information, sought to transmit as much information as efficiently as possible into the small but growing head of the child; in its place progressivists sought to configure educational spaces in which children actively explored materials, working with other youngsters in a socially supported environment, "rehearsing" for life in a democratic society.

New Insights

It has been important to delineate the forces against which the psychological and pedagogical progressives were aligned; we [the authors] share the antipathy of the progressives to adultocentric views of children, on the one hand, and to a transmission view of education, on the other. Indeed, we continue to cherish much of the vision that was forged earlier in the century by such scholars as Dewey and Piaget. Yet in the half century since the canonical "innocent" view was first consolidated, an ensemble of new perspectives has arisen (or, to put it less grandly, some earlier perspectives have received fresh attention). In what follows, we first list the set of ideas that have emerged during recent decades. We then introduce a new approach—the "symbol systems approach"—which purports to preserve the strengths of the canonical view while drawing upon the insights of more recent times. We examine the ways in which views of human development and approaches to education might be reformulated in the light of the symbol systems approach, yielding a new and perhaps more powerful intellectual and practical synthesis.

Among the perspectives that have emerged in the past several decades, we single out for special mention six insights that have pointed the way toward a new perspective.

1. *The existence of domains beyond universals.* The broad spectrum of work in developmental psychology has, perhaps appropriately, begun by examining those conceptions and domains that are part and parcel of the experience of every human being. Thus Piaget focused on the development of conceptions in what might be termed the Kantian realms, such as time, space and causality; and other scholars, like Kohlberg (1969) and Arnheim (1974), have investigated other putatively universal domains, such as morality and the arts.

However, much of what is most valued within a culture is not necessarily esteemed or even shared by other cultures. That literacy which is virtually required within Western culture has until recently not been known in many indigenous cultures (Olson, 1994). And other activities, ranging from the playing of chess to the mastery of calculus to the execution of various dances and rituals, prove peculiar to specific cultures or subcultures. Thanks to the work of David Henry

Feldman (1980), we are far more cognizant of those domains that, while of import in one or several cultures, are not valued universally; and we consider as well the possibly quite particularistic trajectories of development that obtain across these disparate domains.

2. *The importance of specific knowledge and expertise.* Just as there has been increasing recognition of the existence of domains that range beyond the universal, there is growing skepticism about the existence of general knowledge and general skills (Carey and Gelman, 1991; Gunnar and Maratsos, 1992; Resnick, 1989). Rather than there being "general thinking" and "general problem-solving" skills, it is now widely believed that most skills are far more task-specific, with ready transfer across contexts being questionable at best. Individuals acquire expertise by working regularly over long periods of time on tasks and skills in particular domains; and the attainment of high levels of skill in one domain is by no means a guarantor of any significant level of skill in other domains, unless they happen to be quite closely related to one another. While this line of work has some superficial resemblance to the older faculty psychology, the particular faculties possess psychological coherence, and the processes of skill acquisition are described in ways that honor the different "domain-specific" conceptions of expertise (Ericsson and Charness, 1994).

3. *The need to explain individual differences.* The concern with difference across domains and tasks has been paralleled by an interest in the differences among individuals. While such differences have always been noted in both lay and scientific circles, of course, these differences have either been viewed along one dimension (more or less intelligent) or in a very general way (individuals have different personalities, temperaments, styles, and the like).

Of late, however, far more specific proposals have been put forth about differences that may be important. Among those interested in stylistic issues, differences in field dependence or independence (Witkin et al., 1962); among those interested in temperament, differences in shyness or impulsivity (Kagan, 1993). Of special importance for this chapter is the possibility that individuals may differ in their profiles of intellectual strengths. The "theory of multiple intelligences" posits that individuals may foreground quite different sets of mental skills, having disparate strengths and weaknesses, and that these in turn are important for the ways in which individuals learn and the kinds of creative or expert achievements that they may ultimately realize (Gardner, 1993a, 1993d).

4. *The existence of potent, enduring misconceptions.* Part of Piaget's (1929) enduring legacy was his demonstration that young children often exhibit quite distinctive conceptions of the world, including ones that are poignantly animistic, artificial, or otherwise egocentric. Because Piaget was concerned primarily with universal domains, he was able to document the spontaneous disappearance of these misconceptions.

Recent work on the acquisition of disciplinary expertise has established an unsettling phenomenon. Put succinctly, except for experts, most individuals

continue to adhere to early misconceptions, even in the face of considerable tute-
lage and counterevidence (Gardner, 1991). Thus even college physics students
often retain Aristotelian notions of force and agency, just as advanced students in
the humanities and social sciences continue to adhere to the most simplistic forms
of stereotypical thinking. The pedagogical moves needed to dissolve these misconceptions, and to place in their stead more well-grounded, complex, and comprehensive views, turn out to be quite demanding.

5. *The critical role of contextual and mediated experiences.* Every behavioral and
cognitive scientist at least pays lip service to the importance of the surrounding
context. However, in the progressive developmental tradition, such contexts were
discussed only in the broadest terms: because universal properties were of primary
interest; because differences across context were thought to be (and perhaps were)
of lesser consequence; and because there did not exist a conceptual apparatus for
analyzing contextual influences in any detail or with any precision.

Stimulated by the work of Vygotsky and other contextualists, researchers have
now provided convincing documentation that the society into which we are born,
the styles and values of the family in which we live, the procedures of the cultural
and educational institutions of our community, and perhaps especially nowadays
the messages transmitted by the dominant media, exert an enormous influence on
the kind of person that each of us becomes (Bruner, 1990; Collier, 1994; Geertz,
1983; Heath, 1983; Rogoff, 1990). To be sure, there are certain universal cognitive and emotional milestones that may differ little across contexts. But once one
begins to attend to the values held by individuals, the ways in which such individuals organize, reflect upon, and symbolize their experiences, and the manners
in which individuals interact with others, the pervasive role played by contextual
and mediated factors cannot be ignored.

6. *The application of standards in the judgment of work.* Midst the welter of contextual factors and agents that surround every developing human being, one strand
deserves to be singled out for separate mention. We refer here to those individuals
and institutions—sometimes called "the field" (Csikszentmihalyi, 1988)—that
render judgments about the acceptability and quality of human work. Every culture transmits explicit and implicit signals about the products and behaviors that
it values; and these values permeate schools and other educational and cultural
institutions. But within these institutions, there are specific individuals—ranging
from master teachers to admissions officers to prize-givers to encyclopedia writers
—who exert massive influence on who and what gets recognized. Indeed, the set
of standards and values beheld by the next generation is determined largely by the
actions of members of the field in the present generation. Even a handbook like
this one represents an effort to control the signals or "memes" that will be available for digestion by the next generation of researchers and educators.

These six insights, along with others that could have been mentioned, amount
to the legacy that a new generation of workers must encounter, master, and evaluate. To use a Piagetian analogy, it is possible to assimilate these lines of work to

an existing educational or psychological framework. However it is also possible to use these fresh insights as the basis for creating a new synthesis, one which may be better suited for the research and practical issues of today and tomorrow.

The Symbol Systems Approach

We introduce here an approach to the study of human development that grows out of the canonical tradition sketched above but which, in our view, is better able to make use of the new lines of investigation and better suited toward constructing an educational approach that is valid for our times. We term our approach the "symbol systems" approach, and, without making undue claims for its originality, we set forth here its basic assumptions and implications.

For at least a century it has been recognized that a distinctive property of human beings—perhaps *the* distinctive property—has been the species' capacity to employ various kinds of symbol systems: physical or notional elements that refer, denote, express, or otherwise convey various kinds of information, various strands of meaning. Initially, the interest of scholars centered around the symbols of language and of logic—those coherent sets of systems that make possible everyday communication as well as the mastery of the crucial domains of mathematics and the sciences. But since the seminal writings of Cassirer (1953–1957), Langer (1942), and Goodman (1976), the existence of other kinds of symbol systems has also been recognized. While artistic symbol systems may lack the precision and unambiguity of more conventional symbol systems, their capacities to create and transmit powerful and otherwise inexpressible meanings is now appreciated within the scholarly community. Moreover, scholars have become attuned not only to the syntactic and semantic properties of symbol systems but to their uses—their pragmatics; and they have come to note both the potential of symbol systems to be combined with one another and the capacities of human beings to create new personal or even public symbol systems (Feldman, 1980; Gardner and Nemirovsky, 1991).

To mention symbol systems to developmental psychologists is to invoke a widely acknowledged phenomenon. "Symbols" may have a somewhat different meaning to a Freudian than to a Piagetian or a Wernerian; but practitioners of these different strands all recognize the crucial milestone in the life of the child when that individual becomes able to capture and convey meanings not only through direct physical contact or through personal regard but through such mediated vehicles as words, pictures, numbers, and the like.

So much work has been done of late on the nature of symbolization in general, and on the ontogenesis and development of symbolization in particular domains, that one could virtually rewrite developmental psychology—or at least cognitive developmental psychology—in terms of the mastery of symbolic systems. And yet, strangely, the crucial nature of symbol systems and their implications for how we think about children, development, and education has not been sufficiently pondered.

Symbol Systems in the Development of the Child

A focus on symbolization makes profound sense from both a substantive and an analytic point of view. There is a sense in which we can speak of infants as presymbolic: both their interactions with the physical world and their relations with the world of other human beings occur primarily in terms of direct, unmediated contact, using mechanisms that have presumably been programmed into the species. (This statement is neutral with respect to the issue of the forms of mental representations or "mentalese" used by the infant [see Mandler, 1983].) By the end of the first year of life, however, overtly symbolic processes begin to come to the fore and they remain prevalent for the remainder of life. Some of these forms of meaning-making are distinctly personal: every child, every family develops its own forms of signaling and symbolizing (Bruner, 1990). But the vast majority of symbolic forms are public, reflecting modes of meaning-making that have evolved over many centuries within and across cultures and that all children must gradually internalize (Vygotsky, 1978).

Until the age of five or so, assuming a sufficiently rich environment, the development of competence within symbolic systems occurs without the necessity of much direct instruction or crafted mediation. Children are so constructed as species members that they readily pick up the various languages that are expressed around them, and also begin to use them productively and fluently (Heath, 1983). Researchers differ on the extent to which they endorse a single, comprehensive story of symbolization—a so-called "semiotic track"—as opposed to an account that invokes instructive and telling differences in the trajectories of different symbolic competences (Karmiloff-Smith, 1992). (Our own view is that the developmental paths are quite different in matters of syntax but have stronger parallels in their semantic and pragmatic dimensions. (See Gardner and Wolf, 1983.) But whether one is a unitarian or a pluralist, the increasing domination by symbolic codes during the course of early childhood is difficult to dispute (Bates, 1976; Bruner, Olver, and Greenfield, 1966; Olson, 1994; Mandler, 1983; Werner and Kaplan, 1963).

Symbolic development continues throughout childhood but takes on different colors after the first five years of life, and particularly so in a literate culture. Education in the use of the most important symbol systems comes to take place in more formal settings—in apprenticeships, in craft-learning, in religious training, and, of course, in those institutions called schools (Scribner and Cole, 1973, 1981). Some education consists in a refinement of the first-order symbol systems. But literate cultures are defined by their employment of second-order symbol systems— notations/marks that themselves refer to first-order symbolic codes. And in the reaches of higher education, ever more subtle and higher-order symbol systems come to be used, a phenomenon exemplified by complex mathematical and computational systems.

Until this point, we have ignored an important ambiguity in the use of our term "symbol systems." In fact the term has two distinct meanings and disciplinary histories. Within the area of philosophy, and in such allied disciplines as semiotics and linguistics, a symbol system consists of a publicly examinable set of marks, whose syntax and semantics can be identified and dissected by trained analysts. Codes ranging from written language to dance notation to scientific diagrams all function as *external* symbol systems (Eco, 1976; Goodman, 1976). Within psychology and various cognitively oriented disciplines, *symbol systems* are thought of primarily in *internal terms*—as cognitive representations in some kind of mentalese or language of thought (Fodor, 1975; Gardner, 1985; Newell, 1980). Fierce debate obtains about the exact nature and specificity of this internal symbolic representation; but that there exists some kind of mental code is the defining assumption of cognitive science (except, one must note, in its recent, parallel-distributed guise—see Rumelhart and McClelland, 1986; Smolensky, 1988).

Symbol Systems as Analytic Tools

In noting the internal/external contrast in any discussion of symbol systems, we segue to a discussion of the analytic role that can be assumed by a symbol systems perspective. Academic disciplines play an important, indeed indispensable, role in our inquiries and in our institutional life. Yet, few would question the assertion that many important issues do not respect disciplinary boundaries and that a key goal of research is to forge appropriate connections among disciplinary perspectives.

It is here, we claim, that a symbol systems approach exhibits special virtues. Any thorough understanding of the mind of the child and the process of education must span the gamut from human biological and evolutionary heritage, on the one hand, to the operation of human cultural institutions and practices, on the other. Yet the distance between genes and gods is simply too great to be casually bridged.

Consider, however, the role that can be played in such disciplinary conversation by the analytic construct of "symbol systems." As a species, human beings are programmed in their genes and equipped in their nervous systems to become symbol-using creatures. Rather than positing a single general cognitive capacity, however, we find it more useful to think of the nervous system as congenial to the development of a number of different cognitive systems that process different kinds of information; we have elsewhere termed these systems "multiple intelligences."

The multiple intelligences commence as a set of uncommitted neurobiological potentials. They become crystallized and mobilized by the communication that takes place among human beings and, especially, by the systems of meaning-making that already exist in a given culture (Bruner, 1990). It is the existence of spoken language, sung music, and communal number systems, respectively, that convert linguistic, musical, and numerical potentials into discretely operating and interacting intelligences. Here the encounter of brain with sounds, sights, or marks in the world brings about a dialectic between external symbol systems—present for all to behold—and internal symbol systems—the particular variants of mentalese that allow individuals to participate in, make use of, and even come to revise the evolved symbol systems of their cultures.

We may note, from an anthropomorphic perspective, the following assertion: the functioning culture must ensure that it continues to exist—the survival of memes proves to be as important for the culture as the survival of genes is for the species. The culture cannot observe genes, brains, or even intelligences; but it can observe the presence and the use of external symbols. And indeed, the culture determines the extent of its survival by creating institutions that monitor whether, to what extent, and how appropriately symbol systems are being learned, absorbed, utilized, and transformed by the younger members of the society. Put more concretely, responsible adults note the appearance (or nonappearance) in growing children of the myths, adages, rituals, art works, scientific practices, and philosophical systems of the community.

Here, then, we may begin to see the powerful analytical role that can be played by symbol systems in any comprehensive human science. Put directly, symbol systems serve as an indispensable *tertium quid* for the analyst—a safe, respected, and hallowed "middle ground" between the genes and the gods. To look at it schematically, consider the location of symbolic systems within the continuum of the human sciences:

Genes	Brain	Internal Symbol Systems (mental representations in one or more codes)	External Symbol Systems (external marks, patterns, sets of behaviors)	Cultural Roles, Institutions, Field

But how does this symbol systems approach unfold in a concrete fashion, spanning the gamut from early biological predispositions to the preservation and transmission of culture, typically through a formal or informal educational system? In what follows, we examine in some detail the application of the symbol systems approach in two domains: that of musical cognition and that of spatial cognition. In each case we begin by noting the kinds of adult end-states that competent practitioners within a culture might expect to attain. We then trace specimen developmental courses within those domains, taking into account the biological predispositions, the cultural messages, and the ways in which initial apprehensions of the domain may prove insufficient to permit the smooth attainment of expertise. The purpose of these surveys is to indicate the complex trajectory that must be followed for the realization of valued forms of competence, and in the process to suggest that a symbol systems approach may obviate some of the limitations of earlier unabashedly "progressivist" tacks in the disciplines of developmental psychology and education. We turn in the final sections to a more direct concern with pedagogical issues.

Musical Cognition

In Western society, the course of musical development results in a number of end-states. To begin with, individuals become competent to participate in the surrounding music culture; most if not all people develop the ability, for example, to tackle perceptual tasks like distinguishing musical styles and to render a reasonable vocal version of "Happy Birthday." The more widely heralded end-states of musical cognition are, however, in the professional realm—mastery of one of the musical disciplines, which include performance, composition, musicology, and music theory. Professional musicians demonstrate a set of rudimentary skills and literacies (e.g., ear training, notation reading) as well as elements specific to particular disciplines (e.g., instrumental technique).

Designed to encourage individuals toward these end-states, music educational practices are based, often implicitly, on a particular "folk psychology" and "folk pedagogy" of the musical mind. In Western society, the predominant "folk pedagogy" advances a relatively simple model of musical achievement: inborn talent revealed through years of practice. The "talent model" predicts that the individual, given the appropriate genetic gifts and sufficient instruction/practice, will enjoy unproblematic accrual of musical skill.

Below we suggest that the view of a smooth path to musical mastery may be unduly optimistic. By looking at music from the vantage point of symbol systems, we see that different representations of music may conflict with one another, but that particular steps can be taken to address the resulting problems. In order to make this argument, we will briefly summarize the symbol systems approach to music and then discuss its educational implications.

Symbol Systems Approach to Music

Neurobiology of Music   The claim of universal and innate capacities for musical symbolization (elsewhere termed "musical intelligence," Gardner, 1993d) is supported by three lines of research. First, nearly all children reveal remarkable vocal skill early in life. After a period of melodic and intonational as well as phonological experimentation, children begin at the age of about a year and a half to engage in "spontaneous song"—individual explorations relatively untouched by environmental input. Second, infants are able to make impressive intonational discriminations: by one year of age, and perhaps earlier, children can match pitch at better than chance rates and are also capable of imitating intonational patterns (Kessen, Levine, and Peindich, 1978). Third, studies of prodigies (Feldman, 1986) and "savants" with severe learning deficits (Viscott, 1970) document advanced performances not easily attributable to practice or training alone.

Consistent with views of a "modular" mind, other evidence suggests that musical intelligence is largely autonomous—distinct from other intellectual competences, most notably language. Studies of music perception provide evidence that the mechanisms by which pitch is apprehended are different from the mechanisms that process language (Aiello, 1994; Deutsch, 1975, 1982). Moreover, neuropsychological research employing brain-imaging techniques (Sergent, 1993) and studies of individuals with brain damage (Basso and Capitani, 1985; McFarland and Fortin, 1982) suggest "functional autonomy of mental processes inherent in verbal and musical communication and a structural independence of their neurological substrates" (Sergent, 1993, p. 168).

Vast individual differences in musical behavior from the earliest years of life suggest that musical intelligence has high heritability (Gardner, 1982; Torff and Winner, 1994; Piechowski, 1993). Biologically based "talent" *is* a factor in musical achievement; but, as we shall see, cultural and training considerations play an indispensable role as well.

Early Musical Development and the Intuitive Musical Mind   Exposed regularly to recorded music and the singing of adults, the young child in the West is immersed in song. This exposure provides the catalyst for several years of musical development that occur without much formal instruction—development that finds the child increasingly in tune with the particular musical symbol systems embraced by the surrounding culture.

At about the age of two and a half, the child begins to exhibit more explicit and extended awareness of tunes sung by others (Gardner, 1982). The child attempts to reproduce familiar nursery rhymes, initially by matching the rhythmic structure, later by following the contour of the melody, and finally by singing discrete pitches (Davidson, 1994). As "learned song" comes to dominate, "spontaneous song" becomes less frequent and eventually all but disappears.

Picking up expressive as well as contextual meanings from the world around them, children acquire the symbolic forms of the ambient music culture. One example is the linkage of harmonies and moods; in the course of everyday life in Western culture, the child comes to appreciate that major tonalities symbolize happiness while minor tonalities convey sadness. Another example connects music to situations; one tune denotes the onset of *Sesame Street*, another a birthday party or a religious ceremony.

This story of spontaneous musical development draws to a close when the child reaches school age, when everyday immersion in the music culture appears to lose its power to catalyze further. At least in Western culture, there is little evidence to suggest that, in the absence of instruction, musical development continues beyond the age of seven or so (Gardner, 1973a; Winner, 1982). Thus musical intelligence demonstrates the same kind of developmental plateau reached by the "five-year-old mind" in other domains (Gardner, 1991).

The result is a musical mind that is at once powerful and limited. Competent to participate as consumers in a music culture, musically untrained individuals demonstrate impressive abilities on tests of perception (Dowling, 1994; Dowling and Harwood, 1986; Krumhansl, 1990), production (Sloboda, 1994; Swanwick and Tillman, 1986), and representation (Bamberger, 1991; Davidson and Scripp, 1988). At the same time, marked limitations also are evident. First, stereotypes may be forged; for example, research indicates that people value poems with regular meter, rhyme, and an upbeat tone—restrictions disciplinary experts do not embrace (Richards, 1929). As children are typically oriented toward the lyric content of songs and to songs that honor a canonical form (Gardner, 1982; Gardner, 1973b), similar stereotypical predilections seem to prevail in music. Second, misconceptions may emerge, such as the notion that songs must begin and end on same note (Davidson, Scripp, and Welsh, 1988). Finally, should instruction commence, conflicts may emerge between intuitive and disciplinary conceptions of music.

Disciplinary Expertise and Instruction in Music   In music classes and apprenticeships, children confront the concepts and moves of the discipline and become more deeply enmeshed in symbols and symbol systems of the music of their culture. To begin with, first-order symbol systems are elaborated; for example, in typical apprenticeship settings in music performance, coaching of performances yields understanding of more subtle shades of expression or of programmatic aspects of compositions (Davidson, 1989). In addition, second-order symbols come into play; for example, linguistic symbols are seen in performance directives (e.g., "legato") and metaphor (e.g., "like a butterfly"). Finally, notation systems are used in "second order" musical cultures (as opposed to "traditional" cultures and Western subcultures like blues and rock).

Instruction brings the symbol systems of the discipline into contact with the intuitive musical mind. In some instances, the result is a smooth path to disciplinary expertise marked by improved performance/composition, perceptual acuity, and reflective skills. In other cases, however, the transition proves more problematic.

In a revealing line of work, Bamberger (1991, 1994) reports a conflict between intuitive "figural" understandings embedded in particular contexts with "formal" systems such as music notation. Trained and untrained subjects were asked to create an invented notation of the rhythmic pattern of "one, two, pick up shoes, three, four, shut the door." This pattern features two claps (grouping A) followed by three claps (grouping B), followed by a silence (a "rest") that is as long as the time between the two claps in grouping A or between the first and third claps in grouping B.

The untrained subjects typically created notations that group the claps appropriately but ignore the length of the rests:

. . . .

A person attempting to "read" this notation would reproduce groupings of two and three but would fail to reproduce the rests in a consistent fashion. In contrast, trained subjects follow metrical patterns, recognizing how much time is taken by both the pulses and rests:

. / . / . . . / . / . / . . . /

This rendering is literally correct; however, when asked to perform the pattern itself, the trained subjects may fail to recreate the feeling of rhythmic grouping ("phrasing") that is highlighted in the naive notations and performances. Crafting a notation that is metrically accurate but fails to capture the phrasing, the trained subjects produced a "correct-answer compromise" rather than a fully appropriate and comprehensive notation. In Bamberger's terms, "formal" knowledge (the notation system) overwhelmed the intuitive "figural" knowledge of the pattern. While the expert musician is not limited to either the figural or formal interpretation, Bamberger argues, students encounter difficulty matching intuitive knowledge of "how the song goes" to its notation. The culture's formal symbol system clashes with intuitive musical competence.

In a vein similar to Bamberger's work, Davidson, Scripp, and Welsh (1988) report that students demonstrate a conflict between perceptual knowledge and conceptual knowledge in a notation task. Attempting to notate the song "Happy Birthday" using the standard notation system of Western music, the students produced an inaccurate notation. They opted to alter the key of the final phrase of the song, based on the misconception that songs must begin and end on the same note. Asked to sing from their notations, the students reproduced the canonical version of the song, while detecting no errors in their notations. In their notations, the students disregarded accurate perceptual knowledge of the song in favor of misconceived conceptual knowledge; in their singing, they drew on the perceptual knowledge and overlooked the inaccuracy in their notations. According to the authors, the students experience a disjunction between perceptual knowledge of music and the formalism of music notation.

Music Education

The foregoing examples point up tensions that may exist between different forms of representation or understanding in music. Many of these persist despite instruction. The progressive movement encouraged music educators to downplay direct transmission of knowledge (e.g., readings, lectures) about music in favor of experience-based learning. Accordingly, there is a tendency in much music education to place overwhelming emphasis on performance—the immediately audible aspect of musicianship. Often resulting in impressive but essentially unanalyzed performances, typical pedagogy restricts student access to the full range of skills required of disciplinary experts and allows misconceptions to remain unconfronted.

The symbol systems approach reveals how an appropriate pedagogy can result in an *understanding* that goes beyond the intuitive by fostering the skills exemplified by expert musicians. To begin to sketch such a music pedagogy (while making no undue claims that our suggestions are original or comprehensive), we seek to combine the best of the traditional apprenticeship model with emerging ideas about teaching for understanding in music.

Around the world, musicians cut their teeth by apprenticing to a master performer for an extended period. Affording the learner sustained interaction with the disciplinary conventions (e.g., moves, techniques, concepts, values, categories, aesthetics) used by expert musicians, the apprenticeship *contextualizes* learning in several important respects.

To begin with, the teacher is often an active musician who may perform or compose in the lessons; in addition, the learner is often charged to analyze recordings and performances. *Modeling* makes visible to the student procedures and rules that are immediate and overt as well as values and goals that are distant and covert. However, it is not enough that students are simply exposed to models; they must also have ample opportunity to imitate. Thus, the apprenticeship affords the learner the opportunity to engage in *successive approximation*—a two-step sequence in which the learner consults the model and attempts to render a performance similar to the model. As the cycle is repeated, the learner edges closer to the modeled behaviors. In addition, the student benefits from *coaching*—personalized feedback (verbal and musical) adapted to the individual learner by the teacher. Often taking the form of comments and demonstrations concerning the student's performance, coaching focuses on strengths in the learner's performance as well as addressing what to improve and how to improve it.

Beneficial as the traditional apprenticeship may be, the existence of enduring misconceptions points to the need for additional steps designed to teach for genuine understanding in music. Given the all too common overemphasis on performance in contemporary pedagogies, it is essential to specify "Understanding Goals" and "Performances of Understanding" that encourage students to encounter and rethink intuitive conceptions about music (see the discussion below and Gardner and Boix-Mansilla, 1994).

Our own research group has developed Arts PROPEL, an educational approach that seeks to address this goal. The basic idea is that artistic activity involves three interrelated cognitive skills or "ways of knowing": *production* (performance or composition); *perception* (skills of aural discrimination), and *reflection* (focusing critical judgment on perception or production) (Gardner, 1989).

To help students draw together these ways of knowing, Arts PROPEL classrooms feature two principal vehicles. First, "domain projects" are extended curricular sequences based on concepts and practices in the discipline; for example, "Ensemble Rehearsal Critique" sets out a semester-long series of activities in which students listen to recordings of their ensemble's performance and write down critical judgments designed to point up potential improvements for the individual and ensemble (Davidson and Scripp, 1991). The second vehicle for fostering understanding in Arts PROPEL classrooms is an assessment device called the "process-folio"—a portfolio of student works designed to capture the steps and phases through which the student passes in the course of learning to play one or more compositions. These works include recordings, perception activities, and vehicles for reflection such as critique sheets and journals. Enabling learners to assume some distance from their work, the process-folio allows them to see where they are headed and to benefit over time from critical judgments rendered by self, peers, and teachers.

Together with the strengths of the apprenticeship model, Arts PROPEL curriculum and assessment devices (and related projects—e.g., Bamberger, 1991) address some of the problems resulting from a "progressivist" pedagogy that overemphasizes performance. A symbol systems approach acknowledges that multiple systems exist for representing or understanding musical knowledge—internal, psychological systems as well as external, cultural ones. Moreover, these symbols and symbol systems may conflict; in particular, intuitive understandings of music (comprising the five-year-old musical mind) can interfere with the appreciation of important concepts and practices within the discipline.

The pedagogical ideas presented above set out candidate strategies to counter these tensions. Combining the strengths of the traditional apprenticeship model with proactive steps to foster understanding in music, our approach encourages students to encounter disciplinary conventions and confront misleading intuitive conceptions about music, with the goal of moving students toward the genuine understanding epitomized by master musicians.

Spatial Cognition

The Development of Spatial Abilities

In talking about the art works of young children Picasso exclaimed, "When I was their age I could draw like Raphael, but it has taken me a whole lifetime to learn to draw like them" (Gardner, 1993c). Picasso's remark reinforces the popular mythology surrounding artists by leaving the impression that artistic ability does not have to be developed—it has to be unleashed. In such a conception, there seems to be little room for education. A similar point of view seems to apply to many other aspects of spatial development. We are more familiar with the seemingly spontaneous demonstrations of chess prodigies than with the years of preliminary drill and match that lead to championships. More mundane spatial abilities like those evident in the use of maps are assumed to develop relatively easily and without explicit instruction.

The abilities and understandings that are central to the spatial domain certainly originate in tendencies that have become a part of our genetic endowment. However, in order to become a painter or a geographer, or to achieve any one of a number of the "end-states" of spatial development, such predispositions are not sufficient. To become a geographer, one has to overcome a natural tendency to assume an iconic relationship between maps and the aspects of the world they represent. The geographer has to get beyond the surface features—how things look—and come to understand why they look that way. Such an understanding involves mastering the symbols and symbolic relationships that have developed in the discipline. It means that one can do more than recite place names or recall the routes between them, instead demonstrating mastery in such "Performances of Understanding" as reading novel maps and creating new geographical representations.

Similarly, becoming an expert visual artist involves mastering such cultural conventions as perspective drawing. Achievement also depends on the development of the understandings of how color, form, and composition can be used to create aesthetic effects. Further, artists have to go beyond the literal, realistic representations that most people can learn to create; they have to demonstrate their understandings in the way they address and challenge the cultural conventions that obtain in their time. In each case, the developmental course includes some useful predispositions, substantial obstacles, and the possibility of ultimate mastery of the representations, practices, and roles of the spatial domain.

The Biological Origins of Spatial Development   A wide variety of research suggests a strong biological component to such spatial abilities as learning new routes, forming and manipulating mental images, and creating spatial representations. For example, studies have shown that a wide variety of animals and insects—including honeybees, ants and rats—have innate tendencies that help them to carry out such specialized spatial functions as route finding (Cheng, 1986; Dyer and Gould, 1983; Gallistel et al., 1991; Margules and Gallistel, 1988).

Evidence is not limited to nonhuman species, however. In fact, the concordance of findings in research with animals and humans is among the most powerful evidence for the biological basis for spatial abilities. Such investigations have shown that specific parts of the brain (especially regions of the right hemisphere) of both humans and monkeys are "prepared" to carry out particular spatial functions (Stiles-Davis, 1988). In addition, there is extensive evidence of a link between sex differences in human performances on spatial tasks and biological factors like hormone levels and rates of physical maturation (Harris, 1981; Witelson and Swallow, 1988). In a task in which subjects have to find their way through a maze, Bever (1992) has even shown analogous sex differences in the performances of humans and rats. Females of both species rely more heavily on landmarks, while males focus more on the configuration of space.

Overcoming the Initial Challenges of the Spatial Domain   This endowment enables infants to begin their lives ready to explore and exploit the spatial world. As they grow older, however, and encounter the representations and knowledge that have evolved in the spatial domain, young children experience a variety of problems that evolution has failed to anticipate. Maps and perspective drawing are two examples of the challenges that symbolic representations provide for development.

Maps are not simply repositories of place names or references for distant journeys. They are notations that represent the knowledge that has accrued over hundreds of years about relationships that obtain over wide spaces. Although young children—both sighted and blind—can use some simple maps (Landau, 1988; Landau, Spelke, and Gleitman, 1984), mastery of these means of representations involves a variety of achievements. Among the most important is the realization that there is not a direct or iconic relationship between maps and their referents (Bluestein and Acredolo, 1979; Gregg and Leinhardt, 1994; Liben and Downs, 1991). In the absence of such an understanding, children exhibit a host of misconceptions—the most common ones including the belief that islands float on top of the ocean, and that lines separating states and countries are marked on the earth (Gregg and Leinhardt, 1994; Hewes, 1982). Even as they learn the conventional properties of graphic representations, children overgeneralize, assuming that grass in an aerial photograph must be at the bottom of the photograph while the sky must be at the top.

Unfortunately, human biological heritage provides no more reliable preparation for the challenges that visual artists must surmount. The accurate depiction of perspective is a particularly problematic step in the development of spatial abilities.

Not until the Renaissance did human beings figure out how to represent objects and scenes from a unitary viewpoint. Even now that this spatial problem has been solved, it takes most children considerable time before they can accomplish this feat.

In young children's drawings, items that should be on top of one another are likely to be drawn as if they are floating on the page. Only about the age of nine do most children attempt to draw in three dimensions, and not until the teenage years are most able to render perspective somewhat properly in their art works (Willats, 1977). The overall development of children's cognitive abilities in a scholastic environment certainly plays a part in this achievement, but it is likely that some exposure to the art works and conventional solutions evolved in our culture are a necessary part of this development as well (Gombrich, 1960; Goodman, 1976).

Education and Achievement in the Spatial Domain

Even though most people do manage to gain some proficiency in reading maps and drawing in perspective, few of us achieve the kinds of understandings that are required to become expert geographers or artists. Without some informal or formal educational experiences, misconceptions and rote performances are likely to persist.

While most adults have learned that maps are not iconic representations, they continue to manifest a variety of incorrect assumptions about our world and its representation. At least in part, such misconceptions in adults arise from our "common sense" of the way the world should look and a tendency to use simple heuristics to aid in perception and recall (Gregg and Leinhardt, 1994). Thus adults who know that the Atlantic Ocean is east of the Americas and the Pacific is to the west incorrectly assume that the Atlantic entrance into the Panama canal is further east than the Pacific entrance (Stevens and Coupe, 1978). Similarly, many adults, expecting some geographical symmetry, believe that North America is situated directly over South America (Tversky, 1981). Even with a map in front of them, the common association of the shape of Italy with a boot leads people to create representations that are somewhat distorted and gloss over important details (Rock, 1974). Some errors also result from a tendency to use maps without a clear understanding of how they are constructed. For example, those who do not understand that reducing three dimensions to two involves some distortions, fail to recognize that Greenland—which appears quite large on most maps—is actually the size of Saudi Arabia (Liben and Downs, 1991).

Such misconceptions are undoubtedly promoted by conventional approaches to geography in which maps are simply reference tools used to teach place names and locations. Such instruction fails to get at the underlying spatial relationships or the sophisticated reasoning that goes into their representation. In contrast, in an exemplary third-grade geography lesson, a teacher structures her lesson by addressing three generative questions: Where? Why there? So what? (White and Rumsey, 1993). In the process, her students get beyond rote knowledge and gain an understanding of what connects the places on a map. Such an activity provides a key to the robust knowledge that will enable students to demonstrate their understanding by carrying out such tasks as constructing their own maps and interpreting representations of unfamiliar areas.

Gregg and Leinhardt (1994) suggest that Geography in an Urban Age (GUA) (Association of American Geographers, 1965/1979), a curriculum developed in the late sixties, provides an example of how a deeper understanding of maps and geography can be achieved. The GUA curriculum engages students in case studies of real problems. In the process, students are asked to consider a variety of questions including: Where is it? Where is it in relation to others of its kind? How did it get there? What factors influenced its growth in that place? What difference does it make to me, to society, that it is there? What else is there, too? How are these things related to each other in place? How is it connected to things in other places? In pursuing such questions, students encounter a reason for using maps. They are required to carry out performances of their understanding of spatial relationships by finding places, relating them, and representing them.

In the visual arts, many people learn to draw fairly realistic representations that respect rules of perspective, color, and composition. This achievement begins to come about in middle childhood when children grapple with the cultural conventions of the discipline. It is at about this time that children become preoccupied with accuracy and with making their representations "realistic" (Gardner, 1982; Winner, 1982). This "literal stage" is apparent across domains as children become concerned with conforming to the standards and rules of the dominant culture.

Many adolescents and adults never get beyond the literal stage, nor are they likely to get beyond a reliance on simple forms or conventional strategies in using perspective. Those who do become artists have to master well-known techniques as well as invent new ones of their own. They have to hone their understanding of color and form in studies and sketches, constantly assessing the results until desired effects are achieved.

As a young child, Picasso showed considerable spatial skills as he drew constantly, noticed visual details and arrangements and recalled almost every live and painted scene that he had ever witnessed (Gardner, 1993c). But just like music prodigies who must transcend manual virtuosity, Picasso had to develop more than technical skills. Formal education in art school was a part of Picasso's education, but for the most part, he learned in more informal ways. In visits to museums, he explored the works of earlier masters like Goya and Velazquez; in his journals, he tried out new ideas and reflected on them; in countless sketches and studies for paintings like *Les demoiselles d'Avignon*, Picasso played with different shapes, colors, and placements in order to achieve particular aesthetic effects. In collaboration with Georges Braque, he tested traditional modes of representation. Through these experiences, Picasso confronted the conventions of the discipline and came to deeper understandings of how to represent the properties of objects in two dimensions and how to bring out the psyche of his subjects and the emotions underlying scenes of all varieties.

Beyond such "informal" learning experiences, many artists have benefited from apprenticeships similar to those that musicians may undertake. Often, apprentices in the visual arts join the studio of an accomplished master and begin their training simply through observation; as they stretch canvases, mix paints, or carry out other simple tasks, they have the opportunity to see how master artists approach the activity of painting or drawing, how they grapple with the conventions of the discipline, and the moves they make in revising their work. At the same time, the apprentice may also have the opportunity to imitate the master by making copies, filling in sketches, or creating works according to instructions. While it is difficult to know how much coaching actually goes on in the artist's studio, there is ample opportunity for the apprentice to secure some guidance from the master. In addition, the assignment of work of gradually increasing complexity by the master is an act of coaching that scaffolds the apprentice's growing spatial abilities.

Both alone and in collaboration with peers and mentors, artists and geographers develop their abilities as they grapple with the problems and conventions of their discipline. We could argue that our biological heritage prepares us to draw and even to read simple maps. But in our culture artists have to go beyond their initial perceptions of what looks "good" and overcome an unreflective affinity for literal representation in order to master the moves and strategies that contribute to aesthetic achievements. Similarly, geographers have to see beneath the surface similarities that lead to misconceptions and learn how to interpret and use the notations and second-order symbols that represent abstract spatial relationships. Without formal and informal educational experiences that guide young artists and geographers through their disciplines and the symbol systems they encompass, any "natural" talents are likely to remain unrealized.

The View from Education

From one vantage point, it has been argued that scientific findings—including those from psychology—are not strictly relevant to educational practice (Egan, 1992). Nearly every social scientific finding or perspective harbors within it a number of possible educational implications, not all of which are necessarily consistent with one another. Moreover, it is hardly the case that educational practitioners need to peruse scientific journals, avoiding the classroom until they have digested the latest finding from the theorist's study or the experimentalist's laboratory. Plato's Academy introduced quite powerful educational notions without any "research base"; neither Locke nor Rousseau (the ancestors of current educational practice) ever conducted an experiment; and most educators rely as much on careful observation of their own practices (and those of others) as on lectures or monographs.

Yet, even if there is not (and perhaps should not be) a unidirectional path from psychological insights to educational practice, representatives of both lines of work do rightfully participate in constant conversations about principles and practices. Nearly all of the psychologists mentioned above have been interested in educational issues; and few of the educators of influence in this century have proceeded in ignorance of current psychological work. It is perhaps better to think of both psychologists and educators as reflecting the predominant intellectual trends of their time. And in this spirit, many contemporary psychological ideas, including those about symbolization, have come to exert influence on the beliefs and practices of educators.

In our own case, we have tried to forge an approach to educational practice that draws upon the strength of the progressive movement, while cherishing features of more traditional approaches, on the one hand, and being mindful of newly emerging insights about human cognitive functioning on the other. These ideas have been worked out, in part, on the theoretical level. But they have been tested as well within schools—as embodied in experimental programs that we and our colleagues have set up; as parts of model school programs, instituted by practitioners "in the field"; and by recent collaborative work with other educational reformers, most especially in the ATLAS project, a collaboration of our research-and-development group with Theodore Sizer's Coalition of Essential Schools at Brown University, James Comer's School Development Program at Yale University, and the Education Development Center, directed by Janet Whitla (ATLAS, 1994; Comer, 1980; Gardner, 1991, 1993b; Sizer, 1984, 1992).

Sketched in the ideal, what are the principal features of the "new progressivism" in education? To begin with, the goals and processes to be adopted by a school or school system need to be negotiated by the principal stakeholders—educators, families, and community members. Schools are unlikely to be effective unless they reflect input and "stake" of those responsible for the life of the community. These parties—in this case the "field"—need to agree on what kinds of knowledge, skills, and understandings should be exhibited by students when they have completed their education. In our terms, there should be extended conversation and ultimately consensus about the symbolic competences to be achieved and exhibited. And "exhibition" is an operative work here. Students can be said to be educated when they are able to display publicly to an acceptable level of accomplishment what they have been able to understand and to master, whether it be performing a new composition on the piano or creating a map of an unfamiliar region of their community. Of course the adoption of exhibitions as occasions for assessment presupposes at least two conditions: the existence of a community that has developed a sense of what constitutes an acceptable performance; and the constitution of a group of judges who can apply standards in a reliable way.

What should be the focus of such an education? As we see it, all human beings are motivated to understand better certain basic issues and questions: Who are we? To what group do we belong? Where do we come from? Where are we headed? How does our group relate to others? What is the physical world made of? How about the biological and social worlds? What is true, what is beautiful, what is good? Youngsters brings versions of these questions with them to school—and both graduates and older individuals hope that they will be able to come up with satisfactory and satisfying answers to these "essential" questions.

Even the five-year-old mind has constructed an approach to these questions but, as we noted earlier, this approach is limited and flawed. Human beings have over the centuries devised more sophisticated approaches to these "essential questions" and have in a number of ways fashioned more comprehensive and satisfactory responses. The principal path to these privileged approaches is through the mastery of disciplines and domains—organized approaches to knowledge, that make use of the existing symbol systems and that, when necessary, revise those systems, or proceed to devise new ones.

A principal purpose of school—indeed, we would argue, the principal purpose of school—is to acquire facility and fluency in the use of the disciplinary symbol systems, moves, and understanding. Not for its own sake—though the cultivation of such skill can be rewarding—but rather because such accumulated corpora of wisdom represent human beings' hard won efforts to gain leverage on deep and subtle questions and issues. Individuals demonstrate their education by exhibiting understandings of the approaches, and the resolutions, that have been arrived at over the centuries; and to the extent possible, by putting forth their own more personal (though still disciplinary-grounded) responses to these issues. In pursuing this path, they are mastering the symbolic processes and products wrought by those who have worked within and across the disciplines.

So far, this educational regime seems quite traditional, and we make no apologies for that fact. To deny tradition is to turn our backs on the very best work done by countless individuals over many hundreds of years. And yet, while the program of disciplinary mastery is one to which we subscribe, we have little sympathy with most of the established pedagogical moves—for instance, strings of lectures, memorization of text, issuing of short-answer tests as a measure of learning.

Indeed, it is here that we gladly revisit some of the principal practices of the progressive movement, though with a newly cut key. To begin with, youngsters possess different interests and these must be taken seriously if we want to involve them integrally in the primary experiences of exploring the physical and symbolic worlds. Relatedly, they also subscribe to different belief and causal theories, held with varying degrees of explicitness, and these must be taken into account as well. Finally, youngsters also learn in different kinds of ways, exhibiting different profiles and blends of intelligences, which result in different representations of bodies of knowledge. In all of these senses, education must be personalized.

Following a period of initial romance, as Whitehead (1929) termed it, a time when interests are first crystallized, there can be no substitute for years of disciplinary training. The classical apprenticeship, where an individual worked for several years at the foot of a master artist or craftsperson, remains an unequaled route toward mastery of a discipline. Still, there is no reason whatsoever why this experience of skill acquisition needs to be dull or dulling. Individuals can gain disciplinary (and interdisciplinary) skills through working with others, through engagement in rich projects, through public exhibitions of their understanding complete with informative and supportive feedback. Apprenticeships come in many flavors. There is at least as much to be learned from time spent within the institution of the children's museum as from hours at the traditional school, church, or factory. The power of personalization, the miracle of motivation, can be marshaled to the ends of disciplinary mastery.

Nor need mastery occur at the expense of creativity and individuality. Even as there are common elements that need to be mastered by every individual, there are alternative routes to mastery, as well as costs and benefits for every road taken, and every road spurned. As long as both students and masters remain cognizant of these pluralities and these tradeoffs, the goal of creativity can continue alongside the goal of skill development and disciplinary mastery.

Even well-set up educational environments, with exciting materials and stimulating teachers, may not suffice to produce genuine understandings. The research on misconceptions, alluded to earlier, has documented the robustness of early conceptions and the sometimes overwhelming obstacles in the face of genuine disciplinary understanding (Gardner, 1991).

Neither we nor others have discovered a royal road to genuine understanding, but our research has suggested a number of pointers. To begin with, individuals must be brought face-to-face with their misconceptions and stereotypes—they have to be exposed repeatedly to the nonsensical implications of these uncritically held beliefs. At the same time, they need multiple opportunities to develop more complex notions and to see the ways in which these conceptions more adequately address the questions and issues at hand. A combination of exposure to models of understanding, on the one hand, and regular opportunities to work out the consequences of one's own beliefs and conceptions, on the other, seem necessary prerequisites for a deeper understanding.

In collaborative work with David Perkins and Vito Perrone, we have developed an explicit approach to teaching for understanding (Educational Leadership, 1994). This approach begins with the recognition of "Understanding Goals" (of a general sort) and with the identification of specific "Performances of Understanding," which alone can reveal the extent to which understanding is actually evolving. Care is taken in selecting questions and issues that have proved generative for students and that can address students in ways that connect with their own sometimes idiosyncratic motifs and intellectual styles. Thus in the above examples, young musicians can be asked to invent a notation for an exotic set of sounds or budding geographers can be asked to create maps for outer space. Along with publicly recognized instances of performances of understandings, we also call for assessment that is regular and ongoing (Gardner, 1991). Both the symbolic products to be emulated, and the symbolic means for assessing them, need to permeate the educational milieu. Only under circumstances where all involved in the community are aware of the standards that are being honored, of the various valid approaches to the achievement of these norms, and of the relative success of current performances relative to this standard, is there a chance of obtaining deeper understandings over time.

If we wish to teach for understanding, we have to accept a painful truth: it is simply not possible to cover everything. Indeed, the greatest enemy of understanding is "coverage." Only to the extent that we are willing to choose certain topics as worthy of exploration, and then to devote the time that is needed to explore those topics in depth and from multiple perspectives, is there any possibility that genuine understandings will be widely achieved.

So far in this discussion, it may appear that we have sidestepped the most nagging question of curriculum—what topics should be covered, what books should be read, which subjects are mandatory, which optional, which expendable? Particularly when we are calling for a sharp reduction of coverage, it may seem derelict to avoid the listing of the most important topics, subjects, and themes.

Here, we adopt a distinctly nontraditional approach. Once the basic literacies have been acquired, once individuals are comfortable in the crucial symbol systems of reading, writing, and reckoning, we discern no necessity to place a special premium on one subject as opposed to another (biology vs. chemistry; American history vs. world history), let alone particular topics (light vs. gravity) or library works (Homer vs. Hamlet). Far more important, in our view, is the experience of approaching with depth *some* key topics or themes in the broadest disciplinary areas—math and science, history and philosophy, literature and the arts. Students need to learn how to learn and how to probe deeply into one or another topic. Once they have achieved these precious insights, they are in a position to continue their own education indefinitely. And if they have not mastered these lessons, all the facts, factoids, and mandated tests will not save their souls. Assessment should look for evidence of deep understanding; the teacher and student should be afforded wide latitude in the topic that is to be assessed.

Progressive education, in its innocence, had too optimistic a view of education—giving rise to the belief that all students could learn, without much scaffolding, ignoring the conceptual obstacles en route, all too often minimizing the need for disciplinary mastery, skill building, and milestones and markers along the way (Gardner, 1993b; Graham, 1967). For committing these sins of omission, we may cast a critical eye on some of our predecessors. Yet, on the bigger picture—the need to establish interest, the openness to various ways of learning, the conviction that we can benefit from work on rich projects set in context, the perceived relationship in a democratic society between the conditions of learning and the conditions of citizenship—Dewey and his associates arrived at profound and enduring truths.

Closing the Loop: Innocence Recaptured

Even given our ambitious charge, we have sought to cover here a wide terrain—one better suited for monographic than essayistic treatment. We have had to provide indications and clues, leaving for another day the task of working out in detail the implications and nuances of our position.

At the end of the day, what do we hope to have achieved? Scholarship and practice is greatly indebted to the giants of our world: upon the life works of Jean Piaget and John Dewey, who inhabited the same century and adjoining intellectual spheres, there is much to build. While we have devoted at least as much energy to critique, we trust that such criticism has not masked our profound respect for their achievements.

Perhaps as penitence, perhaps as proof, we suggest—admittedly with some timidity—that the developmentalists and the pedagogues of the midcentury would not reject the picture that we have put forth here. Modify perhaps, quibble here and there, raise a few objections and point in a few new directions—but not challenge it in a fundamental way. And that is because, by and large, the fresh insights about human nature and the keener sensitivities to educational complexity in no fundamental way contradict the picture forged at midcentury—instead they deepen and complexify it in relatively congenial ways. Moreover, the emerging dialectic between researchers and school personnel, as epitomized by the themes of this volume, is in its deepest respects congenial to the vision of society and knowledge that was embraced by Piaget, Dewey, and their associates.

In putting forth the symbol system approach, as a privileged perspective for the broad understanding of human development, and as a central element in conceptualizing the purposes of education, we again make no claim for a revolutionary change of direction. Both the psychological and educational traditions have been sensitive to the importance of symbolic vehicles and systems. Yet, we do believe that the picture of symbolization put forth here has the potential to bring about a greater degree of order and a more reliable synthesis of knowledge and practice than has been available heretofore.

It is our deepest belief that the human mind comes prepared—we might even say "well prepared"—to be open to new ideas. It is the obligation of any society in which we would choose to live to maintain that openness and to facilitate the routes to new insights and new understandings. We oppose those psychological and educational approaches that threaten that openness or presume to deny its importance and even its existence. The approaches that we choose to build on are those that share with us this fundamental theme, this "world hypothesis" (Holton, 1988; Pepper, 1942). It is because we believe that creativity is not possible in the absence of disciplines and discipline, and that new knowledge must be based upon a deep mastery of tradition, that we have sought to leaven the more innocent aspects of progressivism—the better to preserve its core vision.

Acknowledgments

Preparation of this manuscript was supported in part by the MacArthur Foundation, the McDonnell Foundation, the Rockefeller Foundation, the Shouse Education Fund, and the Spencer Foundation. We would like to thank William Damon, David Henry Felman, Gerald Holton, Ellen Condliffe Lagemann, David Olson, and Caroline Zinsser for their helpful comments on an earlier draft of this paper.

References

Aiello, R. (1994). Music and language: Parallels and contrasts. In R. Aiello and J. Sloboda (Eds.), *Musical perceptions* (pp. 40–63). New York: Oxford University Press.

Arnheim, R. (1974). *Art and visual perception: The new version.* Berkeley: University of California Press.

Association of American Geographers. (1965/1979). *Geography in an Urban Age.* New York: Macmillan.

ATLAS. (1994). *Authentic teaching, learning, and assessment for schools.* Cambridge: Harvard Project Zero.

Bamberger, J. (1991). *The mind behind the musical ear.* Cambridge: Harvard University Press.

Bamberger, J. (1994). Coming to hear in a new way. In R. Aiello and J. Sloboda (Eds.), *Musical perceptions.* New York: Oxford University Press.

Basso, A. and Capitani, E. (1985). Spared musical abilities in a conductor with high global aphasia and ideomotor apraxia. *Journal of Neurology, Neurosurgery, and Psychiatry, 48,* 407–412.

Bates, E. (1976). *Language and context: The acquisition of pragmatics.* New York: Academic Press.

Bever, T. (1992). The logical and extrinsic sources of modularity. In M. Gunnar and M. Maratsos (Eds.), *Modularity and constraints in language and cognition* (pp. 179–212). Hillsdale, NJ: Lawrence Erlbaum.

Bluestein, N. and Acredolo, L. (1979). Developmental changes in map-reading skills. *Child Development, 50,* 691–697.

Bruner, J. S. (1965). The course of cognitive growth. *American Psychologist, 15* (1), 1–15.

Bruner, J. S. (1990). *Acts of meaning.* Cambridge: Harvard University Press.

Bruner, J. S., Olver, R. R., and Greenfield, P. M. (1966). *Studies in cognitive growth.* New York: Wiley.

Carey, S. and Gelman, R. (1991). *The epigenesis of mind.* Hillside, NJ: Lawrence Erlbaum.

Cassirer, E. (1953–1957). *The philosophy of symbolic forms.* New Haven: Yale University Press.

Cheng, K. (1986). A purely geometric module in the rat's spatial representation. *Cognition, 23,* 149–178.

Collier, G. (1994). *The social origins of mental ability.* New York: Wiley.

Comer, J. (1980). *School power.* New York: Free Press.

Csikszentmihalyi, M. (1988). Society, culture, and person: A systems view of creativity. In R. Sternberg (Ed.), *The nature of creativity* (pp. 325–338). New York: Cambridge University Press.

Davidson, L. (1989). Observing a Yang Chin lesson. *Journal for Aesthetic Education, 23* (1), 85–99.

Davidson, L. (1994). Songsinging by young and old. In R. Aiello and J. Sloboda (Eds.), *Musical perceptions.* New York: Oxford University Press.

Davidson, L. and Scripp, L. (1988). Young children's musical representations. In J. Sloboda (Ed.), *Generative processes in music.* Oxford: Oxford University Press.

Davidson, L. and Scripp, L. (1991). Tracing reflective thinking in the performance ensemble. *The Quarterly of Music Education, 1,* 17–45.

Davidson, L., Scripp, L., and Welsh, P. (1988). "Happy Birthday": Evidence for conflicts of perceptual knowledge and conceptual understanding. *Journal of Aesthetic Education, 22* (1), 65–74.

Deutsch, D. (1975). The organization of short-term memory for a single acoustic attribute. In D. Deutsch and J. Deutsch (Eds.), *Short term memory* (pp. 108–151). New York: Academic Press.

Deutsch, D. (Ed.). (1982). *The psychology of music.* New York: Academic Press.

Dewey, J. (1899/1967). *The school and society.* Chicago: University of Chicago Press.

Dewey, J. (1916). *Democracy and education.* New York: Macmillan.

Dowling, W. (1994). Melodic contour in hearing and remembering melodies. In R. Aiello and J. Sloboda (Eds.), *Musical perceptions* (pp. 173–90). New York: Oxford University Press.

Dowling, W. and Harwood, D. (1986). *Music cognition.* New York: Academic Press.

Dyer, F. and Gould, J. (1983). Honey bee navigation. *American Scientist, 71,* 587–597.

Eco, U. (1976). *A theory of semiotics.* Bloomington: Indiana University Press. *Educational Leadership.* 1994, February. *51* (5), 4–23.

Egan, K. (1992). Review of the Unschooled Mind. *Teachers College Record, 94, 2,* 397–406.

Ericsson, R. A. and Charness, N. (1994). Expert performance: Its structure and acquisition. *American Psychologist, 49,* 8, 725–747.

Erikson, E. H. (1963). *Childhood and society* (2nd edn.). New York: Norton.

Feldman, D. (1980). *Beyond universals in cognitive development.* Norwood, NJ: Ablex.

Feldman, D. (1986). *Nature's gambit.* New York: Basic Books.

Fodor, J. (1975). *The language of thought.* New York: Crowell.

Gallistel, C., Brown, A., Carey, S., Gelman, R., and Keil, F. (1991). Lessons from animal learning for the study of cognitive development. In S. Carey and R. Gelman (Eds.), *The epigenesis of mind: Essays on biology and cognition.* Hillsdale, NJ: Lawrence Erlbaum.

Gardner, H. (1973a). *The arts and human development.* New York: Wiley. Reprinted by New York: Basic Books, 1994.

Gardner, H. (1973b). Children's sensitivity to musical styles. *Merrill-Palmer Quarterly, 19,* 67–77.

Gardner, H. (1982). *Art, mind, and brain.* New York: Basic Books.

Gardner, H. (1985). *The mind's new science: A history of the cognitive revolution.* New York: Basic Books.

Gardner, H. (1989). Zero-based arts education. *Studies in Art Education: A Journal of Issues and Research, 30* (2), 71–83.

Gardner, H. (1991). *The unschooled mind: How children think and how schools should teach.* New York: Basic Books.

Gardner, H. (1993a). *Multiple intelligences: The theory in practice.* New York: Basic Books.

Gardner, H. (1993b, June). *Progressivism in a new key.* Paper presented at the conference on education and democracy, Jerusalem.

Gardner, H. (1993c). *Creating minds.* New York: Basic Books.

Gardner, H. (1993d). *Fremes of mind: The theory of multiple intelligences.* New York: Basic Books.

Gardner, H. and Boix-Mansilla, V. (1994). Teaching for understanding in the disciplines and beyond. *Teachers College Record, 96* (2), 198–218.

Gardner, H. and Nemirovsky, R. (1991). From private intuitions to public symbol systems: An examination of creative process in Georg Cantor and Sigmund Freud. *Creativity Research Journal,* 1991, *4* (1), 1–21.

Gardner, H. and Wolf, D. P. (1983). Waves and streams of symbolization. In D. P. Rogers and J. A. Sloboda (Eds.), *The acquisition of symbolic skills.* London: Plenum Press.

Geertz, C. (1983). *Local knowledge.* New York: Basic Books.

Gombrich, E. H. (1960). *Art and illusion.* Princeton: Princeton University Press.

Goodman, N. (1976). *Languages of art.* Indianapolis: Hackett.

Graham, P. (1967). *Progressive education from arcady to academe.* New York: Teachers College Press.

Gregg, M. and Leinhardt, M. (1994). Mapping out geography: An example of epistemology and education. *Review of Educational Research, 64* (2), 311–361.

Gunnar, M. and Maratsos, M. (Ed.). (1992). *Modularity and constraints in language and cognition: The Minnesota Symposia on Child Psychology* (Vol. 25). Hillsdale, NJ: Lawrence Erlbaum.

Harris, L. (1981). Sex related variations in spatial skill. In L. Liben, A. Patterson, and N. Newcombe (Eds.), *Spatial representation and behavior across the lifespan* (pp. 83–125). New York: Academic Press.

Heath, S. B. (1983). *Ways with words.* New York: Cambridge University Press.

Hewes. D. (1982). Pre-school geography. *Journal of Geography, 81,* 94–97.

Holton, G. (1988). *Thematic origins of scientific thought.* Cambridge: Harvard University Press.

Kagan, J. (1993). *Galen's prophecy: Temperament and human nature.* New York: Basic Books.

Karmiloff-Smith, A. (1992). *Beyond modularity.* Cambridge: MIT Press.

Kessen, W., Levine. J., and Peindich, K. (1978). The imitation of pitch in infants. *Infant Behavior and Development, 2,* 93–99.

Kohlberg, L. (1969). Stage and sequence: The cognitive-developmental approach to socialization. In D. Goslin (Ed.), *Handbook of socialization theory and research* (pp. 347–480). New York: Rand McNally.

Krumhansl, C. (1990). *Cognitive foundations of musical pitch.* New York: Oxford University Press.

Landau, B. (1988). The construction and use of spatial knowledge in blind and sighted children. In J. Stiles-Davis, U. Bellugi, and M. Kritchevsky (Eds.), *Spatial cognition: Brain bases and development* (pp. 343–71). Hillsdale, NJ: Lawrence Erlbaum.

Landau, B., Spelke, E., and Gleitman, H. (1984). Spatial knowledge in a young blind child. *Cognition, 16,* 225–260.

Langer, S. (1942). *Philosophy in a new key.* Cambridge: Harvard University Press.

Liben, L. and Downs, R. (1991). The role of graphic representations in understanding the world. In R. Downs, L. Liben, and D. Palermo (Eds.), *Visions of aesthetics, the environment, and development.* Hillsdale, NJ: Lawrence Erlbaum.

Mandler, J. (1983). Representation. In P. Mussen (Ed.), *Handbook of child psychology* (Vol. 3) pp. 420–494. New York: Wiley.

Margules, J., and Gallistel, C. (1988). Heading in the rat: Determination by environmental shape. *Animal Learning and Behavior, 10,* 404–410.

McFarland, H. and Fortin, D. (1982). *Archives of Neurology, 39,* 725–727.

Mead, G. H. (1934). *Mind, self, and society.* Chicago: University of Chicago Press.

Newell, A. (1980). Physical symbol systems. *Cognitive Science, 4,* 135–183.

Ogden, C. K. and Richards, I. A. (1929). *The meaning of meaning.* London: K. Paul.

Olson, D. (1994). *The world on paper.* New York: Cambridge University Press.

Pepper, S. (1942). *World hypotheses.* Berkeley: University of California Press.

Piaget, J. (1929). *The child's conception of the world.* New York: Harcourt Brace.

Piaget, J. (1962). *Play, dreams, and imitation.* New York: Norton.

Piaget, J. (1983). Piaget's theory. In P. Mussen (Ed.), *Handbook of child psychology* (Vol. 1) pp. 103–128. New York: Wiley.

Piechowski, M. (1993). "Origins" without origins. *Creativity Research Journal, 6* (4), 465–469.

Resnick, L. (Ed.). (1989). *Knowing, learning and instruction: Essays in honor of Robert Glaser.* Hillsdale, NJ: Lawrence Erlbaum.

Richards, I. A. (1929). *Practical criticism.* New York: Harcourt Brace.

Rock, I. (1974). *Orientation and form.* New York: Academic Press.

Rogoff, B. (1990). *Apprenticeship in thinking.* New York: Oxford University Press.

Rumelhart, D. and McClelland, J. (1986). *Parallel distributed systems.* Cambridge: MIT Press.

Scribner, S. and Cole, M. (1973). Cognitive consequences of formal and informal education. *Science, 182,* 553–559.

Scribner, S. and Cole, M. (1981). *The psychology of literacy.* Cambridge: Harvard University Press.

Sergent, J. (1993). Music, the brain and Ravel. *Trends in Neurosciences, 16,* 5.

Sizer, T. (1984). *Horace's compromise.* Boston: Houghton Mifflin.

Sizer, T. (1992). *Horace's school.* Boston: Houghton Mifflin.

Sloboda, J. (1994). Musical performance: Expression and the development of excellence. In R. Aiello and J. Sloboda (Eds.), *Musical perceptions.* New York: Oxford University Press.

Smolensky, P. (1988). On the proper treatment of connectionism. *The Behavioral and Brain Sciences, 11* (1), 1–74.

Stiles-Davis, J. (1988). Spatial dysfunctions in young children with right cerebral hemisphere injury. In J. Stiles-Davis, U. Bellugi, and M. Kritchevsky (Eds.), *Spatial cognition: Brain bases and development.* Hillsdale, NJ: Lawrence Erlbaum.

Stevens, A. and Coupe, P. (1978). Distortions in judged spatial relations. *Cognitive Psychology, 10,* 422–437.

Swanwick, K. and Tillman, J. (1986). The sequence of musical development: A survey of children's composition. *British Journal of Music Education, 3,* 3.

Torff, B. and Winner, E. (1994, August). Don't throw out the baby with the bathwater: On the role of innate factors in musical accomplishment. *The Psychologist,* 25–29.

Tversky, B. (1981). Distortions in memory for maps. *Cognitive Psychology, 13,* 407–433.

Viscott, D. (1970). A musical idiot savant. *Psychiatry, 33,* 494–515.

Vygotsky, L. (1978). *Mind and society.* Cambridge: Harvard University Press.

Werner, H. (1948). *Comparative psychology of mental development.* New York: Wiley Science.

Werner, H. and Kaplan, B. (1963). *Symbol formation.* New York: Wiley.

White, J., with Rumsey, S. (1993). Teaching for understanding in a third-grade geography lesson. In J. Brophy (Ed.), *Advances in research on teaching* (Vol. 4) Greenwich, CT: JAI Press.

Whitehead, A. N. (1929). *The aims of education.* New York: Free Press.

Willats, J. (1977). How children learn to represent three-dimensional space in drawings. In G. Butterworth (Ed.), *The child's representation of the world.* New York: Plenum Press.

Winner, E. (1982). *Invented worlds.* Cambridge: Harvard University Press.

Witelson, S. and Swallow, J. (1988). Neuropsychological study of the development of spatial cognition. In J. Stiles-Davis, U. Bellugi, and M. Kritchevsky (Eds.), *Spatial cognition: Brain bases and development.* Hillsdale, NJ: Lawrence Erlbaum.

Witkin, H., Dyk, R. B., Faterson, H. D., Goodenough, D. R., and Karp, S. (1962). *Psychological differentiation.* New York: Wiley.

4

A Rereading of Dewey's *Art as Experience:*
Pointers Toward a Theory of Learning

MAXINE GREENE

Viewed through the perspectives of pragmatic philosophy, Dewey's *Art as Experience* is a paradigmatic account of lived experience as the basis for human knowledge and understanding. From the vantage points of constructivism, hermeneutics, and narratological approaches to teaching and learning, it may be seen as an inquiry into the making of meanings by learners actively engaged in the world. Granted, the book does not deal explicitly with the young, nor with cognitive development, nor with schoolhouse learning in the ordinary sense. It does, however, deal with the kinds of cognitive, perceptual, and imaginative transactions out of which meanings of many sorts emerge, even as it focuses upon what Dewey called "*an* experience when the material experienced runs its course to fulfillment" (1934, p. 35). The esthetic, for him, meant "the clarified and intensified development of traits that belong to every normally complete experience" (p. 46). The world itself referred "to experience as appreciative, perceiving, and enjoying" (p. 46) rather than as doing or making. When a work of art was considered, nevertheless, the reflective attending dimension could not be cut off from the productive dimension. If a poem or painting or piece of music were to be conceived as artistic, it had to have been created for receptive perception and for some mode of enjoyment. Moreover, the artist had to have been capable of esthetic perception and of a kind of passion that would have prevented the making from being cold and mechanical. "In short," wrote Dewey, "art in its form, unites the very same relation of doing and undergoing, outgoing and incoming energy, that makes an experience to be an experience" (p. 48).

When Dewey spoke of learning in other texts, he was always concerned to challenge dualisms of various kinds: between knowledge as external or objective and knowing as an ongoing quest, a continual posing of questions; between the intellect and the emotions; between mind and body; between theory and action. To speak of "doing and undergoing" in the context of education was to call attention to concrete situations in which method was not separated from subject matter nor the "how" from the "what." In *Democracy and Education*, he wrote: "Experience, in short, is not a combination of mind and world, subject and object, method and subject matter, but is a single continuous interaction of a great diversity. . .of energies" (1916, p. 197). If "doing" referred to thinking, trying out, testing, questioning, wondering, imagining, then "undergoing" referred to the human and physical environment as it involved and affected the learner. Clearly, there are connections between Dewey's view of art as experience and the learning experience; and, indeed, his investigation of art and the esthetic qualities of experience has shed considerable light upon the continuity not only between works of art and everyday lived lives but between subject matter of various kinds and the actualities of child and adult experience.

Thomas F. Green has said that a theory of learning puts together

a series of statements that will help to explain or otherwise give an account of certain empirical phenomena which we recognize as learning. And the type of explanation or account to which a theory of learning should contribute is an empirical explanation. On the other hand, the analysis of "learning" is a conceptual rather than an empirical affair; it is the investigation of the term, its logic, its meaning, or its use. (1971, p. 136)

A confusion of the two, he said, is a fundamental mistake in thinking. Green has made the point that learning is many things, and that its various relationships to knowledge may be responses to different educational goals. The primary concern of the present chapter is neither with a description of certain empirical phenomena nor with conceptual clarification of the term "learning." Nor is its concern with an attempt at treating and accounting for the arts as empirical phenomena or with discovering a single and unarguable definition of "art." We know very well that no definition we can find is likely to account for every phenomenon that has been treated as a work of art over the centuries, nor is it likely to account for artistic phenomena still to come. The same thing may be true about "learning"; but that does not imply that we should not try to expand and deepen its meanings by looking at it in different contexts and from different points of view.

Dewey and "Theory"

Dewey was particularly opposed to "theories which isolate art and its appreciation by placing them in a realm of their own, disconnected from other modes of experiencing" (1934, p. 10). Generally speaking, when writing about art and the esthetic, he confined himself to esthetic theories *per se*. In this domain, he asserted:

Theory can be based *only* upon an understanding of the central role of energy within and without, and of that interaction of energies which institutes opposition in company with accumulation, conservation, suspense and interval, and cooperative movement towards fulfillment in an ordered, or rhythmical experience. Then the inward energy finds release in expression and the outward embodiment of energy in matter takes on form. Here we have a fuller and more explicit case of that relation between doing and undergoing of organism and environment whose product is an experience. (1934, p. 160)

He was interested in tension and release, in the excitement of uncertainty and wonder and in the transient calm that accompanies a sense of consummation, of order and integration and design. We need only think of significant experiences with the arts in our own lives to know what this suggests: the uncertainties and dangers of Huck Finn's and Jim's short-lived journey up the river northward—and the ending, like a deep sigh in the silence: "But I reckon I got to light out for the territory ahead of the rest, because Aunt Sally she's going to adopt me and sivilize me, and I can't stand it. I been there before" (Twain, 1935, p. 650); the desperations north and south in Toni Morrison's *Jazz*, and the ending that is no ending when the music stops: "Look where your hands are. Now" (1992, p. 229). We might recall *Tosca* or Martha Graham's *Appalachian Spring* or the Verdi *Requiem* or even the perceptual journey through Van Gogh's wheatfield with the crows overhead to recall the consummatory moments that are not conclusions, that settle nothing, that mark what Dewey called "*an* experience." For Thomas Green, there is the strange overlapping linked to what he named the "attitude of ignorance which we know as wonder" (1971, p. 201). Out of wonder, he wrote, comes the "joy of the beginner, of the mind always open to what is fresh and new and as yet unknown"; it is the way to further knowledge. Wonder, for Green, is the mother of motivation and the parent of curiosity; and, therefore, it may make reflection, study, and learning itself necessities, "as spontaneous and essential to life as breathing" (p. 202). Curiosity, wonder, problem-posing: that is where the tension is, the passion, the uncertainty. According to this formulation, reflection and study and learning are the release, the momentary calm before the searching begins again.

Mind as a Verb

Crucial to such a notion is a vision of the active mind, to be conceived (as Dewey wrote) as a verb and not a noun, denoting "every mode and variety of interest in, and concern for things: practice, intellectual, and emotional. . .all the ways in which we deal consciously and expressly with the situations in which we find ourselves" (1934, p. 263). Mind signifies, he reminded us, memory, attention, purpose, care, "an activity that is intellectual, to *note* something; affectional, as caring and liking, and volitional, practical, acting in a purposive way" (p. 263). Dewey, from a different philosophical perspective, was anticipating the work of an analytic philosopher like Gilbert Ryle who exposed what he called "Descartes' Myth" or the dogma of "the Ghost in the Machine" (1949, pp. 15–16). This meant, of course, the old dualism, the separation of body and mind; and it carried with it the idea that the mind was made of a different stuff than the body with its mechanical structure. As Dewey put it:

In making mind purely immaterial (isolated from the organ of doing and undergoing), the body ceases to be living and becomes a dead lump. This conception of mind as an isolated being underlies the conception that esthetic experience is merely something "in mind," and strengthens the conception which isolates the esthetic from those modes of experience in which the body is actively engaged with the things of nature and life. It takes art out of the province of the live creature. (p. 264)

Saying that within the context of what might be called an "art world," Dewey may well have illuminated some of the problems that arise when any subject matter is taken out of the province of the "live creature." Ryle, in another essay, wrote about how learners (in the Aristotelian sense) learn to do things by doing them. Learners can, on their own initiative, after a minimum of instruction, better their instructions. He was interested in how people can learn from themselves something that they did not know previously and had not been taught by someone else (1967, p. 112). Warning against wild guessing and haphazard plunging, he stressed the idea "of taking care when taking risks," and about mastering "techniques, *modi operandi*, rules, canons, procedures, knacks, and even tricks of the trade" (p. 114). Using as an example a poet composing a sonnet according to the regulation rhyming scheme and metrical pattern, he made the point that the sonnet will be a new one. "No one ever composed *it* before. His teacher who taught him how to compose sonnets had not and could not have made him compose this sonnet, else it would be the teacher's and not the pupil's sonnet. Teaching people how to do things just *is* teaching them methods or *modi operandi*; and it is just because it is one thing to have learned a method and another thing to essay a new application of it that we can say without paradox that the learner's new move is his own move and yet that he may have learned the how of making it from someone else" (p. 114). And, at the end of the essay, Ryle wrote that what the teacher is involved with is "teaching how to," just as the student is involved with "learning how to." The teacher can introduce the student to ways of doing things; but the student's actual attempts to exercise a craft or competence are his, not the teacher's.

I give you the *modus operandi*, but your operatings and tryings to operate according to this *modus* are your own doings and not my inflictings and the practicing by which you master the method is your exertion and not mine. I have given you some equipment against failing, *if* you try. But that you try is not something I can coerce. Teaching is not gate-shutting but gate-opening, yet still the dull or the scared or the lame calf does not walk out into the open field. (p. 119)

Reflectiveness and Beyond

Dewey's discourse was not quite the same; and Dewey did not speak of a *modus operandi* in speaking about art as experience; but many of the emphases are the same, most particularly the emphasis upon the active mind moving toward reflectiveness and the capacity to go beyond what happens to have been taught. Where encounters with the arts are concerned, it seems altogether clear that no one can guarantee or provide a full experience with a work of art. Where exhibitions or performances or engagements with literature are concerned, individuals must be personally present and, indeed, allow their energies to go out into whatever is the work at hand. Dewey knew perfectly well that the signal experiences he associated with the arts could not happen spontaneously. We have, he continued to remind us, to pitch our energy at a responsive key in order to *take* in whatever we might be hearing, reading, or seeing. But he was fully aware that this did not happen naturally, and that few encounters with the arts could be realized if they were left to odd moments.

The eye and the visual apparatus may be intact, the object may be physically there, the cathedral of Notre Dame, or Rembrandt's portrait of Hendrik Stoeffel. In some bald sense, the latter may be "seen." They may be looked at, possibly recognized, and have their correct names attached. But for lack of continuous interaction between the total organism and the objects, they are not perceived, certainly not esthetically. A crowd of visitors steered through a picture-gallery by a guide, with attention called here and there to some high point, does not perceive; only by accident is there even interest in seeing a picture for the sake of subject matter vividly realized. (1934, p. 54)

Dewey went on to make what some consider a fairly questionable claim—that the beholder, in creating his own experience, must go through the same process of organization that the creator of the work consciously experienced. It seems likely that readers, say, must, in their achieving a text as meaningful, gather together details and particulars into what is for them an integrated whole, responsive as far as possible to the text at what Wolfgang Iser calls the "artistic pole" (1980, p. 21). For Iser, talking about literary texts, "the artistic pole is the author's text and the aesthetic is the realization accomplished by the reader. In view of this polarity, it is clear that the work itself cannot be identical with the text or with the concretization, but must be situated somewhere between the two."

The Role of the Perceiver

Dewey's view of the necessary interaction was similar to this, but Iser makes it clear that what is actualized can never be reduced either to the reality of the text or the subjectivity of the reader. This might well be analogous to what happens with other forms of art. Dewey recognized, however, the perceiver's role in the realization of any art work. As in the case of any encounter that was to become meaningful and make a difference in experience, the beholder or the reader had consciously to exert energy, to lend his or her life to the text, the painting, the musical performance, the dance, the play. Dewey wrote:

There is work done on the part of the percipient as there is on the part of the artist. The one who is too lazy, idle, or indurated in convention to perform this work will not see or hear. His "appreciation" will be a mixture of scraps of learning with conformity to norms of conventional admiration and with a confused, even if genuine emotional excitation. (1934, p. 54)

The attainment of full appreciation depends upon a number of factors. There has to be an awareness of being present to a painting that has been located by a variety of scholars, critics, connoisseurs, and museum curators in what Arthur Danto calls an "artworld" (1981, p. 5), built for a particular period of time through the thinking and writing of aficionados or "experts." The same is true to different degrees with other art forms: Beethoven's Eighth Symphony must be attended to somewhat differently than a blues song or musical comedy overture; Twyla Tharp's "Push Comes to Shove" demands a different address than does a performance of the Rockettes. The energies of the perceivers have to be organized so that they can notice (on their own initiative) the way in which Cézanne's mountain juts out from the pictorial plane, the pattern of sonorities in the Beethoven, the staccato movements in time and space in the Twyla Tharp. The reader, entering the as/if universe of Fitzgerald's *The Great Gatsby*, has to set aside the hope that a meaning is buried in the novel, to be unearthed by anyone reading it properly. Paying heed to figures of speech, to shifting and often clashing perspectives, to images becoming symbols (like the billboard showing Dr. Ekleburg's eyes), the reader—ordering his or her experience in accord with the vantage points made available by the text—renders the valley of ashes, the appealing young "roughneck," the voice that "sounds like money," the strangers at Gatsby's party, the automobiles, the broken nose, the death in the road, the body in the pool, what Dewey called "objects of experience."

Indeed, Dewey wrote at the start of his book that "the actual work of art is what the product does with and in experience" (p. 3). What it does is in large measure a function of the "work" the perceiver chooses to undertake. There must be some understanding that subjective and objective factors work in cooperation. The objective aspect (the paint and canvas, the words printed on a page, the musical sounds, the moving body) become the stuff of art "only as it is transformed by entering into the relations of doing and being undergone by an individual person with all his characteristics of temperament, special manner of vision, and unique experience" (p. 287).

Conscious Intention and Experience

It is helpful to recognize the importance of conscious intention where any experience is concerned. On the simplest level, experience can be understood as the interactions or transactions that continually go on between the "live creature" and the environment. Much of the time it is formless, vague, inchoate. We walk in the street in something resembling a reverie; we are only vaguely aware of the light changing in the city sky, of the lights coming on, of voices in the near distance. There may be peculiar dissonances and tensions: we may feel compelled to go home; but, at once, we may want to go for a run or visit a bar, even though there is a job we want to finish at home. We may decide to stop in a bookstore, then realize there is not enough time; and even that small adventure dwindles away, as we feel ourselves caught between inner lethargy and outside obligation. The difference between that kind of experience and what Dewey called "*an* experience" is that the precarious, the contingent, the unresolved are, in "*an* experience," somehow integrated with the ordered, the settled, the uniform. It is not simply that the material experienced "runs its course to fulfillment." It is marked out from the other experiences in the flux of things, the ongoing stream of consciousness. Whether a game is being played, a problem worked over, an article being written, we have *an* experience when "it is so rounded out that its close is a consummation and not a cessation" (p. 35). Again, we need but think back to the end of a Mozart sonata, of a Faulkner novel, of a ballet, of a fine film like *Citizen Kane*. It does not simply close down. It does not end with a conclusion that can be detached, as a conclusion can from an argument; the last line of the novel or the final take of a film cannot be treated as if it were an inference logically derived from a proposition. The image of a wave, as in the famous woodblock print by Hokusai, is sometimes used to suggest the continuity, the seamlessness, the rise and fall of the movement in a work of art—and the consummation when the wave breaks on the beach.

For Dewey, a human being has to cooperate with the coming-to-be of a work if the outcome is to have a liberating effect, if it is to lead to the making of new connections in experience. Making new connections, new patterns in experience, after all, is a mode of creating meanings. The metaphors we learn to pay heed to enable us to see new relationships. If, for example, we are freed to conceive modern technology in unexpected ways because of the impersonality of the steamboat in *The Adventures of Huckleberry Finn* when it cuts "right through the raft," or because of the ash-grey men holding their shovels in the "Valley of Ashes" in *The Great Gatsby*, our conceptions of a postindustrial world may become more complex, more multifaceted. When we look at Claude Monet's multiple painted versions of Rouen Cathedral, we may find ourselves thinking of objects in time in startlingly new ways and even looking at the changing facades of the cathedral as if they were commentaries on a religion that can become stark and grey at one moment, pink and merciful at another. The recognition of the *kind* of involvement or cooperation needed (at least according to Dewey) depends upon a particular mode of thinking and knowing. To conceive something happening *in* experience is to realize that ideas are arrayed and meanings made within the transactions linking human beings to their environment. The response to the steamboat or the valley of ashes is a response that happens within experience and, as Dewey put it, against a "background of organized meanings that can alone convert the new situation from the obscure into the clear and luminous" (1934, p. 266). The new situation, in this case, may be one vaguely understood, somehow involving technological inventions and expectations that may or may not relate to the one studying them. We can only read a novel, be it Mark Twain's or Henry James's or Toni Morrison's, within a new or present situation. Inevitably, we must read by means of and against meanings we have funded over the years. These meanings, derived as they are from prior experiences, enter into present undergoings; they find their way through what Dewey called the "gateway" of imagination. Indeed, Dewey believed that "the conscious adjustment of the new and old *is* imagination" (p. 272) and that ongoing experience is fully conscious only when "that which is given here and now is extended by meanings and values drawn from what is absent in fact and present only imaginatively." It seems clear that recollections of machines and instruments seen or dealt with in the past extend and deepen what is presently seen and dealt with, and that the past is in some measure remade when it is viewed through the lenses of what has been discovered in the present day.

Grounding in Life Situations

This engagement with situation and lived history was another example of Dewey taking issue with philosophies that presumed the existence of defining essences and/or aesthetic theories in realms isolated from "life." He was trying as well to remove the underpinnings from the old formalisms and from the canonical views that equated products of art with works of art. For him, as we have seen, the products of art were one thing; the works of art referred to what human beings made of them. It was all too customary in this country's schools to fabricate objective categories, arrange them hierarchically, and present for students' passive absorption instances of "fine" art, "high" art, "transcendent" art. Students were asked implicitly to accept as role model or to imitate the docent, guide, or professor, including the reigning attitudes of awe, respect, and specialization. Nothing could be better calculated to ensure the isolation of art works that Dewey so often criticized. Few assumed that the ordinary young person could be equipped to crack the codes that presumably held the secret of great art. Few believed that an ordinary person had the potential for comprehending the spirit or inspiration of those who built the Greek temples or sculpted statues of an adolescent David or found a mode of rendering light as the Impressionists did. Dewey's concern was very like that of Walter Benjamin, the German critical theorist, who used the concept of the "aura" to explain how works of art (ascribed a preciousness and uniqueness) were kept at a distance from the masses (1978, p. 223): "To pry an object from its shell, to destroy its aura, is the mark of a perception whose 'sense of the universal equality of things' has increased to such a degree that it extracts it even from a unique object by means of reproduction." Benjamin believed that the aura would decay because of the spread of "mechanical reproduction" (pp. 217–242)—film, photography, recording, and the rest. Dewey, writing just before the great technological shifts, placed his emphasis upon a transformation of learning into what is sometimes called "experiential learning."

Learning in the arts (as in so many disciplines) tended to signify learning *about*, knowing *that*. It was and is unlikely that people conducted on tours around museums (or listening to the recorded lectures on accutrons) had or have what Dewey called aesthetic experience. This was largely because they were not directly engaged—as individuals and as members of a community—in active transactions with the works around. Dewey noted how few paid any heed to the surface structures of the paintings: the quality of the paint; the contrasts and contraries of color; contours, shadows, forms. Very few even showed interest in the subject matter of the pictures exhibited: the landscapes, portraits, and still lifes and what they presumably depicted. He might well have commented that students in the social and natural sciences are often presented with predefined representations and "objective" explanations without any attempt to involve them in participant interpretation. For Dewey, the perceiver, like the creator, "needs a rich and developed background which, whether it be painting, in the field of poetry, or music, cannot be achieved except by consistent nurture of interest" (1934, p. 266). The implication here is not that discrete pieces of "background knowledge" (Hirsch,

1987, pp. 60–64) should be mastered in the interests of "cultural literacy." E. D. Hirsch Jr. views Dewey, in his particular challenge to rote learning, as a disciple of Rousseau (Hirsch, p. 119) and sees something damaging in the presumed Deweyan preoccupation with the needs of children and their positive self-concepts. It appears clear, however, that in *Art as Experience* Dewey not only made the idea of a "rich and developed background" central; he continued to encourage the kind of active learning that involved questioning, making judgments, giving reasons, drawing inferences, as well as perceiving and imagining.

Interest and Identity

Interest, for Dewey, was not to be equated with a momentary kind of attentiveness of curiosity. In *Democracy and Education* (1916), he wrote that the kind of interest actively taken in something reveals the quality of selfhood that exists. What he said goes far beyond the nurture of "self-esteem" or a "positive self-concept"; and it has extreme relevance in these days of apathy and disinterest in the public schools. "Bear in mind," he said, "that interest means the active or moving identity of the self with a certain object" (1916, p. 408). Conceiving the self as "something in continuous formation through choice of action," he was speaking in terms of a project, an actual life project. The so-called "object" is a kind of attachment to an end in view, something to be pursued, an undertaking requiring a futuring. It is one of the means by which individuals create identities for themselves within the culture or the intersubjective world. In the chapter where Dewey discussed this, his example is that of a physician who continues to serve the sick in a time of plague. He is a doctor so interested in keeping at his work, it becomes clear that his self is found *in* his practice, in his work. We can see the same thing happening, on occasion, in sports: in soccer, for example, or in basketball. In the domains of the arts, it is unlikely to find persons deeply desiring to become dancers or poets or painters *not* identifying themselves with the *process* of becoming artists. This is very different from a mere assertion of self-esteem (due to a sense of being human and therefore a creature of worth) or a self-identification as "dancer" or "poet" or even "rap singer." As Ryle said, like Dewey and so many others have been saying, learning involves a deliberate and conscious doing of what one is learning to do. And this is as true with respect to learning how to perceive, appreciate, and resonate to works of art as it is with respect to any other subject matter or any other *praxis*.

Applied to the classroom, this suggests that "it is interest in the occupation as a whole—that it is this, in its continuous development—which keeps a pupil at his work in spite of temporary diversions and unpleasant obstacles" (Dewey, 1916, p. 410). Computer classrooms, chemistry laboratories, storytelling circles, "whole language" groups, marching band rehearsals: all of these today offer evidence of active learning and a certain rapt, interested relationship to the subject matter at hand. The Deweyan concept of "interest" connotes something far more than an attitude or habit of mind externally motivated or oriented to an extrinsic goal.

In *Art as Experience*, Dewey links interest to sincerity, specifically on the part of the artist who will not fake and compromise. But he makes another point with regard to the creative mind that may well have application to learning as well as thinking. He speaks of how the creative mind may "reach out and seize any material that stirs it so that the value of that material may be pressed out and become the matter of a new experience" (p. 189). He was lashing out at the kind of timidity that often causes the mind to shy away from some materials and refuse to admit them into the spaces of perceptive consciousness or (perhaps we should say) block any clear conceptualization. This description of the active mind comes close to the phenomenological description of the intentional acts of a consciousness thrusting into the world. Intentionality means that all consciousness is consciousness *of something*; it is not simply an interiority filled with intuitions and ideas. It is oriented, at all points, to the world with which it is in contact—and that means the physical world and the human society. Maurice Merleau-Ponty, a phenomenologist with a profound concern for the intersubjective, for the perceptual, and for the arts in their multiple embodiments, wrote much about being located in the world and about the influence of location and situation on the perspectives taken with respect to what lay around. He spoke of what he called "operative intentions" which are those apparent "in our desires, our evaluations and in the landscape we see, more clearly than in objective knowledge, and furnishing the text which our knowledge tries to translate into precise language" (1967, p. xviii). To avoid such an orientation would be to withdraw from connections, to take refuge in passivity and bad faith. For Dewey, it would mean excluding them from the "light of perceptive consciousness" (1934, p. 119).

Again, Dewey's conception of experience derived from a vision of human beings (live creatures all) developing, learning to be human, making meanings through selective engagements with the physical and human environment. What they attach themselves to and become vitally interested in depends a great deal on the ways in which they construct their realities. If, as in many urban schools today, school learning does not appear relevant to what young people hope for and desire, they are simply not going to be interested. If they belong to a minority group, they may take it for granted that they are going to be excluded from the kinds of mainstream activities that lead to what society at large deems success. Alternatively, they may have developed a scorn they share with their friends—a defensive rejection of what appears to reject them. This is one reason why so many young people act as if they were betraying their associates if they break with custom and try to be "good students" in ways defined by the majority. They have often (and with considerable justification) constructed models of social reality that highlight the inequities, the racism, the humiliations associated with the groups they consider dominant today. In consequence, many carve out their own paths in underground economies, on the street, and (if they are talented and fortunate) in entertainment or in sports.

Dewey did not take phenomena of this sort into account, in large measure because minority groups and their distinctive predicaments had not achieved the visibility they have today. Liberal though he surely was, active for some years in the National Association for the Advancement of Colored People, he apparently did not recognize (to use Cornel West's terms) that "race matters" (1993) the way it does in the United States.

The Matter of Social Pathology

Dewey's views on inclusiveness, however, on human rights, and equal participation might well have led to his naming all this as a mode of social pathology if he had been writing after 1927, when he published *The Public and Its Problems*. In that text, he made the point that there was in the country

a social pathology which works powerfully against effective inquiry into social institutions and conditions. It manifests itself in a thousand ways: in querulousness, in impotent drifting, in uneasy snatching at distractions, in idealization of the long established, in a facile optimism assumed as a cloak, in riotous gratification of things "as they are," in intimidation of all dissenters—ways which depress and dissipate thought all the more effectually because they operate with subtle and unconscious pervasiveness. (1927/1954, pp. 170–171)

Dewey's concern for intelligibility and order in *Art as Experience* may be an aspect of his response to what he saw as thoughtlessness. He spoke in that text of "the enrichment of immediate experience through the control over action" that may be exercised by knowledge (p. 290). Pathologies may be countered by reflectiveness, yes, and by social inquiry. They may as well be remedied by the consciousness made possible by the "fusion of old meanings and new situations that transfigures both (a transformation that defines imagination)" (p. 275) and can most likely be found in the esthetic experience.

Indifference, habituation, routines, mindless conformity: all these stand in the way of such experience as they stand in the way of learning. Dewey continually stressed the importance of heightened consciousness of what was happening, and of resistance and tension when it came to making sense of things. Without resistance to what stands in the way, the self would scarcely become aware of itself, since it would feel neither fear nor hope. Resistance to what stands in the way "calls out thought, generates curiosity and solicitous care" (1934, p. 60). It is clear enough that question posing or problem posing begins with a sense of obstacle or unease, a curiosity that could never be felt if there were a perfect fit between the organism and the environment. Dewey made the point that there are many desires and impulses, no matter what the favoring wind, that will be deflected and opposed as persons make their way through life; and this is surely the case where teaching and learning are concerned. There are those who turn away, who cannot even *name* what stands before them as an obstacle. There are others who try to convert obstacles into favoring agencies, as women have done in setting up Women's Studies courses, as African-Americans have done with their great novels and theater pieces, as certain young people have discovered causes and companionship by campaigning against violence and war. Undertaking tasks such as these, the self or the live creature becomes aware of his or her original intention. "The self, whether it succeed or fail, does not merely restore itself to its former state. Blind surge has been changed into a purpose; instinctive tendencies are transformed into contrived undertakings. The attitudes of the self are informed with meaning" (1934, p. 59). This becomes related to the art work in part because it is an instance of the act of expression. There is unlikely to be an act of expression, said Dewey, if the impulse or desire that leads to it is not thrown into some kind of commotion or turmoil. There must be compression, he wrote, if there is to be expression. "The turmoil marks the place where inner impulse and contact with environment, in fact or in idea, meet and create a ferment. . . . To generate the indispensable excitement there must be something at stake, something momentous and uncertain. . . . A sure thing does not arouse us emotionally" (1934, p. 66). There must be excitement about something if there is to be a search for an outlet in action. This brings us back to what was said earlier about uncertainty and problem posing in the learning process: the point has again to do with working toward a resolution by means of thoughtful *praxis*. There must be passion of some kind, anything but mechanism or apathy.

The Rhythms of Problem Solving

Most people are familiar with Dewey's preoccupation with problem solving and with the rhythms associated with an awareness of problems, the processes of deliberation and hypothetical thinking, the provisional solutions, the reaching of plateaus, the moments of release before the restlessness takes over again. The energies that give rise to unease may be transformed, as was said above, into thoughtful action when the person strives to make use of what is at hand to solve the problem that has been defined. The "forward action" that follows is sometimes converted "into reflection; what is turned upon is the relation of hindering conditions to what the self possesses as working capital in virtue of prior experience" (1934, p. 60). Again, we are reminded of the importance of funded meanings, meanings perhaps derived from childhood and now sharpening the awareness of present problems. Reflection, according to Dewey, may not only sharpen the sense of problem; it may make much clearer the end-in-view. Every meaningful experience, he said, is one in which stored materials are given new significance because they are used in meeting a new situation.

Art experiences, informed by imagination as they are, are instances of adjustment of new and old, of stored meanings and present exigencies. There is always a gap, Dewey said, between the here and now and past interactions. "Because of this gap, all conscious perception involves a risk; it is a venture into the unknown, for as it assimilates the present to the past, it also brings about some reconstruction of that past" (1934, p. 272). We need only think of the narratives being shaped and shared in today's classrooms, the stories being told, the life histories being recaptured. In time past, the young were not challenged to tell authentic stories about their own early lives nor to explore the ways in which such telling affected the construction of their present lives, even as it shed new light on what they had undergone in earlier times. To think of children living in time, capable of remembering things past, holds a new significance for learning quite different from the psychological conclusions accumulated with regard to children, most of whom live innocently in the "now." It might be worth recalling Marcel Proust's *Remembrance of Things Past* and summoning up the consequence of the taste of madeleines for the lived present. We might think of Melville's Ishmael in *Moby Dick* finding himself looking at coffin warehouses when he feels "a dark, drizzly November in my soul" and he finds it is time to go to sea. Reading that, many have remembered their own dark Novembers and experienced the risk, not only of assimilating the present to that past, but of remaking the remembered past at the same time. There are the memories stirred up by the poet's return to his original landscape at the beginning of Wordsworth's *The Prelude*, subtitled the "Growth of a Poet's Mind." There are memories, too, conjured up by Virginia Woolf's account of the "shocks of awareness" she experienced as a child, of a "shock-receiving capacity that made me a writer." Again, the past flowed into the present; the present was illuminated; the past was transformed, at least where its meanings were concerned.

Dewey spoke often of the slow processes of generation below the threshold of consciousness and of the often sudden emergence of materials above that threshold. Relating that to the life of emotion, he said that emotions are ill-defined at the start and assume definite shape as they work themselves through a variety of changes in imagined material. He wrote:

What most of us lack in order to be artists, is not the inceptive emotion, nor yet merely technical skill in execution. It is capacity to work a vague idea and emotion over into terms of some definite medium. . .But between conception and bringing to birth there lies a long period of gestation. During this period the inner material of emotion and idea is as much transformed through acting and being acted upon by objective material as the latter undergoes modification when it becomes a medium of expression. (1939, p. 75)

Whether we think of this in terms of the adjustment of past to present, inner to outer, or emotion to idea, it seems to hold considerable relevance to learning, most especially with the emphasis placed upon a "definite medium." Learning, after all, is a reflected-on process that moves on into conscious *praxis* in an unpredictable world.

Continuities in Experience

When *Experience and Education* (1953) is read through the filters of *Art as Experience*, what Dewey called "the principle of continuity of experience" takes on a richer significance. The principle suggests "that every experience both takes up something from those which have gone before and modifies in some way the quality of those which come after" (p. 35). He used continuity as the criterion by which to discriminate between experiences "which are educative and those which are mis-educative" (p. 37). On one level, this means that each experience in learning widens the conditions for subsequent learning, as in the case of learning to speak or to read or to use a microscope. But, as Dewey saw it, continuity works differently if an experience arouses curiosity, strengthens initiative, and sets up desires and purposes "that are sufficiently intense to carry a person over dead places in the future. . ." (p. 38). Without imposing a goal or a direction on learners, teachers are obligated to use enough insight to judge the moving force and the direction of particular experiences. They must be capable of sympathetic understanding, enough to communicate to the learner what conditions and what attitudes might be conducive to what the young person is striving to achieve or to become. Moreover, teachers are charged with knowing something about what feeds into the learner's experience from without and with trying to take from the learner's surroundings that which might contribute to building up worthwhile experiences.

Such charges are more sharp-edged today because of the recognition of so much diversity in the culture and in the classrooms, and because of the unfamiliarity (for most teachers) of street culture, popular culture, and the like. Very often, the traditions brought into classrooms are equally different and strange to the teachers. Many are beginning to recognize the need to enter social realities that have been constituted in ways quite unlike those now inhabited by mainstream adults, most often members of the middle class. The norms of the New England community no longer can be relied upon in the central cities; it is more difficult than it ever was to effect connections between schools and neighborhoods. Dewey knew that the world each person experiences becomes an integral part of the self that acts and is acted upon; and the diversity in experience is not of incidental importance.

Nonetheless, Dewey continued to warn against apathy and torpor. He wrote: "Familiarity induces indifference, prejudice blinds us; conceit looks through the wrong end of a telescope and minimizes the significance possessed by objects in favor of the alleged importance of the self" (1934, p. 104). And then he affirmed: "Art throws off the covers that hide the expressiveness of experienced things; it quickens us from the slackness of routine and enables us to forget ourselves by finding ourselves in the delight of experiencing the world about us in its varied qualities and forms" (p. 104). He ended that section by speaking of the arts as "the only media of complete and unhindered communication between man and man that can occur in a world full of gulfs and walls that limit community of experience" (1934, p. 105). There was at least an awareness of the connection between one-dimensionality of vision and slackness or indifference, even though Dewey did not quite confront the importance of multiple perspectives or of recognition of the marginal point of view.

When Dewey dealt with outright difference of opinion, he made the point that different ideas often have different "feels" or qualitative aspects. Indeed, he believed that, very often, it was the presence of felt qualities that enabled people to know when they were on the right path or the wrong. In truly artistic inquiry, "a thinker proceeds neither by rule nor yet blindly, but by means of meanings that exist immediately as feelings having qualitative color" (1934, p. 120). He made a point applicable to many modes of thinking when he said that, if we have to think out the meaning of each idea discursively, we are likely to lose ourselves in labyrinths without centers or ends.

It is evident enough, as Dewey said, that the word "symbol" is "used to designate expressions of abstract thought, as in mathematics, and also such things as a flag, crucifix, that embody deep social value and the meaning of historic faith and theological creed" (1934, p. 29). Verbally articulated ideas, Dewey seemed to be saying, are clearly different from algebraic symbols, whether in discursive or in nondiscursive contexts. They have more than instrumental significance: They are more than merely stimuli to the execution of operations, although that may be one of their necessary functions. But ideas are the stuff of thinking and learning; and when they find expression in works of art, they take on a certain opaqueness. They need to be cherished sometimes for their qualities, permitted to shine in a variety of connections.

Alison Hawthorne Deming, for example, has written a poem called *Science* (1993). The first three verses, like the rest of the poem, are replete with what might be called ideas (or concepts, or clusters of meaning):

> Then it was the future, though what's arrived
> isn't what we had in mind, all chrome and
> cybernetics, when we set up exhibits
> in the cafeteria for the judges
> to review what we'd made of our hypotheses.
>
> The class skeptic (he later refused to sign
> anyone's yearbook, calling it a sentimental
> degradation of language) chloroformed mice,
> weighing the bodies before and after
> to catch the weight of the soul,
>
> wanting to prove the invisible
> real as a bagful of nails. A girl
> who knew it all made cookies from euglena,
> a one-celled compromise between animal and plant,
> she had cultured in a flask. (p. 3)

The poem could possibly be translated into an argument, a critique of a prideful science in the technological age, laced with the absurd confidence that the "invisible" could be proved to be real. Obviously, it is not an argument; there is no reasoning process, there is no defensible conclusion. Still, the ideas remain. Conscious of it being a poem, we attend not simply to that which the ideas ostensibly refer, but to the rhythm of the words, to the repetition of the letter *c*, to the peculiar linkages, to the dominant image of chrome and cybernetics in the cafeteria, to the one outright figure—"real as a bagful of nails." If it does function as a work of poetic art, we are liable to find the events on the surface awakening resonances below where meanings are being generated and from which they may irradiate the common world of cafeterias and cybernetics and nails and cookies and chrome.

Dewey wrote that, through art (or poetry) the

> meanings of objects that are otherwise dumb, inchoate, restricted, and resisted are clarified and concentrated, and not by thought working laboriously upon them, nor by escape into a world of mere sense, but by creation of a new experience. . . . But whatever path the work of art pursues, it, just because it is a full and intense experience, keeps alive the power to experience the common world in its fullness. (p. 133)

Engagement with a work like the preceding poem cannot but bring into being a "new experience." Like the sonnet Gilbert Ryle mentioned, it cannot but be a fresh experience for everyone who reads it, for all the agreement on the look and feel of most of the objects in the poem. If only because it is a depiction and not a representation of the common world, a refraction in a type of distorting mirror, it breaks with the familiar and the conventional view and may therefore restore fullness to the experience of the world.

Toward the Common World

To speak about the common world is to refer not only to the facts of communication without which no one would be human and without which human communities would not exist. It is also to underline the identification of language and mind and to recognize that the more meanings become articulated by means of the symbol systems available to us, the more multiplex and complex experience becomes. Dewey did not speak explicitly about the social construction of reality; but it is not of small importance that the social phenomenologist Alfred Schutz, who explored in innovative fashion the concept of social reality, refers to Dewey's view that "all inquiry starts and ends within the social cultural matrix. . ." (1967, p. 53). Schutz wrote:

> By the term "social reality" I wish to be understood the sum total of objects and occurrences within the social cultural world as experienced by the common-sense thinking of men living their daily lives among their fellow-men, connected with them in manifold relations of interaction. . . . From the outset, we, the actors on the social scene, experience the world we live in as a world both of nature and culture, not as a private but as an intersubjective one, that is, as a world common to all of us, either actually given or potentially accessible to everyone; but this involves intercommunication and language. (p. 53)

This allows for the possibility that, as Dewey said, the arts are the only media of "complete and unhindered communication."

In *Art as Experience*, particularly in his discussions of encounters with art works, Dewey reaches toward a constructivist view. Because of Schutz's many references to Dewey's work, along with William James's and George Herbert Mead's, he was not only attentive to the overlap between phenomenological and pragmatic approaches, he may have found suggestive hints in their work for his sociology of knowledge. Of particular interest in this context is Schutz's mention of Dewey when he speaks of alternative possibilities of action. "My total biographical situation, that is, my previous experiences as integrated into my actually prevailing system of interests, creates the principally problematic possibilities of conflicting preferences, as Dewey expresses it" (p. 83). And then he made the point that we assume the conduct of human beings must be explained as if occurring in the form of choosing among problematic possibilities. Human beings have to define situations in which alternatives appear; and the only way they can be thought to do this is through the transactional relation between the individual and the world that Dewey continued to describe.

It is through intercourse, through action and communication, that the live creature's native capacities are transformed and become a self, wrote Dewey; and "through resistances encountered, the nature of the self is discovered" (1934, p. 282). Teachers must realize, as they face more and more differentiated groups of young people, that the environment in which they have developed could not have been identical for everyone. For Dewey, "the more deep-seated" shared experience is, the more common it is likely to be. What we know we hold in common is that we inhabit the same world, in spite of the different faces it shows to various ones of us.

There are impulsions and needs common to humanity. The "universal" is not something metaphysically anterior to all experience but is a way in which things function in experience as a bond of union among particular events and scenes. Potentially anything whatsoever in nature or in human association is "common"; whether or not it is actually common depends upon diverse conditions, especially those that affect the processes of communication. (p. 286)

Dewey's view that values and qualities *become* common by means of language and a range of shared activities has as much significance for a conception of education and learning as it does for a conception of the aesthetic experience. Like freedom, like the virtues themselves, community must be achieved; and it can only be achieved by what we might today call a kind of dialogical intelligence. If we attend as well to what is involved in art experiences, we would need to add that intelligence of that sort must be integrated with perception, feeling, and imagination if active learning is to take place, and if there is to be a common world.

Values and Judgments

There remains the matter of judgment, which Dewey raised in his discussion of criticism. He objected, as he had in his writings on education, to the standardized objectivity of "ready-made rules and precedents" (1934, p. 304). At the same time, he objected to the uncontrolled reliance on "subjectivity" in the making of judgments. He used as an example the idea of an impression, taken from impressionist art criticism, and focused on the "total qualitative unanalyzed effects that things and events make on us" (1934, p. 304). All judgments begin with such impressions; but we have to go beyond the initial impressions to talk about the grounds upon which they rest and the consequences to which they lead. The search for grounds may begin with personal history; but Dewey reminds the reader that personal biography is what it is because of "interactions with the world out-side, a world which in some of its aspects and phases is common with that of others" (p. 305). When learners are old and reflective enough, they can reflect on that biography and try to discover the factors that made it what it was. In the work being done on young women's "math anxiety" and the efforts to counter racism, learners are provoked to move beyond their initial impressions and look for the grounds of the judgments they are making. It may be that a careful examination of false statements made, of propaganda, of media formulations—preferably in the context of dialogue—may convert the obstacles to tolerance or compassion into opportunities to pose problems, to try to understand.

There is a need, in the course of all this, to avoid what Dewey called a confusion of categories or values. In the realm of the arts, this might mean a translation of the esthetic into the moral, or a treatment of a historical novel (like *War and Peace*) into a re-editing of historical fact, or a rejection of *Paradise Lost* by an agnostic reader skeptical of the "truth" of Genesis. In Dewey's discussions of all this there is an implicit challenge to positivisms of all sorts, including the screening out of all but empirical judgments or the undervaluing of the "subjective" and even the "esthetic." There is a recognition of multiple modes of awareness of the ways in which these enhance understanding and increase the likelihood of constructing meanings and making connections in experience. In *Experience and Nature*, Dewey wrote that the realm of meanings "is wider than that of true-and-false mean-ings. . . . Poetic meanings, moral meanings, a large part of the goods of life are matters of richness and freedom of meanings rather than of truth; a large part of our life is carried on in a realm of meanings to which truth and falsity as such are irrelevant" (1958, pp. 410–411). When Dewey spoke of truth, he had empirical science in mind; but his notion of the scope of that realm of meanings holds many implications for learning today.

At the conclusion of his discussions of art, he wrote that most value confusion comes from neglect of the intrinsic significance of the medium:

The use of a particular medium, a special language having its own characteristics, is the source of every art, philosophic, scientific, technological, and esthetic. The arts of science, of politics, of history, and of painting and poetry have finally the same material; that which is constituted by the interaction of the live creature with his surroundings. They differ in the media by which they convey and express this material, not in the material itself. (1934, p. 320)

Considered from the vantage point of learning, this may imply that the crucial purpose of learning is to transmute some of the raw material of experience into new objects according to the purpose. The objects, as we have noted, are those things to which experience lays hold, those things that feed into human projects and the shaping of identity.

The "pointers towards a theory of learning" may finally be summarized as those pointers to an attainment of a union of the possible with the actual. In a work of art, wrote Dewey in his own conclusion, perception of such a union is a great good, but the good does not terminate with the immediate and particular occasion in which it is had. The union that is presented in perception persists in the remaking of impulsion and thought. The first intimations of wide and large redirections of desire and purpose are of necessity imaginative. Art is a mode of prediction not found in charts and statistics, and it insinuates possibilities of human relations not to be found in rule and precept, admonition and administration. (p. 348)

The pointers may direct us far beyond.

References

Benjamin, W. (1978). The work of art in the age of mechanical reproduction. In H. Arendt (Ed.) and H. Zohn (Trans.), *Illuminations* (pp. 217–251). New York: Shocken Books.

Danto, A. C. (1981). *The Transfiguration of the Commonplace.* Cambridge: Harvard University Press.

Deming, A. H. (1993). *Science and Other Poems.* Baton Rouge: Louisiana State University Press.

Dewey, J. (1916). *Democracy and Education.* New York: Macmillan.

Dewey, J. (1934). *Art as Experience.* New York: Minton, Balch.

Dewey, J. (1927/1954). *The Public and Its Problems.* Athens, OH: Swallow Press.

Dewey, J. (1953). *Experience and Education.* New York: Collier Books.

Dewey, J. (1958). *Experience and Nature.* New York: Dover.

Green, T. F. (1971). *The Activities of Teaching.* New York: McGraw-Hill.

Hirsch, E. D. (1987). *Cultural Literacy.* Boston: Houghton-Mifflin.

Iser, W. (1980). *The Act of Reading.* Baltimore: Johns Hopkins University Press.

Merleau-Ponty, M. (1967). *Phenomenology of Perception.* Evanston, IL: Northwestern University Press.

Morrison, T. (1992). *Jazz.* New York: Knopf.

Ryle, G. (1949). *The Concept of Mind.* New York: Dover.

Ryle, G. (1967). "Teaching and Training." In R. S. Peters (Ed.), *The concept of education* (pp. 105–119). London: Routledge and Kegan Paul.

Schutz, A. (1967). *The Problem of Social Reality* (Collected Papers I). The Hague: Martinus Nijhoff.

Twain, M. (1884/1935). *The Adventures of Huckleberry Finn.* New York: Harper's.

West, C. (1993). *Race Matters.* Boston: Beacon Press.

5

Changing Views of Knowledge and Their Impact on Educational Research and Practice

ROBBIE CASE

No matter what else may divide them, most educators are agreed on one general point. A central aim of education is to take the knowledge that has been acquired by one generation and create conditions such that this knowledge can be reacquired and extended by the next. Beyond this general point, views on educational aims and methods diverge quite widely. One reason for this divergence, I believe, is that no general agreement exists on the nature of knowledge itself. In the present chapter I describe three different views of knowledge. I also describe the psychological theories to which these views have led, and the impact they have had on educational research and practice. Finally, I describe the dialogue that is currently going on among educators who hold these different views, and draw some conclusions regarding future developments of a theoretical and practical nature.

Didactic Theories of Learning and Their Roots in British Empiricism

The roots of the first view of knowledge lie in British empiricism, as articulated by David Hume (1748/1965). According to the empiricist position, knowledge of the world is acquired by a process in which the sensory organs first detect stimuli in the external world, and the mind then detects the customary patterns or "conjunctions" in these stimuli. Psychologists who have accepted this view have tended to view the study of children's learning as one whose object is to describe the process by which new stimuli are discriminated (perceptual learning), the process by which correlations or associations among these stimuli are detected (cognitive learning), and the process by which the new knowledge is accessed and used in other contexts (transfer).[1]

In the first half of the twentieth century, the major theories of learning to which the empiricist view gave rise were those of Watson (1914), Thorndike (1926), and Hull (1943). In the field of education, this family of theories gave rise to the technology of *programmed instruction* (Skinner, 1954). The object of this latter endeavor was to put instruction on a more scientific footing by applying the following general procedure: (1) the learning objectives of curricula were to be subjected to detailed *behavioral analysis*; (2) the entering behaviors of learners were to be assessed with carefully constructed tests; and (3) a sequence of steps was to be laid out that would take learners from their entering behaviors to the desired behaviors in a direct and logical fashion.

During the early 1960s, behavioral theories of learning came under fire because they failed to do justice to the organization of human behavior, and the complex inner processes that are responsible for generating it. At about the same time, computers were emerging as an economic force, and a new discipline was being created whose province was the design of software for them. In the end, investigators from the newly formed discipline of computer science joined hands with psychologists, linguists, and other social scientists, in an effort to describe the cognitive processes that are necessary to generate and control complex human behavior. The result was a paradigm shift that became known as the "cognitive revolution" (Gardner, 1985).

The first theories of learning that were generated after the cognitive revolution were ones that described human behavior as resulting from a linear problem-solving process. This process was seen as one in which symbols are manipulated in a sequence of steps, each one of which involves some form of elementary transformation. As subjects analyze a problem, they go through such a sequence in one of two directions: forward from a set of givens, or backward from a goal. They also develop heuristics that enable them to alternate between these methods in a flexible manner, as a function of the progress they are making. Specifying these heuristics, and simulating them on a computer, were important early achievements that helped to launch the cognitive revolution and to convince psychologists that the processes involved in human problem solving could be understood (Newell, Shaw, and Simon, 1958; Miller, Gallanter, and Pribram, 1960).

It was not just problem solving that was seen as depending on complex internal processes. Conceptual and learning motivation came to be seen as depending on such processes as well. As Gagné (1968) showed, the optimal conditions for acquiring complex concepts and problem-solving processes are different from those for acquiring simple discriminations and associations. Specifying the high-level processes that children must master, and the conditions that will foster their mastery, became the focus of a newly invigorated science of instructional programming (Gagné and Briggs, 1979; Glaser, 1985).

As the cognitive revolution gained momentum, and a large number of human activities were subjected to detailed cognitive analysis, it became apparent that many complex forms of learning—learning to carry a coffee cup without spilling it, for example, or learning to recognize the sequence of letters that make up a particular word—are not easily simulated by programming a complex sequence of problem-solving acts or building complex conceptual models. Indeed, they are difficult to simulate by programming a linear sequence of symbolic manipulations of any sort (McLelland, Rumelhart, and Hinton, 1987). The easiest way to simulate these forms of learning is by setting up a complex network of associations, each of whose elements applies in parallel—then letting these weights be "attuned" to a set of environmental contingencies in a relatively autonomous fashion. A new class of associationist models was therefore created in which processing was distributed across a wide number of nodes and took place in parallel rather than in sequence (Rumelhart, McLelland, and Hinton, 1987). Even on tasks where a linear sequence of transformations was required (e.g., in mathematics) it became apparent that many of the most efficient strategies were those with a strong associative component (Siegler and Shrager, 1984). Discovering which tasks are better handled by associative models, which by linear/symbolic models, and which by some combination of the two, is a process that is still very much in progress.

A related issue that is still being investigated has to do with the role of domain-specific knowledge. Both for the "game-like" tasks that were the focus of much early cognitive analysis (e.g., chess), and for the more applied tasks that have become the focus of more recent interest (e.g., reading X rays, solving physics problems), it became apparent that high-level performance was at least as dependent on specific knowledge as it was on general problem-solving heuristics (Simon and Chase, 1973; Simon and Simon, 1978). The sheer amount of specific knowledge that is necessary to become a genuine expert in any area turns out to be formidable, and takes a minimum of ten years to acquire (Hayes, 1981). Characterizing this sort of knowledge and contrasting it with the knowledge of novices or children thus became front-line research activities (Bereiter and Scardamalia, 1985; Chi and Rees, 1983; Larkin, 1985; Simon and Chase, 1973; Simon and Simon, 1978).

Looking back on the cognitive revolution, two generalizations may be drawn. The first is that, "after the revolution," cognition came to be seen in a fashion that was far richer and far more complex than had been the case before it. From general problem-solving heuristics and theories through to task-specific models, procedures, and databases, massive strides were made in understanding the cognitive underpinnings on which high-level human performance depends. The second generalization is that the new forms of cognitive analysis were by and large put in the service of an old epistemology. Whether it was learning to detect 10,000 patterns in chess, or learning to recognize and solve tricky vector problems in mechanics, knowledge was still seen as involving the recognition of complex patterns and the mastery of complex techniques. As a consequence, once the desired cognitive outcomes and potential pitfalls had been thoroughly analyzed, the favored educational technique remained one of direct instruction and practice, under conditions designed to optimize motivation and transfer (e.g., Anderson, 1982).[2]

Constructivist Theories of Learning and Their Roots in Continental Rationalism

The empiricist view of knowledge and its acquisition is not the only one that has had an impact on North American psychology and education during this century. A second view is the rationalist view, whose best known early advocates were Descartes (1647/1954) and Kant (1781/1961). In reaction to the British empiricists,

Kant suggested that knowledge is acquired by a process in which order is imposed by the human mind on the data that the senses provide, not merely detected in them. In effect, Kant's proposal was that learning takes place from the inside out, not just from the outside in. Psychologists who accepted this view thought that the study of children's cognition should entail an elucidation of the order-imposing devices (structures) with which children come equipped at birth, and any changes that may take place in these structures with age. Stated differently, their view was that the central phenomenon that had to be understood was not learning from experience but a more endogenous process they called intellectual development.

In fact, children do appear to come equipped with structures of considerable sophistication at birth (Spelke, 1988). Also, great changes do take place in these structures with age. The most influential psychologist to chart the development of these structures in the first half of this century was Jean Piaget. Drawing on a theory first proposed by Baldwin (1896/1968), Piaget (1970) suggested that four general types of such structures may be described, which build on each other in a progressive fashion. In the first two years of their lives, infants' intellectual structures are entirely *sensorimotor*. At about the age of two, these structures are reworked into symbolic format and assume forms that are successively *intuitive* (or prelogical), *logical* (but concrete), and *formal* in nature. Because these structures vary so widely in the type of order that they impose on the data of sensory experience, the experiences from which children can profit at each stage vary widely as well.

Although Piaget readily acknowledged the importance of children's physical and social experience, he believed that most human environments meet children's minimum needs for environmental input of this sort, and thus have equal developmental potential. The major factor he saw as affecting children's intellectual development was the internal mental activity in which they engage as a result of their universal tendency to explore their environment, to build models of it, and to reflect on the adequacy of these models. Given this view, it was natural for him to favor an educational approach whose prime focus was engaging children's natural curiosity, and providing abundant opportunities for exploration and reflection. Educators who were influenced by his work also tended to favor the approach known as *guided discovery*.[3]

As Piaget's theory became known in North America, serious questions were raised about it. The strongest and most persistent of these criticisms were those directed at the points on which empiricist and rationalist theories were in conflict—namely, (1) the assumption that children's knowledge structures are coherent, logical, and/or "system-wide" rather than domain-specific in their nature, and (2) the assumption that children's structures are acquired or modified by processes that are primarily endogenous or internal in nature. As data challenging these two assumptions accumulated, quite a wide variety of new theories were proposed. One of the most important of these was the "theory theory" proposed by Carey (1985), Wellman (1990), and others (Astington, 1994). According to this theory, children are either born with, or very early construct, naive theories about certain very general domains of their experience: domains such as physical matter (Carey, 1985), causality (Spelke, 1988), living things (Carey, 1985; Chi, 1988), number (Starkey, 1992; Griffin, Case, and Siegler, 1994), and intentionality (Astington, Harris, and Olson, 1989). Then, as children mature, their theories are restructured, often in quite a radical fashion, into theories whose content is different and whose form is much more explicit. This process does not take place in all domains at exactly the same time. In many domains, however, the same four general levels of theory may be discerned (Case and Okamoto, in press).

Two generalizations that apply to all modern theories of development in the constructivist tradition are (1) that they acknowledge the importance of structures that are domain-specific, and (2) that they also acknowledge the importance of external factors in determining the rate of cognitive growth. Educators with a constructivist bent have thus been put in a position where they can make suggestions for instruction that are more detailed and content focused (for example, see Griffin, Case, and Siegler, 1994; Noddings and Maher, 1990; Wiser and Kippman, 1988). Once again, however, there has been more change in the specifics of modern theories in this tradition than in the underlying epistemology (Beilin, 1992; Overton, 1983). Knowledge is still viewed as having its own internal structure, for example, and as being under the control of processes with a strong endogenous component. Moreover, the optimum educational process is still seen as being one in which guided discovery, not direct instruction and practice, plays the major role.

Cultural Views of Learning and Their Roots in Sociohistoric Theory

The third general view that has had an impact on North American psychology is rooted in the sociohistoric epistemologies of Hegel and Marx, and the modern continental philosophers who have followed them (Kaufmann, 1980). According to their view, knowledge does not have its primary origin in the structure of the objective world (as empiricist philosophers suggested). Nor does it have its primary origin in the structure of the subject and his spontaneous cogitation (as rationalist philosophers suggested). It does not even have its primary origin in the interaction of the subject's activity with that of the objective world (as Piaget maintained). Rather, it has its primary origin in the social and material history of the culture of which the subject is a part. If we want to understand the knowledge that children acquire in the course of their development, then, we must first examine the technology that the culture has evolved in the course of its history, and the use to which that technology has been put. We must then examine the modes of discourse and belief systems which support this "praxis," and the ways in which children are initiated into them.

Psychologists who have accepted the sociohistoric view have tended to assume that the study of knowledge acquisition should entail an elucidation of the social, cultural, and physical contexts in which human cultures find themselves, the social, linguistic, and practical intellectual tools that they have developed over the years for coping with these contexts, and the way in which these tools are passed on from one generation to the next. In this latter regard, schooling is often assumed to play a particularly important role, since it is one of the primary social institutions for fostering knowledge acquisition, at least in the modern era.

The best known of the early sociohistoric theories was Vygotsky's (1934/1962). According to Vygotsky, children's thought must be seen in a context that includes both its biological and its cultural evolution. Three of the most important features of humans as a species are (1) that they have developed language: this serves as a "second signal system" that "mediates" between them and the stimuli to which they are exposed; (2) that they fashion their own tools, both physical and intellectual; and (3) that they can transmit the discoveries and inventions of one generation to the next, via institutions such as schooling. From the perspective of Vygotsky's theory, the most important milestone in children's early development is the acquisition of language. First, children master language for social (interpersonal) purposes. Next, language becomes internalized and is also used for intrapersonal (self-regulatory) purposes. As the capacity for self-regulation develops, all cultures recognize the change that takes place in children's capabilities, and begin to assign them some form of independent responsibility (Rogoff, 1990). They also begin to provide them with training in the rudiments of the industrial skills that they will be required to exercise as adults.

In the modern era, this training is likely to take place in school, and to involve an initiation into formal disciplines such as science. As children are engaged in scientific activities and conversations by their teachers, a final transformation in their thought takes place, one that gives them the formal capabilities described by Piaget and many other high-level capabilities as well. Although there may be some (unspecified) biological limits in the rate at which these transformations can take place, the important thing for Vygotsky was that interaction with more knowledgeable adults is capable of extending the level of thought of which children would otherwise be capable. Indeed, Vygotsky did not believe that high-level thought could be acquired without this form of interaction.

Early educational movements that drew on Vygotsky's notions were quite varied (see Moll, 1990). Included would be the movement for teaching language across the curriculum (Vacca and Vacca, 1986), the movement devoted to redesigning curricula in keeping with the most recent advances in the broader culture (e.g., Bruner, 1965), and the movement designed to overcome the disadvantages of special groups of children, by providing them with some form of socially mediated learning (Feuerstein, 1980; Diaz, Neal, and Amaya-Williams, 1991).

As was the case with Piaget's theory, Vygotsky's theory became the focus of a lively debate as its tenets became known in North America. Points that received particular attention were: (1) the preeminent position assigned to language in intellectual development (a point disputed by Piagetians); (2) the system-wide transformation in intellect ascribed to schooling (a point challenged by many empiricists); and (3) the superiority of modern scientific thought and schooling over more traditional thought and instructional methods (a point rejected by many anthropologists).

As these discussions took place, anthropologists and psychologists began to work in closer collaboration, and a new group of theories emerged that might loosely be termed "neo-Vygotskian." The proposed modifications to Vygotsky's theory that are of greatest relevance in the present context are the following: (1) physical and intellectual tools are now seen as having specific, rather than general effects on children's intellectual capabilities (Cole, 1991; Frake, 1985; Olson, 1994); (2) notational systems (diagrams, numerical systems, print, etc.) are now acknowledged to be a vital class of intellectual tool (Cole, 1991; Greeno, Smith, and Moore, 1993; Gardner, 1991; Olson, 1994); (3) the process of extending children's thinking is now seen as taking place via a process that is referred to as "scaffolding" (Wood, Bruner, and Ross, 1976); (4) formal education is now seen as having much to learn from traditional forms of learning such as apprenticeship (Rogoff, 1990; Lave and Wenger, 1991); and (5) intelligence is now explicitly viewed as distributed across a social group rather than being localized exclusively in its individual members (Brown and Duguid, 1991).

As was the case with the other traditions, recent educational work founded on sociohistoric assumptions is a good deal different from that of its predecessors (e.g., Graves, 1983; Lampert, 1990; Brown and Campione, 1994). Although it is different in its specifics, however, the general epistemology that underpins it is little changed. The favored educational method also remains the same—namely, creating a community of authentic praxis in the school, and initiating children into it.

A Comparison of Three Views of Knowledge and Their Embodiment in Philosophy and Psychology

The foregoing scheme is not the only one that is possible for classifying the different views of knowledge that have been proposed in philosophy, or for exposing their influence on contemporary psychological and educational thought.[4] One merit of the foregoing account, however, is that it highlights a number of parallel trends that have taken place over the past 30 years, within and across the different schools of thought.

1. Within each of the three traditions that have been described, it is clear that some form of progressive change has taken place across the last few decades in response to developments that have taken place in other fields. In the empiricist tradition, the move has been toward more sophisticated models of the internal processes that are involved in understanding the world, and in solving the problems that it presents. In the rationalist tradition, the move has been toward a more "modular" conception of thought, and the acknowledgment of external influences on it. In the sociohistoric tradition, the move has been toward a more detailed and contextualized account of different forms of representation, the way in which children are initiated into their use, and the role that they play in constraining and/or potentiating adult patterns of activity.
2. Although each tradition has developed a more sophisticated understanding of

human cognition, and the influences to which it is subject, it is clear that each tradition has also retained certain core assumptions about the nature of human knowledge and the manner in which this knowledge is acquired.

3. If we look across the different traditions rather than within them, it is clear that each tradition has taken a close look at the epistemological assumptions of its predecessor, and then rejected one or more of the assumptions that are at their very core. For rationalists, the fundamental problem with the empiricist tradition is that it views human knowledge in a fashion that is far too atomistic, and far too rooted in external as opposed to internal processes. For sociohistoric theorists, the fundamental problem with the rationalist tradition is that it locates human knowledge in the cognitive processes of the individual, rather than the patterns of activity of the human group. The cognitive result of this process is that the progress that has taken place has had a strongly dialectical character. The affective result is that each group has regarded its own particular view as superior to those of its predecessors.

4. A final trend that may be discerned across the three traditions is the gradual move from pure to applied theory. In each tradition, new principles have been proposed first in philosophy. The implications of these principles have then been worked out, at some later period in time, by psychologists and/or educators. As a result, developments in psychology and education have appeared to "recapitulate" those that took place in philosophy a good deal earlier.

The presence of the last two trends raises an interesting question with regard to the future of the empiricist and rationalist positions: namely, to what extent the sociohistoric approach to development and education is likely to replace its predecessors. My own view is that it will not replace it, since the view that it provides of human knowing—while coherent and extremely valuable—is like that of its predecessors in that it is only a partial one, which must ultimately be supplemented with insights from the other two traditions. In order to appreciate the complementarity of the three positions, rather than just the polarized stances that they have taken toward each others' work, it is worthwhile to review the position that each tradition has developed on the major constructs that have classically fallen within the purview of psychology.

In the *empiricist* tradition the core position is as follows: (1) the *mind* is a device for detecting patterns in the world, and operating on them; (2) our *knowledge* of the world is a repertoire of patterns that we have learned to detect and operations that we can execute on these patterns; (3) *learning* is the process that generates knowledge: it begins when we are exposed to a new pattern, continues as we learn to recognize and respond to that pattern in an efficient manner, and does not end until we can recognize the new pattern in other contexts, and generalize our response in an appropriate manner; (4) *development* is cumulative learning; (5) *intelligence* as an individual trait that sets a limit on the maximum rate at which cumulative learning takes place; (6) *motivation* is a variable that affects the deployment of attention and that is subject to external influence; (7) *education* as the process by which the external conditions that affect children's learning and motivation are brought under control, so that socially desirable goals may be achieved; (8) finally, one of the most powerful educational techniques is *direct instruction followed by practice*, under conditions designed to foster high motivation and broad transfer.

In the *rationalist* tradition, the same set of constructs is viewed quite differently: (1) the *mind* is thought of as an organ whose function is the acquisition of knowledge; (2) *knowledge* is seen as something that is constructed by the mind, and evaluated according to rational criteria such as coherence, consistency, and parsimony; (3) *learning* is seen as the process that takes place when the mind applies an existing structure to new experience in order to understand it; (4) *development* is seen as the long-term change that takes place in the structures to which new experience is assimilated. (These structures are viewed as logical systems in classical Piagetian theory, and as conceptual systems in more recent theory, but the general point remains the same); (5) *intelligence* is seen as the adaptive capability that all children possess, to apply and modify their existing cognitive structures in this fashion; it is also seen as something that grows, since the structures of each successive stage of development are more powerful than those of the previous stage; (6) *motivation* is seen as the set of natural tendencies that draw human beings of all ages toward epistemic activity. (Included in this general category is the natural tendency to explore our physical and social environment, the natural desire to make sense of the relationships that are discovered in this process, and a natural dissatisfaction with explanations that are inconsistent or incoherent); (7) in the best of all possible worlds, *education* is seen as a child-centered process: one that involves the provision of an environment that will stimulate children's natural curiosity and constructive activity, and promote active reflection on the results of that activity; (8) finally, it is believed that these goals are far better achieved via *guided discovery* than direct instruction.

A third perspective on these same constructs is offered in the *sociohistoric* tradition: (1) the human *mind* is seen as being distinctive from the minds of all other species in its capability for developing language, tools, and a system of education; (2) *knowledge* is seen as the creation of a social group, as it engages in its daily interaction and praxis, and both adapts to and transforms the environment around it; (3) *learning* is seen as the process of being initiated into the life of a group, so that one can assume a role in its daily praxis; (4) *development* is seen as involving the emergence and training of capacities that make this sort of initiation possible; (5) like knowledge, *intelligence* is seen as being distributed across a group, and as intimately tied to the tools, artifacts, and symbol systems that the group develops; (6) the primary *motivation* for development and learning is seen as being one of identification: that is, the natural tendency of the young to see themselves as being like their elders, and to look forward to the day when they will assume their elders' roles; (7) *education* is seen as the process by which a community takes charge of its young and moves them from a peripheral to a central role in its daily practices; (8) finally, the optimal form of education is seen as one of *initiation into authentic social praxis*.

As will hopefully be apparent, each of the foregoing views is coherent, and largely nonoverlapping with that of its predecessor. It is for this reason that I believe each subsequent view will continue to stand beside its predecessor, rather than replace it. Although there may well be "turf wars" among the three traditions, it seems far more likely that these will lead to further differentiation and/or integration of the three views than the triumph of one over the others.

The Impact of Three Views of Knowledge on Educational Research and Practice

When viewed on a year-to-year basis, educational change may appear to have little rhyme or reason to it. Since education is a social activity, this is hardly surprising. We would expect that each new wind of social change would have some impact on the field, moving it in directions that would be hard to anticipate. Still, as pointed out in the introduction, education is also an activity whose purpose is the transmission of knowledge. Thus we would expect that any historical change in the understanding of knowledge would constitute a deep and powerful force for change itself: an underlying current, if you will, propelling an entire body of water in a constant direction, in spite of surface changes in the wind and waves.

If one surveys the educational scene in North America over the last 30 years, it is possible to observe such a trend. That is to say, it is possible to observe the influence of the three evolving epistemologies that have just been described, with a gradual but incomplete shift taking place from an empiricist, to a rationalist, and most recently to a sociohistoric point of view. In the sections that follow, I present three illustrations of this trend.

Example 1: Educational Assessment and Research

In the 1960s, a variety of factors combined to produce a worldwide recognition of the importance of education in the process of economic and technical development. With this recognition came the realization that there was relatively little hard evidence on the effectiveness of different kinds of educational practice. If education were to be put on the same scientific basis as such practical fields as agriculture and medicine, it was reasoned, then a similar program of basic research and development would be necessary. In the United States, fueled partly by the Soviet launching of Sputnik, the National Institute of Education was established, and federal funding for educational research was made available (Brademas, 1991). In the next two decades there was a surge in educational research, one that produced a tenfold increase in the membership of organizations such as the American Educational Research Association (Gage, 1991). As this research enterprise got underway, changes naturally took place in the way in which a wide variety of substantive problems were understood and investigated. These specific changes took place, however, against the background of change of a more fundamental epistemological nature.

Early Influence of Empiricism   The dominant epistemology at the time the new research effort got started was empiricist. As applied to the conduct of science, this view held that scientific inquiry should begin with careful observation of some empirical phenomenon, and the recording of these observations in an objective, precise, and systematic manner. As observational data were accumulated, the next step should be to formulate a set of tentative hypotheses concerning the factors that produce the phenomenon in question, or that regulate it. Once formulated, these hypotheses should be tested in a series of carefully controlled experiments. Finally, the experimental data should be used to stimulate some further refinement or revision of the hypothesis, which would then motivate a new wave of experiments. In its most extreme form, as developed by the Viennese circle of philosophers known as logical positivists, the view was that any enterprise that did not investigate phenomena in this manner, using variables that could be defined in precise, operational terms, could not be called "scientific."

When Piaget's work was first translated into English (Flavell, 1963), the empiricist view of science was at its apogee. As a result, educational investigators tended to react against the theory, not just because it assigned a weak role to teaching as an instrument of intellectual growth but because the methods that had been used to develop the theory did not seem sufficiently scientific. To the empiricist, Piaget's clinical method of interviewing children seemed subjective and unreliable. The number of subjects that he used also seemed too small, and his sampling procedures too unsystematic to justify the general conclusions that he drew. Finally, the overall theoretical structure that he proposed was seen as too vague to operationalize, and hence untestable. Most early research was thus devoted to checking Piaget's findings with better techniques, or attempting to show that the insights on which he focussed could be taught.

Introduction of a Constructivist Viewpoint   As empiricist epistemology began to decline in its influence, so did the corresponding view of science and scientific research. In the field of education, Thomas Kuhn's *The Structure of Scientific Revolutions* (1962) served as a catalyst for this change, and a handbook for those who participated in it. According to Kuhn, scientific knowledge was not really accumulated in the sort of patient inductive manner that empiricist philosophers had assumed. Rather it took place in waves, with periods of "normal science" being punctuated by scientific "revolutions." Normal science, according to Kuhn, was essentially a problem-solving process. It consisted of attempts to explain a variety of specific phenomena using the general theory that was dominant in the current era. When events appeared that were difficult to reconcile with this theory, a particularly vigorous round of problem solving would be triggered, and a variety of creative explanations for the anomaly would be advanced and tested. No matter how bold or elegant a theory, however, the time eventually came when the experimental anomalies that it had helped to reveal could not be explained away. At that point—by a process that Kuhn did not attempt to explicate—a new theory would be proposed, and a new paradigm for research established. The processes that took place in such a shift were likely to be quite turbulent—hence the term "revolution."

Kuhn's theory seemed better able to describe the major developments that had taken place in modern physics at the turn of the century than views that were more empiricist in nature. It thus received a wide degree of attention among philosophers of science. A philosopher who drew on Kuhn's work and attempted to extend it along rationalist lines was Lakatos (1970). Using the historical record in physics and astronomy, Lakatos attempted to provide a more detailed account of the developmental life cycle of a general scientific theory, one that preserved a role for rational criteria in determining the new problems that it brought to light, the changes that were introduced as a result, and whether or not these changes were regarded as "progressive." The view of science that emerged from his work was of an enterprise that produced knowledge that was never certain but in which the relative adequacy of two different theories could still be determined in a rational manner (e.g., by noting which theory was more capable of generating a program of research that was "conceptually and empirically progressive").

The new view of science had a strong impact on educational research. From a substantive point of view, the effect was to move researchers toward an interest in the constructive activity of students who were engaged in the learning process —in particular, the learning strategies they used and the naive concepts and theories that they constructed (Carey, 1985; Case and Bereiter, 1984; Pressley, 1982). From a methodological point of view, the effect was to move researchers toward an interest in measures that were less superficial and more oriented toward gaining information about children's general level of understanding (cf. Biggs and Collis, 1982; Haertel and Wiley, 1993). Finally, from a theoretical point of view, the effect was to put cognitive developmental theory on an equal footing with learning theory in the field of educational psychology.

In the field of cognitive development, both the method and the models that were developed were often drawn from contemporary biology rather than 19th-century physics (Piaget, 1970). Modern evolutionary biology devotes a great deal of effort constructing, a posteriori, models of the structural changes that have taken place across species over long periods of time. It also devotes a great deal of effort to theorizing about the functional causes or consequences of these changes. Finally, it devotes a great deal of effort to explicating the general theoretical superstructure that gives these structural and functional analyses meaning, and ensuring that local interpretations are consistent with this general structure. As the field developed, the activities began to play a role equal to the observation, induction and operational definition that had been stressed earlier.

Influence of the Sociohistoric Perspective   The rationalist philosophers who followed Kuhn were by no means the only ones who took his work seriously. Other philosophers took his descriptions of scientific change equally seriously, but viewed scientific revolutions in social rather than rational terms (Feyerabend, 1970). This new work had great appeal to the generation of educational researchers who had been brought up on Bruner's and Vygotsky's work, and who looked more toward anthropology than physics or biology for their guidance on appropriate scientific methods. From their perspective, scientific theories were always social creations, and the forces that led one theory to triumph over another were more likely to be social than rational in nature. In order to understand the process by which scientists construct knowledge according to this view, we must first understand the social and historical context in which that construction takes place.

From a substantive point of view, the effect of this position was to interest investigators in exploring the social dynamics of education, including the process by which new meanings are negotiated among children, or between children and their teachers, and the role of new technologies in changing children's social and intellectual life (Cole, in press; Pea, 1987; Greeno, Collins, and Resnick, 1995). From a methodological point of view, the effect was to interest a new generation of educational researchers in the use of ethnographic techniques for describing educational practice (Spindler and Spindler, 1987). Finally, from a theoretical point of view, the effect was to interest investigators in theories that were context-specific rather than general in nature (Lave and Wenger, 1991; Newman, Griffin, and Cole, 1991).

Example 2: The Reform Movement in Mathematics Education

In 1957 the same crisis that led to the establishment of educational research as a major enterprise in the United States also led to a reexamination of curricula that were currently being used in the public schools. To those interested in maintaining America's scientific and technological advantage, the elementary mathematics curriculum seemed little more than an aggregation of algorithms. Worse still, the conceptual foundation on which these algorithms were based seemed superficial, since it took no account of the considerable developments that had taken place in mathematics during the twentieth century. All in all, then, mathematics as it was taught in elementary school seemed more appropriate for training nineteenth-century bank clerks than for training children who would be expected to function in advanced technical and scientific occupations at the end of the twentieth century. To remedy this situation, it was decided that the best minds in mathematics should be brought together with the best minds in education, and that a major curricular reform effort should be initiated (Bruner, personal communication). In fact, just such a series of meetings did take place, and a radically different curriculum was the outcome. The *New Math*, as it became known, made a radical break with the past, in the hopes of producing a better preparation for the future. The curriculum started out by teaching the language and operations of set theory rather than algorithms for performing addition and subtraction. It then went on to introduce children to the discipline of modern mathematics in a principled and well organized fashion.

While the new curriculum represented a great improvement from the point of view of professional mathematicians, it encountered several major problems when it was implemented in the schools. For one thing, classroom teachers were rather intimidated by the new curriculum, since they had not been taught in this fashion themselves, and felt beyond their depth with regard to content. For another thing, parents—although at first excited that their children were learning things that they themselves did not understand—quickly became disenchanted when they discovered that, even after several years in such programs, children still did not appear to have mastered the basic mathematical operations that they needed for their everyday life. Finally, in many instances, the children themselves found the programs rather confusing.

Many of the attempts to remedy these problems were rather superficial. Fueled by a new conservatism on the political scene, they involved little more than a return to the "basics" that had originally been judged to be so problematic. This was by no means universally the case, however. Programs were developed that attempted to address the problems that had arisen with the new math without simply returning to the old content and methods. It is in this cutting-edge work—which became known as the "reform movement" in mathematics—that the influence of a changing epistemology may once again be seen.

Empiricist Approach to the Problem   Consider first a program that was called *Real Math* (Willowby, Bereiter, Hinton, and Rubenstein, 1981). This program brought back an emphasis on arithmetic algorithms to the elementary school curriculum. However, it did so in a fashion that was mathematically rigorous and that was designed to teach children the reason that the algorithms worked the way they did. The program also took into account the most common errors that children made in learning elementary mathematics, and attempted to head these off by building on children's previous knowledge on the one hand, and giving them the tools to understand the difficulty with their incorrect answers, on the other. Finally, the program provided extensive opportunities for children to apply the concepts and algorithms that they were taught to problems of a more challenging nature: problems that were set in imaginary (often humorous) contexts, as well as realistic contexts taken from everyday life. Using the classification scheme that was developed in the previous section, we could say that the general epistemology that underlay this program was empiricist in nature, and that the primary educational technique was direct instruction and practice. Not surprisingly, the program was subjected to a lengthy period of empirical testing before it was marketed. Many of its learning activities were also subjected to detailed task analysis.

Constructivist Approaches to the Problem   Consider next a program called *Math Their Way*, which became popular during the same general time period. Although this program did not explicitly derive from any particular body of theory or research, it fit well with the theory of development that was articulated by Piaget, and that was being explored and taught by developmental psychologists during this time period. One major way in which the program differed from others was that the formal notation of mathematics was greatly delayed. Another way in which it differed was in its emphasis on concrete "manipulatives." Such manipulatives had been used as a vehicle for direct teaching of quantitative mathematical procedures in Real Math. In Math Their Way, however, they played a much more prominent role, since they were thought to be the only real vehicles for providing young children with the opportunity to make discoveries about the world of number. Exploratory activities with manipulatives thus comprised nearly half of the kindergarten year, a third of the first-grade year, and a fourth of the second-grade year. This emphasis fit well with the notion that this was the stage of "concrete operations."

A program in the same general category as Math Their Way was *Cognitively Guided Instruction* (Carpenter and Fennema, 1988). The primary emphasis in this program was not on new curriculum materials. Rather, it was on new methods for introducing teachers to constructivist ideas and methods. Teachers who participated in the program continued teaching in their regular classrooms, but took a class at the university in parallel with their teaching. In the course of their studies, they were introduced to the emerging literature on children's mathematics learning. The focus was on the major types of solution strategies children employ in solving math word problems and the developmental time course that these strategies normally take (Carpenter and Moser, 1984; Riley, Greeno, and Heller, 1983). Teachers were asked to monitor children individually as they moved through these developmental sequences, and to present them with tasks that would support their transition to more sophisticated concepts and strategies. At every step there was a great emphasis on communicating the idea that children's own constructions were valued, and that there are many different strategies that can yield the correct answer to any problem. In its neutral position on the importance of manipulatives, and its emphasis on the solving of conventional word problems, Cognitively Guided Instruction was different from Math Their Way. In its belief that children are active constructors of their own knowledge, however, and that education should support this process rather than adapting a didactic stance, it was similar.

Sociohistoric Approaches to Mathematics Learning   Consider finally two approaches that are of more recent origin still and that have espoused a sociohistoric epistemology. The first is a curriculum designed by Paul Cobb and his colleagues (Yackel, Cobb, et al., 1990). For Cobb, the process of acquiring and using mathematical concepts is presumed to be one of acculturation. The object is not just to get individual children involved in a process of construction but to create a mathematics community in which students are continually sharing their insights and engaging in dialogue on the nature of these experiences, and the form in which they can best be represented with symbols. Students work in small groups on a problem, and then communicate their findings to the whole class. At other times, the teacher leads a discussion in which everyone participates. As the students' understanding of the principles of mathematics grows and changes, so too does their ability to communicate those understandings, and to negotiate new meanings, as a member of a mathematical community.

A second approach in the same general category is the one being developed by Magdalene Lampert (1990, see also Lampert, Rittenhouse and Crumbaugh, this volume, chap. 31). Like Cobb, Lampert is interested in setting up communities of mathematicians. Partly because she works with older children, however, and partly because she takes her model of what real mathematicians do from other sources, her focus is different. Her main emphasis is on setting up socially agreed upon rules for mathematical discussion, inquiry, and proof: rules that will work in the classroom, and that will enable children to engage in the sort of interchange that she presumes is central to the work of real mathematicians. In spite of these differences, her primary method, like Cobb's, can be classified as one of initiating children into a community engaged in authentic social praxis.

Example 3: Early Educational Programs for Children at Risk

A third sequence of events that took place in the 1960s—alongside the new emphasis on educational research and curricular reform—was that a new interest developed in the plight of students who are at risk for school failure for social or economic reasons. Like the previous movements, this one was fueled by political developments that were taking place on a broader stage, which in the United States included the Civil Rights Movement and the War on Poverty.

Empiricist Approach to the Problem   From the point of view of empiricist theory, the problem that children experience in school, if they grow up in poverty, is that they have not been exposed to the sort of social and physical stimulation that is necessary in order to fully master the skills on which successful school performance is dependent. There are a number of skills—from those involving language through to those involving enumeration, problem solving, and sustained attention—which children from advantaged homes do not have to learn, and which are necessary prerequisites for school success. Since children from low socioeconomic homes are demonstrably weak in these skills, what they need is some sort of early remediation, so that they will adapt to school more easily, and begin it on an equal footing with their advantaged peers (Deutsch, 1965). It was this general line of reasoning that was the basis for the creation of Project Head Start and television programs such as Sesame Street. By no means were all programs associated with Head Start academic in nature. However, many of those that were associated with it used a general approach that was empiricist in its assumptions and that involved substantial doses of direct instruction followed by practice under conditions designed to foster high motivation and transfer (Bereiter and Engleman, 1966).

Constructivist Approach to the Problem   As Piaget's theory became widely known, and the constructivist epistemology on which it was based became accepted, the notion that children from certain environments had a set of "deficits" that good instructional programming could "remediate" was called into question. When low SES children were given Piagetian assessments, they appeared to show the same curiosity and desire for knowledge as high SES students. They also appeared to approach the problems they were presented, and to reason about them, in a similar fashion. The notion that they were "culturally deprived" thus appeared to be a myth, and a potentially pernicious one at that (Ginsburg, 1972). Still, the problem of "mismatch" was clearly a serious one (Gaudia, 1972). The curriculum of the school tended to be designed for the mainstream student, and the general conceptual understandings it presupposed were those that mainstream children had constructed by the beginning of first grade. What was needed, it seemed, were school programs that offered a better match to the conceptual structures that low SES children brought with them when they started their formal school experience.

In recent years, programs based on this sort of constructivist analysis have begun to appear. One is a program called Rightstart, which is designed to stimulate children's engagement with mathematics, and foster the development of a general "number sense" that is appropriate for use with existing school curricula (Griffin, Case, and Siegler, 1994). Another is the phonic awareness program designed by Bradley and Bryant (1983). In contrast to programs designed to teach specific skills that children are lacking, these programs are designed to foster the development of a more general understanding on which the learning of specific skills appears to be dependent. They are also designed to do so in a manner that meets the learning needs of low SES populations, using an approach that might best be described as guided discovery.

Sociohistoric Approaches to the Problem   At the same time as the foregoing programs were being implemented and tested, a new generation of programs was also being developed that was rooted in sociohistoric theory. Three general approaches have been implemented so far and are worthy of mention:

1. *Community based learning centers.* This approach has been taken by Cole (1990, in press), who has devised a program that can be instituted by local communities in libraries, Boys' Clubs, YMCAs, etc. Cole's program involves an innovative set of rules for social engagement, the opportunity to interact with computers and other modern technology, and the opportunity for children to participate in electronic networks with children in similar and dissimilar social environments. The idea behind the program is to create conditions for successful development and learning outside school, which will bypass some of the social barriers that are present in conventional schooling and permit skills such as early reading and mathematics to be acquired in a context that is more authentic.

2. *Culturally appropriate curricula.* A second approach is to alter the curriculum and form of instruction of the elementary school, so that it will be rooted in the culture of those who encounter it. This sort of effort is seen as particularly important in certain "gatekeeping" subjects such as mathematics. The prealgebra program developed by Moses (1992) for African-American children has these features, although it also contains a number of more substantive innovations that make it more widely applicable. So too is the movement for mother tongue literacy programs (Cazden, 1992).

3. *Communities of learners.* A final approach is one that stresses the creation of "communities of learners" (Brown and Campione, 1994). This program offers children the realistic possibility of assuming high-level roles, roles that often require they exercise genuine intellectual leadership, even in their first few years of schooling (e.g., teacher, researcher, group leader). Among the techniques that are used for permitting low SES students to assume such roles are: (a) allowing students a genuine role in setting the goals of the curriculum; (b) using "jigsaw learning" to

introduce new content (this is a technique wherein every child is responsible for learning some particular part of the curriculum, and teaching it to others); (c) cross-age tutoring (where older children act as instructors for younger children); (d) the use of student-created examinations (where children analyze their own learning, and create test items to assess it); and (e) reciprocal teaching (where students take turns in teaching and monitoring each other).

Once again, although these three programs differ widely in their details, what they share in common with each other and with other innovative approaches (e.g., Scardamalia, Bereiter, and Lamon, 1994) is a commitment to setting up a community of learners that is engaged in authentic social praxis, and initiating children into such a community in such a fashion that they can play an increasingly central role in it.

Epistemological Influences on Research and Practice   The general point that I have tried to make in this section is a simple one, but worthy of restatement. If we examine the trends in educational research and practice over the last 30 years, we see a pattern that is quite similar to the one that has been observed in psychology and that indeed has been influenced by it. Although many of the developments that have taken place have been in response to changing political, social, or disciplinary conditions, these changes have nonetheless taken place against a background that has included a changed view of knowledge, and the conditions that are likely to optimize its acquisition. The change in question is one that has involved a gradual evolution from an empiricist to a rationalist to a sociohistoric stance. This change has not been complete. The sociohistoric view has not completely replaced the constructivist view, and the constructivist view has not completely replaced the empiricist view. Rather, as in psychology, the new views have come to stand beside the previous ones, and—not without some jostling—come to be accepted as necessary partners in producing educational change of a significant and lasting nature.

General Summary and Conclusion

Three general conceptual frameworks have contributed to our understanding of knowledge and its acquisition during this century: (1) the empiricist, (2) the rationalist, and (3) the sociohistoric. As we have made the transition to the modern era, and grappled with the implications of the revolutions that have taken place (and are continuing) in a number of different spheres, each of these frameworks has undergone a major revision. In addition to the progression that has taken place *within* each conceptual framework, a progression has also taken place *across* frameworks, with each successive framework taking the preceding one as its starting point, moving beyond it in some fashion, and ultimately altering the context in which the previous framework must be understood.

In philosophy, the movement across frameworks took place during the late nineteenth and early twentieth centuries. This movement was then recapitulated in psychology and education during the latter half of the twentieth century. In effect, then, each discipline may now be seen as having three successive frameworks, each of which has some region of overlap with its predecessor, but each of which also has an independent focus and sphere of influence.

Looking to the Future   If the foregoing description is accurate in its general outline, what trends can we anticipate, as we look toward the future? Two possibilities seem particularly likely.

1. The first is that the overall process that has been described will continue, with further advances in epistemology continuing to influence work in psychology and education. As we are all no doubt aware, the last few years have seen a lively debate between classical and "postmodern" philosophers on the relativity of all knowledge, and the possibility of distinguishing scientific from nonscientific knowledge on any grounds other than social ones (Rabinow, 1984; Rorty, 1991; Harvey, 1990). The first prediction we can venture is that—as this controversy moves forward—the results will have the same sort of cascading influence on psychological and educational thought as have previous epistemological debates of a similar nature.

2. The second prediction has to do with the dialogue that can be expected among the three existing perspectives within psychology and education. If there really are regions of overlap among the three positions but each nevertheless has a distinctive core, then it seems likely that there is much to be gained from each tradition becoming aware of the others, and sorting out which issues or domains are common and which are not. If a process of dialogue is initiated, it also seems likely that each tradition will have something special to contribute to the ultimate outcome.

For empiricists, a major question will be whether or not the different traditions suggest propositions whose truth value can be evaluated in some sort of empirical manner. For example, if educators with a sociohistoric perspective assert that collaborative learning is superior to direct instruction, then empiricists might want to know what aspect of learning it is believed to be valuable for, and to test this claim empirically. For rationalists, clarifying the core postulates of each theory is likely to become a priority, as is working toward a synthesis that is conceptually progressive. (For preliminary attempts see Case, 1992; in press; Greeno, Collins, and Resnick, in press.) Finally, for sociohistoric theorists, exposing the metaphorical core of each view, and outlining the social consequences for those who hold it, are likely to be seen as important activities.

I have spoken about continued epistemological advances and a dialogue among different groups of educators and psychologists as two distinct trends, each of which may be extrapolated into the future. In fact, however, these two trends are actually just one. That is, one way of looking at the postmodern debate in philosophy is that it is a process of dialogue among philosophers that has been initiated by sociohistoric claims of exclusive rights to understand knowledge and the process of its acquisition—and that much of the energy that the position generates comes from empirical and rationalist reactions against this territorial claim and the transfer of power that would take place if it were not contested. As we move into the "post-postmodern era," then, it seems possible that territorial issues of this sort will become clearer in all three disciplines and that attempts at boundary delineation and/or synthesis can be anticipated.

One final point is worth making in conclusion. There is a tendency among practitioners to view philosophic debates—especially in an area as abstract as epistemology—as arid and abstruse, if not completely sterile. What I have tried to show in the present chapter is that this is not the case: that epistemological positions have practical consequences that are of great concern to psychologists and educators, and touch them in a direct and vital manner. In recent years, contemporary theorists from several different disciplines have converged on the notion that scientific and technical knowledge are likely to play a more central role in the future than they have in the past, and to become increasingly central to our economic, social, and physical well being (Drucker, 1994; Galbraith, 1967; Keating and Mustard, 1993; Porter, 1990; Rohlen, 1994; Rosenberg and Birdzell, 1986). If this is so, then we may perhaps hazard a more sweeping generalization on the potential impact of epistemological debates as we move toward the "knowledge-based society" of the future. This is that the general way in which we view knowledge and its acquisition is likely to have an increasingly large impact: one that transcends the particular disciplines that have been the focus of the present chapter, and ripples out to touch the full range of disciplines, activities, and institutions by which our social and economic life is bounded.

Acknowledgment

Preparation of this chapter was facilitated by a fellowship from the Canadian Institute for Advanced Research. The author is indebted to John Breuer, Andre Carus, Howard Gardner, and David Olson for their comments on a earlier draft.

Notes

1. A closely related objective has been to study individual differences in each one of these processes (Spearman, 1922; Terman, 1916).
2. For an exception, see Collins (1985).
3. This general approach, coupled with specific content drawn from Piaget's theory, was used in the kindergarten program developed by Kamii and De Vries (1977), and in the science curriculum that was developed by Karplus (1964). The same approach also featured very prominently in the science programs that were developed in the United Kingdom (Nuffield Foundation, 1964).
4. For alternative, though related, schemes see Langer (1969), Overton (1983), or Pepper (1975).

References

Anderson, J. R. (1982). Acquisition of a cognitive skill. *Psychological Review, 89*, 369–406.

Astington, J. W. (1994). *The child's discovery of mind.* New York: Cambridge University Press.

Astington, J. W., Harris, P. L., and Olson, D. R. (1989). *Developing theories of mind.* New York: Cambridge University Press.

Baldwin, J. M. (1896/1968). *Mental development in the child and the race.* New York: August M. Kelly.

Baratta-Lorton, M. (1976). *Mathematics their way.* Menlo Park, CA: Addison-Wesley.

Beilin, H. (1992). Piaget's new theory. In *Piaget's theory: prospects and possibilities* (pp. 1–19). Hillsdale, NJ: Lawrence Erlbaum.

Bereiter, C. M. and Engleman, S. (1966). *Teaching the disadvantaged in the preschool.* Englewood Cliffs, NJ: Prentice-Hall.

Bereiter, C. M. and Scardamalia, M. (1985). Cognitive coping strategies and the problem of inert knowledge. In S. Chipman, J. W. Segal, and R. Glaser (Eds.), *Thinking and learning skills* (Vol. 2) *Research and open questions* (pp. 65–80). Hillsdale, NJ: Lawrence Erlbaum.

Biemiller, A. F. (1993). Lake Wobegon Revisited. *Educational Researcher, 22* (9), 7–12.

Biggs, J. and Collis, K. (1982). *Evaluating the quality of learning: The SOLO taxonomy.* New York: Academic Press.

Brademas, J. (1991). Melding education and politics. In D. L. Burleson (Ed.), *Reflections: Personal essays by 33 distinguished educators* (pp. 24–31). Bloomington, IN: Phi Delta Kappan.

Bradley, L. and Bryant, P. (1983). Rhyme and reason in reading and spelling. *International academy for research in learning disabilities* (Monograph 1). Ann Arbor, MI.

Brown, A. L. and Campione, J. C. (1994). Guided discovery in a community of learners. In K. McGilly (Ed.), *Classroom lessons* (pp. 229–272). Cambridge: Bradford/MIT Books.

Brown, J. S. and Duguid, P. (1991). Organizational learning and communities of practice: Toward a unified view of working, learning, and innovation. *Organization Science, 2*, 40–57.

Bruner, J. S. (1965). *Man: A course of study.* Cambridge: Educational Services.

Carey, S. (1985). *Conceptual change in childhood.* Cambridge: MIT Press.

Carpenter, T. P. and Fennema, E. (1988). Research and cognitively guided instruction. In E. Fennema, T. P. Carpenter, and S. J. Lamon (Eds.), *Integrating research on teaching and learning mathematics* (pp. 2–19). Madison: Wisconsin Center for Educational Research.

Carpenter, T. P. and Moser, J. M. (1984). The acquisition of addition and subtraction concepts in grades one through three. *Journal of Research in Mathematics Education, 15*, 179–202.

Case, R. (1985). *Intellectual development: Birth to adulthood.* Orlando, FL: Academic Press.

Case, R. (1992). *The mind's staircase: Exploring the conceptual underpinnings of children's thought and knowledge.* Hillsdale, NJ: Lawrence Erlbaum.

Case, R. (in press). Classical and contemporary views of children's cognitive structures. In R. Case and Y. Okamoto (Eds.), The role of central conceptual structures in the development of children's thought. *Monographs of the Society for Research in Child Development.*

Case, R. and Bereiter, C. M. (1984). From behaviorism to cognitive behaviorism to cognitive development: Steps in the evolution of instructional design. *Instructional Science, 13*, 141–158.

Case, R. and Okamoto, Y. (in press). The role of central conceptual structures in the development of children's thought. *Monographs of the Society for Research in Child Development*.

Cazden, C. B. (1992). Richmond Road: A multilingual/multicultural primary school in Auckland. In C. B. Cazden, *Whole language plus: Essays on literacy in the United States and New Zealand* (pp. 242–273). New York: Teachers College Press.

Chi, M. T. H. (1988). Children's lack of access and knowledge reorganization: An example from the concept of animism. In M. Perlmutter and F. E. Weinert (Eds.), *Memory development: Universal changes and individual differences* (pp. 169–194). Hillsdale, NJ: Lawrence Erlbaum.

Chi, M. T. H. and Rees, E. (1983). A learning framework for development. *Contributions to Human Development, 9,* 71–107.

Cole, M. (1990, May). *Cultural psychology: Some general principles and a concrete example.* Paper presented at the second international congress of activity theory, Lahti, Finland.

Cole, M. (1991). Cognitive development and formal schooling: The evidence from cross cultural research. In L. C. Moll (Ed.), *Vygotsky and education: Instructional implications and applications of sociohistorical psychology* (pp. 89–110). New York: Cambridge University Press.

Cole, M. (in press). *Culture in mind.* Cambridge: Harvard University Press.

Collins, A. (1985). Teaching reasoning skills. In S. Chipman, J. W. Segal, and R. Glaser (Eds.), *Thinking and learning skills* (Vol. 2.) *Research and open questions* (pp. 579–586). Hillsdale, NJ: Lawrence Erlbaum.

Descartes, R. (1641/1647/1954). *Philosophical writings.* Toronto: Nelson.

Deutsch, M. (1965). The role of social class in language development and cognition. *American Journal of Orthopsychiatry, 25,* 78–88.

Diaz, R. M., Neal, C. J., and Amaya–Williams, M. (1991). The social origins of self regulation. In L. C. Moll (Ed.), *Vygotsky and education: Instructional implications and applications of sociohistorical psychology* (pp. 127–154). New York: Cambridge University Press.

Drucker, P. F. (1994, November). The age of social transformation. *Atlantic Monthly,* pp. 53–75.

Feuerstein, R. (1980). *Instrumental enrichment: An intervention program for cognitive modifiability.* Baltimore: University Park Press.

Feyerabend, P. (1970). Against method. *Minnesota studies in the philosophy of science,* 4. Minneapolis: University of Minnesota Press.

Flavell, J. H. (1963). *The developmental psychology of Jean Piaget.* Princeton, NJ: Van Nostrand.

Frake, C. O. (1985). Cognitive maps of time and tide among medieval seafarers. *Man, 20,* 254–270.

Gage, N. (1991). Reflections on research in teaching. In D. L. Burleson (Ed.), *Reflections: Personal essays by 33 distinguished educators* (pp. 173–187). Bloomington, IN: Phi Delta Kappan.

Gagne, R. M. (1968). *The conditions of learning.* (2nd edn.) New York: Holt Rinehart and Winston.

Gagne, R. M. and Briggs, L. J. (1979). *Principles of instructional design.* New York: Holt.

Galbraith, J. K. (1967). *The new industrial state.* Boston: Houghton Mifflin.

Gardner, H. (1985). *The mind's new science: A history of the cognitive revolution.* New York: Basic Books.

Gardner, H. (1991). *The unschooled mind.* New York: Basic Books.

Gaudia, G. (1972). Race, social class, and age of achievement of conservation of Piaget's tasks. *Developmental Psychology, 6,* 158–165.

Ginsburg, H. (1972). *The myth of the deprived child.* Englewood Cliffs, NJ: Prentice-Hall.

Glaser, R. (1985). Learning and instruction: A letter for a time capsule. In S. Chipman, J. W. Segal, and R. Glaser (Eds.), *Thinking and learning skills* (Vol. 2): *Research and open questions* (pp. 609–618). Hillsdale, NJ: Lawrence Erlbaum.

Graves, D. H. (1983). *Writing: Teachers and writers at work.* London: Heinemann Educational Books.

Greeno, J. G., Collins, A., and Resnick, L. (in press). Cognition and learning. In R. Calfee and D. Berliner (Eds.), *Handbook of Educational Psychology.*

Greeno, J. G., Smith, D. R., and Moore, J. L. (1993). Transfer of situated learning. In D. K. Detterman and R. J. Sternberg (Eds.), *Transfer on trial: Intelligence, cognition, and instruction* (pp. 99–167). Norwood, NJ: Ablex.

Griffin, S. A., Case, R., and Siegler, R. S. (1994). Rightstart: Providing the central conceptual prerequisites for first formal learning of arithmetic to students at risk for school failure. In K. McGilly (Ed.), *Classroom lessons: Integrating cognitive theory and classroom practice* (pp. 25–50). Cambridge: M.I.T. Press.

Haertel, E. H. and Wiley, D. E. (1993). Representations of ability structures: Implications for testing. In N. Frederiksen, R. J. Mislevy, and I. I. Bejar (Eds.), *Test theory for a new generation of tests* (pp. 359–384). Hillsdale, NJ: Lawrence Erlbaum.

Harvey, D. O. (1990). *The condition of post modernism.* New York: Scribner.

Hayes, J. R. (1981). *The complete problem solver.* Philadelphia: Franklin Institute Press.

Hull, C. (1943). *Principles of behavior.* New York: Appleton-Century-Crofts.

Hume, D. (1748/1965). *An inquiry concerning human understanding.* New York: Bobbs-Merrill.

Kamii, C. and DeVries, R. (1977). Piaget for early education. In M. C. Day and R. Parker (Eds.), *The preschool in action.* Boston: Allyn and Bacon.

Kant, I. (1781/1961). *Critique of pure reason.* New York: Doubleday.

Karplus, R. (1964). The science curriculum improvement study. In R. E. Ripple and V. N. Rockcastle (Eds.), *Piaget rediscovered* (pp. 113–118). Ithaca, NY: Cornell School of Education Press.

Kaufmann, W. (1980). *Discovering the mind: Goethe, Kant, and Hegel.* New York: McGraw-Hill.

Keating, D. P. and Mustard, J. F. (1993). Social and economic factors in human development. In D. Ross (Ed.), *Family security in insecure times* (pp. 87–105). Ottawa: National Forum on Family Security.

Kuhn, T. S. (1962). *The structure of scientific revolutions.* Chicago: University of Chicago Press.

Lakatos, I. (1970). Falsification and the methodology of scientific research programmes. In I. Lakatos and A. Musgrave (Eds.), *Criticism and the growth of knowledge* (pp. 91–196). New York: Cambridge University Press.

Langer, J. (1969). *Theories of development.* New York: Holt Rinehart and Winston.

Lampert, M. (1990). When the problem is not the question and the solution is not the answer. *American Educational Research Journal, 27,* 29–63.

Larkin, J. H. (1985). Understanding, problem representations and skill in physics. In S. Chipman, J. W. Segal, and R. Glaser (Eds.), *Thinking and learning skills* (Vol. 2) *Research and open questions* (pp. 141–160). Hillsdale, NJ: Lawrence Erlbaum.

Lave, J. and Wenger, E. (1991). *Situated learning: Legitimate peripheral participation.* Cambridge, England: Cambridge University Press.

McClelland, J. L., Rumelhart, D. E., and Hinton, G. E. (1987). The appeal of parallel distributed processing. In D. E. Rumelhart and J. L. McClelland (Eds.), *Parallel distributed processing: Explorations in the microstructure of cognition* (Vol. 1) (pp. 3–44). Cambridge: MIT Press.

Miller, G. A., Galanter, E., and Pribram, K. H. (1960). *Plans and the structure of behavior.* New York: Holt, Rinehart, and Winston.

Moll, L. M. (1990). *Vygotsky and education: Instructional implications and applications of sociohistorical psychology.* Cambridge, England: Cambridge University Press.

Moses, R. (1992). Multiplying the meagre numbers. *Science, 258,* 1200–1201.

Newell, A., Shaw, J. C., and Simon, H. A. (1958). Elements of a theory of human problem solving. *Psychological Review, 65,* 151–166.

Newman, D., Griffin, P., and Cole, M. (1991). *The construction zone: Working for cognitive change in school.* New York: Cambridge University Press.

Noddings, N. and Maher, C. (1990). Constructivist approaches to mathematics education. *Monographs of the National Society for Teachers of Mathematics Education.* Reston, VA.

Nuffield Foundation. (1964). Nuffield Foundation Science Teaching Project. London.

Olson, D. R. (1994). *The world on paper: The conceptual and cognitive implications of writing and reading.* New York: Cambridge University Press.

Overton, W. (1983). World views and their influence on psychological theory. In H. W. Reese (Ed.), *Advances in child development and behavior, 18,* 191–226.

Pea, R. (1987). Integrating human and computer intelligence. In R. D. Pea and K. Sheingold (Eds.), *Mirrors of minds: Patterns of experience in educational computing.* Norwood NJ: Ablex.

Pepper, S. C. (1975). *World hypotheses.* Berkeley: University of California Press.

Piaget, J. (1970). Piaget's theory. In P. H. Mussen (Ed.), *Carmichael's Handbook of Child Development* (pp. 703–732). New York: Wiley.

Porter, M. E. (1990). The competitive advantage of nations. New York: Free Press.

Pressley, M. (1982). Elaboration and memory development. *Child Development, 53,* 296–309.

Rabinow, P. (1984). *The Foucault reader.* New York: Pantheon Books.

Riley, M. S., Greeno, J. G., and Heller, J. I. (1983). Development of children's problem-solving ability in arithmetic. In H. P. Ginsburg (Ed.), *The development of mathematical thinking* (pp. 153–196). New York: Academic Press.

Rogoff, B. (1990). *Apprenticeship in thinking.* New York: Oxford University Press.

Rohlen, T. R. (1994). *The learning society.* Unpublished manuscript, Stanford University.

Rorty, R. (1991). *Objectivity, relativism, and truth.* Cambridge, England: Cambridge University Press.

Rosenberg, N. and Birdzell, L. E. (1986). *How the west grew rich.* New York: Basic Books.

Rumelhart, D. E., Hinton, G. E., and McClelland, J. L. (1987). A General framework for PDP. In D. E. Rumelhart and J. L. McClelland (Eds.), *Parallel distributed processing: Explorations in the microstructure of cognition* (Vol. 1) (pp. 45–77). Cambridge: MIT Press.

Scardamalia, M., Bereiter, C., and Lamon, M. (1994). The CSILE Project: Trying to bring the classroom into World 3. In K. McGilly (Ed.), *Classroom lessons: Integrating cognitive theory and classroom practice* (pp, 201–229). Cambridge: MIT Press.

Siegler, R. S. and Shrager, J. (1984). Strategy choices in addition and subtraction problems: How do children know what to do? In C. Sophian (Ed.), *Origins of cognitive skills.* Hillsdale, NJ: Lawrence Erlbaum.

Simon, D. P. and Simon, H. A. (1978). Individual differences in solving physics problems. In R. S. Siegler (Ed.), *Children's thinking: What develops?* (pp. 325–348). Hillsdale, NJ: Lawrence Erlbaum.

Simon, H. A. and Chase, W. (1973). Skill in chess. *The American Scientist, 61,* 394–403.

Skinner, B. F. (1954). The science of learning and the art of teaching. *Harvard Educational Review, 24,* 86–97.

Spearman, C. (1992). *The abilities of man: Their nature and measurement.* New York: Macmillan.

Spelke, E. (1988). Where perceiving ends and thinking begins: The apprehension of objects in infancy. In A. Yonas (Ed.), *Perceptual development in infancy: Minnesota symposia in child psychology* (pp. 197–234). Hillsdale, NJ: Lawrence Erlbaum.

Spindler, G. and Spindler E. (1987). *Interpretive ethnography of education: At home and abroad.* Hillsdale, NJ: Lawrence Erlbaum.

Starkey, P. (1992). The early development of numerical reasoning. *Cognition, 43,* 93–126.

Terman, L. M. (1916). *The measurement of intelligence.* Boston: Houghton Mifflin.

Thorndike, E. L. (1926). *The measurement of intelligence.* New York: Teachers College Press.

Vacca, R. T. and Vacca, J. L. (1986). *Content area reading* (2nd edn.). Boston: Little, Brown.

Vygotsky, L. S. (1934/1962). *Thought and language.* Cambridge: MIT Press.

Watson, J. S. (1914). *Behavior, an introduction to comparative psychology.* New York: Holt, Rinehart, and Winston.

Wellman, H. M. (1990). The child's theory of mind. Cambridge: Bradford/MIT Press.

Willowby, S., Bereiter, C. M., Hilton, P., and Rubenstein, J. (1981). *Real Math.* Peru, IL: Open Court Publishing.

Wiser, M. and Kipman, D. (1988). *The differentiation of heat and temperature. An evaluation of the effect of microcomputer models on students' misconceptions* (Report TR88-20). Cambridge: Educational Technology Center, Harvard University.

Wood, D. J., Bruner, J. S., and Ross, G. (1976). The role of tutoring in problem-solving. *Journal of Child Psychology and Psychiatry, 17,* 89–100.

Yackel, E., Cobb, P., Wood, T., Wheatley, G., and McNeal, G. (1990). The importance of social interactions in children's construction of mathematical knowledge. In T. Cooney (Ed.), 1990 *Yearbook of the National Council of Teachers of Mathematics* (pp. 12–21). Reston, VA: National Council of Teachers of Mathematics.

6

Rethinking the Historical Role of Psychology in Educational Reform

BARBARA BEATTY

In 1892 William James informed a group of teachers attending his lecture series in Cambridge, Massachusetts, that "psychology is a science, and teaching is an art; and sciences never generate arts directly out of themselves." Moreover, James added, knowing psychology was not a "guarantee" that someone would be a good teacher. The issue, in James's mind, was not whether psychology *should* be able to give teachers "radical help," but whether it *could*. In his view, qualities such as "tact and ingenuity" that teachers needed to know what to do with real pupils in complex classroom situations were "things to which psychology cannot help us in the least" (James, 1958, pp. 23–24).

Historically, many teachers, particularly high school teachers, seem to have agreed with James. These subject-centered classicists or "humanists," as Herbert M. Kliebard calls them in his history of American school curricula (1987), looked to disciplinary knowledge from the arts and sciences, not to psychology, as the base for education. But many teachers, particularly teachers of younger children, did look to psychology for help in education. The question was which psychology, because from its inception as an outgrowth of philosophy, there have been different psychologies which evolved along separate lines and enjoyed different heydays or ascendancies in American academia and education.

The research of historians of psychology and education converges upon three main varieties of educational psychology and curriculum. Sheldon H. White distinguishes three "visions" of educational psychology: (1) the developmental vision, (2) the engineering vision, and (3) the reconstructive vision. Each vision is in turn associated with a leading psychologist: the developmentalists with G. Stanley Hall at Clark University; the engineers with Edward L. Thorndike at Teachers College at Columbia University; and the reconstructionists with John Dewey during his University of Chicago period. Kliebard describes three curricular models associated with these same three educational psychologies: a developmental model, a social-efficiency model, and a social-meliorist model (White, 1991; Kliebard, 1987). To these three I would add a fourth, a psychoclinical vision that has taken different forms. This fourth vision, which focuses on emotional development, personality, and "adjustment" problems, includes the work of theorists and therapists like Sigmund Freud, Erik Erikson, Abraham Maslow, Carl Rogers, and clinicians who look within the individual psyche and at interpersonal relationships for explanations of behavior and learning.

Changing Models and Hybrids

These visions or models have evolved and changed over time. The work of Jean Piaget, Jerome Bruner, and other cognitivists, for instance, modified and supplanted Hall's more primitive, deterministic developmentalism. This newer, cognitive-developmental vision had great impact on educational reform during the late 1960s and 1970s and remains the dominant model for explaining children's development and learning, particularly in early childhood education.

There have also been variants and cross-typings of these models. In his history of how American teachers have taught, Larry Cuban talks about blends of modes of instruction that he calls "hybrids" (Cuban, 1993). The proliferation and recombining of psychologies and curricula has created hybrids, some of which have come and gone (some of which might be termed "fads"), and some of which remain. One prevalent blending has been that of efficiency engineering or behaviorism and psychoclinicalism, which has produced hybrids like habit training and other approaches that have arisen in response to the need to deal with children's behavioral and emotional problems. There are other hybrids as well and arguments could be made for other models.

What difference has it made in the long and ongoing process of educational reform in the United States which of these models and hybrids have interacted in psychology and education? To explore this large question I have chosen three historical examples: G. Stanley Hall's developmentalist child study movement and the kindergarten in the 1880s and 1890s; John Dewey's social reconstructionism and the Laboratory School at the University of Chicago from 1896 to 1904; and habit training and the nursery school movement in the 1920s. Note that two models—the efficiency engineering vision associated with Edward L. Thorndike and psychoclinicalism—are missing. In their stead I discuss habit training, a hybrid with some characteristics of each.

Though I include no example of Thorndike's efficiency engineering vision, I agree with Ellen Condliffe Lagemann and others who argue that this model, which emphasized direct teaching of basic skills and standardized testing, has prevailed in American public education, especially at the elementary school level (Lagemann, 1989). In the 1910s and 1920s, Thorndike developed an associationistic theory of learning based on experiments with animals. Thorndike hypothesized laws of learning that he then proceeded to quantify. Though few teachers may have consciously based their classroom practice on the law of effect, the myriad educational tests that Thorndike and his colleagues at Teachers College at Columbia University designed to measure learning were enormously influential in shaping education because they provided the first hard, seemingly incontrovertible, "scientific" evidence of children's academic learning, or lack thereof. As psychologists and school superintendents began compiling and disseminating test results, teachers came under pressure to produce higher test scores. As David Tyack and others describe, this quantifiable science of education fit well with the needs of urban school administrators who sought efficient methods of top-down management to control America's burgeoning system of public schools (Tyack, 1974, 1985). As school systems became more "rationally" organized and hierarchical, superintendents and associate superintendents developed increasingly detailed curriculum guidelines specifying the skills and content that teachers were to teach, and teachers increasingly shaped their classroom practice to fit the guidelines and to teach to the tests.

Nor do I include an example of a purely psychoclinical model as these have been rare in mainstream public education, in part because psychoclinicalism developed as a way of dealing with children who were out of the mainstream, children who did not fit comfortably within what David Tyack calls the "one best system" of American public education (Tyack, 1974). Psychoclinicalism grew out of the mental hygiene and child-guidance movements of the turn of the century begun by psychiatrists like Lightner Witmer and William Healy, who started clinics to treat children with school "adjustment" problems. Later other clinicians added theories of personality, emotional development, self-actualization, and so on to the repertoire of strategies for dealing with the "degenerate," "deviant," "depressed," and "disadvantaged" whose problems impeded the smooth running of America's educational and other institutions, whose perceived needs created the need for new institutions, and whose failures, pain, and anxiety were in part caused by the failure of those institutions and of the system (Horn, 1989).

But though omitted here, these models should not be forgotten, particularly the efficiency engineering model as it is the entrenched and most powerful contender in any discussion of educational reform. Nor should the apsychological, subject-centered humanists be forgotten, many of whom are probably quite comfortable with Thorndike's efficiency engineering approach. They prevail at the high school level and have an enormous, if indirect impact on the lower grades. Some would even argue that subject-centered, disciplinary didacticism is the major obstacle to meaningful educational reform (Clinchy, 1994).

Of course, these models I describe are oversimplified generalizations. William James was right. Psychological theories do not directly produce educational practice. There is much interaction, invention, compromise, and confusion. Indeed, Sheldon White argues that the promise of providing useful answers to practical educational questions may have been the impetus for the establishment of psychology departments in colleges and universities around the turn of the century (White, 1991). So educational needs and practices may have indirectly driven theory, and influenced the questions psychologists asked, were asked, and tried to answer. But though the reality of applied psychology and educational reform is infinitely more varied, complicated, and messy than this sketchy typology and three brief case studies can begin to suggest, it is worth re-examining the relationship between these interrelated fields periodically as we may derive useful information about the processes of change and reform within both psychology and education.

Hall's Developmentalism and the Kindergarten Movement

G. Stanley Hall's child study movement, a precursor to modern developmental psychology, had a direct influence on one of the most successful of modern American educational reforms, the kindergarten. Born in 1844, Hall was the first American psychologist to systematically study young children. In 1878 he received the first doctorate in psychology awarded in the United States, from William James in Harvard's Philosophy Department. Hall's developmentalism was an outgrowth of various European psychological, philosophical, and pedagogical movements. He learned about experimental methodology in Carl Ludwig's and Wilhelm Wundt's German psychology laboratories, picked up the idea that ontogeny recapitulates philogeny from the German natural philosopher Ernst Haeckel, and adopted the concept of "culture epochs" from the German pedagogues Tuickson Ziller and Wilhelm Rein. Hall then combined these notions, along with a hefty dollop of Hegelianism and other quasiscientific ideas into an overall theory of "genetic psychology," which he claimed traced the biological origins of human mental development. Thus, Hall believed, human embryos went through a fish stage, young children's play repeated the social organization of "primitive" tribes, and schoolchildren should study the Greeks, then the Romans, and so on, in a developmental-cultural order (Ross, 1972; Strickland, 1973; Kliebard, 1987; White, 1992).

Unlike William James, Hall thought psychology could be of direct use to teachers, and vice versa. Working at a time when the canons of academic psychology and practice were still in formation, Hall used teachers as research assistants and collected data on children through questionnaires sent to teachers. Beginning in 1880, he worked with kindergarten teachers in Boston to interview five- and six-year-olds about their knowledge of the natural world. Hall analyzed the mass of data the teachers collected in a pathbreaking article entitled "The Contents of Children's Minds on Entering School," in which he argued that young children growing up in the city needed to attend kindergarten because their mental development was being stunted by lack of contact with nature. First published in the *Princeton Review* in 1883, Hall's article provided scientific support for the worth of the kindergarten and helped legitimize Friedrich Froebel's German kindergarten philosophy among American psychologists and academics (Hall, 1893; Siegel and White, 1982; Zenderland, 1988; White, 1990; Beatty, 1995).

Hall then began an active campaign to attract kindergarten teachers to his child study movement. Motivated in part by a need to bolster the finances of newly founded Clark University in Worcester, Massachusetts, of which he was president, Hall started in 1892 a summer school at which schoolteachers were taught about psychological theory and research and introduced to research methods. Some of the teachers became Hall's assistants and helped him design a kindergarten questionnaire or "topical syllabus" which was sent to kindergarten teachers around the country (Clark University Summer School, 1899).

As important as this joint research was the way Hall mingled with the teachers socially. The Clark summer sessions included parties and receptions at Hall's house, picnics and outings, and other social events that were attended by the teachers and the psychologists on the staff. Hall even put some prominent kindergarten teachers up at his house. Lucy Wheelock, for instance, the head of what was to become Wheelock College in Boston, remembered pleasant evenings on Hall's porch and stimulating informal discussions of psychology and education. Wheelock was one of the first kindergarten teachers to change her classroom practice based on Hall's ideas and to stop using some of Friedrich Froebel's original German kindergarten "gifts" and "occupations," especially some of the smaller materials and complicated activities that required advanced fine-motor skills, because she thought they were inappropriate for young children (Wheelock, n.d.; "Kindergarten Day at Clark University," 1896; Beatty, 1995).

The impact of Hall's new developmental psychology of child study on the kindergarten movement was especially apparent in the work of Patty Smith Hill, who headed the kindergarten department at Teachers College in New York for many years. Born near Louisville, Kentucky, in 1868, Hill worked as Anna Bryan's assistant in the charity kindergartens run by the Louisville Free Kindergarten Association in the late 1880s and 1890s and attended Hall's Clark University Summer School in 1894. Hill too was concerned about the rigidity and developmental inappropriateness of Froebel's prescientific kindergarten methods and saw the implications of developmental psychology for kindergarten education.

Based on her new understanding of child development, Hill realized that if children developed according to universal "laws" then there should be universal kindergartens. This realization was critical because kindergartens in America had initially been provided for rich and poor children separately, along European, class-segregated lines. Hill asserted in a position paper entitled "The Free Kindergarten as the Basis of Education," published in the 1894–1895 Louisville Free Kindergarten Association report, that psychology revealed "the fact that the Creator has seen fit to develop the mind in all classes of society by the same laws." Whether rich people liked it or not, and even though "the thought might be humiliating to some," she stated, the "minds of the prince and the pauper unfold in obedience to the same divine laws, which, if violated, in either case must inevitably result in evil." Though pedagogical methods might "differ somewhat, according to environment, the principle is the same for both classes," Hill concluded (Hill, 1894–1895, pp. 7–8).

Here was a case of psychology providing an explicit rationale for educational reform. Because young children developed through biologically equal processes, Hill argued they should be educated and treated equally by teachers and society. Furthermore, she thought the same teacher and methods could be effective with children from different class backgrounds and that there were beneficial results to educating young children from different classes in the same classrooms. "It is wonderful to see the extremes of society meet under the guidance of a skillful teacher to unfold and blossom," Hill exclaimed, "not only by the same laws and principles, but even, in some cases, under the same methods" (Hill, 1894–1895, p. 8).

The influence of G. Stanley Hall's developmentalist psychology was also evident in the work of other so-called "radicals" and progressives within the kindergarten movement who, along with Patty Smith Hill, departed from Froebel's traditional kindergarten pedagogy. For instance, when one of Hall's students, Frederick Burk, became superintendent of schools in Santa Barbara, California, he began experimenting to find out what materials kindergarten children themselves would play with if given the choice. In a study conducted in 1898, Burk and his wife, Caroline Frear Burk, found that young children preferred dolls, swings, bean bags, and other toys over Froebel's carefully prescribed, sequenced "gifts" and "occupations." The problem with the kindergarten, the Burks stated, was that children had not been "particularly consulted either in the choice of material, or in the use to be made of it" (Burk and Burk, 1899, p. 81). The Burks began giving children two free-play periods a day, which in later "free-play kindergartens" became the focus of the program. The experiments of the Burks, and Patty Smith Hill, who continued to develop new kindergarten practices and materials including designing her own set of kindergarten blocks, and others led the way away from Froebel's pre-scientific formalism toward the more developmentally oriented modern American kindergarten (Shapiro, 1983; Beatty, 1995). Though there were many other political, economic, and cultural factors behind the universalization of public kindergartens around the turn of the century, developmental psychology played a key supporting role in providing scientific backing for this important and lasting educational reform. G. Stanley Hall's encouragement of teachers to participate in psychological research, whatever his motivation, seems to have helped kindergarten teachers like Patty Smith Hill make connections between psychology, educational reform, and teaching methods. Though William James may have been right that teachers do not need to be psychologists, and right that psychologists "profited" more than anyone else from the educational ferment in America around the turn of the century, popularization had benefits as well as perils and could be a stimulus for new conceptualizations of educational programs and practice (James, 1958, p. 23).

Dewey's Social Psychology and Laboratory School

John Dewey's social recontructionist psychology also had an impact on educational reform, though it did not become as mainstream as Hall's developmentalism in preschool education or Thorndike's efficiency engineering in elementary education. Dewey's ideas influenced the Progressive Education movement at the turn of the century and the Open Education movement of the late 1960s and 1970s, and Dewey is being heard from again more and more loudly in the school reform movement of today.

Best known as a philosopher, Dewey's psychological ideas derived from some of the same sources as Hall's. In fact Dewey studied with Hall at Johns Hopkins and was also influenced by Hegelianism, Herbartianism, and other German pedagogical theories. For Dewey, psychological development, education, and social change were linked. As he stated in his "Plan for the Organization of the University School," probably written around 1895, the "ultimate problem of education is to coordinate the psychological and the social factors." Dewey thought this coordination must happen at the level of the individual school and required "that the child be capable of expressing *himself*, but in such a way as to realize *social* ends (Dewey, 1895/1972, p. 224). Here and in his later works, especially *Democracy and Education* (1916), Dewey was looking for ways to connect individual psychological development with social progress. He saw the school as the key mediating and meliorating institution through which society could be reconstructed in more progressive, democratic ways.

The best example of the application of Dewey's social psychology to educational reform was the Laboratory School of the University of Chicago, which he started as an experiment to test his ideas. The Laboratory School, which first opened in January of 1896 and reopened in October, began with three teachers and 32 students. By 1902 the school enrolled 140 children aged 4 to 16 and at its maximum was staffed by 23 teachers and 10 graduate assistants (Mayhew and Edwards, 1936, pp. 7–9). Dewey was the director, his wife Alice Chipman Dewey served as principal, and Ella Flagg Young, future superintendent of the Chicago Public schools, was supervisor of instruction. The school continued in existence for seven years but suffered from continual lack of funding. After protracted and complicated negotiations with the University of Chicago concerning in part whether Mrs. Dewey would be paid for her work, the school was merged with other laboratory schools, Dewey resigned, and in 1904 he went to Teachers College at Columbia (Cremin, 1961; Kliebard, 1987; White, 1991; Cuban, 1993).

Despite the Laboratory School's small size, experimental nature, and short period of operation, it was an influential model for curriculum reform. Dewey believed the curriculum should be child- rather than subject-centered, but he did not want to abandon academic subject matter. Rather, he hoped to do away with what he saw as the dualism between the child and the curriculum (Dewey, 1902). The way Dewey hit upon to mediate between children's personal experience and academic subject matter was through "occupations," activities like cooking, sewing, and carpentry, an idea he adapted from Friedrich Froebel's kindergarten pedagogy. As Katherine Camp Mayhew and Anna Camp Edwards, teachers at the Laboratory School, described in detail, the children spent time making their own food and other practical things they could use, and in the process acquired academic skills. These simple occupations then led to study of the development of human occupations like metalworking and mining, which eventually led to study of the historical sequence of human culture and to acquisition of knowledge of academic subject matter (Mayhew and Edwards, 1936).

The most radical aspect of Dewey's educational psychology as embodied in the University of Chicago Laboratory School curriculum was the amount of time the children spent in these occupations, manual training activities, and on thematic projects, as opposed to direct instruction in basic skills. Dewey believed that children would learn to read, write, and do arithmetic better if they acquired these skills through activities more related to human life and society. As he put it in an article published in the *Forum* in 1898, "the predominance of learning to read in early school life seems to me a perversion. . .the child learns to read as a mechanical tool, and gets very little conception of what is worth reading" (Dewey, 1898/1972, p. 264). Dewey thought occupations like cooking and sewing were a better vehicle for learning arithmetic as well as reading, even though children might not learn as much about number and arithmetical technique this way as from more direct teaching. Through occupations, as he said in an address to the Pedagogical Club in 1896, the "child may not learn as much of number as by the study of the multiplication table, but he will get an idea of what number really is, instead of the mere technique of number as is the case at present" (Dewey, 1898/ 1972, p. 440). Thus, children taught under the Dewey model, unlike those taught under the Thorndike model, spent relatively little time in direct skill instruction. The five- to seven-year-olds, for instance, spent only $1/2$ hour three times a week or a total of about $1^{1}/_{2}$ hours a week in what Dewey called "techniques." And out of a total of 20 hours a week, the seven- and eight-year-olds spent only 2 hours a week in "techniques" of reading, writing, and arithmetic (Mayhew and Edwards, 1936, pp. 385–386).

Of course, as Dewey argued, the children at the Laboratory School were spending more time on basic skills than this distribution suggests because they were using reading, writing, and arithmetic in many of their other activities. How effective these "occupations" were as a means of acquisition of basic skills is an empirical question, however, and one that is still difficult to answer a century later. Anecdotal comments of graduates of the University of Chicago Laboratory School some 30 years after it closed were almost uniformly positive. Mayhew and Edwards include statements from alumni who thought the school had helped them become more independent thinkers, better able to solve real-world problems, and possessors of "an attitude of confidence toward life." But at least one former student mentioned that he had had a hard time learning how to spell and that he never read a book of his own "free will" until his second year in high school. Though this student attributed his difficulties to the fact the school closed and "the experiment stopped just before we non-book people came to the point where we wanted to read or write," his comments make one wonder how well the Dewey school served less intrinsically motivated students or those with potential learning problems (Mayhew and Edwards, 1936, pp. 404–405).

Though relatively few older students attended the University of Chicago Laboratory School, the curriculum continued Dewey's commitment to child-centered learning and occupations through the high school level. Older students did a lot of photography, for instance, and spent a great deal of time planning and building a clubhouse where they could meet and work on projects. They studied architecture, sanitation, and other subjects as they constructed the clubhouse, which they did with little outside help. The following year, however, the 14- and 15-year-olds took special review courses and prepared for college entrance examinations, the need for which Mayhew and Edwards felt "hampered" the Dewey school curriculum (Mayhew and Edwards, 1936, p. 237).

Despite this relatively small compromise with the entrenched, subject-centered humanistic curriculum model, teachers at the Dewey school had enormous autonomy to experiment, develop, and implement new ideas about curriculum.

Though John Dewey's presence and vision clearly permeated the school, the staff operated as a collegial community. The teachers worked out the curriculum as they went along and published a journal with extensive reports on their work. They saw themselves as professional educators and curriculum developers, not "hands" in an educational factory or followers of a psychologist-king who told them what to do. Even more than Hall, Dewey collaborated with teachers, respected their ability, and, indeed, felt the success of the Laboratory School experiment depended upon their competence (Dewey, 1900).

So, at the University of Chicago Laboratory School, too, educational reform occurred when psychologists and teachers worked together, although in somewhat different ways. Dewey thought educational change happened first at the individual classroom and school level, in a relatively small-sized educational experiment, which needed to be supported for a sustained period of time. As he put it in a critique of existing primary education methods, schools needed time to work out "carefully and definitely the subject-matter of a new curriculum." Larger-scale educational change could then occur when these experiments grew and infused school systems as a whole, but this kind of systemic reform, Dewey knew, was "dependent upon a collateral wider change in the public opinion which controls school board, superintendent, and teachers" (Dewey, 1898/1972, p. 269). But this kind of broad-based educational reform proved difficult for Dewey and his collaborators to achieve.

Habit Training and the Nursery School Movement

The third historical case I want to examine deals with the psychoclinical-behavioristic hybrid of habit training in the nursery school movement in the 1920s and 1930s. By the 1920s psychologies were recombining to form hybrids such as habit training, a method Arnold Gesell and other clinicians and nursery school teachers used to treat preschool children with behavioral and emotional problems. It would be incorrect to identify this behavioristic-affective hybrid specifically with Gesell, however, who also was a student of G. Stanley Hall and is best known for espousing maturationism, a biologically deterministic form of developmentalism. But like many other early psychologists, Gesell was a practitioner with direct links to schools and his practical, clinical work drew upon a variety of methods. Gesell started a child guidance clinic and consulted with the public schools of the state of Connecticut, where he was appointed the country's first school psychologist. Through this clinical work with children with problems, Gesell and other psychologists like Douglas Thom in Boston and Helen Thompson Woolley, whose case studies of nursery school children at the Merrill-Palmer Institute in Detroit show evidence of early psychoanalytic influence, combined behavioristic and affective psychology in ways similar to methods used by many special educators today (Gesell, 1923; Thom, 1924; Woolley, 1925, 1926; Kessen, 1965; Ames, 1989).

This psychoclinical-behavioristic hybrid derived from a number of sources.

Psychologists and psychiatrists working in the mental hygiene and child guidance movements that began in Philadelphia and Chicago around the turn of the century began realizing that many of children's school "adjustment" problems stemmed from family problems. There were "problem parents" as well as "problem children." Psychologists, social workers, parent educators, and teachers working together in the nursery school movement of the 1920s, with the support of funding from the Laura Spelman Rockefeller Memorial, hoped to solve larger social problems in part by using habit training and other approaches to improve parenting (Schlossman, 1981; Horn, 1989; Grant, 1992; Beatty, 1995).

The behavioristic psychology of John Watson was another important source of this hybrid. Watson also focused on parents, particularly mothers, as the cause of children's educational and other difficulties. Watson's book *The Psychological Care of the Infant and Child* (1928), for instance, contained numerous dire warnings about the dangers of excessive "mother love" and instructed mothers to "never hug or kiss" their children or "let them sit in your lap" (Watson, 1928, pp. 81, 87). Like G. Stanley Hall, Watson was an active popularizer and applier of psychology to child rearing and education whose ideas were widely read by parent and nursery school educators.

Habit training was used to treat all manner of conditions from eating and personality disorders, bedwetting, masturbation, temper tantrums, aggressiveness, shyness, and delinquency, to convulsions, psychoses, and retardation. A child who had been identified with one or more of these problems was brought to a clinic or laboratory nursery school where a full case history of the child and family, often including a home visit, was developed. The mother was then asked to sit hidden behind a screen and watch while a specially trained nursery school teacher interacted with the child in a "healthy" way and used psychoclinical and behavioristic methods to correct the child's problems. The mother was supposed to use these methods at home, follow the team's advice about diet, schedule, and other routines, keep detailed records, and report back on changes in the child's behavior (Thom, 1924, p. 36).

Habit training was used in a more or less consistent fashion in a number of nursery schools in the 1920s, including the nursery school at Arnold Gesell's Yale Psycho-Clinic in New Haven, Connecticut. Begun in 1911, the Yale Psycho-Clinic received a grant in 1926 from the Laura Spelman Rockefeller Memorial and began the Guidance Nursery School, which served individual children on a referral, fee-paying basis while they were being studied and treated by the clinic. There was also a small "Regular Group" of about five normal children with whom the problem children were placed "for a period of re-education" (Ames, 1989, pp. 136–137).

The curriculum of the Guidance Nursery School was determined almost entirely by the individual problems and needs of the children attending at any given time. "Thus," as Gesell described in a 1929 national survey of preschool and parental education, "a child who is referred on account of certain problems in relation to the feeding situation may be served luncheon in the nursery alone or with other children; one who is over-dependent upon the presence of the mother may have to undergo separation; or a child who is given to disobedience or temper tantrums may be faced with situations which bring out these responses so that undesirable behavior could be treated" (Gesell, 1929, p. 167).

Habit training was most frequently used with two different populations: children from well-to-do families whose parents were anxious or concerned about their children's behavior and had the financial means and time to buy expert, private help; and poor and immigrant children whose families were deemed deviant, deficient, or pathological and were referred to free, child welfare programs and clinics. The impact of habit training was much felt by well-educated mothers in the 1920s and 1930s who tried assiduously to adjust their child-rearing routines to strictly recommended, regimented guidelines. Later, during the 1940s when a more affectionate mode of child rearing was promoted, in part as an antidote to the stressful effects of war on young children, some of these mothers expressed regret for having followed the experts' stern prescriptions. "If only I had known," one nursery school educator quoted a mother as saying, "how much babies do need to be cuddled, I certainly would have done plenty of it. I wanted to. But I had been warned, 'Now leave your child alone. Don't touch him more than you have to'" (Baruch, 1942, p. 52).

Even more worrisome than these mothers' regrets about dutifully following the experts' advice is the spectre of how habit training and psychological prescriptions to limit affection may have damaged a generation of American children. In fact, there are hints that psychologists themselves should have been able to see some of these ill effects at the time. Gesell, for instance, observed that the problems of "Richard," a child treated in the Yale Psycho-Clinic's Guidance Nursery School, may have been in part caused by his mother's rigidly scheduled forcefeeding due to her "misinterpretation of her doctor's instructions." Gesell saw that some mothers who brought their children to the clinic had "completely lost confidence in their ability to handle the problems presented by their children," but could not see that he and other experts might have contributed to this lack of confidence (National Society for the Study of Education, 1929, p. 168).

Especially troubling are accounts of the effects of habit training on the children of immigrants and the poor. Douglas Thom's Habit Clinic in Boston sponsored programs for preschool and school-age children similar to those at Yale and worked closely with nursery school educators such as Grace Caldwell, whose Play School for Habit Training began in a settlement house in Boston's North End in 1922. Here children from very poor, mainly Italian immigrant families attended a special nursery school designed to change their problematic behaviors and "bad" habits. For instance, accounts of Caldwell's school contain a disturbingly stereotypic description of a little boy whose temper tantrums seemed to be the product of the "overemotional home atmosphere" in his Italian-American family. After being cured of the tantrums through habit training, the boy then started stuttering. Caldwell herself wondered whether "In view of the development of stammering, was the temper tantrum, with its release of emotion, better at his age than regulated group pressure toward more stable behavior?" (National Society for the Study of Education, 1929, p. 210).

These problematic examples of the psychoclinical-behavioristic hybrid of habit training in nursery education and child rearing suggest that it matters very much what psychological ideas are popularized and how they are used. They also suggest that the relationships between psychologists, teachers, and parents matter. In the hierarchy of the nursery school movement, psychologists and pediatricians were the professional experts, nursery school teachers were like nurse practitioners, and children and parents were the patients. Though not all nursery schools functioned in this medical model and some promoted cooperative relations with parents, habit training seems to have contributed to the demoralization of some mothers and may have led them to do things against their own better judgment and will, because the "doctor told them to." It may also have led teachers to apply psychological prescriptions in simplistic ways that were not in the best, long-term interests of children. At the same time, however, habit training provided help and support for some children and families and contributed to awareness of the importance of parent education and parent involvement in education. Teachers were encouraged to see children within the context of their families, and family needs and problems were brought into the sphere of the curriculum. In this hybrid vision, psychology had an enormous role to play in education.

Conclusions

What lessons and warnings for educational reform today can be found in these three brief case studies? The example of G. Stanley Hall's developmentalism and the kindergarten movement shows that psychology can have a lasting impact on educational policy and pedagogy. Kindergartners like Patty Smith Hill, Anna Bryan, and Frederick Burk, all of whom studied with Hall, changed their views on the relationship between social class background and learning and altered kindergarten teaching methods, in part because of ideas about children's development. Hall's energetic popularization of developmentalism and child study methods made teachers generally more aware of the uses of psychology in education.

But the notion of universal laws of development was also problematic. By the early nineteenth century, the concept of normality upon which Hall and other developmentalists built, was being used to posit monolithic norms and stereotypes of one "right" pattern and pace of development, deviance from which was seen as pathological (Hacking, 1990). It took psychologists a long time to describe plural paths of development and see the multiplicity of intelligence. Preschool educators today, for instance, are still struggling with the idea of "developmentally appropriate" practice, and have been critiqued for the rigidity as well as the vagueness with which it is sometimes applied (New and Mallory, 1994; Lubeck, 1994; Beatty, 1995). And, as controversies about the effectiveness of preschool programs have shown, applying developmental psychology to education can be misinterpreted as a "magic bullet" for boosting cognitive development and test scores, thus creating unrealistic expectations and disillusionment with educational reforms like Head Start (Vinovskis, 1995; Zigler and Muenchow, 1992).

The example of John Dewey's social reconstructionist psychology at the University of Chicago Laboratory School shows how a different psychological vision can serve as a catalyst and guide for the design of new curriculum and instructional practices. The Dewey school provides lessons about the processes of educational reform. Dewey and the teachers at the Laboratory School worked as colleagues who respected each others' insights, contributions, and experience. The small size of the experiment and its freedom from educational bureaucracy also undoubtedly added to its success.

But the Dewey school also shows the necessity of long-term financial and administrative support and of reworking the relationship of new curricula to traditional, subject-centered expectations for academic achievement. Given more time, Dewey and his teachers might have designed alternative forms of assessment such as the portfolio method espoused by many in the current school reform movement. Given more time, Dewey might have asked college presidents to consider less standardized evidence of achievement in admissions decisions, as Theodore Sizer and the Coalition of Essential Schools have requested of colleges today. The importance of designing methods to deal quickly and directly with students with potential learning problems is also suggested by the case study of the Dewey school.

The third case study, of the psychoclinical-behavioristic hybrid of habit training, exemplifies an attempt to use psychology in education to treat children's emotional and behavioral problems at home and at school. Though short-lived as a psychoeducational vogue, habit training focused teachers' attention on the relationship between children and their families, provided new strategies for dealing with children's problems, and emphasized the importance of parent involvement and parent education.

But the case of habit training also shows that psychologists and teachers should be wary of telling parents to do things that run against parents' intuitions and common sense about what is good for their children. This is not to say psychologists and teachers should not offer advice or should ignore the existence of problematic situations in homes that can harm children. But care should be taken to avoid crossing the line between enlisting and helping parents, as psychiatrist James Comer does in the educational reform model he has developed in the New Haven public schools today, and intruding into family life and insisting on one best way to raise children (Comer, 1980, 1986).

This brief overview of some historical examples of the relationship between psychology and educational reform is based on the premise that both psychology and education are pluralistic fields with multiple models or visions rather than one "correct" paradigm. Though Thorndike's teacher-centered skill instruction and standardized testing and apsychological, teacher- and-subject-centered humanism have predominated in elementary and secondary education, there has been competition among different models. This competition is healthy in that it reflects human and cultural diversity and diversity of values about the purposes of education, and because it may foster improvement of theory and practice in both psychology and education.

Recently, however, worries have been expressed that two of the main competitors in the current educational reform movement, the Thorndike-like push for higher, more uniform standards and testing, and the Deweyan emphasis on "authentic," more child-centered learning and "deep understanding," may be on a collision course. Linda Darling-Hammond, for one, suggests that the success of the school reform enterprise as a whole may hinge on the implementation of the Deweyan reforms that she and many other educators and psychologists espouse (Darling-Hammond, 1993). Given Dewey's analysis of the potentially energizing nature of crosscurrents in education, if properly directed, and of the importance of broad public acceptance for school reforms to be generalized, now may be an especially critical time for psychologists and educators to talk and work together and to talk and work with teachers and parents (Dewey, 1931/1984). Whether, as Larry Cuban, David Tyack, and others suggest, educational reforms have come and gone again and again because of cyclical or pendulum-like swings, conflicts of political values, the loosely coupled structure of schools as institutions, or the imperatives of classroom structure and teaching as an occupation, psychologists and educators must not forget the need of parents and society to understand psychological theories and educational reforms and see evidence of educational progress (Cuban, 1990; Ravitch and Vinovskis, 1995; Tyack and Tobin, 1994; Tyack, 1995).

If the descriptions of children's roles in actively constructing knowledge represented by much of the research in this volume are correct, then the success of educational reform depends on all participants in the process—psychologists, educators, teachers, parents, and children—having opportunities to experiment with and act upon different ideas. The pluralistic and participatory nature of this process is likely to continue creating new hybrids, as is apparent in the collaboration of educator Theodore Sizer, psychologist Howard Gardner, and psychiatrist James Comer in the ATLAS (Authentic Teaching, Learning, and Assessment for All Students) Communities and New American Schools Projects now underway. Such hybrids should be welcomed as a sign of continuing attempts to resolve the dualism between the child and the curriculum that John Dewey set as his task and ours back at the turn of the century.

Acknowledgments

I am grateful for the suggestions of Emily Cahan, Kenneth Hawes, and David Olson, whose comments on early drafts of this chapter were very helpful, and for the ideas of Larry Cuban, Herbert Kliebard, and Sheldon H. White, upon whose research my typology heavily depends.

References

Ames, L. B. (1989). *Arnold Gesell: Themes of his work.* New York: Human Sciences Press.

Baruch, D. (1942). *You, your children, and war.* New York: Appleton-Century.

Beatty, B. (1995). *Preschool education in America: The culture of young children from the colonial era to the present.* New Haven: Yale University Press.

Burk, F. and Burk, C. (1899). *A study of the kindergarten problem.* San Francisco: Whitaker and Ray.

Clark University Summer School. (1899). *Kindergarten Magazine, 12,* 22. Summer School Records, Clark University Archives, Worcester, MA.

Clinchy, E. (1994). Higher education: The albatross around the neck of our public schools. *Phi Delta Kappan, 75,* 744–751.

Comer, J. P. (1980). *School power: Implications of an intervention project.* New York: Free Press.

Comer, J. P. (1986). Parent participation in the schools. *Phi Delta Kappan, 67,* 442–446.

Cremin, L. A. (1961). *The transformation of the school: Progressivism in American education, 1876–1957.* New York: Vintage Books.

Cuban, L. (1990). Reforming again, again, and again. *Educational Researcher, 19,* 3–13.

Cuban, L. (1993). *How teachers taught: Constancy and change in American classrooms, 1880–1990* (2nd edn.). New York: Teachers College Press.

Darling-Hammond, L. (1993). Reframing the school reform agenda: Developing capacity for school transformation. *Phi Delta Kappan, 74,* 753–761.

Dewey, J. (1895/1972). Plan of organization of the university primary school. In J. A. Boydston (Ed.), *John Dewey: The early works, 1882–1898* (Vol. 5) *Early essays, 1895–1898* (pp. 224–243). Carbondale and Edwardsville, IL: Southern Illinois University Press.

Dewey, J. (1896/1972). The university school. In J. A. Boydston (Ed.), *John Dewey: The early works, 1882–1898* (Vol. 5) *Early essays, 1895–1898* (pp. 436–441). Carbondale and Edwardsville, IL: Southern Illinois University Press.

Dewey, J. (1898/1972). The primary-education fetich. In J. A. Boydston (Ed.), *John Dewey: The early works, 1882–1898* (Vol. 5) *Early essays, 1895–1898* (pp. 254–269). Carbondale and Edwardsville, IL: Southern Illinois University Press.

Dewey, J. (Ed.) (1900). *The elementary school record.* Nos. 1–9, February–December. Chicago: University of Chicago Press.

Dewey, J. (1902). *The child and the curriculum.* Chicago: University of Chicago Press.

Dewey, J. (1916). *Democracy and education: An introduction to the philosophy of education.* New York: Macmillan.

Dewey, J. (1931/1984). The way out of educational confusion. In J. A. Boydston (Ed.), *John Dewey: The later works, 1925–1953* (Vol. 2) (pp. 75–89). Carbondale and Edwardsville, IL: Southern Illinois University Press.

Gesell, A. (1923). *The preschool child.* New York: Houghton Mifflin.

Gesell, A. (1929). The guidance nursery of the Yale Psycho-Clinic. In *Twenty-eighth yearbook of the National Society for the Study of Education.* Chicago: University of Chicago Press.

Grant, J. (1992). *Modernizing motherhood: Child study clubs and the parent education movement.* Doctoral dissertation, Boston University.

Hacking, I. (1990). *The taming of chance.* Cambridge, England: Cambridge University Press.

Hall, G. S. (1893). *The contents of children's minds on entering school.* New York: E. L. Kellogg.

Hill, P. S. (1894–1895). The free kindergarten as the basis of education. In Louisville Free Kindergarten Association, *Report for 1894–1895.*

Horn, M. (1989). *Before it's too late: The child guidance movement in the United States, 1922–1945*. Philadelphia: Temple University Press.

James, W. (1958). *Talks to teachers*. New York: Norton.

Joncich, G. (1968). *The sane positivist: A biography of Edward L. Thorndike*. Middletown, CT: Wesleyan University Press.

Kessen, W. (1965). *The child*. New York: Wiley.

Kindergarten Day at Clark University. (1896). *Kindergarten News, 9,* 36–41.

Kliebard, H. M. (1987). *The struggle for the American curriculum, 1893–1958*. New York: Routledge.

Lagemann, E. C. (1989). The plural worlds of educational research. *History of Education Quarterly, 29,* 185–214.

Lubeck, S. (1994). The politics of developmentally appropriate practice: Exploring issues of culture, class, and curriculum. In Mallory, B. L., and New, R. S. (Eds.), *Diversity and developmentally appropriate practices* (pp. 17–43). New York: Teachers College Press.

Mayhew, K. C. and Edwards, A. C. (1936). *The Dewey school: The laboratory school of the University of Chicago, 1896–1903*. New York: Appleton-Century.

National Society for the Study of Education. (1929). *Twenty-Eighth Yearbook*. Chicago: University of Chicago Press.

New, R. S. and Mallory, B. L. (1994). Introduction: The ethic of inclusion. In Mallory and New, *Diversity and developmentally appropriate practices* (pp. 1–14). New York: Teachers College Press.

Ravitch, D. and Vinovskis, M. (Eds.) (1995). *Learning from the past: What history teaches about school reform*. Baltimore: Johns Hopkins University Press.

Ross, D. (1972). *G. Stanley Hall: The psychologist as prophet*. Chicago: University of Chicago Press.

Schlossman, S. L. (1981). Philanthropy and the gospel of child development. *History of Education Quarterly, 21,* 275–300.

Shapiro, M. S. (1983). *Child's garden: The kindergarten movement from Froebel to Dewey*. University Park: Pennsylvania State University Press.

Siegel, A. and White, S. H. (1982). The child study movement: Early growth and development of the symbolized child. *Advances in Child Behavior and Development, 17,* 233–285.

Strickland, C. (1973). *The child and the race: The doctrines of recapitulation and culture epochs in the rise of the child-centered ideal in American educational thought, 1875–1900*. Doctoral dissertation, University of Wisconsin.

Thom, D. (1924). *Habit clinics for the child of preschool age*. Washington: Children's Bureau.

Tyack, D. B. (1974). *The one best system: A history of American urban education*. Cambridge: Harvard University Press.

Tyack, D. B. (1985). *Managers of virtue: Public school leadership in America, 1820–1980*. New York: Basic Books.

Tyack, D. B. (1995). Reinventing schooling. In D. Ravitch and M. Vinovskis (Eds.), *Learning from the past: What history teaches about school reform* (pp. 191–216). Baltimore: Johns Hopkins University Press.

Tyack, D. B. and Tobin, W. (1994). The "grammar" of schooling: Why has it been so hard to change? *American Educational Research Journal, 31,* 451–479.

Vinovskis, M. (1995). School readiness and early childhood education. In D. Ravitch and M. Vinovskis (Eds.), *Learning from the past: What history teaches about school reform* (pp. 243–264). Baltimore: Johns Hopkins University Press.

Watson, J. (1928). *The psychological care of the infant and child*. New York: Norton.

Wheelock, L. (n.d.). *My life story*. Unpublished autobiography, Archives, Wheelock College, Boston, MA.

White, S. H. (1990). Child study at Clark University: 1894–1904. *Journal of the History of the Behavioral Sciences, 26,* 131–150.

White, S. H. (1991). Three visions of a psychology of education. In L. T. Landsmann (Ed.), *Culture, schooling, and psychological development* (pp. 1–38). Norwood, NJ: Ablex.

White, S. H. (1992). G. Stanley Hall: From philosophy to developmental psychology. *Developmental Psychology, 28,* 25–34.

Woolley, H. T. (1925). David: A study of the experience of a nursery school in training a child adopted from an institution. *Child Welfare League of America, Case Studies, No. 2,* 3–26.

Woolley, H. T. (1926). Agnes: A dominant personality in the making. *Pedagogical Seminary and Journal of Genetic Psychology* (March), 569–598.

Zenderland, L. (1988). Education, evangelism, and the origins of clinical psychology: The child study legacy. *Journal of the History of Behavioral Sciences, 24,* 152–165.

Zigler, E. and Muenchow, S. (1992). *Head Start: The inside story of America's most successful educational experiment.* New York: Basic Books.

7

Rethinking the Concept of Learning Disabilities: The Demise of Aptitude/ Achievement Discrepancy

KEITH E. STANOVICH
PAULA J. STANOVICH

Introduction

The danger of reification is ever-present in many areas of educational psychology, but this is especially true in the area of learning disabilities—a field with a recurring history of concepts getting ahead of the evidence. It is, for example, well known that the field of learning disabilities has had a checkered history. It is littered with contention, false starts, fads, dead ends, and just a little bit of hard-won progress. It seems as though the field is constantly getting into scrapes, is always on probation, is never really secure. Why is this? Surely, one of the reasons is that, when borrowing ideas from allied fields such as developmental psychology, neuropsychology, and cognitive psychology, the LD field has displayed a remarkable propensity to latch on to concepts that are tenuous and controversial. Examples of this tendency are legion, ranging from visual process training to the concept of minimal brain damage. The LD field seems addicted to living dangerously.

In this chapter, we will illustrate this history of reification and hasty theoretical generalization by focusing on reading disability—the most common learning disability. Sadly, similar stories could be told about other learning disabilities (Coles, 1978, 1987; Cole, Dale, and Mills, 1990; Forness and Kavale, 1991; Lyon, 1987; Senf, 1986; Vaughn and Bos, 1987).

The vast majority of children who are labeled learning disabled receive the designation because of failures in learning to read (Gaskins, 1982; Lerner, 1985). Likewise, the bulk of learning disabilities research has focused on reading disabilities. However, despite this research focus, the field is still grappling with such basic issues as the classification criteria for reading disability (e.g., Ceci, 1986;

Morrison, 1991; Rutter, 1978; Siegel, 1988, 1989; Stanovich, 1986a, 1991; Vellutino, 1978). Equally contentious has been the ongoing debate about which information-processing deficiencies are uniquely characteristic of reading-disabled children (e.g., Bruck, 1988, 1990; Morrison, 1991; Olson, Wise, Conners, and Rack, 1990; Siegel, 1989, 1993; Siegel and Ryan, 1988; Stanovich, 1986a, 1988b; Vellutino, 1979; Willows, Kruk, and Corcos, 1993). Such basic issues are still in dispute because of the strange "cart-before-the-horse" history that has character-ized the reading disabilities field (Stanovich, 1991). We might have thought that researchers would have begun with the broadest and most theoretically neutral definition of reading disability—reading performance below some specified level on some well-known and psychometrically sound test—and then proceeded to investigate whether there were poor readers with differing cognitive profiles *within* this broader group. Unfortunately, the history of reading disabilities research does not resemble this logical sequence. Instead, early definitions of reading disability *assumed* knowledge of differential cognitive profiles (and causation) within the larger sample of poor readers and defined the condition of reading disability in a way that actually served to preclude empirical investigation of the unproven theoretical assumptions that guided the formulation of these definitions.

Aptitude/Achievement Discrepancy as a Reified Construct

This remarkable sleight of hand was achieved by tying the definition of reading disability to the notion of aptitude/achievement discrepancy (Ceci, 1986; Reynolds, 1985; Shepard, 1980; Siegel, 1989; Stanovich, 1991). That is, it was assumed that poor readers of high aptitude—as indicated by IQ test performance—were cognitively and neurologically different from poor readers of low aptitude. The term dyslexia, or reading disability, was reserved for those children showing signi-ficant statistical discrepancies between reading ability and intelligence test per-formance. Such discrepancy definitions have become embedded in the legal statutes governing special education practice in many states (Frankenberger and Fronzaglio, 1991; Frankenberger and Harper, 1987) and they also determine the subject selection procedures in most research investigations (Stanovich, 1991).

During the 1960s and 1970s, several proposed definitions of reading disability had considerable influence both on research and in service delivery debates. The definition of the World Federation of Neurology had many features that became canonical for many researchers and practitioners. Specific developmental dyslexia was characterized as "A disorder manifested by difficulty in learning to read de-spite conventional instruction, adequate intelligence, and socio-cultural opportun-ity. It is dependent upon fundamental cognitive abilities which are frequently of constitutional origin" (Critchley, 1970).

This particular definition highlighted the well-known "exclusionary criteria" that subsequently caused much dispute in discussions of dyslexia (e.g., Applebee, 1971; Ceci, 1986; Doehring, 1978; Eisenberg, 1978; Rutter, 1978). These exclusionary criteria were carried over into the definition of learning disability employed in the landmark Education for All Handicapped Children Act (PL 94–142) passed in the United States in 1975:

Specific learning disability means a disorder in one or more of the basic psychological processes involved in understanding or in using language spoken or written, which may manifest itself in an imperfect ability to listen, think, speak, read, write, spell, or to do mathematical calculations. The term includes such conditions as perceptual handicaps, brain injury, minimal brain dysfunction, dyslexia, and developmental aphasia. The term does not include children who have learning problems which are primarily the result of visual, hearing, or motor handicaps, of mental retardation, of emotional disturbance, or of environmental, cultural, or economic disadvantage.

The National Joint Committee for Learning Disabilities responded to criticisms of the exclusionary criteria by proposing that "these disorders are intrinsic to the individual and presumed to be due to central nervous system dysfunction. Even though a learning disability may occur concomitantly with other handicapping conditions (e.g., sensory impairment, mental retardation, social and emotional disturbance) or environmental influences (e.g., cultural differences, or inappropriate instruction, psycholinguistic factors), it is not the direct result of those conditions or influences" (Hammill, Leigh, McNutt, and Larsen, 1981). The committee thus emphasized that the mere presence of other impairments or of environmental deprivation should not exclude children from the LD categorization. The Interagency Committee on Learning Disabilities established by the U.S. Health Research Extension Act of 1985 (Kavanagh and Truss, 1988) accepted the essentials of the NJCLD definition, but included disorders of social skills in the listing of learning disabilities and added that learning disabilities may also co-occur with attention deficit disorder.

Various learning disabilities are defined in a similar way in the Diagnostic and Statistical Manual of Mental Disorders III-R (American Psychiatric Association, 1987). For example, the key diagnostic criterion for developmental reading disorder in DSM III-R is "reading achievement, as measured by a standardized, individually administered test, is markedly below the expected level, given the person's schooling and intellectual capacity (as determined by an individually administered IQ test)" (p. 44). The diagnostic criterion for developmental arithmetic disorder in DSM III-R is analogous: "Arithmetic skills, as measured by a standardized, individually administered test, are markedly below the expected level, given the person's schooling and intellectual capacity (as determined by an individually administered IQ test)" (p. 42).

As Shepard (1980) notes, "All LD definitions, either by connotation or denotation, rest on this discrepancy between achievement and ability. LD children are thereby distinguished from slow learners, who have low achievement but are presumably learning as fast as they are able" (p. 80). For example, one purpose of the so-called exclusionary criteria (ruling out mental retardation, socioenvironmental influences, etc. as causes; see Rutter, 1978) is to screen out generically poor cognitive functioning.

Operationally, researchers and practitioners have turned to the IQ test as the means of screening out generically poor cognitive functioning and as a way of positively identifying selective impairment. Formulas based on IQ test and achievement test performance have been (and continue to be) the main criterion that schools have used in defining this reading disability (Frankenberger and Fronzaglio, 1991; Frankenberger and Harper, 1987; Kavale and Nye, 1981; Reynolds, 1985). Despite repeated admonitions that disability classification should be multidimensional (Johnson, 1988), the formal or informal assessment of IQ/achievement discrepancy has dominated both educational practice and research into reading disability (Frankenberger and Fronzaglio, 1991; Stanovich, 1991).

The critical assumption that was reified in these definitions—in the almost total absence of empirical evidence—was that degree of discrepancy from IQ was meaningful: that the reading difficulties of the reading-disabled child with IQ discrepancy (reading-disabled, discrepant: RD-D) were different from those characterizing the reading-disabled child without IQ discrepancy (reading-disabled, nondiscrepant: RD-N). One reason that the study of reading disability has remained so confused is that, until quite recently, we lacked empirical evidence that validated the foundational assumption that was driving classification of children for purposes of research and educational practice. Ironically, the dominance of the discrepancy assumption has sometimes precluded the collection of the relevant data. Obviously, from the beginning, researchers should have made sure to include both RD-D and RD-N poor readers in their samples so that the discrepancy assumption could be tested. What happened instead was that the discrepancy notion became so quickly reified in practice that researchers often culled RD-N children from their samples in order to attain "purer" groups, thus precluding the critical comparison of RD-D and RD-N children.

For many years, most investigations of reading disabilities lacked RD-N controls. These investigations provided no indication of whether or not RD-N readers would have shown the same cognitive pattern as the RD-D children who were the focus of the investigation. Rutter and Yule's (1975) groundbreaking investigation of differences between RD-D and RD-N children stood alone for nearly a decade. Only recently have a number of converging studies that included RD-N controls been reported (Fletcher, Francis, Rourke, Shaywitz, and Shaywitz, 1992; Fletcher, Shaywitz, Shankweiler, Katz, Liberman, Stuebing, Francis, Fowler and Shaywitz, 1994; Jorm, Share, Maclean, and Matthews, 1986; Shaywitz, Fletcher, Holahan, and Shaywitz, 1992; Siegel, 1988, 1989; Stanovich and Siegel, 1994).

Quite early in the history of research on reading disability, researchers adopted a strong theoretical bias by tying an intuition about differential causation so closely to the notion of aptitude/achievement discrepancy (see Pennington, Gilger, Olson, DeFries, 1992; Taylor and Schatschneider, 1992). It was simply assumed that reading difficulty unaccompanied by low IQ was a distinct entity from other reading problems. But as Pennington et al. (1992) argue, the issue of "whether RD is just the lower tail of the multifactorially determined, normal distribution of reading skill, or whether some cases of RD represent an etiologically distinct disorder" (p. 562) is separable from the issue of whether there are differences between RD-D and RD-N poor readers. We must ask first whether there is evidence that some children within the entire group of poor readers display evidence for distinct etiology. At that point, we are in a position to address the question of whether RD-D children happen to *be* those with distinct etiology. As Pennington et al. (1992) note, "If no cases of RD represent an etiologically distinct disorder or syndrome, then it is pointless to argue about how to define a syndrome that does not exist!" (pp. 562–563).

Are There Distinct Etiologies for Some Cases of Reading Disability?

Genetic epidemiology provides one basis for establishing distinct causation for some cases of reading disability. In several samples, Pennington, Gilger, Pauls, Smith, Smith, and DeFries (1991) found evidence for sex-limited, autosomal additive or dominant transmission of reading disability, although there is evidence for genetic heterogeneity (see Pennington, 1990; Smith, Kimberling, and Pennington, 1991; Stevenson, 1992a). Additionally, twin studies have also consistently indicated a moderate heritability for the group deficit in reading ability displayed by the twin probands—as well as significant genetic covariance between the group deficit and phonological coding and awareness skills (DeFries, Fulker, and LaBuda, 1987; Olson et al., 1990; Olson, Wise, Conners, Rack, and Fulker, 1989; Pennington et al., 1992; Stevenson, 1992a, 1992b). The evidence has been summarized by Pennington, Van Orden, Kirson, and Haith (1991): "These behavior genetic analyses are consistent with the view that the heritable component in dyslexia at the written language level is in phonological coding and the heritable precursor to this deficit in phonological coding is a deficit in phoneme awareness" (p. 183).

Further evidence that reading disability might have distinct etiology comes from neuroanatomical studies (see Galaburda, 1994; Hynd, Marshall, and Gonzalez, 1991; and Hynd, Marshall, and Semrud-Clikeman, 1991 for reviews). For example, both post mortem and in-vivo studies have indicated that atypical symmetry in the planum temporale is associated with reading disability (Galaburda, 1991, 1994; Galaburda, Sherman, Rosen, Aboitz, and Geschwind, 1985; Larsen, Hoien, Lundberg, and Odegaard, 1990; Steinmetz and Galaburda, 1991). Larsen et al. (1990) found that the atypical symmetry was directly associated with the phonological coding deficit that is the primary phenotypic indicator of reading disability (see below). Additional cortical anomalies have been identified in other studies (see Galaburda, 1994; Hynd, Marshall, Gonzalez, 1991; Semrud-Clikeman, Hynd, Novey, and Eliopulos, 1991).

Does Discrepancy Measurement Identify Poor Readers with a Distinct Etiology?

Thus there is some support for a distinct etiology for at least some cases of reading disability. But these genetic and neuroanatomical findings are not enough—in and of themselves—to justify current definitional practice. There is still one critical link missing in the chain of evidence. The phenotypic performance pattern that defines the concept of dyslexia must be reliably and specifically linked with these indicators of distinct etiology. As discussed in the introduction, both research and educationally based definitions of reading disability have incorporated the notion of reading/IQ discrepancy (Stanovich, 1991). This practice arose because of the intuition that children with reading/IQ discrepancies (RD-D) would be more likely to display distinct etiology. Thus, identifying reading/IQ discrepancies was viewed as an easy way of picking out those children characterized by this distinct etiology. The basic assumption was that there were fundamental etiological, neurological, and (reading-related) cognitive differences between RD-D and RD-N children. It is this assumption that is presently without empirical support.

Reading disabled children display a characteristic profile of cognitive skills (to be discussed below); reading disability displays moderate heritability; evidence of a number of different modes of genetic transmission has been found (Pennington, 1990; Stevenson, 1992a); and some reading disabled children display atypical neuroanatomical features. The problem is that there is not one bit of evidence indicating that these characteristics are more true of RD-D children than of RD-N children.

No extant study has systematically related the neuroanatomical correlates of reading disability to degree of reading/IQ discrepancy. There is no evidence in the literature indicating that similar relationships between neuroanatomical features such as symmetry of the planum temporale and reading disability would not be found if reading disability were defined without reference to IQ discrepancy. Equally problematic is the finding that neurological disorders are no more common among RD-D than RD-N children. If anything, the opposite appears to be the case (Ingram, Mason, and Blackburn, 1970; Rutter and Yule, 1975; Silva, McGee, Williams, 1985).

The issue of differential etiology for RD-D and RD-N children has been directly addressed in twin studies of genetic influence. Olson, Rack, Conners, DeFries, and Fulker (1991) did find that the heritability of the group deficit of high-IQ (full scale) reading disabled twins (.67) was higher than the heritability of the group deficit for low-IQ reading disabled twins (.40), but this difference was not statistically significant. A parallel analysis based on verbal IQ rather than full-scale IQ revealed heritability values of .59 and .49, a difference that was again not statistically significant. Pennington et al. (1992) defined two groups of reading disabled children: one using a reading/IQ regression equation and the other using an age-only discrepancy. The group heritability for low scores on the IQ-discrepancy criterion was .46 and the group heritability for low scores on the age-discrepancy criterion was .49. The authors concluded that "These values indicate that approximately 50 percent of the deficit in scores for both diagnostic continua is due to heritable factors. The similarity in values suggests that the estimated proportion of genetic variance contributing to RD is essentially the same, regardless of the manner in which RD is identified. Thus, there is no evidence here for differential external validity of the two phenotypes" (p. 567). Pennington et al. (1992) also found that the genetic covariance between phonological coding ability and the IQ-discrepancy diagnosis (.60) was slightly higher than the corresponding covariance for phonological coding and the age-discrepancy criterion (.47), but this difference was not significant. The investigators concluded that "The heritability analyses are primarily consistent with the hypothesis that the same genes influence each diagnostic phenotype [RD-D vs. RD-N]" (Pennington et al., 1992, p. 570). Other investigations have also failed to provide strong evidence for markedly different heritability of deficits among high- and low-IQ reading-disabled children who are reading at the same level (Stevenson, 1991, 1992b; Stevenson, Graham, Fredman, and McLoughlin, 1987).

IQ-Discrepancy and the Reading Disability Phenotype

It is really not so surprising that genetic and neuroanatomical correlates have not been found to be differentially associated with RD-D and RD-N poor readers. This is because IQ-discrepancy appears to be at best weakly correlated with the primary phenotypic indicators of reading disability. What are those indicators?

Although there may be small groups of children who have specific comprehension difficulties (Oakhill and Garnham, 1988), there is a great deal of converging evidence indicating that most cases of reading disability arise because of difficulties in the process of word recognition (e.g., Adams and Bruck, 1993; Bruck, 1988, 1990; Morrison, 1991; Perfetti, 1985; Share, 1995; Siegel, 1985; Siegel and Faux, 1989; Siegel and Ryan, 1989; Snowling, 1991; Stanovich, 1981, 1986b, 1988b). These difficulties are, in turn, due to deficiencies in processes of phonological coding whereby letter patterns are transformed into phonological codes. Problems with phonological coding lead to the most diagnostic symptom of reading disability, difficulty in pronouncing pseudowords (e.g., Bruck, 1988, 1990; Felton and Wood, 1992; Manis, Custodio, and Szeszulski, 1993; Olson et al., 1989; Rack, Snowling, and Olson, 1992; Share, 1995; Siegel, 1989; Siegel and Ryan, 1988; Snowling, 1981, 1991; Stanovich and Siegel, 1994). In contrast to phonological coding, processes of orthographic coding—where words are recognized via direct visual access—appear to be relatively less impaired in disabled readers (Frith and Snowling, 1983; Holligan and Johnston, 1988; Olson, Kliegl, Davidson, and Foltz, 1985; Olson et al., 1989; Pennington et al., 1986; Rack, 1985; Siegel, 1993; Stanovich and Siegel, 1994; Snowling, 1980).

The precursor to the phonological coding difficulty appears to be a deficit in basic segmental language representation sometimes termed phonological sensitivity (e.g., Bentin, 1992; Bowey, Cain, and Ryan, 1992; Bradley and Bryant, 1978, 1985; Bruck, 1990, 1992; Bruck and Treiman, 1990; Bryant, Maclean, Bradley, and Crossland, 1990; Goswami and Bryant, 1990; Olson et al., 1989; Share, 1995; Stahl and Murray, 1994; Stanovich, 1982, 1992; Stanovich, Cunningham, and Cramer, 1984; Torgesen, Wagner, and Rashotte, 1994; Vellutino and Scanlon, 1987; Wagner and Torgesen, 1987). The development of more finely segmented phonological representations appears to be a prerequisite to rapid reading acquisition in an alphabetic orthography. Lack of phonological sensitivity inhibits the learning of the alphabetic coding patterns that underlie fluent word recognition (Bryant et al., 1990; Goswami and Bryant, 1990; Stahl and Murray, 1994; Stanovich et al., 1984; Tunmer and Hoover, 1992; Tunmer and Nesdale, 1985).

As previously indicated, the most distinctive indicator of the phonological coding deficits that are characteristic of reading disability is difficulty in naming pseudowords (Rack et al., 1992). Reading-disabled children not only perform worse than chronological age peers on pseudoword tasks, but they also underperform reading-level controls; that is, younger nondisabled children equated on word recognition skill. This pseudoword deficit in a reading-level match is one of the most distinctive indicators of the reading-disability phenotype (Olson et al., 1989; Rack et al., 1992; Stanovich and Siegel, 1994). However, several studies that have compared the performance of poor readers with and without reading-IQ discrepancy have found that they display equivalent pseudoword deficits (Felton and Wood, 1992; Fredman and Stevenson, 1988; Share et al., 1990; Siegel, 1988, 1989, 1992; Stanovich and Siegel, 1994). This primary indicator of reading disability does not distinguish disabled readers with IQ-discrepancy from those without such discrepancies (see also Fletcher et al., 1994).

Likewise, measures of orthographic processing, on which reading-disabled children are less impaired, show no differences between poor readers with and without reading-IQ discrepancy (Fredman and Stevenson, 1988; Siegel, 1992; Stanovich and Siegel, 1994). Finally, the spelling-sound regularity effect, often interpreted as an indicator of the relative reliance on phonological and orthographic coding processes (Barron, 1981; Manis, Szeszulski, Holt, and Graves, 1990; Olson et al., 1985) appears to be of a similar magnitude in reading-disabled children and younger reading-level controls. This also appears to be true for both poor readers without (Beech and Harding, 1984; Stanovich, Nathan, and Zolman, 1988; Treiman and Hirsh-Pasek, 1985) and for poor readers with reading-IQ discrepancy (Baddeley, Logie, and Ellis, 1988; Ben-Dror, Pollatsek, and Scarpati, 1991; Brown and Watson, 1991; Bruck, 1990; Holligan and Johnston, 1988; Olson et al., 1985; Siegel and Ryan, 1988; Watson and Brown, 1992; Stanovich and Siegel, 1994).

Thus there is no indication that the nature of processing within the word recognition module differs at all for poor readers with and without IQ-discrepancy. Their relative strengths in phonological and orthographic coding processes, and their relative reliance on these subskills, appear to be nearly the same. The relative tradeoff between phonological and orthographic subskills—one of the most reliable phenotypic behavior patterns associated with reading disability—does not distinguish poor readers with and without reading-IQ discrepancy. This finding is consistent with the lack of evidence for a difference between these two groups in genetic and neuroanatomical studies.

Not surprisingly, there *are* cognitive differences between RD-D and RD-N children outside of the word recognition module (Ellis and Large, 1987; Siegel, 1992; Stanovich, 1988b; Stanovich and Siegel, 1994), because these children differ in intelligence. Some of these cognitive differences may be related to comprehension processes. Thus there may well be reading comprehension differences between

RD-D and RD-N readers who are equated on word recognition ability (Bloom, Wagner, Reskin, and Bergman, 1980; Ellis and Large, 1987; Jorm et al., 1986; Silva et al., 1985), although even this expectation has sometimes not borne out (Siegel, 1988, 1989; Felton and Wood, 1992). These differences might well relate to certain educational issues such as the reading level to be expected of students subsequent to remediation of their primary word recognition problem (Stanovich, 1991). However, it is important to note that any such differences are not indicators of the core processing problem that caused the word recognition deficit that triggered the diagnosis of reading disability in the first place—phonological coding difficulties probably resulting from deficient phonological sensitivity. Thus such differences outside of the word recognition module provide no rationale for a definition of reading disability based on IQ-discrepancy. Such definitions would only give the mistaken impression that children with reading-IQ discrepancy have distinctive genetic/neurological etiology. Although indirect validation of the idea of differentiating poor readers on the basis of reading-IQ discrepancies could be derived from data showing that high- and low-IQ poor readers are differentially sensitive to specific educational interventions, there is currently no body of evidence indicating that poor readers with reading-IQ discrepancy respond differently to various educational treatments than do poor readers without such discrepancies.

Deeper Conceptual Problems: The Issue of Intelligence

The central assumption that underlies the concept of a learning disability is the idea of selective cognitive deficit: the idea that individuals can display deficits in only a restricted domain of cognitive functioning and therefore that educational interventions in Domain A should be different for children who have a deficit only in that domain as contrasted with children who have a deficit in Domain A that is accompanied by a variety of other cognitive dysfunctions. In educational practice, the concept of selective deficit became tied to the construct of intelligence and was operationalized by the use of IQ tests. However, the learning disabilities field has only recently begun to come to grips with the fact that linking the concept of a learning disability to the construct of intelligence automatically transfers all of the empirical and theoretical controversies surrounding the latter to the former (Lyon, 1987; Siegel, 1989; Stanovich, 1989, 1991; Torgesen, 1986, 1991).

The popularity in educational practice of the use of the concept of intelligence as a benchmark in the definition of learning disability is puzzling, however. Surely we would be hard-pressed to find a concept more controversial than intelligence in all of psychology. It has been the subject of dispute for decades, and this shows no sign of abating. Current work on individual differences in intelligent functioning continues to produce exciting findings and interesting theories (Baron, 1985; Ceci, 1990, 1993; Sternberg, 1985, 1988), but no consensual view of the intelligence concept (Sternberg and Detterman, 1986). Even though much progress has been made in both empirical and theoretical domains, quite fundamental disputes remain. For example, some investigators have recently emphasized more contextualized approaches to the study of intelligence (Bronfenbrenner and Ceci, 1994; Ceci, 1990, 1993; Sternberg, 1985, 1988; Sternberg and Wagner, 1986; Voss, Perkins, and Segal, 1991), whereas others have been advocating more decontextualized biological approaches (Carpenter, Just, and Shell, 1990; Mulder, Wijers, Smid, Brookhuis, and Mulder, 1989; Vernon, 1987, 1991).

Yet despite the controversy surrounding intelligence in the cognitive, developmental, and psychometric literature, it was adopted as a foundational construct for definitions of learning disability. Oblivious to the ongoing debates, the learning disabilities field seems to have avoided worrying about the issue by simply adopting a variant of E. G. Boring's dictum and acting as if "Intelligence is what the Psychological Corporation says it is!" The choice of IQ test performance as the baseline from which to measure achievement discrepancies was accepted by teachers, schools, professional organizations, and government agencies in the absence of much critical discussion or research evidence. Until quite recently, the field seems never to have grappled very seriously with the question of why the benchmark should have been IQ. It is thus not surprising that the concept of intelligence is the genesis of so many of the conceptual paradoxes that plague the learning disabilities field (Stanovich, 1986a, 1986b, 1988b, 1991).

Why was professional assent to the use of IQ test scores in the discrepancy definition given so readily? Undoubtedly there were many reasons, but probably one factor was the belief that IQ scores were valid measures of intellectual potential. Certainly an extreme form of this belief can be seen in the promotional activities of many advocacy groups and in media portrayals. The typical "media learning disabled child" is almost always a very bright child who is deeply troubled in school because of a "glitch" (usually assumed to be biologically based, see Coles, 1978, 1987, McGill-Franzen, 1987) that prevents him or her from learning. The subtext of the portrayal clearly implies that the tragedy of the situation is proportionally greater because the child's great "potential" remains unfulfilled.

One major problem, however, is that most psychometricians, developmental psychologists, and educational psychologists long ago gave up the belief that IQ test scores measured potential in any valid sense. Indeed, standard texts in educational measurement and assessment routinely warn against interpreting IQ scores as measures of intellectual potential (Anastasi, 1988; Cronbach, 1984; Thorndike, 1963). At their best, IQ test scores are gross measures of current cognitive functioning (Humphreys, 1979; Detterman, 1982). Indeed, many theorists would dispute even this characterization. Without entering into the details of all of these debates, the point is that an IQ test score is not properly interpreted as a measure of an individual's potential. Thus, to the extent that this misinterpretation contributed to the practice of measuring discrepancies from IQ scores, this practice was misconceived from the beginning. In short, we have been basing systems of educational classification in the area of learning disabilities on special claims of unique potential that are neither conceptually nor psychometrically justifiable.

But this is only the beginning of a set of theoretical problems that surround the use of IQ scores in learning disability definitions. Consider the fact that researchers, let alone practitioners, cannot agree on the type of IQ score that should be used in the measurement of discrepancy. For example, it has often been pointed out that changes in the characteristics of the IQ test being used will result in somewhat different subgroups of children being identified as discrepant and also alter the types of processing deficits that they will display in comparison studies (Bowers, Steffy, and Tate, 1988; Fletcher et al., 1989; Lindgren, De Renzi, and Richman, 1985; Reed, 1970; Shankweiler, Crain, Brady, and Macaruso, 1992; Siegel and Heaven, 1986; Stanley, Smith, and Powys, 1982; Torgesen, 1985; Vellutino, 1978). Yet it is not hard to look in the research literature and find recommendations that are all over the map.

For example, a very common recommendation that one finds in the literature is that performance and/or nonverbal IQ tests be used to assess discrepancy (e.g., Beech and Harding, 1984; Perfetti, 1985, p. 180; Siegel and Heaven, 1986; Stanovich, 1986a; Thomson, 1982) because verbally loaded measures are allegedly unfair to dyslexic children. In complete contrast, Hessler (1987) argues for the use of *verbally loaded* tests because "Using a nonverbal test of intelligence because an individual has better nonverbal cognitive abilities than verbal cognitive abilities does not, of course, remove the importance of verbal processing and knowledge structures in academic achievement; it only obscures their importance and perhaps provides unrealistic expectations for an individual's academic achievement" (p. 46).

Of course, the use of full-scale IQ scores results in some unprincipled amalgamation of the above two diametrically opposed philosophies but is still sometimes recommended precisely *because* the field is so confused and so far from consensus on this issue (Harris and Sipay, 1985, p. 145). Finally, there is a sort of "either" strategy that is invoked by investigators who require only that performance *or* verbal IQ exceed 90 in dyslexic samples (e.g., Olson et al., 1985). As Torgesen (1986) has pointed out, the naturally occurring multidimensional continuum of abilities guarantees that such a criterion ends up creating more discrepancies with performance IQ. A discussion of the implications of these different choices for studies of the information processing problems of reading-disabled children is contained in Stanovich (1991). We will here focus briefly on the fact that there are social implications in these choices as well.

Value Judgments Inherent in Different Indices of "Potential"

It is rarely noted that the use of certain types of intelligence tests in the operationalization of reading disability often conceals conceptions of "potential" that are questionable, if not downright illogical. Consider some of the hidden assumptions behind the often-heard admonition that verbally loaded intelligence tests are unfair to reading-disabled children and that performance IQ measures provide "fairer" measures of the reading potential of such children. Typical arguments are that "The instrument (WISC-R) is confounded and not a true measure of potential. The learning disability itself is reflected clearly in the IQ performance" (Birnbaum, 1990, p. 330) and that "Computing an IQ from items shown to be specifically associated with dyslexic difficulties may be an underestimate" (Thomson, 1982, p. 94). But it is not at all clear—even if we accept the problematic notion of educational "potential"—that the spatial abilities, fluid intelligence, and problem-solving abilities tapped by most performance tests provide the best measures of the potential to comprehend verbal material. To the contrary, it would appear that verbally loaded measures would provide the best estimates of how much a disabled reader could get from written text if their deficient decoding skills were to be remediated.

As Hessler (1987) notes:

There are different types of intelligence, and they predict academic achievement differently. . . . In fact, the performance score accounts for so little academic achievement that there is reason to question its relevance for use as an ability measure to predict academic achievement. It is therefore a mistake to use any test of intelligence as an ability measure for predicting academic achievement in a severe discrepancy analysis simply because it is called a test of intelligence, without demonstrating some ability to predict academic achievement. (p. 45; see also Lyon, 1987, pp. 78–79).

Consistent with this interpretation, van der Wissel (1987) has demonstrated that the extent to which an IQ subtest separates RD-D from RD-N children is *inversely* related to how highly the subtest correlates with reading achievement. It is a paradoxical situation indeed when the indicators that best make this subgroup discrimination are those that do *not* relate to the criterion performance that drew professional attention in the first place—namely, reading failure.

It goes largely unnoticed that when people make the "fairness" argument for the use of nonverbal tests they in fact jettison the notion of "potential," at least in its common meaning. They cannot mean the potential for verbal comprehension through print if the decoding deficit were remediated, since this is not what IQ tests—particularly the performance tests they are recommending—assess. What people who make the "verbal IQ scores are unfair to dyslexics" argument are asserting—implicitly—is that if we had a society that was not so organized around literacy, dyslexics would have the potential to do much better. True. But we must recognize that this is a *counterfactual* premise that contradicts more common usages, to the advantage of some and to the disadvantage of others. It raises the question of how the field so easily fell into adopting a linguistic usage of the term "potential" that requires the assumption that literacy-based technological societies will be totally reconstructed. We seem to find it difficult to use this crude cognitive probe—an IQ score—as a circumscribed behavioral index without loading social, and indeed metaphysical (Scheffler, 1985), baggage onto it. Despite the fact that our textbooks remind us that these tests are merely predictors of school performance, the learning disabilities field finds it remarkably difficult to treat them as such.

A Thought Experiment for the Learning Disabilities Field

To further highlight the value judgments inherent in the use of IQ test scores to define particular children and to single them out for special treatment, Stanovich

(1993) has proposed a thought experiment for the LD field that is designed to illustrate how the somewhat arbitrary composition of IQ tests, as well as changing assumptions about what the concept of intelligence is, can lead to the postulation of new disability categories that perhaps have not been thought of before. The thought experiment was intended to force the field to think through the implications of defining learning disabilities in terms of discrepancies from psychometric IQ.

The key to the thought experiment is the realization that the way that reading and arithmetic have been operationalized in terms of IQ discrepancy invites, by analogy, the recognition of other disabilities when certain behavioral domains are found to be out of kilter with intelligence test performance. For example, in the report of the Interagency Committee on Learning Disabilities, established by the U.S. Health Research Extension Act of 1985 (Kavanagh and Truss, 1988) the analogy has been extended to social skills which, in the Interagency definition, is a domain in which a learning disability can occur. That is, the logic of discrepancy-based classification based on IQ test performance has created a clear precedent whereby we are almost obligated to create a new disability category when an important skill domain is found to be somewhat dissociated from intelligence.

One logical corollary of this past practice is that the less comprehensive IQ tests are, the more such domains there will be; or, conversely, the more comprehensive and exhaustive the set of skills tapped by IQ tests the fewer candidates for additional discrepancy-based disability categories there will be. Unfortunately, there seems every reason to believe that we are in the former situation. Almost all critics of IQ tests make the argument that these instruments ignore many important domains of cognitive/behavioral functioning (e.g., Block and Dworkin, 1976; Ceci, 1990; Davidson, 1990; Evans and Waites, 1981; Gardner, 1983, 1986; Gould, 1981; Hilliard, 1984; Neisser, 1976; Owen, 1985). Such critics often point out that the cognitive domains that these instruments actually assess are only a small subset of the larger set of skills that are folded into the vernacular concept of intelligence. For example, studies of the layperson's concept of intelligence consistently demonstrate that it encompasses practical problem-solving, creativity, and social skills (Sternberg, Conway, Ketron, and Bernstein, 1981)—none of which are tapped by the conventional IQ tests that are used for learning disability classification. Finally, the literature on practical intelligence and recent research on the domain-specificity of cognitive performance both serve to focus attention on the narrowness of the psychometrically defined intelligence concept (see Ceci, 1990; Gardner, 1983; Resnick, Levine, and Teasley, 1991; Rogoff and Lave, 1984; Sternberg and Wagner, 1986; Voss, Perkins, and Segal, 1991).

Thus criticisms of IQ tests are often motivated by the impression that IQ tests are missing important aspects of behavior and cognition. Naturally, these aspects that are missing are logically more likely to be discrepant from IQ than is a domain that is represented on the tests. When a discrepancy occurs in an area that is deemed important, we have the makings of a situation where we may feel pressure to create a disability category. Given the standard way of operationalizing learning disabilities, the field will always be hard-pressed—from a legal or a conceptual point of view—to deny such a request for a new disability category. It is mere hubris to think that our current jury-rigged definitions cover all of the potential domains that a concerned public might view as candidates for educational intervention.

In short, the very narrowness of the cognitive domains tapped by IQ tests could potentially spawn a plethora of disability categories as yet unrecognized if the logic of current discrepancy-based classification continues to be a key feature of the learning disabilities construct in research and in practice. The thought experiment introduced by Stanovich (1993) demonstrates this point by proposing a new disability category. The new psychological disability arises from the possibility of deficits in a set of thought processes, behaviors, and dispositions that are not the same as the capacities tapped on current IQ tests and that therefore can become severely dissociated from IQ test performance. These behavioral dispositions and thought processes are often folded into the vernacular concept of intelligence and thus are deemed to be important by the general public.

The new disability is called dysrationalia. The proposed definition of the disability is as follows:

Dysrationalia is the persistent failure to think and behave rationally despite adequate intelligence. It is a general term that refers to a heterogeneous group of disorders manifested by significant difficulties in belief formation, in the assessment of belief consistency, and/or in the determination of action to achieve one's goals. Although dysrationalia may occur concomitantly with other handicapping conditions (e.g., sensory impairment), dysrationalia is not the result of those conditions. The key diagnostic criterion for dysrationalia is a level of rationality, as demonstrated in thinking and behavior, that is significantly below the level of the individual's intellectual capacity (as determined by an individually administered IQ test).

Stanovich (1993) outlined how this definition could be used to justify a disability category. The theoretical task is simply to operationally define rational thinking dispositions and behaviors and demonstrate that they can become dissociated from traditional psychometric intelligence. Once this has been done (Stanovich, 1993, 1994), the dysrationalia concept can be defended against potential objections. Such a defense has implications for all discrepancy definitions in the learning disabilities field because it immediately becomes apparent that the conceptual problems entailed by admitting a concept of dysrationalia are no more formidable than those inherent in other discrepancy-based categories that have become reified in current professional, legal, and research practice. The choice is to accept dysrationalia as a viable concept or else to have the rationale for currently accepted learning disabilities undermined. Consider the following objections:

Objection: Rationality cannot be measured.

Reply: The dispositions toward rational thought and behavior are, in principle, no less measurable than the capacities traditionally viewed as underlying intelligence. The latter have simply been the subject of much more intense investigation. This is not to deny the difficult problems presented by the concept of rationality (Goldman, 1986, 1993; Kitcher, 1993; Nozick, 1993; Stich, 1990). It must be stressed, however, that most of the "in principle" arguments against the possibility of assessing individual differences in rationality (see Cohen, 1981; Davidson, 1984; Dennett, 1978; Stich, 1990) could be turned against the traditional concept of intelligence. This is particularly so when intelligence is taken to encompass abilities relevant to adapting to the environment or to attaining the organism's goals (Baron, 1985; Stich, 1990). In fact, the "impossibility of measurement" argument has repeatedly been put forth by critics of the intelligence concept. Because the concept of learning disability, as traditionally conceived, is crucially dependent on some notion of intelligence (Siegel, 1989; Stanovich, 1991) it would behoove those who are supporters of our traditional categories of learning disability not to put intelligence in jeopardy by attacking the idea of operationalizing rationality.

Objection: But we have no standardized tests of rational thinking.

Reply: This is true enough, but it is hardly a reason to reject the concept of dysrationalia. In fact, given the myriad criticisms of today's standardized IQ tests— which, for the most part, congealed into their present form decades ago—it is unclear that we should view the lack of established tests of rationality as a drawback. The fact that IQ tests took form *before* the cognitive revolution and the concomitant explosion in information processing assessment methods has been a constant source of grief for the intelligence field. Actually, if we do ever decide to construct standardized devices to assess processes of rational thinking, we will benefit from the extended discussion of the mistakes that have been made in constructing standardized instruments for assessing cognitive capacities.

Indeed, rationality measures will benefit from not having the "cart before the horse" history that characterizes IQ tests. With the exception of a few "critical thinking" tests (Ennis and Millman, 1985; Watson and Glaser, 1980), we lack any history of measuring individual differences in rational thinking via standardized instruments. This means that we will have a chance to get a more conceptually coherent foundation of methods and theory laid down before the construction of standardized instruments begins to limit conceptual development. Preliminary work has been done on many individual components of rational thought. For example, we know a considerable amount about the ability to properly infer causation, to utilize probabilistic information, to detect covariation, to isolate variables, to detect inconsistency in beliefs, to utilize falsification strategies, and to coordinate theory and evidence (see Arkes and Hammond, 1986; Baron, 1985; Dawes, 1988; Evans, 1989; Kahneman, Slovic, and Tversky, 1982; Kuhn, 1991, 1993; Nisbett and Ross, 1980). Relatively reliable operational methods of assessing rational thinking components such as covariation detection (Arkes and Harkness, 1983; Broniarczyk and Alba, 1994; Kunda and Nisbett, 1986; Wasserman, Dorner, and Kao, 1990), the ability to isolate variables (Farris, and Revlin, 1989; Tschirgi, 1980), and the ability to calibrate knowledge (Arkes, Christensen, Lai, and Blumer, 1987; Fischhoff, 1988) have been developed. We know as much about some of these processes as we know about certain cognitive components of intelligence.

Objection: Learning disabilities are related to difficulties in school. Rationality is not an academic subject.

Reply: Neither are social skills, but they are included in the definition of the Interagency Committee on Learning Disabilities (Kavanagh and Truss, 1988). For that matter, neither are "reasoning" or "listening," but they are likewise included in the Interagency definition and in the definition of the National Joint Committee on Learning Disabilities (Hammill, 1990).

Objection: But social skills, reasoning, and listening are critical to functioning in a variety of domains, including functioning in academic settings.

Reply: So is rationality, to some extent. But an important point is being made here. Perhaps it *is* easier for a person with dysrationalia to successfully negotiate their way through our current educational institutions than it is for a person who has some other learning disability. But is this a good thing? Perhaps defining a disability of dysrationalia would focus our schools on areas of thinking that are currently neglected. This point returns us to the issue of the differential privileging of some thinking skills over others that was discussed earlier. For example, Ivy League colleges or selective flagship state universities in the United States are selecting society's future elite (selection mechanisms in other countries have a similar logic despite surface dissimilarities). What societal goals are served by the selection mechanisms (e.g., SAT tests) that they use? Social critics have argued that it is the goal of maintaining an economic and social elite (Aronowitz and Giroux, 1985; Bowles and Gintis, 1976; Oakes, 1985). But the social critics seem to have generally neglected to ask another type of question: "Why select for capacities and ignore rationality? Whose interests are served by our almost exclusive focus on cognitive capacities and who is disadvantaged by our doing so?" For example, it is an interestingly open question whether race and social class differences on measures of rational thinking would be found to be as large as those displayed on tasks tapping cognitive capacities.

Finally, there are examples where dysrationalia *does* seem to very directly interfere with school learning. Wassermann (1987) describes such a case—a sixth grader named Bob. Bob's measured IQ was 116 and he did fine on achievement tests. However, despite his reasonably high IQ, his rigidity and his disposition toward absolutist thinking were creating learning problems. His answers to any questions posed by the teacher that required thought and reflection, rather than rote memory, were startlingly oversimplified and immature for his age and IQ. During a discussion of the situation in South Africa, Bob articulated his puzzlement at why this problem was not solved: "I don't understand it. When there was slavery down South in our country, the northern states fought against the southern states, and the slaves were free. So why don't the people in North Africa go to war against South Africa" (p. 461). Wassermann (1987) explains that Bob's "troubles began only when he was called upon to think for himself—to make purposeful choices, to connect means with ends, to identify similarities and differences in seemingly analogous situations, to suspend judgment in the presence of contradictory data, to design and carry out plans for projects or investigations. At tasks such as these, he functioned at a considerable deficit" (p. 461). This certainly seems to be a case where school learning is being interfered with by a problem in critical thinking dispositions (Baron, 1985; Perkins, Jay, and Tishman, 1993).

Objection: The cognitive capacities of intelligence and the components of rationality might be more intertwined than has been suggested. Discrepancies between these domains might be highly unlikely.

Reply: Of course, the magnitude of the correlations between cognitive capacities and rational thinking processes is an empirical question. Nevertheless, even a substantial relationship would leave enough room for dissociations of the type that would define dysrationalia. Scores on reading comprehension tests and IQ tests can be correlated as high as .60 to .70 in samples of adults (Harris and Sipay, 1985; Stanovich, Cunningham, and Feeman, 1984), yet this still leaves enough room for the dissociations that define reading disability to occur. It is unlikely that cognitive capacities and rational thinking skills correlate any more highly than this. In fact, there does exist some empirical evidence indicating that processes of evidence evaluation can sometimes be strikingly independent of IQ (Ceci and Liker, 1986; King, Kitchener, Davison, Parker, and Wood, 1983; Kitchener and Brenner, 1990; Kitchener and King, 1981; Lesser and Paisner, 1985).

Objection: The definition of dysrationalia presented previously did not contain parallels to the parts of the National Joint Committee on Learning Disabilities (NJCLD) definition indicating that a learning disability must be "intrinsic to the individual," that it be "due to central nervous system dysfunction," and that it not be the result of "extrinsic influences" such as cultural differences or inappropriate instruction. Likewise, the Interagency definition (Kavanagh and Truss, 1988) rules out "socioenvironmental influences" as causes of learning disabilities.

Reply: These parts of the NJCLD definition are remnants of the old "exclusionary criteria" that were once used to define learning disability and that have received voluminous criticism (Ceci, 1986; Doehring, 1978; Rutter, 1978). These particular aspects of the NJCLD definition are problematic because they assume a causal model of learning disability that we simply do not have (Coles, 1987; Senf, 1986; Siegel, 1989; Stanovich, 1991). In fact, they create a conceptual muddle that will continue to bedevil the learning disabilities field if they are not abandoned. For example, it is not clear just what "intrinsic to the individual" means if anything other than a redundant reference to a later part of the definition: that the disability not be the direct result of "extrinsic influences." "Due to central nervous system dysfunction" by itself does not rule out "extrinsic influences" because such influences would ultimately manifest their effects in changing the central nervous system (both genetic and environmental causes will have their proximal influences by way of the nervous system). Without further elaboration that only future research can provide (i.e., what kind of central nervous system dysfunction), the phrasing in the NJCLD definition is little more than a tautology. There is simply not a shred of empirical evidence indicating that children with aptitude/achievement discrepancies caused by "extrinsic" influences differ from "intrinsically" caused learning disabilities in their response to treatment, educational prognosis, or cognitive profile. "Extrinsic influences" are ruled out seemingly by fiat, because the earlier parts of the definition do not provide a principled rationale for eliminating such causes.

In short, "intrinsic to the individual" and "due to central nervous system dysfunction" do no conceptual work at all, and "extrinsic influences" are ruled out in the absence of principled reasons. To put it bluntly, these parts of the traditional definition of learning disabilities are pure hash, and thus it seemed wise not to similarly burden the concept of dysrationalia. To the extent that dysrationalia is free of the conceptual confusion surrounding these parts of the traditional definitions it is actually on *firmer* ground than disabilities deriving their conceptual support from the traditional definitions.

Objection: Should not the absolute level of rationality be important, as well as discrepancy from IQ?

Reply: Yes. Dysrationalia was defined by reference to discrepancy only to highlight its conceptual similarity to other learning disabilities. Discrepancy measurement was proposed only in order to establish the analogy with learning disability: that one could start out with the same "common sense" assumption that the "potential" for rational behavior is higher among those higher in intelligence. But as we have seen, "common sense" in the domain of reading disability has been harder to verify than we might have thought. The same might be true for rationality/intelligence discrepancies. Note that the "common sense" or "folk concept" (Greenwood, 1991) of learning disability probably also involves the vernacular concept of intelligence and the assumption that the IQ test is a comprehensive assessment of the nature of cognitive functioning. That is, the folk model leads us to view discrepancies from IQ in some domain as "surprising" because it is assumed that intelligence reflects something comprehensive and pervasive about cognitive functioning. If, in fact, IQ tests are nothing of the sort—if they reflect only a thin slice of the thinking domain (a small collection of cognitive microcapacities)—then the fact that individuals show up with discrepancies from IQ (in reading or in rational thinking or whatever) becomes much less surprising. The point is that the interpretation of any particular discrepancy from a score on an IQ test rests on a comprehensive theory of what mental components are assessed by the test.

Whither Learning Disabilities?

In short, it is not difficult to define and defend a whole host of "disabilities" by simply taking the idea of aptitude/achievement discrepancy to its logical conclusions. But, when taken to its logical conclusion via such "disabilities" as dysrationalia, the concept of learning disability fractionates into incoherence. Either from a conceptual or empirical point of view, the concept of learning disability appears to be unstable.

For example, with regard to reading disability—the learning disability on which we have the most complete evidence—the research literature provides no support for the notion that we need a special scientific concept of "dyslexia" or "reading disability" separate from other, more neutral, terms such as poor reader, less skilled, etc. Whatever conceptual work terms such as dyslexia or reading disability appear to be doing is more apparent than real.

The concept of dyslexia is inextricably linked with the idea of an etiologically distinct type of reading disability associated with moderate to high IQ. In fact, it appears that (1) reading-IQ discrepancy measurement fails to identify a distinct phenotypic pattern of word recognition subskill deficits; (2) reading-IQ discrepancy measurement does not identify a group of children with significantly different heritability values for core information processing deficits; and (3) there are as yet no indications that the neuroanatomical anomalies that are associated with reading disability are more characteristic of high-IQ than of low-IQ poor readers. As Taylor and Schatschneider (1992) argue, "IQ criteria were imposed primarily as a means of ruling out confounding variables and for assisting in the search for specific cognitive antecedents" (p. 630). It appears that the intuition that IQ discrepancy measurement would provide such assistance is mistaken. IQ discrepancy does not carve out a unique information-processing pattern in the word recognition module that is the critical locus of reading disability. If there are a special group of reading-disabled children who are behaviorally/cognitively/genetically "different" it is becoming increasingly unlikely that they can be quickly picked out using reading-IQ discrepancy as a proxy for the genetic and neurological differences themselves.

Rather than becoming further distracted by the IQ issue, it may well be more fruitful for the field to explore the implications of conceptualizing reading disability as residing on a continuum of developmental language disorder (see Bishop and Adams, 1990; Catts, 1991; Gathercole and Baddeley, 1987; Kamhi, 1992; Kamhi and Catts, 1989; Scarborough, 1990). For example, Gathercole and Baddeley (1987) argue the following:

Although language problems are typically detected prior to the children receiving reading instruction. . . . it is possible that the alphabetic literacy skills required in reading may be more sensitive to the adequacy of speech analytic skills than other aspects of normal linguistic development, such that a mild deficit may only be detectable in reading performance. More severe subjects may result in the more generalized symptom complex associated with developmental language disorder. . . . This is also clearly consistent with the notion that the two populations may quantitatively differ rather than qualitatively. (p. 464)

In light of these attempts to conceptualize reading disability as a milder form of language disability, it is interesting to note that the question of whether a discrepancy-defined disability is different from a disability defined purely in terms of chronological age occurs in analogous form in the area of developmental language disorder (Aram, Morris, and Hall, 1992; Cole, Dale, and Mills, 1990). Cole et al. (1990) describe how prior to more recent concerns about the relation between cognition and language "Any child who demonstrated a discrepancy between chronological age and language age would generally have been considered a candidate for language intervention by speech-language pathologists" (p. 291). However, an assumed tight link between language and cognition has recently led to what is called the Cognitive Referencing model, which has the implication that "Children who have developed language skills at a level equal to their cognitive skills are not considered to be language delayed, even if their language skills are significantly below chronological age" (p. 292). However, just as in the area of reading disability, Cole et al. point out that "it is surprising that there is little or no empirical evidence for evaluating the Cognitive Referencing model" (p. 292).

In summary, the search for neurological, genetic, and information-processing correlates of reading disability is being conducted with vigor in research laboratories around the world. There appears to be no reason for such investigations to restrict their research samples in advance based on reading-IQ discrepancy. Indeed, our ability to map the multidimensional space of reading-related cognitive skills would be impaired by such a procedure. No one disputes the logical possibility of distinct etiologies within the population of poor readers. Obviously, if a group of children were not taught to read and not exposed to print, their reading disability would have a distinct causation different from that in the general disabled population. The point, instead, is that it has yet to be demonstrated that whatever distinct causes actually exist are correlated with the degree of reading-IQ discrepancy.

In the face of such evidence, why has the discrepancy-based notion of learning disability remained so enticing to the education field? We have alluded to some of the reasons in our previous discussion of the emphasis on the "potential" notion. Carrier (1986) and Coles (1987) discuss an even wider range of social and political determinants. For example, Coles (1987) views the learning disability label as a fig leaf behind which society hides the collapse of the learning environments it provides for its children. His book provides a portrait of the middle-class family stretched to the limit by larger economic and social forces, and he sketches a model of how such pressures reduce the mediating learning experiences available to children. As these pressures increase, Coles argues that we become more desperate to find biologically based categories that obscure the dysfunctional nature of many family and learning environments.

In the decade subsequent to Coles' (1987) critique, the competitive pressures of a world economy dominated by corporate power intent on reducing employment security in order to maximize profit (Barlett and Steele, 1992; Greider, 1992) have only served to render the foundations of family and learning environments even more insecure. Coles' (1987) work thus joins a handful of critiques that have revealed social trends that are opaque to many observers precisely because of their very ubiquity. For instance, Greenberger and Steinberg's (1986) research indicates that a gradual trend of the past 20 years—middle-class parents' advocacy of high-consumption lifestyles for their children—has subtly undermined school standards and reduced educational opportunities (Steinberg, Fegley, and Dornbusch, 1993). Such research evidence reinforces Coles' (1987) conclusion that "the nuclear family does not seem to fulfill its obligation to. . .provide all children with satisfactory cognitive development. . . . If families are involved to some extent in the creation of learning disabilities, it is clear that to eliminate the sources of the problem, current family life must not be accepted as a given" (pp. 148–149). Coles' (1987) book thus raises the issue of whether some potent social issues might lie beneath our technical concern with aptitude/achievement discrepancy.

Acknowledgment

The preparation of this paper was supported by Grant 0GP0001607 from the Natural Sciences and Engineering Research Council of Canada to Keith E. Stanovich.

References

Adams, M. J. and Bruck, M. (1993). Word recognition: The interface of educational policies and scientific research. *Reading and Writing: An Interdisciplinary Journal, 5,* 113–139.

American Psychiatric Association. (1987). *Diagnostic and statistical manual of mental disorders* (III-R). Washington.

Anastasi, A. (1988). *Psychological testing* (6th edn.). New York: Macmillan.

Applebee, A. N. (1971). Research in reading retardation: Two critical problems. *Journal of Child Psychology and Psychiatry, 12,* 91–113.

Aram, D., Morris, R., and Hall, N. (1992). The validity of discrepancy criteria for identifying children with developmental language disorders. *Journal of Learning Disabilities, 25,* 549–554.

Arkes, H. R., Christensen, C., Lai, C., and Blumer, C. (1987). Two methods of reducing overconfidence. *Organizational Behavior and Human Decision Processes, 39,* 133–144.

Arkes, H. R. and Hammond, K. (Eds.). (1986). *Judgment and decision making.* Cambridge, England: Cambridge University Press.

Arkes, H. R. and Harkness, A. R. (1983). Estimates of contingency between two dichotomous variables. *Journal of Experimental Psychology: General, 112,* 117–135.

Aronowitz, S. and Giroux, H. A. (1985). *Education under siege.* South Hadley, MA: Bergin and Garvey.

Baddeley, A. D., Logie, R. H., and Ellis, N. C. (1988). Characteristics of developmental dyslexia. *Cognition, 30,* 198–227.

Barlett, D. and Steele, J. (1992). *America: What went wrong?* Kansas City: Andrews and McMeel.

Baron, J. (1985). *Rationality and intelligence.* Cambridge, England: Cambridge University Press.

Barron, R. (1981). Reading skill and spelling strategies. In A. Lesgold, and C. Perfetti (Eds.), *Interactive processes in reading* (pp. 299–327). Hillsdale, NJ: Lawrence Erlbaum.

Beech, J. and Harding, L. (1984). Phonemic processing and the poor reader from a developmental lag viewpoint. *Reading Research Quarterly, 19,* 357–366.

Ben-Dror, I., Pollatsek, A., and Scarpati, S. (1991). Word identification in isolation and in context by college dyslexic students. *Brain and Language, 40,* 471–490.

Bentin, S. (1992). Phonological awareness, reading, and reading acquisition. In R. Frost and L. Katz (Eds.), *Orthography, phonology, morphology, and meaning* (pp. 193–210). Amsterdam: North-Holland.

Birnbaum, R. (1990). IQ and the definition of LD. *Journal of Learning Disabilities, 23,* 330.

Bishop, D. and Adams, C. (1990). A prospective study of the relationship between specific language impairment, phonological disorders, and reading retardation. *Journal of Child Psychology and Psychiatry, 31,* 1027–1050.

Block, N. J. and Dworkin, G. (1976). IQ, heritability, and inequality. In N. J. Block and G. Dworkin (Eds.), *The IQ controversy* (pp. 410–540). New York: Pantheon Books.

Bloom, A., Wagner, M., Reskin, L., and Bergman, A. (1980). A comparison of intellectually delayed and primary reading disabled children on measures of intelligence and achievement. *Journal of Clinical Psychology, 36,* 788–790.

Bowers, P., Steffy, R., and Tate, E. (1988). Comparison of the effects of IQ control methods on memory and naming speed predictors of reading disability. *Reading Research Quarterly, 23,* 304–319.

Bowey, J. A., Cain, M. T., and Ryan, S. M. (1992). A reading-level design study of phonological skills underlying fourth-grade children's word reading difficulties. *Child Development, 63,* 999–1011.

Bowles, S. and Gintis, H. (1976). *Schooling in capitalist America.* New York: Basic Books.

Bradley, L. and Bryant, P. E. (1978). Difficulties in auditory organization as a possible cause of reading backwardness. *Nature, 271,* 746–747.

Bradley, L. and Bryant, P. E. (1985). *Rhyme and reason in reading and spelling.* Ann Arbor: University of Michigan Press.

Bronfenbrenner, U. and Ceci, S. J. (1994). Nature–nurture reconceptualized in developmental perspective: A bio-ecological model. *Psychological Review, 101,* 568–586.

Broniarczyk, S. and Alba, J. W. (1994). Theory versus data in prediction and correlation tasks. *Organizational Behavior and Human Decision Processes, 57,* 117–139.

Brown, G. D. A. and Watson, F. L. (1991). Reading development in dyslexia: A connectionist approach. In M. Snowling and M. Thomson (Eds.), *Dyslexia: Integrating theory and practice* (pp. 165–182). London: Whurr Publishers.

Bruck, M. (1988). The word recognition and spelling of dyslexic children. *Reading Research Quarterly, 23,* 51–69.

Bruck, M. (1990). Word-recognition skills of adults with childhood diagnoses of dyslexia. *Developmental Psychology, 26,* 439–454.

Bruck, M. (1992). Persistence of dyslexics' phonological awareness deficits. *Developmental Psychology, 28,* 874–886.

Bruck, M. and Treiman, R. (1990). Phonological awareness and spelling in normal children and dyslexics: The case of initial consonant clusters. *Journal of Experimental Child Psychology, 50,* 156–178.

Bryant, P. E., Maclean, M., Bradley, L., and Crossland, J. (1990). Rhyme and alliteration, phoneme detection, and learning to read. *Developmental Psychology, 26,* 429–438.

Carpenter, P. A., Just, M. A., and Shell, P. (1990). What one intelligence test measures: A theoretical account of the processing in the Raven Progressive Matrices Test. *Psychological Review, 97,* 404–431.

Carrier, J. G. (1986). *Learning disability: Social class and the construction of inequality in American education.* New York: Greenwood Press.

Catts, H. W. (1991). Early identification of reading disabilities. *Topics in Language Disorders, 12* (1), 1–16.

Ceci, S. J. (1986). *Handbook of cognitive, social, and neuropsychological aspects of learning disabilities* (Vol. 1). Hillsdale, NJ: Lawrence Erlbaum.

Ceci, S. J. (1990). *On intelligence. . .more or less: A bio-ecological treatise on intellectual development.* Englewood Cliffs, NJ: Prentice-Hall.

Ceci, S. J. (1993). Contextual trends in intellectual development. *Developmental Review, 13,* 403–435.

Ceci, S. J. and Liker, J. K. (1986). A day at the races: A study of IQ, expertise, and cognitive complexity. *Journal of Experimental Psychology: General, 115,* 255–266.

Cohen, L. J. (1981). Can human irrationality be experimentally demonstrated? *Behavioral and Brain Sciences, 4,* 317–331.

Cole, K. N., Dale, P. S., and Mills P. E. (1990). Defining language delay in young children by cognitive referencing: Are we saying more than we know? *Applied Psycholinguistics, 11*, 291–302.

Coles, G. S. (1978). The learning-disabilities test battery: Empirical and social issues. *Harvard Educational Review, 48*, 313–340.

Coles, G. S. (1987). *The learning mystique.* New York: Pantheon.

Critchley, M. (1970). *The dyslexic child.* London: William Heinemann Medical Books.

Cronbach, L. J. (1984). *Essentials of psychological testing* (4th edn.). New York: Harper and Row.

Davidson, D. (1984). On the very idea of a conceptual scheme. In D. Davidson (Ed.), *Truth and interpretation* (pp. 183–198). Oxford: Oxford University Press.

Davidson, J. E. (1990). Intelligence recreated. *Educational Psychologist, 25*, 337–354.

Dawes, R. M. (1988). *Rational choice in an uncertain world.* San Diego: Harcourt, Brace Jovanovich.

DeFries, J. C., Fulker, D., and Labuda, M. (1987). Evidence for a genetic etiology in reading disability in twins. *Nature, 329*, 537–539.

Dennett, D. (1978). Intentional systems. In D. Dennett (Ed.), *Brainstorms* (pp. 3–22). Cambridge: MIT Press.

Detterman, D. (1982). Does "g" exist? *Intelligence, 6*, 99–108.

Doehring, D. G. (1978). The tangled web of behavioral research on developmental dyslexia. In A. L. Benton, and D. Pearl (Eds.), *Dyslexia* (pp. 123–135). New York: Oxford University Press.

Eisenberg, L. (1978). Definitions of dyslexia: Their consequences for research and policy. In A. L. Benton and D. Pearl (Eds.), *Dyslexia* (pp. 29–42). New York: Oxford University Press.

Ellis, N. and Large, B. (1987). The development of reading: As you seek so shall you find. *British Journal of Psychology, 78*, 1–28.

Ennis, R. H. and Millman, J. (1985). *Cornell Critical Thinking Test.* Pacific Grove, CA: Midwest Publications.

Evans, B. and Waites, B. (1981). *IQ and mental testing: An unnatural science and its social history.* London: Macmillan.

Evans, J. B. T. (1989). *Bias in human reasoning: Causes and consequences.* London: Erlbaum Associates.

Farris, H. and Revlin, R. (1989). Sensible reasoning in two tasks: Rule discovery and hypothesis evaluation. *Memory and Cognition, 17*, 221–232.

Felton, R. H. and Wood, F. R. (1992). A reading level match study of nonword reading skills in poor readers with varying IQs. *Journal of Learning Disabilities, 25*, 318–326.

Fischhoff, B. (1988). Judgment and decision making. In R. J. Sternberg and E. E. Smith (Eds.), *The psychology of human thought* (pp. 153–187). Cambridge, England: Cambridge University Press.

Fletcher, J. M., Espy, K., Francis, D., Davidson, K., Rourke, B., and Shaywitz, S. (1989). Comparisons of cutoff and regression-based definitions of reading disabilities. *Journal of Learning Disabilities, 22*, 334–338.

Fletcher, J. M., Francis, D. J., Rourke, B. P., Shaywitz, B. A., and Shaywitz, S. E. (1992). The validity of discrepancy-based definitions of reading disabilities. *Journal of Learning Disabilities, 25*, 555–561.

Fletcher, J. M., Shaywitz, S. E., Shankweiler, D., Katz, L., Liberman, I., Stuebing, K., Francis, D. J., Fowler, A., and Shaywitz, B. A. (1994). Cognitive profiles of reading disability: Comparisons of discrepancy and low achievement definitions. *Journal of Educational Psychology, 86*, 6–23.

Forness, S. and Kavale, K. (1991). Social skills deficits as primary learning disabilities: A note on problems with the ICLD diagnostic criteria. *Learning Disabilities Research and Practice*, *6*, 44–49.

Frankenberger, W. and Fronzaglio, K. (1991). A review of states' criteria and procedures for identifying children with learning disabilities. *Journal of Learning Disabilities*, *24*, 495–500.

Frankenberger, W. and Harper, J. (1987). States' criteria and procedures for identifying learning disabled children: A comparison of 1981/82 and 1985/86 guidelines. *Journal of Learning Disabilities*, *20*, 118–121.

Fredman, G. and Stevenson, J. (1988). Reading processes in specific reading retarded and reading backward 13-year-olds. *British Journal of Developmental Psychology*, *6*, 97–108.

Frith, U. and Showling, M. (1983). Reading for meaning and reading for sound in autistic and dyslexic children. *British Journal of Developmental Psychology*, *1*, 329–342.

Galaburda, A. (1991). Anatomy of dyslexia: Argument against phrenology. In D. Duane and D. Gray (Eds.), *The reading brain: The biological basis of dyslexia* (pp. 119–131). Parkton, MD: York Press.

Galaburda, A. (1994). Developmental dyslexia and animal studies: At the interface between cognition and neurology. *Cognition*, *50*, 133–149.

Galaburda, A. M., Sherman, G., Rosen, G., Aboitz, F., and Geschwind, N. (1985). Developmental dyslexia: Four consecutive patients with cortical anomalies. *Annals of Neurology*, *18*, 222–233.

Gardner, H. (1983). *Frames of mind*. New York: Basic Books.

Gardner, H. (1986). The waning of intelligence tests. In R. J. Sternberg and D. K. Detterman (Eds.), *What is intelligence?* (pp. 73–76). Norwood, NJ: Ablex.

Gaskins, I. (1982). Let's end the reading disabilities/learning disabilities debate. *Journal of Learning Disabilities*, *15*, 81–83.

Gathercole, S. E. and Baddeley, A. D. (1987). The processes underlying segmental analysis. *European Bulletin of Cognitive Psychology*, *7*, 462–464.

Goldman, A. I. (1986). *Epistemology and cognition*. Cambridge: Harvard University Press.

Goldman, A. I. (1993). *Philosophical applications of cognitive science*. Boulder, CO: Westview Press.

Goswami, U. and Bryant, P. (1990). *Phonological skills and learning to read*. Hove, England: Lawrence Erlbaum.

Gould, S. J. (1981). *The mismeasure of man*. New York: Norton.

Greenberger, E. and Steinberg, L. (1986). *When teenagers work: The psychological and social costs of adolescent employment*. New York: Basic Books.

Greenwood, J. D. (Ed.). (1991). *The future of folk psychology*. Cambridge: MIT Press.

Greider, W. (1992). *Who will tell the people?* New York: Simon and Schuster.

Hammill, D. D. (1990). On defining learning disabilities: An emerging consensus. *Journal of Learning Disabilities*, *23*, 74–84.

Hammill, D., Leigh, J., McNutt, G., and Larsen, S. (1981). A new definition of learning disabilities. *Learning Disability Quarterly*, *4*, 336–342.

Harris, A. J. and Sipay, E. R. (1985). *How to increase reading ability* (8th edn.). White Plains, NY: Longman.

Hessler, G. L. (1987). Educational issues surrounding severe discrepancy. *Learning Disabilities Research*, *3*, 43–49.

Hilliard, A. (1984). IQ testing and the emperor's new clothes. In C. R. Reynolds and R. T. Brown (Eds.), *Perspectives on bias in mental testing* (pp. 189–220). New York: Plenum.

Holligan, C. and Johnston, R. S. (1988). The use of phonological information by good and poor readers in memory and reading tasks. *Memory and Cognition, 16,* 522–532.

Humphreys, L. G. (1979). The construct of general intelligence. *Intelligence, 3,* 105–120.

Hynd, G. S., Marshall, R., and Gonzalez, J. (1991). Learning disabilities and presumed central nervous system dysfunction. *Learning Disability Quarterly, 14,* 283–296.

Hynd, G. S., Marshall, R., and Semrud-Clikeman, M. (1991). Developmental dyslexia, neurolinguistic theory and deviations in brain morphology. *Reading and Writing: An Interdisciplinary Journal, 3,* 345–362.

Ingram, T., Mason, A., and Blackburn, I. (1970). A retrospective study of 82 children with reading disability. *Developmental Medicine and Child Neurology, 12,* 271–281.

Johnson, D. J. (1988). Review of research on specific reading, writing, and mathematics disorders. In J. F. Kavanagh, and T. J. Truss (Eds.), *Learning disabilities: Proceedings of the national conference* (pp. 79–163). Parkston, MD: York Press.

Jorm, A., Share, D., Maclean, R., and Matthews, R. (1986). Cognitive factors at school entry predictive of specific reading retardation and general reading backwardness: A research note. *Journal of Child Psychology and Psychiatry, 27,* 45–54.

Kamhi, A. G. (1992). Response to historical perspective: A developmental language perspective. *Journal of Learning Disabilities, 25,* 48–52.

Kamhi, A. and Catts, H. (1989). *Reading disabilities: A developmental language perspective.* Austin: PRO-ED.

Kahneman, D., Slovic, P., and Tversky, A. (1982). *Judgment under uncertainty: Heuristics and biases.* Cambridge, England: Cambridge University Press.

Kavale, K. A. and Nye, C. (1981). Identification criteria for learning disabilities: A survey of the research literature. *Learning Disability Quarterly, 4,* 363–388.

Kavanagh, J. F. and Truss, T. J. (Eds.). (1988). *Learning disabilities: Proceedings of the national conference.* Parkston, MD: York Press.

King, P. M., Kitchener, K. S., Davison, M. L., Parker, C. A., and Wood, P. K. (1983). The justification of beliefs in young adults: A longitudinal study. *Human Development, 26,* 106–116.

Kitcher, P. (1993). *The advancement of science.* New York: Oxford University Press.

Kitchener, K. S. and Brenner, H. G. (1990). Wisdom and reflective judgment: Knowing in the face of uncertainty. In R. J. Sternberg (Ed.), *Wisdom: Its nature, origins, and development* (pp. 212–229). Cambridge, England: Cambridge University Press.

Kitchener, K. S. and King, P. M. (1981). Reflective judgment: Concepts of justification and their relationship to age and education. *Journal of Applied Developmental Psychology, 2,* 89–116.

Kuhn, D. (1991). *The skills of argument.* Cambridge, England: Cambridge University Press.

Kuhn, D. (1993). Connecting scientific and informal reasoning. *Merrill-Palmer Quarterly, 38,* 74–103.

Kunda, Z. and Nisbett, R. E. (1986). The psychometrics of everyday life. *Cognitive Psychology, 18,* 195–224.

Larsen, P. J., Hoien, T., Lundberg, I., and Odegaard, H. (1990). MRI evaluation of the size and symmetry of the planum temporale in adolescents with developmental dyslexia. *Brain and Language, 39,* 289–301.

Lerner, J. (1985). *Learning disabilities* (4th edn.). Boston: Houghton Mifflin.

Lesser, R. and Paisner, M. (1985). Magical thinking in formal operational adults. *Human Development, 28,* 57–70.

Lindgren, S. D., De Renzi, E., and Richman, L. C. (1985). Cross-national comparisons of developmental dyslexia in Italy and the United States. *Child Development, 56,* 1404–1417.

Lyon, G. R. (1987). Learning disabilities research: False starts and broken promises. In S. Vaughn and C. S. Bos (Eds.), *Research in learning disabilities* (pp. 69–85). Boston: College-Hill Press.

Manis, F. R., Custodio, R., and Szeszulski, P. A. (1993). Development of phonological and orthographic skill: A two-year longitudinal study of dyslexic children. *Journal of Experimental Child Psychology, 56,* 64–86.

Manis, F. R., Szeszulski, P. A., Holt, L. K., and Graves, K. (1990). Variation in component word recognition and spelling skills among dyslexic children and normal readers. In T. H. Carr and B. A. Levy (Eds.), *Reading and its development: Component skills approaches* (pp. 207–259). San Diego: Academic Press.

McGill Franzen, A. (1987). Failure to learn to read: Formulating a policy problem. *Reading Research Quarterly, 22,* 475–490.

Morrison, F. J. (1991). Learning (and not learning) to read: A developmental framework. In L. Rieben and C. Perfetti (Eds.), *Learning to read: Basic research and its implications* (pp. 163–174). Hillsdale, NJ: Lawrence Erlbaum.

Mulder, G., Wijers, A., Smid, H., Brookhuis, K., and Mulder, L. (1989). Individual differences in computational mechanisms: A psychophysiological analysis. In R. Kanfer, P. Ackerman, and R. Cudeck (Eds.), *Abilities, motivation, and methodology* (pp. 391–434). Hillsdale, NJ: Lawrence Erlbaum.

Neisser, U. (1976). General, academic, and artificial intelligence. In L. B. Resnick (Ed.), *The nature of intelligence* (pp. 135–144). Hillsdale, NJ: Lawrence Erlbaum.

Nisbett, R. and Ross, L. (1980). *Human inference: Strategies and shortcomings of social judgment.* Englewood Cliffs, NJ: Prentice-Hall.

Nozick, R. (1993). *The nature of rationality.* Princeton, NJ: Princeton University Press.

Oakes, J. (1985). *Keeping track: How schools structure inequality.* New Haven: Yale University Press.

Oakhill, J. and Garnham, A. (1988). *Becoming a skilled reader.* Oxford, England: Basil Blackwell.

Olson, R., Kliegl, R., Davidson, B., and Foltz, G. (1985). Individual and developmental differences in reading disability. In G. E. MacKinnon and T. Waller (Eds.), *Reading research: Advances in theory and practice* (Vol. 4, pp. 1–64). London: Academic Press.

Olson, R. K., Rack, J., Conners, F., DeFries, J., and Fulker, D. (1991). Genetic etiology of individual differences in reading disability. In L. Feagans, E. Short, and L. Meltzer (Eds.), *Subtypes of learning disabilities* (pp. 113–135). Hillsdale, NJ: Lawrence Erlbaum.

Olson, R. K., Wise, B., Conners, F., and Rack, J. (1990). Organization, heritability, and remediation of component word recognition and language skills in disabled readers. In T. Carr and B. A. Levy (Eds.), *Reading and its development: Component skills approaches* (pp. 261–322). New York: Academic Press.

Olson, R. K., Wise, B., Conners, F., Rack, J., and Fulker, D. (1989). Specific deficits in component reading and language skills: Genetic and environmental influences. *Journal of Learning Disabilities, 22,* 339–348.

Owen, D. (1985). *None of the above: Behind the myth of scholastic aptitude.* Boston: Houghton Mifflin.

Pennington, B. F. (1990). The genetics of dyslexia. *Journal of Child Psychology and Psychiatry, 31,* 193–201.

Pennington, B. F., Gilger, J., Olson, R. K., and DeFries, J. C. (1992). The external validity of age- versus IQ-discrepancy definitions of reading disability: Lessons from a twin study. *Journal of Learning Disabilities, 25,* 562–573.

Pennington, B. F., Gilger, J., Pauls, D., Smith, S. A., Smith, S. D., and DeFries, J. (1991). Genetic and neurological influences on reading disability: An overview. *Journal of the American Medical Association, 266* (11), 1527–1534.

Pennington, B. F., McCabe, L. L., Smith, S., Lefly, D., Bookman, M., Kimberling, W., and Lubs, H. (1986). Spelling errors in adults with a form of familial dyslexia. *Child Development, 57,* 1001–1013.

Pennington, B. F., Van Orden, G., Kirson, D., and Haith, M. (1991). What is the causal relation between verbal STM problems and dyslexia? In S. A. Brady and D. P. Shankweiler (Eds.), *Phonological processes in literacy* (pp. 173–186). Hillsdale, NJ: Lawrence Erlbaum.

Perfetti, C. A. (1985). *Reading ability.* New York: Oxford University Press.

Perkins, D. N., Jay, E., and Tishman, S. (1993). Beyond abilities: A dispositional theory of thinking. *Merrill-Palmer Quarterly, 39,* 1–21.

Rack, J. (1985). Orthographic and phonetic coding in developmental dyslexia. *British Journal of Psychology, 76,* 325–340.

Rack, J. P., Snowling, M. J., and Olson, R. K. (1992). The nonword reading deficit in developmental dyslexia: A review. *Reading Research Quarterly, 27,* 28–53.

Reed, J. C. (1970). The deficits of retarded readers—fact or artifact? *The Reading Teacher, 23,* 347–357.

Resnick, L. B., Levine, J., and Teasley, S. (Eds.). (1991). *Perspectives on socially shared cognition.* Washington: American Psychological Association.

Reynolds, C. R. (1985). Measuring the aptitude–achievement discrepancy in learning disability diagnosis. *Remedial and Special Education, 6,* 37–55.

Rogoff, B. and Lave, J. (Eds.). (1984). *Everyday cognition.* Cambridge: Harvard University Press.

Rutter, M. (1978). Prevalence and types of dyslexia. In A. Benton and D. Pearl (Eds.), *Dyslexia: An appraisal of current knowledge* (pp. 5–28). New York: Oxford University Press.

Rutter, M. and Yule, W. (1975). The concept of specific reading retardation. *Journal of Child Psychology and Psychiatry, 16,* 181–197.

Scarborough, H. S. (1990). Very early language deficits in dyslexic children. *Child Development, 61,* 1728–1743.

Scheffler, I. (1985). *Of human potential.* New York: Routledge and Kegan Paul.

Semrud-Clikeman, M., Hynd, G. S., Novey, E., and Eliopulos, D. (1991). Dyslexia and brain morphology: Relationships between neuroanatomical variation and neurolinguistic tasks. *Learning and Individual Differences, 3,* 225–242.

Senf, G. F. (1986). LD research in sociological and scientific perspective. In J. K. Torgesen and B. Y. L. Wong (Eds.), *Psychological and educational perspectives on learning disabilities* (pp. 27–53). Orlando, FL: Academic Press.

Shankweiler, D., Crain, S., Brady, S., and Macaruso, P. (1992). Identifying the causes of reading disability. In P. Gough, L. Ehri, and R. Treiman (Eds.), *Reading acquisition* (pp. 275–305). Hillsdale, NJ: Lawrence Erlbaum.

Share, D. L. (1995). Phonological recoding and self–teaching: Sine qua non of reading acquisition. *Cognition, 55,* 151–218.

Share, D. L., Jorm, A., McGee, R., Silva, P., Maclean, R., Matthews, R., and Williams, S. (1990). *Word recognition and spelling processes in specific reading disabled and garden-variety poor readers.* Unpublished manuscript.

Shaywitz, B. A., Fletcher, J. M., Holahan, J. M., and Shaywitz, S. E. (1992). Discrepancy compared to low achievement definitions of reading disability: Results from the Connecticut Longitudinal Study. *Journal of Learning Disabilities, 25,* 639–648.

Shepard, L. (1980). An evaluation of the regression discrepancy method for identifying children with learning disabilities. *The Journal of Special Education, 14,* 79–91.

Siegel, L. S. (1985). Psycholinguistic aspects of reading disabilities. In L. Siegel and F. Morrison (Eds.), *Cognitive development in atypical children* (pp. 45–65). New York: Springer-Verlag.

Siegel, L. S. (1988). Evidence that IQ scores are irrelevant to the definition and analysis of reading disability. *Canadian Journal of Psychology, 42,* 201–215.

Siegel, L. S. (1989). IQ is irrelevant to the definition of learning disabilities. *Journal of Learning Disabilities, 22,* 469–479.

Siegel, L. S. (1992). An evaluation of the discrepancy definition of dyslexia. *Journal of Learning Disabilities, 25,* 618–629.

Siegel, L. S. (1993). The development of reading. In H. Reese (Ed.), *Advances in child development and behavior* (Vol. 24, pp. 63–97). San Diego: Academic Press.

Siegel, L. S. and Faux, D. (1989). Acquisition of certain grapheme–phoneme correspondences in normally achieving and disabled readers. *Reading and Writing: An Interdisciplinary Journal, 1,* 37–52.

Siegel, L. S. and Heaven, R. K. (1986). Categorization of learning disabilities. In S. J. Ceci (Ed.), *Handbook of cognitive, social, and neuropsychological aspects of learning disabilities* (Vol. 1, pp. 95–121). Hillsdale, NJ: Lawrence Erlbaum.

Siegel, L. S. and Ryan, E. B. (1988). Development of grammatical-sensitivity, phonological, and short-term memory skills in normally achieving and learning disabled children. *Developmental Psychology, 24,* 28–37.

Siegel, L. S. and Ryan, E. B. (1989). Subtypes of developmental dyslexia: The influence of definitional variables. *Reading and Writing: An Interdisciplinary Journal, 1,* 257–287.

Silva, P. A., McGee, R., and Williams, S. (1985). Some characteristics of nine-year-old boys with general reading backwardness or specific reading retardation. *Journal of Child Psychology and Psychiatry, 26,* 407–421.

Smith, S. D., Kimberling, W. J., and Pennington, B. F. (1991). Screening for multiple genes influencing dyslexia. *Reading and Writing: An Interdisciplinary Journal, 3,* 285–298.

Snowling, M. (1980). The development of grapheme–phoneme correspondence in normal and dyslexic readers. *Journal of Experimental Child Psychology, 29,* 294–305.

Snowling, M. (1981). Phonemic deficits in developmental dyslexia. *Psychological Research, 43,* 219–234.

Snowling, M. (1991). Developmental reading disorders. *Journal of Child Psychology and Psychiatry, 32,* 49–77.

Stahl, S. A. and Murray, B. (1994). Defining phonological awareness and its relationship to early reading. *Journal of Educational Psychology, 86,* 221–234.

Stanley, G., Smith, G., and Powys, A. (1982). Selecting intelligence tests for studies of dyslexic children. *Psychological Reports, 50,* 787–792.

Stanovich, K. E. (1981). Relationships between word decoding speed, general name-retrieval ability, and reading progress in first-grade children. *Journal of Educational Psychology, 73,* 809–815.

Stanovich, K. E. (1982). Individual differences in the cognitive processes of reading. I: Word decoding. *Journal of Learning Disabilities, 15,* 485–493.

Stanovich, K. E. (1986a). Cognitive processes and the reading problems of learning disabled children: Evaluating the assumption of specificity. In J. Torgesen and B. Wong (Eds.), *Psychological and educational perspectives on learning disabilities* (pp. 87–131). New York: Academic Press.

Stanovich, K. E. (1986b). Matthew effects in reading: Some consequences of individual differences in the acquisition of literacy. *Reading Research Quarterly, 21*, 360–407.

Stanovich, K. E. (1988a). Explaining the differences between the dyslexic and the garden-variety poor reader: The phonological-core variable-difference model. *Journal of Learning Disabilities, 21*, 590–612.

Stanovich, K. E. (1988b). The right and wrong places to look for the cognitive locus of reading disability. *Annals of Dyslexia, 38*, 154–177.

Stanovich, K. E. (1989). Has the learning disabilities field lost its intelligence? *Journal of Learning Disabilities, 22*, 487–492.

Stanovich, K. E. (1991). Discrepancy definitions of reading disability: Has intelligence led us astray? *Reading Research Quarterly, 26*, 7–29.

Stanovich, K. E. (1992). Speculations on the causes and consequences of individual differences in early reading acquisition. In P. Gough, L. Ehri, and R. Treiman (Eds.), *Reading Acquisition* (pp. 307–342). Hillsdale, NJ: Lawrence Erlbaum.

Stanovich, K. E. (1993). Dysrationalia: A new specific learning disability. *Journal of Learning Disabilities, 26*, 501–515.

Stanovich, K. E. (1994). Reconceptualizing intelligence: Dysrationalia as an intuition pump. *Educational Researcher, 23* (4), 11–22.

Stanovich, K. E., Cunningham, A. E., and Cramer, B. (1984). Assessing phonological awareness in kindergarten children: Issues of task comparability. *Journal of Experimental Child Psychology, 38*, 175–190.

Stanovich, K. E., Cunningham, A. E., and Feeman, D. J. (1984). Intelligence, cognitive skills, and early reading progress. *Reading Research Quarterly, 19*, 278–303.

Stanovich, K. E., Nathan, R. G., and Zolman, J. E. (1988). The developmental lag hypothesis in reading: Longitudinal and matched reading-level comparisons. *Child Development, 59*, 71–86.

Stanovich, K. E. and Siegel, L. S. (1994). The phenotypic performance profile of reading-disabled children: A regression-based test of the phonological-core variable-difference model. *Journal of Educational Psychology, 86*, 24–53.

Steinberg, L., Fegley, S., and Dornbusch, S. M. (1993). Negative impact of part-time work on adolescent adjustment: Evidence from a longitudinal study. *Developmental Psychology, 29*, 171–180.

Steinmetz, H. and Galaburda, A. M. (1991). Planum temporale asymmetry: In-vivo morphometry affords a new perspective for neuro-behavioral research. *Reading and Writing: An Interdisciplinary Journal, 3*, 331–343.

Sternberg, R. J. (1985). Implicit theories of intelligence, creativity, and wisdom. *Journal of Personality and Social Psychology, 49*, 607–627.

Sternberg, R. J. (1988). The triarchic mind. New York: Viking.

Sternberg, R. J., Conway, B., Ketron, J., and Bernstein, M. (1981). People's conceptions of intelligence. *Journal of Personality and Social Psychology, 41*, 37–55.

Sternberg, R. J. and Detterman, D. K. (1986). *What is intelligence?* Norwood, NJ: Ablex.

Sternberg, R. J. and Wagner, R. K. (1986). *Practical intelligence*. Cambridge, England: Cambridge University Press.

Stevenson, J. (1991). Which aspects of processing text mediate genetic effects? *Reading and Writing: An Interdisciplinary Journal, 3*, 249–269.

Stevenson, J. (1992a). Genetics. In N. Singh and I. Beale (Eds.), *Learning disabilities: Nature, theory, and treatment* (pp. 327–351). New York: Springer-Verlag.

Stevenson, J. (1992b). Identifying sex differences in reading disability: Lessons from a twin study. *Reading and Writing: An Interdisciplinary Journal, 4*, 307–326.

Stevenson, J., Graham, P., Fredman, G., and McLoughlin, V. (1987). A twin study of genetic influences on reading and spelling ability and disability. *Journal of Child Psychology and Psychiatry, 28*, 229–247.

Stich, S. (1990). *The fragmentation of reason.* Cambridge: MIT Press.

Taylor, H. G. and Schatschneider, C. (1992). Academic achievement following childhood brain disease: Implications for the concept of learning disabilities. *Journal of Learning Disabilities, 25*, 630–638.

Thomson, M. (1982). Assessing the intelligence of dyslexic children. *Bulletin of the British Psychological Society, 35*, 94–96.

Thorndike, R. L. (1963). *The concepts of over- and under-achievement.* New York: Teachers College, Columbia University.

Torgesen, J. (1985). Memory processes in reading disabled children. *Journal of Learning Disabilities, 18*, 350–357.

Torgesen, J. K. (1986). Controlling for IQ. *Journal of Learning Disabilities, 19*, 452.

Torgesen, J. K. (1991). Learning disabilities: Historical and conceptual issues. In B. L. Wong (Ed.), *Learning about learning disabilities* (pp. 3–37). San Diego: Academic Press.

Torgesen, J. K., Wagner, R. K., and Rashotte, C. A. (1994). Longitudinal studies of phonological processing and reading. *Journal of Learning Disabilities, 27*, 276–286.

Treiman, R. and Hirsh-Pasek, K. (1985). Are there qualitative differences in reading behavior between dyslexics and normal readers? *Memory and Cognition, 13*, 357–364.

Tschirgi, J. E. (1980). Sensible reasoning: A hypothesis about hypotheses. *Child Development, 51*, 1–10.

Tunmer, W. E. and Hoover, W. (1992). Cognitive and linguistic factors in learning to read. In P. B. Gough, L. C. Ehri, and R. Treiman (Eds.), *Reading Acquisition* (pp. 175–214). Hillsdale, NJ: Lawrence Erlbaum.

Tunmer, W. E. and Nesdale, A. R. (1985). Phonemic segmentation skill and beginning reading. *Journal of Educational Psychology, 77*, 417–427.

van der Wissel, A. (1987). IQ profiles of learning disabled and mildly mentally retarded children: A psychometric selection effect. *British Journal of Developmental Psychology, 5*, 45–51.

van der Wissel, A. and Zegers, F. E. (1985). Reading retardation revisited. *British Journal of Developmental Psychology, 3*, 3–9.

Vaughn, S. and Bos, C. S. (1987). *Research in learning disabilities: Issues and future directions.* Boston: College-Hill Press.

Vellutino, F. (1978). Toward an understanding of dyslexia: Psychological factors in specific reading disability. In A. L. Benton and D. Pearl (Eds.), *Dyslexia* (pp. 59–111). New York: Oxford University Press.

Vellutino, F. (1979). *Dyslexia: Theory and research.* Cambridge: MIT Press.

Vellutino, F. and Scanlon, D. (1987). Phonological coding, phonological awareness, and reading ability: Evidence from a longitudinal and experimental study. *Merrill-Palmer Quarterly, 33*, 321–363.

Vernon, P. A. (1987). New developments in reaction time research. In P. A. Vernon (Ed.), *Speed of information-processing and intelligence* (pp. 1–20). Norwood, NJ: Ablex.

Vernon, P. A. (1991). The use of biological measures to estimate behavioral intelligence. *Educational Psychologist, 25*, 293–304.

Voss, J., Perkins, D., and Segal J. (Eds.). (1991). *Informal reasoning and education.* Hillsdale, NJ: Lawrence Erlbaum.

Wagner, R. K. and Torgesen, J. K. (1987). The nature of phonological processing and its causal role in the acquisition of reading skills. *Psychological Bulletin, 101,* 192–212.

Wasserman, E. A., Dorner, W. W., and Kao, S. F. (1990). Contributions of specific cell information to judgments of interevent contingency. *Journal of Experimental Psychology: Learning, Memory, and Cognition, 16,* 509–521.

Wassermann, S. (1987). Teaching for thinking: Louis E. Raths revisited. *Phi Delta Kappan, 68* (6), 460–466.

Watson, F. and Brown, G. (1992). Single-word reading in college dyslexics. *Applied Cognitive Psychology, 6,* 263–272.

Watson, G. and Glaser, E. M. (1980). *Watson-Glaser Critical Thinking Appraisal.* San Antonio, TX: Psychological Corporation.

Willows, D. M., Kruk, R., and Corcos, E. (Eds.). (1993). *Visual processes in reading and reading disabilities.* San Diego: Academic Press.

8

Rethinking Readiness for Learning

RITA WATSON

Introduction

A commonsense view of readiness pervades our personal, social, and institutional lives. Every culture has some age- or achievement-related criterion for the transition from childhood to adulthood, and marks it through ceremony, ritual, or the bestowing of rights and responsibilities. In the West, we are ready to be held legally responsible for our actions at the age of majority, or the age of consent, usually around 18. We are ready to drive a car around 16 years of age. Closer to home, there are those ever-moving goalposts of readiness, mysteriously "known" to every parent and infuriating to every growing child: "You're not old enough now, in a few years you'll be ready." Whether it is staying up late or getting your first bike, there is no higher court of appeal when you are five years old and your view of readiness differs from that of your parents.

However these commonly accepted or institutionalized thresholds of readiness are derived, it is clear that they are basic to our commonsense understanding of what it means to grow up. Readiness is a core principle in our "folk developmental psychology" (Stitch, 1983). It is not surprising that it also permeates our folk pedagogy, our commonsense ideas of education. The question of when to teach, the classic readiness question in education (Tyler, 1964), actually conflates several issues.

First, conceptions of readiness derive from broader frameworks of assumptions about children, learning, and teaching. Such frameworks may be scientific, psychological theories of mind or learning that are constructed and tested in a laboratory. More often, they consist of a naive theory, or a folk psychology, as described above: a system of beliefs and principles of explanation that serve the individual in the interpretation of actions, events, and intentions that characterize everyday life. It is thus not likely to be the case that there is only one valid theory of readiness. Both scientific theories and commonsense beliefs about children, learning, and teaching change and re-emerge across different historical epochs and cultures. A reappraisal of readiness is not likely to be useful if it is expressed simply in terms of new, better theories supplanting the old, worn-out ones. Rather, conceptions of readiness should be viewed as relative to a theory, or set of assumptions and explanatory beliefs.

The second issue implied in Tyler's question is that formal instruction is central in a theory of readiness. This is not necessarily so. Children learn virtually from birth, and the informal apprenticeship and social interaction they experience early in life can be construed as modes of instruction. While formal instruction is certainly the primary mode of schooling, readiness to *learn* thus cannot be identical to readiness to engage in formal instruction.

The third issue is the relation of a theory of readiness to a theory of the child. Children do not come to the world as empty vessels waiting to be filled with the wisdom of their elders. They are intellectually and interpersonally engaged, or predisposed to be so, from their earliest hours of life. We need to be certain that our ideas of readiness are not simply grounded in the institutional needs of society. Rather, they must reflect our best understanding of the child's social, emotional, and cognitive states. A view of readiness based on a view of a passive, cognitively inactive child, for example, would be hopelessly flawed. This chapter addresses each of these issues in turn.

The Theory of Readiness

With the possible exception of Thorndike's Law of Readiness (Hilgard and Bower, 1966), no theory of readiness has ever been explicitly formulated in such a way that it could be empirically tested. Rather, theories of readiness are embedded in broader frameworks of psychologies or pedagogies. Some great minds have wrestled with the issue. Large-scale interventions designed to enhance it have been implemented and have been the subject of much evaluative debate (Consortium for Longitudinal Studies, 1983). Yet it is difficult to pinpoint a single, coherent research tradition that could be said to have a theory of readiness as its focus. Rethinking the theoretical aspects of this problem thus requires some exploration of its roots in psychological and pedagogical theory.

Historical Perspectives

It is sometimes easier to see the origins of belief systems in historical eras removed from our own. Evidence that views of readiness are inseparable from philosophical or epistemological framework theories is clear in early views. Comenius (1592–1670) was an early advocate of child-centered education. With all the vigor and optimism of a man with a mission, he pursued his universalist educational vision against the backdrop of plague, personal tragedy, and the Thirty Years' War. In his original works, it is evident that his dedication to "celestial flowers," as he characterized children, is intimately bound up with his faith and his philosophy, the goal of which was to unify humankind through universally accessible education. The nurturing metaphors with which his "School of Infancy" abounds contrast to the authoritarian and pedagogically unsophisticated practices of the time. His creation of picture books for children, and simplified texts on language and other subjects, were meant to render the world of nature and of knowledge more accessible to the tender mind. According to his view, the child was not ready for formal instruction before age six. However, he strongly advocated informal tutoring and nurturing by parents in the crucial preschool years during which time he believed the foundations for the child's character were formed.

In contrast, Rousseau's (1762/1979) romantic nativism held that the deepest aspects of morality, such as the sense of justice, were innate. It was the tampering of ignorant and uncaring people that disrupted the child's early sensibilities. The practice of swaddling, widespread in Rousseau's day, was a case in point: it substantially reduced the advantages of exiting the womb. On Rousseau's view, the child needed to be free to move. He expresses an early account of the importance of action in the emergence of a naive physics and the sense of self:

He wants to touch everything, to handle everything. Do not oppose yourself to this restlessness. It is suggestive to him of a very necessary *apprenticeship*; it is thus that he learns to feel the hotness, the coldness, the hardness, the softness, the heaviness, the lightness, of bodies, and to judge their size, their shape, and all their sensible qualities by looking, feeling, listening, particularly by comparing sight to touch, by estimating with the eye the sensation that they would make on his finger. It is only by movement that we learn that there are things that are not us. . . . (Rousseau, 1762/1979, p. 64)

The early years are critical also on Rousseau's view, but for a different reason. The damaging effects of a corrupt and artificial civilization must be minimized, while the natural categories of knowledge and morality are allowed to unfold in the young mind. The child begins to learn from birth, but learning here is more a response to lived experience than an imposition by a cultural institution: "experience anticipates lessons." Far from denying the importance of parents or other early caretakers, Rousseau emphasized the need for structuring early experience to enable a steady and continuous path toward understanding, strength, and freedom from prejudice and fear. His nativism is evident not only in his intense awareness of the child's early sensitivities and abilities, including prelinguistic communication, but also in his concern with the child's early physiology, and the role of the elements in early experience. Rousseau looked upon formal instruction as a subsidiary to experience. It was not to be imposed until the child's natural sensibilities were sufficiently developed, in late childhood and adolescence. Readiness was determined by the child, not by society's institutional requirements.

The distinctively American pragmatism of Dewey and James offers yet a third framework in which readiness has historically been viewed. James (1939) argued that Rousseau was wrongheaded in thinking the inborn emotions were all necessarily aesthetic and noble, and that impulses such as rivalry and competition were necessarily bad. Rivalry could be noble and generous, the root of social improvement. No runner all alone on a racetrack will fulfill his ultimate capability, and the sight of action in another can motivate action in ourselves. James hated what he called "namby-pamby. . .soft. . .pedagogy. It is a poor compliment to their [children's] rational appetites to think that anecdotes about little Tommies and little Jennies are the only kind of thing their minds can digest" (1939, p. 152). He argued that the teacher should exploit all the basic human emotions and motivations in challenging and stimulating children, including embarrassing them when they did not know their lessons.

Readiness, on James's view, figured largely at all stages of educational practice, although he argued for a late onset of formal instruction. James's characterization of the infant's mental state as "blooming, buzzing confusion" is well-known, and he argued that during the first seven or eight years of life the child is most interested in the "sensible properties of material things," and should be given ample opportunity to experience the world. At this stage, all kinds of activities with all imaginable materials should be encouraged, in the context of both nature and human activities, from the barnyard to the blacksmith's. Only when children reach adolescence are they ready to grasp the abstract principles and causal relations underlying the subjects of mathematics, mechanics, chemistry and biology, and not until late adolescence can sociology and metaphysics be grasped. James even argued against introducing philosophy too early in college. Undergraduates could be permanently disenchanted with the field if forced into it before they were ready.

Dewey (1902/1956) cast children in the mold of his own instrumentalist philosophy. He disagreed with both the romanticization of the child's inherent states, as with Rousseau, and with the use of discipline and external motivators in the reaction against "soft pedagogy," as with James. The former view, with which Dewey identified the child study movement, was in danger of regarding the child's early interests and proclivities as something final and significant in themselves, to be "cultivated as they stand," rather than indicating attitudes toward the possible. Expecting the children to "develop" something out of their own minds, without the benefit of formal instruction in existing knowledge is as unrealistic as expecting philosophers to come up with a comprehensive theory without the benefit of reading the historical works in their field (p. 18).

Formal bodies of knowledge are simply a systematized, abbreviated record of others' explorations and grapplings with the same phenomena that children are apprehending in their own experience. Rediscovering this immediacy in formal knowledge is the key to what Dewey called "psychologizing" the curriculum, or making it more accessible to the child. If a connection is successfully established between the psychological concerns of children and the instrumental uses of formal subject matter, it will be of intrinsic interest to children, and no external bribes or levers are necessary to nudge them into learning. The principles of formal knowledge will be of use in successfully addressing the problems that children are facing in their own experience. Readiness, on Dewey's view, is a function of the interaction between an active, discovering child and a *progressive*, child-centered curriculum in which formal knowledge is rendered accessible to the child. Dewey thought formal instruction in reading should wait until the child reached about eight years of age. In spite of his characterization of the child as an active learner, Dewey conceived of the preschool child's mind as largely undifferentiated and egocentric, even "crude." This is in marked contrast to the views that have emerged in the latter half of this century.

Thorndike's Law of Readiness

In twentieth-century psychology, the notion of readiness emerges in the learning theory of Thorndike. His Law of Readiness described the conditions necessary for learning to occur. "Conduction units" were pseudo-neurological entities that "fired" when a particular stimulus potential was fulfilled. This resulted in a change of state: learning. Hilgard and Bower (1966) argue that Thorndike's law referred to preparatory adjustment in learning, not to growth, and was thus not an anticipation of the concept of maturational readiness as commonly used by educators. This argument may be historically true. Nevertheless, Thorndike's law is a fluid and adaptable notion. Neuronal conduction units "firing when ready" may be an apt metaphor for the varied notions of readiness necessary on current views of mind, reviewed below. It could apply to either a domain-specific or domain-general account. The more familiar maturationist account of a steady progression through various plateaus of domain-general abilities seems, in contrast, limited to a single view.

The Early Maturationist View

The account of readiness that has most influenced educational theory and practice in this century derives primarily from early maturationist psychology and individual differences theory (Tyler, 1964). Durkin (1973) links the origin of the term to the theories of Hall and Gesell in the 1920s. These early characterizations of children's readiness for learning are rich with biological metaphors: children are "ripe" for educational experience, or they are ready to "unfold" like buds ready to bloom. On this view, development is a continuous process, without bursts or irregularities, the rate and course of which are determined by genetic endowment. The child's readiness to learn is determined by a combination of Mental Age and mastery of requisite subskills (Morphett and Washburne, 1931). Any attempt to hasten or interfere with the process of development is held to be seriously, even irretrievably, detrimental. The solution to problems in learning, on this view, is to wait. After some time has elapsed, the child will mature enough to benefit from instruction. A primary and long-lasting consequence of this view for educational practice was the doctrine of educational postponement: failing, or retaining students as it is now more commonly known.

These early maturationist views were domain-general, even species-general, accounts. While not based on behaviorist theory per se, they emerged when learning was thought to be best characterized by a few general laws that held across all domains of knowledge and all kinds of learners. The only difference between a pigeon learning how to bowl, in one of Skinner's more interesting experiments, and children learning how to solve math equations was a matter of degree, not of qualitative difference. Most importantly, early maturationist theories did not ascribe innate cognitive structures or predispositions to the child. Rather, the biological maturity of the child simply set the necessary stage on which the laws of learning acted.

Bruner's Dictum and the "New Look" in Early Cognition

In that revolutionary epoch that began with the 1960s, Bruner advanced the now famous and often misunderstood dictum that "any subject can be taught in some intellectually honest form to any child at any stage of development" (1966, p. 33). The central claim of his argument was that it is the nature and organization of thought, not physiological or psychometric age, that determines how and when a child learns. The important thing was to attune instruction to the mental life of the child. This view found expression in a program of research at the Center for Cognitive Studies at Harvard, in which Bruner, Miller, Trevarthen, and other colleagues began a search for "infant mind" (Bruner, 1983b). The new look in infant cognition, in contrast to earlier views, cast the child as a competent, intentional, thinking being. This seminal period gave rise to a new generation of infancy research, the results of which are still unfolding. Many current research programs can be traced directly or indirectly to the influence of the ideas generated there. The educational consequence of this view is that children are never NOT ready to learn and that learning need only be adapted to the intellectual proclivities of the child.

The temptation in applying these ideas is that if children are indeed so competent so early in life, perhaps we could speed up their progress and raise a generation of geniuses if only we started educating them earlier. Piaget would come to lament this *"question américaine"*: How can we accelerate development (Piatelli-Palmerini, 1980)? Acceleration, however, is not the only implication for readiness that can be drawn from accounts of early cognitive competence. It is an institutionally oriented, curriculum-based response. Competence need not be exploited; it needs only to be recognized and aided.

In the decades since, research in the cognitive tradition has yielded substantial new evidence on the nature of infant cognition. Piaget originally claimed, for example, that infant cognition was based on reflexive, sensorimotor activity, and that object permanence did not emerge until about 18 months. Current evidence suggests that even six-month-old infants perceive objects as stable and three-dimensional and as persisting under conditions of occlusion, much the way that adults do (Spelke, 1991). Piagetian theory also held that children's ability to represent others' beliefs and intentions was quite limited until well into the concrete operational stage—that is, that young children were *egocentric*. It is now widely held that children at about age four understand both their own and others' minds as representational (Astington, Harris and Olson, 1988). There is some controversy over whether findings of early competence can be subsumed under a revised version of existing theory, as Fischer and Bidell (1992) suggest, or whether the Piagetian view of early mental life is simply flawed (Karmiloff-Smith, 1992). But however much Piaget's views are challenged today, his views were a substantial advance over earlier accounts of the child's mental life. The implications of his views for what children may usefully be taught, though, remain somewhat unclear (although see Bruner, 1966).

Nativism and the Later Maturationist View

Recent maturationist claims are more closely identified with nativist accounts of cognitive abilities (Chomsky, 1986; Fodor, 1983). These accounts differ substantially from earlier views. First, and most importantly, they ascribe innate cognitive structure to the child. Chomsky argues that the human capacity for language is a kind of "organ," with a biologically determined developmental path, much as that of other organs, such as the liver. On this view, the environment *triggers* innate structures that are part of the child's native endowment. When the organism is biologically ready, the input has an effect, but not before, and in the case of language, apparently not after (cf. Lenneberg, 1967; Newport, 1990). Children the world over acquire their native tongue, whether it be Japanese or Turkish or Quiche Mayan, at around the same age, with relative ease, and without formal instruction. This is a powerful argument for maturational constraints on the language acquisition capacity. The speed with which this complex domain of knowledge is acquired, usually in the absence of systematic corrective feedback on grammatical well-formedness, is also strong evidence for some form of innate, language-specific knowledge.

A second difference in current nativist theories is that they are domain-specific. Early maturationist-learning accounts, and early cognitive accounts such as Piaget's, were domain-general: learning proceeded across all domains of knowledge according to the same principles and in essentially the same manner. Recent nativist accounts argue that knowledge acquisition and processing takes place according to principles that are unique for each domain of knowledge (Fodor, 1983; Carey and Spelke, 1994). Language acquisition takes place according to language-specific principles, which are assumed to be different from, say, the acquisition of knowledge of physical objects, which is different again from the acquisition of number concepts, and so on. Not all maturationist accounts are entirely domain-specific, however. Newport (1990) argues convincingly that critical periods in language acquisition are influenced by domain-general principles (see also Keil, 1990). The ability to learn language declines at about the same time that other cognitive skills increase. On the "less is more" hypothesis, early domain-general cognitive limitations may actually help the child focus on linguistically relevant input (Newport, 1990).

Current maturationist views are also species-specific: while many species communicate, for example, the human capacity for language is distinct. Honeybees are able to indicate, via certain movements performed at the entrance to their hive, the location of an absent source of honey, but if the source is moved directly upward, they are at a loss, because they have no way of communicating "directly above" (Von Frisch, 1954). Unrestricted absent reference, structure-dependent generativity, and constitutiveness are defining features of the uniquely human language capacity.

In short, current accounts of innate endowment are becoming hard to refute. Cognitive ethologists (cf. Ristau, 1991) can attest to the fact that all higher species are endowed with some form of innate knowledge. It is unlikely that the human

infant is the planet moron, a mere sensate bundle of reflexes and diffuse responsiveness. The educational and cultural implications of the new nativism have yet
to be derived.

The Pedagogy of Readiness

Like most institutions and movements, perhaps more so, the history of early childhood education is the history of personalities, ideologies, and allegiances to particular belief systems, more often than not in the absence of systematic evaluation
or supporting empirical data. The influence of Rousseau, Pestalozzi, and Froebel
was profound on individuals charged with the establishment of early education
programs in the last century and early in this century. Even to the latter part of
this century, early educators have not been universally committed to basing their
pedagogy on new developmental theory or the results of research (Day, 1980).
Attempts to apply scientific research and theory to early education practice have
been spotty. The assumptions about readiness that underlie educational practice
reflect aspects of both commonsense, or folk-psychological theories and scientific
psychological theories.

Folk-psychological Assumptions

Commonsense theories of readiness seem to have changed little over the years.
Early maturationist views persist even to the latter decades of this century. A
recent survey of teacher's beliefs about readiness found that fully half of the teachers surveyed held classic maturationist views, including the belief that readiness
cannot be enhanced by intervention, and the astonishing opinion that in many
cases, "you can tell the first time you see them that they are not ready" (Smith and
Shepard, 1988). This kind of observation is akin to claiming a relation between
certain physical characteristics, such as size, coordination, or anatomical configurations, with mental abilities. There is a long and not very appealing history of this
theory in psychology (see Gould, 1981). It is a good example of the pitfalls of
unexamined folk theories that on the surface seem innocuous or even obvious.
None of us is free from the unexamined assumptions of our own folk psychologies,
and denying that we have such a commonsense theory does not mitigate its
effects.

Current Pedagogical Assumptions and Practices

While no single theoretical view or set of explicit explanatory assumptions in the
scientific sense can be identified universally with the term "readiness" as it is
currently used, the most dominant pedagogy in early education remains, not
surprisingly, one based on some version of the early maturationist view (Range,
Layton, and Roubinek, 1980). While current conceptualizations of the maturationist perspective in the pedagogical literature are somewhat woolly, it consists

of several general assumptions: children develop according to an inherent, "natural," stage-wise progression, the course of which must be supported and enriched, but not interfered with or forced; the "whole child" approach (Simmons, Whitfield, and Layton, 1980) which contends that maturation is global and includes social, emotional, physical, and intellectual factors in an inseparable whole; and the general notion that environmental stimulation does not enhance or speed maturation.

Retention   Several educational practices that derive directly from this view have recently come under attack by educational researchers (Meisels, 1992; Shepard and Smith, 1989). Foremost among these is the practice of retaining students in the early grades, or delaying their entry into kindergarten or first grade. The history of this issue is a long one. Early studies of readiness (Morphett and Washburne, 1931) for many years influenced educational practice virtually unquestioned, and delaying the onset of instruction, or retaining children until they were ready to learn, became commonly accepted. Several recent studies and reviews of this and related practices, including the use of measurement instruments such as the Gesell Readiness Inventory to determine which children are not ready for school entry (Meisels, 1987; Shepard and Smith, 1986, 1987) have yielded telling negative evidence.

In a carefully controlled study, Shepard and Smith (1987) compared children who had been retained one extra year in kindergarten with a matched control group that was not retained. At the end of the first grade, there was no significant academic difference between the group that had an extra year of schooling (or, three years in all) and the control group children (who had two years). As well as showing no academic advantage, the retained children displayed a more negative view of school. These investigators also found that the small measurable differences in academic skills between the youngest children in first grade and the oldest, something on the order of 7 or 8 percentile points (Shepard and Smith, 1986), virtually disappears by the end of the third grade. The authors argue that psychometric instruments widely used to justify delaying onset of educational advancement are in many cases poorly validated and used inappropriately. They find no evidence whatsoever to suggest that educational postponement or retaining children in kindergarten in any way enhances their chances of success, and further suggest that the negative socioemotional consequences can be deleterious to the child's overall functioning (Shepard and Smith, 1989).

Meisels (1992) points out that the increased emphasis on readiness and early testing in recent years results from pressures on educators trying to respond to concerns of falling academic standards, and the desire to protect students from the negative results of failure. However, as he forcefully argues, retention and associated practices such as delaying entry to kindergarten, are not only unsuccessful strategies, they are highly deleterious, from academic, socioemotional, and cultural perspectives. A better solution is designing "developmentally appropriate" curricula. It is difficult to find a match between an increasingly academically oriented curriculum and the inclinations of the child (Bredekamp and Shepard, 1989; Meisels, 1992).

Intervention   A second assumption of the old maturationist view is that intervention does not speed or enhance the child's level of readiness. This also has no empirical support. The watershed era for early intervention was the 1960s. Project Head Start was designed to advance the academic readiness of disadvantaged children, and to head off school failure and resulting social problems in advance (see Zigler and Meunchow, 1992, for a detailed account). No single dominant pedagogy or theory marked this massive national intervention. Numerous different programs emerged, based on theories as diverse as behavioral learning theory (Bereiter and Englemann, 1966) and Piagetian cognitive theory (Weikart, 1967). The pitfalls of moving from theory to practice were such that ostensibly identical programs would often be adjusted to local conditions and teacher preferences, so that consistency even within single programs was often difficult to maintain (Day, 1980). Even now, the program is in the position of needing to play theoretical "catch-up," because of the massive nature of the intervention. While evaluation of this intervention has been controversial (Consortium for Longitudinal Studies, 1983), overall evaluations have been positive. Funds continue to be allocated to it within the United States (Zigler and Meunchow, 1992) and international early intervention programs continue to grow (Lombard, 1994). It is important to remember that the success of such interventions is not always obvious in test scores in the early grades; it is rather reflected in deeper changes in attitudes to school, society, and self. These attitudes may manifest themselves later in life as a higher likelihood of pursuing postsecondary education or careers, and lower rates of delinquency and dropping out (see Zigler and Meunchow, 1992, for personal histories of some Head Start "graduates").

In short, there is certainly no evidence that early intervention is in any way deleterious. The assumption that direct, early instruction in particular knowledge domains somehow violates the notion of the "whole child" who is "globally unready" to learn is not tenable: there is simply no scientific evidence that this is the case. While a reaction against formal education's emphasis on academic skills to the exclusion of other aspects of the child's being, such as social needs, play, emotions, and so forth, is a healthy one, it does *not* follow that children should be denied formal tutoring or instruction in domains in which they show an inclination to learn.

Current maturationist pedagogies of readiness clearly need to be reexamined. Existing evidence suggests that retaining children does not lead to any kind of academic advantage, and that the predictive validity of kindergarten screening tests used to consign children to educational postponement is suspect. There is no indication that early intervention is deleterious. In contrast, there is evidence that retention can harm children's attitudes to school, and that early screening is unlikely to distinguish children who would benefit from formal instruction from those who would not. Early intervention also appears to have positive results. As is evident below, current evidence about children's early competence yields a vastly different picture of the child than that on which the early maturationist view was based.

Rethinking Readiness

Current Evidence of Children's Early Cognitive Competence

New evidence of children's early competence, emerging in the last few decades of this century, has radically changed scientific theories about the nature of initial mental states and early thought. Children are now viewed as cognitively competent, intellectually active, and socially engaged much earlier than previous theories allowed. They are capable of imitation and cross-modal representation from the earliest hours of life (Meltzoff and Moore, 1983), and they show evidence of taxonomic conceptual organization in the first 18 months of life (Bauer and Mandler, 1989). Their understanding of object properties, such as lawfulness of trajectories in movement, figure-ground distinctions, and gravity indicate the presence of a naive physics as early as six months of age (Spelke, 1991). They make complex inductive inferences about biological kinds, and differentiate clearly between some properties of living and nonliving things by the age of four (Wellman and S. Gelman, 1992). Their acquisition of language, perhaps the most impressive and complex of their early cognitive achievements, is largely accomplished by the age of five (Pinker, 1990; Gleitman, Gleitman, Landau, and Wanner, 1988). Most important for a theory of readiness is evidence that, in contrast to earlier characterizations of the child as egocentric and incapable of taking another's point of view until around seven or eight years of age, four-year-old children are now known to be quite capable of inferring another person's beliefs and desires, and of recognizing their own and others' minds as representational (Astington, Harris, and Olson, 1988; Wellman, 1990; see also Astington and Pelletier, this volume, chap. 26).

Domain-Specificity and Theory-based Knowledge

The need for new explanatory frameworks to support these diverse findings is evident. How do children draw the right kind of conclusions about the world so early, manifesting knowledge that has not been explicitly taught? The environment that surrounds them is amenable to many interpretations, yet children seem to make the right ones. Several kinds of principles have been proposed to explain this knowledge. The first is that at least some knowledge is innate. The renascent nativism of Chomsky, described above, was precipitated by the need to explain the child's early impressive feats in the area of language acquisition. While social interaction provides the occasions, intentions, and content of the child's early language, the complex and abstract rule system of grammar is acquired with virtually no formal teaching, and thus must be aided in some way by innate, language-specific knowledge. Fodor (1983) extended this idea to a general theory of mind that claims that much of cognition is *domain-specific*. On this view, different domains of knowledge—such as language, visual perception, knowledge of number and of beliefs, and desires—each seems to have unique explanatory principles associated with it. The development or acquisition of knowledge is *constrained* by principles unique to each domain. That is, the human mind has built-in structure or predispositions (*constraints*) that narrow the range of possible outcomes that can be arrived at, enabling the child to draw the right conclusions from a myriad of competing inputs in the environment: Linguistic constraints guide inferences about language input, perceiving and reasoning about objects is guided by constraints on object perception, and so on.

A second kind of explanation that has emerged is the characterization of early knowledge as *theory-like*. The theory view of children's conceptual development holds that children's early understandings of the world are organized, conceptually coherent, and explanatory in nature: in short, they are like scientific theories (Carey, 1985; Carey and Spelke, 1994; Gopnik and Wellman, 1994). There are many different ways in which the term "theory" is used. Wellman and Gelman (1992) argue for a differentiation between *framework theories* and *specific theories*. Framework theories are broad sets of explanatory principles that define domains, such as physics or biology or person knowledge. They are open systems, that influence and are articulated by specific theories. Specific theories can be as restricted as assertions about specific causal relations between two phenomena, such as the effect of water on salt, or as general as a theory of what constitutes membership in the genus "mammal." Children's early theories, and any theory that is based on commonsense understanding rather than scientific understanding, are *naive theories*.

The current picture of the preschooler implied by new evidence is overwhelmingly one of a cognitively competent child, possessed of highly specific kinds of knowledge, organized in a coherent manner by core principles used by the child to understand the world. This is in marked contrast to historical characterizations of the child discussed at the beginning of this chapter. What do these new views imply for readiness for learning?

First, viewing children's knowledge as theory-based allows a new conception of readiness in terms of prior theories. If early knowledge is theory-based, a rapprochement between children's early understanding of the world, or their *naive framework theories*, and the scientific, or *explicit theories* embodied in the curriculum of the teaching adult becomes much easier to conceptualize (see Olson and Bruner, this volume, chap. 2). Simply discovering the theory-like nature of early thought suggests that the principles that children use to explain the world to themselves are more similar to those of adults than previously thought, in kind if not in content. In what follows, some specific implications of current views are drawn. These are only a few instances of a very large set of potential implications. Whether or not one adopts the explanatory principles of domain-specificity and theory-based understanding, and these are certainly not the only views on offer, the following illustrates how a view of readiness is framed in relation to an overall view of children's thinking and learning.

Implications of Current Perspectives for a Theory of Readiness

Domain-General Readiness   On a theory view of knowledge, children's readiness for formal instruction depends on their possessing the ability to revise naive, commonsense theories and to formulate explicit, "scientific" theories with the benefit of formal instruction. A primary difference between these two kinds of theories is the degree of intentionality involved. Naive theories are acquired unintentionally, or incidentally. They are a consequence of the way the mind works, and the way the world is—they are transparent. They exemplify the kind of learning that goes on without formal instruction.

Explicit theories, in contrast, are opaque. In the language of cognitive science, they are metacognitive. Acquiring explicit theories requires the capacity for intentional learning, which must be in place for the child to begin formal instruction. Children must be able to represent elements of their own naive theories to themselves, to represent the new information in the formal theories being presented in instruction, and to intentionally derive the implications of matches or mismatches between the two. They must bring principles of their naive theories to bear in the intentional acquisition of explicit theories.

Readiness, on this view, thus requires that children recognize beliefs *qua* beliefs—that is, as not synonymous with reality and as subject to revision. The revision of belief is a domain-general, metarepresentational ability that lies at the very core of intentional learning. It underlies the child's ability to intentionally enrich or change the core explanatory principles in a naive theory, and thereby, the ability to learn from formal instruction. Children's recognition of their own mind as representational constitutes the emergence of *metarepresentational* competence, or metacognition. This explicit understanding about the origins and veracity of belief underlies all other forms of explicit, intentional theory change, and in this sense is domain-general. The ability to distinguish between appearance and reality, between one's own past and present beliefs, and to recognize beliefs, desires and intentions in others, all components of a *theory of mind* (Astington, Harris, and Olson, 1988; Wellman, 1990; see also Olson and Astington, 1993), emerge at about four or five years of age.

Domain-Specific Readiness   The division of the curriculum into subjects like geography, physics, mathematics, and literature is not simply an artifact of a rigid and outdated pedagogy as Dewey claimed. It is, in fact, quite consistent with a domain-specific view of mind, and probably reflects some sense of these distinctions in antiquity. The kinds of explanatory principles involved in physics are different than the kinds of explanatory principles involved in language, biology, or other domains, and the way in which learning occurs in each domain is also likely to be different.

This raises several kinds of questions. It is not clear, for instance, whether learning in a given domain consists of the acquisition of a new theory about the content of that domain or rendering an existing theory more accessible and coherent. Some investigators argue the former, that learning results in conceptual change and a *discontinuity* between early theories and later ones (Carey and Spelke, 1994), and some argue the latter, that learning involves increasing skill at accessing and applying the same basic explanatory principles, a *continuity* view of the relation between early and later theories (Fodor, 1992). More important for application is the relation between early naive or commonsense theories and later-emerging scientific theories in a particular domain of knowledge. Such relations must be made explicit in order to enhance the match necessary for the child's successful uptake of new information.

Implications for readiness in several domains of knowledge are drawn below, assuming that the nature of knowledge in each domain is theory-like. The child's early naive theories are characterized as *incidental*, or nonintentional, theories, following the classic distinction in learning theory between incidental and intentional learning (Hilgard and Bower, 1966). Similarly, later-emerging scientific theories are characterized as *intentional*. Note that this distinction is equally apt on both continuity and discontinuity views of theory development.

1. *Naive physics: Incidental and intentional theories.* From the first year of life, the child is an *incidental physicist*. Sensitivity to the continuity and solidity constraints on objects emerges at between two and three months of age, and sensitivity to gravity and inertia begins to emerge at around six months (Spelke, 1991). Naive theories of the physical world begin from these early experiences of object perception and object reasoning. Informal tutoring by others in the child's world, such as parents holding and shaking objects and other children vying for supremacy in toy possession, is likely to occur from very early in the child's experience. But even in its absence, the child can be expected to form some coherent ideas about the causal principles underlying the properties and actions of objects in the world in the first year of life.

Every good preschool is a lab for the incidental physicist: some objects stack and some roll, some can be nested within one another; wet sand and dry sand react differently, and wet sand becomes dry if left alone for a few days; the surface tension of water supports some objects while others sink immediately, water resists objects that are pushed through it, and too many objects will displace enough water to overflow the container. Principles derived from such happy experimentation are too often abandoned when "playtime" is over, and the work of formal instruction begins in school. They will remain inchoate until they are explored and brought to bear on formal principles in subsequent formal instruction about the physical world.

Readiness to become an *intentional physicist* depends on the extent of the match between the core explanatory principles of children's naive physics derived from their interactions with the world and those of the physical theory being taught. A theory could be outside of their direct experience, but if its principles are compatible with those of their existing understanding, it could be comprehended. The first step is to render the child's existing explanatory principles explicit, whether this is done through a question-definition process, diagrams, or even simple formulae. The physical theory to be taught can then be couched in similar terms.

Learning radically discontinuous content may not be possible in the early grades. The explanatory principles underlying the claim of relativity theory that time bends at the speed of light, for example, are discontinuous with the core principles of a six-year-old's naive physics. In naive physics, solid things bend when pressure is applied. It would probably be difficult for young children to conceive of light as something that could bend, and what could cause such a transformation, unless time-space physics could be recast in terms continuous with a five- or six-year-old's existing physics.

Domain-specific readiness in physics thus depends on the degree of match or mismatch between the explanatory principles that children are using in their current understanding of the physical world, and the explanatory principles of the formal physical theory being taught (see also diSessa, this volume, chap. 30).

2. *Naive biology: Incidental and intentional theories.* Preschool children are enthusiastic *incidental biologists*. Their profound interest in living things around them is reflected in a deep understanding about some of the nonobvious characteristics of biological kinds. They make different kinds of inductive inferences about biological kinds than they do about nonliving things (Gelman, 1988; Keil, 1989). They will infer that the same kinds of animals have the same kinds of insides, while something that looks like the animal but is not alive will not have the same insides (Gelman and Wellman, 1991). By age four, children also recognize innate potentials, such that baby cows will moo and have straight tails, even if raised with pigs (Gelman and Wellman, 1991); and realize that leaves change color because of intrinsic rather than extrinsic forces (Gelman and Kremer, 1991). Findings such as these contradict Piagetian claims that childhood animism causes the child to attribute human or biological characteristics, such as feelings or agency, indiscriminately to inanimate or animate objects. Still, Carey (1985) argues that children under the age of ten do not always realize that the domain of living things includes plants. In general, Wellman and Gelman (1992) conclude that naive biology is not as well developed as naive psychology or naive physics, by the time children reach school age. But evidence suggests that children reason about living kinds with domain-specific principles, that cannot be accounted for by domain-general processes like similarity judgments.

The child's readiness to become an *intentional biologist* can thus be expected to differ depending on whether the subdomain in question is animals or plants, since knowledge about animals seems to be more developed at an earlier age. Children are, in comparison, late in developing a coherent, adult-like category of "living things." It may be that children's explanatory principles about plants are developing just as early as their explanatory principles about animals, but that they simply do not include both kinds in one general category (but see Atran, this volume, chap. 28). What adults consider the domain of biology might thus best be broken down for young children into smaller subdomains, such as naive botany or naive zoology. Children's core understanding about the living world is more coherent in subdomains such as these. Readiness for formal instruction about plants or animals depends on the existing forms of understanding children have in these specific subdomains, the ease with which such understanding can be rendered explicit, and the compatibility of the formal theory being taught with the child's existing explanatory principles.

3. *Early theories of number.* Counting objects involves very different principles than perceiving them or naming them. Counting principles must assign to numerically equivalent sets the same numeron, regardless of the perceptual characteristics or names of the objects in the set; and in spite of a constantly changing lexicon, the young child does not confuse names and numbers (Gelman, 1990). R. Gelman (1990) argues that the constraints on count words are different than the constraints on object labels. It has also been argued that small sets of objects can be enumerated by a process of *subitizing*, a global perceptual process distinct from counting (Klahr and Wallace, 1973), but others hold that even enumeration of small sets involves counting (Gallistel and Gelman, 1992). Evidence exists that knowledge of the core principles of numerosity, one-to-one correspondence, and unique serial succession, are innate (Gallistel, 1990; Gallistel and Gelman, 1992). These core principles form the basis for arithmetic reasoning and are grasped by every young *incidental mathematician*. On several current views, then, perceiving and reasoning about large sets of numbers is generally held to be accounted for by a single set of core principles.

Readiness for formal instruction in arithmetic or mathematics would require making these existing core principles explicit, and mapping onto them whatever new principle is being explained. Mathematics has an extremely rich notational system, a "language" of its own. Learning this domain-unique system is a fundamental part of explicating its core explanatory principles. Children who display an understanding of the principles of counting are ready to become *intentional mathematicians*, to begin learning how such principles can be represented in explicit, formal ways with symbols and notations. Explicit theories of number, arithmetic, and basic mathematical principles can then be attempted, if they are framed in terms that are consistent with children's naive understanding.

Rethinking the Pedagogy of Readiness

How is Tyler's (1964) classic readiness question of "when to teach" best understood? Children's readiness to be taught depends more on the *kind* of teaching than on when it begins. Teaching will be most effective when it is easily mapped, not only into the child's existing knowledge as explained above, but also into the child's existing understanding of how knowledge exchange takes place. Formal instruction is simply a particular kind of envelope in which knowledge is delivered. Acquiring information from adults is not an entirely new experience for children. Many such events have impinged on young minds in the five long years prior to kindergarten. Nevertheless, discontinuities do exist between formal instruction and previous forms of knowledge exchange.

Discontinuities with Early Experience

Unlike earlier experience, formal instruction deals with abstract principles separately from the context of their real-world application. Formal instruction is, in short, "decontextualized." This has often been argued to be a source of difficulty for the young child in the transition to schooling. It is, however, a necessary one. It is impossible to conceive of instruction in some domains, such as advanced algebra or philosophy, as ever being fully contextualized or concrete. Formality and abstraction are necessary features of advanced domains of instruction, not a flaw in educational methodology.

It is important to note in this respect that young children's knowledge can also be abstract. Their understanding of language and other domains of knowledge operates according to abstract rules from an early age. The observation that children's grammatical knowledge is resistant to explicit correction (see Brown and Hanlon, 1970; Braine, 1971) is taken as evidence for the robustness of their own inner abstract principles. But these are principles that children derive for and by themselves within a particular domain, and not abstract principles that are taught as such. Thus the difficulty that children experience when encountering "decontextualized" abstract principles in formal instruction does not derive from children being incapable of employing abstract principles. It is rather that they are not used to receiving bundles of new knowledge in abstract packages, so to speak. The kind and degree of abstraction is discontinuous with their early experience.

Continuities with Early Experience

Conveying the structure and content of other people's domain-specific theories to the child, the stuff of formal instruction, can map into the preschool child's experience more smoothly if some continuities are identified between formal instruction and earlier experience. First, most formal instruction, in the early years at least, is *interactive*. A knowledgeable adult provides an interpretive or explanatory structure within which a novice child can learn to function. While in educational contexts this often occurs in a formal and distant manner, it is not fundamentally discontinuous with the structure of interaction that emerges in infancy. Parents, or other caretakers, when feeding, changing, calming, or playing with the child, attribute consciousness and intentionality to their offspring from the very beginning (Stern, 1985). They talk to the child and set up an expectation of a response long before the child seems capable of providing one. The repetitive structuring of these interactions not only gives evident pleasure to the child but also "scaffolds" experience in such a way that it boosts the child's own expressive and cognitive capabilities (Bruner, 1983a). These are early informal instructional events: older, more experienced members of the culture lend form and content to the child's earliest, hesitant inclinations to explore the world. Such intervention is not necessarily intended as instruction. More often the child's learning is aided in a spontaneous or incidental way, in the manner Rousseau (above) referred to as *apprenticeship*. This notion has gained much currency in recent years (Miller, 1977; Rogoff, 1990; Rogoff, Matusov, and White, this volume, chap. 18).

Second, formal instruction usually involves *absent reference*: events and individuals that are not present in the immediate context; but again, this is not unfamiliar to the child. Children's earliest encounters with absent or hypothetical events and individuals usually occur either in pretend play or in narrative. In pretend play, children represent absent objects that are the products of their own experience and imagining. This is an early form of the representational competence that comes to figure in the child's theory of mind (Leslie, 1988). The absent characters and events of narrative, in contrast, are the products of writers' and narrators' minds, rather than of the children's themselves. But far from presenting a difficulty to children, the absent reference of narrative is a source of endless fascination. The naturalness of narrative as a mode of instruction is easily observable in any home or preschool where children are read to. Children's responsiveness to it echoes the primacy of narrative as a history- and culture-bearing form across all human cultures (Bruner, 1986).

Thus the absent topics of formal instruction need not be a source of difficulty in themselves. The explanations and interpretations given to children should take into account the kinds of contexts in which these sorts of topics have been experienced. Similarly, the structured and sometimes distant nature of formal instruction can be more effective if it builds on continuities with earlier forms of interaction. Taking into account both sorts of continuities should render formal instruction more accessible to the young child. Still, the particularities of formal instruction as commonly experienced in western schooling, with its emphasis on explicit, decontextualized and abstract forms, necessarily engender unique experiences and attitudes to knowledge that in turn place unique demands on the child.

Conclusions

Reevaluating the Scientific Basis of Readiness

At the outset of this chapter, it was argued that a theory of readiness is best viewed as relative to a broader theoretical framework, a scientific psychology, philosophy, or a naive, commonsense theory. A general conclusion of this position is that regardless of our theoretical orientation or commonsense beliefs, a first-order move is to make our theoretical framework explicit. Before any theory of readiness is advanced, or any curricula designed, underlying assumptions about children, learning and teaching should be articulated. While these need not be at the same level of detail as a scientific theory designed to advance knowledge, they should at least be consistent with it. It is simply bad practice to maintain a theory, and implement curricula, that are inconsistent with existing scientific evidence.

It is evident from the above that certain ideas about readiness can be seen to recur. These recurring ideas are good candidates for pretheoretical assumptions in developing a coherent theory of readiness. Previously unknown empirical facts about how children's minds function also put us in a better position to evaluate both historical and current positions.

1. *Readiness for learning is a function of the match between the cognitive dispositions of the child and the form of what is to be taught.* From Comenius through Dewey to Bruner and the current theory view of mind, this can be seen to be a recurring principle. This is in stark contrast to the early maturationist view, with its fixed, domain-general assumptions. It is not that biological factors such as maturation have no effect. Clearly they have important effects, but these do not include a global restriction on the child's ability to benefit from instruction. A "matching" view allows for both domain-general and a range of domain-specific principles in explaining readiness for learning. It assumes that the child brings to any learning task an active body of beliefs, expectations, and assumptions, which are best taken advantage of if successful learning is to occur.

2. *Domain-general readiness to engage in formal instruction can be expected to occur at about four or five years of age.* It depends on the child's emerging meta-representational competence, or theory of mind. The ability to represent his or her own mind as representational, and the recognition that beliefs can be revised, underlies the ability to benefit from formal instruction. This age is earlier than the age that would be predicted by, say, classic Piagetian theory. Basing a theory of readiness on the notion of metarepresentational competence also has substantially different implications for pedagogy than the early maturationist account, primarily because it is based on a particular kind of competence—competence with representations—and not on the rather vague notion of maturity. This form of competence is what enables naive theories to be represented in explicit form, across diverse domains and different representational formalisms.

3. *There is more than one kind of readiness.* Readiness to acquire knowledge can be expected to vary across domains, as organizing principles in the child's existing theories vary depending on the kind of knowledge in question. Thus many different schedules of readiness can be expected to occur, depending on the domain of knowledge. On this account, effective teaching is more interpretive than didactic. Children's own inclinations and interests need to be recognized as important indicators of their current naive theories, and taken into account in determining which explicit principles are to be taught, and in what manner. This is particularly important in the early school years, until such time as domain-general strategies for learning are well developed.

In summary, it becomes evident that the readiness question is not simply *when* to teach, as Tyler (1964) argued, but rather *how* and *what* to teach. Reducing readiness to a unidimensional *when* question derives from a maturationist view, one that, as we have seen, has been roundly discredited. It is not accurate to assume that we must wait patiently on the sidelines until children bloom, untouched. It is evident from current research that they are just as likely, or even more likely, to wilt than to bloom. They can benefit from being taught, as long as their existing understanding is taken into account. The *how* and *what* questions about readiness for learning are interpretive and explanatory: they assume that the substance and manner of what is taught are most important in the success of learning. The substance issue (the what question) is a domain-specific one: the accessibility of existing core explanatory principles to revision and/or change on the basis of new information, and the nature of the new information given, will vary according to the domain of knowledge. The manner issue (the how question) is a domain-general one: teaching as explanation and interpretation requires of the child some grasp of the mind as representational, that beliefs are subject to revision. A domain-general understanding of beliefs *qua* beliefs underlies the readiness to engage in formal instruction, and the ability to understand reasons for the revision of belief.

Implementation: Theory and Practice

Some characteristics of theory-practice interaction may account for the persistence of outdated and inadequate theories in educational practice, and the resistance to implementing new theory-based pedagogy.

First, in the process of passing from laboratory to classroom, many theories undergo such drastic changes as to be pale resemblances of their former selves. Second, a theory designed to advance knowledge, like most scientific psychological theories, may not be a good theory for imparting knowledge. Science and teaching are fundamentally different activities (see Dewey, 1902/1956), and a bad metaphysics could be a good epistemology (see Medin, 1989). It is worth noting that Socrates was a renowned teacher, with an effective pedagogy that was not informed by developmental theory. Third, the instructional implications of widely different theories, when translated into recommendations for teachers, sometimes look remarkably similar (see Simmons, Whitfield, and Layton, 1980). Fourth, scientific psychological theories designed to advance knowledge about the nature of cognition and learning are constantly changing. This makes for good science but bad pedagogy. If a particular view turns out to be "wrong," educators have to constantly readjust their practices, which gets time-consuming, expensive, and frustrating. It is also often overlooked that it is highly unrealistic to expect that a teacher, who is not usually a trained scientist, should be able to derive the instructional implications of a theory that even the originator of the theory might have trouble deriving. A final issue is the "graininess" or level of detail in a theory. Most scientific psychological theories address only a subset of human functioning in great detail, while pedagogy has a much wider scope and tends to be less detailed.

All of these points militate against a smooth interface between the laboratory and the classroom. But as the example of school retention makes clear, failing to base educational practice on sound theory can have disastrous consequences for children. No theory answers all pedagogical questions, but maintaining pedagogical practices that directly contradict empirical evidence is indefensible.

It may be the case that some ideas about readiness currently held by educators derive at least partly from the unforgiving nature of institutional life, schools being no exception. The term "school readiness" in place of readiness for learning reflects this. A primary concern of an administrator is whether a given child can function within the school, with its myriad social, physical, and intellectual demands. Institutions are notoriously nonadaptive to individuals. It is the individual who is expected to somehow make the necessary adjustments in order to thrive within a given set of institutional restrictions. "School readiness," on this commonsense account, thus actually describes a "fit" between the individual and the institution's demands. Many factors, such as temperament, personality, cultural background, parental attitudes, even health and nutrition can play a role here. As real as this problem is, to erroneously cast it as an intraindividual learning problem will inevitably lead to wrong solutions being proposed. It is not clear that there will ever be an accurate, streamlined process for separating the "able-to-fit" from the "not-yet-able-to-fit" in the lively and mutable population of five-year-olds, nor is it clear that this would be desirable. The situation is inescapably complex: children are individuals, and a successful educational experience requires mutual adaptability, as problematic as that may be for the institution.

The Child Versus the Curriculum

In spite of the fact that his view of children's early thought was quite at odds with current views, Dewey's ideas are worth revisiting, in light of our new understanding of the child. Dewey argued strenuously that in practice, the curriculum is often either inaccessible to the child because its abstract, logical nature is too removed from the child's immediate experience, or if attempts are made to make it accessible, the subject often becomes "denatured"—robbed of its explanatory principles and reduced from a coherent logical system to a series of isolated facts that must be committed to memory. Neither technique serves in rendering the world more comprehensible to children, nor does it allow them to benefit from the cumulative theoretical knowledge of our forebears in the intentional construction and revision of their own naive theories.

> We are almost fortunate if he does not get actual non-science, flat and commonplace residua of what was gaining scientific vitality a generation or two ago—degenerate reminiscence of what someone else once formulated on the basis of the experience that some further person had, once upon a time, experienced. . . . (Dewey, 1902/1956, p. 26)

No one can accuse today's educators of being insensitive to this issue. The fact remains, however, that finding the middle ground between a curriculum that is too dissimilar from the child's current experience to be grasped, and one that is so simplified as to be robbed of its explanatory dynamism and immediacy, is a tall task. The proposals contained here are only a beginning. The validity of common-sense theories about children and how they learn, particularly those derived from many years of experience working with children, should not be underestimated. But these proposals need examining for flawed assumptions, and stand to be immeasurably enriched by the theories of others who have thought deeply about the child, and about the forms of activity most central to the child's life: the discovery of and engagement with the cultural, social, and physical world.

Acknowledgment

The author gratefully acknowledges helpful comments and suggestions by David R. Olson; responsibility for remaining flaws rests with the author. Thanks also to the Hebrew University of Jerusalem for providing support during the writing of this chapter.

References

Astington, J., Harris, P., and Olson, D. R. (1988). *Developing theories of mind*. Cambridge, England: Cambridge University Press.

Bauer, P. and Mandler, J. (1989). Taxonomies and triads: Conceptual organization in one-to-two-year-olds. *Cognitive Psychology, 21* (2), 156–184.

Bereiter, C. and Englemann, S. (1966). *Teaching disadvantaged children in the preschool*. Englewood Cliffs, NJ: Prentice-Hall.

Braine, M. D. S. (1971). The acquisition of language in infant and child. In C. E. Reed (Ed.), *The learning of language*. New York: Appleton-Century-Crofts.

Bredekamp, S. and Shepard, L. (1989). How best to protect children from inappropriate school expectations, practices, and policies. *Young Children, 44*, 14–24.

Brown, A. Domain-specific principles affect learning and transfer in children. *Cognitive Science, 14*, 107–133.

Brown, R. and Hanlon, C. (1970). Derivational complexity and order of acquisition in child speech. In J. R. Hayes (Ed.), *Cognition and the development of language* (pp. 11–53). New York: Wiley.

Bruner, J. S. (1966). *The Process of Education*. Cambridge: Harvard University Press.

Bruner, J. S. (1983a). *Child's talk*. New York: Norton.

Bruner, J. S. (1983b). *In search of mind: Essays in autobiography*. New York: Harper and Row.

Bruner, J. S. (1986). *Actual minds, possible worlds*. Cambridge: Harvard University Press.

Carey, S. (1985). *Conceptual change in childhood*. Cambridge: Bradford/MIT Press.

Carey, S. (1991). Knowledge acquisition: Enrichment or conceptual change? In S. Carey and R. Gelman (Eds.), *Epigenesis of mind: Studies in biology and cognition* (pp. 257–291). Hillsdale, NJ: Lawrence Erlbaum.

Carey, S. and Gelman, R. (1991). *The epigenesis of mind*. Hillsdale, NJ: Lawrence Erlbaum.

Carey, S. and Spelke, E. (1994). Domain-specific knowledge and conceptual change. In L. Hirschfeld and S. A. Gelman (Eds.), *Mapping the mind: Domain specificity in cognition and culture* (pp. 169–200). Cambridge, England: Cambridge University Press.

Chomsky, N. (1986). *Knowledge of language: Its nature, origin and uses*. New York: Praeger.

Comenius, J. A. (1633/1956). *The school of infancy*. E. Eller (Ed.), Chapel Hill: University of North Carolina Press.

Consortium for Longitudinal Studies. (1983). *As the twig is bent: Lasting effects of preschool programs*. Hillsdale, NJ: Lawrence Erlbaum.

Day, B. (1980). Contemporary early childhood education programs and related controversial issues. In D. C. Range, J. R. Layton, and D. L. Roubinek (Eds.), *Aspects of early childhood education: Theory to research to practice* (pp. 39–86). New York: Academic Press.

DeVries, R. and Kohlberg, L. (1987). *Programs of early education: The constructivist view*. New York: Longman.

Dewey, J. (1902/1956). *The child and the curriculum.* Chicago: University of Chicago Press.

Durkin, D. (1973). What does research say about the time to begin research instruction? In R. Karlin (Ed.), *Perspectives on elementary reading* (pp. 135–143). New York: Harcourt Brace Jovanovich.

Fischer, K. W. and Bidell, T. (1992). Constraining nativist influences about cognitive capacities. In S. Carey and R. Gelman (Eds.), *The epigenesis of mind* (pp. 199–235). Hillsdale, NJ: Lawrence Erlbaum.

Fodor, J. (1983). *Modularity of mind: An essay on faculty psychology.* Cambridge: MIT Press.

Fodor, J. (1992). A theory of the child's theory of mind. *Cognition, 44,* 283–296.

Gallistel, C. R. (1990). *The organization of learning.* Cambridge: Bradford/MIT Press.

Gallistel, C. R. and Gelman, R. (1992). Preverbal and verbal counting and computation. *Cognition, 44,* 43–74.

Gelman, R. (1990). First principles organize attention to and learning about relevant data: Number and the animate-inanimate distinction. *Cognitive science, 14,* 79–106.

Gelman, S. A. (1988). The development of induction within natural kind and artifact categories. *Cognitive Psychology, 20,* 65–95.

Gelman, S. A. and Kremer, K. E. (1991). Understanding natural cause: Children's explanations of how objects and their properties originate. *Child Development, 62,* 296–314.

Gelman, S. A. and Wellman, H. M. (1991). Insides and essences: Early understanding of the nonobvious. *Cognition, 38* (3), 213–244.

Gleitman, L. R., Gleitman, H., Landau, B., and Wanner, E. (1988). Where language learning begins: Initial representations for language learning. In F. J. Newmeyer (Ed.), *Linguistics: The Cambridge Survey* (Vol. 3, pp. 150–193). Cambridge, England: Cambridge University Press.

Gopnik, A. (1993). The "theory theory" of cognitive development. Paper presented at the Society for Research in Child Development, New Orleans.

Gopnik, A. and Wellman, H. M. (1994). The theory theory. In L. Hirschfeld and S. Gelman (Eds.), *Domain-specificity in culture and cognition* (pp. 257–293). New York: Cambridge University Press.

Gould, S. J. (1981). *The mismeasure of man.* New York: Norton.

Hilgard, E. and Bower, G. (1966). *Theories of learning* (3rd ed.). New York: Appleton-Century-Crofts.

James, W. (1939). *Talks to teachers about psychology.* New York: Holt. Republished in 1983 as *Talks to teachers on psychology and to students on some of life's ideals.* Cambridge: Harvard University Press.

Karmiloff-Smith, A. (1992). *Beyond modularity: A developmental perspective on cognitive science.* Cambridge: MIT Press.

Keil, F. (1989). *Concepts, kinds, and cognitive development.* Cambridge: MIT Press.

Keil, F. (1990). Constraints on constraints: Surveying the epigenetic landscape. *Cognitive science, 14,* 135–168.

Klahr, D. and Wallace, J. G. (1973). The role of quantification operators in the development of conservation. *Cognitive Psychology, 4,* 301–327.

Lenneberg, E. (1967). *The biological foundations of language.* New York: Wiley.

Leslie, A. M. (1988). The necessity of illusion: Perception and thought in infancy. In L. Weiskrantz (Ed.), *Thought without language* (pp. 185–210). Oxford, England: Clarendon Press.

Lombard, A. D. (1994). *Success begins at home: The past, present, and future of the home instruction program for young children.* Guilford, CT: Dushkin Publishing Group.

Medin, D. (1989). Concepts and conceptual structure. *American Psychologist, 44,* 1469–1481.

Meisels, S. (1987). Uses and abuses of developmental screening and school readiness testing. *Young Children, 42,* 4–6, 68–73.

Meisels, S. (1992). Doing harm by doing good: Iatrogenic effects of early childhood enrollment and promotion policies. *Early Childhood Research Quarterly, 7,* 155–174.

Meltzoff, A. N. and Moore, M. K. (1983). Newborn infants imitate adult facial gestures. *Child Development, 54,* 702–719.

Miller, G. A. (1977). *Spontaneous apprentices: Children and language.* New York: Seabury Press.

Morphett, M. V. and Washburne, C. (1931). When should children learn to read? *Elementary School Journal, 31,* 496–508.

Newport, E. (1990). Maturational constraints on language learning. *Cognitive Science, 14,* 11–28.

Olson, D. R. and Astington, J. W. (1993). Thinking about thinking: Learning how to take statements and hold beliefs. *Educational Psychologist, 28* (1), 7–23.

Perner, J. and Wilde Astington, J. (1992). The child's understanding of mental representation. In H. Beilin and P. B. Pufall (Eds.), *Piaget's theory: Prospects and possibilities* (pp. 141–160). Hillsdale, NJ: Lawrence Erlbaum.

Piatelli-Palmerini, M. (1980). *Language and learning: The debate between Jean Piaget and Noam Chomsky.* Cambridge: Harvard University Press.

Pinker, S. (1990). Language acquisition. In Posner, M. (Ed.), *Foundations of cognitive science* (pp. 359–399). Cambridge: MIT Press.

Range, D., Layton, J., and Roubinek, D. (Eds.). (1980). *Aspects of early childhood education: Theory to research to practice.* New York: Academic Press.

Ristau, C. A. (1991). *Cognitive ethology: The minds of other animals.* Hillsdale, NJ: Lawrence Erlbaum.

Rogoff, B. (1990). *Apprenticeship in thinking: Cognitive development in social context.* New York: Oxford University Press.

Rousseau, J.-J. (1762/1979). *Emile, or on education* (A. Bloom, Trans.). New York: Basic Books.

Shepard, L. and Smith, M. L. (1986). Synthesis of research on school readiness and kindergarten retention. *Educational Leadership, 44,* 78–86.

Shepard, L. and Smith, M. L. (1987). Effects of kindergarten retention at the end of first grade. *Psychology in the Schools, 24* (October), pp. 346–357.

Shepard, L. and Smith, M. L. (Eds.). (1989). *Flunking grades: Research and policy on retention.* Philadelphia: Falmer Press.

Simmons, B., Whitfield, E., and Layton, R. (1980). The preparation of early childhood teachers: Philosophical and empirical foundations. In D. L. Range, J. R. Layton, and D. L. Roubinek (Eds.), *Aspects of early childhood education: Theory to research to practice* (pp. 1–38). New York: Academic Press.

Smith, M. L. and Shepard, L. A. (1988). Kindergarten readiness and retention: A qualitative study of teachers' beliefs and practices. *American Educational Research Journal, 25* (3), 307–333.

Spelke, E. (1991). Physical knowledge in infancy. In S. Carey and R. Gelman (Eds.), *The epigenesis of mind* (pp. 133–169). Hillsdale, NJ: Lawrence Erlbaum.

Stern, D. (1985). *The interpersonal world of the infant: A view from psychoanalysis and developmental psychology.* NY: Basic Books.

Stitch, S. P. (1983). *From folk psychology to cognitive science: The case against belief.* Cambridge: MIT Press.

Teale, W. H. and Sulzby, E. (1986). *Emergent literacy.* Norwood, NJ: Ablex.

Tyler, F. T. (1964). Issues related to readiness to learn. In E. Hilgard (Ed.), *Theories of learning and instruction. The 63rd yearbook of the National Society for the Study of Education* (pp. 210–239). Chicago: University of Chicago Press.

Von Frisch, K. (1954). *The dancing bees.* London: Methuen.

Wellman, H. M. (1990). *The child's theory of mind.* Cambridge: MIT Press.

Wellman, H. M. and Gelman, S. A. (1992). Cognitive development: Foundational theories of core domains. *Annual Review of Psychology, 43,* 337–375.

Weikart, D. P. (1967). *Preschool intervention: A preliminary report of the Perry Preschool Project.* Ann Arbor, MI: Campus Publishers.

Zigler, E. and Meunchow, S. (1992). *Head Start: The inside story of America's most successful educational experiment.* New York: Basic Books.

9

Language and Literacy Development: Discontinuities and Differences

LOWRY HEMPHILL
CATHERINE SNOW

Literacy and Language

It seems clear from common sense and from a wide panoply of correlations that knowledge of a language relates to literacy in that language, so it is not surprising that the notion of language-literacy continuity is widely held by those who may differ on other principles. Children who score well on measures of language proficiency—on vocabulary tests, for example—are likely to be good readers, and conversely children who encounter problems learning to read often turn out to have preexisting (sometimes subtle) deficits in oral language skill as well. The correlations between skill at oral language and at literacy, which might be interpreted as evidence for some common underlying processes, have been taken by many as an argument that literacy acquisition is just like language acquisition.

Ideas about the relationship between oral language development and literacy have been around as long as modern theorizing about literacy. However, with the Chomskian revolution in language acquisition theory, notions of the dependencies between oral language and literacy development took on new form and achieved more compelling status. Transformational generative grammar reconceptualized language as an abstract system with a deep structure that was not directly accessible from surface structure utterances (Chomsky, 1957). This reconceptualization resulted in an upsurge of research on language acquisition designed to confirm with developmental data the universal and rule-governed nature of language. A corollary of the Chomskian view was that language acquisition was rapid and easy because much of the structure of the system was innate and thus did not need to be acquired, let alone taught. Language was explicitly differentiated from other complex cognitive systems by Chomsky by its feature of universal acquisition in the absence of instruction. Though precisely this feature distinguishes language from literacy, three basic parallels between language and literacy have been nonetheless widely presupposed in much recent thinking about literacy: the notion of ease and speed of learning, the claim that acquisition could proceed without direct teaching, and the presumption that competence emerged from use for authentic communicative purposes (Sydow, 1990). For example, writing in 1977, the Goodmans argued:

The differences between oral and written language result from differences of function rather than from any difference in intrinsic character. . . . We are convinced that oral and written language differ much more in how they are taught than in the way they are learned. (K. Goodman, 1982, p. 55)

Progressivist views on the naturalness of literacy development are much older than the Chomskian revolution and the research program that it inspired (Y. Goodman, 1989; Shannon, 1990; Willinsky, 1990). However, these views acquired new prestige and authority as a consequence of their association with scientific theorizing about language acquisition. The "emergent literacy" notion, for example, is predicated on the natural, inevitable, and universal emergence of early literacy skills and the obfuscation of distinctions between literacy and language as systems to be acquired (Holdaway, 1986; Teale, 1982). Weaver, for example, argues:

Adults cannot actually teach children how to read or write, though they can demonstrate or model reading and writing for them, collaborate with them, demonstrate and discuss reading and writing strategies with them, and guide them in reading and writing. In all of these ways, adults facilitate children's developing ability to read and write. But they cannot effectively teach children to read and write, any more than they can effectively teach babies and toddlers the rules for putting together sounds to make words, and words together to make sentences. (1994, p. 86)

Although this view is a simple extrapolation to literacy of Chomskian arguments for the innate nature of language development, in fact it is a very anti-Chomskian position because Chomsky argues explicitly for the distinction between natural human faculties like language and invented, culturally determined human capacities like literacy.

Facilitative Environments   Emergent literacy theorists and whole language practitioners emphasize strongly the role of a literacy-rich environment in supporting successful literacy acquisition. Children who learn to read "naturally" in the preschool years are children whose homes are full of print, whose parents make wide use of reading and writing themselves, and who involve their offspring in frequent experiences with written text (Hall, 1987; Holdaway, 1986). To reproduce these advantages for all children, and to support this type of natural acquisition of literacy in school, they claim that teachers, like highly literate parents, should immerse children in print and create rich opportunities for engagement with written text (Vacca and Rasinski, 1992; Weaver, 1994). Thus whole language prescriptions for classroom practice emphasize both the naturalness and ease of children's movement into greater competence as readers and writers, and the teacher's responsibility for creating rich and well-supported environments for the development of literacy (Calkins, 1991; Holdaway, 1979; Newman, 1985).

   A basic claim of whole language theory is that surrounding children with literacy will ensure literate outcomes as reliably as surrounding infants with language ensures language acquisition. One version of this view draws on activity theory (Leont'ev, 1979; Wertsch, 1979), seeing literacy as the inevitable outcome of (and indeed as indistinguishable from) engagement in literacy activities. Teale, for example, argues:

By being engaged in activities which have literacy embedded in them and in which the reading or writing, and the oral language which accompanies them, are played out in the social interaction between the child and the more experienced literate person, the child is able to participate in the activity itself, gradually internalize the social relationships, and thereby develop personal competencies in reading and writing. (1982, p. 563)

Communicative Sources of Competence   Another closely related view is that literacy development, like the development of oral language, is driven by the learner's desire to communicate:

Language is not only the most social of human skills, it is the necessary condition for a specifically human society of any kind. It is learned in strongly communal settings and fueled by social satisfactions. Although literacy entails the decontextualizing and abstracting of our linguistic interactions—the distancing of "speaker" from the immediate sensory world, and from the "listener"—reading and writing share in the fundamental social priorities of language. (Holdaway, 1986, p. 69)

In a very similar vein, the Goodmans argue:

We believe that children learn to read and write in the same way and for the same reason that they learn to speak and listen. That way is to encounter language in use as a vehicle of communicating meaning. The reason is need. Language learning, whether oral or written, is motivated by the need to communicate, to understand, and be understood. (Goodman and Goodman, 1979)

Thus the defining characteristic of a good environment for literacy acquisition is the presence of multiple and authentic opportunities for communicating through language (Edelsky, Altwerger, and Flores, 1991; Ruddell, 1992). Just as learners' own communicative intents are thought to drive oral language acquisition (Wells, 1986), the child's communicative purposes around written language serve to motivate and structure development. These purposes are expressed most successfully through early-acquired language forms such as narrative (Bruner, 1986; Nelson, 1986), which highlight the display of personal "voice" (Dyson and Genishi, 1994; Egan, 1987; Gallas, 1994). These views about similarities between oral language and literacy development lead naturally to the implementation of certain practices in early childhood classrooms—for example, writing personal experience stories, rich modeling of literacy practices, avoidance of direct instruction, reliance on group process, and elevation of narrative to a central position.

Conflicting Views   The emphasis on environmental support for acquisition reflects these theorists' incorporation of conclusions from the large body of work on environmental support for language learning—work done to argue *against* an innatist perspective—into an essentially innatist account of development. Work of the past two decades on the social context within which language acquisition occurs has had the explicit purpose of defining environmental sources of information to the language learner that could substitute for hypothesized innate mechanisms. A superficial extrapolation of that work might well lead to the conclusion that a literacy-rich environment that honors children's communicative intents as sources of literacy experience would replicate the circumstances under which language is acquired. In fact, though, a more careful reading of work on the social-interactive context of language acquisition suggests that the environmental sources of language facilitation take very different forms in different social and cultural settings and at different stages of development (Ochs, 1988; see Lieven, 1994, and Snow, 1995, for reviews). The very large body of work on social interactive facilitation of language development (see Gallaway and Richards, 1994, for a review) suggests that facilitation of language development need not start from the child's communicative intent, nor even involve engaging the child in dyadic conversation. Mechanisms for promoting language development are an inextricable part of the local culture of child-rearing, and as such must conform to broader cultural rules defining children's and adults' social roles and relationships (Clancy, 1986; Ochs, 1988; Schieffelin and Ochs, 1986).

Whole language theorists, however, have happily merged applications of innatist views (e.g., that literacy acquisition is rapid and easy) with simplistic interpretations of social interactionist views (e.g., that an enriched literacy environment is necessary for literacy acquisition), while simultaneously rejecting notions implied both by innatist views (e.g., that there might be specific reading disabilities) and by a social interactionist perspective (e.g., that organizing and sequencing exposure to reading materials would enhance learning) (Moorman, Blanton, and McLaughlin, 1994; Ruddell, 1992; Smith, 1983). They have, furthermore, adopted a very oversimplified view of the research on social interactive facilitation of communicative development, one that ignores cultural and situational variation in forms of facilitation.

In summary, the emerging orthodoxy within whole language literacy research and theorizing makes a set of claims about language and literacy development:

1. Language (literacy) acquisition is natural, rapid, and universally successful.
2. Participation in the communicative practices of language- (literacy-)rich communities generates language (literacy) competence, without the need for direct instruction.
3. Language (literacy) competence is a socially situated, not an individual, cognitive, accomplishment.
4. Children learn language (literacy) in order to express their own communicative intents.
5. Preeminent among the language (literacy) forms that children acquire is narrative, a natural, universal form for organizing experience.

The epistemic status of these claims is disparate; some are uncontroversial, while others—for example, the claim that literacy acquisition ought, like language acquisition, to be universally successful—are demonstrably wrong. Our main critique of this collective set of claims is that they represent a distortion of what we know about language acquisition and they lead to a misreading of the particular challenges associated with literacy development and thus to inadequate instructional practices.

Literacy and Language Distinguished

We will argue in this chapter that the view that literacy acquisition is just like language acquisition is too simple, and thus that corollary claims about home-to-school continuities and optimal curriculum design are simply wrong. We will demonstrate that, for middle-class children who do well in school as well as for children at risk of school failure, there are two major and perhaps unavoidable discontinuities that must be confronted in language and literacy practices. The first discontinuity falls within the domain of oral language use, which is itself a complex system whose rules vary widely as a function of context; we will demonstrate abrupt discontinuities in the rules for the use of oral language at home and at school, and echoing Tizard and Hughes (1984) we will furthermore show that children's participation at home is typically more sophisticated and more competent than at school. These discontinuities are, we argue, ubiquitous and as severe for middle-class children as for children from families in which parents have little education. Second, we will demonstrate discontinuities between oral and literate uses of language at school—evidence that a simple transfer of the rules for using language orally to literate contexts will drastically misfire, and thus that attempts to build literacy directly on oral language are misguided. Skilled teachers who take this approach almost inevitably, we argue, are forced into misrepresenting to themselves and to their students what the goal and structure of school literacy activity is.

We also contend that classroom practices that emphasize continuity between home and school or between oral and literate practices risk underestimating children's abilities; children are notably competent practical sociolinguists, capable of understanding from an early age that one shifts linguistic register when addressing a baby or a foreigner or when speaking in the role of teacher or doctor (Andersen, 1990). Children at an early age are sensitive to the differences in the way language is used orally and in writing (Elster, 1994; Purcell-Gates, 1991), and there is no evidence that they find those differences more confusing than they find the differences between talking to an adult and an infant. Of course, there are different rules for talking and for writing at school—but we should not assume that children cannot learn those new rules, or that they would not benefit from explicit teaching of them (Delpit, 1992; Dorr-Bremme, 1990; Walkerdine, 1988). Pretending that the rules are not different, or even creating for temporary use classrooms where they are not, does not help children achieve success in literacy.

A full demonstration of the inevitable discontinuities between home and school or between language and literacy would be well beyond the scope of a brief chapter, so we must satisfy ourselves here with pertinent examples. We have chosen to examine a type of language use which is frequent both at home and at school: narratives, both naturally occurring and elicited, produced orally and in writing. We have examined a variety of sources of home and school conversations and writing, but acknowledge the need for more systematic comparisons and contrasts in future work. We present below examples of oral narratives occurring during interactions at home and at school, as well as children's written narratives and discussion of written narratives at school, in order to demonstrate our major claim in this chapter: that the widely presupposed continuity between home and school narratives and between oral and written narratives is an illusion, undermined by differences of participation structure, of purpose, and of rules for competent performance across these various settings.

Oral Narratives at Home

Personal experience narratives are perhaps the most widely studied genre of connected discourse in children, and are a commonly used form in elementary school curricula attempting to build on continuity between oral and literate language. Thus, for example, oral language forms like sharing time stories are meant to be based on personally experienced events, and are meant equally to display in oral language use many of the features of essayist literacy—for example, focus on a single point, explicit provision of information even about matters that the audience has prior knowledge of, "focused" rather than interactive language forms, and so on (Michaels, 1981, 1991). Personal experience narratives are also used in many classrooms as a basis for early writing productions, and thus also become reading material for other students in those classrooms that use writing process and whole language models of literacy instruction.

Personal experience narratives are also, of course, a common feature of family talk. Blum-Kulka and Snow (1992) have characterized middle-class American dinner tables as forums where children have the right to "tell their day" to the other family members. Ochs and her colleagues (1992), Snow and Dickinson (1990), and others have documented the interactive processes by which adults and older siblings support younger children's tellings.

In evaluating hypothesized continuities between narrative talk at home and at school, an important concern is whether the child competencies displayed are essentially similar in the two settings. A related issue is whether the rules for participating in narratives are the same at home and at school, and whether the purposes that underlie narrative performances are comparable. Representative home narratives presented here come from two main sources: family mealtime conversations recorded by low-income mothers of three- to five-year-olds (De Temple and Beals, 1991) and family stories elicited in the homes of working-class and middle-class five- and six-year-olds (Hemphill, Wolf, and Camp, 1993).

Participation in Storytelling at Home   Although some form of participation is obligatory in more formal contexts for storytelling (even minimal participation of the "I don't know" type), on many occasions within families narrative participation is voluntary and optional.

MOTHER: What did you do at school today?

DEANNA: I don't like this.

MOTHER: That's all right, then don't eat it. What did you do at school today? [Silence.]

MOTHER: Deanna!

DEANNA: I'm not going to tell you.

(working-class four-year-old)

At home, family members can join in constructing a narrative with the child, either at the child's request, as in the example with Carla and her mother below, or uninvited, as in the example of Patrick's narrative. These collaborations can occur when the family member jointly participated in some of the narrated events, as is the case for Carla and her mother, or when the co-narrator has some indirect knowledge of the events to be reported—for example, Patrick's mother's experience with a written "ouch report."

CARLA: One day me and my friend Gwen um um were being kind of wild or something like that. Then I bonked my head into, into the cubbies. And um, then um, none of the teachers um saw it. And then one of the teachers just um just saw me. And then they saw me crying. And then they called my mother. Then. . .[Looks expectantly at mother.]

MOTHER: And then I happened to be home for only about one minute. And they happened to call at that minute and say, "Don't worry, I think Carla will be okay but um there's a slight problem. She had a little accident and it's not that serious but we really feel you should come in and take her to the doctor." And I was really scared. . . .

CARLA: That I would have stitches. But the doctor was so silly and he. . .

MOTHER: It was a very funny man.

CARLA: And it and it was just a little, and it was just a little hole in my head. And um. . . .

MOTHER: Even though there was blood all over her Oshkosh. . . .

CARLA: B'gosh. . . .

MOTHER: Overalls.

CARLA: Purple ones. But we can't have those any more cause it got blood all over them.

MOTHER: We had to throw them away.

CARLA: And um so um I, the doctor said I don't have to have any um stitches. And my mom was like, "Phewww!"

(middle-class six-year-old)

MOTHER: So Patrick got another one of those ouch reports.

MARIA: Oh. What is an ouch report?

MOTHER: Well, it's when you get injured at daycare.

MARIA: Did he?

MOTHER: A little bit, yeah.

MARIA: How?

MOTHER: Is there a story of that, Patrick?
MARIA: How?
PATRICK: And you, and you get dizzy.
MARIA: How?
PATRICK: By running around.
MARIA: How'd Patrick get hurt, Mom?
MOTHER: Well, another kid bopped into him, right? Isn't that the story, Patrick?
PATRICK: No.
MOTHER: No? What happened?
PATRICK: I, Gerald, I was. . .There's no fighting there, Mom.
MOTHER: Not fighting, but didn't a kid bump into you?
PATRICK: No.
MOTHER: On the playground?
PATRICK: No.
MOTHER: That's what the ouch report said.
PATRICK: Gerald crashed his bike into me.
FATHER: Who crashed the bike into you?
PATRICK: Gerald.
FATHER: Carol?
PATRICK: No, Gerald.
FATHER: Gerald?
MOTHER: Yeah.
PATRICK: Crashed the bike into me.
MOTHER: That probably hurt. Gerald's a big kid and he goes fast on the bike.
PATRICK: Yeah. He ran into me when I was standing.

(middle-class three-year-old)

Just as family members can collaborate in telling a narrative, they can also dispute each other's versions of events, as Roland and his mother do during his telling of a fantastic crab story, or as Jerome and his brother do in telling about a school activity.

MOTHER: Why don't you tell me everything you and Fred did yesterday. And Ricky and Richard.
ROLAND: I go to crab. To see cr—
MOTHER: But you went. . .
ROLAND: I see crab and I see crab walking and crab walking. And they bite me and I say ouch! [Acts out events.] Ah! [Acts out events.] Ha ha! And I laugh! And I laugh! And I laugh!
MOTHER: Oh, Roland. I think you made that up. I think you see crab, but I don't think that it bite you!

(working-class three-year-old)

JEROME: I went apple pickin'.
MOTHER: You did?
JEROME: Today, uh-huh.

JASON: Nunh-unh.

JEROME: Uh-huh!

JASON: Nunh-unh.

JEROME: We. . .

JASON: He did not! He told a lie! It's not even summer!

JEROME: Well, I pick—

MOTHER: Well maybe he went make-believe apple picking.

JEROME: Ma! Mommy, I didn't! I'm not makin' believe.

JASON: Yes, you are.

JEROME: Nunh-unh!

MOTHER: That is enough.

(working-class four-year-old)

On other occasions, the narrative itself is told to dispute other family members' versions of events, to argue that "that's not how it was; *this* is how it was." Bianca, for example, tells her story of a visit with family friends to prove her assertion about the visit and disprove her mother's characterization of the visit.

MOTHER: So Frankie and Bianca, how did you like going to Carmela's house? Wasn't that fun? Playing with uh what's his name? Wilfredo? He's a nice boy, huh?

BIANCA: No.

MOTHER: He's not?

BIANCA: He said, "Girls out, boys in." Girls in, boys out! Girls out, boys in! Girls in, boys out.

MOTHER: What was he playing?

BIANCA: He said, "No girls, just boys." No boys, just girls. No boys, just girls.

MOTHER: He didn't want any girls?

BIANCA: Yes boys, yes boy, yes girls. . .

FRANKIE: She's just, she's just tricking you, Mama.

MOTHER: Um maybe you are joking, Bianca?

BIANCA: No!

MOTHER: No?

(working-class four-year-old)

In another family, Richard and his aunt argue about the chain of events that resulted in his staying up late the night before:

AUNT: Now you remember, you're going to bed early tonight 'cause you were awake very late last night. And you had a hard time wakin' up this morning.

RICHARD: I know. But I was tryin' to go to sleep and Matt kept on botherin' me.

AUNT: Lisa told me she heard both of you in there talking.

RICHARD: Well I was cryin' because he put the pillow over my head.

AUNT: Why'd he do that?

RICHARD: Last night.

AUNT: I know when, I said *why*.

RICHARD: I don't know. He always likes to beat me up.
AUNT: Were you awake when Matt went in to go to bed? Just yes or no, Richard, that's all.
RICHARD: Yes.
AUNT: Yes. And you know even *that* is late.
RICHARD: And you know?
AUNT: I know now, don't I?
RICHARD: No, do you know when Matt came in?
AUNT: No, I wasn't there.
RICHARD: Where were you?
AUNT: I went out to do some laundry, remember?
RICHARD: You, why you, why you?
CASS: You could go out to the laundry, yeah.
AUNT: I did. My washing machine's broken, remember.

(working-class four-year-old)

Even within collaborative, co-constructed narratives, children are often most eloquent when the information they are relating represents their own stance on the narrated events, distinct from that of other participants:

MOTHER: And we went with, who'd we go with?
KERRY: David.
MOTHER: David. Who else?
KERRY: And Nana and Papa.
MOTHER: And who else? Daddy went too, didn't he?
KERRY: Yeah.
MOTHER: Yeah. Who else?
KERRY: That's all?
MOTHER: Oh, and Auntie Karen and Uncle Pete, right?
KERRY: Yeah.
MOTHER: And David's two brothers.
KERRY: Mmhm.
MOTHER: We went whale watching and um I think it turned out to be a disaster because it was rough out there and we got kind of seasick. We did see whales, but not as good as we wanted to.
KERRY: I saw one.
MOTHER: Yeah, we saw them. They're big, huh?
KERRY: [Nods.]
MOTHER: How many were there?
KERRY: About thirteen.
MOTHER: About thirteen! There were only two or three!
KERRY: No, there wasn't, because they were runnin' back and forth like fifty times!

(working-class six-year-old)

Purposes of Storytelling at Home   Stories told at home often have the immediate goal of letting other family members in on knowledge of important happenings. What is highlighted, however, in family storytelling is the meaning of the reported events to the child, rather than the simple adequacy of the telling.

MOTHER: How'd you like flying those kites?
ANDRE: Good.
MOTHER: Is it fun?
ANDRE: I like it when it was way up.
MOTHER: [Laughs.]
ANDRE: They couldn't even see us. Right?
MOTHER: I know. Way up high.
ANDRE: Yeah.
MOTHER: [Laughs.] Way up.

(working-class four-year-old)

Family narratives often serve to work out behavioral ethics, "this is how we feel about this kind of situation in our family." Children often volunteer reports that show they understand family expectations for social behavior, as Andre does in this example.

ANDRE: Frankie's fresh the most.
MOTHER: Why? What's he do?
ANDRE: He doesn't do what the teacher says. He gets up at nap. He plays.
MOTHER: Really?
ANDRE: But we don't play. When we're still on the mat.
MOTHER: You do what the teacher says, huh?
BABY: Babababa.
ANDRE: What?
MOTHER: You do what the teacher says?
ANDRE: Yeah. Not the other kids.
MOTHER: Yeah.
ANDRE: The other kids be mean to other kids.
MOTHER: Who's mean?
ANDRE: Oh, the other kids.

(working-class four-year-old)

Parents also elicit stories from children that provide an opportunity for commenting on standards for good behavior, as Eddie's mother does here:

MOTHER: So Eddie, tell me how school was today. We didn't talk about it today at all. What did you do, did you have gym today?
FATHER: He told *me* he had a good day at school.
EDDIE: I didn't have gym.
MOTHER: Did you see his paper?
FATHER: No.

MOTHER: You didn't? You should see his paper!
EDDIE: It's Mr. M-M-M.
MOTHER: And he got an "excellent" on it.
EDDIE: [Sings.] I'm Mr. M, my munchy mouth.
MOTHER: You know what an excellent means?
EDDIE: Mommy!
MOTHER: You know what excellent means?
EDDIE: What?
MOTHER: It means you did the best, the best you could, and she was so pleased
          with it.

(working-class five-year-old)

Family members often contest each other's evaluations of events in the stories they tell, attempting to align ethical perspectives on the reported happenings, as Eddie's father does, later in this story about Eddie's day:

EDDIE: Cause um everybody cheated on the football and I'm the only one who
          didn't cheat.
BABY: [Whines.] Mom.
EDDIE: My team didn't cheat!
MOTHER: Who cheats? Your team didn't cheat, did they?
EDDIE: No, the um um the Pandas cheated.
MOTHER: Oh.
EDDIE: They always cheat so we, so we had, we, we can't have football any day.
          Not even baseball any day. Everybody cheats, but not my team. So only
          our, us can play.
BABY: Rarababa.
FATHER: You guys are the only good guys in the whole school huh?
EDDIE: Yeah.
FATHER: Is that what you're saying? I don't know about that, Eddie. There's a lot
          of good people in that school.

(working-class five-year-old)

Storytelling in the family can serve as an occasion for talking about ways of handling situations in the future, as a guide for action. Thus Devin and his parents discuss two potentially dangerous situations at the playground:

MOTHER: So did you tell Daddy about the little girl on the slide at the playground?
DEVIN: Yeah.
FATHER: Yes, he did. And I said to him, "Geez, that was an *excellent* safety move
          that you made there." Put the brakes on, huh? Before you got to the end.
MOTHER: She was just a little tiny kid and said, "Devin, wait, wait!" Huh?
DEVIN: But they stopped.
MOTHER: Yeah, that's right. You didn't stop, but you grabbed the sides of slide so
          you wouldn't go.
MOTHER: She was just a tiny kid and she wasn't even aware or anything.

FATHER: Mmhm.

MOTHER: She was just barely able to walk huh? What else happened at the playground?

DEVIN: I don't know.

MOTHER: What about that tire swing deal.

DEVIN: You tell him.

MOTHER: Why don't you tell him. He wants to talk to you, too.

DEVIN: You tell him. Please, mommy.

MOTHER: Devin was playing on the tire swing and all of a sudden a whole bunch of kids from a day care came running into the playground.

FATHER: Mmhm.

MOTHER: And Devin and I, Devin was just playin' on the tire swing and kinda twirling around. And I don't like to push other kids when they're on a swing or on the merry-go-round thing with him. Cause if a kid falls off, you know, looks like it's my fault. So I, you know, I said, "Well I'm gonna wait a minute," and then two of the kids came runnin' over and they just jumped on the swing with him. So I said, "Devin I'm not gonna push them," and he got off. And he got mad because those kids kinda took over the swing on him.

FATHER: Oh yeah. Well, well kids. . .

MOTHER: And then two others.

FATHER: Yes.

MOTHER: Hmm?

FATHER: Kids don't know. They just jump on the, they see you having fun so they think they're just gonna join right in. But if one of them got hurt, then Mom or I would um, you know, we would feel kinda bad about that, you know?

MOTHER: Mmm. And then. . .

FATHER: Now we know you're not gonna get hurt, but we don't know if some of the other kids joining in are gonna be all right. [To baby.] Well what do you think about that little Lucas? Huh? What do you think about that? [Kisses baby.] Okay. Okay.

DEVIN: There's um, there's a. . .

MOTHER: Well in the spring when you go to a public playground you have to, you gotta share the things.

(working-class four-year-old)

On another kind of occasion, Tiana's parents closely question her on a happening at preschool, to get clear about possible culpability and to highlight for Tiana how she might handle the situation differently in the future:

MOTHER: Tell Daddy what you told me.

TIANA: Hmm. What one? The arm one?

MOTHER: Yeah.

TIANA: Um, Cindy grabbed me by the arm tight.

FATHER: Cindy who?

MOTHER: Teacher.

TIANA: Cindy my teacher!

FATHER: Why'd she do that?

MOTHER: You don't know?

FATHER: Do you have a reason?

MOTHER: Were you foolin' around and she wanted you to take, take you out of line?

TIANA: No, no, no! I wasn't in the line, I was in the gym. We were cleaning up!

MOTHER: Um.

FATHER: Well, were you cleaning?

TIANA: Mmm. . .

FATHER: Or being a grump sitting in a corner somewhere.

TIANA: Grump!

FATHER: You were being a grump. But that doesn't give her the right to grab you by the arm tightly.

MOTHER: And I told you if she, if anybody. . .

TIANA: If. . .but my time was up!

MOTHER: But you're supposed to tell Cindy. Say, "Cindy, you hurt me when you grabbed me."

FATHER: So in the morning we're gonna call Cindy and we'll talk to her. All right?

TIANA: Well, when I'm sleeping.

MOTHER: I'll tell Cin, I'll tell Cindy not to grab you anymore.

(working-class four-year-old)

Stories at Home Versus School   In summary, stories told by children at home are rarely told just for the purpose of relating happenings; family stories are typically embedded in larger social and rhetorical purposes. These purposes, which vary across occasions for storytelling, determine who can participate in the telling, and what information is relevant to report. The complex purposes that underlie much family storytelling (for example, contesting other family members' versions of events, revealing one's own distinctive stance, or embedding fantasy elements in a real life anecdote) motivate much of the complex language use that occurs in home narratives.

At home, children often do not tell their stories themselves. While other family members may join in the storytelling, children are typically expected to relate information that is uniquely theirs or which conveys their distinctive perspective on the reported events. Parents and other family members are often able to support the child's storytelling through their independent knowledge of the people and events the child's story is concerned with, and through strategic use of questioning, restatement, and probes. The adequacy of the child's telling is judged, not against abstract standards of completeness and informativeness, but rather in relation to the social and rhetorical goals that prompted the telling.

In schools, the implicit rules for storytelling are often different from those operating in family interaction. Young narrators are able to tell stories in school when these fill slots created by particular classroom speech events—for example, circle time, story dictation, and "sharing time." Access to the conversational floor to tell a story at school is achieved typically through teacher nomination, not through the child's own initiative and eloquence, and quite independent of whether the child has something important to tell. Children hold onto the floor in these occasions because the teacher controls access by other participants, not because the story being told is worthy of everyone's undivided attention. Stories at school are rarely co-constructed by other participants, in part because the purposes of school storytelling (preeminently, the display of individual competence) do not authorize multiple participants.

In comparing narrative talk at home and at school, a central issue is whether the competencies acquired at home transfer to school occasions for storytelling. School narratives presented and analyzed here come from two main sources: classroom storytelling recorded by the teachers of low-income three- to five-year-olds (Snow and Dickinson, 1990), and stories occurring during literacy instruction of seven- to ten-year-olds (Snow, Barnes, Chandler, Hemphill, and Goodman, 1991).

Oral Narratives at School

One of the challenges that young narrators face is deciding which lived experiences are reportable. Reportability includes, among other things, the dimensions of audience interest and relevance. Because teachers and children have for the most part *not* jointly participated in the events that children's narratives are potentially concerned with, teachers, unlike parents cannot guide children to choices of reportable events. In this example, Theresa's teacher signals some general expectations of what is reportable when she asks, "Anything special?" However, lacking experience of the events of Theresa's weekend, she cannot guide her to report on happenings that are at all interesting.

TEACHER: What'd you do this weekend at home? Anything special?
THERESA: [Playing with a puzzle.] No, it goes like that. Oops!
TEACHER: Huh? Did you do anything at home this weekend?
THERESA: Yeah.
TEACHER: What?
THERESA: I played.
TEACHER: Who'd you play?
THERESA: I ha—, I have a puzzle at home.
TEACHER: Puzzles at home? Which kind of puzzles?
THERESA: Potato head puzzles.
TEACHER: What kind?
THERESA: [Playing with puzzle.] Oops! It's that way.
TEACHER: Wrong way. Very good. What kind of puzzles you got at home?
THERESA: Potato head puzzles.
TEACHER: Potato head puzzles.
THERESA: Yeah.

TEACHER: What other kinds?
[Long pause.]

(Head Start classroom)

Teachers often define occasions for report-giving where what is reportable is precisely not what is interesting or remarkable. Instead, reportable experiences are those shared by every group member, where everyone can offer an equally adequate account. What is important is not that the experience was particularly compelling, but that the child can offer some kind of account of it.

TEACHER: Who remembers what they had last night for supper to eat?
TEACHER: I had spaghetti.
RICKY: I had long s'ghetti.
TEACHER: You had that long spaghetti?
TEACHER: What did you have Jennifer?
JENNIFER: I had pancakes.
TEACHER: Pancakes?
TEACHER: What did you have Chrystal?
CHRYSTAL: Pancakes.
TEACHER: Pancakes! Mmm!

(Head Start classroom)

Consistent with the general goal for this kind of report-giving, that everyone be able to participate, the teacher does not ask for the kinds of highly specific elaboration of events that would mark them as unique or as having some special meaning to the narrators. Instead, she asks everyone for the same type of elaboration, and then comments on the similarity in experiences.

TEACHER: What did you put on them? Just had them plain or. . .
JENNIFER: Uh. . .
TEACHER: What did you have on yours, Jennifer?
JENNIFER: Syrup.
TEACHER: What did you have on your spaghetti, Ricky?
RICKY: Cheese.
TEACHER: Cheese?
TEACHER: Mmm-mmm. What else?
TEACHER: Anything else?
RICKY: Uh-uh.
TEACHER: No?
RICKY: And sauce.
TEACHER: Sauce. Mmm-mmm.
TEACHER: That's what I had, too.

(Head Start classroom)

Although teachers' narrative elicitations typically result in much shorter and structurally less complex narratives than children can produce at home (Snow and Dickinson, 1990; Tizard and Hughes, 1984), teachers have other goals for children's storytelling. In particular teachers, much more than parents, value explicitness, that children put into words and make literal what they are trying to communicate. Explicitness as a goal in itself is virtually absent from family story-telling, although parents will press children to provide details that are crucial to the interpretation of an event sequence (as Richard's aunt and Tiana's mother and father do) or that force the narrator to go on record about particular happen-ings (as Eddie's father and Andre's mother do). At school, however, explicitness exists as an important goal, even when it does not advance the informativeness of a child's narration.

TEACHER: What did you do? Did you watch TV?
TINA: [Nods.]
TEACHER: Answer.
TINA: I was watchin' TV, sit down, lay down.
TEACHER: And you watched the TV and lied down? You didn't do anything else?
TINA: I was watchin' TV and lay down. And play toys. Color. Play games.
TEACHER: Did you play with your baby sister?
TINA: [Nods.]
TEACHER: Yes? Say "yes"! Answer me.
TINA: [Very softly.] Yeah.
TEACHER: Huh?
TINA: Said "yeah".
TEACHER: You did?
TINA: Yeah.

   (Head Start classroom)

However, efforts to elicit more explicit contributions from children do not neces-sarily result in child reports that are linguistically complex or sustained, autono-mous productions. In a lengthy kindergarten sharing-time session, Edwin's teacher uses school pictures to initiate reminiscences about experiences the children have had during their kindergarten year.

TEACHER: What do you think I have in back of me?
LISETTE: A picture of Edwin.
EDWIN: A picture of me.
TEACHER: A picture of you. Would you like to see it? Show it to your friend. Would you call that a play school picture or a beach picture or a school picture?
CHILDREN: School picture!
TEACHER: Oh, are you guys Edwin? Whose turn is it now?
GILBERT: Edwin.
TEACHER: Let's give Edwin a turn now.
EDWIN: A school picture.
TEACHER: What did you say, Edwin, excuse me?
EDWIN: It's a school picture.

TEACHER: It's a school picture and what grade would you say that was? Do you
            think it's preschool? What grade are you in? Do you know what that
            means, Edwin, when I say what grade are you in? Okay, Edwin are you
            in kindergarten, first grade, second grade, third grade? Which grade?

EDWIN: I don't know.

TEACHER: You don't know? Okay. Well, you can read what it says up there, can
            you? Well, the bulletin board says "Kindergarten in Bloom." Okay? This
            over here says "kindergarten" and it means all the flowers are bloom-
            ing. And who are the kindergartners in this classroom?

CHILDREN: Us!

TEACHER: Edwin, who are the kindergartners in this classroom?

EDWIN: The kids.

TEACHER: The kids, very good. Okay, so are you one of them?

EDWIN: Yes.

TEACHER: Are you one of them? Sure. So does that mean you're in kindergarten,
            too? Do you know what the kindergarten in bloom really represents?
            All of you people because you all are ready to be. . .

CHILDREN: First grade.

TEACHER: Well, some of you will be going to first grade, yes. So what grade are
            you in, Edwin? What's this classroom? What would you say, what would
            you call this classroom, is it first grade? Is this a first grade classroom?
            Can you say "kindergarten"?

EDWIN: Kindergarten.

TEACHER: I can't hear you, Edwin.

EDWIN: Kindergarten.

TEACHER: Kindergarten, thank you.

(kindergarten "circle time")

Edwin's teacher works so hard to get him to articulate accurate background
information (he was in kindergarten at the time a photograph was taken), that
she never succeeds in eliciting the intended narrative from him. Classroom demands that children produce targeted elements of narrative structure (for example, the orientation information, "When I was in kindergarten") result in heavily
adult-mediated forms of narration. Teachers typically reject peer attempts at collaboration ("Oh, are you guys Edwin? Whose turn is it now?"), although in classrooms as in families, these might help get the story out and allow for elaboration
of more important information. The strategies that teachers use to elicit the information they consider important include hints ("Would you call that a play school
picture or a beach picture or a school picture?"), logical deductions ("Are you one
of them? Sure. So does that mean you're in kindergarten, too?"), and direct prompts
("Can you say 'kindergarten'?"). Paradoxically, although the goal of this kind of
questioning is the production of autonomous, decontextualized text, children respond to this type of adult scaffolding with language that is elliptical and compressed. Teachers struggle in part because the pragmatic conditions that underlie
production of the targeted elements (for example, the need to distinguish your

own story from dissimilar ones told by preceding speakers, or the need to claim the floor for your own telling) are often absent from classroom contexts for storytelling. Since everyone in the sharing time session has been telling stories about experiences in kindergarten, Edwin might well feel no particular obligation to ground his narrative in an initial orientative assertion, "When I was in kindergarten" or in an abstract, "I had an exciting thing happen to me one day in kindergarten." And since he has been assigned a turn at storytelling rather than volunteering, it is not clear whether he even has a narrative in mind to tell. Although his teacher succeeds, finally, in eliciting the word "kindergarten" from him, the effort has exhausted Edwin's sharing time turn and the information about kindergarten is never integrated into a sustained narrative performance.

In summary, teachers use oral narratives in classroom settings for a variety of purposes, which often include laying the foundation for children's transition from oral to literate language uses. The belief underlying this particular practice is, in part, that narratives are easy, natural, and familiar. We see, though, that in the ways that narratives are used, and in the ways that children participate, narratives at school are quite different from those at home. We do not criticize those differences, and we certainly do not intend to portray teachers who let such differences emerge as incompetent. We argue, rather, that such differences are inevitable, and that failing to acknowledge them puts children at risk of looking incompetent in school language performances, where rules for participation may be unfamiliar. The presumption that school narratives are just like home narratives might seduce us into a belief that children who do not participate effectively at school are also incompetent at home—a presumption that turns out to be quite wrong. Teachers of students like Tina and Edwin often conclude that these children "have no language" or that they lack specific narrative competencies and thus in critical ways have failed to acquire the prerequisites for literacy. Unfortunately characteristics of classroom occasions for telling personal narratives—audiences that lack direct knowledge of the events that child is attempting to narrate, participation acquired through formal turn allocation rather than through having a story worth telling, focus on the facts of the story rather than their interpretation—work against the display of children's most mature narrative skills. In addition, because teachers are rarely explicit about the elements they value in school narrative performance, children may have difficulty assessing what kind of performance counts as adequate in classroom storytelling. As a consequence, children may conclude that minimal participation or nonparticipation is the safest strategy.

Written Narratives at School

Writing Stories Fictional narratives form the backbone of materials for learning to read in most classrooms; narratives, either fictional or personal experience, are the written genres that children's earliest composing efforts are directed toward. Pedagogical practices assume a seamless transition between offering oral reports of personal experience and producing and comprehending written narratives; thus in the early years of school, children are encouraged to dictate reports of personal experience to an adult scribe, and then notate these reports themselves, using drawings as well as invented and, later on, conventional spellings and punctuation. Children's early efforts at school writing, however, result in texts that often differ markedly from their oral stories and reports, as this example from a whole language kindergarten illustrates:

> THIS IS A HWS
> THE SUN
> WL SHIN
> ND MI
> GRDN
> WL GRO

(middle-class five-year-old)

Though this is ostensibly a personal account ("my garden"), it accompanies a drawing of an idealized, storybook house, surrounded by a straight line of sunflowers and tulips. The author, an urban child, in fact has no garden. The text reflects the child's attempt to reproduce the linguistic forms and the characteristic content of the kinds of written texts that he has encountered in school: in this case, simple informational books about the world of young children. Although the text is the work of a beginning writer, it includes some of the formal characteristics of this written genre, specifically topicalization through indefinite introduction of the central referent (this is *a house*) and parallel sentence structure (the sun *will shine* and my garden *will grow*). The text also incorporates a theme that is common to this type of simple informational book (seasonal change and growing things) and a perspective that is not rooted in any particular time or place.

The child's purpose in this kind of early writing is not to relate a unique perspective on events that an audience has not experienced. It is also not the child's purpose here to explore the kinds of social conflicts that play or fantasy narratives typically are concerned with, and that personal experience anecdotes are often embedded in. Instead, this kind of early writing serves as an apprenticeship in school literacy; trying out the forms and perspectives that are typical of the written texts each child will be reading and writing in the years to come.

A fictional narrative produced by a somewhat older child in a progressive first grade shows additional characteristics of early school writing:

The Long Grass

There was a little boy and he was playing in the grass and he came to a tall patch. He wondered what to do about the grass being so tall, because he wanted a bigger space to play in. The little boy got the lawnmower and tried to mow the grass but the grass was too long to cut. The boy put the lawnmower back. He then got the saw and he tried to saw the grass down but the grass was so long that it just bent over as he tried to cut. He went to get his daddy. His daddy tried the same things the little boy had tried but of course they didn't work. So he asked his mommy but his mommy couldn't come because she was in the kitchen cooking. So the little boy went to get his dog. He asked his dog to bite down the grass for him. The dog bit down the grass and they played happily together until they went in for dinner.

(middle-class six-year-old)

Unlike oral fictional narratives produced by six-year-olds, this written narrative shows a striking lack of elaboration, which serves to highlight instead the narrative's basic and very traditional structure. The written story adheres closely to the conventions of classic European fairy tale narratives: beginning with the statement of problem (the problem itself is not so consequential, but it is a given of the form that the problem has to be accepted as important), multiple attempts to solve the problem, involving multiple agents; and a happy, although unexpected resolution.

In contrast to oral narratives produced by six-year-olds, the narrator-audience relationship in this written story is reduced. The events are told from a fixed viewpoint—that of a distanced, authoritative narrator ("but of course they didn't work"). The content is heavily influenced by the kinds of cultural archetypes that Carolyn Baker and Peter Freebody (1989) have noted in beginning reading materials: the little boy, the tall grass, the physically competent father and domestically preoccupied mother, the happy pet and master. These reflect not the everyday social world of this particular child, but the world that is portrayed in conventional reading material for children.

Like the younger child, this early writer is striving to display mastery of the conventions of school literacy—in this case, the conventions of traditional fictional narratives written for children. The kind of early writing exemplified in these two texts draws on very different competencies from those displayed in oral narratives, either at home or at school. In fact, though, we would argue that the competencies displayed by these two writers are quite relevant to school success and to eventual literacy accomplishment. They can be seen as representing a way in which language and literacy acquisition are similar—that both result from a tendency on the part of children to replicate important adult forms. These writings do not represent the kinds of authentic communication that many writing teachers exhort children to produce—they represent precisely the inauthentic communications that are salient artifacts of their literate cultures.

Talk About Written Narratives at School   Talk about written narratives, and in particular written narrative retelling, is ubiquitous in early literacy instruction. Teachers ask for story-retellings to check on whether children have read and understood an assigned text, to elicit story information that may have been confusing and thus may require discussion and commentary, to highlight story content that may be relevant to particular pedagogical objectives (e.g., distinguishing fact from fiction, interpreting figurative language), and to make connections between story content and children's personal experiences. These diverse goals for eliciting story-retelling are reflected in differentiated expectations for the kind of narrative that should be provided. If the goal is to check on whether children have really read and understood the fictional narrative, teachers expect a thorough but not heavily elaborated retelling, focused on central events and characters.

TEACHER: Good reading! Now what was the story about?

BOBBY: A boy who doesn't know how to whistle and then in the story he says that his mother whistles and his father whistles. . .

TEACHER: Now don't give us the whole story!

BOBBY: And he couldn't whistle. And then he heard a bird, and then, I don't know, somehow he could whistle.

TEACHER: Good.

(fourth-grade reading group)

If the goal is to provide links between story content and some other aspect of the text, the retelling is expected to be less comprehensive but more elaborated, and elaborated in ways that reflect characteristics of the other valued information (for example, those elements of the story that challenge its interpretation as factual):

TEACHER: Something strange happened to Mrs. Ellsworth on Saturday.

YVROSE: She went away.

TEACHER: What did she take with her?

YVROSE: A suitcase?

TEACHER: Right, and when she came back?

YVROSE: It was heavier.

(third-grade reading group)

Because these literacy goals for telling are frequently not made explicit, children often provide retellings that fail to match teacher expectations. In this excerpt from an individual reading conference, Craig offers a summary of a book passage that is both an accurate reply to his teacher's question, and a full account of a section of the fictional narrative. Craig's teacher, however, presses him for a much more compressed retelling, that explicitly states the information she is seeking.

TEACHER: Okay, the cat in the story was called Scat. Why?

CRAIG: Because he's a street cat. And he always used to come up to people and they didn't like, people didn't like what they did to him. What he did to them.

TEACHER: And so what would people tell him all the time?

CRAIG: Scat.

TEACHER: And what does that mean?

CRAIG: Go away.

TEACHER: Yeah. So he got the name Scat because people were always telling him to go away.

(second-grade reading lesson)

Thus, although retellings of fictional narratives can draw on many of the same competencies as personal experience narratives (for example, skill at introducing story participants, reporting key happenings, describing participants' mental and physical states), the pedagogical goals of school occasions for these retellings demand very specialized kinds of narrative performances. Children become skilled at meeting these new expectations for narration through learning to recognize the *literacy* goals that motivate particular teacher requests for retellings (for example, the goal of producing an abstract of a story, rather than the story itself, or the goal of highlighting fictive elements of a story). These require new narrative forms, however, and the competencies that children have developed in out-of-school occasions for storytelling (for example, displaying the narrator's personal stance toward the reported events) are often irrelevant to success at retellings of fictional narratives.

Literacy Practices at School   In the course of several hours, a six-year-old may move from a sharing time session where she is asked for a loosely defined account of events from her weekend, to a personal writing session where she might choose to compose a fictional narrative, to a small group discussion of a fictional story she has been reading, where the teacher is emphasizing contrasts between fictional and realistic story elements. Success in this kind of classroom environment for literacy learning is predicated not on a simple transference of home narrative skills to school but rather on the child's ability to shift skillfully among very different kinds of discourse productions and understandings. The factors that are likely to support her success are familiarity with a broad range of narrative text types, both oral and written, rich internalized representations of the distinctive features of these text types, interest and confidence in experimenting with diverse text productions, and sociolinguistic insight into the kinds of text productions that are valued in particular school contexts. Although most children enter school with wide linguistic repertoires that include differentiated genres such as scripts, personal anecdotes, fictional stories, explanations, and descriptions (Hemphill, Feldman, Camp, Griffin, and Wolf, 1994; Hicks, 1990; Hudson and Shapiro, 1991; Hyon and Sulzby, 1992), primary school classrooms do little to capitalize on and further develop these understandings. Ideas about reading for different purposes and writing for different audiences are usually reserved for the later stages of elementary schooling, when expository forms begin to dominate the curriculum. During all the years that children are acquiring fluency and confidence in reading and writing, their discourse productions are judged by complex sets of genre standards that form part of the hidden curriculum of most primary classrooms (Delpit, 1992; Gee, 1990). Children are typically not provided with a vocabulary for talking about differences among personal anecdotes, fictional stories, and reports, nor are they often even given clear guidelines about which of these genres is expected in response to particular classroom assignments. As a consequence, schools end up reproducing the social advantages of children from highly literate families, who are heavily exposed to diverse forms of written texts outside of school, and who participate in frequent talk with adult family members about characteristics of different types of written texts.

Literacy and Language Revisited

We have presented examples illustrating the degree to which oral language and literacy practices are subject to discontinuities that undermine simple attempts to build literacy curricula on home-based oral language abilities. We also contend that much of the rhetoric surrounding the design of literacy curricula in whole language and other "progressive" educational settings is based on a romantic and misconceived view of the nature of language acquisition. The descriptions of natural language acquisition that seem to inform attempts to design comparable literacy curricula derive from descriptions of language acquisition in a rather particular setting—the middle-class Western model in which the language-learning child is treated as a conversational partner by the parent, who empowers the child's every action or vocalization as an attempt at communication. A basic notion here is that child language development is driven by the child's communicative intentions and is facilitated by appropriate adult responses to those communicative intentions. Children in the process of expressing their intentions generate data about the nature of the language system, in the form of adult responses. These responses are usable as data about the language system because they map onto the child's focus of attention and express meanings the child can understand independent of the utterances. This description of optimal environmental conditions for language acquisition correctly characterizes what goes on in some places during some periods of development—but it certainly does not provide a universal or a developmentally differentiated view of how language is acquired. The notion that children should be treated as conversational partners whose every burble requires an interpretation is rejected by adults in many cultures (Crago and Eriks-Brophy, 1994; LeVine et al., 1994; Ochs, 1988, 1992); furthermore, even among Western groups in which adult-lowering is a process intrinsic to child-raising, such indulgence becomes less common as children get older. Even highly child-centered middle-class American parents provide explicit language instruction to post-toddlers, about word meanings, politeness forms, conversational rules, and so on, and acknowledge older children's capacity to follow an adult agenda by no longer limiting themselves to child-initiated topics.

Furthermore, the romantic view of language development as driven by child communicative needs misrepresents the degree to which young children are active agents in their own development—active not just as motivated communicators but also as problem solvers, trying to figure out the language system even in its details that have no communicative significance. For example, both Karmiloff-Smith (1979) and Bowerman (1982) give examples of how children who have achieved errorless control of a linguistic subsystem (French possessive pronouns and intransitive versus causal verbs respectively) subsequently start making errors with those systems because they analyze and reorganize their own stored knowledge. In Karmiloff-Smith's terms (1992), the initial phases of language production are driven largely by access to input, but development in later stages (after about age three, the age at which emergent literacy acquisition typically begins) is driven by children's taking their own knowledge as a problem space susceptible to analysis and restructuring.

If this view of children as autonomous creators of linguistic problem spaces and self-motivated oral language problem solvers is correct, then the romantic view of language development has clearly overemphasized the degree to which communication drives acquisition. Acquisition seems to be at least in part a product of children's capacities to analyze systems and of their desires to replicate the cultural forms of their parents, quite independent of the short-term communicative efficacy of those forms. If this is true for oral language learners aged four and five, then it may be even more the case for somewhat older children acquiring literacy. Thus linking literacy acquisition to children's particular communicative intents may be neither necessary nor optimally efficient. Yet, the romantic view of language development and the view that literacy is just like language impose precisely that strategy. For example, journal writing that mimics conversational exchange in the literate mode is seen as an appropriate transition to more formal literacy, and children are encouraged to write about personally meaningful experiences, rather than about topics that extend beyond their firsthand experience (Edelsky, Altwerger, and Flores, 1991; Graves, 1983). In process approaches to writing, discussion of topics and drafts with the eventual audience is a crucial part of writing (Calkins, 1991; Graves, 1983). While such approaches have clear appeal when compared to traditional, highly prescriptive writing pedagogy, they also presuppose excellent oral communication between the emergent writer and the teacher, and shared communicative purposes—conditions that do not always obtain (Michaels, 1987; Ulichny and Watson-Gegeo, 1989). McCarthey (1994), for example, documents a case where the teacher who thought she knew what her fifth-grade student should write about risked pushing the child into exposing sensitive family issues that she could not deal with emotionally; the result in the case McCarthey documents was competent student sleight of hand to avoid teacher pressure, and escape into the sort of fictively authentic communication that we argue is much too common in such classrooms.

Another major strategy of the whole language movement has been devising practices that make school more like home. Although this solution appears to be a positive response to the finding that children often participate more competently in home discourse contexts (Snow and Dickinson, 1990; Tizard and Hughes, 1984), it has a number of disadvantages: first, because of institutional constraints, in particular differences in social participation structures and in goals, it is very difficult to make classroom communication like home communication; second, attempts to introduce homelike interactions into school setting can produce hybrid social settings that leave children more confused and less able to act competently than they would be if they had simply been taught the new, school-specific rules; third, increasing continuities between home and school can detract from the effectiveness with which elementary teachers prepare children for the very different institutional settings they will eventually face.

Pleas for use in curriculum of "natural" and "universal" language and literacy forms like the narrative are clearly also related to the notion that such forms show optimal continuity with ways of thinking and of speaking that all children may be familiar with, thus building on strengths that all children possess (Bruner, 1986; Dyson and Genishi, 1994; Egan, 1987; Gallas, 1994). Such pleas have had a massive impact on curriculum, despite the absence of evidence that children understand narrative forms more easily than other genres, or that they require narrative forms in order to learn to read or to acquire information. In fact, Pappas (1993) has reported that information from expository texts is as likely to be learned and recalled as information from narratives. In addition, the narrative forms and conventions that children learn in out-of-school settings may vary dramatically across cultures, challenging the notion that children enter school with a single, universal conception of narrative (Minami and McCabe, 1991).

If we view children as skilled linguistic problem solvers, as form masterers, and as flexible sociolinguists, what view of literacy acquisition might we adopt? First, we would expose children to a wide range of spoken and written language genres, involving children in producing as many different varieties of spoken and written language as possible. Second, we would provide activities to develop children's capacities consciously to analyze those genres and how they differ, acknowledging that children can treat language as an object of contemplation, not just as a tool for communication. Third, we would recognize that the rules for producing extended discourse are arbitrary, language-specific, community-specific, and situation-specific, and we would abandon the notion that some forms are natural, universal, and directly accessible.

References

Adams, M. (1990). *Beginning to read: Thinking and learning about print*. Cambridge: MIT Press.

Andersen, E. (1990). *Speaking with style: The sociolinguistic skills of children*. London: Routledge.

Baker, C. and Freebody, P. (1989). *Children's first school books*. Oxford, England: Basil Blackwell.

Blum-Kulka, S. and Snow, C. (1992). Developing autonomy for tellers, tales, and telling in family narrative events. *Journal of Narrative and Life History*, 2, 187–217.

Bowerman, M. (1982). Reorganizational processes in lexical and syntactic development. In E. Wanner and L. Gleitman (Eds.), *Language acquisition: The state of the art*. Cambridge, England: Cambridge University Press.

Bruner, J. (1986). *Actual minds, possible worlds*. Cambridge: Harvard University Press.

Calkins, L. (1991). *Living between the lines*. Portsmouth, NH: Heinemann.

Chomsky, N. (1957). *Syntactic structures*. The Hague: Mouton.

Clancy, P. (1986). The acquisition of communicative style in Japanese. In B. Schieffelin and E. Ochs (Eds.), *Language socialization across cultures* (pp. 213–250). Cambridge, England: Cambridge University Press.

Crago, M. and Eriks-Brophy, A. (1994). Culture, conversation, and interaction: Implications for intervention. In J. Duchan and R. Sonnenmeier (Eds.), *Pragmatics: From theory to practice* (pp. 43–58). Englewood Cliffs, NJ: Prentice-Hall.

Delpit, L. (1992). Acquisition of literate discourse. *Theory into Practice, 3,* 296–302.

De Temple, J. and Beals, D. (1991). Family talk: Sources of support for the development of decontextualized language skills. *Journal of Research in Childhood Education, 6,* 11–19.

Dorr-Bremme, D. (1990). Contextualization cues in the classroom: Discourse regulation and social control functions. *Language in Society, 19,* 379–402.

Dyson, A. and Genishi, C. (Eds.). (1994). *The need for story: Cultural diversity in classroom and community.* Urbana, IL: National Council of Teachers of English.

Edelsky, C., Altwerger, B., and Flores, B. (1991). *Whole language: What's the difference.* Portsmouth, NH: Heinemann.

Egan, K. (1987). Literacy and the oral foundations of education. *Harvard Educational Review, 57,* 445–472.

Elster, C. (1994). "I guess they do listen": Young children's emergent readings after adult read-alouds. *Young Children, 49,* 27–31.

Gallas, K. (1994). *The languages of learning: How children talk, write, dance, draw, and sing their understanding of the world.* New York: Teachers College Press.

Gallaway, C. and Richards, B. (1994). *Input and interaction in language acquisition.* Cambridge, England: Cambridge University Press.

Gee, J. (1990). *Social linguistics and literacies: Ideology in discourses.* London: Falmer.

Goodman, K. (1982). *Language and literacy: The selected writings of Kenneth S. Goodman* (Vol. 1). London: Routledge.

Goodman, K. and Goodman, Y. (1979). Learning to read is natural. In L. Resnick and P. Weaver (Eds.), *Theory and practice of early reading* (Vol. 1, pp. 137–154). Hillsdale, NJ: Lawrence Erlbaum.

Goodman, Y. (1989). Roots of the whole-language movement. *Elementary School Journal, 90,* 113–127.

Graves, D. (1983). *Writing: Teachers and children at work.* Exeter, NH: Heinemann.

Hall, N. (1987). *The emergence of literacy.* Portsmouth, NH: Heinemann.

Hemphill, L., Feldman, H., Camp, L., Griffin, T., and Wolf, D. (1994). Developmental changes in narrative and non-narrative discourse in children with and without brain injury. *Journal of Communication Disorders, 27,* 107–133.

Hemphill, L., Wolf, D., and Camp, L. (1993, April). *Narrative competence: Local patterns of usage.* Paper presented at the biennial meeting, Society for Research in Child Development, New Orleans.

Hicks, D. (1990). Narrative skills and genre knowledge: Ways of telling in the primary school grades. *Applied Psycholinguistics, 11,* 83–104.

Holdaway, D. (1979). *The foundations of literacy.* Sydney: Ashton Scholastic.

Holdaway, D. (1986). The structure of natural learning as a basis for literacy instruction. In M. Sampson (Ed.), *The pursuit of literacy: Early reading and writing* (pp. 56–72). Dubuque, IA: Kendall Hunt.

Hudson, J. and Shapiro, L. (1991). From knowing to telling: The development of children's scripts, stories, and personal narratives. In A. McCabe and C. Peterson (Eds.), *Developing narrative structure* (pp. 89–136). Hillsdale, NJ: Lawrence Erlbaum.

Hyon, S. and Sulzby, E. (1992, April). *Black kindergartners' spoken narratives: Style, structure, and task.* Paper presented at the annual meeting of the American Educational Research Association, San Francisco.

Karmiloff-Smith, A. (1979). *A functional approach to child language.* Cambridge, England: Cambridge University Press.

Karmiloff-Smith, A. (1992). *Beyond modularity: A developmental perspective on cognitive science.* Cambridge: MIT Press.

Leont'ev, A. (1979). The problem of activity in psychology. In J. Wertsch (Ed.), *The concept of activity in Soviet psychology* (pp. 37–71). Armonk, NY: Sharpe.

LeVine, R., Dixon, S., LeVine, S., Richman, A., Leiderman, P., Keefer, C., and Brazelton, T. (1994). *Child care and culture: Lessons from Africa*. New York: Cambridge University Press.

Lieven, E. (1994). Crosslinguistic and crosscultural aspects of language addressed to children. In C. Gallaway and B. Richards (Eds.), *Input and interaction in language acquisition* (pp. 56–73). Cambridge, England: Cambridge University Press.

McCarthey, S. (1994). Authors, text, and talk: The internalization of dialogue from social interaction during writing. *Reading Research Quarterly, 29*, 200–231.

Michaels, S. (1981). Sharing time. *Language in Society, 10*, 423–447.

Michaels, S. (1987). Text and context: A new approach to the study of classroom writing. *Discourse Processes, 10*, 321–346.

Michaels, S. (1991). The dismantling of narrative. In A. McCabe and C. Peterson (Eds.), *Developing narrative structure* (pp. 303–354). Hillsdale, NJ: Lawrence Erlbaum.

Minami, M. and McCabe, A. (1991). Haiku as a discourse regulation device. *Language in Society, 20*, 577–599.

Moorman, G., Blanton, W., and McLaughlin, T. (1994). The rhetoric of whole language. *Reading Research Quarterly, 29*, 309–329.

Nelson, K. (1986). *Event knowledge*. Hillsdale, NJ: Lawrence Erlbaum.

Newman, J. (Ed.). (1985). *Whole language: Theory in use*. Portsmouth, NH: Heinemann.

Ochs, E. (Ed.). (1988). *Culture and language development*. Cambridge, England: Cambridge University Press.

Ochs, E. (1992). Indexing gender. In A. Duranti and C. Goodwin (Eds.), *Rethinking context: Language as an interactive phenomenon* (pp. 335–358). Cambridge, England: Cambridge University Press.

Ochs, E., Taylor, C., Rudolph, D., and Smith, R. (1992). Story-telling as a theory-building activity. *Discourse Processes, 15*, 37–72.

Pappas, C. (1993). Is narrative "primary"? Some insights from kindergartners' pretend readings of stories and information books. *Journal of Reading Behavior, 25*, 97–129.

Purcell-Gates, V. (1991). Ability of well-read-to kindergartners to decontextualize/recontextualize experience into a written narrative register. *Language and Education, 5*, 177–188.

Ruddell, R. (1992). A whole language and literacy perspective: Creating a meaning making instructional environment. *Language Arts, 69*, 612–620.

Schieffelin, B. and Ochs, E. (Eds.). (1986). *Language socialization across cultures*. Cambridge, England: Cambridge University Press.

Shannon, P. (1990). *The struggle to continue: Progressive reading instruction in the United States*. Portsmouth, NH: Heinemann.

Smith, F. (1983). *Essays into literacy*. London: Heinemann.

Snow, C. (1995). Issues in the study of input: Fine-tuning, universality, individual and developmental differences, and necessary causes. In P. Fletcher and B. MacWhinney (Eds.), *The handbook of child language* (pp. 180–193). Oxford, England: Blackwell.

Snow, C., Barnes, W., Chandler, J., Goodman, I., and Hemphill, L. (1991). *Unfulfilled expectations: Home and school influences on literacy*. Cambridge: Harvard University Press.

Snow, C. and Dickinson, D. (1990). Social sources of narrative skills at home and at school. *First Language, 10*, 87–103.

Sydow, K. (1990). The oral language acquisition analogy in early literacy research. *ERO, 14*, 43–50.

Teale, W. (1982). Toward a theory of how children learn to read and write naturally. *Language Arts, 59,* 555–570.

Tizard, B. and Hughes, M. (1984). *Young children learning.* Cambridge: Harvard University Press.

Ulichny, P. and Watson-Gegeo, K. (1989). Interactions and authority: The dominant interpretive framework in writing conferences. *Discourse Processes, 10,* 309–328.

Vacca, R. and Rasinski, T. (1992). *Case studies in whole language.* Fort Worth, TX: Harcourt Brace Jovanovich.

Walkerdine, V. (1988). *The mastery of reason.* London: Routledge.

Weaver, C. (1994). *Reading process and practice: From socio-psycholinguistics to whole language* (2nd edn.). Portsmouth, NH: Heinemann.

Wells, C. (1981). *Learning through interaction.* Cambridge, England: Cambridge University Press.

Wells, C. (1986). *The meaning makers.* Portsmouth, NH: Heinemann.

Wertsch, J. (Ed.). (1979). *The concept of activity in Soviet psychology.* Armonk, NY: Sharpe.

Willinsky, J. (1990). *The new literacy: Redefining reading and writing in the schools.* New York: Routledge.

10

Accommodating Diversity
in Early Literacy Learning

MARIE M. CLAY

"The small child goes into school and finds that the school did not have him in mind," wrote Henry Levin (1990), designer of the Stanford Program for Accelerated Schools. The mismatch between what schools require and the individual diversity of learners has been accepted as inevitable and institutionalized in school systems. The delivery system for education is group or whole class instruction, not individual instruction, which societies believe they cannot afford. Classes are instructed but classes do not learn; only individuals learn. To adjust for any mismatches, education provides special programs, special education, counseling, psychological services, home schooling and innumerable special policies for the extremes of diversity. Recent developments in cognitive psychology describing how individuals learn make it imperative that we reconsider how teaching might accommodate diversity among learners. The use of the term diversity here refers to any and all the variants of individual difference and is not limited to cultural, ethnic, or linguistic diversity.

Societies and educators agree on certain paths that "all" children are supposed to traverse: the scheme, the curriculum, the method, the textbook series, the laws and principles of psychology, the educational or developmental sequences described by research. These define average performance for age or time at school, and assessment standards mark the average levels to be attained. Diversity of any kind does not fit well within such expectations. Can educational practice escape from expectations of "average for age" and the assumptions that children must take common paths to common outcomes? Modern societies may find it essential to address the learning of individuals in order to raise skill levels in a whole population. Modern societies claiming to value diversity, and wishing to mainstream learners who were previously kept apart, need ways of escaping from the tyranny of the average.

One program, called Reading Recovery, has made such an escape. It brings diverse individuals by different routes to full participation in the mainstream of their classroom activities and has been used successfully in the education systems of five countries. This intervention seeks to eliminate literacy learning difficulties in hard-to-teach children, and to reduce literacy problems in schools during a "window-of-opportunity" in the second year in school. It selects children who are hard to teach for many different reasons and it accommodates diversity through one-on-one lessons lasting 30 minutes a day. Teaching interactions that are specifically tailored to each child's strengths follow an idiosyncratic path—which means that what is done in Reading Recovery cannot be mimicked or translated into classroom practice. The assumption that "what works well for the hardest to teach children would be the best adaptation for most learners" is an example of how we fail to accommodate diversity. In this chapter a close analysis is made of Reading Recovery in the context of current debates about cognition and learning because that intervention's results negate commonsense predictions about "slow learners."

From recent publications we have a better understanding of how learners construct their cognitive processes (although only some of that construction is self-conscious, deliberate, and reflective) and cognition is now understood to be constructed in particular activities, rather than powered by some reservoir of general ability. This creates interest in how learners contribute to their own learning. In a classroom each learner enters into new learning with different prior experience, and effective teaching may need to be "differentiated teaching" (Hansen and Robenhagen, 1993). I have argued that when societies begin to teach literacy in schools most children rather quickly construct an "inner control" over a wide range of reading and writing processes by means of which all later literacy learning is learned (Clay, 1991). At beginning ages, which range from five to seven years, 80 to 90 percent of children in industrialized countries construct this control quite easily in programs generated by distinctly different theories, and delivered in different languages. Country by country, children do become literate by traveling different paths to a common outcome.

Reading Recovery research from English-speaking countries provides evidence that among the lowest-achieving children, most can also become readers and writers if the conditions of learning are changed (Clay, 1993). Accounts describe how, as if in slow motion with exaggerated moves, such children shift from passive novices to active information processing, and apparently from acting on the information in print to an awareness of what they need to do. Some do begin to talk about what they do although their program does not require them to do this.

Different Routes to Common Outcomes

Reading Recovery teachers claim to design individual lessons for each child. Is that possible? Yes, if one assumes that literacy learning is complex and that complexity, like a drive to a large city, might begin at any one of several different starting points and be approached in any one of several different ways. Studies of what preschool children know about literacy show that they are attending to different aspects of literacy and enter kindergarten or school with islands of knowledge that are highly specific with surprisingly little overlap from child to child.

Such idiosyncrasy is not well served by two pervasive expectations in education: we either expect students to make some kind of average response or action like those we encounter most of the time (Assumption 1) or we group students according to stereotypes that apply to some subgroup (Assumption 2). Children entering school are measured with the yardstick of the "average five- or six-year-old" (A1) or categorized by socioeconomic, ethnic, cultural, linguistic, or maturity stereotypes (A2) and societies and educational systems provide special education for some subgroups. Learners making very different responses for any number of reasons do not fit the average or stereotypic descriptions, and in my role as clinical child psychologist I have had to find special help for such children. Reading Recovery evolved out of my concern to maximize educational outcomes for children who fit neither the "normal" nor the "stereotypical" categories.

Reading Recovery provides supplementary assistance for the lowest achievers in literacy learning in the age group after the first year at school, not excluding any children in an ordinary classroom for any reason, and as soon as it can be reliably determined that what the school provides is allowing these learners to fall further and further behind their age peers. It is assumed that children will need supplementary help for different reasons and that prior learning and other contributing causes will differ from child to child. Rejecting the search for a single, important cause or chain of causes for reading and writing difficulties, Reading Recovery recognizes two types of multiple causation: within the group any conceivable cause or causal chain may occur, and a particular learner may have difficulty for several different reasons. Low achievement may arise from lack of learning opportunities, or because the child chose to attend to other things, or because a child has the fine-motor skill and language level of a much younger child. Life events and crises in the preschool or early school years may also contribute to low achievement. If the learner is to read and write, every attempt must be made to help the child to attend to and learn basic literacy responses. Working with individual strengths may make this possible, although it will require more and different teaching interactions.

Multiple causation makes it highly unlikely that a prescribed sequence of instruction would suit all children with low literacy achievements. Yet historically literacy difficulties have been addressed by prescriptive programs, with irrational decisions such as a predetermined sequence of instruction for brain-damaged children, regardless of the site or extent of damage, or a severely reductionist attention to letter-sound relationships, no matter how limited the child's language or knowledge of the world. Gittleman (1985) concluded that we have little evidence that such programs work. Most learners in literacy remediation programs make meager gains while continuing to fall further and further behind their classmates.

Diverse children all with extremely low achievements in literacy bring to their first Reading Recovery lessons profiles of competencies that differ in level and pattern. Extreme limitations in prior knowledge or response repertoires make it imperative that the teacher tap every available response among those competencies. To create a trajectory of progress in slow learners, the teacher must begin with what each child can already do and then must work with that to bring each learner by different routes to the common outcome of effective performance as quickly as possible. First lessons in Reading Recovery include only what a child already knows (which is limited but different for each child), and call upon learners to move with flexibility around their own current competencies, challenged by meeting what they know in new juxtapositions.

The end of supplementary help in Reading Recovery comes as soon as learners are judged to be ready to make continuing progress at average levels in their own classes without supplementary support. Learners need to work among their peers, relatively independent and indistinguishable from them. Becoming a competent silent reader by mid-elementary school gives children the resources they need to cope with other school subjects. The goal of independent survival with a self-extending literacy system thus becomes both realistic and necessary. The common goal of Reading Recovery is the survival of every child back in the classroom. Levels of success with the hardest to teach children are high although they vary across countries, education systems, populations of children, social class divisions, curricula, dialects, languages and teachers. Cost-effective results only come with quality implementation of Reading Recovery at the level of the education system. Yet the day-to-day teacher-child interactions are a critical part of such success.

The Tyranny of the Average and Other Mind-Traps

Research studies hide the complexity of child learning by reporting group averages, but a pooled average may not describe any individual. Case studies and in-depth ethnographies in contrast may describe superbly what exists in a few individual cases and yet this knowledge may not help us accommodate to diversity.

As a consequence of thinking about teaching a class, we reason as if it were the class that learns, when in fact it is only individuals that learn. The tyrannies of common concepts discussed in this section—the average learner, the curriculum, the stages of development, the sequences of learning, and the poor/slow learner—these are concepts related to teaching that get in the way of individuals having appropriate opportunities for learning.

Classroom teachers have a sense of high, average, and low progress over time, and they can recall exceptional routes taken by a few individual students. From New Zealand research, I can draw two illustrations. In 1978 children close to entering high school completed a national survey about the daily news (Clay and Oates, 1985). When children were asked to write down the meanings of some cryptic newspaper-type headlines it was not surprising that items like WORKERS OUT—FACTORY BLACK, or DOLLAR DROPS AGAIN were only partially understood by some children. Low-, middle-, and high-level responses, and exceptional statements were reported. For DOLLAR DROPS AGAIN, an illustrative low-level response was "A man keeps losing his money," a middle-range response was "It's not worth having a dollar any more because it's not worth anything," and a high-level response was

"The American dollar has dropped 2.7 percent against the Swiss franc today," (from a New Zealand child). Some responses could not be fitted into preselected categories because they were so divergent. To say that such differences stem from differences in general intellectual ability is not informative; the teacher's challenge is not to predict from an IQ score but to move each child along from where he or she is today. The teacher needs to know what strengths each learner can bring to working on this kind of problem.

Similarly, in a study of high school students' confusions about meanings in school texts (Nicholson, 1985), I was struck by the lack of opportunities for students to negotiate the various meanings they assigned to those texts. Knowing what 13-year-olds could "read" on the average would be no help in addressing the understanding and misunderstanding of these students.

Another disjunction between theory and practice results from collapsing data across age groups and historical time. All children change rapidly but on somewhat different time scales in different learning domains. With such diversity does it help a teacher's responses to a learner to know that all five- to seven-year-olds are at a particular "stage of development"? A stage sketches some general educational landscape but does not help teachers move diverse learners into new territory. When the findings of psychology are used to predict individual change or generate teaching interactions with an individual learner they are always at risk of being inappropriate.

I have found administrators and teachers emphatic about the factors that will prejudice or facilitate a child's progress, taking their predictions from groups, and some intuitive averaging of their personal experience, and not acknowledging that such claims are very often wrong for individuals. Commonly their own school's delivery system has contributed to the effects they are observing.

Psychology's search for general laws that apply to behaviors of human beings of all ages has been as problematic as the tyranny of the average when applied to education. Psychologists have tried to uncover laws to account for sequences of change in children's behaviors; societies create sequences of expectancies and learning opportunities for children; and educators like to have variability squeezed into a standard sequence because it makes it easier to think about curricula, outcome standards, and what will be taught each day. I have been unable to find a fixed sequence in the development of young children's writing and believe that children enter that complex activity from many different starting points. Some researchers, such as Gentry (1978), have reported sequenced learning stages for writing and spelling, and some curricula such as the IBM "Writing to Read" program have been built from such descriptions.

Yet recent experiments with young children in Israel (Levin and Tolchinsky-Landsmann, 1989; Levin and Korat, 1993) report lack of sequence. Some basic understandings may in fact be learned sequentially, but in any complex learning it is often impossible to specify a fixed sequence of acquisition. Shephard (1991) questions the search for developmental sequences in school learning—like averages, subgroup stereotypes, and psychological laws—and educators should consider them as potential mind-traps. A teacher considering a particular child needs to believe that descriptions of average/typical/normal achievement or sequences for learning are always surrounded by error, generate their own exceptions, and do not necessarily constrain what can be true of individuals.

Along with a commitment to normal distributions of competencies there comes an assumption that toward the "low" end of the normal curve we encounter simple kinds of limitations. In fact, to the contrary, as we move from average to low achievers we encounter individuals who know less and less that can be related to the learning task and show several weak spots in their functioning, all of which make teaching them more complicated. It is not a matter of surmounting a particular hurdle of language, cognition, perception, motor skill, or phonemic awareness; it is a matter of multiple weaknesses in the learner creating greater complexity of inappropriate responding and producing less predictability for the teacher about how to proceed.

The clinical child psychologist who works with individual development knows that what is good practice in interacting with most children is often wrong for a particular child. I have tried to face each of my clients as a new challenge and have never assumed that normal performance, or categories of special problems or my previous experience with other clients, would tell me anything about this client. I would say to myself "this client may look like another you have seen but forget that; try to assume that this client is unique." I brought that view to my longitudinal research of literacy development and into the development of Reading Recovery.

Today we are better than we used to be at accepting cultural difference, language difference, and gender difference. Nevertheless, because we frequently do not acknowledge diversity in ways of learning, we have been open to blunders in this area. The average, typical or normal distribution and the curriculum or developmental sequence may give teachers a sense of the direction in which learners need to move. However, when sequence and prescription emerge from scientific studies of groups, we can predict all kinds of mismatches between the prescription and the most facilitating route for particular individuals. We cannot teach well from descriptions of what occurs on the average: it may be a place to start our thinking but it has little scope for fine-tuning. It is not enough to reveal the learners' knowledge as scores on assignments or tests, for we need to understand in some specific way how they negotiate and construct new meanings in particular contexts.

Can education empower each individual or do we have to settle for simplified descriptions that apply only to groups of children? Fortunately for schools and for society, most individuals become constructive learners who can, on their own, get to successful performance despite the fact that there is noise, error, or mismatch between the prescriptive curriculum and their prior learning. It is in the diverse group of low achievers that we find those for whom the presciption was so far from what they needed that they could not engage with the learning process in the classroom. There is some evidence that, supported by responsive and reflective teaching interactions, even these children can do surprising things. With good teaching interactions, learners can be helped to construct their cognitions and get good outcomes where poor predictions would have typically been made. If that occurs on a large enough scale, teachers can spoil the correlations on which much educational practice is predicated.

The Negative Critique of Policies for Dealing with Diversity

Many of the arguments in this section and some of the wording come from Shephard's (1991) important analysis and excellent critique of policies for dealing with diversity. She reviewed U.S. educational practices such as special placements for the mentally retarded, diagnosing children as learning disabled, holding them back to repeat a grade, and special kindergarten placements for "unready children." Urging the rejection of current practices, she wrote:

These placement policies can be seen as part of a recurring pattern in the U.S. educational system to deal with children who have trouble learning by assigning them to a special place where, despite good intentions, they receive systematically poor instruction that lessens their chances for important learning gains. (p. 279)

Against the background of an increasing concern for children of ethnic and linguistic minorities in the United States, she reported that "children from non-mainstream cultural and linguistic backgrounds are disproportionately the victims of these ineffective instructional practices." The intention of the practices was to accommodate diversity by providing instructional help targeted to the needs of an individual. In retrospect we see that these practices still target groups, not individuals. Negative side effects accrue as soon as students are assigned a special place to receive help. Assessment and diagnosis become ways of sorting diverse children into categories and segregating them in special placements. Those labeled as slow learners are given a "dumbed-down instruction."

Most of Shephard's criticisms were avoided in the design of the Reading Recovery intervention in 1977, as if I had first listened to the critique before developing Reading Recovery. This is explained by the fact that my work as a trainer of educational psychologists kept me close to the frailties of special education. So Reading Recovery did not prescribe special placement but provided for supplementary teaching for children who remain in, and are brought to full participation in, the activities of their classrooms. "Lowest achiever status" relative to peers of the same age group was established through observation tasks (with the qualities of tests) that expose the literacy response repertoire of the learner to the prospective teacher. The same systematic observations are used by an independent evaluator to decide when the supplementary program should be withdrawn. Children spend a minimum of time in Reading Recovery, 30 minutes per day for a limited time, varying according to need from 12 to 20 weeks. This need to lift the child's level of performance to that of most classmates in the shortest possible time is incompatible with a simplified, sequenced, or massively analytic curriculum. Help is discontinued by a procedure that predicts reliably that a child will be able to perform in his or her classroom with a particular teacher and her curriculum. Progress in the following few months is monitored, and competent classroom performance is sustained by high percentages of the children who enter.

Children from nonmajority cultural and linguistic backgrounds are selected into Reading Recovery only when they fall into the lowest achiever category. Then their cultural and linguistic diversity can be accommodated because the planning and delivery of instruction is on an individual basis. Shephard's comments on particular practices sharpen the account of Reading Recovery.

Tracking

Grouping by intellectual ability developed early in this century as schools moved from educating a homogeneous, elite group to an intake of children with more heterogeneous learning levels. It was expected that achievement would improve when teaching could be tailored to what students were capable of learning. Research evidence shows that such expectations were seldom met, that children in the middle and slow groups generally lost academically, that their self-concepts were negatively affected, and teachers delivered a simplified curriculum to low-ability classes. These are the consequences of labeling. Other studies show that teachers prefer to teach high-ability students for whom they hold higher expectations, expect more homework, and ask more challenging questions.

Reading Recovery works in opposition to tracking: It seeks to move diverse children from extremely low achievements at entry to full participation in an unstreamed classroom.

Special Education Placement

Originally designed to serve the deaf, blind, and mentally retarded, special education provided special instruction that acknowledged and accommodated a child's disability. It then expanded to serve larger populations with less severe problems that were more vaguely defined. Yet research shows that students received a watered-down curriculum and therefore lost ground academically compared with control children in ordinary classrooms. The negative effects were greatest for the less severely handicapped students and minority students were disproportionately represented. The numbers identified grew markedly from 1975 to 1990, especially in the learning disabilities (LD) category. Criticisms supported by research studies were that tests are technically inadequate, that diagnostic signs that occur among successful learners are interpreted as signs of disorder, that the costs of assessment and staffing leading to LD placement involve an average of six different professionals, with little attempt to reconcile the findings of these professionals in the design of a program to be delivered to the child. Categorizing or labeling a child changes the nature of the classroom teacher's responsibility for that child's learning.

More than half the children labeled LD in schools do not match clinical definitions and are more accurately described as slow learners, children from non-English backgrounds, children from highly mobile families or those with frequent absences, naughty children, and average achievers in high-achieving districts. It is as if the clinicians have abandoned a scientific definition of LD and ask instead, "Does this child need special help? If so he must be LD" (Shephard, 1991; see also Clay, 1987).

There are no categories of children in Reading Recovery. Individual histories and characteristics are not ignored, but the only selection criteria are low achievement indicators that suggest the need for supplementary help. There is minimal dependence on testing, and test results are double-checked with observations of complex processing on authentic tasks, and with performance in classrooms. Costs of selection are low because the Reading Recovery teachers survey the child's competencies with observation tasks (which operate like standardized measures) and use what they find out on these authentic tasks in planning the child's first lessons. As the child's curriculum expands and task difficulty increases, new competencies become available; the positive effects are most rapid for the least handicapped but the greatest distance is covered by the most handicapped.

A well-run program could lead to fewer students being classified for special education provisions outside mainstream education. The school's Reading Recovery team tune the program to serve that school's own population because the school accepts responsibility for its own diverse children. The children selected for supplementary help remain in their classes and move gradually to average band performance in a short period of time. If a child remains in the program for about 20 weeks and has not reached average band performance, the child's progress should be reviewed by the school's Reading Recovery team and a decision may be taken to refer the child for an individual appraisal from a specialist professional, who would probably recommend that the education system provide assistance of a somewhat different kind for a longer period. Most but not every child can succeed in this program; in New Zealand 1 percent or less of the age cohort are referred.

Grade Retention

Nonpromotion was the nineteenth century's answer to diversity, so the practice is older than tracking and special education. Grade retention is the intervention of choice in the United States for children who lack prerequisite skills for the next grade but whose problems are not serious enough to trigger special education placement. Beliefs about the efficacy of retention are strong even though research shows that repeating a grade does not improve achievement, that retained students have lower achievement than control students who went directly on to the next grade, and retainees are 20 to 30 percent more likely to leave school without graduating than similar students who had never been retained. There is a negative effect on personal adjustment in the majority of studies.

A special form of retention occurs at the kindergarten level. Solutions designed to ensure more success and less stress among first-grade children stem from Gesell's theories in the 1950s and similar developments in the 1980s in the United States. They took a variety of forms, had different philosophies, and differ in the type of children defined as children at risk. They include repeating kindergarten, two-year programs such as developmental kindergarten before kindergarten, and transition rooms before first grade (also called junior-first, prefirst, and readiness rooms).

Children are given the "gift" of another year, which is used in one of three ways: (1) it provides wait-time until readiness occurs; (2) it provides remediation following a curriculum that closely resembles readiness skills tests; or (3) it merely provides a second run through the same kindergarten program. Children may be selected for immaturity or academic deficiences; boys are a target group. The results are not positive.

A review of 16 controlled studies now available shows typically no difference academically between unready children who spend an extra year before first grade and at-risk controls who went directly on to the first grade. (Shephard, 1991, p. 287)

There is also a tendency to group "unready children" together in kindergartens, so all children who need the resource are placed in one classroom, with a curriculum in these special rooms dominated by drill on isolated readiness skills.

Reading Recovery cannot work alongside such early retention practices. If children were retained in kindergarten and given a Reading Recovery program, there would be no activities in the kindergarten to support what they were learning in their lessons, and when they were ready to be discontinued there would be no suitable classroom program to extend and support their continued learning. They need a first-grade classroom to support their first-grade competencies. It would waste resources to hold children in kindergarten and put them through Reading Recovery. The contract must be to promote (rather than to retain) children and to place them in Reading Recovery. Indeed, we should ask why the kindergarten program is creating a call for retention.

Shephard concludes that millions of public school children in many countries are failing because of, not in spite of, the concerted effort vested in special programs. Sorted and labeled by fallible tests and teacher judgments, children are assigned to treatments that were intended to provide better instruction for homogeneous groups and matching instruction to student ability. Analysis of these policies shows that children segregated under special arrangements with special curricula are likely to receive poorer instruction delivered at a slow pace with overemphasis on elements and neglect of complexity, and that children from linguistically and culturally different backgrounds are more likely to be selected.

Older Psychological Theories

Shephard describes how older psychological theories about human ability and learning supported these unsatisfactory special education practices. Two types of theories from the past, which were used to sort children into categories, led to the old accommodations to diversity described above.

Psychology began as a study of individual differences with particular emphasis on differences in human intellectual capacity. (Tracking, described above, is predicated on sorting children by measured "potential" intelligence.) The theory of intelligence as inherited, which did not allow for much influence of past learning on current status, has been strongly challenged and discredited by the criticisms of IQ tests, by the evidence of the influence of environment on observed capacities, and by demonstrations that children can be taught to think intelligently. Scientists have steadily revised their estimates of the relative influence of heredity downward but, according to Shephard, teachers and the public "have not kept pace with the research insights from cognitive psychology, sociology, or cultural anthropology." The simple, public view is that heredity plus environment "or the sum of these two contributions sets fairly firm limits on how much children can learn" (p. 290).

A newer environmental theory has taken the place of the theory of heredity in the minds of many teachers. While most teachers would find it socially and politically unacceptable today to talk about a child's limited genetic endowment for school learning, they often substitute an environmental explanation for school failure that denigrates the child's home experiences, a view that has come to be known as the deficit model. They talk about this environmentally determined inability as though it were relatively permanent and unalterable, yet they rarely respond to missed opportunities to learn with make-up opportunities. To be specific, a child who enjoys regular bedtime stories acquires book knowledge that is helpful in learning to read; a child who has no such experience needs a rich and accelerative set of encounters to make up for missed experience. Similarly, a child who has never noticed people writing, or explored with a pencil or "danced with a pen" (Learning Media, 1992), will need make-up opportunities to watch writers writing and to try out this activity. This is not an indictment of the child's home but of the schools that do not provide the make-up opportunities.

Reading Recovery never used measured intelligence for selection of children because (1) too many errors arise in using it to predict individual success with learning literacy, (2) we cannot predict the interaction of environment with heredity even if we could locate a problem in the genes, and (3) a system-wide early intervention program must depend on selection by teachers rather than by psychologists. So, whatever the hereditary, physical, or cultural limitations of the child, the Reading Recovery teacher provides the low achiever with a second chance to learn. By working with the learning opportunities of the present, by assuming that responses that are the consequence of environmental learning are alterable, effective literacy learning responses can be drawn out of idiosyncratic response repertoires irrespective of attributed cause. With supplementary instruction, the teacher tries to bring the learner to independent problem solving in under 20 weeks; for a very small percentage of children, such intensive efforts do not produce the desired outcome and longer-term help is sought. The challenge of accommodating diversity is met by temporary and time-limited teaching that is idiosyncratically responsive to the learner.

Shephard also identified the dominant theory of learning in the United States since the 1950s as a theory responsible for poor results in special education. Educators assumed that complex learning could be broken down into constituent skills and taught to students in fragments in a prescribed sequence, from the simplest to the more complex (Resnick and Resnick, 1990; Stallman and Pearson, 1990). Once learned, these separate elements were supposed to transform themselves into complex competency and little attention was given to how constituent parts were to be integrated to achieve conceptual understanding. This reductionist model led to particularly poor results for learners who could not spontaneously combine the separate elements (i.e., without instruction). The teaching of constituent skills usually took place out of the contexts to which it was to be applied (e.g., the long-standing and widely spread practice of occupying children with workbook exercises).

Problematic in these practices was the common assumption that the development of "high-order" skills like thinking and comprehension could be postponed until after students had mastered the elements of learning. Despite overwhelming evidence from cognitive psychology that complex learning involves thinking, including how a three-year-old negotiates the meaning of a simple story, instruction predicated on the old model resulted in some programs that denied students opportunities to think until they had mastered prerequisites. Meanwhile, successful students made the practices look good because they created their own opportunities for complex learning.

Such interpretations of learning theory had numbing effects on the quality of instruction delivered to low-achieving students and became translated into the expectations held by their teachers. Allington (reviewed in Shephard, 1991) found that good readers were expected to be self-directed and their assignments implied that the purpose of reading was the comprehension of meaning. Poor readers, on the other hand, were taught in a markedly different way, emphasizing externally controlled fluent decoding; teachers interrupted poor readers more often, asked poor readers fewer comprehension questions, and assigned more skill-in-isolation work (p. 346). As my thesis would be that teachers need many different ways of interacting with diversity to meet the needs of low-achieving students, I find a prescriptive and sequential bit-by-bit learning model inappropriate for Reading Recovery children.

New Theories, New Practices, and General Principles

New theories have emerged in cognitive psychology, in constructivist developmental psychology, and in the broader framework of sociocultural theory for understanding learning. All stress that learning, social or academic, is an active, constructive process, but the multiple meanings of constructivism make it hard to define. To illustrate how these newer theories relate to Reading Recovery, I will discuss some teaching implications of two constructivist principles reported by Shephard.

1. *Intelligence and reasoning are developed abilities.* According to Shephard's account, humans learn how to think based on the models of thinking they have the opportunity to try out. Metacognitive processes are constructed by the learner.

Planning and evaluating during problem solving, self-checking for comprehension during reading, developing a mental representation of a problem, drawing analogies to previously learned concepts are all learned, some "naturally," some in interaction with a more expert person, and some in more formal tutoring situations. Some learning-to-learn strategies can be quite content-specific. Cognitive researchers are concerned primarily with the construction of meaning that goes on inside an individual's head (for example, the building of knowledge structures, the linking of related information, and the strategic learning of how to work with content specific solutions). Most acknowledge that such learning is socially constructed (Bruner, 1990). Anthropologists, sociologists, and developmental psychologists (Valsiner, 1987; McNaughton, 1995) are interested in the co-construction and negotiation of meaning among individuals in a culture.

Teachers can teach with constructiveness in mind if they create more effective teaching interactions, and the new theory of cognitive development should direct attention to how teachers can critique their teaching interactions with students on their own and with colleagues. Some suggestions for changes in teaching interaction can be made.

(a) *Observe individual learners closely.* What the learner contributes to the teaching-learning interaction is likely to be different, child for child, signalling the constructing of the understanding. Change will begin at different starting points for different learners; it will proceed in different ways and at different rates, and teachers must come to understand that each learner is taking new learning aboard by the very processes that make each child different! If a teacher can ever find a homogeneous group, good teaching should rapidly make the participants heterogeneous.

(b) *Tune in to individual differences.* For decades, teachers have thought about the physical, age, and personality differences between learners, and they have adjusted in small part to the huge implications of having a different sociocultural upbringing. The improvement of teaching interactions requires something additional; it requires the teacher to tune in to the way the learner takes in new information, the individual nature of the process of learning. The teacher will consider many questions, among them: How does this child work in the literacy domain? communicate with the teacher? get a sense of mastery and assurance? In what contexts does the learner work well? Certain questions are of immediate importance: What is this learner attending to within the complexity of the current task? Does the learner catch miscues and mismatches and initiate problem solving? What specifically makes this task so difficult for the learner to understand? What would make a difference to how this learner works at this activity? In sum, the expert teacher acknowledges differences that recur in teaching interactions and uses them constructively.

(c) *Converse with individual learners.* While managing all of the above, teachers must create opportunities for individuals to negotiate what they do not understand with someone who does. The one-room schoolhouse, so successful in teaching individuals, provided just this opportunity for learners to talk about their work with the teacher. Today's theories on how learners construct their understanding call for talking through, playing back, and rounding out understanding in conversation.

On the other hand systematically managed individualization in many content areas that came to schools with specially developed materials and technology in the form of programmed learning and then computer learning rarely provides for the negotiation of understanding with the teacher/instructor. Today the term individualization is an ill-defined term, glibly used, and it does not refer to teaching individuals. As Scriven (1975) wrote: "I see it swinging especially between the exaggeration of its value in order to keep up with each new fashion and the inevitable disheartening recognition that the promised marvels have not been flawlessly achieved in classrooms."

(d) *The teacher must interact with "the constructive child."* What is a constructive child? Two decades of research on language acquisition left us with excellent descriptions of how a child learns to speak, and with the conviction that young children work out what they need to learn in order to be understood without direct teaching but through negotiations of meaning that take place in conversations. The miracle of language acquisition occurs as parents and siblings who know the individual well talk with the individual child. Nothing like the "group delivery" of the classroom occurs. From those interactions, children take what they want, constructing their own cognitive competencies.

Conversations that negotiate meaning provide a starting point for thinking about how to improve teaching interactions in classrooms, displacing much current and unsatisfactory teacher talk (Cazden, 1988). We must learn how to enlist the constructiveness of children in the interests of their own progress, and having done this we need to know how to pass the initiative to learners so they can be on their own much of the time and do without us as teachers. We do not have to solve the problems of teaching with diversity entirely on our own: we have the constructive learner as our strongest ally.

Cazden (1992) highlights the need not only to talk with the child but to personalize the conversation or assignment; she illustrates with an example of a Samoan boy in a social studies lesson asked to compare his life with that of a Neanderthal man. He asked the teacher "Which of my three lives should I compare?" and explained these as his island life in Samoa, his city life in Auckland, and his church life. Giving learners opportunities to reveal their range of experience will allow their personal constructions of meaning to enter into the teaching interaction. This point is stressed in Shephard's article.

2. Instruction should allow students to use what they already know to arrive at new understandings. If learning is to be a constructive process, then learners should engage in tasks that have meaning for them (i.e., that are situated in comprehensible contexts) and allow what a learner already knows to enter into new learning (both strategic and knowledge-based). Prior knowledge is not just prior prescribed school learning; it includes all the images, language patterns, social relations, and personal experiences that a student relies on to make sense of something new.

(a) *Develop tasks with scope.* Change will need to occur in the policies of administrators, in research department evaluations, in curriculum design, and in teacher expectations, but I want to emphasize that a theory of the constructive learner demands an essential change in lesson delivery. We have to escape from notions of stepwise progressions of learning new concepts in set sequences. Any prescribed sequence of instruction leaves some children behind early in the sequence without providing any means for catching up. In one sense, Reading Recovery provides just such an opportunity to return again.

A valuable and different approach that should be part of a teacher's repertoire is the use of "tasks with scope," a term I had to invent. These allow children to enter a classroom task with whatever they bring to it, using the task as a vehicle for learning to problem-solve and construct new knowledge. If the teacher designs the task so that all children can enter at their own level (as in "write a story about what we did" or "reread the text to discover something you did not notice the first time"), then there is scope for learners to move from where they are to somewhere else as a result of the encounter. This occurs routinely in conversation. In contrast, tasks directed to the learning of items of knowledge, skills or concepts in a prescribed order do not allow for different starting points and the sequence of the curriculum does not allow for different routes to different outcomes. On rare occasions prescribed learning may be necessary, but whereas formal sequencing has become the predominant mode of delivering education, the prime emphasis needs to be placed on constructive learning in early education. Tasks with scope also provide the opportunity for serendipitous learning when active learners learn much more than the teacher had expected.

Reading Recovery has a framework for lessons that some critics have mistaken for prescriptive teaching. Each required segment of the lesson is a task with scope within which teachers create learning opportunities for individuals who are coming to complex learning from different directions. In every lesson a child (1) reads familiar books, (2) rereads yesterday's book, (3) does a few minutes of work with letters singly or in making and breaking up words, (4) composes and writes a story, (5) reassembles that story as a puzzle from its parts, (6) is introduced to a new reading book, and (7) reads that book for the first time. What occurs in each slot of the lesson increases in difficulty on an individual schedule until the activities are as advanced as those completed by most children in the learner's classroom. The tasks can remain "whole" because the teacher shares any part of the task needed to support the learner's participation, sometimes completing some part of the task. It would be possible for teachers to use this framework prescriptively but training helps the teacher to provide scope for the constructive child.

(b) *Change the delivery variables.* Appropriate instruction for diverse pupils in Reading Recovery required a different delivery system, and a change in the design of the learning opportunities. The lessons are individually designed by teachers who have additional training over and above their classroom expertise, and who can use a wide range of alternatives for working with the limited response repertoires of the children. This results in learning at a faster rate than classmates, producing the necessary accelerated progress needed to catch up to them. The teacher's daily records of child responses (1) demonstrate the idiosyncratic paths to success, (2) can be used by a school's Reading Recovery team to ensure that the program is effective, and (3) are available for research analysis.

When classroom teachers try to teach all children as individuals, they cannot find enough time for individual teaching. Consequently sessions become too widely spaced. New biases develop. Teachers can hear several good readers read in the time they can hear one who is struggling, so distortions of attention develop. Individual teaching is not a preferred way to teach in classrooms, but individual interactions with learners and between learners throughout the school day in conversations which construct knowledge are essential if we are to accommodate individual differences.

Three programs with atypical delivery systems aspire to change and improve schooling and share a belief in the learning abilities of all children, in building on strengths, and in the empowerment of both teacher and learner with decision-making roles and with responsibility for results: (1) Henry Levin, leader of the Accelerated Schools project, is working to change whole schools, (2) Stan Pogrow's Higher Order Thinking Skills program (1990a, b) delivers supplementary help to upper elementary students in math and science, and (3) Reading Recovery targets individual children at a critical time in literacy learning during "a window of opportunity."

In each case the whole school is involved in supporting the change and the purpose of intervention is always to serve the local education system and the individual learner.

A drastic change in the delivery system is the hardest part of the change process, but the importance of organizational and delivery contributions to teaching-learning changes cannot be underestimated.

(c) *Tolerate different routes to desired learning outcomes.* Given a diverse group of learners with multiple weak spots in some complex area of cognitive activity, how can teachers bring them to some satisfactory level of functioning? Because they ignore how much learners bring to their tasks, fixed sequences of instruction create impediments in many areas of education, especially for immigrants and adults.

Reading Recovery selects children who are noticeably and reliably at extremely low levels of performance for their age group. They form a diverse group who must learn faster than their classmates if they are to escape from that diversity, but they travel by different routes and need different learning conditions in order to achieve the school's common outcome for the age group.

Constructing Cognitions About Complex Tasks

Once literacy competencies are constructed, there seems to be nothing to reading; it is an easy task that allows attention to go to meanings. Writing continues to offer challenges. Both reading and writing require that a complex set of competencies be put in place in the first two to three years of literacy instruction.

Attempting a Complex Task

Learning a language is complex yet young children successfully learn to talk (Lindfors, 1987). Individual "tuition" takes place in conversations without formal instruction. Homes use language differently; vocabulary, structures, dialects, content, interaction style, exposure to different genres, and opportunities to talk differ from child to child. Children differ in the use they make of their available opportunities. Yet, from this diversity, children learn the forms of English, the rules for constructing utterances, and ways of extending their language competencies out of the control they have already. They come by different routes to two general outcomes: (1) understanding how their language works and (2) knowing how to extend their own control over it.

In Reading Recovery, literacy learning occurs in a somewhat analogous way. Teachers assume that literacy learning is complex learning and they help each child to attend to those aspects of the task that challenge him or her. They arrange complex tasks in a tentative gradient of difficulty, assuming that what the child is able to do at any one time is an organized totality. Initial and primitive responses can be used to construct more complex responses (Lewin, 1954). Authentic tasks like reading stories and writing messages are sufficiently meaningful to allow learners to recognize whether the ways in which they are working are successful or not.

Close observation of children reading stories and writing messages in the daily lessons of Reading Recovery reveal to the teacher the points at which a particular child struggles. So the teacher puzzles this out. What, within the complexity, is making this task difficult for this child? The teacher knows the child's performance repertoire (recorded in the teacher's detailed daily records) and performance history (over the short-term supplementary program), and this is a sound basis for thinking through where and how to help the child move forward. So the analysis of the complexity of the task and what might be needed is carried out during every interaction. Teachers may devise a trial task or two to test their assumptions. A big step forward is achieved not by adding some items of new knowledge but by learning how to select from multiple sources of information (world knowledge, cognition, perception, language, and movement) to arrive at one decision.

Reading Recovery teachers work from a common model of children's decision making about continuous texts derived from research on children learning to read and write successfully (Clay, 1991). This model assumes that children need to attend to (and work with) a network of information in written texts in order to make choices among possible responses. Through experiences with texts, meanings, words, letters, and sounds, learners build reservoirs of item knowledge but these will not, of themselves, enable readers to understand what they read. In addition to the general perceptual, cognitive, and linguistic strategies used in all conscious activity, the literacy learner must develop strategic behaviors for working with language presented visually in printed continuous texts. Developing phonemic awareness and phonological links to visual texts are known to be special challenges. Young learners in classrooms build these strategic behaviors out of their experiences gained in reading texts and writing texts, and the processing systems that they construct change to cope with new occurrences.

Classroom teachers operating from a constructivist theory support the completion of whole tasks in which the children handle some of the complexity and the teachers in various ways share the tasks and introduce challenges for the learners. But Reading Recovery teachers have a theory of progress in complex learning that is more specific and detailed than classroom teachers need. It is a dynamic theory open to change as new information becomes available, and it is used as a tool until better tools become available. If new ideas can establish their credibility (1) in practice, (2) under research conditions, and (3) among the professional networks, they may be accepted among the alternative routes for Reading Recovery teaching.

Can We Ask Learners How They Think?

If teachers need to know where particular learners are and how those learners are thinking, can they just ask them? No, not in Reading Recovery, because learners who can engage in that kind of dialogue are indeed ready to leave the program. This claim warrants further analysis.

Neo-Piagetians saw this requirement—asking children to verbalize the logic of their thinking—as one of the limitations of Piaget's work, for he asked children to explain how they were thinking, and not all learners can do that. Older children are better than younger children at telling us what they are thinking, and those who are so articulate are no longer novices to turning an introspective eye on their own products and processes. Most teachers recognize that there are individual differences in how easily young children can give a metacognitive commentary on their thinking, learning, remembering, forgetting, and understanding. Sometimes theorists attribute "thinking about learning" to what is merely the ability to talk one's way through a lesson using the same words as their teacher. Reading Recovery children can learn to mimic the teacher's talk; however when faced with metacognitive processing, they have first to learn some ways of working effectively with print, and then to move from effective acts in reading and writing tasks to awareness of how they are working on text in both activities. We know when they are becoming aware of how they are responding because we can watch them problem solving "the hard bits" in the texts, and this has its own way of making a learner aware. If we listen to the children verbalizing about what they are doing, it is not easy to determine whether learners are merely mimicking the teacher's talk or reflecting on the productive responding. Some children reveal their thinking to the teacher; others learn well but find the reflection difficult. Hard-to-teach children often begin as passive learners, but as independence in problem solving increases, they begin to talk about what they are doing and reveal to the teacher the generative links between their experience and their literacy work. Once children begin to comment on what they are doing and why, using some of the language of the lesson, the dialogue between teacher and learner about how the tasks can be carried out improves. But with novice learners who have little successful experience in related domains, a direct call to articulate how they think and learn is very likely to result in refusals to initiate responses or in attempts to oblige the teacher. The early shifts in young children are from acts to awareness as productive responding increases to strategic use of what is learned; in some children this leads to metacognitive reflection. Perhaps this is another example of a language-specific aspect of cognitive functioning.

It is particularly inappropriate to ask learners what they are thinking about when what has to be learned involves fast perceptual decision making with minimum attention, or smooth and fast execution of skilled actions such as the visual-motor learning of directional behavior, and the visual perception of letters, letter clusters, and words. While I accept the Brunerian notion that the processes involved in perceptual and cognitive domains are similar (Bruner, 1957), young readers and writers must choose within a second which of the perceptual cues to use; there is no time for a slow cognitive debate and self-reflection. What the teacher hears is a comment that is an outcome of the child's thinking not the process itself. Examples abound: the boy who queried a test booklet with changed-around letter and word order, saying "Did you buy this book at a regular book-shop?" and the boy who found *and* in *landed* as well as in *sandwiches* and who said, in surprise, "Wow! there it is again, just like in the other book," as if he were just discovering how to work with letter clusters. Perceptual-motor aspects of literacy acquisition are impeded by an overdose of cognitive attention prompted by unnecessary teacher talk about "remembering" and "thinking", which can distract the human processor from the real purpose of the reading (Johnston, 1985). The successful learner with fast perceptual responding is free to give attention to the messages. Teachers might ask learners who are diverse and competent what they think they are doing or trying to do, but to ask hesitant nonachieving children to be metacognitive about their processes is unproductive. Reading Recovery teachers infer how children are working on print from recorded observations of behavior, and they must be tentative and wary of the errors in their inferences. What children say and how they understand or misunderstand the teacher provides interesting information, as do their commentaries on the stories they are reading and writing. The teacher may even arrange situations that reveal the ways in which the learners are thinking (Cazden, 1992).

Features Specific to Reading Recovery

What is necessary for Reading Recovery in addition to a theory of constructiveness? Beginning the program close to the onset of confusion, and limited variation of time allowed for the program (12 to 20 weeks) are specific to literacy learning. There is a growing sense among experienced trainers of Reading Recovery teachers that "a lesson every day" is essential if both teacher and learner are going to be able to tap yesterday's learning trace and consolidate it. On the other hand teachers must strive for generative outcomes: They want each child to learn how to work with certain features of print, and they require that once a "how to" is established, the learner, working independently but not without nudging, will apply it to new encounters with print. If teachers were to break the complex task into parts, taught separately, this would prevent the opportunity for complex decision making and orchestrating complex skilled actions. Teachers cannot proceed through a set sequence of learning if they are to allow the diverse learner to leap forward up the gradient of difficulty as soon as that child's processing strategies will permit this (which should be allowed to happen in good classroom teaching also).

Reading Recovery teachers work collaboratively with learners who are reading and creating printed texts; they explore the stories, prompt the children to problem-solve the detail and recall known responses, support the learner in meeting new challenges, foster independent attempts, accept approximations as moves toward new achievements, acknowledge shifts toward correct responding, applaud "mastery" because it frees attention for problem solving at the boundaries of knowledge, and raise task difficulty gradually. Throughout the program, the teacher knows that for ultimate success even the learner's weak areas of functioning must also contribute to performance. Teachers must ward off a student's dependency and release that student as an independent thinker and learner.

Teaching Individuals with Diversity in Mind

We are surrounded by human variability. When our own personal characteristics or those of our loved ones do not fit described stereotypes or sequences, we say, aha, yes, individuals vary. We think daily about divergence from normality when it comes to superiority—from sporting prowess and high intelligence, to talent and giftedness in art, music, and figure skating. We also accept differences in personal attributes: looks, physique, reaction time, need for sleep, visual perception, auditory perception, sight, hearing, muscle power, singing ability, and so forth. And we do this so readily that identical twins are strange and even disturbing to think about. We grossly underrate how different each child's history of learning opportunities has been, how much families differ, and how we have each been closed out from certain experiences in life. In this sense literacy instruction must be culturally responsive.

Education has responded to diverse learners by slowing down the pace of learning and simplifying the content. But techniques have also been invented to teach complex things to diverse learners. In literacy learning this means helping learners to perform complex activities, moving up a steep gradient of difficulty while maintaining success. In addition to a constructivist view of cognition, we need a theory that views literacy learning as a complex task directed to messages in continuous texts. In particular, knowing what successful learners learn to do as they move up a gradient of difficulty in texts would allow teachers to help diverse students make the same kinds of shifts, although not necessarily through similar lessons.

If hard-to-teach children are also to become literate, we also need (1) theory about the psychological competencies that make up the substructure of effective performance (including language learning and perceptual learning), (2) theory about the influence of social contexts on learning and about teaching interactions, (3) theory about training teachers to use large teaching repertoires from which they select for diverse learners, and (4) theories about implementing effective programs in education systems. Delivery of an effective early intervention program like Reading Recovery draws upon large bodies of such theory.

Reading Recovery teachers accept all as potential learners and find each learner's starting point. They observe how children work on easy tasks when everything goes well; they spend extended time responding to children's initiatives and interacting with their thoughtfulness; they observe learners closely as they work on novel things, always prepared to be surprised by talent they had not predicted. This personalized analysis includes identifying strengths that will provide the "firm ground" on which to build while tentatively exposing the learner to challenge in the weak areas. The activities, the books, the progressions made by the children have to remain free to vary with the idiosyncratic progress of a particular child, and the lesson framework is designed to allow for this. Emphases in tomorrow's lesson will arise out of today's observations but will be used in the context of the child's engagement with tomorrow's authentic tasks of reading and writing stories. Teaching interactions change from one child to another so that all these activities will be realized differently by a teacher with each of the four to six pupils taught daily.

Reading Recovery teachers need a vast repertoire of alternative teaching moves to bring diverse children to classroom competencies and further independent literacy learning. That calls for training over and above that required for quality classroom teaching. The principles of constructivism and an enhanced repertoire of teaching alternatives are new to most Reading Recovery teachers when they begin training: They need to become interactive experts who support children who are constructing a literacy system. Their year-long in-service course runs in parallel with their first year of working with hard-to-teach children. It takes a year of practice and discussion for their teaching to become responsive to diversity in their pupils. Faced with a puzzling pupil, they brainstorm possible ways to work with that child. How can such teachers be kept at a peak level of tentativeness and flexibility in designing their lessons for diverse individuals? The average expectations and subgroup stereotypes that creep back into the thinking of Reading Recovery teachers have to be challenged to prevent them from doing what they do so well—which is to search for common characteristics and disregard the uncommon. It is imperative that teachers remain responsive to the individual variability of children, and that they teach in response to this variability. Their decisions need to be tentative judgments that they can readily change in response to interactions with learners. Tentativeness and flexibility are bywords of the program. This is why Reading Recovery encourages communication networks between teachers, schools, tutors, trainers, and countries—professionals who support each other in the ongoing processes of problem solving.

Classroom teachers are probably correct in arguing that the demands and ambiguities of classroom instruction cannot be informed by what goes on in such special delivery conditions. Fortunately, classroom teachers have many constructive learners among their students who work with, rather than against, the teacher to negotiate understanding. If the newer theories of cognitive development lead to more focus on the quality of teacher-child exchanges in classrooms and on individual differences, then the experience of Reading Recovery may be more generally applicable. For example, the experience of Reading Recovery might inform some shift toward more personalized teaching interactions in the classrooms of the future and encourage a closer monitoring of learners at the time they begin to work on new subjects such as foreign languages, particular sciences, and branches of mathematics. But the Reading Recovery model of accommodating diversity has the most to offer in fields of special education, where inclusion or mainstreaming policies operate for the hard-of-hearing, for those labeled by "someone" as "dyslexic," "learning disabled," or "slow."

References

Allington, R. (1984). Content coverage and contextual reading in reading groups. *Journal of Reading Behavior, 16,* 85–95.

Bruner, J. (1957). On perceptual readiness. *Psychological Review, 64,* 123–152.

Bruner, J. (1990). *Acts of meaning.* Cambridge: Harvard University Press.

Cazden, C. B. (1988). *Classroom discourse: The language of teaching and learning.* Portsmouth, NH: Heinemann.

Cazden, C. B. (1992). *Whole language plus: Essays on literacy in the United States and New Zealand.* New York: Teachers College Press.

Clay, M. M. (1982). *Observing young readers.* Portsmouth, NH: Heinemann.

Clay, M. M. (1985). Reading Recovery: Systemic adaptation to an educational innovation. *New Zealand Journal of Educational Studies, 22* (1), 35–58.

Clay, M. M. (1987). Learning to be learning disabled. *New Zealand Journal of Educational Studies, 22* (2), 155–173.

Clay, M. M. (1990). Developmental learning puzzles me. *Australian Journal of Reading, 14* (4), 263–276.

Clay, M. M. (1991). *Becoming literate: The construction of inner control.* Auckland, New Zealand: Heinemann Education.

Clay, M. M. (1993). *Reading Recovery: A guidebook for teachers in training.* Auckland, New Zealand: Heinemann Education.

Clay, M. M. and Cazden, C. B. (1990). A Vygotskian interpretation of Reading Recovery. In L. B. Moll (Ed.), *Vygotsky and education* (pp. 203–222). New York: Cambridge University Press. Reprinted in Cazden (1992).

Clay, M. M. and Oates, R. E. (1985). Round about twelve: Studies of Form 2 children in 1978. Auckland, New Zealand: University of Auckland Education Department.

Ferreiro, E. and Teberosky, A. (1982). *Literacy before schooling.* Portsmouth, NH: Heinemann.

Gaffney, J. and Anderson, R. (1991). Two-tiered scaffolding: Congruent processes of teaching and learning. Technical Report No. 523, Center for the Study of Reading, University of Illinois at Urbana-Champaign.

Gentry, J. R. (1978). Early spelling strategies. *Elementary School Journal, 79,* 88–92.

Gittleman, R. (1985). Controlled trials of remedial approaches to reading disability. *Journal of Child Psychology and Psychiatry, 26,* 843–846.

Hansen, V. R. and Robenhagan, O. (1993). *Abdullah's genuine Indonesian curry powder.* Copenhagen: The Danish National Institute for Educational Research.

Johnston, P. H. (1985). Understanding reading disability: A case study approach. *Harvard Educational Review, 55,* 153–177.

Learning Media. (1992). *Dancing with a pen.* Wellington, New Zealand: Ministry of Education.

Levin, H. (1990). Building school capacity for effective teacher empowerment: Applications to elementary schools with at-risk students. Stanford, CA: Stanford University School of Education.

Levin, I. and Korat, O. (1993). Sensitivity to phonological, morphological and semantic cues in early reading and writing in Hebrew. *Merrill-Palmer Quarterly, 39* (2), 213.

Levin, I. and Tochinsky-Landsmann, L. (1989). Becoming literate: Referential and phonetic strategies in early reading and writing. *Merrill-Palmer Quarterly, 12* (3), 369–384.

Lewin, K. (1954). Behavior and development as a function of the total situation. In L. Carmichael (Ed.), *Manual of child psychology.* New York: Wiley.

Lindfors, J. W. (1987). *Children's language and learning.* Englewood Cliffs, NJ: Prentice-Hall.

McNaughton, S. (1995). *Patterns of emergent literacy: Development and transition.* Auckland, New Zealand: Oxford University Press.

Nicholson, T. (1985). Experts and novices: A study of reading in the high school classroom. *Reading Research Quarterly, 19* (4), 436–451.

Pogrow, S. (1990a). Challenging at-risk students: Findings from the HOTS program. *Phi Delta Kappan* (pp. 389–397).

Pogrow, S. (1990b). A Socratic approach to using computers with at-risk students. *Educational Leadership* (pp. 61–66).

Resnick, L. B. and Resnick, D. P. (1990). *Tests as standards of achievement in schools.* Proceedings of the Educational Testing Service Invitational Conference on the Uses of Standardized Tests in American Education. Princeton: ETS.

Scriven, M. (1975). Problems and prospects for individualization. In H. Talmage (Ed.), *Systems of individualized education* (pp. 199–210). Chicago: National Society for the Study of Education Yearbook.

Shephard, L. (1991). Negative policies for dealing with diversity: When does assessment and diagnosis turn into sorting and segregation. In E. Hiebert (Ed.), *Literacy for a diverse society: Perspectives, practices and policies* (pp. 279–298). New York: Teachers College Press.

Stallman, A. and Pearson, D. (1990). Formal measures of early literacy. In L. M. Morrow and J. K. Smith (Eds.), *Assessment for instruction in early literacy* (pp. 7–44). Englewood Cliffs, NJ: Prentice-Hall.

Stanovich, K. E. (1986). Matthew effects in reading: Some consequences of individual differences in the acquisition of literacy. *Reading Research Quarterly, 21* (4), 360–406.

Valsiner, J. (1987). *Culture and the development of children's action.* Chichester, England: Wiley.

11

Writing and Learning to Write

GUNTHER KRESS

Introduction

Questions of literacy may be dealt with in a variety of ways: from a formal, linguistic point of view; from a historical point of view; comparatively; ethnographically, anthropologically; and so on. In an educationally and developmentally focused approach to the issues of writing and the learning of writing, a social and cultural theory of representation is an essential context. It provides the possibility of an understanding of the actions of children in their engagement with the conventionally saturated system of representation of writing, and, at the same time, a possibility of understanding the crucial characteristics of the challenges which they face in doing so. Both are prerequisites for the development of curricula of writing and the pedagogies best suited for their implementation. The theoretical approach that I adopt is a social semiotic one. It treats the making of signs as an action most plausibly explained in terms of the social structures and cultural systems in which makers of signs act in communication. Crucially, this approach has to deal seriously with the complex matter of *affect*, as a central, continuous modalization of all semiotic activity.

There are several points I wish to focus on. Two are fundamental. First, children come to writing as thoroughly experienced makers of meanings and of signs in any medium that is at hand. The huge range of semiotic media which they employ as a matter of course is not taken up in schooling, where there is instead a focus on the single medium of lettered representation—"literacy"—with some attention to and perhaps encouragement of (though less and less so through the years of schooling) other forms, such as painting, drawing, building, and play of various kinds. Second, children's signs are motivated conjunctions of meaning and form; that is, the forms (and materiality) of signs made by children are, for them, sufficiently expressive of the meanings which they intend to make. They are, literally, *full* of meaning. With that disposition they come to writing, which has, to the learner, all the aspects of a system of arbitrarily constructed signs. This is at odds with their own sense of what signs are and how they work. Moreover, those whose task it is to facilitate their path into writing share a now firmly entrenched common sense about the arbitrariness of signs and of language in particular.

Not surprisingly, this presents some child-learners with a huge barrier. I will

Figure 11.1   *"This is a car." Drawing by a three-year-old boy.*

deal with aspects of that problem, focusing on the characteristics of signs, and on the child's disposition or habitus to signs. The question of the assumed arbitrariness of signs, especially in writing, is one central issue. A second issue arises for the child at this point of transition, and often lasts late into periods of schooling and into adult life: the issue of the distinctively different syntactic and textual organization of speech and writing, and its effects on the learning of writing. My approach is to treat children as competent and practiced makers of signs in many semiotic modes; and to attempt to understand, from that point of view, the problems they encounter in learning to write.

The topic of this chapter is *writing.* However, there exists by now a relatively secure consensus that writing cannot be understood or theorized without an understanding of reading, for reading provides the occasion for children's learning how others in the culture use signs. Reading and writing are aspects of a single cognitive and semiotic complex. My reasons for including a brief section on reading are, simply, to reassert that continuity, and to give some brief indication of what place that cognitive/semiotic complex has in my account. Importantly, there is for me the crucial question of what evidence one can get for "readings"; and what that evidence can then be used for.

A Social Semiotic Theory of Representation

The drawing presented in Figure 11.1 was made by a three-year-old boy. Sitting on his father's lap he talked about the drawing as he was doing it. "Do you want to watch me? I'll make a car. . .got two wheels. . .and two wheels at the back. . .and two wheels here. . .that's a funny wheel." When he had finished, he said "This is a car."

I had become interested in understanding visual representations and had begun to keep the drawings, doodlings, etc., of our two children. I had begun to take photographs of arrangements of toys, Lego-block constructions, spaceships made from chairs and blankets and cushions. This was the first time that the three-year-old had named a drawing, and it was this which initially proved puzzling to me. How was this a car? Of course, he had provided me with the key to an understanding of this drawing, through his commentary—"Here's a wheel. . . ." For him a car, clearly, was first and foremost defined by the criterial characteristic of having wheels. His representation focused on that aspect of the object to be represented, and he had the means available to him for representing the criterial features of *car*, namely wheels, or "wheelness."

Wheels may in any case be a plausible criterial feature of cars for many three-year-olds. A three-year-old's gaze is likely to fasten on wheels as he or she walks up to a car; the wheel's action—on a toy car as on a real car—is perhaps the most prominently describable feature; and so on. So a three-year-old's *interest* in cars may plausibly be condensed into and expressed as an interest in wheels. Wheels are plausibly represented by circles, both in terms of their physical visual appearance and in terms of a mimetic representation—the circular motion of the hand in making the circle mimetically repeating the action of the wheel in going "round and round."

This is the first time that I have seen a car represented in this form. My hypothesis is that all three-year-olds (and indeed everyone else) in drawing a car (or anything else) act precisely in this fashion; a representation/sign arises out of their *interest* at that moment, and in its formal aspects it plausibly represents those features of the object that the child regards as criterial of that object at that moment. This interest is always, even at this early stage, complex, arising out of physiological, psychological, emotional, and cultural factors, and it is focused by specific factors in the context in which the sign is being made. These aspects of the object are taken as being fully, adequately, or sufficiently representative. It is never "the whole object" which is represented, but only ever certain criterial aspects. These are represented in the most apt, plausible available fashion in and with some representational medium (drawing; chairs and blankets; Lego-blocks; language; etc.).

This is the process of the constitution of metaphor, in two steps; "a car is (most like) wheels," and "wheels are (most like) circles." The semiotic means whereby these structures are established is that of analogy; the result is a (double) metaphor: circles are ([like] wheels; wheels are [criterial of]) a car. Signs are the result of metaphoric processes in which analogy is the constitutive principle. Analogy is a process of classification: X is like Y (in criterial ways). Metaphors are classificatory statements, and as such are crucial in cultural, social, and cognitive ways. Existing social relations, particularly of power, between makers of sign/metaphors govern what metaphors carry the day and pass into semiotic systems as "natural," neutral expressions. Children are, like adults, ceaselessly engaged in the construction of metaphors; unlike adults they are, on the one hand less constricted by culture, by already existent metaphoric arrangements, and on the other hand, usually in a position of lesser power, so that their metaphor/signs are less likely to carry the day.

Signs are motivated conjunctions of signifiers (forms) and signifieds (meanings). Makers of signs use apt forms for the expression of their meaning, in any medium in which they make signs. When children treat a cardboard box as a pirate ship, they are making a sign in which the material form (the box) is an apt medium for the expression of the meaning (the pirate ship), because what they regard as the criterial aspects of "pirate ship"—"containment," "mobility," etc., are aptly expressed in the form of the box. Language is no exception; all linguistic form is used in a motivated (nonarbitrary) manner in the expression of meaning. For children in the preschool years, there is both more and less freedom of expression. More, because they have not yet learned to confine the making of signs to the culturally and socially facilitated media; and more, too, because they are relatively unconstrained in the making of signs through being unaware of convention. Less, because they do not have the rich cultural semiotic resources available with which to make signs.

So when a boy, laboring to climb a steep slope, says, "This is a heavy hill," he is constrained by not having the word "steep" as an available semiotic resource. The same is the case with the semiotic resources of syntax, and of textual form. "Heavy" in "heavy hill" is, however, a motivated sign; the child has focused on particular aspects of climbing the hill ("it takes a lot of energy, it is exhausting") and uses an "available form" which is apt as an expression of his meanings.

Making use of "what is available" is the ruling strategy for children, and one way for the parent, teacher, or educator/theorist of viewing their activity. But that is both too limiting a view, and a distortion which misses the central aspect of all sign making, especially that of children. "Availability" as the central focus is not the issue. In its usual senses it belongs to an "acquisition" model of language learning. Children—like adults—make their own resources of representation *out of* what is available: They are not acquired but *are made* by the individual sign maker. Putting it differently: "Availability" either as simple repetition or as imitation, is a misperception of the child's action. "Imitation" is always a remaking, however slight. The available resources constitute the stuff from which we constantly refashion our representations.

Even the simple representation of the car above has a history of constant remaking and transformation, from initial "circular scribbles," via a gradual generalization toward "circular shape," to the production of circles. The movement from "circular scribbles" to circles is clear enough, in the drawings produced over a ten-month period, as is the cognitive, conceptual, transformative work done by the child in that time. The child *developed* the representational resources which were then "available" to him when he came to do the car drawing. This also suggests why "circles" had such an aptness as a means of expressing his meaning; the expressive, energetic motion of circular scribbles, the physicality of this motion, persists in the child's development/transformation of this representational resource, so that (circular) motion is still a part of the meaning of circle/wheel, and of the wheels/car.

Children are the makers of their "own" representational resources, as a part of the constant production of signs of any kind, of any size, in which previously produced signs are transformed into new signs, and previously produced "sign-substance" is transformed in the production of new signs. As children are drawn into culture, their transformative practice is more and more applied to materials that are already culturally formed and which are encountered through reading and writing. In this way, children are the agents of their own cultural and social construction. The transformative, productive stance toward the making of signs is at the same time a transformation of the signmaker's subjectivity. Certain of the sign-making practices of children are noticed by adults around them; and certain of these (i.e., language, drawing, building) are valued. Many are not noticed, and not valued, or are relegated to the category of "play," for instance. Those which are valued become subject to the regulatory intervention of culture and of society. Of these, the child's encounter with language and literacy receive the most attention from adults, and these are therefore most subjected to regulation. The child's semiotic habitus is not recognized in most institutional settings. Worse, the folk-theoretical notions which most adults (including teachers, academics, and professionals in the health and welfare field) bring to these questions can lead to pedagogies and to curricula which are fundamentally mismatched with the dispositions of the child-learners.

Of course, this field is in any case always subject to the regulatory forces of social systems: to forms of political organization and their ideological effects.

Characteristics of Speech and of Writing

One of the insights of socially oriented theories of language is the variation of linguistic form with variation of social context. Accounts differ, ranging from correlation—"linguistic feature x or language form x correlates with social context y"—to determination—"linguistic feature x or language form x is produced by social actors y or by social context y." A social semiotic approach takes the latter position, which can be characterized as follows.

1. The requirements of *communication* are such that the participants in communication will wish to make their messages maximally understandable for a particular situation. This necessitates that each participant chooses forms of expression which are potentially maximally transparent to the other participants. As communication is a social action, it takes place in social structures which are inevitably marked by power-difference. This affects how each participant understands the notion of "maximal understanding." A participant who is able, through excessive power, to force others, willfully, into greater efforts of interpretation, has a different notion of "maximal understanding" than a participant who makes every effort to produce messages/signs which require minimal efforts of interpretation or to a participant who through lack of command of the resources of the representational system—a child, or a learner of a new language—produces messages/signs which take greater effort of interpretation. In the latter case the possibility rests with the other participants either to make the effort or not, to make the effort required to interpret that message/sign, whether this is in a school, or in a railway station in a country where one does not speak the language.

The effects of communication act as constant pressure in this, for children as for adults: "success" and "failure" each have their effects on the next making of signs, in differing ways.

2. The requirements of *representation* are that I, as the maker of a representation/sign, choose an apt, plausible form for the expression of my meaning—a form for the representation of the object, event, state of affairs that I have in mind. The earlier examples are instances: circles to stand for wheels, and wheels to stand for car; "heavy" to stand for "significant effort," and "significant effort" to stand for the action required in climbing the steep slope of the hill. When I as a learner of French attempt to express myself, my lack of syntactic and lexical knowledge leads me, with the same strategy, into exactly the same situation: I choose the nearest most plausible form that I have for the expression of the meaning that I have. My assessment of my success or failure acts as a pressure to find more apt means of expression—from my phrase book, from my French grammar, or from a helpful bystander.

The requirements of representation in usual circumstances are no different; they are simply less apparent. The *interest* of the makers of the representation/sign at the moment of the making of the sign leads them to choose an aspect, or a bundle of aspects, of the object to be represented, as being criterial at that moment, for the representation of an object, and they then choose the most plausible, the most apt available *form* for its representation.

These two aspects of a message, the communicational and the representational, are central to any understanding of the representations made by children, right through their years of schooling; they provide insights into their actions, and into the difficulties which they face in their engagement with schooling. They are central in understanding the processes of learning. More immediately, they explain the differences in the formal organization of language in the spoken and in the written mode and the meanings expressed in these formal differences. For the child-learner, the two concerns—here separated as the differential organization of language in speech and writing, and the production of sign-messages—are at all times connected, in learning and in everyday communication. The central consideration in both is the *interest* of the producer of the message, and the interests of communities of producers of messages which express themselves as the (histories of) conventions of codes. Learning to write is a matter of bringing both kinds of interest together.

The social contexts of speech and writing differ in fundamental ways, and so do their psychological, cognitive contexts. The materiality of the semiotic medium of representation is an additional issue. These factors have, over longer historical periods, given rise to a broad coincidence of features of the spoken unit: a unit of not too great a length given the limitations of short-term memory; from the point of view of the physiology of speech production, the breath-unit. This forms the basis of the informational unit, which relies on pitch variation, "lowering and raising the voice" to mark information of greater or lesser prominence. Because of the knowledge structures characteristic of participants in spoken interactions, this prominence is usually used to mark information which is treated as *new* to the interlocutor as more prominent (by being "new" rather than assumed to be shared, "given"). Lastly, this unit is *about* something; it encodes some event, or a relation between objects in the world which is represented. In languages such as English this is always a unit consisting of some verbal process joined with one or more nominal entities, presented as a coherent, single conceptual entity: "Last night it rained a lot" (with three nominal entities related more or less directly to the process "rained"), in other words, a *clause.*

The materiality of the medium of sound entails that *succession,* the sequence of one element after another temporally, is the fundamental semiotic factor of speech. This forms the organizational logic of speech: One thing has to be said after another. Whatever conceptual structures a speaker has in mind, he or she is bound by the logic of sequence in time. Oral cultures invent elaborate devices to overcome or circumvent this fundamental factor, but this simply illustrates the semiotic effort necessary to do so. (In some literate Western cultures, the major semiotic effort of the "cultured person" consists in using the hierarchical structures of writing in speaking.)

These coincidences produce a characteristic formal organization of language in the spoken mode (always assuming the absence of circumventory strategies) of *a single clause*; which functions as an *information unit*; joined by various means (intonation, and often lexically through conjunctions of various kinds) to the next unit of *single clause/information unit.* Characteristically, these tend to be, in monologic speech-genres, quite long "chains," with overarching conceptual/textual structuring—speech-paragraphs. In speech-genres of a dialogic kind, the structures are formed by all the participants, always in accordance with generic rules which are well understood (though not necessarily adhered to!) by fully competent speakers.

Conceptual development takes place by sequence, elaboration, restatement, and repetition nuanced by a complex system of conjunctive devices of which intonation may be the most developed and elaborated one. Although most mainstream linguistic theories (and folk-linguistics) still focus primarily on sentences, language always occurs as discourse. Children meet language, always, as discourse. An early question for a literacy curriculum is therefore about the typical speech-genres, and their formal characteristics, which a particular child or group of children or community of children bring as their linguistic resources to the learning of writing. Children who typically participate more in dialogic speech-genres at home or in their peer groups may be disadvantaged in relation to children who have experience of genres of a more monologic kind, in a society which values writing above speech and therefore values broadly monologic forms above the dialogic.

For writing, the limitations of temporality and sequence are far less significant, and often replaced by processes of complex syntactic design, such as embedding, developed through careful editing. The limitations on the size of the unit in speech imposed simultaneously by physiology, psychology, and sociology are thus more or less absent. I say "more or less," because on the one hand for very many speakers the structures of speech continue to form a substratum of writing—as evidenced in patterns of punctuation, for instance (see Kress, in press); on the other hand, it is to some significant extent a matter of individual discretion as to where, on a hypothetical continuum between more speech-like and more writing-like structures, writers wish to locate their writing (or their speech, for highly literate speakers). The materiality of the medium of writing is visual; and temporality is replaced by spatiality. The logic of temporal sequence is replaced by the logic of (an abstract) spatial arrangement: hierarchy. Conceptual development takes place by the production of complex, hierarchical interrelations of clausal units, with embedding rather than conjunctions being the characteristic mode.

To make this point more concrete, consider the following sequence, which illustrates the gradual stages of integration of clausal units into a syntactically integrated sentence. It is based on an actual example from a text on mass communication, which appears as (3) in this series of transformations:

1. "That rejection casts us out to sea on the question 'What might that relationship be?'"
2. "That rejection casts us out to sea on the question 'What might that relationship be.'"
3. "That rejection casts us out to sea on the question of what might that relationship be."
4. "That rejection casts us out to sea on the question of what that relationship might be."
5. "That rejection casts us out to sea on the question what that relationship might be."

The sequence from the (hypothetical) initial form, where the two clauses are brought into loose conjunction, via the actual example through a succession of small steps, in each of which the two clauses are somewhat more closely integrated, to the final structure in which one clause is clearly subordinated to the other, represents cognitive and semiotic work which is typical of writing. There is another point which I will simply touch on: What has caused the writer of form (3) to stop the process of integration at precisely this point? What cognitive/intellectual position is coded by this form?

These characteristically hierarchical structures, sentences, have a motivation of two kinds. One is the writer's wish to produce a conceptual structure adequate to his or her intention: "What I regard as the appropriate conceptual and communicational entity." The other is the need to produce entities which are appropriate to the larger generic textual structures which the writer is developing. The sentence arises out of the contingencies of two logics: one is the logic of overall textual development; within this there is the second logic of the conceptual development of the constituent elements of the text—namely, the sentence.

Writing is the medium of overtly monologic genres. The requirements of the reader in writing unlike in speech, are not a primary consideration. The knowledge structures obtaining between participants in a communicational situation recede as a significant element and are replaced by the requirements of the appropriate hierarchical conceptual structure of the text.

Technological developments are bringing about fundamental changes in some of the hitherto relatively stable social contexts of speech and writing. At the same time, certain social developments have, over the last two or three decades, made aspects of generic forms dependent on stable configurations of power less stable. These changes are producing effects on the structures of writing; they are difficult to foresee but need to be borne in mind in the design of literacy curricula. To mention two: (1) electronic forms of communication are producing what until now seemed a paradoxical situation—namely, the physical separation but communicational copresence of two interlocutors; and (2) the increasing prominence of visual communication is having effects not only on the social status of writing—which is becoming less central in many contexts—but also on the formal aspects of writing. The change in the status of writing, from a central medium of information to the medium of commentary on the visual, is producing far-reaching changes in genres of writing, and through these on formal aspects of writing, including its syntax.

Children come to writing with the formal resources of speech, unequally, with different experiences of generic forms of speech; some are more usable as platforms for the production of the signs of writing than others. Agency lies with the individual in writing, and with a group (of at least two) in speech. Above all, the child's *interest* in the making of signs in writing has to be fostered or produced; often children are expected to produce writing when their interest is not in that direction.

Writing initially presents itself as (and indeed *is* at one level) a system of signs of arbitrary construction. Given that children come to this stage as makers of motivated signs, this is incomprehensible to the child. The fact that this problem is not recognized is yet another barrier. I will take this up in detail later in this chapter.

In the previous section I pointed out that the most useful metaphor for the child's learning in the domain of representation is that of (own) production rather than that of acquisition. The learning of writing proceeds in that fashion: employing the strategy of using the most apt available form of expression for a particular meaning—in making motivated signs—children use such representational means as they have available for making that meaning. This allows us to see children's signs as arising from their interest in using what they have as available representational means, and as therefore *fully* meaningful in every sense; and to understand children's actions as being productive/transformative of their own representational resources. The role of the teacher and of the literacy curriculum is to make available new representational resources for child-learners to use in their transformative making of new resources. This is how teachers "move children on," in a Vygotskian and Freirian sense. This is also how children are drawn into culture, and actively produce their path into culture using the resources of an existing culture.

Let us take, as an example, one child's developing understanding of the two connected matters of textual structures and of the sentence. The resources which she brings to this task are those of language as speech. This includes generic structures, such as texts of sequenced events—"stories," narratives, accounts of happenings, understandings of narrative structures of the kind she may have learned from being read to—and also texts of an interactive, dialogic kind; it also includes the resources of "text-internal" grammatical structuring, of clause-chains, and of clause-internal structures. These are discussed at some length in *Learning to Write* (Kress, 1994). Here I will give two brief examples of what is at issue. The text below was written by an eight-year-old girl.

Birds

(1) I have not got a bird but I know some things about them. (2)—The have tow nostrils and They clean Ther feather and They eat seeds, worms, bread cuddle fish, and lots of other things. (3) and they drink water. (4) When he drinks he Puts his head up and it gose down. and a (5) A budgie cage gets very dirty and peopel clean it.

Three questions can be asked of this text: (1) What representational, literacy resources does this writer have available to her, as her available means for written representation? (2) How does this writer use these resources to make new signs? (3) What changes happen—that is, what new representational resources are produced by her as a result of her sign-making activity? She has available the resources of the grammar of speech: simple clauses, simply conjoined. She uses this resource to make the new sign of sentence: she joins clauses to produce rudimentary sentences. The principle for this clause-conjunction seems to be to put topically integral elements into one unit. This has a potential effect on sentence structures, so that at a later stage closer clausal integration can take place—for instance, by deleting repeated pronouns: "They clean their feathers and (they) eat seeds." There is evidence of her thinking about this precise issue of what constitutes a sentence, in the transition from sentence 4 to sentence 5. She had conjoined "and they drink water" to sentence 2 but then decided that "eating" is an action significantly different from "drinking," so that on her own principle of classification "and they drink water" deserves to be a sentence in its own right.

We can thus ask, "Are the grammatical resources of the grammar of speech apt, suitable for the expression of the conceptual and textual meaning which she wishes to construct?" The answer is: "They are the most apt, the best available resources at this stage—and in the process of the making of the new grammatical sign of sentence (and the new semiotic signs of these particular units of meaning) she is fashioning new representational and semiotic resources."

The next example is an extract from a text produced as part of a "project" by a nine-year-old girl.

Building Material

The building material was very simple because Mylor has lots of gold mines they soon found that stone was available in lots of placese and easy to get.

Another comonx common building material was wood because the amount of tressx trees around Mylor most of the land around was full of tressx trees and they were easy to get.

But they needed xsomething to Ix put inbetween the stone and wood they found mud but you could only get it in the winter so they looked harder then they found clay which was the best.

The clause-grammar used by this writer is similar to that of the text just discussed in many respects. The principle of sentence construction is topical integrity; and generally there are simple clauses either adjoined and/or intonationally linked in the child's prior or simultaneous spoken representation: "the amount of trees around Mylor most of the land around was full of trees. . ."; or linked by conjunctions: "around was full of trees *and* they were easy to get."

The transitions between the sentences are semantically stronger here than in the previous example; that is, the *internal* coherence of units within sentences is stronger than coherence of units across sentence boundaries.

There are however also marked differences between this and the preceding example. Conjunctions such as "because" show a conceptual development, from sequence (of whatever kind—temporal or listing) to causality. The sentence "Most people think that Goyder was the founder of Mylor but he wasn't" has three clauses, with one clause ("that Goyder was the founder of Mylor") syntactically embedded to its main clause "Most people think" and the last clause conjoined by the adversative conjunction "but." "Syntactic embedding" describes, at the level of form, conceptual and cognitive processes of a hugely significant kind, ranging from the distinction of "my thought versus other's thought" to the complex interpenetration of both, to the development of "distance" (of perspective), which itself is crucial in the development of metalanguages.

This is a shift of a significant kind from the "Birds" example, and similar to the incorporation of the complex noun phrases "the drainage of the South East," "the planting of Pinus Radiata" from a part not quoted above. These nominalizations are complex in their overt structure (the result of transformations from fuller clausal structures "The South East was drained by him"); and even though they are "lifted" from the model text which has been provided by the teacher (a brief local amateur history), they make the point about the extension of the set of available resources very well. They are more than merely lifted: the awkwardness of their use here shows an incorporation by a child-writer of a *part* of another text into her own text. It is both a novel use for this writer, and a change to her set of available resources.

Model	*Child's Text*
(1). . .the then South Australian Surveyor-General, Mr. Goyder. . .	(1). . .Goyder was the founder of Mylor.
	. . .He was South Australia's Surveyor General.
(2). . .his interest in drainage in the South East and the planting of the Pinus Radiata were also recommended by him.	(2) The drainage of the South East and the planting of Pinus Radiata.
	It was recommended by him.

This brief example points to a change of what a sentence is and can be for her. The writer who can use these sentence forms, and who is beginning to engage the complex syntax of forms such as "the drainage of the South East" has pretty adequate control of the syntactic literacy resources of adult writing. In that process she has transformed herself in fundamental ways; she has also, and this is less obviously so and certainly less visible, transformed the representational resources which had been made available to her by her teacher.

Representational Resources and Subjectivity

The reigning view of language during this century has been a particular reading of Saussure's *Course in General Linguistics*: language as a system beyond the effect of the individual language user, who makes use of the system (*langue*) but, who, in its use (*parole*) does not produce any changes in the system. Although Saussure himself was intensely interested in history, those who produced the hegemonic reading of Saussure's ideas focused on the ahistorical aspects of Saussure's theory, thus enabling, indeed legitimating, the production of a century of mainstream linguistic work in which language was severed from history and society, and from the effective action of individual language users. Of course, this is not an adequate description of the full range of linguistic work during this period (it ignores the work of Hjelmslev, of Prague School linguistics, of Firth and Halliday, and of American anthropologists and ethnographers such as Sapir and Hymes), but it will serve as an extremely rough but nevertheless usable sketch of the largely American mainstream in linguistics.

This hegemonic view has underpinned the notion of language acquisition by assuming (as in the varying models produced in the Chomskian school, which continue to be dominant) the existence of an innate mental predisposition to language more or less articulated (for instance, the influential notion of the "Language Acquisition Device"), in relation to which a specific language provides merely stimulus, input, context, or whatever metaphor expresses the specific view best. The task of the language learner is then to acquire this instance-language.

One constant effect of these approaches is precisely that implied in the acquisition metaphor, which on the one hand treats the system to be acquired as independent of the acquirer, and on the other treats the role of the acquirer as relatively inert: simply that of acquisition. There are more profound implications of this model, including its implicit notions of asocial individuality, of particular forms of sociality, and of subjectivity. "Acquisition" remains a dominant even if often implicit metaphor in psychology, pedagogy, etc.

An alternative view sees language as predominantly a socially, culturally, and historically produced system. While not denying that the particular structure of the brain makes human language possible, this alternative view holds that individual users of language—or of any other human system of representation—are users and *(re)makers* of that system of representation, out of their social and cultural histories and present positions, and out of their affective dispositions, their *interests* at the point of making signs. Individual interest, itself a condensation in complex ways of the interests of social groups, is constantly at work in the making

of each individual sign, and in the shaping of the individual's system of representation. Consequently the systems of representation are both the product of individual actions and the effect of the socially and culturally available resources. The
systems of representation of any social and cultural group are the effects of the
collective actions of individual makers of signs. Social and individual semiotic,
communicative, and representational activities are thus linked in a complex but
tightly integrated mesh.

The individual's semiotic work is cognitive work. It is transformative work in
the context of a constant "reading" of the relevant aspects of the semiotic environment. The context, so called, is semiotically speaking a rich texture of signs in
different semiotic modes, which is constantly *read* by an individual in terms of
constantly revised organizations of relevance. This highly focused, selective reading of complexes of signs forms part of the information which leads to the establishment of the individual's *interest* at any particular moment, which is criterial in
the production of signs as representation and as communication. The cognitive/
semiotic process of sign making constantly alters the conceptual repertoire of the
individual, and in doing so alters the potential of cognitive action of the individual;
and the cognitive state of the individual. What is changed is the individual's *subjectivity*. The child who has produced the representational resource of "circles" is,
in a cognitive sense, not the same as the individual who previously had available
to him "circular scribbles." His potential for producing meaning has increased and
altered; a change has occurred in who he *is* and who he *can be*; a change produced by the child for himself. Changed subjectivities entail changed potentials for
identity—where "identity" indicates the production of a relatively stable external
display, a "persona," from a particular configuration of internal resources or states,
out of a given subjectivity. Representational resources are thus an alternative
aspect of subjectivity. A formal description of the semiotic repertoire of an individual is a description of the characteristics of subjectivity. "Development" has to
be seen in intimate connection with the possibilities of representation.

In the context of schooling it becomes important to understand the representa-
tional/cognitive potentials of the different semiotic modes, to understand both the
assembly of representational modes available to and used by children, and their
potentials of interaction. It has usually been assumed in mainstream educational
theories that cognition rests on language; or, if different representational modes
have been considered (painting, drawing, dancing, music, "play," etc.), it has been
assumed that each remains a discrete area of cognition and of individual action.
In nonmainstream theories and practices—in the work, for instance, of Steiner
and Montessori, among others—an integrated approach has formed the basis of
the foundation of schooling through teaching and learning.

"Mode of representation" and "subjectivity" are mutually interacting and interdependent. The potentials and limitations, the degree of development and articulation of each medium, make possible the individual's differential production of
subjectivity. Subjectivities are the products of the use of complexes of representational and communicational modes, and of their interaction, suffused by the
modalities of affect. This interaction is an effect of public regulations and valuations,

though individual dispositions are a significant factor: Despite the school system's emphasis on language and on writing in particular, some children grow up to be cartoonists, dancers, carpenters, physicists, painters, musicians, architects, designers, mathematicians; they insist on using other modes of representation as their favored modes of expression, representation, and communication.

The school's valuation of modes of representation and of communication meshes differentially with the value systems which different children bring to school. If a school values writing most highly, it may be less sensitive to the forms of language which children bring with them from backgrounds more oriented to the spoken form. The problems of a child's future path in the valued representational forms of schooling can be traced to these early periods, to their assessment by the child, and their effect on the child. The speech-writing difference—on a larger level the distinction between oral and literate cultures—is one major issue even in so-called literate societies, and it is slowly being recognized and theorized. The differential uses and valuations of other modes of communication and representation is less recognized; but it is an equally significant issue.

In multicultural societies, this problem is vastly increased, though not necessarily fully acknowledged. The formation of cohesive, if not unified societies rests, among other economic and political matters, on a full recognition of this factor— and schooling has a central part in this.

This "alternative account" places the production of subjectivity in the center, between social and cultural possibilities, and it forces on the one hand available resources and structures of power and on the other the individual's action in the making of signs. An issue such as gender-specific forms of communication can find an explanation here, resolving the paradoxical positions of "imposition" and "internalization" for instance. Children produce signs which reflect and encode their interests. It includes their "reading" of the semiotic environment; their criteria of relevance—which is where family structures, for instance, become so significant; and their interest in possibilities of communication. It may range from dispositions called "conformity" to "resistance"; it may be subversive or solidary. Whether in solidarity or in subversion, the production of the representational resources of children are intimately connected, in a relation of reciprocity, with *their* production of their subjectivity. The following two extracts (from economics essays written by two students in their final year of high school in the New South Wales education system) may provide some suggestions of the ongoing development of previously produced and learned gendered subjectivities; they are put forward here as one possible means of understanding these issues.

It is sometimes assumed that a more technically oriented school subject such as economics might suit boys better than girls (where "suit" is a complex and euphemistic term for the histories of gender arrangements in relation to school subjects). Yet the writer of Extract B, a young woman, produces a text that is more "fluent," than that of the male writer of Extract A. The female writer was given a grade of 18 out of 20; the male writer a grade of 12 out of 20. The "content" of each, the competence in the subject matter, was judged to be about the same by several economics teachers to whom I showed the two essays.

Extract A: Need for Tax Reform in Australia

The main pattern of the Australian tax system is a heavy reliance on income tax, it has a tendency to cause inflation. It also has relied on partly the Keynesian policies, the equity of the system has left something to be desired causing uneven income distribution and other problems. Recent suggestions for improving the system, which were outlined in the Sydney Morning Herald in "Tax and You" are a capital gains tax, Broad Based Indirect tax system, Retail tax, wealth tax and Gift and Death duties. All of the above taxes have major problems in trying to implement them.

The heavy reliance on personal income tax is because of the decreasing reliance on other taxes and it is a big revenue collector. From 1948 to 1983/84 it has increased approximately 9.2 percent, i.e. from 42 percent–51.2 percent. A decrease in company tax from 15.4 percent in 1948 to 10 percent in 1983/4 is because the government has tried to get the companies to increase production, eventually leading to an expanding economy.

The reason why this system causes inflation is because they tried to adopt old methods for different and new problems, i.e. Keynesian policies which were to get the government to increase revenue to companies in form of investment which needs increased production leads.

Extract B: Need for Taxation Reform in Australia Year 12

The recent call for taxation reform in Australia has been prompted by the fact that Australia's taxation system is becoming less equitable. Therefore, the major consideration for tax reform in Australia is the equity of the new system.

At present, Australia's tax system relies fairly heavily on the tax receipts from PAYE taxpayers. The past 35 years has seen an increasingly heavy burden bourn by income taxpayers. Their share of the total taxation revenue has increased from 42 percent in 1948/49 to 51.2 percent in 1983/84. This has been combined with a fall in taxation revenue from Company tax and customs duty. This heavy burden bourne by personal income taxpayers in Australia has been one of the major reasons for the call for tax reform. So, at present, we have a tax system that relies heavily on income tax.

The equity of Australia's tax system has also been questioned. Twenty years ago you had to earn 17.6 times the average weekly earnings (AWE) before you fell into the then top tax bracket of 66c in the dollar. Today this figure has fallen to approximately 2 times the AWE. This has meant that people in the middle income groups have fallen into the top tax bracket. So, in the past a pay rise for all Australian workers left the poor generally better off, didn't affect the rich much, but the middle income groups "got it in the neck." Their incomes (by no means gigantic) pushed them into the top bracket.

Without going into great descriptive detail here (for a fuller description, see Andrews, 1988), my account is as follows. The relative (social/gendered) valuations of speech and writing are different for young men and young women. In the peer groups of the young men, the (working-class) values attaching to speech are higher than those attaching to writing: whole clusterings of values around masculinity, identification with (oppositional) subgroupings (in relation to school, for instance), may dispose the male writer to feel uncomfortable with the syntax of written language. That unease emerges in the speech-like clausal syntax of the first two sentences of Extract A: the two clauses in the first sentence are weakly integrated, so are the first clause and the second (main) clause in the second sentence. Both sentences are fine when spoken, when intonation provides appropriate linking. To turn each of the two sentences into "proper" sentences very little needs to be done: A semicolon would mark an adequate writing-like relation; so would the conjunction "because." A broad constellation of sets of social values "means" that working-class speech in particular expresses values of masculinity. This makes it harder for the young man to produce for himself the full representational resources of written language; the kind of subjectivity associated with these are not what he wishes to develop. However, this is only one part of the case. His competence in and use of the technicist aspects of economics discourse—the technical terminology—is, if anything, greater than that of the young woman writer. (My account here is, I think, broadly in line with those of Trudgill, 1974, and Willis, 1978.)

The situation for the young woman may be that in her peer group there is no resistance to the production of the syntactic-grammatical forms of writing, and of its broader valuation. On the contrary, there may be value systems which are supportive of these. She produces for herself the full representational resources of the syntax of written language, in this instance in the school subject economics. With this comes a complex of conceptual/cognitive possibilities and of social values. In a sense, the grade is a reward for that at least as much as for her competence in economics. An analysis of this text reveals a fine, nuanced attention to interpersonal aspects of the social situation of writing and to modal discriminations in her argument. To give just an indication, the first two paragraphs are "formal" in tone, until the introduction in the last sentence of "we." This personalizing touch is confirmed in the use of "you" in the second sentence of the third paragraph; it is also intensified in the less formal "the poor," "the rich," and the " 'got it in the neck' " nicely distanced through the use of scare quotes. The effect is an address of the reader both formal and familiar, conveying an ease with the subject matter, and a confidently articulated position for the writer vis-a-vis her readers. Her use of "we" at the end of the second paragraph—after she has established a securely "objective" tone—and the use of "you" at the start of the third paragraph both prepare the way for the increasingly informal tone: for example, "left better off," "didn't," and the distanced yet informal " 'got it in the neck.' " It may be that these characteristics, too, have "feminine" valuations in her cultural group and society.

There are large consequences for the construction of curricula and for the development of pedagogies. Curricula as much as pedagogies are designs for subjectivities. This moves the whole debate from the "now" to the future, from questions of skills to questions of subjectivity, citizenship, and forms of society.

Learning to Write and Learning to Mean: Rethinking Preliteracy

While many educational thinkers and practitioners have been fully aware of the possibilities of cognitive development in representational modes other than language, a residual and basic commonsense position remains, equating, however implicitly, cognitive development with the development of language, spoken or written. Given another residual commonsense position in linguistic theory as in folk linguistics, which equates language with language in its written form ("grammar" as the grammar of language in its written form), there remains a deep-seated assumption that cognitive development, ability, equates with control of language in its written form: variants of "learning to write as learning to mean." I want to argue directly against this position. Cognitive development takes place through all forms of oral and written linguistic development, *and* through a vast range of many other representational means as well. Let me sketch some aspects of this alternative by means of two examples. To a large extent this is sketching an agenda for theorizing and research.

My first example consists of six drawings, made by a five-year-old boy, some commentary by him on these drawings (see Figure 11.2); and of a page from a school exercise book (see Figure 11.3).

The context in which they came about is as follows. On a summer Sunday afternoon, our five-year-old took a small, square notepad from next to the telephone, and, out in the garden, drew a picture on each of six pages. I had not taken any real notice of this, until I came across him in the hallway of our house, putting the cards "in order" on the floor, in pairs, as shown in Figure 11.2. When I asked him what he was doing, he said (for pictures 1 and 2 together): "The boy is in life//and the dog is in life//so that's alright"; (for 3 and 4): "The plane is in the air//and the flying bomb is in the air//so that's alright"; and (for 5 and 6) "The patterns are together."

Some two weeks later, at the end of that summer term, he brought home his exercise books. Among them was the page shown in Figure 11.3.

The task at issue here is classification; it had preceded the making of the images and their ordering, at home. What interests me is the sequence of production, transformation, and development. My hypothetical reconstruction of this series is something like this: the teacher *speaks* with the children about the task (language/speech); she introduces the book/page and *shows* them what is at issue ("demonstrating" with the physical object/the visual mode); the children use their pencils to *draw* the connecting lines (*an energetic manual action* as much as a semiotic act—as anyone who has seen a five-year-old holding a pen and making a line will appreciate). All this takes place in the classroom with the child in a particular affective state, which has its effects on how this activity is "read" and taken up by the child (with the *affective* as a modality on cognitive/semiotic processes). There may then be further *spoken* discussion by the teacher with the children; and some evaluatory comments. The school task is then completed. This is followed by a period of "silence"—at least two weeks when nothing is "seen" or "heard," but during which a complex series of transformative acts by the child continues "internally." This internal activity then becomes visible, literally, through the child's unprompted production of the drawings again, in a particular affective state, his unprompted classificatory activity, and his spoken commentary in response to his parent's question.

(a)

(b)

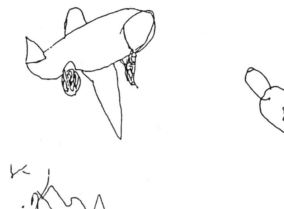

(c)

Figure 11.2 *Drawings by a five-year-old boy showing visual and spatial classification.*
(a) "Me and the dog are in life, so they're in the correct order." (b) "The flying bomb is in the air and the plane is in the air, so they're in the correct order." (c) "The patterns are in the correct order."

There is constant cognitive activity, involving a series of differing representational media, including, of course, "internal representations." The child is constantly productive, transformative; here this happens in part in response to resources made available by and tasks prompted by the teacher. This activity is not confined to the medium of language, and probably does not have language at its center as the major representational resource. The function of language lies not in cognition so much as in communication: from teacher to children; in internal

MIC HAEI

Draw a line to join the things which are the same.

Figure 11.3 *Joining like with like. Classification in a school exercise book.*

"dialogue," including dialogue and "traffic" between differing media; across different cognitive domains; from child to parent. This is a view of language not as the central medium of cognition, but as a necessary translation medium and as the medium of communication, as a kind of universal semiotic solvent.

In the end it is crucial to know what medium in this sequence of cognitive/semiotic transformations has what semiotic, cognitive possibilities, and has what effects. The complexities encoded in the images and in their classification might have been beyond the child's capacity of expression (or of conception/formulation) in spoken language. The visual medium offers possibilities of realization/expression and of cognition ahead of those available in the verbal. Once expressed, and classified in the visual, the meanings become available, in some part at least, for verbal expression. But their "expression" in the verbal mode constitutes a transformation precisely in terms of the categories of the verbal mode, in speech or writing.

The question of the representational and cognitive potential of the different modes and forms of representation is at the center of issues of learning, cognition, and subjectivity. If science is shifting, as it has done over the last two decades, from verbal to visual representation, in textbooks for instance, several questions arise. What is the effect of the mode of representation on the epistemology of science? Are different accounts of natural phenomena facilitated, made possible, or ruled out? In other words, are theoretical accounts linked to modes as well as to forms of representation (see Olson, 1994)? Another question is again about subjectivity. The implied reader of "new" science textbook pages is a reader with characteristics fundamentally different from those of the reader of the older, largely printed page. Readers who have become habituated to the contemporary textbook page with its cartoon characters, caricatures, line drawings, photographs, not only have a different conception of what science is but also of what (being) a scientist is. They have different notions of authority relations, of the status of science as a discipline, of epistemological positions, just as the makers of the page have conceptions of these questions different from those of the makers of the "older" page.

Crucial, though, for the issue of writing and the learning of writing is the status of written language in such pages. In "older" pages language is the foundational medium; it is the medium of information. Images have the function of illustrating the argument which is carried by the written word—that is, of presenting the contents of the written language in a transparent medium. In the older example, the subjectivity of the reader is formed in the formal organization of the mode of written language. It is a subjectivity which treats language naturally as the medium of information, and of truth transmitted relatively transparently in the syntax of writing. It is a subjectivity habituated to sustained, concentrated analysis, and to information constructed in the hierarchically organized syntax of (scientific) writing, based on concentration, attention, analysis, reflection. In contrast, we see in the new page that images are the central medium of information; the role of language has become that of a medium of commentary. Images (including the layout of the page) carry the argument. The subjectivity of the reader is formed in a mix of semiotic modes, in which the visual is probably dominant; formed by its formal organization, its potentialities. It is a subjectivity which is habituated to being informed through entertainment, to the ready apprehension of the transparently presented visual. The immediate apprehension of facts has displaced the concern with more deliberate analysis, with a strong use of the affective aspects of pleasure in entertainment.

The shift is based on changed relations of power and authority in social valuations of scientific knowledge, where the authority of science can no longer be taken for granted, and education, where the authority of the transmitters of social and cultural values equally can no longer be taken for granted. Authority has to be *achieved* rather than taken for granted. The subjectivity of the student/reader in relation to power and authority is changed from that of an earlier form, which had accepted social valuations of both science and education even when, in the case of many students, they turned away from internalizing them as their own.

All of this is of course connected with changes in public communication: with the dominance of visual, electronic media; with the dominance of the visual in many organs of the print media. A revealing indicator are the prospectuses produced by universities: Their use of modes of communication reveals both their changed perceptions of the subjectivities of the prospective students to whom they appeal, and their uncertainties about their status, that of their disciplines, and of their social roles and functions.

This is a revolution which has swept across the semiotic landscape of western societies in the last 20 years, and considerations of language, writing, and the learning of writing ignore it at their peril. The new situation reveals what has always been the case: Language, whether in speech or writing has always existed as just one mode in the totality of modes invoked in the production of any text, spoken and written. A written text is written on something, some material—paper, wood, vellum, stone, metal, rock, etc.; it is written with something—gold, ink, engravings, dots of ink, etc.; the letters are formed in systems influenced by aesthetic, psychological, pragmatic, and other considerations; the text has a layout on the material substance, whether on the page or on a rockface or on a polished brass plaque. Each of the modes is semiotically formed and rich in meanings which contribute to the complex of the text.

The selective concentration on the (abstracted) medium of grammatical formation of (written) language has had its effects particularly tellingly in educational considerations of what has come to be called "preliteracy", a term that construes the period prior to the child's full engagement with literacy as proleptically structured by an abstracted notion of literacy. It is a massive distortion of the child's semiotic agenda produced by the superimposition of the concerns of an adult agenda on that of the child. Children are makers of signs in any medium at all—the varied media covered by the term "toys," in the hugely varied semiotic activity covered by the term "play," with a cardboard box, or with old clothes and blankets, through the medium of sound organized as "music," in a room or in a corner in a garden, or silently in a corner of their minds in a corner of a room. Each of these modes offers different potentials for cognitive activity.

Literacy enters into this differentially for each child. The voraciously enquiring eyes of children engage with the stuff of literacy just as they engage with all other cultural semiotic stuff around them. And just as they transform cultural semiotic stuff in their signmaking, so they transform the material stuff of literacy. Children's early explorations with writing—whether of their name, of a story, of any material—are just that. These instances are well known: below I discuss two, simply to indicate what I have in mind. Figure 11.4 presents a set of transformations produced by a child over a period of one year and one month on the representations of (the letters of) her name. Figure 11.5 shows the transformations produced by two children, an older brother and a younger sister, of the genre of "newspaper."

The engagement with (or imposition of) literacy is not neutral, or innocent: Whether via the cultural and social anxieties of parents, or the necessities of schooling, it is not, nor could it be, a domain of free experimentation for the child. Two reasons work against that possibility. One is the deeply entrenched commonsense view of language, in which I include most theoretical positions. The other is the fact that the accretions of conventions in the system of writing over three millennia or more make it impossible to be "successful" by treating it as a system of motivated signs until the user of this semiotic system is fully within it. Linguists, educators, and parents come with a theory of language which meets, in total inversion, the child's own notions derived from personal experience. Children will attempt to make sense of this in terms of their individual dispositions—for instance, in the case of what are called "invented spellings," as just one example: *neclse/necklace; racder/recorder; patnan/pattern; washas/watches*. These show, as has frequently been pointed out, careful attempts to match sound to formal realization in *plausible fashion*, signified to signifier. The response of adults (already coded by labels such as "invented spelling") is based on their common sense, which is used as the yardstick of measuring success. Children cannot make sense of this new system; teachers or parents cannot understand the child's problem because they understand neither the child's semiotic disposition, nor the semiotic construction of language.

These problems between teachers and students are in the end resolved for most children due to their perseverance and willingness to continue to engage in transformative activity. Teachers, linguists, and educational theorists stay with their common sense, reassured and fortified by the seeming success of both their theories and practices for the larger proportion of children. Factors of social organization, such as class, gender, ethnicity, provide ready explanations for the failure of the rest, and legitimations for the continuation of practices and theories. Teachers have to rely on available theories, and they face significant problems in bending officially endorsed theories to the insight of their own practical experience and the more informal theoretical positions which they construct from that.

The sequence in Figure 11.4 reveals an intense analytic engagement with print/writing as a multisemiotic medium. It is analyzed by the child into at least the following features: (letter) shapes; spatial orientation of elements; ordering of letters; sequence of letters; overall configuration of "units" words; directionality; and "style." In each of these there is a period in which more than one of these comes under analytic scrutiny. In (1), at age 4 years 1 month, for instance (1c) has the "correct" number of elements in the configuration, while (1b) and (1a) do not. Spatial orientation of letters is an issue, particularly in the case of *E*; so are the letter shapes. (How many "bars" are there on an *E*?) Sequence of elements seems less of an issue: the important issue seems rather to be that of the presence of an adequate number of characteristic elements/ letters; because of this it is difficult to know whether "directionality"—left-right or right-left—is an issue. However, both sequence and directionality are (seemingly settled) issues in 2, one month on. Here "appropriate number of elements" is an issue, though having the "correct" elements is not. The bars on the *E* range from six to four: it seems that at this stage it is sufficient to signal "multiplicity," "plurality."

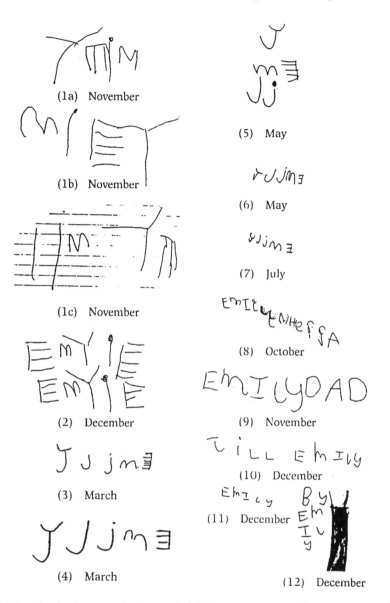

Figure 11.4 *The development of writing. A child's representation of her name, November 1993–December 1994.*

These are evidence of "reading" as much as of writing; that is, the child attempts to assimilate, come to terms with, construct *her signs* from cultural resources that have (been given) great significance for her. Hence her reading of *E* implies (as just one instance of the principles and features involved in the analysis), that there is one single lengthy line, to which a multiple of lines are attached at right angles. In (2), "spatial orientation" is "correct" in adult terms. By (6), six months on, *E* is established; though (5), contemporaneous with (6), shows that this is still a relatively transitional stage as far as linear sequence and letter shape are concerned; it can be unsettled. In (5) the name appeared in the top-left side of a painted self-portrait, and it may be the confined space that leads both to the interruption of linear sequence (though it is very likely that in writing the name the child has written the letters in the correct sequence but has felt free (or constrained) to break the spatial, linear, configuration of the "word" and to return, temporarily, to the former *E*.

Both (6) and (7) show the settling of letter shapes, *and* the issue of "style"—which is a feature at all stages—for example, at (1) and (2). In (8), where the appropriate left-right sequence and directionality are established, there is a problem with "orientation": the "hook" on the *l* goes in the same direction, to the right, as does the "hook" on the "y" (as it does in 3, 4, 5, 6, 7 except that they point left). By (9) that is sorted out; the briefly experienced problem of "orientation" of the letters *l* and *y* in (8) shows just what complex achievements are coded in these superficially simple structures. In (9) too, a problem has been untangled: the three successive left-orientated hooks of *i*, *l*, and *y* in (7) and (6) are now sorted out: *l* points right, *y* points left, both correctly, and *i* has been deprived of its hook, by using the capital form of the letter. It is important to stress the complexity of the semiotic analysis performed in this sequence, over eight months. From (3) to (8) the principle at work is that the hooks go in the same direction as the direction of the letters: first to the left, and then, when the child has discovered the conventional directionality of writing, to the right. This is quite an achievement, as all of these are written left-handedly. In (9), finally, there is left-handed writing, left-to-right directionality, and variable directionality of the "hooks."

There tends to be a period of relative stability for a particular style, so much so that we can date particular forms of writing by a child quite precisely: the style of (1) and (2); of (3), (4), (5), (6), and (7); of (9), (10), (11). I say "relative stability" because there is constant transformative activity. During (9), (10), and (11) for instance, there is experimentation with the *m*. And during this period, while certain features are stable, others are relatively fluid: when writing accompanies a drawing, as in (5), spatial linear horizontal orientation goes, and is supplanted by vertical orientation here; and left-right horizontal directionality is replaced by vertical directionality.

One central point is that the child "reads" in terms of the notion of the motivated sign and she has one implicit question: What can be the plausible underlying motivations of these forms? Her readings are acts of sustained analysis and produce incessant transformations, of existent cultural materials. In this constant reading-transformation-production the child engages with culture, remakes some of it, and remakes herself and her representational resources *with* this cultural material. Individual action and production is totally drawn into the social and cultural.

As my second example of explorations with writing, Figure 11.5 presents a brief series of transformations at the level of *text*, with newspaper genres. The two children, brother and sister, produced these newspapers at an interval of six months, at the ages of 4.9 and 5.3 years and 7.0 and 7.6 years respectively. At that age

Figure 11.5   *A newspaper page, created by a girl aged five years, three months, and the child's (spoken) caption: "In John Princes Street somebody got dead."*

newspapers are familiar to many children, though what precisely they might be is a question. These productions give us some idea both of what sense they make of the genre, what they read them to be, and what they can themselves produce from that sense as their own signs.

The early examples of the younger child consist of some "writing" where the regularity of layout and the bold letters may be one indication of genre, and the conjunction of verbal text with visual image is another.

A second newspaper, not illustrated here, contains verbal text only: "They were having a conference in America. There was...a burglar broke into somebody's window."

The older brother's newspaper at this first stage consisted of a drawing, to which he supplied a caption which the parent transcribed. Two instances were: "No. 10 Downing Street got taken away by a hurricane" and "Someone is hanging out too much washing. Do you know who it is ? If you find her/him call: (his home telephone No)." Both were spoken in "Newscaster tone."

Six months later, both their papers consist, physically, of folded sheets of $8^1/_4'' \times 11^3/_4''$ paper, and therefore of a front-page, two inside pages, and an (unused) back page. The girl's paper had her father's and her own name on the front, a drawing and some writing on the inside page, and the words "Christmas time" on the third page. Her spoken gloss on the second page was "Christmas time is coming," and on the third page: "Christmas time has been." Her earlier newspapers had engaged very much with news-type content and perhaps with her transformation of "newspaper language"; now the physicality, the materiality of newspapers, the semiotics of shape and layout are more foregrounded.

The older child's papers have this format ("invented" by him), have a clear front page (in one case headed *The Sun* with a very large picture of the sun with an airplane traversing it), an inside page showing a weatherchart, and a third page headed "News.War"; and a drawing of two planes firing at each other, and one plane crashing. Figure 11.6 shows the other instance.

A number of features give insight into this child's understanding of the newspaper genre. There is, for instance, the notion of headings/headlines; of different content material—sports, "news"; of language as comment—"Airplane cashas." There is also the technical terminology involved, the register specific language "The mach of the day," "The Big day." Perhaps the most significant indicator may be the child's assessment of the place of language in the "semiotic landscape"; and in that, visual images seem more important than writing.

The project implied in my comments so far was always essential, but it is crucial now given the revolution in forms of public communication. The cognitive, cultural potentials of the different modes must become part of the curricula of representation in schools. At the moment, drawing, painting, movement, tactile making, slowly fade from the concerns of schooled representation; yet under the influences of pluriculturalism, technology, globalization of economies, and of the media, they are moving into the centre of public communication. The theories underpinning the writing curricula are seriously flawed; in relation to the needs of children now in or entering school, the representational curricula of the school are already anachronistic.

Reading

The decisive distinctions between reading and writing are neither cognitive nor semiotic but rather social and cultural; they do, however, have cognitive and psychological effects and through these further social and cultural effects. The distinctions have to do with the social and cultural status of written text; with

Figure 11.6 *"The Big Day." Newspaper created by a boy aged seven years, six months.*

differential access to producing texts and to reading texts. These are themselves effects of social and economic histories and of present social configurations. The learning of writing is hugely influenced by the kind of access to the forms of language which is most characteristic in the social group in which a child grows up: this access provides an initial and often ultimately decisive structuring of the child's path into writing.

Semiotically speaking, there is a continuity between reading and writing: Writing is the production of new signs from existing and available resources, and so is reading. In Peircean terms, reading is the construction of an "interpretant," which constitutes the *internal* production of the new sign for the reader (or viewer, or sensor) from the externally available sign, the sign that is read. Writing is the *external* production of signs, for a readership usually consisting of more than one reader.

Reading is the means whereby new semiotic materials become available to me. Whether I have access to certain semiotic materials, and what kind of materials these are, affects what kinds of transformative processes I will engage in, and around what kinds of semiotic structures these transformative processes occur. Cognitively, there is a crucial difference between the possibilities of producing signs in reading only, and the production of external signs. The latter has the social consequences of making me a participant in my group's constant reproduction of its representational resources; it also has the crucial cognitive and subjective consequences of making me the producer of my own resources of representation in what still remains society's most valued mode. This is neither more nor less than the entirely common experience had by any writer that "writing it down" makes this "it" newly and productively usable in ways in which it was not, prior to "its" being written down. Externalization and objectification are central processes in cognitive development.

In the social semiotic theory of writing which I have put forward in this chapter, reading is the process whereby new materials can be "assimilated" and can be transformed and become transformative in terms of an individual's existent set of resources, and thereby of her or his subjectivity.

Theories of reading, and practices of reading deriving from these, are crucial both in the formation of subjectivity and in the possibilities of new production of signs. If texts are multimodal, reading is a complex activity in which the reader attends to the different modes in which signs are produced and has to integrate complexes of signs from the different modes into a single, coherent reading. Different practices of reading entail different subjectivities. Theories which stress a single mode, which stress closely defined units with impermeable boundaries, which hold to a decoding view rather than one of transformation, will envisage and encourage a specific kind of subjectivity. A theory which stresses the multimodality of texts and the reader's power in setting the boundaries of the unit to be read and which sees reading as a process of transformation will envisage and encourage a different subjectivity.

Evidence for the processes and effects of reading is always indirect. Direct observation is impossible, and although observing readers reading can provide material

THANK YOU

Thank you : "Look I've done it"

Figure 11.7   *Parent's model and child's "reading."*

for speculation, it remains just that. The evidence which I have begun to focus on is somewhat different. It consists of signs produced by a reader following some reading, usually immediately, but not necessarily so. Take, for instance, the example shown in Figure 11.7.

The four-year-old child had asked her parent to write "thank you," in order to write it herself on a card for a friend. When she had produced the sign in the figure, she showed it to her parent, excitedly, "Look, I've done it!" The sign shows that a fundamental principle employed in reading as much as in writing is that of the motivated sign. Here the motivation for joining signifier and signified might be "linked elements go together," (later) generalized to the broader notion of "coherence." This enables her to read the initial two elements in the parent's carelessly written THANK YOU as a single unit. The child's complex *interest* provides the motivation for the production of the (assumed/inferred) internal sign: wishing to be able to write "thank you" leads her to seek the principles of the constitution of units in the model.

The singular focus and concentration on linguistic representation, and on the written in particular, has led to an obscuring of more general questions that need to be asked, in relation to reading as to writing. Two final examples are shown in Figure 11.8.

One would be regarded, conventionally, as a "drawing," in this case of a wooden model of the skeleton of a Tyrannosaurus rex, the other would be called "early writing." I wonder how the three-year old who produced both saw it. I half suspect that in a quite real sense she was "reading" the wooden model *and* the lines of print in quite similar ways. To put it provocatively, let me say that she was drawing the writing, and writing the model. Or to put it more accurately, as "drawing" already represents a distinction of semiotic modes made by adults, she was representing both writing *and* wooden model in the same fashion.

Futures

Human semiotic systems are social and cultural, and therefore historical. Here I have put forward a position which allows me to relate individual human semiotic action to the larger cultural and social configurations in which human actors,

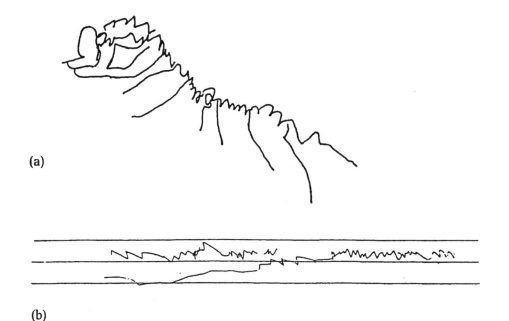

(a)

(b)

Figure 11.8   *(a) "Writing" a model of a Tyrannosaurus Rex, and (b) "drawing" two lines of writing.*

child or adult, act and to their making of their subjectivities. In this way I have also related the microhistories of individual *interaction* to the histories of semiotic systems—spoken language, writing (painting, gesture, music, etc.) and, a task for others, to relate these histories of representational systems to the larger histories of cultural and social groupings.

The decades in which we now live have seen the sudden, nearly cataclysmic impact of the accumulations of two centuries' changes in the "West"; in technologies of transport or of information; in the globalization of economies; in the disintegration of political structures such as the nation-state, under the impact of changes in large part due to economic and technological transformations. Such changes have led to still increasing multiculturalisms, whether intra-nationally or trans-nationally. Forms and modes of representation are being affected in fundamental ways, partly discernible, partly unknowable. For me the most urgent question is: What literacy curriculum *within* a much extended curriculum of representation and communication is appropriate for young people now in school? The answer, I feel certain, lies in an account something like that put forward here, in which socially and culturally located individuals are seen as agentive in the production of their systems of representation.

Acknowledgments

I wish to thank Denise Newfield and David Olson for their detailed and most helpful comments, and Yvette Sutton for her great skills, efficiency, and good humor in dealing with a difficult script. Errors of whatever kind are attributable to myself alone.

Bibliography

Andrews, R. (Ed.). (1988). *Narrative and argument*. Milton Keynes: Open University Press.

Bachmair, B. (1991). From the Motorcar to the Television: Cultural-historical Arguments on the Meaning of Mobility for Communication. *Media Culture and Society, 13*, 521–533.

Bakhtin, M. M. (1986). *Speech genres and other essays*. Austin: University of Texas Press.

Bernstein, B. (1990). *The structuring of pedagogic discourse—class codes and control* (Vol. 4). London: Routledge.

Bissex, G. L. (1980). *Gnys at work: A child learns to write and read*. Cambridge: Harvard University Press.

Bourdieu, P. (1991). *Language and Symbolic Power*. Cambridge, England: Polity Press.

Bruner, J. S. (1983). *Child's talk: Learning to use language*. New York: Norton.

Bruner, J. S. (1990). *Acts of meaning*. Cambridge, England: Cambridge University Press.

Ferreiro, E. (1985). Literacy development: A psychogenetic perspective. In D. R. Olson, N. Torrance, and A. Hildyard (Eds.), *Literacy, language, and learning* (pp. 217–228). Cambridge, England: Cambridge University Press.

Ferreiro, E. and Teberosky, A. (1982). *Literacy before schooling*. New York: Heinemann.

Freire, P. (1972). *Pedagogy of the oppressed*. New York: Herder and Herder.

Halliday, M. A. K. (1979). *Language as social semiotic*. London: Edward Arnold.

Halliday, M. A. K. (1985). *An introduction to functional grammar*. London: Edward Arnold.

Hodge, R. I. V. and Kress, G. R. (1993). *Social semiotics*. Ithaca, New York: Cornell University Press.

Kalantzis, M. and Cope, W. (1993). The powers of literacy. A genre approach to writing. London: Falmer Press.

Kress, G. R. (1988). Textures and meaning. In R. Andrews (Ed.), *Narrative and argument* (pp. 9–21). Milton Keynes: Open University Press.

Kress, G. R. (1989) *Linguistic processes in sociocultural practice*. Oxford: Oxford University Press.

Kress, G. R. (1994). *Learning to write*. London: Routledge.

Kress, G. R. (in press). *Before writing: Rethinking preliteracy*. London: Routledge.

Kress, G. R. and van Leeuwen, T. (1995). *Reading images: The grammar of visual design*. London: Routledge.

Lakoff, G. (1987). *Women, fire and dangerous things: What categories reveal about the mind*. Chicago: University of Chicago Press.

Olson, D. R. (1994). *The world on paper*. Cambridge, England: Cambridge University Press.

Olson, D. R., Torrance, N., and Hildyard, A. (Eds.). (1985). *Literacy, language, and learning*. Cambridge, England: Cambridge University Press.

Ong, W. (1982). *Orality and literacy: The technologizing of the word*. London: Methuen.

Peirce, C. S. (1940/1965). *Collected papers*. Cambridge, MA.: Belknap Press.

Ricoeur, P. (1986). *The rule of metaphor*. London: Routledge and Kegan Paul.

Trudgill, P. (1974). *The pronunciation of English in Norwich.* Cambridge, England: Cambridge University Press.

Saussure, F. de (1974). *A course in general linguistics.* London: Fontana.

Voloshinov, V. N. (1973). *Marxism and the philosophy of language.* New York: Seminar Press.

Vygotsky, L. S. (1978). *Mind in society.* Cambridge: Harvard University Press.

Willis, P. (1978). *Learning to labour.* London: Saxon House Press.

12

Rethinking the Role of Emotions in Education

KEITH OATLEY
SEEMA NUNDY

Introduction: The Importance of Affect in Education

Traditionally, research on how students learn has centered on memory, thought, reasoning, perception, and language. Less has been done on the emotional aspects of learning. Recent theorizing on the nature of education has focused on models of learning based on the child's conception of the world, including the world of other minds, in which it has become yet clearer that children are not just clean slates waiting to be written upon by educators. Rather, each student entering the classroom already has a set of beliefs and is engaged in a developmental sequence of organizing and reorganizing skills and knowledge. Emotions and attitudes are also part of what the child brings to school, derived in part from experience at home, and derived too from the interaction of the child's goals with those of school.

Intuitively, the importance of the emotional realm in education is obvious. People speak of how liking or hating a teacher has influenced their choice of a course or even a career, how the suicide of a peer or the death of a loved one has affected their learning, of how anxiety or boredom has influenced their achievement. More formally too there is evidence of how factors such as peer pressure or a discordant home can have long-term consequences that affect learning. There are, however, few integrative accounts in which children's emotional lives are understood in relation to education. Although empirical contributions to this field are scattered, we aim to offer in this brief outline some steps toward an integrated account.

We will take the view that education in any society, including societies with formal schooling for the majority of children, is a process of enculturation. By culture we mean a set of beliefs, ideas, attitudes, and skills that a group of people hold in common. We can divide enculturation roughly into two components. The first is cognitive. In industrialized societies it includes cultural skills such as reading, writing, mathematics, oral presentation, practical skills, and declarative knowledge of material that one might find in an encyclopedia. Such skills provide people with access to income, to influence, to the ability to contribute to society, to a sense of self, as well as to certain forms of creativity. The second component is affective: It consists of emotions, attitudes, interests—what students feel about a teacher, or about being in a school, whether they are happy or depressed, and how actively they are engaged in doing this or that. In this chapter we will argue that it is the affective component that guides a student's attention and is the primary determinant of achievement in school.

Because research on emotions has grown considerably in the last 30 years, we give here a small vocabulary of terms used in the affective domain. These terms, although not exactly technical, have acquired fairly clear meanings.

Affect, though it has an old-fashioned sound, is often used as a general term covering concepts such as emotion, mood, and the others given below.

An *attitude* is an evaluative tendency—typically a like or dislike—toward something, someone, or some social issue.

An *emotion* is a mental state lasting usually for minutes or hours that changes priorities of goals or concerns, that makes ready a particular repertoire of actions, and that biases attention and memory. It is defined relationally: An emotion is elicited by evaluating an event in relation to a goal or concern. So an emotion typically points to a goal: If a child is sad, we may infer a loss of something important to that child. The terms "emotion" and "emotional" are also used more generally to cover moods, emotional disorders, and sometimes the whole affective realm.

An *emotional disorder* is a state typically lasting for months or years that includes a predominance of some mood. In children these are divided into externalizing disorders, marked by aggression and based on anger, and internalizing disorders characterized by withdrawal and based on anxiety, sadness, or both.

A *mood* is an emotional state usually lasting hours or days. Whereas episodes of emotion are associated with changing from one sequence of actions to another, as when a child becomes angry when reprimanded, moods are sustained emotional states that resist intrusion of events incompatible with them: When anxious, children do not attend to anything except the concerns of their anxiety.

A *value* is an attitude toward some broad mode of conduct held by a group or community.

A basic reference on emotions is Lewis and Haviland (1993), and on attitudes Eagly and Chaiken (1993).

The rethinking that we believe is necessary about the role of affect in education is prompted by two considerations. One is the hypothesis that the emotional realm is primary rather than secondary in educational concerns and neglecting its influence distorts our understanding of the cognitive processes of education. The other is the fact that in the last 30 years a great deal of new research on emotions and their effects has been accomplished, with important implications for education.

How Children Spend Their Time

We start this chapter with larger scale (sociological) processes and then move to individual (psychological) processes.

In the civilizations of the East and West, the family is the most important agency

Table 12.1 *Estimates of hours spent per week and per year in different activities by an average 10- to 11-year-old child (grade 5) in North America*

	Per week	Per year
Sleeping (at 10 hours per day)	70	3640
At school	30	1044
At school doing academic work	19.2	668
Playing	20.2	1050
Homework	4.2	146
Watching television	15.3	796
Reading books outside school	1.2	62

Note: Estimates of time spent sleeping, at school, at school doing academic work, playing, and doing homework are from Stevenson and Lee's (1990) figures for fifth graders in Minneapolis; time watching television is from Anderson, Wilson, and Fielding (1988); time reading outside school is from Stanovich (1994). Yearly estimates of school-based activities derive from a school year of 34.8 five-day weeks (i.e., Stevenson and Lee's estimate of the school year of 174 days in Minneapolis), while other activities are estimated in terms of 52 seven-day weeks.

of enculturation. Second to this, also with very considerable importance, is formal schooling. Much research has shown that home has a larger influence than school on children's overall academic achievement (Good and Brophy, 1986). This itself is an indication of the importance of affective variables, since it is at school that most hours of formal instruction in cultural skills are spent.

Let us distinguish purely cognitive aspects of education—aimed at passing on cultural skills and defined in research terms as the acquisition, representation, transformation, and use of knowledge, from the affective aspects, defined in terms of emotions and attitudes to such knowledge and to the teachers who make it available. In this chapter we point to evidence for the view that the two aspects of enculturation, cognitive and affective, are inseparable: the acquisition of cultural skills cannot be divorced from emotions and attitudes toward these skills, or toward the adults and institutions that transmit them.

It is estimated that a child spends about 15,000 hours in school education from age 5 to 17 (Rutter et al., 1979). During this time, children learn not only to read, write, and do arithmetic but to make plans, to carry out purposeful actions, and to interact with others. They come to feel confident or defeated by academic matters, to join in with or become defiant toward school and the society it represents.

We can become oriented to our subject by looking at Table 12.1, a simple outline of the amounts of time involved in education and other activities for children. For example, notice, in terms of influences of enculturation how, in the course of a year, time spent watching television is about the same as time spent on academic work in school plus homework. From work on expertise (Ericsson, 1990) we know that what it takes to become an expert in any cognitive, artistic, or athletic pursuit, is about ten years or 10,000 hours of intense and involved application. Arguably, then, children would have the time and opportunity to become experts at what goes on in school during their careers there—perhaps to become expert learners. But this would depend on them being attentive and emotionally engaged during this time, enjoying and actively organizing the knowledge required for such expertise—matters of the affective realm for both children and teachers. If not actively engaged in becoming experts in transforming knowledge, children spend their time doing something else—for instance, learning how to avoid academic activities.

Emotional Disorders Among Children

Table 12.1, and much of the discussion of education, is based on data about average children. But there are large individual differences. Is some proportion of children at school seriously impeded by emotional factors? The psychiatric definition is that an emotional disorder is a state that substantially interferes with ordinary life. For children, this means that it substantially interferes with the benefit a child can derive from schooling.

The first major study of the epidemiology of child psychiatric disorder was by Rutter, Tizard, and Whitmore (1970). They contacted parents or guardians of all the ten-year-old children on the Isle of Wight, an island three miles off the south coast of England. The ten-year-olds were first screened by asking parents and teachers to complete a questionnaire about their behavior and emotions. Then children who had many problems, and a sample of those who had few, were interviewed.

Since then a number of epidemiological surveys have been done in Europe and North America, and the prevalence of psychiatric disorders among school-age children has been estimated at between 12 percent and 18 percent (National Academy of Sciences, 1989; Offord, Boyles, and Racine, 1989). It is also known what the risks for such disorders are. They include temperamental factors as well as six situational factors: (1) low family income, (2) overcrowding in the home, (3) having a depressed mother, (4) having a father who indulges in antisocial behavior, (5) parental discord or separation, and (6) the child having to be removed from home (Rutter, 1989). With only one such factor, the risk of emotional disorder is not substantially raised, but with two the risk is fourfold, and with four of these factors the risk is twentyfold.

Psychiatric disorder is a term applied to children who are disadvantaged when it comes to learning in school. These children absorb a share of school's limited resources that is disproportionate to their numbers. They also provoke negative reactions in teachers, and pose problems for management. When an event that triggers an emotion at school is clear, and when the emotion triggered is considered socially appropriate, it is easily understood and easily managed by a teacher. But when an emotion is inappropriate to the immediate flow of events, it tends to be considered in terms of emotional disorder. If, for instance, a child frequently hits other children for no apparent reason, the child is seen as disturbed, and referred for psychological help. The inference is that hitting has more to do with a schema learned at home than with current events (Jenkins and Oatley, 1995). Children who exhibit such behavior are difficult for teachers, because the causes of their emotions (e.g., their home life) are remote from the situation in which these emotions are expressed.

The psychiatric approach not only helps in identifying problems and hence in referrals, but it suggests processes by which emotional disorders affect schooling. For instance, the most widely used screening questionnaire for child psychiatric disorders is the Achenbach, Conners, and Quay Child Behavior Checklist (Achenbach et al., 1991). For externalizing disorders, items include stealing, truancy, vandalism, bullying, destroying others' things, disobedience, and fighting. For internalizing disorders, items include refusal to talk, shyness, staring into space, headaches, nausea, overtiredness, feeling worthless, self-consciousness, and fear/anxiety. For these and other items it is easy to see how such emotionally based patterns can disturb a child's schooling. Though the amount of time spent doing academic work seems a simple index, it enables us to compare general factors (such as the amount of homework set in a school, cf. Table 12.1), with individual factors such as a particular child's attendance at school. Attendance is a good affective measure, a behavioral indicator of whether children are attracted to school or are avoiding it. Truancy, which is one of the features of externalizing disorder, can be thought of as the extreme end of poor attendance. In a longitudinal study of London schools, Maughan, Pickles, and Rutter (1990) found that some schools were particularly poor on this measure, but one school was able to improve its attendance figures from very poor to very good over a five-year period following the appointment of a new principal to the school.

Children with externalizing disorders not only diminish their own educational possibilities, but also tend to disrupt the education of others, causing them to spend less time than they might in academic activities.

It is also known that achieving recognition in some domain at school helps protect children from the risk of psychiatric disorder due to home circumstances (Jenkins and Smith, 1990). By contrast, not doing well at school exacerbates such disorders, as is implied by some of the studies to be reviewed next.

Emotions and the School Ethos

Until recently it was not known how large the influence of school was, or how it was mediated. The research that has gone a long way toward answering these questions was begun in two large-scale projects in inner-city London, one on 12 high schools (Rutter et al., 1979), and the other on 50 elementary schools (Mortimore et al., 1988). The research has become known in terms of school effectiveness. Its object was not the individual child, but the school—what are the characteristics of schools that are effective as compared with those that are not?

There were two sets of variables. One set was of predictor variables, such as number of children per class, teaching style within the school, rewards and punishments, social conditions for students, the level of responsibility and independence that was granted to them. Then there were outcome variables for the children in both skill-based academic subjects, such as reading, mathematics, and oral presentation, and affective outcomes, such as children's attitudes toward learning, emotional disorders, rates of attendance, and delinquency in the school. One important accomplishment of this research is that the outcome measures were not just raw, like league tables in which schools in a city are ranked in terms of which gets the best results on standardized tests, or the worst attendance. Outcomes were assessed in terms of the change for each child in skills and affective outcomes over the years during which the child attended the school. Thus the influence of home and background of the children entering the school could both be assessed and then subtracted out.

Affective factors were important both as outcomes and as predictor variables. As shown in Rutter et al. (1979), the high schools that were successful in promoting better levels of academic achievement were also successful on affective measures, such as children's affective disorders, attendance, and delinquency.

Some schools were much poorer at promoting good outcomes in both cognitive and affective domains. In a study of 50 elementary schools, Mortimore et al. (1988) found that 14 of these schools showed outcomes that were good in both cognitive and affective areas, whereas five were ineffective in both areas—generally there was an association between cognitive and affective outcomes.

In terms of predictor variables, the most general result of Rutter et al.'s (1979) study was that the greatest effect on both cognitive performance and on affective outcomes, when students' different abilities and home backgrounds had been taken into account, was the school ethos. This was made up from a composite of predictor variables that included the system of praise and punishments in the school, teachers' degree of organization in the classroom, teachers' level of preparedness for classes, expectations of the children, the extent to which teachers agreed among themselves on values and approaches. Good schools were well-functioning social communities, and they promoted beneficial changes fairly evenly among all their pupils, not just the brighter ones. Similar results were found by Mortimore et al. in elementary schools, though they isolated more specific predictor variables of school culture and organization, ranging from the effects of the principal and deputy principals, to involvement of staff members, to a sense of order and purpose in the classroom, and an atmosphere of praise and encouragement rather than criticism and punishment.

School is primarily effective as a social institution that influences and shapes a child's academic and emotional model of the world. According to findings by Rutter et al. and Mortimore et al., as well as research in North America (Good and Brophy, 1986), the school's interactive and social environment can provide even the most disadvantaged children with a strong and protective atmosphere whereby they can learn to adapt and function to the best of their abilities.

Cultural Differences: Home and School

An important piece of research on school effectiveness has involved comparisons of schools, and of attitudes of parents, in three countries: the United States, China, and Japan (Stevenson and Lee, 1990; Stevenson, 1992).

Stevenson and Lee (1990) studied 1,440 children, comprising 240 first graders and 240 fifth graders each from Minneapolis in the United States, from Taipei in Taiwan, and from Sendai, Japan. The researchers measured the IQ of children in the three cities, and found that there were no large differences. What they did find, however, was that the proportion of Minneapolis children who in grade 5 could not meet the criteria for reading at the grade 4 level was 31 percent. In Taiwan the corresponding proportion was 12 percent, and in Sendai it was 21 percent, despite the fact that Japanese is notoriously the world's most difficult language to read and write. When it came to mathematics the differences were even larger. The children were given a standard test of mathematical achievement. Then the scores for the fifth-grade children of the three countries were considered together: of the 100 lowest scores, 67 were from American children; of the 100 highest scores only one was from an American child whereas 89 percent were from Japanese.

How can these huge differences be explained, and what is their relation to academic and nonacademic factors? The attitudes of Japanese and Taiwanese mothers toward education differed greatly from those of their North American counterparts, where attitudes were measured in terms of the values placed on education, and beliefs regarding how learning could be enhanced. In Japan and Taiwan parents take their children's education much more seriously than in North America. Academic achievement was a central concern among Japanese mothers, and they held higher standards for their children's performance. By contrast academic achievement was not a central interest among American mothers: They were more interested in their children's general development. And, in contrast to the realistic appraisals of their children's abilities by Japanese mothers, American mothers overestimated their children's abilities. Japanese mothers thought that ability was important, but they believed more strongly in the importance of effort than American mothers. These differences in attitude were borne out by the fact that despite the amount of living space in Japanese families being much smaller than that of American families, nearly all the Japanese children had a quiet place to work. Whereas 98 percent of Japanese fifth graders had a desk at home, only 63 percent of the American fifth graders had one.

Other differences occurred at school: whereas American fifth graders were observed to be taking part in academic activities for 64 percent of the time at school, Japanese fifth graders were occupied in such activities for 92 percent of the time. In Japan the number of hours in the school year is greater, and as compared with the American children, Japanese children received more than double the number of hours of instruction in mathematics.

Measures of achievement also agreed with affective measures—for example, higher achievement scores corresponded to lower scores of affective disturbance. Further studies by Stevenson and his colleagues have included schools in Chicago and Beijing (Stevenson, 1992). Thus, for instance, as compared with children in Chicago, those in Beijing fidgeted less in school, were more attentive, did less contact seeking, had fewer psychosomatic complaints (tiredness, headache, stomachache—all symptoms from Achenbach's checklist indicating internalizing problems), and they had less desire to avoid school.

Even if we wished to do so, we could not import an Asian educational system as we import a television set. It is part of a cultural system and, as we stressed at the beginning of this chapter, education is enculturation. But there are some lessons to be learned. One is that as compared with our Asian cousins, North Americans give less value to effort and academic attainment, and to home and school-based social support for effortful work. It is possible that the North American educational experience, with its emphasis on social interaction and individuality, has a broader range than the Japanese one. On the other hand, perhaps the schools in Western society, the second most important enculturation agents, are less coherent and less effective than they might be in passing on the values of a society and the skills necessary to be contented and productive members of that society.

Discrepancies Between the Cultures of Home and School

Patterns of emotional interaction are primarily learned at home; indeed, we can think of them as adaptations to the culture of home. Moreover, if the culture at home is very discrepant from the culture at school, "the contrast between school and home experiences [can] deeply affect the child's psychosocial development, and thereby shape. . .academic achievement" (Comer, 1988). As Comer points out, one of the major difficulties that schools have is their refusal to acknowledge the variation in students' cultural backgrounds. We can conceptualize the general culture in which Americans, or Italians, or Danes, grow up as the mainstream. But not all students come from mainstream society. The more inhomogeneous the society the more difficult this problem becomes.

In schools where the values and expectations of home differ markedly from those of the school mainstream, or where emotional development has been impeded at home, successful learning does not take place in school (Stevenson, Chen, and Uttal, 1990). Without commonality between the ethos of home and that of school, children find it difficult to bond with the teacher; hence school-based development and learning are impeded. Moreover, when there are overt threats in the environment outside of home, as occurs with prejudice, then performance deteriorates. Gougis (1985) had 45 black college students study material that was accompanied by antiblack racially prejudiced verbal and visual material. A control group was asked to study the same material but accompanied by pleasant information. The experimental group experienced more emotional stress than the control group. As a result, they spent less time studying the target material and consequently their recall was poorer than that of the controls. High levels of emotional stress due to discrimination, maltreatment, bullying, or other stressors interfere with the cognitive processes that are involved in learning at school.

The work of Comer (1980, 1988) is important because he developed an intervention project in two elementary schools which in terms of their academic performance, and affective measures such as attendance, were among the worst in the city of New Haven, Connecticut. At the start of the project in 1968 the staff had low morale and there was a 25 percent turnover rate. Ninety-nine percent of the children were black and virtually all of them were poor—almost 70 percent were receiving Aid to Families with Dependent Children. Comer's intervention project brought these two schools to the point where they ranked near the top of the city's schools. By 1980, on the Iowa Test of Basic Skills, they came to rank third and fourth highest in the city, and by the early 1980s one of the schools came to rank first or second in the city on attendance. By 1975 behavior problems had started to decline, and in 1988 Comer wrote that "there have been no serious behavior problems at either school in more than a decade." Despite the general perception that emotional disorders in children are partly constitutional, and in any case very hard to treat, these outcomes are remarkable testimony that well-functioning schools can have highly beneficial effects on children's mental health. All this was without any change in the economic status of the families from which the children came into these schools.

The intervention was very extensive and covered many aspects: It included a mental health team working with the teachers, and—most important of all—engaging parents with teachers in school governance and decision making, involving parents as classroom assistants, and involving them also in school events. In this way parental values and school values were able to come into register. Interventions of the same design have also been implemented in other U.S. schools. Other research too has been successful in showing that schools can improve as effective, happily functioning, and cooperative organizations within the larger community (Maughan et al., 1990), with good cognitive and affective outcomes.

Research on Emotions as Individual Psychological Processes

We move now to a different area of research—the individual and interpersonal functions and effects of emotions—as yet poorly integrated with sociological studies. Understanding of emotions and their role in life has been slow to take its place alongside consideration of perception, memory, thought, and language. Within the context of education, it is almost as if such matters have been exorcised. Vygotsky (1987) caught the idea in an apt way by commenting that on the basis of Darwin's (1872/1965) work, we could get the impression that among human psychological characteristics, emotions were a "dying tribe." The implication is that as education and our understanding of educative processes become more successful, emotions will indeed become finally extinct. Here we put the opposite view, that the emotional domain is at the center of psychological life, including education. The question, as Vygotsky has put it, is this: "Why is every critical moment in the fate of the adult or child colored by emotion?" (1987, p. 335).

Emotions and Causal Attributions

Attribution theory is one of the few theories of emotions that have reached textbooks of educational psychology (e.g., Gage and Berliner, 1992). According to Weiner (1983), one of the most important aspects of cognition is causal attribution, or the "individual's search for understanding, seeking to discover why an event has occurred. . . . Causal search is not confined to any single motivational domain." Like learning, causal attribution is a process of making meanings that influences the emotions we experience. Weiner (1983, 1990) outlines three dimensions of the attributions we make concerning the causes of events: locus, stability, and controllability. Locus can be internal, as when we attribute some event to our own doing, or external, as when we attribute a cause to something outside ourselves. Causal stability refers to the temporal aspect of an attribution; ability is long-lasting, whereas luck is more temporary. As to controllability, it is generally considered that the amount of effort expended can be controlled, whereas, for instance, developmental stages can not be controlled by the individual.

Different attributional patterns lead to different emotions based on outcomes of success and failure. Attributing a success to the internal and stable source of ability results in a feeling of pride and competence, but attributing failure to this source of ability leads to a sense of incompetence and over the longer term to depression. For instance, Metalsky et al. (1993) have shown how students' internal attributions of failure in an examination can lead to depressive symptoms. By contrast, attributions of success to the controllable source of effort leads to relaxation if successful but to guilt or shame if one fails. An attribution of one's success externally to others leads to gratitude, whereas attributions of one's failure to others leads to anger. The attribution to the unstable source of luck results in surprise plus happiness when there is a successful outcome, but leads to surprise plus frustration when there is failure.

According to Weiner (1983), the emotions of pity, anger, and guilt are critical in the classroom. Pity is experienced when one sees that another has lost control of his or her environment. Anger, in terms of attribution theory, is the result of negative outcome, when the factors controlling that outcome are attributable to another. Guilt results from negative outcome, where the factors controlling that outcome are within one's own control.

The importance of attribution theory in the classroom is that teachers and students are constantly making attributions to people and events. As Weiner points out, however, these attributions need not always be explicit—subtle cues can often inform the students as to the teacher's perception of them. The teacher's perception of students often forms the basis of their self-perception and the instructor's attributions are often adopted by students to rationalize reasons for their success or failure (Weiner, 1983). Thus, when a teacher pays little attention to students who failed at an easy task, those students infer that they are of low ability; if, on the other hand, the teacher pays inordinate amounts of attention and expresses a lot of praise at the success of an easy task, students may again interpret that they are of low ability.

When a teacher displays anger in the classroom, this signals to the student that something ought to have been done; when there is a display of pity, then this indicates a lack of ability on the part of student, but it also suggests a lack that is beyond the student's control. If adopted by the student, this type of reaction would tend to curtail effort on the part of the student. Thus, from an educational perspective, the attributional approach to emotions helps us to understand how models of the self are developed, which in turn lead to the development of particular patterns of motivation. For instance, Dweck (1986) has shown how these ideas can be used to explain gender differences in motivation and attainment in mathematics and verbally based subjects. In the cross-national studies of Stevenson and Lee (1990), Chinese and Japanese parents and children use the controllable attributional concept of effort significantly more than Americans, who in turn prefer the internal and stable concepts of ability and developmental stages as explanations.

Functional Approaches to Emotions

Attribution theory is an account of the causal explanations people give, and of how emotions are a product of these explanations. During recent years, interest has also grown in emotions as such, and in the question "What are the functions of emotions?" Three different approaches have been developing rapidly. Among these a remarkable unanimity has developed. Emotions have come to be thought of as not just disruptive, regrettable, or obsolete, as had been assumed by researchers at the beginning of this century, and as we might think if we only paid attention to data on emotional disorders. Emotions are functional and indeed central to mental and social life.

First, in developmental psychology, starting with the work of Bowlby (1951), emotional development has been seen as the foundation on which everything else is built. Putting this crudely, love between caregiver and child provides outline structures for all social relations with others, including relations with peers and teachers. Early emotional interactions with caregivers, siblings, and friends, provide, as it were, the important schematic structures for social understandings on which culture and individuality depend (Dunn, 1988). In his intervention project in New Haven, Comer (1988) describes how essential it is that poor minority children acquire affectional bonds with their predominantly middle-class teachers.

Second, in cognitive psychology, at least since the work of Simon (1967), researchers have begun to see emotions not so much as irrational elements in human cognition but as processes that manage attention and the control of action. The argument is this: Fully rational behavior is possible only in the most restricted environments like an end-game in chess. In general, humans operate in a world for which their mental models are imperfect and their resources are limited. Emotions function to manage these limited resources as demands change and as different goals become important. It is not so much that emotions are irrational elements in human mental life but that they are biologically based heuristics that help us bridge the ubiquitous situations in life for which we have insufficient knowledge, or no plans that are developed enough for us to behave with full rationality (Oatley, 1992).

Third, in evolutionary psychology, emotions are no longer seen as the equivalent of exotic but extinct fossils. They are seen as threads of continuity through evolution in which outline repertoires of action have been selected for recurring and important situations (Tooby and Cosmides, 1990)—responses to cooperation, to threat, to loss, to frustration. Such response repertoires have the quality of providing their possessors not with fixed action patterns as some of the older ethological literature had suggested, but with start-up programs, selected as useful during evolution and capable of being built upon culturally and individually. Indeed, one of the goals of education is to build a culturally useful understanding of emotional understanding and interaction.

In all three different areas, emotions are seen as related to action and the management of action. Emotions are about connections: They connect what happens in the external world (events) to elements of the mind (goals and beliefs). They are the means by which people become ready for particular kinds of action, and shift attention from one goal or plan to another. Moreover emotions are the primary means by which people relate to others: happiness is the emotion of cooperation, anger the emotion of conflict, fear (or anxiety) the emotion of preoccupation with safety and danger.

Goals are established by individuals within the context of their culture. These goals are value laden and are structured hierarchically. When unexpected events occur, goals need to be reordered. Emotions serve as signals that prioritize particular goals. Thus fear (or anxiety) prioritizes safety. It stops the current action, makes ready a response repertoire of wary vigilance and avoidance, and devotes attention almost exclusively to issues of danger. For an anxious child, this sets an agenda that is independent of anything a teacher might consider preferable. Similarly, liking and affection will make attractive certain attitudes and styles of behavior, whether these derive from a mainstream culture or from an alternative one.

The objects to which emotions are directed are people and events, but students' connections to these objects are mediated by mental models, or schemata (Oatley and Johnson-Laird, 1995). For instance, when a child becomes frightened of a teacher, that teacher becomes what in ordinary parlance is known as an authority figure, invested with a set of powers and intentions that are partly known by the child in terms of his or her history with other such figures. Such models are often inaccurate, but some inaccuracy is typical, because mental models are always incomplete: Their function is to allow outline responses to fragmentary information. The inaccuracies and incompleteness of our information about the world are what make emotions necessary. Emotions are processes by which we manage incomplete knowledge.

Effects of Emotions

Apart from providing repertoires of readiness and action to certain types of situations that have recurred in the life of our species (such as attainments, losses, frustrations, threats), each emotion also has a cognitive effect: It influences our interpretations of our environment, and makes available certain cognitive resources that allow individuals to reformulate their current plans and actions. Happiness, for instance, is the emotion of cooperation and of subgoals being achieved; it signals that no large change in the current plan or interaction is necessary. Engagement in an active plan in this way is not only productive but experienced as creative and satisfying (Csikszentmihalyi, 1990).

There is now a good deal of empirical research on the effects of happiness. In a problem-solving task, Isen, Daubman, and Nowicki (1987) found that happiness increased creativity. Subjects were asked to solve a problem invented by Duncker (1945, to fix a candle to a wall when provided with a box of thumbtacks), and to take a remote associates test. Significantly more subjects in whom happiness was induced solved Duncker's candle task within ten minutes than those in a neutral or negative mood. Subjects in a happy mood were also more creative in word associations in that they allowed for more atypical categories of response than did the control group. In another study, Isen et al. (1978) found that negative experiences, such as defeat and failure, facilitated access to negative material in memory. Thus by influencing the amount and type of material that one has access to and by facilitating this access, emotions affect the "way in which material is processed, rather than just the amount of capacity present" (Isen et al., 1987). Happiness generally broadens the range of attention, and biases access toward positive material in memory; such material tends to be more complex and extensive. Happy moods, as compared with sad or anxious moods, also allow more relations to be formed among objects, thereby increasing creativity.

Schwarz and Bless (1991) also found that positive moods gave more access to diverse knowledge and procedures for action, and therefore led to increased creativity, since in a positive state there are fewer perceived threats to the self. Since the environment is considered safe, the individual will be more prone to take action with a high number of unknowns regarding the outcome.

By contrast sadness has generally been found to decrease access to diverse knowledge, and to lessen creativity. Sad moods have, however, been found to encourage more systematic processing of a problem, as compared with happiness, which can be associated with the use of short cuts and easy heuristics (Schwartz and Bless, 1991; Clore, 1992). Although happy as compared with sad moods may encourage simpler processing strategies from an educational point of view, their bringing to mind of more procedures probably compensates for this.

Findings of the effects of happiness connect with research on interest (Hidi, 1990; Hidi, Reninger, and Krapp, 1992). Interest can be thought of in two ways: as an enduring predisposition toward certain topics (individual interest) and interest generated by an object (situational interest). It has been found that material congruent with individual interests is processed more deeply and creatively than other material, and that engaging with such material is accompanied by happy emotions. Readers remember better a text that they find interesting, and it has also been found that the quality of writing was better for students writing on topics that were personally interesting. Motivation to achieve in mathematics is highly correlated with an interest in mathematics. One needs to be cautious though because such an interest can sometimes interfere with learning processes by "providing the learner with a false sense of understanding" (Hidi et al., 1992). Moreover, because interests vary widely, this issue is not always easy to manage in the classroom.

In terms of situational interest, interesting passages of text lead to better performance on tests of reading comprehension. Some kinds of material in textbooks have become known to researchers as "seductive details"; they are more interesting than other pieces of text and it is found that they are better remembered, but their superior memorability does not extend to nearby material in the textbook.

By contrast with emotions of happiness and sadness, the effects of which have been studied only quite recently, the emotion of fear and its corresponding mood of anxiety have long been known to have debilitating effects on many aspects of school performance: Hembree (1988) has reviewed 562 studies in the area. Debilitating effects of anxiety occur especially among average students, and especially when the work or performance required is seen as difficult.

What is new in research on fear is its conceptualization. Fear and anxiety signal the presence of anything perceived as a danger, and they have particularly strong effects on attention. To give one example of recent laboratory studies, Mathews and MacLeod (1985) found that anxiety states in individuals selectively affected their focus of attention in a modified version of the Stroop color-naming task. In this task the subject is asked to name as quickly as possible the color in which each word is printed, when words are presented one at a time. The task involves disattending the meaning of the word, and people cannot do this so easily; they are distracted by the meanings of the words. In the experimental task some words were chosen to represent a social or physical threat while other words were not threat-related. The results were that anxious subjects (as opposed to the nonanxious subjects) were slower in naming the colors in which all the words were printed, and they were especially slow in naming the colors of words that had anything to do with threat. In subsequent studies it has been shown that the effect extends also to words that are synonyms of safety (Mathews and Klug, 1993). The effects are especially marked when the words match a subject's particular anxieties. The conclusion is that anxiety induces attentional bias. Despite the demands of the task, attention of anxious individuals is drawn toward anything concerned with their own safety and danger, distracting them from other matters, even when the attentional shift itself increases anxiety, in a vicious cycle. These effects have been found in tasks ranging from the simple, like naming colors, to the complex, such as taking tests and examinations.

This kind of effect has been confirmed in many studies (Mathews and MacLeod, 1994). Safety of the self becomes primary, at the expense of any other task or problem. Thus anxiety in a student shifts focus to ignore the learning task at hand and to allocate cognitive resources to issues of safety and danger. At the very least, anxiety steals time from other matters, and there is good evidence that it dissuades people from challenges. Anxiety thus makes it hard for a child to focus on goals set by a teacher. From this perspective, school needs to provide a protective environment for students so that academic learning can take place as easily as possible. Results on laboratory studies of the attentional effects of anxiety link to the sociological studies such as that of Mortimore et al. (1988), in which it has been shown that schools in which there is a predominance of punishment and the concomitant anxiety it arouses, tend to have generally worse academic and affective outcomes than those in which a positive atmosphere is provided, including firm classroom management together with praise and encouragement.

Conclusion

Emotional factors are critical to the development of any educational process. In rethinking the role of emotions in human interaction and their effects on learning, problem-solving, and the other processes of education, it becomes clear that it is not sufficient to look at human cognition from a purely analytic perspective, as if any knowledge can be acquired, in any circumstance, and that the issues for educators involve merely the ways in which this knowledge can be organized and transformed. It is important to look at human thought in intellectual terms, but it is equally important to examine the process in terms of emotions and motivation. Answering the question of what goes on in a child's mind while learning to solve a differential equation is not more important than answering the question of why the child might or might not be prepared to study mathematics.

As compared with our understanding of the knowledge structures involved in development and learning (Case, 1991), or of skilled use of conceptual thinking, research on emotions in education is fragmentary and dispersed. For too long we have looked at schools largely as institutions for disseminating information and for acquiring knowledge. As Rutter et al. (1979) point out, however, schools are social institutions where the educational values of the school reflect those of society. The primary purpose of instruction in a school is to allow a child to learn both cognitively (cultural skills such as reading and mathematics) and also affectively (values, attitudes, trust, and affection for other people). Cognitive and affective processes cannot be disentangled; emotional processes make all the difference in determining how easily even the most abstract of skills are acquired.

Acknowledgment

Keith Oatley gratefully acknowledges a grant from the Social Sciences and Humanities Research Council of Canada (# 410–93–1445) which assisted in the preparation of this chapter.

References

Achenbach, T. M., Howell, C. T., Quay, H. C., and Conners, C. K. (1991). National survey of problems and competencies among four- to sixteen-year-olds. *Monographs of the Society for Research in Child Development, 56*, serial no. 225.

Anderson, R. C., Wilson, P. T., and Fielding, L. G. (1988). Growth in reading and how children spend their time outside of school. *Reading Research Quarterly, 23*, 285–303.

Bowlby, J. (1951). *Child care and the growth of love*. Harmondsworth, England: Penguin.

Case, R. (1991). *The mind's staircase*. Hillsdale, NJ: Lawrence Erlbaum.

Clore, G. L. (1992). Cognitive phenomenology: Feelings and the construction of judgment.

In L. Martin, and A. Tesser (Eds.), *The construction of social judgments*. Hillsdale, NJ: Lawrence Erlbaum.

Comer, J. P. (1980). *School power: Implications of an intervention project*. New York: Free Press.

Comer, J. P. (1988, November). Educating poor minority children. *Scientific American, 259*, pp. 42–48.

Csikszentmihalyi, M. (1990). *Flow: The psychology of optimal experience*. New York: Harper-Collins.

Darwin, C. (1872/1965). *The expression of the emotions in man and animals*. Chicago: University of Chicago Press.

Duncker, K. (1945). On problem solving. *Psychological Monographs, 58* (5, Whole No. 270).

Dunn, J. (1988). *The beginnings of social understanding*. Cambridge: Harvard University Press.

Dweck, C. S. (1986). Motivational processes affecting learning. *American Psychologist, 41*, 1040–1048.

Eagly, A. H. and Chaiken, S. (1993). *The psychology of attitudes*. Fort Worth, TX: Harcourt Brace Jovanovich.

Ericsson, K. A. (1990). Theoretical issues in the study of exceptional performance. In K. J. Gilhooly, M. T. J. Keane, R. H. Logie, and G. Erdos (Eds.), *Lines of thinking: Reflections on the psychology of thought: Skills, emotion, creative processes, individual differences and teaching thinking* (Vol. 2, pp. 5–28). Chichester, England: Wiley.

Gage, N. L. and Berliner, D. C. (1992). *Educational psychology* (5th edn.). Boston: Houghton Mifflin.

Good, T. L. and Brophy, J. E. (1986). School effects. In M. C. Wittrock (Ed.), *Handbook of research on teaching* (pp. 570–602). New York: Macmillan.

Gougis, R. A. (1985, August). *How a prejudice-based stressor disrupts the emotional state and academic achievement of Black-American students*. Paper presented at the Summer Institute for Cognition–Emotion Interrelations, Winter Park, Colorado.

Hembree, R. (1988). Correlates, causes, effects, and treatment of test anxiety. *Review of Educational Research, 58*, 47–77.

Hidi, S. (1990). Interest and its contribution as a mental resource for learning. *Review of Educational Research, 60*, 549–571.

Hidi, S., Renninger, K. A., and Krapp, A. (1992). The present state of interest research. In K. A. Renninger, S. Hidi, and A. Krapp (Eds.), *The role of interest in learning and development*. Hillsdale, NJ: Lawrence Erlbaum.

Isen, A. M., Daubman, K. A., and Nowicki, G. P. (1987). Positive affect facilitates creative problem solving. *Journal of Personality and Social Psychology, 52*, 1122–1131.

Isen, A. M., Shalker, T. E., Clark, M., and Karp, L. (1978). Affect, accessibility of material in memory, and behavior: A cognitive loop? *Journal of Personality and Social Psychology, 36*, 1–12.

Jenkins, J. M. and Oatley, K. (1995). The development of emotion schemas in children: The processes underlying psychopathology. In W. Flack and J. Laird (Eds.), *Emotions and psychopathology*. New York: Oxford University Press.

Jenkins, J. M. and Smith, M. A. (1990). Factors protecting children living in disharmonious homes: Maternal reports. *Journal for the American Academy of Child and Adolescent Psychiatry, 29*, 60–69.

Lewis, M. and Haviland, J. M. (Eds.). (1993). *Handbook of emotions*. New York: Guilford.

Mathews, A. and Klug, F. (1993). Emotionality and interference with color-naming in anxiety. *Behavior Research and Therapy, 29*, 147–160.

Mathews, A. and MacLeod, C. (1985). Selective processing of threat cues in anxiety states. *Behavioral Research and Therapy, 23,* 563–569.

Mathews, A. and MacLeod, C. (1994). Cognitive approaches to emotion and emotional disorders. *Annual Review of Psychology, 45,* 25–50.

Maughan, B., Pickles, A., and Rutter, M. (1990). Can schools change? Outcomes at six London primary schools. *School Effectiveness and School Improvement, 1,* 188–210.

Metalsky, G. L., Joiner, T. E., Hardin, T. S., and Abramson, L. Y. (1993). Depressive reactions for failure in a naturalistic setting: A test of the hopelessness and self-esteem theories of depression. *Journal of Abnormal Psychology, 102,* 101–109.

Mortimore, P., Sammons, P., Stoll, L., Lewis, D., and Ecob, R. (1988). *School matters.* Berkeley: University of California Press.

National Academy of Sciences, Institute of Medicine. (1989). *Research on children and adolescents with mental, behavioral, and developmental disorders.* Washington: National Academy Press.

Oatley, K. (1992). *Best laid schemes: The psychology of emotions.* Cambridge, England: Cambridge University Press.

Oatley, K. and Johnson-Laird, P. N. (1995). The communicative theory of emotions: Empirical tests, mental models, and implications for social interaction. In L. L. Martin and A. Tesser (Eds.), *Goals and affect.* Hillsdale, NJ: Lawrence Erlbaum.

Offord, D. R., Boyle, M. H., and Racine, Y. (1989). Ontario child health study: Correlates of disorder. *Journal of the American Academy of Child and Adolescent Psychiatry, 28,* 856–860.

Rutter, M. (1989). Isle of Wight revisited: Twenty-five years of child psychiatric epidemiology. *Journal of the American Academy of Child and Adolescent Psychiatry, 28,* 632–653.

Rutter, M., Maughan, B., Mortimore P., and Ouston, J. (1979). *Fifteen thousand hours: Secondary schools and their effects on children.* Cambridge: Harvard University Press.

Rutter, M., Tizard, J., and Whitmore, K. (1970). *Education, health and behavior.* London: Longman.

Schwarz, N. and Bless, H. (1991). Happy and mindless, but sad and smart? The impact of affective states on analytic reasoning. In J. P. Forgas (Ed.), *Emotion and social judgments.* Oxford, England: Pergamon.

Simon, H. A. (1967). Motivational and emotional controls of cognition. *Psychological Review, 74,* 29–39.

Skinner, E. A., Wellborn, J. G., and Connell, J. P. (1990). What it takes to do well in school and whether I've got it: A process model of perceived control and children's engagement and achievement in school. *Journal of Educational Psychology, 82,* 22–32.

Stanovich, K. (1994). Does reading make you smarter? Literacy and the development of verbal intelligence. In H. Reese (Ed.), *Advances in Child Development and Behavior, 24.* New York: Academic Press.

Stevenson, H. W. (1992, December). Learning from Asian schools. *Scientific American, 267,* pp. 70–76.

Stevenson, H. W., Chen, C., and Uttal, D. H. (1990). Beliefs and achievement: A study of black, white, and Hispanic children. *Child Development, 61,* 508–523.

Stevenson, H. W. and Lee, S.-Y. (1990). Contexts of achievement: A study of American, Chinese, and Japanese children. *Monographs of the Society for Research in Child Development, 55,* serial no. 221.

Tooby, J. and Cosmides, L. (1990). The past explains the present: Emotional adaptations and the structure of ancestral environments. *Ethology and Sociobiology, 11,* 375–424.

Vygotsky, L. S. (1987). Emotions and their development in childhood. In R. W. Rieber and A. S. Carton (Eds.), *Collected works of L. S. Vygotsky* (Vol. 1, pp. 325–337). New York: Plenum.

Weiner, B. (1983). Some thoughts about feelings. In S. G. Paris, G. M. Olson, and H. W. Stevenson (Eds.), *Learning and motivation in the classroom.* Hillsdale, NJ: Lawrence Erlbaum.

Weiner, B. (1990). History of motivational research in education. *Journal of Educational Psychology, 82,* 616–622.

Biological and Cultural Foundations of Pedagogy

13

Pedagogy and Imitation in Monkeys: Yes, No, or Maybe?

ELISABETTA VISALBERGHI
DOROTHY M. FRAGASZY

> The more closely we examine teaching, in the full sense, the more we see can be achieved without it.
>
> S. A. Barnett, "The 'Instinct to Teach,'" 1968

The aim of this chapter is to highlight the depth of the differences existing between humans and their closest living relatives, nonhuman primates, in the processes of cognition and the power of social learning. These differences have everything to do with education: Why we experience it; why animals do not; what can only be achieved with pedagogy; what can be achieved with formal "training"; what can be achieved merely by being in the right place at the right time with others or with the right opportunities to work on something by oneself. Examining the differences in social learning from a comparative perspective allows us to appreciate better to what extent interpretive aspects of learning and teaching, as seen in humans, apply to other species.

We believe that many people do not appreciate the vast differences between humans and other species in social learning. The problem of appreciating the differences between humans and other animals is broader than the domains of teaching and learning. It is a general problem that arises whenever people attempt to describe the internal states of knowledge or feeling of other species. Even cautious observers (including scientists) can easily and inadvertently overinterpret what they see animals doing. Wildlife documentaries on television, popular books, and the general print and film media almost inevitably provide "juicy" interpretations of animal behavior, perhaps because they do not know better, or perhaps because these interpretations are appealing to their audience, even if unwarranted. They often discuss maternal pride, childish disappointment, parental interest in their offspring's progress in learning a task, and so forth. When we describe the behavior or internal states of other species with the words used to describe humans, we inevitably grant the animals feelings, expectations, intentions, knowledge, planning, and other aspects of emotion and cognition that are implied by such words. This is not a trivial deviation from scientific accuracy; by casual use of these terms for other species, we obscure the fundamentally important characteristics of our own species of which we should all be aware. The solution to this problem is vigilance on the part of educators and researchers: vigilance that they themselves are appropriately precise in their use of language, and vigilance that they point out to others when unwarranted casual use of terms creeps into conversation and writing.

We shall focus in this chapter on two words, and on the assumptions that go with them: imitation and teaching. By using several examples with monkeys[1] we illustrate some cases of overinterpretation, made by laypersons and scientists alike, and some cases in which critical consideration of similar behaviors suggests a different interpretation. We also present examples from apes, to highlight the differences between monkeys and apes in these capacities. Second, these examples will be discussed to highlight the differences across humans, apes, and monkeys in the nature of learning from others. The differences between humans and monkeys are striking; apes appear to occupy an intermediate position. We will show that nonhuman primates have a distinctly nonhuman perspective on their social lives and the physical world around them. In any case, it is not easy, perhaps impossible, for humans to "think" like another species, and it seems highly unlikely that other species "think" like humans.

Imitation

Imitation has a long and illustrious history in philosophy, psychology, and animal behavior. The idea that nonhuman primates are proficient imitators is also evident in the convergence of the words that many languages use to label nonhuman primates, and copying. For example, *scimmiottare* in Italian, *singer* in French, *macaquear* in Portuguese, *nachaffen* in German, *majmuna* in Bulgarian, *obez'janstvovat'* in Russian, *majmol* in Hungarian, *matpowac'* in Polish, and last but not least, *to ape* in English all mean "to imitate," and all rely on the same stem linguistic root that in that particular language labels primates.

Imitation can have several meanings (e.g., Galef, 1988). For example, Heyes (1993) distinguishes between imitative and nonimitative social learning.

In non-imitative social learning, observers learn about stimuli, objects, or events in the environment either to distinguish them from other classes of stimuli, or to attach to them a positive or negative value by virtue of their relationships with other objects and events. . . . In imitative learning, on the other hand, observers learn as a direct result of conspecific observation about responses, actions, or patterns of behavior. (p. 1000)

For us, to be useful in studies with nonhumans and in descriptions of their behavior, imitation can only be claimed to have occurred when an individual demonstrates that it has *learned* a *new* skill (Visalberghi and Fragaszy, 1990). Imitation in this sense has several important features relevant to education and learning. First, it can be a quicker way of learning than individual trial-and-error experiences, and, of course, it is safer in some circumstances than learning on one's own (that an animal is a predator, for example). Second, it allows the transmission of information and behaviors across individuals, a component of culture in its human form (although imitation is not sufficient for culture—see Heyes, 1993). Third, it is an inherently social process, involving observation of one individual (an "expert") by another (an "observer"). In this sense, it may be a component of education (meaning structured learning to achieve a culturally defined outcome). This is a restricted usage of "imitation"; it excludes, for example, behavioral matching where A follows B in engaging in the same familiar behaviors.

In order to provide compelling evidence that imitation has occurred, we must demonstrate both that some novel behavior has been performed and that performance depends critically on the observation of a model.

We present below seven cases in which imitation has been inferred or has been denied in monkeys. In some of them, a cautious use of language and a parsimonious interpretation of the data are evident. In others, an opposite tendency is evident. These cases illustrate the difficulties of interpreting the behavior of nonhuman primates in everyday circumstances, where there are many shades of novelty and many aspects of behavioral similarity. It is not always easy to determine if, or what, the observer has learned from an expert. We believe that one must be unfailingly cautious in interpreting animals' behavior, and therefore we follow each example with a synopsis of how we interpret the data from our conservative perspective.

The Monkey's Puzzle

One capuchin monkey (*Cebus apella*, a South American species) watches another solve a mechanical puzzle, in which several parts must be handled to lift the final part covering a bit of food. First, a pin has to be pulled out, then the hasp lifted, and finally, the hinged piece covering the food has to be lifted. The monkey watches the expert doing this many times, and he also has several opportunities to handle the puzzle when the expert is not present over the course of several days. But when he eventually gets a turn at the puzzle right after watching the expert, he does not touch the correct parts of the puzzle in order. Instead, he goes straight to the last part of the puzzle, pulling unsuccessfully on the piece that covers the food, even though it cannot be lifted. Touching this part of the puzzle was the most closely connected in time with uncovering the food in his experience. But he has apparently not understood that undoing the other parts is necessary to make moving the last part possible (Adams-Curtis and Fragaszy, submitted for publication).

What has the monkey learned from the expert? Something, clearly, as it directs its contacts selectively to the last part of the puzzle. This is the part most closely connected in time and space with the appearance of the food. Has the monkey learned how to solve the task? Not in any functional sense. Has the monkey imitated? Not in our sense of the word.

Snakes and Other Frightening Things

A rhesus macaque (*Macaca mulatta*, an Asian species) is shown a snake. This monkey, having had no previous contact with snakes, gives no outward signs of excitement or distress; just mild interest. Later, this same monkey watches another monkey responding fearfully (making specific facial expressions, vocalizations, and postures) to a snake. After this experience, upon its next encounter with the snake, it too responds with expressions of fear and threat (Mineka and Cook, 1993).

What has the monkey learned from the expert? That snakes are frightening. Is this imitation? Not in our sense of the word, because fear behaviors are not new. The monkey has learned the "value" of a new kind of object. This is obviously significant, biologically, and clearly the processes underlying this learning are important in everyday social learning, but it is not imitation. The authors of these studies interpret their results in a classical conditioning model, in which the model's behavior serves as an unconditioned stimulus eliciting an unconditioned (emotional) response in the observer. Afterward, the snake serves as the conditioned stimulus, eliciting the conditioned (emotional) response in the subject (Mineka and Cook, 1993). This is an appropriately conservative interpretation, in our view. Suboski (1990) has recently described a general process through which animals are capable of rapidly acquiring emotional responses to a stimulus from observing a conspecific giving the same emotional response to the same stimulus. The relation between emotion and learning in social situations is an important topic that we take up again below.

A Wrinkle in Time

A group of capuchin monkeys is given several objects, which prompt a flurry of activity. One monkey carries a piece of cloth up into the branches of a tree. In the course of handling the cloth, the monkey spreads it over a limb of the tree, and strokes it in a way that results in smoothing out some wrinkles. This is a distinctive behavior, and the observer believes it is also a novel behavior for this individual.

Two months later, several objects are given again to the same group of monkeys, and a piece of cloth is included in the set. A different monkey picks up the cloth this time, and goes up the tree. It also handles the cloth in various ways, including at one point placing it over the limb of the tree and stroking the cloth, with the effect of smoothing out some wrinkles. A half an hour later, a third monkey does the same (Chevalier-Skolnikoff, 1989, p. 571).

Do the behaviors of the second and third monkeys reflect an influence from observing the first one? This is an unanswerable question. We do not know, and the author does not mention, several critical things: (1) if the behavior was novel for any of the individuals, (2) if the monkeys watched each other, and

(3) if watching the expert was necessary for the observers to exhibit the behavior. In fact, the implication was that the first individual "invented" the behavior. If that is so, then it is just as likely that the other individuals also invented it as that they copied the behavior of the first individual. The author cannot address this point, as she has no way to rule out prior experience with cloth, or the necessity of watching the model. She observed a group of animals that had lived in a zoo for many years, and her observations spanned only a few hours. Is this case an example of imitation? We do not think so.

"Food Washing"

Many people are familiar with the impressive history of the Japanese macaques (*Macaca fuscata*) living in Koshima Islet, Japan (reviewed in Nishida, 1987). These monkeys have been the subject of many documentaries for television, and their behavior has been cited over and over again as the best example of "culture" among monkeys. The story goes like this: Many years ago, sweet potatoes were given on a regular basis to a group of monkeys at a feeding site along the sandy shore of a small volcanic island. At that time, sweet potatoes were a new kind of food for these monkeys. The standard description of what happened is that one individual "discovered" that dipping potatoes into the salty water was desirable, either to clean the sand or dirt from it and/or to improve its taste. Eventually, other members of the social group began to do the same. The behavior consisted of placing the potato in shallow water, and rubbing it between the hands. The common interpretations of this sequence of observations are that (1) "food washing" was a beneficial behavior, and (2) observation of some monkeys performing food washing prompted its emergence in other individuals.

But let us consider for a moment how the special behavior of "washing" fits into the normal pattern of handling food in this species. Two points seem particularly relevant. First, Japanese macaques, like many other species of monkeys, habitually rub food items between their hands. They do this whether the food is clean or dirty, wet or dry, familiar or novel. We can envision the general value of such behaviors in removing debris that is either unpleasant to have in the mouth (such as grit) or potentially unhealthful to ingest (such as molds or parasites). In any case, the monkeys seem motivated to rub small objects, even inedible small objects such as pebbles, in their hands no matter what their initial conditions.

Second, Japanese macaques, like other macaque species, habitually dip foods into water. They do not do this to clean foods. For example, monkeys are as likely to dip peanuts that are then shelled before eating, as they are to dip foods that are put directly into their mouths. Wheatley (1988) even reported an instance in which an adult long-tailed macaque dipped a sealed plastic bag of peanuts in a puddle, and then opened the bag and ate the peanuts. At Jigokudani Monkey Park, in the mountains west of Tokyo, we saw macaques repeatedly dipping firm, clean apples into a stream. Why were the monkeys doing this? Dipping the apples into fresh water did not change their flavor. If monkeys are inclined to rub food and to dip food into water, then the use of the verb "to wash" to describe these actions is misleading, as it implies an intention to clean. There are no experimental data that demonstrate that food washing is performed for its beneficial effects.

The second interpretation has to do with the processes responsible for the spread of this behavior. We think that an assumption of imitative learning is unwarranted in this case. As we have just noted above, macaques are prone to dip things into water. There are several physical features at Koshima Islet which would make dipping provisioned foods into water likely. Given the habitual preference of the monkeys to sit at the rocky edges of the shore where tidal pools form in small depressions in the rocks (in part because few other places to sit above the sand are available), and the frequent presence of water in the depressions of the rock, it is almost inevitable that monkeys will pick up pieces of food from the water. Also, young monkeys chasing each other often run into the surf, carrying bits of food with them. These conditions provide a supportive physical and social environment in which individuals can acquire the habit of dipping food into water. Moreover, the extraordinarily slow and constant rate at which this behavior spread among members of the social group argues against an imitative learning process (see fig. 1, p. 89, in Galef, 1990; and Visalberghi and Fragaszy, 1990). If imitation were responsible for the spread of the behavior, then "the rate of spread. . .should increase with an increase in the number of its practitioners" (Galef, 1990, p. 89).

We will never know for certain how this behavior appeared, because the observational records of this population were intermittent. We only know the order in which the behavior appeared in the population and not precisely how *any* individual began to do it. This example should caution us to be careful in our acceptance of reports that monkeys display imitative learning.

Tool Use: The Value of "Lessons"

A capuchin monkey watches while her two cagemates use a stick to push a food treat out of a clear horizontal tube (see Figure 13.1). They do so again and again. Although the monkey also is interested in the food, she does not pick up a stick and use it herself. Later, analysis of videotapes made during these "lessons" shows that she did not attend to the actions of the others more while they were solving the task than when they were simply near the task, but not engaged in moving the food out of the tube. The experts in this case did not make any attempts to gain her attention either. She did, however, put the stick against the tube more often after the "lessons" than before. She placed the stick against the tube, not near the opening but all along its length (Visalberghi, 1993). Last but not least, she is only one of many capuchins that, when presented with this task or other similar simple tool-using tasks that her conspecifics could solve, did not learn to solve by watching an expert cagemate (Fragaszy and Visalberghi, 1990). Subsequent to these observations, two other capuchins participated in a similar regime of "lessons" with the same results: no success at learning the task (Visalberghi, 1993).

What did the three subjects learn from the "lessons"? The only significant change in their behavior was an increase in the actions involving the stick and the tube with getting the food. These actions were, however, already present before the

Figure 13.1   *Carlotta, a capuchin monkey, is solving the tube task while another is attentively watching her solution. In a series of experiments carried out by Visalberghi and co-workers (for a review see Visalberghi and Limongelli, in press), capuchins did not learn by imitation how to solve the task.*

lessons took place. The precise orientation of the connection between the tool and the opening of the tube, which is fundamental for solution of the task, was not learned. Was this imitation? Clearly not.

Fishing for Termites

A chimpanzee sits at a termite mound, using a long stem of grass to probe into the mound. The termites respond to this action by swarming onto the stem. The chimpanzee withdraws her stem, sweeps off the termites with her hand, and swallows them. Her infant is with her, fiddling around with bits of grass nearby, sometimes taking some termites from her mother's stem, sometimes paying no attention at all to her activity. Eventually, she will also fish for termites, like her mother.

Fishing for termites was the first instance of tool use reported in wild chimpanzees (Goodall, 1964), and it is justifiably famous for this reason. It obviously is a behavior that requires a great deal of practice for proficiency. It is tempting to say that infants learn this skill "from their mothers" by imitation. Is this a warranted conclusion? No. There is no evidence to date that infants acquire this skill through imitation. There is, on the other hand, a wealth of descriptive information suggesting that mother chimpanzees allow their infants to remain near them during termiting, and that infants are allowed to touch their mothers' tools, to take termites from them, and to participate with the mother in her activities in other ways. As in monkeys, the social milieu supports the infants' learning through means other than imitation. Moreover, as infant chimpanzees start on this learning journey at very young ages, it is likely that their earliest exposure to others' fishing for termites occurs before they are able to profit from the experience. We have argued else-where (Bard, Fragaszy, and Visalberghi, in press) that, as is the case for human children, there is no advantage to chimpanzees of observing a model when the task is too far beyond their capabilities—that is, when the observers are too young. Thus, if imitation did occur, it would happen later in childhood and therefore be impossible to distinguish from learning through individual activity.

Novel Gestures

A researcher teaches two young (4.5 years old) chimpanzees a game: Repeat the action she performs, and for this receive praise and a small food treat. She shapes this behavior first by mimicking them: she uses behaviors that they perform fre-quently, such as slapping the floor. Eventually, they are good mimics of her ren-ditions of their actions. Then, she asks them occasionally to reproduce actions that they have never performed before, such as touching their elbows in a distinctive way. The young chimpanzees are able to do this with many different actions, even though their initial attempts are often not oriented very precisely (Custance, Whiten, and Bard, 1994; see also Tomasello, Savage-Rumbaugh, and Kruger, 1993).

Is this imitation? It fits our requirements: novel actions, performed only after observation of a demonstrator. It is not "natural," in the sense that it was not spontaneous, and the demonstrator was a human, not another chimpanzee. But it is still imitation. It should be noted that the chimpanzees in this study were youngsters. There is accumulating evidence that several related cognitive achieve-ments appear later in apes than they appear in human children (Bard et al., in press; Lin, Bard, and Anderson, 1992). It seems likely that the study reported above would not have worked with younger chimpanzees (say, two years of age or younger), even though human children of the same age would be able to imitate an adult demonstrating a novel action.

Imitation: So What?

What general conclusions can be drawn from these examples of purported, assumed, or investigated cases of imitation in monkeys?

1. Most obviously, that the phenomenon, far from being robust, is in fact as far as can now be determined, actually *absent* when a novel combination of actions has to be learned. Monkeys have not been shown to imitate, as we use the word, in any carefully observed situation.

2. Monkeys are, however, exquisitely sensitive to the display of fear by other monkeys, demonstrating a matching affective display after observing another in-dividual for a very short time (as discussed earlier in this chapter in the section on snakes and other frightening things). This can more accurately be called "obser-vational conditioning" (Mineka and Cook, 1993), and can be adequately explained as a variation of classical conditioning. In observational conditioning, the observer acquires from the conspecific an emotional response to a particular stimulus. This

form of social learning is likely to have fundamental biological significance and to exist broadly in the animal kingdom (see the discussion on the octopus, *Octopus vulgaris*, in Fiorito and Scotto, 1992). Mobbing of predators, food recognition, parental care, and many other species-typical behaviors may be passed from individual to individual in this way. There is currently a debate as to the details of the conditioning process (compare Mineka and Cook, 1993, and Suboski, 1990), but the generality of the process is not in dispute.

3. Monkeys are sensitive to the activities of others, in the sense that they modify their behavior in one way or another as a consequence of observing another (see the first and last examples in the previous section). This is also a fundamental aspect of social sensitivity relevant to learning. Animals that attend to one another, that associate with one another, and that can learn even simple associations from each other, can benefit from information provided by others, even if they cannot imitate. We take up later the issue of how information is provided to one individual by another individual.

Why is it that a monkey can sit right in front of another one, closely watching the other busily pounding nuts with a tool, and not learn to use the tool itself? The observer has the same motor skills, the same objects available, and the same desire to eat the nuts. What is it lacking?

It seems that witnessing the same events does not provide the human observer and the monkey observer with the same information. We accept this when the comparison is between child and adult, partly because we think of the child as motorically limited, and also because we realize that the child may not attend to the details of our actions or understand the causal principles involved in events that we are producing. We cannot assume that all individuals comprehend the same things from viewing the same events. This simple point is self-evident when we think of our own species but often forgotten when the subject is nonhuman.

One difficulty that monkeys face in learning new skills from observing others is that they have a limited comprehension of the dynamics of what they see happening among objects. Imitation in an instrumental situation can be aided by comprehension (Koehler, 1925; Piaget, 1962). Recent findings have shown that even individual monkeys that can use tools proficiently in a particular task do not comprehend the causal relations among the objects involved and the actions performed in the task (Visalberghi and Limongelli, 1994, in press). If the model does not master these concepts, why should the observer? Without practice, and without selective attention to the proper features, the observer is not able to channel its actions to reproduce the relevant parts of the demonstrator's behavior.

We cannot at present explain why monkeys do not imitate in other situations in which comprehension of causal relations is not involved—say, if the actions are gestural. There are no sound examples of imitation in monkeys regardless of the nature of the action to be copied. Our understanding of the cognitive processes supporting imitation in humans is still unclear, and it is therefore not surprising that we cannot fully explain its absence or its presence in other species. Why a parrot can be a much better mimic than a monkey in both vocal and gestural modalities (see Moore, 1992) is still a mystery.

What about apes? They stand at the borders of this mystery. Imitation is more likely to be involved in several different behaviors known to vary across populations of wild chimpanzees, but it is impossible from field reports to know exactly how these behaviors are acquired. In the example of termite fishing, imitation would be impossible to distinguish from individual experience. On the other hand, there are now a few reports from carefully controlled laboratory experiments with chimpanzees observing a human demonstrator which indicate that chimpanzees from the age of about four are able to reproduce gestures upon request and to orient objects correctly to use them as a tool (Custance et al., 1994; Nagell, Olquin, and Tomasello, 1993; Tomasello et al., 1993). Russon and Galdikas (1993) provide evidence of imitation by orangutans of behavioral routines they observed being performed by human companions. Even so, imitation in apes is rather crude and difficult to elicit compared to human children.

Teaching

For teaching, the problem is reversed from that faced by one learning through imitation. The task for the teacher is to convey information in a form that can be comprehended and used by the learner, so that behavior is altered. Teaching, as we recognize it in humans, is a general feature of human interaction that can be applied potentially to every aspect of life. It implies intentions on the part of the teacher to convey information or to influence behavior, and attribution by the teacher of the learner's state of knowledge or skill (Cheney and Seyfarth, 1990a). Intention and attribution are unobservable components, however, and they cannot be assumed to guide the behavior of other species. Fortunately, it is possible to define teaching in objective terms that do not rely upon the (unobservable) intentions of the teacher to impart information or alter the behavior of the learner. Caro and Hauser (1992) have provided such a definition:

An individual actor A can be said to teach if it modifies its behavior only in the presence of a naive observer, B, at some cost or at least without obtaining an immediate benefit for itself. A's behavior thereby encourages or punishes B's behavior, or provides B with experience, or sets an example for B. As a result, B acquires knowledge or learns a skill earlier in life or more rapidly or efficiently than it might otherwise do, or that it would not learn at all. (p. 153)

In short, cases of teaching must include evidence that an activity was undertaken in a way that would impart information to another that would not be obtained through the normal performance of that activity alone—i.e., that some special activity occurred to foster learning. This definition was developed to enable objective comparisons of behavior across taxonomic groups, without privileging human forms of teaching and without making teaching reliant on inferences of intention. Therefore it can be considered a broader definition of teaching than is usually used and the most likely to include examples from nonhuman species. As the authors point out, if functional teaching occurs in the animal kingdom, this is important to know about, and the mechanisms supporting it are worthy of study.

However, even using this objective, functional definition of teaching, at present there is no species in which there is strong evidence (1) that the actor modifies its behavior in the presence of the naive observer, (2) that there is a demonstrated cost to the actor, and (3) that a benefit to the naive observer has been demonstrated. In short, according to Caro and Hauser (1992) there are few cases of strong evidence of teaching in nonhuman species, and there are no cases of teaching in monkeys, and extremely few in apes. Apart from chimpanzees, the best evidence of teaching comes from domestic cats, and cheetahs. Below, we give examples of cases in which teaching has been suggested or observed, and cases in which teaching might have been useful but was absent.

Food Avoidance as a Private Affair

In many species of animals, monkeys included, foods that have been associated with gastrointestinal distress are subsequently avoided for a long time (Garcia and Koelling, 1966). This phenomenon is called food aversion learning, and it has been widely demonstrated in animals, including humans (for an overview, see Galef, Mainardi, and Valsecchi, 1994). It would seem that if a monkey knew that a particular food item was noxious, it would attempt to stop others from eating it or to inform them in some way to avoid this food. This can be seen as similar to the situation encountered when a potential predator appears, and alarm calls alert all members of the social group within hearing range of the presence of danger. Giving alarm calls in the face of danger is widely documented in social animals, including primates.

Does a monkey provide information to others, like a form of alarm call, if one monkey is about to eat something that another has learned is noxious (produces illness)? This question was examined by Hikami (1991) in a series of controlled experiments with group-living macaques and with mother-infant pairs, and by Fairbanks (1975) with macaques and spider monkeys, and by Jouventin, Pasteur, and Cambefort (1976) with baboons. The results of all these experiments have been similar: the knowledgeable individual did nothing to prevent the naive individual from eating the noxious food, nor did the knowledgeable individual's avoidance of the food result in the naive individual avoiding the food. Food avoidance must be learned through individual experience, it seems. Hikami (1991; Hikami, Hasegawa, and Matsuzawa, 1990) showed that even when the knowledgeable individual is a dominant male (to which group members pay a lot of visual attention) feeding in the presence of his group mates and their offspring, or when the knowledgeable individual is a mother feeding with her young infant, the knowledgeable individuals make no effort to stop others from eating the noxious food. Thus, even in biologically compelling situations (i.e., the potential safety of one's own kin), active intervention is not observed, nor is learning by the naive individual from the other's avoidance of the food. Rather, if one individual has learned that a certain food is noxious, and it spends time feeding with another that is eating that food, its own aversion can be diminished: it will eat the food again. This is in line with the finding that it is easier to learn from the presence of activity or information than from its absence (see below).

Alarm Calls

Vervets produce three specific vocalizations to indicate the appearance of each of three kinds of predators (snake, leopard, and raptor). Young vervets are repeatedly exposed to adults' alarm calls and initially produce alarm calls in an indiscriminate fashion (giving raptor calls to vultures, for example). Later they become very selective, rarely producing incorrect vocalizations. One might surmise from this sequence that infants learn from adults what calls to give to what predators. Might this happen because adults give alarm calls to "teach" the young individuals? Do adult vervet monkeys adjust their behavior in accord with the state of knowledge or the state of ignorance of the other individuals they care for?

While it is virtually impossible to answer these questions in natural situations, it is possible to carry out specific experiments. This is exactly what Cheney and Seyfarth (1990a) have done. In an experiment with captive Japanese and rhesus macaques, females were shown food or a predator, either in the presence of their offspring or alone, to determine whether the mothers would attempt to alert an ignorant offspring more than a knowledgeable one. The mothers did not appear to alert their offspring to the presence of either food or a predator, not even by gaze or other relatively subtle changes in their behavior. The authors concluded that the females' behavior did not depend on their audience's knowledge.

Parents Sharing Food with Their Offspring

Golden lion tamarins (genus *Leontopithecus*) are small South American monkeys that live in close-knit family units. Within these family units, parents (especially fathers, who exhibit a lot of nurturant behaviors toward their offspring, including carrying them for the greater part of the time) frequently share food with their younger offspring. Particular vocalizations are also sometimes used by the adults to attract offspring to them in conjunction with offering food. Infants often beg food from parents in the absence of the special "invitation" behaviors of the adults. These seem a possible species and a context in which parents could "teach" their offspring about what foods to eat.

Price and Feistner (1993) showed that infant tamarins received more foods from their parents than they acquired for themselves. However, adults did not act in a way that would help infants learn about the edibility of foods. When novel foods were presented, infants begged for food at the same rate as when the foods were familiar, but their begging attempts were less effective than when the foods were familiar. Adults were more likely to share with infants, however, if the food was rare than if it was abundant. Adult tamarins, rather than adjusting their behavior to impart information to their offspring, apparently adjust their behavior in accord with the availability of the food.

The way food sharing is organized in these monkeys works well to ensure that infants receive adequate amounts of foods that are rare or perhaps difficult to acquire, and this is surely biologically significant. It does not, however, help the infants to learn from more experienced individuals about the edibility of food. As in the previous case, infants are potentially able to learn from being around others, but the precise discovery (of edibility, in this instance) is a product of individual experience, rather than directed efforts on the part of others to impart information.

Expert Witness

At the Primate Cognition Project of Ohio State University (Boysen, 1992), Darrell, a male chimpanzee that is an expert at solving a particular tool-using task, watches Sarah, another chimpanzee, working at the same task with mixed success. As Sarah prepares to make an irreversible error, Darrell gives a low bark indicating mild alarm. Sarah makes the error. The same sequence is repeated twice more just before Sarah makes the error, and not on the other four trials in which Sarah makes no errors (Limongelli, Boysen, and Visalberghi, 1995). Darrell's behavior indicates that he seems to have anticipated the negative outcome of her impending actions, and responded with an affective expression. There is no way of knowing if he intended to alarm Sarah about the imminent loss of the reward before she made the error. To be sure, Sarah did not change her behavior as a consequence of Darrell's bark. She did not appear to notice he had given it. A case like this could be interpreted as a display of emotion by Darrell due to his anticipation of failure, even if the failure did not affect him. It could also be interpreted as an example of attempted teaching, in the sense that Darrell "wanted to warn" Sarah that what she was doing was not correct. We think this would be an unwarranted interpretation, even though we believe that the episode provokes interesting questions about Darrell's motivations to "comment" on another's actions that did not affect him.

Nut Cracking in Wild Chimpanzees

Chimpanzees in West Africa use stones or other hard objects as tools to pound open very hard nuts. Typically, females pound nuts more frequently and are more efficient nut crackers than males, and infants remain with their mothers for several years. Young chimpanzees acquire nut-cracking skills over several years. They practice this activity at the same sites where their mothers are cracking nuts. They begin by pounding nuts on the ground directly, or pounding the tool on the ground. It is only very gradually that they combine the tool and the nut in an appropriate manner by pounding the nut with the tool and by orienting the nut correctly. Nut cracking has been observed closely for many years in one forest in the Ivory Coast by Boesch and Boesch (1983, 1990, 1993). In all these years, the Boesches have observed only a few cases in which the mother appeared to have intervened actively while her offspring was attempting (ineffectively) to crack nuts (Boesch, 1991). Boesch called this "active teaching." While the significance of at least these few cases can be appreciated (as they are the only evidence of something close to "teaching" in a nonhuman primate species ever to have been observed), the fact remains that it is clearly a *rare event*. Moreover, we do not know if maternal interference in the long run aided the young individual's acquisition of the skill— that is, we do not know if teaching was effective.

Despite the rarity of "active" teaching of nut cracking (as defined by Boesch, 1991), social circumstances undoubtedly fostered the infant's acquisition of this skill. Mothers stimulated the infants' activity with tools and nuts, and facilitated the infants' acquisition of the skill once elements of nut cracking appeared. The mothers' behaviors varied in accord with the infants' ability to open the nuts. For example, mothers often left the younger infant with hammers and unopened nuts at the site while they collected more nuts. Females without infants did not leave nuts or tools when they went off to search for more nuts. Older infants (who were able to use the tools, although inefficiently) were allowed to use tools and to crack nuts their mothers had brought to the site. These actions no doubt facilitated the youngsters' explorations with the appropriate objects and their opportunities to practice cracking nuts with appropriate tools. However, they are not "teaching" in the usual sense of the word (implying guidance).

The development of nut cracking among the chimpanzees living in the Taï forest is an elegant example of how a complex skill is acquired with social assistance but largely without active teaching. We have no reason to suppose that active teaching plays an important role in the development of other behaviors in chimpanzees, or in other nonhuman species. Yet, one hears often about how mother chimpanzees teach their offspring to pound nuts, dip for termites, make nests, or any other interesting behavior performed by adult chimpanzees. People apparently are willing to assume that chimpanzees routinely teach their offspring these actions because the chimpanzees display so many other aspects of complex social behaviour (Goodall, 1986; de Waal, 1982, 1989).

The Interpreter   We have been impressed by a spontaneous sequence of interactions between an adult bonobo (Kanzi) and his juvenile sister (Tamuli) and a human partner (Sue Savage-Rumbaugh) filmed by the Japanese broadcasting company, NHK, and included in a television documentary they produced. The bonobos live at the Language Research Center of Georgia State University. Kanzi comprehends spoken English at about the level of a 2.5 year-old-child, and can also comprehend and use a keyboard system of symbolic communication (Savage-Rumbaugh et al., 1993). Tamuli, although equally familiar and comfortable with human partners as Kanzi, does not have the same comprehension of language (spoken or keyboard) as Kanzi. In the filmed sequence, Sue asks Tamuli to slap Kanzi (a common element of play between the two siblings). Tamuli does not respond. Kanzi, seated right next to Tamuli and observing the proceedings, reaches over to Tamuli and thumps her on the back a few times. Then, Sue asks Tamuli to hug Kanzi. Again, Tamuli does not respond to the request. Kanzi reaches over and hugs Tamuli. Finally, Sue asks Tamuli to groom Kanzi. This time, Kanzi takes Tamuli's hand and places it on his chest, and tucks his chin down until her hand is held gently in place against his chest by his chin, in a very distinctive position.

Despite Kanzi's actions, Tamuli did not "catch on" to what she was supposed to do.

The unmistakable impression gained from this sequence is that (1) Kanzi understood what was requested of Tamuli, and (2) that he understood that Tamuli was responding inappropriately to the request. His actions appeared to be intentionally helpful in two cases because he performed for Tamuli (literally, on her body) what she was requested to do to him, and in the third case, because he helped her to perform the requested action on him.

Because of the very special rearing experiences of these individuals, it cannot be taken as typical of apes; however, it is a striking example and it does indicate that apes possess some degree of pedagogical disposition. This behavior suggests at least that one individual acts to complete a request made to another, and in the third example acts in a manner that involves switching roles.

Teaching: So What?

As normally defined, teaching is nearly by definition a uniquely human activity. Barnett (1968) pointed out that teaching was unlikely in animals, but that other learning processes were so effective that its absence was not obvious to human observers. Caro and Hauser (1992) have made a renewed effort to consider teaching in nonhumans from an evolutionary perspective. Caro and Hauser's review of the comparative literature suggests, however, that guided instruction is indeed very rare in the animal kingdom. As Barnett suggested, there are many convergent mechanisms that have evolved to produce homogeneity of learned behaviors across generations, and teaching or guided instruction is one of the least frequent of these. As we have seen, nonhumans seem unable to alter their behavior in accord with the knowledge state of another, even when the other is their own infant. Instead, what happens is that experienced individuals do what they would do anyway, whether or not they have a certain audience, and by doing so, their activity often provides situations, objects, leftovers, motivational influences, etc., that can aid a less experienced individual to learn for itself the important features of the task at hand.

Apes may be a possible exception to this general statement. Apes both in captivity and in natural settings occasionally exhibit some abilities to attribute knowledge to others and to adjust their behavior accordingly (Povinelli, Nelson, and Boysen, 1990; Premack and Woodruff, 1978). But even in apes, it is not the usual way in which young individuals acquire information or skills. Thus, while there is no unbridgeable chasm between humans and nonhuman primates in this domain, there is a functionally important difference in the impact of teaching and its precursors in the overall behavioral achievements of individuals in the various species.

Now we turn to further aspects of learning/teaching that are conspicuously present in humans and absent or attenuated in nonhumans: (1) learning by absence; (2) comprehension and production of negation; (3) emotional expressiveness; and (4) causal understanding. All of these components may affect learning in social contexts.

Learning from Absence

Recognizing and learning from absence, deletion, and nonoccurrence are surprisingly difficult. Animals and people, it seems, accentuate the positive. (Hearst, 1991, p. 432)

Hearst (1991) provides many examples drawn from animal and human experimental studies showing that it is much easier for an individual to detect presence than absence, and easier for an individual to learn something from the arrival of a stimulus than from the removal of a stimulus. Let us consider the implications of this phenomenon for social learning. In a social context, an individual can enhance the observer's attention or interest in a stimulus that is present, but of course cannot (in the absence of language) draw the observer's attention to a stimulus that is absent. Similarly, an individual can draw an observer's attention to what it is eating but not to what it is not eating (that is, what it is avoiding). Seen in this way, it is trivial that animals do not learn what to avoid from watching others avoid particular foods (see the section on food avoidance earlier in this chapter). There is only one way an animal can learn to avoid a food from watching another: by seeing the other individual spitting out the food or vomiting. Illness and/or distaste are otherwise invisible to an observer (in part because nonhumans do not have facial expressions indicating disgust at the taste of food), or they are too distantly related in time or space to the causal event to be learned effectively if not experienced directly. In short, absent behaviors cannot influence an observer; and a social partner cannot make absent stimuli more salient. This is the situation in nonhuman animals. Social context can only enhance learning from events or about things that are present unless sophisticated communication and comprehension enable one to draw another's attention to something that is not present. Humans are able to manage this task because they can talk about absent events as well as about past and future. Thus a whole dimension of pedagogy is available to humans that is not available to nonhumans.

Humans incorporate the general principle "learning is easier through presence than absence" into many didactic situations, especially in Western culture (although not necessarily in all cultures to the same extent; see Rogoff, 1990). Consider the case of an absent behavior: avoiding eating something poisonous. Cautious Western parents do not assume that children will learn from their parents' avoidance of poisons (say, soaps under the kitchen sink) to avoid the soaps themselves. Rather, they actively tell the children to avoid the bottles of soap in advance of the children approaching it, and often place a distinctive visual label on poisons to help the children remember their instructions.

Negation in Learning and Teaching

One way to draw attention to what should not be done is to intervene or to punish when the undesirable activity occurs. This can be seen as a behavioral instantiation of negation. Negation is a ubiquitous linguistic form in human cultures, and one that emerges very early in development. Every parent can vouch that "No!"

is one of the first words produced by his or her child. Humans universally have some word that means "No!" and a whole vocabulary of phrases that relate to negation of past, present, and future actions and events.

The child's comprehension of others' use of negations (i.e., parental directives to stop, or "No!") proceeds through a process of elaboration. As we know that comprehension precedes production, we can use the child's production of negations as a window into its comprehension of this linguistic form. In the human child, negation first appears as a gesture or a word in the context of stopping an ongoing action or event or refusing further participation: "No!" as in "I won't eat it." In linguistic terms, it is used to negate an imperative statement, and it is related to ongoing action. Later, "no" is used in an anticipatory way, before an event happens. For example, the child says "no" as the mother prepares, in her familiar manner, to leave the child. Eventually, it is used to comment about situations that were present a long time age ("No more candy"), absent items or conditions ("the sky is not cloudy"); and about their own intention not to perform some action ("I don't go to bed. . .") (Volterra and Antinucci, 1979).

Consider the problem facing a nonhuman lacking language in informing another not to do something. Nonhumans must convey negation through behavior alone (intervention or punishment of ongoing behavior). Obviously, nonhumans are for all practical purposes limited to messages about the present. It is not possible, through the forms of the vocal, gestural, and postural signals that nonhumans use, to convey information about the past or the future, beyond the very immediate past and future. The most common and obvious forms of negation seen in nonhumans involve interruption of undesirable activity, as by a mother monkey nipping her offspring if it bothers her through boisterous activity on her body, or when she wants it to dismount from her body. A clearly missing form is the use of negation to warn or to prevent, as when a human calls to a child "No!" if the child is about to walk into the street. We do not call in this way to every *car* going by—we call to the *child*, and only when it appears headed for the street. A monkey in this situation could only give alarm calls for every car. It cannot understand which car presents a danger to another, and it has no way to signal to a specific individual that *it* should be wary of a specific danger that is not general to others. Monkeys notify others through vocalizations, gestures, and postures of the presence of danger or food, but they do not guide another individual's activity. They do not intervene in another's efforts to perform any specific action that may be dangerous, such as eating unpalatable foods or moving toward a dangerous area (see also Cheney and Seyfarth, 1990a).

Negation is critical in human teaching. For example, when an individual is learning to perform a task with many steps, it is extremely useful to know from the teacher's signal at the time an error is made, rather than finding out at the end that failure has occurred. In humans, negation with the intent to intervene is also critical to early parental teachings about safety—the "Don't do *that!!*" commands, for example. These are forms of negation that do not require sophisticated linguistic abilities. They do not refer to absent events or objects or intentions. They refer to immediate, ongoing actions occurring in that time and place. We can think of no impediment to the use of these forms of negations in nonhumans; but they simply do not use them.

We do not claim that teaching is absent in nonhumans merely because negation is severely limited in complexity. Simple negation in the form that nonhumans do display it (as immediate punishment) could still be a powerful way of teaching. Rather, our purpose is to use this limitation as an illustration of nonhumans' inability to behave in ways that could instruct another in a very simple form, such as merely interrupting another making a mistake or preventing another from making a mistake.

Emotions in Social Learning

Social intelligence in humans includes expressing and reading emotions as well as behavior and minds, taking into account how others feel as well as what they do and know, and behaving in ways that influence how others feel. Often emotions are more important than propositional objective "facts" in human interactions.

Social learning can be linked to emotion via the concept of emotional intelligence, defined by Salovey and Mayer (1989–1990) as "the ability to monitor one's own and others' feelings and emotions, to discriminate among them, and to use this information to guide one's thinking and actions" (p. 189). Emotional intelligence in humans allows them to use their own and others' emotions in constructive ways. Emotional intelligence, as other labeled aspects of intelligence, seems to differ among humans, and also to differ dramatically between humans and nonhuman primates.

What do we know about the expression and perception of emotion in social learning in other species? Almost nothing. In fact, we know little about emotion as a topic in other species, let alone how it relates to social learning. Scientists have shied away from the topic of emotions in animals for many years, but the contemporary climate seems to call for a renewed investigation into emotions of nonverbal individuals, both human and nonhuman. It is clear that intensive emotional displays do lead nonhuman primates to learn important things from each other, such as what to fear (Mineka and Cook, 1993; Boccia and Campos, 1987). However, comparative researchers have not examined whether the ordinary displays of moderate emotion present during daily routines of nonhuman primates (such as vocalizations when food is discovered, or the grimaces and vocalizations accompanying courtship) contribute to social learning by others. We do not know, for example, whether species with more expressive displays are themselves more sensitive to the modulation of the displays or whether they are more likely to learn something from the displays of others than species with less expressive displays or less frequent displays.

The contemporary focus on social cognition in terms of computation and inferences about knowledge misses a fundamental point: An essential component of social learning, and the first to appear ontogenetically and phylogenetically, is sensitivity to the emotions of others. The combination of emotional and objective information is precisely what is special and powerful in social learning. Contemporary "theory of mind" writings (e.g., Whiten, 1991) concentrate largely upon the propositional aspects of information used in social learning, not focusing on the intertwining of feeling and objective information (for a review dealing with nonhuman primates, see Povinelli, 1993). Surely, differences across species in emotive processes are associated with differences in the form and efficiency of social learning. In humans, emotions are fuel for the engine of social learning. Indeed, humans derive pleasure from learning, especially when that learning is a way of sharing with or pleasing others. We need to investigate to what extent this is true for other species.

Causal Understanding and Social Learning

Causal understanding is present when an individual comprehends the necessary relation between two physical events (e.g., the ball moves because I hit it). Children use certain fundamental physical concepts (solidity of objects, continuity of movement, inertia, momentum) to interpret what they observe even in the first year (Spelke, 1991; Leslie and Keeble, 1987). Nonhuman subjects' comprehension of these fundamental principles has not been tested. However, recent work with apes (chimpanzees) and monkeys (capuchins) with a tool-using task has shown that whereas apes are able to plan the effect of their actions on the movement of an object, monkeys are not (Visalberghi and Limongelli, 1994; Limongelli et al., 1995). On the other hand, both monkeys and apes are able to solve other tasks involving planning movements in both near space (as in captive studies with mazes presented via computer monitor; see Washburn, 1992) and far space (as in moving through a home range; see Sigg and Stolba, 1981). The differences in the task demands that result in these contrasting findings require further clarification.

Comprehension of physical principles is relevant both to imitation and to teaching. It is enormously useful to the individual learning an instrumental action from watching another to understand why the other's actions are effective or ineffective. Comprehension of causation allows the observer to monitor the model's actions more effectively, as it channels the observer's attention toward the relevant actions and objects or parts of objects. Without such an understanding, the individual would have to rely on memorizing all of the actions and events observed.

Teaching requires comprehension of the task on the part of the teacher. How otherwise could teachers assist pupils to improve their knowledge or competence? For example, the teacher that understands why a pupil is failing at a task (e.g., using a tool incorrectly) can focus didactic efforts on the specific segments of the task where the failure occurred. The fact that apes at least occasionally display comprehension of physical causality makes it possible for them to teach one another. Monkeys, on the other hand, have not yet been shown to possess concepts of causality, nor to teach one another.

It has been argued that social attribution involves comprehension of causality (for example, an observer concludes that an individual can or cannot know something depending on whether the individual has seen the critical event) (Wimmer and Weichbold, 1994). Social attribution is relevant for teaching what the pupil has not seen and therefore does not know through experience. This capacity has been experimentally demonstrated in some ape subjects (Povinelli et al., 1990; Povinelli, Nelson, and Boysen, 1992a), but not in monkeys (Povinelli, Parks, and Novack, 1991; Povinelli, Parks, and Novack, 1992b). By the same logic, causal understanding can also be used for inferring the external cause of an emotional state of an individual, or the reverse, the emotional state experienced as a consequence of an external event. Such inferences all require the ability to reason about causation. It may be that understanding physical causation emerges in human ontogeny before understanding that information causes knowledge; nevertheless, humans master both tasks in the first years of childhood. We think the joint occurrence of these phenomena (causal understanding, teaching, imitation, social attribution) in children and, to some extent, in adult apes, and their joint absence in monkeys at any age is not coincidence. This point has major implications for the way in which we should describe and interpret their behavior.

Conclusions

It is often assumed implicitly (and anthropomorphically) that imitation and teaching are necessary components of a rich social life, and that they contribute to the sophisticated behavior reported in monkeys and apes. However, monkeys do quite well without imitation and teaching. Social context supports individual learning so effectively for the things that monkeys do that we have been fooled for a long time into thinking that they were teaching and imitating one another. One has to look closely to see that monkeys see and understand the world in a way that is different from humans (Cheney and Seyfarth, 1990b). Monkeys have a markedly different sense of causality, for example, and they do not exhibit empathy in any recognizable fashion toward others, even those to whom they are emotionally attached, such as their own close relatives. With a different constellation of comprehension and affect, imitation and teaching in a human sense are absent.

Apes represent an intermediate case. They show some abilities to understand the state of knowledge of others, and to adjust their behavior accordingly. Also, they seem to be more responsive to affect displayed in others, and to have a wider range of expressions than monkeys. Imitation is possible in apes, although not common. Teaching is also possible, although again, not common. Comprehension of causality has been demonstrated in at least one study (Limongelli et al., 1995; see also Premack, 1976). However, as in monkeys, the social context in which apes live supports well individual learning of the majority of things, and all of the important things, that apes do. Imitative and pedagogical capacities are apparently unimportant to their normal subsistence activities, so far as is now known.

In contrast to nonhuman primates, humans have extra "gears" in both cognitive and affective domains that enhance social learning. They have many ways of communicating "no" and pointing out absence, a rich repertoire of emotional expressions, and an ability to modulate emotional expressions and to read them in others. Moreover, they have an elaborated sense of physical causality, which allows them to connect causes and effects, and thereby to relate and interpret events. Imitative capacities and teaching in nonhuman primates do not approach those of humans in any sense. In humans, imitation is ubiquitous and apparent perhaps from birth (Meltzoff and Moore, 1977). Imitation aids learning new skills, but this is not its only important role. Imitation is also used socially—for example, to initiate play in two- and three-year-old children and perhaps for more fundamental activities in very young infants. Meltzoff and Gopnik (1993), for example, argue that human neonates and young infants make use of imitation to check the match between expected and observed reactions of others to their actions, in the normal course of developing a sense of personhood. Imitation is thus used as a probe in social interactions.

An understanding of this point is evident in Steven Spielberg's movie *E.T.*, about the interaction between an extraterrestrial (E.T.) and a human child (Elliott). In an early scene, Elliott, like the viewer, wants to find out if E.T. is intelligent and friendly, and despite his strange appearance, like himself. In depicting Elliott's efforts to figure out how similar E.T. is to a human, Spielberg could have tried several things. Speech would have been too obvious. And tool use would seem too adult in its appeal, and out of place in a child. The director instead had a brilliant idea which has greater visual power without involving language at all. The scene is set by having Elliott seem perplexed by his predicament as caretaker of this unknown being. Absentmindedly, Elliott rubs his nose with his hand while looking at E.T. He is surprised when E.T. duplicates the action. As each watches the other intently, the child touches his lips with a finger, and E.T. tentatively repeats the same movement. Still unsure, the child touches his temples with his fingers, spreads his fingers on one hand, and finally, points with an index finger. E.T. faithfully reproduces each movement in turn. Both the child and E.T. appear happy and relaxed by this exchange. The tension is broken. From this point on, they share an intense empathy. For both the child and the alien, the odd-looking other individual, by virtue of its ability to match his actions, becomes a peer.

In the art of film making the film director can play "god" and give an essence of human nature to an alien being. However, in real life, anthropomorphism—attributing human characteristics to nonhumans—is a more complex process. One reason the layperson overinterprets animal behavior in terms of emotions and sophisticated social knowledge is in part because informed scientific explanations of these aspects of behavior, so compelling to the human observer, are not available. If science has nothing to say of interest or relevance to the layperson about a particular topic, then "folk science" will fill the gap.

Note

1. Monkeys, apes, and humans, together with prosimians, all belong to the order Primates. There are 30 genera of monkeys found in South America, Asia, and Africa. Genera mentioned in this chapter include vervets, macaques, capuchins, and tamarins.

There are many fewer genera of apes: three of great apes (orangutans, gorillas, and chimpanzees), and two of lesser apes (gibbons and siamangs). Apes occur only in Asia and Africa. Only chimpanzees are mentioned here. Phylogenetically, apes are more closely related to humans than are monkeys.

References

Adams-Curtis, L. E. and Fragaszy, D. M. (submitted for publication). The influence of a skilled momdel on the behavior of conspecific observers in capuchin monkeys (*Cebus apella*).

Bard, K., Fragaszy, D., and Visalberghi, E. (in press). Acquisition and comprehension of a tool-using behavior by young chimpanzees (*Pan troglodytes*): Effects of age and modeling. *International Journal of Comparative Psychology*.

Barnett, S. A. (1968). The "instinct to teach." *Nature, 220*, 747–749.

Boccia, M. L. and Campos, J. J. (1987). Social attentional processes in human and non-human primate infants. *Primate Report, 18*, 3–10.

Boesch, C. (1991). Teaching among wild chimpanzees. *Animal Behaviour, 41*, 530–532.

Boesch, C. and Boesch, H. (1983). Optimisation of nut-cracking with natural hammers by wild chimpanzees. *Behaviour, 83*, 265–286.

Boesch, C. and Boesch, H. (1990). Tool use and tool making in wild chimpanzee. *Folia Primatologica, 54*, 86–99.

Boesch, C. and Boesch, H. (1993). Transmission of tool use in wild chimpanzees. In K. R. Gibson and T. Ingold (Eds.), *Tools, language and cognition in human evolution* (pp. 171–183). Cambridge, England: Cambridge University Press.

Boysen, S. (1992). Pongid pedagogy: The contribution of human–chimpanzee interaction to the study of ape cognition. In H. Davis and D. Balfour (Eds.), *The inevitable bond* (pp. 205–217). Cambridge, England: Cambridge University Press.

Caro, T. M. and Hauser, M. D. (1992). Teaching in nonhuman animals. *The Quarterly Review of Biology, 67*, 151–174.

Cheney, D. and Seyfarth, R. (1990a). Attending to behavior versus attending to knowledge: Examining monkeys' attribution of mental states. *Animal Behaviour, 40*, 742–753.

Cheney, D. and Seyfarth, R. (1990b). *How monkeys see the world*. Chicago: University of Chicago Press.

Chevalier-Skolnikoff, S. (1989). Spontaneous tool use and sensorimotor intelligence in *Cebus* compared with other monkeys and apes. *Behavioral and Brain Sciences, 12*, 561–627.

Custance, D. M., Whiten, A., and Bard, K. A. (1994). The development of gestural imitation and self-recognition in chimpanzees (*Pan troglodytes*) and children. In J. J. Roeder, B. Thierry, J. R. Anderson, and N. Herrenschmidt (Eds.), *Current primatology: Selected proceedings of the Fourteenth Congress of the International Primatological Society, Strasbourg. Vol. 2. Social Development, Learning and Behaviour* (pp. 381–387). Strasbourg.

Fairbanks, L. (1975). Communication of food quality in captive *Macaca nemestrina* and free ranging *Ateles geoffroyi*. *Primates, 16*, 181–189.

Fiorito, G. and Scotto, P. (1992). Observational learning in *Octopus vulgaris*. *Science, 256*, 545.

Fragaszy, D. M. and Adams-Curtis, L. E. (1991). Generative aspects of manipulation in tufted capuchin monkeys (*Cebus apella*). *Journal of Comparative Psychology, 105*, 387–397.

Fragaszy, D. M. and Visalberghi, E. (1990). Social processes affecting the appearance of innovative behaviors in capuchin monkeys. *Folia Primatologica, 54,* 155–165.

Galef, B. G. (1988). Imitation in animals: History, definition, and interpretation of data from the psychological laboratory. In T. R. Zentall and B. G. Galef (Eds.), *Social Learning* (pp. 3–28). Hillsdale, NJ: Lawrence Erlbaum.

Galef, B. G. (1990). Tradition in animals: Field observations and laboratory analyses. In M. Bekoff and D. Jamieson (Eds.), *Interpretation and explanation in the study of animal behavior* (pp. 74–95). Boulder: Westview Press.

Galef, B. G., Mainardi, M., and Valsecchi, P. (Eds.). (1994). *Behavioral aspects of feeding: Basic and applied research on mammals.* Chur, Switzerland: Harwood Academic Publisher.

Garcia, J. and Koelling, R. A. (1966). Relation of cue to consequence in avoidance learning. *Psychonomic Science, 4,* 123–124.

Goodall, J. (1964). Tool-using and aimed throwing in a community of free-living chimpanzees. *Nature, 201,* 1264–1266.

Goodall, J. (1986). *The Chimpanzees of Gombe.* Cambridge: Belknap Press, Harvard University Press.

Hearst, E. (1991). Psychology of nothing. *American Scientist, 79,* 432–443.

Heyes, C. M. (1993). Imitation, culture and cognition. *Animal Behaviour, 46,* 999–1010.

Hikami, K. (1991). Social transmission of learning in Japanese monkeys (*Macaca fuscata*). In A. Ehara, T. Kimura, O. Takenaka, and M. Iwamoto (Eds.), *Primatology Today* (pp. 343–344). Amsterdam: Elsevier.

Hikami, K., Hasegawa, Y., and Matsuzawa, T. (1990). Social transmission of food preferences in Japanese monkeys (*Macaca fuscata*). *Journal of Comparative Psychology, 104,* 233–237.

Jouventin, P., Pasteur, G., and Cambefort, J. P. (1976). Observational learning of baboons and avoidance of mimics: Exploratory tests. *Evolution, 31,* 214–218.

Koehler, W. (1925). *The mentality of apes.* London: Routledge and Kegan Paul.

Leslie, A. M. and Keeble, S. (1987). Do six-month-old infants perceive causality? *Cognition, 25,* 265–288.

Limongelli, L., Boysen, S., and Visalberghi, E. (1995). Comprehension of cause and effect relationships in a tool-using task by common chimpanzees (*Pan troglodytes*). *Journal of Comparative Psychology, 109,* 18–26.

Lin, A. C., Bard, K. A., and Anderson, J. R. (1992). Development of self-recognition in chimpanzees (*Pan troglodytes*). *Journal of Comparative Psychology, 106,* 120–132.

Meltzoff, A. and Gopnik, A. (1993). The role of imitation in understanding persons and developing a theory of mind. In S. Baron-Cohen, H. Tager-Flusberg, and D. Cohen (Eds.), *Understanding other minds.* Oxford, England: Oxford University Press.

Meltzoff, A. and Moore, M. (1977). Imitation of facial and manual gestures by human neonates. *Science, 198,* 75–78.

Mineka, S. and Cook, M. (1993). Mechanisms involved in the observational conditioning of fear. *Journal of Experimental Psychology: General, 122,* 23–38.

Moore, B. R. (1992). Avian movement imitation and a new form of mimicry: Tracing the evolution of a complex form of learning. *Behaviour, 122,* 231–263.

Nagell, K., Olguin, R. S., and Tomasello, M. (1993). Processes of social learning in the tool use of chimpanzees (*Pan troglodytes*) and human children (*Homo sapiens*). *Journal of Comparative Psychology, 107,* 174–186.

Nishida, T. (1987). Local traditions and cultural transmission. In B. Smuts, D. Cheney, R. Seyfarth, R. Wrangham, and T. Struhsaker (Eds.), *Primate societies.* Chicago: University of Chicago Press.

Piaget, J. (1962). *Play, dreams, and imitation in childhood*. New York: Norton.

Piaget, J. (1971). *The construction of reality in the child*. New York: Ballantine Books.

Povinelli, D. J. (1993). Reconstructing the evolution of mind. *American Psychologists, 48,* 493–509.

Povinelli, D. J., Nelson, K. E., and Boysen, S. T. (1990). Inferences about guessing and knowing by chimpanzees (*Pan troglodytes*). *Journal of Comparative Psychology, 104,* 203–210.

Povinelli, D. J., Parks, K. A., and Novak, M. A. (1991). Do rhesus monkeys (*Macaca mulatta*) attribute knowledge and ignorance to others? *Journal of Comparative Psychology, 105,* 318–325.

Povinelli, D. J., Nelson, K. E., and Boysen, S. T. (1992a). Comprehension of role reversal in chimpanzees: Evidence of empathy? *Animal Behaviour, 44,* 633–640.

Povinelli, D. J., Parks, K. A., and Novak, M. A. (1992b). Role reversal by rhesus monkeys, but no evidence of empathy. *Animal Behaviour, 43,* 269–281.

Premack, D. (1976). *Intelligence in ape and man*. Hillsdale, NJ: Lawrence Erlbaum.

Premack, D. and Woodruff, G. (1978). Does the chimpanzee have a theory of mind? *Behavioral and Brain Sciences, 1,* 515–526.

Price, E. C. and Feistner, A. T. C. (1993). Food sharing in lion tamarins: Tests of three hypotheses. *American Journal of Primatology, 31,* 211–221.

Rogoff, B. (1990). *Apprenticeship in thinking*. New York: Oxford University Press.

Russon, A. E. and Galdikas, B. M. F. (1993). Imitation in free-ranging rehabilitant orangutans (*Pongo pygmaeus*). *Journal of Comparative Psychology, 107,* 147–161.

Salovey, P. and Mayer, J. D. (1989–1990). Emotional intelligence. *Imagination, Cognition and Personality, 9,* 185–211.

Savage-Rumbaugh, E. S., Murphy, J., Sevcik, R. A., Brakke, K. E., Williams, S. L., and Rumbaugh, D. (1993). Language comprehension in ape and child. *Monograph of the Society for Research in Child Development*, serial no. 233.

Sigg, H. and Stolba, A. (1981). Home range and daily march in hamadryas baboon troop. *Folia Primatologica, 36,* 40–75.

Spelke, E. (1991). Physical knowledge in infancy: Reflections on Piaget's theory. In S. Carey and R. Gelman (Eds.), *The epigenesis of mind* (pp. 133–169). Hillsdale, NJ: Lawrence Erlbaum.

Suboski, M. D. (1990). Releaser-induced recognition learning. *Psychological Review, 97,* 271–284.

Tomasello, M., Savage-Rumbaugh, S., and Kruger, A. C. (1993). Imitative learning of actions on objects by children chimpanzees, and enculturated chimpanzees. *Child Development, 64,* 1688–1705.

Visalberghi, E. (1993). Capuchin monkeys: A window into tool use activities by apes and humans. In K. Gibson and T. Ingold (Eds.), *Tools, language and cognition in human evolution* (pp. 138–150). Cambridge, England: Cambridge University Press.

Visalberghi, E. and Fragaszy, D. M. (1990). Do monkeys ape? In S. T. Parker and K. R. G. Gibson (Eds.), *"Language" and intelligence in monkeys and apes* (pp. 247–273). Cambridge, England: Cambridge University Press.

Visalberghi, E. and Limongelli, L. (1994). Lack of comprehension of cause–effect relationships in tool using capuchin monkeys (*Cebus apella*). *Journal of Comparative Psychology, 108,* 15–22.

Visalberghi, E. and Limongelli, L. (in press). Action and understanding: Tool use revisited through the mind of capuchin monkeys. In A. Russon, K. Bard, and S. Parker, *Reaching into thought. The minds of the great apes*. Cambridge, England: Cambridge University Press.

Volterra, V. and Antinucci F. (1979). Negation in child language: A pragmatic study. In E. Ochs and B. B. Shieffelin (Eds.), *Developmental pragmatics* (pp. 281–303). New York: Academic Press.

de Waal, F. (1982). *Chimpanzee politics*. London: Jonathan Cape.

de Waal, F. (1989). *Peacemaking among primates*. Cambridge: Harvard University Press.

Washburn, D. A. (1992). Analyzing the path or responding in maze-solving and other tasks. *Behavior Research Methods, Instruments and Computer, 24*, 248–252.

Wheatley, B. P. (1988). Cultural behavior and extractive foraging in *Macaca fascicularis. Current Anthropology, 29*, 516–519.

Whiten, A. (Ed.). (1991). *Natural Theories of Mind*. Oxford, England: Basil Blackwell.

Wimmer, H. and Weichbold, V. (1994). Children's theory of mind: Fodor's heuristics or understanding informational causation. *Cognition, 53*, 45–57.

14

Why Animals Lack Pedagogy and Some Cultures Have More of It Than Others

DAVID PREMACK

ANN JAMES PREMACK

Pedagogy, the teaching of one individual by another, appears to be a biological novelty, an activity largely confined to humans. If this is true, what are the psychological mechanisms on which pedagogy depends?

Pedagogy is not a neutral achievement; it permits the evolution of culture and the possibility of history—that sequence of changes through which a species passes while remaining biologically stable. These changes are cultural changes, each stage incorporating important aspects of the past. The means for preserving and transforming culture are primarily pedagogical. The more rapid the social changes, the more they are dependent upon pedagogy.

While a vast number of histories of these cultural changes have been written about human beings, one could not write a history of the chimpanzee, or of any other animal. We could perhaps write a history of how humans have treated the chimpanzee, or the beaver or pigeon, but not one of the animal itself, for animals have not undergone significant cultural change while remaining biologically stable. For example, basic social practices in the chimpanzee have remained the same: The female leaves the natal group today, as she did, so far as we know, five million years ago. The "technology" of nest building—so far as we know—is the same now as it was five million years ago. Observed differences among contemporary chimpanzee groups are minor and are restricted to such things as one group eating nut A, another nut B; one group cracking a nut by striking it with a rock, another by slamming it against a tree; one group peeling the bark from twigs to be used in fishing for insects, another not, and so on.

History is not, however, an automatic by-product of the human brain; nor is it an inevitable concomitant of culture. A group whose members are equipped with a human brain may have a culture but no history—that is, no discernible record of cultural change. The concept of "traditional culture" was advanced to cover just such cases.

Many writers outside of anthropology find the concept of culture vague but nonetheless ask, "Do animals have culture?" thereby sidestepping the question of

"What is culture?" The question is reformulated as "How is animal behavior transmitted?" If a "tradition" is transmitted across generations by "appropriate social mechanisms," then the behavior is deemed to be cultural (e.g., Galef, 1992). E. O. Wilson (1975, p. 168) claims that "culture, aside from its involvement with language, which is truly unique, differs from animal tradition only in degree."

But animals have neither culture nor history (Premack and Premack, 1994). Furthermore, language is not the only difference between, say, chimpanzees and humans: A human is not merely a chimpanzee to which language has been added. Anthropologists have underestimated the significance of the differences.

In this chapter we first compare the social transmission of information in humans and animals. Second, we will show that humans have pedagogy while animals do not and we will identify a condition that makes pedagogy essential for the human, though not for the animal. Finally, the role of pedagogy in culture will be examined and a theory of aesthetics advanced to account for the presence of pedagogy in humans and its absence in animals.

The Social Transmission of Information in Humans and Animals

In the social transmission of information, one generation imparts its skill or knowledge to another, accomplishing in one afternoon what might have taken generations under biological transmission. Although this quick, flexible transformation is best seen in human cultural inheritance, the same social transmission of information is found in animals (in what might be called protocultural inheritance). Note that this transmission is not confined to apes and monkeys, and can even be found in the rat. The first solid food a rat eats is likely to be one whose odor it encountered in its mother's milk (Galef, 1981). After weaning, social guidance continues. The rat develops a map of the food sources in its area, so that it can use the food odors it detects on the bodies of its peers as cues for finding particular foods (Galef, 1981).

None of this implacably social transmission of information depends on pedagogy. Simple associative learning will explain all of it. Moreover, more complex cases, such as those seen in monkeys—for instance, the well-known improvisations in food technology in the Japanese macaques—can be accounted for by adding observational learning. The washing of sweet potatoes and winnowing of grain, introduced by the gifted young female, Imo, diffused through the colony, largely on the basis of observational learning (Kawamura, 1959). The fastest diffusion took place among animals that looked at Imo and at one another—her peers—whereas the slowest took place among animals that apparently did not look at Imo or at any other young animal—the old males (Itani, 1958; Kawamura, 1959).

Imo's innovations have a further characteristic. They lie well within the competence of her species in this sense: They were acquired without any assistance. Other members of Imo's group needed only an opportunity to observe Imo, or a member that had already observed her, along with the opportunity to try out what they had observed. That is, they needed only a passive model, not an active or judgmental one who would oversee their learning and correct their errors.[1]

Suppose, however, that an appreciable part of the innovations of gifted individuals did not fall within the competence of the species. That is, suppose that most of the population could not acquire the innovations of its gifted members without assistance. In such a case, innovations would not be self-propagating, diffusing through the group, socially transmitted across generations. They would die with the innovator.

Is Pedagogy Confined to Humans?

In imitation, the novice observes the model, copying the model's behavior, but the model does not return the observation. The model may never even know that the novice is there, and, indeed, were the novice not there, the model's behavior would not change. Pedagogy is immediately distinguishable in that observation goes in both directions: novice to model but also model to novice. In addition to observing, the model judges the novice according to internal standards, and intervenes actively to modify the novice's performance should it depart from the model's standards. Pedagogy thus consists of a combination of observation, judgment, and intervention.

In addition, we may ask about the motivational basis of pedagogy. As we shall see, it is best described as follows: the pedagogue acts so as to reduce the disparity between the acts of the novice that are being observed and the pedagogue's internal standards.

In deciding whether pedagogy is confined to humans, we must take into account the parental investment in progeny that is found in many animals. For instance, there is a well-known correlation between the complexity of a bird's food technology and the length of time the parent remains with the fledgling (Brown, 1975). Birds whose diet depends on cracking open mollusks remain longer with the parents than do those that eat simple seeds and insects (Norton-Griffiths, 1969).

A more dramatic example of parental investment is that of the live mice (brought to infant kittens by their parents) which the growing kittens soon come to stalk with increasing efficiency. This "assistance" is not confined to domestic cats, of course, but is found in many carnivores (Ewer, 1969; Leyhausen, 1979). Why is this parental investment not pedagogy?

In the first place, the parental investment of nonprimates is largely confined to one domain (food technology), a limitation that should already arouse suspicion, for human pedagogy has no such restriction—it applies to every conceivable domain. It is a hallmark of human cognition that already indicates the flexibility that often sets the human apart from the animal.

In addition, the animal's investment shows no apparent sensitivity to feedback from progeny. Consider these rhetorical questions: If a kitten were inept, falling behind the littermates, would the parents give it additional training, bringing extra mice and delaying the kitten's departure until it caught up with its peers? Or suppose, upon releasing the kittens from the nest, parents found one to be an inadequate hunter, would they reclaim it for further training? In brief, does a parent judge the quality of an infant's performance and modulate its "training" accordingly?

The lack of such evidence is not the result of a failure on the part of human observers. On the contrary, cases can be found where the animals have been closely observed, where the description of their interactions is fine-grained, as is Ewer's account of parental training in the domestic cat (1969). In this acutely described case, the closest approximation to "parental judgment" is this: A mouse that escaped was recaptured by the parent and returned to the kittens. Note this is a reaction to the mouse, not to the kittens (and it is not the mouse the cat is "training" but the kittens).

Closer approximations of human pedagogy can be found in nonhuman primates. Both monkey and ape mothers have been observed to remove from the mouths of their infants leaves of plants not eaten by the species. Gorilla and chimpanzee mothers have been observed to hold their infants away from them and to encourage them to walk toward them (Yerkes, 1943). Unlike the previous cases, these examples are not species-specific, do not apply only to food technology, and though exceedingly simple, have something of the flavor of pedagogy. Yet, even if complex, these examples could be ignored because of their sheer infrequency. Wrangham and Nishida, two distinguished field-workers, report only two instances of removal of leaves from infants' mouths after approximately 150 hours of field observation (personal communication, 1986). Human pedagogy could be ignored, too, were it equally infrequent.

A more frequently observed example consists of "toilet training" in the monkey. When an infant voids while being carried by its mother, she is likely to pull the infant away until it stops. The infant screams when first torn from its comfortable perch, though in time the two animals improve their reading of each other's signals, so that the infant is anticipated, and released before it voids. Is this pedagogy? No, because no matter how subtle the communication may become in this dyad, the mother's response is little more than a simple reaction to an aversive stimulus.

The macaque weans her infant in much the same manner. At first she simply pulls the infant from her breast and denies it further access, though if the infant persists, she may strike it (Barnett, 1968). Punishment is apparently the prime mechanism animals use in modifying one another, and the macaque's manner of weaning her infant is a good example. Punishment, from the recipient's perspective, is a painful stimulus received just when it is doing what it most wants to do, whereas from the sender's perspective it is a natural reaction to an aversive condition. One individual's painful stimulus is another individual's cathartic response.

We can find appreciably more complex cases that, nonetheless, remain responses to aversive stimuli. For example, when the Hamadryas baboon bites the nape of the female's neck if she wanders too far afield (Kummer, 1971), the male's reaction is again largely an innate response to a negative state of affairs. When the chimpanzee mother intervenes to terminate the excessively rough play that caused her infant to shriek (Goodall, 1988), she provides another example of basically the same kind. Finding the infant's shrieking aversive, she acts to terminate it. The infant may benefit from its mother's intervention, but protection is not pedagogy. One can help or protect another without training it in any way.

The issue is not whether animals modify one another. They do. When one animal has been defeated in a dominance fight, its behavior has been undeniably modified. But not all modification is pedagogy. In pedagogy, one individual has a mental representation of properly executed behavior, compares the actual behavior of the other one with the representation, and trains the other one to bring its behavior into conformity with the representation. One does not *know* that the individual has mental representations and engages in planned action. Mental representations (and planning) cannot, of course, be observed. However, the complexity of the observed training warrants the assumption.

Complex Examples from the Laboratory

A most complex case of pedagogic-like behavior in animals occurred in our laboratory, not as the product of an experiment but as a spontaneous action. Captive animals, when properly maintained, often show forms of behavior that are more complex than can be seen in the field. Though complex, these cases are rare. In more than 20 years of observation, we have seen only three or four such cases. Here is the first of two examples.

Among captive chimpanzees, one of the prerogatives claimed by the dominant animal is that of being accompanied when changing locations. While submissive animals change locations alone, dominant animals demand company. By stationing themselves in front of the submissive animal, they lead the latter to abandon its current enterprise—foraging, grooming, or resting. The two then move off together to a new location chosen by the dominant.

Before moving, the submissive animal connects itself to the dominant in either of two ways: grasping the other around the waist from behind, or lining up alongside and putting an arm around the other's shoulder.

Sadie and Jessie were among the four juvenile animals that had lived in a group in the lab for more than three years, but they were not a natural pair. They did not choose one another's company, had never before been placed in the compound (a walled half-acre field) by themselves, and had no history of walking together.

When first placed together, Jessie ran off whenever Sadie approached. Sadie's first job was thus to calm an extremely skittish Jessie. She accomplished her purpose by patience and steadfast calm. Over and over, Sadie approached Jessie, slowly, peaceably, until finally Jessie did not run off. Now Sadie stood before Jessie and actually patted her shoulders and head. Her next step was to position herself alongside Jessie. Then Sadie took Jessie's arm, lifted it up, and, ducking her head, dropped Jessie's arm around her shoulder. Why didn't Sadie simplify matters by placing her own arm around Jessie? We have no idea, though in fact that is not the normal arrangement. In this social exchange, the submissive animal makes the connection, placing its arm around the dominant one, and it was this canonical form that Sadie taught Jessie.

Once Sadie had placed Jessie's arm where it belonged, the two animals set off. All would have been well, except that Jessie was too short for Sadie. Her arm slipped from Sadie's shoulder, down along Sadie's back until finally both her arms and full weight lay across Sadie's back and Sadie stopped. Whereupon Jessie ran off. Sadie did not hotly pursue her, but reinstated the whole cycle, beginning with the slow, patient approach. At the end of about two hours, Jessie was perfectly trained. Not only was all skittishness gone, she carried out perfectly the services of the submissive animal. When Sadie approached, Jessie abandoned her current enterprise, lined up beside Sadie, placed an arm around Sadie and the two set off together. The problem caused by Jessie's relative stature had not been solved, of course, and after a short distance, Jessie slumped across Sadie. The two stopped. But now rather than running off, Jessie righted herself and the two set off again.

This case has been described in full to show that on occasion we can find, in the chimpanzee, training that has the cognitive complexity of the human case. Sadie's behavior has everything that could be wished for in order to argue that the trainer has in mind a representation of a desired state of affairs concerning the behavior of the other one, and carries out a highly deliberate set of planned acts to bring about the representation. Sadie's acts are not simple reactions to an aversive stimulus. On the contrary, she successfully inhibited the disposition to strike or attack the originally uncooperative Jessie, substituting calm and even a few pats for the inhibited aggression, and putting Jessie's body into the desired position, a beautiful act of passive guidance, also differs from chasing a fleeing female or from a mother pulling a voiding infant from her body. Lifting another chimpanzee's arm and placing it around her own shoulder probably has no base frequency. That is, it probably does not occur in any other setting. The act is designed for this occasion.

In every respect save one, Sadie's training of Jessie was a perfect example of pedagogy. What was the exception? The training was carried out for the trainer's benefit. Can we prove this? In principle, quite easily. The distinction could be drawn in this manner: Allow Sadie to train two animals, Jessie and a female twin, Leslie. In the case of Leslie, allow Sadie not only the opportunity to train but also to benefit from training, whereas in the case of Jessie allow the training but not the benefits. Does Sadie train both of them or rather concentrate her efforts on Leslie, ignoring Jessie evermore? If in the long run Sadie trains only Leslie, we can be reasonably confident that the point of the training was to benefit the trainer.

By contrast, a pedagogue, tested in the same way, would not differentiate between the two sisters, but would seek to bring the performance of both into conformity with the pedagogue's standards. This outcome, as we noted earlier, is the goal of pedagogy. Suppose that the goal of the training were to change, becoming that of benefiting the trainer. The main consequence of such a change would be to limit the occasions on which the pedagogy occurred. No longer keeping an eye on the young, surveying their performance in the light of standards, the pedagogue would train only those whose improved performance was of benefit. For instance, the pedagogue would not train the young simply to climb trees—thereby producing a well-formed act—but train only those whose climbing brought fruit to the pedagogue.

In the case of Köhler's star pupil, Sultan, we find another animal whose pedagogic-like behavior would probably also fail on motivational grounds, though in a slightly different way. Köhler (1925) reported that Sultan watched his less gifted peers struggle with problems that he had already solved, and often went to their aid, apparently to assist them. For example, on one occasion, Sultan stacked the boxes they had failed to stack, reached the banana, brought it down and then departed, leaving the banana behind. Although this may look like pedagogy, it can probably be shown that it is not. Allow Sultan to observe the failure of his peers to solve the problem, but remove the peers before allowing Sultan to enter. Will Sultan nevertheless enter, stack the boxes and leave the banana behind? If he does, then Sultan's behavior does not qualify as pedagogy. More likely, Sultan has observed a state of affairs that he finds nonoptimal, that he is therefore disposed to modify. But modifying the condition of the inanimate world is not pedagogy. Note that changing the inanimate world can have only an indirect effect on the future. By contrast, pedagogy, in improving the competence of the next generation, has a direct effect. In training the young, the pedagogue effectively arranges for a world that will be brought into an optimal state even though he is no longer present to make the change.

Theories of Mind and the Sharing of Experience

The behavior of the captive chimpanzee shows that it has the cognitive capacity to carry out pedagogy. In addition, the captive chimpanzee has been shown to have a "theory of mind" (Premack, 1988; Premack and Woodruff, 1978), which may be regarded as a major prerequisite for pedagogy. Beings with a theory of mind attribute mental states to others and understand their behavior in terms of these states (Leslie, 1987; Perner, 1991; Wellman, 1990; Wimmer and Perner, 1983). For example, if shown an individual reaching for inaccessible food, they understand that the individual *wants* food and is *trying* to get it. Furthermore, if shown an individual whose view of food is obstructed, they understand that the individual cannot *see* the food. This knowledge would enable one being to alleviate the problems faced by another—to obtain food for the one, to remove the obstruction for the other.[2]

To teach effectively, one individual must understand what another *sees, knows, wants*, and *is trying* to achieve. Recent laboratory evidence demonstrates, surprisingly, that the chimpanzee has such knowledge to some degree, though not to the degree that is present in humans (Premack, 1988, 1993). It is not found at all in the monkey (e.g., see Povinelli, Parks, and Novak, 1991).

The captive chimpanzee demonstrates the capacity for pedagogy, and its unexpected theory of mind, yet the wild chimpanzee demonstrates no evidence of pedagogy. Why? There are two principal reasons. One has to do with an aesthetic factor that is extremely strong in humans but is either weak or absent in animals. For instance, humans not only train others, they also train themselves (Premack, 1984, 1991). They devote hours to honing their skills—that is to *practicing*—not primarily for extrinsic reward but for the intrinsic satisfaction of mastering a skill. The sense of standards or excellence implicit in practicing also operates in pedagogy and is responsible for the *imperative* of human pedagogy, for the fact that the intervention is not desultory (as in the chimpanzee) but pursued until the child attains a standard. Practicing—the training of self—and pedagogy—the training of others—go hand in hand. The one is never found without the other.

Second, chimpanzees have no discernible disposition to "share experience." In humans, this is a major disposition, detectable from early infancy. For instance, a 6-month-old infant, clinging to a teddy bear, makes eye contact with an observer, then glances at its teddy bear, inviting the observer to share with it the presence of the bear and of the child's possession of it. In children of 11 or 12 months, who are likely to have a few words, the evidence takes a more overt form. When children point excitedly to an object, almost always a moving one—a bus, truck, fish swimming in a bowl, even an ant crawling on the ground—they call the name repeatedly, avidly seeking eye contact with the observer at the same time (Bates, 1979; Premack, 1990b). The child is not requesting the object, as tests have shown (Premack, 1990b), but is inviting the recipient to share the excitement of the object that the child has encountered. No comparable behavior has been reported in chimpanzees, neither visual behavior analogous to that of the preverbal child, nor combined visual-verbal behavior (in the language-trained animal) analogous to that of the older child. The disposition to share experience is, to our knowledge, unique to humans.

This pedagogical disposition is likely to have played a key role in the evolution of the human species. Since language and pedagogy are independent—as demonstrated by Sadie's elaborate nonverbal training of Jessie—the combination of these two separate competencies could, in principle, have resulted in four kinds of species: those with both language and pedagogy, those without either, and those with either one or the other. But, in fact, we do not find "mixed" cases, of species having language without pedagogy, or pedagogy without language; rather, we find species with either both competencies or neither.

This restriction on the range of logical possibilities can be explained by the disposition to share experience. Given this factor, both language and pedagogy are likely to evolve; without it, neither is. The common code, or the sharing of symbols that language presupposes, is unthinkable without a disposition to share experience. Such a disposition seems equally essential for the evolution of pedagogy, for pedagogy involves bringing others into conformity with the standards one applies to oneself. The absence of this disposition might well explain the absence of both language and pedagogy in the chimpanzee. It is a high price to pay for the lack of what, on the surface, would appear to be an entirely secondary factor!

Adult chimpanzees do not engage in activities that young chimpanzees cannot acquire for themselves by a combination of maturation and learning. Moreover, the offspring's learning largely repeats that of the parent, because, as we have seen, chimpanzees do not significantly change their environments: parent and offspring grow up in virtually the same world. By contrast, adult humans engage in numerous activities that children cannot acquire without assistance. They could not, in ancient times, have acquired advanced lithic tool-making skills by themselves; nor can they, today, acquire reading, writing, or arithmetic in this way. Moreover, children's learning does not repeat that of parents, for, as we have seen, parents and children do not grow up in the same world.

Two features of human intelligence—its modular character and the presence of large individual differences—put an additional premium on pedagogy. These features make for more specialized competence than is found in other species— resulting in "gifted" toolmakers, hunters, cooks, shamans, and the like. The innovations introduced by these gifted individuals are unlikely simply to diffuse through the group; they must in fact be taught to others. Pedagogy plays two roles in human culture: that of transmitting existing skills and also that of preserving the innovations of gifted members.

Culture and Belief

Earlier we observed that nonanthropologists tend to deal with the issue of "animal culture" by focusing on how culture is transmitted, not on the question of the *content* of culture. This is regrettable, for the content of culture illuminates certain distinguishing facets of human beings, while the mode of transmission does not. In particular, a focus on content requires that we attend to the nature and sources of *belief*.

Belief comes in two varieties: weak and strong. Weak belief arises when we simply question the veracity of our own perceptions: Did I really see a snake? Was that a red dot, or only a reflection from the sun? And so on. Perception normally leads directly to action, but in this case action is suspended while we question the veracity of a perception. If I verify the perception and therefore *believe* it, I will act. This form of belief is weak because it still depends heavily on evidence and is only a small step removed from perception.

The strong form of belief is far removed from perception; its relation to evidence is no longer simple but now quite complex. The complexity is well demonstrated by religious beliefs. Consider, for instance, the relation between the evidence and the belief that Jesus is the son of God, that the consumption of pork is evil, that the devil is a fallen angel. Let it not be assumed that the relation between belief and evidence is complex only in these cases. Take such beliefs as that germs cause disease, or that the universe began with a big bang. Though these beliefs are widely accepted, most of us do not hold them because of the evidence on which they stand. What proportion of those who believe unswervingly in the germ theory of disease have ever seen a germ, or even requested to see one as a condition for their belief?

A theory of disease is one of the standard components of human culture. The germ theory is a replacement for an earlier theory that distinguished between the body and the soul, holding that illness was caused by the soul leaving the body, so that the healer's task was to recover and return it. The big-bang theory is a version of yet another universal component of human culture, an origin myth, an account of how the world began. No human culture lacks such an account.

We hardly need a comprehensive list to observe that beliefs of this kind are not found in nonhuman animals. Although the weak form of belief might possibly be found, there is no evidence presently for the strong form. A strong belief is essentially an informal theory, concerned, for example, with how the world began, the elements of which it is made, what holds these elements together, what causes disease, and so on. It therefore raises all the questions concerning evidence that are raised by more formal theories.

On what do these cultural beliefs or informal theories depend? Ultimately, of course, on language, for they could not be propagated without it. But language is both ontogenetically and phylogenetically a late prerequisite, applicable only to a developed stage of belief. There are earlier prerequisites, such as the existence of a set of categorical domains into which the infant is primed to divide the world— physical object, mind, biological kind, and number being presently recognized examples. There is increasing evidence that the infant divides the world into such domains, entertaining hypotheses not only on what constitutes a member of the domain but also the privileged changes to which members of a domain are subject (Hirschfeld and Gelman, 1993).

For instance, inanimate objects are distinguished from animate ones by the character of their movement. The former move only when acted upon by other objects, whereas the latter start and stop their own motion—that is, they are self-propelled. The infant assigns different interpretations to the two kinds of movement. Induced motion—for example, one object launching another—is interpreted as caused (Leslie and Keeble, 1987), whereas self-propelled motion is interpreted not as caused but as intentional (Dasser, Ulbaek, and Premack, 1989; Premack, 1990a). In addition, children consider biological kinds to have special properties, which include growth and reproduction as well as disease. Strong beliefs (or informal theories) as to what causes disease are, as we have already seen, an invariant component of culture. The kinds of theories of which cultures are composed are likely to bear a close relation to the different domains recognized by the infant. In every case, cultural theory may represent an attempt to explain the changes that are specific to a domain—or that an infant considers to be specific to it.

Nonhuman animals lack culture not only because they do not propagate their traditions by imitation or pedagogy but also because they are without the foundations on which cultural belief depends. In other words, it is not just the lack of language that prevents them from holding theories about the world: more fundamentally, it is the fact that they lack the categorical distinctions that are the principal prerequisites for theory building. Perhaps they are not primed, as is the infant, to divide the world into categories whose members undergo distinctive kinds of changes.

What conception does the chimpanzee have of biological kind? Does it understand—as young children do (Keil, 1989)—that members of such a kind grow (as inanimate objects do not), undergoing appreciable physical transformation while at the same time preserving their identity? Although highly testable, by means of the same nonverbal procedures that are applied to infants, these questions have not been answered. Animals, we can speculate, will either prove to recognize no domains, or their domain recognition will be less well formulated than that of human infants. This could itself explain the animal's lack of culture, for the seeds of culture lie in the human infant's domain recognition.

In holding theories about the world, humans are beset by the questions to which these theories lead. Disposed to share experience, they pursue these questions together. The initial environmental changes that humans made, and which set history in motion, were all changes arising from practical matters—a shift to agriculture, large settlements, permanent shelters. Practical interventions continue to give rise to environmental changes, but more recent changes have come from another source. What are the basic particles of which the world is made? What forces hold them together? How did it begin? Concerted attempts to answer these profoundly theoretical questions brought about the nuclear revolution, a more momentous change than any brought about by practical concerns. Indeed, the rate of historical change linked directly to practical concerns is meager compared with that resulting from attempts to answer theoretical questions. All the questions for which special sciences have been developed are adumbrated in informal theories of culture. In addressing these questions, human beings have quickened the pulse of history and widened their gulf from the animals.

What Is the Need for Pedagogy?

Although forms of behavior resembling pedagogy are to be seen in animals, they fall short of the human form on several grounds. Those that qualify in even some respects are extremely infrequent, whereas those that have the desired complexity are not only infrequent but motivationally incorrect, clearly done solely for the trainer's benefit.

Is pedagogy more effective than unassisted learning? Will it enable individuals to learn skills and acquire knowledge that they do not learn otherwise? Though the answer is emphatically "yes," discussion of that question will be delayed for a later section. Let us return now to the question of the need for pedagogy, and how such a need could have arisen.

A need for pedagogy could have been brought about by a sufficient increase in the variability of intelligence within a species. When individual differences in intelligence reached a sufficient magnitude, then innovations by the gifted members might lie beyond the range of the less gifted; the latter could acquire such innovations only with assistance.

Human intelligence is indeed more variable than that of animals. However, it differs from that of animals not only in having greater within-species variability but also in being more divisible into separate or specialized components. This modularity is only hinted at in animals. We do not find the chimpanzee that is strong on verbal factors but weak on quantitative ones; high on social skills but low on spatial. And if we do find such profiles in animals they are certain to be less pronounced than they are in humans. Among humans, there are individuals who are capable of significant innovation in one component but incapable, without assistance, of acquiring even existing knowledge in another component. This is not a condition likely to be found in an animal.

Is the variability and modularity of human intelligence sufficient to make pedagogy a necessity? Presently it is. Scientists provide examples of this kind of innovation every day. So, for that matter, do homemakers. A close look at the kitchens of the world would reveal new ways of preparing food that only expert cooks could acquire on an observational basis. Most of the population would require pedagogy! So much for the present.

But when did this condition first arise? When did the divisibility of human intelligence into specialized components attain a magnitude that would make pedagogy beneficial, not to pedagogues, of course, but to their kin (who would be the principal beneficiaries in any case)? Though the definitive answer to this question must be left to appropriate scholars, prehistorians, and others, we can speculate about these matters from the already known variability in tools. For instance, the transition from the protractedly unchanging tool kit of *Homo erectus* to the subsequent rapid growth suggests the kind of change we are looking for (Jelinek, 1977). The transition may mark both the change in intelligence that would make pedagogy advantageous and the emergence of pedagogy itself.

In summary, whenever an appreciable proportion of a group cannot acquire the innovations of its gifted members by the usual combination of imitation and learning, a need for pedagogy arises. It is not necessary, of course, that the innovator do all the teaching. At most, he or she need teach only one other individual, or not even one, for the population may include others who, though incapable of producing the innovation themselves, understand it, and could teach it to others.

The Role of Pedagogy in Culture

Advantages of Pedagogy

Earlier we asked whether pedagogy is more effective than unassisted learning. Our answer was an emphatic "Yes," for the following reasons.

1. Pedagogues provide superior feedback. They know what the ideal product should look like and judge novices accordingly. By contrast, the novice, being ignorant of what the ideal looks like, may settle for a decidedly inferior product, a tool that "works" but with suboptimal efficiency. In this connection, one author is reminded of the cooking of two generous young anthropologists who guided him through the Kalahari, sharing their food with him. Though both had had ample opportunity to observe their colleagues cooking in the field, and thus to learn the basics of this discipline, certain details had escaped them. They neither preheated their cooking utensils nor lubricated them. Steak was

placed in a cold pan and eggs cracked into one that was neither heated nor greased. Somehow, the wayward products that emerged from their campfire never led them to question their procedures. In fact, not until the peculiarity of their cooking was pointed out to them did they recognize the inadequacy of the food they had been eating for months or perhaps years. Yet when pedagogy exposed them to preheating and lubrication, they immediately adopted these practices. Which is to say, often the first contribution of the pedagogue is to teach the novice how things are supposed to be.

2. Pedagogues may encourage novices. They may know, as novices do not, that a period of intermediate achievement, a plateau, intervenes at a certain stage, but that the novice has only to persevere in order to achieve final excellence. Pedagogues may also encourage the novice, simply by subdividing the task, astutely assigning the novice subgoals that can be reached and that will therefore encourage continued effort.

3. At a more advanced level, the pedagogue can explain the purpose of an act or an artifact to the novice, so that the novice need no longer learn by a kind of blind mimicry. In understanding the causal intent of the device, the novice can modify constructions in the light of that intent. Indeed, the novice may even innovate, departing somewhat from the pedagogue's model.

4. When language is added to pedagogy, the novice can be given the benefit of explicit definitions. Now, the pedagogue can go beyond ostensive definitions, for example, in the case of the kinship system, beyond pointing to cousins or aunts, and provide the novice with formal definitions of these classes.

5. Novices may be taught that they are better at some things than others, that it may be a waste of time to make any investment at all in certain skills, that it would be better to devote efforts to skills where they appear to have some talent. Novices can then trade their products with those of other individuals whose skills complement their own. Although these are judgements that lie well beyond a novice, they could readily be made by a pedagogue.

6. Finally, although the novice in some cases may not learn at all without pedagogy, in other cases the advantage may reduce to one of efficiency, a reduction in error. Even this advantage should not be underestimated, however; while in the laboratory the cost of error is often small, in the real world it can be substantial. Sometimes the novice is not given a second trial.

Origins of Culture

Cultural evolution is said to have fueled biological evolution (e.g., Maynard-Smith, 1972; Mayr, 1982; Tinbergen, 1964). According to this analysis, behavior, once a neglected part of evolutionary theory, has emerged as a major source of natural selection. Conjectures concerning protohumans (e.g., Isaac, 1978; Washburn, 1963) are compatible with this view. At a time when the protohuman brain was little larger than that of contemporary ape, protohuman behavior already differed from that of ape. Upright posture, stone tools, home base, and possibly food sharing distinguished protohumans. Individuals who lived in semipermanent shelters (as opposed to nests constructed each night), made stone tools (rather than stripped twigs), and shared food (rather than scrounging from one another) are likely to have formed social organizations whose complexity would put a premium on intelligence and therefore lead to selection of mutations making for a larger brain.

There is no doubt that the ability to communicate through language can greatly increase social complexity, thus applying pressure for the evolution of intelligent forms. However, pedagogy can have a comparable effect. Any procedure such as pedagogy that increases the diffusion of innovations of gifted individuals, will increase the complexity of the group in which the innovations occur. Moreover, this effect does not depend on language. Even the passive guidance that Sadie used in training Jessie shows how effectively training can proceed without language. In addition, simply being competent in language does not itself ensure that the competence will be used for pedagogical purposes.

Anthropologists, who commonly point out that a certain level of tool making cannot be acquired without assistance, stress that language is therefore essential for a group to attain this level (e.g., Harris, 1975; Jelinek, 1977; Leroi-Gourhan, 1964). The confounding of language with pedagogy is a common error; what anthropologists mean is that since the skill cannot be acquired without assistance, pedagogy is needed to diffuse the skill. But pedagogy, as we have seen, does not require language.

The Anthropology of Pedagogy

Do all human groups engage in pedagogy, as the present account requires? Data on pedagogy are surprisingly hard to find. Pedagogy is not an official anthropological category: No catalogue lists the pedagogical practices of different groups. It is possible to find ethnographies that contain pertinent sections—for example, material on socialization—as well as the occasional monograph devoted to child education. But the questions for which we want answers—for example, Who are the pedagogues: parents, older children, and so on? How much pedagogy is verbal? How much reliance is there on passive guidance? Is the pedagogy used in teaching social practice the same as that used in teaching technology or are there systematic differences? Do cultures differ in the domains to which they apply pedagogy?—these questions are left unanswered by the information presently available. The anthropology of pedagogy is largely nonexistent; its proper study has yet to begin.

The !Kung San or Kalahari Bushmen may be an exception to this pessimistic conclusion. The infants and children of this group have been extensively observed (e.g., Draper, 1976; Konner, 1976), and some of this observation has even led to the impression that pedagogy is not to be found among the Bushmen. It is said that the foraging technology of the !Kung is simple, and that it is not taught to children. When parents forage, young children are not taken along; they are left behind in camp in the presence of other adults and older children. However, not all !Kung technology is simple. Collecting melons may be simple but making jewelry, poisoning arrows, butchering, and so forth, are not. Bushman technology is of variable complexity. For instance, the !Kung make their jewelry from ostrich egg-shell pieces, each of which is pierced and rounded to a more or less uniform shape before being strung in one of several characteristic fashions. How do children learn this skill, or that of making and poisoning arrows, or butchering the several large ruminants that the group eats?

How can it be determined whether or not a group is pedagogical? Perhaps we can simply watch for a time, and if no pedagogy appears, conclude that there is none. But how long must we watch before drawing this conclusion? How many pedagogical interventions does the average parent make in a day? Without some basis for estimating these rates, watching without a specified target may be un-informative. It is better to observe children as they actually acquire the technologies and social practices of their culture.

Furthermore, we know that there is a domain in which the !Kung infant is subjected to intensive training. The domain is one in which we do not train our children, for we do not believe that the ability to sit, stand, or walk requires train-ing. Bushmen believe otherwise, however, and train their infants intensively in these early motor skills (Konner, 1976).

The connection between Bushman beliefs about child development, and their practice of pedagogy is informative, for it suggests how pedagogy may operate in all human groups. Most human dispositions, no matter how strong their innate component, are not reflexes; they are affected by cognitive factors, by the beliefs an individual holds. Thus groups that hold different theories about child develop-ment may be expected to direct their pedagogy at different targets. Although we do not teach our children to walk, we do teach them how to eat. Bushmen are likely to do the opposite: teach their children how to walk, not eat.

The human need for pedagogy is sometimes demeaned on the grounds that important competencies such as that of language can be acquired without in-struction. We do not teach our children grammar—we do not, it is said, even correct their grammatical errors (e.g., Brown and Hanlon, 1970). Incidentally, this claim cannot be entirely correct, for the literature provides amusing counterexamples—for instance, a case in which a child, though repeatedly cor-rected for grammatical error, retains the error while changing virtually every-thing else (Cazden, 1965, 1968). Of course, if grammatical correction really never occurs, we can hardly discover that it does not work. But this case is intriguing from the present point of view for a different reason: Even where pedagogy does not work, some parents still apply it.

Not *every* human activity is subject to pedagogy in *every* culture, nor does *every* human competence require pedagogy. Language is distinctive because it does not require pedagogy, though language is not alone in this regard. Attributing causal relations to inanimate objects, as well as attributing states of mind to others ("theory of mind," Premack and Woodruff, 1978) are evidently also natural competencies; they, too, develop without instruction.

On the other hand, much of what humans learn is not derived from natural competence. At stake here are not only the technologies and social practices that characterize every culture but also the theories that every human group entertains. These theories, detailing how the world began and how it works, are all transmitted by instruction, the cosmologies that trace the world's origins to, for example, a benevolent snake, no less than the scientific theories that replaced them. Although the predilection to hold such theories is not taught, the theories themselves are.

Pedagogical targets will vary among cultures, influenced not only by actual need but also by the theories cultures hold as to how competencies are acquired. Although the acquisition of some human competencies obviously requires more instruction than others, to recognize a need for pedagogy is hardly to endorse a *tabula rasa* view of human knowledge.

Aesthetics: The Motivational Basis of Pedagogy

Although the pedagogue may appear to judge the novice on grounds of efficiency, in most cases such a judgment would require a complex computation of which the pedagogue is incapable. The efficiency of an act or product is likely to be highly correlated with its appearance, but the judgment itself, which is typically quick and unstudied, is based on appearance alone.

In describing pedagogical judgment, we have referred to "internal standards," suggesting that these standards motivate and direct the pedagogue, that all discrepancies in the novice's behavior are computed relative to them. We need an account of these standards, their origins, and their content.

We also need an account of these standards to explain why the chimpanzee does not engage in pedagogy. The extreme simplicity of examples from the field (e.g., the removal of leaves from the infant's mouth) may suggest that the animal is cognitively incapable of pedagogy. But this is repudiated by examples from captive animals. Though cognitively capable of training another chimpanzee in elaborate ways, on those rare occasions when the chimpanzee engages in such training, it does so for its own benefit. The "internal standards" driving the human do not appear to drive the chimpanzee.

In the theory we will present here, aesthetics is ultimately granted broad social consequences. It emerges as an integral part of pedagogy, and therefore affects what one individual does to another. Nevertheless, we first encounter aesthetics not in social but in individual behavior—in the human investment in self-betterment, in the practice of one activity or another in which humans recurrently engage.

Practice

We can expect to see little pedagogy—little correction of another—in a species whose individual members do not correct themselves. Pedagogy starts at home, with self-correction. In speaking of self-correction, self-betterment, or the like, we should keep in mind what is meant when speaking of practice, as in the practice of musical instruments, sports, cooking, speech, or any of the infinitely many activities in which humans pursue excellence. Practice should not be confused with learning. Members of all species learn or eliminate errors, obtaining the pellet more efficiently, but that is not what is meant by practice. There is no pellet in "practice," no consequence extrinsic to the act itself.

Practice is so rare in the nonhuman that when one author first saw what appeared to be a case, he ceased to do any counting or recording, and simply watched. Here was the same Jessie of the earlier example, once again in the compound, evidently practicing somersaults. Most of her attempts were successful, achieving a proper form and carrying the animal straight ahead. But occasionally she failed, twisting off to the side as children do when they first learn to somersault.

The failures were interesting. They appeared to lead Jessie to "try" again, where by try we mean that following a bad somersault, Jessie produced the next somersault more quickly and with greater vigor. A defense of this impression could have been initiated, simply by counting the number of times the chimpanzee quit (did not somersault for, say, 5 seconds) following good and bad acts respectively. If the conditional probabilities were appropriate, they could have defended the idea that animals do "practice"—that is, that they engage in acts that have no extrinsic consequences, actively discriminate good form from bad, and try to produce one while avoiding the other. By themselves they could not have proved the claim— additional data would be needed—but they could have begun the proof.

Practice presupposes three factors: (1) The behavior is done without extrinsic consequences; (2) good can be distinguished from bad on some criterion; and (3) individuals act to maximize the good and minimize the bad. How the third factor is carried out may vary according to individuals and/or occasions. Following a bad act, one individual may respond more vigorously and after a shorter latency (as appeared to be the case with Jessie); on another occasion, the same individual may respond with less vigor and after a longer interval, taking time to "think things over" and responding with special care or delicacy. What is essential is that there be systematic differences in the behavior following good and bad acts.

We see little practice in nonhuman animals. The somersault case, because it appears to realize all three factors, is rare. Chimpanzee stone throwing is more typical. Though chimpanzees are robust (if inaccurate) stone throwers, they are accurate enough to endanger visitors on the observation platform. Chimpanzees never practice stone throwing. They throw only when someone is there.

Play, though common in vertebrates, does not qualify as practice because, while the first factor obviously applies, it is not clear that either the second or third does. That is, there is no serious evidence that animals, when playing, reject bad forms, even to the extent of being more likely to quit after a good act than a bad one, thus providing differential conditional probabilities of the kind described here. Perhaps birdsong is more nearly an example of practice, though here too it is not clear whether either the second or third factor applies. Moreover, the mere elimination of wrong notes, as may occur in the development of birdsong, does not automatically qualify as practice. Indeed, the elimination of errant forms is neither a necessary nor sufficient condition for practice. On the one hand, an individual may try repeatedly to perfect a form of movement, fail completely, and nonetheless be said to practice. On the other, even if errant forms that do not conform with a template are eliminated automatically, this still does not constitute practice. Finally, we must question any improvement that results from practice when, as is apparently the case with birds, only *one* activity is subject to "practice." Humans show no such restriction, one behavior being as likely a target of practice as another.

A more provocative example is afforded by placing mice in a square wheel. When placed in such a wheel, mice of some varieties run more than normal (Kavanau, 1966). Though Kavanau gives these data a simple interpretation, they can be interpreted more liberally. We could say that the mice run until their increasing mastery of the square corner enables them to restore a more or less normal form of running. The same procedure might have a comparable effect on other species. Stones placed in a bird's mouth, weights tied to a horse's leg, a clothespin attached to a pike's fin—these impediments could heighten responding, leading the animal to respond until it had more or less restored the species-specific form of the act.

The investment induced by the impediment would simulate human practice; but it would depart from the practice in two essential respects: First, human practice does not depend on impediments. A human might, in the course of practicing, place a stone in his or her mouth, but only to sharpen the challenge; the act of practicing does not depend on the stone or any other impediment (moreover, no bird would put a stone in its own mouth). Second, the acts that humans practice do not have species-specific forms. Stereotypical form and rate of responding are a characteristic of the rat and of other nonprimates. Not only do rats lick at a fixed rate (see Schaeffer and Premack, 1961, for evidence of fixed lick rate in neonatal rats licking for the first time), they also eat, groom, copulate, run, executing all recurrent behaviors at a fixed rate (e.g., Premack and Collier, 1962). But this is not a characteristic of primate behavior, human or nonhuman. Hitting a ball, diving, driving a car, carving a stick, whistling, riding a horse, playing the piano, shooting an arrow—none of these acts or the untold others that humans practice has species-specific form; they practice to achieve a "best possible" form. It is the sense of this ideal, rather than an external impediment, that goads the human.

Practice is a response to an aesthetic constraint under which all humans operate. Although naturally of variable magnitude, the constraint is present in some degree in all humans. The near-absence in the chimpanzee of either practice or pedagogy is compatible with the overall evidence. Not all human competencies can be found in the chimpanzee (e.g., language), and those that can be found are profoundly weaker than the human counterpart. The chimpanzee's aesthetic competence is evidently commensurate with its other faculties, too weak a device to give rise to more than a suggestion of either practice (self-betterment) or its social counterpart, pedagogy.

Conclusion

We can distinguish three grades of socially transmitted information, depending on the degree of intention in the system. A system is made up of at least one novice and one model, and in the lowest grade of transmission information is exchanged without intention by either party. For instance, a rat often eats as its first solid food an item having an odor encountered in its mother's milk. The information exchanged here was not exchanged intentionally; the neonate did not seek the information nor did the mother seek to impart it.

In the intermediate grade, the novice behaves intentionally, though the model remains unintentional. This is traditional imitation or observational learning. For instance, a monkey, ape, or child observes a model, acquiring a new technology, but the model behaves in the same way whether the novice is present or not.

In the highest grade, both novice and model act intentionally. Not only does the novice seek information but the model also seeks to impart it. The novice observes the model, as in imitation, but now the model returns the observation, in fact, not only observing the novice but also judging and correcting when he or she fails to conform with a standard. This is pedagogy, the most efficient form of social information exchange.

Though precursors of pedagogy can be found in animals, the full-fledged activity is found only in humans. The absence of pedagogy in the chimpanzee cannot be explained on cognitive grounds; it requires a motivational explanation, one we provided in the form of a theory of aesthetics. The theory consists of two assumptions. First, all three levels on which humans describe humans—appearance, behavior, character—are subject to aesthetic judgment. Every culture characterizes a positive and negative value on each level. Second, humans believe that the three levels are interconnected, associatively at least and in some cases even perhaps causally.

Though animals show preferences of an aesthetic kind, either these preferences are based on mechanisms too weak to give rise to pedagogy, or on mechanisms different from the human ones, mechanisms that will not give rise to either practice or its social counterpart, pedagogy. The former is apparently the case with the chimpanzee, the latter with the Japanese quail.

Because differences in intelligence among animals are relatively small, innovations of gifted individuals can be transmitted by ordinary learning and imitation—that is, by a combination of the first and second grades of social transmission of information. But this is not true among humans. Given the greater variability and modularity of human intelligence, most humans cannot acquire the innovations of gifted members by the ordinary combination of learning and imitation. They require assistance. This is one of the advantages of pedagogy for the human species.

Notes

1. Recent evidence, casting doubt on observational learning and suggesting that simple learning will account for the Koshima data, is fully compatible with our point. The dietary practices lie within the competence of the species: They can be acquired without any assistance.

2. Chimpanzees can look at another chimpanzee, observe what he cannot do (and they want done!) and not only train the other to do it but train him in an impressively efficient way. Modifying the behavior of the other (to bring it into conformity with one's desires) does not, we think, lean heavily on the attribution of belief; such training has cognitive presuppositions but attribution of belief is not one of them. No doubt attribution of belief figures importantly in human pedagogy—it figures in all human affairs!—but it is not a necessary condition.

References

Barnett, S. A. (1968). The "instinct to teach." *Nature, 220,* 747–749.

Bates, E. (1979). *The emergence of symbols: Cognition and communication in infancy.* New York: Academic Press.

Brown, J. L. (1975). *The evolution of behavior.* New York: Norton.

Brown, R. and Hanlon, C. (1970). Derivational complexity and order of acquisition in child speech. In J. R. Hayes (Ed.), *Cognition and the development of language* (pp. 155–207). New York: Wiley.

Cazden, C. B. (1965). *Environmental assistance to the child's acquisition of grammar.* Doctoral dissertation, Harvard University, Cambridge.

Cazden, C. B. (1968). The acquisition of noun and verb inflections. *Child Development, 39,* 433–448.

Dasser, V., Ulbaek, I., and Premack, D. (1989). The perception of intention. *Science, 243,* 365–367.

Draper, P. (1976). Social and economic constraints on child life among the !Kung. In R. Lee and I. Devore (Eds.), *Kalahari hunter-gatherers* (pp. 199–217). Cambridge: Harvard University Press.

Ewer, R. F. (1969). The "instinct to teach." *Nature, 222,* 698.

Galef, B. J., Jr. (1981). The ecology of weaning. In D. J. Gubernick and P. H. Klopfer (Eds.), *Parental care in mammals* (pp. 211–241). New York: Plenum.

Galef, B. G. (1992). The question of animal culture. *Human Nature, 3,* 157–178.

Goodall, J. (1988). *The chimpanzees of Gombe Stream.* Cambridge: Harvard University Press.

Harris, M. (1975). *Culture, people and nature.* New York: Crowell.

Hirschfeld, L. and Gelman, S. (Eds.). (1993). *Domain specificity in cognition and culture.* Cambridge, England: Cambridge University Press.

Isaac, G. L. (1978). The food-sharing behavior of proto-human hominids. *Scientific American, 238* (4), 90–108.

Itani, J. (1958). On the acquisition and propagation of a new food habit in the natural group of the Japanese monkey at Takasakiyama. *Primates, 1,* 84–98.

Jelinek, A. J. (1977). The lower paleolithic: Current evidence and interpretations. *Annual Review of Anthropology, 6,* 11–32.

Kavanau, J. L. (1966). Wheel-running preferences of mice. *Zeitschrift für Tierpsychologie, 23,* 858–866.

Kawamura, S. (1959). The process of sub-culture propagation among Japanese macaques. *Primates, 2,* 43–60.

Keil, F. (1989). *Concepts, kinds, and cognitive development.* Cambridge: MIT Press.

Köhler, W. (1925). *The mentality of apes.* London: Routledge-Kegan.

Konner, M. J. (1976). Maternal care, infant behavior and development among the !Kung. In R. Lee and I. DeVore (Eds.), *Kalahari hunter-gatherers* (pp. 218–245). Cambridge: Harvard University Press.

Kummer, H. (1971). *Primate societies.* Chicago: Aldine.

Leroi-Gourhan, A. (1964). *Le geste et la parole: Technique et langage.* Paris: Albin Michel.

Leslie, A. (1987). Pretense and representation: The origins of "theory of mind." *Psychological Review, 94,* 412–426.

Leslie, A. and Keeble, S. (1987). Do six-month-old infants perceive causality? *Cognition, 25,* 265–287.

Leyhausen, P. (1979). *Cat behaviour: The predatory and social behaviour of domestic and wild cats.* London: Garland.

Maynard-Smith, J. (1972). *On evolution.* Edinburgh: Edinburgh University Press.

Mayr, E. (1982). *The growth of biological thought: Diversity, evolution and inheritance.* Cambridge: Harvard University Press.

Norton-Griffiths, M. N. (1969). Organization, control, and development of parental feeding in the oystercatcher. *Behavior, 34,* 55–114.

Perner, J. (1991). *Understanding the representational mind.* Cambridge: MIT Press.

Povinelli, D. J., Parks, K. A., and Novak, M. A. (1991). Do rhesus monkeys (*Macaca mulatta*) attribute knowledge and ignorance to others? *Journal of Comparative Psychology, 105,* 318–325.

Premack, D. (1984). Pedagogy and aesthetics as sources of culture. In M. Gazzaniga (Ed.), *Handbook of cognitive neuroscience* (pp. 15–35). New York: Plenum Press.

Premack, D. (1988). "Does the chimpanzee have a theory of mind?" revisited. In R. W. Byrne and A. Whiten (Eds.), *Machiavellian intelligence* (pp. 94–110). Oxford, England: Clarendon Press.

Premack, D. (1990a). The infant's theory of self-propelled objects. *Cognition, 36,* 1–16.

Premack, D. (1990b). Words: What are they, and do animals have them? *Cognition, 37,* 197–212.

Premack, D. (1991). The aesthetic basis of pedagogy. In R. R. Hoffman and D. S. Palermo (Eds.), *Cognition and the symbolic processes: Applied and ecological perspectives* (pp. 303–325). Hillsdale, NJ: Lawrence Erlbaum.

Premack, D. (1993). Prolegomenon to evolution of cognition. In T. A. Poggio and D. A. Glaser (Eds.), *Exploring brain functions: Models in neuroscience.* New York: Wiley.

Premack, D. and Collier, G. (1962). Analysis of non-reinforcement variables affecting response probability. *Psychological Monographs, 75* (whole no. 524).

Premack, D. and Premack, A. J. (1994). Why animals have neither culture nor history. In T. Ingold (Ed.), *Companion encyclopedia of anthropology: Humanity, culture and social life* (pp. 350–365). London: Routledge.

Premack, D. and Woodruff, G. (1978). Does the chimpanzee have a theory of mind? *Behavioral and Brain Sciences, 1,* 515–526.

Schaeffer, R. W. and Premack, D. (1961). Licking rates in infant albino rats. *Science, 134,* 1980–1981.

Tinbergen, N. (1964). Behavior and natural selection. In J. A. Moore (Ed.), *Ideas in modern biology.* New York: Natural History Press.

Washburn, S. L. (1963). Behavior and human evolution. In S. L. Washburn (Ed.), *Classification and human evolution* (pp. 190–203). Chicago: Aldine.

Wellman, H. (1990). *Children's theories of mind.* Cambridge: MIT Press.

Wilson, E. O. (1975). *Sociobiology: The new synthesis.* Cambridge: Harvard University Press.

Wimmer, H. and Perner, J. (1983). Beliefs about beliefs: Representation and constraining function of wrong beliefs in young children's understanding of deception. *Cognition, 13*, 103–128.

Yerkes, R. M. (1943). *Chimpanzees: A laboratory colony*. New Haven: Yale University Press.

15

Humanly Possible:
Education and the Scope of the Mind

MARGARET DONALDSON

In the first part of this chapter a psychological theory of the mind's development is outlined. In the second part some educational implications are considered. The theory gives equal prominence to emotion and cognition. The two are recognized to be closely interconnected most of the time, though the relations between them vary. The extent to which they may in the end become separable is a focus of interest.

The notion of a developmental stage in the Piagetian sense is replaced by that of a mode of functioning. Modes, like stages, follow a regular sequence but whereas stages are held to be passed through and left behind, modes, once established, remain available for use. It follows that the notion of a single final developmental goal, such as formal operational thought, is replaced by that of a modal repertoire. Three kinds of development may then be distinguished: (1) extension of the repertoire, (2) within-mode learning, and (3) enhancement of repertoire control.

The role of education in these developments is discussed. Some kinds of development are recognized as mandatory for ordinary participation in any society. Beyond that there is emphasis on the opening of possibilities and the exercise of choice. But who is to do the choosing? Discussion of this leads to the conclusion that both child-centered and culture-centered conceptions of education have very serious drawbacks if taken to extremes. A case is made for a thoroughly decentered education that will respect the legitimate interests both of individuals and of the social groups to which they belong.

Background

Science is a communal enterprise and thus much open to social influence. From time to time, the collective nose smells something intriguing, and there is a rush to follow the fashionable trail. These chases are needed, I suspect, for the enthusiasm they generate. They are fun, they are stimulating, and they may bring new understanding that sets off sustained inquiry and yields a lasting gain. But there are dangers. Highly selective attention entails selective neglect. So it is good to pause now and again and ask what we have been overlooking.

In developmental psychology over the past half-century there has been one dominant direction of attention. This has not excluded other interests but it has certainly drawn to it many inquiring minds. Along with it has gone a fundamental assumption that has remained largely unexamined. Both, oddly enough, find expression in a single quotation that antedates the discipline by almost two millennia: "When I was a child, I spake as a child, I understood as a child, I thought as a child, but when I became a man I put away childish things" (Corinthians I:13, 11).

Notice in this quotation the emphasis on cognition. And notice the claim that "becoming a man" means putting away childish things. This claim is taken for granted very widely, not only by those who study development. It is part of our cultural common sense.

I shall be arguing that while certain "childish things" are indeed left behind by most people, much more remains with us for life and is needed throughout life than is usually acknowledged. That is, we are closer to children than we think we are. Also I shall propose that an adequate account of development must not give undue and distorting prominence to cognition.

Why has this cognitive emphasis become so marked in psychological theorizing today? Why is it so fashionable? I do not really think we can attribute this to Pauline influence. After all, beyond the quotation's immediate theme of understanding lies the more general theme of "charity" or love. But whatever the remoter historical origins there can be little doubt that, within developmental psychology, the immediate and strongest source is Piaget. He picked up the scent and blew his horn, drawing many after him. For the avoidance of misunderstanding, I had better start by trying to make clear how I differ from him in the account I shall be giving.

Piaget (1983) argues that intelligent thought in its most highly developed forms originates in certain kinds of direct acting upon the world that give us what he calls logico-mathematical experience. This is a very specific, narrow kind of experience, as we shall see. According to the theory, the actions that yield it—actions like ordering and sorting objects—are later internalized so that they can be performed covertly, "in the head" as it were. They are also organized to form certain tightly defined structures. When this is accomplished, they become the operations that Piaget considers to be the very stuff of which adult intelligence is made. Operational structures are held to be the means by which we reason.

Now Piaget believes that the building of these structures is achieved through processes of active self-regulation. He consistently rejects the idea that the developing mind is passive. He rages against the notion that learning of the kind that fundamentally matters can be simply impressed upon children. Perhaps this is why so many people have failed to see what a limited account he gives of the human mind. It took me a long time to realize how very much he chooses to ignore.

Here is the heart of the matter: expressly, and at times explicitly, Piaget chooses to ignore our ordinary, rich "lived experience" (Piaget, 1971, p. 68). He does not take this to be any part of his concern as a psychologist, and sometimes he treats with scorn the very idea of studying it. For him, there is a crucial distinction between "lived experience" in all its diversity and the "common mechanisms" that underlie it. It is with these mechanisms, stemming from the very limited logico-mathematical kind of experience, that his theorizing mainly deals; and these mechanisms pertain to what he calls the *epistemic subject*, not to the *psychological subject* as usually understood. Indeed, it is only in a very odd sense that the epistemic subject can be thought of as a subject at all. It (and notice that one must say "it", not "she" or "he") is a curious kind of cognitive average constituted by the mechanisms claimed to be common to all subjects at a given level. Piaget suffers greatly from the fact that he did his work before the computational age was here. He would not have had so much trouble explaining what he meant by the epistemic subject if he had been able to give it "embodiment" in a computer.

Thus in relation to what Piaget saw as his great task, the complex richness of psychological subjects was more of a nuisance than a challenge. It was liable to get in the way.

Now it is true that we cannot give an account of any developmental pattern without leaving aside a great deal of diversity. The question is whether Piaget's epistemic subject is so shorn of the essentials of human functioning—even of human cognitive functioning—that the theory is quite inadequate. I have come to believe that this is so. I have therefore looked for commonality of a different kind.

This search has led me to conclude, first, that any adequate account must give a central place to emotion. This would be true, by reason of the ways in which thought and emotion are connected, even if we were just interested in a theory of thought. But the links with thought are not the only justification for according importance to emotion. In other words, I do not include it in a subsidiary role. This must be emphasized, for in giving emotion its own place within a developmental framework, I am departing from custom. In modern Western culture there is an overwhelming tendency to give pride of place to reason and to regard emotion as a lower function that interferes.

Revaluing Emotion

The starting point for a revaluing must be to take a fresh look at the nature of emotion. Has this been well understood? On the whole I think not. Let me begin, then, by asking if we can say anything quite general about the conditions that favor emotion. When does it tend to occur? When does it tend not to occur? The latter question, which is not frequently asked, turns out to be the more revealing. We are so often emotional that it can be hard to discern similarities in the evoking circumstances.[1] But a common feature is much easier to detect where emotion is absent: We feel no emotion in response to that which is unimportant. We shrug our shoulders. What is that to us? What difference does it make? We do not care.

Emotion arises only when we do care. It is a response to *that which matters*. Recognition of this is the first step to a better understanding of the place of emotion in human lives.

However, there is a distinction to be drawn without which the argument will run into confusion as many others on this topic have done before. It is possible for human beings to assess importance in a way that is mainly intellectual. We can under certain circumstances make dispassionate value judgments.

These are expressly meant not to be emotive (though to be wholly dispassionate about anything that matters at all is never easy). An example of such a judgment would be the decision about whether a work of art is genuine or a forgery. Another is my attempt in this paper to assess the importance of emotion within a theory of development.

How then are emotions to be distinguished from the other kind of judgment of value or significance? The best way is to recognize that emotions are value *feelings*. They are apprehensions of importance felt in the body—in the chest and the gut and the limbs and along the spine—and often felt very strongly.

Now to stress that emotions are value feelings and to distinguish them by this means from dispassionate value judgments is not to say that emotions are independent of our cognitive capacities. It is frequently taken to imply this, but it does not. They may sometimes be irrational, as indeed our thoughts often are. But emotions are not by their nature cut off from judgment.

Consider the following. We interpret the world that we encounter, we struggle to make sense of it, and this interpretive activity is a large part of what we mean by cognition. It yields what we call understanding. How could it be divorced from the question of what we take to matter and what emotions then arise? If we *mis*interpret something, inappropriate emotions may well follow and the outcome of that may be seriously undesirable.

The point is that emotions, most of the time, are not disjoined from what we think and believe. Indeed, the relationship is so close and intimate that to study human cognition without taking emotion into account is really an odd enterprise. How can we have come to take it as normal? Only by concentrating on a narrow cognitive bandwidth, not much in use, and ignoring all the rest.

This has seemed to be a justifiable research strategy because of the power of a modern Western fable: the fable of Reason. The story goes like this. Reason is the great glory and crowning achievement of the human mind. It is logical, precise, hard-nosed, and compatible with the materialistic worldview. And it is chiefly to be found among adults, especially males, who have had a lengthy, traditional, Western education. These people—the members of this small group—have the distinction of being able to function rationally most of the time. Regrettable lapses do occur, even in them; but such lapses are commonly due to the interference of emotion, which is an altogether lesser function. So emotion, if it is felt, is better not displayed. To feel it is unworthy. To display it is more unworthy still.

This fable—this quite unreasonable yarn—has been a kind of background murmur in Western culture for centuries, often only half heard, a widely taken-for-granted refrain. It has been clearly heard by some, of course, and challenged by some, but it has not been ousted. In its terms the leaving out of emotion from the study of cognition does not seem strange at all. It looks like the "reasonable" thing to do. Accordingly it has been done.

Now it is not wrong to say that emotion interferes with thought. So it often does, and very seriously too. But that is not the whole story. Emotion also empowers thought. If nothing mattered, how much would we think at all? And again it is not nonsense to say that thought can interfere with emotion. The fact is that the relations between the two are complex and variable. I believe the best way to gain understanding of them is through a study of how they develop. This study must be made within a new conceptual framework, quite different in its most fundamental assumptions from the Piagetian one that has been dominant for so long.

The Modal Theory of Development   The new framework must make provision for dealing with the rich complexity of lived experience. Where do we start? It is helpful to start from the fact that the mind typically directs itself toward some object of interest or concern. That is, mental activities are always *about* something.

The recognition that being about something is characteristic of the mind's functioning is no new idea. Its history goes back at least to the Scholastic philosophers of the Middle Ages. However, it was Franz Brentano (1874/1973) who brought it into use within psychology. Like the Scholastics, Brentano used the word "intentionality" to name the quality of "aboutness." Today, since we have come to use "intentionality" in a narrower sense, the word "concern" seems a better choice. Let us say, then, that a mind's concern, at any given moment, is what its activities are about. That is the most general way to put it.

Now the concerns that are possible for a human mind are of great diversity. So if *our* concern, as psychologists, is to find pattern in all this variety, we need to take a step further. And, if we are in search of developmental patterns, that step must have regard to the changes that take place as people grow older.

One highly significant change from this point of view is the increase in spatiotemporal scope. The arena for our concerns enlarges vastly. And as it does so a number of points can be discerned at which, fairly suddenly, new openings of possibility occur. Let us call these *advents*. Advents mark the start of a new *mode*.

During the period shortly after birth, a baby can deal only with what is present here and now, though that already gives much scope for active, emotional, thoughtful concern. The first advent—or break-out, as one might say—comes with the onset of the capacity for dealing with what lies elsewhere in space-time. The mind, no longer confined to *here and now*, begins to move into the vastness of *there and then*.

However, a notable restriction remains and will stay for a while longer. Concern continues to be about specific happenings just as it was in the earliest months of life. The difference is that the happenings may now lie in a past that is ordered in time or in a future conceived as possible. It is a big difference. An even bigger one is to follow.

The next advent consists in a striking movement from specificity to generality: from *there and then* to *somewhere, sometime* or *anywhere, anytime*. The mind starts to be able to concern itself with the general nature of things, with the way the world is ordered.

Once this new kind of concern is established, it may seem as if we have reached a limit. For what can follow—on this dimension of change—except a further gradual enlargement of the conception of space-time? There is more, however.

The next great extension of the range comes with the advent of concerns that have no locus in space-time at all—concerns that transcend space-time, we may say. Clear and familiar examples of these are to be found in mathematics and logic. Concern here is with relationships—more particularly with the systematic study of patterns of relationships. These patterns may have an *instantiation* in space-time, but when we study formal logic or "pure" mathematics concern lies with relations themselves, considered in complete independence of any spatio-temporal existence. A line, for Euclid, is breadthless length. We cannot, strictly, imagine such a thing, for we never meet with it. But the mind can ultimately work with the idea.

I have discussed elsewhere in some detail the evidence about the advents of the modes (Donaldson, 1992), and I shall not rehearse it here. What is important for the present argument is just the basic fact that we can discern four modes of functioning defined by spatio-temporal *locus of concern*. In the mode first available to the child, the locus of concern is here and now. This is called the *point mode*. As development proceeds, there is added a second mode: the *line mode*. The child is now able to be concerned with specific events recalled from the past or anticipated in the future. After this comes the *construct mode*: a mode in which concern has shifted from the specific to the general. The child can now think about, have emotions about, the ways things are in the world, which includes the very important matter of how the self fits into this world. In this mode the constructive activities of the imagination, already important in the line mode, come to have very special parts to play. Then lastly there follows—or may follow—the development of the *transcendent mode*, in which concern is no longer with things and happenings in space-time at all. The example of logical and mathematical thinking serves to illustrate the general nature of the transcendent mode by reference to intellectual functioning. The question of emotion in this mode will be considered later.

So far this is obviously a quite sketchy account. There will be more to say about the nature of the modes and especially about their critically important subdivisions. Before we proceed to further detail, however, it is essential to make one point clear: The modes follow one another developmentally, but they do not replace one another. Once available, they remain available throughout life, unless there is some damage to the functional integrity of the brain. Thus they are fundamentally different from Piagetian stages. It is true that both stages and modes follow an order of appearance that is invariant. But there the resemblance ends. To make this quite clear, let me spend some time on the dissimilarities.

Within the Piagetian system, each stage is characterized by its own organization or structure. Movement onward to the next stage is held to entail the breaking up of this organization so that for a time there is bound to be a measure of disequilibrium in the system. But because it is in the nature of the individual organism to engage in certain kinds of self-regulation, there then ensue processes that work toward the establishment of a new state of equilibrium that will be "better" in certain ways than the one it replaces. Specifically, a state of improved equilibrium is one that can handle successfully a greater number of contingencies, as well as being more permanent, more mobile, and more stable. According to this view, then, as each stage builds on its predecessor, the predecessor effectively disappears. It is engulfed. It does not remain as an option available for further use.

In these respects stages and modes are sharply different. A mode is not broken up in order that its successor may be formed. It is not subsumed into the form of its successor. It is not replaced or "put away," to quote Saint Paul's words again. It continues to function with no diminution of importance. The appearance of a new mode does not mark even the completing, let alone the superseding, of its predecessors. For the advent of new modes is not the only way in which development of the mind takes place.

One way, certainly, is by the addition of new modes, and we shall call this *expansion of the repertoire*. A second, however, is by widening the scope of competence within an existing mode, as when, having already become capable of some mathematical thinking, we extend our understanding. This is *within-mode learning*.

There remains a third kind of development that is often entirely overlooked both in theory and in educational practice. This is the development of the ability to decide in which mode—or modes—one is going to function at a given time and for a given purpose. Let us call this *control of the repertoire*. It is of very great significance. Its cultivation—for it needs to be cultivated—should have a central place in the devising of educational strategies.

If the aim were only to give an account of the development of cognition, this fairly simple outline might serve as a framework. But if the mind is to be understood not just as a thinker, then there are further complexities to reckon with.

So far, in trying to correct the current overemphasis on thought, it is emotion that I have stressed as having suffered neglect. But if we are going to come at all close to lived experience, we must provide a framework that deals also, at the very least, with action and perception. What this means, in effect, is that we must allow for subdivision of the modes according to the components of mental activity that are active. Consider, for instance, the point mode, where the locus of concern is here and now. The most usual case when the mind is occupied with some feature of the present is for perception, thought, emotion, and direct action all to be implicated in some degree. This is certainly normal for young children. For them, the various aspects of the mind's functioning are so closely interwoven that separation is barely possible. There is an all or none quality about a young child's involvement that is striking to observe. Later, however, the possibility of some separation begins to arise. The child can, for instance, control the extent of motor activity so as to sit still and watch. As development proceeds further, the degree of possible separation of components increases. Thus in the line mode we have thoughts and emotions about events in the past and in the future but we can have no direct perception of these (unless we allow for some form of extrasensory perception), and we do not act except in the present.

It is true likewise in the construct mode that direct acting and perceiving drop out. The giving up of continual reliance on them is part of the process by which the scope of the mind's concerns comes to be enlarged. To this extent the line and construct modes are alike. The difference between them lies, as we have already seen, in the movement from specificity to generality. With the advent of the construct mode the mind starts to be actively and consciously concerned about the ways in which the world (including, very importantly, the personal and social world) is organized.

Within the construct mode three subdivisions must be recognized. These are called the core construct mode, the intellectual construct mode, and the value-sensing construct mode. They arise out of the varying relations that occur between thinking and emotion. Sometimes—indeed usually—thoughts and emotions in this mode are as thoroughly and consistently interwoven as in the ordinary functioning of the point and line modes. When this is so, the mind is functioning in the *core construct mode*. This is the arena for most of politics, ideology, and national feeling and for much religion. Here, too, belong all concerns about one's self-image. Whenever thoughts and emotions are closely bound together in a single experience, the term *core mode* will apply. Thus the line and point modes in the forms already described fall into this category together with the core construct mode.

The same is not true of the remaining two subdivisions of the construct mode, for here the process of "dropping out" or separation reaches the point where it affects not only action and perception but emotions and thinking too. It becomes possible to suspend either one of them for a while, at least to some degree. However, this suspension seems to be rarely, if ever, complete. Certainly we can function in a way that is mainly cognitive. We can try for—and in some measure achieve—dispassionate thought. But even here emotion is not often entirely absent. For one thing, the urge to understand necessarily entails some apprehension of importance; and even if the problem is trivial, this urge is seldom quite cool. Where the emotional warmth of interest is altogether absent in someone who is nevertheless *required* to think, we have a situation, uncomfortably familiar to educators, where thinking is unlikely to be at its most effective. Einstein described himself as passionately curious, and the emotional power of a real desire to understand has to be allowed for in specifying the nature of even the most thought-dominated division of the construct mode. This division, where thought is strongly dominant, is the *intellectual construct mode*. Yet in it there occurs, as a normal feature of the activity, the delight that comes when one glimpses a feasible solution or sees a new pattern emerging. This kind of emotion is integral to the intellectual endeavor. But notice that whenever emotions of other alien kinds, such as concern for personal standing, break in, then one is no longer in an intellectual mode. Such motives, when present, shift the activity into a core mode, however intellectual it may seem. This is so by definition.

We have now considered two of the three divisions of the construct mode: one where thought and emotion mingle and interweave freely, and one where thought is dominant though certain kinds of appropriate emotion accompany it—and, indeed, support it. What of the third? In the third, which is the *value-sensing construct mode*, emotion is dominant; and thinking, though not absent, has a secondary part to play.

This kind of mental functioning has not been a focus of interest within developmental psychology, a fact that presents some problems for a developmental theorist who becomes aware that a gap exists in a theoretical structure. The first question following this awareness must be: Do people indeed have as part of their mental repertoire, anything that fills it? For in principle it might turn out to be empty.

Let us look to see. But first we had better be quite clear about how we would know what we are looking for if we were to find it. The value-sensing modes are so defined as to run, in some sense, parallel to the intellectual modes. And just as the word "intellectual" distinguishes some kinds of thinking from others, so the word "value-sensing" marks out some kinds of emotion. The distinction is this: Value-sensing emotions must, like intellectual thoughts, have certain impersonal qualities. Of course, there is always a person doing the feeling or the thinking but the thoughts and feelings must be *about* some more general concerns if they are to belong in these modes. Do people then, in fact, respond emotionally to concerns that transcend the personal? Do they experience emotions that are not about specific events such as the success or failure of some purpose, not about being praised or blamed, loved or hated, not about the status of their person or their own social or ethnic group or their own religion? Do emotions occur that are not in any way about one's own fortunes or the fortunes of those one cares about?

As soon as the question is formulated in this way the answer is obvious: of course they do. Certain quite common types of response to art and to music, and certain kinds of religious or spiritual experiences clearly satisfy the criteria. These experiences are strongly felt in the body and they mark an apprehension of value or importance. Thus they are emotions. But the values apprehended do not derive from the personal life. There are certainly personal prerequisites for the recognition of such values but emotions felt in response to them are not about the personal life at all. Notice that the analogy with intellect holds well in that there are personal prerequisites for intellectual activity but the activity itself must achieve independence from personal concerns.

A word of caution is in order, though: It is not the case that all artistic, musical or spiritual experiences belong in the value-sensing modes. We may feel emotion in listening to a piece of music precisely because we associate it with something that happened to us in the past or because it has some special significance for our football club, say, or for our country, as anthems do. In the case of religion we may have emotions that are about the hope of heaven or the fear of hell. Or we may have feelings that are closely bound up with sectarian thinking. These belong in the core modes beyond any doubt.

Thus it is necessary to be careful in deciding what satisfies the criteria for the value-sensing modes. But exactly the same is true of the intellect. Much that passes for intellectual activity properly belongs in the core modes because of the prominence in it of personal concerns.

One further important question arises about how far the intellectual/value-sensing analogy will go. There is, as we have seen, a distinction to be drawn between the intellectual division of the construct mode and the intellectual transcendent mode. The distinction we are considering hinges on the role of imaging derived from our experience of space-time. In the intellectual transcendent mode, where the locus of concern does not lie in space-time at all, we have to be able to stop relying on such imagery though it is freely used and heavily relied on in most other thinking. Is there a comparable distinction on the value-sensing side?

When we turn to emotional development, the distinction between *construct* and *transcendent* seems less clear-cut but it is, I think, still there. For a discussion of this complex topic see Donaldson (1992). One difficulty should be noted here: As emotions cease to be about the vicissitudes of individual lives they become harder—sometimes almost impossible—to talk about. They are commonly described as ineffable. However, this is no excuse for neglecting them when considering the mind's scope. We all know about them really. We have just not given them a place within a framework that could help us to relate them systematically to other things. The branch on which they flourish is firmly attached to the main trunk but this attachment has been somehow concealed, or camouflaged. Or else we have simply turned our eyes the other way.

Some Educational Implications

Let us turn now to educational implications, recalling for a start the three ways in which development may proceed. First there is *expansion of the repertoire*—that is, the advent of a mode not previously available. Then there is *within-mode learning*, which consists in some extension of competence in a mode already established. And finally there is *control of the repertoire*, by which I mean the development of the much-neglected skill that enables us to determine from moment to moment how to use the mental capacities we already possess.

Now this theoretical analysis contrasts sharply with any account that presents development as moving toward a single goal, such as formal operational thought. And the most obvious immediate difference is this: The new theory, instead of focusing narrowly, invites even-minded consideration of a wide range of developmental possibilities. At the same time it offers a structure which, by revealing how these possibilities are related, enables reflection about them to proceed somewhat systematically.

The recognition that possibilities for development are many and complex does not mean that anything goes, and so it does not remove the need for judgments of importance. On the contrary, the need to make them—and keep on making them—becomes all the more clear. To be aware that many possibilities are open is to be aware also before long of conflicts arising between them. These conflicts are often such that to realize one possibility is to close off others, if only because the attempt at excellence generally takes time. It takes time to become a good mathematician. It takes time to become a good guitar player, or a good athlete, or to learn to write good prose. We may combine many different developed skills, of course, but we cannot have them all. What becomes actual in a life necessarily stands against the vast, unknowable ground of what might have been.

Thus the constricting idea that potential is something fixed and determinate, able to be assessed as we sit with a child in a classroom—or anywhere else—will not do. A person's potential is not to be thought of as a kind of stop sign on a road, still less as a stop sign that someone else can see ahead from afar. This notion, which belongs with the view of mental development as moving toward a single goal, is deeply damaging. It can cause children to be written off at early points in their lives, with severely harmful long-term consequences.

Of course, there are some people who resist being judged like this. A few may even be strengthened and helped by the process of resisting. But many accept the judgment that their potential is low in some ill-specified sense and go on believing this for the rest of their lives.

However, dangers at the opposite extreme can as usual be found; and the opposite extreme in this case is the belief that anyone may very well do anything. Not so. People differ. They differ in aptitudes and they differ in preferences or personal style. Some like to be in libraries, some like physical action, some enjoy performing in public. Educational choices that go against the person's grain can lead to much suffering and failure.

Yet, though these choices are matters in which individuality must be respected, they are social matters too in a double sense. First, no individual, except in the most rare and wretched circumstances, develops without being profoundly influenced by other people. And second, other people have legitimate interests in the competences that we acquire, in the possibilities that we bring into actuality. What we do with our lives is not a matter of indifference to the social group to which we belong.

Now it is evidently the case that societies, like individuals, differ. They differ, for example, in the immediate difficulties they face at any given period and they differ in the traditional ways of coping that they bring to present problems. What they look for in their members will vary accordingly. There will be encouragement and discouragement. There will be prohibitions and requirements.

Let us consider the question of requirements, for it is of great educational importance. And let us ask first whether we can find anything common to all human social groups in this regard, in spite of the diversity.

This much at least can be said: To function normally, a mature member of any human group must have the three core modes in the repertoire and freely available for use. Even if harsh physical circumstances lead to an emphasis on the teaching of skills needed for immediate survival, these will never be the only concern. There will always be cultivation of the skills of memory and planning, and there will always be a corpus of emotionally rich beliefs—beliefs about the general nature of human beings and animals, about the world, about the cosmos—into which the young members of the group will be initiated. What it is deemed normal and necessary to learn within the core modes may vary greatly, but the modes themselves are universally required. This may perhaps seem too obvious to need saying. But the point is that the same is not true of the advanced modes, and this leads on to a critically important educational distinction.

The kind of development within the core modes that we have been considering is clearly an educational process. Young members of the social group are being taught the kinds of understanding and competence that older members can pass on. However, this is normally done in a quite informal and spontaneous way. There are no systematic objectives, no curricula, no assessments. Above all, there is no special time set aside for the activity. Teaching occurs when a moment for learning happens to arise.

The moment for learning may come when the adult sees the need, or at least the chance, to explain or to demonstrate, which is often when the child has shown some kind of perplexity—a perplexity that may or may not be expressed as a direct request for help. But even this amount of deliberate purpose is often lacking from the encounters that yield the learning. Children seem to pick much of it up in a quite unplanned, effortless way. The most distinctive thing about this early kind of core-mode learning is its easy spontaneity. It uses what the moment affords. It arises out of ongoing events, out of the circumstances of daily life together.

As a model of how to teach and learn, this has proved very appealing. And many educators have tried to adapt it for use in more systematic settings, enjoying the lack of struggle and finding satisfaction in the escape from kinds of teaching that force children to comply. However, a question then arises that should be faced directly but is often evaded: Can the kind of spontaneous education that works so easily in the early core modes serve equally well for learning in the advanced modes? Do they, like the first three, enter the repertoire in an easy, effortless way? And, once they are available, can specific sorts of learning within them be achieved in the same old casual style?

Notice that these questions cannot even be formulated until the distinctions between the modes have been clearly drawn. Lack of this articulation has led to much confused thought and futile debate.

As to the entry of advanced modes into the repertoire, I think it is clear that something changes. The intellectual modes are not within the scope of all members of present-day societies, and I am sure that in this we are not unusual. It seems quite improbable that there has ever been a society in which all the members have developed intellectual competence, even of a modest kind. And the same is surely true of the value-sensing modes, even in societies that set great store by them.

The conclusion seems inescapable: The core modes "come naturally" to us in a way that the remainder do not. If we live in a society where cultivation of the advanced modes is held to matter, the implications for education are then very great, and we must recognize the special nature of the difficulties that the enterprise will bring.

At this point, I want to guard against misunderstanding. When I say that the core modes "come naturally," I am not claiming that they unfold in some automatic way untouched by social influence or personal experience. Not at all. This should be clear from what has gone before, but sometimes it is wise to be explicit. The core modes "come naturally" in the sense that ordinary human life in society regularly yields them by unplanned means, given only that the child is not severely abnormal genetically or in some way seriously damaged early on. If all goes normally, then by the age of four or five a child will have these modes in the repertoire, freely available for current use and for much further development in the form of within-mode learning yet to come. And this will have been done without conscious goal-setting either by child or by adult.

Of course, it does not follow that all learning in the early years takes place in this way. Deliberate teaching and learning do also occur and can be intensively pursued. The point is to note how much is achieved spontaneously. Then, having noted it, we need to move on to the recognition that certain kinds of human achievement demand something other. They demand substantial disciplined study; and they will never come to pass unless there is a plan and a dedication to that plan. Thus we enter the realm of deliberate education in the pursuit of a conscious goal.

Learning that is consciously planned and followed through is of critical importance in the establishment and development of the advanced modes, for reasons already considered. Yet we must not forget that it occurs in all the modes. Think of becoming a highly skilled singer, for instance. There is no way to develop the full power of the human voice without long, disciplined practice. Also the contribution of good, systematic teaching is very great.

Concerning this example, and many others like it, there will, I think, be little dispute. However, when it comes to the development of the intellect, matters are curiously different. Over recent years, the opinion that spontaneous learning is the ideal has proved powerfully influential, particularly in regard to the learning of literacy, where the idea that written language can—and indeed should—"emerge" in the same way as spoken language has won widespread and enthusiastic support. But the appeal of spontaneity has not been confined to literacy learning. There has been a general trend to think it unenlightened to *teach* anything within the traditional intellectual domains in deliberate systematic ways, especially in the early school years. This has gone so far that many teachers who really know better have fallen into line, for fear of the scorn they will encounter.

This curious and damaging resistance to disciplined study seems to derive in part from a fundamental failure to appreciate the nature of the difference between the core modes and the intellectual modes. Skilled activity in the latter demands a kind of control over the relations between thought and emotion that is alien to activity in the former. So if we are to develop the intellectual competences, we must learn to regulate our minds in new ways—in ways that are difficult for everyone, ways that are quite strange and mysterious for children on first encounter. Unless we face up to this fact and try to give children the right sort of help with the new kind of learning, then we fail them. In such circumstances, if they then fail to learn, who is to blame?

I do not want to imply that "the right sort of help" is easy to determine. Giving it is a very delicate matter—a matter of treading a narrow path with equally dangerous pitfalls on either side. Let us consider first two obstacles that often block the way. One has to do with adverse circumstances, material and social. The development of the intellectual competences takes a great deal of time and a great deal of sustained attention. The enterprise is unlikely to go well unless the learner is leading a life that is reasonably comfortable and stable, not liable to sudden crises, perturbations, or alarms. I do not say that things cannot ever go well educationally in the absence of a tranquil, secure life, but the chances are much reduced. If a child is hungry or cold or tired or frequently afraid, how is calm, concentrated attention to be expected? And if calm, concentrated attention cannot be achieved over reasonably sustained periods of time, how is "educational failure" to be avoided?

The second obstacle may be less easy to recognize. It has to do with security also but of a more inward kind. The advanced modes demand of us the ability to hold certain kinds of emotion in check, specifically the kinds that derive from quite personal concerns. Now it is characteristic of human beings that many of our most vexing personal concerns have to do with the self-image: the picture we each have of the kind of person we are. This image begins to be constructed during the preschool years and grows in complexity thereafter. If it is negative in important respects, then it will worry us. If it persistently worries us, then it will be hard to lay aside. If it cannot be laid aside at least for a while, then instead of applying our minds cheerfully to an intellectual task, we will be worrying about whether we can do it. Or instead of just wanting to find the solution to a problem, we will be wanting to prove that we can solve it. Such things inevitably interfere with the development of the intellectual modes. They are at least as likely to interfere with the development of the value-sensing modes, though it is less probable that anyone will notice.

It cannot be denied that events in school can damage a child's self-image. But the sense of personal worth has its roots elsewhere, in the home and the community. Being wisely loved and regarded with respect at home is the best of all beginnings. However, even if this advantage is present, things are harder for children when they belong to a social subgroup that is generally disparaged. There is then much more to overcome in the establishing of a self-image that can be comfortably neglected for a while.

I see some resemblance here to that stage in early development when a baby who has a secure relationship with a trusted mother will happily explore a new environment, ignoring her as she sits in the background. Her presence is an important source of reassurance, but the exploration can proceed as if she were not there, so long as she does not interfere. Similarly, in favorable circumstances the self-image can fade into the background for a time, making room for other concerns.

The two obstacles that we have been considering are not rare and they are not easy to remove. Certainly, it is often not within an educator's power to clear them away. Let us assume, however, that whatever can be done about them has been done. And let us go on now to discuss what positive means teachers can use to help in the deliberate cultivation of advanced mode skills.

Every theory of education takes a stand, explicit or implicit, on the relation that should obtain between the best interests of a child and the best interests of the culture within which that child lives. The culture offers education, formally or informally, with more or less insistence on certain kinds of acceptance and compliance. The child responds in ways that may range from enthusiasm to stubborn rejection.

When the culture insists harshly on compliance, this is of course apt to generate resistance, and a grim and cruel fight may ensue, an outcome that has not been rare and is certainly never profitable. Distaste for this and a recognition of its fruitlessness have contributed to the development of theories of education of the sort that we now call "child-centered." The opposite extreme may appropriately be called "culture-centered," though the term is less often used. Child-centered theories minimize the role of the culture except as a provider of opportunities. In their extreme forms they allow society no right to prescribe goals or procedures and no right to require anything of the child by way of response. The child's individuality is placed center stage. "What does the child want to learn now?" becomes the guiding question.

These ideas are powerfully appealing and in many respects they are well-founded. The teacher should indeed always be concerned about this child here now—and how best to help this child here now. To do so requires an ability to take the child's point of view, to appreciate imaginatively how it all looks to the learner at a given point along the way. Education has to be a shared enterprise, and unless it is felt to be so by both teacher and learner it will never succeed. But on the other hand, the child's point of view is limited. Children do not know the possibilities that lie far ahead. They cannot judge the distant outcomes of choices made now. They cannot tell what later options are being currently opened up or excluded. Of course, no one can tell this with any certainty. But the teacher is so placed as to know more than the child about what lies ahead, about the doors that are likely to be opened or closed.

What these considerations imply is that a single point of view will not serve. Why should we expect it to, when we know how often the coordination of different points of view is called for in affairs of any complexity? Certainly we need to have regard for the child's point of view at the time of learning. To neglect it is to fail as a teacher. But we need to ask also how the things we do now will seem to the same child grown older and looking back. What of the risk that too much child centering may come to look like a betrayal?

To acknowledge that the learner's point of view will change is clearly important, but it is still not enough. I want to argue that the cultural group, too, has a point of view that must not be ignored. It matters to any group how its new members grow up, what skills and values they develop, what kinds of people they become. It matters legitimately. Society has the right to have some say. And beyond this still, I believe we must recognize the legitimacy of yet another point of view, though it is more remote, harder to take stock of. The whole of humanity can in principle be affected by what our child becomes. The outcomes of education anywhere are matters of proper concern to us all.

To say that we need to consider different points of view is to advocate what Piaget called *decentering*. To decenter is to be able to see how things look to others and then to bring the different perspectives into relationship. It is to achieve some kind of overview. Piaget was apt to underestimate what children can do themselves by way of decentering, but we must not make the mistake of overestimating it. In particular, children cannot do much decentering themselves in regard to the guiding of their own education. How could they? The outcomes lie too far ahead. Children do not know what it will be like to grow up and look back. And they cannot be aware in advance about their cultural heritage, either as to the constraints inherent in it or as to the richness of its resources. We should not expect it of them.

The conclusion must be that both the child-centered and the culture-centered extremes are dangerously limited. Culture-centered education, because it neglects the child's point of view, is over-inclined to impose requirements. It values obedience and conformity. Standards are to be reached and that is what matters. There is to be no stepping out of line. Thus the child's capacity for imagination, for exploration, for novel thinking is discouraged. At the same time there is a failure to recognize how much rebellion will be generated, and how much boredom.

On the other hand, if children are left to find their own way, without a map, where they have never been before, then much wandering around in circles is to be expected. And this can be deeply confusing and unsatisfying for the learner. Children are not well equipped to direct the course of their own studies, particularly when these are in preparation for remote ends. It follows that they need well-thought-out help in this regard. And not only do they need it, they generally welcome it, if it is not harshly forced on them by someone who cares very little whether they like it or not. It is part of our humanity to be interested in accepting new challenges from others and in achieving new forms of mastery to which, if left to ourselves, we would never have aspired.

Bruner (1965) has drawn our attention to the fact that children are on the whole better at solving problems than at finding them. In this they are like most adults, for it is never an easy matter to think up a whole new problem. Of course, there are some kinds of problems that force themselves on us, but others are more elusive and you have to seek them out. The ability to do this in adulthood—in science, say, or in philosophy—is often acknowledged to be the mark of a strongly innovative mind. Certainly there are children who show the beginnings of the same ability quite early, but even they will not be harmed by having challenges set for them, new purposes offered to them. A human culture is a rich storehouse of purposes, and it is no small part of the function of education to propose these to the young.

However, a difficulty then arises—a difficulty of central importance for any education that aims to foster the advanced modes. It is that purposes differ in the visibility of their ends. In some cases the goal is displayed in such a way that even young children can perceive it. They may have little idea of what it would be like to work toward it or to achieve it, but they can to some extent comprehend its nature. It is at any rate not deeply mysterious. For instance, they can directly see what it is to be a brilliant ice skater. They can do this even if they have never had skates on their own feet, though they will surely appreciate the achievement more if they have had a go on the ice themselves.

The early appreciation of such displayed goals is helped along if the child comes in close and sustained contact with an expert. When the expert is one of the child's parents, there is sometimes precocious development. For instance, a Chinese girl called Yani whose father was an artist was allowed to watch him at work in his studio and she began to try to copy him at the age of two. Over the next few years she produced a series of paintings that were amazingly skilled (*Yani's monkeys*, 1984). It seems that her efforts were strongly encouraged from the start, so that even when she smeared charcoal over one of her father's paintings she was not chased away. She was in effect accepting a purpose highly valued by her culture. There was a visible goal, an opportunity to try, an enthusiastic teacher. The paintings are distinctively her own, but they are also remarkably sophisticated products of the Chinese tradition.

It is not rare for a child to take some admired and beloved person as a model and thus shape a life. But this is less likely to happen—or at least to happen early and easily—if the kind of activity in which the potential model engages is less visible and comprehensible. What if there are few outward signs of what is going on? For instance, how is the activity of sitting still and thinking to be recognized as offering any sort of purpose to a young child?

So if a culture values purposes of this more remote, less observable, less immediately attractive kind, then deliberate steps need to be taken that will lead toward their communication. Also, of course, any purpose that matters cannot be left to depend on the chance presence of a suitable model. The proposing of important purposes has to be part of an educational plan.

Now it is not possible to legislate for the transfer of a purpose from one human being to another. This is one thing that insistence on compliance cannot achieve, however harsh the regime. You may force someone to comply with your purpose, but if you want to have your purpose genuinely adopted that is another matter.

One may ask whether it is enough that a purpose be complied with, and there are some advocates of culture-centered education who seem at times to think that this will do. I take it as fundamental, however, that education fails if this is all that is achieved. Unless learners adopt purposes as their own, then the pursuit of them will last no longer than the circumstances that induce compliance.

Adopting a purpose as your own entails understanding it, seeing the point, foreseeing the goal, and appreciating its value. Advocates of child-centered education tend to argue that what children learn should always be relevant to their lives. The intuition underlying this opinion is entirely sound. It is that children ought not to be forced into doing what seems pointless. However, insistence on making everything directly relevant to life as it is can be a trap, for it can lead to neglect of the fact that education is about *changing* lives. It is about opening up new directions in which the life may move and thus enlarging the range of relevance. It is about proposing new purposes, new desires.

If this is agreed, what is to be done? How can we give children a sense of remote achievements not readily displayed? If we want to propose to them the ultimate attainment of high levels of competence in the value-sensing or intellectual modes, how can we get them to see the point well enough to be willing to make the long, disciplined effort that will surely be needed?

It is not an easy problem, as anyone who tries soon discovers. There is no magic telescope that can instantly bring the distant goals clearly into view. But there are at least two things that may make the enterprise more likely to succeed.

The first is good planning. It is the teacher's job not only to know what lies ahead but to have a well-thought-out conception of how to get there. There are many intermediate goals that can be offered so as to set appropriately intriguing challenges and give opportunities for the experience of conscious mastery, than which there are few things more rewarding for human minds.

The other influence is of a very different kind. It has to do with the spirit and prevailing mood of the culture at a given time. It has to do with what is generally respected and valued in the community. Children are sensitive to adult values even when they do not understand the reason for them. Indeed the more puzzling these values are, the more they may attract interest. Think of the traditional holy man in India. Suppose that such a person comes to a village where the children observe his treatment. They see that this man, who does no work and is in no obvious way useful, is made most welcome. Scarce supplies of food are shared with him and if he decides to settle nearby this is cause for rejoicing, even though the drain on food will now be a continuing one. The children see, in short, that this man is valued. He is treated with reverence. And thus one very clear message is conveyed: There is more to this valuing business than you can always immediately see. It is a most important message for children to receive early in life. It prepares them in a powerful, subtle way for the later extension of their aspirations.

Jean-Paul Sartre tells us in his autobiography how this notion was first communicated to him (Sartre, 1964). Before he could read, he was in the habit of watching his grandfather handling the books in his library. He saw the care with which it was done, the reverence shown for these mysteriously precious objects. What were they for? Why did they matter? Sartre had no idea. However, though he could not read books, he could read his grandfather's behavior. He understood its emotional significance. He got the message, and it powerfully affected the future course of his life.

When an educational goal is remote and mysterious, willing movement toward it depends on an act of trust: trust that the enterprise is worth the effort. The person of the teacher may encourage—or discourage—this trust but is not the only source of it. Society does likewise through its prevailing attitudes as apprehended by the child. So what can be said about these attitudes and their effects today? In particular what general cultural message concerning the value of the advanced modes is being conveyed? Do children learn early to respect them even if they do not understand them? I think not.

It is true that we demand universal schooling; and through it we attempt at least to introduce all our citizens to the intellectual modes, which is no small matter. Considered in the context of human history, it is indeed a great novelty, a highly ambitious and costly affair. We do not aim to make everyone highly proficient in the intellectual skills, which would in any case be undesirable because it would lead to the neglect of other kinds of development. But we do set out to equip all our children with some skill in the handling of written language and of number, with some basic understanding of science and with some capacity to think rationally and systematically about general themes. The law says that this is to be done, and there is public concern over any evidence that we are not managing to do it. All of this may give the impression that the intellectual competences are widely held in respect. Unfortunately the impression is misleading. It is possible to insist on the teaching of basic literacy and numeracy yet neither to understand the intellect nor to value it.

How can this be? The explanation is that skill in handling words and numbers is often valued for purely line-mode reasons. It helps people "get on" in life. This was already appreciated in ancient Egypt, where the scribe was generally the boss and where an old text exhorts children to study written language by threatening them with accounts of the dreadful toil in which they will otherwise have to spend their lives (Pritchard, 1955). Things have not so greatly changed. Literacy is still valued more for its line-mode usefulness than for its contribution to the development of the mind.[2]

If we turn now from the intellectual modes to the value-sensing ones, we come immediately upon a striking difference: the cultivation of the latter at elementary levels does not improve chances of material prosperity. It does not move people into the middle classes or keep them there.

This has two consequences. The first is that, when these modes *are* cultivated, it is likely to be for reasons more appropriate to their nature. Thus there may be fewer distorting pressures. The second result, however, is that total neglect becomes more common. Certain sections of society, particularly in the inner cities, have become in this regard acutely deprived (Ahern, 1990), but some measure of deprivation is widespread. Many people are aware of something missing from their lives without knowing what it is they feel they lack.

It would be quite wrong to attribute the neglect entirely to the question of line-mode usefulness. The relative absence of effects on material prosperity may explain why there is no popular clamor about educating our value-sensing capacities, but there are much deeper and more complex causes for our attitudes, reaching back into our history. It is the case that for a long time our most influential thinkers and writers have taken the view that reason is our highest capacity. This has been the orthodox opinion, at least since the Enlightenment of eighteenth century Europe. It is the accepted wisdom. Thus our value-sensing capacities have been put in second place. Emotion, even of the highest kind, is not placed in the same league as the intellect.

Why not? I think it is because of sustained, systematic failure to make the appropriate comparison. That is, advanced mode thought is normally compared not with its true counterpart but with core mode emotion. The very idea that emotion can be genuinely on a par with rational thought has not been taken seriously.

This kind of failure to compare like with like will go undetected, with much resultant confusion of thought, so long as the relevant distinctions are not drawn. It is the general theme of this chapter that a number of distinctions of great educational importance have not been widely recognized, partly for lack of a theoretical framework within which they can be presented and considered.

To draw good distinctions you need an eye for where to cut (which means, at the least, a wide and detailed knowledge of the subject matter), a sharp knife (that is, conceptual and linguistic equipment capable of yielding adequate precision), and a steady hand (that is, an ability to hold on to what you are about). This is a lot to ask of anyone! Even so, the making of the cuts is only a first step. However, it is an essential one, for it has to precede the study of relatedness. You cannot lay bare the structure of relations obtaining among things that remain fudged. Equally, if you cut too often or in the wrong places the articulation of the system will not be properly revealed. There is much risk of misjudgement; and the account of modal structure that I propose here is no doubt susceptible to improvement. I offer it as having certain provisional advantages. Let me now summarize what I see as the main ones, especially as they relate to education.

The modal theory ranges more widely than has been customary in accounts of development. In particular it brings emotion in from the cold, stressing its positive importance. This revaluing is done partly by taking stock of the nature of emotion in a way that shows it to be neither inherently irrational nor yet wholly assimilable to cognition.

A consideration of the developmental evidence reveals that thinking and emotion are not related in one single or simple way; and the modal framework provides an overview of the different kinds of relationships between them that come— or may come—into existence as we grow older.

One change of critical educational importance is shown to occur with the advent of movement beyond the core modes. The marking of this change draws attention to the difference between spontaneous and deliberate learning and suggests some rethinking of the arguments about child-centered education.

Lastly, the modal analysis provides a way of putting reason in its place. However, that place turns out to be good and secure. No disparagement of the intellect is implied, nor any denial that rationality is possible for human beings. Indeed, putting reason in its proper place may even afford it some protection from those who, sensing that it has been given a false pre-eminence, would like to pull it down. Yet it is evident that strict rational thought is very hard for us and must be cultivated if it is to be attained more than momentarily. On the other hand, putting reason in its proper place helps to show that the intellect neither is nor should be the sole great achievement. Many are open to us. In particular, developments analogous to those of the intellect find their place in the value-sensing modes; and it then emerges that attainment in these modes needs a similarly disciplined cultivation if they are to enter effectively into the repertoire of the mind.

Notes

1. The heterogeneity of emotions has been used as an argument against giving them what Oatley calls "coherent psychological status." He himself rejects this argument (Oatley, 1992).

2. On the topic of literacy and the development of the mind see, for instance, Olson (1977, 1986).

References

Ahern, G. (1990). *Spiritual and religious experience in modern society: A pilot study*. Oxford, England: Alister Hardy Research Centre.

Brentano, F. (1874/1973). *Psychology from an empirical standpoint*. London: Routledge and Kegan Paul.

Bruner, J. S. (1965). The growth of mind. *American Psychologist, 20*, 1007–1017.

Donaldson, M. (1992). *Human minds: An exploration*. London: Allen Lane/Penguin Press.

Oatley, K. (1992). *Best laid schemes: The psychology of emotions*. Cambridge, England: Cambridge University Press.

Olson, D. R. (1977). From utterance to text: The bias of language in speech and writing. *Harvard Educational Review, 47*, 257–281.

Olson, D. R. (1986). The cognitive consequences of literacy. *Canadian Psychology, 27*, 109–121.

Piaget, J. (1971). *Structuralism*. London: Routledge and Kegan Paul.

Piaget, J. (1983). Piaget's theory. In W. Kessen (Ed.). *Handbook of child psychology*. New York: Wiley.

Pritchard, J. B. (Ed.). (1955). *Ancient near eastern texts*. Princeton: Princeton University Press.

Sartre, J.-P. (1964). *Words*. London: Hamish Hamilton.

Yani's monkeys. (1984). Beijing: Foreign Languages Press.

16

Acceptable Ignorance, Negotiable Disagreement: Alternative Views of Learning

JACQUELINE J. GOODNOW

Analyses of learning typically start from a focus on what is acquired and how this comes about. I propose to start from the other side of the coin: from knowledge, skill, and views of the world that might be expected to occur but do not. That starting point might be expected to lead into an analysis of "delayed development" or "problems of motivation." I shall use it instead to bring out the way learning takes place within a framework of social values and social relationships.

The approach is an extension of some earlier analyses of the social values implicit in judgments about "good" or "intelligent" cognitive performances (e.g., Goodnow, 1976, 1986, 1990a). Initially, my interest in values as part of cognition was prompted by a lack of fit between what I observed in the course of some cross-cultural comparisons and the explanations offered by the dominant "folk psychology" within psychology and education. When cultural differences emerged on academic tasks, for instance, the most frequent explanations were in terms of a difference in capacity or in the availability of the conceptual tools and supports needed to solve a problem. My own sense was that the differences often reflected differences in what was regarded as the "smart" or the "reasonable" thing to do in a testing situation (Goodnow, 1976). On that basis, the definition of the task and of appropriate task behaviors offered the more meaningful explanation of one group doing "less well" than another.

At a later point, a similar sense of doubt about standard explanations emerged in connection with three other instances of "failure" to learn or to achieve. One of these instances had to do with gender and achievement in mathematics. The initial explanations for women's lower interest or lower achievement emphasized variables firmly located within females: their "fear of success," their belief in a lower degree of "natural" ability, their sense that mathematics was not "relevant" to their lives. The emphasis was also on women's responses as a form of avoidance. It was only later that discussions were phrased in terms of differential access, differential encouragement, and women's active choice of alternatives (e.g., Eccles, 1986; Eccles and Jacobs, 1986; Walkerdine, 1989). The second instance had to do with studies of expert-novice dyads. Here the surprise for me was the extent to which explanations revolved around the competence of the expert. With rare exceptions (e.g., Verdonik, Flapan, Schmit, and Weinstock, 1988), most explanations implied that learning would take place once the expert knew how to provide an appropriate scaffolding for the novice's performance (Goodnow, 1990a). That expectation, however, assumes that experts are willing to teach and learners are eager to learn. Neither assumption may be valid. Experts are not always willing to give away all that they know. Novices are not always eager to take over responsibilities as soon as they have the competence to do so. What people bring to any situation involving the acquisition or display of knowledge and skill—what is in "the mind" of both teacher and learner—must surely be both more complex and more interesting than the level of competence they display in teaching or in learning.

The third and last instance raising questions for me had to do with agreement or congruence across generations. Most of the studies on this issue focus upon the extent to which parents and their children hold the same views on a variety of issues: issues ranging from the importance of doing well at school to the kind of occupation one should aim for, the value of obedience, or the importance of commitment to what one undertakes. The usual expectation is that agreement should occur; values should be "handed on." What needs to be explained, given this assumption, are the occasions when agreement does not occur. The majority of explanations favor two variables. One is again in terms of the older generation's competence: the extent, for instance, to which they have offered a clear and appropriate rationale for what their children should do. The other has to do with the warmth of the relationship between parent and child. Taken together, these conditions—proper rationales and a warm relationship—should lead to agreement. It is only recently that questions have begun to be raised about whether agreement, or compliance in situations where parents issue directives, is what parents actually want or expect and whether nonagreement, or noncompliance, should be conceptualized in terms other than terms of "failure" (e.g., Goodnow, 1992; Kuczynski and Kochanska, 1990).

Discontent with prevailing explanations, however, is only a first step. I began to look for explanations as to why we, as psychologists, have acquired such a strong orientation toward explanations phrased only in terms of capacity. I also began to look for alternative ways of conceptualizing learning, with a particular interest in cases of "failure to learn."

On the first issue (a focus on capacity alone), part of the explanation appeared to lie in a particular borrowing from Piagetian theory. When we present children, or adults, with problems that have little or no social value (there is, for instance, little or no social pressure to acquire an understanding of conservation), then the variance among individuals is likely to stem from differences within the individual: differences, for instance, in their logical capacity or their intellectual curiosity (Goodnow, Knight, and Cashmore, 1985). We seem to have taken less heed—or to have segregated into an area labeled "moral development"—everything Piaget had to say about there being content areas where children are not left to think things out for themselves or encouraged to do so. They are instead presented with versions of the world they are expected to accept without reflection. In these content areas, only one's peers might offer challenges and demands for thinking through any differences in viewpoint, and even they might not do so.

On the second issue—alternate conceptualizations—I began to look for accounts of learning and cognition that took more strongly into account the fact that the social context is not neutral in its ideas as to what we should come to know or not know. That decision led toward a more active reading of some anthropologists (e.g., D'Andrade, 1981) and some sociologists, in particular Bourdieu, Foucault, and Habermas (a 1990 review—Goodnow 1990b—summarizes much of what I found relevant for cognitive psychologists).

I began also to look for ways of thinking about "failure to learn" that took both parties into account. That search led me to look again at studies of cross-generation agreement (Goodnow, 1992, 1995). It led me also to pay particular attention to accounts of "noncompliance" or "nonagreement" that emphasized the presence of negotiations between adult and child: a reconceptualization offered especially by Kuczynski (cf. Kuczynski, 1993; Kuczynski and Kochanska, 1990) and by Smetana (cf. Smetana, 1988a, 1988b). In short, I began to consider more carefully occasions where people do *not* acquire the knowledge, skills, or viewpoints that might be expected of them, but where explanations in terms of the incompetence of the teacher or the intellectual weakness of the learner could not be easily used.

To develop an alternative view, I shall draw from formal studies and from everyday experience. I shall also draw from material based upon comparisons of social groups: looking across cultures, looking back in time, or contrasting males and females. These are the comparisons that help us become aware of values and expectations that we otherwise take so much for granted that they seem matters of "nature" and invite little or no reflection. It is appropriate then that, within this book, this chapter is part of a section on the cultural context of development and education.

With this much introduction, I begin by taking a look at the nature of ignorance or incompetence, with an emphasis upon the way that—far from being deplored on all sides—it is often functional, is often tolerated or encouraged, and often serves as a marker of one's social place.

Acceptable Ignorance/Incompetence

For all of us, there are areas of ignorance and incompetence. I, for instance, seldom know the distance from one place to another: I am in fact surprised to find a question about distance (from New York to Paris) on the Wechsler Adult Intelligence Scale—Revised. I type poorly, iron badly (on the rare occasions that I do so), forget birthdays, have practically no understanding of what makes a car run, seldom know where north is, etc. Being the product of a girls' school that did not see science as a relevant part of its curriculum, I have the most minimal knowledge of physics, chemistry, or biology (mathematics was fortunately required by the state), and I have shed the knowledge of Latin that was for some reason seen as an appropriate alternative. (I did retain some knowledge of French and German, and a fondness for English literature.) Once in a while I feel, or others feel, that these deficiencies should be remedied but the effort is usually short-lived. For my part, I am surprised when I find that there are people—people I think of as "competent"—who lack a skill I take for granted. Intellectually, for instance, I understand why some friends of mine do not drive a car but in my heart of hearts I find it extraordinary that they have not wanted to acquire a skill that seems so "basic," and have been able to avoid doing so.

Such areas of ignorance and incompetence may seem strange within a cultural climate that emphasizes the importance of a skilled, enlightened citizenry and the value of constant self-improvement. How do they come about? That question, I propose, not only sheds light on some particular areas of nonlearning. It also helps one move toward a different perspective upon the general nature of learning or development.

The Sources of Acceptable Ignorance/Incompetence

Ignorance/Incompetence as Functional   Three examples will make this point. The first comes from Garvey's (1975) analysis of preschool conversations. When one child wants another to abandon a request (a request, for instance, to join in some activity or to yield something the other wants), what is the most effective turn-off? The most effective is the answer "I can't."

The second example comes from a study of disclaimers (Hewitt and Stokes, 1975). It is often helpful, their argument runs, to present a critical comment with a disclaimer of knowledge. "I'm no expert but. . ." is such a disclaimer. So also is the opening I heard at a recent meeting: "I'm not familiar with the history of this problem, but is this perhaps a case of. . .?" The speaker is, in fact, often knowledgeable. Pleading ignorance, however, allows one to have a defense line to fall back upon, or to be "flat-footed" in a way that admitting to knowledge would not easily allow.

The third example comes from analyses of household tasks. "I can't" is again very much to the fore, along with "you do it so much better." The prominence of such pleas, it has been proposed, often stems from the unacceptability of saying that one is unwilling (especially if the tasks being declined are tasks one is willing to have someone else do). The function of "can't" on these occasions is then one of preserving the appearance of "voluntarism" (Backett, 1982). Phrases such as "I would if I could," "I would if I were asked," "I would if I had time," Backett argues, provide a "fabric of explanation" that disguises a lack of willingness or an inequity that a couple prefers not to face. The fabric, she continues, is one to which both partners contribute; neither wishes to have unwillingness be part of their own or their partner's image.

Backett's argument is supported by Goodnow and Bowes (1994). In their sample of couples who share household tasks, open admissions of unwillingness and open refusals do occur ("there are some things I won't do," to cite one man: "dusting and washing the car"). These assertions, however, are from people who feel sure that they are contributing their fair share or are ready to balance an open refusal of one task with the willingness to do another. Among them, pleas of incompetence may even be regarded as a source for mirth. To quote another of the men interviewed: "Ah yes, she's afraid of electricity; that's what she says. She just doesn't want to change fuses."

These examples may make it sound as if it is only the display of ignorance or incompetence that is functional. That is sometimes the case. There are, however, also occasions when "ignorance is bliss," when it is advantageous not to acquire information or skill in the first place, when it is useful to say to others, "don't tell me."

These examples may also make it sound as if ignorance/incompetence is always a matter of choice. Quite the contrary: It may be expected and encouraged.

Ignorance/Incompetence as an Expected Part of a Social Position   We are accustomed to the idea that acquiring knowledge and skill is the access route to a variety of social positions. Passing tests of various kinds entitles us to move from one school grade to another, to become accredited, to become regarded as "adult." The reverse, however, may also hold. The absence of knowledge or skill (at least the absence of its display) may be what is called for, what is regarded as appropriate.

For one such example, I am indebted to Bourdieu's (1977) comments on the extent of "don't know" answers from women in opinion surveys. For an item such as "France should help Algeria," for instance, the number of "don't know" answers was sizable. In contrast, the number was far lower for a further item: "France should help countries that are less well developed." (The incidence of "don't know" answers for men did not vary across the two items.) The first kind of item, Bourdieu comments, implies political knowledge: not the traditional province of women. The second kind of item, in contrast, is one upon which all women—those "specialists of the heart" in Bourdieu's phrase—may feel that they can freely express a view: in fact, should hold a view in line with the supportive, help-the-needy image that is traditionally theirs.

The second example draws again from analyses of gender in relation to knowledge. It has to do with "knowing a little bit" about many things, but nothing in depth. The ideal held out for many women is that they should know enough to be able to converse intelligently with a variety of people, to "draw them out" on *their* favorite topics. The aim of the "finishing schools" of Europe, for example, was to produce generalists rather than specialists. Special knowledge, intense hobbies: These could wait until marriage. Then a woman could adopt as her own her partner's specialties: his occupational interests and his hobbies. Narrowing her interests too early—that is, before marriage—could reduce a woman's charm, diminish her value on the marriage market. The old arguments for women having portable skills (nurses, teachers, secretaries) had a similar basis. These arguments, I am told informally, are still present but they need not be restricted to low-level skills and are not restricted to gender. Males whose skills are in computing, clinical psychology, or emergency medicine (skills much in demand and easily moved from one place to another) are looked upon with favor by women whose specialization narrows their choice of place.

For a third and last example, I shall turn to a report by Albert (Albert, 1972, cited by Ochs, 1990, p. 297):

In many societies. . .lower-status persons talking to higher-status persons are expected to exhibit confused speech or to otherwise index that they do not know as much as their addressees.

Who could be unfamiliar with such a phenomenon? It is apparent, for instance, in the "confusion" or hesitancy often found "charming" in children or women. And it is, as the English television series, "Yes, Minister," repeatedly indicates, the essence of a good private secretary to encourage his minister to discover for himself what the secretary already knows, and then to applaud the minister's perspicacity.

Ignorance/Incompetence as Promoted   The examples in the previous section come close to the argument that ignorance (in the form especially of some degree of "lesser knowledge") may be encouraged as a way of turning out people whose knowledge, or whose display of knowledge, is appropriate to their role. They know "no more than they should" or than they "need to know." In those examples, however, knowledge is not ruled out. It is simply moderated. For examples of stronger sanctions against knowledge, let me again pull out three from a diversity of reports. As a further contrast to the earlier examples, none of these three involve gender.

The first comes from comments on "precocity." In most English-speaking societies, the usual view of a child who speaks, reads, or walks at an age before its peers is positive. It is "the late bloomer" for whom one has to hunt around for positive descriptions or positive examples ("Einstein was a late talker," for instance). This positive view of precocity, however, is not universal. Blount (1972), for instance, reports that, among the Luo, a child who speaks at an age earlier than most of its peers is cause for concern. In fact, witchcraft is likely to be suspected. Nor has the view of precocity always been positive in English-speaking groups (Kett, 1978). Even in current times, "precocious" sexual knowledge, or a "precocious" awareness and understanding of money or any "seamy" side of life, seems incompatible with the "innocence" (in essence, the ignorance) that is usually part of the current folk image of childhood.

The second example comes from a study by Valsiner (1984). In standard fashion, Valsiner began by looking at the interactions of mothers and young children (toddler age) with an eye to observing the way mothers encouraged children to move toward skill in feeding themselves and in becoming mobile. The study was sparked by an interest in the concept of "zones of proximal development"—zones stretching between a state of being able to operate only with help to a state of being able to act alone. Valsiner did observe mothers offering the kind of guidance that fits the expected picture. He also observed, however, actions that led him to propose three zones: one of proximal development (promoted actions), one of tolerated performance, and one of prohibited actions. Self-feeding, for instance, was often discouraged, or tolerated only after the mother judged the child to have already eaten a fair amount. Sooner or later, the child was allowed to feed itself and to explore the stairs. The mother, however, displayed no great rush to promote skill as soon as the first signs of interest and competence emerged.

Such delays of knowledge and skill, of course, are not limited to toddlerhood. "You'll learn about that when you're older" (or when you're 16, or 18, or 21, when you're married): Comments of this type are frequent. Nor are they limited to the family. "You don't do decimals until third grade" a second-grader I know was firmly told, when he solved—with pride—an arithmetic problem by a technique he had learned from an older sibling. In such cases, it is not only the marking of the learner's social place that prompts the withholding of knowledge. The expert's social position is also protected. Distance between novice and expert can be preserved and the expert can keep control of the agenda.

The third and last example is one to which I shall give special space. It has a particular relevance to the emphasis in this handbook upon theories of mind: teachers' theories, children's theories. Skill in understanding the intentions and mental state of others—as well as those of oneself—is clearly regarded as a valuable skill to acquire. As Ochs puts it, with reference to "Western European societies":

Members of these societies devote considerable attention to speculating about what is or was in someone else's mind. Our legal system, for example, assesses the gravity of an action in terms of mental states and allows speculation concerning the premeditation of actions and the mental fitness of the actor at the time of the action. Further, a major pedagogical procedure in these societies is to get novices to explicitly guess what the instructor is thinking about. This procedure is codified in the test question, where the questioner knows the information and is eliciting from others the information the questioner already has in mind. The interest in this sort of mind probing is also evident in riddles and in games such as "Twenty Questions" and "I Spy," which require others to verbally hypothesize about what is in the speaker's mind. (Ochs, 1990, p. 298).

This freedom to speculate about what another person "means" (indeed, the requirement to do so) leads also to particular ways of responding to statements that are unclear or that indicate an "uncertain state of mind":

Dozens of times a day caregivers in middle-class mainstream communities explicitly guess at unclearly formulated thoughts of young children. The caregivers make a wild or educated guess at what these children may have in mind and ask them to confirm or disconfirm their hypotheses. (Ochs, 1990, p. 299)

Added to the guesses and the queries ("Is that what you meant?") are other probes into the nature of a child's mental state: "Do you know what we're doing? We're having a tea party" or "Do you know what that was? That was a nurse" (Ochs, 1990, p. 291).

Is there an alternate view of what seems to "Western Europeans" so natural and so essential? The alternate view is one that Ochs has reported for Samoa and

Schieffelin for the Kaluli of New Guinea (e.g., Ochs, 1982; Ochs and Schieffelin, 1984). These societies "strongly disprefer verbal speculation on what someone else might be thinking or feeling":

> In the traditional Samoan households, interlocutors do not typically pose test questions nor do they engage in mind-reading games or riddles. Legal assessments of wrongdoing do not rely on properties of mental states, and verbal conjectures on this topic are not part of legal proceedings. When Samoan caregivers hear an unclearly expressed thought of a young child, they do not engage the child in hypothesis testing vis-a-vis that thought. Rather, as in other societies, Samoan caregivers prefer to elicit a more intelligible reformulation of the thought—asking "What did you say?" for example—or terminate the topic. (Ochs, 1990, p. 299)

This is not to say that speculation is not encouraged or that expressions related to uncertainty are absent in Samoa:

> Rather, they are dedicated to speculating about reported events, actions, and conditions. Speculation in these cases addresses the accuracy of the report and poses possible alternative accounts. (Ochs, 1990, p. 299)

What does not happen, however, is the encouragement of skill in exploring the other's state of mind: what they might have meant, what they intended. Competence in this particular area is, to use Ochs's term, "dispreferred."

Implications for General Views of Learning

Documenting the acceptability of ignorance or incompetence is all very well as a way of highlighting an aspect of learning and development that has been neglected. Does it go beyond that? It carries, I shall now propose, two kinds of implication. The first is for the views we hold about the nature of what is known or developed. The second is for our views of how learning takes place: for the ways in which we come to be possessors or nonpossessors of knowledge and skill. I shall discuss each of these kinds of implication in turn.

Implications for "What" Is Learned   We are accustomed to thinking of cognitive change in terms of the acquisition of general logical capacities or of domain-specific expertise (knowledge about limited areas). Thinking about ignorance, however, and combining attention to ignorance with attention to contrasting areas (knowledge or skill that one *must* have), suggests a different view of what is acquired. As a minimal first step, we are encouraged to look beyond the explicit curriculum when we ask what children are learning. An example of such a step is Mehan's (1979) analysis of changes over the course of a school year in the way third graders performed in a classroom. What does it take, Mehan asked, to be regarded as a "competent" member of the classroom? Over the course of the year, he pointed out, children acquired not only the knowledge that was part of an explicit curriculum. They also came to know the question-and-answer formats that the teacher expected, the times when you could talk, the times you should raise your hand.

On a larger scale, we can lay out four propositions that every new member of a social group (children, immigrants, anyone whose social membership has changed) needs to learn in order to be judged as a competent, mature, or reasonable member of the group:

1. Areas of knowledge and skill have varying social value (both positive value and negative value).
2. These values are not equivalent for all people: the values vary with the person, with social position.
3. Styles of learning, thinking, and problem solving have varying social value (both positive value and negative value).
4. These values are not equivalent for all people: they also vary with the person or with social position.

Each proposition can be briefly concretized as follows.

The Varying Values of Different Content Areas. The presence of values is readily signaled by the way we speak, with reference to schooling, about "basics" and "extras" (or "frills," a term that lowers the value of "extras" or "electives" still further). Values are signaled also by the way we refer, in research, to "significant" problems and "trivial" topics. As Anne Oakley (1974) was quickly told, the sociology of housework was not at that time regarded by "mainstream" sociologists as a "significant" research topic. It has gained in respectability since then, especially if renamed as research into "the domestic economy" (the term economists prefer; see England and Farkas, 1986).

The assertion of value, however, cannot be left without asking: What gives rise to such variations? Part of the answer may lie in the perceived strategic utility of particular areas. Taking advanced mathematics in the Australian school system, it is often argued, carries (by way of scaling procedures) extra weight when the final score is assigned in the competitive statewide examinations. The argument is regularly responded to by assertions that advanced levels in any content area carry the same degree of privilege, or that no such privilege exists, but each year the local newspapers carry the same debate. The belief is clearly entrenched.

Part of the answer must also lie in the degree to which an area of knowledge or skill is associated with people of power or prestige. On this basis, "men's activities" usually have preference over those of women. As Margaret Mead put it some time ago: "You may cook or weave or dress dolls or hunt hummingbirds, but if such activities are appropriate occupations of men, then the whole society, men and women alike, votes them as important" (Mead, 1949, p. 168). The association of some skills with *lower* levels of prestige must equally be expected to be a powerful factor. To be assigned to "C-stream" subjects when students regard themselves as "A-stream" students is hardly pleasant. The suggestion that students might learn to type, to repeat an example I have used once before, carries a very different implication in schools where only the lower streams learn to type than it does in schools where all students, regardless of stream or of gender, are expected to learn to type (or learn "word processing") just as they are expected to learn to read (Goodnow, 1990a).

Variations in Persons. The example of typing has pointed to the way the value of a particular area of knowledge or skill can vary from one historical time to another. It has also foreshadowed the fact that the value of a particular form of knowledge or skill is not seen as being the same for all members of a group. The classic current example is the perceived relevance of mathematics (or the "hard" natural sciences) for females. Mathematics, for instance, is still perceived by many, at least in the Western world, as more relevant and more useful for boys than for girls (Parson, Adler, and Kaczala, 1982).

Such variations by gender, however, need to be added to in two ways. One is by noting that gender is not the only source of variation. The perceived "brightness" of a learner is a further source. To take an example from Jackson and Marsden (1966), there was a time (not so long ago) when "the classics" (Latin and Greek) were regarded as the special province of the top scholars (male or female) in the English school system. The "sciences" were for lower streams, and "art" was for a lower stream still. A further addition lies in noting that variations can occur within gender groups, on grounds other than brightness. Among the boys in the Detroit high school that Eckert (1991) studied, taking science (an elective promoted by the school) was regarded by the boys as "OK for the burn-outs" (the ones who were no longer struggling against the system) but not for "the jocks."

The Varying Values of Different Performance Styles. The presence of these values is again made easily apparent when we stop to consider the adjectives we use so readily in commenting on academic performances. We speak positively, for instance, of good questions, interesting answers, and elegant solutions, reserving for what we dislike or disapprove of such adjectives as plodding, pedestrian, a recital of facts, unoriginal. The most detailed analysis of such values undoubtedly comes from Bourdieu (1979). Our judgments of academic performance, he proposes— like our judgments of food and of bodies—display the presence of ideas about "good taste" or "good form." Among the middle class, Bourdieu argues, one particular aspect of taste consists of giving a higher value to form than to content. At the least, both need to be present for an academic performance at university level to be judged as "good." The proposal may seem particularly "French": France, Kristeva (1992) has argued, is marked especially by the value it places on written work that involves, at one and the same time, both a new idea and "stylistic inventiveness." There is no doubt, however, that our comments on academic productions (whether they are on the side of "all facts and no form" or on the side of "all style and no substance") reflect the presence of values with regard to the way problems are solved or knowledge is reported (Goodnow, 1990a).

Variations by Persons. I have remarked already on the expectation that people of lower status should be hesitant rather than assertive in their expressions of knowledge. Let me add at this point an example from Cazden (1993) that is of particular interest. Like Wertsch (1991), Cazden is interested in Bakhtin's concept of "voice," and in the way schooling presents some types of voice as "better" or more "privileged" than others. In classroom discussions of science, for example, children learn that the way to be listened to or praised is to speak with the voice of "true" or "official science": to refer, for instance, to the "scientific" properties of a rock brought in for "show and tell" rather than to the "personal" history of where it came from and how it has been looked after to avoid its breaking (Wertsch, 1991). In classrooms, Cazden (1993) points out, pupils also encounter the expectation that they will come to use a teacher's "voice" to speak as he or she does, although with less authority. This teacher's voice, however, is often at odds with being what Willis (1981), in England, once termed "one of the lads." "Lads" do not talk the way teachers do. What happens then, Cazden asks, when a "lad" wishes to impress both a teacher and his peer group? The skill developed by some, she comments, is a version of Bakhtin's "multivocalism." The boy who says, for instance, "La Paz ain't the capital of Peru, Miss," signals his status as one of the schoolsmart boys by displaying his knowledge of geography. At the same moment, his deliberate use of "ain't" signals his membership in a group that is unimpressed by proper school speech.

Two last comments are needed on the issue of intellectual performance as a matter of "taste" (Bourdieu, 1979) or "intellectual manners" (Goodnow, 1976). The first is that the expected style of learning or thinking varies not only by persons but also by content area. Stodolsky's (1988) analysis of the way mathematics and social studies are taught in U.S. schools brings out very clearly the expectation that children will learn mathematics by prescriptive procedures (this is what you "do"), whereas social studies can come to be learned and understood by projects and by independent thought. The second comment is that issues of style—issues we might be tempted to set aside as "trivial"—have in fact serious consequences. Not to understand the way learning, thinking, and problem solving should proceed, not to understand the way in which knowledge should be presented, is to invite the risk—a risk especially marked in the case of minority groups or of newcomers to a society—of being judged not simply as inexperienced but as of lesser intelligence or capacity (Bourdieu and Passeron, 1977; Goodnow, 1984; Mehan, 1979; Perret-Clermont, 1991; Schubauer-Leonie, Perret-Clermont, and Grossen, 1992).

Implications for "How" Learning Takes Place   I have been dealing so far with implications for our ideas about "what" is to be learned. A focus upon ignorance or incompetence, however, also carries implications for the way we understand "how" learning takes place. Suppose we start from the view that some forms of knowledge and skill are encouraged, while others are tolerated (with amusement or with disapproval) and still others are actively discouraged or prohibited.

That view of what is acquired immediately makes one wonder how far such social realities are represented in theories of human development or of school education. I have come, for instance, to see Piagetian theory—a type of theory for which I have considerable sympathy in many respects—as usually based on the assumption that the learner operates in a "free market". The information needed is assumed to be present, to be sufficient, and to be readily available. The only source of variation among individuals must then be their capacity to make use of what is available for all to take. The settings in which such a "free market" (Goodnow, Knight and Cashmore, 1985; Goodnow, 1990b) holds, however, must be relatively rare. In real life, as Glick (1985) has pointed out, they are likely to be the exceptional cases.

What then is an alternate view? Suppose we set aside the notion that cognitive change comes about by individuals who construct, by themselves and from readily available information, ideas about the way the world works. What is one to put in its place?

Regulation from Above. One strong alternative is a "regulated" view of knowledge. Children, Piaget points out, are not always encouraged to try out their ideas, to ask questions, or to take a contrary view. Whenever such curiosity or challenge runs counter to the demand for "obedience" or "morality," they are likely to find adults issuing few invitations to develop their own contrary positions (Piaget, 1965).

That type of argument is taken further by scholars such as Bourdieu (1979) and Foucault (1980). Knowledge, they point out, is a commodity, distributed by some to a restricted set of others. In effect, the flow of knowledge is actively and selectively controlled by individual teachers and by institutions, by way of decisions about who meets their "prerequisites" and may be admitted or initiated into knowledge. As the economic metaphor suggests, there will also be some who attempt to establish monopolies, to "corner the market" in particular areas of expertise. This kind of alternative to assumptions of "free education," "free knowledge," or "open knowledge" is more familiar among sociologists than among psychologists. A knowledge of such views, however, can add considerably to psychologists' approaches to the way development or education proceeds (Goodnow, 1990b). This type of viewpoint may, in fact, be becoming part of general culture. I have now seen a ten-year-old wearing a T-shirt with a slogan that would have delighted Foucault especially: "Knowledge is power."

Regulation from Below. It is easy to be carried away by a vision of knowledge and skill as regulated from above: by experts or monopolists who decide what shall be made available—freely, in trickles, or at a price. Any such vision of one-way control, however, is likely to be inadequate. There must be a place for pressure also from below: from a consumer who, far from being a passive and eager absorber of what is offered, takes a more active stance—demanding some forms of knowledge or skill, choosing among alternatives, turning away from or resisting what is offered.

Once again, standard theories of cognitive change tend to give short shrift to these forms of pressure. To repeat an earlier comment, one rarely finds, within Vygotskian-style analyses of learning, accounts of expert-novice interactions that depart from a picture of "willing teachers, eager learners." The kind of analysis offered by Valsiner (1984) or by Verdonik et al. (1988) is unusual. Valsiner's analysis, as noted earlier, draws attention to what is tolerated or prohibited as well as to what is encouraged. The analysis by Verdonik and his colleagues draws attention to the differences in power between adult and child that structure task formats: that determine, for instance, who gets to ask the questions or to set the pace.

It is not enough, however, to simply say that the learner is also making demands, decisions, or choices. That statement immediately provokes further re-thinking. Take, for instance, the proposal that the learner, or the person being socialized in any way, is making some active choices with regard to what will be learned, what will be worked on, what will be believed. There must then be some alternatives in what is "out there"; there cannot be some single position that is to be either accepted or rejected.

That is, in fact, the position urged by many analysts of social contexts. Any society, many anthropologists and sociologists argue, contains more than one viewpoint to most issues (see Quinn and Holland, 1987, for one account). Contemporary Western society, for instance, contains both formal medicine and "alternative medicine," both formal education and "alternative" education. One viewpoint may be "dominant," the other "recessive," to use Salzman's (1981) distinction. The presence of more than one viewpoint, however, is the norm. Moreover, asking about the way alternative viewpoints are related to one another provides a basis for differentiating among societies, among content areas, and among learning situations. What one looks for in all these occasions are differences in terms of the extent to which alternatives are present, are known about, have differential status, and openly compete with one another. In effect, we now need to ask not only about the learner's interests but also about the nature and status of the available alternatives.

The notion of "regulation from below" also prompts questions about the way variations in the nature of the information "out there" mesh with variations in the quality or interests of the learner. That is, in fact, a weak part of the concern with "multiple" or "plural" cultural models of knowledge: models that tend to concentrate on aspects of what is "out there." The gap gives a special interest to a proposal that Foucault (1980) has offered. Analyzing the rise of interest in alternatives (alternative medicine and education especially), Foucault suggests that people turn to alternatives as a way of criticizing and expressing their dissatisfaction with the standard offerings. When the turning to alternatives becomes sizable, he continues, then the formal systems move to incorporate part or all of the alternatives, wooing the dissidents back into the fold until such time as dissatisfaction again increases. In the course of this wooing, a more open view is taken of alternatives once set aside as too much "on the fringe." Schools begin to offer more freedom (or more structure as the case may be); formally trained physicians begin to learn acupuncture, etc.

In those examples, however, the proponents of the majority view come to see a certain value, even a certain self-interest, in finding a way to accommodate the dissidents, and the dissidents find it easy to return to the majority position, now modified. Such accommodation may not occur so easily once the two positions come to be matters of identity. It is easier, for example, to merge proposals for formal and alternative schooling than it is to merge proposals for colonial and native law. It is not only that some of the basic assumptions are incompatible. It is also that the proponents of both systems see yielding on matters of law as involving a loss of identity.

Let me bring that argument of identity closer to the area of human development and education. Within that area, there are often expressions of surprise that some people seem to refuse what is offered. There is, for instance, surprise at the way Australian aboriginals progress in white schools up to a certain point and then "abandon" all they have learned of "white" skills (Seagrim and Lendon, 1981). There is also surprise at the way minority groups retain a patois, an accent, or a "distortion of syntax" even though they have had ample opportunity to hear and to learn majority speech (e.g., Shapira, 1978). The "failure," these authors have proposed, lies not in any lack of capacity to learn but in the perception of learning, or further learning, as too much of a compromise or too much of a loss of one's separate identity. These refusals are different from the impositions or expectations of ignorance/incompetence I gave earlier in the section on ways by which others mark one's social place. Now not knowing is a choice made to mark a person's difference. There may still be aspects of imposition: the options from which a choice is made are still socially structured. The presence of active choice by both "learner" and "teacher," however, is a reminder that in any occasion of socialization or education, the interests, demands, choices, and resources of all parties need to be considered.

Negotiable Disagreement

Up to this point, I have started from instances of ignorance/incompetence, using them as a starting point for reconsidering what is learned and how learning takes place. I now wish to alter the starting point a little. In its general quality, it is again an instance where a "novice" group does not acquire the viewpoints of the "experts." In its specific form, however, the phenomenon is one of children not taking on board the viewpoints of adults: not following their directions, not agreeing with their opinions, not going along with their agenda. These negatives reinforce some of what was brought out by analyses of ignorance or incompetence, and add some further points. The research I shall cite comes predominantly from the literature on adult-child interactions within households. It is, however, readily extendable to classrooms. In fact, it fits well with some analyses of the way pupils and teachers negotiate what will be learned, how order will be maintained, or what room will be found for the different agendas that pupils and teachers often bring to a classroom (e.g., Davies, 1989; Martin, 1976; Mehan, 1979).

The area often called *compliance* provides a first case. For some time, psychologists have framed a child's refusal to do what its parents have directed as "noncompliance" and have regarded such noncompliance as "dysfunctional." A shift in perspective involves perceiving occasions of noncompliance as occasions in which children try out a variety of strategies and in which parents—North American parents at least—teach children about the more or less acceptable ways to phrase a dissent or to negotiate a compromise (Kuczynski, 1993; Kuczynski and Kochanska, 1990). Kuczynski's proposals stem mainly from observing the interactions of preschoolers with their mothers. Smetana's (1988a, 1988b) observations, however, point to the same kind of phenomenon in later years (adolescence).

A child's challenge to a parent's rules, she observes, is less likely to escalate into an unhappy conflict when the child offers reasons or arguments that in their sophistication are like those of the adult.

The studies by Kuczynski and by Smetana are North American (Canada for Kuczynski, the United States for Smetana), and they lead us to wonder when other cultures approve a child's negotiating rather than complying, and when they provide early practice in this skill. Australia is certainly in the same cultural group as North America, as Leonard's (1993) study of preschool negotiations indicates, and as is suggested by the application to a child of the Australian term "bush lawyer" (that is, a self-taught but skilled maker of arguments and counter-arguments). To say that a child is a "bush lawyer" is by no means a sign of disapproval, however wearing the process of argument may be for the parent. Australia provides also an interesting classroom example of children coming to learn that they could negotiate in some classrooms but not in others. In this school, some classrooms were officially tagged as "open plan" or "teacher directed": terms that came to be part of the children's vocabulary (e.g., "I was supposed to be put in TD but I changed to OP"; see Davies, 1989, p. 142). In OP, you could work out your own projects or redefine one that a teacher had set; in TD you did the assignment that was set: a distinction that caused the children no difficulty until a TD-style teacher took over, on a temporary basis, a class used to negotiations and revisable contracts.

The area known as *cross-generation agreement* provides the second case. Here again, psychological theory has tended to start from the expectation that agreement represents the outcome that is both desirable psychologically and desired by the adults involved. The phenomenon to be accounted for is then the phenomenon of difference or nonagreement, approached again as a failure in socialization or instruction (Goodnow, 1992).

What is the alternative? One way to approach this question is to consider a range of instances in which children and their parents do not agree. That step brings out first of all the fact that instances of disagreement are not alike. They do not come about in identical ways, and they are not all responded to in the same way.

To start with, there are instances in which children are aware of differences from their parents and instances in which they are unaware; they assume their parents' view is like their own. That difference among instances of dissimilar views is one underlined by Cashmore and Goodnow (1985). There are also instances where the child or the parent is aware of the difference but regards it as unimportant or amusing: No one needs to act upon this awareness, to attempt any change or updating of the other. In contrast, some differences call for action to reduce the gap: Either I will change, you will change, or we will both move to agree on a compromise (Goodnow, 1992). There are as well instances where the child takes a different view, the parent is aware and regards the difference as important but applauds it. In effect, rather than always wishing or working for similarity, as a parent I may hope to see a child go further than I have done: take a different view of the world or of what is possible (Goodnow, 1995). Finally—another version of not closing the gap—there are instances in which children are determined to maintain a difference. When a parent moves to accept their position, the child stakes out another area of difference in a continuing assertion of dissimilarity (Goodnow, 1995). Any view of what is being acquired or not acquired in these situations will clearly need to take account of nonagreement stemming from a variety of sources rather than being a simple failure to achieve agreement.

Implications for General Views of Learning

Just as considering examples of ignorance/incompetence brought out their several forms and functions and served as a base for rethinking what is learned and how this occurs, so also do instances of disagreement, dissent, or—to use a more neutral term—a lack of congruence in viewpoints. The instances of ignorance/incompetence served especially as a base for proposing that what is learned is the varying social value of particular areas of knowledge and skill, and of various kinds of task performance. They served also as a base for proposing that learning consists only occasionally, if ever, of individuals constructing schemas by themselves, drawing upon information that is freely available. More often, perhaps always, the flow of data and of the resources we need is regulated by others and by the newcomers' demands upon those holders of knowledge.

Considering instances of nonagreement reinforces and adds to those shifts in framework. I shall again start by considering what is to be learned and then move to implications about how learning takes place.

Implications for What Is to Be Learned   Let me start from the point of view of the learner, child or adult. Suppose that you have been presented with the explicit demand or with the expectation that you acquire some particular viewpoint, that you act in a particular way. The new research on compliance and cross-generation congruence suggests that a significant part of what is learned has to do with the quality of this expectation. What can you ignore? How far is this matter negotiable? How close do you need to get to what has been proposed for you?

The new views of noncompliance underline especially the variety of negotiation strategies that children acquire: strategies such as deferral ("later, OK?"), offering a compromise, offering a reason for not complying, acting as if no directive or request has been made (Kuczynski and Kochanska, 1990; Leonard, 1993). The same studies make it clear that children need to learn that any one strategy varies in its effectiveness with the occasion: variations that include the adult's mood.

From these several strategies, I shall draw out some specific aspects of what is to be learned. To start with, a learner needs to know when a demand need not be met at all. It may be sufficient to "turn a deaf ear" or to offer some noncommittal acknowledgment. Judging the degree of importance of an expectation to the other—recognizing when "they really mean it"—is a critical first acquisition.

Once an expectation is accepted, what needs to be learned is the degree to which the expectation needs to be met. There are some areas of learning and problem solving where, to be counted as "correct," a performance must fall within a very narrow range. To use an analogy with a dartboard or a rifle target, the "hit" must be right on the central spot, the bull's eye: Anything else is not counted. Arithmetic problems in which answers have to be "spot on" rather than "close" provide one example. Class-based accents—accents designed to exclude imitators—provide another. In contrast, there are areas of learning where approximations are received positively, or—the extreme—where reward is attached to effort, no matter how far off the answer.

In addition, the meeting of expectations can vary in the extent to which substitute performances are acceptable. The nonperformance of household tasks has drawn my attention especially to this phenomenon. Nonperformance of one task will be discounted by many Australian mothers if some other task is adequately performed: either some other household task (the child, for instance, is "useless inside the home but loves to work in the garden") or some task outside the household (e.g., the child does well in school). I am far from understanding what marks the distinction between times when substitute performances are acceptable and times when they are not. The difference, however, is one that I now perceive as important for many teaching or socialization situations.

In short, a major part of what we need to learn has to do with how much "give," "slack," or "stretch" (Rodman, 1963) a situation allows: learning that involves coming to know how strongly others feel about an expectation, when substitute performances are more versus less acceptable, and what the limits are to any degree of noncompliance, nonagreement, or substitution. How does this learning come about?

Implications for the "How" of Learning

Up to this point, most of my comments on noncompliance and nonagreement have been about what needs to be known. As was the case with ignorance/incompetence, however, there are as well implications for how such understanding is acquired. The implications I wish to draw out have to do with the need to ask: What are the goals of the person who presents the expectation? And what are the possible ways by which these expectations end up not being met?

The importance of reexamining goals emerges from studies of both noncompliance and noncongruence. Goals need to be distinguished in terms of their importance to the adult and in terms of whether they are adult-centered or child-centered, that is, whether they revolve around meeting the adult's needs and interests or the child's needs and interests as the adult perceives them (Dix, 1992). Goals also need to be distinguished in terms of their relationship to time. Researchers, it has been pointed out, need to distinguish between the goals of short-term and long-term compliance (Kuczynski, 1984). In an alternate phrasing, researchers need to recognize that adults may be more concerned with maintaining a pleasant relationship—a goal important over the long run—than they are with getting their way on a specific occasion, having a child agree with them on a specific topic, or having a child acquire a particular skill (Goodnow, 1992; Grusec and Goodnow, 1994).

For the several ways in which a lack of agreement between adult and child may come about, the more elaborated discussion of possibilities is to be found in analyses of congruence across generations. These analyses bring out especially the need to consider any outcome in terms of more than a single step.

In one pair of possible steps, the first has to do with the receiver's perception of the message being sent: the receiver's perception of the demand, the directive, or the expectation. For a variety of reasons (e.g., the sender's message is not clear, the receiver lacks the inferential capacity to decode what is heard), this perception may be accurate or inaccurate. The second step within this pair then has to do with the acceptance or rejection of the perceived message. In Cashmore and Goodnow's (1985) analysis, a lack of agreement across generations may stem from one or both of two sources: inaccurate perception or rejection. In addition, the two steps are regarded as influenced by different conditions. Information-relevant conditions (e.g., the clarity or redundancy of the original message) are especially relevant to the first step. In contrast, the warmth of the relationship is seen as being more relevant to the second step: acceptance versus rejection (Cashmore and Goodnow, 1985; Goodnow, 1992; Grusec and Goodnow, 1994).

A second pair of steps presents a different scenario for how it is that a situation ostensibly designed for teaching and learning may not result in what was officially intended. The first step of this pair again has to do with awareness: in this case, awareness that the other has not complied, not learned, not agreed. Within families or classrooms, for instance, the people involved may or may not be aware that they hold different views on an issue. The second step within this pair then has to do with whether one or both parties feels responsible for closing the perceived gap (e.g., Collins, 1995; Goodnow, 1992). Some differences may simply be "lived with" rather than attracting any attempt at resolution. We do not yet know the conditions that make some people, in some situations, feel that they should live with a difference, as against attempting to reduce the gap by changing their own position or attempting to change that of the other person. It is clear, however, that we often find acceptable or tolerable occasions of difference, occasions that to an observer might well appear to call for action, with inaction stemming only from "abdicated responsibility."

Neither pair of steps, I should note, considers a third that is largely neglected within studies of congruence. This is a step in which learners cease to be aware of the sources of their ideas and come to regard them as their own, as self-generated. In this step, it has been proposed, the critical factor is likely to be the degree of pressure applied for acceptance (the less pressure, or the less overt the pressure, the more likely a learner is to regard a position as self-generated; e.g., Hoffman, 1986). Occasions where the difference across generations takes the form of one person seeing ideas as "handed on" while the other perceives only self-construction ("all my own work") strike me as an especially challenging point from which further analyses of differences might well begin.

Are these several proposals, it may be asked, relevant beyond the learning that takes place in households? What are the comparable phenomena in classrooms? I have already mentioned one example of children coming to identify the teachers and the classrooms that offered more versus less room for negotiating the work that would be done, for exploring the degrees of freedom allowed in redefining the work that a teacher has set (Davies, 1989). Let me now add to that source another detailed analysis of negotiations in classrooms. This is Mehan's (1979) account of the way classrooms involve the interweaving of two agendas: that of the teacher and that of the students. Both Davies (1989) and Mehan (1979) bring out the work that pupils put into uncovering the teachers' agenda (what is really wanted is often far from clear). Both bring out as well the variety of strategies that children use to bring the two agendas together (how can you both "follow the rules" and "have fun"), to define in an agreed-upon way an item that is on both agendas ("learn things"), and—when agreement is difficult—to bend the teacher's agenda (in Mehan's phrase, to "derail" it) so that the balance tips toward the child's preference. In effect, negotiated areas of difference from an adult's position are far from being restricted to parent-child interactions or to households. They are well and truly present in classrooms; the analysis of what occurs in households simply sharpens our ideas about what to look for in other settings.

A Final Comment

To provide an alternate perspective upon what is learned and how learning takes place, I have started from negative instances: from cases where what is acquired is less than one might expect on the basis of capacity and opportunity. That starting point has led me to consider occasions of ignorance or incompetence, and occasions of noncompliance or nonagreement between generations. That starting point has led me also to propose that learning, or any form of socialization, takes place within a framework of values and social relationships.

My final comment takes the form of a question: Where might we find a comparable type of argument? It would, after all, be extraordinary if this type of argument had not been made before in some form or other. There is, to start with, clearly some overlap between what I have proposed for the negotiation of competence and agreement and what some classroom analysts have proposed for the maintenance of order. Order, the argument runs, is not so much imposed as it is negotiated between teachers and pupils (e.g., Martin, 1976).

A second area of overlap is with analyses of ways of speaking. In this area of inquiry, there is an explicit recognition of the extent to which learning involves coming to know the social value placed upon particular ways of speaking in particular interactions. (The comments by Higgins, McCann, and Fondacaro, 1982, on the "communication game" provide an overview.) In this area of research, there has also been some explicit concern with the extent to which children are aware of a gap between their understanding of a message and another's understanding, and with the attributions of responsibility that they make when such a situation arises (e.g., Robinson, 1981).

More broadly, the argument may be offered that all attempts at inquiry, persuasion, or instruction involve questions about what is regarded as legitimate or proper to know or not to know, and how people negotiate the giving or the refusal of information. Barnes (1979, p. 15) presents the following argument:

Social inquiry may. . .be seen as a process of interaction and negotiation between scientist, sponsor, gatekeeper and citizens. These negotiations will be facilitated [if there is a recognition of] not only. . .diverse interests and. . .powers over one another, but also. . .diverse perceptions of the objectives and likely outcome of the inquiry. This assumption of legitimate diversity. . .is, in my view, a necessary condition for social science to flourish. . .a necessary condition for the recognition of the right to privacy, for the need to balance the scientist's and sponsor's interest in finding out against the citizen's interests in preventing them from doing so; privacy may also include the right to remain in ignorance about himself. (p. 24)

In effect, any occasion of inquiry, persuasion, or instruction may be seen as an occasion of negotiations among parties with diverse interests. Among those interests, the maintenance or promotion of ignorance, of particular differences and disagreements, needs to be recognized as often present and as an intrinsic part of what learning involves.

Acknowledgments

Acknowledgments typically specify a few particular people. I shall more broadly express my debt to all those—too many to name—who in person or by their writing have encouraged me to ask in any content area: "Is this all there is to be said? What is missing here?"

References

Backett, K. C. (1982). *Mothers and fathers*. London: Macmillan.

Barnes, J. A. (1979). *Who should know what? Social science, privacy, and ethics*. Cambridge, England: Cambridge University Press.

Blount, B. G. (1972). Parental speech and language acquisition: Some Luo and Samoan examples. *Anthropological Linguistics, 14*, 119–130.

Bourdieu, P. (1977). *Outline of a theory of practice*. Cambridge, England: Cambridge University Press.

Bourdieu, P. (1979). *Distinction: A social critique of the judgment of taste*. London: Routledge and Kegan Paul.

Bourdieu, P. and Passeron, J.-C. (1977). *Reproduction in education, society and culture*. Beverly Hills: Sage.

Cashmore, J. and Goodnow, J. J. (1985). Agreement between generations: A two-process model. *Child Development, 56*, 493–501.

Cazden, C. (1993). Vygotsky, Hymes, and Bakhtin: From word to utterance and voice. In E. A. Forman, N. Minick, and C. A. Stone (Eds.), *Contexts for learning* (pp. 197–212). New York: Oxford University Press.

Collins, W. A. and Luebker, C. (1993). Resolving discrepancies in parents' judgments of adolescence. In J. Smetana (Ed.), *Parents' sociocognitive models of development: New directions* (pp. 65–80). San Francisco: Jossey-Bass.

D'Andrade, R. G. (1981). The cultural part of cognition. *Cognitive Science, 5,* 179–195.

Davies, B. (1989). *Life in the classroom and playground: The accounts of primary school children.* London: Routledge and Kegan Paul.

Dix, T. H. (1992). Parenting on behalf of the child: Empathic goals in the regulation of responsive parenting. In I. E. Sigel, A. V. McGillicuddy-DeLisi, and J. J. Goodnow (Eds.), *Parental belief systems: The psychological consequences for children* (pp. 319–346). Hillsdale, NJ: Lawrence Erlbaum.

Eccles, J. S. (1986). Gender-roles and women's achievement. *Educational Researcher, 15,* 15–19.

Eccles, J. S. and Jacobs, J. E. (1986). Social forces shape math attitudes and performance. *Signs: Journal of Women in Culture and Society, 11,* 367–380.

Eckert, P. (1991). *Jocks and burnouts: Social categories and identity in the high school.* New York: Teachers College Press.

England, P. and Farkas, G. (1986). *Households, employment and gender.* New York: Aldine.

Foucault, M. (1980). *Power-knowledge: Selected interviews and other writing.* Brighton, England: Harvester.

Garvey, C. (1975). Requests and responses in children's speech. *Journal of Child Language, 2,* 41–63.

Glick, J. (1985). Culture and cognition revisited. In E. Neimark, R. DeLisi, and J. L. Newman (Eds.), *Moderators of competence* (pp. 99–115). Hillsdale NJ: Lawrence Erlbaum.

Goodnow, J. J. (1976). The nature of intelligent behavior: Questions raised by cross-cultural studies. In L. Resnick (Ed.), *The nature of intelligence* (pp. 169–188). Hillsdale, NJ: Lawrence Erlbaum.

Goodnow, J. J. (1984). On being judged intelligent. *International Journal of Psychology, 19,* 193–205.

Goodnow, J. J. (1986). The socialization of intelligence: Comments on Sternberg and Suben. In M. Perlmutter (Ed.), *Intelligence: Minnesota Symposium on Child Development* (pp. 237–251). Hillsdale, NJ: Lawrence Erlbaum.

Goodnow, J. J. (1990a). The socialization of cognition: Acquiring cognitive values. In J. Stigler, R. Shweder, and G. Herdt (Eds.), *Culture and human development* (pp. 259–286). Chicago: University of Chicago Press.

Goodnow, J. J. (1990b). Using sociology to extend psychological accounts of cognitive development. *Human Development, 33,* 81–107.

Goodnow, J. J. (1992). Parents' ideas, children's ideas: The bases of congruence and divergence. In I. E. Sigel, A. V. McGillicuddy-DeLisi, and J. J. Goodnow (Eds.), *Parental belief systems: The psychological consequences for children* (pp. 293–318). Hillsdale, NJ: Lawrence Erlbaum.

Goodnow, J. J. (1995). Acceptable disagreement across generations. In J. Smetana (Ed.), *Parents' models of development: New directions* (pp. 51–64). San Francisco: Jossey-Bass.

Goodnow, J. J. and Bowes, J. A. (1994). *Men, women, and household work.* Sydney/New York: Oxford University Press.

Goodnow, J. J., Knight, R., and Cashmore, J. (1985). Adult social cognition: Implications of parents' ideas for approaches to development. In M. Perlmutter (Ed.), *Social cognition. Minnesota Symposia on Child Development* (pp. 287–324). Hillsdale, NJ: Lawrence Erlbaum.

Grusec, J. E. and Goodnow, J. J. (1994). The impact of parental discipline methods on the child's internalization of values: A reconceptualization of current points of view. *Developmental Psychology, 30,* 4–19.

Hewitt, J. P. and Stokes, R. (1975). Disclaimers. *American Sociological Review*, 40, 1–11.

Higgins, E. T., McCann, C. D., and Fondacaro, R. (1982). The "communication game": Goal-directed encoding and cognitive consequences. *Social Cognition*, 1, 21–37.

Hoffman, M. L. (1986). Affect, cognition, and motivation. In R. M. Sorrentino and E. T. Higgins (Eds.), *Handbook of motivation and cognition* (pp. 244–280). New York: Guilford.

Jackson, B. and Marsden, D. (1966). *Education and the working class*. Harmondsworth, England: Penguin.

Kett, J. F. (1978). Curing the disease of precocity. In J. Demos and S. S. Boocock (Eds.), *Turning points: Historical and sociological essays on the family* (pp. 183–211). Chicago: University of Chicago Press.

Kristeva, J. (1992). *Nations without nationalism*. New York: Columbia University Press.

Kuczynski, L. (1984). Socialization goals and mother–child interaction: Strategies for long-term and short-term compliance. *Developmental Psychology*, 20, 1061–1073.

Kuczynski, L. (May, 1993). *Evolving metaphors of bidirectionality in socialization and parent–child relations*. Paper presented at the annual meeting of the Canadian Psychological Association, Montreal.

Kuczynski, L. and Kochanska, G. (1990). Development of children's noncompliance strategies from toddlerhood to age 5. *Developmental Psychology*, 26, 398–408.

Leonard, R. (1993). Mother–child disputes as arenas for fostering negotiation skills. *Early Development and Parenting*, 2 (3), 157–167.

Martin, W. B. W. (1976). *The negotiated order of the school*. Toronto: Macmillan.

Mead, M. (1949). *Male and female*. New York: Morrow.

Mehan, J. (1979). *Learning lessons: Social organization in the classroom*. Cambridge: Harvard University Press.

Oakley, A. (1974). *The sociology of housework*. London: Martin Robertson.

Ochs, E. E. (1982). Talking to children in Western Samoa. *Language in Society*, 12, 157–169.

Ochs, E. E. (1990). Indexicality and socialization. In J. W. Stigler, R. A. Shweder, and G. Herdt (Eds.), *Culture and human development* (pp. 287–308). Chicago: University of Chicago Press.

Ochs, E. (1992). Indexicality and socialization. In J. W. Stigler, R. A. Shweder, and G. Herdt (Eds.), *Cultural psychology* (pp. 287–308). Cambridge, England: Cambridge University Press.

Ochs, E. and Schieffelin, B. (1984). Language acquisition and socialization: Three developmental stories. In R. Shweder and R. LeVine (Eds.), *Cultural theory: Essays in mind, self, and emotion* (pp. 276–326). Cambridge, England: Cambridge University Press.

Parsons, J. E., Adler, T. F., and Kaczala, C. M. (1982). Socialization of achievement attitudes and beliefs: Parental influences. *Child Development*, 53, 310–321.

Perret-Clermont, A.-N. (1991). The social construction of meaning and cognitive activity in elementary school children. In L. Resnick, J. M. Levine, and S. B. Teasley (Eds.), *Perspectives on socially shared cognition* (pp. 41–62). Washington: American Psychological Association.

Piaget, J. (1965). *The moral judgment of the child*. New York: Free Press.

Quinn, N. and Holland, D. (1987). Culture and cognition. In D. Holland and N. Quinn (Eds.), *Cultural models in language and thought* (pp. 3–42). Cambridge, England: Cambridge University Press.

Robinson, E. J. (1981). The child's understanding of inadequate messages and communication failure: A problem of ignorance or egocentrism? In W. P. Dickson (Ed.), *Children's oral communication skills* (pp. 167–188). London: Academic Press.

Rodman, H. (1963). The lower-class value stretch. *Social Forces, 42,* 205–215.

Salzman, P. C. (1981). Culture as enhabilmentis. In L. Holy and M. Stuchlik (Eds.), *The structure of folk models* (pp. 233–256). London: Academic Press.

Schieffelin, B. (1990). *The give and take of everyday life: Language socialization of Kaluli children.* Cambridge, England: Cambridge University Press.

Schubauer-Leonie, M. L., Perret-Clermont, A.-N., and Grossen, M. (1992). The construction of adult child intersubjectivity in psychological research and in school. In M. von Cranach, W. Doise, and G. Mugny (Eds.), *Social representations and the social bases of knowledge* (pp. 69–77). Lewiston, NY: Hogrefe and Huber.

Seagrim, G. and Lendon, R. (1981). *Furnishing the mind: Aboriginal and white.* New York: Academic Press.

Shapira, E. C. (1978). The non-learning of English: Case study of an adult. In E. M. Hatch (Ed.), *Second language acquisition: A book of readings* (pp. 246–255). Rowley, MA: Newbury House.

Smetana, J. G. (1988a). Concepts of self and social convention: Adolescents' and parents' reasoning about hypothetical and actual family conflicts. In M. Gunnar and W. Collins (Eds.), *Minnesota Symposia on Child Development* (pp. 79–122). Hillsdale, NJ: Lawrence Erlbaum.

Smetana, J. G. (1988b). Adolescents' and parents' conceptions of parental authority. *Child Development, 59,* 321–335.

Stodolsky, S. (1988). *The subject matters: Classroom activity in mathematics and social studies.* Chicago: University of Chicago Press.

Valsiner, J. (1984). Construction of the zone of proximal development in adult–child joint action: The socialization of meals. In B. Rogoff and J. Wertsch (Eds.), *Children's learning in the zone of proximal development* (pp. 65–76). San Francisco: Jossey-Bass.

Verdonik, F., Flapan, V., Schmit, C., and Weinstock, J. (1988). The role of power relationships in children's cognition: Its significance for research on cognitive development. *Quarterly Newsletter of the Laboratory of Comparative Human Cognition, 10,* 80–85.

Walkerdine, V. (1989). *Counting girls out.* London: Virago Press.

Wertsch, J. (1991). *Voices of the mind.* Cambridge, England: Cambridge University Press.

Willis, P. (1981). *Learning to labor: Working class kids get working class jobs.* New York: Columbia University Press.

17

Cultural Learning and Learning Culture

ANN C. KRUGER

MICHAEL TOMASELLO

The universals and cultural variations of human development have been the focus of fruitful study by anthropologists for decades. In recent years psychologists also have directed their attention, long overdue, to understanding development in cultural context. There are striking differences among psychologists, however, in the approaches they take to culture and development. Most markedly, Cole (1989) distinguishes two very different theoretical perspectives on cultural psychology and its approach to human development. In one perspective the focus is on culture as a collective enterprise (e.g., Gauvain, in press; Shweder, 1990; Super and Harkness, 1986). There is no need in this view for focusing on the individual development of individual children since all important forms of learning are socially distributed; children simply become more skillful over time at participating in various collective activities (Lave and Wenger, 1991). Indeed, in some versions of this more sociological view of cultural psychology the focus on the cultural collective is so strong that there is really no justification for reference to the development of individuals at all: "Individual, interpersonal, and sociocultural processes constitute each other and cannot be separated" (Rogoff, Chavajay, and Matusov, 1993, p. 533).

The other perspective on cultural psychology is more in line with traditional psychological approaches to the individual person in culture. In this view, it is important to distinguish individual children and the cultures into which they are born. A central focus of this approach is the competence that children bring to the process of enculturation and how this competence contributes to their internalization of various aspects of their cultures (Vygotsky, 1978). In this view an exclusive focus on the collectivity to the neglect of individuals makes it impossible to understand the cognitive development of such individuals as autistic children, who never become very skillful at participating in collective activities, and non-human primates, who do not grow up in cultures at all (Tomasello, 1990).

Our own previous work has been decidedly within this more psychological, and less sociological, orientation to human development in cultural contexts. In 1993, for example, we and Hilary Ratner proposed a theory of cultural learning that attempted to explain how children's developing social cognition leads to new forms of participation in cultural activities and thus to new ways of internalizing important aspects of their cultures (Tomasello, Kruger, and Ratner, 1993). For instance, we hypothesized that it was not until children could understand other persons as mental agents, with thoughts and beliefs that differed from their own, that they could engage in the kinds of internal dialogues of private and self-regulating speech that Vygotsky (1978) described some years ago—since such dialogues often presuppose two distinct mental perspectives on the same situation.

We have seen no data and heard no arguments to dissuade us from our more psychologically based view of cultural psychology. However, based on the responses to our ideas that we have received, especially from cultural anthropologists and cultural psychologists, it is clear that our theory of cultural learning as we originally formulated and presented it focused too narrowly on the cognitive capacities of the individual child. For a more balanced and complete theory, we need to complement our focus on what the child brings to the culture with a focus on what the culture brings to the child. We believe that there are two aspects of culture that will be especially important in formulating a more complete account.

First, it is important to emphasize, as we did not in our original account, the role in children's development of the preexisting structure of the culture: its games, institutions, rituals, cultural models, intentional scripts, and communal activities —in brief, its "habitus" (Bourdieu, 1977). Children are born into some version of this structure and these activities, and the particular version they are born into potentiates some forms of development and constrains or even disallows other forms of development. In many domains children develop culturally specific ways of acting that they do not explicitly set out to learn and that no one explicitly sets out to teach them; they simply participate in forms of activity structured by the culture and learn some ways of behaving and thinking as a result. Our previous account did not give adequate attention to the ways in which cultural patterns structure children's lives, and thus for many anthropologists it was woefully incomplete (Ingold, 1993). We mostly agree with this criticism.

Second, it is important to emphasize that culture sometimes imposes itself on children in the form of intentional instruction. In our previous account of instructed learning we explicitly took the child's point of view, defining instructed learning essentially as the child's internalization of adult instructions. We do not wish to change this perspective here, but it is necessary to supplement it with a fuller account of the process of instruction. In particular we need to respond to the criticism of our theory that we portrayed adult instruction in an excessively Western fashion. On the one hand, Rogoff et al. (1993; see also Foreman, 1993) argued that in some cultures there is basically no intentional instruction of children, and thus our entire treatment of instructed learning as the internalization of adult instruction was misguided. Olson and Astington (1993), on the other hand, simply pointed out that our treatment of instruction did not adequately explicate the adult side of the interaction, not taking into account the different types of instruction that exist in different cultures and the cognitive abilities that these require of the adult. We do not agree that there are cultures that do not intentionally instruct their young, as we hope to demonstrate in this paper, but we do agree that there are differences in the type of instruction employed in different cultures, and that these will have important consequences for children's development.

In this paper, we attempt to make our theory of cultural learning more complete by giving an account of the process of cultural learning not from the point of view of the child, but from the point of view of the culture. In the process, we try to address the two shortcomings of our theory just elaborated. First, we briefly discuss the role of preexisting cultural patterns as an important part of the enculturation process. We are brief on this score because there is no controversy here; we only wish to appropriate the ideas of many anthropologists who have emphasized this aspect of learning culture (e.g., Quinn and Strauss, 1994; Shweder, 1990). Second, we deal with instruction and instructed learning. In this case we must go into more detail because we have disagreements here with other cultural psychologists on several important issues, even over such fundamental points as the definition of intentional instruction. We conclude with brief discussions of the role of intentional instruction in cognitive development and the implications of our theoretical approach for processes of education.

Individual Learning of Culture

Tomasello, Kruger, Ratner (1993) went to great lengths to distinguish cultural learning from individual learning, but also, importantly, from other forms of social learning. For example, we argued that many animals are exposed to some learning situations that they otherwise would not be exposed to because they follow their mothers and other group members. Sometimes the changes of state in the world that adults bring about through their individual efforts (e.g., opening nuts) reveal to the developing youngster affordances of the environment that it previously did not know existed (e.g., that nuts can be opened and have something edible inside). We call this emulation learning.

Our definition of cultural learning, however, singles out those instances of social learning in which the child learns something more deeply social than the physical fact that nuts can be opened. In cultural learning children learn not just about affordances of the inanimate environment but also something about the intentional states of adults—what they intend to do in performing certain actions or, perhaps, the strategy they are using or thoughts they are thinking. In cultural learning the child does not learn *from* the adult's actions, but the child learns *through* the adult's perspective in a truly intersubjective fashion. It is also important in our definition of cultural learning that on many occasions children internalize adults' intentional attitudes from such encounters and make them their own. Within this definitional framework we identified three types of cultural learning: imitative learning, instructed learning, and collaborative learning. The fact that these three types of learning emerge in human ontogeny in an invariant developmental sequence—imitative, instructed, collaborative—was explained through references to the different levels of understanding of the intentional states of others that children of different ages are able to employ—specifically, the understanding of others as intentional agents, mental agents, and reflective agents.

In our original paper we were quite explicit that cultural learning may only account for a few of the child's learning experiences. Its importance lies in the fact that it enables many uniquely human cultural activities and artifacts—for example, the learning and use of conventional symbols and language. However, it is clear that children learn many other things about culture in ways that do not invoke such intersubjective forms of interaction and learning. Following Bourdieu (1977), Quinn and Strauss (1994) refer to the habitus of culture, the cultural "schemas" that lead children down certain culturally specific developmental pathways. For example, children in traditional hunter-gatherer societies are exposed to a particular set of practices during infancy, one of which is being carried in close contact with their mother's body throughout the day. At a very young age the babies become familiar with the smell of their mother's skin, the sensation of being carried as she walks, the warmth of the sun on their scalps, the touch of the sack they are carried in, and the taste of breast milk. As the babies develop, their experiences multiply, but those experiences are always delimited. For children growing up in various cultures, what will become familiar or "second nature" will be based on the particular set of experiences that define their young lives. The habits, attitudes, and ways of looking at the world that these experiences engender are not something that the adult sets out to teach or something the child sets out to learn. They are just a part of the habitus of a particular society that the child, over time, joins.

It is interesting that other species also may learn the patterns of their social group in this same way. Thus many behavioral ecologists refer to chimpanzee "culture" (e.g., see Wrangham, McGrew, deWaal, and Heltne, 1994). What they are describing with this term is a number of intergroup differences in the behavior of chimpanzees in the wild, differences in habits such as foods eaten and tools used. But, as argued before (Tomasello, Kruger, and Ratner, 1993), based on a wide variety of evidence, it is not very likely that chimpanzees engage in cultural learning narrowly defined (see also Tomasello, 1994). However, it is possible that they are learning the habitus of their group, which, like the human counterpart, includes all of the group's habitual ways of acting. Thus a chimpanzee youngster in one group follows its mother to a termite mound and finds holes containing sticks with termites crawling on them, while a youngster in another group follows its mother to nut trees and finds stones and half-opened nuts. The point is that many animals are excellent individual learners, and if different groups of a species adopt different behavioral practices as adaptations to their particular local ecologies (or for whatever reasons), then their offspring will experience different sets of learning experiences.

Nevertheless, the way humans engage in this process may still have two species-specific features. First, and perhaps more importantly, children have not just the physical environment as their habitus but also various social activities and even cultural institutions that lead them to have highly specific learning experiences. For example, children in some cultures grow up in the company of a large extended family; life is communal and materials and activities are shared with siblings, cousins, grandparents, and others. Other children grow up in cultures in which individuals possess private property and in which many activities are performed with just a few others, or even alone. The communal or private structures of these cultures channel children's experiences in particular ways.

Second, human children "soak up" not just the outward practices of their group but also, by inference, the values and attitudes of their group. For example, in cultures in which children sleep in the same room with their parents, children may deduce the importance of closeness and communality, without anyone explicitly expressing those values. In cultures in which children sleep in their own rooms, children may infer respect for individuality and privacy, all on their own. It is possible that other animal species do not have such inferencing capacities, which means that the transmission of the habitus of the group to the developing individual has a wider range of influence in the human species.

Through this discussion of habitus, then, we wish to supplement our theory of cultural learning with an account of the individual learning of cultural patterns. It is very likely that, if quantification of such matters were possible, the individual learning of culture contributes "more" to the differences among members of different cultures than cultural learning in our very specific definition. Nevertheless, we maintain that many uniquely human abilities are only possible through cultural learning as we originally defined it. Moreover, we must also point out that many of the cultural patterns that children individually learn in the habitus of their cultures are patterns that were originally created through processes of cultural learning, especially collaborative learning. That is to say, such things as farming practices that a child may come to learn more or less individually through participation, were first invented by individuals collaborating with one another in an intersubjective manner.

Intentional Instruction of Culture

Our earlier work was also criticized for implying that intentional instruction is a human universal (Rogoff, Chavajay, and Matusov, 1993). The contention is that many traditional societies do not practice intentional instruction since their education is informal: children learn by observing their elders' activities and by their own practice in the flow of everyday life (Bruner, 1972; Childs and Greenfield, 1980). It is children who assume the responsibility for learning; adults do not intentionally teach them (Greenfield and Lave, 1982).

We believe that this position is untenable, both definitionally and factually. Definitionally, we contend that informal education is also an instance of intentional instruction, and so our proposal that intentional instruction is a human universal is clearly true. But in addition, we contend, factually, that all cultures engage in formal education; it is just that some of them do so only in a few, circumscribed contexts. To support these contentions we will (1) propose a definition of intentional instruction, (2) identify three different processes of intentional instruction, and (3) provide evidence that all cultures engage to some extent in all three of these processes.

Intentional Instruction in Comparative Perspective

Adults in our nearest primate relatives do all kinds of things that serve to promote the acquisition of particular skills. For example, chimpanzee mothers often walk away from their young infants at the age at which they are just beginning to self-locomote (Goodall, 1986). If the infants do not follow, the mothers stop, look back, and sometimes make noises of frustration. If the infants now follow the mother, it can be said that she has encouraged their self-locomotion. But it could also be said that she wishes to travel and is frustrated that the infant is not following as it should. Thus it can be said that the mother's intentions are that the baby follow her, not that the baby learn something. The same can be said of the well-known example of chimpanzee mothers taking poisonous leaves away from their infants (Goodall, 1986): She intends for them to refrain from eating the leaves, not for them to *learn* to refrain from eating the leaves.

The point is that teaching is a behavior that can only be adequately defined by its intention. We can refer to all behaviors of one animal that serve to facilitate some behavior by another as "teaching" (e.g., as Caro and Hauser, 1992), but it then loses all of its meaning. Teaching is a behavior in which one animal intends that another learn some skill or acquire some bit of information or knowledge that it did not have previously. Such an intentional definition is not hopelessly unverifiable; rather it is quite easily identified. The teacher needs to behave in ways that are adapted to the skill level of the learner, for example, providing more and different kinds of instruction when the skill level is low, changing as the learner becomes more skillful, and ceasing when the skill level becomes self-sufficient. In any case, if we restrict our definition of teaching to intentional forms—or if we posit a subcategory of teaching termed intentional teaching—then the most serious candidates from the nonhuman world are those that have been recently reported by Boesch (1991, 1993).

For almost a decade Boesch has been observing chimpanzees in western Africa as they crack and eat nuts—which they do on a daily basis during certain seasons of the year. They place one of several varieties of nut on some type of rigid substrate such as a stone or root (called the anvil) and then pound it with either a stone or hefty stick (called the hammer). It is not an easy skill for youngsters to learn and it typically takes them several years of practice (during the one- to five-year age range) before they attain adult-like skill levels. In this context Boesch has observed a number of ways that the behavior of mothers serves to facilitate the nut cracking of their offspring. In line with an intentional definition, he has divided his observations into "facilitation" and "active teaching." Observations of facilitation are fairly common and consist mainly of mothers allowing their infants to use their hammers or nuts (which they tend not to let other animals do). This behavior is consistent with mothers allowing children to take food from their hands (which they also do not allow others to do). In his decade of observation Boesch has seen only two instances of what he considers active teaching. They are important enough that we will cite them each at some length (paraphrased from Boesch, 1993, pp. 176–177).

(1) A mother was cracking some very hard nuts, with her son eating most of them. The son then tried to crack some nuts for himself, with limited success. At one point he placed a partly open nut on the anvil in a way not conducive to successful opening. Before he could strike the nut, however, his mother picked it up, wiped off the anvil, and placed it on the anvil in the correct position. The son then successfully struck and opened the nut.

(2) A daughter was attempting unsuccessfully to open nuts with an irregularly shaped hammer. Her mother then joined her. The daughter pushed the poor hammer to the mother. The mother then, in a very deliberate manner (for over one minute), rotated the hammer into its best position for pounding the nut. She then successfully opened a number of nuts, with both mother and daughter eating them. The mother then left and the daughter proceeded to make attempts on her own, with mixed success but always with the hammer in the orientation her mother had used.

Boesch claims that in the first example the mother anticipated her son's impending failure and intervened to ensure his success. Perhaps. But it is also possible that she noticed from her own previous experience that the nut was not correctly positioned and positioned it for herself, which her son then exploited. Boesch interprets the second example as the mother correcting her daughter's mistake and demonstrating the correct method. Again, perhaps this is correct, but it is also possible that the mother was simply using the hammer to crack nuts for herself as she normally would. The only behavioral evidence for the instructional interpretation of this observation is that the mother very slowly rotated the hammer into the most efficient position for her own cracking attempts. And even if the mothers were intending that their infants successfully crack a nut on these singular occasions, the intention that the child succeed is still different from the intention that they learn. In any case, these two isolated observations would be much easier to interpret if they fell into a larger pattern of instructional activity in this and other contexts in the chimpanzees' lives. For now, we remain skeptical that the mothers' intentions were to help their infants *learn* to crack nuts efficiently.

Overall, the difference between human intentional instruction and all of these examples from nonhuman primates is that human adults do whatever is necessary so that children will learn skills for themselves, and then, when children attain a certain level of skill, withdraw. If a child is not successful initially, the adult keeps at it, adjusting instruction as necessary, with the child's self-sufficient competency as a goal. Moreover, as Bruner (1993) points out, in many situations of human life there is an onus placed on children: Children are *expected* to learn from the instruction, perhaps so that they can eventually be helpful to adults, and are dealt with harshly if they do not. Human pedagogical intentions thus make themselves manifest both in adults' propensity to show children how to do things, and in the adults' expectation that children will become more self-sufficient and competent as a result.

Three Processes of Intentional Instruction

Although all human societies expect their children to learn, what varies both within and between cultures is the adults' beliefs about how this learning will take place and about the degree to which active instruction is necessary. We hypothesize three types of adult theory of child learning and consequent level of adult involvement in education. These hypothesized types are actually prototypes, hypothetical pure cases. We recognize that real life is less pristine than our theory; indeed, the nature of these adult beliefs as they actually exist may resemble our prototypes, or they may be on the borderline between two types or a mixture of types. We take the risk of oversimplification for the heuristic benefits that accrue, and we argue that to some degree these three types are present in all human societies.

First, adults believe that children "come up" to master some skills on their own. They assume that children are competent learners just as they are competent growers. This expectation arises from the theory that nature provides for learning, just as it does for growing, and that adult participation is not required in either process. Adults in these cases are not indifferent to children's learning; in fact, their interest in learning is profound enough to produce a theoretical understanding that guides practice. Should their theory prove faulty in some instances, adults will adapt both theory and practice to make sure that children learn. For example, in most Western cultures the skill of walking is expected to develop naturally, but if it does not, adults intervene in the process. This expectation of learning, and the intention to provide for it if the need arises, distinguishes human adults from the adults of other primate species, as described above. The adults' approach to education in these cases may be called laissez-faire, and it is present when the skill to be learned is not highly valued or when it is simple. We call this educational style *expected learning* because adults anticipate that children will learn on their own, that learning will happen naturally.

Second, adults believe that children need guidance to learn complex or valued tasks, that they need to "bring up" their children to master certain skills. They feel that although children might eventually learn such skills on their own, their intervention enables children's acquisition of challenging skills more rapidly and efficiently. In some cases the adult requires the child to observe a particular practice at a particular time. In other cases the adult allows the child to participate in the task to the extent to which the child is currently able. The adult might simplify the task, adding more demonstration or explanation when necessary, and increase difficulty and reduce assistance as the child progresses. This type of practice is easily distinguishable from "teaching" by other primates because it is so clearly intentional; the adult persists in the practice until the child is successful. This level of adult involvement may be called scaffolding; it requires sensitive observation of

Table 17.1   *Three types of intentional instruction and their associated adult beliefs and activities*

	Adult beliefs	Adult activities	Types of tasks	Types of practice
Expected learning	Learning occurs through maturation	Laissez-faire	Simple or not valued	Informal
Guided learning	Learning needs assistance	Scaffolding	Moderately complex or valued	Semiformal
Designed learning	Learning needs insistence and direct instruction	Teaching	Highly complex or valued	Formal

the child's performance and attention to the child's experiences to enhance learning. This type of practice is semiformal, falling between informal and formal in the quantity and quality of structure provided. We call this educational style *guided learning*, because children's efforts at learning benefit from adults' assistance.

Third, adults believe that in some situations learning must be created, that they must effortfully "pull up" their children to certain skills and standards. They assume that children alone will never be able to master highly complex, abstract, or valued tasks and that precise instruction is necessary to prepare for eventual mastery. The adult understands the uniqueness and importance of the tasks and understands that it is virtually impossible to learn these tasks by methods other than those that are the most motivating and persuasive. Consequently, the adult's level of involvement is high, designing a special setting for the learning and communicating the information in a systematic way. This type of practice is formal, and the adult's activity may be termed teaching. We call this educational style *designed learning*, emphasizing the responsibility of the adult to effortfully create the learning situations. While designed learning is not used by all cultures in all situations, it is used by all cultures in some domains, as we show in the section that follows. A summary of these three types of instruction appears in Table 17.1.

Intentional Instruction in Different Societies

To check for the presence of these three levels of adult involvement in the education of children, we surveyed the anthropological literature for several human societies. These societies have a wide geographic distribution and range in polity types from camps (foragers like the !Kung San of Botswana) to chiefdoms (traders like the Puluwatans of the Western Caroline Islands) to people living within states (like the Chaga living on the slopes of Mount Kilimanjaro). Nearly all are nonliterate societies. More specifically, these cultures were selected to test the hypothesis that even the smallest-scale society features intentional teaching of children, if only for a few and special tasks.

Expected Learning   People living in small-scale societies are widely believed to have a hands-off attitude toward the education of children. This is true for many tasks and skills, often because they are assumed to develop naturally. For example, the Tallensi of Taleland in northern Ghana, West Africa, live in a small-scale farming society. According to Fortes (1970), life skills (e.g., chopping, carrying, washing) are acquired via the Tallensi children's participation in the ongoing flow of activity. The adults assume that skills develop with practice, just as the body grows with time. Children are thought to be capable and desirous of learning, so the adults stay out of the process. About child development, the adults remark, "*Naawun mpaan ba* [heaven teaches them]" (p. 37). Similarly, the Manus people of New Guinea (Mead, 1930) assume that physical skills, and even grace, develop naturally. Although their world presents many physical challenges to young children, they are never taught. The children learn to swim, to walk over treacherous wooden slats, to canoe, and many other skills by straightforward immersion and participation in the activities.

On the island of Samoa, adults believe that children learn best when they are left alone to observe and adopt adult behaviors over time. Consequently, adults make few accommodations to young children. For example, Samoan parents do not simplify their speech when they address their sons and daughters. Instead, they expect the children to come up to adult speech standards on their own. The adults believe that for children "the way to knowledge and power is to serve (i.e., attend)" (Ochs, 1988, p. 205). The !Kung San of the Kalahari Desert in Botswana (Konner, 1982) claim that infants cry because they have no "sense." There is no use for adults to try to stop the babies from being senseless. The !Kung believe that when the babies grow older they will develop sense on their own. This expectation of maturation constitutes a belief about how the child changes with age. It is important to note, however, that if the belief is violated by experience, as when a child fails to learn on its own an important task, such as food gathering, adults behave differently. They adjust their theory and become more assertive about the need to learn. In such an instance, !Kung adults make a piquant comment, such as, "Maybe this child doesn't like to eat" (M. Konner, personal communication, 1994). The implication of this usually requires no further elaboration for the child. As we see in this example, the societies that possess maturational theories of child development and who sometimes practice laissez-faire education also have other theories about development and other levels of involvement, depending on the particularities of the individual, the task, and its domain.

Guided Learning   There is evidence that adults in all cultures believe children need a careful, graduated program of guidance to learn at least some more complex skills. In these circumstances, adults expect children to eventually learn, but they scaffold the child's acquisition of ability nevertheless. For example, Tallensi young people serve as apprentices to skilled practitioners, such as leatherworkers.

Although the apprentices learn mostly by observation and participation in the practice, they also are given explanations by the masters when necessary (Fortes, 1970). Mayan mothers simplify the task of tortilla making for their daughters; they give pointers, make demonstrations, provide suggestions, and adjust the task to increases in skill (Rogoff, 1990). Early in their career, Liberian apprentice tailors are allowed to work on parts of clothing that are inexpensive (in case they botch the job) and on pieces of the material that do not show (Greenfield and Lave, 1982). With time and improved skills, they are given more important work, eventually being trusted to make entire articles of clothing. In Mexico, Zinacanteco girls learn to weave by observation and active participation, but they receive simplified situations, corrections, and help from the adults (Childs and Greenfield, 1980), and the support supplied by adults varies inversely with the skill level of the learner. Adult structuring of learning situations can be quite subtle. In some cases adults simply encourage observation generally; in other cases they may point out certain events for particular notice (Rogoff et al., 1993). Scaffolding also can be nonverbal, as when a Rotuman parent in Melanesia simply adjusts a child's body position during a task (Howard, 1970), or when a parent makes a tiny bow for a little boy to practice hunting or a tiny bucket for a young girl to use in carrying water (Fortes, 1970).

These are examples of semiformal, scaffolded interaction, in which the adult intervenes to prevent the learner from going hopelessly off track, from ruining a piece of work, or from becoming discouraged. The adult's expertise is valuable to the child, and the child's productivity is valuable to the adult. The children are not expected to reinvent weaving or tailoring or leatherworking on their own, or to learn them perfectly by observation and practice. Part of the adult's motivation is economic, no doubt, but this economic need for a productive helper coincides with their theoretical and empirical understanding of what will happen if the apprentices are left to their own devices.

It is our contention that scaffolding is intentional instruction. The adults expect the children to learn, but they also expect that they will have to intervene in order to produce a skilled helper. The adults provide help in a graduated manner that reflects their monitoring of the child's developing capacity for more independent work. Thus the adult's behavior reflects a theory that the learner must be active in the flow of practice from the beginning, but that the learner's perspective on the task will be immature. The expert must then carefully structure the learning experiences to match the child's changing perspective.

Designed Learning   There is evidence that highly valued skills are carefully taught, even in traditional societies. Super (1981) reports that valued physical skills such as sitting and walking are deliberately taught to babies in most traditional African cultures. For example, sitting is taught by placing the infant in the upright position supported by cloths, or by placing the infant in a shallow hole that supports the sitting position. This teaching takes place every day for several months before the expected age of performance. Clearly, these adults in traditional, nonliterate cultures are not only practicing laissez-faire education or even scaffolding. They are actively, intentionally teaching their infants these skills, outside the casual practice of them, even before the infant can attempt these skills alone.

The practice of hunting among the !Kung is both highly valued as a food source and highly complex in the skills required. Boys are given tiny bows for practice, and they are allowed to tag along and participate with the adults as they can. However, their hunting education also includes periods of storytelling and question-and-answer sessions conducted by experts, back in camp (Konner, 1981). These are times for hunting instruction that are set apart from the everyday practice of these skills. The adults behave in a way that reflects their belief that their knowledge is important, abstract, and essential to the hunting education of the children.

One of the most impressive displays of teaching can be found among the Puluwat people of the South Pacific (Gladwin, 1970). The Puluwats design and build ocean-going canoes and navigate vast expanses of open ocean by dead reckoning. Their skills are formidable, and they pass them on to the next generation in a highly formal manner. Apprenticeship in navigation is open only to the candidates who are most promising, and it lasts about 20 years. Usually a boy is apprenticed to a male relative. Boys without relatives in the practice pay dearly for the privilege of being instructed. Less than half of those who volunteer to apprentice actually complete the course of training and become navigators. Even fewer are capable of navigating a long solo trip. The apprenticeship is conducted first on land, during lessons in which the learners must memorize large amounts of information, such as the pattern of rising and setting stars for countless routes. Not only is star information taught, but dozens of other topics as well, such as currents, conditions, waves, positions, reefs, weather, and sealife. There is a special hut for these lessons, and mats and stones are used flexibly to represent different relevant environmental elements. Lessons on land are followed by years of practice at sea, in a graduated program of guided practice. The program of apprenticeship for the Puluwat navigators might be seen as most similar to the modern, Western system of medical education.

Although a variety of cultures use intentional instruction as the method of education for the acquisition of valued economic skills, the use of intentional instruction is even more clearly evident in the education of manners, religion, and other socially designed practices. As Fortes (1970) observed, when children learn practical skills, they have their own objective achievement as an evaluation of their progress. However, when the child is learning prayers or humility or magic, the only test for educational progress is the reaction of other people. Other people possess all the information about taboos, charms, terms of address, and all the many and complex aspects that make up the social rules and identity of a people.

Among the Tikopia of Polynesia, parents are considered responsible for the instruction of children in manners, customs, and polite speech (Firth, 1970). In North America Hopi parents strive to create "good hearts" in their children, the feelings that motivate appropriate behavior (Eggan, 1970). In Wogeo, New Guinea, parents believe in *singara*, "steering" their children's moral development (Hogbin, 1970). Parents of the Chaga tribe in Tanzania begin drilling their three-year-olds in the three classes of names that all family members have. By six years of age the children have been taught terms of address and new and elaborate manners (Raum, 1970). In Uganda etiquette is also drummed into the children of the Ganda people. They must master phrases of greeting and farewell, polite gestures, and the rules of gift giving; errors are severely punished (Mair, 1934). The Tallensi people place a high value on their ancestor cult and acknowledge the positive obligation they have in transmitting it to the next generation. One chief informed Fortes, "This is my child, and I am teaching him uprightness. If he is about to do anything that is not seemly I tell him, so that when he grows up he will know upright ways" (Fortes, 1970, p. 23).

Initiation rites are clearly an example of the intentional teaching of adolescents. During adolescent initiation, Chaga boys must endure the adults' relentless repetition of ethical teaching (Raum, 1970). Special isolation, taboos, and vocabulary instruction are required of the apprentice shamans among Eskimo boys (Bernhard, 1988). For the vision quest of the North American Sioux, adults require that boys experience four days of fasting while alone and naked in a small, deep pit. Once a boy has survived the initiation, an elderly teacher informs him that he is now a man and may take a new name (Lame Deer and Erdoes, 1972). The boys of the Sambia people in the New Guinea Highlands are required to undergo a strict initiation that lasts from 7 to 17 years of age. During these years initiates are totally isolated from uninitiated males and from all of the females of the community. Adult males teach the initiates by telling them ritualized stories concerning masculine values and taboos. They also stage horrible events to deliberately frighten the boys so that they will listen even more carefully. Furthermore, the men demand that the boys participate in nightly ritualized homosexual activities throughout this multiyear period in order to develop masculinity (Herdt, 1981). In these and other initiation rites it is clear that adults are intentionally orchestrating experiences to create a deep impression on the children, one that will last a lifetime.

Mead (1930) reports that although Manus parents expect the natural development of physical grace, they intentionally teach two important cultural values: property rights and modesty. For example, since the rules of possession are extremely important to adults, they directly and repeatedly instruct children in them. Children are explicitly taught not to touch articles they do not own. Just one act of damage to another's property results in a major public scene. It begins with drumming to the entire community, alerting everyone that a meeting will soon take place. At that time the crimes of the errant child are announced, and the young offender is denounced and shamed, humiliated before the entire Manus community. This is not learning about cultural values by inference. This is learning by direct, intentional instruction about the rules of society.

Similarly, Lutz (1983) reports that the Ifaluk of Micronesia have a cultural value of cooperation and nonaggression. Parents see themselves as responsible for ensuring that their children are worthy members of society. They use lectures and long discussions on Ifaluk customs and correct behavior as one tool of instruction. Another tool is the elicitation of the emotion they call *metagu*. Children are encouraged to feel *metagu* in the presence of strangers, or whenever they should feel shame. If a child does not demonstrate the appropriate *metagu* reaction to a situation, her parents issue a call to a ghostly figure (*tarita*), beseeching her to come forward from her inland hiding place. The child knows that this phantom kidnaps and eats little children, and the child understands that her parents have called the ghost because of her misbehavior. The dreaded ghost (a female household member in horrific disguise) appears outside the house, on cue, and the terrified child clings for parental protection. This emotional state in the child is considered to be a very good moment for instruction in the experience of *metagu*.

The examples cited above show adults engaging in formal, intentional instruction of children. These are verbal encounters, separate from the daily flow of activity and repeated as necessary until the children's behavior reaches some preestablished criterion. The adults have requirements, and they enforce them. This behavior by adults reflects a belief that children, for some activities and standards, must be trained in the ways of the culture. Obviously, not all ways require teaching, but when the cultural practice is highly valued, complex, or abstract, adults use intentional instruction to ensure that their children will not embarrass them. They want their children to be appropriate, respectable members of society, and so they stay with the children, teaching them the upright ways. In the ethnographies reviewed, covering numerous and far-flung societies, every society used intentional teaching, at least for some very important aspects of cultural life.

The Effect of Intentional Instruction on Cognitive Development

We have argued and presented evidence that adults in all cultures have beliefs about what children know and how they learn. Adults are motivated to act on those beliefs, whether out of the tender desire for their offspring to be well adjusted, or out of the practical need for their children's help with the economic burdens of life. For love or money, the motivation to affect children's development results in adult involvement in the learning process. Thus the human child, and only the human child, is born into a developmental niche populated by educators. Intentional instruction is a key ingredient in the recipe that creates a normally developing human being.

We see intentional instruction as making its contribution to human development in two main ways. One effect of instruction is to enhance or even enable the child's acquisition of many culturally relevant skills. As we have seen, scaffolding and teaching lead to more effective learning in many domains and with many tasks. To acquire a new skill, children often rely on adults to direct their attention to the right things and to give them feedback about how they are doing. Adults provide the boost children need to learn important cultural tasks efficiently and appropriately.

However, there is a second and more profound effect of intentional instruction. In certain instructional situations, the adult intends for the child to learn in a special way, to adopt a new, more adult-like perspective. Children comprehend the intention of the adult with respect to their own intentions and appropriate the adult's understanding. Thus, children experience instructed learning; they have a new understanding that retains the intersubjectivity of the learning situation. As we argued in Tomasello, Kruger, and Ratner (1993), when a child internalizes an adult's intentions, there are dramatic effects on cognitive development.

The origins of this effect on cognitive development can be seen in the earliest days of infancy, when adults treat children as if they have intentions toward other people. Western mothers and their babies engage in a reciprocal smiling and vocalizing game that resembles the turn taking of conversation (Trevarthen, 1979); this rhythmical interaction is richly supported by the mother's structuring, and the baby's behavior is lavishly interpreted by the mother as intentional (Kaye, 1982). Mothers on the Marquesas Islands, by contrast, hold their infants facing out to others in the household, intending the babies to be interactive partners with older children (Martin and Kilpatrick, 1981). Kaluli mothers in Papua New Guinea will occasionally "speak" for their infants in high-pitched voices to entice teenagers to chat with them (Schieffelin, 1990). Around the world the intentional treatment of young children also includes adults' references to entities in the environment. Adults demonstrate the uses of materials, point out features of the environment, and highlight cause-effect relations by gesturing, vocalizing, presenting, and emoting. The adult intends for the child to attend to the object of interest. In these situations adults are behaving as if their babies were mature interactive partners with the intention of conversing. Eventually, as a result of living in this world of intentions and expectations, and being treated accordingly, the child comes to understand the adult, and the self, as intentional: hence, the so-called nine-month-miracle, when for the first time human infants look where adults are looking (joint attention), feel what adults are feeling (social referencing), and do what adults are doing (imitation). By figuring out the intentions of the other people in their world, and by adopting these intentions as their own, children are cognitively changed. The new understanding of persons as intentional agents enables older infants to acquire more complex abilities, such as the use of symbols (Tomasello, in press), and perhaps to form a self concept (Tomasello, 1993).

The effect of intentional instruction does not stop at the end of infancy. Around the age of four years, the child understands that other people have unique, subjective perspectives, ones that often differ from her own. This development in the child's social cognition supports even more elaborate cultural learning, often in the context of one of the forms of intentional instruction. For example, the child may understand that she and her mother have different minds and different perspectives on a task, and they converse about the task in a dialogue exploring these differences. The two work together, in a manner controlled by the adult, to reach a meeting of the minds. The adult intends to affect the child's understanding, the child is aware of this intention, and the child works to create a new understanding of the task, one based on the adult's intentions. In true instructed learning the child leaves the interaction with an internalized dialogue that represents a coordination of the participants' mental representations during the instructional process (Vygotsky, 1978).

As an aside, we should also mention that intentional instruction of the type we have been describing can also have profound effects on the cognitive development of other animal species. For example, when apes receive intentional instruction from humans—of a type they do not experience in their natural habitats—some significant changes take place in the nature of their cognitive and social cognitive skills (Tomasello, Savage-Rumbaugh, and Kruger, 1993; see Call and Tomasello, in press, for a review).

Implications for Education

We have focused here on the beliefs and practices of educators. However, it is important to recognize that in any instructional encounter there are at least two different individuals present—teacher and learner—with different comprehensions of the task, different plans about how to proceed, different understandings of the other person and of what that person understands. In past educational practice, only one of these differences between teacher and learner was emphasized: their mismatched comprehension of the task. For generations it was held that the teacher understands, the learner is ignorant, and the goal of education is to pass under- standing from the teacher to the learner. This view of the empty-headed pupil has been abandoned by many lately in favor of a more generous alternative. Gardner (1991), for example, argues that children construct naive theories of how the world works. Their so-called unschooled minds are not empty, just less developed than those of more educated people. This variation on the Piagetian view of the child's mind must now be expanded to include children's naive theories of other persons as an important part of the process, as we emphasized in our original formulation of the theory of cultural learning. What we have attempted to empha- size here is that to understand and enhance educational practice, this fuller model of the child's mind must be considered in tandem with a model of the instructor's theory of children, and their minds and learning skills, and how this affects their choice of pedagogical method.

In Olson and Astington's (1993) view, instruction involves complex social cognitive processes. For teachers to be effective, their thinking must integrate a representation of the goal of the task with a representation of the learner's under- standing, and they must continuously monitor the effect of feedback and prompts on the learner's progress. This instructional process also may be different for dif- ferent kinds of tasks. If the point is to teach the learner how to *do* something, such as prepare tortillas, then teachers must craft their physical demonstrations, moni- toring, and feedback accordingly. If the point is to teach the learner how to *think* about something, such as how to judge whether the current and wind speed favor a long sailing journey, then teachers must craft interpersonal interactions such as discussions with the learner which will prompt the learner to consider and criti- cize alternatives. A further distinction may be made between teaching students to think about *facts* and teaching them to think about *perspectives*. Phelps and Damon (1989) argue that when faced with the challenge of learning facts, such as the multiplication tables, no shift in a learner's perspective is really needed. The facts of multiplication are "out there" in the culture; the learner just needs to get them. This information can thus be learned more or less individually, assuming the culture makes it available. However, when the task requires shifts in perspective-taking, such as understanding the concept of proportion (this is *relative* to that), children learn the concept much more efficiently and deeply through an intersubjective interaction with another person. Learning concepts that rely on perspective is facilitated by the comparison and negotiation of different points of view in social interaction. Thus the more important it is for the child to adopt a second perspective, to see things in a new way—the cultural way—the more likely it is that the adult will intentionally instruct. Instructors' theories of domains of learning, and how these interact with children's learning skills, are therefore an important part of the picture as well.

In our theory of cultural learning (see Tomasello, Kruger, and Ratner, 1993) we emphasized the aspect of the process that we felt cultural psychology had neglected: the child's cognition, especially social cognition. This led us to under-emphasize the structuring role of culture and the important part played by intentional instruction. We have attempted to redress the balance here by explicitly describing some of the ways that cultures shape the development of human children, especially through the intentional instruction of others. As a species-universal and species-specific developmental niche, culture is an integral part of the process whereby human children become human adults.

References

Bernhard, J. G. (1988). *Primates in the classroom: An evolutionary perspective on children's education.* Amherst: University of Massachusetts Press.

Boesch, C. (1991). Teaching in wild chimpanzees. *Animal Behavior, 41,* 530–532.

Boesch, C. (1993). Aspects of transmission of tool use in wild chimpanzees. In K. Gibson and T. Ingold (Eds.), *Tools, language, and cognition in human evolution.* New York: Cambridge University Press.

Bourdieu, P. (1977). *Outline of a theory of practice.* Cambridge, England: Cambridge University Press.

Bruner, J. S. (1972). Nature and uses of immaturity. *American Psychologist, 27,* 687–708.

Bruner, J. S. (1993). Do we "acquire" culture or vice versa? *Behavioral and Brain Sciences, 16,* 515–516.

Call, J. and Tomasello, M. (in press). The role of humans in the cognitive development of apes. In A. Russom, K. Bard, and S. Parker (Eds.), *Reaching into thought: The minds of the great apes.* New York: Cambridge University Press.

Caro, T. M. and Hauser, M. D. (1992) Is there evidence of teaching in nonhuman animals? *Quarterly Review of Biology, 67,* 171–174.

Childs, C. P. and Greenfield, P. M. (1980). Informal modes of learning and teaching: The case of Zinacanteco weaving. In N. Warren (Ed.), *Studies in cross-cultural psychology* (Vol. 2) (pp. 269–316). London: Academic Press.

Cole, M. (1989). Cultural psychology: A once and future discipline? In J. Berman (Ed.),

Nebraska symposium on motivation, 1989: Cross-cultural perspectives (pp. 279–335). Lincoln: University of Nebraska Press.

Eggan, D. (1970). Instruction and affect in Hopi cultural continuity. In J. Middleton (Ed.), *From child to adult: Studies in the anthropology of education* (pp. 109–133). Garden City, NY: Natural History Press.

Firth, R. (1970). Education in Tikopia. In J. Middleton (Ed.), *From child to adult: Studies in the anthropology of education* (pp. 75–90). Garden City, NY: Natural History Press.

Foreman, E. A. (1993). What is the difference between cognitive and sociocultural psychology? *Behavioral and Brain Sciences, 16*, 518–519.

Fortes, M. (1970). Social and psychological aspects of education in Taleland. In J. Middleton (Ed.), *From child to adult: Studies in the anthropology of education* (pp. 14–74). Garden City, NY: Natural History Press.

Gardner, H. (1991). *The unschooled mind: How children think and how schools should teach.* New York: Basic Books.

Gauvain, M. (in press). Thinking in niches: Sociocultural influences on cognitive development. *Human Development.*

Gladwin, T. (1970). *East is a big bird: Navigation and logic on Puluwat Atoll.* Cambridge: Harvard University Press.

Goodall, J. (1986). *The chimpanzees of Gombe: Patterns of behavior.* Cambridge: Harvard University Press.

Greenfield, P. M. and Lave, J. (1982). Cognitive aspects of informal education. In D. Wagner and H. Stevenson (Eds.), *Cultural perspectives on child development* (pp. 181–207). San Francisco: Freeman.

Herdt, G. H. (1981). *Guardians of the flutes: Idioms of masculinity.* New York: Columbia University Press.

Hogbin, H. I. (1970). A New Guinea childhood: From weaning till the eighth year in Wogeo. In J. Middleton (Ed.), *From child to adult: Studies in the anthropology of education* (pp. 134–162). Garden City, NY: Natural History Press.

Howard, A. (1970). *Learning to be Rotuman.* New York: Teachers College Press.

Ingold, T. (1993). A social anthropological view. *Behavioral and Brain Sciences, 16*, 526–527.

Kaye, K. (1982). *The mental and social life of babies: How parents create persons.* Chicago: University of Chicago Press.

Konner, M. (1981). Evolution of human behavior development. In R. H. Munroe, R. L. Munroe, and B. B. Whiting (Eds.), *Handbook of cross-cultural human development* (pp. 3–51). New York: Garland STPM Press.

Konner, M. (1982). *The tangled wing: Biological constraints on the human spirit.* New York: Holt, Rinehart and Winston.

Lame Deer, J. and Erdoes, R. (1972). *Lame Deer, seeker of visions.* New York: Simon and Schuster.

Lave, J. and Wenger, E. (1991). *Situated learning: Legitimate peripheral participation.* New York: Cambridge University Press.

Lutz, C. (1983). Parental goals, ethnopsychology, and the development of emotional meaning. *Ethos, 11*, 246–262.

Mair, L. P. (1934). *An African people in the twentieth century.* London: Routledge.

Martini, M. and Kirkpatrick, J. (1981). Early interactions in the Marquesas Islands. In T. M. Field, A. M. Sostek, P. Vietze, and P. H. Leiderman (Eds.), *Culture and early interactions* (pp. 189–213). Hillsdale, NJ: Lawrence Erlbaum.

Mead, M. (1930). *Growing up in New Guinea.* New York: Mentor.

Ochs, E. (1988). *Culture and language development: Language acquisition and language socialization in a Samoan village.* New York: Cambridge University Press.

Olson, D. R. and Astington, J. W. (1993). Cultural learning and the educational process. *Behavioral and Brain Sciences, 16,* 531–532.

Phelps, E. and Damon, W. (1989). Problem solving with equals: Peer collaboration as a context for learning mathematics and spatial concepts. *Journal of Educational Psychology, 81,* 639–646.

Quinn, N. and Strauss, C. (1994). *A cognitive framework for a unified theory of culture.* Unpublished manuscript.

Raum, O. (1970). Some aspects of the indigenous education among the Chaga. In J. Middleton (Ed.), *From child to adult: Studies in the anthropology of education* (pp. 91–108). Garden City, NY: Natural History Press.

Rogoff, B. (1990). *Apprenticeship in thinking: Cognitive development in social context.* New York: Oxford University Press.

Rogoff, B., Chavajay, P., and Matusov, E. (1993). Questioning assumptions about culture and individuals. *Behavioral and Brain Sciences, 16,* 533–534.

Schieffelin, B. B. (1990). *The give and take of everyday life: Language socialization of Kaluli children.* Cambridge, England: Cambridge University Press.

Shweder, R. A. (1990). Cultural psychology—what is it? In J. W. Stigler, R. A. Shweder, and G. Herdt (Eds.), *Cultural psychology: Essays on comparative human development* (pp. 1–43). New York: Cambridge University Press.

Super, C. M. (1981). Behavioral development in infancy. In R. H. Munroe, R. L. Munroe, and B. B. Whiting (Eds.), *Handbook of cross-cultural human development* (pp. 181–270). New York: Garland STPM Press.

Super, C. M. and Harkness, S. (1986). The developmental niche: A conceptualization at the interface of child and culture. *International Journal of Behavioral Development, 9,* 545–569.

Tomasello, M. (1990). Cultural transmission in the tool use and communicatory signaling of chimpanzees? In S. Parker and K. Gibson (Eds.), *Language and intelligence in monkeys and apes: Comparative developmental perspectives* (pp. 274–311). New York: Cambridge University Press.

Tomasello, M. (1993). On the interpersonal origins of self-concept. In U. Neisser (Ed.), *The perceived self* (pp. 174–182). New York: Cambridge University Press.

Tomasello, M. (1994). The question of chimpanzee culture. In R. Wrangham, W. McGrew, F. deWaal, and P. Heltne (Eds.), *Chimpanzee cultures* (pp. 301–317). Cambridge: Harvard University Press.

Tomasello, M. (in press). Joint attention as social cognition. In C. Moore and P. Dunham (Eds.), *Joint attention: Its origins and role in development.* Hillsdale: Lawrence Erlbaum.

Tomasello, M., Kruger, A. C., and Ratner, H. H. (1993). Cultural learning. *Behavioral and Brain Sciences, 16,* 495–552.

Tomasello, M., Savage-Rumbaugh, S., and Kruger, A. C. (1993). Imitative learning of actions on objects by children, chimpanzees, and enculturated chimpanzees. *Child Development, 64,* 1688–1705.

Trevarthen, C. (1979). Communication and cooperation in early infancy: A description of primary intersubjectivity. In M. Bullowa (Ed.), *Before speech: The beginning of interpersonal communication* (pp. 321–347). Cambridge, England: Cambridge University Press.

Vygotsky, L. S. (1978). *Mind in society.* Cambridge: Harvard University Press.

Wrangham, R., McGrew, W., deWaal, F., and Heltne, P. (1994). *Chimpanzee cultures.* Cambridge: Harvard University Press.

18

Models of Teaching and Learning: Participation in a Community of Learners

BARBARA ROGOFF
EUGENE MATUSOV
CYNTHIA WHITE

The aim of this chapter is to distinguish theories of development that cast learning as a community process of *transformation of participation* in sociocultural activities from theories that cast learning as a one-sided process in which only teachers or learners are responsible for learning, either through *transmission* of knowledge from experts or *acquisition* of knowledge by learners by themselves. To distinguish these perspectives and highlight the theoretical stance of transformation of participation, we take a developmental approach by examining the transformation in understanding that occurs as adults who have been used to functioning in institutions employing transmission theories attempt to understand a new institution employing a participation theory.

Our examination of these theoretical positions makes use of observations of models of instruction held by parents who become participants in a public elementary school program (the "OC" of the Salt Lake City School District) that functions as a community of learners. In this optional program, parents are required to spend three hours per week (per child) working in the classroom.

The contrasting instructional models used by parents in the program correspond with theoretical discussions regarding who is responsible for learning. The parents' views that education should be *"adult-run"* correspond with theoretical notions that learning is a process managed by experts who transmit knowledge to learners; the views of those who argue that education should be *"children-run"* correspond with theoretical notions that learning is the province of learners who acquire knowledge through their active exploration; and the views of those who propose a *"community of learners"* involving both active learners and more skilled partners who provide leadership and guidance correspond with the theoretical stance that learning involves transformation of participation in collaborative endeavor. Thus the notions involved in the theoretical perspectives of learning as transmission, acquisition, and transformation of participation are associated with instructional models that differ in how participants' responsibilities for promoting learning are seen.

We are distinguishing here between theoretical perspectives on learning regarding how learning occurs (transmission, acquisition, and transformation of participation) and models of instruction that are aligned with these three theoretical perspectives but focus more on issues of how to promote learning (by adults controlling the process, children controlling the process, or collaboration in a community of learners with varying responsibilities). Both the theoretical perspectives on learning and the instructional models involve cohesive conceptual frameworks, although the instructional models can be seen as based on the theoretical perspectives on learning (rather than vice versa). Both conceptual frameworks—the theoretical perspectives on learning and the instructional models—can be distinguished from "practices" that people carry out and that can in some sense be described without reference to their conceptual basis. Indeed, often a particular practice can serve different models of instruction. However, when clusters of practices are examined together, in context, they can reveal the conceptual basis that ties them to one or another model of instruction. So, in our terminology, coherent patterns of instructional practices are based on instructional models, and instructional models are based on theoretical perspectives on learning.

In the following sections we describe how all three instructional models can be analyzed from the perspective of a participation theory (Lave and Wenger, 1991; Rogoff, 1990, 1995), then describe the three instructional models in more detail, and then turn to our observations of parents' use of the three instructional models as they transform their participation in a public elementary school based on a community of learners model.

A Participation Theory Analysis of Learning in all Three Models

Two of the models, adult-run and children-run instruction, are often cast as opposite extremes of a pendulum swing between unilateral control and freedom. The idea of this pendulum swing can be seen frequently in ongoing discussions among researchers focusing on freedom and control in classrooms and families as well as on issues of restructuring schools and evaluating child-centered versus didactic approaches (see Eccles et al., 1991; Giaconia and Hedges, 1982; Greene, 1986; Stipek, in press). We argue that the adult-run and children-run models are closely related, in that they both involve a theoretical assumption that learning is a function of one-sided action (by adults or children, respectively, to the exclusion of the other).

The community of learners instructional model supersedes the pendulum entirely; it is not a compromise or a "balance" of the adult-run and children-run models. Its underlying theoretical notion is that learning is a process of transformation of participation in which both adults and children contribute support and direction in shared endeavors (Newman, Griffin, and Cole, 1989; Rogoff, 1990; Tharp and Gallimore, 1988; Wells, Chang, and Maher, 1990). However, it is difficult for people with a background in one-sided models of learning (such as many of the new parents in the school we are studying) to avoid assimilating the community of learners model to the adult-run/children-run dichotomy.

We apply theoretical notions of the transformation of participation perspective to analyze learning not only in a community of learners instructional model but also in adult-run and children-run instructional models, although their conceptual roots involve alternative theoretical notions of learning as being the product of transmission or acquisition, respectively. Thus, although we view the three instructional models as based on the three theoretical perspectives on learning, any of the theoretical perspectives on learning can be used to examine the learning that occurs in activities structured according to any of the three instructional models. (This is commonly done when measures based on the acquisition theory of learning are used to evaluate learning regardless of the instructional model used in the community or program.)

We argue that learning occurs in any situation, but different instructional models involve different relations of learners to the information and its uses in sociocultural activities. This view is based on the theoretical perspective of transformation of participation, which takes as a central premise the idea that learning and development occur as people participate in the sociocultural activities of their community, transforming their understanding, roles, and responsibilities as they participate (Lave and Wenger, 1991; Rogoff, 1995; Rogoff, Baker-Sennett, Lacasa, and Goldsmith, 1995; Rogoff, Baker-Sennett, and Matusov, 1994).

From a transformation of participation perspective, the difference between the three instructional models is not a matter of whether one involves learning and the others do not, but a matter of what is learned through the kind of participation that occurs in learning activities structured according to the different models. Instructional approaches based on the transmission, acquisition, and transformation of participation theories have different conceptions of what is involved in learning the academic subject matters of school; in their varying approaches to structuring learning, learners come to participate in (i.e., learn) different aspects of use of the information being taught.

We argue that the three instructional models all stimulate learning of the subject matter but that, in the diverse roles they play in the process of instruction, students also learn varying aspects of the uses of the information. For example, in instruction based on a transmission theory of learning (adult-run instruction), students learn the information to be able to demonstrate that it has been encoded and retained, in response to tests evaluating the transmission piece by piece. In instruction based on an acquisition theory of learning (children-run instruction), students learn the information as they explore in idiosyncratic ways that are not necessarily connected to the uses to which the information is historically or currently put in the adult world. In instruction based on a transformation of participation theory of learning (community of learners instruction), students learn the information as they collaborate with other children and adults in carrying out activities with purposes connected explicitly with the history and current practices of the community. In all three instructional approaches, the students learn the subject matter; however, in each, they learn a different relation to the subject matter and to the community in which the information is regarded as important, through their varying participation in the process of learning.

Pendulum Swing between One-Sided (Adult-run and Children-run) Models

The adult-run and children-run models can be viewed as different versions of one perspective that treats learning as one-sided, in that only one "side" of a relationship is active. Both treat adults and children as being on opposite sides of a relationship, not in a mutual process of collaboration between active participants. Both attribute responsibility for learning to one or the other, with the one that is not regarded as responsible having a passive role in the process of learning.

In the adult-run instructional model, which prevails in U.S. elementary schools (Bennett and LeCompte, 1990; Cuban, 1984; McDermott, 1993) and in U.S. middle-class parenting (Greene, 1986), learning is viewed as a product of teaching or of adults' provision of information.[1]

In most classrooms. . .the teacher sits or stands at the front of the room, dispensing "inert ideas" to his passive students, as if they were so many empty vessels to be filled. (Silberman, 1970, p. 148)

Adults are seen as responsible for filling children up with knowledge, as if children are receptacles and knowledge is a product. The children are treated as receivers of a body of knowledge but not active participants in learning. The children have little role except to be receptive, storing the knowledge that adults dispense. Figure 18.1 shows graphically a conception of a successful child as a receptacle of knowledge.

The adult-run model seems to be a feature of the U.S. public school system, attributable to the nature of educational philosophy and practices from educational policy makers, administrators, teachers, and parents. We do not see it as usually deriving from an explicit choice of instructional models by individuals but rather as an inherited model in which most middle-class U.S. adults have been educated (in elementary, secondary, and higher education, including teacher training), for reasons that extend beyond issues of education.

The role of broader forces on classroom instruction is particularly apparent in an extreme version of the adult-run model that appeared with the factory model of education that was central to the "scientific" efficiency movement in U.S. education in the early 1900s and has been extremely influential in public schooling since. In this movement, school superintendents responded to public pressures to run schools on the model of efficient factories, with a passive role for learners and management by experts and with cost reduction placed ahead of learning (Bennett and LeCompte, 1990; Callahan, 1962). Callahan chronicled the emulation of factory efficiency as fostering the development of standardized tests for measurement of the "product," of clerical work by teachers to keep records of costs and progress at the expense of teaching, and of "management" of teaching by central district

Figure 18.1   *An illustration of learning as the filling of a receptacle, from the lead article titled "Psychology's input leads to better tests,"* American Psychological Association Monitor *(1994, June, vol. 25, p. 1). Note that the information is portrayed as simply stored in the child's skull, and given access to seeing inside, the adult can assess whether or not the knowledge is possessed by the child. (Reproduced by permission of the illustrator, Sheila Harrington.)*

authorities who had little knowledge of educational practice or philosophy. That period led to the development of a separate profession of school administration, focusing on fiscal rather than educational issues, inspired by such leadership as that provided by Elwood P. Cubberley, Dean of the School of Education at Stanford, whose 1916 textbook was described as the most influential book on school administration of the generation. Callahan quoted Cubberley:

Our schools are, in a sense, factories in which the raw products (children) are to be shaped and fashioned into products to meet the various demands of life. The specifications for manufacturing come from the demands of twentieth-century civilization, and it is the business of the school to build its pupils according to the specifications laid down. This demands good tools, specialized machinery, continuous measurement of production to see if it is according to specifications, the elimination of waste in manufacture. . . . (Cubberley, *Public School Administration*, 1916, pp. 337–338, cited by Callahan, 1962, p. 97)

An example of a teacher espousing an extreme factory model of instruction, based on a transmission theory of how learning occurs, is provided by a chemistry teacher recently quoted by McRobbie and Tobin (1995):

The way the lessons are run at the moment they are completely teacher directed. . . . If I maintain control we will make progress through the work program, students will learn more, and learn more efficiently. I'm setting out to get this information into the kids' brains as efficiently as possible (although sometimes the schedule has to be adapted to meet the learning needs of the students), and by a transmissive model of teaching I can guarantee that there will be a greater percentage of students with the desired quantity of knowledge at the end. We are trying to meet timelines, and we are intolerant of digression. The greatest part of my teaching is geared to keeping the students moving along and on task. Getting the work done according to strict timelines is very important to us because we have negotiated to cover a certain amount of chemical science in a set amount of time as set out in the accredited work program and we also have to meet the external requirements of the certification processes for student achievement.

I believe I have all the knowledge the students need for their course. I see the learner as absorbing knowledge and I transfer some of that knowledge by having the students taking down notes. . . .

In order to get understanding you've got to be able to remember the basic facts that you are investigating. If you can't remember basic facts you can't get to the next step of sorting out relationships between facts. Almost every student is capable of being taught how to memorize large bodies of information quickly and I believe I can teach them that. . . . If students don't understand they should memorize the important information regardless and allow understanding to occur later in its own good time. I'm sure the brain will make the connections that are necessary if they have the basic knowledge memorized even if it may take a while. (pp. 7–8)

This extreme factory version of the adult-run model would probably not be espoused by other teachers who employ an adult-run model. For example, not all teachers who use an adult-run model would agree that rote memorization is so appropriate for teaching scientific concepts.

However, the guiding principle of the adult-run model is apparent in the example: unilateral defining of tasks, means, and goals for students by teachers. The students' role is to enter the adult-defined inquiry rather than to share inquiry with others. Students learn how to solve problems but not how to set them. They can produce correct answers but do not have experience examining how to determine what is correct. They learn how to participate in tasks that are not of their own personal interest and how to be motivated by the teacher but not how to build on or develop their own interests to extend to new and difficult inquiries. Students learn how to be led through tasks but not how to manage themselves or others in inquiry. They learn how to behave according to procedures and rules set by the teacher but not how to develop working procedures for managing the processes of interpersonal or material aspects of learning.

The teacher's job in the adult-run model is to prepare the knowledge for transmission and to motivate children to make themselves receptive. Often this is a matter of subdividing tasks into small mechanical units and applying incentives (or threatening punishment) for students to get through them. In a pure adult-run model, there is no necessity for the children to understand the purposes to which the knowledge is to be put or to become interested in the material for its own sake, since the children's role is simply to receive the information. The teacher does not rely on mutual engagement to help guide instruction, but instead must plan the amount, segmentation, and timing of instruction that will be necessary for transmission of the information. The teacher seeks pedagogical tricks to motivate students to be willing to accept the information, and uses standardized measurement devices to determine the quantity of knowledge that the students possess and their capacity to learn, by comparing them with each other. These teaching agendas emerge from the assumptions that learning results from one-sided transmission of knowledge and skills from those who possess them to those who do not.

The students' job in the adult-run model is to be receptive. This, of course, is not an entirely passive role; however, the kind of activity it involves is not one of leadership in the cognitive activity or in the "transmission" of information. The children are not collaborators with the teacher in intellectual inquiry or in the process of managing learning. Their role may be "cooperation" with the teacher's agenda, but it does not include helping to shape the agenda, or even necessarily understanding the agenda. Rather than participating in a shared endeavor, their role is to carry out the actions that the teacher designates for them. Although the teacher's and students' actions are in some sense coordinated with each other, they are compartmentalized in a way that differs from collaboration in which people's ideas and interests mingle.

Minick (1993) described such compartmentalization in which teachers' introduction of directives do not provide a rationale and inherent motive for actions required from the students. For example, in a classroom lesson, an elementary school teacher introduced the concept of mirror symmetry by asking children to perform separated actions with mirrors and geometric shapes. The children were not told the purpose of the manipulations, on what they should focus, or what the teacher wanted them to learn. The teacher's motive for the lesson was unavailable for the students; the students' purpose was limited to finding the actions that satisfied the teacher, almost like a guessing game. To complete the picture, it is necessary to mention that the lesson's motive is often unavailable to the teacher as well, because the teacher is only a part of the institutional chain of transmission of knowledge from the "higher" experts to the students.

The adult-run model of instruction, based on a transmission philosophy of how people learn, is nicely summarized in Kliebard's (1975) discussion of metaphorical roots of curriculum design. He referred to the metaphor of production as follows:

> The curriculum is the means of production, and the student is the raw material which will be transformed into a finished and useful product under the control of a highly skilled technician. The outcome of the production process is carefully plotted in advance according to rigorous design specifications. (p. 84)

In reaction to the adult-run model, various scholars and practitioners have proposed switching to a model that involves a more active role for the children as learners. Usually, this takes the form of a pendulum swing to children-run instruction, the opposite one-sided approach in which children are active constructors of knowledge and adult involvement is seen as a potential impediment to learning. In the children-run model, children discovering reality on their own or through interaction with peers is the ideal; children become the active agents in learning and the adult world is either seen as a passive source of materials or as a negative influence that can stunt the budding of children's own potential. Children are expected to discover and extend the knowledge, skills, and technologies of human history among themselves; adults may set up learning environments for the children but should otherwise avoid influencing children's "natural" course of learning. Graubard (1972) argued that many of the "free schools" of the 1960s and 1970s were characterized by an attitude that children would learn best if adults merely stayed out of their way. The challenge with the children-run model is to get the "natural" course of learning to somehow correspond with the skills and standards that the community values for the children.

An example of the pendulum swing between adult-run and children-run models, with the ideal being some sort of balance between the two extremes of freedom and control (Silberman, 1970), appears in a 1975 newspaper editorial quoted by Gold and Miles (1981) in their study of an open education elementary school that was under community pressure to return to basic skills training. The editorial proclaimed, "Basics are Back!" but also expressed concern about the pendulum swing:

Teachers, students and parents have all complained that language arts skills are sadly lacking in many "bright" students who graduate from the local high school with top scores. Good high school age writers often don't know the difference between the use of the words "threw" and "through"; spelling among many high school students is atrocious. Parents of elementary age students complain their children's spelling is not corrected because teachers fear correction will stifle creativity.

So now the pendulum swings back. The rote learning of the past is called into the present to save the citizens of the future. Admittedly the swing could turn into a destructive backlash. The move of the 1960's toward meaningful, creative, relevant, innovative education should not be lost in this age of recession. (pp. 204–205)

Freedom and control are thus conceived as opposites on a single dimension on which one partner holds the active position and the other partner is passive (for alternative conceptualizations see Kohn, 1993; Mosier and Rogoff, 1994). Together, the adult-run and children-run models constitute the one-sided philosophy of instruction in which adults and children are seen as contesting for control, with the side that does not have control being passive; these models can be seen as narrow alternatives to each other.

Curriculum debates in this country from at least the 1880s have reflected concern with the one-sided alternatives. According to Kliebard (1987), William Torrey Harris, an editor who had provided early encouragement for John Dewey in his youth, in 1880 advocated that the curriculum should build on the great resources of civilization, not on children's spontaneous impulses. Harris added an emphasis on the importance of "guiding direction" to the maxim arguing for learning to do by doing. Dewey, as he entered the debate over the importance of interest (corresponding to the children-run model) versus effort (corresponding to the adult-run model) in 1896, suggested that both were guilty of the same fallacy.

[Dewey] argued that the choice did not lie between engaging the child in mere amusement on the one hand, and forcing the child to pursue disagreeable tasks as part of the training of the will. . . . [Both sides] proceeded, according to Dewey from the identical assumption:

"the externality of the object or idea to be mastered, the end to be reached, the act to be performed, to the self.". . . Dewey was struggling with the possibility that the apparent opposition between the curriculum and the child could be not so much reconciled as vitiated. The problem was not one of choosing between two existing alternatives as it was reconstructing the questions so as to present new ones. (Kliebard, 1987, pp. 55–57)

Dewey (1938) criticized the *"Either-Or* philosophy" that prevails when educators simply "reject the ideas and practices of the old education and then go to the opposite extreme. . . . to make little or nothing of organized subject-matter of study; to proceed as if any form of direction and guidance by adults were an invasion of individual freedom" (p. 9). He argued that

Because the older education imposed the knowledge, methods, and the rules of conduct of the mature person upon the young, it does not follow, except upon the basis of the extreme *Either-Or* philosophy, that the knowledge and skill of the mature person has no directive value for the experience of the immature. (p. 8)

Consistent with Dewey's call for going beyond the dichotomy (see also Cahan, 1994), we argue that the community of learners model is not on the one-sided pendulum track; it removes the assumption of learners being on the other "side" from teachers, recasting them as mutually involved in shared endeavors.

Community of Learners Model

The community of learners model is not a balance or "optimal blend" of the two one-sided approaches, but rather a distinct instructional model based on a different philosophy. One type of evidence for its distinctness is the difficulty experienced by individuals who attempt to see its structure from the perspective of transmission or acquisition theories of learning (or adult-run or children-run instructional models), as is frequently the case for new parents entering the OC.

In a community of learners, all participants are active; no one has all the responsibility and no one is passive. Children take an active role in managing their own learning, coordinating with adults who are also contributing to the direction of the activity, while they provide the children with guidance and orientation. (And the children sometimes do likewise for the adults.) Adults support children's learning and development through attention to what the children are ready for and interested in as they engage in shared activities in which all contribute. In a community of learners, children and adults together are active in structuring the inquiry, though usually with asymmetry of roles. Children and adults collaborate in learning endeavors; adults are often responsible for guiding the process and children also learn to participate in the management of their own learning (Brown and Campione, 1990, 1994; Dewey, 1916; Newman, Griffin and Cole, 1989; Rogoff, 1994; Rogoff, Mistry, Göncü, and Mosier, 1993; Silberman, 1970; Tharp and Gallimore, 1988; Wells, Chang, and Maher, 1990).

The approach to learning in many communities in which children learn informally through active observation and participation in ongoing community activities with mutuality and support from more skilled community members is consistent with the community of learners model, though less focused on instruction than a school necessarily is (Lamphere, 1977; Rogoff, Mistry, Göncü, and Mosier, 1993). Schools organized as communities of learners are more self-consciously organized to promote children's learning, with more reflection and attention to the learning process, than are many informal learning practices, where the structure is less self-conscious and the purpose may focus more on actual contribution to community economic and other functions (Rogoff, 1994).

In a classroom functioning as a community of learners, organization involves dynamic and complementary group relations among class members who learn to take responsibility for their contribution to their own learning and to the group's functioning. Instead of a teacher attempting to address and manage many students as one recipient of instruction, trying to treat them as a unit, the organization involves a community working together with all serving as resources to the others, with varying roles according to their understanding of the activity at hand and differing (and shifting) responsibilities in the system. The discourse is often conversational, in the sense that people build on each other's ideas on a common topic guided by the teacher's leadership, rather than one way, with children's contributions considered to be interruptions.

We argue that it is consistent within the community of learners model for adults under some circumstances to provide strong leadership or extensive explanations to assist the group, and for children under some circumstances to have primary responsibility. This would not involve a patchwork of adult-run and children-run events. Although a community of learners model does not imply a precise format of instruction, it does assume a collaborative system in which whoever has the responsibility for leadership is still carefully coordinating with and assisting the others in a shared endeavor.

A community of learners model differs from the idea of piecemeal incorporation of innovative techniques into an otherwise conflicting fabric of the instructional model. An example of the latter is the use of cooperative learning techniques in an isolated fashion, where often only small portions of the day in school are allocated to group projects, and the rest of the day follows the adult-run model with all communication and decisions happening through the teacher. If during most of the day, only one child speaks at a time, and only to the teacher, the exceptional times when children tutor each other or work in cooperative groups do not correspond to a community of learners that is itself coherently structured as a cooperative system.

There are sometimes clashes that make the contrast quite clear, as Deering (1991, 1994) articulated in his descriptions of one teacher who emphasized competition and individual achievement, and tried to coerce students into cooperating. Changing practices in a piecemeal fashion, such as adding a cooperative learning session to an otherwise adult-run classroom structure, does not amount to transforming the underlying model of instruction (Cremin, 1962; Deering, 1991, 1994). Attempts to incorporate piecemeal cooperative learning practices reveal the prevalence of viewing one-sided models as the only alternatives, and show the difficulty for holders of those models to understand the coherence of an alternative such as the community of learners model. Trying to understand the community of learners model from a background in the one-sided (either adult-run or children-run) models requires a paradigm shift like that of learning how to function in another culture.

It is important to note, however, that any functioning institution will include variations rather than "pure" exemplars of the models. For some models, this is because institutions have multiple constituencies and responsibilities and interactions with other institutions that require compromises. With the community of learners model specifically, variety of practices (e.g., in the extent of asymmetry between people in different roles and in the kind of leadership provided) is a resource for the community's continued learning. If all teachers used just the same practices at all times, this would indicate that the community as a whole had stopped developing and making use of variations to continually spark ideas. A community of learners is always in a process of transformation, especially with the inclusion of newcomers who may not understand the traditions and who may also contribute to transforming them into revised traditions, even as new newcomers enter and continue the process.

Within the OC, the teachers refer to the issue of necessary variations on a theme in terms of the diverse approaches across classrooms while still maintaining a "common thread" throughout the program. Coherence of the philosophy in this school involves both commitment to the idea that all members of the community continue to learn through their varying roles in shared endeavors and commitment to the value of variations in participants' particular practices within this shared theme.

Newcomers Moving from Adult-Run to Community of Learners Models in School

Attempts to use the community of learners model in U.S. schools meet with unique challenges because most U.S. teachers and parents have been "raised" in a one-sided model of teaching and learning (usually adult-run; Matusov and Rogoff, 1995). In the OC, this difference between newcomers' educational background and the school's philosophy (i.e., the community of learners model) often makes for culture shock as adults who are newcomers try to align themselves with the new system. Until they develop an understanding of the community of learners model, it is difficult for newcomers to understand how the practices of the school fit together.

In our ongoing study, we are investigating how children, parents, teachers, and an educational institution transform in the process of developing and sustaining a public school that is structured as a community of learners, and how new generations and events contribute to changes in the community's practices. The challenges faced by the community in newcomers' developing understanding of a community of learners model illuminate both the developmental process involved in a paradigm shift and the nature of the community of learners and one-sided models of learning.

The OC was started 18 years ago by a group of parents and teachers who wanted to form a public elementary school with an innovative educational philosophy. It continues to be run cooperatively by parents and teachers (and sometimes administrators), with parents spending three hours per week (per child) in the classroom contributing to instruction, curriculum decisions, and classroom management as "co-opers." A large part of co-opers' time in the classroom is spent leading small groups of three to six children in activities devised by the co-opers (or sometimes the teachers) in the curriculum area for which they are responsible. There are six or seven classrooms of about 30 students each, from kindergarten through sixth grade, blended in groups of two or sometimes three grade levels per classroom.

Our statements in this chapter about the program are based on extensive participation of the first two authors as parent "co-opers" in the program and of the three of us as researchers, recording ongoing classroom activities and discussions of philosophy and practices in teacher and parent meetings, studying program newsletters and documents available since the inception of the program, talking with participants about their understandings of philosophy and classroom practices, and surveying co-opers' reflections on their own development and OC philosophy and practices. The quotations from parents reported in the following pages are taken from our four-page survey of co-opers' reflections on their own development and OC philosophy and practices, in 20 mostly open-ended questions. The survey was completed by 79 percent of the children's co-opers; all survey quotes are taken from co-opers participating in the fourth through sixth grades.

The OC functions with a coherent system of practices integrated in a largely tacit underlying philosophy corresponding to a community of learners model of instruction, which differs from schools that most adults in the OC have attended, in which learning is generally seen as the filling of children (as receptacles) with knowledge. Parents' initial involvement in the OC often involves confusion as they attempt to fit into a new value system and its practices. Their efforts to implement the practices in the classroom are often tentative and awkward as they puzzle out the philosophy through their own participation and observation of and discussion with others. New teachers face similar questions in their own career development and work with both children and parents in the classroom.

For many new members of the community, coming to participate in this program requires a long period of being "legitimate peripheral participants" (to use Lave and Wenger's term, 1991)—provided with some direct instruction but mainly with opportunities to observe, discuss, and participate. They struggle to understand the new philosophy tying together specific practices of a community of learners. Their issues are often based on coming to understand that the practices embody a distinct and coherent philosophy of learning rather than a pendulum swing between adult-run and children-run instruction or simple adoption of a few new pedagogical techniques. At first, new adults in the community often see daily events as unstructured and chaotic.

In describing similar school programs, Silberman (1970) provides an account of the initial impression:

Understandably, in view of all the sound and motion, the first impression may be one of chaos. In most schools, it is a false impression. "You always have to assess the nature of the noise," the headmistress of the first school the writer visited helpfully explained. "Is it just aimless chatter, or does it reflect purposeful activity?" And as the visitor becomes acclimated, it becomes clear that the activity usually is purposeful. . . . As the strangeness wears off, one becomes aware of many things. One becomes aware, for example, of the teacher's presence: in contrast to the first moments of wondering where she is, or whether she is even there at all, the visitor begins to see that the teacher is very much there and very much in charge. She seems always to be in motion, and always to be in contact with the children—talking, listening, watching, comforting, chiding, suggesting, encouraging. . . . One becomes aware, too, of the sense of structure. (pp. 225–226)

The process of becoming aware of the structure and the teacher's role is not rapid; for many newcomers to the OC, it takes several years (Matusov and Rogoff, 1995). A co-oper in his fifth year in the program remarked on our survey that over the years he had noticed more structure, and added that the teachers, who are superb, "have constructive activity in what sometimes appeared a chaotic environment."

Newcomers to the OC first begin to see particular practices in isolation as routines and attempt to follow them, but without comprehending how they fit together. They often assume that the new practices are opposite to the adult-run model with which they are familiar, swinging to the other one-sided model—the children-run model—and trying to implement new practices as simply the opposite of the old.

The attempt of many newcomers to assimilate the new model by simply switching which "side" (adults or children) is active makes sense. Marris (1986) suggested that in adult development, we attempt to cling to the familiar, for the more an innovation challenges existing understanding, the more threatening change is. Marris referred to Piaget's ideas on assimilation and accommodation:

Assimilation depends upon the pre-existence of organising structure sufficiently developed to incorporate the experience. The process of assimilation may lead to modifications of structure (accommodation), but only within limits of continuity. As John H. Flavell says (1963, p. 50):

Assimilation is by its very nature conservative, in the sense that its primary function is to make the unfamiliar familiar, to reduce the new to the old. A new assimilatory structure must always be some variant of the last one acquired and it is this which insures both the gradualness and continuity of intellectual development.

. . . It is slow, painful and difficult for an adult to reconstruct a radically different way of seeing life, however needlessly miserable his preconceptions make him. In this sense we are all profoundly conservative, and feel immediately threatened if our basic assumptions and emotional attachments are challenged. (p. 9)

Certain aspects of the community's functioning are difficult for newcomers to see until they have begun to really align themselves with the direction and philosophy of the program. Former OC teacher Pam Bradshaw (in press) points out that a central qualification for adults (and children) to participate skillfully in the program is willingness and readiness to "align" oneself with the direction in which the group is moving.

OC teacher Leslee Bartlett (in press) describes stages of development for newcomers to the OC in terms of movement from seeing only chaos, to seeing small parts of the routine, to seeing the structure surrounding one's own activity, to seeing the structure of the program. The process occurs through the newcomer personally becoming a part of the structure, in widening fields of participation. Co-opers who are partway there carry out their own activities with understanding; subsequently, co-opers can lead others through a "tour" of the OC; some go on to be able to be responsible for the whole classroom or larger parts of the program. Bartlett describes how, as teacher, she removes herself from the classroom for short periods to give co-opers whom she regards as ready the opportunity to take this responsibility; she can tell upon return to the classroom how things have gone.

Such learning involves the whole program in a continual process of renewal and change within continuity, as new generations come to play the roles of newcomers and oldtimers[2] in the community, becoming part of the structure. As Bartlett points out, one is never "done" learning; she and other teachers report that their reason for remaining involved with this high-commitment program is that they continue to learn. In fact, one indicator of alignment with the philosophy of a community of learners in a school seems to be regarding oneself as a learner, continually. Experienced co-opers, in response to a request in our survey for advice for new co-opers, often offered these suggestions: expect to learn yourself and concentrate on improvement rather than perfection.

Newcomers to the OC first begin to notice the morning or the afternoon routine: The whole class meets several times (in "circle") for planning activities and for whole-group instruction, but much of the day involves small groups of children working at an activity led by a co-oper or the teacher. The children choose which activity they will engage in during the different activity times, from among some required activities that they can complete according to their own schedule and others that are optional.

Newcomers easily notice the following features of the OC that do not require them to understand the community of learners philosophy:

- The active role of children and prevalence of hands-on, experiential learning
- The adult-child ratio, with about three parents in addition to the teacher in the classroom
- The families' commitment to education and involvement in the curriculum that provides enrichment from the expertise of each family and support for children's learning at home
- The nurturant environment and respect for individual interests and rates of progress (with avoidance of much ability grouping)

These items were the most commonly listed characteristics of the OC in our survey; most co-opers listed several of them, especially in responding to our question regarding why they chose to send their children to the OC in the first place.

In contrast, newcomers often have trouble understanding many OC practices that are based on the community of learners model. These they frequently attribute to the "permissive" end of the pendulum swing, as they turn from adult-run structure to children-run "lack" of structure. The developmental process involved in coming to understand the community of learners model is apparent from the remarks of a parent who had co-oped for 11 years. When asked in our survey how her co-oping skills and understanding of classroom procedures had changed with experience, she wrote, "I first relaxed and 'let go' of my memory of 'school' and let it teach you—be flexible and absorbent, trying not to push a concept but being aware of learning and teaching moments." She also referred to the differences between adult-run and children-run approaches and the community of learners approach:

Some parents are academic oriented, others want freedom, and these groups clash. I'm a fence sitter—I want a spider's web. A structure so fine and strong you don't know you're on it. It allows freedom of choice and those choices have been designed to provide learning experiences that are subtle and provide strong basic academic foundations w/o being forced or rote.

Newcomers struggle especially with issues central to the OC community of learners approach, which they often assimilate to their preconceptions of the permissive, children-run alternative to their own adult-run schooling experiences. Some of these central issues, elaborated below, include the instructional emphasis on the process rather than just the products of learning with adults serving as leaders and facilitators rather than direct instructors; the emphasis on teaching that builds on children's inherent interests; the evaluation of student progress through working with the child and observing; and the collaboration that occurs throughout the whole program. Only as they break free of the adult-run/children-run one-sided dichotomy do newcomers begin to understand the community of learners philosophical model underlying these practices.

Emphasis is on the process of learning, with adults supporting children's learning. The emphasis is on learning as an ongoing process (rather than only the production of finished products) in activity-based learning situations with meaningful purposes, conceptual approaches including both problem finding and problem solving, integration across curriculum areas, and planned flexibility of curriculum in order to build on student contributions. As former OC teachers Marilyn Osborne and Monica Solawetz (July 1993, personal communication) pointed out, often the process extends past the completion of a product, as when children continue to read about a topic of interest sparked by their research for a class report.

At first newcomers have trouble recognizing the process of learning without the more familiar format of texts, workbooks, tests, and divisions of the curriculum into self-contained domains, and they expect rigidly preplanned instructional units. However, as teacher Carolyn Goodman Turkanis (in press) points out, whole curricula can be built on students' curiosity or concerns about things happening around them if adults are prepared to be flexible, teaching to the moment.

In our survey, when asked for advice to help new co-opers, many co-opers advised taking a flexible approach. They suggested preparing in advance but not expecting to use much of what was prepared, because it is important to go with kids' interests and build on the many "teaching moments" beyond co-opers' structured goals. They advised new co-opers to "listen to the kids." A co-oper in her sixth year of co-oping advised, "When planning curriculum—don't have it set in stone—kids may change it a little—or think of other ways to learn from it that you hadn't thought of—and that's OK."

In this emphasis on flexible process, adults serve as leaders and facilitators for students and each other, not as authority figures. At first the teachers' leadership is not seen and newcomers think the teachers are simply permissive. Newcomers wonder who is in charge, how the classroom is organized, whether it should be more organized or more structured with more teacher control, and so on. An issue frequently raised in the surveys by co-opers in their first three years in the program was a desire for teachers to be more explicitly directive. A first-year co-oper offered this answer to a question regarding the OC philosophy: "It is too free and do what you want. More *structure*!!!" A co-oper in her second year stated, "It is somewhat distractive when so much is going on—the small groups are nice but I'd like to see more structure as a whole."

Relatedly, newcomers worry that without such adult-run control, "academics" may not be happening, since they associate learning with being taught in a controlling fashion. They often do not see the teachers' subtle ways of helping children make responsible choices or of monitoring the children's learning over the day. Some parents swing to the other one-sided extreme and argue that children should be left to their own creative freedom, not conceiving the possibility that children can still make choices in the presence of adult guidance, as in the community of learners approach.

A co-oper in her fourth year reflected on her perennial concerns with coverage of academics, and the reassurance from more experienced members of the community and from observing graduates:

Each year I observe the classroom and read the notes each week. Then I worry "Do these kids learn enough Academics?" I check assignments, and tests, record keeping, talk to parents, teacher(s). Somehow these kids do learn the basic stuff along with all the other things going on. Maybe they learn it in a different way and at a different rate than kids at the neighborhood schools. But I see, and the parents I've talked to have told me, by the time they graduate they have it, and they had fun getting it. It certainly works for my daughter.

Co-opers seem to develop as participants in a community of learners as they manage their small group activities (Matusov and Rogoff, 1995). In a study examining co-opers' approaches to their classroom instruction, many new co-opers were observed to use an adult-run approach, taking over decision making and ownership of the activity, providing leash-like guidance. Co-opers who had participated in the program for a few years were less likely to use the adult-run approach. They were more likely to use the community of learners approach, in which the co-oper and children participate in the activity with shared interest and mutuality and a learning attitude, with leadership provided by the co-oper in initiating the activity and helping the children manage the process so that instruction is embedded in children's inquiry. For parents who had co-oped more than four years, the community of learners was the most prevalent approach. However, some long-time co-opers used adult-run or children-run approaches effectively as well; their contributions in the classroom were also valued. The community of learners model involves some diversity of approaches coordinated within the overall "common thread" of mutual engagement in shared endeavors, with varying responsibility from different community members at different times.

Inherent motivation is fostered along with development of responsibility for one's choices. At first newcomers whose background is in the adult-run model see the children's leeway to make choices and follow their interests as an attitude of emphasizing play and fun at the expense of school WORK (which is not supposed to be fun). They are concerned that insufficient discipline is provided by adults, and that children waste time and make poor choices.

However, with the curriculum aim of children becoming responsible for managing their own learning (and developing a love of learning), it is necessary for children's involvement in activities to build on motivation inherent in the activity as opposed to coming from promises or threats of candy bars, grades, stars, or scoldings. In characterizing the OC philosophy in our survey, many co-opers (especially the more experienced ones) referred to children learning responsibility for their own learning, learning to manage their time and set their own goals, and learning *how* to learn—developing a love of learning, daring to fail, and becoming a lifelong learner.

Due to the emphasis on inherent motivation, OC students often think that they have no homework. When they have a project at school, they read and prepare for it at home but having chosen their project, they are invested in it and it is not an *assignment.* (In addition, at the OC, school and home are not bounded off from each other, so projects and involvements at school and home are not so distinct.)

Along with making choices, it is necessary for children to learn responsibility for their own choices, with the support of the people around them helping them see when they have made effective choices or when they have wasted their time and run out of time for something that they would really have liked to accomplish. Ideally, the consequences of children's choices are inherent to the activities. For example, when there was an Invention Convention in each classroom, some of the children developed a quality project while others treated their project more casually. They could see the difference in people's interest in their projects when the other classrooms came to visit. The children who took the invention project more casually had a chance to think that the next time they had an opportunity to work on such a project, they would give themselves a little more time to work on it, plan ahead a little more so they could finish, or make the project so it was clearer to others. (And the adults in the classroom helped them to notice the consequences of their choices and to think through how they could handle a future occasion.)

It is easy for adults with a background in the adult-run model to step in and "fix" children's problems in ways that keep children from finding out what happens when they do not make good choices. As OC teacher Donene Polson (in press) points out, such "false rescue" can come from either adults controlling situations so children cannot make choices or from adults saving children from the consequences of their choices. For example, adults sometimes take over children's projects for them or prepare what needs to be brought to school the next day or provide quick answers when children would benefit from becoming increasingly responsible for their own activities and finding (and escaping from) dead ends in their path of thinking.

A switch to the children-run model would leave students in the position of unsupported exploration. Children would not have guidance in noticing the consequences of their choices for themselves and others, or developing responsibility for managing their activities in ways that are consistent with the goals of schooling and of participation in a community.

In a community of learners model, neither extreme—neither control nor free choice—is applicable. Individuals assist each other in learning to be responsible, making choices and solving problems in ways that fit their individual needs while coordinating with the needs of others and with group functioning. For example, the children clean up the classroom not with threats of punishment or offers of bribes but through developing the understanding—supported by the teacher— that their next project will be easier if they have room to work or that they need to put one set of materials away before they can begin the next (interesting) activity. One of the teachers pointed out, "When they leave stuff out, the tables are messy and they have no place to work and no place to put their things. So it's really to their own advantage."

Building on the motivation inherent in children's involvement in the activities at hand of course requires that the children be interested in the activities. When we asked children what advice they might give a new co-oper to make their learning activity effective, their first response was usually, "Make it fun." When asked what makes an activity fun, children often elaborated, "when we get some choice in how to do things." Sometimes the children added, "The co-oper needs to have fun with it too."

Supporting the idea that instruction is enhanced if all participants enjoy the activity, a co-oper in his eighth year responded to our survey question asking for advice for new co-opers by suggesting, "Do something you like to do, adjust it in response to the kids' reaction, and build a repertoire." The enjoyment for adults can involve the topic on which they are working as well as the relationships and involvement with the children. A co-oper in his third year suggested, "take a real interest in the children and actively participate with them." Many of the most experienced co-opers characterized their own development as co-opers in terms of learning how to make learning fun for the children along with finding ways to contribute from their own interests and skills; they often indicated that these aspects of co-oping had initially given them difficulty.

Evaluation of student progress occurs through working with children and observing. Teachers, co-opers, and students attend to and reflect on children's progress and need for improvement in the context of children's learning activities; grades are avoided. This is often not understood as providing detailed information on learning until much later in a co-oper's development.[3] A co-oper in her fourth year, whose child had transferred from a neighborhood school, noted, "I used to say 'What did you do in school today?' Now I know what's going on and I can say 'Did you do your rough draft today?' 'Are you finished with your book?' I guess I can keep track of specific things."

The emphasis is on children's own improvement, rather than on comparison of children with others. Daily involvement of adults in children's processes of learning, along with periodic reflection, provide opportunities for evaluation and planning for improvement. (This approach also helps students treat each other as resources and collaborators rather than as adversaries, and adults as helpers rather than as judges.)

For example, in helping a child write a report, an assisting adult is able to observe the extent to which the child needs help with formulating ideas, using resources to search for information, putting ideas in their own words, and understanding the mechanics of spelling and punctuation, in the process of providing instructional support in these areas. In addition, this involvement of the adult provides key information on the extent to which children are learning to manage their own motivation to enter and sustain involvement in the particular activity, and to seek and provide help effectively.

Evaluation of student progress involves students joining with their teacher and parents in conferences that focus on students evaluating both their own progress and goals for the next months. These are worked out with the teacher's assistance in reflecting on which aspects of classroom functioning are easy and hard for each child, and on which areas the children feel they should focus for improvement. Most students become skilled in such self-evaluation with teachers' assistance, and their written goals for the coming months serve as a resource in the students' decision making in the classroom and in the adults' support of the children's daily activities. Some students for whom this self-monitoring and management is more of a challenge develop a more specific "contract" with the teacher and their parents to help them learn to manage their daily decision making.

Collaboration occurs throughout the whole program, among all members. Children work in collaboration with other children and adults throughout the day in ways that are intended to promote learning to lead and support group processes as well as to make use of others as resources. At first, newcomers may see this as permissiveness and may not see skills in contributing to interpersonal problem solving and group processes as relevant to "academic" learning. In our survey, the more experienced co-opers frequently indicated the importance of learning interpersonal problem-solving skills and learning to work with others as both leaders and group members.

The children's learning how to build on each others' ideas collaboratively is supported by a study by Matusov, Bell, and Rogoff (1994) that found that pairs of OC children were more likely to work together with consensus, building on each other's ideas collaboratively, and to assist each other collaboratively in structured out-of-class tasks than were children from a neighborhood traditional school that had less emphasis on collaboration.

The children are also collaborators with the adults, rather than adversaries of the adults or mere products of the system. Although newcomers worry, with so many activities and changing adults in the classroom, where the continuity is from one day to the next, an important source of continuity is collaboration with the children. For example, if children are reading novels in shared-reading groups with different co-opers on successive days, it is not necessary for each co-oper to be on top of what happened (in the book or in the group) before the day begins. The children can tell the co-oper what is going on. Such reflection on the reading and the group's efforts provides the children with the opportunity to summarize for a nonartificial purpose (i.e., the co-oper needs the information, rather than simply testing the children on whether they understand the story). A co-oper who asks the children "What are we supposed to be doing today?" provides the children with a chance to reflect on the purpose of their activity and to report their difficulties in understanding in ways that an adult who is thus informed can help them to manage. If adults only were in charge of things and "in the know," children would not need to reflect on what they did yesterday and how it relates to what they are going to do today.

The collaborative nature of the program applies to the adults involved, not just the children. Ideally, the teachers are closely involved with each other across classrooms, and the teachers and parents in each classroom build on each other's efforts. Newcomers often worry that they need to make sure that each child is receiving their instruction equally; oldtimers begin to see that overall the children balance out in their involvements in different activities with different people. They help the teacher stay abreast of children who may be having difficulties, but otherwise trust that the teacher is monitoring the bigger picture for each child's learning.

In a community of learners, the whole is greater than the sum of the parts and different people have differing roles. A resource of a community is that each person has multiple opportunities to get involved with the subject matter, connecting with different individuals. One child may get excited about writing commercials about children's books while another may hit it off with another co-oper's activity and begin their writing career with enthusiasm about creating poems about food. As a co-oper in her sixth year suggested in response to our survey question asking for suggestions to help new co-opers learn how to co-op, "Recognize that *some* projects will give some children a lot. Other projects or co-opers will probably reach the ones missed by one's own."

Learning New Practices through Participation

The paradigm shift experienced by adult newcomers who begin to understand a community of learners is promoted by the same processes for the adults as is the children's learning of the curriculum of the school: emphasis on the process of learning with facilitation by those who understand, inherent motivation with responsibility for choices, evaluation during the process of participation, and collaboration. As pointed out by the former OC principal, Carol Lubomudrov (in press), and former OC teachers Marilyn Johnston, Theresa Cryns, and Marcy Clokey-Till (in press), the collaborative decision making and learning processes among the adults in the program mirror the processes that the community of learners is intended to produce with the children.

Often, community members express frustration at the extent to which committees and classrooms need to revisit decisions and procedures that have already been devised ("reinventing the wheel"). However, just like each new classroom of children needs to participate in the *process* of learning to read and do arithmetic and solve problems together (rather than having knowledge "transmitted" to them in an adult-run model), each new generation of adult participants needs to participate in the *process* of learning to lead in a community of learners. Neither the children nor the co-opers discover the process on their own (as in a children-run model); with their participation with others in ongoing structured activities they begin to see and become part of the continually dynamic structure of practice. This process is consistent with Tharp and Gallimore's (1988) description of the necessary collaborative arrangements between teachers and administrators in school restructuring.

By encouraging involvement with respect for differing perspectives, experienced OC teachers assist the development of adult members of the community who may work from adult-run and children-run models. In the process of participation with teachers guiding *them* according to the community of learners model, newcomers can begin to work within it and to transform their participation. For example, Leslee Bartlett, a seasoned OC teacher, reported that when she helps a co-oper in their activity with children, she does not try to convert them to her own model but instead helps them from the point of view and philosophical model the co-oper seems to use (July 1994, personal communication). By helping with the *co-oper's* problems in classroom activity with the co-oper's own teaching approach, the seasoned OC teacher collaborates with the co-oper and supports participation in the community of learners model. The teacher involves the co-oper in collaboratively reflecting on why, for example, there was "a disciplinary problem" (from the perspective of the adult-run model) in the activity or why the children refused to do as they were told. Through this collaboration with the teacher, the co-oper thus has the opportunity to learn how to collaborate with the children. A similar but more detailed description of how a seasoned educator collaborates with a new teacher to improve her teaching is provided by Tharp and Gallimore (1988).

The facts that the community of learners philosophy is difficult for many middle-class researchers, teachers, and parents to understand at first glance, and that it is commonly assimilated to the more familiar one-sided dichotomy, provide evidence that the community of learners model is a different paradigm than the one-sided adult-run and children-run models. The observation that newcomers to the community of learners model often seem to need to participate themselves in the practices to align their thinking with the philosophy is consistent with the idea that learning itself is a process of transformation through participation in shared endeavors.

The process of learning through participation is often overlooked in efforts to produce change in adults' understanding, even by people who recognize its importance in children's learning—for example, as in school reform efforts. R. Gallimore (personal communication, June, 1994) provides an example as he discusses efforts to change teachers' practices. In Gallimore's case, the aim is to encourage more conversational classroom discourse formats (a reform effort with some relation but not just the same as creating a community of learners):

Historically, teachers have tended to control discourse in ways that greatly restricted students' participation. Efforts to diversify classroom discourse have often sought a more conversational, discursive style found in teaching/learning activities outside of school. Certain kinds of literacy functions cannot be taught through disjointed, question-answer sequences. In more conversational exchanges, children learn to critique multiple interpretations of texts, to take multiple perspectives, and marshal and weigh evidence. As long as involvement in the activity is high, even silent participants get a "cognitive work-out." They are "participant-observers in the activity," a stage that precedes actual practice.

Since at least the 1920s, there have been major efforts to diversify teacher discourse to include more conversational interactions. Yet most of these efforts have failed, and they failed because the focus was exclusively on the experiences of the students. Most of the training was based on the same model of instruction that the innovators were trying to diminish in the teachers' classrooms. The trainers asked the teacher to do as they said, not as they did.

But when the trainers do as they ask the teachers to do, better results are obtained. . . . It is a reflexive phenomenon. Teachers were not "trained" or "taught" how to conduct conversational lessons. Conversational instruction and learning is not only an end, but the means to that end.

As can be seen in Gallimore's description, what it takes for adults to change their way of thinking about teaching and learning is the kind of participation that is more widely seen as important for children's own learning.

Examining the Three Models from the Perspective of a Theory of Participation

This chapter has argued that the community of learners model of instruction differs in principled and coherent ways from two versions of one-sided instructional models—adult-run and children-run learning. The community of learners model is based on a consideration of learning in terms of people's transformation of participation, and conceives of participants as having shared responsibility for learning, with guidance in joint endeavors provided by some participants. In contrast, the one-sided adult-run and children-run models are based on conceptualization of learning as transmission of knowledge by an expert or acquisition of knowledge by a novice, with a passive role assumed for people other than the one responsible for learning. In adult-run instruction, adults devise and manage learning activities, attempting to make children learn, while the children's role is limited to being willing to accept the information delivered; in children-run instruction, children develop activities spontaneously, while adults attempt to stay clear or simply provide an enriched learning environment. The three models thus differ in their working assumptions, with the community of learners model being based on mutuality that is likely to involve some asymmetries in roles and responsibilities, and the two one-sided models being based on assumptions that only one side (the adult or the child) is active in promoting learning.

All three models can be examined from the perspective of a transformation of participation theory to consider what is learned in each. If learning and development are conceived of as processes of transformation of participation (Rogoff, Baker-Sennett, Lacasa, and Goldsmith, 1995), school or family engagements based on any of the three models can be examined for the learning that would accompany the process of participation in each. In other words, it is not only in a community of learners model that learning would occur. But the learning of participants in a community of learners would differ in principled ways from that of participants in adult-run or children-run models.

There appear to be few differences in learning of the academic matter of school between students from U.S. schools organized according to the community of learners and adult-run models. (However, graduates of the OC have the reputation of showing greater conceptual understanding of mathematics, oral and written expression, science, and social science, and sometimes less attention to mechanics such as spelling and punctuation than do graduates of their more traditional adult-run neighborhood schools.)

The differences between a school based on a community of learners model and one using the traditional adult-run model appear to be greatest in other aspects of the students' learning that have to do with the nature of their participation: In communities of learners, students appear to learn how to coordinate with, support, and lead others, to become responsible and organized in their management of their own learning, and to be able to build on their previous interests to learn in new areas and to sustain motivation to learn. In adult-run models, students learn how to manage individual performance that is often measured against the performance of others, to carry out tasks that are not of personal interest and may not make sense to them, to demonstrate their skills in the format of basal text answers and test questions, and to figure out the criteria by which adults will judge their performance to be better than that of others.

Clearly, both kinds of learning can be seen to have a place in preparing children for the adult world; judging the worth of the two requires value judgments related to how one sees the adult worlds for which the children are preparing. In addition, judging the value of the two models requires consideration of the other functions and special interests that schools and curricula serve in the nation's political and economic system, such as selecting children who will receive opportunities for special programs or higher education.

Rogoff et al. (1993) suggested that individuals can become "fluent" in more than one philosophy of learning and its practices. Indeed, Toma (1993, personal communication) has suggested that in Japanese child development an important aspect of learning is becoming skilled in several models of learning, and coming to understand the different circumstances of each (with Japanese elementary education structured similarly to a community of learners and after-school study "juku" classes structured more as adult-run instruction).

The point of this chapter has been to articulate the philosophical differences between the community of learners and the adult-run and children-run instructional models for consideration and to argue that whatever choices are made, learning is a matter of how people transform through participation in the activities of their communities. Children learn to read, write, perform computations, etc., through their transforming participation in shared endeavors in which these processes are useful. Likewise, adults who are newcomers to a philosophy of teaching and learning come to understand it through their transforming participation as they engage in shared endeavors with other people in which the philosophy is used.

The distinctness of the community of learners model from either one-sided model is supported by the difficulties that newcomers face in understanding the coherent basis of a new philosophy of learning. For many researchers, practitioners, and parents—more familiar with the adult-run model—coming to understand the community of learners model, and the theory of transformation of participation on which it is based, seems to require the same sort of participation in shared endeavors that is often cited as important for children's learning.

Acknowledgments

We are grateful to the Spencer Foundation and the National Institute of Mental Health for their support of the research and thinking reported here, and to Leslee Bartlett, Carolyn Goodman Turkanis, and Brewster Smith for their comments on a previous draft of this paper. We are especially indebted to the teachers, parents, and students of the OC in Salt Lake City for the opportunity to learn from their insights, and to the Salt Lake City School District. Some portions of this chapter overlap partially with two articles by Rogoff (1994; in press).

Notes

1. Of course, there is variation from classroom to classroom and from family to family. Our aim here is to draw attention to a prevailing pattern that operates at a structural level, widely regarded as defining what instruction *is* (or what learning depends on) in U.S. middle-class schools and families.
2. Again, thanks to Lave and Wenger (1991) for the terms and the ideas they represent.
3. Although the philosophy of learning used in the OC does not correspond with that of the assessment procedures of traditional tests, OC students usually perform at or above the level of the students in the other schools. The reputation of OC graduates among

junior high school teachers is that the students are especially well prepared in conceptual aspects of mathematics and writing, oral expression, management of their own learning, effective use of teachers as resources, social maturity, and group and community leadership. Interviews with recent graduates and their parents are consistent in reporting that OC students are especially well prepared in academic skills, managing their time and resources, motivation to learn, and leadership (Rogoff, Matusov, and White, unpublished data).

References

Bartlett, L. (in press). Seeing the Big Picture. In B. Rogoff, L. Bartlett, and C. Goodman Turkanis (Eds.), *Sharing circles: Principles of learning in a community.* New York: Oxford University Press.

Bennett, K. P. and LeCompte, M. D. (1990). *The way schools work: A sociological analysis of education.* New York: Longman.

Bradshaw, P. (in press). What does being qualified mean? In B. Rogoff, L. Bartlett, and C. Goodman Turkanis (Eds.), *Sharing circles: Principles of learning in a community.* New York: Oxford University Press.

Brown, A. L. and Campione, J. C. (1990). Communities of learning and thinking, or a context by any other name. In D. Kuhn (Ed.), *Developmental perspectives on teaching and learning thinking skills* (Vol. 21). *Contributions to Human Development* (pp. 108–126). Basel: Karger.

Brown, A. L. and Campione, J. C. (1994). Guided discovery in a community of learners. In K. McGilly (Ed.), *Classroom lessons: Integrating cognitive theory and classroom practice* (pp. 229–270). Cambridge: MIT Press/Bradford Books.

Cahan, E. D. (1994). John Dewey and human development. In R. D. Parke, P. A. Ornstein, J. J. Reiser, and C. Zahn-Waxler (Eds.), *A century of developmental psychology* (pp. 145–167). Washington: APA Press.

Callahan, R. E. (1962). *Education and the cult of efficiency.* Chicago: University of Chicago Press.

Cremin, L. A. (1962). *The transformation of the school: Progressivism in American Education, 1876–1957.* New York: Knopf.

Cuban, L. (1984). *How teachers taught: Constancy and change in American classrooms, 1890–1980.* New York: Longman.

Deering, P. D. (1991, November). *Show me that you want to work in groups: An ethnographic study of cooperative learning in a multiethnic middle school.* Paper presented at the meetings of the American Anthropological Association, Chicago.

Deering, P. D. (1994, April). *Is "cooperative learning" either, both, or neither? Tales from three middle school classrooms.* Paper presented at the meetings of the American Educational Research Association, New Orleans.

Dewey, J. (1916). *Democracy and education.* New York: Macmillan.

Dewey, J. (1938). *Experience and education.* New York: Macmillan.

Eccles, J. S., Buchanan, C. M., Flanagan, C., Fuligni, A., Midgley, C. and Yee, D. (1991). Control versus autonomy during early adolescence. *Journal of Social Issues, 47,* 53–68.

Giaconia, R. M. and Hedges, L. V. (1982). Identifying features of effective open education. *Review of Educational Research, 52,* 579–602.

Gold, B. A. and Miles, M. B. (1981). *Whose school is it, anyway? Parent–teacher conflict over an innovative school.* New York: Praeger.

Goodman Turkanis, C. (in press). Creating curriculum with children. In B. Rogoff, L. Bartlett, and C. Goodman Turkanis (Eds.), *Sharing circles: Principles of learning in a community.* New York: Oxford University Press.

Graubard, A. (1972). *Free the children.* New York: Pantheon Books.

Greene, M. (1986). Philosophy and teaching. In M. C. Wittrock (Ed.), *Handbook of research on teaching* (3rd edn.) (pp. 479–501). New York: Macmillan.

Johnston, M., Cryns, T., and Clokey-Till, M. (in press). Teacher collaboration. In B. Rogoff, L. Bartlett, and C. Goodman Turkanis (Eds.), *Sharing circles: Principles of learning in a community.* New York: Oxford University Press.

Kliebard, H. M. (1975). Metaphorical roots of curriculum design. In W. Pinar (Ed.), *Curriculum theorizing: The reconceptualists* (pp. 39–50). Berkeley: McCutchan.

Kliebard, H. M. (1987). *The struggle for the American curriculum, 1893–1958.* New York: Routledge and Kegan Paul.

Kohn, A. (1993, September). Choices for children: Why and how to let students decide. *Phi Delta Kappan,* 8–20.

Lamphere, L. (1977). *To run after them: Cultural and social bases of cooperation in a Navajo community.* Tucson: University of Arizona Press.

Lave, J. and Wenger, E. (1991). *Situated learning: Legitimate peripheral participation.* Cambridge, England: Cambridge University Press.

Lubomudrov, C. (in press). Who is responsible?: Decision-making in a community of learners. In B. Rogoff, L. Bartlett, and C. Goodman Turkanis (Eds.), *Sharing circles: Principles of learning in a community.* New York: Oxford University Press.

Marris, P. (1986). *Loss and change.* London: Routledge and Kegan Paul.

Matusov, E., Bell, N., and Rogoff, B. (1994). *Collaboration and assistance in problem solving by children differing in cooperative schooling backgrounds.* Unpublished manuscript.

Matusov, E. and Rogoff, B. (1995). *Newcomers and oldtimers: Educational philosophy of parent volunteers in a community of learners school.* Unpublished manuscript.

McDermott, R. P. (1993). The acquisition of a child by a learning disability. In S. Chaiklin and J. Lave (Eds.), *Understanding practice: Perspectives on activity and context* (pp. 269–305). Cambridge, England: Cambridge University Press.

McRobbie, C. and Tobin, K. (1995). *Restraints to reform: The congruence of teacher and student actions in a chemistry classroom.* Submitted for publication.

Minick, N. (1993). Teachers' directives: The social construction of "literal meanings" and "real words" in classroom discourse. In S. Chaiklin and J. Lave (Eds.), *Understanding practice: Perspectives on activity and context* (pp. 343–374). Cambridge, England: Cambridge University Press.

Mosier, C. and Rogoff, B. (1994). *Young children's autonomy and responsibility within the family: Cultural variations.* Unpublished manuscript.

Newman, D., Griffin, P., and Cole, M. (1989). *The construction zone: Working for cognitive change in school.* Cambridge, England: Cambridge University Press.

Polson, D. (in press). Responsible choices. In B. Rogoff, L. Bartlett, and C. Goodman Turkanis (Eds.), *Sharing circles: Principles of learning in a community.* New York: Oxford University Press.

Rogoff, B. (1990). *Apprenticeship in thinking: Cognitive development in social context.* New York: Oxford University Press.

Rogoff, B. (1994). Developing understanding of the idea of communities of learners. *Mind, Culture, and Activity,* 1, 209–229.

Rogoff, B. (1995). Observing sociocultural activity on three planes: Participatory appropriation, guided participation, and apprenticeship. In J. V. Wertsch P. del Río, and A. Alvarez (Eds.), *Sociocultural studies of mind* (pp. 139–164). Cambridge, England: Cambridge University Press.

Rogoff, B. (in press). Finding the "common thread": Learning through participation in a community. In B. Rogoff, L. Bartlett, and C. Goodman Turkanis (Eds.), *Sharing circles: Principles of learning in a community.* New York: Oxford University Press.

Rogoff, B., Baker-Sennett, J., Lacasa, P., and Goldsmith, D. (1995). Development through participation in sociocultural activity. In J. Goodnow, P. Miller, and F. Kessel (Eds.), *Cultural practices as contexts for development* (pp. 45–66). San Francisco: Jossey-Bass.

Rogoff, B., Baker-Sennett, J., and Matusov, E. (1994). Considering the concept of planning. In M. Haith, J. Benson, R. Roberts, and B. Pennington (Eds.), *The development of future-oriented processes* (pp. 353–373). Chicago: University of Chicago Press.

Rogoff, B., Mistry, J. J., Göncü, A., and Mosier, C. (1993). Guided participation in cultural activity by toddlers and caregivers. *Monographs of the Society for Research in Child Development, 58,* 7, serial no. 236.

Silberman, C. E. (1970). *Crisis in the classroom: The remaking of American education.* New York: Random House.

Stipek, D. J. (in press). Is child-centered early childhood education really better? In S. Reifel (Ed.), *Advances in early education and day care.* Greenwich, CT: JAI Press.

Tharp, R. G. and Gallimore, R. (1988). *Rousing minds to life: Teaching, learning, and schooling in social context.* Cambridge, England: Cambridge University Press.

Wells, G., Chang, G. L. M., and Maher, A. (1990). Creating classroom communities of literate thinkers. In S. Sharan (Ed.), *Cooperative learning: Theory and research* (pp. 95–121). New York: Praeger.

19

The Individual-Society Antinomy Revisited: Productive Tensions in Theories of Human Development, Communication, and Education

JAMES V. WERTSCH
WILLIAM R. PENUEL

"Development" is a term used constantly when talking about children's lives in families, day-care settings, and schools. Although it might seem that there is general agreement about what we mean when we speak of development in children, closer examination reveals major differences, if not confusion, among discussants in their understanding and use of the term. Indeed, many of us have discovered that it is quite easy for a single individual to hold contradictory ideas on this topic.

Trying to make sense of this apparent confusion is obviously important for professionals concerned with human development, and not surprisingly, they have expended great effort in creating explicitly formulated accounts of it (e.g., Piaget, 1971; Vygotsky, 1978; Werner, 1948). It is also important for us as laypeople as we employ "cultural models" (D'Andrade, 1990; Holland and Quinn, 1986) about development in deciding how to raise children, organize educational systems, and carry out a host of other tasks.

The goal of this chapter is to examine a major issue that divides theories of human development into two general categories. After having outlined this division, we shall argue that it may be grounded in values rather than fact or rational argument, and we shall propose that an appropriate theory of communication can lead us out of the untenable position that such a bifurcation produces. The upshot is a set of constructs that can hopefully build new bridges between major developmental theorists such as Vygotsky and Piaget.

Two Models of Development

There are many ways that we can categorize accounts of human development. For example, they can be classified on the basis of the "telos," or ideal endpoint, they assume (Kaplan, 1983), the general area of human functioning they address (e.g., biological, psychological), or the kind of theoretical orientation they presuppose within an area such as psychology (e.g., Freudian, Skinnerian). In this chapter we shall focus on yet another criterion—how a theory assigns "analytic primacy" to one or another factor.

Specifically, we shall be concerned with social and individual factors, and we shall argue that the analytic primacy assigned to one or the other provides the basis for distinguishing between two broad categories of theories of human psychological development. On the one hand, social processes may be given analytic primacy, and individual, psychological functioning may be viewed as derivative. Conversely, analytic primacy may be assigned to individual, psychological functioning, and social processes may be assumed to be derivative.

In at least some instances, differing views on this issue reflect disciplinary orientation. For example, there is a tendency among many psychologists to assume that we can explain social and cultural phenomena by appealing to psychological processes in individuals, whereas there is a tendency among many sociologists to assume that we can explain psychological phenomena by appealing to large- or small-scale social processes. Regardless of whether it is grounded in disciplinary orientation or something else, analytic primacy is often implicitly assumed rather than explicitly addressed. It is perhaps the exception rather than the rule for an account of human development to take an explicit, reflective stance on whether social or individual processes are given this status.

We would argue nonetheless that just about any developmental account makes some assumption on this matter. Instead of being part of the explicit theoretical formulation, the assumption may surface in the methods or line of reasoning employed in empirical studies, but this of course makes it no less present. Indeed, the fact that assumptions about analytic primacy are often implicit and hence unexamined, rather than clearly spelled out, usually serves to make them more powerful than they might otherwise be. In our view, a great deal of confusion and bogus disagreement in discussions about development can be traced to the influence of implicit, unexplored assumptions on this issue.

As an example of a theoretical perspective that gives analytic primacy to social processes, consider the writings of L. S. Vygotsky (1978, 1981a, 1981b, 1987). Reflecting in part his goal of formulating a Marxist psychology, he argued for the need to recognize social factors as underlying psychological processes of the individual. His position on this was quite explicit and was reflected in statements such as the following: "the social dimension of consciousness is primary in time and in fact. The individual dimension of consciousness is derivative and secondary" (1979, p. 30).

What might be called Vygotsky's "social formationism" perhaps shows up most clearly in his "general genetic law of cultural development."

Any function in the child's cultural development appears twice, or on two planes. First it appears on the social plane, and then on the psychological plane. First it appears between people as an interpsychological category, and then within the child as an intrapsychological category. This is equally true with regard to voluntary attention, logical memory, the formation of concepts, and the development of volition. . .[I]t goes without saying that internalization transforms the process itself and changes its structure and functions. Social relations or relations among people genetically underlie all higher functions and their relationships. (1981a, p. 163)

In this view individual ("intrapsychological") mental functioning derives its existence and form from social ("interpsychological") processes, and as a result such individual functioning retains an essentially social character.

[Higher mental functions'] composition, genetic structure, and means of action—in a word, their whole nature—is social. Even when we turn to mental [i.e., intrapsychological] processes, their nature remains quasisocial. In their private sphere, human beings retain the function of social interaction. (Vygotsky, 1981a, p. 164)

As can be seen from this quote, an important aspect of Vygotsky's insight into the relation between social and individual functioning was that these two planes are not differentiated in any simple, static manner. Instead, there are essential parallels and interrelations between the two planes in form and function, a point reflected in his analysis of phenomena such as social, egocentric, and inner speech (Vygotsky, 1987).

The key to understanding these parallels and interrelations for Vygotsky was that the same basic "means of action," or "mediational means" (Wertsch, 1985) are used on both planes. This applies to language in particular in Vygotsky's view. This assumption clearly underlay his analyses of concept formation and the emergence of inner speech, but it operated throughout the rest of his framework as well. In all cases, his point was that children's use of sign systems, which are produced and encountered in social life, have a powerful transformatory role on speaking, thinking, and other forms of human action. It has been argued that the basic unit of analysis in this approach is "mediated action" (Wertsch, 1985, 1991; Zinchenko, 1985), and it is by bringing action increasingly under the influence or control of sign systems that children come to be incorporated into a community.

Vygotsky's comments about internalization in the formulation of the general genetic law of cultural development reveal that he did not understand intramental functioning as a simple copy, or mirror image, of intermental processes that is somehow imposed on passive individuals. Instead, processes carried out by the active individual were also viewed as playing a role in the formation of psychological functioning. However, what these processes were and how they contributed to development were issues that Vygotsky did not address in any detail, a point that is consistent with characterizing his theoretical perspective as giving analytic primacy to social processes.

As Bruner (1962) noted some time ago in a discussion of Vygotsky, a very similar line of reasoning about giving analytic primacy to social processes can be found in the writings of the American pragmatist George Herbert Mead (1934). Although Mead and Vygotsky were contemporaries and although Vygotsky was familiar with the writings of Mead's colleague and teacher John Dewey, it seems that neither Mead nor Vygotsky was directly acquainted with the other's work. Nonetheless, the following quote from Mead bears striking similarities to Vygotsky's claim that "the social dimension of consciousness is primary in time and in fact" (1979, p. 30).

We are. . .forced to conclude that consciousness is an emergent from such [social] behavior; that so far from being a precondition of the social act, the social act is a precondition of it. The mechanism of the social act can be traced out without introducing into it the conception of consciousness as a separable element within that act; hence the social act, in its more elementary stages or forms, is possible without, or apart from, some form of consciousness. (Mead, 1934, p. 18)

A clearer assignment of analytic primacy to social processes could hardly be desired.

Partly because they were quite clear about the assumptions that guided their thinking, figures such as Vygotsky and Mead can sometimes serve as good targets when criticizing accounts that rely heavily on the strategy of giving analytic primacy to social processes. They run the risk of "oversocialization" (Westbrook, 1991, p. 289), or a tendency to focus so heavily on social forces that the contributions of active individuals to human mental development may be lost. At least in the case of Vygotsky, however, it is worth pointing out that he noted the importance of taking the active individual into account, a point that makes it difficult to pigeonhole him in any simple way as a social reductionist. Attributing to him a tendency toward oversocialization has more to do with the focus of his concrete theoretical and empirical research than with his general claims.

Standing in contrast to Vygotsky and Mead with regard to where analytic primacy is assumed are theorists such as Chomsky (1966, 1972) and Piaget (1966). These two figures contrast with Vygotsky and Mead in quite different ways. Chomsky is committed to a Cartesian rationalist view and assigns analytic primacy not just to the individual but to the neurological makeup of the individual. Specifically, he argues that any adequate account of human language and mind must begin with the "innate ideas" as shaped by neural makeup. Such a position has parallels in contemporary cognitive science in the "connectionist" school, a school that readily accepts the need for reductionism (e.g., Churchland, 1988). In general, such views accord social processes little role in development other than as stimuli that may serve to trigger underlying, innate cognitive structures.

Piaget differed sharply from Chomsky on many points. He specifically rejected the assumption that the roots of human knowledge can be traced to innate ideas, thereby rejecting the kind of Cartesianism and reductionism that can be found in the writings of Chomsky and some contemporary cognitive scientists. Piaget also rejected the notion that the roots of human knowledge can be traced solely to input from the environment, thereby rejecting the path of empiricist approaches that surface in contemporary psychology—for example, in behaviorism.

Instead of accepting either of these two positions, Piaget argued for an *interactional* approach (Cole and Cole, 1989). In this view, neither the individual nor the environment (i.e., neither "nature" nor "nurture") in isolation can account for the emergence of human knowledge. Instead, it is only in the process of the individual's *interacting with the environment* that such knowledge can emerge. Piaget's basic focus on the "schema" as a generalized pattern of action, where action necessarily involves both the individual and the environment (especially the physical environment), reflects this interactional perspective.

Although Piaget's focus was on how individuals engage in "learning on one's own, or. . .learning by invention" (Bruner, 1986, p. 127), he did not ignore the influence of social processes on psychological development. For example, he began a chapter on social factors in intellectual development by stating:

The human being is immersed right from birth in a social environment which affects him just as much as his physical environment. Society, even more, in a sense, than the physical environment, changes the very structure of the individual, because it not only compels him to recognize facts, but also provides him with a ready-made system of signs, which modify his thought. . . .

Certainly, it is necessary for sociology to envisage society as a whole, even though this whole, which is quite distinct from the sum of individuals composing it, is only the totality of relations or interaction between individuals. (1966, p. 156)

Such statements should not be taken to indicate that Piaget accepted any kind of analytic primacy of social over individual processes. Indeed, if anything, his formulation suggests an implicit acceptance of the notion that the existence of individuals is, to quote Mead, a kind of "precondition" for social processes, but not vice versa. In this regard, note Piaget's statement that society is "only the totality of relations or interaction between individuals," or his statement elsewhere that society's " 'collective representations,' as Durkheim calls them, still presuppose the existence of a nervous system in each member of the group" (1971, p. 368).

Piaget explicitly raised the issue of the analytic primacy of individual and social processes in passages such as the following:

One question now arises which is inescapable: is the "grouping" the cause or the effect of co-operation? Grouping is a co-ordination of operations, i.e., of actions accessible to the individual. Co-operation is a co-ordination of viewpoints or of actions emanating from different individuals. Their affinity is thus obvious, but does operational development within the individual enable him to co-operate with others, or does external co-operation, later internalized in the individual, impel him to group his actions in operational systems? (1966, p. 163)

Piaget addressed this opposition by arguing that social and individual psychological functioning are both manifestations of a more general, underlying logic: "Internal operational activity and external co-operation are merely. . .two complementary aspects of one and the same whole, since the equilibrium of the one depends on that of the other" (1966, p. 166). This reflects his orientation, at least during the latter part of his career, toward examining the general logical dimensions of "genetic epistemology" (1970) rather than examining ways in which logic is manifested or realized in individual or social practice.

While recognizing all this, however, we would still argue that there is a strong, if implicit tendency on Piaget's part to give analytic primacy to the individual in the sense of treating individual processes as "preconditions" of social ones. As noted above, this is evidenced in some of the formulations he provided, but it is also manifested in many of the ways that he collected and interpreted empirical findings.

One of the ways this emerges is in the methodological procedures Piaget used when analyzing the form and function of social interaction. In his analyses, there is a strong tendency to interpret social processes from the perspective of their role in generating challenges to, and disequilibria in, an individual's thought. It is almost as if social processes are considered solely from the perspective of how they might foster growth in individual mental functioning. The general nature of this relationship has been outlined by Rogoff (1990) as one in which "social influence fosters change [i.e., in individual cognitive structures] through the induction of cognitive conflict and the logical operations carried out by children attempting to reconcile their differing views to achieve equilibrium in their [individual] understanding" (p. 140).

When analyzing children's social interaction with family members, Piaget outlined the process as one in which "the child will at every moment see his thought approved or contradicted, and he will discover a vast world of thought external to himself, which will instruct or impress him in various ways" (1966, p. 159). Again, the methodological strategy is to characterize and assess social processes from the perspective of individual cognitive processes. Such statements reflect a general tendency in Piaget's writings to assign analytic primacy (as reflected through methodological procedures in this case) to individual processes in that these processes provide the metric for characterizing and assessing social interaction.

Another, even clearer indication of Piaget's tendency to assign analytic primacy to the individual emerges in his claims about how social processes can influence individual mental functioning. In his view, the very possibility for a child to engage in social processes or for those social processes to have an influence on individuals' mental functioning depends on the developmental level of the individual. In this connection Piaget argued that "however dependent he may be on surrounding intellectual influences, the young child assimilates them in his own way. He reduces them to his point of view and therefore distorts them without realizing it" (1966, p. 160).

Piaget's comments on the primary instrument of social communication—language—provide related evidence about his tendency to assign analytic primacy to individual processes. In his view, the process of coming to use the socially organized instrumentality of language does not result in a qualitative transformation of mental functioning as it does for figures such as Vygotsky (see Vygotsky, 1978, p. 24). Instead, the mastery of language becomes possible only when a preexisting, more general "semiotic function" has already emerged in the child. As Olson (1995) notes:

For Piaget, as I understand him, children's mastery of the symbolic world—the world of representations—was not basically different from their mastery of the natural world. Language did not create a representational or symbolic function; rather the representational function that was based on the ability to hold objects in mind in their absence made language learning possible. (pp. 96–97)

Thus, here again we see Piaget's tendency to assume that social phenomena can have an impact on individuals' mental life only when the groundwork has been laid by individual cognitive development.

Hence while Piaget's explicit theoretical formulations focused on issues of logic and genetic epistemology, a focus that he argued allowed him to avoid having to choose between a psychological or sociological perspective, we would argue that his concrete methodology and empirical studies indicated an assignment of analytic primacy to individual factors. In particular, his tendency to view social processes from the perspective of individual cognitive functioning and his insistence that children can participate in social processes only when they are capable of assimilating others' perspectives reflect this view.

The Role of "Valuation" in Assigning Analytic Primacy

In one way or another differences over whether to assign analytic primacy to individual or social processes have been a part of debates that are decades if not centuries old. The fact that there seems to be no end in sight to this debate suggests something—namely, that differences over whether to give social or individual processes analytic primacy reflect a deeper debate of some kind, a debate that may not be amenable to resolution through rational argument or empirical studies. The debate we have in mind concerns fundamental ethical and political issues having to do with the relationship between the individual and society.

Among the commentators on this relationship, Elias (1991) has provided an account that is particularly relevant to our line of reasoning. According to Elias, the debate at issue here involves an antinomy and resembles a "curious party game that certain groups in western society are apt to indulge in over and over again" (p. 54). The two opposing groups he had in mind endlessly engage in encounters of the following sort.

One says, "Everything depends on the individual," the other, "Everything depends on society." The first group says: "But it is always particular individuals who decide to do this and not that." The others reply: "But their decisions are socially conditioned." The first group says: "But what you call 'social conditioning' only comes about because others want to do something and do it." The others reply: "But what these others want to do and do is also socially conditioned." (p. 54)

Elias suggested that this "debate" is likely to go on endlessly and fruitlessly because it is not really one based on empirical fact or rational argument. In his view it is grounded instead in "valuations" of individual and society. These valuations take a particular form having to do with what one takes to be means and what one takes to be ends.

In their most popular form, the professions of one side present the "individual" as the means and the "social whole" as the supreme value and purpose, while the other regard "society" as the means and "individuals" as the supreme value and purpose. And in both cases these ideals and goals of political thought and action are often presented as facts. What one side says *should* be is thought and spoken of as if it *is*. For example. . .members of groups in which it is loyal to demand and wish that the claims of individuals *should* have priority over those of the group, often believe they can observe that individuals are the true reality, that which actually exists, while societies are something that comes afterwards, something less real and perhaps even a mere figment of thought, an abstraction. . .In short, what one understands by "individual" and "society" still depends to a large extent on the form taken by what people wish for and fear. (pp. 83–85; italics in the original)

Among other things, Elias's account of the individual-society antinomy is instructive in that it brings into clear focus the presence of values ("valuations")— often veiled as simple assertions of what *is*—that guide research in the human sciences. His formulation is also useful in that it clearly suggests that this is not simply a matter of academic debate. Indeed, it would seem to be a matter of value stances that are part of public discussion and cultural models more generally.

Our claim with regard to Vygotsky and Piaget is not that either one of these "modern titans of developmental theory" (Bruner, 1986, p. 136) fell neatly or unreflectively into one of the two valuation perspectives outlined by Elias. Although they had leanings in one direction or another as we have outlined, both of these theorists were too sophisticated to subscribe totally or unreflectively to one or the other of these valuation perspectives.

The point has of course been made that Soviet Marxism did end up viewing individuals as means and society as the end, often with very tragic consequences. However, there are many indications that Vygotsky was quite concerned with the contributions that active individuals make to psychological and social development. His is not a position that can simply be categorized as social reductionism, and he was clearly opposed to a telos of mindless conformity by individuals to societal goals. Conversely, even though Piaget's perspective is often referred to as one in which the child is viewed as an independent inventor or discoverer (see Bruner, 1986), he clearly did not think that individuals somehow exist in a vacuum. Nor did he formulate what *should* be or actually *is* in terms of the individual as the sole end and society as a means.

Given these caveats, how do we resolve the still striking differences between Vygotsky and Piaget on the issue of analytic primacy? Was one simply right and the other wrong? To say this would almost certainly be to slip into the mistake of taking what we believe should be for what is. Were they both right and both wrong to some degree? To follow this line of argument is likely to involve some degree of unprincipled eclecticism, another sort of muddle that we believe wise to avoid. Instead of following any of these paths, we believe a principled resolution to these questions can be found in the way that communication processes underlying both perspectives are formulated.

Communication Theories: Utterances as Univocal Transmission versus Utterances as "Thinking Devices"

Both Vygotsky and Piaget recognized communication as the essential social process involved in the development of human mental functioning. This is obvious in the case of Vygotsky with his assignment of analytic primacy to semiotically mediated social processes, especially speech, but it is also the case for Piaget, who found it "very difficult to understand how the individual would come to grasp his operations in any precise manner. . .without the interchange of thought" (1966, p. 164), an interchange that occurs through communication.

As is the case with the notion of development, any attempt to understand the notion of communication in these two theorists' perspectives must begin by considering their explicit and implicit assumptions. And here again, there are some important differences between the two figures. We shall begin our analysis of these differences by considering where the two theorists stood with regard to a basic and pervasive cultural model of communication, a model based on the notion of transmission.

As authors such as Reddy (1979) have suggested, there is a strong tendency among theorists as well as laypeople to understand communication in terms of transmitting information from one person (or more generally, from a "sender") to another (or more generally, to a "receiver"). Reddy suggests that at least for speakers of English, this reflects a basic set of metaphors that shape the ways that we speak and think about communication. In this connection he reviewed a wide range of metaphors concerned with communication in English such as the following:

(1) Try to get your thought across better; (2) Whenever you have a good idea, practice capturing it in words; and (3) Can you actually extract coherent ideas from that prose?

On the basis of his analysis, he outlined an underlying "conduit metaphor," which in its "major framework" version, consists of the following points:

(1) Language functions like a conduit, transferring thoughts bodily from one person to another; (2) in writing and speaking, people insert their thoughts or feelings in the words; (3) words accomplish the transfer by containing the thoughts or feelings and conveying them to others; and (4) in listening or reading, people extract the thoughts and feelings once again from the words. (p. 290)

In general, Reddy sees the metaphors about communication in English as being so heavily weighted in favor of conduit notions that "Practically speaking, if you try to avoid all obvious conduit metaphor expressions in your usage, you are nearly struck dumb when communication becomes the topic" (1979, p. 299). He also believes that the power of this basic metaphor is largely responsible for the misinterpretation and misapplication of information theory. Because "English has a preferred framework for conceptualizing communication" (Reddy, 1979, p. 285), it ends up being "its own worst enemy" (p. 286) in this respect.

The transmission model of communication that springs from the conduit metaphor is often represented schematically in terms such as the following:

```
              Signal                      Signal
            transmitted                  received
Sender  ──────────────── >  Channel  ──────────────── >  Receiver
```

One of the most common criticisms of the transmission model thus schematized concerns the unidirectionality of the arrows involved. Because they point only one way, the receiver is viewed as being passive (note the very term "receiver"). The alternative would seem to be some kind of model in which the receiver is viewed as playing at least as active and important a role as the sender. In such an alternative the receiver would be an active interpreter, if not constructor or coconstructor, of the message.

An approach that takes into consideration the claims of both the transmission model of communication and the alternative just suggested can be found in the writings of Lotman (1988, 1990). His view assumes a "functional dualism of texts in a cultural system" (1988, p. 34). The two basic functions he sees texts fulfilling are "to convey meanings adequately, and to generate new meanings" (1988, p. 34). The first of these is very similar to the function presupposed by the transmission model of communication.

The first function is fulfilled best when the codes of the speaker and the listener most completely coincide and, consequently, when the text has the maximum degree of univocality. The ideal boundary mechanism for such an operation would be an artificial language and a text in an artificial language. (p. 34)

Lotman notes that this text function, which we will term the "univocal transmission" function, has been at the core of a great deal of contemporary language study. One of the reasons for this is that "it is this aspect of a text that is most easily modeled with the means at our disposal" (1988, p. 35). The means he had in mind are theories used by linguists, psychologists, and communication scientists, theories reflecting a pervasive "literate" mode of thought in the post-Renaissance West (Olson, 1994). The overriding influence of these theories has been such that the univocal function has "at times. . .been identified with a text as such, obfuscating the other aspects" (Lotman, 1988, p. 35).

In contrast to this first function of a text, Lotman outlined a second function that can be termed "dialogic."

The second function of text is to generate new meanings. In this respect a text ceases to be a passive link in conveying some constant information between input (sender) and output (receiver). Whereas in the first case a difference between the message at the input and that at the output of an information circuit can occur only as a result of a defect in the communications channel, and is to be attributed to the technical imperfections of this system, in the second case such a difference is the very essence of a text's function as a "thinking device." What from the first standpoint is a defect, from the second is a norm, and vice versa. (1988, pp. 36–37)

In discussing these issues, a central point for Lotman throughout is that *both functions of text are present in any act of human communication.* This is not to deny that one or the other function may dominate in certain contexts, but the very term "functional dualism" indicates his commitment to the notion that both functions are always at work. Hence while univocal transmission models of communication, such as those suggested by the conduit metaphor, are not viewed as incorrect from this perspective, they are incomplete in an essential way. Communication is *always* a matter *both* of transmitting information and of actively interpreting the utterance by taking it as a "thinking device."

Lotman's analysis of communication has some major implications for Vygotsky's and Piaget's accounts of communication and development. The first point to make in this regard is that both theorists seem to have had a view of communication that is limited from Lotman's perspective of the functional dualism of utterances. This is not to say that either one of them held the view that communication is simply or strictly a matter of univocal transmission, something that perhaps reflects the fact that neither was a native speaker of English, with its basically misleading conduit metaphors as outlined by Reddy. However, this reason alone is undoubtedly insufficient to account for their more complex views, among other things because Russian and French have at least some tendencies toward conduit metaphors of their own.

If one of the two theorists we are examining did have a tendency toward taking communication to be a matter of univocal transmission, however, it was clearly Vygotsky. This is consistent with the position he took on analytic primacy as outlined earlier. More concrete evidence of this tendency can be seen in his statements about the development of concepts, or word meanings.

Adult speech, through its stable, well-defined meanings, determines the developmental course taken by generalizations;. . .it determines the child's complexive formations. The child does not choose the meaning of the word. It is given to him through verbal interaction with adults. The child is not free to construct his own complexes. . . . The child receives in completed form a series of concrete objects generalized by a given word. . . . Stated simply, the child does not create his speech but learns the developed speech of the adults around him. (1987, pp. 144–145)

Vygotsky's focus in this passage is actually on concept development rather than on communication. Nonetheless, the line of argument he outlines is quite consistent with a notion of communication grounded in the univocal transmission function of utterances. In this connection, note in particular his mention of how the child "receives" information.

Having said this, however, it is important to point out that Vygotsky left room for notions that sound more like Lotman's dialogic function of language. Specifically, he noted that although the conceptual and preconceptual ("complexive") structures that children develop are "determined" by what adults provide, there remains an essential sense in which adults' messages are treated as thinking devices. Namely, the fact that adults use certain words with conventionally organized meanings when communicating with children does not guarantee that children "receive" them in the form understood by adults. Hence, children were not viewed simply as passive receivers of information.

As he moves along this predetermined path [i.e., the one provided by adults' word meanings], the child thinks in correspondence with the characteristics of a particular stage in the development of intellect. By addressing the child in speech, adults determine the path along which the development of generalizations will move and where that development will lead, that is, they determine the resulting generalizations. However, the adult cannot transfer his own mode of thinking to the child. (1987, p. 143)

Thus Vygotsky recognized *both* the importance of transmission of a certain sort from adults and the process whereby adults' utterances are actively taken up by children as thinking devices.

Such a formulation would seem to meet the requirements of Lotman's account of "functional dualism" where the univocal transmission function and the dialogic function of text always operate in tandem. And at a general level it does. Within the framework of an approach based on functional dualism, however, there remains an imbalance in the way that Vygotsky conducted his theoretical and empirical research. For example, while he went into considerable detail about the kinds of communicative messages children receive, he said virtually nothing about the constraints imposed by "a particular stage in the development of intellect."

In sum, then, Vygotsky outlined an account of communication that is consistent with Lotman's claims about functional dualism at a general level, but the overwhelming focus of his theoretical and empirical research was on how utterances and communication can be viewed from the perspective of their univocal, transmission function. The difference here between Vygotsky's abstract formulation for what a theory should address and the way he translated such a formulation into concrete theoretical and empirical research problems is what Davydov and Radzikhovskii (1985) had in mind when they distinguished between "Vygotsky the methodologist" and "Vygotsky the psychologist" and argued that the latter did not always live up to the former's aspirations.

If there is a tendency in Vygotsky's writings to emphasize the univocal, transmission function in communication, there is the opposite tendency in Piaget's approach. As suggested by earlier quotes from his writings, Piaget acknowledged the importance of both the univocal transmission function and the dialogic function of utterances, at least in general theoretical terms. As was the case for Vygotsky, however, we would argue that he focused on one of these and largely ignored the other in his concrete theoretical and empirical research. Specifically, he tended to approach communication primarily from the perspective of how messages are received and actively interpreted by the individual—i.e., from the perspective of how messages can serve as thinking devices, to use Lotman's terminology in describing the dialogic function. For Piaget, this meant that the focus was on what a child can "assimilate."

Language conveys to the individual an already prepared system of ideas, classifications, relations—in short, an inexhaustible stock of concepts which are reconstructed in each individual after the age-old pattern which previously moulded earlier generations. But it goes without saying that the child begins by borrowing from this collection only as much as suits him, remaining disdainfully ignorant of everything that exceeds his mental level. And again, that which is borrowed is assimilated in accordance with his intellectual structure; a word intended to carry a general concept at first engenders only a half-individual, half-socialised pre-concept (the word "bird" thus evokes the familiar canary, etc.). (1966, p. 159)

In this passage, Piaget begins by noting the importance of transmission in communication but then goes on to attribute primary importance to the issue of assimilation, which involves a form of taking an utterance as a thinking device.

Thus, like Vygotsky, Piaget recognized both the notion of transmission and the notion of active interpretation—especially the limitations imposed by assimilation in such interpretation—in communication. However, in contrast to Vygotsky, who emphasized the notion of transmission and mentioned the developmental limits of understanding only in passing, Piaget emphasized the importance of active assimilation on the part of the child and gave much less emphasis to what is transmitted when dealing with the role of communication in development. In short, Vygotsky's account of the role of communication in development focused on what is sent; Piaget's focused on what can be assimilated.

Theories of Development and Theories of Communication

In our review of Vygotsky and Piaget, we have emphasized how they held contrasting views on several issues. In particular, we have focused on how Vygotsky tended to assign analytic primacy to social processes, whereas Piaget assigned it to individual functioning. Furthermore, we have argued that Vygotsky focused on the univocal transmission function of utterances, whereas Piaget focused on the dialogic function. At each step along the way we have noted that both theorists made general assertions recognizing the importance of both sides of these oppositions but nonetheless went on to focus on one side in their concrete theoretical and empirical research.

In general, the theoretical frameworks of both Vygotsky and Piaget are too sophisticated and broad to fit into neat bifurcations of contradictory perspectives, but clear differences in orientation nonetheless do show through. One way of thinking of these differences is to view them as reflecting alternative ways to choose an "entry point" into a swirl of complex and complexly interacting forces. We "have to start somewhere," and Piaget and Vygotsky can be interpreted as choosing to begin from different sides of the picture in order to get their research enterprises underway.

But we have suggested that the differences in their orientations may also be indexes of fundamentally different systems of valuation, as outlined by Elias. This raises a host of questions about the value orientations that guided Vygotsky and Piaget, questions that are very broad and certainly go beyond what we hope to accomplish here.

As a preliminary gloss, however, it is worth noting that although both Vygotsky and Piaget were deep believers in Enlightenment rationality, they translated this belief into research agendas in quite different ways. For Vygotsky, it was translated into an interest in how to revolutionize society and the mental functioning that would go along with new societal forms, whereas for Piaget this belief was translated into the study of how individuals' interactions with the environment give rise to a set of universal logical structures that govern human action and thought. Bruner (1986) brings the contrast we have in mind into sharp focus in a statement about Piaget: "There is neither reform nor liberation in the Piagetian canon" (p. 141).

In addition to the points we have raised about Vygotsky, Piaget, and other figures concerned with development and communication, there is a more general issue that emerged out of what we have said. In our discussion we have formulated positions in terms of oppositions, antinomies, bifurcations, and other dichotomies. We have focused on the tendency to assign *either* social processes *or* individual functioning analytic primacy and on the tendency to emphasize *either* the univocal transmission *or* the dialogic function of utterances in communication. To some degree this tendency toward bifurcation reflects our own analytic and presentational strategies of course, but it also reflects tendencies that are very much in evidence in the theoretical perspectives we have reviewed, something that is hopefully evident from the citations we have used.

This strong tendency toward either/or oppositions reveals something important about the ideas of Piaget and Vygotsky in our view, but it may also have implications for theories and cultural models of development and communication more generally. Specifically, it may index a broad tendency for theories and cultural models of development and communication to have an either/or form. And this in turn raises the question of whether we *must* formulate theoretical positions on development and communication in terms of oppositions such as those we have outlined.

One point we have made in this connection derives from Elias's comments on the individual-society antinomy. Elias makes a convincing case that this antinomy is not so much one grounded in rational argument or empirical fact as one based on valuations, on mistaking "what should be" for "what is." In an analogous manner, the tendency we have noted to organize theories and cultural models of development and communication in terms of an either/or dichotomy may not be so much a fact about the power or appropriateness of analytic tools as a fact about valuations that may not have been made explicit. In this case we have in mind not valuations concerned with the individual-society antinomy outlined by Elias but instead valuations having to do with what constitutes an adequate, sophisticated, or elegant scientific theory or cultural model. This issue is related to the notion of "cognitive values" as recently outlined by Goodnow (1990).

In our review of Lotman's ideas we saw that while he organized his account around the analytic distinction between a univocal transmission function and a dialogic function of utterances, he insisted that *both* functions *always* characterize an utterance. He viewed them as existing in a kind of dialectic or "irreducible tension" (Wertsch, 1991, 1995) that is inherent in the phenomena under examination. If Lotman was correct, then to the extent that Vygotsky and Piaget incorporated claims about communication into their accounts they may be interpreted as being committed to a line of reasoning that militates against the kinds of tendencies toward bifurcations we argued they occasionally fell into. By introducing Lotman's account of functional dualism into the picture, we are introducing a kind of check on what might otherwise be all too common tendencies toward dichotomization.

In this connection it is important to emphasize that the distinction Lotman made between functions is *analytic* in nature and should not be mistaken for an ontological commitment to phenomena that exist in distinct form in reality. His approach to this issue follows very much in the tradition of figures such as Bakhtin (1986) and Vygotsky (1987) who insisted that the most basic analytic units we can envision cannot be reduced further into elements. In contrast to the acceptance of irreducible tensions in the basic unit of analysis, a powerful, and often quite debilitating aspect of many accounts of development and communication in circulation today is the tendency to try to do exactly what figures such as Lotman, Bakhtin, and Vygotsky said we should not do—i.e., reduce a basic unit of analysis with its inherent dialectic of forces into some kind of more basic elements.

We would argue that the tendency to follow such a reductionistic path is pervasive in theories encountered in academic discourse as well as in cultural models employed by laypeople. It is a tendency that probably can be traced to a kind of valuation, or cognitive value that generally guides contemporary western discourse about models, or theories of development and communication. This cognitive value assumes that it is not appropriate, or aesthetically acceptable for the most basic unit of analysis to involve an irreducible tension. Instead, there should be a search for a way to break such a unit down further into elements.

In contrast to this pattern of valuation, figures such as Bakhtin and Lotman assumed that the units of analysis we employ will almost always involve some kind of "functional dualism" or "dialogicality." Among such analysts there is a kind of ready acceptance, or comfort with this assumption that stands in sharp contrast with many contemporary Western theorists. One's stance on this, as reflected in both explicit statements and implicit assumptions, is an important factor in understanding the shape of any theory or cultural model on issues such as development and communication.

Both Piaget and Vygotsky made explicit claims to the effect that dialectical processes in one form or another are at the heart of their approaches. As we have seen, however, they (or in some cases perhaps their interpreters) nonetheless had difficulty keeping this point in mind when carrying out their concrete theoretical and empirical research. It seems to us that the most effective way to avoid falling into the traps that arise when we formulate issues in an either/or form is to formulate or reformulate a central theoretical construct in the approach in such a way that the either/or tendency is held in check. This is what we suggested may be possible by introducing Lotman's account of communication, an account grounded in functional dualism, into Vygotsky's and Piaget's theoretical discussions.

In the realm of education, one prescription that follows from a more dialogical approach is that instruction be viewed as a both/and process. In this view instruction involves both transmission of information and the production of new meanings. What takes place in classroom communication from this perspective may not be much different from other settings, yet classrooms are often presumed to be sites where only transmission occurs. All too often researchers and teachers employ a transmission model of education for assessment, testing, and evaluation, even when they explicitly reject such a model. For example, Strauss and Shilony (1994) have found that teachers overwhelmingly subscribe to the transmission model in thinking about teaching.

An example of an instructional approach grounded in the functional dualism we have outlined can be found in the writings of Nemirovsky (in press). He rejects the dominant view within mathematics education that "learning mathematics is learning new symbolic rules as well as abandoning 'wrong' rules" (p. 3). Citing Brown and Burton (1978) and Matz (1982) as examples, Nemirovsky (in press) argues that such an approach leads to the assumption that the role of the teacher ought to be to transmit to students the correct rule or procedure that must be used in various contexts when approaching mathematics problems of a particular type. What is lost in this approach, argues Nemirovsky, is that the rules and procedures are descriptions of symbolic processes that take place within a particular situation. In the terms we have outlined in this chapter, what is missing is the sense in which rules are not simply truths to be transmitted but thinking devices for students to incorporate into their ongoing activity.

Nemirovsky (in press) calls the activity of coming to understand how rules operate within dynamic processes "learning a way of symbolizing" (p. 6). From his perspective, learning something like graph analysis

is not a matter of being able to replicate a certain symbolic procedure. It involves developing a point of view about the meanings of graphical shapes and about the situation represented by the graph, from which a style of symbol-use emerges as a natural, fruitful, and meaningful action in a specific context. (p. 6)

This development of a point of view, moreover, does not come only from the teacher. Students come to the classroom with their own theories and quite adequate representations of everyday lifeworlds. Students do not approach mathematics or other forms of inquiry "from an empty state of mind" but often have "clear and far-reaching expectations" (p. 37) of what they will find. Nor are these expectations "wrong" when considered from the point of view of the lifeworld in which students operate, even if they are inadequate as mathematical explanations.

What teachers do provide in this context of learning mathematics concepts are interpretations of symbolic behaviors that students must interpret for themselves; behavior that does not always conform to the expectations of students. It is through encountering "conflictive and senseless symbolic behaviors" (Nemirovsky, in press, p. 39) from the students' perspectives that they have the opportunity to use the rules of mathematical sign systems in a way that makes sense to them. The best teachers and learning environments, according to Nemirovsky, offer "opportunities of symbol-use that encourage the learner to revise what she already knows and expects in order to make sense of what, for her, is a strange and puzzling symbolic behavior" (p. 40). Within this process, teachers are neither solely transmitters of knowledge nor simply partners in dialogue. They play a crucial role in providing meaningful activity in which students learn to use mathematical rules.

What makes this approach "dialogic" or an example of an approach that uses a "functional dualist" model of communication is that it takes both the transmission and thinking device functions of communication as central. In keeping the educational goal of "learning mathematics" at the center of instruction, Nemirovsky's approach reflects the tenets of a transmission model. In arguing that mathematical "rules" only make sense insofar as students come to use them within meaningful activity, he takes rules to be "thinking devices" rather than simply part of a system of stable meanings. Moreover, this particular approach reveals what is productive about the tension involved in a both/and perspective with regard to communication. By seeing students' own intentions and purposes as important parts of mathematical thinking, rules come to have a value greater than their standard definition. Students move beyond comprehending the definition of mathematical rules to learn how to use symbols such as graphs and charts to accomplish their own ends within an inquiry guided activity.

Some may argue that we have not identified the right candidate to resist the either/or tendencies in Piaget and Vygotsky or the right example of an instructional process that illustrates our claims. Regardless of one's position on these matters, however, we would continue to argue for the need to consider more general questions such as the following: Do either/or tendencies underlie our theoretical and cultural models of development and communication? If they do, how can we most effectively resist the tendency to formulate accounts in this form? It seems to us that until we address these questions we will find it difficult to formulate many of the most pressing theoretical and practical issues in education and developmental psychology in such a way that will not mistake what should be for what is.

Acknowledgments

The writing of this chapter was assisted by a grant from the Spencer Foundation to the first author. The statements made and the views expressed are solely the responsibility of the authors.

References

Bakhtin, M. M. (1984). *Problems of Dostoevsky's poetics* (C. Emerson, Ed. and Trans.). Minneapolis: University of Minnesota Press.

Bakhtin, M. M. (1986). *Speech genres and other late essays* (C. Emerson and M. Holquist, Eds.; V. W. McGee, Trans.). Austin: University of Texas Press.

Brown, J. S. and Burton, R. B. (1978). Diagnostic models for procedural bugs in basic mathematical skills. *Cognitive Science, 2*, 155–192.

Bruner, J. S. (1962). Introduction to L. S. Vygotsky. *Thought and speech* (pp. v–x). Cambridge: MIT Press.

Bruner, J. (1986). *Actual minds, possible worlds*. Cambridge: Harvard University Press.

Chomsky, N. (1966). *Cartesian linguistics: A chapter in the history of rationalist thought*. New York: Harper and Row.

Chomsky, N. (1972). *Language and mind*. New York: Harcourt Brace Jovanovich.

Churchland, P. (1988). Reductionism, connectionism, and the plasticity of human consciousness. *Cultural Dynamics, 1*, pp. 29–45.

Cole, M. and Cole, S. R. (1989). *The development of children.* New York: Scientific American Books.

D'Andrade, R. (1990). Some propositions about the relations between culture and human cognition. In J. W. Stigler, R. A. Shweder, and G. Herdt (Eds.), *Cultural psychology: Essays on comparative human development* (pp. 65–129). Cambridge, England: Cambridge University Press.

Davydov, V. V. and Radzikhovskii, L. A. (1985). Vygotsky's theory and the activity-oriented approach to psychology. In J. V. Wertsch (Ed.), *Culture, communication, and cognition: Vygotskian perspectives* (pp. 35–65). New York: Cambridge University Press.

Elias, N. (1991). *The society of individuals.* (M. Schroter, Ed.; E. Jephcott, Trans.). Oxford, England: Blackwell.

Goodnow, J. (1990). The socialization of cognition: What's involved? In J. W. Stigler, R. A. Shweder, and G. Herdt (Eds.), *Cultural psychology: Essays on comparative human development* (pp. 259–286). Cambridge, England: Cambridge University Press.

Holland, D. and Quinn, N. (1986). *Cultural models in language and thought.* New York: Cambridge University Press.

Kaplan, B. (1983). Genetic-dramatism: Old wine in new bottles. In S. Wapner and B. Kaplan (Eds.), *Toward a holistic developmental psychology* (pp. 53–74). Hillsdale, NJ: Lawrence Erlbaum.

Lotman, Yu. M. (1988). Text within a text. *Soviet Psychology*, Spring, *26* (3), 32–51.

Lotman, Yu. M. (1990). *Universe of the mind: A semiotic theory of culture.* Bloomington: Indiana University Press.

Matz, M. (1982). Toward a process model for high school algebra errors. In D. Sleeman and J. S. Brown (Eds.), *Intelligent tutoring systems* (pp. 25–50). New York: Academic Press.

Mead, G. H. (1934). *Mind, self, and society from the standpoint of a social behaviorist.* Chicago: University of Chicago Press.

Nemirovsky, R. (in press). On ways of symbolizing: The case of Laura and the velocity sign. *Journal of Mathematical Behavior.*

Olson, D. R. (1994). *The world on paper: The conceptual and cognitive implications of writing and reading.* Cambridge, England: Cambridge University Press.

Olson, D. (1995). Writing and the mind. In J. V. Wertsch, P. del Rio, and A. Alvarez (Eds.), *Sociocultural studies of mind* (pp. 95–123). New York: Cambridge University Press.

Piaget, J. (1966). *The psychology of intelligence.* Totowa, NJ: Littlefield, Adams.

Piaget, J. (1970). *Genetic epistemology* (E. Duckworth, Trans.). New York: Columbia University Press.

Piaget, J. (1971). *Biology and knowledge: An essay on the relations between organic regulations and cognitive processes.* Chicago: University of Chicago Press.

Reddy, M. J. (1979). The conduit metaphor: A case of frame conflict in our language about language. In A. Ortony (Ed.), *Metaphor and thought* (pp. 284–324). Cambridge, England: Cambridge University Press.

Rogoff, B. (1990). *Apprenticeship in thinking: Cognitive development in social context.* New York: Oxford University Press.

Strauss, S. and Shilony, T. (1994). Teachers' models of children's minds and learning. In L. A. Hirschfeld and S. A. Gelman (Eds.), *Mapping the mind: Domain specificity in cognition and culture* (pp. 455–473). Cambridge, England: Cambridge University Press.

Vygotsky, L. S. (1978). *Mind in society: The development of higher psychological processes* (M. Cole, V. John-Steiner, S. Scribner, and E. Souberman, Eds.). Cambridge: Harvard University Press.

Vygotsky, L. S. (1979). Consciousness as a problem in the psychology of behavior. *Soviet Psychology, 17* (4), 3–35.

Vygotsky, L. S. (1981a) The genesis of higher mental functions. In J. V. Wertsch (Ed.), *The concept of activity in Soviet psychology* (pp. 144–188). Armonk, NY: M. E. Sharpe.

Vygotsky, L. S. (1981b). The development of higher forms of attention in childhood. In J. V. Wertsch (Ed.), *The concept of activity in Soviet psychology* (pp. 189–240). Armonk, NY: M. E. Sharpe.

Vygotsky, L. S. (1987). *The collected works of L. S. Vygotsky.* (Vol. 1) *Problems of general psychology.* (N. Minick, Trans.). New York: Plenum.

Werner, H. (1948). *Comparative psychology of mental development.* New York: International Universities Press.

Wertsch, J. V. (1985). *Vygotsky and the social formation of mind.* Cambridge: Harvard University Press.

Wertsch, J. V. (1991). *Voices of the mind: A sociocultural approach to mediated action.* Cambridge: Harvard University Press.

Wertsch, J. V. (1995). The need for action in sociocultural research. In J. V. Wertsch, P. del Rio, and A. Alvarez (Eds.), *Sociocultural studies of mind* (pp. 56–74). New York: Cambridge University Press.

Westbrook, R. B. (1991). *John Dewey and American democracy.* Ithaca, NY: Cornell University Press.

Zinchenko, V. P. (1985). Vygotsky's ideas about units of analysis for the analysis of mind. In J. V. Wertsch (Ed.), *Culture, communication, and cognition: Vygotskian perspectives* (pp. 94–118). New York: Cambridge University Press.

20

Some Educational Implications of Genre-Based Mental Models: The Interpretive Cognition of Text Understanding

CAROL FLEISHER FELDMAN
DAVID A. KALMAR

It has seemed to some observers of the field (see especially Bruner, in press) that after the cognitive revolution, cognitive psychology took a rather specialized turn toward those aspects of cognition most amenable to computer modeling—those that were context (and *a fortiori* culture) independent, were not consciously experienced, and were syntactic rather than based on semantics or meaning. Other cognitive processes that were of immense interest to some psychologists because they seemed central to the everyday experience of culturally situated actors were difficult, or impossible, to capture satisfactorily in computer models, chiefly because they so centrally involved the meaning of things. This general view has been widely shared among both computer enthusiasts (Fodor, 1980) and detractors (Searle, 1984), but not by all observers. For example, Boden (1990) thinks computer models of thinking are suitable to capture the main outlines, at least, of the meaning-based processes of everyday life.

It may be of some interest to note that Boden hopes for a computer-based account of these processes because it is only in such terms that she can imagine a cognitive psychology being genuinely scientific. The notion that only computer-based research can give scientific respectability to the interpretive processes of everyday life is one that is very widely shared among both cognitive scientists and also philosophers of science with an interest in cognition, though there are important exceptions, among them Nagel (1986), Searle (1992), Penrose (1990), Putnam (1990), and Toulmin (1990). The upshot is that until very recently, the cognition of meaning making was given very little attention in psychology (Bruner, 1990).

There were deep philosophical, indeed metaphysical, difficulties that stood in the way of such a project. The mainstream of informed opinion in both empirical psychology and philosophy has adopted as an article of deep religious/scientific faith, sometimes without real inspection, a metaphysics of physical monism—the view that the only real things in the world are physical. The more likely of the two obvious alternatives, now that idealism has virtually disappeared from scholarly life, is a Cartesian dualism that assigns equally real standing to mind and body. But it has dropped so far in respectability in current philosophical theory that it is chiefly encountered as a term of opprobrium, an accusation of fuzzy-mindedness.

Thus minds, thoughts, and understandings are seen as naught but illusion until, and only insofar as, their physical underlying reality is identified (e.g., see Stich, 1983; Dennett, 1991). Notwithstanding the end of behaviorism, then, positivism is still very much with us, demanding that cognition be given a material representation—sometimes in the brain, more often in a machine, or, more metaphorically, in the programs that run them. For these reasons, then, the turn to cognitive science was overdetermined—by a widely shared positivist *Zeitgeist* that dominated philosophical and psychological thinking alike.

Even an important strain of contrarian opinion in cognitive psychology (e.g., Gergen, 1991; Shweder, 1991), one that takes the experience of everyday life as *the* central cognitive matter in need of scholarly attention, tends to agree with philosophical mainstream opinion—not that interpretive experience is unreal, but that it must forever elude systematic scientific scrutiny because it is forever shifting with changes in perspective. This has led the "perspectivalists" to see certain kinds of research efforts as irrelevant to their enterprise. What might seem at first a strange concession to the physicalists makes somewhat more sense once we consider that a powerful *Zeitgeist* defines the terms of agreement and disagreement alike.

In our view there is no reason why an empirical psychology of interpretive cognition cannot be carried on in scientifically useful terms, and, moreover, without continuing to rewrite the phenomena of interest right out of the story. But it will take some new work in a nonpositivist philosophy of science—not necessarily an oxymoron—to make philosophical sense somewhere down the road of this presently feasible empirical work.

Anthropology has been interested in systems of meaning making for longer than most of us. Interesting work in that discipline (e.g., d'Azevedo, 1962; Duranti, 1993; Ochs, Smith, and Taylor, 1989; Rosaldo, 1980; Sansom, 1982), developing an approach that was brought into the mainstream by Geertz (1973), has plowed ahead with *its* kind of scientific description of meaning-making processes. In psychology proper, a good many people are trying to develop paradigms that blend anthropological textual sensitivity with psychological method. Our laboratory has been one such center of effort.

Toward a Cognitive Psychology of Understanding

Within a cultural psychology, the central processes are acts of meaning (Bruner, 1990). Leaving unresolved for the moment the metaphysical status of such mental acts so worrying to orthodox philosophy and psychology alike, we can nevertheless proceed empirically to ask what the processes are that people go through when they interpret, or make sense of, events in the world. We have noted elsewhere (Feldman, 1994) that in contrast with the forward focus of better understood reasoning processes, interpretation tends to be backward looking and not predictive.

But the fact that the mental events to be scientifically described are not *themselves* scientific does not imply that they may not be described in scientific terms, a matter that is very commonly misunderstood in our literature. This misunderstanding amounts to a (generally unanalyzed) belief that only scientific cognition can be approached for scientific study. But this conclusion comes of conflating two different levels of thought—the thinking of the scientist/theorist and the thinking of the subjects being studied. It may be of interest to note that this general problem has been with us since before cognition ever turned to the problem of meaning making.

For even in the Piagetian era, Feldman and Toulmin (1976) noted a confounding of these levels in, say, claims about formal operational theory. Was it the scientific description of adolescent scientific thought that Piaget claimed had the form of the logician's four-group, or was it the adolescents' own descriptions? Often, the two were not carefully distinguished. Nevertheless, in the Piagetian context, with its interest in children's *scientific* thinking, the confusion did lead to doubts about the feasibility of a scientific cognitive psychology. On the other hand, for interpretive or narrative cognition, with its interest in observing nonscientific forms of thought, the confusion of levels make the whole scientific project look impossible, even oxymoronic.

Once we disentangle acts of meaning their apparent scientific inscrutability disappears. Though meaning making itself may follow narrative patterns very different from those of scientific thought, scientists may hope to describe it in their own ways. Not that these other ways are unproblematic—for, it is plain that scientific accounts of meaning making will not be a case of scientific business as usual. Nevertheless, it should be possible to preserve core features of scientific description in the new context. For example, even if meaning making is itself a backward-looking process, it should be possible to give a predictive scientific account of it.

Where the predictive accounts of scientific thinking, for example, can be seen as attempts to *explain*, the backward-looking interpretive accounts of everyday life can be seen as attempts to *understand*. This distinction, which was discussed most interestingly by von Wright (1971), was also the premise of Lewin's much older (1935) *A Dynamic Theory of Personality*. And both von Wright and Lewin attribute them to Galileo and Aristotle, respectively. In that context, the two modes are seen as alternate forms of *scientists'* theoretical accounts, while, for our present purposes, we wish to extend them to a new domain: the forms of everyday mental life. This extension is not simply metaphoric, for as with artfulness more generally, scientists' accounts are imitated by lay explanations in everyday life. And, in this case, formal science may be influenced by everyday life as well. For Aristotelian and Galilean theory types no doubt enshrine at a more abstract level modes of thought natural to people in general. In any case, both are certainly used by laypersons as different kinds of accounts of everyday life. Our central interest, put in von Wright's terms, is this: We are asking psychological science to give us a Galilean account of ordinary people's Aristotelian understanding of events in everyday life. We turn now to meaning making as a central cognitive activity.

Understanding Texts in School

One field where cognitive processes of understanding are of central, indeed compelling, interest is in education, and, especially, in the teaching of reading. The problem of literacy is a pressing one, and the nature of that problem, in particular, is of educating children to read with understanding, and not in some other way. But what is understanding? And how can it be taught? These are not easy questions, and they have captured the attention of some of the most thoughtful people in education today (see, especially, Snow and Dickinson, 1992; Palincsar and Brown, 1984).

What is involved in understanding a text? We can begin by considering the experts—professional literary critics—and what they do. The textual understanding of children who will never be literary critics might reasonably be expected, indeed asked, to share features in whatever form it can with that professional apparatus of understanding. But the professionals master technical tools for narrative interpretation. This is a step that is almost never taken in our ordinary schools. Indeed, it seems to conflict with deeply held commitments in educational policy, a matter we shall return to below.

Snow (1990) reports discovering quite by chance how a shift from description to storytelling changed the way details were understood. Though subjects were given a picture description task, some of them spontaneously began telling a story about the picture, something they had recently been doing a lot of in school. This shift can readily be understood as a genre-like shift from description to narration. Snow noted that although some details dropped out, the remaining details were weighted more correctly, and the central point more often conveyed.

A related finding was reported by Palincsar and Brown (1984), who created a reading program where novice readers faced with technical prose passages were required to figure out exactly what question the passage is an answer to. Once the right question was asked, it was easy for readers to keep track of details and to distinguish important details from less important ones. Question asking can be looked at as having imposed a narrative frame suitable for interpretation.

Genres are basically narrative categories, or narrative types, that are assigned to texts by interpreters as an aid to understanding the specific events within them. To give an example that involves our own data to be reported more fully later in this chapter, deciding how to interpret the meaning of an invitation to a birthday party (with disreputable looking Russians, who insist on sharing their ghastly bootleg liquor) is impossible until one decides whether the story is fiction or autobiography. The fictional frame makes the invitation fun, while in an autobiography it is threatening. Moreover, in the fictional context, the invitation is the story's turning point to a day of fun, while in the autobiography context it is not the turning point at all. Rather, there, the turning point is the moment when the drinking starts; it is the drinking itself that destabilizes a steady state and turns the day into one of fear.

Narrative events without any genre frame are basically unintelligible. But the situation is not unique, for isolated scientific statements or observations without a framing theory are in the same boat. This is because details within a discourse frame are always exemplifications of something else. The discourse frame gives instructions, in a sense, for what meaning they bear. If the genre (or question, or theory) they exemplify is unknown and undiscoverable, we ask the reader to make sense where no sense can be made.

Literary Genres as Cognitive Models

The forms that genre taxonomies have taken have ranged widely. The *fons et origo* of serious genre theory was Aristotle's discussion of tragedy. In the modern era, the most important genre theorist was Northrop Frye (1957), whose taxonomy distinguished between lyric, epic, drama, and fiction, on the basis of different discourse patterns between speaker/writer and audience/listener. There has been some historical change in genres (for example, the fairly recent appearance of the first novel), but, in general, in every era, definitions of particular genres have been sufficiently widely accepted to serve as compositional norms (Cuddon, 1991; Fowler, 1982).

But in a sense Frye's was the last genre taxonomy, for since then the locus of genre, to put it roughly, has been shifted from text to cognition, and from writer to reader. Genres are seen as brought by readers to the task of construing texts, indeed, even as constructing texts along the lines of the reader's understanding— or, as Fowler notes, more like the pigeon than the pigeonhole. But what cognitive genres readers may have in mind surely cannot be completely divorced from the patterns of literature they see in their cultural surround; indeed, they must come from it. Perhaps all that has changed is the force we assign to canonical types— that we see them now as descriptive rather than prescriptive.[1] In any case, for our purposes, it is enough to note that in some sense genres exist both out there in the text itself, and in the mind of the enculturated reader, chiefly because they permeate the culture and so inform the writer and the reader who live within it.

As others have noted (e.g., Bakhtin, 1986), the whole set of narrative genres can, with profit, be seen as a subclass of discourse types—namely, those discourse patterns that are found in our written literature. Seen this way, the universe of discourse types would also include other kinds of written texts, such as the scientific writing so central to classroom instruction. In addition, it should include oral discourse types, which can also rise to the level of literary art in certain strictly oral cultures; for example, as oratory among the Ilongot (Rosaldo, 1980). And, finally, it would include the more prosaic oral discourse patterns of classroom talk.

All of these discourse types are candidates for becoming cognitive models that guide interpretation. For if discourse of any type follows a certain pattern, and readers read it, the pattern becomes part of the reader's knowledge, "going underground" to become a cognitive model, or a framework for construal. Through this process, the genres of literature, as well as, for example, the discourse patterns of ordinary conversation, or scientific writing, or even classroom talk can become mental models that guide interpretation. If the genres of written literature in this culture are an especially central case of such frames, it is perhaps because they have for centuries interested a professional group of scholars, with the result that they have become marked throughout the culture (that is, even in the lay culture) as distinctive, and even canonical, forms.

Genre Instruction in Schools

Not very commonly, but in some high school English classes, genre types are noted, examples are read, and, sometimes, their signature patterns are taught. We wish there were more of it. In this context, the strangely bereft vocabulary of genre that we have noted in our subjects is not surprising. They rarely have any idea what to say when we ask them what kind of story they have heard. They often cannot remember what kind of a story we said it was at the start. Nevertheless, lexicon or no, our college-educated subjects do have canonical, and distinct, story types in mind.

Aside from such focal attention to literary genres, the classroom could provide a rather steady stream of information about genre types as teachers and students shift from one subject and task to another in the normal course of things. For each task and subject has something of a distinctive discourse frame of its own. The teacher could make these frames explicit, actually teaching the rules of each discourse pattern as a mode of construal. This would be as relevant, we believe, for science as for art, for mathematics as for history. *All classroom work takes place within a discourse frame.*

There is a tendency among teachers to think of the usual varieties of teacher and student talk in the classroom as genreless, and also of basic reading materials that way. But classroom genres are highly patterned for objectivity. In earlier research (Feldman and Wertsch, 1976), it was noted that modal verbs that were very common in teachers' speech outside the classroom were largely deleted from their classroom discourse. Latour and Woolgar (1986) note that the discourse of scientific paper and laboratory talk differ in a similar way. Classroom discourse patterns are supported by a widely shared educational ideal in favor of eliminating rhetoric from the classroom, and focusing classroom talk (and text) on the information it is seen as "containing."

And there is an additional problem. Whether because teachers see them as genreless, or for some other reason, classroom discourses are not usually marked as writing or talk of a certain kind, so that children in the classroom rarely know what genre they are working in, until by trial and error they get it right. Children, then, have to try to understand the "information contained within" without the "genre" instruction that would make it plain.

Perhaps inconsistently, these classroom language forms, whilst being seen as genreless, are also seen as the best, or highest, kind of discourse (e.g., most abstract, most context independent). But, the context-independent discourse types found in the classroom may not be the only, or even the best, kind of language to support scientific thought, or abstract thought more generally. Among nonliterate people, oral forms of art develop in support of abstract thought (Feldman, 1991), as they do in this culture among some young people (Feldman, 1992). The corollary notion, that bad genres can drive good genres out of the child's mind, is surely mistaken. (The same sort of reasoning prevailed for decades with respect to the two dialects of Hawaii's schoolchildren; see Feldman, Stone, Wertsch, and Strizich, 1977; see also Dyson, 1995.) In short, we have been so worried about context-independent discourse and scientific writing that we have failed to support the other genres around them that might make them more intelligible.

Most important, we have failed to teach any discourse frames, including the few we actually do use in schools, as the rule governed interpretive frames that they really are. It should be no surprise, then, that penetrating the mystery of discourse pattern comes more easily to children with more culturally enriched home lives that could assist them to see the texts of the classroom as *texts of a certain kind*. Their exposure to a wider array of genres is, we believe, the real origin of the middle-class child's linguistic advantage, and not simply that home talk includes more of the special, context-independent genres of teachers' classroom talk, as has often been supposed. Educated middle-class families are more likely to produce context-independent talk around the house, and it seems likely that exposure to such talk at home would be helpful when children hear it in school. But the explanation seems to us incomplete. For, in fact, middle-class children also have a much wider genre exposure, along with the whole literacy based cultural tool kit of modern life.

How do we think the middle-class child's exposure to a range of genres at home would help in school, and how especially given that the same, specific genres are not likely to be encountered in school? We suggest that *awareness* of genre and frame would be raised by such exposure, and that this would, in turn, equip children to identify different discourse types in classroom talk. This is especially likely to be facilitative because the children usually have to figure these matters out for themselves, as even the limited range of classroom discourse is usually untaught and even unmarked.

The teaching of classroom discourse frames, and of a wider array of literary genres, would surely benefit their less privileged peers. One hears that these problems of understanding are now creeping their way up the social-class ladder. Certainly it cannot be a coincidence that it is at a time when the variety of oral genres in everyday life is shrinking, when parents of the middle class are home less, and when even the ritual of dinnertime conversation is fast disappearing from many middle-class families. We return to these problems later in this chapter.

In the next section, we report a series of studies that give some exemplifications of mental models for understanding texts. In the following studies, we were working our way into an empirical exploration of the cognitive patterns of genre knowledge. No one of them alone delineates the nature of such interpretive cognition, nor even the collection of them taken all together. Rather, taken together, they may be seen as giving a preliminary report of some of the kinds of things scientific research may hope to discover in this domain. Along the way, a host of methodological issues arose, and our handling of those may also be of some interest to others who would like to extend the procedures of science into the domain of meaning making. We offer these studies, then, with all modesty, and as an early step toward an empirical cognitive psychology of understanding.

Some Empirical Studies of Genre Knowledge

Simply giving a story a genre label is enough to shift the way subjects will understand and interpret it. For example, as we will report below, we found patterned differences in interpretation when adult subjects were told that a story was autobiographical or told that it was fictional. Similarly, Kalmar (1996) found differences in adults' interpretation when stories were labeled as either a spy story or a travelogue. When genre labels alone are adequate to guide the ways subjects understand stories, it seems reasonable to believe that subjects "know" the pattern of the genres when they come to the task.

There are in fact at least two routes through which people can be asked to access the genres in their cognitive tool kit. One route is through a genre label, as in the research described above. The second route is through textual features that are characteristic for a genre. Here, the reader may see or hear such genre-distinctive features early in a tale (e.g., "Once upon a time there lived. . ."). We imagine that the reader then selects the suitable genre pattern from a set of available cognitive models. An example of how textual features can guide the way a story is understood was reported by Feldman, Bruner, Renderer, and Spitzer (1990). They began by describing two different landscapes written into modern stories. One landscape is the landscape of action—the patterned sequence of action events that are reported in a story. The other landscape is the landscape of consciousness—the world as perceived, felt, and conceived by each of the characters in the story. Such textual features can serve to construct different types, or genres, of stories.

In their research, they used two different versions of the same story. The story as originally written served as one version, called the "conscious" version. It included both a landscape of action and a landscape of consciousness. The other version (the "nonconscious" version) was created by editing out the mental words bearing the landscape of consciousness. Comparisons between subjects listening to the two versions of the story revealed intriguing differences. Subjects listening to the conscious version patterned their interpretation of the story around the psychological states of the protagonist. They also gave a more temporal account and reported more information beyond the given. In contrast, subjects listening to the nonconscious version focused on action. They also saw the action as plotted and recognized a pervasive authorial presence.

In this chapter we shall report several studies that evoke cognitive genre models in subjects of different ages. Some studies use genre labels, others textual triggers, as means of evoking them. In every study, each subject listens to a story read aloud to them alone and answers a variety of interpretive questions, such as, "What was the most important thing in the story?" Usually, they are also asked to tell the story back. In every case, subjects' responses were tape-recorded, and a verbatim transcription made that could be analyzed by various methods for clues to the subjects' understanding of the story. In the first study, we explored the effects of labeling a single narrative as one of two different genres: "Autobiography" or "Fiction."

Thirty-five undergraduates were read an excerpt from Primo Levi's *The Monkey's Wrench*. In the story, two tourists, Falcone and an unnamed narrator, while traveling in Russia, decide to take a boat trip. While waiting for the boat, they meet a Russian named Rasnitsa. Rasnitsa tells them that it is his birthday, and he invites the tourists to join him as his guests. Once on the boat, the tourists are introduced to Rasnitsa's ominous-looking friends, who urge the tourists to drink to excess. The story ends with the narrator growing increasingly intoxicated and increasingly anxious about it.

Half (18) of the subjects were told, "This is autobiographical. It's an excerpt from a memoir." The other half (17) were told, "This is fictional. 'It's an excerpt from a novel." After the story was read, subjects answered the following eight questions:

1. First, I'd like you to tell it back to me, using your own words, and filling in all the details of how you saw it.
2. What do you think came *before* this?
3. And why do you think that came before?
4. What do you think will come next?
5. Why do you think so?
6. How do you imagine these characters? What kind of people are they?
7. What do you think they are after in this scene? What do they want?
8. What do you think the *author* was trying to accomplish with this scene?

Questions 1, 6, and 8 give subjects an opening to mention the text's genre, if it is seen as relevant. When responses to these questions are examined, it is seen that more autobiography than fiction subjects mention a genre, chi-square (1) = 7.44, $p < .01$, suggesting that "fiction" is the unmarked case for our subjects, and conversely that the autobiography label evokes a more specific genre.

	Genre mentioned	
Label	*No*	*Yes*
Autobiography	8	10
Fiction	15	2

Responses were also coded for whether the subjects believed that the story was true or fictional.

Label	Type of story	
	True story	*Fictional story*
Autobiography	7	11
Fiction	2	15

While subjects predominantly view the story as fictional, there is a bias on the part of "autobiography" subjects to see the story as true. This effect was marginally significant, chi-square $(1) = 3.37$, $p < .07$. At most, it only suggests that for these subjects, autobiography may be merely reportorial, rather than a crafted narrative form. But, the next code makes the same point more clearly.

This code reflects the subject's assessment of the type of writing presented by the author, as it appears in answers to any of the questions. Did the story represent reporting, or was it more constructed, representing a "making"?

Label	Perceived narrative style	
	Reported	*Made*
Autobiography	12	6
Fiction	5	12

Whereas subjects told the story is an "autobiography" tend to see the author as merely reporting events, "fiction" subjects tend to view the story as created, chi-square $(1) = 4.86$, $p < .05$.

Now we may note how labeling the text as autobiographical, as opposed to fictional, affected whether subjects noted features of the situation that situated it in the real world when describing the characters (question 6). One key feature of this kind is the national/cultural identities of the characters (i.e., Russian, American).

Label	Nationality mentioned	
	No	*Yes*
Autobiography	15	3
Fiction	9	8

The result is at first surprising. Autobiography subjects, who tend to see the story as true, do not note such landscaping details. The difference was only marginally significant, chi-square $(1) = 3.75$, $p < .06$, but it received further support below.

Subjects completed a questionnaire that asked them to rate the relevance of a list of potential genre features after they responded more discursively to the questions reported above. There were 22 items, each testing a feature that might discriminate between the two genres. They were rated as relevant or not on a four-point scale—for example, "1: Is mostly about action and adventure" to "4: Is mostly about people's thoughts and feelings." It is of some interest in its own right that only one item, that concerning character development, was significantly different between the groups, for it suggests that knowledge about narrative patterns may itself be encoded in a narrative form, from which it is accessed most readily by highly narrativized tasks.

The one significant feature ranged from "1: Characters are developed fully and in depth" to "4: Characters are thinly sketched." Fiction subjects (mean = 1.82) saw the characters as more richly developed than autobiography subjects did (mean = 2.67; $t(33) = 2.68$, $p < .05$). For the fiction subjects, seeing the story as constructed may provide inferential triggers to flesh out more about the characters than is actually told. Now, note that the autobiography subjects find the characters thin, and recall that above we reported that they do not mention their nationality. We begin to suspect a common mechanism: that autobiography subjects are so closely identified with a protagonist who is unmediated by an authorial presence, that they do not see him as a character to be concerned about, and who needs development. We will have more to say about this below.

The upshot of the analyses so far is some hints that do not add up to a clear picture of the *patterns* typical of the different modes of understanding induced by the two instructional sets. To this point, all we have is *features*. This led us to want to look at the subject's actual talk in answering the questions *as a text* to see whether we would find patterns of construal that differed between the groups. We hoped to find their mental genre models by looking at their renarration of the text as a text in its own right. We approached this by looking for distinctive word usage patterns in the subjects' talk.

We began with a word count for each group, and then compared the two groups in order to identify each group's distinctive words, before examining their usage in context.[2] Thirteen words appeared significantly more often in the answers of the autobiography group, 11 in the answers of the fiction group.

The words are as follows:

Autobiography	Fiction
another	a
around	birthday
between	each
coming	go
drank	invited
information	little
is	more
men	names
Nicolai	on
picture	people
someone	time
tall	
wrapped	

An examination of their usage in context enabled us to look at what kind of story subjects in each group prototypically told. For the fiction group, as our tourist protagonists approach a dock to *go on* a boat trip, they are *invited* to join in a *birthday* party by some Russian *people* (they do or do not know *each* other), whose *names* have been forgotten, where they have a (good or bad) *time*, *more* or less (*little*). In this story about a party, the turning point comes with the invitation. In the autobiography group, after our travelers (not tourists, for they are in search of *information*) approach the dock, *Nicolai*, who is *someone* unusual, *another* sort of person or from *another* country, presses them to join him and his friends on the boat. There are two more *men*, one of them was *tall*. They sat down with one of the foreigners *between* them, and one of them produced some food ominously *wrapped* in newspaper and a large quantity of bad wine. They all *drank* to excess, and the Russians pressed the narrator to drink more, but no one was *coming* to his aid. In this story about entrapment by sinister characters, the turning point comes when the drinking starts.[3]

This analysis, by permitting us to reconstruct from word usage the way that subjects in the two groups tell stories about this story, allows us to ask about the genre of the subjects' own narrativization. For the fiction subjects, it is *A Day at the Races*—a playful encounter built around a birthday party with some new friends where everyone has a good time, more or less. For the autobiography subjects, it is a bad trip, a near abduction where men altogether unlike oneself move in too close and force feed bad liquor to the point of illness.

In a second study, we explored the parallel text manipulation—readers' understanding of texts told in first- versus third-person voices. The choice between writing in the first person and the third person is one that is often consciously made by a writer. Some writers have found the difference between the two styles so compelling that they have rewritten their work from one perspective into the other. Gottfried Keller, for example, published a third-person version of the novel *Der grüne Heinrich* ["Green Henry"] in 1854, and 25 years later published a first-person version of the same story (Romberg, 1962). Similarly, Franz Kafka began writing *The Castle* in the first person, but 42 pages later rewrote his draft into the third person (Cohn, 1968). Controversy over genre definitions often arises out of puzzles over how genre effects would be expressed in what Wellek and Warren (1962) have termed the "outer form": the specific meter and structure of the text. Nevertheless, the distinction between first-person and third-person writing is very basic (Botheroyd, 1976). Roughly speaking, it corresponds to the genre distinction between autobiography and fiction.

The question here then was whether first- and third-person versions, corresponding roughly to autobiography and fiction labels, would also affect the way subjects construe a story, and affect it in a similar way. In this study, 36 undergraduate subjects heard one of two versions of an excerpt from Kafka's *The Castle*. Half of them heard it in the third-person voice; the other half, in the first-person.

After the story was read, subjects answered the following eight questions:

1. What happened in the end?
2. Why did it happen that way?
3. What was the turning point in the story?
4. Tell me some things about the character that I haven't told you. What was he like?
5. What was the character's plight? I mean, what was he up against?

6. What was the author trying to say—that is, what is the meaning of this story?
7. What *kind* of story is this? It's not a mystery, it's not a folktale—what would you call it?
8. I'd like for you to tell me the story now—the same story I told you, but in your own words.

An accuracy measure, comparing the two groups' reports of 12 basic plot events in question 8 retellings, found eight on average in each.

Answers to question 4 indicate that the two groups describe the protagonist differently. Third-person subjects gave many more descriptions of the protagonist's psychological states, $t(34) = 2.00$, $p < .06$; first-person subjects were significantly more likely, $t(34) = 2.38$, $p < .05$, to attribute habitual states to the protagonist (e.g., "He was a man who didn't want to explain everything"). Third-person psychological responses include, "He seems to be planning some strategy." While first-person subjects feel they know the person, and especially know his general character, third-person subjects are more attentive to (and inventive about) what he is thinking (perhaps as opposed to saying or seeming to be) at each moment. They do not know what he is really like so they are constantly on the lookout. This first-person intimacy echoes autobiography subjects' identification; the third-person psychological focus echoes the richness of character fiction subjects experienced.

Subjects' responses to question 6, the author's intention in telling the story, tended to fall into one of six categories: don't judge a book by its cover; question authority; declare yourself, be honest; manipulation works; documentary. Interestingly, whereas the first-person subjects tended to fall into the category, "Don't judge a book by its cover," third-person subjects tend to give responses of the form, "Manipulation works," chi-square $(1) = 5.619$, $p < .05$. The interesting origin of this finding is the pervasive nonskepticism of the first-person subjects, virtually none of whom express doubt about whether K is really a land surveyor, in the teeth of the textual evidence that he is not.

The first-person version tends to be far more sympathetic to the land surveyor, who is seen as caught in a plight not of his own making. The third-person version attributes him with a psychological complexity bordering on craftiness, an author rather than victim of his circumstances. Third-person subjects, then, both identify less with the protagonist, and see more psychological complexity in him, as did subjects receiving the parallel fiction label.

A related analysis examined the certainty with which subjects responded to this same question. Third-person subjects were more uncertain of their responses than were first-person subjects, $t(33) = 2.37$, $p < .05$. It is interesting that third-person subjects, who in fact drew a great many inferences that went beyond the text, actually felt they were on the shaky ground of inference, while first-person subjects, who felt they had unmediated knowledge of what the character is really like but also saw less information beyond the given, were more confident. In sum, the protagonist is distal and unclear, but interesting, in the third person, while he is proximal and clear, but dull, in the first.

Discourse analyses were conducted, as above, based on each subject's answers to questions about the story. Seven words appeared significantly more often in the answers of the first-person group, and 17 in the third-person group, as follows:

First person	Third person
and	although
bed	corner
room	course
treated	has
walked	having
who	inside
without	K.
	or
	phone
	remember
	sense
	sudden
	talking
	therefore
	though
	time
	whether

To begin with, third-person words were used to mark plot structure—*sudden* was used in "all of a sudden," which marks a turning point in the plot, *although*, *therefore*, and *though* were used to arrange plot elements in a structured way. And many plot elements (*talking, phone, corner*) were noted. This parallels the finding that fiction subjects see the story as crafted. The first-person words, in contrast, tell of a sad man who asked for a *room* and got a *bed* on the floor instead, and was *treated* badly because no one knew *who* he really was and he was *without* the necessary permit. Moreover, and this is most interesting indeed when we consider Kafka's authorial purposes, the first-person version raised no suspicion that the man presenting himself as the land surveyor may not really have been one.

Obviously, Kafka succeeded in writing a far more mysterious story by shifting to the third person. If the first-person character is nearby, the third-person one is distal. This same distancing process is reflected in codes that show subjects see K. as living in a narrative frame within a crafted structure, while, conversely, first-person subjects responded to the character simply as a person encountered, even met. In both cases, we can see the parallel to the patterns of interpretation evoked by the autobiography and fiction labels reported above. So the two different experimental manipulations—labeling and textual variation—seem in this case to evoke similar interpretive models.

The Feldman et al. (1990) study found that textual manipulations could lead subjects to interpret a story in different ways. A story containing both a landscape of action and a landscape of consciousness led subjects to interpret the story in terms of the psychology of the characters. In contrast, a story containing only a landscape of action led subjects to interpret the story in terms of the actions and events in the story. If these different patterns in fact represent genre-like distinctions, then labeling manipulations such as those reported above should also successfully trigger *these* genre models. The next study was designed to address this hypothesis. All of the subjects listened to the same story, but half of the subjects were told that the story would be psychological, while the other half were told that it would be about action. We asked whether the pattern of results would be similar to that obtained for the two story versions. A psychology label and a conscious version should lead to one pattern of construal, while an action label and nonconscious version should lead to another.

Forty undergraduate subjects, with a mean age of 19;6, were individually read the original version of "Truth and Consequences" (Gill, 1961) used by Feldman et al. (1994),[4] who describe the story as follows:

> [It is] about a young man who, on the eve of entering a seminary to train for the priesthood, goes off to a summer resort for a holiday with his mother, who has from the beginning wanted him to enter the profession. At the resort he is drawn to an attractive and bold young woman with a lame leg and a penchant for swearing. He and the girl talk about their plans—his to be a priest and hers to get married. She asks him whether he really has a calling. The story ends as his mother approaches them heavily in the gathering dusk. (p. 256)

Psychology-label subjects were told, "It's a story about a young man's psychological development." Action-label subjects were told, "It's a story about important events in a young man's life." The experimenter then read the story to the subjects. After reading the story, the experimenter repeated the genre label. Then subjects were asked the following six questions:

1. What is the gist of the story?
2. What was most important in the story?
3. What was the turning point in the story?
4. What happened in the end?
5. Why did it happen that way?
6. What kind of story is this? It's not a mystery, it's not a folktale—I don't know, what would you call it?

Some interesting interpretive effects were found in the codes for question 4. Responses were analyzed for whether subjects stated that the story came to a close at the end and was resolved, or that the story was open-ended. Action-label subjects mostly described the ending as resolved, while psychology-label subjects described it as open, chi-square (1) = 4.286, $p < .05$.

	Type of ending	
Label	*Open*	*Resolved*
Psychology	9	11
Action	3	17

Question 5 asked *why* the story ended the way it did. Responses were categorized as explaining the ending in terms of either the character's or the writer's intentions. An example of character's intentions is ". . .perhaps because the girl had kind of like told him the total truth. And he was just going to be like really topical with her, but then he kind of felt like he had to really tell her how he really felt about things and she kind of pressured him into it. Not pressured him into it, but made him feel like he could really tell her." An example of explaining the ending by reference to the writer's intentions is ". . .the writer was trying to say that a conversation could change one's whole life." The more generative psychology-label subjects tended to appeal to characters' intentions, while the action-label subjects cite writer's intentions, chi-square (1) = 5.227, *p* < .05.

Label	Writer's	Character's
Psychology	4	16
Action	11	9

A discourse analysis was also undertaken. Five words were distinctive to the psychology-label group, and six words to the action-label group (*p* < .05), as follows:

Psychology	Action
also	a
else	after
find	everything
not	man
wasn't	to
	young

The action list suggests a story defined by what happens at a moment when the protagonist meets with a crucial, and destabilizing, experience—and the plot reaches a turning point. *After* he meets a girl, a *young man* on his way to the seminary questions his calling, and *everything*. The presence of a structural feature in the turning point, and the subject's use of "and everything," which turns particular events into tropes that stand for whole categories of experience, both suggest that this construal sees the story as crafted into a particular form.

The psychology list suggests a story defined by the character's progressive mental life: what he *finds* out about whether he really wants to be a priest, or *not*, what *else* life has to offer. He *wasn't* really sure of his calling. In short, the landscape is entirely an interior one, and its pattern is given by the atemporal logic of psychological conflict that seems to take place outside the bounds of all story frames, in the person himself.

Our favored explanation to account for any observed genre label effect is that the different genre labels trigger different mental genre models. One alternative explanation, however, is that such genre labels only serve to foster alternative selections among the propositions that structure the story. Under that theory, subjects listening to the story with one genre label will attend to, select out, or remember one subset of the basic events of the story, while subjects given a different genre label will focus on others.

To test this "propositional difference" hypothesis, a sentence selection task was used. Subjects were given three sentences that described the three most basic plot elements of the story:

1. Charles is on vacation with his mother.
2. Charles is about to enter a seminary.
3. Charles takes the girl's hand as his mother approaches.

Then they were given eight other sentences that contain basic (psychological or action) plot elements of the story, and asked to select four to complete the story. The two groups did not differ in which propositions they used to complete the story outline.

To provide another test of the propositional difference hypothesis, responses to the "gist" question (question 1) were analyzed. Each response was coded for the presence of each of four basic story propositions:

1. Charles is going to be a priest.
2. Charles's mother wanted him to be a priest.
3. The girl influences Charles.
4. Charles realizes he doesn't know if he really wants to be a priest.

There were no group differences for subjects including these propositions in their gist summaries of the story. There was no overall difference between groups, nor did the groups differ on any of the individual propositions. This result also suggests that subjects were using the same basic propositional structure in their understanding of the story. We think then that our interpretive effects were not connected with basic plot understanding; they were purely a matter of interpretation.

The next study reports a parallel text manipulation. Twenty-four adults from the literate middle class were tested. The mean age was 30;3. Two versions of the story "Truth and Consequences" were used, as described in Feldman et al. (1990). The original, or "conscious," version included features of both action and consciousness and was comparable with the psychological label. The "nonconscious" version was the same story but with the psychological language deleted; it was comparable to the action label.

Each subject was read one version of the story. In this study, the reading was interrupted at fixed points, to ask the subjects questions about their interpretation of it. One-quarter of the way into the story, they were asked:

What is the most important thing I've told you so far?
Why?

One-third of the way into the story, those questions were asked again. Halfway through the story the following three questions were asked:

What are the directions this could be going?

Which way do you think it will go?
Why?

Just before the end of the story, they were asked the last three questions again.

After the story was finished, subjects were asked the final questions:
Tell me some things about this character that I haven't told you. What is he like?
Tell me the story now—the same story I told you, but in your own words.

Since the results from codes have been reported elsewhere (Feldman et al., 1990), we will just mention the main results here, and then move on to a new discourse analysis. First, conscious version interpretations are driven by the protagonist's psychological states, while action versions are not. Second, conscious versions are more temporal or diachronic, while thinking about the nonconscious version tends to be atemporal. Third, the conscious version interpretations contain more information beyond the given, and especially, more information about the protagonist and his development. Finally, although the versions elicited interpretive differences, retellings from the two groups contained the same number of basic plot events.

For a more detailed understanding of the subject's cognitive models, and particularly of what pattern they saw in the story versions, we turn now to a discourse analysis along the same lines as reported above. Seven words were significantly associated with the "conscious" group and seven with the "nonconscious" group ($p < .05$), as follows:

Conscious	Nonconscious
Charles	'cause
feeling	had
haven't	keep
herself	moment
named	questions
open	show
this	well

The conscious version elicited mental words (*feeling* and *open*), and a focus on character (*Charles*, *named*, and *herself*). The nonconscious version, in contrast, directs subjects' interest to narrative structure: *'cause*, *had*, *moment*, *questions*, *show*, and *well*. This division of labor is notably similar to the psychology/action label results reported above.

We next turn to how the same matters are handled by teenagers. Fourteen high-school-age subjects, with a mean age of 16;6, were recruited from a literary private high school. The same procedure was used as for the adult sample. Eight words were attributed to the "conscious" group, and 11 to the "nonconscious" group at $p < .05$.

Conscious	*Nonconscious*
actually	hair
Charles	hand
he'd	obviously
realize	off
realizes	outside
understanding	red
wanted	though
wants	together
	walk
	were
	which

The two versions are sharply different from one another, as they were in the adult sample, and they are distinguished along similar lines. But the specific form the distinction takes is very much affected by the relative youth, and, perhaps, interpretive inexperience. The conscious version again elicits Charles's name and a perhaps even more heavily psychological focus, seen in: *realize*(s), *understanding*, and want (*wants, wanted*). As was seen in the adults, narrative structure words appear in the nonconscious version (*were, which*). But they do not dominate the picture as before. Instead, it is dominated by the more concrete carriers of plotted action: *hair, hand, red, outside, together,* and *walk*.

Evidently, the adult psychological genre is an earlier acquisition than the adult action genre. For at this age, plot breaks down into very little more than its constituent specific actions. We will see this same precocity of psychological genres in still younger children, below. It suggests that mastering the narrative tools for the specific purpose of understanding other people's interior lives is something children are very motivated to do. And that is not so surprising when we consider that narrative patterns are really the only way of coming to a full understanding of the mental lives of others.

Both teenage versions are marked with hedges. The conscious version's *actually* is used to mark how the protagonist really feels inside. The nonconscious version's use of *obviously* and *though* marks an emergent understanding of the plot and of how earlier events constrain the range of possibilities for later ones. All the same there is a definiteness about *obviously* that can easily be seen as bravado in the face of confusion. It is almost as though we can hear the struggle in the effort after the nonconscious version's meaning in subjects of this age.

Finally, we explore the same matters in children. Twelve 10- to 12-year-old subjects, with a mean age of 11;8, were recruited from the same private local preparatory school as the teenagers were. The same procedure was used again. Eight words were attributed to the "conscious" group, and 11 were attributed to the "nonconscious" group ($p < .05$).

Conscious	*Nonconscious*
at	can
didn't	hand

everything	important
himself	make
how	they're
made	who's
maybe	
on	
realizes	
seem	
type	
up	
what's	

The children also distinguish the versions, but along only somewhat familiar lines. The conscious version has the only mental words, *realizes* and *didn't* (which modifies mental words), though they add up to a much thinner psychological interpretation. Moreover, the children's use of *himself* marks the boy as object (as well as his more obvious role as subject) of such thought. And the pattern has the flavor of a logical puzzle, as seen in the use of *how*. For these reasons, this genre is not well defined, nor entirely familiar. In fact, it contains some elements of the teens' nonconscious versions—e.g., the heavy use of prepositions (*at, on, up*) used to situate specific actions. (Conversely, the children's nonconscious version does not include the teens' action details.) Moreover, the children are very uncertain about what is happening in the protagonist's mind, and it shows up in their heavy use of hedges of uncertainty *maybe* and *seem*. They use *everything* and *type* to mark specific events as members of a not specifically labeled class or category of the plot. This suggests, among other things, that they are still hard at work on *constructing* the cultural canon for the conscious version at this age. Their uncertainty, then, would be because, as we have seen in the way their model mixes elements from the adult's conscious and nonconscious model, they have not yet mastered the culture's lexicon of canonical genres.

Though anomalous by adult standards, the children's construal of the conscious version nevertheless shows that they have something definite in mind—perhaps, something about how feelings are patterned in terms of classes and categories and the logical relations between them. Though surprising, this is not entirely implausible, for we have seen something of this kind in the crib speech of a three-year-old named Emmy as well (Feldman, 1989). It certainly suggests that the mental models for narrative interpretation are harder, or at least later acquired, than those for prediction in the physical world. It is as if, for children, the Galilean, rather counterintuitively, preceded the Aristotelian. That this is a general problem and not due to the special difficulties of understanding other people's mental states is suggested by the fact that for the action focused nonconscious version, the children's interpretations seem even more immature, indeed rather minimally structured, and only very faintly resemble adult models.

The children's words for interpreting the nonconscious version all refer to the same rather simple story about kinds of *people*, what they *can* do, what they are like (*who's* about to become a priest), and what *they're* up to together. Perhaps these categorical structures for people types are the crucible for later adult plot structure, which at its simplest is also categorical, though the categories in, for example, the structure of the folktale go way beyond such human types.

Educational Implications

We have tried, with this tour of the horizon, to give some empirical exemplification of the possibility of an empirical cognitive psychology of interpretive processes of knowing. Naturally, we are aware that these data are at best suggestive and illustrative, but they do tell us a few things we did not know before. It is plain that our subjects' interpretations are patterned, and that the interpretive patterns our subjects use are already part of their cognitive tool kit when they arrive at the testing room. Therefore we can think of their interpretations as being guided by mental (or cognitive) models (or patterns). Moreover, we can see that these mental models bear a striking resemblance to the genre patterns of literature in our subjects' cultural surround. The models that have become part of the cultural tool kit constrain what may go together, along some lines that can be thought of as principles of good construction (Goodman, 1978) or good form (see Koffka, 1935 for a discussion of the Gestaltist notion of *prägnanz*). Patently, there are many, and diverse, patterns of this kind available to the adult, far more than we have seen here; for it is extremely improbable that we just happened to stumble onto all of them.

That these mental models seem to correspond at many points to the literary principles for writing literature of the same kind is not surprising. The culture's generic tool kit is bound to influence our forms of understanding. That these mental models can be triggered by most minimal information from outside, whether given as label or by textual signals, leaves no doubt that they are known by the subject before encountering the text. And the fact that the same, or similar, models can be triggered in these two ways—by genre label and by textual signal, as well as by different stories—further suggests that the models are general or abstract. Finally, that the various models (to varying degrees) permit subjects to tell us things about the character we have not told them—that is, to generate information beyond the information given—tells us that they are generative.

There is reason to suppose that these interpretive models are rather late developmentally. Ten- to twelve-year-old children have genre models that look very little like those of adults, though they can be seen as a plausible, if somewhat confused, precursor. Moreover, there are seemingly age-related ways of interpreting conventional genres, with adolescent interpretation, particularly, finding the human condition more fatalistic than adults do (Feldman et al., 1994). Finally, interpretive models evoke different meanings without affecting the learning of the "bare facts" of the story, or their recall. What they affect is something more like weighting and placement, significance and sense.

The results of the various genre studies reported here, then, lead us to propose that genre instruction should be made much more explicit in the classroom, and in several ways. First, and most important, the variety of genres or, more generally, frames used now implicitly in the classroom should be marked by the teacher with explicit descriptions and terms that label them. This would be useful for two sets of frames commonly encountered in the classroom: (1) those related to different subject matters (math talk versus history talk; news reporting versus news interpreting), and (2) those related to different classroom tasks (recall for us what you read, digest it for us, interpret it in relation to what we said today, invent a fantasy world that incorporates its principles, create an artistic product that displays its mood). Based on the preservation of core events in the various genres of retelling reported above, there seems little reason to fear that being more explicit about such matters would divert effort away from mastery of the constituent facts. On the contrary, by making the frame explicit, and even seeing some sets of facts in the context of multiple frames, certain confusions about which facts are optional style markers and which essential might be resolved and lead students to a clearer sense of those elements constituting the core facts.

Marking the frame makes it possible at last to mark the core facts framed by it *as* facts. Thus the objective focus that we know teachers strive for would perhaps be assisted by clearer marking of a variety of frames. For at the moment, with unmarked frames, or a putatively "objective" frame (masking other frames in the background), the desirable goal of a focus on objective facts is displaced from the facts themselves onto the framework within which they are situated instructionally. Moreover, the effort to make content accessible with a neutral or frameless frame it seems to us could, for many sorts of material, make it much harder to learn, for it turns coherent bodies of knowledge into a list of disconnected *Jeopardy* items. This would be especially true of any knowledge that is by nature the result of an interpretive process, which is a surprising preponderance of classroom knowledge, certainly by junior high school. For example, bare facts of American history, such as the rupture of the country by the civil war, depend on understanding the interpretive frame with which the same events were viewed by multiple groups of contemporary actors. But it could be true of the less interpretive instruction of elementary school as well.

As adults we situate or locate facts in an interpretive framework (or theory) from which very often they are deeply connected by having been derived from it in the first place. We adults understand objective facts by being able to situate them in their era, their genre, their theory—in short in the framework that gives them life. We do this by acquiring knowledge of the culture, which is where knowledge frames are found that constitute culture itself. What the teacher's "neutral" frame does is to *conceal* the relevant adult interpretive framework (which would be the teacher's own as well) behind a mask of neutrality.

We believe that making use of the variety of school-relevant genres to offer the information contained within them would improve access to it for children much as it does for adults. School frames would be much simpler. Perhaps they should be seen not so much as constituents of the adult culture as constituents of the culture of the classroom, which, as many important observers have noted, has a culture of its own, with its own tasks and forms of life. We think that even in elementary school, some kind of simpler framing could be useful. We all know stories of children who describe being in a fog in those early years, unclear what the teacher's agenda was—in math, in writing, in civics. Sometimes students even say they understood what they were supposed to do on exercises enough to get them right, but they did not understand what they were *doing* when they did them. In a sense, this is an appeal for some frame information from the teacher, information about what form of life or purpose drives the low-level, and largely uninterpretive, tasks of early elementary school.

Would presenting such frames just confuse things further?[5] Would they just go onto the list of disconnected facts as one more fact? They would if they were not seen as frames. Is there an age before which they cannot be so seen? Or an age by intelligence interaction? And how would they be taught or offered? Obviously, there are questions in need of research here, and some real instructional problems since frame deletion is virtually the cardinal sign of expertise at present. There are some working examples around in this country (often those schools we think of as the "best" ones—including some inspired private schools, but also such outstanding models as Deborah Myers's in an unwealthy New York public school, already being replicated elsewhere). And there are more literary models elsewhere in the Western world. For example, the standard (and highly uniform) French high school curriculum considers important the interpretive modes of the adult culture.

If the relevant genre frames of the elementary classroom are rather simple, the relevant genre frames get more and more demanding as education progresses, and as interpretive sophistication, rightness, and skill become part of the required competence demanded of students. But the *habit* of genre removal and distrust that pervades American teaching carries right into the high school literature classroom and into modern algebra, where it is essential to any real competence. Now we ask for a variety of approaches without telling students what the various approaches are called or what the rules for their correct construction are. Good students may pick them up between the lines, good teachers may slip them in between the facts, but they are not taken seriously as what should be taught. And there is a real problem on the obverse face of this: without teaching the rules of good interpretive form, perhaps we give students the impression that only one reaction is a competent interpretation, or, its equally problematic obverse, that *any* reaction is. We hear that this latter view has injected itself into some postmodern curricula. At its most misleading it can suggest that interpretation is just a matter of how one happens to feel—that no informed critical thinking about interpretation is necessary or, at worst, even possible.

So with respect to high school, we believe that genres, theories, and frames of all sorts should be taught as cultural forms of construal that informed much literature and literary response in the past, as much by their orthodox expression as by the power to inform that comes from deviations from a known canon. And that canons are invented forms that become canonical when they are widely shared. We sketch some of these details here simply to note that neither genre, nor canon, is a straitjacket unless someone uses it that way and gets away with it. It should, we think, be obvious that being aware of the genre in use *as a genre in use*, something we might hope would result from more genre instruction, would be the best defense against such abuses.

With respect to lower grades, we suggests that the explicit marking or naming of the various classroom discourse frames that are used now implicitly in different subject areas and tasks would help the child begin to prepare for later interpretive instruction in genres in high school. We think it would, in addition, have benefits in the ease with which material is acquired in the early grades, for it would allow children to see the nature of each overall project more clearly, establish a separation of approach from content, and permit a clearer marking of the objective constituents to be mastered. It might even help some children begin to see how contents are related under a covering model.

Acknowledgments

This research took place in collaboration with Jerome Bruner. We acknowledge with gratitude the support of a grant from the Spencer Foundation, "Studies in Cultural Psychology," to Jerome Bruner.

Notes

1. Though even about this one may wonder. Canons have evolved all through literary time, each great artist pushing the old forms to new patterns. We might even suppose that canons have always had as their chief value that they make use of a recognized pattern chiefly so that they will be able to communicate deviations from it to the knowledgeable reader. The meaning making of literature, in this view, would rely largely on *deviations* from canon. But deviations, and their meaning, are presumably only appreciated by enculturated readers who know the canon they deviate from.
2. Two subjects were dropped from this analysis because they were outliers in the number of words per subject; that is, they talked much longer than the other subjects. For further details about the mechanics of this procedure, see the methodological appendix to Feldman et al. (1994).
3. Nearly all the words that were differently used by the two groups are used up by this account; there are only five words that did not fit into it, and these are generally too ambiguous to put anywhere. Of those words, *around* and *is* are from the "autobiography" group, while *a* and *on* are from the "fiction" group. They were of multiple and therefore indeterminate use. The only other word is the "autobiography" subjects' use of *picture*, which may have reflected something rather interesting, if it was not just an echo of something in one of our questions. It suggests that these subjects "see" the scene in the mind's eye, as they answer the questions. It suggests a more iconic, perhaps less highly symbolized, approach.
4. For further methodological discussion, see Feldman et al. (1994).

5. Olson (1994, pp. 229–230) points out that one can disguise content by adopting the style of a different genre. Defoe, he suggests, wrote *Robinson Crusoe* adopting the reportive style used by Robert Boyle for describing his experiments with the vacuum pump.

References

Bakhtin, M. (1986). *Speech genres and other late essays*. Austin: University of Texas Press.

Boden, M. A. (1990). *The creative mind: Myths and mechanisms*. New York: Basic Books.

Botheroyd, P. F. (1976). *Ich und er: First and third person self-reference and problems of identity in three contemporary German-language novels*. The Hague: Mouton.

Bruner, J. S. (1990). *Acts of meaning*. Cambridge: Harvard University Press.

Bruner, J. S. (in press). Does the cognitive revolution ever stop? In D. Johnson and C. Erneling (Eds.), *Reassessing the cognitive revolution: Alternative futures*. Oxford, England: Oxford University Press.

Cohn, D. (1968). K. enters *The castle*: On the change of person in Kafka's manuscript. *Euporion, 62*, 28–45.

Cuddon, J. A. (1991). *A dictionary of literary forms and literary theory* (3rd edn.). Oxford, England: Blackwell Reference.

d'Azevedo, W. L. (1962). Uses of the past in Gola discourse. *Journal of African History, 3* (1), 11–34.

Dennett, D. C. (1991). *Consciousness explained*. Boston: Little, Brown.

Duranti, A. (1993). Truth and intentionality: An ethnographic critique. *Cultural Anthropology, 8* (2), 214–245.

Dyson, X. (1995). Writing children. *Written Communication, 12*, 4–46.

Feldman, C. F. (1989). Monologue as problem-solving narrative. In K. Nelson (Ed.), *Narratives from the crib* (pp. 98–122). Cambridge: Harvard University Press.

Feldman, C. F. (1991). Oral metalanguage. In D. Olson and N. Torrance (Eds.), *Literacy and orality* (pp. 47–65). Cambridge, England: Cambridge University Press.

Feldman, C. F. (1992). On reading Paley. Special issue on Vivian Paley. F. Kessel (Ed.). *Quarterly Newsletter of the Laboratory for Comparative Human Cognition. 14* (3), 73–77. La Jolla: University of California at San Diego.

Feldman, C. F. (1994). Genres as mental models. In M. Ammaniti and D. N. Stern (Eds.), *Psychoanalysis and development: Representations and narratives* (pp. 111–121). New York: New York University Press.

Feldman, C. F., Bruner, J. S., and Kalmar, D. A. (1993). Reply to Olson and Salter's discussion. *Human Development, 36* (6), 346–349.

Feldman, C. F., Bruner, J. S., Kalmar, D. A., and Renderer, B. (1993). Plot, plight, and dramatism: Interpretation at three ages. *Human Development, 36* (6), 327–342.

Feldman, C. F., Bruner, J. S., Kalmar, D. A., and Renderer, B. (1994). Plot, plight, and dramatism: Interpretation at three ages (with a methodological appendix). In W. Overton and D. Palermo (Eds.), *The nature and ontogenesis of meaning*. Hillsdale, NJ: Lawrence Erlbaum.

Feldman, C. F., Bruner, J. S., Renderer, B., and Spitzer, S. (1990). Narrative comprehension. In B. Britton and A. Pellegrini (Eds.), *Narrative thought and narrative language* (pp. 1–78). Hillsdale, NJ: Lawrence Erlbaum.

Feldman, C. F., Stone, A., Wertsch, J., and Strizich, M. (1977). Standard and nonstandard dialect competencies of Hawaiian Creole English speakers. *TESOL Quarterly*, *11* (1), 41–50.

Feldman, C. and Toulmin, S. (1976). Logic and the theory of mind. *Nebraska Symposium on Motivation, 1975*, 409–476.

Feldman, C. F. and Wertsch, J. (1976). Context-dependent properties of teachers' speech. *Youth and Society*, *7* (3), 227–258.

Fodor, J. A. (1980). Methodological solipsism considered as a research strategy in cognitive psychology. *Behavioral and Brain Sciences*, *3*, 63–110.

Fowler, A. (1982). *Kinds of literature: An introduction to the theory of genres and modes*. Cambridge: Harvard University Press.

Frye, N. (1957). *Anatomy of criticism: Four essays*. Princeton: Princeton University Press.

Geertz, C. (1973). *The interpretation of cultures*. New York: Basic Books.

Gergen, K. J. (1991). *The saturated self: Dilemmas of identity in contemporary life*. New York: Basic Books.

Gill, B. (1961). Truth and consequences. In R. B. Goodman (Ed.), *Seventy-five short masterpieces: Stories from the world's literature*. New York: Bantam.

Goodman, N. (1978). *Ways of worldmaking*. Indianapolis: Hackett Publishing.

Kalmar, D. A. (1996). The effect of perspective on recall and interpretation of stories. Doctoral dissertation, Yale University.

Koffka, K. (1935). *Principles of gestalt psychology*. New York: Harcourt Brace and World.

Latour, B. and Woolgar, S. (1986). *Laboratory life*. Princeton: Princeton University Press.

Lewin, K. (1935). *A dynamic theory of personality*. New York: McGraw-Hill.

Nagel, T. (1986). *The view from nowhere*. New York: Oxford University Press.

Ochs, E., Smith, R., and Taylor, C. (1989). Dinner narratives as detective stories. *Cultural Dynamics*, *2*, 238–257.

Palincsar, A. S. and Brown, A. L. (1984). Reciprocal teaching of comprehension-fostering and comprehension-monitoring activities. *Cognition and Instruction*, *1* (2), 117–175.

Penrose, R. (1990). Précis of *The emperor's new mind: Concerning computers, minds, and the laws of physics*. *Behavioral and Brain Sciences*, *13*, 643–705.

Putnam, H. (1990). *Realism with a human face*. Cambridge: Harvard University Press.

Romberg, B. (1962). *Studies in the narrative technique of the first-person novel*. Stockholm: Almqvist and Wiksell.

Rosaldo, M. Z. (1980). *Knowledge and passion: Ilongot notions of self and social life*. Cambridge, England: Cambridge University Press.

Sansom, B. (1982). The sick who do not speak. In D. Parkin (Ed.), *Semantic anthropology* (pp. 183–195). London: Academic Press.

Searle, J. R. (1984). *Minds, brains and science*. Cambridge: Harvard University Press.

Searle, J. R. (1992). *The rediscovery of the mind*. Cambridge: MIT Press.

Shweder, R. A. (1991). *Thinking through cultures: Expeditions in cultural psychology*. Cambridge: Harvard University Press.

Snow, C. E. (1990). *The correlations of imponderables: Assessing relations between language proficiency and academic achievement*. Unpublished manuscript, Harvard University, Graduate School of Education.

Snow, C. E. and Dickinson, D. K. (1992). Skills that aren't basic in a new conception of literacy. In E. Jennings and T. Purvis (Eds.), *New conceptions of literacy* (pp. 179–218). Albany, NY: SUNY Press.

Stich, S. (1983). *From folk psychology to cognitive science: The case against belief*. Cambridge: MIT Press.

Toulmin, S. (1990). *Cosmopolis: The hidden agenda of modernity.* Chicago: University of Chicago Press.

von Wright, G. H. (1971). *Explanation and understanding.* Ithaca, NY: Cornell University Press.

Wellek, R. and Warren, A. (1962). *Theory of literature* (3rd edn.). New York: Harcourt Brace and World.

21

Habits of Mind for a Learning Society: Educating for Human Development

DANIEL KEATING

Education is fundamental to the success of any modern society. It is particularly central during periods of social transition, when the flexibility and adaptability of populations and institutions are most seriously challenged. In these circumstances, a society's ability to foster new skills, new concepts, and new patterns of learning depends heavily on its ability to renew educational institutions and practices.

There can be little doubt that we now face such challenges, arising from profound shifts in economic and social paradigms. Responding to these challenges requires that we understand three core dynamics. The first is the nature of the techno-economic paradigm shift that creates pressures and opportunities for social change. Although we cannot predict specific economic and social patterns with great confidence, we can learn much from the historic interplay between technological and social innovation (Keating, 1995b; Keating and Mustard, 1993).

The second core dynamic addresses the nature of educational institutions themselves. We need to understand how the current structures and practices evolved, and particularly how they may function as a system resistant to change. Our ability to guide educational transformation in a positive direction is dependent upon our ability to identify the points of leverage for such change (Keating, 1995a).

The third core dynamic focuses on our shifting understanding of the nature of human development. This dynamic is the key focus of the current volume. To the extent that our conceptual structures for thinking about human development and learning are incomplete or misguided, our ability to renew social and educational institutions in a progressive fashion is compromised. As the evidence accumulated in this book attests, the conceptual frameworks for understanding human development are undergoing significant revision (Keating, in press b, c; Task Force on Human Development, 1992). The fundamentally social nature of cognition and learning, the mutual feedback between individual and collective human development, and the role of developmental history in the shaping of human diversity are central themes in this revised understanding. Our ability to make significant progress in education depends on a fundamental shift in society's "folk psychology" of development and learning (Bruner, 1990).

These three core dynamics—social and economic transformation, education's role in that transformation, and our conceptual grasp of fundamental processes of human development—interact to define society's capacity for learning and adaptation. Together they comprise a complex social system that is difficult, but perhaps not impossible, to comprehend. Comprehension is made easier to the extent that we have a broad conceptual framework within which each dynamic is embedded, along with their interrelations. Comprehension of the full system is likely to be essential to progressive change in key social institutions, especially in periods of rapid change. We have been exploring the notion of a learning society as a potentially valuable conceptual framework for this task, including the question of how to build such a society (Keating, 1995a, b, in press a; Keating and Mustard, 1993; Task Force on Human Development, 1992).[1]

In this chapter, I briefly explore each of these key dynamics using the framework of a learning society as a focus. Based on this analysis, one major issue that requires rethinking is our understanding of human diversity, and how we should address that diversity in educational institutions.

Our traditional views of diversity are not only too limited in their scientific scope, but they are also an inadequate basis for building a learning society (Keating, 1995a, b, in press c). We need to find ways to encourage greater breadth and depth of competence throughout the population, in order to support a knowledge-based economy. We also need to accommodate the increasing human diversity arising from population dynamics that generate multicultural and metropolitan aggregations, and from political dynamics that highlight demands for more meaningful inclusion of previously marginalized sectors of the population.

The Information Revolution: Continuing Experiments with Civilization

The rapid social and economic changes we are encountering as we approach the twenty-first century present complex and unprecedented challenges to contemporary societies (Keating, 1995b; Keating and Mustard, 1993). Societies now must cope simultaneously with global economic competition, the demand for new competencies in the population, the provision of opportunities for health and well-being across the population, and the maintenance of the social fabric for nurturing, socializing, and educating the next generation. How well these requirements are met forms the foundations for future population health and competence, and hence economic prosperity.

The pace, magnitude, and complexity of social change are often perceived as overwhelming and uncontrollable. This perceived lack of control may in turn distort other perceptions, further diminishing our ability to respond and adapt to change. This core dynamic—accelerating change and decreasing sense of control—makes thoughtful planning and reform difficult to achieve.

Breaking this cycle may be aided by a combined evolutionary and historical perspective that takes note of the fundamentally social nature of *Homo sapiens* and of the highly variant patterns of organizing human social life.

We are a social species. We play, work, interact, learn, and reproduce in social groups throughout our lives. We develop in social relationships from the earliest period of life, and we remain dependent longer on caretaking for our survival than any other primate. At our core, then, we need social groups to survive. Our early experiences—most of which occur through social interactions—play a critical role throughout life in how we cope, how we learn, and how competent we become. The nature of the social environment in which we develop is thus a key determinant of our quality of life. Diverse life outcomes—positive and negative— are closely associated with identifiable differences in early social experiences.

In turn, the quality of the human social environment is a function of the competence that is available within the society. The nurture, education, and socialization of new members of the group depend on the skills and commitment of more mature members, and on social arrangements that facilitate high quality interactions between generations.

Although these demands are not historically new, we face additional challenges unknown even to our recent ancestors. Although we share much in common with our primate cousins, humans are unique in having developed the capabilities of conscious self-reflection, cultural transmission of skills and knowledge through language and other symbolic means, cumulative technological development, and civilization. In evolutionary terms, these are quite recent changes in our lives (Keating, 1995b; Keating and Mustard, 1993).

We can get a better sense of this recency using a calendar-year analogy. If we take 100,000 years as an estimate of the time elapsed since the emergence of fully modern humans, and place it on the scale of a single year, we would note that our species first moved into small urban centers, supported by agriculture, about the end of November, and started an industrial revolution on the afternoon of New Year's Eve. Just a few minutes ago, we launched experiments in instantaneous global communication, information technology, and multicultural metropolism. This recency is further exaggerated if we start our hypothetical year with the appearance of the tool-making hominid line from which we derive, in which case the correct baseline is in the millions of years.

The origins and mechanisms of this evolutionary process remain controversial, but several important features have gained fairly broad consensus. To grasp the first feature, consider the social sophistication of nonhuman primates. Our complex social arrangements and behaviors are not merely a function of cultural experiences; other primates are also skilled social strategists (Tomasello, Kruger, and Ratner, 1993). Much of our intuitive understanding of how to function in groups thus has a lengthy evolutionary history. We added new language capabilities to this already rich social mix, yielding apparently infinite potential for complex communication. Language enables much more complex social communication, and perhaps arises initially out of a need to maintain cohesion in larger groups (Donald, 1991; Dunbar, 1992). The larger group size may have contributed economic benefits of organization and specialization of work, permitting more effective exploitation of harsh habitats and a primitive form of shared risk.

The teaching and learning of special skills were also enhanced by language, and technological development ensued. This unification of instrumental and symbolic functions is apparently unique to *Homo sapiens*. Vygotsky (1978) proposed this unification of language and tool use as the starting point of fully human intelligence, both phylogenetically and ontogenetically. Humans drew on their increasing symbolic and instrumental sophistication (that is, language and tool use) to establish connections *between* troops and tribes. We can date the origins of this pattern rather precisely to about 40,000 years ago (Stringer and Gamble, 1993), using as evidence the remarkable explosion of symbolic forms (particularly art) and the rapid spread of more complex stone technologies, which had been previously unchanged for a million years or more.

The accelerating pace of technological and social change is thus based on our unique penchant for collaborative learning across formerly rigid group boundaries. Our ability to encode and enhance this learning through progressively more efficient cultural means—oral histories, formal instruction, writing, and now information technologies—contributes directly to this acceleration. Changes in the means of communication have nontrivial consequences for cognitive activity—how we think, what we know, and how we learn.

A well-understood example is the connection between the practice of literacy and the development of logic, argument, reflection, and metacognitive understanding (Cole and Scribner, 1974; Olson, 1994). As literacy spreads, so do literate habits of mind.

Modes of teaching and learning also evolve in response to these broad social and technological shifts, as in the ascendance of "book learning" over hands-on apprenticeship. Because evolutionary changes are by definition trial and error, we cannot be assured that any given historical trend in education is beneficial rather than harmful. Dewey's (1963) cogent criticism of formal education as overly abstract and insufficiently practical spoke to this concern, a concern echoed in many contemporary educational critiques (Bruner, 1960; Lave, 1988; Rogoff, 1990). As the pace of change accelerates, there may be insufficient time for societal adaptation by trial and error. In these circumstances, understanding the core dynamics in order to guide progressive change becomes more critical.

The combination of a new technology for communication with new capabilities in the population creates a potent new medium for discourse among previously isolated groups and individuals, and thus new opportunities for innovation. In concert with changes in social communication (such as language, literacy, and information technology), we have continued to discover new means for extracting material subsistence from the earth. The agricultural revolution first made possible the congregation and settled existence of large groups of humans in specific places over a long period of time (that is, cities). The production demands of agricultural societies were such that a relatively large proportion of the population was needed to provide physical energy directly into the system. Thus only a small portion of the population was directly involved in the acquisition and expansion of knowledge that was potentiated by the agricultural revolution. Literacy and numeracy, for example, remained rare skills over long historical periods—and into the present in less affluent societies.

The next major revolution in social forms occurred very recently. The industrial revolution removed human labor from the direct energy loop required for material production (Rosenberg, 1986) but created a demand for ever more complex arrangements for the division of labor. We see again that the technological innovations were dependent upon concomitant changes in social structures and practices.

These examples illustrate the ongoing, mutually causal interplay between technological and social innovation. This may be difficult to visualize initially, as we are more accustomed to linear or main-effect models, in which an isolated cause yields a specific outcome (Keating, in press c; Senge, 1990). But as we trace four major transformations in our species' history, we can see that changes in technology generate demands and opportunities for changes in societal functioning, and changes in society generate demands and opportunities for technological innovation:

1. Language and complex social communication (100 to 50K years before present [BP]; Donald, 1991)
2. Intertribal communication and cultural exchange (about 40K years BP)
3. The agricultural revolution and settled urban civilizations (10K years BP)
4. The industrial revolutions (0.5 to 0.1K years BP), from steam to electrical.

Another such transformational moment seems to be upon us, in the form of existing information technologies—instantaneous global communication, unlimited knowledge storage and retrieval, sophisticated techniques for data analysis and simulation, and artificially intelligent design with robotic manufacture.

Unique among species, then, we have created what systems theorists call an iterative feedback loop between our ways of using material resources and the ways in which we organize our social lives. This new pattern of cultural and social change continually reshapes the ecological habitats in which we live and work—and in which subsequent generations will develop (Keating and Mustard, 1993). Developing an educational system to respond to these demands requires us to attend simultaneously to the broad historical forces that have shaped human development, to the fundamental processes of individual and collective human development, and to the nature of contemporary educational practices.

The Transformation of Education

Criticism of contemporary education in North America has become commonplace, sometimes growing to seemingly desperate levels. Yet little substantive change has occurred. This can be attributed to several sources.

First, and too often overlooked, is the inherent stability of large and complex self-organizing systems. This inertia arises not from the complicity or apathy of educators, as often believed, but rather because the institutions and practices that have evolved over a long period are interlocking and self-sustaining. Our loyalty to a credentialing function, for example, makes it difficult to adapt instruction in ways that would be beneficial to the development of expertise (Keating, 1990a,

1991). Thus making changes to any part of the system implies changes to many other aspects of the system.

This leads directly to the second obstacle: the proliferation of simplistic or faddish solutions that engage energy but ultimately fail to make a difference. One example can be found in programs designed to enhance critical thinking as a simple set of teachable skills—rather than as a coherent way of engaging the world that requires such skills, plus content knowledge, personal dispositions, emotional commitments, and productive patterns of social interaction (Keating, 1990c, 1991). Limited solutions such as these appear to be based on exclusive consideration of main effects—if only this aspect could be changed, then other problems would be solved. Addressing these complex issues requires instead that we understand the dynamics of the full system as it actually functions.

A third obstacle is that proposed solutions often focus on the past rather than the present and future. Conscious adaptation requires anticipation, and will likely fail if changes are designed to solve historic rather than contemporary dilemmas, and if they do not recognize the opportunities for innovation afforded by ongoing technological and social revolutions.

One further and quite major obstacle is the perceived conflict between two ways of identifying the core problem. This conflict is usually portrayed as a forced choice between excellence and equity. Defenders of excellence usually focus on declining standards in education as the culprit, whereas proponents of equity usually see those very standards as the source of the problem.

Back to Basics

The first group focuses on how well we are doing as a society in developing the expertise and learning skills that we will need to be globally competitive in an economic sense. The striking differences between North America and Asia in mathematical achievement—a cornerstone skill of the new knowledge-based economies in the view of many observers—are particularly troubling (Stevenson and Stigler, 1992). In addition the apparent downward secular trend in overall academic performance across successive cohorts of North American students in the past several decades has raised concerns about potential deterioration of educational standards.

One popular response to this concern can be described as "back to basics." The identified culprit is that academic standards have been diluted in several ways: the inclusion of groups who are not well prepared for instruction delivered in the traditional way; the inclusion of topics involving personal or social life experiences, taking time away from academic fundamentals; and the increasing social resistance to any form of grading or judging that could diminish a student's sense of self-esteem, as in the use of "social promotions" for students who have not mastered the material at their current grade level.

This critique is frequently paired with a belief that mainstreaming of special education students is a particular burden, both in how it affects classroom dynamics and in how it draws scarce resources away from children without identified special needs. The preferred solution in this view is to return to a perceived past in which educational practices were undiluted in these ways. The golden past to which this view alludes never existed in quite the way it is remembered.

In any case, merely recreating the *status quo ante* is unlikely to be sufficient for future needs, not least because the substantive demands are increasing. Facility with rapidly shifting information technologies is an obvious example of a new expectation. Furthermore, our existing educational system was built on the premise that we would likely need only a small elite with the skills to guide the efforts of the mass of population, which needed only a modicum of familiarity with formal learning.

The new economies may well depend on a much greater depth and breadth of population competence in order to function well. When limited skills were economically adequate, a high discard rate could be tolerated—economically, if not humanely. Failure to develop our human resources as fully as possible in the future, however, may hamper our potential to become a knowledge-based economy.

Standards as the Culprit

The competing view sees schools as the core of the problem, rather than as any possible route to a solution. In this view, it is the schools themselves that dampen an innate desire for learning, through a relentless message of comparative failure. Historically less powerful groups are systematically told they are less competent, or even incompetent, relative to mostly arbitrary performance standards.

Since the standards are themselves biased, according to this view, the sense of failure is largely illusory and serves mainly to reproduce existing power relations in society. The core problem, then, is too much emphasis on standards, not too little; too much emphasis on excellence and elites, and too little concern with equity and diversity.

The current educational crisis surrounding the teaching of exceptional learners is a prime example of the need for a revised understanding of diversity in human development, and how we can address that diversity productively in formal education (Keating, 1990a, 1991, 1995a; see also M. Clay, this volume, chap. 10).

Several basic assumptions sparked the special education movement that has had a dramatic impact on shaping educational practice since the mid-1960s. The first was a fundamental human rights issue, that all children should have access to appropriate educational experiences. The second arose from the fact that most excluded students could be readily identified by organic deficits, particularly mental retardation, sensory impairments, and physical disabilities. Flowing from this was the adoption of a deficit model, in which special arrangements would be needed to accommodate these previously excluded students.

The provision of special educational resources represented one of the few growth areas in educational budgets. This coincided historically with a growing concern over the increased numbers of children who were performing lower than expected or desired but who did not suffer any overt disability in the organic sense.

The unforeseen consequence of this conjunction of events—quite understand-able retrospectively—was a movement to expand the notion of special education to include a much broader range of underperforming students. To qualify for the newly available resources, it was necessary to posit some specific deficit internal to the child. The research on learning disabilities has historically been driven more by this political agenda than by sound scientific evidence (Keating, 1995a; see also Stanovich and Stanovich, this volume, chap. 7).

One dramatic illustration of this peculiar dynamic was the political aggregation of parental pressure groups whose primary goal—securing adequate educational resources for their children—was transformed into an actual goal of having their children declared deficient in some specific fashion, so as to gain access to the resources. That this historical transformation could have occurred so readily is a testimony to the seeming "naturalness" of internal deficit models.

Reconstructing the historical logic is relatively straightforward: Normative educational practices are adequate to accommodate normally developing children. The exclusion of children with overt disabilities is unacceptable; to include them, however, requires the provision of additional educational resources. At the same time, we become concerned with the lack of performance among many children who do not have overt disabilities. If, however, they do not benefit from normative educational practices, then we can assume that they have some covert disability. If we construct such a category of covert disability, then we can justify the provision of resources to those children.

These distortions do not occur only on the political level, however. One of the most frequent research designs in the area of learning disabilities is the comparison of normal children with those who are identified as learning disabled (categorized in that way using widely divergent criteria across studies). Such comparisons usually entail the administration of some cognitive task or test to both groups, with the virtually inevitable result that the LD children are significantly worse. The result then leads to two simultaneous inferences: (1) the LD category is valid; and (2) the observed differences can be causally attributed to the deficiency.

Stated in this simple (but not oversimplified) fashion, the fatuity and tautology of the inferences are obvious. Children who are identified as performing more poorly than average on most tasks will perform more poorly than average on a related task. Very few studies are designed to test a specific hypothesis about the origin or nature of the presumed disability. When more rigorous criteria are used, the proportion of labeled LD children who appear to have specifiable cognitive processing differences is much smaller.

This critique does not imply that children are identical in their fundamental attentional or learning processes. Such differences surely exist, and just as surely are a conjoint product of organic factors (such as infant temperament and attentional processes) in interaction with diverse social and interpersonal environments, beginning with the earliest interpersonal interactions.

But diversity exists throughout the population, not just as a unilinear criterion of competence versus deficit. Our predilection to arrange educational practices as if this unilinear model were actually true is a function of historical contingency, not scientific evidence.

Table 21.1 *Characteristics of education in the industrial and information ages*

	Industrial age	Information age
Pedagogy	Knowledge transmission	Knowledge building
Prime mode of learning	Individual	Collaborative
Educational goals	Conceptual grasp for the few, basic skills and algorithms for the many	Conceptual grasp and intentional knowledge building for all
Nature of diversity	Inherent, categorical	Transactional, historical
Dealing with diversity	Selection of elites, basics for broad population	Developmental model of lifelong learning for broad population
Anticipated workplaces	Factory models, vertical bureaucracies	Collaborative learning organizations

Source: Keating (1995a).

A similarly misguided belief system operates among some proponents of a mainstreaming model of education. This is an unanalyzed hope that mere inclusion of students who have been previously excluded will solve their problems, and have only beneficial impact on the student population as a whole. We need to recognize, instead, how complex a task it is to design a working system that supports developmental progress for all students. It is a task that requires considerable research and innovation on many related fronts (Keating, 1990a, 1995a). This is as true for meeting the needs of developmentally advanced students as it is for students with a wide array of learning difficulties (Keating, 1991, 1995a).

From the perspective of a learning society, we can recognize the legitimate concerns of those who identify excellence or equity as the key issue. We can go a step further, however, and examine ways in which excellence and equity are complementary rather than competing pressures. This is assisted by a revised understanding of human learning and development. Such a revision would focus on the developmental supports for learning that each child requires, and on the fundamentally social nature of learning that affords collaborative learning opportunities to individuals at different levels of expertise (Bereiter and Scardamalia, this volume, chap. 22; Keating, 1990a, 1991).

We can perhaps grasp the impact of these broad social forces for contemporary educational practice through a comparison of educational perspectives that evolved in the industrial age with those that may serve us better in an information age. Table 21.1 summarizes some of the key contrasts (Keating, 1995a).

Information technology, especially networking, reduces the absolute value of acquired knowledge, because it is so readily available (Keating, 1995b). Advantages thus accrue to those whose goal is knowledge building (Scardamalia and

Bereiter, 1993). This is further enhanced when the knowledge building is collaborative rather than strictly within the individual.

The goals of course are quite different. In an industrial era, only a few people were required to plan and innovate (the "heads"), whereas the masses were expected merely to execute repetitive tasks (the "hands"). An educational system in such a regime ideally functions as an honest selection mechanism, to ensure that the best and brightest become heads. This never worked well in practice. Schools are deeply embedded in society and thus tended to reproduce social class distinctions based on nonrelevant factors, especially social class and gender.

In any case, this selection mechanism may be far less relevant in an information age. Positions in bureaucracies are far less stable, credentials are less valuable as a guarantee of social status, and the nature of work is changing rapidly. The decimation (or more) of middle management in both the private and public sectors is but one example of this. Enterprises and organizations capable of adapting to rapidly shifting conditions will become more dominant.

To support this, we need to expand competence more broadly and deeply through the population than we have been able to do previously. In this regard, the tensions between excellence and equity, between proponents and opponents of traditional standards, and between regular and special education, take on a new character. We need to base *all* education on a more explicit and conceptually sophisticated developmental model.

The Sources of Diversity: Traditional Versus Developmental Views

In a previous discussion, I summarized the core conceptual distinctions in this way:

Those individuals who give evidence of being best *adapted* to current social and educational practices, revealed in test scores and school performance, are defined in the categorical model as most generally *adaptable* (that is, intelligent) due to a more optimal underlying design. A consequence of this conflation of two quite different meanings is the assumption that educational difficulty is legitimately explained as a failure of adaptability of the student.

From a developmental perspective, we would recognize that success in a particular ecological. . .niche is not necessarily a sign of adaptability to a wide range of niches. Moreover, we are more likely to look for ways in which the instructional environment has failed to adapt to the developmental diversity that differential histories inevitably generate. By shifting the onus from a lack of adaptiveness in the child to a lack of adaptiveness in the setting, we can begin a close examination of the ways to design better learning environments, rather than simply demarcating presumed design flaws in the child. (Keating, 1990a, p. 264).

Theories of human intelligence that place the greatest emphasis on the heritability of individual differences stress the importance of evolutionary history (and thus the contextual factors that operate through natural selection) in shaping the distribution of genetic factors that influence phenotypic (observed) diversity

(Eysenck, 1988; Galton, 1892/1962). In contrast, theories of intelligence that focus on the diversity that arises from different life experiences emphasize the contextual contingencies that operate on individuals (Hunt, 1961).

This traditional dichotomy between nature and nurture—that is, inheritance or genetic accounts versus environmental or experiential accounts—has often obstructed understanding. Given the stark contrast between these two views of the world, it is not surprising that the conflict between them has been heated, in all spheres—scientific, political, cultural. What is more disheartening is that the scientific argument has not moved much beyond the political one in many respects, even though the inaccuracy of this bipolar debate has been recognized for some time (Anastasi, 1958). Apportioning variance between these competing factors has become more complex as the precision of these estimates increases (Plomin and Thompson, 1988).

For the functioning organism, of course, these influences are never dichotomous, but instead are fully integrated during ontogenesis. A good example of this integration arises from current work that demonstrates the key impact of experiential history on the sculpting of fundamental neural, immune, and hormonal patterns (Cynader, Shaw, Prusky, and Van Huizen, 1990; Suomi, 1991). Historically, less effort has gone toward the construction of robust developmental accounts of *how* these two substantive influences give rise to the observed diversity in human intellectual performance.

To do so, researchers of both persuasions need to shift their focus beyond the apportionment of isolated effects, toward the more complicated task of describing the dynamic interaction of multiple influences over the course of human development (Anastasi, 1986; Bronfenbrenner and Ceci, in press; Green, 1992).

Some past confusion can also be traced to the failure to distinguish between contextual factors in ontogenesis that are associated with intellectual development in general versus those that are associated with the observed diversity in intellectual accomplishment.

A useful distinction can be drawn here between capacities and capabilities, a distinction that is masked by the omnibus term "mental abilities." Literacy offers a helpful example. It is obvious that the vast majority of humans have the capacity to become literate, given the appropriate experiential contingencies. Previously illiterate populations demonstrate high proportions of literacy with the advent of schooling, rapidly becoming capable of reading.

Due to theoretical assumptions prevailing in the early history of empirical research on human intelligence (for example, Terman, 1916), these two constructs—capacity and capability—were conflated, in the belief that attained capabilities were reliable estimates of fundamental intellectual capacity (Keating, 1990c). Recent efforts to disentangle these notions, in order to achieve purer, more reliable estimates of fundamental capacity *independent* of ontogenetic influences—such as information-processing capacity or neural efficiency—have generated mixed results (Ceci, 1990; Hunt, 1978; Sternberg, 1990).

We have argued that the case for "pure" information-processing parameters has yet to be made successfully (Keating, List, and Merriman, 1985; Keating and

MacLean, 1987). The natural processes of developmental integration make it difficult to disentangle these influences, stressing again the need to examine in much greater detail the nature of human diversity as a developmental phenomenon (Gardner, 1983; Keating, in press b, c).

In summary, the debate in this area has operated as a reverberating cycle between positions labeled as "nature" versus "nurture." Our increasing understanding of the fundamental inseparability of these two broad categories—that is, organisms have built-in structure arising from phylogenetic history; ontogenesis always occurs in a physical and social environment that impacts on development—the continuing devolution of an important question into an either/or decision likely reflects the presence of hidden barriers to progress in our understanding.

Some of the barriers that impede our understanding of human diversity in intellectual functioning arise from overly simple ideologies and methodologies. Theoretical advances in our understanding of developmental processes, and methodological progress in our ability to study such processes empirically, create the opportunity to move these questions beyond the traditional dichotomies.

In so doing, we should first acknowledge the robust empirical evidence about human diversity that we have acquired using traditional models. Among the best established empirical findings in the behavioral and social sciences are the robust covariance structures of performance on a wide range of cognitive and intellectual tasks (Keating and MacLean, 1988). We may usefully remind ourselves how pervasive these covariance patterns are. In a sufficiently heterogeneous population, positive correlations across a wide variety of cognitive tasks are virtually assured. As well, mean increases in performance with age during the childhood and adolescent years are observed on virtually all cognitive tasks (Case, 1992).

In addition to these robust patterns of individual and age covariance, there are of course stable group differences on many measures of cognitive performance. Patterns associated with demographic indicators, including social class, ethnicity, and gender, have been regularly reported. Organic trauma or genetic anomalies, such as brain lesion or Down syndrome (Cicchetti and Beeghly, 1990), are also reliably related to cognitive performance differences. Patterns of individual differences have also been grouped into diagnostic categories, such as learning disability.

What are the sources of this diversity? The empirical regularity of the patterns described above has contributed to a presumption—among some scientists and the public at large—that a simple and overarching design principle must be responsible. Often, this presumption takes the form of a belief in underlying organismic differences (such as neural efficiency, capacity, or power) as the fundamental source of observed differences.

We should hesitate to make this inferential leap. Empirical efforts to isolate cognitive processing variance from knowledge-base variance, and vice versa, have encountered substantial methodological obstacles. The evidence for uncontaminated measures of either hypothetical source remains unpersuasive (Keating and Crane, 1990; Keating, List, and Merriman, 1985; Keating and MacLean, 1987; Morrison, Morrison, and Keating, 1992). Covariance patterns alone, no matter how robust, are insufficient to demonstrate the operation of any specific mechanism.

This example illustrates the confusion that often arises between data structures and inferred mental structures. The two are not the same. Presumably, robust patterns in cognitive performance data must reflect some coherent source, but this does not necessarily imply that there is an organismic structure homologous with any particular data structure. Borrowing from evolutionary logic, we observe the surface similarity but structural dissimilarity between, say, bats and birds, and the surface dissimilarity but structural homology between spiders and crabs.

To get at homologies, we need to uncover the underlying processes and their histories (Keating, 1990a). This entails one further understanding: the impact of experience is also constrained by internal structures that are shaped by both phylogeny and ontogeny. In other words, humans are not infinitely plastic, and remedial experience is not always fully effective.

The historical conflict between dichotomous positions has unnecessarily constrained theory, practice, and research methods that seek to address important questions about human diversity. We need to know more than how to apportion the amount of influence exerted by two competing categories, each of which is so broad as to be almost wholly uninformative. We need to know *how* human competence and human coping actually develop as self-organizing dynamic systems. We need to move beyond these traditional dichotomies in order to generate a coherent conceptual understanding of developmental diversity that is methodologically rigorous, empirically sound, and practically useful for educational transformation.

Research Methods: Toward Developmental Integration

The inherited ability and the environmentalist positions on human diversity have often been interpreted as though the main effects were the ones that truly mattered. But both interpretations ignore the central reality: The only truly causal pathways are embedded in the transactions between the organism and the environment over time.

Both [correlational and experimental] methods favor main effects over interactions, whereas the development of all aspects of life. . .involves an interaction of heredity with environment. But dissecting that interaction will require a level of detail and precision not now available. (Green, 1992, p. 331)

One problem in pursuing this research agenda is thus its seemingly overwhelming complexity. The number of potentially important factors and their interactions expands exponentially as we take higher-order interactions into account, and even more so if we examine the multiplicative interactions of those factors across time. Beginning with even a small set of factors, we rapidly approach an effectively infinite set of possible causal arrangements, at least some of which will be indistinguishable on the basis of statistical fit to a model (Glymour, Scheines, Spirtes, and Kelly, 1987).

Can we hope to deal with this level of complexity? We must learn to do so, if we hope to address pressing theoretical and practical questions. Specifically, we need to create a developmental methodology for integrating analyses from many sources in a robust fashion (Gould, 1986; Keating, in press c).

Paradoxically, dissecting the interaction should be as interesting to pure nature as to pure nurture types. To be viewed as causal, behavior genetic accounts ultimately require a developmental account of how that genetic variation is translated into behavior. In other words, available behavior genetic evidence speaks to the fact *that* genetic variation is implicated in behavioral variation, not with *how* that connection is established.

One possible explanation is that genetic variability codes directly for neural efficiency in some way. Given the fascinating evidence now emerging on neural sculpting and reorganization that occurs as a function of the transaction of the organism with the environment, direct coding for size, capacity, or efficiency is an assumption that no longer seems tenable (for example, Chang and Greenough, 1982; Cynader et al., 1990; Turner and Greenough, 1985). It is also worth noting that heritability varies with the age of the group in which it is examined, suggesting that the developmental routes of genetic expression are unlikely to preserve one-to-one correspondence with particular phenotypic characteristics (Plomin and Thompson, 1988).

Another behavior genetic candidate for the understanding of diversity in competence is temperament, which does show stable variation very early in infancy. But again, the temperament of the infant interacts with characteristics of the primary caregiver (usually the mother), so that a one-to-one correspondence between infant temperament and later behavioral outcome seems implausible. Genetically controlled experimental studies of *Rhesus macaques* show this interaction quite clearly, in that genetically hyperreactive (and thus highly vulnerable) infant monkeys cross-fostered to experienced and highly nurturant mothers are more likely than normal infants to become group leaders (Suomi, 1991).

To advance our understanding of human diversity, then, we shall need to examine in greater detail the history of interactions between the organism and the environment. In this investigation, our evolutionary heritage, especially our primate histories, are directly relevant. Numerous examples come quickly to mind.

The socially shared nature of much cognitive activity, of increasing practical importance (Resnick, Levine, and Teasley, 1991), implicates interpersonal relationships and social competence. Our primate history as a social species thus plays an important role in competence and productivity (Suomi, 1991). In addition, the major role of emotional aspects in cognition has been emphasized in recent work (Oatley and Jenkins, 1992), which in turn invoke psychoneuroimmune links (Kiecolt-Glaser and Glaser, 1991).

Integrating human development so as to encompass all these histories—evolutionary, cultural, ontogenetic—requires that many specific methods be used. Each of these methods needs to be critically examined for its ability to permit robust inferences, but we should not assume that we can define robustness with paradigmatic criteria.

Progress in methodology has changed the way we can investigate human intelligence (Keating, in press c). To reflect this shift, I often use the term developmental diversity as a more inclusive one than individual differences, which implies a primary origin within the individual, rather than a historical transaction between the person and a cognitively socializing habitat.

What shape might a developmental integration on human intelligence take? Recognizing that history is always contingent, contextualists never predict the future with certainty. But odds now favor efforts to weave these strands into a coherent story of human development, in all its diversity. Our attempt to tell a developmentally integrated story (Keating, 1990c; Keating and MacLean, 1988) begins with the premise that human intelligence is a dynamic system, at two major levels: populations and individuals.

It grows increasingly clear that knowledge of all types—practical, scientific, theoretical—is always a social and cultural product. As advanced information technologies spread, the social nature of knowledge becomes ever more apparent. The emerging picture of science as a collaborative and cumulative discourse captures the essence of one key self-organizing social system. Differences among societies in how well they are able to make use of the social nature of knowledge may determine, in part, how effective they will be in building successful, innovation-based economies.

In other words, socially distributed intelligence may become increasingly central to societal success. It depends in turn on the diversity of talent available in the population *and* on the ways in which human groups interact to become units of learning.

Human intelligence is also a self-organizing system at the individual level. A handful of critical elements are essential to the story (Keating, 1990c; Keating and MacLean, 1988). A first principle of dynamic systems—behavioral, biological, or physical—is that they display the capacity to become organized over time, even from ill-formed or chaotic origins. An important corollary is that infinitely elaborate and formally elegant structures can arise from simple feedback processes operating over time. This arises from four central features of dynamic systems, two of them describing functions and two others describing the operational context: (1) the process must iterate routinely; (2) the process must have a feedback loop; (3) the context includes internal constraints that shaped the system—for organisms, their phylogenetic and the ontogenetic history to date; and (4) the context sets the external constraints that limit and shape the actual self-organization that takes place (Keating, 1990b; Keating and MacLean, 1988).

These principles can then define a general developmental function. The history of developmental interactions is incorporated into organismic structures. As in the evolution of species, an individual's future is never fully determined by the past, but it is always constrained by it. Several consequences follow from the nonlinear nature of dynamic systems. We should expect causes and effects to be multidimensional, and often mutually causal. Also, the magnitudes of causes and effects will not always be commensurate. Indeed, the timing of even minor events may lead to a cascade of other events whose outcome for the individual was far greater than the seeming magnitude of its origin.

Habits of Mind: Developmental Diversity in Competence and Coping

One of the crucial discoveries in recent studies of cognitive development is the fundamental nonindependence of cognitive activities from their content and context. An equivalent, more positive term for this nonindependence is connected, or perhaps even better, integrated cognitive activity. To locate homologous structures in cognitive activity, we need to study its ontogenesis along with its current functioning. This requires much more than looking at the correlation of age with cognitive performance, since that reflects in large part the averaging effects of cognitive socialization environments. We need to study the dynamic interactions among emerging cognitive structures and the cognitive socialization niches within which they develop (Ceci, 1990; Keating, 1990c; Resnick et al., 1991; Rogoff and Lave, 1984). For some time, we have been exploring the developmental processes—especially in infancy, childhood, and adolescence—that underlie competence, both in specific expertise and in general habits of mind.

In seeking to account for the early growth of conceptual knowledge, we need to be aware of Gibsonian phenomenological priors that constrain how we see the world, and how these pre-attuned perceptual patterns are shaped by experiences during infancy into basic conceptual structures (Keating and MacLean, 1988; MacLean and Schuler, 1989). Intuitive conceptions and misconceptions acquired early in life interact differentially with schooling experiences; these interactions are another potent source of developmental diversity (Gardner, 1983; Keating and Crane, 1990).

Understanding these interactions is aided by detailed investigations into the role of automaticity; the organization and content of procedural and declarative knowledge; the function of self-regulating cognitive activities (like metacognttive strategies or control processes); and social, emotional, and motivational factors, all of which influence the development of intelligence. The links among emotion regulation, attention regulation, and performance appear to emerge quite early in development, during the first year of life (Lewis, 1993; MacLean, Keating, Miller, and Keenan, 1995).

We need to study how these various aspects of cognitive activity become coordinated over time as individuals develop expertise and competence (Keating, 1990a; Keating, List, and Merriman, 1985; Keating and MacLean, 1987). One potential outcome of an integrative approach is the detailed description of pathways to the development of expertise (Keating, 1990a). The long-lived controversy between general and specific theories of intelligence, seen in developmental terms, becomes productive rather than unresolvable (Keating and Crane, 1990). For example, even among adolescents who are in the top 5 percent of the general intelligence dimension, there are diverse and highly consistent patterns of competence (linguistic, social, technical) that are also strongly associated with "noncognitive" factors such as goals, future aspirations, out-of-school activities, and perceived self-competence (Matthews and Keating, 1995).

In this context, the metaphor of habits of mind may have several advantages over traditional notions of mental abilities or capacity. First, it presumes no particular structural outcome. Rather than reducing diversity to fit an a priori pattern, it encourages the observation of what fits with what over time. In so doing, it allows appropriate degrees of freedom to the operation of contingent history. Second, it strikes a better balance between the inevitably closed or fixed quality of structures and the apparent plasticity of development. We know a bit about habits—the longer we have them, the harder they are to change—but they are very flexible in the early stages, and are never completely rigid. Third, habits of mind incorporate dispositional, emotional, motivational, and personality variability, a clearly desirable goal (Keating and Crane, 1990; Sternberg, 1989).

We have found it useful to identify two kinds of habits of mind: those that relate to domain-specific expertise and those that are more domain-general. More general habits of mind are those that guide the customary, or more automatic, ways in which individuals engage the world. Predilections for perception, thinking, learning, and interacting with others have a significant impact on how individuals acquire and use competence. Even in infancy, such patterns appear to be associated with performance. Nine- and twelve-month-olds who are successful in an object permanence task demonstrated patterns of attention and emotion regulation that are different from those who did not succeed (MacLean et al., 1995). Moreover, these patterns are predictive of cognitive competence and self-regulation four to five years later (Miller, 1995). Later in development, variability in cognitive activities such as attending to and learning from errors (Shafrir, Ogilvie, and Bryson, 1990; Shafrir and Pascual-Leone, 1990), reflective or critical thinking, and intentional learning and knowledge building (Bereiter and Scardamalia, this volume, chap. 22) become central to the growth of competence. These dispositions likely have their origins in early development as well.

These developments are probably closely linked with other important habits of mind, namely coping skills and orientations (Menna and Keating, 1992). These, too, are not merely cognitive but also social and emotional. We may well discover that habits of coping that are most important for health and well-being—maintaining social connectedness and exercising reasonable control over one's choices—are similar to, and perhaps even homologous with, the broad habits of mind that shape the acquisition of competence.

It is likely that the most developmentally sensitive period for laying the groundwork of later competence and coping occurs during the infant's earliest social interactions, probably in the first two years of life. Basic habits of mind that guide how we interact with others, how we attend to the world, what we focus our attention on, and how we learn to deal with new situations, are shaped in the context of these key social relationships (MacLean et al., 1995).

Competence in particular domains of experience begins to accrue as well, most likely in the form of self-organizing systems (Keating, 1990b). The observation that expertise is domain-specific has been well documented by many researchers represented in this volume. The tension between accounts that focus on generality versus specificity is a productive one, if we take a developmental perspective (Gardner, 1983, 1991; Keating, 1990a; Keating and Crane, 1990). The developmental interplay between emerging habits of mind of the general sort with the acquisition of specific expertise is the key area of research for understanding human diversity in competence and coping.

In simplest terms, traditional models of human diversity have focused on the question of who had more or less competence, and to what those differences should be attributed. We need to move now toward a developmental model, whose focal questions are different. How are the universal human capacities—for language, social interaction, forward planning, and abstract thinking—translated into attained capabilities? And perhaps most important, how can we arrange the human social environment so as to maximize competence and coping in the population, maintain the valuable diversity of domains of expertise, and create the social frameworks that facilitate productive networks for collaborative learning?

At the most general level, we need to understand how to support the development of habits of mind that are central to building a learning society. Viewed from a broader historical and cultural perspective, it seems likely that engendering those habits of mind will require substantial institutional innovation, especially in education. Linking these changes with other important social innovations is likely to be necessary, especially those which embed educational activities in the community and in the broader social environment (Keating, 1995b, in press a).

Note

1. This conceptual framework has been and continues to be developed as a collaborative effort of the Human Development Program of the Canadian Institute for Advanced Research. I thank CIAR for their generous support in this activity, and the program members of this interdisciplinary team for their generous collaboration: Jeanne Brooks-Gunn, Robbie Case, Max Cynader, Barrie Frost, Clyde Hertzman, Dan Offord, Alan Pence, Chris Power, Tom Rohlen, Steve Suomi, Richard Tremblay, and Doug Willms.

References

Anastasi, A. (1958). Heredity, environment, and the question "How?" *Psychological Review, 65,* 197–208.

Anastasi, A. (1986). Experiential structuring of psychological traits. *Developmental Review, 6,* 181–202.

Bronfenbrenner, U. and Ceci, S. J. (in press). Heredity, environment, and the question: "How?" In R. Plomin and J. McClearn (Eds.), *Nature, nurture, and psychology.* Washington: American Psychological Association.

Bruner, J. S. (1960). *The process of education.* Cambridge: Harvard University Press.

Bruner, J. (1990). *Acts of meaning.* Cambridge: Harvard University Press.

Case, R. (1992). *The mind's staircase: Exploring the conceptual underpinnings of children's thought and knowledge.* Hillsdale, NJ: Lawrence Erlbaum.

Ceci, S. J. (1990). *On intelligence. . .more or less.* Englewood Cliffs, NJ: Prentice-Hall.

Change, F. and Greenough, W. T. (1982). Lateralized effects of monocular training on dendritic branching in adult split-brain rats. *Brain Research, 232,* 283–292.

Cicchetti, D. and Beeghly, M. (Eds.). (1990). *Children with Down syndrome: A developmental perspective.* New York: Cambridge University Press.

Cole, M. and Scribner, S. (1974). *Culture and thought: A psychological introduction.* New York: Wiley.

Cynader, M., Shaw, C., Prusky, G., and Van Huizen, F. (1990). Neural mechanisms underlying modifiability of response properties in developing cat visual cortex. In B. Cohen and I. Bodis-Wollner (Eds.), *Vision and the brain: The organization of the central visual system* (pp. 85–108). New York: Raven Press.

Dewey, J. (1963). *Experience and education.* New York: Collier Books.

Donald, M. (1991). *Origins of the modern mind: Three stages in the evolution of culture and cognition.* Cambridge: Harvard University Press.

Dunbar, R. (1992). Why gossip is good for you. *New Scientist, 136,* 28–31.

Eysenck, H. J. (1988). The concept of "intelligence": Useful or useless? *Intelligence, 12,* 1–16.

Galton, F. (1892/1962). *Hereditary genius: An inquiry into its laws and consequences.* Cleveland: World Publishing.

Gardner, H. (1983). *Frames of mind: The theory of multiple intelligences.* New York: Basic Books.

Gardner, H. (1991). *The unschooled mind.* New York: Basic Books.

Glymour, C., Scheines, R., Spirtes, P., and Kelly, K. (1987). *Discovering causal structure.* Orlando, FL: Academic Press.

Gould, S. J. (1986). Evolution and the triumph of homology, or why history matters. *American Scientist, 74,* 60–69.

Green, B. F. (1992). Exposé or smear? The Burt affair. *Psychological Science, 3,* 328–331.

Hunt, E. (1978). Mechanics of verbal ability. *Psychological Review, 85,* 109–130.

Hunt, J. McV. (1961). *Intelligence and experience.* New York: Ronald Press.

Keating, D. P. (1990a). Charting pathways to the development of expertise. *Educational Psychologist, 25* (3 and 4), 243–267.

Keating, D. P. (1990b). Developmental processes in the socialization of cognitive structures. In *Development and learning: Proceedings of a symposium in honour of Wolfgang Edelstein on his 60th birthday.* Berlin: Max Planck Institute for Human Development and Education.

Keating, D. P. (1990c). Structuralism, deconstruction, reconstruction: The limits of reasoning. In W. F. Overton (Ed.), *Reasoning, necessity, and logic: Developmental perspectives* (pp. 299–319). Hillsdale, NJ: Lawrence Erlbaum.

Keating, D. P. (1991). Curriculum options for the developmentally advanced: A developmental alternative for gifted education. *Education Exceptionality Canada, 1,* 53–83.

Keating, D. P. (in 1995a). Educating for a learning society: The transformation of schooling. In J. Lupart, A. McKeough, and C. Yewchuk (Eds.), *Schools in transition: Rethinking regular and special education* (pp. 119–139). Toronto: Nelson.

Keating, D. P. (1995b). The learning society in the information age. In S. A. Rosell (Ed.), *Changing maps: Governing in a world of rapid change* (pp. 205–229). Ottawa: Carleton University Press.

Keating, D. P. (in press a). Families, schools, and communities: Social resources for a learning society. In D. Ross (Ed.), *Family security in insecure times* (Vol. 2). Ottawa: National Forum on Family Security.

Keating, D. P. (in press c). Habits of mind: Developmental diversity in competence and coping (with commentary and reply by the author). In D. K. Detterman (Ed.), *Current topics in human intelligence: The role of the environment.* Norwood, NJ: Ablex.

Keating, D. P. (in press d). Understanding human intelligence: Toward a developmental synthesis. In C. Benbow and D. Lubinski (Eds.), *From psychometrics to giftedness: Essays in honor of Julian Stanley.* Baltimore: Johns Hopkins University Press.

Keating, D. P. and Crane, L. L. (1990). Domain-general and domain-specific processes in proportional reasoning. *Merrill-Palmer Quarterly, 36,* 411–424.

Keating, D. P., List, J. A., and Merriman, W. E. (1985). Cognitive processing and cognitive ability: A multivariate validity investigation. *Intelligence, 9,* 149–170.

Keating, D. P. and MacLean, D. J. (1987). Cognitive processing, cognitive ability, and development: A reconsideration. In P. A. Vernon (Ed.), *Speed of information processing and intelligence* (pp. 239–270). Norwood, NJ: Ablex.

Keating, D. P. and MacLean, D. J. (1988). Reconstruction in cognitive development: A post-structuralist agenda. In P. B. Baltes, D. L. Featherman, and R. M. Lerner (Eds.), *Life-span development and behavior* (Vol. 8, pp. 283–317). Hillsdale, NJ: Lawrence Erlbaum.

Keating, D. P. and Mustard, J. F. (1993). Social economic factors in human development. In D. Ross (Ed.), *Family security in insecure times* (Vol. 1, pp. 87–105). Ottawa: National Forum on Family Security.

Kiecolt-Glaser, J. K. and Glaser, R. (1991). Stress and immune function in humans. In R. Ader, D. L. Felten, and N. Cohen (Eds.), *Psychoneuroimmunology* (2nd edn., pp. 849–867). New York: Academic Press.

Lave, J. (1988). *Cognition in practice: Mind, mathematics, and culture in everyday life.* Cambridge, England: Cambridge University Press.

Lewis, M. D. (1993). Emotion–cognition interactions in early infant development. *Cognition and Emotion, 7,* 145–170.

MacLean, D. J., Keating, D. P., Miller, F., and Keenan, T. (1995, April). *Emotion and attention regulation in object permanence performance.* Paper presented at the meeting of the Society for Research in Child Development, Indianapolis.

MacLean, D. J. and Schuler, M. (1989). Conceptual development in infancy: The understanding of containment. *Child Development, 60,* 1126–1137.

Matthews, D. J. and Keating, D. P. (1995). Domain-specificity and habits of mind: An investigation of patterns of high-level development. *Journal of Early Adolescence, 15,* 319–343.

Menna, R. and Keating, D. P. (1992, June). *Coping with emotions in adolescence and early adulthood: Developmental changes.* Paper presented at the meeting of the Canadian Psychological Association, Quebec City.

Miller, F. (1995). *Attention regulation, emotion regulation, and competence from infancy to school entry.* Master's thesis, Brock University, St. Catharines, Ontario.

Morrison, G. R., Morrison, S. R., and Keating, D. P. (1992). On estimating processing variance: Commentary and reanalysis of Kail's "Developmental functions for speeds of cognitive processes." *Journal of Experimental Child Psychology, 54,* 288–307.

Oatley, K. and Jenkins, J. M. (1992). Human emotions: Function and dysfunction. *Annual Review of Psychology, 43,* 55–85.

Olson, D. R. (1994). *The world on paper: The conceptual and cognitive implications of writing and reading.* Cambridge, England: Cambridge University Press.

Plomin, R. and Thompson, L. (1988). Life-span developmental behavior genetics. In P. B. Baltes, D. L. Featherman, and R. M. Lerner (Eds.), *Life-span development and behavior* (Vol. 8, pp. 1–31). Hillsdale, NJ: Lawrence Erlbaum.

Resnick, L. B., Levine, J. B., and Teasley, S. D. (Eds.). (1991). *Perspectives on socially shared cognition*. Washington: American Psychological Association.

Rogoff, B. (1990). *Apprenticeship in thinking: Cognitive development in social context*. New York: Oxford University Press.

Rogoff, B. and Lave, J. (Eds.). (1984). *Everyday cognition: Its development in social context*. Cambridge: Harvard University Press.

Rosenberg, M. (1986). Self-concept from middle childhood through adolescence. In J. Suls and A. G. Greenwald (Eds.), *Psychological perspectives on the self* (pp. 107–136). Hillsdale, NJ: Lawrence Erlbaum.

Scardamalia, M. and Bereiter, C. (1993). Technologies for knowledge-building discourse. *Communications of the ACM, 36* (5), 37–41.

Senge, P. M. (1990). *The fifth discipline: The art and practice of the learning organization*. New York: Doubleday.

Shafrir, U., Ogilvie, M., and Bryson, M. (1990). Attention to errors and learning: A cross-task and a cross-domain analysis of the postfailure reflectivity measure. *Cognitive Development, 5*, 405–425.

Shafrir, U. and Pascual-Leone, J. (1990). Postfailure reflectivity/impulsivity and spontaneous attention to errors. *Journal of Educational Psychology, 82* (2), 378–387.

Sternberg, R. J. (1989). Domain-generality versus domain-specificity: The life and impending death of a false dichotomy. *Merrill-Palmer Quarterly, 35*, 115–129.

Sternberg, R. J. (1990). *Metaphors of mind: Conceptions of the nature of intelligence*. New York: Cambridge University Press.

Stevenson, H. W. and Stigler, J. W. (1992). *The learning gap: Why our schools are failing and what we can learn from Japanese and Chinese education*. New York: Summit Books.

Stringer, C. and Gamble, C. (1993). *In search of the Neanderthals: Solving the puzzle of human origins*. London: Thames and Hudson.

Suomi, S. J. (1991). Early stress and adult emotional reactivity in rhesus monkeys. In *The childhood environment and adult disease*. (Ciba Foundation Symposium 156). Chichester, England: Wiley.

Task Force on Human Development (1992). *The learning society*. Canadian Institute for Advanced Research, Research Publication #6. Toronto: CIAR.

Terman, L. S. (1916). *The measurement of intelligence*. Boston: Houghton Mifflin.

Tomasello, M., Kruger, A. C., and Ratner, H. H. (1993). Cultural learning. *Behavioral and Brian Sciences, 16*, 495–552.

Turner, A. and Greenough, W. T. (1985). Differential rearing effects on rat visual cortex synapses: Synaptic and neuronal density and synapses per neuron. *Brain Research, 329*, 195–203.

Vygotsky, L. (1978). *Mind in society: The development of higher psychological processes*. M. Cole, V. John-Steiner, S. Scribner, and E. Souberman (Eds.). Cambridge: Harvard University Press.

SECTION III

Schooling Minds

22

Rethinking Learning

CARL BEREITER
MARLENE SCARDAMALIA

The term "learning" has always covered a wide range of phenomena—from schoolchildren learning their multiplication tables to deans learning that their budgets have been cut. Suddenly, in just the last few years, the range has gotten much wider—by orders of magnitude, it seems. We now have learning corporations, even learning societies, institutional memory, and distributed expertise. Marshall McLuhan's catchy phrase, "learning a living," has been resurrected as a characterization of what life will be like in the fiber optics age.

Traditional conceptions of learning do not comfortably embrace these newer notions. The fact that people are able to talk about them is mainly a testimony to· the remarkable flexibility of language. The term "learning" has been extended metaphorically, but it does not follow that our basic understanding of learning has changed.

The conception of learning that has guided education through recent millennia is grounded in what has come to be called "folk psychology" (Bruner, 1990; Stich, 1983). To say this is no particular aspersion on educators, for the same could be said about all the other professions and disciplines in which considerations of human mental activity are involved—law, psychiatry, theology, even contemporary work in artificial intelligence.

A number of new views of learning have begun to have an impact on education. "Constructivist," "situated," and "sociocultural" are labels much in evidence. These labels do, in fact, point to new possibilities. Often, however, the new ideas are grafted on to the unexamined assumptions of folk psychology, thus losing much of their innovative potential. Our objective in this chapter is to examine the basic assumptions about learning that come to us as part of folk psychology and to propose an expanded set of concepts that we believe are necessary in order to move educational thought and practice significantly beyond where they are today.

Folk Theory of Mind: Mind as Container

Folk psychology is simply the psychology a person acquires through growing up in a human society. The psychology acquired growing up in a modern western society posits, for each individual, a mind. This mind contains things such as beliefs, desires, intentions, and memories of past events. These mental contents determine behavior, in the strong sense that if you knew the contents of someone else's mind you would be able to predict their behavior.

The idea of the mind as an immaterial entity, distinct from the brain, has been bothersome to some scientists. There have been recurrent efforts to eliminate it as a scientific concept. The most notable effort was behaviorism, but recent advances in neuroscience have led to renewed proposals for elimination (e.g., Churchland, 1986). Whether such proposals have scientific merit is an issue that lies outside this chapter. Our concern is with developing a conceptual framework that is adequate to advance educational thought. We can perfectly well admit that the mind is a fiction. The question is whether it is a useful fiction. Do we really need it? Is it useful throughout or only for certain purposes? Does it lead to pitfalls that we must be on the watch for?

Such otherwise dissimilar thinkers as Jerome Bruner (1990) and Zenon Pylyshyn (1984) agree in arguing for the necessity of a mentalistic level of description. Without it, they show, the accounts we can give of human behavior are simply too impoverished to permit us to make sense of it. We find their arguments compelling. On the assumption that most readers will be of similar persuasion, we shall not review those arguments here. Instead, we shall take it as given that education needs a concept of mind. The question we shall pursue from that starting point is whether education needs or must be limited to the concept of mind that comes to us from folk psychology.

In folk psychology, the root metaphor is mind as container (Lakoff and Johnson, 1980). Beliefs and desires have been the items of mental content most interesting to those studying the development of folk theory of mind in children (Astington, Harris, and Olson, 1988). But folk psychology places no particular restrictions on the kinds of things the mind may contain. When Freud proposes unconscious motives or Piaget proposes *structures d'ensemble* or Newell and Simon propose production systems, folk psychology has no trouble admitting any of these as objects that may populate the mind. Some objects have only a fleeting presence in the mind, whereas others reside there more or less permanently. Learning is any process by which these more enduring objects get into the mind. Again, folk psychology is quite permissive regarding the processes by which new objects get into the mind. It can tolerate such shortcut notions as knowledge transmission— knowledge passing from the mind of the teacher to the mind of the student via the spoken word. But it can equally well accommodate the constructivist notion that knowledge is produced within the mind through mental activities of the learner. And there is no fundamental objection to the Vygotskian idea of internalization, although it is likely to appear obscure. As for the so-called "cognitive revolution," its main effect for educators and related kinds of practitioners has been to reinstate folk psychology from its exile by behaviorists (Carroll, 1976).

Given all this versatility, one might suppose that folk psychology would be safe from complaints that it stands in the way of grasping and applying new ideas. Yet that is the complaint we shall make. It may be true that with sufficient effort one can think anything that needs thinking, without violating the premises of folk psychology. But folk psychology does have its biases. Some ways of thinking are much easier to pursue than others, some ways seem more natural. Generally, it appears that people are most comfortable dealing with cognitive issues when they are formulated in ways that fit with the mind-as-container metaphor. Hence:

- Knowledge is most readily conceived of as specifiable objects in the mind, such as discrete facts, beliefs, ideas, or intentions. Less specifiable sorts of knowledge, such as intuitions or understandings, are harder to hang on to, and so are any sorts of knowledge not assignable to individual minds, such as the "state of knowledge" in a discipline.
- Mental abilities are defined in terms of doing specifiable things with specifiable mental objects. Memory involves retaining and retrieving such objects. Classification and sequencing abilities (favorite components of thinking skills programs) involve arranging mental objects, and reasoning abilities involve new mental objects (conclusions) resulting from combinations of existing objects. Mental abilities that cannot be thus specified tend to be neglected, treated as mysterious, or reduced to specifiable operations on specifiable objects.

There are important kinds of learning that do not readily fit the container metaphor. They are difficult to teach by ordinary methods, because pedagogy has evolved as a craft for cultivating mental content. They are difficult to test, because educational testing of course depends heavily on the container metaphor; it is a matter of inventorying mental contents. Because they are unspecifiable in mental content terms, they may also be difficult to defend as educational objectives. At the same time, there are important kinds of mislearning or problematic learning that ought to be taken into account in education but that are difficult to come to grips with unless they are reduced to mental content. Finally, there is the whole matter of the advancement of knowledge. It often takes the form of specifiable objects—theories, inventions, discoveries, and the like—but these tend to take on a life of their own that is difficult to reconcile with these same objects being considered as content inside individual minds.

In the following sections we shall elaborate on these kinds of learning that do not fit the container metaphor. They prove to cover much more educationally important territory than we might at first imagine. At the same time we shall try to show how concepts drawn from connectionist approaches to artificial intelligence, sociocultural theory, and philosophy of science provide ways out of the mind-as-container trap, enabling us to better comprehend human learning in its full range.

Mind Without Mental Content

There are kinds of learning that cannot be reduced to specifiable objects or actions. There is a large class of learnings that we may describe as "learning one's way around in" some physical or abstract domain. The salient example is place learning (Woodworth, 1958), which means knowing some physical environment well enough that one is never lost in it and can quickly find one's way from one place to another by an efficient route. Experienced taxi drivers have it, and so do rats or mice in a building. Such learning is sometimes spoken of as acquiring a "mental map" (thereby identifying it with an object in the mental container). But mental maps would seem to characterize an early stage of place learning. At high levels of place learning, one does not have to consult a map, mental or otherwise.

Closely analogous to place learning, and more immediately relevant to educational concerns, is number sense. Number sense is "knowing one's way around" numerical domains. It manifests itself in the ability to make flexible, efficient, and almost effortless use of mathematical facts—for example, that 63 is closer to 100 than it is to zero but closer to 50 than to 100, that it is odd, that it is divisible by 7 and 9, that adding 7 to it makes 70—as they are encountered in situations that call for their arithmetic manipulation. It is the basis for shortcuts, error checking, approximation, and taking advantage of situation characteristics. Scribner (1984), for instance, found dairy truck loaders taking advantage of the row-and-column layout of packing cases and basing their calculations on those. Any particular number facts and operations can be accounted for by the relatively small number of principles constituting arithmetic, and these might plausibly be regarded as items of mental content. But to account in this way for the flexibility and situatedness of normal quantitative skills, we would have to posit an inordinate number of little context-sensitive rules. And even then we would have trouble accounting for how number sense works in new situations.

"Creativity" is a name applied to all kinds of productive thinking that cannot be explained by rules and items of information in the mind (Bereiter and Scardamalia, 1993, chap. 5). Hence the perennial belief in inspiration, attributing creativity to a source (possibly divine) outside the mind. But human intelligence exhibits creativity almost continuously, in countless small ways that hardly justify divine intervention. In conversation we frequently start a sentence without knowing how we will finish it. Sometimes we get into trouble and have to start over, but more often we improvise effortlessly, producing a sentence that is both grammatical and faithful to our intent. Such mundane creativity, which represents the typical rather than the exceptional workings of the human mind, similarly defies explanation in terms of specifiable mental content.

Another major kind of learning not suited to the container metaphor is that occurring in the study of literature. People who appreciate literature themselves seldom question its value in the curriculum, but they have trouble defending it during back-to-basics crazes. They can claim that literature enriches life, makes one a better person, changes the way one sees the world—but what, precisely, is learned that could give substance to these claims? The dilemma shows up most clearly when it comes to testing. Students can be tested on their knowledge of text content or facts about the author and the historical context, or they can be asked to interpret passages or write critical essays—but what is the learning that is supposed to be reflected in such tasks? The teaching of literature tends similarly to vacillate between teaching specific but incidental information and becoming an occasion for students to talk about whatever reading has brought to mind.

The container metaphor is thus severely limited in its applicability to human learning and intelligence. But what alternative is there? As recently as 1985, Jerry Fodor could say of cognitive theory based on the container metaphor, that it is "the only game in town" (p. 90). A year later, however, a monumental two-volume work firmly established a second game, now generally known as connectionism (McClelland, Rumelhart, and PDP Research Group, 1986; Rumelhart, McClelland, and PDP Research Group, 1986).

As with folk psychology, the scientific status of connectionism is not of immediate concern. We may look on it as simply providing a new metaphor for the mind. But connectionist achievements in artificial intelligence (AI) are important in making the metaphor plausible—indeed, in making the metaphor even comprehensible. Traditional AI is fully consistent with the mind-as-container metaphor. The builder of an AI implementation can tell you exactly what rules and items of information are contained in the simulated mind. But a connectionist AI program does not contain any rules or facts. A connectionist program consists of a set of abstract objects that interact with each other and with the outside world according to purely quantitative schemes. It is essentially a pattern detection device. Give it patterned input, such as spellings of English words (irregular as well as regular) or different portraits of the same people or information on animal characteristics and it will begin to act as if it is making progress in figuring out the underlying patterns, categories, defining rules, and so on. But such pieces of knowledge are nowhere to be found. As Rumelhart (1989, p. 135) put it, "all the knowledge is in the connections"—and these connections are merely quantitative.

The connectionist mind can thus be *knowledgeable* without *containing knowledge* (Bereiter, 1991). It will act in ways that we normally attribute to mental content, as we do with human beings, but in this case we know the content is not really there. More importantly for our purposes, to the connectionist mind, place learning, number sense, and linguistic creativity are all perfectly normal *capabilities* that it may acquire, and there is nothing mysterious about claiming that literature alters the way we see the world. It is exactly what we expect of a mind that attunes itself to pattern in the information it receives.

The new metaphor suggested by connectionism is *mind as pattern recognizer.* There have been important proposals along this line that preceded the rise of connectionism (Lakoff, 1987; Margolis, 1987; Shaw and Turvey, 1981), but it required connectionism to provide a conception of how such a mind could actually work. For the idea is not that the mind stores up patterns and matches new experiences to them (that is how folk psychology would conceive of it). The idea is that the mind acquires abilities and dispositions to recognize and respond in various ways to various patterns, but the patterns are not *in* the mind. We can say that the patterns are in the environment or, more cautiously, that the patterns are a way for us as observers to describe relations between the mind and the environment.

None of this seems as easy or natural as defining learning in terms of mental content, but until educators can begin to think about learning in this way, we believe, many of the most important kinds of human learning will remain in the shadows.

Knowledge Embedded in Practice

In Rome, to cross a wide thoroughfare where automobile traffic flows endlessly, pedestrians will step out boldly and proceed at a steady pace while the automobile traffic parts like the Red Sea around them. Trying that in a North American city would create a horrendous traffic jam, if not much worse. To attribute the difference to the superior skills and versatility of individual Roman motorists is hardly adequate. What we see in Rome is an evolved motoring practice that adapts to pedestrian cross-traffic. No amount of individual training of motorists would produce it. There is, indeed, probably no way to get such a motoring practice established in places where it does not already exist. It would have to have started long ago, when cars were few and not very fast, and become progressively refined as traffic grew denser and faster. Thus we are looking at a learning trajectory that extends over several generations and for which the necessary initial conditions no longer exist. Today's Roman motorists are collectively executing a skilled performance that is more than a combination of their individual driving skills. They are participants in a social practice with a learning history of its own, growing out of the activities of drivers now gone, who probably had no idea what they were contributing to.

Some cultural practices, such as school teaching and social drinking, have longer learning histories. Others run their course very quickly, as when flood or earthquake victims create a temporary society in emergency accommodations. In all cases, however, we witness learning that cannot be fully accounted for at the level of individual minds, connectionist or otherwise. The cultural practice itself is a kind of knowledge and the evolution of that practice is a kind of learning.

The idea of knowledge and learning inhering in cultural practice now enjoys considerable currency, as an aspect of situated cognition. Accordingly, we will not elaborate on it to the extent that we did on connectionism. Several other chapters in this book develop the idea more fully and in various contexts (see Case, this volume, chap. 5; Rogoff, Matusov, and White, this volume, chap. 18). Instead, we shall focus on the conceptual requirements for dealing effectively with this idea in education.

Collaboration and teamwork are very much in the air these days, and have been ever since management experts began attributing much of the success of

Japanese industry to teamwork and group loyalty. "Ability to work in groups" is now appearing as an educational objective almost on a par with literacy and numeracy. How do we address or think about such an objective?

Situated learning has caught on so easily and quickly among educators that it seems safe to assume that most have found a way to assimilate it within folk psychology. Knowledge and learning beyond the individual level can be treated as metaphorical extensions of "real" learning—as occupying a larger container, so to speak. And the skills embodied in cultural practices can be treated as individual social skills, which are skills like any others, except that they are learned through social experiences.

There is nothing dramatically wrong with these folk versions, but they do reduce the likelihood of any very profound change taking place in educational practice. Thomas Rohlen (1989) has studied Japanese socialization practices from kindergarten to the workplace. The story he tells is not simply one of children acquiring social skills at school, which they carry with them into adult life. Rather, schools foster the development of certain group practices, related to internal maintenance of discipline and performance standards, which are replicated in the adult workplace. Thus an important part of what passes from school into society is the practices themselves, not just the individual knowledge that goes with them.

Social practices evolve in all schools, of course. Some of them, such as recitation, are so salient that children often start school already knowing them, having learned them through playing school at home. But such practices have little transfer value beyond school. Unfortunately, the social practices that seem most likely to have transfer value outside school are of the more subversive sort that develop without official sanction. It has been observed, for instance, that students evolve subtle and coordinated ways of lowering the level of teachers' work demands. This is clearly more than a collection of individual skills. Individual students may not even be aware of the point of the collective activity they are engaged in (that is not uncommon in social practices). Yet the practice itself may well be transferable to other situations, with other participants, where it may serve similar purposes of workload reduction.

What if schools could foster the development of cultural practices that have broad applicability to situations in the outside world that call for working productively with knowledge? It sounds like just what the "Education for the Twenty-first Century" and the "Global Competitiveness" pundits keep urging upon us, except that they never quite put it that way. Instead they talk about higher-level thinking skills and group participation skills. Later we shall argue for "knowledge building" as such a transferable cultural practice. But in order to grasp the general concept, we have to recognize that promoting individual learning (whether it is done individually or through group processes) is one thing and fostering knowledge embedded in transferable social practices is another. These represent two jobs for schools, not one, even though they are closely intertwined. The second job receives virtually no attention in educational thought and practice, because our folk conceptual framework offers essentially no support for doing so.

Knowledge as Object

Although folk psychology treats knowledge as objects in individual minds, there is another way of treating knowledge, which has a long and respectable past. In the history of knowledge (which includes the history of ideas and the history of science), knowledge has been treated implicitly as consisting of objects that exist in some sense independently of individual knowers. It matters, of course, that various people believe or disbelieve, understand or misunderstand an idea. That is much of what the history of ideas is about. But essential to such history is the idea itself, the object of people's attitudes and actions. Thus phlogiston, an idea, plays a role in the history of chemistry in much the same way that Charles II, for instance, plays a role in the political history of England.

For the most part, historians as well as less specialized thinkers about knowledge have been little bothered by the problem of reconciling the two views—one a subjective view, regarding knowledge as a mental state, the other an objective view, regarding knowledge as something in its own right. Educators have lived comfortably with this dualism. One moment the teacher wears the hat of a biologist or space scientist, and knowledge is treated as something brought before the class to be discussed and understood. The next moment the teacher puts on a pedagogical hat and asks questions to probe knowledge, now regarded as stuff hidden away in the minds of individual students.

This casual dualism obviously works, up to a point. We believe, however, that education is now at a point where it needs a more disciplined approach to knowledge. We believe, as everyone is saying, that education will have a crucial role in determining how successful societies are in negotiating a shift from manufacturing-based to knowledge-based economies (Drucker, 1994). Successful societies will be those whose citizens are most adept at creating and elaborating the uses of new knowledge. In industrial societies, there is not much problem distinguishing knowledge from what it is applied to. If you are educating aeronautical engineers, say, then the knowledge you are concerned with is knowledge of the kind conventionally located in the mind of the engineer. The objects to which the knowledge is applied are huge metal contraptions that would never be confused with things inside people's heads. But if you are educating a knowledge worker, then you again have knowledge conventionally located in the mind of the worker, but what that knowledge is applied to is also knowledge. Now there is considerable risk of confusion between workers' knowledge and the objects to which it is applied.

If educators are going to play more than subservient roles in a knowledge-based society, they are going to have to be able to negotiate flexibly and without confusion between several different ways of conceptualizing knowledge, appropriate to its different roles. At present, this is a bit like negotiating a complex business arrangement between four companies that are all named General Motors. We do not have distinctive terms for various senses of the word "knowledge," and the term "learning" is applied indiscriminately wherever a knowledge-related verb is required.

Philosophers of knowledge, although living in a less complicated world than modern educators, have had to wrestle with related conceptual problems. Perhaps the most fully developed effort to get knowledge problems sorted out was that of Sir Karl Popper, building on work of Gottlob Frege. Popper (1972) identified three separate though related worlds: World 1, the physical world; World 2, the subjective world, the world inside our minds; and World 3, the world of what he called, to the confusion of many, "objective knowledge." What he meant was not "objectively true" or "free of subjective bias." He meant, simply, *treatable as an object.* Thus phlogiston theory clearly belongs in World 3, although no one any longer would claim it to be true. Indeed, it has no possible home other than World 3. It does not belong in World 1, because according to present knowledge no such substance as phlogiston exists in the natural world. And, assuming that no living person believes in phlogiston theory, it cannot be said to exist in World 2 either. But as an object in World 3, it survives as a historically important theory. It can be studied, its history can be told, people can judge its effects on the progress of chemistry, analyze its appeal, and so on.

As with connectionism and knowledge embedded in practice, we do not put Popper's three-worlds schema forth as something forced upon us because of its truth or universal desirability. We put it forth as having something to add to a conceptual framework that education needs in order to advance. However, in this case the addition to the conceptual framework is mainly of value in helping education to develop better connections with the outside world. In the past this connection has been a simple one. The world outside the classroom is the source of knowledge (this outside world, of course, includes the sciences and scholarly disciplines; it is not just the world of practical affairs). The teacher's job is to get some of this knowledge into the heads of students. Some small number of students may eventually become producers of knowledge themselves, a possibility that begins to receive attention at the university level, but this is seldom a concern of the schools. In Popperian terms, the traditional job of the schools is to select objects from World 3 and get them transformed into objects in World 2, the minds of individual students. But if that is all there is to it, we hardly need Popper's framework. The ordinary language of curriculum planning should suffice.

The implication of the term "knowledge-based economy," however, is that wealth generation throughout the economy depends on creating and transforming knowledge (Romer, 1990). (*Using* knowledge does not distinguish a knowledge-based economy; all economies, including the most primitive and stagnant, rely on vast amounts of knowledge.) It would seem that this rise in prominence of knowledge should have some educational implication, even if it is not clear what. Perhaps the least controversial implication is that educators ought to be thinking seriously about what the implications are. They should not be jumping directly to conclusions—that more knowledge should be taught, or less; that computer and media literacy are the answer, or lifelong learning dispositions; that it all comes down to information search skills, or, alternatively, promoting curiosity and creativity or cooperative learning skills; that we must teach knowledge-processing skills. (Fine, but what are they? Are they just yesterday's thinking skills with the dust blown off?) These are all ideas (possibly good ones) arising from word associations. Where is the kind of thinking that arises from deep analysis? We suggest very little of it is going on, and that a major reason is the lack of conceptual tools for doing the analysis. Popper's three-worlds schema is not exactly a precision instrument, but compared to what folk theory has to provide, it gives a significant boost to analytic powers, as we shall try to show in later sections.

An Expanded Set of Concepts for an Expanded Approach to Formal Education

Ideally, education should have a comprehensive theory of mind and knowledge that can deal in a coherent way with the various ideas touched on in preceding sections. Lacking that, however, we can at least assemble a group of concepts that in combination allow necessary distinctions to be made and that support the development of new ideas. We believe the essential concepts can be assembled out of Popper's three-worlds schema, ideas coming from connectionism and situated cognition, and other ideas retained from folk psychology. This may strike some as naively eclectic; for there are situated cognition proponents who sneer at the mention of Popper, upholders of folk psychology who regard connectionism as a throwback to behaviorism, and connectionists who think the idea of mind is obsolete. But there are fundamentalists everywhere, and we need not be swayed by their exclusionary passions. The fact is that we need a patchwork of concepts, because no single approach can handle all the ways in which knowledge needs to be considered by modern educators. There is no reason to get spiritually agitated about this. Most people who work in applied sciences, whether they deal with water quality, highway safety, or telecommunications, find themselves in a similar situation.

Although it does so in a rather heavy-handed manner, Popper's three-worlds schema lays down what seem to us fundamental distinctions necessary for clear thinking about educational processes. An exemplary classroom discourse is likely to be *about* World 3 objects—ideas, theories, interpretations, and the like—but these objects *refer to* World 1—experiments, observations, remembered experiences, and so on. However, the classroom discourse is orchestrated by the teacher *for the purpose of* producing changes in World 2, the mental states of the students. Leave out World 3 and you either have naive realism, in which students' beliefs (World 2) are to be brought into conformity with the true nature of things (World 1), or else you have the relativistic gabfest, in which students "share" thoughts out of their respective Worlds 2, with no basis for comparing or improving them. Leave World 1 out of consideration and you have the verbalism academic discourse is prone to. Leave World 2 out of consideration and you leave out personal meaning and the intuitive wellsprings of progress in World 3.

Popper's schema must be augmented, however, by what could be called World

2.5. It is the world of knowledge embedded in practice. As we have already seen, this is knowledge that cannot be reduced to World 2, individual minds. But it is not part of World 3, either. Being embedded in practice means, in fact, that knowledge has not been abstracted as objects that can be discussed, compared, hypothetically modified, and so on. In addition to recognizing knowledge embedded in practice, situated cognition theorists also recognize knowledge embedded in tools (such as measuring devices) and artifacts (including books). These may be physical embodiments of World 3 knowledge, but they are not World 3 knowledge itself. If students are discussing a theoretical article, they are of course not discussing the pieces of paper it is printed on; but generally they are not discussing the text of the article, either. They are discussing the theory presented in the text. That is the World 3 object, and it is important that it be distinguishable from its wrappings. It is the theory itself, not the text through which it is presented, that students will argue is true, false, interesting, trivial, applicable or inapplicable to the problems that concern them.

The importance of the World 3 concept becomes most evident when we consider knowledge in relation to goals of education. Correspondingly, the difference between connectionist and folk conceptions of mind takes on special importance when considered in relation to World 3. If we take the folk psychological view of mind, then World 2 is a container of representations of World 1 and World 3; education is concerned with the adequacy of those representations; but the distinction between World 1 and World 3 can for the most part be ignored. We may, for instance, want students to know where Egypt is, but it is rather a pedantic issue whether this means knowing where Egypt is physically situated on Earth (World 1) or whether it means having it properly located on a world map (the result of a World 3 construction).

If we take a connectionist view of mind, however, then the relation of the student's World 2 to Worlds 1 and 3 becomes more complex and the difference between 1 and 3 takes on more significance. The student's mind is seen as adapting to patterns, both as these are experienced in the physical world and in social practices. That kind of adaptation to pattern, however, characterizes the learning of social animals as well as human beings. It is what we described earlier as "learning one's way around" in physical and social environments. A distinctively human aspect of cognition is learning related to World 3. Educated people learn their way around in this world, as well. That is, they learn their way around in a world of ideas, explanations, problems and issues, theories, stories, histories, critiques, and models of various kinds. To reduce this, as folk psychology does, to acquiring mental copies of these objects, is to omit most of what is important in acquiring such knowledge. It is knowing how to function effectively in this world that counts, appreciating what is to be found and experienced there, feeling at home in a World 3 that is continually expanding as one explores more of it.

There is another distinctly human aspect to cognition, which folk psychology tends also to neglect, and in which it is important to recognize the several different worlds that individual minds can relate to. This is the creative, constructive capacity of human cognition. We do not just learn our way about in the physical world as it is, we modify that world, sometimes drastically, to our purposes. We devise new social arrangements and practices as well. We do not necessarily take World 3 as given, either. We keep adding new objects to it and modifying or reevaluating old ones. In the context of creative activity, World 3 has a special significance. Some changes that we bring about in the physical and social worlds evolve gradually and unconsciously, but those that are the products of deliberate thought and imagination are often worked out first in World 3. They originate as ideas, plans, or designs, which are discussed and modified in their abstract form before they are enacted concretely. What it means to have a knowledge-based society is that a very large part of productive activity goes on in World 3 in comparison to the amount that is directly engaged with physical things and overt practices.

Although schooling is extremely limited in its means for supporting students' activities in the physical world and for enabling them to participate in real-life social practices, it is well designed to support activity in World 3. That, of course, has been its traditional role—to transmit the knowledge contained in books. Dissatisfied with that limited role, educators throughout this century have strived to bring more of the physical and social worlds into schooling. Although these efforts have not been without effect, schooling continues to provide only a severely cramped and often distorted range of experience with natural and social phenomena. How much more promising would it be for educators to try instead to provide students a richer and more rewarding involvement in World 3!

Advocates of liberal education have always claimed much more for formal education than merely stocking the mental warehouse. The benefits they have claimed for immersion in the world of books and ideas have included wisdom, imagination, and character (e.g., Barzun, 1944). But these larger benefits have been shadowy ones, easily lost sight of. The conception of learning provided by folk psychology provides no realistic way of talking about how students might get wisdom, imagination, or character out of a book. They might learn specific lines of verse, or specific ideas and arguments, and conceivably these might be retrieved on important occasions and used to some purpose. But we know that is unlikely and that it furthermore misses the point.

From a connectionist standpoint, the retention in memory of particular items of text or information is incidental and a challenge to explain. The natural and expected result of sustained exposure to a culture's classics would be very general kinds of pattern learning, which would be manifested in ways such as the following:

1. A familiarity with, a feeling of being at home in and in harmony with the attitudes, objects of interest, and ways of thinking pervading the classical body of work.
2. A change in the way we see the world, through what amounts, in Lakoff and Johnson's (1980) terms, to a change in the "metaphors we live by."
3. A change in our intuitive standards of moral and aesthetic judgment. In short, the primary educational results would be in such attributes as wisdom, imagination, and character.

At one level of educational planning these more profound outcomes of schooling are taken very seriously. They are much at issue in the controversies that have been swirling around university English departments and public school boards concerning multiculturalist movements to revise the literary canon. The disputes are over what culture students are to feel at home in, what ways of seeing the world they are to internalize, whose moral and aesthetic judgments are to serve as standards. But at the level of pedagogy—the level of classroom lessons, projects, and tests—all this tends to be forgotten. And that is to a considerable extent, we believe, due to the conceptual impoverishment of the folk psychological view of learning.

If the mind-as-container metaphor fails to do justice to the deeper outcomes of reading and discussing the received works of World 3, it fails even more conspicuously to do justice to education's potential role in developing people who are active constructors of and workers within World 3. We will elaborate on that issue in the next section. To round out the present discussion, however, we need to recognize the continuing value of certain aspects of folk psychology as part of a conceptual framework for educational thought.

There are two ideas grounded in folk psychology that seem indispensable to a modern pedagogy. One idea is probably as old as folk psychology itself. The other has only been fully developed within the past two decades. The old idea is intentionality. Defenders and critics of folk psychology agree on its centrality. Folk psychology makes sense of and predicts people's behavior on the basis of inferred intentions. It is hard to imagine a teacher carrying on any reasonable schooling process without attention to the students' own goals, and folk psychology provides the only practical basis for doing so. The newer idea is mental models (Gentner and Stevens, 1983; Johnson-Laird, 1983). A mental model is a more systematic version of the traditional idea of *belief*. Mental models are especially applicable in cases where students' behavior appears to have some logic to it, but not of the conventional or intended kind—when they commit nonrandom errors in arithmetic, for instance, or ask strange questions, such as "What keeps gravity from leaving the earth?" In these cases, a useful strategy for the teacher is to imagine a theory or rule that might be entertained by students and that would give rise to the observed behavior. Folk psychology and its modern variants encourage teachers to believe that they are making inferences about mental models that are really there in the minds of students, although not directly observable. From a connectionist viewpoint, such conjectured models serve only a heuristic purpose for the teacher, but they can be quite useful in that role.

In this section, we have not introduced any new educational vision. We have merely taken educational ideas variously advanced by traditionalists, constructivists, socioculturalists, and just plain folks, and tried to show how an expanded set of concepts of knowledge and learning is necessary in order to do justice to them. The existing conceptual framework leads to a dreadful discontinuity between big ideas and day-to-day pedagogy. At a high verbal level, we can spin out grand ideas of what education might be, but at the classroom level we are bound to a psychology far older than any of the big ideas, a psychology ill-suited for coming to grips with what it means to understand or to invent. In later sections, we shall try to show how an expanded set of concepts better enables us to tackle such higher concerns, and how this in turn can begin to generate new educational vision.

Understanding Newton's Dog: A Connectionist View of Understanding

"Learning with understanding" is one of the catch phrases of educational reform at present. What does it mean? With the kind of partly systematized folk theory usually applied to such a question, quite different accounts are given, depending on whether we are talking about what it means to understand Newton's theory, for instance, or about what it means to understand Newton's dog. A more enlightened theory of mind, we argue, will eliminate this discrepancy.

A common present-day account of understanding Newton's theory would run something like this: Through everyday experience, the student has already acquired a mental model of the physical world and how objects move in it. On studying Newtonian mechanics, any of several things may happen. The student may acquire a new cognitive structure suitable for answering test questions and solving textbook problems related to Newton's laws, while the student's original mental model remains unchanged. This will be revealed by presenting novel tasks, such as describing the path of an object dropped from an airplane. Alternatively, the student's mental model may undergo changes so that it becomes more like the model that was in the mind of Isaac Newton (or in the mind of a certified physicist, acting as surrogate). Teachers are now being encouraged to look for such shifts by having the students draw actual maps of their conceptual structures (networks of concepts and relationships), which may then be compared to maps prepared by experts (cf. Novak and Gowan, 1984). What it means to understand, accordingly, is to have the thing that is in your mind correspond to what is correct or to what is in the minds of people who are already assumed to understand. This is folk theory of mind, through and through, no matter how it may be dressed up with contemporary cognitive science terminology.

Understanding Newton's dog, however, is viewed in a more commonsensical way. In the first place, we would all recognize that Newton's dog could be understood in various ways, that there is no privileged way that ought to be expected of everyone. Not everything will pass as understanding, however. In judging whether someone understands Newton's dog, we would look for the following:

1. The ability to act intelligently with respect to the dog. Acting stupidly with respect to it would cast doubt on a person's understanding. Again, it is not a matter of there being just one way to act that is intelligent, but judgments can be made.
2. The ability to explain problematic aspects of the dog. We would not require a lecture on dog neurology, unless it happened that Newton's dog exhibited neurological peculiarities. In short, the ability to explain is relative to what it is about the dog that seems to need explaining.

3. An awareness of the limitations in the two previously mentioned abilities, and a disposition to improve them. Claiming to know all there is to know about the dog would likely be taken as a sign of limited understanding, as would a disinterest in knowing more.

These commonsense criteria, as we see, make no reference to mental models of dogs or any other sorts of objects in the mind. Understanding inheres in the kinds of things a person is able or inclined to do with respect to the object in question. If the object in question is something like Newton's theory, however, folk theory treats understanding as a characteristic of something in the learner's mind. Understanding no longer inheres in abilities and dispositions; it is instead a matter of correspondence between what is in the learner's mind and external reality or what is in someone else's mind.

Through a combination of connectionism and Popper's conception of World 3, however, we can approach the understanding of Newton's theory in the same sensible way that we approach the understanding of Newton's dog. Popper's World 3 is a world in which Newton's theory is as real as Newton's dog is in World 1. In the connectionist view of mind, there is no mental content to talk about. There are only abilities and dispositions. Abilities and dispositions, as we have seen, are all we need to talk about in judging understanding of Newton's dog. If we treat Newton's theory as an equally real thing, albeit an immaterial one, then the same approach may be taken.

Applying the same criteria as before, we would judge a person's understanding of Newton's theory on the basis of (1) how intelligently the person acts with respect to Newton's theory, (2) ability to explain whatever is judged to need explaining in the theory, and (3) awareness of and interest in doing something about shortcomings on the first two criteria. Of course, similar criteria might be used by a folk cognitivist in assessing a student's understanding. The difference is that the folk cognitivist is using observations as clues for inferring the theory hidden away in the student's mind, which is to be compared with the kind of theory hidden away in the mind of the physicist; whereas we are saying that understanding just is these abilities and dispositions. There is not something else hidden away in the mind that is our real target, if we but knew how to get at it.

The bottom line of the connectionist view is that if we could open up the mind and probe its depths we would not find anything we could make sense of. The sense is in the dispositions and abilities, of which we of course always have only partial information. We never know for sure what a person will do under other circumstances, or indeed under the same circumstances at another time. But such uncertainty is built into the cognitive system and its relations to the environment. It is not a result of the mind's inaccessibility to observation.

An immediate advantage of this approach to understanding is that it permits liberality without a total collapse into relativism. Science educators these days agonize over what to do about students' naive theories via-a-vis authoritative knowledge. Folk theory of mind ensures that this will remain a muddy problem. If theories are just things in the mind, then who is to say that the thing in the student's mind is inferior to what is in the physicist's mind and should be altered accordingly? If we appeal to truth, we get into one kind of trouble, and if we appeal to elite consensus we get into another; but if we maintain that the student's theory is as good as Newton's, we come off sounding plain ignorant.

Treating Newton's theory like Newton's dog, however, we can approach the matter of instruction in a more forthright way. Newton's theory has won a place in science curricula, whereas Newton's dog has not, because of its importance in a vast range of human concerns. So it is an object students ought to come to understand, in the sense of learning to act intelligently with respect to it and to be able to explain what needs explaining. Acting intelligently with respect to Newton's theory could include being able to recognize it in various guises, to discuss it knowledgeably, to make use of it in various ways, and to recognize what it is and is not good for. Being able to explain its problematic aspects would include, for instance, being able to explain how it can be asserted that a body in motion will continue in motion unless acted upon by a force when all the moving objects we observe eventually come to a halt unless acted upon by a force. The issues of truth and authority, so vexatious to educators of a postmodern persuasion, need scarcely arise. We do not insist that there is some true or correct understanding, but neither do we say that anything goes. Actions and explanations can be criticized, improvements can be urged. All that has happened is that understanding Newton's theory has joined the natural order of human activities, so that it can be treated in the same humane, liberal, and constructive ways that we try to treat all other human activities.

Knowledge Building Distinguished From Learning

Let us use the term "knowledge building" to refer to the production of knowledge objects—objects that in Popper's scheme occupy World 3. The term is intentionally broad in its denotation, so as to include what scientists and scholars do and at the same time to include similar productive activity on the part of students. Were it not for the inclusion of students, the question of how knowledge building relates to learning would likely not arise. If you ask scientists or scholars at work what they are doing, you do not expect "learning" to be the answer. They will tell you what they are trying to find out, explain, prove or disprove, or what problem they are trying to solve. Of course, they learn things in the process, but that goes without saying.

From time to time, however, the scientist's or scholar's answer to "What are you doing?" would be "learning." Often the response would take the form of "I'm *trying* to learn" such and such—to use a new piece of software, to carry out a difficult experimental procedure, to master a language or a body of mathematics, and so on. Usually the learning would be seen as instrumental to the person's work, the actual work being knowledge production. Thus in the world of knowledge building, learning plays an important, even if occasional role. But it is not perceived as the same thing as knowledge building.

Interestingly, if you ask school students what they are doing, you are not likely to get either a learning answer or a knowledge-building answer. Researchers who have asked the question find that students tend to answer by referring to the work they are doing (Doyle, 1983; Lancy, 1976a; Lancy, 1976b). But unlike scientists and scholars, the work, as perceived by students, does not involve the production of knowledge. Rather, it centers around the production of pieces of writing or other artifacts, the completion of assigned problems, and other sorts of schoolwork or self-chosen activity. Learning occurs, of course—that is the point of the activities. But as far as students' goals are concerned, what distinguishes students from practicing scholars and scientists is not that they are focused on learning but rather that they are not focused on either learning or knowledge building.

Neither folk theory nor sociocultural theory makes a distinction between knowledge building and learning. Popper's three-worlds model provides a basis for such a distinction, although it leaves the nature of learning entirely open. Knowledge building is activity directed toward changes in World 3. Learning is directed toward changes in World 2.

Learning as Complementary to Knowledge Building

The lack of a distinction between knowledge building and learning has caused needless dilemmas for educational innovators. One innovative group reported with dismay that teachers who were seemingly committed to a constructivist approach to mathematics and were doing fine work in getting students to, in effect, reinvent mathematics, nevertheless started each class session with mental arithmetic drills. It seems to us that these teachers had intuited a distinction that went beyond their adopted constructivist theory.

We have encountered teachers who would never stand in front of a class and explain the difference between restrictive and nonrestrictive clauses and who would be appalled at the thought of teaching young children how to sound out words; yet, when introducing a new software application to their students, they do not hesitate to deliver direct lessons, complete with explanations, diagrams, and demonstrations, accompanied by exercises of graduated complexity. Somehow, teaching software use falls outside their strict constructivist philosophies. It is just something the students need to learn in order to get on with their constructivist work.

With a better-elaborated epistemology, such teachers might find that a great deal more of school learning fell into the category of "just something the students need to learn in order to get on with their constructivist work"—their constructivist work being knowledge building. The so-called "basic skill" components of reading, writing, and arithmetic might well fall into this category. So might various kinds of factual knowledge that are presupposed in reading material students will use— knowledge of countries' locations, for instance, and the many items that have been catalogued in the name of "cultural literacy" (Hirsch, 1987). It is not our business to make recommendations about curriculum content here. It is always debatable whether something should be addressed as a learning objective or whether it should be left to be picked up incidentally in the course of knowledge building. Should students be explictly taught principles such as control of variables and the distinction between hypothesis and evidence? The important thing is that teachers should be able to discuss this as a strategic issue and not as a test of loyalty to the constructivist faith.

Practical educators implicitly recognize the kind of distinction we are trying to make here, but, operating within the conceptual framework of folk theory, they tend to express it in misleading and antagonizing terms. They will say, for instance, "I believe in constructivism, but some things still need to be learned by rote." Such a statement is incoherent. If we believe in constructivism, then we should believe that even rote learning is a constructive process. Implicitly, the position being advanced is one that could be stated more accurately as, "I believe that knowledge building should be the principal activity in school, but some things need to be deliberately pursued as learning objectives." Within the conceptual framework of folk theory of mind, however, such a statement is uninterpretable. That is why we need a conceptual framework that distinguishes between working in World 2 and working in World 3.

"Constructivist Learning" and Knowledge Building

"Constructivist learning" is a name attached these days to a very large range of classroom activities that do not have very much in common except for the absence of direct instruction. What it means can vary considerably, however. The differences become evident if we compare various approaches according to the extent of actual construction of World 3 objects—that is, instances of knowledge treated as objects to be considered, criticized, improved. The following are observable varieties that are all typically classified as constructivist:

1. *Messing around.* Students are provided with equipment or materials and encouraged to do whatever they feel like. A set-up for studying light and shadow, for instance, may end up being used to make shadow puppets (Smith and Neale, 1987). Although learning goes on in such activity, as it does in any deliberate activity, there is likely to be no objectification of knowledge whatever, except possibly by the teacher.

2. *Hands-on learning or guided discovery.* Here there is guidance in what to do, often with the aim of discovering some particular mathematical or scientific principle. Ideally, a World 3 object—the principle in question—should end up being constructed by the students, with the teacher providing such help as is needed to produce it. In less fortunate cases it can lead to results like that reported by a young student quoted by Roth, Anderson, and Smith (1987): "I already knew that plants need light to live, and now I know it again." Even in the more substantial examples that we have seen, there is a tendency to focus on the process rather than on the knowledge emerging from it, to abandon inquiry as soon as the principle has been found, and to keep the work isolated from the body of knowledge already developed and accessible through books. All of this, we would suggest,

reflects the folk view that recognizes only World 1 (physical action on physical objects) and World 2 (mental processes and content).

3. *Learning through problem solving.* Students are engaged collaboratively in some problematic task that might be anything from a complicated mathematics problem to doing an environmental impact study. A popular task these days is planning a space trip. In the course of planning the voyage, students must deal with a host of problems that space travel entails, and they are expected, as a result, to learn much about outer space, the solar system, human biology, rocket science, and general physics and mathematics. Such activity can be called knowledge building in only a marginal sense. The World 3 object that the students are objectively building is a plan for a space mission. Although they may *make use of* a variety of World 3 objects, such as scientific theories and accepted facts, the actual object they are building—the plan—is not an object of value in its own right. It is really a pedagogical vehicle for producing learning. Thus, the real point of the activity is the incidental learning that results, rather than the building of knowledge.

4. *Curiosity-driven inquiry.* Driven by their own curiosity, perhaps stimulated by challenging questions from the teacher, students gather information from reading, observation, or empirical research in an effort to satisfy their curiosity and answer the questions. Such activity counts as knowledge building insofar as it results in creating World 3 objects of value. Typically the main focus of attention is not World 3 but World 1—the animals, electrical circuits, or whatever that are the actual objects of curiosity, plus the report or presentation that is the concrete product of the activity. World 3 objects do get produced—explanations, summaries of received knowledge, hypotheses, and the like—but they are seldom deliberately evaluated and improved in the course of inquiry. Instead, it is left to the teacher to evaluate them, after the activity is ended. Efforts by teachers to get students to test hypotheses and to weigh evidence run into difficulties that are usually attributed to the students' inadequate conceptions of theory, evidence, and scientific method (Kuhn, 1989). However, it should be noted that such efforts to foster scientific thinking presuppose a World 3 focus that the structure of the inquiry activities may do little or nothing to support.

5. *Theory improvement.* Inquiry again begins with students' questions and puzzlements, but the focus is immediately shifted to World 3 by having the students propose initial theories (we shall call them "theories" because that is what they are called in the classroom, although "conjectures" would be a more accurate term). The focus of inquiry and discussion then becomes improvement of these theories. Pursuit of information may go on much as in the preceding approach, but the information obtained is applied to theory improvement and its relevance is judged in that context. Scientific thinking does not grow out of efforts to test or substantiate certain beliefs but out of trying to show how a revised theory is an improvement over its predecessor (Scardamalia, Bereiter, Hewitt, and Webb, in press).

Although educational approaches within the range of these five levels are often treated as merely procedural variations on the same constructivist theme, they actually represent fundamental differences. There are differences in assumptions about students' motives and abilities, about how knowledge is created, and about what learning needs to receive deliberate attention and what should be allowed to develop in its own way through experience. These differences add up to radically divergent views of what schooling can or should be.

To gain a better perspective on knowledge building in schools, it is necessary to go further into the implications of constructivism than is usually done. The first implication is that learning-by-discovery, no matter how hands-on it may be, is not primarily a matter of discovering what the natural world has to reveal. It is a matter of discovering a World 3 object—a principle or theory—that makes sense of what is observed. These objects, of course, are not originally discovered; they are created by people trying to make sense of observations similar to those being made by the students. The second implication is that, from the learner's point of view, there is hardly any difference between creating a new theory or explanation and understanding one that has already been established. Popper made this point explicitly:

What I suggest is that we can grasp a theory only by trying to reinvent it or to reconstruct it, and by trying out, with the help of our imagination, all the consequences of the theory which seem to us to be interesting and important. . . .One could say that the process of understanding and the process of the actual production or discovery of. . .[theories, etc.] are very much alike. Both are making and matching processes. (Popper and Eccles, 1977, p. 461)

Thus the learning side and the knowledge-building side of formal education merge in cases where the World 3 object that is being produced in the classroom is an interpretation, critique, or derivation of one or more culturally recognized World 3 objects. A powerful way of "getting to know" a World 3 object (and here we part company with the analogy to Newton's dog) is to create another World 3 object based upon it. This is how science, scholarship, and to an important degree the arts as well (Gombrich, 1959) progress. With an improved conception of knowledge and learning, it becomes easier to see how this kind of progressiveness can be brought into schools.

Learning and Knowledge Building in Schools: The Case of Elementary Mathematics

Research institutes and laboratories have knowledge as their end product. High-tech companies have knowledge as an intermediate product, something created on the way to producing the advanced goods or services that are their source of income. What is the status of the knowledge students produce in school? Is it merely an intermediate product, created in the service of learning? Essentially, yes, although the relation between the knowledge and the learning is more complicated than a simple affirmative suggests.

No matter how much a school might be restructured to function like a research laboratory, society is unlikely to accept World 3 knowledge as its end product. What society thinks it is paying for and sending its offspring to school to obtain is World 2 learning: the personal knowledge and competence that students will carry away with them in their own minds. Whatever schools do in the way of promoting the building of World 3 knowledge will, accordingly, have to be justified on the basis of its contribution to World 2. To a large extent, this is true even of universities, where the production of new World 3 knowledge is part of their role. Periodic complaints that research is receiving too much emphasis are answered by claims that research improves the quality of education.

We would like to see a less restrictive attitude, with schools being recognized as having a dual role, the way universities do. This would not mean expecting scientific advances to come out of elementary schools. It would, however, mean seeing knowledge creation as a worthy societal activity that young students have some part in and seeing this activity as continuing and advancing to higher levels as students proceed to higher levels of schooling. Lacking this broader conception, the conventional view leads to an unfortunate devaluation of students' knowledge-building activities. They are reduced to learning activities. They are an alternative route to learning academic content—learning by discovery, as opposed to learning from direct instruction—or they are a kind of academic role playing.

We are not arguing for the opposite here—for devaluing learning and making it a mere adjunct to knowledge building. Rather, our claim is that by failing to distinguish between learning and knowledge building, educators fail to do full justice to either. This can be shown most clearly in the case of elementary mathematics.

From a World 3 standpoint, mathematics is the purest of cases. Formal mathematical knowledge consists of World 3 objects, but, unlike scientific knowledge, the objects do not refer to the physical world (Popper's World 1). Rather, they refer to other World 3 objects; in the case of arithmetic, they refer to numbers, which are also immaterial objects, constructions of the human intellect.

But school mathematics is not wholly concerned with World 3. Indeed, in its typical versions, school mathematics has scarcely anything to do with World 3— the world of mathematical ideas treated as improvable human constructions. Instead, it is occupied with the individual acquisition of skills (World 2), supplemented to a greater or lesser extent by activities involving World 1 objects, known as "manipulatives." Of course, manipulatives, such as base 10 blocks, are chosen because they embody important mathematical ideas, but children are famously insensitive to the ideas and inclined to treat the physical objects as just physical objects (Resnick and Omanson, 1987). New approaches to school mathematics are emerging that do engage students in World 3 activity (Lampert, Rittenhouse, and Crumbaugh, this volume, chap. 31). Skills of some kind continue to be recognized as important, but the old skills of executing paper-and-pencil computations have declined in importance. Problem-solving skills have risen in prominence; but are these skills in the same sense, and are they teachable in anything like the way long division, for instance, is teachable? School mathematics is thus a challenging testbed for concepts of learning. In this discussion, we shall not presume to resolve any of the controversies surrounding school mathematics, but only to show

how the enlarged set of concepts we have been proposing serves to draw useful distinctions.

Situated Quantitative Abilities

There is a growing and fascinating body of research carried out under the situated cognition label that examines the informal quantitative skills of street vendors, truck loaders, garment workers, and the like (reviewed in Lave and Wenger, 1991). The research shows that people with little or no formal education in mathematics learn how to carry out quite impressive computations, using methods that are typically more efficient than those employing formal algorithms—methods that take advantage of peculiarities of the work and of the environment in which it is carried out. Not surprisingly, this research has created a pressure on schools to include more real-life kinds of quantitative activities in the mathematics curriculum. But is this a reasonable conclusion? A better grounded conclusion would be that schools should not bother with this sort of skill at all, because there is no way they can foster it to good purpose. What the research reveals is knowledge embedded in cultural practices. Each kind of practice has its distinctive knowledge, which is acquired through extended and increasingly full participation in a particular community of practice. As an environment for fostering such skills, one would have to go some distance to design a worse one than the common school. To feel comfortable rejecting such obviously desirable learning objectives, however, educators would need a clear view of other kinds of learning to pursue as alternatives. For that, we need to see knowledge embedded in practice as one among several kinds of knowledge, others of which may be equally valuable and more suitable to the conditions of schooling.

Number Sense

We earlier defined number sense as "knowing one's way around" in numerical domains. It is a facility with numbers themselves, not with the quantitative aspects of particular environments or practical activities. Number sense, thus conceived, has been found to vary greatly among people, even if they are equally proficient in some situation-bound quantitative activity (Stigler and Baranes, 1988). It has also been found to vary greatly with socioeconomic status and to be highly predictive of progress in school mathematics (Griffin, Case, and Siegler, 1994). Most mathematicians, we may assume, have an abundance of number sense; yet one may look in vain through the guidelines and textbooks produced by mathematicians for anything that addresses the development of number sense in a knowing way. They do not seem to distinguish it from mathematical understanding. Within Popper's three-worlds framework, however, the two are quite distinct. Mathematical understanding relates to World 3—the world of mathematical principles. Number sense is pure World 2. It is a property of the individual mind.

As we suggested earlier, the reason number sense is hard to get hold of conceptually is that it does not lend itself to the mind-as-container metaphor. If we are bound to this metaphor, then we look for mental objects to constitute number sense, and the obvious candidates are textbook principles, as replicated in the minds of students. But number sense cannot be found in any textbook. To be sure, any particular demonstration of number sense can be *justified* by appealing to recognized mathematical principles. But a student could thoroughly grasp the principles and yet lack number sense.

Although number sense thus appears as something mysterious and elusive from the standpoint of folk psychology, it appears as something quite natural from the standpoint of a connectionist view of mind. It is a variety of pattern learning. It is just what we would expect a connectionist network to acquire after extensive and varied involvement with numerical relationships. Rightstart, the most successful and fully developed program for teaching number sense that we know of (Griffin, Case, and Siegler, 1994), provides just this kind of experience and can best be understood as tuning the whole cognitive system to numerical relationships rather than as implanting any particular sorts of objects in the mind.

Knowledge Building in Mathematics

Drawing on the distinction made earlier between learning and knowledge building, we can confidently identify the development of number sense as learning. What, then, would constitute knowledge building in school mathematics? What are the World 3 objects students might create? The obvious answer is that knowledge building would mean producing the kinds of things mathematicians produce—theorems, structures, algorithms, proofs, along with such subsidiary objects as explanations and justifications. Generally speaking, that is what goes on in the new constructivist approaches to school mathematics (Lampert, Rittenhouse, and Crumbaugh, this volume, chap. 31; Yackel, Cobb, Wood, Wheatley, and Merkel, 1990). Identifying this as knowledge building, a World 3 activity, has the virtue of setting it off as a distinctive kind of enterprise whose relationship to the rest of school mathematics needs to be considered. It leaves us free to ask a question that is difficult to put clearly in the language of folk psychology: What is learned as a result of this knowledge building? That question is important for determining to what extent knowledge building may replace other kinds of educational activity in mathematics and to what extent it supplements or reinforces them. Or is what is learned through knowledge building off on another dimension and of little relevance at all to traditional objectives? (See Ohlsson and Rees, 1991, for an analysis and theoretical model that addresses questions of this kind.)

Popper's distinction between World 1 and World 3 also has a useful bearing on knowledge building in school mathematics. It helps us to understand why it is so much harder to motivate than knowledge building in empirical domains. We have found students to generate productive and challenging questions when invited to state what they wonder about in all sorts of areas of natural and social science (Scardamalia and Bereiter, 1992). But these same students tend to be dumfounded when asked what they wonder about in mathematics. They do not see that there is anything to question or wonder about with regard to mathematics.

One fifth-grade student tried to explain this lack of problematicity. "Say I have a problem about whether I have enough wood to make shelves in my closet. That's a problem for me, but it isn't a problem for anyone else. Somebody else might have a problem about gas for their motorbike, but what do I care about that?"

The unstated contrast here is with problems in the empirical sciences, where students believe, with good reason, that a question that interests them is likely to interest others as well. Questions like "How do electromagnets work?" and "What causes people in the same family to look alike?" have generality, whereas questions about shelf length in a closet or fuel consumption in a motorbike do not. But, of course, questions about shelf length and fuel consumption are not mathematical questions. They are questions about particulars of a real or imagined World 1, which mathematics may serve as a tool in answering. But they are not very interesting questions.

One approach to this motivational problem is to introduce more interesting World 1 situations. These can range from bringing real-life commerce into the school (e.g., Richmond, 1973) to presenting complex fictional situations, as in the *Jasper Woodbury* videos (Cognition and Technology Group at Vanderbilt, 1992). Although this approach may motivate more extensive and meaningful uses of mathematics as a tool, it is not clear that it brings students any closer to the construction of World 3 mathematical objects. The other approach is to make numbers themselves sufficiently real to children that they begin to wonder about them, form conjectures, dispute, and investigate. It amounts, virtually, to making numbers a part of World 1, the natural world, so that they are no longer just attributes of physical things but are things in themselves, capable of arousing puzzlement and wonder. This, it would seem, is an essential part of the approach taken by Lampert and others, who engage students in the public construction of mathematical knowledge. We do not want to judge one approach against the other, only to point out that they are radically different, and that their being lumped together under the label of "constructivism" is a testimony to the need for an enriched conceptual framework.

Procedural Learning

In discussing mathematics learning, we have so far slighted the kind of learning that often makes up virtually the entire mathematics program in elementary schools (and sometimes high schools as well). This is the learning of step-by-step procedures—commonly, procedures for adding, subtracting, multiplying, and dividing, first with small whole numbers, then larger numbers, then fractions and decimals; later, procedures for solving equations of various kinds. Our leaving this kind of learning until last should not be taken as a judgment on its importance. There were two reasons for putting it last. One was to make the point that there are very significant kinds of mathematics learning that are neglected in traditional school mathematics, and that this neglect is at least in part traceable to a prevailing folk theory of knowledge and learning. The other reason is that, when it comes to procedural learning of the kind commonly pursued in elementary mathematics, learning theories grounded in folk theory seem to be on solid ground.

In the prevailing usage within cognitive science, procedural learning and skill learning are synonymous. What is learned consists of rules in the mind—"production systems," in the most fully developed theory of skill learning (Anderson, 1983; Anderson, 1987; Anderson, Conrad, and Corbett, 1989). The difference between learning to execute a multidigit subtraction algorithm and acquiring number sense, according to this view, is entirely a matter of the size and complexity of the rule system to be learned. Because we see them as importantly different, we would prefer to limit the term "procedural learning" to learning of the first kind, where explicit procedures are involved, and to use the term "skill learning" more broadly to refer to acquiring the vast range of human competencies—everything from walking to creative writing—that go beyond what can be reduced to explicit procedures.

With cognitive theories grounded in the mind-as-container metaphor, learning multidigit subtraction is relatively easy to explain and number sense is difficult. We already know the rules for doing multidigit subtraction right, and so it only remains to account for the various erroneous rules that students may concoct (Brown and Burton, 1978). Number sense, by contrast, is baffling because there seem to be countless context-sensitive rules. From a connectionist standpoint, the opposite is the case. Number sense is just the finely tuned adaptation to environmental conditions that all sorts of learning are expected to exhibit. Learning how to execute a fixed procedure under the guidance of explicit rules, however, raises difficult problems about how a cognitive system can in some fashion consult rules stored within it (Beer, 1991). It may be remarked that this seems to be the right order of difficulty. Any organism credited with an intelligence exhibits adaptive capabilities similar to number sense, whereas the consulting of explicit rules may be unique to human intelligence.

Accordingly, folk psychology, with its modern derivatives, is at its best when dealing with procedural learning that involves rules that are explicitly stated or demonstrated. Even if connectionist learning theory is eventually able to account adequately for such learning, systematized folk theory is likely to remain more practical for dealing with it instructionally. When a student is doing the wrong thing, but in a seemingly deliberate and orderly fashion then a practical first step in helping the student is to try to cast the student's behavior in the form of rules (some of which the student may be able to report explicitly) and then consider what might have prompted such rules, what their adaptive value might be in the instructional context, and what might be required to get the student to abandon those rules in favor of more satisfactory ones. Although from a connectionist standpoint such rule-based models are fictions and will usually provide only an approximate fit to the student's actual behavior—behavior that often deviates even from rules that the student explicitly claims to be following (Nisbett and Wilson, 1977)—they can be useful fictions in dealing with problems of procedural learning. They can also be useful for dealing with problems of learning bodies of knowledge already explicitly formulated, as in textbook physics. They can be dangerous fictions, however, when applied to more complex and intuitive kinds of skill and understanding, such as number sense.

Conclusion

Central to Western folk theory of mind is the metaphor of mind as container. Until recently, this metaphor has shaped every theory in which mind figures as a concept. Learning, accordingly, has been conceived of as the introduction and modification of objects in people's minds, with theories differing as to the processes involved. We have argued that the container metaphor is too limiting, and that education needs an expanded set of concepts if it is to do full justice to the various roles of knowledge in modern life. There are important kinds of learning that cannot be reduced to objects in the mental container. To do justice to them, we can make use of the new connectionism, which offers us the conception of a mind that can act knowledgeably and logically without itself having content. Sociocultural theories offer us a conception of knowledge that inheres in cultural practices and artifacts and that cannot be reduced to either the contents or the capabilities of individual minds. Popper's three-worlds schema offers a unifying framework in which we may conceive of a connectionist mind (World 2) acting knowledgeably and logically with respect to knowledge objects that have a kind of autonomous existence outside both individual minds and cultural practices. It is these objects, constituting Popper's World 3, that are created, evaluated, revised, and otherwise operated upon in the advancement of science and, more generally, in what is coming to be called "knowledge work."

Within this expanded conceptual framework, a distinction between knowledge building and learning becomes possible. Knowledge building is activity directed outward toward World 3; learning is activity directed inward toward changes in World 2, one's own mental abilities and dispositions. Both are valuable, and it now becomes possible to consider questions such as the following: How much of schooling should be devoted to knowledge building and how much to learning? What is learned from particular knowledge-building activity? How can each support the other? In the preceding section we elaborated such questions as they arise with respect to school mathematics, but they are questions of importance in any area. Yet they are questions that tend to get lost in the kinds of conceptual soup dished up under labels such as "constructivist learning" or "higher-order thinking and learning."

It is not only educators who could benefit from a more elaborated conception of knowledge and learning. As Olson and Bruner propose (this volume, chap. 2), students' own conceptions of knowledge and learning are important. If there is a more profitable way to conceive of knowledge and learning than the way offered by folk theory, students ought to be let in on the secret. If today's students are to be making careers out of working with and adding value to knowledge, they too need a conception of knowledge and learning that does not confuse knowledge objects (World 3) with mental states of knowing (World 2). This is not an unrealistic goal, even at the elementary school level. Students in one class heavily committed to knowledge building (Scardamalia, Bereiter, Hewitt, and Webb, in press) were asked individually how they knew when they had learned. The most articulate response was given by a fifth-grade girl, but other responses were along the same lines. She said:

I think that I can tell if I've learned something when I'm able to form substantial theories that seem to fit in with the information that I've already got; so it's not necessarily that I have everything, that I have all the information, but that I'm able to piece things in that make sense and then to form theories on the questions that would all fit together.

We doubt if Karl Popper would have put it much better.

Acknowledgments

Most of this chapter was written while the authors were scholars-in-residence at the American Institutes for Research Palo Alto Research Center. We are grateful to AIR and its staff for their hospitality and support and to the James S. McDonnell Foundation, which funded the research that made it possible for us to be there.

References

Anderson, J. R. (1983). *The architecture of cognition*. Cambridge: Harvard University Press.

Anderson, J. R. (1987). Skill acquisition: Compilation of weak-method problem solutions. *Psychological Review, 94*, 192–210.

Anderson, J. R., Conrad, F. G., and Corbett, A. T. (1989). Skill acquisition and the LISP tutor. *Cognitive Science, 13*, 467–505.

Astington, J. W., Harris, P. L., and Olson, D. R. (Eds.). (1988). *Developing theories of mind*. New York: Cambridge University Press.

Barzun, J. (1944). *Teacher in America*. Boston: Little, Brown.

Beer, R. D. (1991). *Intelligence as adaptive behavior*. Cambridge: MIT Press.

Bereiter, C. (1991). Implications of connectionism for thinking about rules. *Educational Researcher, 20*, 10–16.

Bereiter, C. and Scardamalia, M. (1993). *Surpassing ourselves: An inquiry into the nature and implications of expertise*. La Salle, IL: Open Court.

Brown, J. S. and Burton, R. R. (1978). Diagnostic models for procedural bugs in basic mathematical skills. *Cognitive Science, 2*, 155–192.

Bruner, J. S. (1990). *Acts of meaning*. Cambridge: Harvard University Press.

Carroll, J. B. (1976). Promoting language skills: The role of instruction. In D. Klahr (Ed.), *Cognition and instruction* (pp. 3–22). Hillsdale, NJ: Lawrence Erlbaum.

Churchland, P. S. (1986). *Neurophilosophy: Toward a unified science of the mind-brain*. Cambridge: MIT Press.

Cognition and Technology Group at Vanderbilt. (1992). The Jasper experiment: An exploration of issues in learning and instructional design. *Educational Technology Research and Development, 40*, 65–80.

Doyle, W. (1983). Academic work. *Review of Educational Research, 53,* 159–199.

Drucker, P. F. (1994, November). The age of social transformation. *Atlantic Monthly,* pp. 53–80.

Fodor, J. A. (1985). Fodor's guide to mental representation: The intelligent auntie's vade-mecum. *Mind, 94,* 76–100.

Gentner, D. and Stevens, A. L. (1983). *Mental models.* Hillsdale, NJ: Lawrence Erlbaum.

Gombrich, E. H. (1959). *Art and illusion: A study in the psychology of pictorial representation.* London: Phaedon Press.

Griffin, S., Case, R., and Siegler, R. S. (1994). Rightstart: Providing the central conceptual prerequisites for first formal learning of arithmetic to students at risk for school failure. In K. McGilly (Ed.), *Classroom lessons: Integrating cognitive theory and classroom practice* (pp. 25–50). Cambridge: MIT Press.

Hirsch, E. D., Jr. (1987). *Cultural literacy: What every American needs to know.* Boston: Houghton Mifflin.

Johnson-Laird, P. N. (1983). *Mental models: Toward a cognitive science of language, inference and consciousness.* Cambridge, England: Cambridge University Press.

Kuhn, D. (1989). Children and adults as intuitive scientists. *Psychological Review, 96,* 674–689.

Lakoff, G. (1987). *Women, fire, and dangerous things: What categories reveal about the mind.* Chicago: University of Chicago Press.

Lakoff, G. and Johnson, M. (1980). *Metaphors we live by.* Chicago: University of Chicago Press.

Lancy, D. F. (1976a). *The beliefs and behaviors of pupils in an experimental school: Introduction and overview* (Technical Report No. LRDC-1976/3). University of Pittsburgh, Learning Research and Development Center.

Lancy, D. F. (1976b). *The beliefs and behaviors of pupils in an experimental school: The science lab* (Technical Report No. LRDC-1976/6). University of Pittsburgh, Learning Research and Development Center.

Lave, J. and Wenger, E. (1991). *Situated learning: Legitimate peripheral participation.* Cambridge, England: Cambridge University Press.

Margolis, H. (1987). *Patterns, thinking, and cognition.* Chicago: University of Chicago Press.

McClelland, J. L., Rumelhart, D. E., and PDP Research Group (Eds.). (1986). *Parallel distributed processing: Explorations in the microstructure of cognition* (Vol. 2). *Psychological and biological models.* Cambridge: MIT/Bradford.

Nisbett, R. E. and Wilson, T. (1977). Telling more than we can know: Verbal reports on mental processes. *Psychological Review, 84,* 231–259.

Novak, J. D. and Gowin, D. B. (1984). *Learning how to learn.* Cambridge, England: Cambridge University Press.

Ohlsson, S. and Reese, E. (1991). The function of conceptual understanding in the learning of arithmetic procedures. *Cognition and Instruction, 8,* 103–179.

Popper, K. R. (1972). *Objective knowledge: An evolutionary approach.* Oxford, England: Clarendon Press.

Popper, K. R. and Eccles, J. C. (1977). *The self and its brain.* Berlin: Springer-Verlag.

Pylyshyn, Z. W. (1984). *Computation and cognition: Toward a foundation for cognitive science.* Cambridge: MIT Press.

Resnick, L. B. and Omanson, S. F. (1987). Learning to understand arithmetic. In R. Glaser (Ed.), *Advances in instructional psychology* (pp. 41–95). Hillsdale, NJ: Lawrence Erlbaum.

Richmond, G. (1973). *The micro-society school: A real world in miniature.* New York: Harper and Row.

Rohlen, T. P. (1989). Order in Japanese society: Attachment, authority, and routine. *Journal of Japanese Studies, 15*, 5–40.

Romer, P. M. (1990). Endogenous technological change. *Journal of Political Economy, 98*, 158–161.

Roth, K. J., Anderson, C. W., and Smith, E. (1987). Curriculum materials, teacher talk, and student learning: Case studies in fifth-grade science teaching. *Journal of Curriculum Studies, 19*, 527–548.

Rumelhart, D. E. (1989). The architecture of mind: A connectionist approach. In M. I. Posner (Ed.), *Foundations of cognitive science* (pp. 133–159). Cambridge: MIT Press.

Rumelhart, D. E., McClelland, J. L., and PDP Research Group (Eds.). (1986). *Parallel distributed processing: Explorations in the microstructure of cognition* (Vol. 1) *Foundations*. Cambridge: MIT Press.

Scardamalia, M. and Bereiter, C. (1992). Text-based and knowledge-based questioning by children. *Cognition and Instruction, 9* (3), 177–199.

Scardamalia, M., Bereiter, C., Hewitt, J., and Webb, J. (in press). Constructive learning from texts in biology. In K. M Fischer and M. Kirby (Eds.), *Relations and biology learning: The acquisition and use of knowledge structures in biology*. Berlin: Springer-Verlag.

Scardamalia, M., Bereiter, C., and Lamon, M. (1994). The CSILE project: Trying to bring the classroom into World 3. In K. McGilly (Ed.), *Classroom lessons: Integrating cognitive theory and classroom practice* (pp. 201–228). Cambridge: MIT Press.

Scribner, S. (1984). Studying working intelligence. In B. Rogoff and J. Lave (Eds.), *Everyday cognition: Its development in social context* (pp. 9–40). Cambridge: Harvard University Press.

Shaw, R. and Turvey, M. T. (1981). Coalitions as models of ecosystems: A realist perspective on perceptual organization. In M. Kubovy and T. Pomerantz (Eds.), *Perceptual organization* (pp. 343–415). Hillsdale, NJ: Lawrence Erlbaum.

Smith, D. C. and Neale, D. C. (1987, April). *The construction of expertise in primary science: Beginnings*. Paper presented at the annual meeting of the American Educational Research Association, Washingon.

Stich, S. P. (1983). *From folk psychology to cognitive science: The case against belief*. Cambridge: MIT Press.

Stigler, J. W. and Baranes, R. (1988). Culture and mathematics learning. *Review of Research in Education, 15*, 253–306.

Woodworth, R. S. (1958). *Dynamics of behavior*. New York: Henry Holt.

Yackel, E., Cobb, P., Wood, T., Wheatley, G., and Merkel, I. (1990). The importance of social interactions in children's construction of mathematical knowledge. In T. Cooney (Ed.), *1990 Yearbook of the National Council of Teachers of Mathematics* (pp. 12–21). Reston, VA: National Council of Teachers of Mathematics.

23

The Development of Understanding

KIERAN EGAN

It has long been obvious that students in the process of their education recapitulate in some way the inventions and discoveries that constitute their cultural history. The young child learning to write and read recapitulates techniques invented a few thousand years ago; the student learning history recapitulates a way of making sense of experience whose development in the ancient Near East we can trace in some detail. That educational development is connected with cultural development is as obvious as it has proven difficult to specify just how. I want to try here to specify just how, drawing on an idea of Vygotsky's. The connection concerns the development, in cultural history and in education, of a set of intellectual tools that profoundly influence how their users can understand the world and make sense of experience.

"Vygotsky defined development in terms of the emergence or transformation of forms of mediation" (Wertsch, 1985, p. 15). That is, Vygotsky argued that intellectual development could not be adequately understood in terms of the accumulation of knowledge or in terms of a sequence of psychological stages like Piaget's. Rather it requires an understanding of the role played by the intellectual tools, the forms of mediation, available in the culture into which a person is born. It is these tools that mediate between knower and known and that determine the kind of understanding that develops in the knower about the known. Vygotsky focused particularly on the development of oral language as a distinctive sign system, concluding that the "*system of signs restructures the whole psychological process*" (1978, p. 35, his emphasis).

In this chapter I want to push this idea a little into the broader field of cultural material. The forms of mediation I will consider are layers of linguistic sophistication, including oral language, literacy, theoretic abstraction, and extreme reflexiveness. If Vygotsky was right, these somewhat distinctive layers of complexity in our major system of signs should have detectible implications for the kind of understanding experienced by their users, whether those users lived long ago or are students today.

I shall try rather briefly to sketch sets of implications that follow from developing oral language, literacy, theoretic abstraction, and extreme reflexiveness. The sets of implications constitute somewhat distinctive kinds of understanding that I call, respectively, mythic, romantic, philosophic, and ironic. I will also mention briefly a fifth kind, which I call somatic.

What I will be sketching, then, is the outline of a new kind of recapitulation theory. In the late nineteenth century, many recapitulation theories were formed, attempting to bring the scientific backing of evolutionary theory to the obvious intuitive sense that the child's education recapitulated the culture's development. Herbert Spencer was one of the more energetic promoters of evolutionary ideas to explain pretty well everything in sight. He compactly expressed the basis for a cultural recapitulation theory of education in the following claim:

If there be an order in which the human race has mastered its various kinds of knowledge, there will arise in every child an aptitude to acquire those kinds of knowledge in the same order.... Education should be a repetition of civilization in little. (1861, p. 76)

This might be called the "folk-recapitulation" position. To become more scientific, a recapitulation theory had to show some precise causal connection between past cultural development and present educational development. The challenge was to show exactly what was recapitulated and why there should arise in every child the aptitude Spencer claimed. If that could be done, then, in the words of another enthusiast, recapitulation "when explored and utilized to its full extent will reveal pedagogic possibilities now undreamed of" (Hall, 1904, Vol. 2, p. 222).

There were two general kinds of recapitulation theories formed, which may be called epistemology-based and psychology-based. They mirrored, not coincidentally, the general kinds of theories formed to account for cultural development on the one hand and educational development on the other. The first kind was based on the observation that knowledge has developed gradually in cultural history and the "order in which the human race has mastered its various kinds of knowledge" exposes a logic that in turn can be used in designing a curriculum. We have only to repeat that order in the curriculum and we have laid out a logical path that the mind of the developing child can follow with maximum ease and a guarantee of finishing up at the peak of "modern" understanding. A significant assumption of these theories was that the mind was largely made up of the knowledge it accumulated; consequently the particular privileged knowledge that had carried "the race" to its rational understanding of reality should form the curriculum.

Psychology-based theories tended to draw more directly on evolutionary theory and its biological sources (Gould, 1977). The recapitulation in these theories was assumed to be from the primitive psychological condition of "savages" to that of sophisticated Victorian adults. John Dewey was supportive of such theories, at least to the degree that they broke the prevailing conventional schemes, and because they provided "the first systematic attempts to base a course of study upon the actual unfolding of the psychology of child nature" (1911, p. 241). A more modern attempt to identify a common psychological sequence in cultural and individual development is made by Hallpike (1979), using Piaget's theory. A significant assumption of these theories was that the mind, in normal interactions with the environment, goes through a regular sequence of developmental stages, and that, for pedagogical purposes, knowledge must be made to conform with these putative stages if it is to be meaningfully learned.

The high hopes of these recapitulation theories came to nothing, or to very little. Most practitioners tried to combine aspects of the epistemology-based and psychology-based theories. The resulting "culture-epoch" curricula seemed plausible when dealing with history and literature, beginning with the study of "primitive" people and their folktales and myth stories. But no amount of ingenuity (see, e.g., Ziller's arguments in Seeley, 1906) could make recapitulation seem a sensible way of dealing with mathematics or science. If the epistemological principle stumbled over how to avoid confusing children with a Ptolemaic view of the cosmos, the psychological principle was coming to grief as recapitulation ideas in biology, to which it was closely allied, were being abandoned (Gould, 1977; Richards, 1992). So, instead of providing a precise causal connection between the order in which the human race has mastered its various kinds of knowledge via logic or psychology, recapitulation reverted to a rather vague though suggestive folk principle, and then it just faded away as far as educational thinking was concerned: "nothing much is left of this radical notion now" (William Kessen, in Philips and Kelly, 1975, p. 354).

So how does Vygotsky's idea help resuscitate recapitulationism? Well, drawing on Vygotsky we can identify what is recapitulated in terms of neither knowledge nor psychological processes but rather in terms of mediating intellectual tools and the kinds of understanding they generate. We can see, too, that Spencer's way of framing the problem did not help; it is not that something that occurred in cultural history causes an aptitude in every child to acquire knowledge in the same order, but rather that by acquiring specific intellectual tools the modern individual generates similar kinds of understanding as existed for people who invented or used these tools in the past. That is, the mistake of past recapitulation theories was to look for some x in cultural history that caused some y in education today; rather we should look for some a—the mediating intellectual tools—that causes both x and y. So we can consider cultural and educational development connected by the intellectual tools that generate common kinds of understanding in both processes.

It might reasonably be objected that this attempted marriage of Vygotsky and recapitulationism is improper, since Vygotsky rejected recapitulation on the ground that ontogenesis involves the natural maturation of the brain, something that plays no part in the course of cultural history (Wertsch, 1991, p. 23). I have three responses: first, it is far from clear how the natural maturation of the brain affects individuals' understanding compared with the acquisition of mediating tools, and we might reasonably argue that the influence of the tools is sufficient to explain the evident changes in kinds of understanding without resort to influences from some putative maturation process; second, Vygotsky and Luria distinguished between bifurcated lines of development in the child, calling one "natural-psychological" and the other "cultural-psychological" and identifying in the latter the major reformulations of mental functioning (see Wertsch, 1985, p. 23), a move compatible with the scheme to be outlined here; and, third, the conceptions of recapitulation Vygotsky would have had in mind were those nineteenth-century kinds dismissed above to which his objection would be destructive in a way that it is not to what follows.

"Kinds of understanding" is not a familiar category in educational discourse. What do such kinds look like? Well, that is what I will try to show in the following sections. But "understanding" is a useful category that may help us past some of the problems education has suffered, drawing on epistemological and psychological traditions and trying to merge them in various ways. These problems largely follow from these somewhat distinct traditions differently identifying the dynamic or primary cause of the educational process; in the former case, it is identified in the accumulation of knowledge and in the latter in an internal developmental process. Of course, probably no one holds to one position exclusively, but holding one or the other as more causally important has given us those persisting battles between child-centered and subject-centered education, between traditionalists and progressivists, and between neoconservatives and neoprogressivists. The category "understanding" has a psychological component, in that restructuring process which Vygotsky claims results from the sequential emerging of mediating sign-sytems. It also has an epistemological component, in that understanding cannot exist without something to understand. This might seem trivial, but attempts to compromise between the dominant epistemological and psychological positions, and their conceptions of the dynamic of the educational process, tend to produce flaccid compromises in which each is allowed scope only to undermine the other; as attempted compromises between child-centered and subject-centered curricula have not given us the best of either world.

Using the category of "kinds of understanding" involves no longer identifying the dynamic of the educational process either in accumulating knowledge or in some process of psychological development; it rather identifies with the generative feature of the human mind that invents or learns to use new intellectual tools. That is, this scheme, and the category of "kinds of understanding," identifies the dynamic in the imagination. This may seem no great step forward as we have very little sense of what the imagination is, but it has the virtue of not ignoring what we do not understand in favor of what we have a better grasp on. So the dynamic that goes with this new category is like a troika: imagination is the "efficient" cause and accumulating knowledge and psychological development are "material" causes, to use Aristotle's terms; that is, imagination is that somewhat mysterious generative feature of the human mind that is the prime causal dynamic of the processes of cultural and educational development, and the logical sequences in which knowledge can be accumulated and the process of psychological development are the enabling constraints that shape what is possible for the generative imagination. The mistake has been to think of as causes what are properly constraints.

I shall now try to characterize the kinds of understanding that are products of using the particular intellectual tools invented and developed in Western cultural history, and I shall indicate very briefly a few implications these have for education today. I shall begin with mythic understanding, which I associate with the invention and development of oral language, whether in cultural history or in children today.

Mythic Understanding

One implication of being an oral language user is a responsiveness to stories. How the beginnings of language led to extensive narratives raises questions I cannot answer here, and could not answer anywhere; it is enough for present purposes to note that the development has been, as far as we can tell, a universal one. All oral cultures that we know of have developed and used stories. Shaped by logical and psychological constraint, the invention of language seems to imply the inevitable development of stories.

But what are stories? How are they distinguishable from other narratives? If I say, "He shot Tom," you will likely have no particular or precise response (unless, perhaps, your name is Tom). If I elaborate this narrative and add that "he" is a handsome, well-groomed young man who loves his grandmother, and that Tom is generally scruffy, bearded, picks his nose in public, and uses foul language in front of children, you may begin to feel glad that "he" shot Tom—given the conventions of fiction today. But if the narrative is extended further, telling you that "he" and the grandmother are leaders of a drug-pushing operation who specialize in selling to kids outside schools, and that his love for his grandmother is of a kind that suggests an unspeakable relationship, and also that Tom, despite his unprepossessing exterior, has a heart of gold and is taking terrible risks to stop the grandmother's and her grandson's nefarious operations. . . . Well, you will properly begin to feel sorry that he shot Tom (unless, of course, a perverse taste for the deaths of heroes has been stimulated in you by the kind of stories Plato so disapproved of). When we know securely how to feel about "He shot Tom," we know we have reached the end of the story.

Stories, then, are narratives that fix our affective orientation to the elements that make them up (Egan, 1978). No other narrative form can do this. We ascribe affective meaning to events, and to people, and to our own lives, by plotting them into provisional or partial stories. We orient ourselves emotionally to our environment by stories. Myth stories are prominent in all oral cultures because they do two things. First, they make their contents more memorable than they could be made in lists or in nonstory narratives—and the preservation of the tribe's lore in living memories is vitally important. Second—and the reason why we might reasonably consider the story as the most important social invention—they orient the emotions of their hearers to their contents. So the initiate into the group becomes emotionally committed to the social, economic, and political conditions of the tribe as iterated in the sacred stories that help to determine the intellectual cosmos and the sense of identity of the individual members.

We can, of course, make sense of our experience in a number of other modalities, but to whatever degree our emotional orientation is involved, then the plotting of events into partial or provisional or overarching stories will be involved. We are creatures who understand an important dimension of our experience and our world in story shapes.

If we briefly consider the kinds of stories that seem to engage young children, we see the transformed folktales of old as readily enjoyed. A number of their features are common to oral cultures of old and to preliterate children today. (This is not, to emphasize, that there is some general "primitive" similarity in their minds but rather that their minds, which are in no significant ways different from those of the most sophisticated Western scholars, use particular intellectual tools and not others, or, rather, use some prominently and others very little.) Myth stories, folktales, and young children prominently employ fantasy. Fantasy, that is, is another universal implication of being a language user.

What is fantasy, and where does it come from? Perhaps the various competing psychoanalytic explanations have some validity, but a much more parsimonious explanation is available if we reflect on fantasy as a universal product of the intellectual tool of oral language use. Consider how young children linguistically grasp the phenomenal world around them. In dealing with temperature, they learn first "hot" and "cold." There is a kind of necessity to this as "hot" means "hotter than my body's temperature" and "cold" means "colder than my body's temperature." In other words, they are the terms for the first and most general discriminations children make and learn to label: similarly with hard/soft, wet/dry, big/little, sharp/blunt, fast/slow, bitter/sweet, and so on and on. Now this approaches contentious issues that are ideological leftovers from structuralism's exaggerated claims, but I want here to make only a limited point. "Logically, we express. . .elementary differentiation in the form of contradictories, A and not-A, and it is certainly true that the ability to distinguish. . .is basic to all cognitive processes" (Hallpike, 1979, pp. 224–225). Or, as Edmund Leach puts it: "Binary oppositions are intrinsic to the process of human thought. Any description of the world must discriminate categories in the form 'p' is what 'not-p' is not" (1967, p. 3). This might be more accurate if the reference to "the process of human thought" is changed to the influence on human thought of the development of oral language. Bruno Bettelheim relatedly refers to the "manner in which [children] can bring some order into [their] world by dividing everything into opposites" (1976, p. 74).

Ogden elaborates the point: "When once an opposition is established and its principle understood, then either opposite, or any intermediary term, can be at once defined by opposition or degree" (1976, p. 20). These oppositions are not necessarily, or even often, made up from genuine logical or empirical opposites; rather they are set up as opposites for conceptual purposes of orientation to complex phenomena, bringing them under some initial conceptual control. So, for example, once the opposition hot/cold is grasped, intermediary words like "warm" or "cool" can be defined and understood in terms of them. This works very well for the continua of the physical world, but it becomes problematic when it goes to work on discrete oppositions like life/death, nature/culture, human/animal. What happens in cases like these? Well, fantasy happens. The intermediary categories between hot/cold and so on, exist and can be perceived, but intermediaries between life and death have to be generated. The use of the intellectual tool of forming binary opposites and intermediaries is very successful in building a conceptual grasp over the phenomenal world, but when it is applied to discrete oppositions like life/death it generates intermediaries like "ghosts." That is, a ghost is to life and death as warm is to hot and cold. The intermediary category is a coalescence of the opposites. So human/animal oppositions generate intermediaries like yetis and Sasquatches. The nature/culture opposition generates those talking animals that fill the myth stories of the world and fill children's stories and their own play-narratives. (Stated so briefly, this may seem starkly speculative, and so it obviously is to a degree. Can we really dispense with the complex mechanisms of the subconscious of Freud and Jung and other psychoanalysts and see fantasy instead as simply a product of an overgeneralized linguistic technique? It has, at least, the virtue of being a more parsimonious speculation.)

In his book *The child's concept of story* (1978), Arthur Applebee argues that the ability of very young children to follow stories is due to familiar features in the stories. This conforms with the general progressivist principle that we should begin with content familiar to the child. Applebee argues that the "sort of familiarity which a child demands in a story is often a social one, a doing of things which the child expects to have done. Thus Peter Rabbit is a manageable story for Carol at two years eight months because of its familiar family setting" (1978, p. 75). But if it is the familiarity that makes the story accessible and meaningful to young children, we must ask why is Peter a rabbit. Also we must wonder why the wild wood is safe and the cultivated garden is dangerous, and death is so close, and so on. The appeal of the story might be better explained as dramatized meditations on security/danger, wild/cultivated, life/death, nature/culture, and obedience/disobedience, and we might see the familiarity that provides access to the story rather in the emotions, the intentions, the hopes and the fears that are familiar to children. It might be a strange world, but it is understandable.

If we reflect on the kind of fantasy-stories young children enjoy so readily, we see that they are built on relatively stark oppositions between security/danger, good/bad, courage/cowardice, and so on. Two features of these are notable for present purposes: one is that they are powerfully affective and the second is that they are abstract. In a simple sense, language implies abstraction: "Language creates distance between the self and the object; language generalizes, transferring a unique perception into a common one; language transmutes realities into abstractions" (Coe, 1984, p. 253). In a more complex sense, it has been argued that abstractions do not develop as a result of encountering concrete objects that are to be named or "enlanguaged." Rather it is only by deploying abstractions that concrete particulars become recognizable: "Concrete particulars are the product of abstractions which the mind must possess in order that it should be able to experience particular sensations, perceptions, or images" (Hayek, 1972, p. 311). Well, this can become a refined neo-Kantian argument, hard to get a secure handle on. But the prevalence of the view that young children and people in oral cultures are "concrete thinkers"—further encouraged by Piaget's theory and its developmental categories—has obscured the sense in which they are also, and perhaps primarily, abstract thinkers.

Hayek suggests that what we mean by abstractions might be better thought of as "operations of the mind," and which I would call another implication of the development of language. Abstractions become conscious, become concepts, Hayek argues, as a result of the mind's reflection on its own operations. The formation of abstract concepts, then, is not itself the mark of their new arrival in some developmental process so much as reflection disclosing what children have been using since they mastered language. So the absence of the awareness of abstractions in young children, or their lack of articulation of, or ability to consciously manipulate, abstractions is not a sign that abstractions are not at work in their thinking. The absence signifies that their language has not developed the tools of reflexiveness that will lead to greater awareness of their own thinking and language use. So the later appearance of abstractions in our language development is not due to their genetically following the concrete, but it represents discoveries of our long active mental operations by reflection on them.

This set of implications of oral language use, these forms of mediation, these "bons-à-penser," to use a Lévi-Strauss term, these intellectual tools, provide the mind using them with a particular kind of "take" on the world and experience, with a particular kind of understanding. They also provide us with a somewhat distinctive way of characterizing children's minds. In turn they can provide us with somewhat distinctive approaches to the curriculum (Egan, 1988) and to teaching (Armstrong, Connolly, and Saville, 1994; Egan, 1989). To give a single abbreviated example, these implications of oral language use suggest a framework to assist teachers to plan lessons or units that might be engaging and meaningful to children. It would be an alternative to the dominant objectives/content/methods/evaluation forms derived from Ralph Tyler's work (1949), and indirectly from industrial procedures used in planning the manufacture of refrigerators and automobiles (Callaghan, 1962). So we can draw up a planning framework like the following:

1. **Identifying importance**
   What is it about the topic that matters to children? What is affectively engaging about it?
2. **Finding binary opposites**
   What powerful binary opposites best catch what is important about the topic?
3. **Organizing the content into a story form**
   3.1. What content dramatically embodies the binary opposites and provides clear access to the importance of the topic? What vivid images can this generate in children's minds?
   3.2. What content best articulates the content into a developing story form?
4. **Conclusion**
   What is the best way of resolving the conflict inherent in the binary opposites? What intermediary positions can be established?
5. **Evaluation**
   How can we know whether the topic has been understood, its importance grasped, and the content learned?

(Examples of using frameworks like this are available most elaborately in Armstrong et al., 1994, and more sketchily in Egan, 1989.)

Romantic Understanding

The intellectual tool whose development leads to what I am calling Romantic understanding is literacy. "Literacy" is meant as a kind of shorthand or code word, referring to much more than the isolable skills of writing and reading. There is, of course, a huge and contentious literature on the implications of literacy (Olson, 1987). I am using the term here to mean also the set of uses to which reading and writing were put, particularly in Greece. I will indicate some of these wider implications below, but in general I mean the invention and development of a technology for representing ideas directly, rather than simply for producing the graphic echo of speech (Donald, 1991).

If you tell a typical five-year-old the story of Cinderella, you are not likely to be asked "What means of locomotion does the Fairy Godmother use?" Nor are you likely to be quizzed about where she is and what she does when she is not active in the story. But if you tell a ten-year-old the equally fantastic story of Superman, you will need to explain his supernatural powers by reference to his birth on the planet Krypton and to the different molecular structure of our Sun from that of his home star, and so on. (A better scholar would have taken the time to consult appropriate authorities at this point.) For the younger audience, magic is entirely unobjectionable, as long as it moves the story forward. Peter Rabbit's world does not make the accommodations with reality that are necessary for the rabbits Hazel and Bigwig in Richard Adams's *Watership Down*; Hazel could not bring Bigwig a nice cup of camomile tea, for instance, as his paws would not be able to hold it.

What happens between five and ten that causes this difference? A folk-psychological response is that it is simply a matter of accumulated experience informing the child's understanding of which regularities tend to be more reliable. It just takes some time to grasp the conditions of reality that exclude Jack Frost and the Tooth Fairy but include computer programmers and monks. But the gradual accommodation with prosaic reality cannot be a sufficient explanation, because it is the accommodation itself that needs to be explained. There are cultures in which this transition from a world in which fantasy and magic perform explanatory work does not take place in anything like the way that is common in the West. And, of course, we can easily overestimate how common this transition is in the West. A cursory glance over the widely selling tabloids available at supermarket check-outs suggests caution in making strong claims about how participants in literate Western societies make some marked transition from the ready acceptance of fantasy and magic in making sense of the world.

Once written records began to accumulate in ancient Greece, it became necessary to coordinate family histories that claimed descent from a god five generations back with accounts that claimed gods had not had intimate relations with humans for a dozen generations and with travellers' tales from Egypt where there were lists of more than a hundred generations of mortal high priests. Criteria were needed to sort out which of the competing claims were more reliable. From such intellectual activity, history was born.

Herodotus, father of history, was also called the "father of lies" because he wrote about what he could not have witnessed. One of the prominent early uses of literacy was to make accounts of reality problematic. Indeed, the concept of reality, as something to be inquired into and discovered, seems to have been one of the implications of literacy. What literacy seemed to allow was a more reliable record of what had really happened, one that would displace the fantastic myths. So Hecataeus of Miletus began his *Genealogies* with the claim that what he wrote was true whereas "the stories of the Greeks are many and, in my opinion, ridiculous." Thucydides tells us that he is writing an account of the Peloponnesian War "to prevent it sliding over into myth," as had the Trojan War, having been left to oral poets.

The initial focus of the *logographoi*—writers of rational prose—is most fully exemplified by Herodotus' *Histories*. His focus is on the *mega ergon*—the great thing done. He describes the great achievements of the Persian Empire, and the other eastern kingdoms, but saves his longest section for the Egyptians: "I am about to lengthen my *logos* on Egypt because Egypt has the largest number of wonders, more than all the rest of the world. And of all the countries of the world, it is Egypt that contains *erga* which actually surpass their reputation" (*The Histories*, II, 35). It reads like a Guinness Book of Ancient World Records.

Open up *The Histories* at random, as I do now, and learn about the black pygmies who carried off a group of Lybian explorers, or about the 22 tons of gold used in building the figure of Bel (the Biblical Baal) in Babylon, or the weirdnesses of the Egyptians whose women attend market and do business while the men stay home and weave *and* whose women stand up to urinate whereas the men squat down, or how to catch crocodiles, or how Amazon women came to settle with a detachment of Scythian young men but preserved such customs as not marrying until killing an enemy in battle, and in the endless stories of outstanding cunning, daring, cruelty, prophecies, sexual misbehavior, and so on. Much of the text bears more than a passing resemblance to those papers at the supermarket check-out.

The initial literacy-driven exploration of reality is of its extremes, of the strange, the bizarre, the wonderful. It is not just coincidental that one of the world's most popular books with newly literate children is the *Guinness Book of Records*, with its Herodotus-like fascination with the *mega ergon*, or that the best-selling publications are tabloids such as the *National Inquirer*. If you are a teacher with a choice of two lessons you can take into a Friday afternoon class of eleven-year-olds whose interests you want to engage, do you take the one on "The structure of your local neighborhood" or the one on "Torture instruments through the ages"? The answer is obvious. (This is not a curriculum recommendation.) But a part of the folklore of teaching is that students' exploration of the world will be more enthusiastic if we begin with what is immediate and relevant to their everyday experience. But we can readily observe that their interest is most commonly and energetically engaged by the exotic, the strange, the wonderful, by the limits of reality and the extremes of experience.

While the exploration of this newly problematic reality can be exciting, it can also be threatening. The threats can be significantly relieved by associating with someone or something that seems best able to overcome them. So associations are formed with embodiments of those human qualities that transcend the everyday constraining and threatening world; whether it is an association with the outrageousness of a pop-singing Madonna or with the skill and power of a Maradona or with the courage of tiny democratic Athens facing the enormous might of the tyrannous Persian empire.

(Herodotus heroizing Athens, the girl heroizing Madonna, and the boy heroizing a football team are involved in a curious psychological act. The heroized object is imbued with a transcendent quality—courage, wonderful disregard of conventional constraints, power and skill—while the object is nevertheless recognized as being constrained by reality. It is the classic ambivalence of romance: seeking to transcend constraints that are recognized as ultimately not transcendable. Associating with these heroes is psychologically quite unlike the admiration, or whatever, that might have been felt for great Hector, tamer of horses, or for wily Ulysses, or for lord of men Agamemnon. Their actions are tied to the choices, deeds, whims of the gods. While Achilles might seem to have a lot in common with the sports hero on strike for more pay because his pride has been hurt by a paltry contract offer, the place of Achilles in a supernatural scheme makes him inaccessible to the ambivalent romantic association the literate boy might form with a sports hero. We can, of course, make Achilles or Hector into romantic heroic figures, but at the cost of making the gods into merely psychological forces and removing them all from the oral world they originally inhabited.)

These kinds of implications of early literacy can in turn imply curricula for evoking, stimulating, and developing the kind of understanding they make possible (Egan, 1990)—and in constructing our curriculum some might prefer to move closer to Herodotus' exemplification of Romantic understanding than to the *National Inquirer*'s. We can thus construct another framework that might help teachers ensure that they design lessons and units likely to be more meaningful and engaging to students during their early years of literacy:

1. **Identifying transcendent qualities**
   What transcendent qualities can be felt as central to the topic? What affective images do they evoke?
2. **Organizing the content into a narrative structure**
   2.1. **Initial access**
        What content, distinct from the students' everyday experience, best embodies the transcendent qualities most central to the topic? What limit of reality or extreme of experience does this expose?
   2.2. **Structuring the body of the lesson or unit**
        What content best articulates the topic into a clear narrative structure?

2.3. **Humanizing the content**

How can the content be shown in terms of human hopes, fears, intentions, or other emotions? What aspects of the content can best stimulate wonder and awe? What ideals and/or revolts against conventions are inherent in the topic?

2.4. **Pursuing details**

What content best allows students to pursue some aspect of the topic in *exhaustive* detail?

3. **Conclusion**

How can we best bring the topic to satisfactory closure, while pointing on to further dimensions or to other topics? How can the students *feel* this satisfaction?

4. **Evaluation**

How can we know the topic has been understood and has engaged and stimulated students' imaginations?

Philosophic understanding

The dominant linguistic development that stimulates philosophic understanding, I am suggesting, is theoretic abstraction. Again, this is a code or shorthand phrase to cover much more than an isolable intellectual skill. In this case, in particular, it implies also communities that support this peculiar kind of thinking. It is not something that is easy to sustain apart from institutions devoted to sustaining it.

I call it philosophic primarily because it received decisive development in the program that Plato and Aristotle brought to a refined pitch and bequeathed to the ancient and modern worlds with such a weight of intimidating intellectual authority. They were magisterial combatants on behalf of "philosophy, or rather of one particular style of philosophizing, as the sole repository of the truth in opposition to all comers" (Lloyd, 1990, p. 128). This style reached a further distinctive pitch after the ancient Greeks' texts became again widely accessible and influential during the European Renaissance.

And what about those communities? This theoretic thinking is not easy, nor is it obvious how such an abstracted language use can be an effective route to dealing with practical problems. We do see examples of this kind of thinking in other ancient civilizations and in oral cultures, but what seems unique to ancient Greece is the systematic cultivation of this level of discourse and the assertion that it is the only form of language that can capture what is real and true about the world and experience. The difficulty of learning and sustaining this theoretic discourse was in part overcome by communities dedicated to it. Among the earliest was the Pythagorean community at Crotona in southern Italy. It had political and religious aims as well as, or combined with, philosophic and protoscientific interests: a combination that would have been recognized without any sense of anomaly by the founders of the British Royal Society, though the dietary and hygiene rules might have seemed a tad alien in seventeenth century England. The diffuse community of Hippocratic practitioners and writers, trying to forge a rational, protoscientific approach to medicine, was also prominent in developing theoretic thinking, as were the argumentative law courts of the Ionian cities and of Athens. There developed in the latter systematic methods for publicly establishing and verifying the truth about cases, and this discourse was carried to and fro between law courts and the disputatious democratic assemblies, where the work of developing knock-down arguments against opposing positions was carried on with urgency (Lloyd, 1990; Vernant, 1982). Communities are important to this kind of understanding because it is carried only in part by philosophic texts; it is "oral discourse about written texts that provides such fertile ground for modern skeptical, interpretive thought" (Olson and Torrance, 1991, p. 1).

This kind of understanding becomes evident in students who engage in systematic academic work and whose language development has been quite sophisticated. Commonly around age 15 or 16 we see such students begin to use such words as "society," "evolution," "culture," "the environment," and so on. These kinds of terms signal the development of a recognition of the theoretic realm. It seems to happen relatively suddenly, and such "portmanteau" words, as Walter Ong calls them, are commonly deployed with a new self-conscious sense of their valency and potency.

Earlier the "romantic" students connected themselves with history, for example, primarily by association with its heroic figures, dramatic events, with the bright bits and pieces. The developing theoretic language helps to generate, or is a symptom of, a significantly different perspective in which the bright bits and pieces are seen increasingly as parts of general wholes, of systems, of processes, and that whatever truth is to be found in history is to come from understanding the nature of the historical process as a whole. The students' connection with history is not any longer through romantic associations; increasingly they see themselves as parts of a single historical process, as agents not transcendent players. They come to recognize of themselves that "I am born with a past" (MacIntyre, 1981, p. 205) and that that past in some significant way has already significantly constituted the student's "self," and it shapes and constrains the student's possibilities for the future.

A related feature of students' educational development, which occurs commonly in late high school or during the college years, is the development of general schemes: ideologies, notions of the process and direction of history, social theories, metaphysical schemes. In these general schemes, whether a Marxist theory of history and society or a liberal social ideology of evolutionary amelioration, students locate truth "with a capital T," as William James put it. The kind of understanding supported in communities like Pythagoras's or Plato's or in parts of modern higher educational institutions, is one in which abstract theoretic schemes are central and are seen as repositories of truth. It is not without its ironies that the most energetic and uncompromising critics of the Platonic/Aristotelian project—identified rather vaguely as central to "Western thinking"—frame their critiques in the kind of abstract theoretic terms those Greeks proposed.

The inappropriate sense of certainty that can come with philosophic understanding in an individual's education is observed with disapproval from the classical period to the present. Plato recognized it as a danger point in his educational program: "You must have seen how youngsters [late teens], when they get their first taste of it [dialectic and the *dianoia* curriculum], treat argument as a form of sport solely for purposes of contradiction. . .delighting like puppies in tugging and teasing anyone who comes near them" (*Republic*, VII, 539). The distress of over-confident youths is loud through the Enlightenment: "It is a frequent and growing Folly of our Age, that pert young Disciples soon fancy themselves wiser than those who teach them" (Watts, 1741, pp. 102–103); or "Young people never show their folly and ignorance more conspicuously, than by this over-confidence in their own judgement, and this haughty disdain of the opinion of those who have known more days" (More, 1777, pp. 92–93). In a more psychologically alert age, like our own, the observation may be put into this form: "The tentativeness implicit in the adolescent condition makes youth vulnerable to ideological certainty" (Spacks, 1981, p. 262).

The "expanding horizons" general scheme that has had so much influence on teaching and the curriculum, especially in North America and Australia, implies that in the last years of high school the student is able to deal with content entirely distant from "the self," knowledge of the self being the educational starting point of that scheme. But there is a sense in which philosophic understanding represents a new and closer apprehension of the self. Educational development, I am suggesting, is a process whose focus of interest and intellectual engagement begins with little concern for reality but rather with a mythlike construction of the world, then "romantically" establishes the boundaries and extent of reality, and then "philosophically" maps the general features of the world with general organizing grids. In this "philosophic" activity, students recognize themselves as parts of complex processes and set about establishing the truth about them with some psychological urgency, because in establishing the truth about the processes they discover the truth about themselves.

The problem with these general theoretic schemes is that they are never able to account adequately for all the relevant particulars. However comprehensive the general scheme, however rigorously scientific, there seem to be always some particulars that are anomalous. Thomas Kuhn's claims about anomalies in science (1962) can, with appropriate disclaimers, be used to indicate how particulars in all areas of inquiry in which general schemes are formed present difficulties in simply accepting the general scheme as reflecting the truth. Either we can simply deny the existence or relevance of the anomalous particulars, in which case we become uncompromising ideologues, or we recognize that the accumulation of anomalies indicates that the general schemes have a troubling epistemological status. They may be useful, but they cannot sustain the expectations held for them by the polemical Greeks, by the Baconian early scientists, by the Enlightenment *philosophes*, or by the positivists.

The ideal teacher of "philosophic" students will require qualities of flexibility, sensitivity, and tolerance in abundance. The teacher needs to be supportive of the students' developing general schemes, even when those schemes will seem simplistic, and perhaps even offensive; the teacher needs to be sympathetic with students' occasional overconfidence and must be ready to support them at those moments of fearful insecurity when a general scheme threatens to be inadequate; and the teacher must gradually introduce anomalies and dissonance at appropriate times, encouraging greater sophistication in students' general schemes. This last activity seems most important pedagogically during this period of education. Usually simply pitting one general scheme against the one held by the student will be less effective in encouraging greater sophistication than the gradual presentation of anomalies to the scheme. In general the procedure is one that will lead to the recognition of the inadequacy of locating truth in such general schemes. But what educational institution can afford such a paragon of pedagogical tact? Clearly we can get by with something less than the ideal.

This is an abstract and rather sterile language, used to try to characterize very briefly some complex features of our educational development. Anyone who has dealings with intellectually energetic students will readily be able to translate this abstract talk of disturbances to general schemes into the very real emotional crises and difficulties they encounter; angst, tears, depression, suicide, and pills are among the real-world correlates of the process. It is a lucky student who makes this intellectual journey buoyed constantly by the excitement of discovery without the distresses and emotional turmoil consequent on the recognition of inadequacy in the schemes used to make sense of the world and experience.

Yet the initial excitement of philosophic understanding comes from a belief that our general schemes disclose the truth about reality, often in pellucid and simple forms that draw together everything we know. It is as though the dark glass has been drawn away, and at last we really *understand*. In his autobiography W. H. Hudson describes such a change at age 15 in these terms: "It was as though I had only just become conscious; I doubt that I had ever been fully conscious before" (1918, p. 292). It is something that nearly all educated people I have surveyed recognize, though some recall it as having more dramatic impact than others. To inquisitive creatures, it can come with the force of revelation. As the years go by, and as irony develops, we may forget the ardor of early philosophic understanding, and, of course, it comes to some only partially, as a feeble glow rather than as a lightning flash. But it can feel like what Faust sold his soul for. We do not see too much of the lightning flash or Faustian contracts in our schools and universities—but we do see some, and we might see more.

We might construct another framework to help teachers focus in their planning on those features of knowledge that might make it more accessible and meaningful to "philosophic" students:

1. Identifying relevant general schemes

What general schemes seem best able to organize the topic into some coherent whole? What are the most powerful and clear relevant general theories, ideologies, metaphysical schemes?

2. **Organizing the content into the general scheme(s)**

   What relevant content can be used to most clearly embody the general scheme? How can this be most vividly introduced to the students?

3. **Introducing anomalies to the gneral scheme(s)**

   What content is anomalous to the general scheme? How can we begin with minor anomalies and continue increasingly to challenge the students' general scheme(s)?

4. **Presenting alternative general schemes**

   What alternative general schemes can coherently organize the topic? Which can best be used to help students best see the contingency of such schemes?

5. **Conclusion**

   How can we ensure that the students' general schemes are not destroyed or made rigid but are recognized as having a different epistemological status from the facts they are based on? How can we ensure that the decay of belief in the truth of the general scheme does not lead to disillusion and despair?

6. **Evaluation**

   How can we know that the student learned and understood the content of the unit and also developed, elaborated, and recognized the limits of a comprehensive general scheme?

Ironic and Somatic Understanding

The decay of belief in general schemes, particularly in the humanities, seems commonly to be brought about by the development of a new reflexiveness on the nature of the language in which they are expressed. The reflection that leads to ironic understanding involves recognizing that words cannot adequately capture things, that the philosophic rationality that had promised to deliver the truth simply cannot, because of the recognized disparity between linguistic forms and what they try to represent. This puts it simplistically, of course, but the Enlightenment project to gradually ameliorate the brutality of human beings and their awful lives by the application of reason began to founder by the late nineteenth century. Alert observers began "rising up against civilization as a disease, and declaring that it is not our disorder but our order that is terrible." (Well, no, that isn't Michel Foucault; it's Bernard Shaw expressing admiration for the insight of Charles Dickens's *Hard Times* [in Cunningham, 1994, p. 6]).

Nietzsche is the apostle of the radical ironic distrust of claims to knowledge and truth: "That there should be a 'truth' which one could somehow approach—!" (Nietzsche, c.1883–1888/1968, p. 249). Mere mythologies were made up to comfort the weak and simpleminded; people forgot that these modern myths had been made up, then forgot that they had forgotten. The confusions were embedded in the very language we have inherited ("We are not rid of God because we still have faith in grammar," as he famously put it in *The Twilight of the Idols*). The claim of some to pursue the truth for its own sake sickened him; the claim is nothing other than a mask for the desire to control, conquer, appropriate; the pursuit of truth is driven only by "wanting to be superior" (p. 249).

His violent irony is a distorted reflection of the more humorous and buoyant irony of Socrates. Thrasymachus irritatedly accuses him of habitual irony (*Republic*, I. 336). Our sense of irony is largely derived from Socrates' peculiar stance in the world. It is made up primarily of what Vlastos calls "Socrates' renunciation of epistemic certainty" (1991, p. 4). Quintilian and Cicero, who elaborated the concept of *ironia*, both refer to Socrates in the process, and the most influential discussion of irony in the modern world, Kirkegaard's, is derived from an extended meditation of Socrates' peculiar character. What infuriated Thrasymachus was "not just [Socrates] not saying what he means but his refusal to mean anything at all" (Bruns, 1992, p. 32).

Richard Rorty, among others, recommends that we strive for something like this condition as an aim of education. His "liberal ironist" accepts the "contingency of. . .our most central beliefs and desires," and abandons "the idea that those central beliefs and desires refer back to something beyond the reach of time and chance" (Rorty, 1989, p. xv). The meanings we contingently construct are to be recognized as having no privileged claim on reality over anyone else's meanings, and their purpose is to enable us to form "solidarity" with others, for the purpose of living well and not harming others.

The sense of ironic understanding I want to suggest draws on the postmodern sense of irony but not on its dismissive certainties. When a postmodern theorist, such as Lyotard (1979), for example, expresses incredulity in the face of all philosophic general schemes or metanarratives and frames a theoretically elaborate manifesto of systematic incredulity, his work takes the shape of a new metanarrative or general scheme and runs the self-refuting risks of such bold claims as "All generalizations are false!"

The resistance in ironic understanding to the postmodern dismissal of the Enlightenment project, and to the confident belief that knowledge, truth, and objectivity are confined only to contingent agreements among the likeminded, and to the claim that Western science and rationality are discourses no more privileged that any others in terms of access to reality, is based on the persistence within ironic understanding of somatic understanding.

This scheme is one in which we accumulate intellectual tools. Becoming literate does not mean that we cease to be oral language users, as becoming oral language users does not mean that we cease to have a distinctive human and prelinguistic "take" on the world. That is, very young children, illiterate deaf-mutes in the past, and certain people with unusual neurological conditions experience the world as human beings who do not use language. They give us clues to the range of prelinguistic human intelligence. It is important to recognize that prelinguistic understanding does not go away when language develops, as oral language does not go away with the development of literacy. They coalesce to some significant degree. Somatic understanding involves a wide range of competences that remain with us throughout our lives and coalesce in various ways with the competences stimulated by the intellectual tools of developing language that we have considered briefly above. What I mean by somatic understanding coincides significantly with what Merlin Donald characterizes as "mimetic" (1991), and includes such capacities as "intentionality, generativity, communicativity, reference, autocueing, and the ability to model an unlimited number of objects' (Donald, 1991, p. 171); it is the basis of whatever common sense we have.

Much postmodern theory is built on the assumption that human understanding is essentially languaged understanding. As Rorty puts it: "For it is essential in my view that we have no prelinguistic consciousness to which language needs to be adequate, no deep sense of how things are which it is the duty of philosophers to spell out in language" (1989, p. 21). This is "the current *doxa* which unites the various schools" of advanced thinking (Norris, 1993, p. 289). Somatic understanding, however, is a prelinguistic consciousness, and it is prelinguistic not simply in the temporal sense, but it remains with us, as a part of our understanding, throughout our lives.

The characteristics of ironic understanding do not lead to a simple planning framework. They point rather to a recognition that we are parts of a conversation. The pedagogical principles we might draw involve modesty about the security of our epistemological grasp of the content to be taught, a sensitive ear for the understanding of our students—whom we will consider, rather, as colleagues—playfulness in acknowledging and exploring diverse perspectives, and all the other old academic virtues. Pedagogy is, of course, the wrong word for teaching people who engage knowledge in a significantly ironic way; they draw on the entire set of intellectual tools developed with each kind of understanding and have become full members of the complex conversation that constitutes intellectual life in the West.

Conclusion

This sequence of cumulative, partially coalescing, kinds of understanding—somatic, mythic, romantic, philosophic, ironic—offers an alternative way of looking at educational development. If we consider the purpose of education as evoking, stimulating, and developing each of these kinds of understanding, more or less sequentially, we will have an educational process that mirrors in one significant dimension the development of Western culture. (The implications and problems for such a scheme in modern multicultural societies cannot be addressed here. Far from it being a fatal objection, however, I think it will be clear that this scheme, ironically, shows us ways of valuing and building on the variety of tools provided by the various cultural backgrounds from which children arrive at school.)

By focusing on mediational intellectual tools rather than on knowledge or on psychological processes, it has at least been possible to generate a somewhat distinctive kind of developmental scheme. It is one that, when elaborated and fleshed out with curricular and teaching implications, also can succeed in the postevolutionary ambition of showing how education can become "a repetition of civilization in little." Our current epistemology-derived and psychology-derived conceptions of education, and attempts at mixing them, have not been so notably successful that an alternative recapitulation scheme should be casually ignored.

References

Applebee, A. N. (1978). *The child's concept of story*. Chicago: University of Chicago Press.

Armstrong, M., Connolly, A., and Saville, K. (1994). *Journeys of discovery*. Melbourne: Oxford University Press.

Bettelheim, B. (1976). *The uses of enchantment*. New York: Knopf.

Bruns, G. L. (1992). *Hermeneutics: Ancient and modern*. New Haven: Yale University Press.

Callahan, R. (1962). *Education and the cult of efficiency*. Chicago: University of Chicago Press.

Coe, R. (1984). *When the grass was taller*. New Haven: Yale University Press.

Cunningham, V. (1994, February 18). Fight, fight, and fight again. *Times Literary Supplement*, p. 6.

Dewey, J. (1911). Culture epoch theory. In P. Monroe (Ed.), *A Cyclopedia of Education* (Vol. 2, pp. 240–242). New York: Macmillan.

Donald, M. (1991). *Origins of the modern mind*. Cambridge: Harvard University Press.

Egan, K. (1978). What is a plot? *New Literary History, 9* (3), 455–473.

Egan, K. (1988). *Primary understanding: Education in early childhood*. New York: Routledge.

Egan, K. (1989). *Teaching as story telling*. Chicago: University of Chicago Press.

Egan, K. (1990). *Romantic understanding: The development of rationality and imagination, ages 8–15*. New York: Routledge.

Egan, K. (1992). *Imagination in teaching and learning*. Chicago: University of Chicago Press.

Gardner, H. (1991). *The unschooled mind*. New York: Basic Books.

Gould, S. J. (1977). *Ontogeny and phylogeny*. Cambridge: Harvard University Press.

Hall, G. S. (1904). *Adolescence* (2 vols.). New York: D. Appleton.

Hallpike, C. R. (1979). *The foundations of primitive thought*. Oxford, England: Clarendon Press.

Hayek, F. A. (1972) The primacy of the abstract. In A. Koestler and J. R. Smythies (Eds.), *Beyond reductionism* (pp. 309–333). New York: Macmillan.

Hudson, W. H. (1918). *Far away and long ago*. London: Dent.

Kuhn, T. S. (1962). *The structure of scientific revolutions*. Chicago: University of Chicago Press.

Leach, E. (1967). Genesis as myth. In J. Middleton (Ed.), *Myth and cosmos* (pp. 1–13). New York: Natural History Press.

Lloyd, G. E. R. (1990). *Demystifying mentalities*. Cambridge, England: Cambridge University Press.

Lyotard, J.-F. (1979). *The postmodern condition: A report on knowledge* (G. Bennington and B. Massumi, Trans.). Minneapolis: University of Minnesota Press.

MacIntyre, A. (1981). *After virtue*. Notre Dame, IN: University of Notre Dame Press.

More, H. (1777). *Essays on various subjects, principally designed for young ladies*. London: Wilkie and Cadell.

Nietzsche, F. (c.1883–1888/1968). *The will to power* (W. Kaufmann, Ed.; W. Kaufmann and R. J. Hillingdale, Trans.). New York: Vintage.

Norris, C. (1993). *The Truth about Postmodernism*. Oxford, England: Blackwell.

Ogden, C. K. (1976). *Opposition*. Bloomington, IN: Indiana University Press.

Olson, D. R. (Ed.). (1987). Understanding literacy. Special issue of *Interchange, 18,* 1/2.

Olson, D. R. and N. Torrance (Eds.). (1991). *Literacy and orality*. Cambridge, England: Cambridge University Press.

Philips, D. and Kelly M. (1975). Hierarchical theories of development in education and psychology. *Harvard Educational Review, 45* (3), 351–375.

Richards, R. J. (1992). *The meaning of evolution*. Chicago: University of Chicago Press.

Rorty, R. (1989). *Contingency, irony, and solidarity*. Cambridge, England: Cambridge University Press.

Seeley, L. (1906). *Elementary pedagogy*. New York: Hinds, Noble, and Eldredge.

Spacks, P. M. (1981). *The adolescent idea: Myths of youth and the adult imagination*. New York: Basic Books.

Spencer, H. (1861). *Education: Intellectual, moral and physical*. London: G. Manwering.

Tyler, R. (1949). *Basic principles of curriculum and instruction*. Chicago: University of Chicago Press.

Vernant, J.-P. (1982). *The origins of Greek thought*. Ithaca, NY: Cornell University Press.

Vlastos, G. (1991). *Socrates: Ironist and moral philosopher*. Cambridge, England: Cambridge University Press.

Vygotsky, L. (1978). *Mind in society: The development of higher psychological processes*. M. Cole, V. John-Steiner, S. Scribner, and E. Souberman (Eds.). Cambridge: Harvard University Press.

Watts, I. (1741). *The improvement of the mind: Or, a supplement to the art of logick*. London: James Brackstone.

Wertsch, J. V. (1985). *Vygotsky and the social formation of mind*. Cambridge: Harvard University Press.

Wertsch, J. V. (1991). *Voices of the mind: A sociocultural approach to mediated action*. Cambridge: Harvard University Press.

24

The Learner's Experience of Learning

FERENCE MARTON
SHIRLEY BOOTH

In this chapter learning in various educational contexts is characterized as a change in the way in which the learner sees, or experiences, some aspect of the world. Learning has two aspects that are inextricably intertwined: (1) the "what" aspect, which refers to the content of learning, and (2) the "how" aspect, which refers to the way in which learning takes place. It is found empirically that whatever it is that learners learn (the "what" aspect), a qualitative variation is to be found in the outcome, and, correspondingly, whatever learning tasks are undertaken (the "how" aspect), there is a qualitative variation in the ways the learners approach them, or go about them. There is a degree of consistency in the nature of the variation in the "how" aspect, in that there is an overall pattern of deep and surface approaches. A deep approach to a learning task is characterized by the learner's intention to find meaning in the content through tackling the task, whereas in a surface approach focus is rather on meeting the demands of the task as such. Empirical evidence is presented for the existence of a relationship between the nature of the approach and the quality of the outcome of learning, which is elaborated into a functional relationship through a consideration of the simultaneity of human awareness. Generalizations over age groups, subject areas, and cultures are discussed, and implications for teaching are drawn out.

Alternative Perspectives on Learning

If you have read this far in the book, you should have a good idea of what learning is. But one of our principles is that nothing should be taken for granted—so we will begin with a short definition, an authoritative characterization from Hilgard and Bower (1981).

Learning refers to the change in a subject's behavior or behavior potential to a given situation brought about by the subject's repeated experiences in that situation, provided that the behavior change cannot be explained on the basis of the subject's native response tendencies, maturation, or temporary states (such as fatigue, drunkenness, drives, and so on). (p. 11)

Now consider this extract from a conversation between a colleague of ours, Eva Ekeblad, and a little boy who is working at a computer program:

EVA: Mmm. . .This about learning—is it something that just happens while you are working?

G: Well. . .it's if you couldn't. . .then you can after.

This is what we believe learning is about: the transition from *not being able to* to *being able to*. In Ingrid Pramling's investigation of children's learning, there are a number of examples of eight-year-olds who describe the transition between *not being able* and *being able*—to do, to know, to understand—something, through something happening—doing something or listening to someone or watching something (Pramling, 1983).

We want to take our starting point in this simple view of learning, constituted from two particular aspects, which lead to two questions:

What is learned?

and

How is it learned?

If we start to examine these fundamental questions, we have to consider ways of tackling them. There are ways used by other people. The prototypical case of learning that comes up when you talk to preschool children, in Sweden at least, is learning to ride a bicycle.[1] Our two questions can be tackled simply by watching the children learn. The "what" of learning is quite clear—now there is balance where before there was none—and the ways they do it—the "how" of learning—follow visible patterns of failure and correction, disappointments and rewards. If we want to explain this learning, we can explain it by its consequences.

The prototypical case of learning when it comes to schoolchildren and university students is more likely to be that of reading a book or listening to a teacher. We can ask them questions to find out the extent to which the text has been understood in the way expected, or set problems to see how well the new information can be used, thus probing the "what" aspect. But if we really want to find out what is going on when they read or answer questions or solve problems—the "how" aspect—then we have to look further. Maybe we could look *into* them, to find out what is going on in their minds. Or we could ask them to look into their *own* minds for us, tell us what is going on there. Or we could observe them and by probing in some way try to *infer* what is happening. Such an approach to inquiring into learning is grounded in a belief that human acts are determined internally, and what is on the inside corresponds in some way to the reality that is to be found on the outside. An explanation for observed change has to be made in terms of changes of internal states and processes in response to stimuli of external origin.

Our line of reasoning is somewhat different; it is based on the assumption that in order to understand how people act in the world we have to take account of the world as they see it. We cannot assume that the text is the same for each learner, since they each read it in their own ways, from their own perspectives, against the background of their own lives. Nor can we assume that the learner sees the world in the same way as the researcher does. Our project is to see learning through the eyes of the learner. This leads us to explain changes in the ways learners act in terms of changes in their ways of experiencing the world.

Experience as the Object of Research

Our research is oriented toward investigating learning, and it is experience that is the subject matter of this research. As the chapters of this book illustrate, experiential data—interviews and think-aloud protocols—are currently in wide use. However, as a rule they are used not with the aim of studying experience itself but instrumentally to reveal hidden entities such as mental models, or mental constructs and procedures, which are in turn related to cognitive activity, including learning. As should be obvious from the explanatory model we are arguing for— that learning is explained by the changes in the way learners experience the world—we believe that experience has to be studied in its own right, and the very experience of learning has to be made the subject of research.

There is, of course, a well-established science of experience, phenomenology, which has been one of the main schools of philosophical thought of this century. It is generally recognized as being founded on the work of the German mathematician and philosopher Edmund Husserl. From the beginning, it has focused on the development of a single theory of experience by using a particular method which— befitting a philosophy—is a philosophical method; philosophers engage in investigating their own experience.

Our orientation, in contrast, is empirical. We are interested in studying other people's experiences, and in particular the different ways in which people experience phenomena in the world around them. We have coined the name *phenomenography* for this research orientation (Marton, 1981). Thus phenomenography and phenomenology both belong to a field of knowledge defined by the criterion of having experience as the subject of study, but they differ in the ways they go about that enterprise.

When we do research aimed at exploring the experience of learning, via the experience of learners, we face a fundamental ontological question: "What kind of thing is an experience?" We shall attempt to address this question now.

To start with, an experience is always an experience of something. Experiences of interest to us have been the experience of a text being read, the experience of tackling a problem of some sort, and the experience of learning itself. Think of a text in a typical textbook. We can think of it as, on the one hand, just a text, and on the other hand, as the learner's way of experiencing or understanding it. You might find it reasonable to view the text as being quite independent of both the learners who read it and the ways in which they understand it: The object (text) and subject (learner) are then totally separate entities. Such a view continues as follows: the learner receives information about the object via the senses and forms a representation of the object in the mind. Experiences, or what can also be called conceptions, are then simply these mental representations that make up an internal, subjective world that corresponds, more or less, to the external, objective world. Finally, studying experiences of a text, or the understanding of a text, means studying how the "text in itself" is represented in the learner's mind; the researcher predetermines what the text really is and compares the learner's image of it with this norm. This way of addressing the question "What sort of thing is an experience?" rests on the belief that object and subject are separate and independent—i.e., on a *dualistic ontology*.

Now consider a *non-dualistic ontology*, in which object and subject are not separate. There is no "text in itself"—a text is always understood by someone in some way, and it thus has no independent existence. From our non-dualistic ontological perspective there are not two worlds, not a real objective world on the one hand and a subjective world of mental representations on the other hand. There is only one world, a real existing world that is experienced and understood in different ways by human beings; it is both objective and subjective at the same time. An experience is now a relationship between object and subject that encompasses them both. The experience is as much a part of the object as it is of the subject. "Experience" (or we can call it conception, understanding, perception, apprehension, etc.) is thus used in phenomenography in the sense of a relation between object and subject, as "something seen in some way by someone," or equivalently, as "someone seeing something in some way." Although the relation is neutral to the distinction between object and subject, someone's way of experiencing something can be seen in two contexts: either in relation to the ways in which others experience the same thing or to the same individual's way of experiencing other things. The former context—which is in line with our overall research approach of looking for variation between students—means stressing the object aspect, while the latter context—which we will be exploring in this chapter in a search for a dynamic description of individual change—means stressing the subject aspect.

Let us reiterate: phenomenography rests on a non-dualistic ontology and thus contradicts the commonsense view (or folk psychology), that experiences are experiences of phenomena that have an objective and independent existence,[2] experience being a relationship between phenomenon and person. For the phenomenographer, the one who experiences the phenomenon and the phenomenon that is experienced are involved in an internal relationship. The two components (knower and known, learner and learned, experiencer and experienced) are poles in the relation, and they are *modified by*, but *not defined by*, the relation. When we say that the poles are "modified by" the relation, we mean that neither pole would be the same without the relation because the relation is a part of the mutual meaning of both poles. When we say "not defined by," we mean that each component is of itself greater than the pole of the relationship: on the one hand, someone's experience of a phenomenon is but an aspect of the whole phenomenon, and on the other hand, the one who is experiencing the phenomenon is greater than that experience alone.

Now consider the two poles of the relation—the phenomenon and the person—

from the point of view of the logic of the internal relation. We need to ask, what is a phenomenon and what is a person when they are seen as constituent parts of the internal relation? Let us consider the phenomenon first. The thesis that an object of experience is *not* independent of the way in which it is experienced does not imply that we see the object as identical with the way in which it is experienced. We hold that the object has to be seen as a complex of all the different ways it *might be experienced*. We emphasize "might be experienced" inasmuch as for our purposes the object—or the phenomenon—must be seen as an abstract entity not only of the ways in which it is currently being experienced but also of all the ways in which it could potentially be experienced—at other times, in other situations, by others. "A way of experiencing something" is then simply a subset of the different aspects together constituting that which is experienced. An experience of an object is thus not just a subjective shadow of the real object but a part of the whole that is both subjective and objective at the same time.

Let's look at the other pole of the relationship: the person, and her *awareness* of the phenomenon.[3] If we want to understand more about learning, then it is the subject pole of experience—the learner—that we must focus on. Taking this focus involves putting the person's experience of a phenomenon into a context of, and into relation with, her experience of other phenomena. We ask the following question: "Is the person who is experiencing the phenomenon of interest in fact experiencing different phenomena simultaneously and, if so, how is she experiencing them?" The totality of a person's simultaneous experiences and her relatedness to the world will be referred to as her awareness.

We could use the terms "consciousness" and "awareness" synonymously (but prefer "awareness" to maintain an aloofness from the overwhelmingly dualistic usage of "consciousness"). In contrast with the way in which these words are usually used, we eschew their usual dichotomous sense in favor of the idea of a structural differentiation of awareness. Let us elaborate on that. We are used to thinking of consciousness as being the opposite of unconsciousness, awareness as being the opposite of lack of awareness. We may think we are aware of one, or a few, things at a time and unaware of all other things—for the time being at least.

It does not demand more than a brief reflection on the experiencing of things—such as the situation you are in at this moment—to illustrate that the idea of being aware of only one thing at a time simply does not ring true. As you, the reader of this text, read this actual line you are aware of the topic of this sentence, you are aware of the book of which this is a chapter, and you are aware, at least to some extent, of the gist of the argument leading up to this particular bit of text. You probably have some previous familiarity with the topic being dealt with, with learning in some sense, at least, and those previous experiences make up the background to your reading. You are aware of why you are reading the chapter, and how you feel as you are reading it. You are aware of who you are, where you are sitting, the season of the year, the day of the week, the time of day, and what you plan to do later in the day. You are aware of your name, whether or not you are married and have children, if your parents are alive, and so on. Although you are aware of innumerable things at the same time it would be wrong to imagine that you are aware of everything in the same way. Your awareness has a structure to it. Certain things come to the fore—they are figural, thematized—while other things recede to the ground—they are tacit and unthematized. And there again, there are not two categories of awareness—figure and ground, thematized and unthematized, or explicit and implicit. There are rather different degrees of how figural, thematized, or explicit things or aspects are in your awareness.

When you read this text we hope, but cannot guarantee, that the meaning of the text is in the focus of your awareness. While reading the text, things that are related to its content come to the fore of your awareness. Gurwitsch (1964) makes a distinction between the object of focal awareness, the theme, and those aspects of the experienced world that are related to the object in which it is embedded, the thematic field. In the example we have just embarked on, the text is the theme and the issues such as phenomenography, phenomenology, the nature of experience, and research into learning belong to the thematic field. The same theme can, of course, be seen against the background of different thematic fields. Furthermore, there are things that are temporally and spatially coexistent with the reading of the text, such as all those details of place, time, and state we mentioned above. Gurwitsch uses the term "margin" to refer to all that is coexistent with the theme without being related to it by dint of the content or meaning. We would go further than Gurwitsch does in drawing a clear distinction between the thematic field and the margin, and see them as having different degrees of relatedness to the theme.

The theme and thematic field are not stable and static structures in awareness. Quite the opposite; as the person's relationship with the object continues and develops, one theme replaces another, being drawn from the thematic field and landing back in the thematic field, in what Gurwitsch calls the stream of consciousness.

Qualitative Differences in the Experience of Learning

We have expounded on what we mean by learning from our experiential perspective—the transition from *not being able to* to *being able to*, as a result of doing something, or as a result of something happening—and we have stated two main questions about learning: (1)What is learned? (2) How is it learned? Furthermore, we have raised the question of what it means to have experience as our object of research, in order to be able to tackle our questions about the experience of learning. Now we will describe two research studies that have been carried out with these questions in focus. The most striking result in both cases was the qualitatively different ways in which learning was experienced.

The Experience of Learning by Reading

The first investigation we shall describe was carried out by Roger Säljö (Säljö, 1982), in which 90 volunteers belonging to six distinct categories of educational and vocational background were interviewed about learning in general and about their learning in reading a particular text. The text itself is about forms of learning, doubtless giving the whole description a somewhat convoluted nature. The text starts with a dramatic quote and then continues with about eight pages of text describing three major forms of learning: classical conditioning, instrumental conditioning, and verbal learning. In Figure 24.1, the quote and a paraphrased version of the rest of the text are given; the last part is actually a foretaste of the rest of this chapter. It can be assumed that this is generally unfamiliar territory for the subjects of the study.

What is the text, actually? As we touched on earlier, in research into verbal learning, researchers look at how their subjects learn a text in terms of how they themselves understand it, lending to the text an assumed objective reality. In order to take such a stance, researchers have to determine in advance just what the text is, what its component parts are, and how they are structured into a whole. Is it reasonable to believe that there is one unique sense to a text and its structure? Our own standpoint, already stated, is clearly and distinctly different from theirs, in that we assume that different readers have differing experiences of a text. Researchers might be very sensitive and scholarly readers, but they are nonetheless readers among other readers. When we look at what people learn from texts, we deliberately avoid having preconceived ideas about the text's "true meaning." And it is by looking at the way they make sense of the text that we address the first main question: *What* do they learn by reading a text?

Säljö (1982) asked the participants in his study, "What is the text about?" and found that there were two principal ways in which the text was understood. One is as a text about forms of learning—classical conditioning, exemplified by a method of torture and Pavlov's dogs; instrumental conditioning, exemplified by Skinner's rats; verbal learning exemplified by Ebbinghaus on the one hand and the Göteborg group on the other. The other way of understanding it is as a text about torture, *and* classical conditioning, *and* Pavlov's dogs, *and* instrumental conditioning, *and* Skinner's rats, *and* verbal learning, *and* Ebbinghaus, *and* the Göteborg group, etc. For example, when asked about the introductory part, Dave said:

D: It began with an introduction, a quote. . . . A Greek who was being tortured by the Greek junta and this was being used as an example of classical conditioning [. . .] This I suppose is an example of classical conditioning which was investigated and discovered by Pavlov. . . . (p. 97)

whereas Suzy listed instead the bits she recalled:

S: There was a lot about Skinner, and, for instance, Ivan Pavlov and the psychologist Ebbinghaus and research results. That's always fun to read about. . . . And then there was something about the torture methods of the Greek junta and you sort of got bad feelings when you read about that kind if thing, even if it's interesting. (p. 97)

That same day they applied the electrodes in a novel way. Instead of putting them on in the ordinary way, behind my ears, they attached them over my whole body—arms, legs, everywhere. It felt like I had a drill inside me and it was drilling on and on until I was nothing but bits. Like tumbling in the heart of a whirlwind, like a straw in a threshing machine. One of the leather straps burst and then they stopped. I was terrified. One of them checked my heart. He said something to me but I didn't understand. Then they put me on a stretcher. I couldn't get myself together. I couldn't think about anything. Lethargy.

I don't remember if it was Karagounákis who arrived then, I only remember the stretcher and the leather bench. New devices. This time I had the feeling that absolutely everything was electrified. I got an electric shock as soon as I saw the electrodes, even before they touched me with them. The guy who held me was surprised. He was only waving the electrodes in front of my eyes and all the time I was feeling the electricity. He moved them behind my head so that I couldn't see them: then I didn't feel the electricity. Then he touched me with the electrodes lightly on the back of my head and I gave a start. The others came closer to watch. They tried the electrodes from different angles. It was just the same wherever they applied them, but as soon as they came into my field of view I could feel the current. They didn't come with any more questions that day. They put me on the stretcher and carried me back to my room.

This description of a very disturbing event in one of the torture chambers of the Greek Junta at the end of the sixties describes a form of learning, albeit in a very dramatic way. It is not normal to feel an electric shock when you only see electrodes or electric contacts of some kind. The prisoner in the story, however, had had experiences which made him react in a different way than he would if he had never been tortured with electric shocks. It can be said that the reaction was learned. This form of learning is called *Classical Conditioning*.

Contact with the live electrodes (unconditional stimulus) originally gave an electric shock (unconditional response), which is natural for the human body. By first seeing the electrode (conditional stimulus) and then feeling it immediately a few times, it becomes sufficient merely to show the electrode in order to give an electric shock (conditional response).

The discovery of conditional response is associated with the Russian scientist Ivan Pavlov, who studied digestive processes and remarked that a dog's gastric juices began to flow at the mere sight of his usual food. The starting point in his famous experiment was that a dog will salivate as an unconditional response to food in the mouth (unconditional stimulus). If a number of times a bell was rung (unconditional stimulus) shortly before the dog got its food, then the dog began to salivate (conditional response) as soon as it heard the bell.

Classical conditioning can explain some types of behavioral change, especially how certain responses are given to stimuli other than those which originally gave rise to them. Such learning is, however, limited to reflex responses. *Instrumental conditioning*, studied by B. F. Skinner, concerns how the probability of a response, of any kind, is influenced by the consequence of the response. Thus instrumental conditioning concerns responses under the control of the will, of which there are considerably more kinds than the reflex responses which are needed for classical conditioning.

Classical and Instrumental conditioning can be used to explain the causes of some behavior, and since the explanations rest on changes in organisms, we are talking about forms of learning.

Most of our learning after early childhood is concerned with widening and deepening our understanding of the world and its nature, and then mostly through writing and reading. This is a question of learning through language, which, strangely, has been researched only to a slight degree in the natural form. Verbal learning has for the most followed the pattern of Ebbinghaus who tried to study "pure" learning by excluding earlier experience and using meaningless syllables. Learning was seen as the genesis of associations between things which occurred in temporal proximity, and researchers looked for ways in which structuring of such material resulted in retention.

Since what one knows already and how it is organized has decisive significance for meaningful learning, such studies lose entirely what distinguishes everyday learning, which is to interpret new experiences in terms of earlier ones, and relate new information to existing knowledge, and thus lacks any explanatory power for why, from the same presentation, some people learn more, or get a deeper understanding, than others.

Our research group in Gothenburg has shown in a number of studies that the quality of learning correlates closely with the orientation of attention while reading. Those who learn better focus more deeply into the text—they look for its meaning, what it is about, relating it to their world picture

Figure 24.1 *Summary of the text used in Säljö's investigation.*

(this is called a deep approach to learning)—while others focus on the surface of the presentation—they look at the text itself, passively trying to memorise it for later recall (surface approach).

In one of our studies the subjects were asked to read a newspaper article criticising a proposed university reform (UKAS); the author made a counter-argument based on facts shown in several tables. The subjects were afterwards asked what they remembered of the article, what the author was trying to say, and to answer questions about how they had gone about the learning process.

Here are two responses which illustrate what we mean by deep and surface approaches to learning (I = Interviewer):

ı: Did you happen to think of anything that wasn't in the text, that was outside the situation? Did anything come to mind?

ᴅ: . . .Yes, I related it to what I had already read, it was. . .UKAS was mentioned wasn't it. You know about that, don't you, so you think about it, what it's really about, and you sort of reflect sort of thing, what you already know about UKAS and what you found out here.

and:

ı: Did you happen to think about anything that wasn't in the text?

s: I didn't think about anything. . .well, you're thinking the whole time of course, that you've got to remember, . . .what I've been reading, like, How am I going to remember this? and, I'm never going to be able to remember this! I thought like that several times.

As already stated, there was a high degree of correlation between these approaches to learning and the quality of what was actually learned. For example, those with a deep approach to learning were very likely to discuss it in terms of being an argument against the proposed blanket changes and in favour of specific and discriminating changes—the author's intent—and those with a surface approach tended to see it as being about the proposed reform in general.

In this chapter we have tried to illustrate some different types of learning, i.e., changes in an organism caused by its experience. Of course, there are many other forms than those taken up here, but the essential thing is that what is decisive for learning depends on the kind of learning in question.

Figure 24.1   (cont.)

In the first way of understanding the text, referred to as D and illustrated in Figure 24.2, there is an overarching theme in terms of which all the different parts of the text are related together—namely, that the text is about forms of learning. The relations within this kind of structure are called organic, meaning nonarbitrary, being based on the content.

In the second case, referred to as understanding of type S, the relations reflect the ordering of the text—one bit follows the other, as illustrated in Figure 24.3.

The readers showing an S understanding find it difficult to come up with a single answer when asked about the text's main theme. Exactly the same themes appear, but their structural roles differ considerably, and the structural differences are mirrored by differences in the meanings assigned to the themes. For example, the first part of the text is understood either as being an example of a form of learning or as being about torture and/or political oppression by those expressing respectively D and S understanding. Thus in D it is seen as being subordinate to the theme of a form of learning, as exemplifying classical conditioning, while in S it stands alone, in its own right, as an undifferentiated piece of the whole text.

Here we have given two different ways in which a particular text was understood by learners, an example of phenomenographic research, in which qualitatively different ways of understanding are described. A principle of phenomenographic work is that whatever phenomenon is at the focus of learning, a limited number of qualitatively different ways in which the learners understand or

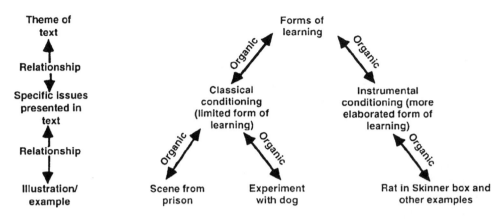

Figure 24.2 *Graphical illustration of structure imposed on the first two sections of the text in a D understanding (Säljö, 1982, p. 166).*

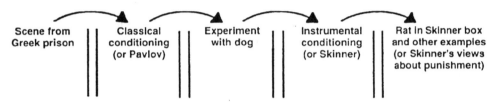

Figure 24.3 *Graphical illustration of structure imposed on the first two sections of the text in an S understanding (Säljö, 1982, p. 167).*

experience or conceptualize it can be described. This provides us with a model for describing qualitative differences in the outcome of learning, the "what" aspect of learning.

When we have, as now, arrived at distinctly different ways of understanding a text, we naturally ask ourselves, how can we account for such a difference? Why is it that some people end up with one kind of understanding and others reach another? Returning to what we said earlier, that our models of explanation have to do with the ways in which people *experience* their world, we will account for the difference in terms of the ways the act of learning was *experienced*.

We thus found two radically different understandings of the text, a text well within the reach of all the participants in the study. We see these different understandings as being part of the total ways in which reading the text was experienced by the subjects, the total situation of sitting and reading for the purposes of being interviewed on it. And the *explanation* for this difference in the ways they understand the text is that they relate themselves to—they experience—the situation in different ways—they *approach* the task of reading in ways that bring about different understandings. These different approaches to learning are known as *deep* and *surface* approaches, and they had been identified prior to Säljö's study—in fact, as we have already seen, they are described as part of the text from Säljö's study.

Before we elaborate on the deep and surface approaches and their functional relation with the outcomes of learning, we should say that they were identified in many studies, as early as 1974 (Marton, 1974, 1975; Dahlgren, 1975; Säljö, 1975; Marton and Säljö, 1976, 1984) and have been replicated also in learning situations other than reading texts—Laurillard (1984) in problem solving; Hounsell (1984) in writing essays; Hodgson (1984) in attending lectures; Whelan (1988) in diagnosing medical cases; Booth (1992) in writing programs—and found to be closely related to the quality of outcomes of learning. Now we shall establish the functional relationship between approaches and outcomes.

We can state succinctly that the main difference between a surface and a deep approach is that in the former it is the *sign* that is focused on and in the latter it is what is *signified*. In learning by reading a text, the former means that the learner focuses on the words of the text and in the second the learner focuses on what the text means. A corresponding distinction has been drawn by Svensson (1977, 1984b) between an atomistic and a holistic approach; the former refers to tackling the text in isolated pieces and the latter refers to maintaining an integrated whole. The difference can be seen even in the two quotes that Säljö included in his text extract (see again Figure 24.1). The second example (S) experiences reading the text as trying to remember its words, in isolation from all else, while the first example (D) treats reading the text as looking beyond it and setting its whole meaning in a wider reality.

What is life normally like for these people who find themselves reading a text in an educational experiment? They surely experience many different situations where they are simultaneously aware of the various things that are present—they are aware of being in a particular place, and of speaking to some friend, and at the same time they are aware of the food on the table between them, and even of how the grapes there taste rather sour. While some particular aspect of the situation is thematic in awareness, other aspects constitute the thematic field, and there is a dynamic switching between themes with a corresponding restructuring of thematic fields, all according to an overall experience and experienced relevance. Now some of them are aware of the text in a similar way: They are aware of different aspects of the text at the same time, each theme being associated with field and theme replacing theme, field replacing field. Others, on the other hand, experience it in a distinctly different way in that simultaneity is lacking: They read it bit by bit and never build up an overall understanding of the text in which aspects of the meaning of the text are present at the same time. For them, awareness lacks a dynamic that keeps themes and thematic fields in a state of a constant restructuring of awareness. Looking back to Figures 24.2 and 24.3, the similarity can be immediately seen. There we were illustrating the way in which parts were related to one another in the course of recall—i.e., to the outcome of learning— and now we are saying that the same sort of structural relationship is to be found in the sense of simultaneous awareness when readers tackle the task of reading.

For some, there is a main theme that is always present, overarching the sense in which other parts of the text are being read: This is why the examples are recalled as examples of forms of learning, because the overall theme, forms of

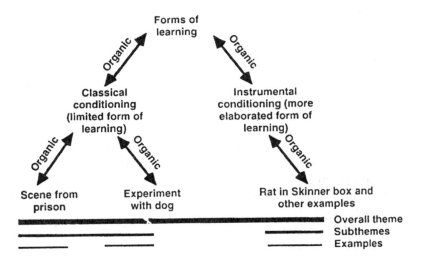

Figure 24.4   *The significance of the imposed structure for awareness of the point of the text as overarching theme and examples.*

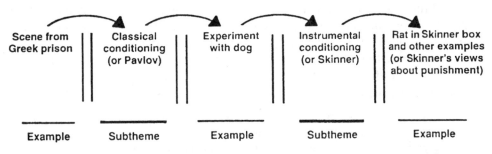

Figure 24.5   *The significance of the imposed structure for awareness of the point of the text as a sequence of items.*

learning, is present to these readers all the time. We illustrate this in Figure 24.4, which is the same as the right-hand part of Figure 24.2 but augmented by lines at the bottom of the diagram that indicate the extent of awareness of the various items and themes.

Others, in contrast, lose sight of the overall theme and the parts of the text are present to them with equal weight and are assigned equal significance, as illustrated in Figure 24.5. The themes and items pass in and out of awareness, and the whole is never in focus. If we ask, in general terms, "Where is the point of the text?" we can see that the reply must be "The point of the text is everywhere," if the text is to take on a rich and full meaning to the reader. The former kind of reading maintains that overall awareness of the point of the text, while the latter kind never glimpses the point but glosses over it in favor of a flat view of the textual elements.

Now we have established that the approach to reading a text is one with the outcome of the reading, united in the total experience of reading. But what is it that brings about the different experiences? We would suggest that the people who are sitting and reading the text see the situation through their different biographies. They have all been there before—reading a text with the expectation of being asked about it—and they made one sort of sense or another of the situation. They have different conceptions of what learning is, as already described, and since they define this situation as a learning situation, it takes on different meanings for them. Some have a history of seeing reading as an imposition, and they make sense of the task as such, learning as something external to themselves, as a task to perform for later recall. Others see reading as a means of finding out about the world around them—the text is a window to reality, as it were—and they treat the current text accordingly. While the former see the text as something separate from and unrelated to themselves, the latter see the text as part of their greater world.

We have evidence of this in Roger Säljö's study. As we stated earlier, each subject was drawn into a dialogue with the researcher about learning in general, prior to being asked to read the text. After reading the text, they were interviewed immediately about their understanding of it, and their experience of the situation. Now, if we refer again to Figure 24.1, we will see that toward the end are described the results of a similar study. None of the subjects who adopted a surface approach saw that part of the text as being relevant to their own situations, while those who adopted a deep approach recognized themselves in what they read there—readers drew the text into their own reality, and their own reality into the text. An interesting case is Dora, who in the initial interview had two contradictory views of learning, or in Roger Säljö's words, she seems to illustrate:

through her statements. . .two competing realities with rival definitions. One is attending to written or spoken discourses as such and on their own terms as documents. . .conveying insights and meanings. The other is attending to them in a way appropriate when factors external to the meaning of the text (e.g., the demands of the assessment system) assume great importance. (p. 86)

After she had read the text, she was asked about her experience of reading it:

Oh, well, first when I read it I sort of thought like this: right, now I'll try to remember as much as possible. . .and then I went on, and the more I read. . .when coming to the end of the article I could have burst out laughing 'cause there they described the type of person I'd been myself at first, those who were trying to learn as much as possible. . .and then there were certain hints about. . .that you should try to find the meaning behind it all, so when I read it once again, I tried to make it make sense in quite a different way.

This is pretty convincing evidence that Dora makes the text part of her own reality, switching from one competing reality to the other, switching from her initial surface approach to a deep approach, affected by what she had read. This is without doubt a significant learning experience for Dora, who shifts from not being able to see approaches to learning in a particular way—i.e., deep and surface—to being able to see them in that way.

The nature of surface and deep approaches and their interconnectedness with the outcomes of learning had been well established in the earlier study, which was referred to in the text (Figure 24.1) used in Säljö's study (Marton and Säljö, 1976). The results have been replicated in several studies. In particular, the work of van Rossum and Schenk (1984) has illustrated approaches, outcomes, and their relatedness, as well as the fact that the adopted approach to learning springs from the learner's underlying ideas about learning.

The Experience of Learning Clinical Diagnosis

In the example we have been considering we have looked exclusively at learning through reading texts, and our descriptions of the approaches to learning are specifically related to such learning. In other tasks of learning the same general qualitatively distinct approaches to other tasks and their interrelatedness with the outcomes of learning can similarly be discerned. Their details and exact descriptions, however, might differ, depending on the specific nature of the content of the task.

One skill that medical students have to learn in the course of their studies is that of clinical diagnosis; faced with a patient who is displaying some combination of symptoms, the qualified doctor has to be able to determine the medical cause, the illness that can be treated. Many practitioners believe that this is a skill acquired naturally (Whelan, 1988); some medical schools take it seriously and build it into medical education either as an element of several courses or as a course in its own right, but it is mostly a skill that is incorporated into other courses, without being emphasized.

Whelan, dismayed by the apparent stabs in the dark that students made when faced with the need to diagnose an illness, studied the problem systematically. He designed two descriptions of cases that could, in principle, be diagnosed according to basic science concepts and asked a number of first-year clinical students (in the fourth year of their medical studies) to discuss them.

Again, distinctly different approaches to the task were seen. What Whelan identified as the approaches of "ordering" and "structuring" refer to the directedness of the students' awareness to the problem, and correspond very closely to the surface and deep approaches already discussed. On ordering, Whelan makes the following observation:

If symptoms were discussed individually without relating to one another, if symptoms were ignored, if parts of the problem were ordered and grouped but if the groupings were not put together into a whole, if the process used distorted the structure of the problem and dislocated the content from its meaning, if the student was unable to describe what she/he was doing, the extracts were considered to characterize an ordering (or atomistic) approach to clinical problem-solving. Students using this approach usually did not discover a solution that satisfactorily accounted for all the information given. (p. 205)

He also comments on structuring:

If the student maintained the underlying structure of the problem, if extracts illustrate that the student used evidence to support his or her ideas and related ideas to previously learned basic science, then these extracts were considered to characterize a structuring (or holistic) approach to clinical problem-solving. (p. 205)

1. A male electrician, aged 23 years, presents complaining of progressively worsening tired-ness and weakness of three weeks' duration. He has difficulty climbing the stairs, he believes that this is due mainly to weakness but he has noticed that he has trouble breath-ing whenever he attempts to walk up more than one flight. Three months ago he first noticed the onset of diarrhea. This occurs on most days varying from four to six bowel actions daily. He has lost approximately 10 kilograms in weight over this time.

   Physical examination reveals a thin male consistent with his stated weight loss. There are no other physical signs of disease—specifically, none of his abdominal organs are en-larged. There is no guarding or tenderness.

2. A 55-year-old female, widowed for two years, presents complaining of shortness of breath on exertion for six months. She has also experienced three episodes of shortness of breath at night. These have been associated with a dry cough and wheeze. Attacks last from 20 minutes up to several hours. Her distress was eased by sitting up. She reported smoking 25 cigarettes a day for 20 years but ceased 13 years ago. Another doctor, several years ago, prescribed Lasix for swollen ankles. There are no abnormal physical symptoms on examination.

Figure 24.6   *Two cases used in the study by Whelan (1988).*

Students adopting the ordering approach look at the list of symptoms in them-selves, while those with the structuring approach look for the meaning of the symptoms in relation to an underlying cause.

But this study has led to a more complex analysis of approaches, which we are interpreting in terms of another dimension—namely, the ways in which the stu-dents actually went about the task. Subordinate to the ordering approach, stu-dents were found to tackle the case either by using *pattern matching* in which a diagnosis was attempted based on one or more clinical features found in the case, or *exclusion*, in which diagnoses were eliminated according to the absence of clini-cal features present in the potential diagnosis but not in the case described. The structuring approach, on the other hand, found students who used *diagnostic in-tegration* to reach a diagnosis. Such students interpreted symptoms in terms of conceivable underlying causes rather than jumping directly to diagnoses, thereby developing a hypothesis via a logical sequence of pathophysiological mechanisms.

Figure 24.6 shows the two case descriptions used in the study. We can see pattern matching very clearly in quotes from two students who describe their approaches to a diagnosis of case 1:

As soon as I read he was tired and weak I thought of anemia. . .I thought, was that in a list (of causes) they gave us concerning such and such a disease?

I thought that the problem was tiredness and weakness and from that I went on to think that the diarrhea was something unrelated or superimposed.

These students are focusing on one symptom and ignoring others. Compare this quote, dealing with case 2.

She probably had some sort of problem with her heart which is unable to cope with main-taining a good circulation. It could be due to hypertension. . .because she is a smoker, hypertension and atherosclerosis could be interrelated. . .The heart has got to the stage where it can't cope with increased demand such as with exercise.

Clearly, in the latter quote the meaning of the symptoms described is being dealt with while in the former quotes the symptoms are being used as a launching pad for diagnosis.

Seen as a learning experience, this diagnostic session led to distinctly different learning outcomes. The students were asked to describe the diagnosis they reached and this was analyzed in terms of the extent to which it demonstrated understanding in terms of their basic knowledge of medical science. *Understanding* was ascribed to the diagnosis if "the clinical features were explained in terms of pathophysiological links, if causal chains with explanatory intermediate steps between clinical features and diagnosis could be recognized, and if both positive and negative links were included (i.e., items for and against the chosen diagnoses were discussed)" (p. 206). If in contrast, mere *description* was the main feature of the diagnosis, in which "the discussion was characterized by short causal (associative) links between symptoms and diagnoses, if the outcome was given only in descriptive terms or if the student was unable to make a diagnosis" (p. 206), then the student was judged not to have based a diagnosis on medical science.

Now the outcome of this learning opportunity has to be seen in the context of the students' whole education, especially the earlier studies of basic science and the clinical experience to come. The outcome of such a diagnosis exercise lies in the form of the understanding arrived at—in Whelan's terms, understanding or description. Out of the 48 students who took part in this study and the two cases they were asked to diagnose, in the overwhelming majority of instances (83) an ordering approach was adopted; only six students reached an outcome that could be classified as understanding. On the other hand, the seven students who adopted the structuring approach reached understanding on all occasions. Again, the approach and the outcome are seen to be clearly related.

If we liken the symptoms to a text about the patient who exhibits them, then we can see the similarity between the ordering approach to diagnosis and the surface approach to reading a text—focus is on the sign rather than the signified, focus passes from one bit to another, as in Figure 24.5, without relating each bit to the whole, and so on. If we continue this metaphor, we can say that students adopting a structuring approach are reading the symptoms as a window into the underlying disease they wish to diagnose, whereas those with an ordering approach read the symptoms for their own worth. The structure of awareness in the case of the ordering approach is one symptom after the other with no sense of the simultaneity of the symptoms. The structuring approach, in contrast, implies an awareness of the symptoms simultaneously and the diagnosis is also there all the time. The ordering approach does not move away from the level of the symbols included in the written case description, whereas the structuring approach sees the case as a real-life entity. In the structuring approach, each symptom is seen by itself, *and* in relation to the other symptoms, *and* in relation to the diagnosis. In the case of students learning from a text, we asked, "Where is the point of the text?" and replied, "The point of the text is everywhere." We now ask, "Where is the intended diagnosis of the case?" and the reply has to be, "The diagnosis is everywhere in the description of the case."

Generalizability of Approaches to Learning

A large number of studies have been carried out in which approaches to learning and outcomes of learning have been described. Two of them have been described in some detail, and the general structure of the approaches are seen to be generalizable across content areas, while retaining distinctive features of the specifics of the area. Now we shall consider the extent to which these results are generalizable in other respects.

Generalizability Across Age Groups

The ideas that we presented at the start of this chapter, on learning as a change in the way in which phenomena are experienced, and the examples we have elaborated demonstrate that there is an internal relationship between the approaches that students adopt to their learning and the outcome of that learning. Furthermore, the approaches described in our examples, and those arrived at in studies of other forms of learning tasks, share a general similarity in their nature. Deep and surface approaches can be taken as generic names—but the specific forms of approach have to be sought in the specific learning tasks and content domain.

The studies we have described pertain to college students, where the surface approach is clearly seen as an artifact of the demand structure of the educational setting. It might be thought that our arguments are confined to adult students, but that is not the case. Pramling (1986) argues that we can observe the origin of the difference between approaches to learning even in the preschool, among children five to six years old. She illustrates this in an observational study of a group of children learning about colors and shapes—at least, that was what the teacher intended. The teacher tried to develop an understanding of the distinction between basic colors and blended colors, knowledge of different colors, the idea of shades of a color. Furthermore, she wanted the children to develop the idea of different shapes, such as the circle, square, triangle, and to gain insights into the relationship between big and small on the one hand and between narrow and wide on the other (p. 29). The children worked and played with different colors and shapes, and the teacher explained the concepts in words. Pramling identified two distinctively different focuses on the situation among the children, the difference resembling the difference between the surface and the deep approach.

Some children focused on the activities themselves (not on what the teacher hoped they would learn from the activities). For instance, when Christopher is asked by the interviewer (I), he responds (p. 33) in the following way:

I: You say you've been painting. Why's that?
c: I think it's fun.
I: But why did the teacher want you to?
c: Because I wanted to paint. So as there'd be a lot of groups.
I: But why have you got to paint with a red color?
c: 'Cause I thought it was fun.

I: What do you think the teacher wanted you to think about?

C: I don't know.

In other cases the children focus on the phenomenon they were supposed to learn about through the activities they had been involved in. For instance, in Birgitta's interview we read:

B: We've talked about colors now. . .so we're learning about colors. . .different colors and which ones you can mix.

I: Why have you done that?

B: Mm. . .I don't know.

I: Why do you think the teacher wants you to learn about different colors?

B: Which colors you can mix, and all that.

Ann Ahlberg (1992) has studied ten-year-olds and their approaches to tackling problems, both overtly and covertly mathematical as well as nonmathematical in nature. She found two different approaches to tackling mathematical problems, again akin to the deep and surface approaches we have been describing here. In the first (deep) kind of approach, children were seen to be mainly directed toward grasping the problem. They are captured by the problem-solving process, they try different ways of solving problems, they put forward hypotheses and they can vary their perspectives on presented problems. They are oriented toward seeing some or all of the parts of the problem and the numbers in the problem and investigating the internal relationships between them. In the second kind of approach (surface), children try to apply a well-known method of solution that they have used before and solve the given problem according to a given pattern. They are not captured by the problem-solving process, but the process of solving problems has set into a definite shape. They do not try alternative methods. They might concentrate primarily on the numbers in the problem, making estimates without making calculations, or they might also focus on the operations they identify there and then focus on carrying out calculations.

Both of these studies indicate the adoption of deep and surface approaches to learning from an early age, and that it is not a concept exclusively useful in studies of adults learning in higher education.

Generalizability Across Situations

We cannot emphasize strongly enough that we do not see approaches to learning as personal learning styles or personal traits. In the two main examples we have described, the students adopted approaches to the tasks they undertook according to their experience of that specific occasion, regardless of how they went about learning tasks on other occasions. The outcomes of those tasks were associated with the approaches adopted there, specific to that situation. There are studies that have indicated that individual students do indeed take different approaches to particular tasks. Other researchers, however, have found it reasonable to make the assumption that individuals have a predominant approach when tackling the

---

Statements to be responded to according to a 5-point scale

DEEP APPROACH

- I generally put a lot of effort into trying to understand things which initially seem difficult.
- I often find myself questioning things I hear in lectures or read in books.
- I usually set out to understand thoroughly the meaning of what I am asked to read.
- When I'm tackling a new topic, I often ask myself questions about it which the new information should answer.

SURFACE APPROACH

- I find I have to concentrate on memorizing a good deal of what we have to learn.
- The best way for me to understand what technical terms mean is to remember the textbook definitions.
- Often I find I have read things without having a chance to really understand them.
- Lecturers seem to delight in making the simple truth unnecessarily complicated.

Figure 24.7   *Typical items from the Lancaster Inventory.*

tasks of learning, and they have tried to determine the extent to which they adopt such an approach to their studies in general. At Lancaster University Entwistle and Ramsden (1983) developed an inventory primarily to investigate relationships between the academic context of university departments and the approaches to study adopted by their students. Sample items used for such measurement are shown in Figure 24.7. A systematic relationship was found between certain departmental attributes and approaches; for example, perceptions of heavy workloads, poor student-teacher contact, lack of choice of content and method, and examinations that demanded reproduction, all correlate with students taking surface approaches to learning. On the other hand, perceptions of good teaching, particularly help with study through good contact between staff and students, and freedom to choose what and how to study, all correlated with deep approaches to learning.

Furthermore, features of learning that are typically associated with deep and surface approaches were used by Biggs (1987a, b) in developing questionnaires to identify how students generally approach their study—at the secondary school level the Learning Process Questionnaire (LPQ) and at the tertiary level the Study Process Questionnaire (SPQ). These are used mainly in Australia and Southeast Asia.

Generalizability Across Cultures

More recently, some apparent paradoxes have arisen as a result of investigations using the LPQ and/or the SPQ, relating to two stereotypes of the Asian learner or, more particularly, the Chinese learner. The first stereotype, the "brainy Asian," is principally a result of the success of the ethnic Chinese students within higher education in Australia and the United States. This success is evident in comparisons of achievement in mathematics and natural sciences in which students from Hong Kong (and also from Japan) performed particularly well (Torney-Purta,

1990). The second stereotype, the "Asian learner as rote learner" (Biggs, 1990; Kember and Gow, 1991), is primarily related to Chinese students, but it is also related to Asian students in general.

These stereotypes of the brainy Asian and Asian learner as rote learner are felt to be incompatible, especially within the framework we have been developing in this chapter. An orientation to rote learning is negatively correlated with achievement, with the exception of reproduction of trivial details (Biggs, 1979). If both of these stereotypes can be demonstrated to be valid, we are left with a paradox— namely, how is it possible that students with an orientation to rote learning achieve as highly as the brainy Asians are seen to?

Research results obtained with the use of the LPQ and SPQ suggest that Asian students (for instance, in Hong Kong and Nepal) at both the secondary and tertiary levels are more oriented to deep approaches and less oriented to surface approaches than Australian students at corresponding levels (Biggs, 1990; Watkins and Regmi, 1990; Watkins, Regmi, and Astilla, 1991; Kember and Gow, 1991). However, these results rely on characterizing a surface approach by the presence of rote learning, while a deep approach is equated with understanding, an interpretation that is an oversimplification of the deep and surface approaches as we have presented them here. While a surface approach may be associated with rote learning in some contexts, it is not *characterized* by this form of learning. Rather, a surface approach is characterized by a focus on the learning material or task itself, not on the meaning or purpose underlying it, as would be the case for the deep approach.

In oversimplifying the deep/surface distinction, the results of the LPQ and SPQ studies fail to indicate the extent to which a deep or surface approach is emphasized by the Chinese and Australian students. No studies had then been carried out of Chinese students' approaches to learning, with the goal of determining what qualitatively different approaches they actually adopt in their learning, but the distinction looked for was based entirely on the approaches to learning that European students had been found to adopt. As Biggs (1990) has pointed out, the deep/surface distinction may not be the most appropriate one for describing the learning of Chinese students.

The paradox of the Chinese learner appears to remain, however. The reason that Asian learners are believed to be oriented toward rote learning is due to the notion that teaching philosophy and practice in Asia (and particularly in the Chinese culture) is directed toward memorization. This notion is confirmed by, for example, Johnson and Wen (1990). In Western countries there is a belief, strengthened by the sorts of studies we have described, that memorization does not enhance understanding but, rather, the two are generally considered to be mutually exclusive. If it is the case that educational systems in Asian (and particularly Chinese) countries are directed to memorization, how is it possible that Asian students demonstrate such high achievement?

This apparent paradox has been the subject of study by Marton, Dall'Alba, and Tse (1993). In describing the Säljö study earlier we pointed out that the learner's approach to learning and the learner's conception of the meaning of learning are inextricably interwoven. In the study of Chinese learners this distinction has not been made at all, in that it was the overall meaning of learning that was being investigated, as well as the experience of learning tasks.

The LPQ and SPQ questionnaires draw the distinguishing line between deep and surface approaches as being between understanding and memorization. The results of the study show, however, that for the Chinese learner the line has to be drawn between, on the one hand, memorization with intention to understand and, on the other hand, mechanical memorization. Thus the source of the paradox is revealed: the Chinese learner who is taking a deep approach to learning *is* indeed making an effort to memorize, and is *at the same time* intending to gain understanding.

The results of the study by Marton et al. shed light on the relationship between memorization and understanding for the Chinese learner. In the process of memorizing, the text being memorized is repeated several times, which may be outwardly suggestive of rote learning. However, a number of the subjects in the study, all teacher educators, explained that the process of repetition contributes to understanding and is different from the mechanical memorization that characterizes rote learning. When a text is being memorized, it can be repeated in a way that deepens understanding; different aspects of the text are focused on with each repetition. The notion of deepening understanding with repetition is not totally foreign. In earlier studies of Western students, some of the participants described how several readings of a passage of text serve to bring about improved understanding. Furthermore, some participants described how each reading of a passage might be done in a different way, focusing on different aspects or reading from a different perspective (e.g., see Marton, Asplund-Carlsson, and Halász, 1992).

In the process of repeating and memorizing in this way, the meaning of the text is grasped more fully. As one subject says: "In the process of repetition, it is not a simple repetition, because each time I repeat, I would have some new idea of understanding, that is to say I can understand better" (Marton, Beaty, and Dall'Alba, 1993). It is upon this use of memorization to deepen understanding that the resolution of the paradox of the Chinese learner rests.

The study by Marton, Dall'Alba, and Tse (1993) was carried out with 18 teacher educators from different parts of mainland China; the results have been replicated in an interview study by Wen and Marton (1993) with 30 university students from Nanjing Teachers University. A third study, by Marton, Watkins, and Tang (1995), carried out with high school students in Hong Kong, again with the distinction between conceptions of learning and the experience of learning somewhat blurred, the difference between rote memorization and memorization in order to understand comes to light quite clearly, as well as deep and surface approaches in the sense modified through the studies with Chinese learners.

In a fourth study in progress, Pramling, Asplund, and Wen (personal communication) have been able to show how orientation toward memorization *and* understanding is reflected in Chinese children's learning a story and their learning *from* a story. The story used in this investigation, Shel Silverstein's (1964) *The giving tree* had been used earlier in another of Pramling's studies in which one group of children participated in an experiment conducted on phenomenographic

Table 24.1 *Percentage of forms of recall among Swedish and Chinese children*

	Swedish group	Chinese group
Fragments	20	17
Structure of tale	30	83
Central theme	50	—
n	40	30

Source: Pramling, Asplund, and Wen (personal communication).

principles and another acted as a control group (Pramling, 1994); that earlier study is also described in her chapter, which follows in this volume. The tale is of a boy and a tree who are very, very close friends. As time goes by the boy's needs change, and his relationship to the tree changes. Little by little the tree gives all he has to the boy—leaves to make a crown, apples to eat and to sell to make money, branches to build a house and the trunk to build a boat to sail far away—until all that is left is a stump. But by that time the boy—with teeth too bad to eat the apples, too busy to swing in the branches, too tired to climb the trunk—only needs to sit and rest in peace and quiet. The stump is perfect for that and so the tree is happy to the end.

Thirty Chinese preschool children in the age range of five to six years listened to their teacher reading the story to them. Afterward they were interviewed individually about what they remembered of it and what they had learned from it. Compared with a group of Swedish six- to seven-years-olds in Pramling's study (her control group), the Chinese children retold the story at greater length and more accurately than did the Swedish children, despite their being younger. Pramling had found three qualitatively different forms of the children's recall. They might mention scattered *fragments* without any coherence; or they might *follow the structure* of the tale with a beginning, a middle with several episodes, and an end; or they might organize their recall around some *central theme*. In Table 24.1 we can see that most of the Chinese children followed the structure of the tale.

The Chinese children were seen to be more "locked into the words of the tale." When, in the course of the interviews, they tried to remember what was said, if they could not remember the actual expressions used they preferred to say, "I don't know," rather than express the same thing in a different way. And still they were better at understanding the story than the Swedish children were. When asked what they could learn from the tale, only 5 percent of the Swedish group (the control group of the study) showed an understanding that the story had a moral, such as, you should listen to the voice of your conscience, or that you should not let your friends down. For example, Christopher said:

C: Everybody should be friends, and not quarrel, and you should give everything to your friends.

I: Ahah, hmm.

C: And you should be real friends as well.

I: Yes, that's good. Can you learn anything else?

C: Yes, that you don't need to look like one another to be friends 'n' that. . .that it doesn't matter if you come from another country 'n' things. (Pramling, 1994, p. 163)

Over 44 percent of the Chinese group showed such an understanding, while even the corresponding figure for the experimental group that participated in Pramling's intervention program based on phenomenographic principles was only 26 percent (Pramling, 1994, p. 230).

In all these Chinese studies the dichotomy between memorization as rote learning and memorization for understanding is somewhat oversimplified. The fact is, however, that the Chinese language itself is more differentiated on the concept of memorization than the Swedish and English languages (Wen and Marton, 1993). The very fact that the Chinese language is picture-based also gives food for thought in this connection. The Chinese results can be contrasted with the results of a study carried out by Nagle and Marton (1993) in which 30 Uruguayan students were interviewed about learning, in which a greater differentiation appears within the ways they comprehend understanding than has been found elsewhere.

To conclude this section on the generalizability of our arguments about the experience of learning, we can say that similar fundamental differences in the approaches to learning are to be found for learning in different content domains, for different age groups, in different situations and different cultures. The fundamental difference is thus generalizable. Furthermore, since we have established the functional relationship between approaches to learning and the quality of the outcomes of learning—through the structure of human awareness—we can also generalize that to different content domains, age groups, situations and cultures. But having said that, in specific content domains, age groups, situations and cultures, the specific *meaning* of the difference has as a rule to be found anew, in each case, on its own premises.

The Educational Significance of the Learner's Experience of Learning

What Is Learned?

The question that is fundamental in the context of our work, but is too often overlooked is, *What is it that is learned?* If we address this question in connection with the studies we have presented, we find a distinct kind of outcome—namely, becoming able to see something in a particular way. Readers of the text in Säljö's study—which we described earlier—could have achieved the learning outcome of seeing learning in a new way; Whelan's medical students had the potential to understand the relation between case descriptions and underlying pathophysiological conditions. Such learning outcomes as these comprise, we firmly believe, the most important type of learning outcome.

We have presented ample evidence that such learning outcomes occur but rarely. Dora, who read Säljö's text, actually describes such a change taking place (as we have quoted above), but that does not happen often. In the Säljö study it was found that there was a high degree of correlation between approaches to learning and the participant's conception of what learning *is*. Those who had what Säljö then called a taken-for-granted or flat conception of learning also tackled their learning task with no clear idea of what they might get out of it—they were closed to the potential for seeing things in a new way; those who had a thematized or deep conception of learning, on the other hand, went about their tasks with more of a clearcut goal of learning—they were prepared for a change of view.

Approaches and Conceptual Change

A study conducted by Prosser and Millar (1989) set out to investigate the relation between approaches to learning and conceptual change (which they take to mean "coming to see something in a particular way"). It was based on a six-week course that included a topic known to be conceptually difficult for physics students— force and motion. Newton's first law states that a body remains in its state of rest or uniform motion unless a force is applied to change it. This draws a critical distinction between, on the one hand, rest or uniform motion implying the net absence of force and, on the other hand, change in uniform motion (acceleration or deceleration) implying the net presence of force. In common belief, and as formulated by Aristotle, the distinction occurs between *rest implying no force* and *motion implying force*, an understanding that proves particularly resistant to change. Earlier studies, such as that by Johansson, Marton, and Svensson (1985), have shown that while students can learn to apply and manipulate the formulas derived from Newton's laws, they tend to retain the qualitative understanding of Aristotle. Conceptual change was emphasized in the teaching inasmuch as qualitative understanding rather than a manipulative facility was sought, students were encouraged to discuss their work with one another to reveal the variation in understanding, and laboratory sessions were arranged to favor problem solving over "cookbook" experiments. Students were interviewed some time before and after the course, both to test their understanding of the key concepts and, on the second occasion, to reveal their approaches to learning.

One example used in the pre- and posttest concerns the typical question: A car is driven at a high constant speed along a straight line on a highway. What forces act on the car to let it travel like this? The Newtonian description is of forces in balance—motive force balancing resistance—while the Aristotelian description is of a net force in the direction of motion—motive force exceeding resistance. No students indicated the Newtonian understanding in tackling the problem prior to the course, while 4 of the 14 participants indicated it afterward. This is not a very impressive result from the point of view of the teaching (although it is in fact impressive when compared with other reports of the outcome of learning about force and motion).

On the basis of the interviews about the students' experience of their studies,

Table 24.2   *Summary of development of conception broken down by approach to learning*

	Approach		
	Clearly deep	*Unclear*	*Clearly surface*
Did develop	8	6	2
Did not develop	1	3	21

Source: Summarized from Prosser and Millar (1989).

carried out after the course was completed, they were classified as having had a deep or a surface approach to their learning in the course as a whole, rather than on a single occasion. In the context of this topic and this course, they describe students with the surface approach as trying to "categorize and memorize disconnected pieces of material so that they could increase the amount of knowledge they had and meet course requirements." Those with the deep approach were trying to "abstract meaning from, change their understanding of, and develop a personal commitment to the material being studied so that they could explain and better understand reality." Three students were unclear cases, indicating traits of both approaches.

Further analysis reveals that those four students who indicated a more developed conception on that problem in the posttest were, remarkably, the only four who had clearly expressed a deep approach to learning. Table 24.2 summarizes their results pooled over four tasks and excluding those students who had the most advanced conception from the start. This study thus suggests that conceptual change is contingent on approach to learning.

Developing the Learners' Approaches

If deep approaches to learning are so decisive for quality outcomes of learning, why don't we try to mold the learners to take deep approaches? In connection with the earliest studies on learning from texts, we attempted to do just that. We observed that in applying deep approaches the successful learners ask themselves questions, and we accordingly interjected oral questions while the participants were reading, in an attempt to encourage all the readers to adopt the habits of the successful readers (Marton, 1976). For example, questions were posed while the text was being read, with the intention of focusing readers' attention on finding structure in the way that readers with deep approaches did spontaneously. The results were disastrous; such interventions were found to have an effect the reverse of that intended. An erosion effect was noted as a result of the technification of the reading process; the readers actually learned less, as a result of merely mimicking the deep approach by seeking only structure and losing sight of the content, thereby adopting an extreme surface approach.

This and other studies point out the futility of training or attempting to induce particular approaches to study regardless of the content. Contrast that with another study (Martin and Ramsden, 1987). They compared the results of two programs designed to raise students' learning skills, one of which used generic material separate from the curriculum content while the other, called learning how to learn, made use of material drawn from the current history curriculum. The students in the latter group were seen to develop more advanced conceptions of learning, in accord with a deep approach, and in addition got better grades on essays and achieved better examination results. Thus separating the *what* from the *how* of learning and attempting to train the how without reference to the what is doomed to failure.

Principles for Teaching

What can we conclude from the above for methods of teaching? What methods of teaching can we devise to bring about the deep approaches with their quality learning outcomes? The answer is at hand—there is no such method, in the sense of generally applicable rules and criteria.

What we can say, however, and with great emphasis, is that the overarching principle of achieving quality outcomes is to thematize both the act and the content of learning in the very act of teaching. The teacher has to be aware of the content of learning—not as a content in itself, encapsulated in a disciplinary framework, but rather as content as it is and as it should be understood by the learners. The teacher has to take an analytical stance to the phenomena to be taught about and identify those educationally critical aspects of it which might otherwise be taken for granted. The teacher has to ensure that learners reveal their various ways of going about the tasks of learning and the various ways in which they understand that which is learned—the how and the what of learning—and subject them to reflection. By becoming aware of the possibility of a variation in ways of experiencing a phenomenon and by considering that variation, the learner becomes open to the possibility of change, and thereby more likely to undergo the sort of conceptual development that Prosser and Millar (1989) were referring to. We explain learning as a change in the way the learner experiences the world, and the teacher has to ensure that the tasks of learning are integrated into that world; that means that the relevance of the task has to be seen to transcend the task in itself and to have some personal meaning for the learner.

One aspect of Ann Ahlberg's work, referred to earlier, addressed the last of our set of principles, to embed the learning task in the learner's own world. She introduced ten-year-olds to mathematics problems through a succession of other sorts of problems, early ones that had no mathematical content, then some with a covert mathematical content, and finally conventional mathematical problems to be found in any textbook. In this way she grounded the problems in the children's own worlds of adventure stories and events in the home, and integrated the mathematical problems into the world of problems as a whole. The problems were formulated such that the children could bring reading and writing, storytelling and drawing into the solution process, in varying degrees. In this way she integrated the mathematical aspects of problem solving into the world of school as a whole. The children also worked in groups and chose from alternative solutions to present to the class, thus revealing and reflecting over the variation of the act and the content of working with the problems. In all of these ways Ahlberg contrived to embed the children's experience of solving mathematical problems in their worlds at large, and learning to solve such problems became a change of experience much greater than merely being able to apply the rules of arithmetic in given situations. The children proved to do better at solving novel problems of the conventional type than children in a control group. Thus, over the period of this study the children had become better problem solvers, and it is of special interest to note that it was the poorly achieving girls who made greatest progress.

In the chapter that follows, Ingrid Pramling gives examples of how these principles have been applied in preschool teaching. The remarkable result is that Pramling has demonstrated convincingly that her initiatives have developed a competence for children to learn more effectively in novel learning situations, and this has been replicated in a wider study. Moreover, it appears that such interventions in preschool have effects on learning later on, when children get to school.

Teachers' Experiences of Teaching

If we look at the two examples we have described, the work of Pramling and the study of Ahlberg, we see that what they have in common is not a particular method but an attitude toward teaching that implies a focal awareness of the learner and the learner's world. In this last section we have at times taken a normative tone, laying down principles for teaching according to our view of learning. But we want to say again that this does not imply the possibility of a particular method being developed out of those principles. Rather each teacher has to tackle the principles and appropriate them within the context of his or her own teaching. There is a dimension of attention in teaching—some teachers, especially in the lower grades, focus on the child at the expense of the content the child is learning, while others, notably in higher education, focus on content at the expense of the student (Marton, 1993). What we are advocating is that teachers should not pay attention primarily to either the learner or the content, but totally to the content as it is being learned by the learner, or to the learner as he or she is learning the content.

But even teachers who are distinctly oriented toward students mastering—or understanding—a particular content in a particular way may still differ widely on what this understanding should look like (and hence also in relation to how this understanding should be achieved). First, the content itself can be understood differently and hence taught differently by different teachers. Tullberg, Strömdahl, and Lybeck (1994), for example, gives a very convincing illustration of the radically different ways in which chemistry teachers in secondary school, and even at the college level, understand the mole in chemistry, and how these differences are reflected in their teaching. Second, the very nature of the subject can be understood differently by different teachers. Patrick (1992) shows how physics assumes different meanings for different teachers, and how they establish different curricula at the classroom level and teach accordingly. They may see physics as being primarily about developing students' understanding of the physical world around them, about enculturating students into the scientific practices of physics—theory, observation, experiment etc.—or about making students capable of handling mathematical relationships and manipulating variables. She demonstrates how differences in the way in which physics is conceptualized are reflected in the way a particular content—in her case harmonic motion—is taught. Furthermore, there may be differences on an even more general level. Teachers do have different views of what teaching is all about and again these differences are frequently reflected on the level of the teaching of the specific content (see Prosser, Trigwell, and Taylor, 1994).

We have now dealt with the teacher in the same way that we dealt more extensively with the learner in the earlier parts of this chapter. There are various more or less general aspects of teaching, the aims of teaching, curricular issues, and so on, on which teachers differ considerably, and which are inherently and simultaneously present in the teacher's awareness, albeit not thematically so, whenever a specific piece of content is taught. Thus teachers' awareness is oriented toward the act of teaching. Our argument is that each teacher's awareness should be focused above all on learning—the learners learning the content and the content being learned. Such an awareness inherently lends an insight into the variation of ways the content is being tackled and an insight into the ways the content is being understood. Then the learner engaged in the act of learning is strongly thematic in the teacher's awareness. If this is the case, then it increases the likelihood that learning will become strongly thematic in the learner's awareness.

We have argued throughout this chapter for a focus on the learner's experience of learning. We believe that good teaching always has to have such a focus. Or to put it differently: in order to teach well, it is imperative to learn continuously from the learner.

Acknowledgments

The authors wish to acknowledge financial support in writing this chapter through grants which they each received from the Swedish Council for Research into the Humanities and Social Sciences.

Notes

1. In Sweden, preschool is for children aged five to six years.
2. Although important distinctions could be made between the terms "object" and "phenomenon," we are using them interchangeably in this chapter.

3. The Swedish word for person (*människa*) retains the archaic feminine pronoun forms—she, her, etc. We will reflect this Swedish linguistic history in this chapter.

References

Ahlberg, A. (1992). *Att möta matematiska problem* [Meeting mathematical problems]. Göteborg, Sweden: Acta Universitatis Gothoburgensis.

Biggs, J. B. (1979). Individual differences in study process and the quality of learning outcomes. *Higher Education, 8,* 381–394.

Biggs, J. B. (1987a). *Student approaches to learning and studying.* Hawthorn, Victoria: Australian Council for Educational Research.

Biggs, J. B. (1987b). *The Learning Process Questionnaire (LPQ): Manual.* Hawthorn, Victoria: Australian Council for Educational Research.

Biggs, J. B. (1987c). *The Study Process Questionnaire (SPQ): Manual.* Hawthorn, Victoria: Australian Council for Educational Research.

Biggs, J. B. (1990, November). *Approaches to learning in secondary school and testing students in Hong Kong: Some comparative studies.* Paper presented at the seventh annual conference, Hong Kong Educational Research Association, University of Hong Kong.

Booth, S. A. (1992). *Learning to program: A phenomenographic perspective.* Göteborg, Sweden: Acta Universitatis Gothoburgensis.

Dahlgren, L. O. (1975). *Qualitative differences in learning as a function of content-oriented guidance* (Göteborg studies in Educational Sciences, 15). Göteborg, Sweden: Acta Universitatis Gothoburgensis.

Entwistle, N. and Ramsden, P. (1983). *Understanding student learning.* London: Croom Helm.

Gurwitsch, A. (1964). *The field of consciousness.* Pittsburgh: Duquesne University Press.

Hilgard, E. R. and Bower, G. H. (1981). *Theories of learning* (5th edn.) Englewood Cliffs, NJ: Prentice-Hall.

Hodgson, V. (1984). Learning from lectures. In F. Marton, D. Hounsell, and N. J. Entwistle (Eds.), *The experience of learning* (pp. 90–102). Edinburgh: Scottish Academic Press.

Hounsell, D. (1984). Learning and essay writing. In F. Marton, D. Hounsell, and N. J. Entwistle (Eds.), *The experience of learning* (pp. 103–123). Edinburgh: Scottish Academic Press.

Johansson, B., Marton, F., and Svensson, L. (1985). An approach to describing learning as change between qualitatively different conceptions. In L. H. T. West and A. C. Pines (Eds.), *Cognitive structure and conceptual change* (pp. 233–257). New York: Academic Press.

Johnson, K. and Wen, Q. F. (1990). A pilot study of beliefs about EFL learning in China. Unpublished manuscript, Department of Education, University of Hong Kong.

Kember, D. and Gow, L. (1991). A challenge to the anecdotal stereotype of the Asian student. *Studies in Higher Education, 16,* 117–128.

Laurillard, D. (1984). Learning from problem-solving. In F. Marton, D. Hounsell and N. J. Entwistle (Eds.), *The experience of learning* (pp. 124–143). Edinburgh: Scottish Academic Press.

Martin, E. and Ramsden, P. (1987). Learning skills, or skill in learning. In I. T. E. Richardsson, M. W. Eysenck, and D. W. Piper (Eds.), *Student learning* (pp. 155–167). Milton Keynes, England: Open University Press.

Marton, F. (1974). Some effects of content-neutral instructions on non-verbatim learning in a natural setting. *Scandinavian Journal of Educational Research, 18,* 199–208.

Marton, F. (1975). On non-verbatim learning. I: Level of processing and level of outcome. *Scandinavian Journal of Psychology, 17*, 41–48.

Marton, F. (1976). On non-verbatim learning. II: The erosion of a task-induced learning algorithm. *Scandinavian Journal of Psychology, 17*, 41–48.

Marton, F. (1980). Innehållsrelaterad pedagogisk forskning—en programförklaring. I *Innehållsrelaterad pedagogisk forskning* [Content related educational research—a manifesto]. Stockholm: Skolöverstyrelsen.

Marton, F. (1981). Phenomenography—Describing conceptions of the world around us. *Instructional Science, 10*, 177–200.

Marton, F. (1993, August). *On the structure of teachers' awareness*. Keynote address delivered at the sixth international conference on teacher thinking, Göteborg, Sweden.

Marton, F. (1994). Phenomenography. In T. Husén and T. N. Postlethwaite (Eds.), *The International Encyclopedia of Education* (2nd edn.). London: Pergamon Press.

Marton, F., Asplund-Carlsson, M., and Halász, L. (1992). Differences in understanding and the use of reflective variation in reading. *British Journal of Educational Psychology, 62*, 1–16.

Marton, F., Beaty, E., and Dall'Alba, G. (1993). Conceptions of learning. *International Journal of Educational Research, 19*, 277–300.

Marton, F., Dall'Alba, G., and Tse, L. K. (1993, August). *The paradox of the Chinese learner*. Paper presented at the fifth European Association for Research on Learning and Instruction conference, Aix-en-Provence.

Marton, F. and Säljö, R. (1976). Qualitative differences in learning. I: Outcome and process. *British Journal of Educational Psychology, 46*, 115–127.

Marton, F. and Säljö, R. (1984). Approaches to learning. In F. Marton, D. Hounsell, and N. Entwistle (Eds.), *The experience of learning* (pp. 36–55). Edinburgh: Scottish Academic Press.

Marton, F., Watkins, D., and Tang, C. (1995, August). *Continuities and discontinuities in the experience of learning: An interview study of high school students in Hong Kong*. Paper presented at the sixth European Association for Research on Learning and Instruction conference, Nijmegen, The Netherlands.

Nagle, A. and Marton, F. (1993, August). *Learning, knowing, and understanding: Qualitative changes in student teachers' views of the relationship between some educational phenomena during the first term of pre-school teacher education in Uruguay*. Paper presented at the fifth European Association for Research on Learning and Instruction conference, Aix-en-Provence.

Patrick, K. (1992, November). Teachers and curriculum at year 12: Constructing an object of study. Paper presented at the 1992 joint conference of the Australian Association for Research in Education and the New Zealand Association for Research in Education, Deaking University, Geelong, Victoria.

Pramling, I. (1983). *The child's conception of learning*. Göteborg, Sweden: Acta Universitatis Gothoburgensis.

Pramling, I. (1986). *Barn och inlärning* [Children and learning]. Lund, Sweden: Studentlitteratur.

Pramling, I. (1990). *Learning to learn*. New York: Springer Verlag.

Pramling, I. (1994). *Kunnandets grunder: Prövning av en fenomenografisk ansats till att utveckla barns sätt att uppfatta sin omvärld* [The foundations of knowing: Trialing a phenomenographic approach to developing children's ways of experiencing their worlds]. Göteborg Studies in Educational Sciences 94. Göteborg, Sweden: Acta Universitatis Gothobergensis.

Prosser, M. and Millar, R. (1989). The "how" and the "what" of learning physics. *European Journal of Psychology of Education, 4*, 513–528.

Prosser, M., Trigwell, K., and Taylor, P. (1994). A phenomenographic study of academics' conceptions of science learning and teaching. *Learning and Instruction, 4*, 217–232.

Silverstein, S. (1964). *The giving tree*. New York: Harper and Row.

Svensson, L. (1977). On qualitative differences in learning. III: Study skill and learning. *British Journal of Educational Psychology, 47*, 233–243.

Svensson, L. (1984a). *Människobilden i INOM-gruppens forskning: Den lärande människan* [The image of man in the research of the INOM-group: Man as learner]. Report 1984:03 Pedagogiska institutionen, Göteborgs universitet.

Svensson, L. (1984b). Skill in learning. In F. Marton, D. Hounsell, and N. J. Entwistle (Eds.), *The experience of learning* (pp. 56–70). Edinburgh: Scottish Academic Press.

Svensson, L. (1985, August). Contextual analysis—The development of a research approach. Paper presented at the second conference on qualitative research in psychology. Leiden, The Netherlands.

Säljö, R. (1975). *Qualitative differences in learning as a function of the learner's conception of the task*. Göteborg, Sweden: Acta Universitatis Gothoburgensis.

Säljö, R. (1979). *Learning in the learner's perspective. I. Some common-sense conceptions*. Reports from the Department of Education, no. 76, University of Göteborg.

Säljö, R. (1982). *Learning and understanding: A study of differences in constructing meaning from a text*. Göteborg, Sweden: Acta Universitatis Gothoburgensis.

Säljö, R. (1988). Learning in educational settings: Methods of inquiry. In P. Ramsden (Ed.), *Improving learning: New perspectives* (pp. 32–48). London: Kogan Page.

Torney-Purta, J. (1990). International comparative research in education: Its role in educational improvement in the US. *Educational Researcher, 19*, 32–35.

Tullberg, A., Strömdahl, H., and Lybeck, L. (1994). Students' conceptions of 1 mol and educators' conceptions of how they teach "the mole." *International Journal of Science Education, 16*, 145–156.

van Rossum, E. J. and Schenk, S. M. (1984). The relationship between learning conception, study strategy and learning outcome. *British Journal of Educational Psychology, 54*, 73–83.

Watkins, D. and Regmi, M. (1990). An investigation of the approach to learning of Nepalese tertiary students. *Higher Education, 20*, 456–469.

Watkins, D., Regmi, M., and Astilla, E. (1991). The Asian-learner-as-a-rote-learner stereotype: Myth or reality? *Educational Psychology, 11*, 21–34.

Wen, Q. (1990). *Learning approaches of successful and unsuccessful Chinese EFL learners and their relation to traditional Chinese educational philosophies and practices*. Doctoral dissertation. Department of Education, University of Hong Kong.

Wen, Q. and Marton, F. (1993, August). *Chinese views on the relation between memorization and understanding*. Paper presented at the fifth European Association for Research on Learning and Instruction conference, Aix-en-Provence.

Whelan, G. (1988). Improving medical students' clinical problem solving. In P. Ramsden (Ed.), *Improving learning: New perspectives* (pp. 199–214). London: Kogan Page.

25

Understanding and Empowering the Child as a Learner

INGRID PRAMLING

This chapter takes the same point of departure as the previous one by Marton and Booth. People's experience and their awareness are seen as the main object of research, and experience is viewed as a relationship between object and subject, which encompasses them both. The research approach here, however, applies to children in the context of early childhood education.[1]

The assumption that this approach is based on is that we act in relation to our way of understanding the world around us (Marton, 1988). How children conceptualize, experience, discern, see, and understand the world around them is the foundation on which their skills and knowledge are based. This implies that in early childhood education we should focus primarily on the different ways children are capable of being aware of the various phenomena in the world around them. Above all, we should find out the critical, and usually taken-for-granted, aspects of their ways of experiencing the world around them and on which their ability to deal with the world rests. Learning from this perspective is learning to experience the world in particular ways.

The idea underlying this chapter is that if we want to understand children's learning better we need to find out what characterizes children's learning. If we want to know what characterizes children's learning, we must know how they see it from their own perspective. And if our knowledge about children's learning should make children better "learners," we must develop their understanding of their own learning. Finally, since learning always has an act and a content aspect, developing children's learning means developing both of these aspects.

Approaches to Early Childhood Education

The philosophy in early childhood education is mainly either play-oriented, where children are expected to learn according to their own free activity, or instructional and "school-like," where children work on tasks repeatedly to finally remember the content (Elkind, 1988a). In different countries and different classrooms one can see varying degrees of one or the other of these two contradictory approaches.

The Swedish early childhood education system is based on an antischool view. The methods emanate from Froebel, who introduced play to educate young children (Johansson, 1992). The idea behind this approach is that when children's "inner life" is transformed into action, they will develop their understanding. The teacher's role is to help children to experience phenomena, by taking them to visit places, by telling them stories, by giving them roles to act out in plays, by creating an environment that stimulates play, etc. Experience from such situations and tasks are then expected to influence children's activities and ways of acting, which are supposed to make them capable of understanding the world around them. The children create their own knowledge from their activities according to their level of maturity.

The opposite view is that understanding is created by the children when they already have all the facts and knowledge as a base. The teacher's role here is to have "lessons" and give children academic tasks to solve. There are "preschool books" spread all over the world as an expression of this approach to learning. Children are supposed to learn to understand through repetition, practice, and paper exercises. Knowledge is transferred to children from the surrounding world. This view may also be based on the "top-down" model, where learning is a question of first knowing the facts and later being able to come to conclusions and understand something (Brown, 1980; Smith, 1986).

Preparing children for later schooling from the first of these two perspectives means viewing everything that happens in early childhood education as preparation for school. From the second perspective, it means covering the same subject matter as in school but at an easier level or more slowly—that is, practicing the alphabet, writing numbers, doing simple arithmetic, etc. These two perspectives are based on different views of what learning is about (Pramling, 1992).

Within most early childhood education classrooms in Sweden today, it is common to see both approaches for developing children's learning and understanding of the world around them. Children are supposed to have free play time in which to develop, but they are also supposed to acquire a body of facts, which teachers present to them using school-like books in which they can practice the 3 Rs. Singer (1992) claims that this contradiction was built into the preschool program from the very beginning in an attempt to integrate home and school. The ideology was to make the environment in preschool like home and to see the good mother as the model for the teacher (Johansson, 1992). At the same time, there was an emphasis on preparing children for school. These two views have still not been integrated into the heart of early childhood education.

Today there are other approaches (e.g., see Schweinhart and Waikart, 1980; Katz and Chard, 1990) in which a great effort is made to find a third way. These are, however, only small islands within the field. I would also like to maintain that these approaches are based on theories of children's general development—that is, on the thesis that children in a specific age group are at a certain level of development to which educational tasks are supposed to be applied. In the field of early childhood education, knowledge about children's development has always been important for teachers. But knowledge about children's development has been used in a variety of ways when applying it to a curriculum (Evans, 1982; Spodek, 1991; Weikart, 1992). The most common perspective is to view children's development in terms of general hierarchical stages, and use these stages as a basis for activities.

If we use the theoretical approach on which this chapter is based, we cannot use children's general development as a base, since children's understanding is related not to a specific age but to the experiences of the child. It means that learning becomes dependent on *content and context*. Child development still plays, and should play, a very important role within early childhood education as we can see that the notion "developmentally appropriate programs" is in focus when talking about good programs for the early years (Cullen, 1993). From the perspective presented in this chapter, however, it is not the children's developmental level that should be the focus for education but *how to develop children* (Clay, 1991). From this idea, it follows that we need to go into the content and context of learning and to learn from particular children's reactions and expressions.

What, then, can we learn from observations in preschool? When we look carefully at what is going on in the classrooms of early childhood education, it soon becomes obvious that teachers often have the intention of teaching children facts (Pramling, 1987b). They use a lot of concrete material and claim that children learn by concrete activities, but still the intention of the teacher is to transfer a body of knowledge. In one of my studies (Pramling, 1986) I observed a teacher whose goal was to teach five- and six-year-olds about time. Among other things, they worked on making clocks. When the children were asked what they had learned during the project, most of them claimed that they had learned to make clocks, since their conception of learning was "learning to do something." The same thing happened when seven-year-olds worked on the topic of temperature and made thermometers. They claimed that they had learned to make thermometers (Pramling, 1986). Teachers have probably learned during their training that children learn by concrete manipulation of materials, but at the same time their own experience from schooling has led them to assume that learning is learning to acquire a body of facts about something.

There is a strong tradition in preschool of believing that concrete action will develop children's understanding on a general level. In trying to teach children about the notion of shape, for example, it was found that they were taught by being introduced to specific shapes and by practicing remembering them. Children's ideas of shapes became ideas of those shapes specifically talked about, and the notion of shape, as such, was not at all developed (Pramling, 1986). As has been seen from earlier studies, it is not always the case that children generalize from concrete and specific examples, so a structure was introduced in the following studies that focused teachers' attention in another way and was expected to influence children differently.

Children are sensitive to teacher expectations (Veinstein, 1986); as Hundeide (1989) says, they try to read the social context. What we know from research in early childhood education is that teachers spend most of their planning time on the activities for circle-time or theme projects. We also know that they tell children about different things during this period and then ask questions to check whether or not the children remember anything (Rubinstein-Reich, 1993). When children in a study were asked how they would teach other children who did not know the things they had learned, they all said that they would tell children verbally. Even though they had worked in many different ways themselves to learn specific content, the children tended to see verbal transference as the only way to learn to know (Pramling, 1987b).

The most common spontaneous view of learning that children have is that they learn to do. However, when they are asked specifically about knowledge, they relate learning to transferring information verbally. This means that teachers and children have somewhat different taken-for-granted ideas about learning, but also that teachers develop an outdated view of learning in children, such as learning to take over a body of knowledge constructed by someone else. This discovery should be viewed in comparison with what most researchers agree upon today— that is, that learning is a process of construction and making sense in a social and cultural context (Bruner, 1988; Rogoff, 1990; Vygotsky, 1972).

What we can learn from observations in the classroom is that teachers' ideas of children's learning are not always in accordance with the ideas of children. Teachers' actions are based on "old" theories of child development; new research pointing to the importance of intervention for developing children is not really taken into consideration within education. The task for education is to develop the child's understanding of various phenomena in the world around them, which leads to the question, "How can we become able to do this?"

It is from this third perspective on early childhood education that the phenomenographically oriented approach has developed.

A Phenomenographically Oriented Approach to Early Childhood Education

In the previous chapter, Marton and Booth refer to *phenomenography* as the empirical study of the qualitatively different ways in which people experience and understand various aspects of the world around them. The approach to early childhood education described in the present chapter focuses on how children experience and become aware of phenomena in, and aspects of, the world around them. Hence, I call it a phenomenographically oriented approach to early childhood education. It rests on five principles:

1. *In learning, both an act and a content aspect are emphasized.* Although the content varies in different classrooms or situations, it should always be dealt with in relation to the act, and vice versa. The content as well as the act have to be thematized. Both the starting point and the goal for education are children's thoughts about both the content and the act—the *what* and the *how* aspects of learning. The act, from this approach, has a metacognitive character—that is, it requires that children focus attention on their own way of thinking about the content.

2. *The focus is on the taken-for-granted aspects of different phenomena in the surrounding world.* If the child has not become aware of a phenomenon, then it is

impossible to learn about it (Elkind, 1988b). The goal of the learning must appear to the child as relevant.

The point here is that, irrespective of whether it is the teacher or the child who first focuses attention on something in the world around them, it is teachers who are aware of what to direct the child's awareness toward, and it is their task to make it visible and relevant for the child to learn about. Different phenomena are visible to children in everyday life to varying extents. In one study (Pramling, 1994) I discovered how preschoolers have conceptions of numbers although they have not worked on them; at the same time, certain aspects of nature, for example, are totally invisible to five- and six-year-olds as long as no one has brought them to their attention.

In recent years, metacognitive researchers have increasingly held the view that metacognitive skills or knowledge are central to children's learning. Many researchers claim that children become better learners if their metacognitive skills, such as the regulation and control of their thinking, are developed (Brown, 1985; Brown and Reeve, 1985), while others seem to have the view that metacognitive knowledge is something embedded in more general cognitive development (Flavell, 1977). From the perspective adopted in this chapter, metacognition is the child's experiential view of metacognition (Pramling, 1987a). The ideas that come to mind when they are asked about their own learning are the taken-for-granted approach to learning of the child. If, for example, a boy says that he has learned to ride his bike or wash his hands, that is what he is aware of. A teacher or a researcher can, however, trace this child's level of awareness according to what he expresses or does. Children talk about specific things they learn and not about learning more generally. To develop children metacognitively means, here, to raise their awareness of their own learning. What will happen, then, if we can raise children's level of awareness so that they can focus on the same thing as the teacher—that is, so that we develop the child's conception of learning, as a question of learning to know or learning as understanding? In other words, what will happen if we can develop children's metacognitive level and understanding of their own learning better?

3. *Reflection is used as a method in education.* To get children to talk and reflect, they must become involved in activities (material, situations, play, tasks, etc.) that allow them to talk and think about what they are doing and learning.
4. *Variation of thought is used.* The teacher must expose the ways in which children are thinking and use these ideas as the content in education. The teacher must then be aware that children learn from one another, which means that the differences instead of the similarities between children are focused on. Exposing children to variation of thought can be achieved in many different ways—for example, through drawing, drama, play, and discussion as well as through alternative ways of saying things.
5. *Learning is to be viewed as a part of the total world of experience.* This means that the total world of experience influences every new experience. Experiences have formed an awareness that can help or hinder children in grasping a meaning

or in relating things to one another. Different meanings "stand out" for children in different ways.

These five principles represent both what teachers' perspectives should be focused on and what they need to do in practice. I have elaborated on these principles elsewhere (1994).

The Teacher's Knowledge and Skills   To the above principles a certain competence has to be added if the teacher is to act in accordance with the intentions of this approach. Since there is no simple method to adopt, the teacher's awareness should be directed toward the following:

1. *Becoming informed about existing research on children's thinking.*[2] Here, the results of phenomenographic research—i.e., the outcome space—constitute a description of the variation of ways of thinking about a specific phenomenon (Pramling, 1995). This is a knowledge base that provides the teacher with tools for working in line with the present approach.
2. *Developing methodological knowledge and skills.* The main area within methodology is to become skilled in interviewing children (Doverborg and Pramling, 1993). This means both being able to put questions other than the normal ones in classrooms and also following up the children's ideas as far as possible. In other words, to become skilled at letting the children expose their ideas and also at getting the children to feel that they want to share their ideas with the teacher and the other children. Children must feel it is enjoyable to express themselves and to be thrilled by others' ideas. To achieve this means that both the teacher and the children must learn to communicate on equal terms and to share their experiences.

A second aspect of the teachers' methodological knowledge is the way they plan for a theme or a topic and carry it through in practice (Doverborg and Pramling, 1988). The planning must include the aim of the theme, in terms of what the children's awareness should be directed toward. When planning in preschool takes place, it is quite common that teachers take the goal aspect for granted and begin to plan what kind of activities to have with children after choosing the theme or topic; they thus never reflect on what they should try to develop an understanding about (Toshach, 1983).

Thematizing different contents and making them visible to children means not only introducing a specific content but also being able to utilize everyday situations and children's interest. Children should be given the opportunity to become aware of different phenomena in the world around them and to develop their own questions and ideas about them. For the teacher, this approach implies becoming aware of what type of understanding to develop in children, and then using every given situation to explore the varieties of ideas among the children. This means confronting children with the same questions, phenomena etc. in several different contexts.

The knowledge base for the teacher and the principles developed above have been used in two research studies (Pramling, 1990, 1994). In Study 1 it is the teachers themselves who choose the content, while in Study 2 the content is defined by the researcher in a developed "curriculum."

Study 1: Learning to Learn

The aim of Study 1 was to implement and evaluate a phenomenographically oriented approach to learning. The basis for it is a description of children's concepts of their own learning (Pramling, 1983). The description is derived from interviews with children aged three to eight. The *what* and *how* aspects of learning were revealed by asking children the following two questions:

1. Tell me something you have learned! (in many different contexts in preschool, such as during circle time or play).
2. How did you go about learning that? (related to the thing children suggested they had learned).

Children's awareness of *what* they learned was described in terms of learning to do, to know, and to understand. *Learning to do* means that children perceived learning as learning a skill, activities, or how to behave—for example, "I have learned to ride my bike." *Learning to know* meant that children perceived learning as knowing facts or receiving information about something—for example, "I have learned that there is a country called Canada." *Learning to understand* meant that children related their own learning to a changed way of thinking, that their way of thinking had changed qualitatively—for example, "Although I knew about cars when I was three years old, I did not know anything about traffic."

Children's conceptions of what they learn not only change but also expand, so that children gain access to an increasing number of different ways of thinking as they get older. Even among eight-year-old children, only about a quarter of them have developed the idea that learning can be to know something. The idea of learning as learning to understand was held by only a very small number of eight-year-olds.

At each of the levels of thinking about what was learned, there were qualitatively different ways of thinking about *how* the learning came about. For the youngest children, learning was not differentiated from *doing*. Many young children denied learning and said: "I just did it!" At the next level of awareness, children related their learning to *age*—that is, at a certain age they think they will be able to do something. Children can say, for example: "When I am five, I will be able to ride my bike." And finally, at the most advanced level, children understand that they have to get some *experience* in order to learn.

The view of experience as a source of learning to do could be related either to an event—that is, you do something and one day you certainly will be able to master the skill—or to something you could influence by practicing. This means that in the first case, learning is embedded in time, while in the second, learning is related to the child's own control—that is, the child can decide to practice more

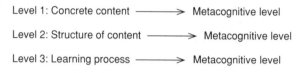

Figure 25.1   *The teacher's structure of teaching in the experiential approach.*

in order to learn something faster or better. In other words, the child sees a particular activity as the source of learning.

When questioned if they have understood that learning to do something depends on themselves, positive responses come from about 33 percent of the five-year-olds, 66 percent of the six-year-olds, 89 percent of the seven-year-olds, and 96 percent of the eight-year-olds. Thus the meaning of learning changes according to the age of the child (Enerstvedt, 1988).

Design and Implementation

To evaluate a phenomenographically oriented approach to learning, four groups of five- and six-year-olds (76 altogether) in middle-class areas were studied during one school year. The four teachers were chosen on the recommendation of the teacher training college, for whom they functioned as supervisors. Two of the teachers were asked to work in the way they usually did, and the other two were asked to apply an experiential approach to learning. The experiential approach mainly involved making use of the principles described above and also using a specific structure of teaching, shown in Figure 25.1.

The structure of the experiential approach involves working at three levels of generality: (1) the concrete content, (2) the structure of the content (relations), and (3) the learning process. At each level, the teachers were asked to raise the content talked about to a metacognitive level, which meant that they were to try to make the children aware of the variety of ways of thinking about the concrete content, the structure, and the learning process. This means that the phenomenon or aspect of the world that is the focus of the learning is always considered as a part of a whole. When, for example, learning is focused upon, it is always learning about something special, a content. To work at the three levels of generality means that, in practice, it is sometimes a question of moving from the specific to the more general and sometimes the reverse. On certain occasions, attention is focused on all three levels at once, on other occasions first on one level then on another.

One example of creating a situation on which to reflect is that of the theme "rain and water." Four children at a time sit in a room with the teacher. They are each given a piece of paper that they are asked to fold in half. They are given the task of making a drawing on one side showing good weather, and one on the other side showing bad weather. When they are ready, they are allowed to compare their drawings and then discover with the help of the teacher's questions the relativity of what is fine and bad weather. To a mother, on the one hand, bad weather may be when she has to pull little brother in his stroller through the snow (someone has drawn this). The children, on the other hand, think of this weather as fine, because they can build snowmen and go tobogganing. Another example of such relativity is that a flower is happy when it rains, while an adult might get annoyed when he is splashed by a passing car. The teacher's message that there is neither good nor bad weather except in relation to someone or something then becomes apparent to the children. Here, the children not only reflect on the phenomenon good or bad weather, but also on how different children think in different ways, as expressed in their drawings.

As we have seen in the example about weather, the children first have to *use their imagination and form an idea about something*. In the next stage, the children are made aware of each other's ideas, or in other words, the variation in their ways of thinking is brought out. This method of alternating between the cognitive and metacognitive levels is one that permeates most of the school-year's program. When we draw children's attention to the diversity and the different levels of generality, the children come to realize that each and everyone thinks in different ways.

On another occasion, the children are given the task of trying to find out what snowflakes look like and then to draw them. They compare them and see that all snowflakes have six points, but despite this they all have different patterns, just as people are all different. When the teacher asks, "If you think about what we talked about in the autumn, how the rain comes, how do you think, then, that we get snow in the winter?" someone replies, "The water drops clump together and turn into ice crystals." Someone else says, "Well, it's the same cycle as the rain." The teacher continues, "And then there's snow instead of rain just because it is colder in the winter." They all look at the wall chart of the cycle of rain and water that they have made on a previous occasion. Now their attention is focused on the *structure* in the form of relationships (the cycle). "How is it that we get rain and snow, really?" asks the teacher. The children have to solve this problem in small groups. The different solutions are discussed and compared. "Shall we see how many different ways of thinking about why we get snow and rain there are in your solutions?" Attention is now focused on the metacognitive level—i.e., how they think about structures.

The next step comes on another occasion when the teacher asks, "Have you ever wondered how we get drinking water into our houses?" Someone says, "Through the pipes." "It comes to the purifying plant first," says another. The teacher then asks, "Where does it come from to the purifying plant?" "From the sea, I think," a child replies. "The pipes go down in the ground." The teacher then asks, "Why are they buried?" "So we don't trip over them and so they don't get broken," suggests a pupil. The teacher wonders whether they remember that a water pipe sprang a leak last year so that nobody in the neighbourhood had any water. They talk about this for a while. The teacher asks what they use water for and the children make suggestions: washing, doing the dishes, drinking, flushing the toilet, etc. They observe that they have thought of many different things. The teacher asks, "Where does the water go to then?" "Out into the sea," someone says. "Do they purify it?" asks the teacher. "Yes, you have to because it is poisonous." Teacher: "What would happen otherwise?" The discussion takes up the problems of the fish dying and the factories not always purifying their water. While the children are talking about how this purification is done, the teacher draws it on a large sheet of paper on the wall so that the cycle can be seen clearly. First, attention has been paid to how children think about water, then again to the structure as a cycle.

Many days are then spent in creating a picture of a town with all of its "underworld" (water pipes and drains). At regular intervals the teacher pauses to let the pupils ponder over how the water goes round in the same way as they talked about in their previous discussions. They have also experimented with steam to illustrate and create situations to reflect upon. While they are doing the experiments the children have to think about why they are doing them and whether they could do them in another way to find out about rain and water (the learning aspect).

To get children to reflect on their own *learning* and on how they think about it, they were asked on one occasion to ponder over what the weather would be like the following day. After their reflections they were given the task of finding out, for the following day, different ways of forecasting the weather. The next day, after they had given an account of various observations and signs that can be found in nature for predicting the weather, the teacher asked them how they had found out about these things. One had asked his mother, another his grandfather, Per had read a book, Ulla had seen a program on TV, and Elin said she had "worked it out" by herself. The teacher then pointed out to the children how many different ways they had been able to think of for finding out what the weather would be like. "Are there any other ways of finding out what you want to know?" The reflections were then at a metacognitive level—that is, at a level showing how the children think about how they learn, remember, and know.

Some aspects of the theme "rain and water" can be summarized in accordance with the three levels of generality:

1. The children present their reflections on and conceptions of rain and water (content) in combination with experiments. The teacher helps them notice the variation in their ways of thinking (in words or with pictures).
2. The children's attention is directed toward the structure in the form of the cycle; they present their reflections on this.
3. The children's attention is directed toward what they are experimenting with, talking about and drawing, how and why they are doing it, and whether there are any other ways of learning (thinking out, finding out, doing, obtaining information, etc.). That is, their attention is directed toward their own learning.

At all three levels the children change their perspective from time to time, with the teacher's help, by reflecting on how they think about the content, structure, and learning. The same stages recur in relation to the water supply and sewers in a town.

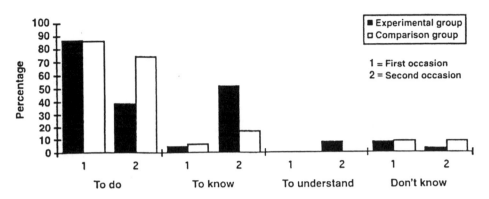

Figure 25.2 *The change of ideas of learning in the experimental and comparison groups.*

The theoretical assumption behind this approach is that the generality is always an aspect of the more specific and vice versa. And it does not mean that children learn the general by operating with the concrete. Rather, it is by getting children to reflect on concrete activities and trying to illustrate the ideas that the source of understanding develops. Children in the study discussed above were expected to learn by adopting a reflective approach to learning at different levels of generality—that is, to explain their learning as well as the topic.

Results

To find out whether the children had changed or not, in terms of their different ways of making sense of their reality, all of them (experimental and comparison groups) were interviewed at the beginning and at the end of the school year about their conceptions of their own learning. During the last month of the school year, the children were also involved in three learning experiments, two of which involved listening to stories and a third that involved visiting the natural science museum and having a "lesson" there about the ecological cycle. The children were then interviewed individually about the different topics in the stories and the "lesson" by an interviewer who did not know what the children had been involved in. The learning experiments were supposed to find out if children who have been involved in the present approach had developed their capacity to learn and to think about their learning.

The overall results show a great difference in children's understanding of their own learning depending on whether they had been involved in the phenomeno-graphically oriented approach to learning (here called the experimental group), or not involved (the comparison group). As shown in Figure 25.2, these children did develop metacognitively—that is, they developed their awareness of their own learning. Most of the children from both the experimental and comparison groups had the idea of learning as "learning to do" at the beginning of the school year, while the children in the experimental group changed to a large extent toward thinking about learning as "learning to know." Furthermore, a few of these children developed the idea of learning as "learning to understand," which is very advanced for children of this age.

After studying the children's metacognitive capability, the following question arose: "Are these children better able to learn from a totally new content?" This was then studied in three learning experiments:

Learning experiment 1: "The Red Apple," a story about two apples that got mixed up with each other, was read to the children in each group. The apples were transferred from character to character and event to event, altogether 11 times. In the children's retelling of the story the number of events recalled was recorded. In the experimental groups, 27 out of 38 children retold between 5 and 11 events, while 27 out of 36 of the children from the comparison groups only retold 1 to 4 events. The children who had participated in the phenomenographically oriented approach in preschool learned to grasp the structure of the story in much greater detail.

Learning experiment 2: A story similar to the one read in the first experiment was read to the children. But the structure of the story was quite different. Entitled "On the Other Side of the River," the story presented the idea of reciprocity between people who lived in a city located on the two banks of a river. The children's spontaneous expression of the plot of the story showed that 16 out of 37 children from the experimental groups grasped the mutual dependence of the people on both banks of the river, while none of the children in the comparison groups did so. In response to a more explicit question about why people built a new bridge over the river, 29 of the experimental children and 12 of the comparison children suggested that they needed each other. Thus children who had participated in the group in which the approach advocated here was used grasped the meaning of the story to a greater extent than children who came from more traditional preschool programs.

Learning experiment 3: This was based on teaching children about an ecological cycle during a visit to a museum of natural history. A lecturer told the children about different animals and plants and then constructed an ecological cycle on the floor, putting arrows between the objects in order to illustrate the cycle. What emerged were qualitatively different ways in which the children had grasped the lecturer's message, which could be categorized as naming parts, grasping fragments, the food chain, and the cycle. The different categories represented more or less extended relationships between the objects in the cycle. The analysis showed that 26 out of 35 children from the comparison group just named parts or perceived fragments of the cycle, while 32 out of 38 children from the experimental group accounted for the food chain or were able to relate all the objects to a total system—that is, to the ecological cycle. This result showed that children from the experimental group also understood the message of the lesson at the museum at a much more advanced level than the comparison group did.

Such results clearly indicate that children who have been involved in a phenomenographically oriented approach to learning have developed both metacognitively and cognitively compared to children of the same age from traditional preschool programs, with their combination of free play and learning tasks structured by the teacher. Critical to the phenomenographic approach are both the structure of the information and a related dimension of how children come to know.

Study 2: The Foundation of Skills and Knowledge

Study 2 has several similarities to Study 1. The main purpose in both cases was to apply and evaluate a phenomenographically oriented approach to learning in preschool. The content in the second study was, however, defined by the researcher, while in the first it was defined by the teachers. The content was also much more extended, since it was supposed to form a basis for future learning in the different content areas in primary school. The principles for acting, however, were the same, as was the structure in terms of different levels of generality—that is, the content, the structure (relations) and learning, and the metacognitive approach at each of these levels. The act and content are both considered in a recent study (Pramling, 1994).

Design

The six preschool teachers who were chosen for the study had a wide range of experience, having worked in the field from 5 to 27 years when the project began. They taught in a broad variety of socioeconomic areas within a large city, three in day care and three in kindergarten.[3]

During the first year, a curriculum, to be discussed in the next section, was developed. These six teachers were also involved in in-service training once a month, where they discussed the research literature in the curriculum area and the principles for teaching. The teachers were also supervised in their classroom settings roughly every third week, when the project leader made observations of what was happening in the classroom. These observations then formed the object of discussion for developing the approach to learning.

The second year began with interviews with all the children about the content areas they were to study. The teachers then began to implement the curriculum in their classrooms, and continuous observations were made of the work in every group. The program continued in this way for two years with children five and six years old. The children who were six at the beginning left preschool after one year and transferred to primary school while the five-year-olds stayed in the program for two years. Before this happened, however, they were all interviewed again about the same content as the first time. They were also involved in a learning experiment, which meant that they listened to a fairy tale about which they were later interviewed.

At the same time as the first group of children were interviewed, six comparison groups were chosen in which the children were given the same interview and the same learning experiment. The groups were chosen on the basis of the criteria that the teachers had experience comparable to that of the teachers involved in the project, and also that they worked in the same socioeconomic areas. Thus similarity of preschool context and home background could be assumed. These teachers were also interviewed about the content and the methods used in their work. They were considered as fairly good "traditional" preschool teachers. A total of 77 children were exposed to the approach developed in this second project, 58 for one year and 15 for two years (4 children moved). In the comparison groups there were 38 children.

"Curriculum" and Implementation

In the present study a curriculum was developed based on research on children's thinking and understanding of different aspects of reading and writing, numbers and counting, natural science, society, and learning. This preschool curriculum focused on phenomena in the surrounding world and was partly oriented toward the subject matter taught in school but not identical with the school curriculum. In school, children's learning is directed at the skills of reading, writing and counting or remembering facts of the natural and social sciences. This alternative approach focused on providing children with conditions for understanding the basis for learning. The following is a brief description of the content, illustrated by examples from its implementation in preschool.

Learning   One focus of Study 2, as it was in Study 1, was children's understanding of their own learning—that is, making them aware of both what they learn and how this learning comes about (Pramling, 1983). The description of children's awareness of their own learning described earlier (see p. 571) was used as a basis for developing children's understanding of their own learning. Let us look at an example from the implementation, where a group of children is focused on the theme "growing new plants."

    A boy in one group asked, "Which is larger, the earth or the sun?" "Well, what do you think?" asked the teacher.

MARCUS: The earth, because there is air there!
ISAURA: The sun, because it can shine so far away.
ZANDRA: They are the same size, because the sun shines all over the earth.

The teacher pointed out that the sun cannot be both larger, smaller and the same and asked them how they would go about finding out the answer to the question.

STINA: Call the radio. They ought to know since they have a space rocket for finding out about the weather.
STIG: Call TV. People there go up to the sky and study the weather. They can look. . .or you can go there yourself.
MARCUS: I can ask Håkan. He goes up into space sometimes.
GABI: I will think about it.
ZANDRA: Read it in a book. My mother can read for me.
NANETTE: I'll read in a book, too.

In the afternoon, when the children were picked up by their parents, the teacher talked with the parents and the children about what each child should find out for the next day. The parent whose child wanted to call the radio seemed very embarrassed, and the teacher said to her: "If you find it difficult, you can find out the telephone number, and we can call them from here, tomorrow." When each of the seven children brought their answers the next day, the teacher drew three diagrams of the sun and the earth: one with them the same size, one with the sun as the largest, and a third with the earth as the largest. Every child had to give his or her answer and the teacher ticked off their answers beside the diagram. After a while they realized that they all now knew that the sun was the largest. The teacher then changed the focus again to the learning aspect and asked each child how he or she had found out. She finished this short session by bringing to the children's attention the many different strategies they used to get their answers.

The teacher tried to make children aware of their own learning by taking a question by one of the children and creating a situation in which they all had to think and reflect and then to follow up their ideas in practice. And finally, once again, they could see the variation between different ways of finding something out. The four new topics for this study will now be described.

Reading and Writing   Within the field of reading and writing, children are made aware of the skills themselves, which are made visible to them as part of their own experience. In addition to this, the relation between verbal and written language is made visible: how the flow of speech is divided into words, what the functions of being able to read and write are, what a symbol means.

Support for this kind of content is found in Dahlgren and Olsson's study (1985) of how children conceptualize reading. They showed that children who did not have any ideas about why they ought to read, or of how to go about reading, developed learning problems in school. In contrast, all the children who had the idea that reading would enable them to read books and messages rapidly learned to read in primary school. Their conceptions of these activities had a strong bearing on what they actually learned there.

One example of working with this type of content occurred when a teacher asked children to make symbols for good and bad weather. Children made their own symbols—that is, they created their own meaning. They then compared and discussed which one was the most informative or easiest for others to understand. Another day, the children were talking about mushrooms and a little girl suggested that there are poisonous mushrooms. The teacher then took the opportunity to ask how she could tell other people that some particular mushrooms are poisonous. She suggested making a picture of a poisonous mushroom with a cross over it. On another occasion, the teacher suggested that the children make their own notes for remembering which songs they were going to sing and in which order they were to be sung, for the performance planned for parents to celebrate Christmas. In her mind the teacher knew what she wanted the children to become aware of—that is, that one aspect of the written language is that we share symbols. The teacher thematized this aspect, which is often taken for granted, for children to reflect on. She also had a clear idea about what to develop and took the opportunity to let the children be active and to notice and reflect on the variation in thinking.

One notion used in the program was to "play-write" (Hagtvet-Eriksen, 1990), which gives children the signal that you can write and express yourself in whatever way you are able to. It is a wonderful notion, since children know that in play they can change goals and features for any reason. Children who are used to this learning approach and teachers using the notion of "play-writing" sometimes focus their own attention on the written text and make comparisons by themselves. The following is an observation of four children drawing pictures and "writing."

ALEXANDER [3 years]: I can't write!

MUHAMMED [5 years]: I can show you. [He writes by pretending to write on Alexander's picture.] Now it says Alexander there!

DANKA [4 years]: [Starts to scribble.] Look, I have written that this is a bus on its way to Stockholm.

ALEXANDER: But look at Christina, she writes in another way!

CHRISTINA [6 years]: I write with letters, but it is okay to scribble or "play-write."

There are many ways to write. But in school you have to learn the alphabet.

Experience of Numbers   Another area we have studied is the experience of numbers, which is not the same as carrying out counting procedures. We believe that mathematical skills are developed by getting children to grasp the meaning of numbers and their meaning in different aspects of counting.

Neuman (1987) has shown in her research on children's mathematical abilities that when children in school have difficulties with number problems, it is not because of a lack of counting procedures but because of a lack of a basic understanding of numbers and the counting activity. Neuman claims that children who have not grasped the meaning of numbers and the meaning of counting in different forms will run into difficulties when they have to work with higher numbers (over 10) later on. To be able to do this, children must be able to imagine numbers and see the structure of the whole number and how it can be split up into different combinations. According to Neuman, learning to imagine numbers can be done by getting children to conceptualize patterns—for example, "finger-pictures." A similar view of basic mathematics can be found in Japanese preschool, where mathematical problem solving is not seen as a question of letting children manipulate and do exercises with symbols but as imagining mathematics problems in a dialogue between the teacher and the children within a group activity (Gordon, 1987).

Doverborg (1987) studied children's development of mathematical skills in two preschools. At one of the schools, teachers worked in a school-oriented fashion and taught different number skills during lessons. At the other, they utilized numbers as they were encountered in everyday contexts—for example, when laying the table or when they did needlework, baked, or cooked. The evaluation showed that children who had been involved in the latter approach to mathematics were better at solving problems than children who had worked in a more instructive, school-like manner.

One aspect of number concepts is division. Earlier studies have shown that pre-school children solve division problems from the perspective of sharing, in the sense of sharing equally in social terms (Doverborg, 1987; Neuman, 1987). Children therefore have problems when they are asked to divide odd numbers. However, what they are asked to divide is of great importance to their capability of solving the problem. We saw in one of the groups how 12 children solved the problem of dividing a cake into eight pieces. Three children divided the whole cake into eight pieces, while eight children cut eight similar pieces and then commented on the rest of the cake by saying "That's left over." One child did not share equally at all but put eight marks straight on to the cake and cut it into nine pieces.

The teacher then focused the children's attention on these three different ways of solving the problem. First, the children were shown how the problem was solved in different ways, and then they were asked to express how they felt about their own way of solving it. Dividing up a cake is a very good example of making the child's understanding of the world become visible. A cake can be cut into pieces, but the pieces do not need to be equal, since grown-ups can eat bigger pieces than children; furthermore it is totally realistic to save some cake.

Order is another aspect of arithmetic. Children in a group were requested to make a drawing of the life cycle of a butterfly, after having worked on this topic for a while. The teacher asked them to think carefully about how they would make the order of the stages in which the butterfly develops visible to people who do not know about it. Some children drew pictures from left to right, explaining that this is the way to read. Other children put an arrow between the egg, the caterpillar, the pupa and the butterfly and others numbered the stages. One child put the pictures in a column, and a few could not remember all the stages or understand what a sequence was. Afterward they put the drawings on the wall and talked about their different ways of thinking about order.

The Natural World   A third topic was to understand aspects of the natural world, which could involve making children aware of the ecological cycle (Pramling, 1990); growth (Russel and Watt, 1990); living and dead things (Stepans, 1985); the change of seasons and changes in nature (Maurice, Staeheli, and Montangero, 1990); time (Dionnet and Montangero, 1990); or aspects of science (Driver, 1982; Lybeck, 1981). Within each area, the aim is not that children should focus on the facts but rather that they should develop their ways of thinking.

In one project a group of children and their teacher went for a walk in a meadow with instructions to choose at least five different objects to take back with them. When they got back to school, they were given the task of categorizing their objects into living and dead things. They were then asked to draw pictures of the living things on one piece of paper and the dead things on another. The children then had to tell each other which were living and which were dead and why they thought so.

Five-year-old Stina started: "The cup is living, since it isn't broken. Birch-seed and mushrooms and moss and oak-leaves and ferns are living. I do not think any of it is old. It will fade when I become old. The string, the handle and the plastic fish-thing, they can die, but I do not know how. They are man-made things." All the drawings were put on the wall the next day, and the children realized that some objects were found in the groups of both living things and dead things. A new discussion with new arguments opened up.

Six-year-old Pelle offered this comment: "The willow leaves are green. They are alive. The pinecone is dead. It was alive when it grew on the tree. Corn was alive when it was green. The stick isn't alive, because sticks which live are on trees, but this one isn't. The rowan-berries are alive. When they become shriveled they are dead."

Society   A fourth topic was to understand aspects of the manmade world, like our surroundings, from a perspective of time (history) and space (cultural and geographical aspects). This could be learned by looking at phenomena in society, such as shops (Pramling, 1991), professions (Furth, 1980), social interactions (Damond, 1977), cooperation (Klerfelt, 1991), artwork (Gustavsson, 1992). One example in this study concerned changes in society. After having worked on different social changes, the children were given a problem to solve that had not been discussed earlier in the group. They were divided into small groups of four or five children and were given two small cards on which to draw how and where people lived. They were also asked if they knew how people began to live together. Every child knew that people had lived in caves, as they had built one in the basement earlier in the year. The teacher then asked children to describe how we live today. The children were told to use one card for the cave and one for the house they lived in today. They were then asked to think carefully about other ways people may have lived and to take as many cards as they wanted to on which to draw people's houses.

One child suggested a cave, an igloo, a log cabin, a straw house, and a "normal" house. Another drew a cave, a wooden hut, a cottage, and a block of flats. Other children suggested other combinations. They invented their own ideas of historical homes. The next day, they looked at all the different ideas together and the children had to explore their thinking about how people's homes have changed and about how their own thinking has changed.

We now have a taste of the "curriculum" and how it was implemented in practice. What happened, then, to the children who for one or two years were involved?

Results

The general trend in the results shows that children from the experimental group—i.e., those who have been involved in the approach to learning developed here—understand most of the topic areas at a more advanced level than the comparison group. A more advanced level means different things, depending on the question. The children received approximately 30 questions within the five areas of the

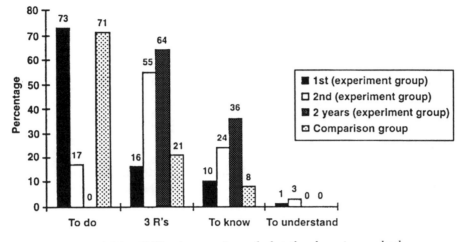

Figure 25.3   *Children's conceptions of what they learn in preschool.*

curriculum, and three questions related to the fairy tale. Let us look at one or two examples from each topic area.

Within the area of *understanding their own learning*, we can see in Figure 25.3 that from the category of learning to do there is a specific category focusing on the skills of reading, writing, and counting, which becomes an obvious content in these children's minds. In the figures, we can see that the children in the comparison group, who are six to seven years old, are at the same level as the experimental group at the first interview—that is, when they are five to six years old. When the children have participated in the phenomenographically oriented program for a year, more than half of them (55 percent) are aware of the fact that they learn to read, write, and count in preschool, compared to 21 percent of the comparison group. One quarter of the experimental group are aware of knowing, while only 8 percent of the children in the comparison group are. When the children have been involved in the special program for two years, these figures are even higher.

The children's capacity to learn a new content was studied in connection with their hearing the *fairy tale* "The Giving Tree," by Silverstein (1964), a study that was referred to in the previous chapter, by Marton and Booth. One of the questions asked of the children was, "What can you learn from this story?" The five qualitatively different ways of dealing with the question were to claim that one learns (1) to read and write (the alphabet, the skill, etc.); (2) the story, as such (to tell it by heart); (3) about stories (they are not true, trees can speak, etc.); (4) episodes from the story (to sell apples, to build a boat, etc.); (5) an understanding of the message in the story (moral, values, etc.). The following interview illustrates what it means to experience learning as a question of understanding:

ELISABETH: You can learn that. . .you shouldn't, for example, just use up a bunch of trees without paying for them, or like, if you learn how you're supposed to do this way and that way with things.

INTERVIEWER: Hmm. What do you mean?

E: Well, that you should take the apples if you think you hear, if you think you hear a voice which says so, or if you feel that you should, so you do what you feel like doing.

I: Yes?

E: That's what you usually do.

I: Is there anything more to learn?

E: You can also learn that you shouldn't do that.

I: You said that you could do what you feel like doing.

E: Yes.

I: Can you tell me more about that?

E: Yes, you might think that you can throw away a little shampoo, because there isn't much left of it. And you shouldn't do that, because you should try to save it.

I: Hmm.

E: So, you think twice before you do something.

As we have seen in the interview with Elisabeth, she talks about the voice of her conscience. For children to relate learning from the fairy tale to an understanding means to go beyond the text and interpret it with their own meaning, a meaning that has to be constructed by the child, since it is not explicit in the text (Pramling, Asplund Carlsson, and Klerfelt, 1993).

It has to be pointed out that this fairy tale was criticized for being too difficult for children when it was published. Yet 26 percent from the experimental group related their learning to an understanding, compared with only 5 percent of the comparison group.

In addition to children's understanding of their own learning and their ability to learn from a fairy tale, children's understanding of the four different areas of content in relation to the "curriculum" was also tested. Children from the comparison groups had also had some experience of these areas of content, but in a more traditional way.

Another question put to the children asked, why are you supposed to *learn to read and write?* The categories of conceptions that arise on analysis of what the children express are the activity as such, the future (school or adult), or the message. The category that is considered the most advanced is that of being aware of the message as a reason for learning to read and write. In the experimental group, 50 percent of the children were aware of the message in relation to reading after one year and 64 percent after two years; in the comparison group, only 21 percent of the children were aware of this message. When it came to being aware of the message as a reason for learning to write, the difference was even larger: 69 percent and 79 percent of the children in the experimental group were aware after one and two years respectively, while only 18 percent of the comparison group were aware of the meaning of writing as giving someone a message.

When the children were asked to write a letter to someone, 19 percent of the children from the experimental group wrote full sentences after one year, and 47 percent after two years, while 8 percent of the comparison children did.

In the area of *numbers and counting*, children were asked both to solve problems and to express their ideas of different aspects of arithmetic. One question was, "Why is it valuable to be able to count?" Different categories of conceptions were found in the responses to this, but the one valued most highly was that of the children being aware of the fact that counting is something for use in everyday life, which indicates the ability to see a function related to one's own experience. In the experimental group 40 percent of the children express this awareness after one year and 57 percent after two years. In the comparison group, only 18 percent of the children seem to be aware of the everyday use of counting.

The result of solving simple arithmetic problems—such as $2 + 7 = \_$, $10 - 7 = \_$ and $3 + \_ = 7$—presented as everyday situations shows a similar trend, indicating that a larger number of children in the phenomenographic group solve the problem than in the comparison groups. It should be noted, however, that the differences between the experimental and comparison groups are not as great in the other areas after one year as after two.

The most interesting question in this area is the "guessing game," developed by Neuman (1987), in which nine buttons are hidden in two boxes. Neuman first made sure that each child could count out nine buttons. After the child had counted, she told them that she would put the buttons into two boxes, and they had to guess how many there were in each. The differences in the present study are mainly that in the experimental group 60 percent of the children solved the problem correctly after one year and 67 percent did after two years; only 32 percent of the comparison group did so. This was a task requiring children to keep the wholes and the parts in their minds simultaneously in order to arrive at a correct solution.

In the topic that is focused on, *society*, one question began by showing the children two pairs of pictures representing "now" and "then" and then asking them to describe the pictures. An example of the pictures is shown in Figure 25.4. As shown in Table 25.1, 81 percent of children from the experimental group spontaneously suggested that the pictures represented "now" and "then," but only 26 percent of the comparison children did. The follow-up question concerns why the object in the pictures has changed. The interviewer focuses the children's attention on the fact that the pictures are about former times and the present, for those who do not see this themselves. The children express qualitatively different understandings of this change. Some of the children cannot go beyond the pictures as such, and talk about colors, etc. Other children relate the change to the fact that people were poorer in former times and are richer today. Still another conception is to understand the change in terms of people's needs, which have also changed. In none of these categories is there any sense of time. This, however, we find in the most advanced category where the children express the understanding that people have invented and developed things in society. In the special program 57 percent of the children express this idea while only 18 percent of the children in the comparison group do.

The last topic area was *nature*. One problem for the children to solve was to sort out the relation between pictures representing objects in an ecological cycle. The

Figure 25.4 *A pair of pictures representing "now" and "then."*

Table 25.1   *Children's conceptions of "now" and "then" and the reason for change in society*

	Percentage of experimental group		Percentage of comparison group
	Begin	1 year	
Spontaneous discovery	23	81	26
Why?			
No difference	13	2	16
The picture as such	25	5	32
Rich and poor	29	16	29
Changed needs	21	21	5
People invent	13	57	18

different categories in which the children's understanding could be described were (1) no relationship, (2) animals eat each other and plants, (3) the biodegradable process and (4) the cycle. The critical factor is eliciting understanding of the relationship between events. In the experimental program 59 percent of the children related the pictures to each other in a cycle, while none of the children in the comparison group did so.

In summary, we can establish that there are differences between the experimental and comparison groups with respect to the answers to most of the questions. The seven-year-olds from the comparison group, who have been in preschool for at least one year, were at the same level as the five- and six-year-olds, who have not yet been involved in schooling but are in the experimental groups. The children involved in the phenomenographically oriented approach have developed an understanding of phenomena that is believed to form a basis for later learning in school. The differences between the experimental and comparison groups in practicing counting and writing skills are minor for the children who have been involved for one year. But when the children have been involved for two years, they are far better than those of the comparison group at both solving mathematical problems and writing. It seems as if children, after one year's exposure to a phenomenographically oriented approach to learning, have developed an awareness and motivation that influences the further development of their skills in writing and solving mathematical problems.

Conclusions

How can the above approach to learning be interpreted? First, the question of what counts as high quality learning is problematized and defined as basic taken-for-granted aspects of the children's "life world." The aspects of the child's world refer both to a content and an act dimension, since it has been shown earlier in research that it is not enough to thematize the act aspect. Second, learning is a question of understanding or making sense. Bruner and Haste (1990, p. 1) point out that "making sense, is a social process; it is an activity that is always situated within a cultural and historical context." They also claim that the emphasis today is on the achievement of meaning, within psychology and other sciences. The meaning is focused upon both individually and culturally, and there is also a realization that these two aspects are inseparable. I maintain, however, that this kind of research has still not been implemented in school practice.

In one study (Pramling, 1988) three preschools with five- and six-year-old children worked with the theme "the shop," for two to three weeks. Two teachers (A and B) organized the content in the same way, which means that during one period they taught about the shop (from the customer's perspective), and during another period about how the shop functions (from the perspective of the shop). The third teacher (C) worked with the theme in her own way. Besides the specific structure shared by teachers A and B, teacher A was asked to problematize and thematize the aspects of learning, which she did by asking questions about the what, when, and why of what they were doing; she used "metacognitive dialogues" (Pramling, 1990). This means that she altered the perspective and focused children's attention on their own thinking about the topic and learning at hand. The teacher did not take the learning for granted but tried to make it visible to the children by means of reflections on the different activities they were involved in.

The results showed that after three weeks the children had developed their awareness of both what they learned and how the learning came about. When they were asked what they had learned from the theme, the children in the experimental group suggested that they had learned why shops used advertisements or what shops used to be like—that is, they had learned to know or understand something. Children from the other two groups suggested that they had learned to play shop or to go shopping—that is, they learned to do something. But in spite of the fact that the children in group A raised their metacognitive level of thinking about their own learning, they did not become better learners; they did not generally understand the content worked on, the shop, at a more advanced level.

Although the children in the above study did not become better learners, they developed their awareness of their own learning. Studies 1 and 2, which were presented earlier, show how children developed both their cognitive and metacognitive abilities. This means that education for young children needs to focus on their understanding both specific topic areas and their own learning. When this is done, children in the experimental groups become more able both to learn to understand a new message and to understand their own learning at a level far beyond the children from good "traditional" programs. In other words, it seems as if the present approach to learning works. Marton and Booth (this volume, chap. 24) present examples of this approach, but there are also studies from Australia in which the present approach has been adopted and similar results have been reached (Allen, 1993).

Children's understanding of the world around them and their own learning develops, as the teacher utilizes a metacognitive approach by giving them opportunities to change perspectives from thinking about different phenomena to how they think about a specific phenomenon. Children's attention alternates between the content and the act aspect.

In general, the problem with intervention studies is to know what difference they will make to the participants in a long-term perspective. Will the effects last? What will the effects look like in the future? As Weikart (1992) has shown, long-term effects of preschool programs can be found, but they are sometimes quite different from what was expected. What will happen in the future to the children involved in Study 2? We do not know, but the first results from the follow-up study (still in progress) of these children in primary school shows that after one year they are still ahead of their classmates in the various subject areas (Pramling, Klerflet, and Williams-Graneld, 1995). In one of these follow-up studies, after seven months at school, the children watched a video film about the water cycle. One of the questions that were put to each child individually was, "What did you learn from this film?" The difference was that between 38 percent and 60 percent of the children who were involved in the phenomenographically oriented approach in preschool expressed that they had understood the water cycle, while only 0 to 36 percent of the comparison groups expressed this kind of understanding of the message in the film. The variation in percentage comes from different school classes.

What then is demanded of the teacher in order to apply the present approach to learning to young children? Besides knowing what children think about different areas and topics and being skilled in actively engaging children and their thinking, the teachers *must know what they want the children to achieve.*

These goals are formulated in terms of understanding, which means that the teacher knows what kind of understanding to work toward with individuals as well as with groups of children. The teacher has to become aware of the aspects of the world around the children that are taken for granted. A skillful teacher knows what sorts of experience to provide children with as well as which aspects to develop and which ones to make visible. From this perspective, it is the teacher's act of consciousness that should be directed toward a specific content, which in turn effects how children experience the phenomena (Alexandersson, 1994).

At the same time as the teacher directs the children's attention toward the understanding she wants them to develop, she *constantly learns from the children.* To participate in such guided intervention, the teacher must understand the child's way of thinking. Without an understanding of how the children experience the task that is being worked on, this approach is impossible. The teaching is guided, directed, and inspired by the children's understanding, but it is based on children's interactions with the teacher and with each other.

Notes

1. Which here means up to the age of 7.
2. For some examples, see the following section, which discusses the curriculum in Study 2.

3. Day care and kindergarten in Sweden have the same guidelines and education requirements for teachers.

References

Alexandersson, M. (1994). *Metod och medvetande* [Method and consciousness]. Göteborg,
Sweden: Acta Universitatis Gothoburgensis.

Allen, L. (1993). *Facilitating metacognitive awareness in early childhood: A classroom intervention with year one children*. Master's thesis, Murdoch University.

Brown, A. (1980). Metacognitive development and reading. In R. J. Spiro, B. Bruce, and
W. Brewer (Eds.), *Theoretical issues in reading comprehension* (pp. 453–481). Hillsdale, NJ:
Lawrence Erlbaum.

Brown, A. (1985). *Teaching students to think as they read: Implications for curriculum reform*.
Paper presented at the American Educational Research Association, Washington.

Brown, A. and Reeve, R. (1985). Metacognition reconsidered: Implications for intervention research. *Journal of Abnormal Child Psychology, 13* (3), 343–356.

Bruner, J. (1988). *Actual minds, possible worlds*. Cambridge: Harvard University Press.

Bruner, J. (1990). The transactional self. In J. Bruner and H. Haste (Eds.), *Making sense*
(pp. 81–96). London: Routledge.

Bruner, J. and Haste, H. (Eds.). (1990). *Making sense*. London: Routledge.

Clay, M. (1991). Developmental learning puzzles me. *Australian Journal of Reading, 14*,
263–276.

Cullen, J. (1993). Why retain a developmental focus in early childhood education? In E.
Mellor and K. Coombe (Eds.), *Issues in early childhood services: Australian perspectives*
(pp. 53–64). Dubuque, IA: Wm. C. Brown.

Dahlgren, G. and Olsson, L. E. (1985). *Läsning i barnperspektiv* [Reading from children's
perspective]. Göteborg, Sweden: Acta Universitatis Gothoburgensis.

Damond, W. (1977). *The social world of the child*. San Francisco: Jossey-Bass.

Damond, W. (1984). Peer education: The untapped potential. *Journal of Applied Psychology,
5*, 331–343.

Dionnet, S. and Montangero, J. (1990, August). *The development of diachronic thinking in
children: Intuitive physics: time and causality*. Poster presented at the fourth European
conference on development psychology, Stirling, Scotland.

Doverborg, E. (1987). *Matematik i förskolan?* [Maths in preschool?]. Publication no. 5.
Institutionen för pedagogik. Göteborgs universitet.

Doverborg, E. and Pramling, I. (1988). *Temaarbete. Lärarens metodik och barns förståelse*
[Topic work. The teacher's methods and children's understanding]. Stockholm: Utbild-
ningsförlaget.

Doverborg, E. and Pramling, I. (1993). *Understanding children's thinking: Methods for interviewing children*. Report no. 5. Department of Methodology in Teacher Education, University of Göteborg.

Driver, R. (1982). Children's learning in science. *Educational Analysis, 4*, 2.

Elkind, D. (1988a). The Resistance to developmentally appropriate education practice with
young children: The real issue. In C. Wanger (Ed.), *Public school early childhood programs*.
Alexandria: Association for Supervision and Curriculum Development.

Elkind, D. (1988b). Early childhood education on its own terms. In S. L. Kagan and

E. Zigler (Eds.), *Early schooling: The national debate* (pp. 98–115). New Haven: Yale University Press.

Enerstvedt, R. T. (1988). *Barn virksomhet og mening* [Children's activity and meaning]. Oslo: A/S Falken Forlag.

Evans, E. D. (1982). Curriculum models and early childhood education. In B. Spodek (Ed.), *Handbook of research in early childhood education* (pp. 107–134). London: Macmillan.

Flavell, J. (1977). *Cognitive development.* Englewood Cliffs, NJ: Prentice-Hall.

Furth, H. (1980). *The world of grown-ups.* New York: Elsevier.

Gordon, B. (1987). Cultural comparison of schooling. *Educational Research, 16, 6.*

Gustavsson, E. (1992). *Barn och konstbilder. En didaktisk utvecklingsstudie* [Children and art: A didactic developmental study]. Uppsats PEF 30. Institutionen för pedagogik. Göteborgs universitet.

Hagtvet-Eriksen, B. (1990). *Skriftspråksutveckling* [Written language development]. Stockholm: Natur and Kultur.

Hundeide, K. (1989). *Barns livsverden* [The child's experience of the world]. Oslo: Cappelens Forlag.

Johansson, J.-E. (1992). Metodikämnet i förskollärareutbildningen. [Methods in teacher education]. Göteborg, Sweden: Acta Universitatis Gothoburgensis.

Katz, L. and Chard, S. (1990). *Engaging children's minds: The project approach.* Norwood, NJ: Ablex.

Klerfelt, A. (1991). *Barns uppfattningar om samarbete* [Children's conceptions of cooperation]. Uppsats från PEF 30, Institution för pedagogik. Göteborgs universitet.

Lybeck, L. (1981). *Arkimedes i klassen* [Archimedes in the classroom]. Göteborg, Sweden: Acta Universitatis Gothoburgensis.

Marton, F. (1988). *Revealing educationally critical difference in our understanding of the world around us.* Paper delivered at the American Educational Research Association, New Orleans.

Maurice, D., Staeheli, F. S., and Montangero, J. (1990, August). *The development of "diacromic thinking" in children: Intuitive biology: Forest damage.* Poster presented at the fourth European conference on development psychology, Stirling, Scotland.

Neuman, D. (1987). *The origin of arithmetic skills.* Göteborg, Sweden: Acta Universitatis Gothoburgensis.

Pramling, I. (1983). *The child's conception of learning.* Göteborg, Sweden: Acta Universitatis Gothoburgensis.

Pramling, I. (1986). *Barn och inlärning* [Children and learning]. Lund, Sweden: Studentlitteratur.

Pramling, I. (1987a). *Vad är metakognition?* [What is metacognition?]. Publikation från Institutionen för pedagogik nr 7, Göteborgs universitet.

Pramling, I. (1987b). Entrance to the world of knowledge. In R. Säljö (Ed.), *The written code and conceptions of reality* (pp. 151–160). New York: Springer-Verlag.

Pramling, I. (1988). Developing children's thinking of their own learning. *British Journal of Educational Psychology, 58,* 266–278.

Pramling, I. (1990). *Learning to learn: A study of Swedish preschool children.* New York: Springer-Verlag.

Pramling, I. (1991). Learning about "the shop": An approach to learning in preschool. *Early Childhood Research Quarterly, 6,* 151–166.

Pramling, I. (1992). To be six years old in Sweden in the 1990s. *Early Years, 12* (2), 47–50.

Pramling, I. (1994). *Kunnandets grunder* [Becoming able]. Göteborg, Sweden: Acta Universitatis Gothoburgensis.

Pramling, I. (1995). Phenomenography and practice. *New Zealand Journal of Educational Studies, 30* (2), 227–239.

Pramling, I., Asplund Carlsson, M., and Klerfelt, A. (1993). *Lära av sagan* [Learning from a fairy-tale]. Lund, Sweden: Studentlitteratur.

Pramling, I., Klerfelt, A., and Williams-Graneld, P. (1995). *Barns möte med skolans värld.* [Children's meeting with primary school]. Rapport från Institutionen för Metodik, Göteborgs universitet.

Rogoff, B. (1990). *Apprenticeship in thinking.* Oxford, England: Oxford University Press.

Rubinstein-Reich, L. (1993). *Samling i förskolan* [Circle-time in preschool]. Stockholm: Almqvist and Wiksell International.

Russel, T. and Watt, D. (1990). *Growth.* Primary SPACE project. Liverpool, England: Liverpool University Press.

Schweinhart, L. and Weikart, D. (1980). *Young children grow up: The effects of the Perry preschool programs on youths through age 15.* Ypsilanti, MI: High/Scope Press.

Silverstein, S. (1964). *The giving tree.* New York: Harper and Row.

Singer, E. (1992). *Child care and the psychology of development.* London: Routledge.

Smith, F. (1986). *Insult to intelligence.* New York: Arbor House.

Spodek, B. (1991). Early childhood curriculum and cultural definitions of knowledge. In B. Spodek and O. N. Saracho (Eds.). *Issues in early childhood curriculum.* New York: Teachers College Press.

Stepans, J. (1985). Biology in elementary schools: Children's conceptions of life. *The American Biology Teacher, 47* (4), 222–225.

Toshach, I. (1983). *"Barn med behov av särskilt stöd" och förskollärarens planeringsarbete* [Children with special needs and preschool teachers' planning]. Rapport från Institutionen för pedagogik, Göteborgs universitet. Nr. 132.

Veinstein, R. (1986). The teaching of reading and children's awareness of teacher expectations. In T. E. Raphael and R. Reynolds. (Eds.). *The context of literacy.* New York: Longman.

Weikart, D. (1992, November). A developmentally appropriate program to young children. Paper delivered at the EDC-CARE conference, Copenhagen.

Vygotsky, L. S. (1956/1972). *Tænking og språg 1 og II.* [Thinking and language]. Copenhagen: Mezhdunarodnaja Kinga og Hans Reitzels Forlag A/S.

26

The Language of Mind:
Its Role in Teaching and Learning

JANET WILDE ASTINGTON
JANETTE PELLETIER

In this chapter we explore the association between language and theory of mind, moving beyond the recent focus on the development of a theory of mind in the preschool years (Astington, Harris, and Olson, 1988) to discuss relations among children's theories of mind, teachers' theories of children's minds, and the linguistic interactions between children and their teachers. A great deal has been written about the relations among language, learning, and schooling. Obviously we would be taking on too much if we were to consider all of these issues. Our focus is on how language serves to relate children's theory of mind to their experience of learning.

Language in Learning and Teaching

In Chapter 2 of this volume Olson and Bruner link theories of mind to models of learning and teaching. Building on the work of Tomasello, Kruger, and Ratner (1993), they describe four different conceptions of learners' minds held by teachers that lead to different kinds of pedagogical practice: (1) conceiving of children as unable to do something leads adults to provide demonstrations for them to imitate; (2) conceiving of children as ignorant of something leads adults to provide them with information about it; (3) conceiving of children as having their own ideas about something leads adults to engage them in discussion of it; (4) conceiving of children as knowledgeable members of the culture leads adults to engage them in reflection on what is known in the world beyond what the children themselves know. Implicitly, if not explicitly, these four models represent a developmental progression on the part of the learner. That is, children first benefit from demonstration, then from didactic instruction, then from participation in collaborative discourse, and finally from participation in a world of "objective" knowledge. These benefits cumulate, rather than replace one another, so that eventually learning can occur in any of these ways. Indeed, perhaps our most thorough learning engages all of these ways.

Our concern is with the role that language plays in Olson and Bruner's four models. In Model 1 (*imitation and the acquisition of "know how"*) it may have little or no role. Learning proceeds by imitation that can be carried out without language. Infants engage in intentional communication and imitation before they have any verbal language. This is how both language and a first awareness of other minds are acquired (Meltzoff and Gopnik, 1993). Equipped with some language children are in a position to be told about things and to learn from instruction, as in the second model. Model 2 (*didactics and the acquisition of propositional knowledge*) requires the ability to comprehend language, to converse about the world, but it requires no talk about the mind. Learning occurs by being told about things. Even though what they are told is something in the teller's mind, it is presented as a fact about the world. As children acquire facts about the world they discover that what they know about the world may be unknown or differently thought of by another person. As they acquire this understanding they acquire terms in which to talk about these things. "I used to *think* a bat was a bird but now I *know* it's a mammal." Such terms make explicit reference to the mind and are essential for teaching and learning in the third and fourth models.

Model 3 (*collaborative discourse and the development of intersubjective knowledge*) sees children as understanding that different people may have different beliefs about the world and that beliefs are subject to change; this is what makes learning by collaboration possible and valuable. Participation in such collaborative discussion would seem to require some mentalistic language in order to talk about and to work out mutual understandings and misapprehensions. In the later preschool years children begin to use a range of terms (e.g., *think, know, believe, expect, wonder, guess, remember*) that can be used to refer to their own and their collaborators' mental states.

In the school years children learn to read and begin to encounter and learn from ideas belonging to people not known to them personally, even people no longer alive whose ideas live on in their writing. Model 4 (*the management of "objective" knowledge*) focuses on such learning from text. Here there is no gesture or intonation to support the sense, as in collaborative discourse; it must all be conveyed in language. Now, as well as mental state terms, speech act terms are required in order to distinguish what the author said—that is, the words of the text—from what he or she meant by it, in order to construct an interpretation.

Thus each subsequent model of learning—from imitation, to didactic instruction, to collaborative discourse, to participation in the world of objective knowledge—depends on linguistic development. This occurs first through the acquisition of language itself, and then through the acquisition of explicit terms for referring to mental states and speech acts. That is, we argue that progression through Olson and Bruner's four models is premised on an increasingly explicit and sophisticated "language of mind."

The Language of Mind

In one sense, all of language is the language of mind. Whenever people communicate verbally with one another they express their mental state in the speech act.

For example, when we convey information about the world to another person, we communicate our beliefs about the world. However, in this sort of information exchange our focus is on the world, on the information exchanged, not on our mind, on the fact that we believe it. We draw attention to our mental state in cases of uncertainty or disagreement: you may *think* it's x but I *know* it's y; that's just your *opinion*; I'm *sure*; you're *undoubtedly* wrong; and so on. We also refer to mental states other than belief; for example: I *want* it; it's his *plan*; you look *happy*; he spoke *angrily*; and so on. In using the phrase "language of mind" we are referring to the explicit use of such semantic terms to refer to people's mental states—to beliefs, desires, intentions, and emotions. The terms may occur in any of the open classes: verbs (e.g., *think, know, want*), nouns (e.g., *opinion, plan*), adjectives (e.g., *sure, happy*), or adverbs (e.g., *undoubtedly, angrily*) (Tager-Flusberg, 1993). Obviously, they form a large part of English vocabulary. Roget's thesaurus (1852/1966) has six major classes: *abstract relations, space, matter, intellect, volition,* and *affections*. The last three, comprising more than half of the total entries, include many terms belonging to the language of mind, although other terms are included in these classes too.

An important question is: What is the structure of this semantic field? How is the language of mind organized in the subjective lexicon? Componential analysis decomposes the meaning of a word into a set of elementary units, which at least some investigators presume are abstract, universal, innate features that are realized in specific lexical items during the acquisition of a particular language (Bierwisch, 1970). Kay and Samuels (1977), examining how componential analysis might be used as the basis for a thesaurus classification scheme simpler than Roget's, provide an analysis of about 300 items under the category *mind* in terms of such a set of semantic primitives (their other suggested categories are *world, body,* and *society*). Within the category *mind* there are six divisions based on the components *cognize, say, want, feel, have,* and *do,* but at least some of these are themselves part of the language of mind. Perhaps componential analysis is of more use to linguists concerned with the meaning relations within language, than to psychologists concerned with the relations between lexical items, concepts, and their referents. Procedural semantics, used by Miller and Johnson-Laird (1976) to analyze *inter alia* verbs of vision and communication, is similar to componential analysis but its approach is more psychological, linking lexical knowledge with world knowledge and perceptual processes. Their theory is detailed and explicit but they analyze only a limited number of terms. Even though some of these are part of the language of mind, they include many other terms too. We are seeking an analysis that considers the whole semantic field of the language of mind from a psychological perspective.

A number of different classification schemes have been provided by philosophers and linguists working within the general framework of speech act theory. Such schemes are based on the individual theorist's systematic analysis of ordinary language usage, a method advocated by J. L. Austin (1961, chap. 8) who used it to illuminate the structure of some fundamental concepts, including reality, truth, intention, meaning (Austin, 1961, 1962b) and, notably, performatives or speech acts (Austin, 1962a). Austin's classification of performatives (1962a, lecture XII) certainly includes some terms from the language of mind, but its focus on speech acts misses much of what we want to include. However, as Searle (1983) points out, the performance of a speech act is necessarily the expression of a corresponding mental state. Hence, speech act classifications can provide a template for classifications of the language of mind. As Vendler (1970) puts it: "the same things that can be asserted, suggested or denied in words, can be realized and understood, believed, suspected or doubted in thought...what one may decide to do, want, wish or intend to do in thought, one also can promise, vow or pledge to do in words...." (Vendler, 1970, pp. 87, 89). Vendler then gives a taxonomy of speech act verbs, roughly based on Austin's (1962a), and for each class he identifies the corresponding mental verbs, which he describes in two groups: mental state and mental activity.

Similarly, Searle's taxonomy of speech acts (1979a, chap. 1) provides a basis for the classification of mental states. The difference between the two is that Vendler bases his taxonomy on the speech act, claiming that "speech is the primary phenomenon, thought the derivative one" (1970, p. 89); whereas for Searle, the intentionality of the mental state is imposed on the speech act, making speech the derivative phenomenon (Searle, 1979b). Thus Searle uses the "sincerity condition" of the speech act—that is, the underlying psychological mode expressed in the speech act—as the major dimension in his classification: beliefs are expressed as assertives, desires are expressed as directives, intentions are expressed as commissives, and emotions as expressives.

Philosophers' taxonomies are not based on empirical evidence but on their own intuition and systematic analysis of ordinary language use. Developmental psychologists who are interested in children's acquisition of this semantic field have examined large corpora of natural language in order to determine when and how children use mental terms. Inevitably, they need a taxonomic scheme to organize their analyses and, like ordinary language philosophers, they seem to rely on their own linguistic intuitions in devising such a scheme.

Bretherton and her colleagues (Bretherton and Beeghly, 1982; Bretherton, McNew, and Beeghly-Smith, 1981) were probably the first to assess children's use of the language of mind, which they construed broadly in terms of language about "internal states", which were divided into six categories: perception, cognition, volition, morality, emotion, and physiology. All other investigators use at least some of these categories. Gearhart and Hall (1982) divided the field into cognitive, perceptual, affective, and also metalinguistic terms. Shatz, Wellman and Silber (1983) were concerned with only mental (that is, cognitive) terms. Brown and Dunn (1991) used three categories: mental state (that is, cognition), desire, and feeling state (that is, emotional and physiological states). Tager-Flusberg (1992) has three categories similar to Brown and Dunn's—cognition, desire, emotion— and a fourth one, perception. Bartsch and Wellman (1995) examine cognition and desire terms. Generally, these taxonomies are just used to investigate children's acquisition of the terms and are not themselves subjected to theoretical analysis.

Laid over all of the taxonomies, whether proposed by linguists, philosophers, or developmentalists, we can discern three major classes of mental state. Some analysts make further divisions within these three, and some empirical investigators do not look for all three. However, the three are clear and they exhaust the logical possibilities concerning the relation between mind and world. Searle (1983) describes this in terms of "direction of fit." Beliefs must fit the world; a false belief is made true by changing the belief. But for desires the fit is in the other direction—the world must fit desires; an unfulfilled desire is satisfied if the world changes to fit it. Emotions have no direction of fit of their own, in Searle's terms, although they presuppose desires and beliefs that do have directions of fit. All taxonomies acknowledge these three states—belief, desire, and emotion. In fact they reflect Roget's three classes: *intellect, volition,* and *affections.*

Can we assume that theoretical analyses of the language of mind resemble the representation of this semantic field in the mental lexicon? It is important to know whether people's intuitions concerning meaning relations among the terms reflect these analyses. There is, however, little relevant empirical work. A study by a cognitive anthropologist, D'Andrade (1987), is sometimes cited as providing empirical support, but he first conceived a theoretical analysis (based on Vendler and Searle) and then interviewed five students, reporting that "none of the interview material from the five informants contradicted the model. . .although some of the material could not be derived from just the model" (D'Andrade, 1987, p. 115). Rips and Conrad (1989) had adult subjects make either taxonomic or partonomic judgments about many different pairs of mental terms; for example, remembering is *a kind of* thinking, or imaging is *a part of* loving (for all instances of the named activities). They found that for mental verbs, unlike for object categories, taxonomic and partonomic relations are reciprocal—that is, one activity is judged part of another and at the same time the second is judged to be a kind of the first (for example, thinking is a part of remembering and remembering is a kind of thinking). However, the data were reduced and analyzed in two separate sets of only seven verbs each, analytic and nonanalytic; this division was imposed, not discovered by the investigators, as Schwanenflugel and her colleagues imply it was (Schwanenflugel, Fabricius, Noyes, Bigler, and Alexander, 1994).

Schwanenflugel et al. provide the most extensive empirical study to date, but only in the area of cognition; they examined how adults organize a set of 30 verbs by asking subjects to make similarity judgments between pairs of verbs, and to select the mental verbs involved in descriptive scenarios (e.g., "making up your mind about what to watch on TV"). They found that subjects distinguished verbs along a dimension of certainty (e.g., *know, think, guess*) and in terms of three components: input (e.g., *observe*), processing (e.g., *reason*), and memory (e.g., *remember*). They conclude that the adult folk theory of cognition is a naive information-processing model with interactive and constructive components. Interestingly, Strauss (1993; Strauss and Shilony, 1994) found that teachers' implicit models of children's minds and learning more resembled an information-processing model than the Piagetian and Vygotskian models they had heard about in their teacher education courses, which suggests that teachers rely more on their naive theories than on explicit instruction.

We are concerned with ways of classifying the language of mind because we are interested in assessment of children's and teachers' use of this language. As we have seen, there is general agreement that the field includes terms for (1) cognition (perhaps including perception), (2) desire and intention, and (3) emotion. There is also agreement on prototypical terms within each class. Disagreement arises, however, over class boundaries—for example, are *hope* and *disappointment* cognition or desire terms?—and more importantly, over the boundary to the field. For example, Hall and Nagy (1986) exclude *trick, deceive,* and *mislead* from their list of mental terms because these words focus on the activity resulting in a mental state rather than on the mental state itself. However, Kay and Samuels (1977) do include *deceive* and *mislead* in their analysis, and Shatz et al. (1983) and Tager-Flusberg (1992) include *trick* in their list of children's cognitive terms. What is included and what is not included is an important issue if we are attempting to evaluate hypotheses concerning relations between individuals' vocabulary of the language of mind and other variables; for example, Hall and Nagy hypothesize that "perhaps size of internal state word vocabulary will correlate with greater readiness for, and success in, school" (Hall and Nagy, 1986, p. 27).

This leads to a related issue concerning usage. Not all uses of mental terms necessarily make reference to mental states—for example, "You *know* what?" said to attract attention or "Do you *want* to take out the garbage?" said as a request. If individuals use a term only in this nonmental way, should the item be counted as part of their vocabulary of the language of mind? Bretherton and Beeghly (1982) included all uses, but Shatz et al. (1983) argued that idiomatic and conversational uses should not be counted. Similarly, Hall and Nagy (1986) distinguished semantic and pragmatic usage and argued that only semantic use should be counted. Again, prototypical nonmental uses are easily defined, as in the examples above, but there are difficult coding problems in deciding what is and what is not a mental use. As Ortony (1987) and Scholnick (1987) argue, pragmatic uses should not all be automatically ruled out because they may be referring to mental states. There are no easy answers. It is important that investigators are aware of the issues involved and explicitly clear about their own coding rules.

In this section we have discussed the language of mind in some detail, although there is much more that could be said. We are interested in explicit talk about mental states because we argue that it is characteristic of some but not all models of teaching and learning. Children start to use such terms during the preschool years as they acquire a theory of mind, a development that has been the focus of much investigation during recent years.

Children's Theories of Mind

The Preschool Years

A theory is an integrated set of concepts, used to predict and explain phenomena in a domain; a theory of mind predicts and explains human action by appealing to mental states (Perner, 1991; Wellman, 1990). A theory undergoes change over time when faced with evidence counter to its predictions. We thus refer to children's "theories" rather than "theory" of mind, recognizing that the theory evolves over time. During the preschool years, children come to understand human activity by attributing mental states to people. They come to see themselves and others as mental beings—that is, as people who hold mental states of belief, desire, intention, and emotion. Children acquire an integrated set of such concepts, allowing them to interpret human behavior in sensible ways. By the time they are five years old, children understand that people's beliefs represent, and may sometimes misrepresent, the world, and that it is people's representation of the world that determines what they say or do (Astington, 1993).

We would not claim that a theory of mind is innate, but developments early in life underlie its acquisition. From a very young age, infants respond differently to persons and to objects, and seek to communicate with other people. They share attention with others, pointing things out to them and turning to look where the other is looking (Bretherton et al., 1981). Remarkable changes in behavior come around 18 months of age when language and pretend play develop. Soon, children start to talk about the mind or, at least, about what they and others *see*, *want*, and *feel*, and they show some understanding of these states in their interactions with familiar others (Bartsch and Wellman, 1995; Dunn, 1988). At the same time, in experimental tasks, two- and three-year-olds show an understanding of perception, desire, and emotion in their ability to predict what people will do (Wellman, 1990). Three-year-olds start to talk about what they and others *think* and *know*, and show some understanding of the link between seeing and knowing.

Around four years of age, children show the critical understanding of false belief; that is, they recognize that people may act in a way that frustrates their desire because their belief is false. In the classic task (Wimmer and Perner, 1983) a story character puts an object into a location from which it is moved during his absence; when he returns, the child is asked where the character will look for the object. By about four years of age, children predict that he will look in the original location, where he thinks the object is. Three-year-olds usually predict that he will look in the new location—after all, he wants the object, and that is where it is! Four-year-olds also understand that another person will expect to find the usual contents in a familiar container. If they have just discovered that there are pencils in a familiar candy box, they predict that someone else, who does not look in the box, will think it has candy inside, whereas three-year-olds predict that he or she will think it has pencils inside (Perner, Leekam, and Wimmer, 1987). Four-year-olds can remember their own earlier mistaken beliefs, so they recall that when they first saw the box they thought it had candy inside, but three-year-olds cannot: They say they thought it had pencils inside (Gopnik and Astington, 1988). Four-year-olds, but not three-year-olds, also recognize the distinction between appearance and reality: They understand that it looks like a box with candy in it, but it is really a box with pencils inside (Flavell, 1986).

Experimental work had also documented children's increasing competence with the metacognitive language that is used to make these distinctions. In the 1970s and early 1980s numerous studies reported children's developing comprehension of what were generally referred to as "mental verbs." This work preceded theory of mind research; indeed, the first false belief task reported in the literature was a pretest condition in a study of preschoolers' comprehension of the terms *think* and *know* (Johnson and Maratsos, 1977). The focus of these studies was on children's comprehension of the precise meaning of a term—for example, *remember* implies prior knowledge, *guess* implies absence of knowledge—which was assessed by their ability to distinguish between a set of related terms (e.g., Johnson and Wellman, 1980; Miscione, Marvin, O'Brien, and Greenberg, 1978; Wellman and Johnson, 1979). Although children start to use these terms in the preschool years, they do not sort out all the distinctions between them until the early school years. More recent psycholinguistic research has established the close ties between children's understanding of mental states and their acquisition of the language of mind (de Villiers, 1995; Moore and Furrow, 1991).

Children's Theory of Mind in the School Years

Even though they may not make all the appropriate distinctions between closely related cognitive verbs, by five years of age children do understand that people act on their representation of the world, even in situations where it misrepresents the real situation. That is, at the time their formal education begins, children can represent and reason from people's first-order beliefs: *X believes p*. The main development occurring after five years of age that has been examined so far in children's theory of mind is their ability to deal with embedded or second-order representations: *X believes that Y believes that p* (Perner and Wimmer, 1985). By six or seven years of age children are able to reflect on their own and others' beliefs. They can then not only represent someone's ignorance or false belief as the four-year-old can, but they can see the other's belief from his or her point of view. That is, they understand that a person with a false belief takes the belief to be true—in other words, thinks he or she knows. They also realize that when they themselves held a false belief, although they did not really know the truth, they thought that they did (Homer and Astington, 1995).

The development of this second-order understanding has not received as much attention in the literature, although we might argue that it is of equal significance to first-order understanding, since much of our social interaction depends on what people believe about other people's beliefs. The importance of second-order understanding has been shown in relation to children's ability to distinguish between speech acts such as lies, jokes, and irony (Leekam, 1991; Winner and Leekam, 1991) and in relation to their judgments of responsibility for accidents (Yuill and Perner, 1987).

The ability to manage higher-order representations may also underlie children's epistemological development and their understanding of the epistemic concepts of evidence, inference, and truth. For example, young schoolchildren can distinguish between hypothetical beliefs and evidence, and they know how to put hypotheses to the test (Sodian, Zaitchik, and Carey, 1991). They can also give reasons why people take their beliefs to be true; that is, they have some understanding of the evidence people use in forming beliefs (Astington and Homer, 1995). However, at this stage, they still hold to the idea that there is some absolute truth in the world. Only later do they come to understand that different interpretations may be equally true when viewed from different theoretical perspectives (Chandler, 1987).

Work by Fabricius and Schwanenflugel (1994) and their colleagues is relevant here. They have studied eight- and ten-year-olds' concepts of a range of mental activities, including memory, attention, inference, and comprehension (Fabricius, Schwanenflugel, Kyllonen, Barclay, and Denton, 1989; Schwanenflugel, Fabricius, and Alexander, 1994). They found that eight-year-olds do not distinguish between attention and comprehension and ten-year-olds still confuse comprehension with memory. They argue that children of this age focus more on the outcome of mental activities than on the mental processes involved, and conclude that a truly constructivist theory of mind, which sees that different outcomes can result from differential processing of the same input, does not develop until adolescence.

Certainly, the adolescent years see great development in students' comprehension of metacognitive terms that are used to characterize constructivist mental activity (Astington and Olson, 1990; Booth and Hall, 1994). The school years are also a time when children's production and comprehension of speech act terms develops (Astington, 1988a; Astington and Olson, 1990). Preschool children use only the terms *say*, *ask*, and *tell*, and these last two are confused until the school years (Chomsky, 1969). Indeed, children may not have a concept of the speech act, independent of the mental state underlying it, until the early school years (Astington, 1988b).

Relation of Theory of Mind to Schooling

There is very little empirical work relating theory of mind to schooling. However, many school activities, from interpreting the intentions of unfamiliar others to forming and revising beliefs about the world, may be easier for children whose theory of mind is well developed, and who can talk with their teachers about intentions and beliefs. When they first come to school, children will differ in the extent to which they have experienced family talk about people's motivations and thoughts. A contrast is often made between two styles of parenting: one that punishes bad behavior and demands obedience, and another that reasons with the child and explains people's different points of view in a situation (Baumrind, 1971). Talking about different viewpoints in the family may well help children understand that people have beliefs about the world, that their beliefs may be different from those of others, and that beliefs may change when a person acquires new information. Such everyday metacognitive understanding may well help children make sense of school. If knowledge is not simply transmitted from teacher to children but constructed by children's forming and revising their beliefs about the world, such activity may be easier for children who have participated in family talk about people's thoughts.

However, we do not yet know whether children's theory of mind bears any relation to their formal educational experiences, although a number of suggestions have been made along these lines. There are strong claims regarding the importance of theory of mind development for children's social behavior generally (Moore and Frye, 1991), which is relevant to school performance, although these claims have rarely been empirically tested. We do know that individual differences in false belief understanding are related to some aspects of children's natural behaviors in a pretend play setting, independent of their age and language ability (Astington and Jenkins, 1995) and to teachers' ratings of children's social behavior (Lalonde and Chandler, 1995). Certainly, social maturity is an important aspect of success in school. Perhaps more directly relevant is the proposal by Tomasello et al. (1993) that there is a relation between the level of children's theory of mind development and their cultural learning via instruction and collaboration. It also seems likely that children require some understanding of mind in order to "self-monitor" their cognitive activities in school settings (Meichenbaum and Biemiller, 1992). In relation to particular subject areas, we suggested earlier that there may be links between children's theory of mind and their development of scientific reasoning. Suggestions have also been made concerning the role of a theory of mind in young children's production of stories (McKeough, 1992) and older students' interpretation of literary and historical texts (Gardner, 1991). Indeed some time ago, Light (1979) found that reading skill at five and a half years correlated with perspective-taking ability at four years of age, which is an aspect of understanding others' minds, but not with IQ at four years.

We would argue that all of these suggested relations depend on development of the language of mind. Such language is required for social maturity in order to explain and excuse oneself, and for collaborative learning in order to talk about mutual understandings and conflicts. But, it may be argued, it is also required in order to monitor one's own cognitive activity, to generate and test scientific hypotheses, to talk about what story characters are trying to do, and to discuss literary and historical characters' motivations. For all these purposes, children need a language that is mentalistic and reflective, that gives reasons and asks for explanations. It therefore seems likely that children's success in school will depend, at least in part, on their acquisition of the language of mind—this is their theory of mind, made explicit in language. There is a need for empirical investigations of the relations between children's understanding of mind, their language of mind, their experience of schooling, and their school success.

Children's Use of the Language of Mind

We have begun to examine children's talk in various school-like situations in relation to their understanding of mind. We recorded their use of terms about cognition (*think, know, guess, remember, forget, understand, describe, explain, mean, learn, teach*), terms related to school activities (*read, write, spell, say, count*), and terms related to styles of learning and teaching: imitation (*show, watch*), instruction (*tell, ask*), and collaboration (*help*). Although *help* is not a term exclusive to the language of mind, its use by children in this study indicated the child's recognition that he or she plays an active role in learning, assisted by teachers and peers. Thirty-six children participated: 12 junior kindergarten[1] children from a public school in a mixed-income city neighborhood (mean age 4 years 9 months), 14 junior kindergarten children from a university lab school (mean age 4 years 9 months), and 10 first graders from the lab school (mean age 6 years 10 months).

The children's understanding of false belief was assessed in two tasks. One was the standard change in location task referred to earlier (Wimmer and Perner, 1983): a story character leaves an object in a place from which it is moved during his absence and when he returns the child is asked to predict where the character will look for the object. In the second task children discovered that a familiar crayons box actually contained a small doll and they were asked what their friend would think was in the box before he or she had opened it (Perner et al., 1987). Correct responses for each group were: public school JK, 36 percent, lab school JK, 75 percent, and first grade, 100 percent. In both tasks the first graders were given an additional question to measure their understanding of second-order beliefs: 78 percent of their responses were correct.

In order to measure children's language use, we set up three situations that were progressively more structured: (1) pairs of children played at school together in a miniature classroom containing school-like props and doll schoolchildren; (2) individual children played school with one of us using a toy school and small dolls, with the child playing the role of the teacher and the adult one of the schoolchildren; (3) we used a lot of metacognitive terms while teaching individual children to play a game, and then they taught another child to play. In the first situation the children's talk was completely *spontaneous*, in the second the child's talk was *prompted* by our questions, and in the third we provided a *model* of metacognitive talk as we taught the child to play the game. Children were videotaped in the three situations, always spontaneous first, then prompted, then modeled. The videotapes were transcribed and coded for cognitive, school activity, and learning/teaching terms used.

In the first (*spontaneous*) situation the children readily "played at school" when we invited them to, and they had fairly elaborate school scripts to call on. However, they produced very little metacognitive talk, although they did talk about school activities, such as reading, writing, and spelling, due to the school-like props they were provided with. They talked a lot about the teacher's role, mainly in assigning or accepting it, but they never spoke about teaching or learning. They used the term *know*, and very occasionally *think, remember, forget*, and *mean*. There were no differences between the three groups. Their use of *know* was mainly conversational, although they did use *know how* in relation to school activities—for example, "I know how to read this book" and "Do you know how to spell 'yes'? " We may recall that Olson and Bruner's Model 1 emphasized procedural knowledge and "*know how.*"

In the second (*prompted*) situation, the child first set up a classroom with toy furniture and dolls and then, in the role of teacher, made up a narrative with the help of one of us in the role of schoolchild. Using this technique, the children could be asked standard questions in an individualized and meaningful context. When the classroom was set up, we (as "schoolchildren") asked, "What are we going to do today?" and "What do kids do in school?" The props included an ABC book and a counting book, and we endeavored to have our doll get hold of them at some point, so that we could ask about reading and counting—for example, "I can't read this book, what shall I do?" or "How can I learn to read it?" or "How do kids learn to count?" At one point our doll asked the teacher doll (that is, the child subject) why kids go to school and what teachers do. Admittedly, we did ask rather a lot of questions. In one exchange, when one of us asked, "How do kids learn to count?" a JK child said, "Just listen to me, just don't keep talking and you'll maybe learn"—a more didactic than collaborative view!

In this pretend play with an adult the children used more metacognitive talk than when they played together, though not a great deal more, but there was much more talk about teaching and learning and about school activities. Because we were talking to the children in this way, they used the terms that we were using. There was a small difference between children in the different groups in the way they talked about teaching and learning. All three groups used *show* and *watch* about equally, the lab school JK children used *tell* and *ask* more than the other groups did, and the lab school first graders used *help* more than the others did.

In the third (*modeled*) situation, one of us taught the child to play a game, and then he or she taught a friend to play. The game was based on a traditional communication game (Kraus and Glucksberg, 1969) in which there were two identical sets of cards, and the two players had to pick exactly the same card to put side by side in a little box. Players hid their cards behind a screen, so each could see their own set but not the other set. Then they took turns to describe a picture so that the partner could pick the same one. In teaching the game we used as many metacognition, perception, and communication terms as we could—for example, "I *can't see* your pictures and you *can't see* mine. I don't *know* which one you're *thinking* about, and you don't *know* which one I'm *thinking* about. . . .Now you can choose one. But *remember*—I *can't see* it, so I don't *know* which one it is. You have to *tell* me which one you've picked, so I can pick the same one. You *can't show* it to me, you've got to *tell* me which one. OK? And you have to *tell* me very carefully. If you just *say* 'red girl,' I won't *know* which one you *mean* because there are lots of red girls." The child then taught a friend how to play the game, and we recorded their talk in that situation. The children, particularly in the older group, did use proportionally more metacognitive talk than the younger ones, presumably in imitation of us. They also used more words in total to explain the game. The younger children, especially those who had failed the false belief task, did not really explain the game at all. They seemed not to understand that their friend did not know what to do. One JK child played with one of us, listening to all our wordy instructions, then when she had to teach her friend, she gave him his cards and said, "Your turn"—with no further explanation.

We became particularly interested in the children's conception of learning, as it was revealed in these episodes—in the way they played and talked about school, and in the way they went about teaching someone—and how this related to their understanding of the mind as measured by their performance on the false belief tasks. While playing the role of teacher in the toy school, all the children were asked, "Why do children go to school?" and most of them said "to learn." Some of the younger ones said they did not know, or they said kids had to go, or needed to because the mommies and daddies were at work. If a child said "to learn," we asked (if we could) "How do they learn?" The commonest response, especially from the older children, was to say "the teacher teaches." Then we asked, "What does the teacher do?" Children said that the teacher shows, or tells, or helps—perhaps reflecting the three conceptions of learning and teaching that we referred to earlier: imitation, instruction, and collaboration. The numbers in our sample are too small for us to make strong claims, and more important, the three groups of children had three different teachers and their responses may have reflected their own teacher's style. However, with these caveats in mind, we did find a trend related to different levels of theory of mind understanding. Only the older children said that the teacher helps you learn. One first grader gave a description of collaborative learning thus:

ADULT [as schoolchild]: Why do kids go to school?
CHILD [as teacher]: To learn things.
ADULT: How do they learn things?
CHILD: Well, by help, then doing things together, and stuff like that.

We set out earlier in this chapter three levels of understanding that enable children to participate in different types of learning episode: (1) understanding people as intentional agents, which allows children to learn by imitation; (2) understanding people as mental agents, which enables children to learn from instruction; and (3) understanding people as reflective agents, which enables children to learn collaboratively (Olson and Bruner, this volume, chap. 2; Tomasello et al., 1993). Our data suggest that not just participation but children's conception of learning and teaching may be related to their level of understanding of mind. That is, when children have no representational understanding of mind (i.e., when they fail first-order false belief tasks), they conceptualize teaching as showing; when children have a representational theory of mind (i.e., when they pass first-order false belief tasks), they conceptualize teaching as telling; and when children have a reflective or recursive understanding of mind (i.e., when they pass second-order false belief tasks), they conceptualize teaching as helping or collaborating.

Table 26.1, Part A shows children's scores on the false belief tasks. Part B shows the terms children used in the three categories of learning/teaching style: (1) imitation (*show, watch*), (2) instruction (*tell, ask*), and (3) collaboration (*help*), as a proportion of the total number of these terms. *Show/ watch* is the highest proportion for the children who score low on the false belief tasks—that is, those who do

Table 26.1　*Children's theory of mind and their understanding of learning and teaching*

	City/JK (n = 12)	Lab/JK (n = 14)	Lab/Gd. 1 (n = 10)
A. Understanding false belief			
First-order	36%	75%	100%
Second-order	x	x	78%
B. Learning/teaching terms used in pretend play (child as teacher doll in toy school) shown as proportion of total learning/teaching terms (raw score in parentheses)			
(1) Imitation	.53	.12	.16
(*show/watch*)	(8)	(5)	(6)
(2) Instruction	.33	.74	.45
(*tell/ask*)	(5)	(31)	(17)
(3) Collaboration	.13	.14	.39
(*help*)	(2)	(6)	(15)
Total terms produced	15	42	38
C. Amount of talk in teaching friend to play game			
Mean number of words per teaching episode	155	262	387

not yet understand others' beliefs; *tell/ask* is the highest proportion for the JK lab schoolchildren who do pass false belief tasks; and then *help* comes in, about equal in proportion to *tell/ask* for the first-grade children who have a recursive—that is, a second-order—understanding of belief. Part C shows the mean number of words a child in each group produced when they were teaching their friend to play the game. The number of words used increases as the understanding of mind increases; the children who do not understand false belief *show* rather than *tell*.

　　These preliminary findings suggest that as children's understanding of other people's minds develops, their understanding of learning shifts from a focus on imitation, to a focus on verbal instruction, and later to a focus on collaboration. Of course, many factors affect the vocabulary children use but the present evidence supports the view that progressive shifts in understanding the mind are reflected in children's understanding of learning and the way they set about teaching something to someone. In a similar way, teachers' everyday understanding of people's minds will be reflected in the way they talk about teaching and learning and in their teaching style. However, we might expect that this would also be influenced by their professional education and experience.

Teachers' Theories of Children's Minds

Strauss's work, cited earlier in this chapter, suggests that teachers may be as much guided by their naive theories of mind as they are by more explicit instruction in the psychology of mind. Recall that Strauss and Shilony (1994) reported that teachers' theory of learning resembled the information-processing model that Schwanenflugel, Fabricius, Noyes, Bigler, and Alexander (1994) had found was characteristic of adults' folk theory of cognition. Strauss and Shilony interviewed experienced and novice teachers in the sciences and humanities, asking them how they would teach a topic of their own choice to 7-year-olds, 12-year-olds, and 17-year-olds. The teachers talked about learning in terms of knowledge "flow" from the outside world into the child's mind. It was their responsibility to make the topic material manageable and interesting so that it would enter the child's mind, and to help the child to store it appropriately once it was there. Even though other work (Yaakobi and Sharan, 1985) shows that teachers of sciences have a relatively more objective view of knowledge than teachers of the humanities do, Strauss and Shilony did not find differences between the models of teachers in the different subject areas, nor did the models of more experienced teachers differ from those of novices, which again suggests that teachers were accessing their naive commonsense theories. This information-processing model was inferred from how the teachers said they would set about teaching a topic to children of different ages, not from their answers to direct questions about the mind and learning. Teachers were expressing their naive beliefs about children's minds, and their theory of learning and teaching, not something they had been taught in their teacher preparation courses. On a broader scale within the education literature, teachers' commonsense beliefs about learning are traditionally discussed in terms of different philosophical orientations to knowledge and its acquisition (Case, this volume, chap. 5).

Traditional Views of Teachers' Theories

The education literature is replete with examples of three traditional philosophical perspectives attributed to teachers: (1) the maturationist, or nativist view, (2) the behaviorist, or instruction view, and (3) the constructivist view, which encompasses both cognitive developmental and sociocultural perspectives (Pelletier, 1994). The origins of these beliefs remain obscure but perhaps they derive from experiences in and out of school as well as from explicit educational theories. Some recent initiatives in "teacher narrative" and "reflective practice," have begun to examine the complexities of teachers' theories about learning (Connelly and Clandinin, 1988; Gomez and Tabachnick, 1992). Belief systems have been described as "filters" that interpret new information about teaching in a way that reinforces preexisting beliefs and causes teachers to become more comfortable with their views (Kagan, 1992). Ultimately, this leads to the formation of a cohesive belief system, or folk pedagogy, that teachers can readily support through their practices. These theories translate into program objectives, then into curriculum selection and program evaluation. First, we consider the three traditional views of teachers' theories and then relate them to recent discussion of theories of mind.

Maturationist Theories

Maturationist theories have been variously labeled as the romantic model (Spodek, Saracho, and Davis, 1991), the dynamic model (Evans, 1982), and the authority-sharing model (Oakes and Caruso, 1990). These models have grown out of the writings of Rousseau (1762/1969) and Gesell (1945). Children are born with abilities and capacities that unfold with development and need only a supportive and healthful environment in order to mature. A teaching approach that follows a maturationist model attempts to match curriculum activities to a child's maturational level so that the child will avoid confronting errors resulting from "hopeless confusion" (Brophy and Good, 1986) and will experience success, which in turn satisfies the affective goals of this approach. This approach to teaching is often adopted by teachers who believe that young children's development must not be "hurried." Teachers design their programs to encourage children's play and to steer away from instruction. It is believed that children will learn skills through observation and attempts to imitate adult behavior. This approach is not often considered conducive to skill instruction with older children.

Behaviorist Theories

Among the labels given to the behaviorist orientation are the model of cultural training (Schwarz and Robinson, 1982), the direct instruction approach (Bereiter and Engelmann, 1966), academic or formal instruction (Fromberg, 1989), the authority-controlling model (Oakes and Caruso, 1990), environmental determination (Evans, 1982), mastery learning (Puleo, 1986), and the learning theory approach (Spodek and Clark Brown, 1993). Behaviorist models have grown out of learning theory that employs reinforcement principles as explanations of discrete behavioral change. Learning occurs sequentially; thus curriculum implications involve a hierarchy of goals, skill development, and direct instruction. The errors a child makes are seen as the result of incomplete learning or inattention by the child, and the teacher works to correct those errors (Brophy and Good, 1986). Carefully sequenced instructional programs do not leave learning to chance and remain under teacher direction. Many teachers believe that this approach is optimal for teaching the basic skills to children, to set the stage for later "higher-order" learning. Indeed, this form of schooling comprises the bulk of teaching behavior in today's schools. Nevertheless, other teachers, whose philosophical orientations are more child-centered, believe that children can acquire skills in ways that do not rely so heavily on direct instruction.

Constructivist Theories

Constructivist theories acknowledge the active role children play in building their own knowledge structures. Cognitive constructivists place more emphasis on the child's interaction with the physical environment and social constructivists on the child's interaction with other people. Cognitive theories include the neo-Piagetian structuralist model (Case, 1985; Siefert, 1993), the cognitively oriented model (Hohmann, Banet, and Weikart, 1979), the open framework model (Schweinhart, Weikart, and Larner, 1986) and the progressivism model (Spodek et al., 1991). In these models, children's learning occurs as previously acquired cognitive structures become coordinated and form new superordinate structures. Initially, structures develop from concrete experiences, such as those provided in "hands-on" school activities. Children's thinking remains concrete until the superordinate structures guiding concrete operations become coordinated, allowing for the beginning of more abstract thought. In the classroom, children should be afforded many opportunities to make discoveries through manipulation and experimentation. These opportunities are carefully planned by the teacher, and observations of the child's success in these learning contexts serve to guide the teacher in planning the next learning experience.

Social constructivist or sociocultural models of teaching have their roots in Vygotskian theory, which holds that cognitive development is a socially mediated process. The models include scaffolding children's learning (Wood, 1986), guiding children's discovery in a community of learners (Brown and Campione, 1994), and cognitive apprenticeships (Collins, Brown, and Newman, 1989). Children's participation in discussion with teachers and fellow students promotes the development of new and adaptive behaviors that are relevant to cultural expectations of what children should learn. As children engage in these cooperative dialogues during the performance of a task, the communication or "Vygotskian dialogue" (Tomasello et al., 1993) is gradually incorporated into children's thinking so that they become able to accomplish similar tasks on their own. The acquisition of knowledge and skills that are deemed necessary for success in a particular culture is determined through the process of social interaction between learner and teacher. Whereas maturationist theory views learning as an unfolding of development, and behaviorist theory views learning as a product of instruction, constructivist theory views learning as the result of interaction between learner and teacher, and the coordination of perspectives.

We have reviewed three different theoretical views that have been used to distinguish among teachers' belief systems. However, it is rare for a teacher to adopt one particular theoretical stance and oppose all others. Intangible constructs such as belief, theory, or folk pedagogy are not easily defined, nor are they easily contained within boundaries. Overlap does occur, although there is generally a predominance of one belief system, or theory, over another. The issue is one of degree; varying degrees of eclecticism across both beliefs and practices are not uncommon, yet programs most often reflect one predominant folk theory that guides a teacher in setting goals and implementing a program (Evans, 1982; Pelletier,

1994). In relating theory to practice, the most widely recognized difference among approaches is the extent of child-centeredness (Evans, 1982).

What remains problematic in pedagogical practice is that teachers are often unaware of their beliefs about how children learn (Pelletier, 1994). They do, however, describe their particular approaches to teaching, which are generally based on their personal experiences as students themselves, their experiences with children, and on programs that are advocated by their particular schools or boards. Interestingly, the three different theoretical perspectives that we have discussed can be related to recent work within developmental psychology generally and theory of mind in particular. We would argue that education needs to move in a direction that views teaching approaches in relation to understanding the minds of learners and that makes these understandings explicit for practicing teachers (Astington, in press).

Connecting Traditional Views with an Explicit Understanding of Mind

Educational practice has, of course, always been based on some understanding of children's minds (Walberg and Haertel, 1992). However, what we suggest is a move away from pedagogical practice based on teachers' *implicit* assumptions about learning to one in which teachers make *explicit* their understanding that children too have assumptions about learning, knowing, thinking, and many other forms of mental activity. Furthermore, teachers must recognize that children's assumptions about knowledge and its acquisition change as they grow and develop.

The teachers' folk pedagogies we have described in terms of traditional views of teacher belief relate in a systematic way to the literature on theories of mind. Teachers' beliefs about learning map in a relatively direct way to assumptions about mind as set out, for example, in the recent work of Kruger, Tomasello, and their colleagues (Kruger and Tomasello, this volume, chap. 17; Tomasello et al., 1993). From the maturationist perspective, learning is viewed as coming to "do." Kruger and Tomasello term this "expected learning"—that is, it will happen naturally. This view assumes that "children are competent learners just as they are competent growers" (Kruger and Tomasello, this volume, chap. 17, p. 376). Children will learn on their own how to do things, without much intervention from adults. Olson and Bruner (this volume, chap. 2) would add that children can be *shown* how to do something, but that the learning does not involve the acquisition of propositional knowledge or understanding. From the behaviorist perspective, learning is viewed as coming to "know." The child is viewed as a passive learner to be filled with knowledge transmitted directly from the teacher. Facts can be relayed by telling (Olson and Bruner, this volume, chap. 2) and the acquisition of facts assessed through formal testing. Kruger and Tomasello (this volume, chap. 17) describe this approach as "designed learning" in which the teacher brings the child up to a specified level of skills and standards. In order for mastery to occur, teachers must employ precise instructional methodology. From a constructivist perspective, learning is viewed as coming to "understand." Kruger and Tomasello describe this approach as "guided learning." The child's learning is facilitated by the teacher as he or she carefully observes the child's performance. Teacher intervention is increased or decreased as needed. Olson and Bruner's description of the Model 3 learner fits well with the constructivist view of teaching. Children are seen as thinkers who have their own points of view and who construct their own models of the world. The teacher helps or guides children to understand and to make their views explicit through discussion and collaboration.

Thus, in both the traditional teacher belief literature and in the new literature based on theory of mind, teachers' conceptions of minds and learning appear to fall into three general categories: (1) the child learns "to do"; teachers need only serve as models, whether intentionally or not; (2) the child learns "to know"; teachers must instruct by teaching specific skills necessary for mastery learning; and (3) the child learns "to understand"; teachers guide children by way of discussion as they share their understandings with others. Finally, the child comes to share in "objective" understandings of authors, past and present.

Earlier, we outlined children's use of mentalistic talk as a function of developmental change and different conceptualizations of teaching and learning. We have also investigated teachers' use of mentalistic talk in classroom settings in relation to their different philosophical orientations or theories of teaching and learning.

Teachers' Use of the Language of Mind

In a study of kindergarten teachers' beliefs and practices and children's understanding of school in regular and French immersion classrooms (Pelletier, 1994), teachers' use of metacognitive talk was examined in two contexts: (1) from observations of their regular teaching practices with children, and (2) from a transcript of an interview conducted by an adult. Each session lasted approximately one hour. Ten regular English language and ten French immersion kindergarten teachers participated. The metacognitive verbs used by teachers during teaching were *guess, know, think, learn, forget, remember, remind, pretend, promise,* and *prove*. French immersion teachers used the French equivalent of these terms. The following metacognitive verbs were used by teachers during the interviews (which were all conducted in English): *think, know, teach, learn, understand, remember, believe, guess, mean, realize, discover, convince, wonder, expect, figure, presume, remind, imagine, concentrate, assume, ignore,* and *pretend*. It was found that teachers use more metacognitive verbs more often during an interview with an adult than they do during teaching. Specifically, only 12 of 20 teachers used any metacognitive terms at all during teaching, and of those 12 teachers, there were only 31 terms in all, that is an average of 2.6 terms each. In contrast, during the interviews, all teachers used metacognitive terms, with a total of 922 metacognitive verbs—an average of 46.1 terms each. This finding supports an earlier study by Feldman and Wertsch (1976) who found that teachers are more likely to use certain forms of mental talk with their colleagues than with students in the classroom.

In order to determine whether teachers' use of metacognitive talk was related to their personal theories about teaching and learning, teachers' beliefs and practices were rated according to whether they fell primarily into maturationist,

Table 26.2   *Teachers' use of metacognitive verbs during observations of teaching*[a]

	Maturationist (n = 6)	Behaviorist (n = 5)	Constructivist (n = 9)
French immersion	0	6[b]	0
English	0	6[c]	19[d]
Total	0	12	19

[a] The terms used included *guess, know, think, learn, forget, remember, remind, pretend, promise,* and *prove.*
[b] One French immersion teacher used five French metacognitive verbs.
[c] One English teacher used all six metacognitive verbs.
[d] All English teachers used metacognitive verbs.

behaviorist, or constructivist orientations, as outlined earlier. Inter-rater reliability for teacher beliefs and practices ranged from 84 to 95 percent. Some teachers were rated as having more eclectic approaches—that is, their pedagogy was characterized by similar ratings in more than one approach. Nevertheless, all teachers had a higher score in one of the three categories and were therefore described, for the purpose of the study, as primarily adopting that approach. In total, there were six "maturationist" teachers (three French immersion, three English), five "behaviorist" teachers (three French immersion, two English) and nine "constructivist" teachers (four French immersion, five English).

During the observations of teachers in the classroom, maturationist teachers used *no* metacognitive verbs in teaching. Behaviorist teachers used 12 metacognitive verbs; however one French immersion teacher used five of those verbs and one English teacher used six of those verbs. Constructivist French immersion teachers used *no* metacognitive terms at all; however *all* constructivist English teachers used metacognitive verbs, with a total of 19 terms (see Table 26.2).

What is of interest among the English teachers is the more frequent use of metacognitive verbs in the constructivist category. All teachers in this category used metacognitive terms in their teaching and used them more frequently than teachers in the other groups. Although this finding has limited interpretation due to the small sample of teachers, the possibilities for interpretation are intriguing. That is, if teachers who favor a constructivist approach to pedagogy conceive of learners as "coming to understand" through discussion and collaboration, it is perhaps not surprising that the use of the language of mind is higher in this group. Similarly, it is not surprising that teachers who favor a maturationist approach are less inclined to use this type of language during teaching, as pedagogy in this orientation follows the child's lead by encouraging play with peers rather than instruction by and discussion with adults. Teachers who favor a behaviorist orientation might be expected to use some metacognitive terms during direct instruction; however, their use of these terms would depend on their learning goals for skill development.

The picture was different during the interviews. Teachers across all three

Table 26.3 *Teachers' use of metacognitive terms during interview*[a]

	Maturationist (n = 6)		Behaviorist (n = 5)		Constructivist (n = 9)	
	Total	Teacher mean	Total	Teacher mean	Total	Teacher mean
French immersion	164	54.7	120	40.0	191	47.8
English	164	54.7	106	53.0	177	35.4
Total	328	54.7	226	45.2	368	40.1

[a] The terms used included *think, know, teach, learn, understand, remember, believe, guess, mean, realize, discover, convince, wonder, expect, figure, presume, remind, imagine, concentrate, assume, ignore,* and *pretend.*

approaches used a variety of metacognitive terms when speaking with an adult. The pattern related to teacher belief category, described above for the observations, was not detected in the interviews. There were only small differences in the use of metacognitive verbs by teachers in the three groups (see Table 26.3).

What are we to infer from these findings? One interpretation is that teachers adjust their use of metacognitive language when interacting with children as opposed to adults. This suggests that teachers' use of the language of mind is based on implicit assumptions that children's minds and adults' minds are different. Thus teachers are more apt to use the language of mind when speaking with an adult whom they believe can more readily share this language with them. Another interpretation is that teachers adjust their use of metacognitive language with children as a function of their beliefs about how children learn. When children are believed to learn by "doing," teachers use less metacognitive talk. When children are believed to learn by "coming to know," teachers use limited metacognitive talk, and when they do, it is in the context of direct instruction and skill development. When children are believed to learn by "coming to understand," teachers use metacognitive talk to facilitate an understanding of minds; thus more metacognitive talk is necessary to meet this goal. These possibilities are compelling; however, much more empirical work is needed to substantiate these interpretations.

Implications for Teacher Education

Teachers' knowledge of learners' minds is itself a product of education. That is, in order to make explicit one's understanding of the mind, one engages in talk about the mind. This kind of talk generally does not occur in teacher education programs; thus teachers' knowledge about children's minds often remains implicit. Therefore current teaching practices most often reflect a folk pedagogy based on teachers' tacit beliefs and past experiences. Teachers generally grow comfortable with a more traditional theory, one that reflects a familiar set of experiences and beliefs rather than a set of mentalistic understandings. Teachers often remain bound to their folk theories about how children learn and how best to teach. Maturationist, behaviorist, or constructivist orientations remain implicit folk pedagogies, never challenged, and rarely a topic of reflection. It is only through change in teacher education that implicit theories will be made explicit and connected to new understandings of the mind (Astington, in press).

Conclusion

Models of learning associated with these different models of mind form a developmental sequence that occurs in a predictable order. With the emergence of more complex social understanding, earlier forms of learning are subsumed by new forms of learning. As we have discussed here, as children acquire more advanced theories of mind and a more complex metalanguage that makes explicit their understanding, they are able to profit from more complex methods of instruction. Teachers and learners become increasingly able to use language to exchange ideas and to develop a shared understanding. Although children may become able to learn in increasingly complex ways, they nevertheless do not lose their earlier systems of learning. Thus children may continue to learn via imitation long after they have acquired an understanding of belief and the ability to learn from instruction. Furthermore, once they acquire a recursive understanding of belief, children may continue to learn some concepts more effectively through instruction, rather than through collaborative learning experiences. Teachers are responsible for choosing their method according to their goals for children and according to the concept being taught. Certainly, some concepts are more easily taught via imitation than via collaboration. On the other hand, unfortunately, many teachers continue to use instruction as a teaching method when the focus could be on children's knowledge building through collaborative learning experiences. This form of pedagogy requires teachers to acknowledge that learners can reflect on their own and others' beliefs and do have theories that organize their learning.

Integration of research in children's theory of mind and research into teacher beliefs may lead to a new conception of the reciprocity of teaching and learning. If child and teacher share the same understanding of mind, of knowledge and its acquisition, and if they share a common language in which to discuss them, their classroom interactions may be fundamentally more satisfactory and successful.

Acknowledgement

Janet Wilde Astington thanks the Spencer Foundation for support of the research reported here through a National Academy of Education postdoctoral fellowship.

Note

1. In Ontario, children are eligible to enter junior kindergarten, where it is available, in September the year of their fourth birthday.

References

Astington, J. W. (1988a). Children's understanding of the speech act of promising. *Journal of Child Language, 15*, 157–173.

Astington, J. W. (1988b). Promises: Words or deeds? *First Language, 8*, 259–270.

Astington, J. W. (1993). *The child's discovery of the mind.* Cambridge: Harvard University Press.

Astington, J. W. (in press). Reflective teaching and learning: Children's and teachers' theories of mind. *Teaching Education.*

Astington, J. W., Harris, P. L., and Olson, D. R. (Eds.). (1988). *Developing theories of mind.* New York: Cambridge University Press.

Astington, J. W. and Homer, B. (1995, April). *Children's understanding of second-order beliefs and its relation to their ability to distinguish between causes and reasons.* Paper presented at the Annual Meeting of the American Educational Research Association, San Francisco.

Astington, J. W. and Jenkins, J. M. (1995). Theory of mind and social understanding. *Cognition and Emotion, 9*, 151–165.

Astington, J. W. and Olson, D. R. (1990). Metacognitive and metalinguistic language: Learning to talk about thought. *Applied Psychology: An International Review, 39*, 77–87.

Austin, J. L. (1961). *Philosophical papers.* J. O. Urmson and G. J. Warnock (Eds.) Oxford, England: Oxford University Press.

Austin, J. L. (1962a). *How to do things with words.* Cambridge: Harvard University Press.

Austin, J. L. (1962b). *Sense and sensibilia* (Reconstructed from the manuscript notes by G. J. Warnock). Oxford, England: Clarendon.

Bartsch, K. and Wellman, H. M. (1995). *Children talk about the mind.* New York: Oxford University Press.

Baumrind, D. (1971). Current patterns of parental authority. *Developmental Psychology Monographs, 4* (1, Part 2).

Bereiter, C. and Engelmann, S. (1966). *Teaching disadvantaged children in the preschool.* Englewood Cliffs, NJ: Prentice-Hall.

Bierwisch, M. (1970). Semantics. In J. Lyons (Ed.), *New horizons in linguistics* (pp. 166–184). Harmondsworth, England: Penguin.

Booth, J. R. and Hall, W. S. (1994). Role of the cognitive internal state lexicon in reading comprehension. *Journal of Educational Psychology, 86*, 413–422.

Bretherton, I. and Beeghly, M. (1982). Talking about internal states: The acquisition of an explicit theory of mind. *Developmental Psychology, 18*, 906–921.

Bretherton, I., McNew, S., and Beeghly-Smith, M. (1981). Early person knowledge as expressed in gestural and verbal communication: When do infants acquire a "theory of mind"? In M. E. Lamb and L. R. Sherod (Eds.), *Infant social cognition* (pp. 333–373). Hillsdale, NJ: Lawrence Erlbaum.

Brophy, J. and Good, T. (1986). Teacher behavior and student achievement. In M. Wittrock (Ed.), *Handbook of research on teaching* (pp. 328–375). New York: Macmillan.

Brown, A. L. and Campione, J. C. (1994). Guided discovery in a community of learners. In K. McGilly (Ed.), *Classroom lessons: Integrating cognitive theory and classroom practice* (pp. 229–270). Cambridge: Bradford Books/MIT Press.

Brown, J. R. and Dunn, J. (1991). "You can cry, mum": The social and developmental implications of talk about internal states. *British Journal of Developmental Psychology, 9,* 237–256.

Carter, K. (1990). Teachers' knowledge and learning to teach. In R. Houston (Ed.), *Handbook of research on teacher education* (pp. 291–310). New York: Macmillan.

Case, R. (1985). *Intellectual development: Birth to adulthood.* Orlando, FL: Academic Press.

Chandler, M. J. (1987). The Othello effect: Essay on the emergence and eclipse of sceptical doubt. *Human Development, 30,* 137–159.

Chomsky, C. (1969). *The acquisition of syntax in children from 5 to 10.* Cambridge: MIT Press.

Collins, A., Brown, J. S., and Newman, S. E. (1989). Cognitive apprenticeship: Teaching the crafts of reading, writing, and mathematics. In L. B. Resnick (Ed.), *Knowing, learning, and instruction: Essays in honor of Robert Glaser* (pp. 453–494). Hillsdale, NJ: Lawrence Erlbaum.

Connelly, M. and Clandinin, J. (1988). *Teachers as curriculum planners: Narratives of experience.* Toronto: Ontario Ministry of Education.

D'Andrade, R. (1987). A folk model of the mind. In D. Holland and N. Quinn (Eds.), *Cultural models in language and thought* (pp. 112–148). Cambridge, England: Cambridge University Press.

de Villiers, J. G. (1995, March). *Steps in the mastery of sentence complements.* Paper presented at the biennial meeting of the Society for Research in Child Development, Indianapolis.

Dunn, J. (1988). *The beginnings of social understanding.* Cambridge: Harvard University Press.

Evans, E. (1982). Curriculum models and early childhood education. In B. Spodek (Ed.), *Handbook of research in early childhood education* (pp. 107–134). New York: Free Press.

Fabricius, W. V. and Schwanenflugel, P. J. (1994). The older child's theory of mind. In A. Demetriou and A. Efklides (Eds.), *Intelligence, mind, and reasoning: Structure and development* (pp. 111–132). Amsterdam: Elsevier.

Fabricius, W. V., Schwanenflugel, P. J., Kyllonen, P. C., Barclay, C. R., and Denton, S. M. (1989). Developing theories of mind: Children's and adults' concepts of mental activities. *Child Development, 60,* 1278–1290.

Feldman, C. and Wertsch, J. (1976). Context dependent properties of children's speech. *Youth and Society, 7,* 227–258.

Flavell, J. H. (1986). The development of children's knowledge about the appearance–reality distinction. *American Psychologist, 41,* 418–425.

Fromberg, D. (1989). Kindergarten: Current circumstances affecting curriculum. *Teachers' College Record, 90,* 329–403.

Gardner, H. (1991). *The unschooled mind.* New York: Basic Books.

Gearhart, M. and Hall, W. S. (1982). Internal state words: Cultural and situational variation in vocabulary usage. In K. Borman (Ed.), *The social life of children in a changing society* (pp. 219–252). Hillsdale, NJ: Lawrence Erlbaum.

Gesell, A. (1945). *The embryology of behavior.* New York: Harper and Row.

Gomez, M. and Tabachnick, B. (1992). Telling teaching stories. *Teaching Education, 4,* 129–138.

Gopnik, A. and Astington, J. W. (1988). Children's understanding of representational change and its relation to the understanding of false belief and the appearance–reality distinction. *Child Development, 59,* 26–37.

Hall, W. S. and Nagy, W. E. (1986). Theoretical issues in the investigation of the words of internal report. In I. Gopnik and M. Gopnik (Eds.), *From models to modules: Studies in cognitive science from the McGill workshops* (pp. 26–65). Norwood, NJ: Ablex.

Hohmann, M., Banet, B., and Weikart, D. (1979). *Young children in action: A manual for preschool educators.* Ypsilanti, MI: High/Scope Press.

Homer, B. and Astington, J. W. (1995, March). *Children's understanding of second-order beliefs in self and other.* Paper presented at the biennial meeting of the Society for Research in Child Development, Indianapolis.

Johnson, C. N. and Maratsos, M. P. (1977). Early comprehension of mental verbs: Think and know. *Child Development, 48,* 1743–1747.

Johnson, C. N. and Wellman, H. M. (1980). Children's developing understanding of mental verbs: Remember, know and guess. *Child Development, 51,* 1095–1102.

Kagan, D. (1992). Implications of research on teacher belief. *Educational Psychologist, 27,* 65–90.

Kay, C. and Samuels, M. L. (1977). Componential analysis in semantics: Its validity and applications. *Transactions of the Philological Society, 1975,* 49–81.

Krauss, R. M. and Glucksberg, S. (1969). The development of communication: Competence as a function of age. *Child Development, 42,* 255–266.

Lalonde, C. E. and Chandler, M. (1995). False belief understanding goes to school: On the social-emotional consequences of coming early or late to a first theory of mind. *Cognition and Emotion, 9,* 167–185.

Leekam, S. R. (1991). Jokes and lies: Children's understanding of intentional falsehood. In A. Whiten (Ed.), *Natural theories of mind: Evolution, development and simulation of everyday mindreading* (pp. 159–174). Oxford, England: Blackwell.

Light, P. (1979). *The development of social sensitivity.* Cambridge, England: Cambridge University Press.

McKeough, A. (1992). Testing for the presence of a central social structure: Use of the transfer paradigm. In R. Case (Ed.), *The mind's staircase* (pp. 207–225). Hillsdale, NJ: Lawrence Erlbaum.

Meichenbaum, D. and Biemiller, A. (1992). In search of student expertise in the classroom: A metacognitive analysis. In M. Pressley, K. Harris, and J. Guthrie (Eds.), *Promoting academic competence and literacy: Cognitive research and instructional innovation* (pp. 3–53). New York: Academic Press.

Meltzoff, A. and Gopnik, A. (1993). The role of imitation in understanding persons and developing a theory of mind. In S. Baron-Cohen, H. Tager-Flusberg, and D. Cohen (Eds.), *Understanding other minds: Perspectives from autism* (pp. 335–366). Oxford, England: Oxford University Press.

Miller, G. A. and Johnson-Laird, P. N. (1976). *Language and perception.* Cambridge: Harvard University Press.

Miscione, J. L., Marvin, R. S., O'Brien, R. G., and Greenberg, M. T. (1978). A developmental study of preschool children's understanding of the words "know" and "guess." *Child Development, 49,* 1107–1113.

Moore, C. and Frye, D. (1991). The acquisition and utility of theories of mind. In D. Frye and C. Moore (Eds.), *Children's theories of mind* (pp. 1–14). Hillsdale, NJ: Lawrence Erlbaum.

Moore, C. and Furrow, D. (1991). The development of the language of belief: The expression of relative certainty. In D. Frye and C. Moore (Eds.), *Children's theories of mind* (pp. 173–193). Hillsdale, NJ: Lawrence Erlbaum.

Oakes, P. and Caruso, D. (1990). Kindergarten teachers' use of developmentally appropriate practices and attitudes about authority. *Early Education and Development, 1,* 445–457.

Ortony, A. (1987). Cognitive development and the language of mental states. *Discourse Processes, 10,* 193–199.

Pajares, M. (1992). Teachers' beliefs and educational research: Cleaning up a messy construct. *Review of Educational Research, 62,* 307–332.

Pelletier, J. (1994). *Children's understanding of school and teachers' beliefs and practices in French immersion and regular English language kindergarten.* Doctoral dissertation, University of Toronto (Ontario Institute for Studies in Education), Toronto.

Perner, J. (1991). *Understanding the representational mind.* Cambridge: Bradford Books/MIT Press.

Perner, J., Leekam, S., and Wimmer, H. (1987). Three-year-olds' difficulty with false belief: The case for a conceptual deficit. *British Journal of Developmental Psychology, 5,* 125–137.

Perner, J. and Wimmer, H. (1985). "John thinks that Mary thinks that. . ." Attribution of second-order beliefs by 5- to 10-year-old children. *Journal of Experimental Child Psychology, 39,* 437–471.

Puleo, V. (1986). *Application of mastery learning theory to full and half-day kindergarten research.* ERIC Document Reproduction Service No. ED 286 623. Kingston, NY.

Rips, L. J. and Conrad, F. G. (1989). Folk psychology of mental activities. *Psychological Review, 96,* 187–207.

Roget, P. M. (1852/1966). *Roget's thesaurus.* R. A. Dutch (Ed.), Harmondsworth, England: Penguin.

Rousseau, J. J. (1762/1969). *Emile* (B. Foxley, Trans.). London: Dent.

Scholnick, E. K. (1978). The language of mind: Statements about mental states. *Discourse Processes, 10,* 181–192.

Schwanenflugel, P. J., Fabricius, W. F., and Alexander, J. (1994). Developing theories of mind: Understanding concepts and relations between mental activities. *Child Development, 65,* 1546–1563.

Schwanenflugel, P. J., Fabricius, W. F., Noyes, C. R., Bigler, K., and Alexander, J. M. (1994). The organization of mental verbs and folk theories of knowing. *Journal of Memory and Language, 33,* 376–395.

Schwarz, S. and Robinson, H. (1982). *Designing curriculum for early childhood.* Boston: Allyn and Bacon.

Schweinhart, L., Weikart, D., and Larner, M. (1986). Consequences of three preschool curriculum models through age 15. *Early Childhood Research Quarterly, 1,* 15–45.

Searle, J. R. (1979a). *Expression and meaning.* Cambridge, England: Cambridge University Press.

Searle, J. R. (1979b). Intentionality and the use of language. In A. Margalit (Ed.), *Meaning and use* (pp. 181–197). Dordrecht, Holland: Reidel.

Searle, J. R. (1983). *Intentionality: An essay in the philosophy of mind.* Cambridge, England: Cambridge University Press.

Shatz, M., Wellman, H. M., and Silber, S. (1983). The acquisition of mental verbs: A systematic investigation of the first reference to mental state. *Cognition, 14,* 301–321.

Siefert, K. (1993). Cognitive development and early childhood education. In B. Spodek (Ed.), *Handbook of research on the education of young children* (pp. 9–23). New York: Macmillan.

Sodian, B., Zaitchik, D., and Carey, S. (1991). Young children's differentiation of hypothetical beliefs from evidence. *Child Development, 62,* 753–766.

Spodek, B. and Clark Brown, P. (1993). Curriculum alternatives in early childhood education: A historical perspective. In B. Spodek (Ed.), *Handbook of research on the education of young children* (pp. 91–104). New York: Macmillan.

Spodek, B., Saracho, O., and Davis, M. (1991). *Foundations of early childhood education: Teaching three-, four-, and five-year-old children* (2nd edn.). Englewood Cliffs, NJ: Prentice-Hall.

Strauss, S. (1993). Teachers' pedagogical content knowledge about children's minds and learning: Implications for teacher education. *Educational Psychologist, 28,* 279–290.

Strauss, S. and Shilony, T. (1994). Teachers' models of children's mind and learning. In L. A. Hirschfeld and S. A. Gelman (Eds.), *Mapping the mind: Domain specificity in cognition and culture* (pp. 455–473). New York: Cambridge University Press.

Tager-Flusberg, H. (1992). Autistic children's talk about psychological states: Deficits in the early acquisition of a theory of mind. *Child Development, 63,* 161–172.

Tager-Flusberg, H. (1993). What language reveals about the understanding of minds in children with autism. In S. Baron-Cohen, H. Tager-Flusberg, and D. Cohen (Eds.), *Understanding other minds: Perspectives from autism* (pp. 138–157). Oxford, England: Oxford University Press.

Tomasello, M., Kruger, A., and Ratner, H. (1993). Cultural learning. *Behavioral and Brain Sciences, 16,* 495–552.

Vendler, Z. (1970). Say what you think. In J. L. Cowan (Ed.), *Studies in thought and language* (pp. 79–97). Tucson: University of Arizona Press.

Walberg, H. J. and Haertel, G. D. (1992). Educational psychology's first century. *Developmental Psychology, 84,* 6–19.

Wellman, H. M. (1990). *The child's theory of mind.* Cambridge: Bradford Books/MIT Press.

Wellman, H. M. and Johnson, C. N. (1979). Understanding mental processes: A developmental study of remember and forget. *Child Development, 50,* 79–88.

Wimmer, H. and Perner, J. (1983). Beliefs about beliefs: Representation and constraining function of wrong beliefs in young children's understanding of deception. *Cognition, 13,* 103–128.

Winner, E. and Leekam, S. (1991). Distinguishing irony from deception: Understanding the speaker's second-order intention. *British Journal of Developmental Psychology, 9,* 257–270.

Wood, D. (1986). Aspects of teaching and learning. In M. Richards and P. Light (Eds.), *Children of social worlds* (pp. 191–211). Cambridge, England: Polity Press.

Yaakobi, D. and Sharan, S. (1985). Teacher beliefs and practices: The discipline carries the message. *Journal of Education for Teaching, 11,* 197–199.

Yuill, N. and Perner, J. (1987). Exceptions to mutual trust: Children's use of second-order beliefs in responsibility attribution. *International Journal of Behavioral Development, 10,* 207–223.

27

Schooling and the Acquisition of Theoretical Knowledge

FRANK C. KEIL

CHANA S. SILBERSTEIN

The Rise of Theory

A theme central in the history and philosophy of science for over a quarter of a century has now come to occupy center stage in cognitive science as a whole: we cannot fully characterize how concepts are represented and learned without also characterizing the larger systems of explanation in which they are embedded. Whether we use concepts to categorize the world, to make inductions about properties, or to justify a belief, such mental events make essential use of systems of explanations, or intuitive theories. A hallmark of human thought is the great flexibility provided by theories when categorizing and understanding new phenomena. Associationist accounts, relying as they do on similarity and common features, are inadequate for describing these reasoning abilities, both because they often fail with novel stimuli and because the selection of features that are relevantly similar are themselves theory-driven (e.g., Hirschfeld and Gelman, 1994; Rips, 1989; Barsalou, 1985). Evidence for an explanation-based component to concept structure can be seen in illusory correlations (Chapman and Chapman, 1969; Medin, 1989), conceptual combinations (Murphy, 1993), patterns of induction (Gelman, 1988; Gelman and O'Reilly, 1988), patterns of concept acquisition (Keil, 1989), patterns of conceptual change at all ages (Carey, 1985), and in a wide variety of judgments made about categories (Medin, 1989).

Although the new "concepts-in-theories" view has now been extensively discussed in several places (e.g., Medin, 1989; Neisser, 1987; Murphy and Medin, 1985; Gopnik and Wellman, 1994), there has been surprisingly little work on how this theoretical knowledge is structured and represented, how it relates to other sorts of knowledge, and how it is related to explicit instruction. There is of course a large literature on misconceptions, often in science, and how those misconceptions influence learning and instruction (e.g., Krist, Fieberg, and Wilkening, 1993; Kaiser, McCloskey, and Proffitt, 1986; Mintzes, Trowbridge, Arnaudin, and Wandersee, 1991; Vosniadou and Brewer, 1992; Vosniadou, 1991; Smith, Carey, and Wiser, 1985), but the accounts of those misconceptions usually involve only a highly concrete and specific false belief; only rarely do they involve a different theory with a large set of interconnected beliefs that is at odds with adult norms. There is increasing discussion of mental models in both the child and the teacher and the need to bring these into congruence (e.g., Strauss and Shilony, 1994), but here too the models tend to be highly concrete bounded "visualizations" of specific phenomena and not a theory. The contrast between models and theories is developed further at a later point in this chapter.

Whereas the emphasis on "theory" holds true for many realms of human experience, such as the functional aspects of artifacts or the goal-based organization of a database, nowhere are the theories as richly developed as they are with regard to natural kinds. All children throughout the world come to develop elaborate and highly structured sets of beliefs about natural phenomena, such as plants, animals, and natural substances, and do so at surprisingly early ages. A surge of research in the last decade has documented how even preschoolers come to understand different causal patternings that hold for natural kinds as opposed to manmade artifacts, and also start to understand fundamental differences among sorts of natural kinds, such as living kinds vs. inorganic ones (Atran, 1987, 1994; Gelman and Wellman, 1991; Gelman and Markman, 1987; Keil, 1989, 1994). Much of this knowledge is acquired implicitly through naturalistic observation of the world.

At present there is still intense debate on how these theories and explanations are to be mentally represented. Are they qualitatively distinct from other sorts of knowledge? Does theory emerge late in development after the brute force facts have been recorded, or is some element of theory needed from the start to guide the recording of fact? Can theories be implicit or is our intuitive knowledge of a fundamentally different nature than the explicit theories that guide our thinking? This chapter considers these issues in the context of educational practice.

Theories and explanations of natural kinds existed long before the development of a technological society, and so it seems fitting to ask how beliefs in this area might emerge and be related to schooling. For many natural phenomena, children construct intuitive theories without any obvious instruction and then later interpret explicit instruction in light of those intuitive constructions. Discussions of theoretical conceptions in general, and the understanding of natural kinds in particular, have been relatively sparse in writings about schooling, despite their universal prevalence. This neglect rises at least partly from the gross preponderance of time spent in the elementary school classroom on instruction that is largely divorced from the natural, preliterate world. Learning to perform basic arithmetic operations, learning to read, and learning to write occupy an enormous percentage of the elementary school years.

Even when instruction does focus on other topics, it is most often not in the form of scientific explanation about natural phenomena. History is frequently a list of who did what when, rather than an examination of why people acted in a certain way. Geography and science too are often learned as a set of facts with little or no explanation given. Countless schoolchildren have learned taxonomies of plants and animals and seashells, but depressingly few are taught anything about the causal forces responsible for the patterns that they so effortfully memorize.

Basic cognitive science research on concepts of natural kinds bears on educational issues in several ways. (For a systematic overview of the powerful relevance of basic cognitive science in general research to educational practice, see Bruer, 1993.) First, it asks if theories and explanations for natural kinds might have different structures than those for either the technological world or social constructions and conventions. Second, it asks how explicit instruction relates to implicit learning. Finally, it asks how any sort of instruction involving everyday concepts of natural phenomena needs to take into account intuitively developed theories.

Theory and Association—An Essential Hybrid

Although debates about the precise formats of intuitive theories and explanations continue, it is increasingly evident that any adequate model will have to reflect the interplay between at least two fundamentally different representational systems: theory and association. There are both principled and empirical reasons for suspecting a hybrid structure for concepts of natural kinds. At the principled level, it becomes quickly obvious that no theory can ever hope to explain all patterns of covariation that are relevant to a class of phenomena. We might have causal explanatory reasons for why birds fly, or why plants are green, but when any of these explanations are pressed for further detail, they soon run out of causal justifications. Thus we might argue that birds fly because they have wings. Wings help flight because they have a shape, substance, and weight that allows them to generate lift in air. The shape, substance, and weight generate lift because—and somewhere about this point most people run out of explanations. Experts go a few steps further, but they too soon run of explanations for widely observable patterns. Yet even as our causal explanations run out steam, there are still patterns of covariation that we notice and remember—for example, that robins have red breasts and ducks make a particular sound. These patterns often become the motivations for later developing more elaborate theories that partially explain them. These patterns of covariation seem to be learned and stored in a manner that is much closer to classical association or to some of the more basic connectionist models (e.g., Cleeremans, 1993).

Often, theory development seems to proceed by gradually expanding the network of causal explanatory beliefs to explain more and more of the patterns of covariation that have been stored previously on the basis of frequency and/or correlation values. To continue with the same example, someone who is just beginning to learn about birds might simply notice that feathers covary strongly with animals capable of flight but have no idea of how feathers might causally contribute to flying. That pattern of covariation is nonetheless stored as a kind of data set for the theory that comes later.

The storage of covariation patterns as a basis for later theory building suggests a complementary need for an explanatory component as part of natural kind concepts from the start as well. This is especially true for natural kinds where causal structure is usually richer and thus requires a great deal more explanation. Although it is necessary to store some patterns of covariation and frequency of occurrence without full explanation of those patterns, it is impossible to store all possible patterns of covariation. There is an indefinitely large number of possible correlations between properties to notice, and we obviously selectively favor some over others (see also Keil, 1981). We do not notice, for example, whether things that fly do so from trees with odd versus even numbers of branches. We do not notice whether things that fly tend to do so on sunny versus cloudy days (although some level of correlation may well exist there for some species of birds). We are saved from the immense computational load of monitoring vast numbers of correlations by intuitive notions of what sorts of patterns are likely to be relevant, and we use these notions to avoid tabulating the huge universe of possible covariations that are not likely to be of any real explanatory value.

This filtering out of explanatorily irrelevant correlations is obviously essential to setting up a useful covariation database for later theory building, but it also can lead to serious oversights, as in those cases where a significant pattern of covariation is consistently overlooked because it is erroneously assumed to be irrelevant; it can also lead to the recording of illusory correlations where the explanatory preconceptions are so strong as to see correlations in randomness (e.g., Chapman and Chapman, 1969). A theory-based component also may be essential from the start of knowledge acquisition simply because no successful models have been able to show how notions such as cause and mechanism can emerge out of simple tabulations of property frequencies and covariation patterns. A radically different sort of representation seems to be needed to capture even the most basic intuitions concerning mechanical causality and functional properties. These ideas create a compelling sense of explanation, as opposed to the sense of pattern recognition that is produced by associative learning.

In short, the hybrid nature of natural kind concepts has powerful consequences for how we understand their representation and acquisition, and any discussion of the teaching of such concepts must take into account both the associative and explanation-based components. Far too often the associative components have been emphasized, either because they were assumed to be sufficient, or because it was assumed that they were developmentally prior to the explanation-based structures. We argue that both assumptions are wrong and lead to inappropriate educational strategies.

What Theories Are Not: Defining by Negatives

Our focus in this chapter is on the theoretical, or explanation-based, component of natural kind concepts, for several reasons. First, this component has been far more neglected that the associative parts. Second, it is more closely linked to the distinctive nature of natural kinds whereas the associative component may work in much the same way for all kinds of things. Third, it may be where the most effective educational interventions are possible. But to make progress on understanding theory, we need to be clearer on what qualifies as theoretical knowledge. As with so many difficult problems, it is often easier to try to gain an understanding of what theories are by showing how some possible candidates are inadequate. With theories in particular, a number of quick definitions come to mind, which upon reflection turn out to be unworkable. One claim is that theories are mental representations or states that take us beyond the phenomenal or the obvious (Gopnik and Wellman, 1994; Wellman and Gelman, 1992). The motivation for that claim comes from a series of recent studies in which surface or phenomenal similarity seems to be overridden by a deeper similarity that is structured by theoretical convictions. Some of these studies come from the infancy literature, where infants dishabituate to events that are more similar on a surface level than distractors, but less similar when interpreted in terms of the principles of a naive mechanics (Baillargeon, Kotovsky, and Needham, 1995; Spelke, Breinlinger, Macomber, and Jacobson, 1992). Other studies have looked at patterns of induction in the preschool years, where surface similarity is overridden by category labels in driving inductions (Gelman and Markman, 1986, 1987). Similarly, adult experts in academic physics sort physics problems in ways that do not correspond to the phenomenal similarities seen by novices (Chi, Feltovich, and Glaser, 1981).

The idea of a deeper theoretical similarity is not a new one and is perhaps best described by Quine (1977) in his essay on natural kinds, where he posits a developmental shift from surface or phenomenal similarity, what he also calls "the animal sense of similarity," to a deeper sense of similarity formed by theoretical kinds and relations.

The problem with this sort of characterization of theories is that other nontheoretical types of structures can also come to override surface similarity. For example, in many areas of perceptual expertise, the expert sees sets of perceptual relations that are not at all apparent to the novice, relations that nonetheless do not have any flavor of theory or explanation. The expert chicken sexer who sorts newborn chicks on the basis of criteria that remain opaque to the novice, has simply learned to pick up subtle perceptual clues that are not apparent to the casual viewer; the information is inherent in the visual stimuli, and no real theory is needed (Gibson, 1969). Similarly, the expert chess player may come to see underlying patterns that a novice cannot see, while not encoding such patterns so much in explanatory terms as in terms of their empirical consequences. Finally, logicians may come to see patterns in proofs that allow them to see similarities based on omitted deductive chains, while nowhere having any real sense of explanation or mechanism. Of course, expert similarity dimensions are often driven by theoretical knowledge that in turn guides what perceptual information is noticed, but this is in no way necessary and is certainly not always the case.

Even outside the realm of pattern recognition, surface similarities can be overridden by nontheoretical aspects of knowledge. Consider, for example, what happens in some complex card games, where experts come to know which hands are more similar to others in terms of payoffs even though other patterns may seem more similar for novices. In many cases, expert poker players are no better than novices in explaining their strategies. Rather, they have implicitly tabulated the results of many trials and have a sense of what has worked in the past and what sort of information is a better predictor of success. In short, although theories usually allow one to see similarity relations that were not otherwise apparent, they are not the only way in which new similarity relations are apprehended.

In addition, although theory may sometimes be fully congruent with phenomenal similarity, it need not make appeals to hidden variables or unobservables, or at least such appeals need not result in any restructuring of the similarity space. For example, we might have a theory that the orbits of the planets are explained by a math based on a heliocentric universe versus a geocentric one, and although one set of calculations may in the end be much more efficient, it is is less clear that our phenomenal experience of heavenly bodies will be any different. So theories cannot be neatly demarcated as those mental states that enable us to go beyond the obvious; much of cognition and perceptual expertise can do that without the accompanying air of explanation.

Another claim often made about theories is that they are the knowledge structures that enable predictions. Here too, however, the characterization seems inadequate. There are certainly many cases where we can predict future events without theories; predictions may be based solely on probability calculations or purely logical noncausal inferences. For example, many classical and operant conditioning paradigms illustrate how a wide range of species can predict likelihoods of future events based on prior patterns (Schwartz, 1979).

More important is the surprising possibility that good, useful theories might nonetheless rarely be used to make predictions. This claim seems counterintuitive since successful prediction is often regarded as a critical test of a theory in science, but naturalistically, we often seem to use intuitive theories in ways that do not result in specific predictions at all. Consider how our folk theories of psychology often seem to work. We rarely make detailed predictions about the behaviors of others. This lack of predictions probably springs from the extraordinary number of interacting factors that determine human behavior and the extent to which small initial differences can result in massively different outcomes. Like so many nonlinear dynamic systems that have been the recent preoccupation of mathematicians in such areas as chaos theory, human behavior is intrinsically difficult to predict on many occasions. Yet we seem to possess rich and elaborate theories about people and their dispositions to behave. Why?

A little reflection on how we use such theories most of the time helps to reveal a different function that they serve. Much of the time we attempt to explain events that have already occurred, whether it be an eccentric uncle's behavior at Thanksgiving dinner, or a recent conflict with a boss. Humans seem to spend endless amounts of time on such after-the-fact explanations. The question is: why engage in such behavior if it rarely results in predictions? One possible answer is that such explanations may not allow for better predictions in the future but may allow more accurate interpretations of future events and the ability to respond more quickly and appropriately to them. For example, if we come to understand that Uncle Harry went into a rage at Thanksgiving because of an endogenous physiological imbalance that is randomly triggered, on future occasions we might not take such outbursts too personally. We are not predicting Harry's behavior in any real sense; rather we are learning how to better react when Harry does something. Being able to know how to interpret events more accurately when they or similar ones recur so as to be able respond more effectively does not necessarily involve any direct predictions, even though causal explanations and theories may be essential to such a process. Explanations can also provide a vastly more powerful storage and retrieval system to aid in the interpretation of future events, thus enabling us to assess better whether a particular event should be construed as dangerous and to be avoided or desirable and to be sought out. At some level, seeking out the event again involves a very weak sort of prediction, but most of the power of explanation lies in interpreting what has already happened and its consequences.

A related misconception is the notion that theories must be defeasible, or able to be disproved by anomalous evidence (Gopnik and Wellman, 1994). While this is a necessary criterion of scientific theory, whose purpose is the advancement of knowledge, it seems unnecessary to the more informal theories that organize our daily experience. A theory about an eccentric uncle is useful if it results in a response that makes Thanksgiving dinners less traumatic; the ability to medically confirm or disconfirm this fact may not necessarily affect the theory's usefulness. Thus, though a theory may be unproven, or even false, so long as it plausibly suggests appropriate responses to the environment, it may be a worthwhile theory to entertain.

For this reason, it is inappropriate to think of theories as structures that always provide correct or accurate explanations of events. Everyone knows that the phlogiston theory of fire was widely held for many years even though it turned out to be completely false. Countless other examples from astrology, alchemy, and the natural sciences can also be offered. There is no single story for why such false theories exist, often surviving for centuries. In some cases the false theory may have an important grain of truth that results in enough successes to keep the theory alive. In many other cases, however, the theory leads to no predictive successes beyond chance and sometimes even causes predictions to more often be wrong than right. The reasons for theory persistence here may be varied as well. Perhaps the theory is inappropriately extended from a domain where it does work; perhaps a few very salient cases in the domain drive theory construction even though the vast majority of cases in the same domain are at odds with that model. A host of social and cultural factors can often lead people to favor theories that have no empirical merit, sometimes merely because they increase consistency with other bodies of belief ranging from religion to political doctrine. An incorrect theory may also simply be more cognitively "compact," making it easier to store and recall. It is not possible or necessary to explore here the full range of reasons why theories can exist and survive without empirical support; it suffices that the phenomenon be recognized and its implications for teaching understood.

Black Boxes, Intuitions, and Theories

Theoretical knowledge need not necessarily be fully stateable. We can have power-ful explanatory notions and insights without having ever verbally expressed them. Certain forms of mechanical or musical theory may be examples of this kind. Some mathematicians report thinking in images as opposed to words, and this kind of manipulation may be an acceptable way of dealing with causal relevance. Kekule's well-known image of a snake biting its tail as a metaphor for chemical structure is another example of a scientific theory that is in some significant way embedded in nonlinguistic thought (Kekule, 1858).

However, in endorsing some kinds of nonverbal knowledge as theoretical, there is the danger of embracing any behavior that conforms to a set of theoretical constructs as evidence for an implicit theory. Many species of animals are able to anticipate physical events in ways that we could explain by possession of an ap-propriate theory. The kingfisher that dives on underwater prey at an angle that incorporates the optical distortions produced when light travels across the junc-tion between two different optical media might seem to possess an intuitive "theory" of optics. So too, the spider that adjusts its jump trajectories as a consequence of the amount of web fluid it has used up might seem to have an intuitive theory of classical mechanics. We want to reject these mental states as "theories" and say that they are more like built-in computational "black boxes," much as police offi-cers who have radar detectors in their cars need not understand much of anything about how the detectors work beyond that they give values corresponding to the recent velocities of nearby vehicles.

Likewise, the infant's intuitions and predictions about simple physical mechan-ics, while systematic in nature, cannot really be termed a theory. It has been extensively demonstrated that infants in the first half year of life have reliable and strong expectations about the behaviors of simple bounded physical objects (Spelke, 1991; Leslie, 1994; Baillargeon, 1987), expectations that seem to be so well struc-tured and rapidly emerging, and so loosely connected with direct experience, that they appear to reflect innate capacities. Many of these expectations also have a striking continuity with beliefs held by all human adults: that objects travel on spatio-temporally continuous paths, that they are solid and cannot interpenetrate, and that they cannot be in two different locations at once. Yet there is no reason to believe that these intuitions reflect more than psychological primitives that have been hardwired in. Nor is there any reason to suppose a deep explanatory structure underlying and connecting these assumptions in the richly structured manner that we normally attribute to theories.

Yet the infant's naive mechanics is much closer to a notion of theory than that of the spider. As mentioned above, the database that is the growth of later theory must itself be guided by some theoretical constructs. It appears that infants are innately prepared to be sensitive to information regarding such notions as gravity and continuity, and to use this predisposition to gather the associations that will eventually form the base of a full-fledged theory. Thus the innate frameworks allow immense elaboration and growth within their constraints. We might consider these to be pretheoretical modes of construal rather than theories themselves (see Keil, 1994).

To take another recent example from the developmental literature, children are said to have a theory of mind, an understanding of wants and desires and intentions, and, from about age four, a clear ability to understand that two people may have conflicting beliefs about a single event (Wellman, 1990; Perner, 1991; Astington, 1993). Precursors to this ability are a notion of representation—namely, knowing that what one thinks about an event is different than the actual event. This ability is clearly present by the second year of life. Also important is an understanding of the existence of mental life: an understanding that infants seem predisposed to develop by their preference for gazing at human faces, their sensitivity to contingent human responses to gurgling and babbling, and the early growth of the ability to look at the object of a parent's point or gaze. It would be presumptuous to take this behavior as evidence of an elaborated theory, but clearly, without these systematic predispositions, it would be difficult for a full-blown theory of mind to develop.

This point clarifies another reason why even young children have developed sophisticated notions of natural kinds. Although we are able to theorize about a huge universe of objects, clearly some kinds of reasoning are more integral to our notions of what it is like to be human. Biology, physics, and psychology are among the basic modes of construal of the universe around us, and we appear to be born with the tools that allow us to expand our understanding of these domains with great rapidity and sophistication.

Schooling readily allows children to contrast the difference between these domains of knowledge and some of the other domains in the modern school curriculum. Every normal child can learn to identify and classify with ease huge numbers of faces and animals, from a variety of positions and orientations. Yet the instruction of a mere 26 letters and their correspondences is a very lengthy process that often stretches over two or three years of early childhood education, and in a significant portion of the population is met with its own peculiar dysfunction, dyslexia. These problems occur even though printed letters, as opposed to real-life images, have the advantage of having distinct edges clearly demarcated from the background, with relatively little variation in shape, form, and orientation.

Although knowledge of natural kinds can be contrasted with other types of schooled and explicit knowledge in terms of its ease of acquisition and the sophistication of its causal explanations, it would be a mistake to assume that this necessarily applies to all natural endeavors. Certainly, there are many things that humans become expert at that rarely become explicitly theorylike at all. Language, perhaps, is one example, where by the age of three or four, children speak with great proficiency, yet have little theoretical understanding of the nature of syntax or pragmatics. Procedural and action tasks are another example of richly developed behavior, which, although analyzable in terms of theory, are not commonly accessible to us. Thus it is immensely difficult to describe the principles governing trajectories of objects, even though we may intuitively reach appropriately to catch them. Some finer-grained distinctions about the kinds of knowledge accessible to the theoretical processes is necessary.

In addition to guiding the basic parameters of theories, implicit information can guide theories in another way. We have discussed the importance of associations and covariation for theories. Much of this associationistic knowledge is gathered without any conscious awareness, influencing and affecting theories in subtle ways. Thus subjects may be implicitly aware of even very small deviations from randomness. They react extremely sensitively to contingencies, though they can often give no theoretical explanation as to why they intuitively select a certain response (Reber, 1993; Berry and Dienes, 1993).

These implicit learning processes are particularly sensitive to covariation, contingency relationships, and relative frequencies. Implicit learning can be expected to be effective if there is a powerful rule governing the data and if the structure of the rule can be approximated by one of these low-level relationships. If a novel formal rule is too complex to be generated by explicit hypotheses yet is approximated well by one of the implicit processes, implicit learning can be expected to surpass explicit learning (Hayes and Broadbent, 1988), creating strong intuitions that may well be at odds with explicitly taught theories. Frequently, these intuitions begin to be incorporated in theorylike knowledge, taking on explanatory roles and helping to carve up the world. On other occasions, implicitly generated theories may take on a life of their own quite distinct from those that are taught by explicit instruction.

Whereas intuitively developed theories are likely to account well for the associations in the natural world, schooled theories, although accepted by the child, often coexist with conflicting intuitions that the child may not even be explicitly aware of.

Consider as a first example, work on intuitive physics that has developed dramatically in the last decade. About 15 years ago a series of influential studies began to document that most adults held sets of beliefs about the movements of simple physical objects that were at odds with the real behaviors of many of those objects (McCloskey, Washburn, and Felch, 1983; Kaiser, McCloskey, and Proffitt, 1986). Adults often seemed to make incorrect predictions about the trajectories of objects such as balls that emerged from a circular spiral or projectiles dropped from airborne vehicles. Several researchers posited that most adults shared versions of an intuitive belief known as "naive impetus theory," which was seen as similar to some classical, more explicit theories of motion, such as that put forth by Aristotle.

Although there continue to be debates about the nature of those theories, there does seem to be a consensus that these theories are truly implicit or intuitive. Thus some adults seem to have the idea that objects have an impetus that is imparted to them by a motive force and which then gradually dissipates over the course of a trajectory thereby initially preserving the trajectory it traveled before the moment of release. This knowledge appears implicit in that people are often unaware that it is guiding their judgments until it is explicitly pointed out to them. Interestingly, this occurs although there is another level of implicit knowledge at which the behavior of objects is anticipated in a more automatic and atheoretical manner. Thus there are indications that subjects will sometimes anticipate trajectories of objects in terms of a motor pattern (e.g., catching a thrown object) while using the erroneous intuitive theory when predicting trajectories. One reason that this intuition is so resistant is that it seems to be able to account well for the most frequent kind of physical phenomena, physics in high friction environments, without any seeming contradiction. Thus it is likely that it becomes the source for a generation of a second, naive theory of physical motion. Because covariational information repeatedly reinforces this notion, the intuition may be almost impossible to override. By clarifying the source of the conflicting information, however, it becomes possible for the adult to develop more elaborated theories that can recognize how the intuitions are erroneous and lead to contradictions.

Two other examples of incorrect intuitions help to illustrate their widespread prevalence. One comes from the personality and attribution literature where it has been assumed for some time that people hold systems of beliefs about what makes others disposed to act in certain ways. Such theories can also depart from accurate predictions and explanations, thereby resulting in errors in performance. For example, there is a widespread implicit belief that the behavior of others is largely a consequence of their internal dispositions, not of environmental influences (Nisbett and Ross, 1980). That people act in this way is well documented, yet despite being told this idea in explicit terms in an introductory class in social psychology, scores of sophomores continue to parse their social world in terms of people's enduring character traits.

A second domain involves notions of perception. Many people seem to think about visual perception as a process in which their eyes project out beams that scan the environment in a way that recovers information, rather than being trackers of reflected light. They will answer a host of questions indicating such a set of explanatory beliefs about the nature of perception, but again they may be quite surprised to learn that they hold such beliefs.

A closer look at these and other examples starts to suggest some possible contrasts between implicitly generated and explicitly taught theories. One difference may center around the degree to which internal contradictions and inconsistencies are tolerated. All too often we find that when we write down a vague hunch or intuition, its intuitive elegance falls short because of contradictions and inconsistencies that emerge when we try to express it in written propositional form (see also Olson, 1977, on cognitive consequences of schooling). Beyond writing, it may be that in general expressing intuitive notions in explicit propositional form for communication to others also highlights many of the most glaring problems. It certainly does not capture all such problems, as even venerable complex theories in the natural sciences have been shown to have internal contradictions after years of unquestioning acceptance by the vast majority of scientists, but in these cases the order of complexity of the theories is vastly greater.

With implicitly developed theories, the clashes may be more dramatic. Beliefs and intuitions may begin to accrue over long periods of time, based on experience and exposure. With time, each of these beliefs may become more theorylike, yet the pieces are rarely combined into an integrated theoretical whole. Consider, for example, that many college undergraduates explain the seasonal changes in temperature by saying that the earth is farther away from the sun in the winter, and yet also report that seasons in the northern hemisphere are the opposite of those in the southern half of the earth (Chinn and Brewer, 1993). Quite remarkably they can hold both of these beliefs for years and yet not be aware of the contradiction until both beliefs are elicited in juxtaposition to each other. Until they have to explicitly address these questions at the same time in one coherent framework, they may never recognize the contradiction.

Two other possible differences between implicit developed and explicit taught theories depend on a fuller characterization of theories and their relations to natural kinds. One is that implicit theories may have a smaller part that could be described in terms of laws concerning specific relations among particular properties and a larger part that could be characterized in terms of the causal powers of properties. The idea of causal powers is gaining increasing support with the recognition that an underlying set of hunches guides much of contemporary science (Salmon, 1989; Harré, 1988). In their day to day practices, scientists frequently operate on hunches that specify what sorts of properties are likely to be causally efficacious in a domain, without having a clear idea of specific mechanisms or laws. Only when those hunches become translated into explicit proposals do they come to have a much more lawlike structure that comes closer to the classical nomological-deductive format. It seems that for nonscientists, these notions about causal powers may play an even larger role, especially for natural kinds where the true sets of laws are so complex and interconnected that for laypersons, notions of causal powers may provide a suitable alternative.

A second difference between explicit and implicit theories may be that the intuitive theories are more fully assimilated into a small handful of fundamental modes of construal or forms of understanding, whereas explicit theories can take on more of a life of their own as their formal structure becomes increasingly complex and interconnected in a propositional and deductive framework. In the intuitive frame, it appears that a half dozen or so basic ways of understanding the world undergird most of our untutored attempts to spontaneously make sense of the world. These basic modes allow us to decide very quickly if a novel entity is a living kind, an artifact, a nonliving natural kind, or a psychological entity and then to strongly interpret all other properties and potential causal relations in light of that initial grounding of the entity into a particular mode of understanding.

Theories versus Scripts, Schemas, and Skills

Cognitive science has adopted other ways of talking about mental structures responsible for explanation and prediction; and it is important to see why these structures are not the same as theories. The two most important cases involve scripts and schemas, which in many ways seem similar to theories in that they attempt to make sense of local domains of knowledge (e.g., Schank and Abelson, 1977). There is often not enough explicit information in a situation for us to properly make sense of what is happening. In such cases, an awareness of context may enable us to find coherence in a series of apparently disparate facts. The question "How do you feel?" elicits markedly different responses when asked by a neighbor, boss, internist, or therapist. We have all developed sets of established protocols that apply to frequently recurring types of situations, and we use these protocols to interpret events in those situations. For this reason, identical events in isolation can be interpreted in radically different ways when embedded in different conceptual schemas. These protocols have often been called scripts, and they have been extremely popular notions in certain areas of cognitive science and social psychology.

Despite the powers of scripts to aid in the prediction and interpretation of events, there are ways in which such scripts seem to be strikingly impoverished mental structures relative to theories, especially with respect to providing rich explanations. Consider, for example, the popular restaurant script (Schank and Abelson, 1977). It has been proposed that all of us develop scripts for what to expect in restaurants; and that indeed we may subdivide a general restaurant script into subscripts with sets of expectations about such things as coffee shops, family restaurants, fast-food restaurants, and places of fine dining. These scripts provide expectations about certain "actors," such as waiters, cooks, and maitre d's, and about certain "props," such as tables, counters, food, and bills. In doing so, the scripts led to local expectations about what actors are likely to do with what props. They do not, however, ask some of the most fundamental questions about why the restaurant is structured as it is. Questions about why we eat in restaurants, why we pay for service, what we eat, and indeed why restaurants should exist at all, are left unanswered even though they might seem at the core of knowing what a restaurant really is.

We can have mental structures that lead to local expectations and perhaps even represent causal relations, but that nonetheless do not provide any sense of deep explanation. Our scripts only seem to explain isolated event sequences near the "surface"; they do not explain why the event or entity should exist and why it has the properties it does. Scripts are also strongly biased toward interpreting events, as opposed to objects. Their abilities to understand even the most familiar objects, such as a dog, are strongly limited to knowing how that entity fits into various scenarios, a way of understanding that can lead to insights but is hardly a full account.

Some have argued that scripts may have a privileged status early in development and may even dominate the child's construction of concepts and representations of categories (e.g., Nelson, 1985). There are ways in which young children can be very sensitive to recurring event patterns; but there is much less evidence suggesting that this form of representation is really developmentally privileged or somehow the cradle of later theories (Keil, 1986).

The notions of schemes or schemas have been used in many ways throughout the history of psychology (e.g., Bartlett, 1932; Piaget, 1952), making any simple comparison to theories impossible. In general, however, they seem to fall to the same criticism as scripts. They lead to local expectations and anticipations and may provide ways of using contexts to enhance the perception and interpretation of an event. They do not, however, provide the deeper sense of explanation that allows us to understand why a class of things is the way it is. The same can be said for various well-developed skills, whether it be chess playing, Nintendo wizardry, or plumbing. The specific skill itself seems not to be enough to model the full sense of explanation, even though it may critically depend on some broader theoretical constructs. Scripts, schemas, and skills can take a body of information in a domain and allow us to make sense of it in ways that go beyond the correlational; but such an ability to go beyond immediate patterns of correlation is not enough to qualify as having a theory.

Skill can bring with it "blind spots" and lack of flexibility. The classic example is "set," in which a series of problems are solved in a particular way, and then a much simpler problem is presented that ends up being solved in the same convoluted manner because the learner is primed to consider all problems as solvable according to the same underlying structure. For example, subjects have been asked to generate a particular volume of liquid using three containers of a particular size. After solving a number of problems where the correct response involves pouring from the first container into the second and then pouring from the second container twice into the third, subjects have great difficulty solving a problem that can be solved much more directly by pouring from the first container directly into the third (Luchins, 1942). Many routines have this flavor, whether it be extraordinary difficulty in saying the alphabet backward, or the difficulty in adjusting to driving on the other side of the road, an arbitrary difference at a conceptual level, but one that can be much more complex at the level of skill. In general, automatization of skill, although organizing knowledge in meaningful ways that enhance memory capacity, also has the price of being closely bound to the sequence and conditions under which it was acquired. When parts of a theory become so automatic, they tend to leave the realm of theory altogether.

The power of theory lies in its ability to be responsive to data and develop further as a result. It tends not to move toward a crystallized and encapsulated form that is automatically executed, but rather to continuously evolve in ways that can encompass more and more relevant instances and better explain the old ones. Karmiloff-Smith (1992) describes school-age children who were told to balance various blocks. Unknown to the children, some of the blocks contained hidden weights that made them balance off-center. The youngest children utilized a data-driven response, using proprioceptive knowledge to balance the blocks. Older children attempted to stick to the principle that all blocks balanced in the center and would simply put aside the weighted blocks as anomalies not to be dealt with, and focused their efforts on the blocks that were consistent with the principle. This principle was too isolated and inflexible to be effective. The oldest children dealt with the anomalous data by incorporating notions of torque into their representations, thereby having more flexible structures that seemed more like true theories. Only the oldest children behaved in truly theory-like manner because only they recognized the need for a rich set of interconnected principles that enabled them to flexibly respond to new data. The younger children seemed to be more bound to schemes and local skill routines.

We have stressed a central role to mechanism and explanation in a theory. The oldest children in the Karmiloff-Smith study were not simply tabulating experience and coming up with a single blind principle. Rather than simply concluding that the center is always the balancing point, they were able to conclude what it is about the center that makes it the usual balancing point and under what conditions (e.g., on a seesaw) the center will not be the balancing point. By grasping the underlying mechanism more fully, they developed a much richer, more flexible, and theory-like structure. It may well be in such cases that we want to think of a continuum from very simple schemes and skills to more complex scripts to theories, where theory does not suddenly emerge at a magical point but becomes more and more compelling as the mental representations elaborate into a rich set of principles that capture a general mechanism applicable to a truly representative range of events.

Theories are therefore inherently incompatible with "black box" models of the mind, models that have children simply predicting the proper outcome of behavior without any real understanding of the process. The extreme black box cases are seen in other species where trajectory anticipation is obviously done without any understanding of classical mechanics and aerodynamics, or sonar guidance is performed without any understanding of acoustics. People have such black boxes as well, both innate and acquired through heavily practiced and automatized skills, but they can also explain and understand their worlds in richer, deeper, and more flexible terms. For related reasons, theories are more than a "reading off" of reality that is done by simulating the situation in the mind and then predicting what will occur (Harris, 1991). Children who anticipate trajectories of balls may well use black box routines to help them catch a ball (although adults may well have such routines much better developed and automatized); but they also have deeper theorylike understandings of the ball's movement, an understanding that may well diverge somewhat from contemporary physics and aerodynamics but which is a theory nonetheless. It is thus quite likely that in many cases, the child may interact with objects in ways that rely more on an intuitive theory and less on a highly automatized, heavily practiced routine that is much more black box-like in nature. This developmental sequence is directly at odds with many first impressions of how knowledge of objects might develop. Thus early motor actions on objects may be purer and more direct reflections of intuitively developed theories than later actions that are often simple executions of encapsulated black box routines. Another indication of this kind of shift occurs when stroke patients or other victims of neurological damage have to relearn motor activities such as walking. Under those circumstances, they are forced to once again consider theoretical aspects of the task.

Theories, Experience, and Expertise

Discussions of scripts, schemas, and theories invariably bring up questions of how knowledge becomes organized in areas of expertise. In talking about the emergence of cognitive competence, it is important to recognize the difference between experience and expertise. Experience can often lead to lack of flexibility and mindless automaticity, but true expertise can be conceived of as transcending that inflexibility. Bereiter and Scardamalia (1993) develop an account where the expert does more than merely fit new circumstances to the most similar past experience. The expert is always expanding the frontiers of his or her knowledge and considers ways in which a new experience might require a different kind of conception.

In the sense meant here, experienced nurses will find that they have fewer and fewer questions that require consultation with others, and that in general, the nursing job becomes more and more routinized as the years go on. The true expert, on the other hand, will still see new problems and challenges, but they will be changing and evolving over the years as a reflection of underlying conceptual change. While some aspects of the job no longer tax the expert's abilities, other aspects that were not even issues in prior years become more fully addressed.

Expertise itself might require many years to develop if it is defined as requiring both ample experience and the ability to handle novel situations; but expert-like behavior can be exhibited by both novices and children. In such cases the learner is constantly trying to construct new and better knowledge structures for handling a problem, rather than merely trying to shoehorn the problem into older conceptions. This contrast of course is reminiscent of Piaget's contrast between accommodation and assimilation. The contrasting styles of learning have been observed in countless studies. For example, when music learners are presented with a style of music they have not previously encountered, some students try to find parallels with older forms that they know (Ghent, 1989), much as the children in Karmiloff-Smith's study tried to fit weighted blocks with their center of gravity rule. The expert learners, on the other hand, are able to create a new category to fit the novel style and try to incorporate it on its own terms. They are willing to expand the limits of their previous knowledge and adapt the knowledge to fit the data.

A primary goal of education is to enable students to think for themselves and to expand the horizons of their lives and societies rather than repeat blindly and in lockstep fashion that which has been presented to them. Just as important as teaching a particular body of knowledge is equipping children to interact with that knowledge in deep and meaningful ways. If we want to teach children to be more expertlike in this sense, intuitive theories about natural kinds are an especially good place to start. For as we shall see, here the insights are essentially unbounded and the learner can constantly explore new frontiers of causal understanding. There is no pat set of things to be learned but an essentially unbounded set of rich and increasingly deep causal patternings to uncover. For those reasons, teaching and learning about natural kinds may promote the kind of flexible, exploratory learning more than any other type.

Theories and Natural Kinds

Intuitive theories may have initially developed primarily to explain natural kinds. For most of human history, the natural world so dominated daily human experience that natural kinds were a major focus of theories (Atran, 1987, see also this volume, chap. 28). Such a heavy focus almost certainly also exists today, but it may be masked somewhat by a world filled with artifacts and social constructions. Because schooling has so much more emphasized learning about socially constructed information, such as written language and arithmetic, and because even learning in many traditional cultures revolves around apprenticeships concerning expertise with artifacts, it may seem that, in an educational context, thought about natural kinds is uninteresting or irrelevant; or at the least, that the way most instruction is done for other sorts of kinds could easily be extended to natural kinds. This pattern of assumptions is risky, for intuitive theories about natural kinds are likely to have a distinct kind of structure that is intimately related to what natural kinds are themselves. For that reason, it is important here to talk about what natural kinds are and are not (see also Keil, 1995).

Natural kinds are not simply naturally occurring classes of things; for such classes include groups that seem to be defined by arbitrary collections of properties that make no theoretical sense. For example, things whose mean temperature was below freezing or above boiling temperatures of water on July 11, 1994, may represent a naturally occurring class of objects, but hardly one that would seem to be a theoretically coherent group that supports rich induction. We can proliferate other such meaningless but naturally occurring classes endlessly: things whose English name contains two or more vowels, things that conduct electricity and are symmetrical on two orthogonal axes, or even red things. Natural kinds are more than such classes because they correspond to things that have a much richer set of causal relations governing their properties and property interactions.

Natural kinds also need not currently exist, as is the case for extinct species of plants and animals; indeed they may not even have yet existed, such as a class of galaxy types that will only occur when the universe is five billion years older. The reason that both nonexistent things can be considered natural kinds is that at some point in time they did exist or will exist as a consequence of naturally occurring causal patterns.

The same physical entity can be a member of more than one natural kind. This key point is often overlooked and can lead to gross misunderstandings of what natural kinds are, how they should be studied, and how we might teach another about them. The human being is perhaps the best example. A person can be understood as a brute physical object subject to the laws governing all solid objects. A person can also be understood as a biological kind individuated by genetic and physiological factors. And finally, the same person can be understood as a psychological kind. Many other examples can also be offered.

Natural kinds may rarely if ever have real essences in terms of a set of singly necessary and jointly sufficient features. In spite of frequent assumptions of such essences for both living kinds and many compounds and elements, such assumptions are usually wrong. For example, there is no fixed nucleotide sequence that corresponds to tigerhood. Tiger DNA is a distribution of sequences in which there is huge overlap among all tigers but perhaps no fixed sequence that all tigers must have. At the same time, tigers are far more than a simple family resemblance structure of properties. Tigers form a natural kind because their properties tend to form a stable unit such that similar clusters are perpetuated over time both within and across lifetimes. There are converging causal forces in the world that result in many properties of tigers supporting the presence of others, such that the full complex of features becomes a stable entity. Those causal convergences are much closer to the real essence of natural kinds than is any list of properties. It has been suggested that we think of these mutually supporting properties as a property "homeostasis" model, much like homeostasis in living kinds (Boyd, 1984). The homeostasis notion does help capture the idea that the property clusters exist because of a kind of dynamic equilibrium (Keil, 1995).

These distinctive properties of natural kinds raise the very real possibility that theories about natural kinds might emerge differently in children and end up being importantly different in adults. If natural kinds exist independently of human activities, and if their property clusters are the result of stable causal patternings, any successful theory of natural kinds must gain at least a partial insight into those causal patternings, patternings that would seem to have a distinctive nature different from those for artifacts or various social constructs. Some have argued that natural kinds themselves are the product of arbitrary human categorizations and individual and societal needs (Dupré, 1981); but such an argument fails to explain the real occurrence of natural kinds and adopts a kind of antirealist stance that questions the ability of any science to make progress (Keil, 1989; Salmon, 1989).

To understand the potentially distinctive aspects of instruction about natural kinds, we start with the more general question of how we might involve intuitive theories in instruction, and based on that discussion we turn to the case of theories of natural kinds. We assume that intuitive theories of the richest and most prevalent types are those we see for natural kinds.

Educational Implications and Consequences

Natural kinds offer an ideal playing field for the nurturance and instruction of theoretical/explanatory thought. Much of the groundwork is already present in the form of intuitive theories. Young preschoolers already have some explanatory biases about a wide range of natural phenomena, whether they be plants, human personality, or substances. It seems obvious that instruction should seize on this structure and exploit it, so that children get a sense of continuity between their own spontaneous inquiries about the world and those inquiries that are guided by instruction. Instruction should clearly be concerned with enhancing theoretical and explanatory knowledge; in practice, however, it rarely is.

The expertise literature does not offer an easy answer on how to gain theoretical insight. It typically emphasizes the role of knowledge and experience in the

efficacy of the expert, with ten years of experience said to be needed for true expertise in such varied areas as chess, music performance, art, and medicine. Sheer
expertise can enable tremendously speeded performance on tasks of enormous
apparent complexity, whether it be sorting of physics problems or contemplating
chess moves. Though often correlated, great expertise and theoretical depth are
not the same or necessarily dependent on each other. Often they are related because expertise allows access to a large and efficiently organized database of information that then can be used much more powerfully to develop theoretical insights.
But the phenomenon of expertise does not in itself explain what it means to have
theoretical insight, and as argued earlier, great expertise can often exist and operate very effectively without any real evidence of an underlying theory. Conversely, we can come to a profound theoretical insight in an area where we may
have only modest experience. Thus, in science, the most profound discoveries are
often made by very young scientists, who are able to take a fresh look at a problem
precisely because they have not yet developed the massive numbers of implicit
correlations that tend to skew their thinking in a particular direction.

Again, we have here a reminder of a past point. The associative part of cognition can capture much of what many forms of expertise seem to be; but it cannot
capture theory and explanation even when that is an important part of expertise
or takes us beyond a highly speeded skill.

The frameworks provided by naive theories of natural kinds often make otherwise computationally impossible tasks tractable. There are incalculably many
correlations and patterns to notice in any natural event, and it is often our theories that sharply constrain what we think is relevant for further analysis. This
may be one sense in which situated cognition is of some help. While cognition
may not spontaneously emerge out of an environment, in many natural environments, the context triggers a theoretical framework that greatly reduces the complexity of the problem (Norman, 1993). Consider, for example, a decision about
how to ford a potentially dangerous stream. The range of possible actions is unlimited, and the simple presence of a goal—to get to the other side—is not a
sufficient constraint because an enormity of possible actions still remains. Powerful constraints, however, are provided by what is believed about the support and
strength properties of various objects such as tree limbs and stones, about the
velocity of the stream and its physical consequences on a human body, and so on.

One of the reasons that it may be so difficult to design a robot that can intelligently navigate the environment may be precisely because so little account is
taken of the natural constraints of the environment. A child does not have to be
taught not to walk through walls or off cliffs; even children know that they must
place their feet on solid ground to move forward, and they automatically constrain their navigational choices to ones that the environment supports.

For these reasons, the classical account of the highest level of natural scientific
reasoning, formal operations (Inhelder and Piaget, 1958), may be of little use.
The endpoint of learning is not becoming a systematic tester; as our knowledge
advances the number of possible things to test proliferates at exponential or even
geometric rates. One makes the problem tractable by pruning the search trees by

means of theories. Invoking the relevant theories can do this to an enormous extent. Instruction can be enormously effective when it recognizes the value of helping the learner see and exploit such relevancy relations. Nowhere is this instructional strategy likely to be more effective than with natural kinds.

Contrast this sort of "relevancy" instruction with the more common "canned experiment" used in most science curricula. Tasks are often chosen for their immediate perceptual appeal—hence the great popularity of science "magic" demonstrations, where the "oohs" and "ahs" are thought to provide the motivation for later instruction. But such tasks usually do not lead to enhancement of exploratory strategies.

A teacher, for example, who splits the stem of a white carnation and dyes half of it red by dipping it into red ink illustrates the uptake of liquids through stems in an attention-getting manner, but unless the study is extended past this point, it offers little that is conceptually richer than a textbook account. Yet the experiment raises many questions. Do some kinds of stems work better than others? Are there natural habitats that "dye" their plantlife in this way? Are there analogues in other living kinds? How long does it take for the dye to be transmitted? How can this process be speeded up? Slowed down? Over what distance will this work? Why? How can we find out the answers to these questions? Suddenly, the original experiment becomes important as a baseline for knowledge and theorizing. If the teacher thinks these particular questions are not important to the subject at hand, then the original experiment is also one that had little pedagogical purpose.

Another problem with canned experiments, and for that matter, with mathematical exploration programs—both touted as making learning come alive with their hands-on approach—is that the teacher knows the questions and the answers and is merely guiding the child to the answer the teacher wants to reach. There is no real problem to solve, so there is no need to deal with the matter theoretically. There is no need to develop a sense of what avenues might be fruitful, and which ideas are worth spending time on. In the end, these explorations become no more than fancy ways of storing knowledge.

A further point is that experiential programs too often focus on children discovering findings on their own. In fact, as mentioned above, theory is rarely used in our daily life to make predictions. Surely, not all children will grow up to be scientists, and even those that do will become expert in only a small corner of the universe of knowledge. The goal of education, then, is not to systematically test, and attempt to disprove, all the facts that we encounter. Rather, it is important to develop criteria for evaluating the conclusions of others.

We must teach children to see what arguments are plausible on the basis of what they know. If something sounds too good to be true, maybe it is false! If children read a claim about apes mastering language, what experience can they draw on to evaluate this claim? What do they know about their own pets' understanding of language? In what way do they think thought is related to language? What kind of performance would they be willing to consider as language? The most useful and efficient kinds of experiments to run in many instances may be armchair speculations.

Children's experience, intuitions, and theories about natural kinds offer a ripe ground for them developing criteria for the evaluation of knowledge. It is a rich area for having them consider how plausible or useful an explanation is, and the power and potential of a particular theoretical approach. It tells them what sort of properties and what kinds of causal patternings are likely to be fruitfully explored.

Natural kinds, by virtue of their rich causal structures, are an excellent domain for teaching expertlike analysis and thoughtful evaluation, but these approaches can later be applied to other parts of the curriculum as well. History and literature lend themselves naturally to social theories. Which theories give coherent accounts for historical events? When should we suspect bias or propaganda in an explanation? There is no laboratory for the systematic testing of historical revisionism, but children can learn to sharpen their abilities for detecting distortions. An understanding of an age can allow them the ability to recognize anachronistic approaches. In addition to deepening understanding and evaluative skills, a theoretical approach can also enhance memory by linking many disparate facts into a coherent whole.

In sum, as educators, we should recognize first that thinking is often guided by innately determined modes of construal. Teaching consists of showing the relevance of already known systems of explanation, and then fleshing them out in each instance. We rarely build up totally new modes of explanation, though revision of older concepts may be necessary.

Second, the powerful capacity of the mind to chart associations, frequently without conscious awareness, can be a source of deep intuition. In some cases, these intuitions will be of immense value in helping theoretical notions to advance; in others, the intuitions may be at odds with explicitly learned theories. It is helpful to recognize that these misconceptions are not so much errors as a reflection of a particular subset of experience. The teacher can then help place these intuitions into an appropriate context, so that they will advance the general theories rather than conflict with them.

Third, the notion of "essence" as reflecting a deep causal structure is a useful one in developing evaluative abilities over a large variety of educational experiences. Although it is impossible to study or test in detail all of the knowledge in an area, we can give children the tools to evaluate the kinds of information that are likely to be true. Children should know that biological arguments should appeal to physical and chemical processes, and that social arguments should appeal to psychological entities like intention and beliefs. While they may not be able to spell out a process in detail, they should, and do, have a sense of what a reasonable process should look like. The teacher, in calling a child's attention to these abilities, gives the child a powerful tool for navigating schooling and later learning.

The study of natural kinds, with an emphasis on the nature of theories, thus becomes a powerful gateway for the development of expertlike growth. We can teach children to think about the underlying assumptions they hold, probe their implications, evaluate truth claims, and ultimately, further the boundaries of knowledge in the areas that capture them most.

Acknowledgments

We gratefully acknowledge David Olson for his extensive comments on an earlier draft of this paper. Much of the research reported in this paper was supported by NIH grant R01-HD23922, awarded to Frank C. Keil, and an NSF graduate fellowship and Olin graduate fellowship awarded to Chana S. Silberstein.

References

Atran, S. (1987). *Cognitive foundations of natural history.* New York: Cambridge University Press.

Atran, S. (1994). Core domains versus scientific theories: Evidence from systematics and Itza-Maya folkbiology. In L. A. Hirschfeld and S. A. Gelman (Eds.), *Mapping the mind: Domain specificity in cognition and culture* (pp. 316–340). Cambridge, England: Cambridge University Press.

Astington, J. W. (1993). *The child's discovery of the mind.* Cambridge: Harvard University Press.

Baillargeon, R. (1987). Young infants' reasoning about the physical and spatial characteristics of a hidden object. *Cognitive Development, 2,* 179–200.

Baillargeon, R., Kotovsky, L., and Needham, A. (1995). The acquisition of physical knowledge in infancy. In D. Sperber, D. Premack, and A. Premack (Eds.), *Causal cognition: A multidisciplinary debate* (pp. 79–116). Oxford, England: Oxford University Press.

Barret, S. E., Abdi, H., and Murphy, G. L. (1993). Theory-based correlations and their role in children's concepts. *Child Development, 64* (6), 1595–1616.

Barsalou, L. W. (1985). Ideals, central tendency, and frequency of instantiation as determinants of graded structure in categories. *Journal of Experimental Psychology: Learning, Memory, and Cognition, 11,* 629–654.

Bartlett, R. C. (1932). *Remembering: A study in experimental and social psychology.* Cambridge, England: Cambridge University Press.

Bereiter, C. and Scardamalia, M. (1993). *Surpassing ourselves: An inquiry into the nature and implications of expertise.* Chicago: Open Court.

Berry, D. C. and Dienes, Z. (1993). *Implicit learning: Theoretical and empirical issues.* Hove, England: Lawrence Erlbaum.

Boyd, R. (1984). *Natural kinds, homeostasis, and the limits of essentialism.* Paper presented at Cornell University.

Brown, A. L., Bransford, J. D., Ferrara, R. A., and Campione, J. C. (1983). Cognitive development. In J. H. Flavell and E. M. Markman (Eds.), *Handbook of Child Psychology* (pp. 77–166). New York: Wiley.

Bruer, J. T. (1993). *Schools for thought: A science of learning in the classroom.* Cambridge: MIT Press.

Carey, S. (1985). *Conceptual change in childhood.* Cambridge: MIT Press.

Carey, S. (1991). Knowledge acquisition: Enrichment or conceptual change? In S. Carey and R. Gelman (Eds.), *The epigenesis of mind: Essays on biology and cognition* (pp. 237–256). Hillsdale, NJ: Lawrence Erlbaum.

Chapman, L. J. and Chapman, J. P. (1969). Illusory correlation as an obstacle to the use of valid psychodiagnostic signs. *Journal of Abnormal Psychology, 74,* 272–280.

Chi, M. T. H., Feltovich, P. J., and Glaser, R. (1981). Categorization and representation of physics problems by experts and novices. *Cognitive Science*, 5, 121–152.

Chinn, C. A. and Brewer, W. F. (1993). The role of anomalous data in knowledge acquisition: A theoretical framework and implications for science instruction. *Review of Educational Research*, 63 (1), 1–49.

Cleeremans, A. (1993). *Mechanisms of implicit learning: Connectionist models of sequence processing*. Cambridge: MIT Press.

Dupré, J. (1981). Biological taxa as natural kinds. *Philosophical Review*, 90, 66–90.

Gelman, R. (1990). First principles organize attention to and learning about relevant data: Number and animate–inanimate distinction as examples. *Cognitive Science*, 14, 79–106.

Gelman, R., Spelke, E. S., and Meck, E. (1983). What preschoolers know about animate and inanimate objects. In D. Rogers and J. A. Sloboda (Eds.), *The acquisition of symbolic skills* (pp. 48–64). New York: Plenum Press.

Gelman, S. A. (1988). The development of induction within natural kind and artifact categories. *Cognitive Psychology*, 20, 65–95.

Gelman, S. A., and Markman, E. (1986). Categories and induction in young children. *Cognition*, 23, 183–209.

Gelman, S. A. and Markman, E. (1987). Young children's inductions from natural kinds: The role of categories and appearances. *Child Development*, 58, 1532–1541.

Gelman, S. A. and O'Reilly, A. W. (1988). Children's inductive inferences with superordinate categories: The role of language and category structure. *Child Development*, 59, 876–887.

Gelman, S. A. and Wellman, H. M. (1991). Insides and essences: Early understandings of the non-obvious. *Cognition*, 38, 213–244.

Ghent, P. (1989). *Expert learning in music*. Master's thesis, University of Toronto.

Gibson, E. J. (1969). *Principles of perceptual and cognitive development*. New York: Appleton-Century-Crofts.

Gopnik, A. and Wellman, H. M. (1994). The theory theory. In L. A. Hirschfeld and S. A. Gelman (Eds.), *Mapping the mind: Domain specificity in cognition and culture* (pp. 257–293). New York: Cambridge University Press.

Harré, R. (1988). Modes of explanation. In D. J. Hilton (Ed.), *Contemporary science and natural explanation: Commonsense conceptions of causality*. Brighton, England: Harvester Press.

Harris, P. L. (1991). The work of the imagination. In A. Whiten (Ed.), *Natural theories of mind: Evolution, development and simulation of everyday mindreading* (pp. 283–304). Oxford, England: Blackwell Publishers.

Hayes, N. A. and Broadbent, D. (1988). Two modes of learning for interactive tasks. *Cognition*, 28 (3), 249–276.

Hirschfeld, L. A. and Gelman, S. A. (1994). Towards a topography of mind. In L. A. Hirschfeld and S. A. Gelman (Eds.), *Mapping the mind: Domain specificity in cognition and culture* (pp. 3–35). New York: Cambridge University Press.

Inhelder, B. and Piaget, J. (1958). *The growth of logical thinking from childhood to adolescence*. New York: Basic Books.

Kaiser, M. K., McCloskey, M., and Proffitt, D. R. (1986). Development of intuitive theories of motion: Curvilinear motion in the absence of external forces. *Developmental Psychology*, 22 (1), 67–71.

Karmiloff-Smith, A. (1992). *Beyond modularity: A developmental perspective*. Cambridge: MIT Press.

Keil, F. C. (1981). Constraints on knowledge and cognitive development. *Psychological Review, 88*, 197–227.

Keil, F. C. (1986). The nonrepresentative nature of representational change: Some possible morals to draw from Nelson's Making Sense. *Cognitive Development, 1*, 281–291.

Keil, F. C. (1989). *Concepts, kinds, and cognitive development*. Cambridge: MIT Press.

Keil, F. C. (1994). The birth and nurturance of concepts by domains: The origins of concepts of living things. In L. Hirschfeld and S. Gelman (Eds.), *Mapping the mind: Domain specificity in cognition and culture* (pp. 234–254). Cambridge, England: Cambridge University Press.

Keil, F. C. (1995). The growth of causal understandings of natural kinds. In D. Sperber, D. Premack, and A. Premack (Eds.), *Causal cognition: A multidisciplinary debate*. Oxford, England: Oxford University Press.

Kekule, A. (1858). Über die Konstitution und die Metamorphosen der chemischen Verbindungen und die chemische Natur des Kohlenstoffs (On the constitution and metamorphasis of chemical reactions and the chemical nature of carbons). *Ann Chem u Pharm, 106*, 129–159.

Krist, H., Fieberg, E. L., and Wilkening, F. (1993). Intuitive physics in action and judgment: The development of knowledge about projectile motion. *Journal of Experimental Psychology: Learning, Memory, and Cognition, 19* (4), 952–966.

Leslie, A. (1994). Tomy, Toby, and agency: Core architecture and domain specificity. In L. Hirschfeld and S. Gelman (Eds.), *Mapping the mind: Domain specificity in cognition and culture* (pp. 119–48). Cambridge, England: Cambridge University Press.

Luchins, A. S. (1942). Mechanization in problem solving: The effect of einstellung. *Psychological Monographs, 54 (Whole No. 248)*.

Mandler, J. M. and McDonough, L. (1993). Concept formation in infancy. *Cognitive Development, 8*, 291–318.

McCloskey, M., Washburn, A., and Felch, L. (1983). Intuitive physics: The straight down belief and its origin. *Journal of Experimental Psychology: Learning, Memory, and Cognition, 9* (4), 636–649.

Medin, D. L. (1989). Concepts and conceptual structure. *American Psychologist, 44*, 1469–1481.

Mintzes, J. J., Trowbridge, J. E., Arnaudin, M. W., and Wandersee, J. H. (1991). Children's biology: Studies on conceptual development in the life sciences. In S. Glynn, R. Yeany, and B. Britton (Eds.), *The psychology of learning science* (pp. 179–202). Hillsdale, NJ: Lawrence Erlbaum.

Murphy, G. L. (1993). Noun phrase interpretation and conceptual combination. *Journal of Memory and Language, 29*, 259–288.

Murphy, L., and Medin, D. L. (1985). The role of theories in conceptual coherence. *Psychological Review, 92*, 289–316.

Neisser, U. (1987). Introduction in U. Neisser (Ed.), *Concepts reconsidered: The ecological and intellectual bases of categorization*. Cambridge, England: Cambridge University Press.

Nelson, K. (1985). *Making sense: The acquisition of shared meaning*. Orlando, FL: Academic Press.

Nisbett, R. E. and Ross, L. (1980). *Human inference: Strategies and shortcomings of social judgment*. Englewood Cliffs, NJ: Prentice-Hall.

Norman, D. (1993). *Things that make us smart: Defending human attributes in the age of the machine*. Reading, Mass.: Addison-Wesley.

Olson, D. R. (1977). The languages of instruction: The literate bias of schooling. In R. C. Anderson, R. J. Spiro, and W. E. Montague (Eds.), *Schooling and the acquisition of knowledge* (pp. 65–89). Hillsdale, NJ: Lawrence Erlbaum.

Piaget, J. (1952). *The origins of intelligence in children.* New York: Norton.

Perner, J. (1991). *Understanding the representional mind.* Cambridge: MIT Press.

Quine, W. V. O. (1977). Natural kinds. In S. P. Schwartz (Ed.), *Naming, necessity, and natural kinds* (pp. 155–175). Ithaca, NY: Cornell University Press.

Reber, A. (1993). *Implicit learning and tacit knowledge: An essay on the cognitive unconscious.* New York: Oxford University Press.

Rips, L. J. (1989). Similarity, typicality, and categorization. In S. Vosniadou and A. Ortony (Eds.), *Similarity and analogical reasoning* (pp. 21–59). New York: Cambridge University Press.

Salmon, W. C. (1989). *Four decades of scientific explanation.* Minneapolis: University of Minnesota Press.

Schank, C. C. and Abelson, R. P. (1977). *Scripts, plans, goals and understanding.* Hillsdale, NJ: Lawrence Erlbaum.

Schwartz, B. (1979). *Psychology of learning and behavior.* New York: Norton.

Smith, C., Carey, S., and Wiser, M. (1985). On differentiation: A case study of the development of the concepts of size, weight, and density. *Cognition, 1985, 21* (3), 177–237.

Spelke, E. (1991). Physical knowledge in infancy. In S. Carey and R. Gelman (Ed.), *The epigenesis of mind: Essays on biology and cognition* (pp. 133–169). Hillsdale, NJ: Lawrence Erlbaum.

Spelke, E., Breinlinger, K., Macomber, J., and Jacobson, K. (1992). Origins of knowledge. *Psychological Review, 95,* 605–632.

Sperber, D. and Wilson, D. (1986). *Relevance: Communication and cognition.* Oxford, England: Blackwell Publishers.

Strauss, S. and Shilony, T. (1994). Teachers' models of children's minds and learning. In L. A. Hirschfeld and S. A. Gelman (Eds.), *Mapping the mind: Domain specificity in cognition and culture* (pp. 455–473). New York: Cambridge University Press.

Vosniadou, S. (1991). Conceptual development in astronomy. In S. Glynn, R. Yeany, and B. Britton (Eds.), *The psychology of learning science* (pp. 149–177). Hillsdale, NJ: Lawrence Erlbaum.

Vosniadou, S. and Brewer, W. F. (1992). Mental models of the earth: A study of conceptual change in childhood. *Cognitive Psychology, 24,* 535–585.

Wellman, H. M. (1990). *The child's theory of mind.* Cambridge: MIT Press.

Wellman, H. M. and Gelman, S. A. (1992). Cognitive development: Foundational theories of core domains. *Annual Review of Psychology, 43,* 337–375.

28

From Folk Biology to Scientific Biology

SCOTT ATRAN

Introduction: The Cognitive Universality of Biology

Humans everywhere, it appears, have similar folk-biological schemata composed of essence-based species and rank ordering of species into lower-order and higher-order groups. To some extent, these groups within groups represent the routine products of innate "habits of mind," naturally selected to grasp relevant and recurrent "habits of the world." They are not as arbitrary, and hence not as variable across cultures as, say, the gathering of stars in constellations.

In the history of biology, or natural history, a series of taxonomic types emerged to provide a system of reference for the comparative study of organisms. It is by developing notions of species, genera, families, and classes that natural historians managed to progressively standardize what was already—at least to some extent—common to the viewpoints of ordinary people everywhere. Ultimately, this framework would provide a practical basis for the comprehensive survey of living beings the world over, and a conceptual foundation for the theoretical elaboration of their interrelations. This elaboration would finally embrace all living kinds—including humankind—into a *theory* of biology.

The Folk Species Concept

All human beings, it appears, classify animals and plants into basic groupings that are "quite as obvious to [the] modern scientist as to a Guaraní Indian" (Simpson, 1961, p. 57). This is the concept of the (folk) species. It provides the primary locus for thinking about biology among laypersons the world over. Historically, it provided a transtheoretical basis for scientific speculation about the biological world in that different biological theories—including evolutionary theory—have sought to account for the apparent constancy of species and for the apparent similarities and differences between species (Wallace, 1889, p. 1; cf. Mayr, 1969, p. 37).

Modes of Causal Thinking

The human mind seems to be endowed with domain-specific schemata—that is, with fundamentally distinct modes of causal thinking about the world. A distinct mode of causal thinking is a distinct way of thinking about the (necessary and sufficient) conditions that relate causes to effects. The focus here is on one particular natural-category domain: nonhuman living things—that is, kinds of animals and plants.[1]

The idea of different modes of causal thinking is not new, of course. Aristotle, for example, argued that ordinary modes of causal attribution differ for naturally occurring physical substances and living kinds, on the one hand, and artifacts, on the other. For Aristotle, the causal connections governing the interactions and changes in the states of substances and living kinds are determined by causal principles (*aitia*) intrinsic to their underlying physical natures (*physis*). By contrast, the causal schema that determines what (kind of) thing an artifact is is necessarily (although perhaps not sufficiently) determined by external agencies, including the intentions emanating from the soul (*psyche*) of the artisan or user (Atran, 1985).

Descartes (1681) held that the mechanical causes (*mécanisme*) governing the behavior of bodies (*corps*) were of a fundamentally different ontological sort than those that produced and agitated the mind (*esprit*). Kant (1790/1951) argued that judgment (*urteilskraft*) about the nature of living kinds is unavoidably teleological (*teleologisch*), whether or not the only true causal mechanisms that pervade the cosmos are in fact contingent and mechanical. Arguably, such distinct modes of causal attribution are good candidates for what Hume (1758/1955) called "that original stock of ideas" that the mind is never altogether free of (even the mechanically minded scientist). As Geoffrey Lloyd (1990) suggests, the unitary notion of "cause" in Western science, like that of "nature," may have no directly corresponding notions in Classical China or in other historical traditions, and is thus an unlikely concept of universal common sense.

Although modern science strives to unify all kinds of causal processes under a single system of contingent, mechanical relationships (push/pull, clockwork, etc.), recent work in cognitive anthropology and developmental psychology suggests that even people in our own culture initially do not spontaneously reason this way, and may never do so. Thus from very early childhood and through all of adult life, people seem to think differently about different domains (Atran and Sperber, 1991; Wellman and Gelman, 1992), including the domains of "naive physics" (Baillargeon, 1986; Spelke, 1990; Carey et al., 1992), "naive biology" (Atran, 1987; Keil, 1989; Gelman and Wellman, 1991), "naive psychology" (Leslie, 1995; Astington and Gopnik, 1991; Avis and Harris, 1991), and "naive sociology" (Turiel, 1983; Cosmides and Tooby, 1992; Hirschfeld, 1994). People attribute *contingent* motions to inert object substances, spontaneous actions and *teleological* developments to species of animals and plants (e.g., internally directed growth and inheritance of related parts and whole), *intentional* relationships to one another's beliefs, desires, and actions, and group assignments (e.g., kinship, race) that specify a range of *deontological* obligations and contractual actions.

The Perception of Living Kinds: The Role of Teleology

Each of these "conceptual modules"—folk physics, folk biology, folk psychology, and folk sociology—targets a somewhat different database as input in order to structure it in a distinct way as output (i.e., as domain-specific representations). For example, the categorization of an organism as a kind of living thing, such as a dog, involves selective attention to certain perceptible features of the world. The selected features may involve various aspects of the object's shape, size, movement, texture, sound, and smell. But the selection process itself is driven, at least in part, by a set of causal presumptions to the effect that the living world categorically divides into well-bounded types, regardless of the degree of morphological variation that may actually exist or be observed within or between different kinds: for example, DOG (including puppies, poodles, and huskies), TOAD (including tadpoles), OAK (including saplings and bonsais) and TIGER (including cubs, dwarfs and three-legged albino mutants).

By constraining input in these ways, such teleological schemata generate categories of living things that more or less correspond to biological species (or genera of closely related species). These teleological presumptions invariably correlate some or all of the following: spontaneous movements, functional relationships between perceptibly heterogeneous parts, canonical patterns of behavioral or morphological change, visibly variable outsides as indicators of less variable but largely imperceptible insides, reproduction and inheritance of all the above. Consider the following.

In the first year of life, children clearly pay special attention to an animal's spontaneous movements at unpredictably odd angles, rather than to the externally directed and predictably contingent motions that drive perception of inert solid objects. Moreover, children just as obviously expect that animals that disappear from sight will move and interact as animals are wont to, and not as they expect billiard balls to (Spelke et al., 1992; Mandler, 1992). General aspects of movement, shape, and size, however, are not the only "perceptual" features "selected" by the causal schema for living kinds. Sound, color, smell, and tactile sensibilities are also involved in subtle ways.[2]

Different species trigger different ways of causally weighting the contributions of various sorts of perceptual stimuli in recognizing different living kinds (Boster and D'Andrade, 1989). In some cases, movement and shape are secondary or irrelevant: for example, canopy birds of the rain forest may be recognized and taxonomically diagnosed by their song pattern alone, whereas the intermediate classification of different cactus plants typically involves color, contour, and tactile dimensions rather than size or bounded form (e.g., a mature, three-inch-high cactus ball with four-inch spikes may be classed with a three-branched, seven-foot-high slender cactus with barely perceptible prickles).

By the age of three or four, children will even "perceive" morphologically very different tokens of an animal kind (e.g., caterpillar, chrysalis, and butterfly) or plant kind (e.g., saplings and mighty oaks from acorns grow) as being states of the *same* complex, self-preserving being (Springer and Keil, 1989; Hickling and Gelman, 1992). A reasonably "correct" appreciation of allowable morphological variation within a folk species may take a few years of environmental observation to learn. But the fact that young children mistakenly assent to the possibility of a biological transformation between morphologically distinct species, far from indicating a general failure to essentially distinguish biological species, could well indicate the child's continuing search for allowable expressions of nonobvious morphological variation.

For example, children who "incorrectly" allow that beetles become frogs (Keil, 1989; Jeyifous, 1985) may thus be relying on the same ability that allows them to adduce that tadpoles become frogs. A three-year-old Mayan child who erringly believes that "a young *karanto* vine, growing under the spreading branches of an *'iw* tree which it in no way resembles [may be] called *yal 'iw* [baby 'iw]" (Stross, 1973, p. 132), thereby understands that (1) a "baby" sapling, living in the environment of a "parent" tree, will grow up to be that tree; and (2) saplings in general are not herbs but trees, although they may look like herbs. In this way, a Mayan or an American child comes to much the same taxonomic understanding that a Tobelorese child in Indonesia comes to: for example, the ability to judge "of a particular small sapling...this is not a (member of the) herbaceous weed class [*o rurubu*], it is a tree [*gota*]" (Taylor, 1979, p. 224).

Even very young children will tend to attribute the rich characteristic structure of living things to very "abstract," informationally poor stimuli that clearly go beyond the information given. For example, they may readily take as representations of living things closed two-dimensional figures that have irregular protruding parts. For a given drawing, children will ask what the protruding part is purposively "for" if they are primed to believe that the drawing represents a prickly plant rather than, say, a prickly mineral (Keil, 1994). The teleological presumption of living things as organized hierarchies of complementary functions that serve the species is a psychologically crucial element to understanding: the relations between physiology and morphology, disease as the derangement of function, and the systematic relationships between living kinds (ultimately including evolutionary theory).

The Folk Species Concept: Its Bearing on Cognitive Evolution

From the standpoint of hominid evolution, the concept of such a deep kind plausibly represents a balancing act between what our ancestors could and could not afford to ignore about their environment. Humans evolved in a world where knowing whether a locally occurring species of animal or plant was harmful or beneficial was necessary for survival: They could eat antelopes, they could be eaten by lions. By knowing that all antelopes are essentially of one kind and that all lions are essentially of another kind, people could go on to learn that since lions also eat antelopes, then by tracking the lion they could survive competition with it by scavenging the remains of the lion's feast—perhaps by breaking the bones of an antelope with stones and intelligently scraping out the nutritious marrow that the lion would have found too troublesome to extract.

The concept of the folk species allows us to perceive and predict many important properties that link together the members of a biological species that are actually living together at any one time, and to categorically distinguish such "nondimensional" species from one another. For each species, people commonsensically presume that its various members share a unique underlying nature, or essence. This allows people to integrally link together the disparate properties of a species without having to know the precise causal relationships between those properties: people believe that tigers are by nature striped, carnivorous, and roaring quadrupeds and that there is presumably something "in" tigers that is the common cause of them having stripes, eating meat, and roaring.

Notice that the concept of underlying nature or essence is not simply the linguistic notion of a defining property, which applies to any noun (object or substance term). Thus CHAIR may be defined in terms of the human function it serves, and MUD may be defined in terms of its physical properties, but the referent of neither word has a deep essence because neither is necessarily presumed to be the unique outcome of an imperceptible causal complex. Nor is the notion of essence merely the notion of a common physical property. RED THINGS, for example, comprise a superficial natural class; however, such things have little in common except that they are red, and they presumably have few, if any, features that follow from the fact that they are red.

People the world over presume that the initially imperceptible essential properties of a species are responsible for the surface similarities they perceive. People everywhere strive to know these deeper properties but also presume that the whole nature of a species may never be known in its entirety. This cognitive compulsion to explore the underlying nature of species provides the focus for a continuing and perhaps endless quest to better understand the surrounding natural world. The essentialist presumption underlying this quest furthers appreciation of the biological makeup of local environments, such as those in which our hominid ancestors evolved and in which many "traditional" cultures develop.

From a scientific vantage, however, the concept of folk species is woefully inadequate for capturing the graded relationships that characterize the evolution of species over geologically vast dimensions of time and space—dimensions for which human minds were not directly designed (naturally selected) to comprehend. That is why the creationist view of timelessly separate and well-distinguished species may seem so much more "commonsensical" than the evolutionary idea that there are no fixed boundaries between species that extend indefinitely back in time: Whereas today antelopes and deer, lions and tigers, or apes and humans appear strikingly different, they all have common ancestors that do not clearly belong to any of these contemporary kinds nor to any wholly different kinds.

Only by painstaking, culturally elaborated conceptual strategies, like those involved in science, can minds transcend the innate bounds of their phenomenal world and begin to grasp nature's graded subtleties. To do so, however, requires continued access to the intuitive categories of common sense, which anchors speculation and allows more sophisticated knowledge to emerge.

Folk Taxonomy

As our forebears began to spread out over the face of the earth, the ability to group similar species into larger groups would enable them to project their knowledge of familiar species to unfamiliar species of the same group. As a result, people could predict the behavior and properties of unfamiliar species without having to learn everything about them by trial and error: If people know a lot about antelopes and lions, and surmise that antelopes and deer comprise one natural group and that lions and tigers comprise another, then they will "automatically" know a lot about how to relate to deer and tigers and how deer and tigers relate to one another.

Thus, in addition to the spontaneous arrangement of local fauna and flora into specieslike groupings, these basic groupings have "from the most remote period in...history...been classed in groups under groups. This classification is not arbitrary like the grouping of stars in constellations" (Darwin, 1859, p. 431). This further taxonomic arrangement of species into higher-order "groups under groups," which is common to all people, provides the principal framework for thinking about similarities and differences between species and for exploring the varied nature of life on earth.

(Folk) Biological Ranks

Ethnobiology is a branch of cognitive anthropology concerned with studying the ways members of a culture apprehend and utilize local flora and fauna. More than a century of ethnobiological research has shown that even within a single culture there may be several different sorts of "special-purpose" folk-biological classifications, which are organized by particular interests for particular uses (e.g., beneficial versus noxious, domestic versus wild, edible versus inedible) (cf. Hough, 1897; Gilmore, 1932). Only in the last quarter-century, however, has intensive empirical and theoretical work revealed a cross-culturally universal "general-purpose" taxonomy (Berlin et al., 1973) that supports the widest possible range of inductions about living kinds (Atran, 1990).

This includes indefinitely many inductions about the plausible distributions of initially unfamiliar biologically related traits over organisms given the discovery of such traits in some organism(s), or the likely correlation of known traits among unfamiliar organisms given the discovery of only some of those traits among the organisms. For example, the discovery of breast cancer in monkeys could warrant the initial induction that mammals are susceptible to breast cancer, but not birds or fish, because only mammals have mammary glands. And the knowledge that wombats have mammary glands would warrant the induction that they also have many of the other external and internal traits associated with mammals, such as fur and warm blood (Warburton, 1967; Rips, 1975).

This "default" folk-biological taxonomy, which serves as an inductive compendium of biological information, is composed of a fairly rigid hierarchy of inclusive classes of organisms, or taxa. At each level of the hierarchy, the taxa, which are mutually exclusive, partition the locally perceived biota in a virtually exhaustive manner. Lay taxonomy, it appears, is universally composed of a small number of absolutely distinct hierarchical levels, or *ranks*: such as the level of folk kingdom (e.g., ANIMAL, PLANT),[3] life-form (e.g., BUG, FISH, BIRD, MAMMAL, TREE, GRASS, BUSH, MUSHROOM),[4] folk species (e.g., GNAT, SHARK, ROBIN, DOG, MAPLE, WHEAT, HOLLY, TOADSTOOL),[5] and folk subspecies (COLLIE, RETRIEVER; SUGAR MAPLE, RED MAPLE).[6]

Intermediate levels also exist between the levels of the folk species and life-form. Taxa at these levels usually have no explicit name (e.g., rats + mice but no other rodents), although sometimes they may (e.g., felines, legumes). Such taxa—especially unnamed "covert" ones—tend not to be as clearly well-delimited as folk species or life-forms, nor does any one intermediate level always constitute a fixed taxonomic rank that partitions the local fauna and flora into a mutually exclusive and virtually exhaustive set of broadly equivalent taxa. Still, there is a psychologically evident preference for forming intermediate taxa at a level roughly between the scientific family (e.g., canine, weaver bird) and order (e.g., carnivore, passerine) (Atran, 1983; Berlin, 1992).

The Significance of Rank

Classes of organisms, or taxa, are identified by clusters of readily perceptible features. These taxonomic clusters of features are maximally covariant, with each such cluster separated from others of its rank by a distinct gap where clusters share few, if any, features (Hunn, 1976). Ranking is a cognitive mapping that places taxa in a structure of absolute levels, which may be evolutionarily designed to correspond to fundamentally different levels of reality. Thus the rank of folk kingdom—the level at which organisms are classified as ANIMAL or PLANT—may be determined, a priori, by our innate ontology (cf. Donnellan, 1971). In other words, we can know that something is an organism if and only if we know that it is either ANIMAL or PLANT.

The rank of folk species—the level at which organisms are classified as DOG, OAK, etc.—corresponds to the level at which morphological, behavioral, and ecological relationships between organisms maximally covary. It is the rank where people are most likely to attribute biological properties. This includes characteristic patterns of inheritance, growth, and physiological function as well as more "hidden" properties, such as hitherto unknown organic processes, organs, and diseases. The rank of folk subspecies—the level at which organisms are classified as BEAGLE, SUGAR MAPLE, etc.—corresponds to ranges of natural variation that humans are most apt to appropriate and manipulate as a function of their cultural interests.

The level of life form—the level at which organisms are classified as BIRD, TREE, etc.—may correspond to a partitioning of the local ecological landscape, to which we assign species roles in the "economy of nature" as a function of the way their specific morphology and behavior is fitted to those roles. For example, the morphology and behavior of different birds corresponds to a partitioning of the ways vertebrate life competitively accommodates to the air. The morphology and growth pattern of different trees corresponds to a partitioning of the ways single-stem plants competitively access sunlight in the earth's gravitational field (a 100-foot-tall multiple-stem bush would be physically impossible on earth). These divisions not only share readily perceptible features and behaviors that are related to habitat, but they also structure inductions about the distribution of underlying properties that presumably relate biology to the local ecology.

The significance of rank is to allow generalizations across classes of taxa at any given level. For example, the living members of a taxon at the level of the folk species generally share a set of biologically important features that are functionally stable and interdependent (homeostasis) and can generally interbreed with one another but not with the living members of any other taxon at that level (reproductive isolation). Taxa at the life-form level generally exhibit the broadest fit (adaptive radiation) of morphology (e.g., skin covering) and behavior (e.g., locomotion) to habitat (e.g., air, land, water).

The generalizations that hold across taxa of the same rank (i.e., a class of classes) are thus of a different logical type than generalizations that apply to only this or that taxon (i.e., a class of organisms). *Termite*, *pig*, and *lemon tree* are related to one another not by virtue of any simple relation of class inclusion or connection to some common hierarchichal node, but by dint of their common rank—in this case the level of folk species.

Notice that a system of rank is not simply a system of hierarchy. Hierarchy— that is, a structure of inclusive classes—is common to many cognitive domains, including the domain of artifacts. For example, CHAIR is often included under FURNITURE but not VEHICLE, and CAR is included under VEHICLE but not FURNITURE. Nevertheless, there is no ranked system of artifacts: There is no inferential link, or inductive framework, that spans both CHAIR and CAR, or FURNITURE and VEHICLE, by dint of a common rank, such as the artifact SPECIES or the artifact FAMILY. In other words, in many domains there is hierarchy without rank, but only in the domain of living kinds is there always rank.

Living kinds, then, exhibit a dual structure that is nowhere apparent in any other cognitive domain (except in easily noticed cases of explicit borrowing): namely, that any given organism is necessarily associated with more than one hierarchically distinguished rank and necessarily belongs at each rank to one and only one taxon. Biological ranks, be they folk or scientific, are a relatively stable class of classes (e.g., species, family, kingdom) whose elements are taxa (e.g., lion, feline, animal). Ranks seem to vary little, if at all, across cultures as a function of theories or belief systems.

The Rank of Folk Species vs. the Basic Level

By far, the majority of taxa in any folk-biological classification belong to the level of the folk species. It is this level that people in most societies privilege when they see and talk about biological discontinuities. Comparing the relative salience of folk-biological categories among Tzeltal Maya Indians and other "traditional" societies around the world, anthropologist Brent Berlin and his colleagues (Berlin et al., 1974) find that folk species (genera) are the most basic conceptual groupings of organisms (see Hays, 1983, for New Guinea). Folk species represent the cuts in nature that Maya children first name and form an image of (Stross, 1973), and which Maya adults most frequently use in speech, most easily recall in memory and most readily communicate to others (Hunn, 1977).

Yet, in a series of experiments conducted by psychologist Eleanor Rosch and her colleagues (Rosch et al., 1976), the most salient category cuts in the folk-biological classification of urban American folk do not uniformly correspond to the level of the folk species (see Zubin and Köpcke, 1986, for Germany). Only folk species of the life form MAMMAL, such as DOG and HORSE, consistently fall within the "one level of abstraction at which the most basic category cuts are made." By contrast, the other life forms tested—TREE, BIRD, and FISH—are themselves treated as basic categories. These life form categories—and not subordinate folk species like OAK, ROBIN, and SHARK—turn out to be the most inclusive category for which a concrete image of the category as a whole can be formed, the first categorization made during perception of the environment, the earliest category named by children, and the categories most codable, most coded, and most prevalent in language.

Cross-cultural evidence suggests that the most basic level in Rosch's sense is a variable phenomenon that shifts as a function of general cultural significance and individual familiarity and expertise (Dougherty, 1978). Thus, urban folk in industrial societies generally have little distinctive familiarity with, knowledge of, and use for various species of trees, fish, and birds. Such folk generally have far fewer named descriptions or images for species than do rural and traditional peoples, who must be intimately aware of the local flora and fauna upon which their lives depend. Only for mammalian species, which retain appreciable cultural importance in industrial societies (often through storybooks and nature programs on television), is there comparable linguistic, perceptual, and mnemonic saliency across cultures.

By contrast, ranks primarily represent *absolute levels of biological significance* and not just *relative levels of linguistic, perceptual, and mnemonic codability*. Thus it is prima facie more plausible that all oaks or robins will be susceptible to some disease—that will stunt their growth, deform their limbs, or derange their functioning—than are all trees or birds. For example, whereas urban American or German subjects appear to treat FISH, BIRD, and TREE as basic-level categories, Itzaj and Tzeltal Maya Indians seem to treat them as superordinate to the basic level. Nevertheless, in a series of inference studies, American subjects perform much as do Itzaj subjects in maximizing inductive potential at the folk-species level. Both Midwestern Americans and Itzaj Maya are much more likely to infer that, say, oak trees have a disease (or a given enzyme, protein, etc.) that white oak trees have, than to infer that trees have a disease that oak trees have (Coley, Medin, Atran, and Lynch, in press). This result cannot be simply attributed to the fact that subjects are more likely to generalize to a more specific category. Indeed, subjects in both cultures are no more likely to infer that, say, white oak trees have a disease that spotted white oak trees have, than to infer that oak trees have a disease that white oak trees have. The same findings apply in cases of inferences to particular folk species of fish or birds as opposed to inferences to fish or birds in general.

Such findings cannot be explained either by appeals to cross-domain notions of perceptual "similarity" or to the structure of the world "out there." On the one hand, if inferential potential were a simple function of perceptual similarity—or the "basic level" in Rosch's sense—then Americans should inductively privilege the life-form level. Yet, the Americans privilege the species level just as Maya do.

On the other hand, objective reality—that is, the actual distribution of biological species within groups of evolutionarily related species—does not substantially differ in the natural environments of Midwestern Americans and Itzaj Maya. Unlike Maya, however, Americans perceptually discriminate life-forms more readily than species. True, there are more locally recognized species, say, of trees in the Itzaj Maya area of Peten, Guatemala, than in the Midwest United States. Nevertheless, the readily perceptible evolutionary "gaps" between species are roughly the same in the two environments (e.g., a clear majority of tree genera in both environments are monospecific). If anything, one might expect that having fewer trees in the American environment allows each species to stand out more from the rest (Hunn, 1976). Likewise for birds, the relative distribution of evolutionarily related species also seems to be broadly comparable across temperate and rain-forest environments (Boster, 1988).

These observations suggest that fundamental categorization processes in folk biology may be rooted in domain-specific conceptual presumptions rather than in domain-general perceptual heuristics. People from traditional versus high techonology cultures may differ in terms of the level at which names readily come to mind, or knowledge about biological kinds, but they may nonetheless presume that the same rank is privileged for biological reasoning. Linguistic patterns in folk-taxonomic nomenclature may indicate which rank is privileged (Gelman and Coley, 1991). Language alone, however, would not suffice to induce the expectation that little or poorly known species are more biologically informative than better known life-forms for Americans. Why presume that an appropriately tagged item is the locus of a "deep" causal nexus of biological properties and relationships? As indicated earlier, cross-cultural and developmental evidence strongly suggests that it is the a priori assumption of essence, or inherent underlying nature, that spontaneously justifies and motivates expectation, inferences, and explorations relating to little known or nonobvious aspects of a presumably fundamental biological reality.

In sum, ranks are domain-specific phenomena peculiar to the biological realm, whereas Rosch's "levels of abstraction" are domain-general heuristics. The latter can apply to many sorts of objects, including artifacts, and to the same objects in different ways depending on context (e.g., TOMATO may be basic when viewed as a type of VEGETABLE but subordinate when perceived as a kind of BUSH). Relative and absolute levels can, and traditionally do, coincide: The most easily accessible criteria for object recognition and communication are the most efficacious indicators of unseen properties of deeper biological significance. But in the degenerate environmental conditions of urbanized societies, domain-general cues may not coincide with domain-specific conceptual presumptions. This does not mean that more general perceptual cues have no inferential value when applied to the folk-biological domain. On the contrary, Americans are still more likely than Maya to infer that, say, trees in general have a disease that oak trees have. This points to a significant role for domain-general cues in targeting basic-level life-forms as secondary foci for inferential understanding in a cultural environment where biological awareness is relatively poor.

From Folk to Scientific Systematics

Readily perceptible properties of taxa (morpho-types) are generally good predictors of deeper, underlying shared properties and may originally provide the basis for living kind categories. Initially, the underlying essential structures are unknown, and merely presumed to (teleologically) cause the observable regularities in biological categories. Attention to this causal link and a cognitive endeavor to know it better leads to awareness that this correlation between surface and deep features is not perfect. Added knowledge about these deeper properties may then lead to category modification. For example, most adult Americans categorize whales and bats as mammals despite the many superficial properties shared with fish and birds, respectively.

Despite the "bootstrapping" revision of taxonomy implied in this example, notice how much did not change: neither the abstract hierarchical schema given by folk taxonomy, nor—in a crucial sense—even the kinds involved. Bats, birds, whales, mammals, and fish did not just vanish from common sense to arise anew in science like Athena springing from the head of Zeus. There was a redistribution of affiliations between antecedently perceived kinds. What had altered was the construal of the underlying natures of those kinds, with a consequent redistribution of kinds and a reappraisal of properties pertinent to reference.

The Transformation of Ethnobiological into Biological Ranks

At intermediate taxonomic levels, which are often not uniformly ranked, we may have no difficulty inferring that a biological property found in a pair of organisms in an intermediate group (e.g., a cat and a jaguar) likely belongs to all organisms in the group (i.e., all felines). This is because for intermediate levels, which often approximate the level of the biological family (for larger vertebrates and trees) or order (for less salient vertebrates and trees), an abstract image can still be readily formed of the taxon as a whole. In other words, there is morphologically apparent support for inductions about underlying biological properties at these levels.

Extending presumptions of an underlying essential nature to taxa at ranks higher than the folk species and intermediate levels, such as BIRD and TREE, may not be nearly so "automatic." Thus to infer that a biological property found in a pair of organisms belonging to two very different looking species (e.g., a chicken and an eagle) likely belongs to all organisms in the lowest ranked taxon containing the pair (e.g., BIRD) may necessitate a reflective elaboration of causal principles that are not related to behavior, morphology, or ecological proclivity in any immediately obvious way. Such a basis could then justify the presumption that all organisms belonging to a taxon at a given rank share equally some internal structure regardless of apparent differences between them.

Such predictions lead to errors as well as to new discoveries. This sets into motion a "bootstrapping" reorganization of taxa and taxonomic structure, and of the inductions that the taxonomy supports. For example, upon discovery that bats bear and nurture their young more like mammals than birds, it is a reasonable step to then exclude bats from BIRD and include them with MAMMAL.

This bootstrapping enterprise in Western science began with Aristotle, or at least with the naturalistic tradition in Ancient Greece he represented. For Aristotle, the task was to unite the various foundational forms of the world—each with their own special underlying nature" (*physis* in the implicit everyday sense)—into an overarching system of "Nature" (*physis* in an explicitly novel metaphysical sense). In practice, this meant systematically deriving each basic-level folk species (*atomon eidos*) from the causal principles uniting it to other species of its life-form (*megiston genos*). It further implied combining the various life-forms by "analogy" (*analogian*) into an integrated conception of life. Theophrastus, Aristotle's student and successor at the Lyceum, conceived of botanical classification in much the same way.

Aristotelian life-forms are distinguished and related through possession of analogous organs of the same essential function (locomotion, digestion, reproduction, respiration). For example, bird wings, quadruped feet, and fish fins constitute analogous organs of locomotion. The folk species of each life-form are then differentiated by degrees of "more or less" with respect to essential organs. Thus all birds have wings for moving about and beaks for obtaining nutriments. But, whereas the predatory eagle is partially diagnosed by long and narrow wings and a sharply hooked beak, the goose—owing to its different mode of life—is partially diagnosed by a lesser and broader wingspan and flatter bill. The principled classification of biological taxa by "division and assembly" (*diaresis* and *synagoge*) ends when all taxa are defined, with each species completely diagnosed with respect to every essential organ (Atran, 1985).

This first sustained scientific research program failed because it was still primarily local in conception and geared to explaining the familiar order of things. Aristotle knew that there were species not present in his own familair environment, but he had no idea that there were orders of magnitude of difference between what was locally apparent and what existed worldwide. Given the (wrong) assumption that a phenomenal survey of the naturally occurring kinds was pratically complete, Aristotle hoped to find a true and consistent system of essential characters by the trial and error method. He did not foresee that the introduction of exotic forms would undermine his quest for a discovery of the essential structure of all possible kinds.

Nevertheless, by inquiring into how the apparently diverse natures of species may be causally related to the nature of life, Aristotle established the theoretical program of natural history (as biology was called before evolutionary theory). An indispensable tool of this program was the introduction of a causally principled doctrine of taxonomic essentialism. This enabled the concept of rank to provide the framework for induction in systematics—that is, the science of classifying animals and plants by degrees of biological relatedness.

As in any folk inventory, ancient Greeks and Renaissance herbalists contended with only 500 or 600 local species (Raven et al., 1971). Phenomenally salient basic taxa often correspond to scientific species (*dog, coyote, lemon tree, orange tree*).

But frequently a scientific genus has only one locally occurring species (*bear, red-wood*), which makes species and genus perceptually coextensive. This occurs regularly with the most phenomenally salient organisms, including mammals and trees (Atran, 1990). For example, in a comparative study, it was found that 69 percent of tree genera in both the Chicago area (40 of 58) and the Peten rain forest of Guatemala (158 of 229) are monospecific.

In Western science, basic folk taxa eventually "fissioned" into species (Cesalpino, 1583) and genera (Tournefort, 1694). During the initial stages of Europe's worldwide "Age of Exploration," the number of species increased an order of magnitude. Foreign species were habitually joined to the most similar European species—that is, to the generic type, in a "natural system."

A similar "fissioning" of intermediate folk groupings occurred when the number of species encountered increased yet another order of magnitude, and a "natural method" for organizing plants and animals into families (Adanson, 1763) and orders (Lamarck, 1809) emerged as the foundation of modern systematics. By looking to other environments to complete local gaps at the intermediate level, naturalists sought to discern a worldwide series that would cover all environments and again reduce the ever-increasing number of discovered species to a mnemonically manageable set—this time to a set of basic, family plans. Higher-order vertebrate life-forms provided the initial framework for biological classes, while plant life-forms such as TREE were abandoned as being intuitively and ecologically "natural," but "philosophically lubricious" (Linnaeus, 1751). Finally, the concept of phylum became distinguished once it was realized that there is less internal differentiation between all the vertebrate life-forms taken as a whole, than there is within most intermediate groupings of the phenomenally "residual" animal life-form, INSECT (bugs, worms, etc.).[7]

Taxonomy: A Prior Condition for Theory-Formation in Biology

If this scenario is anywhere near correct, then an integrative (folk-)biological theory—however rudimentary—*cannot be* the cognitive mechanism responsible for the ontology of living kinds, as some researchers have proposed (Murphy and Medin, 1985; Carey, 1985; Keil, 1989; Gelman and Coley, 1991). In other words, it is not the elaboration of a theory of biological causality that progressively distinguishes people's understanding of the (folk) species concept as it applies to (nonhuman) animals and plants, from their understanding of concepts of inert substances, artifacts, or persons. Rather, there seems to be a universal, a priori presumption that species constitute "natural kinds" by virtue of their special (initially unknown and perhaps unknowable) teleological natures, and that species further group together naturally into ranked taxonomies. This spontaneous arrangement of living things into taxonomies of essential kinds constitutes a prior set of constraints on any and all possible theories about the causal relations between living kinds. Recent cross-cultural evidence indicates strongly that this is in fact the case.

A Comparison with Itzaj Maya Folk biology

The Itzaj are the last Maya Indians native to the Peten rain forest, once an epicenter of Classic Maya civilization. Although the cosmological system of the Itzaj was sundered by the Spanish conquest and subsequent oppression, their folk-biological knowledge—including taxonomic competence as well as practical application—remains strikingly robust (Atran, 1993). This is not surprising; for, if the core of folk knowledge about the biological world is spontaneously emitted and transmitted by minds, then it should be largely independent of (historically and culturally specific) institutionalized modes of communication.

Itzaj Taxonomy

Itzaj Maya folk biology provides evidence for generalizations about the specific taxonomic structure that delimits the universal domain of folk biology, but also for the influence of local ecology and culture. There is no common lexical entry for the plant kingdom in Itzaj; however, the numeral classifier *teek* is used only with plants (e.g., *jun-teek ixi'im* = "one-plant corn"). Plants generally fall under one of four mutually exclusive life-forms: (1) *che'* (trees); (2) *pok~che'* (undergrowth such as herbs, shrubs, bushes); (3) *ak'* (vines); and (4) *su'uk* (grasses). Each life-form is distinguished by a particular stem habit, which is believed to be the natural outgrowth of every primary kind of *pu(k)sik'al* (species-essence) included in that life-form. A number of introduced and cultivated plants, however, are not affiliated with any of these life-forms and are simply denoted *jun-teek* (literally, "one plant"), as are many of the phylogenetically isolated plants, such as the cacti. Arguably, some may be thought of as *monospecific life-forms*, in much the same way that the aardvark is the only known species representing its scientific order. All informants agree that mushrooms (*xikin~che'* = "tree-ear") have no *pu(k)sik'al* and are not plants, but they take life away from the trees that host them. Lichens and bryophytes (mosses and liverworts) are not considered to be plants, or to have an essence or to live.

The Itzaj term for animals (*b'a'al~che'* = "forest-thing") polysemously indicates both the animal kingdom as a whole (including invertebrates, birds, and fish), and also a more restrictive grouping of quadrupeds (amphibians, reptiles, and, most typically, mammals). The quadrupeds are divided into two mutually exclusive life-forms: "walking animals" (*b'a'al~che' kuximal* = mammals except bats) and "slithering animals" (*b'a'al~che' kujiltik ub'aj* = herpetofauna, i.e., amphibians and reptiles). Birds (*ch'iich'* including *sotz'* = bats) and fish (*käy*) exhibit patterns of internal structure that parallel those of the mammals (Coley et al., in press).

For the life-form of invertebrates (*mejen b'a'al~che'*), whose morphology and ecological proclivity is very different from that of humans and other vertebrates, correspondence of folk to modern systematics blurs as one descends the ranks of the scientific ladder, and violations of scientific taxonomy tend to be more pronounced. Still, in this respect as in others, the categorical structure of Itzaj folk biology differs little from that of any other folk-biological system, including that which initially gave rise to systematics, including evolutionary systematics.[8]

Like other folk around the world, the Itzaj also have a number of relatively stable intermediate categories, both named and unnamed. Examples of named intermediate categories include *aak* (turtle), *kan* (snake), *kab'* (bee), and *xa'an* (palm trees). Examples of unnamed intermediate categories include locally occurring fragments of biological families, such as Cebidae (monkeys), Dasypractidae (agoutis and pacas), and Meliaceae (mahogany and tropical cedars). A number of intermediate categories are also polysemously named after a protoytpical species: *b'alum* (jaguars in particular, and large felines in general), *juj* (iguanas in particular, and lizards in general), *ya'* (chicle trees in particular and Sapotaceae trees in general).

Cross-Cultural Constraints on Theory Formation: The Case of Reproduction

If different cultures have different theories or belief systems about the relations between biological categories, shouldn't there be clear differences in biological reasoning? Not necessarily. Because of initial universal taxonomic constraints on theories or belief systems about biological categories and relationships, there should be predictable stability and cross-cultural consistency to theory-related inferences. For example, different cultures may have very different beliefs about reproduction but their judgments about whether or not two species could interbreed may well show the same decreasing function of taxonomic distance.

Thus for Aristotle, offspring are considered "unnatural monsters" to the extent that they fail to resemble their fathers, and in direct proportion to the number of nodes in the "common Greek's" taxonomic tree that must be climbed to encounter a likely progenitor (Atran, 1985). Similarly, a preliminary study with the Itzaj Maya led to the discovery of a highly structured taxonomy that enjoys a strong cultural consensus and is strongly correlated with notions about the likelihood of mating between intermediate group animals that do not normally interbreed (Atran, 1994). For example, the jaguar's even temperament, the mountain lion's aggressiveness, and the margay's small size generally disallow mating between these three members of the Itzaj taxon of large felines (*b'alum*). Nevertheless, Itzaj are readily inclined to believe that even these matings could occur under certain imaginable situations, and which we experimentally manipulated (e.g., animals that were were caged, dwarfed, or drugged).

Given Itzaj explanations of how reproduction works, actual fulfillment of these conditions can never be empirically confirmed or disconfirmed. The Itzaj believe that offspring are preformed before birth in their same-sex progenitors. Because daughters resemble mothers and sons resemble fathers, there is no empirical counterevidence to unlikely but imaginable crossings. Aristotle's theory of reproduction and generation is markedly different from that of the Itzaj, but the same sorts of taxonomic constraints operate on both. Indeed, evolutionary theory itself initially had to meet many of the same conditions.

American and Mayan Mammal Taxonomy

As further illustration of the general framework of folk biology, consider recent experimental findings that my colleagues and I obtained among University of Michigan students raised in rural Michigan and among the Itzaj. Our working hypothesis was that if the same kinds of folk-biological constraints on taxonomies and inductions describe performances of people in such different cultures, then we have reason to believe that the underlying cognitive processes are part of human nature.

What follows is a brief account of findings in regard to all mammals represented in the local environments of the Itzaj and Michigan groups, respectively. For Itzaj we included bats, although Itzaj do not consider them mammals. For the students we included the emblematic wolverine, although it is now extinct in Michigan. Each group was tested in its native language (Itzaj and English), and included six men and six women. No statistically significant differences between men and women were found on the tasks below, which were designed to probe two general questions.

To what extent are different folk-biological taxonomies correlated with one another and with a corresponding scientific (evolutionary) taxonomy of the local fauna and flora? Elsewhere (Atran, 1994), I describe the sorting procedures for eliciting individual taxonomies as well as mathematical techniques for aggregating individual taxonomies into a "cultural model" of the society's folk-biological system. Results indicate that the individual folk-biological taxonomies of the Itzaj and of students from rural Michigan are all more or less competent expressions of comparably robust cultural models of the biological world. To compare the structure and content of cultural models with one another, and with scientific models, we mathematically correlated each group's aggregate taxonomy with an evolutionary taxonomy (for details, see López, Atran, Coley, Medin, and Smith, in press).

The overall correlations were quite high between both evolutionary and Itzaj taxonomy ($r = .81$) and between science and the folk taxonomy of Michigan students ($r = .75$). Somewhat surprisingly, the Itzaj came even closer to a scientific appreciation of the local mammal fauna than did Michigan students. A comparison of higher-order taxa only (i.e., excluding folk species) still showed a strong correlation both for Itzaj ($r = .51$) and Michigan subjects ($r = .48$).

The overwhelming majority of mammal taxa in both cultures corresponded to scientific species, and most of these taxa also corresponded to monospecific genera: 30 of 40 (75 percent) basic Michigan mammal terms denote biological species, of which 21 (70 percent, or 53 percent of the total) are monospecific genera; 36 of 42 (86 percent) basic Itzaj mammal terms denote biological species, of which 25 (69 percent, or 60 percent of the total) are monospecific genera. At higher levels, Itzaj and Michigan folk taxonomic trees compared favorably to one another (see Figures 28.1 and 28.2) and to science (Figure 28.3), both in terms of number of nodes and levels at which nodes are formed. Agreement between the higher-order folk taxonomies and science is maximized at the level of the scientific

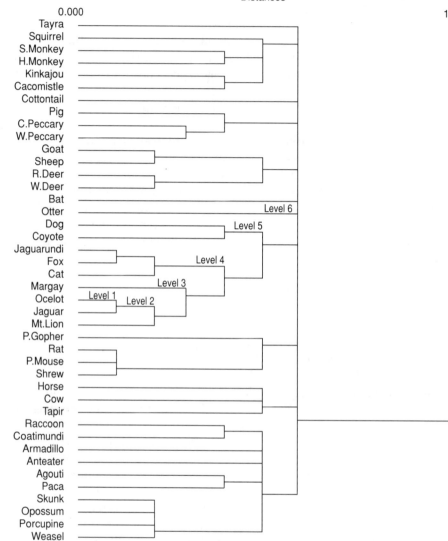

Distances

0.000   10.000

Figure 28.1   *Intermediate levels in sample mammal taxonomy for one Itzaj female subject*

As exhibited by average link cluster analysis (the preferred clustering technique in systematics), this tree shows that the folk-biological taxonomy of mammals for the subject has a total of six levels, with only three groups of mammals at Level 1: Fox and JAGUARUNDI, JAGUAR and OCELOT, and POCKET MOUSE, RAT and SHREW. It also shows that MOUNTAIN LION goes together with JAGUAR and OCELOT at Level 2, with MARGAY at Level 3, with CAT, FOX and JAGUARUNDI at Level 4, with COYOTE and DOG at Level 5, and with the rest of the mammals at Level 6 (e.g., OTTER). The lowest level at which two given mammals go together in the taxonomy represents the taxonomic distance between them. Thus low taxonomic distance corresponds to high folk-biological relatedness. In the example, MOUNTAIN LION is closely related to JAGUAR (2), fairly related to CAT (4), and not very related to OTTER (6). Note that the topological structure of the corresponding scientific tree for Itza mammals in Figure 28.2 resembles this individual's tree and that the correlation of "topological distance" between these trees is 0.5.

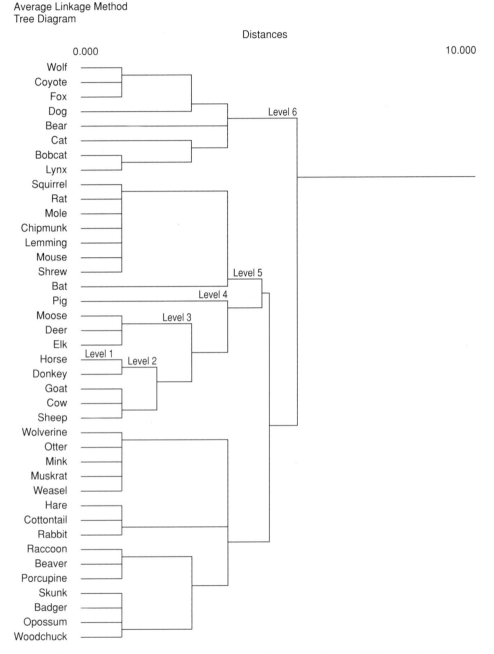

Figure 28.2 *Intermediate levels in sample mammal taxonomy for one Michigan male subject*

Note the linkage between OPOSSUM and SKUNK at Level 1, whereas in Figure 28.4 they are maximally distant in the corresponding scientific tree. The bovids (GOAT. COW. SHEEP) are linked to the equids (HORSE. DONKEY) at Level 2, and to the cervids (MOOSE. DEER. ELK) at Level 3; scientifically, however, bovids and cervids but not equids are ruminants. The bat is linked to the rodents and SHREW at Level 4. Level 5 links this group to all other mammals save canines and felines. Canines and felines are linked at Level 4, and with the rest of the mammals at Level 6.

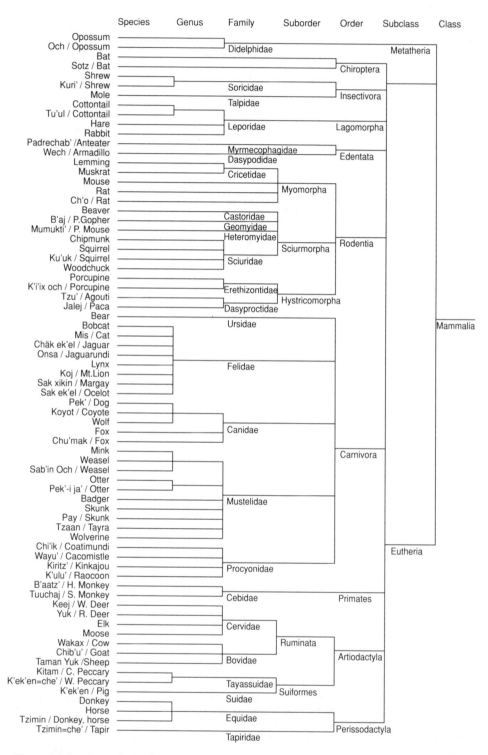

Figure 28.3   *Scientific (evolutionary) taxonomy of all mammals used in studies*

suborder (i.e., the level between family and order), both for Itzaj and Michigan subjects, indicating that there is indeed an intermediate level in the folk taxonomies of both cultures.

On the whole, taxa formed at this level are still imageable. For example, taxa formed at Level 3 in Figure 28.1 (the Itzaj counterpart of scientific rankings at the level of the suborder or below) are not only representable by an abstract image, but they are sometimes named as well. At Level 3, for example, *b'alum* includes the large felines (margay, ocelot, jaguar, and mountain lion). At Level 2, *och* includes the skunk, opossum, porcupine, and weasel, which are morphologically and behaviorally close (in Figure 28.1) but scientifically distant (in Figure 28.3).

A closer comparison of the folk groupings in the two cultures suggests that there are at least some universal cognitive factors at work in folk-biological classification that are mitigated or ignored by science. For example, certain groupings, such as felines and canines, are common to both the Itzaj and Michigan subjects, although felines and canines are phylogenetically further from one another than either family is to other carnivore families (e.g., mustelids, procyonids). These groupings of large predators indicate that size and ferocity are salient classificatory dimensions in both cultures (see Henley, 1969; Rips et al., 1973). These are dimensions that a corresponding evolutionary classification of the local fauna does not markedly exhibit.

Other factors in the divergence between folk taxonomies and science are related both to the latter's incorporation of a worldwide perspective in classifying local biota and to its reliance on biologically "deep," theoretically weighted properties of internal anatomy and physiology. For example, the opossum is the only marsupial present in North and Central America. Both the Itzaj and Michigan subjects relate the opossum to skunks and porcupines because it shares with them numerous readily perceptible features of morphology and behavior. From a scientific vantage, however, the opossum is taxonomically isolated from all the other locally represented mammals in a subclass of its own. Thus, if we exclude the opossum from the comparison between the folk taxonomies and science, the correlation rises notably for the Itzaj (from $r = .51$ to $r = .60$) and the Michigan students (from $r = .48$ to $r = .55$).

One factor mitigating the ability of all subjects to appreciate the opossum as scientists do is that there are no other locally present marsupials to relate the opossum to. As a result, the most readily perceptible morphobehavioral difference between the opossum and other local mammals—carrying its young in a pouch—cannot be linked to discoverable differences that would connect the opossum to other marsupials and help to differentiate them from nonmarsupials. The opossum's pouch appears as just another characteristic morphobehavioral feature, like the porcupine's quills or the skunk's smell. Both the Michigan students and the Itzaj are apparently unaware of the deeper biological significance of the opossum's lack of a placenta.

To what extent do the culturally specific theories and belief systems, such as science, shape folk-biological taxonomy?   A striking folk bias is evident in the Itzaj classification of snakes (*kan*). Questioning shows that people fear certain snakes. Only some of these are actually poisonous, but all those feared are nevertheless thought to sprout wings and extra heads, and to fly off to the sea with their last victims—a likely cultural survival of the Precolumbian cult of *kukul~kan* ("feathered serpent"). In-depth interviews suggest that supposed danger is an overriding factor in preliminary snake sortings, and supports one interpretation of a multidimensional scaling of these sortings (Figure 28.4).[9]

A first interpretation of the phenomenon might be that in some cases the biological target is more determined by culturally specific interests than by readily perceptible phenotypic gaps in the distribution of local biota. Evidence from biology and social history, however, indicates a more complex story. Humans everywhere, it seems, are emotionally disposed to fear snakes (Seligman, 1971) and to socially ritualize this phobia (Marks, 1987) in recurrent cross-cultural themes, such as "the cult of the serpent" (Munkur, 1983).

The fact that people are spontaneously more inclined to exhibit and express fear of snakes than fear of much more lethal cultural artifacts—like swords, guns, and nuclear bombs—intimates an evolutionary explanation. Such naturally selected phobias to resurgent perils in ancestral environments may have provided an extra margin for survival, whereas there would be no such direct natural selection of cognitive responses to the more recent dangers of particular cultural environments. To some extent, then, Itza snake classification seems an exception that proves the rule: folk taxonomies are more or less naturally selected conceptual structures—"habits of mind"—that are biologically "pretuned" to capture relevant and recurrent contents of those natural environments—"habits of the world"—in which hominid evolution occurred.

Nevertheless, perception of snakes as poisonous or nonpoisonous may itself be a partial product of culturally conditioned interests. Preliminary findings suggest that perceptual analogy with lethal vipers (Crotilidae) and visibly different but equally deadly corals (Elapidae) strongly influences which other snakes are classified as poisonous. Yet snakes which, like people, kill or eat other snakes tend to be classified as nonpoisonous unless they morphologically mimic the vipers or corals. Thus cultural interest may affect attention, which in turn affects patterns of perceived similarity.

The best candidate for the cultural influence of theory in American folk biology is science of course. Yet, the exposure of Michigan students to science education has little apparent effect on their folk taxonomy. From a scientific view, the students taxonomize no better than do the Itza. Science's influence is at best marginal. For example, science may peripherally bear on the differences in the way the Itzaj and the Michigan students categorize bats. The Itzaj deem bats to be birds (*ch'iich'*), not mammals (*b'a'al~che'*).

Like the Michigan students, the Itzaj acknowledge in interviews that there is a resemblance between bats and small rodents like rats and mice. Because Itzaj classify bats with birds, they consider the resemblance to be only superficial and not indicative of a taxonomic relationship. By contrast, Michigan students "know" from schooling that bats are mammals. But this knowledge can hardly be taken as evidence for the influence of scientific *theory* on folk taxonomy. Despite learning

Coordinates in 2 Dimensions: stress of final configuration is .10861; proportion of variance (rsq) is: .93985.

Variable	Plot	Dimension 1	Dimension 2	
aj-chäk~tzitzi'	A	1.16	1.04	*Ninia sebae* (red coffee snake)
= aj-suk'in kan ("fasting snake")				*Imantodes cenchoa/Leptodeira septentrionalis*
ch'elpat	B	−.78	.09	*Porthidium nummifer* (jumping tommy pitviper)
aj-ek'~u-nej	C	.21	−.74	*Drymarchon corais* ("black-tail")
aj-ek'~xux	D	−.62	.45	*Xenodon rabdocephalus* (false fer-de-lance)
				Senticollis triaspis (juveniles only)
u-kan-il~ja'	E	−.69	−1.03	*Thamnophus proximus* ("water snake")
ix-koraal	F	−.77	.36	*Micrurus diastema/M. nigrocintus* (coral)
including "false corals," e.g.				*Oxyrhopus petola/Sibon sartori/Tintilla moesta*
aj-kuy zumbadora	G	.53	−.56	*Coniophanes schmidti/Tantilla canula*
including species variable				*Dryadophis melanalomas/Drymobius margeriitif./*
in color and cross-classified				*Stenorrhina freminvillei*, etc.
aj-k'än k'ok'o'	H	−.94	.35	*Bothrops asper* ("yellow fer-de-lance")
aj-ya'ax k'ok'o'				*Botreichis schlegeli* ("green fer-de-lance")
miikaj	I	.38	.21	*Spilotes pullatus* ("rat snake" = aj-kan~ch'o')
aj-och~kan	J	.58	−.84	*Boa constrictor* ("opossum snake")
ix-soj~b'ach kan	K	1.60	.02	*Oxybelis aeneus* ("dry-bone snake")
= kan-il ak' "vine snake," e.g.				*Oxybelis fulgidus* ("green vine snake")
aj-tz'aab' kan	L	−.92	.26	*Crotalus durissus* ("rattle snake")
ix-ya'ax kan	M	.25	.40	*Leptophis ahaetulla* ("green snake")

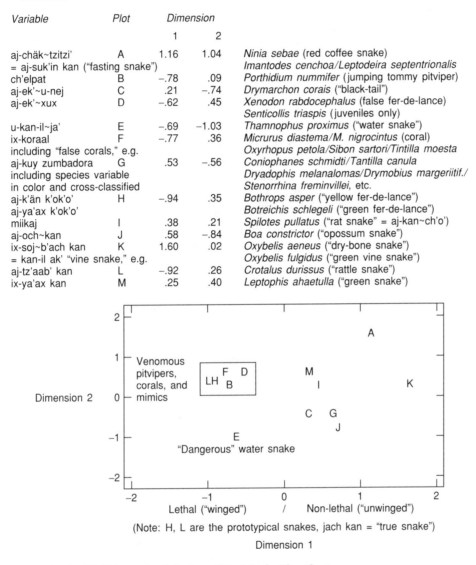

Figure 28.4 *Multidimensional Scaling of Itzaj Snake Classification*

that bats are mammals, the students go on to relate bats to mice and rats just as the Itzaj might if they did not already "know" that bats are birds. From an evolutionary stand, however, bats are taxonomically no closer to rats than to cats. The students, it seems, pay little or no attention to the deeper biological relationships science reveals. In other words, the primary influence of science education on folk-biological knowledge may be to fix category labels, which in turn may affect patterns of attention and induction.

The influence of science education on folk induction may also reflect less actual knowledge of theory than willing belief that scientific theory supports folk taxonomy. The high concordance between folk taxonomy and science, especially at the level of the folk species, provides Michigan students prima facie support for believing that their folk taxonomy is more or less on a scientific track. Given their belief that science has a causal story to tell, they assume that the same story pretty much holds for their folk taxonomy. This belief steers them into inductive errors, but also to the realization that eliminating such errors leads to a closer accord with science—albeit a modest one.

For example, given that a skunk and opossum share a deep biological property, Michigan students are less likely to conclude that all mammals share the property than if it were shared by a skunk and a bear. From a scientific standpoint, the students are using the right reasoning strategy (i.e., diversity-based inference), but reaching the wrong conclusion because of a faulty taxonomy (i.e., the belief that skunks are taxonomically further from bears than from opossums). But if they are *told* that opossums are phylogenetically more distant from skunks than bears are, then the students readily revise their taxonomy to make the correct inference. Still, it would be misleading to claim that the students thereby use theory to revise their taxonomy, although a revision occurs in accordance with scientific theory.

The Michigan students and the Itzaj both project biological properties from typical taxa to superordinate groups, as determined by the lowest mean taxonomic distance (calculated in terms of the intervening number of hierarchical nodes between a given taxon and every other taxon in the superordinate group). Thus, when people learn that an unknown biologically related property, such as a disease, is possessed by a typical species that shares many properties with other members of the same taxonomic category, they are then more likely to generalize than if the same fact had been learned about some atypical species (see Rips, 1975). Nevertheless, the Itzaj and the Michigan students differ in their appreciation of what counts as a typical taxon.

For example, large felines appear at the bottom of American typicality ratings and at the top of Itzaj ratings, although the actual frequency of occurrence and encounter with large felines is nowadays roughly comparable in rural Michigan and central Peten (Lopéz et al., in press). By contrast, frequently encountered squirrels and raccoons appear toward the top of the American typicality ratings but toward the bottom of Itzaj typicality ratings. This is true for typicality ratings indirectly derived from the taxonomy itself (mean taxonomic distance), or from direct subject ratings of how "typical" (on a seven-point scale for Americans) or how "true a representative" (*jach* for Itzaj) each species is of the mammals in general. Similarly birds at the top of Rosch's (1975) typicality list for Americans (e.g., plain-colored passerines such as sparrows) are never considered "true representatives" (*jach*) of BIRD (*ch'iich'*) for Itzaj, whereas birds at the bottom of Rosch's typicality list are (e.g., galliformes such as turkeys). This is the case despite the fact the frequency of occurrence and encounter with plain-colored passerines is about the same in rural Michigan and central Peten, and always greater than frequency of occurrence and encounter with galliformes.

In one study, we asked both Midwestern Americans and Itzaj to indicate the "truest" birds among a series of 104 scaled color drawings of the birds of Peten. The Americans invariably placed passeriformes, such as flycatchers and orioles, at the top of their list and galliformes, such as the ocellated turkey, crested guan, and great curassow, at the bottom. Itzaj did just the reverse. When asked which birds were more likely to share a disease with other birds, Americans and Itzaj both strongly preferred their respective "truest" birds. In justifying choices, Americans argued that the less remarkable and more frequently encountered passeriformes were more like most other birds than the remarkable galliformes were like most other birds. In other words, the passeriformes had a higher maximum average similarity to the birds as a whole. By contrast, Itzaj tended to argue that diseases of the galliformes would have greater impact on other living things in the forest, including other birds. This is supposedly because of their remarkable size, behavior, and value (in the food-chain) to other salient birds (predators), mammals (large carnivores), trees (large nut and fruit trees), and humans.

In each case for which we have direct Itzaj typicality measures, the most typical folk representatives are large, perceptually striking, culturally important, and ecologically prominent: the jaguar and its allies for the mammal life-form, the ocellated turkey and its allies for the bird life-form, the fer-de-lance and its allies for the named intermediate category of snakes, the cabbage palm and its allies for the unnamed intermediate category of palms. Each can grow large but is not the largest of its category (cows are bigger than jaguars, certain vultures are bigger than ocellated turkeys, boa constrictors are bigger than fer-de-lance, corozo palms are more massive than cabbage palms).

The three dimensions of perceptual, cultural, and ecological salience are all seemingly necessary to a determination of typicality, but none alone appears to be sufficient. Nor is there any one criterion, or well-defined group of criteria, that determines any one dimension. Each typical representative is otherwise physically striking, but in a different way (the jaguar's luxuriant coat, the ocellated turkey's magnificent feathers, the fer-de-lance's yellow throat, the young cabbage palm's broadleaf cover of the forest floor and the mature cabbage palm's strikingly tall and leafless trunk). Each is culturally important but in a different way (jaguars are lords of the forest, ocellated turkeys define the country's bounty, the fer-de-lance is the most feared creature of all, cabbage palms provide the thatch for all types of shelter).

Each is salient to the forest's ecological composition and to the place of humans in it, but in a different way (the jaguar's habitat—some 50 square kilometers—determines the extent of a forest section, the ocellated turkey's presence indicates where game is abundant, where the fer-de-lance strikes determines where people should fear to tread, where there are cabbage palms human settlement is possible). Indeed the three dimensions seem to be so bound up with one another that it is difficult, if not impossible, to completely distinguish them for any particular case. In other words, typicality for the Itzaj appears to be an integral part of the human (culturally relevant) ecology.

Ecological Understanding Through Folk Taxonomy　Concern with ecology is also one likely reason for Itzaj "failure" to apply the so-called "diversity principle" to biological reasoning. According to this principle, when things are equal (e.g., when taxa are equally typical), then a biological property shared by two taxonomically close taxa (e.g., a wolf and a coyote) is less likely to be shared by a superordinate group of taxa (e.g., mammals) than a property shared by two taxonomically distant taxa (e.g., a wolf and a gopher). The diversity principle corresponds to the fundamental principle of induction in scientific systematics: a property shared by two organisms (or taxa) is likely shared by all organisms falling under the smallest (or lowest ranked) taxon containing the two.

Thus American subjects seem to use their biological taxonomies much as scientists do when given information that is unfamiliar to infer what is likely in the face of uncertainty: If informed that goats and mice share a hitherto unknown property, they are more likely to project that property to mammals than if informed that goats and sheep do. By contrast, the Itzaj tend to use similarly structured taxonomies to search for a causal ecological explanation as to why such an unlikely event should occur: For example, bats may have passed on the property to goats and mice by biting them, but a property would not likely need an ecological agent in order to be shared by goats and sheep.

In the absence of a theory—or at least the presumption of a theory—of causal unity underlying disparate species, there is no compelling reason to consider a property discovered in two distant species as biologically intrinsic or essential to both. In such circumstances it may make more sense to consider the counterintuitive presence of a property in dissimilar species as the likely result of an extrinsic or ecologically "accidental" cause. It is not that the Itzaj do not understand the diversity principle. In tests involving diversity-based reasoning in other domains, they performed successfully as a group. For example, when asked whether a person should spend a fixed amount of time visiting one part of a forest or many parts in order to determine if that forest should be settled or cultivated, the Itzaj invariably opted for the latter alternative.

Note that in both the American and Itzaj cases similarly structured taxonomies are providing the distance metrics over which biological induction takes place. For the Americans, taxonomic distance indicates the extent to which underlying causes are more likely to predict shared biological properties than are surface relationships. For the Itzaj, taxonomic distance suggests the extent to which ecological agents are likely to be involved in predicting biological properties that do not conform to surface relationships. A priori, either stance might be correct. For example, diseases are clearly biologically related; however, the distribution of some hitherto unknown disease among a given animal population could well involve epidemiological factors that essentially depend on both inherent biological susceptibility and ecological agency.

More generally, what "counts" as a biological cause or property may reflect one thing for the Itzaj, who necessarily live in intimate awareness of their biological surroundings, and another for Americans, whose awareness is less necessary and intimate. For most Itzaj, awareness of biological causes and properties may be directly related to ecology, whereas for most Americans the ecological ramifications of biological causes and properties may remain obscure. Historically, the

West's development of a worldwide scientific systematics explicitly involved disregard of ecological relationships, and of the colors, smells, tastes, and textures that constitute the most intimate channels of recognition and access to the surrounding world of organic beings.

Between Folk Biology and Scientific Biology: The Failing of Compromise   With their ranked taxonomic structures, and their essentialist understanding of species, it would seem that the Itzaj would require no great cognitive effort to recursively essentialize the higher ranks as well, and thereby avail themselves of the inductive power ranked taxonomies provide. But contrary to earlier assumptions (Atran, 1990), empirical studies now show this is not the case. The Itzaj, and probably other traditional folk, do not ranks: They do not establish causal laws at the higher folk-biological levels, and they do not presume that higher-order taxa share the kind of unseen causal unity that their constituent species do. An implicit use of ranks to organize ecologically significant relationships between species does seem clear and consistent. But the cognitive benefit of converting these implicit organizing schema into explicit second-order categories (law-supporting ranks)—and the consequent reconstrual of the causal relationships between their first-order categories (law-abiding taxa) that this would entail—would not outweigh the cognitive cost. In other words, it would not be relevant. It might also prove maladaptive (cf. Sperber and Wilson, 1986).

There seems, then, to be a sense to Itzaj "failure" in turning their folk taxonomies into one of the most powerful inductive tools that humans may come to possess. To avail themselves of this tool, the Itzaj would have to suspend their primary concern with ecological and morphobehavioral relationships in order to disregard them for deeper, hidden properties of greater inductive potential. But this potential, which science strives to realize, is to a significant extent irrelevant, or only indirectly relevant, to local ecological concerns. To suspend or forsake the reasoning that people use to fit together their local environment, for the promise of some greater cosmic understanding, encourages a casual concern with what is happening in the world around. This is a luxury some can ill afford.

For the most part, Americans—including many university students—are not really scientists after all. Although they may reason formally as a scientist might, their conclusions are often spurious. This is because the taxa American folk employ are less properly scientific taxa than they are folk taxa. Scientists use diversity-based reasoning to generate hypotheses about global distributions of biological properties so that predictions can be tested against experience, and the taxonomic order is subsequently restructured when prediction fails. This leads scientists to radically reconstrue, transform, and even forsake their prior folk-based categories when those categories fail to support the predictive theories that science develops (i.e., when the categories fail to function successfully as the natural-kind predicates of biological laws). By contrast, American folk do not have the biological theories to support diversity-based reasoning that scientists do. If they did, these folk would not have the categories they do.

For example, we find that American students use TREE as if it were a theory-based category, and reason about the supposed distribution of biological properties among different tree species despite the fact that TREE cuts across evolutionary lines. From an ecological standpoint, however, TREE remains a valid category: trees determine how other plants will grow and how animal species will interact. Thus, when Itzaj reason about the relationships between trees in terms of ecological causes and agents rather than in terms of some presumptive underlying causal unity, their reasoning has local validity. To be consistent, American folk should either abandon TREE, to correctly reason as scientists do, or retain TREE as an ecological category, and reason more or less as Itzaj do.

Increasingly urbanized Americans are caught in a bind: intuitively, TREE retains a powerful hold on the minds and lives of people, but its use as an organizing concept has lost many of its local implications and it is treated as if it had the global or cosmic (theoretically driven) significance that scientists require of biological categories. Americans are educated to be sensitive to these requirements, without having to understand them. Nowadays, when American students are asked to identify kinds of TREE, they are more apt to be able to analytically explain in what ways angiosperms differ from gymnosperms than to tell the difference between beech trees and elms. As a people's understanding falls through the cracks between folk and scientific awareness, so may any meaningful comprehension of the biological world they live within.

In sum, Itzaj and American subjects use similarly structured taxonomies in somewhat different ways in order to extend understanding of the world in the face of uncertainty. In principle, either way might succeed. For centuries, the Itzaj have managed to use their folk-biological structures to integrate and maintain a fairly stable, context-sensitive ecological order. In a different way, scientists who use taxonomies as heuristics for reaching a more global, context-free understanding of biological relationships, generate important new discoveries of properties that do not conform to surface appearances. American folk unwittingly pursue a compromise of sorts: maintaining ecologically valid categories, but reasoning about them as if they were theory-based. Irrelevancy often results.

Science and Common Sense

Aristotle was the first in the West (or anywhere else, it seems) to advance the theoretical presumption of overarching causal unity and underlying lawful uniformity for domains of "natural kinds," including biological kinds as well as kinds of inert physical substances. This strategy eventually enabled Western science to extend these "natural" domains from just local relationships among their respective kinds to the whole planet and cosmos. It took more than two thousand years, however, before scientists began to articulate principles that were explicitly designed to go beyond common sense.

In what is widely regarded as the first "true-to-nature" herbal of the post-Renaissance, a keen historian of science has noted:

The plant was taken out of the water, and the roots were cleansed. What therefore we see depicted is a water lily without water—isn't this a bit paradoxical? All relations between the plant and its habitat have been broken and concealed. (Jacobs, 1980, p. 162)

Only by isolating organisms from their local habitats and describing them in the sense-neutral tones of written discourse could a worldwide system of biological comparisons and contrasts develop. This meant sacrificing the local "virtues" of folk-biological knowledge, including cultural, ecological, and sensory information.

From Linnaeus to the present day, biological systematics has used explicit principles and organizing criteria that traditional folk might consider secondary or might not consider at all (e.g., the geometrical composition of a plant's flower and fruit structure, or the numerical breakdown of an animal's blood chemistry). Nevertheless, as with Linnaeus, the modern systematist initially depends implicitly, and crucially, on a traditional folk appreciation. As Bartlett (1936, p. 5) noted with specific reference to the Maya region of the Peten:

A botanist working in a new tropical area is. . .confronted with a multitude of species which are not only new to him, but which flower and fruit only at some other season than that of his visit, or perhaps so sporadically that he can hardly hope to find them fertile. Furthermore, just such plants are likely to be character plants of [ecological] associations. They are often gigantic trees of which flowers are not easily detected from the ground; or lianas, whose leaves, even, are inaccessible in the tops of trees; or palms extremely difficult to collect adequately; or bamboos, very seldom found in flower. When confronted with such a situation, the botanist will find that his difficulties vanish as if by magic if he undertakes to learn the flora as the natives know it, using their plant names, their criteria for identification (which frequently neglect the fruiting parts entirely), and their terms for habitats and types of land. (cf. Diamond, 1966, for zoology)

For scientific systematics, traditional folk biology may represent a ladder to be thrown away after it has been climbed. But those who lack traditional folk knowledge, or implicit appreciation of it, may be left in the lurch. For an increasingly urbanized and formally educated people, no amount of cosmically appropriate scientific reasoning skill may be able to compensate for a loss of ecological awareness that threatens everyday survival.

Trees and Birds: Not Scientific but Not Outworn

Enlightenment naturalists, such as Joachim Jungius and Caroli Linnaeus, effected a further separation of scientific biology (natural history) from its cognitive moorings in human ecology. They banned from botany the intuitively "natural," but scientifically "lubricious," life-forms, such as TREE and GRASS. To be sure, TREE constitutes no unitary phyletic line (e.g., legumes are variously trees, vines, bushes, etc.). Only now are evolutionary theorists beginning to question the "reality" of longstanding zoological life forms such as BIRD and REPTILE, and of the whole taxonomic framework that made biology conceivable in the first place. For example, if the first birds descended from dinosaurs, and if crocodiles but not turtles are also directly related to dinosaurs, then it follows that crocodiles and birds form a group that excludes turtles; or crocodiles, birds, and turtles form separate groups; or all form one group. Whatever the case, the traditional separation of the classes BIRD and REPTILE is no longer scientifically tenable.

Yet, Linnaeus no less than any contemporary field biologist, would continue to rely on popular life-forms like TREE to collect and understand local species arrangements. People who live intimately with nature ignore such ecologically salient kinds only at their peril. And even when people become largely ignorant of local ecological relationships, as they do in our urban Western culture, they continue to cling to life-forms, such as TREE (or BIRD or REPTILE), as unforgettable parts of their lives and the evolutionary history of the human species.

The Enduring Nature of Vitalism and the Taxonomic Tree of Life

Vitalism is the belief that biological kinds—and their maintaining parts, properties, and processes—are not reducible to the contingent relations that govern inert matter. The cultural expression of vitalism varies (see Hatano and Inagaki, 1994). Within any given culture people may have varying interpretations and degrees of attachment to this belief: Those who are religiously inclined may think that a "spiritual" essence determines biological causality; ancient Greek atomists as well as those with a more scientific temperament may hold that systems of laws that suffice for physics and chemistry do not necessarily suffice for biology. Many, if not most, working biologists (including cognitive scientists) implicitly retain at least a minimal commitment to vitalism: They acknowledge that physico-chemical laws should suffice for biology, but suppose that such laws are not adequate in their current form and must be enriched by further laws whose predicates (i.e., "natural kinds") are different from those of inert physics and chemistry.[10]

Moreover, it is not at all clear how the complete elimination of teleological expressions (concepts that are defined functionally) from biological theory can be pursued without forsaking a powerful and fruitful conceptual scheme for understanding physiology, morphology, disease, and evolution. In cognitive science, the belief that biological systems, such as the mind/brain, are not wholly reducible to electronic circuitry, like computers, is a pervasive attitude that implicitly drives considerable polemic but also much creative theorizing. Thus, even if this sort of vitalism represents a lingering folk belief that science may ultimately seek to discard, it remains an important and perhaps indispensable cognitive heuristic for regulating scientific inquiry.

The use of taxonomic hierarchies in systematics reveals a similar point. By tabulating the ranges of extant and extinct genera, families, classes, and so on, systematists can provide a usable compendium of changing diversity throughout the history of life. For example, by looking at just numbers of families, it is possible to ascertain that insects form a more diverse group than tetrapods (i.e., terrestrial vertebrates, including amphibians, birds, mammals, and reptiles).

Furthermore, by calculating whether or not the taxonomic diversity in one group varies over time as a function of the taxonomic diversity in another group, evidence can be garnered for or against the evolutionary interdependence of the two groups. For example, recent comparisons of the relative numbers of families of insects and flowering plants reveal the surprising fact that insects were just as taxonomically diverse before the emergence of flowering plants as after. Consequently, evolutionary effects of plant evolution on the adaptive radiation of insects are probably less profound than previously thought (Labandeira and Sepkoski, 1993). The heuristic value of (scientifically elaborated) folk-based strategies for cosmic inquiry is compelling, despite evolutionary theorists being well aware that no "true" distinctions exist between various taxonomic levels.

The Limited Effects of Science on Everyday Thought

Wholesale replacement of "core" commonsense knowledge may even be impossible in some cases. There may be (innately determined) natural limits on assimilation of new knowledge to basic domains when no ready intuitive sense can be made of it. Regarding folk physics, for example, it is doubtful that any complete physical interpretation—much less phenomenal intuition—can be given to the equations of quantum mechanics. In a crucial sense that is unlike the case for classical mechanics, understanding quantum mechanics just is understanding the mathematics. There is little doubt that people—even quantum physicists— understand and negotiate their interactions with everyday physical objects without ever using, or being able to use, concepts derived from quantum equations.

Take Eddington's two tables: On the one hand, there is the hard, solid everyday table upon whose stability even the most devoted quantum physicist depends for eating meals and writing up research. On the other hand, there is the same table conceived from a cosmic vantage, with much empty space and relatively little matter, whose parts move at such great and variable speeds and which are impossible, in principle, even for the most discerning instrument ever to locate or observe. Imagine the paralyzing difficulty of being compelled to *calculate*, in quantum terms, a response to "Could you please pass the salt down the table?"

In certain respects, evolutionary understanding of species is as counterintuitive, and as difficult to teach and understand, as quantum mechanics (Hull, 1991). No hard and fast rule categorically distinguishes a race or variety from a species in time, although failure to interbreed is a good rule of thumb for distinguishing (some) groups of organisms living in close proximity. No laws of molecular or genetic biology consistently apply to all and only species.

Nevertheless, many philosophers, and scientists, continue to discuss species taxa as if they were enduring natural kinds. Indeed, some take the notion of the species as a natural kind as a scientific given, and purport to show from this that there is not only a progressive continuity between common sense and science, but that this "scientific" notion of species as natural kind is the ultimate reference for the commonsense meaning of living kind terms (Kripke, 1972; Putnam, 1975; Schwartz, 1979). If anything, modern science shows as much the reverse: There is marked discontinuity between evolutionary and preevolutionary conceptions of species, while the lingering notion of the species as a natural kind in science indicates that certain basic notions in science are as much hostage to the dictates of common sense as the other way around.

Such basic "common sense" may remain *psychologically valid* for everyday understanding of the world but perhaps not *epistemically valid* for the vastly extended or reduced dimensions of modern science. To be sure, our "metacognitive" abilities, which allow us to represent and integrate the outputs of more basic modules, can generate new types of information. Some of this elaborated knowledge can be manipulated so as to meet the input conditions of basic conceptual modules—for example, in the presentation of pictures and stories of animals rather than the animals themselves. By thus altering databases (stimulus inputs) and influencing data structures (representational outputs), even aspects of "core" knowledge may change, but within limits.

For example, even young children in our society appear to comprehend modern notions of the earth and other heavenly objects as spherelike objects (Vosniadou and Brewer, 1987), although they are likely unaware that such notions resulted from laborious scientific discoveries involving mathematics. Similarly, our children may believe that whales and bats are mammals, despite only the vaguest awareness of the anatomical insights that made these identifications possible (Medin, 1989). Even when there are demonstrable and pervasive effects of metacognitive (e.g., scientific) reasoning on basic conceptualization, the effects are not likely to be uniform nor such as to have commonsense structures wholly replaced by new structures (e.g., theories) (see Dupré, 1981; diSessa, 1988).

The commonsense knowledge underscored by basic cognitive dispositions can—and in the most counterintuitive cases must—remain somewhat separate from more sophisticated scientific conceptions despite the subtle and pervasive interactions between the two kinds of knowledge. These innately determined limits may be such as to preserve enough of the "default" ontology and structure of the core domain to make the notion of domain-specific cross-cultural universals meaningful. This leads to a strong expectation that core principles guide learning in much the same way across cultures. The genesis and understanding of cultural variation, including science, depends on it.

Conclusion: The Anthropology of Science

Specific "modular" habits of mind, it appears, evolved to capture recurrent features of hominid environments relevant to species survival. It is not surprising, therefore, that such core-compatible ideas, once emitted in a cultural environment, will spread "contagiously" through a population of minds. They will be little affected by subsequent changes in a culture's history or institutions. They are learned without formal or informal teaching and, once learned, cannot be easily or wholly unlearned. They remain inordinately stable within a culture, and are by and large structurally isomorphic across cultures.

Although there appears to be a highly structured, domain-specific, and cognitively universal basis to folk-biological knowledge, there may be considerable individual and cultural variation in how people put to use what they know in what they do. For example, the Itzaj Maya, who must live in intimate awareness of their local environment, seem to use their taxonomies of living kinds to reason through and better understand the ecological relationships between species. By contrast, American folk, who are less intimate with their local environment and culturally influenced by science, tend to reason as scientists do in order to make deeper biological connections among species than surface appearances would intimate.

University students who take survey courses are generally exposed to the explicit criteria of science, but not to the implicit criteria that are indispensable to actually doing the science. Consequently, their consistent use of scientific, rather than traditional, reasoning is as often as not a consistent matter of blind faith rather than sophistication. By contrast, the Itzaj's consistent neglect to reason according to, say, the diversity principle may reflect less a failure to reason correctly than a consistent appreciation of the irrelevance of such reasoning to understanding the everyday world around them.

A science of living kinds, first as natural history and then as biology, developed to better comprehend what could not be so easily grasped at a glance. Vast numbers of new species exposed during Europe's Age of Exploration stretched commonsense ways of thinking to the limits. More recently discovered aeons, with their indeterminately many fossilized forms, finally caused an epistemological rupture between science and common sense. This rupture is not between what is "true" or "false." Rather, it is between how the world (ideally) is in itself, independent of human observers, versus how it must appear to people, whatever science holds to be reality. A research task of "the anthropology of science" is to comprehend the emergence of this division of cognitive labor between science and common sense: to find the bounds within which commonsense thinking stands up and to show us where our ready perceptions no longer hold the promise of truth.

Acknowledgments

The comparative studies reported here received support from the National Science Foundation (No. SBR-931978) and the French Ministry of Higher Education. Participants in this project on biological categorization and reasoning across cultures include Ximena Lois (CREA, Ecole Polytechnique), Alejandro López (Max Planck Institute), Douglas Medin, John Coley, and Elizabeth Lynch (Northwestern University), Edward Smith and Paul Estin (University of Michigan), Brian Smith (University of Texas, Arlington), and Valentina Vapnarsky (Université de Paris, X, Nanterre).

Notes

1. There are no cultures in the world, except those exposed to Aristotle, that consider humans and nonhuman living kinds to belong to the same ontological category. Nor do people ordinarily process information about human beings in the same way that they process information about (nonhuman) living kinds. Thus "for the Kayapó

(Indians of the Amazon) all things are divided into four categories: (1) things that move and grow, (2) things that grow but do not move, (3) things that neither move nor grow, and (4) man, a creature that is akin to all animals, yet unique and more powerful than most animals because of his social organization" (Posey, 1981, p. 168).

2. Even within the visual modality, specific channels for color and shape processing are specialized subcomponents that underlie finer-grained visually based semantic representations. For example, in differentiating fruits (e.g., berries) *color* rather than *shape* may be critical. For flowers (e.g., tulips), *shape* rather than *color* information may be crucial (Warrington and McCarthy, 1987).

3. It makes no difference whether or not these groups are named. English speakers ambiguously use the term "animal" to refer to at least three distinct classes of living things: nonhuman animals, animals including humans, and mammals (the prototypical animals). The archaic term "beast" seems to pick out nonhuman animals in English but is seldom used today. The English term "plant" is also ambiguously used to refer to the plant kingdom, or to members of that kingdom that are not trees. Mayan languages generally have no name for "plant" as such, although these languages do permit a clear distinction to be made between plants and all other things by other means (e.g., by assigning a particular numeral classifier to all and only plants).

4. Life-forms may differ somewhat from culture to culture. For example, cultures such as the ancient Hebrew or modern Rangi (Tanzania) include the herpetofauna (reptiles and amphibians) with insects, worms, and other "creeping crawlers" (Kesby, 1979). Other cultures, such as the Itzaj Maya and (until recently) most Western cultures, include the herpetofauna with mammals as "quadrupeds" (Atran, 1994). Some cultures, such as the Itzaj Maya, place phenomenally isolated mammals like the bat with birds, just as the Rofaifo (New Guinea) place phenomenally isolated birds like the cassowary with mammals (Dwyer, 1976). Whatever the particular constitution of life-form groupings, or *taxa*, the life-form level, or *rank*, universally partitions the living world into broadly equivalent divisions.

5. Botanists and ethnobotanists prefer to emphasize morphological criteria and to identify this basic folk-biological level with the scientific genus (Bartlett, 1940; Berlin, 1972), whereas zoologists and ethnozoologists tend to emphasize behavioral (especially reproductive) criteria and identify these with the species (Diamond, 1966; Bulmer, 1970). The scientifically "ambivalent" character of basic taxa has led me to dub them *generic-species*—a somewhat cumbersome term that I have replaced here with the less accurate but more convenient notion of *folk species*. Invariably, basic-level groupings are mutually exclusive. They also represent virtually exhaustive partitionings of the local fauna and flora in the sense that hitherto unknown or unfamiliar organisms are generally assigned to a basic taxon when attention is directed toward them.

6. Folk subspecies are generally polynomial, while folk species are usually labeled by a single lexical item. Foreign organisms suddenly introduced into a local environment are often initially assimilated to basic taxa as subspecies. For example, the Lowland Maya originally labeled the Spanish horse "village tapir," just as they termed wheat "Castilian maize." Similarly, the Spanish referred to the indigenous pacas and agoutis as "bastard hares," just as they denoted the Mayan breadnut tree "Indian fig."

7. Actually, it was Cuvier who in 1829 first reduced the vertebrates to a single "branch" (*embranchement*) of the Tree of Life.

8. Thus, for Linnaeus, the Natural System was rooted in "a natural instinct [that] teaches us to know first those objects closest to us, and at length the smallest ones: for example, Man, Quadrupeds, Birds, Fish, Insects, Mites, or firstly the large Plants, lastly the smallest mosses" (1751, sec. 153).

9. Only the prototypical species of the most frequently cited Itzaj snake taxa are represented in Figure 28.4. We have yet to determine the full extension of these folk-biological taxa. Itzaj use other snake categories as well, but our biological inventories of them are too incomplete to allow their inclusion at this time.

10. Aristotle first proposed that both living and inert kinds had essential underlying natures. Locke (1689/1848) deemed these unknowable kinds, nature's "real kinds," and claimed that their underlying features could never be completely fathomed by the mind. Mill (1843) referred these kinds to nature's own "limited varieties," and thereby considered them to be the predicates of scientific laws. He dubbed them "natural kinds," including biological species and the fundamental elements of inert substance (e.g., lead, gold). Cross-culturally, it is not clear that inert substances comprise a cognitive domain that is conceived in terms of underlying essences or natures. Nor is it obvious what the basic elements might be across cultures, since the Greek EARTH, AIR, FIRE and WATER are not apparently universal. In other words, the conception of "natural kind," which supposedly spans all sorts of lawful natural phenomena, may turn out not to be a *psychologically* real predicate of ordinary thinking (i.e., a "natural kind" of cognitive science). It may be, instead, simply an *epistemic* notion peculiar to Western science and philosophy of science.

References

Adanson, M. (1763). *Familles des plantes*, 2 vols. Paris: Vincent.

Astington, J. and Gopnik, A. (1991). Theoretical explanations of children's understanding of the mind. *British Journal of Developmental Psychology, 9*, 7–31.

Atran, S. (1983). Covert fragmenta and the origins of the botanical family. *Man, 18*, 51–71.

Atran, S. (1985). Pre-theoretical aspects of Aristotelian definition and classification of animals. *Studies in History and Philosophy of Science, 16*, 113–163.

Atran, S. (1987). Constraints on the ordinary semantics of living kinds. *Mind and Language, 2*, 27–63.

Atran, S. (1990). *Cognitive foundations of natural history: Towards an anthropology of science.* Cambridge, England: Cambridge University Press.

Atran, S. (1993). Itza Maya tropical agro-forestry. *Current Anthropology, 34*, 633–700.

Atran, S. (1994). Core domains versus scientific theories. In L. Hirschfeld and S. Gelman (Eds.), *Mapping the mind: Domain specificity in cognition and culture* (pp. 316–340). New York: Cambridge University Press.

Atran, S. and Sperber, D. (1991). Learning without teaching: Its place in culture. In L. Tolchinsky-Landsmann (Ed.), *Culture, schooling and psychological development* (pp. 39–55). Norwood, NJ: Ablex.

Avis, J. and Harris, P. (1991). Belief-desire among Baka children. *Child Development, 62*, 460–467.

Baillargeon, R. (1986). Representing the existence and location of hidden objects: Object permanence in 6- and 8-month-old infants. *Cognition, 23*, 21–41.

Bartlett, H. (1936). A method of procedure for field work in tropical American phyto-geography based on a botanical reconnaissance in parts of British Honduras and the Peten forest of Guatemala. *Botany of the Maya Area, Miscellaneous Papers I.* Carnegie Institution of Washington Publication No. 461.

Bartlett, H. (1940). History of the generic concept in botany. *Bulletin of the Torrey Botanical Club, 47*, 319–362.

Berlin, B. (1972). Speculations on the growth of ethnobotanical nomenclature. *Language and Society, 1*, 63–98.

Berlin, B. (1992). *Ethnobiological classification: principles of categorization of plants and animals in traditional societies.* Princeton: Princeton University Press.

Berlin, B., Breedlove, D., and Raven, P. (1973). General principles of classification and nomenclature in folk biology. *American Anthropologist, 74*, 214–242.

Berlin, B., Breedlove, D., and Raven, P. (1974). *Principles of Tzeltal plant classification.* New York: Academic Press.

Boster, J. (1988). Natural sources of internal category structure: Typicality, familiarity, and similarity of birds. *Memory and Cognition, 16*, 258–270.

Boster, J. and D'Andrade, R. (1989). Natural and human sources of cross cultural agreement in ornithological classification. *American Anthropologist, 91*, 132–142.

Brown, C. (1984). *Language and living things: Uniformities in folk classification and naming.* New Brunswick: Rutgers University Press.

Bulmer, R. (1970). Which came first, the chicken or the egg-head? In J. Pouillon and P. Maranda (Eds.), *Echanges et communications: Mélanges offerts à Claude Lévi-Strauss* (pp. 1069–1091). The Hague: Mouton.

Carey, S. (1985). *Conceptual change in childhood.* Cambridge: MIT Press.

Carey, S., Klatt, L., and Schlaffer, M. (1992). Infants' representations of objects and nonsolid substances. Unpublished manuscript, MIT.

Cesalpino, A. (1583). *De plantis libri XVI.* Florence: Marescot.

Coley, J., Medin, M., Atran, S., and Lynch, E. (in press). Does rank have its privilege? Inductive inferences within folkbiological taxonomies. *Cognitive Psychology.*

Cosmides, L. and Tooby, J. (1992). Cognitive adaptations for social exchange. In J. Barkow, L. Cosmides, and J. Tooby (Eds.), *The adapted mind: Evolutionary psychology and the generation of culture* (pp. 163–228). New York: Oxford University Press.

Darwin, C. (1859). *On the origin of species by natural selection.* London: Murray.

Descartes, R. (1681). *Les principes de la philosophie* (4th edn.). Paris: Theodore Gerard.

Diamond, J. (1966). Zoological classification of a primitive people. *Science, 151*, 1102–1104.

diSessa, A. (1988). Knowledge in pieces. In G. Forman and P. Pufall (Eds.), *Constructivism in the computer age* (pp. 49–70). Hillsdale, NJ: Lawrence Erlbaum.

Donnellan, K. (1971). Necessity and criteria. In J. Rosenberg and C. Travis (Eds.), *Readings in the philosophy of language* (pp. 42–52). Englewood Cliffs, NJ: Prentice-Hall.

Dougherty, J. (1978). Salience and relativity in classification. *American Ethnologist, 5*, 66–80.

Dupré, J. (1981). Natural kinds and biological taxa. *The Philosophical Review, 90*, 66–90.

Dwyer, P. (1976). An analysis of Rofaifo mammal taxonomy. *American Ethnologist, 3*, 425–445.

Gelman, S. and Coley, J. (1991). Language and categorization: The acquisition of natural kind terms. In S. Gelman and J. Byrnes (Eds.), *Perspectives on language and thought: Interrelations and development* (pp. 146–196). New York: Cambridge University Press.

Gelman, S. and Wellman, H. (1991). Insides and essences: Early understanding of the non-obvious. *Cognition, 38*, 214–244.

Gilmore, M. (1932). Importance of ethnobotanical investigation. *American Anthropologist, 34*, 320–327.

Hatano, G. and Inagaki, K. (1994). Young children's naive theory of biology. *Cognition, 50*, 171–188.

Hays, T. (1983). Ndumba folk biology and the general principles of ethnobotanical classification and nomenclature. *American Anthropologist, 85*, 489–507.

Henley, N. (1969). A psychological study of the semantics of animal terms. *Journal of Verbal Learning and Verbal Behavior, 8*, 176–184.

Hickling, A. and Gelman, S. (1992). Young children's understanding of seed and plant growth. Paper presented at the conference of human development, Atlanta.

Hirschfeld, L. (1994). The child's representation of human groups. In D. Medin (Ed.), *The psychology of learning and motivation: Advances in research and theory* (Vol. 31). San Diego: Academic Press.

Hough, W. (1897). The Hopi in relation to their plant environment. *American Anthropologist, 10*, 33–44.

Hull, D. (1991). Common sense and science. *Biology and Philosophy, 6*, 467–479.

Hume, D. (1758/1955). *An inquiry concerning human understanding*. New York: Bobbs-Merrill.

Hunn, E. (1976). Toward a perceptual model of folk biological classification. *American Ethnologist, 3*, 508–524.

Hunn, E. (1977). *Tzeltal folk zoology*. New York: Academic Press.

Jacobs, M. (1980). Revolutions in plant description. In J. Arends, G. Boelema, C. de Groot, and A. Leeuwenberg (Eds.), *Liber gratulatorius in honorem H.C.D. De Wit* (pp. 155–181). Wageningen, Netherlands: H. Veenman.

Jeyifous, S. (1985). Atimodemo: Semantic conceptual development among the Yoruba. Doctoral dissertation, Cornell University.

Kant, I. (1790/1951). *Critique of judgement*. New York: Hafner Press.

Keil, F. (1989). *Concepts, kinds, and cognitive development*. Cambridge: MIT Press.

Keil, F. (1994). The birth and nurturance of concepts by domains. In L. Hirschfeld and S. Gelman (Eds.), *Mapping the mind: Domain specificity in cognition and culture* (pp. 234–254). New York: Cambridge University Press.

Kesby, J. (1979). The Rangi classification of animals and plants. In R. Reason and D. Ellen (Eds.), *Classifications in their social contexts* (pp. 33–56). New York: Academic Press.

Kripke, S. (1972). Naming and necessity. In D. Davidson and G. Harman (Eds.), *Semantics of natural language* (pp. 253–355). Dordrecht, Netherlands: Reidel.

Labandeira, C. and Sepkoski, J. (1993). Insect diversity in the fossil record. *Science, 261*, 310–315.

Lamarck, J.-B. (1809). *Philosophie zoologique*. Paris: Dentu.

Leslie, A. (1995). A theory of agency. In D. Sperber, D. Premack, and A. J. Premack (Eds.), *Causal cognition* (pp. 121–141). New York: Oxford University Press.

Linnaeus, C. (1751). *Philosophia botanica*. Stockholm: G. Kiesewetter.

Lloyd, G. (1990). *Demystifying mentalities*. Cambridge, England: Cambridge University Press.

Locke, J. (1689/1848). *An essay concerning human understanding*. London: Tegg.

López, A., Atran, S., Coley, J., Medin, D., and Smith, E. (in press). The tree of life: Universals of folkbiological taxonomies and inductions.

Mandler, J. (1992). How to build a baby. II: Conceptual primitives. *Psychological Review, 99*, 587–604.

Marks, I. (1987). *Fears, phobias, and rituals*. New York: Oxford University Press.

Mayr, E. (1969). *Principles of systematic zoology*. New York: McGraw-Hill.

Medin, D. (1989). Concepts and conceptual structure. *American Psychologist, 44*, 1469–1481.

Mill, J. (1843). *A system of logic*. London: Longmans, Green.

Munkur, B. (1983). *The cult of the serpent: An interdisciplinary survey of its manifestations and origins*. Albany: State University of New York Press.

Murphy, G. and Medin, D. (1985). The role of theories in conceptual coherence. *Psychological Review, 92,* 289–316.

Posey, D. (1981). Wasps, warriors and fearless men: Ethnoentomology of the Kayapó Indians of Central Brazil. *Journal of Ethnobiology, 1,* 165–174.

Putnam, H. (1975). The meaning of "meaning." In K. Gunderson (Ed.), *Language, mind and knowledge* (pp. 131–193). Minneapolis: University of Minnesota Press.

Raven, P., Berlin, B., and Breedlove, D. (1971). The origins of taxonomy. *Science, 174,* 1210–1213.

Rips, L. (1975). Inductive judgments about natural categories. *Journal of Verbal Learning and Verbal Behavior, 14,* 665–681.

Rips, L., Shoben, E., and Smith, E. (1973). Semantic distance and the verification of semantic relations. *Journal of Verbal Learning and Verbal Behavior, 12,* 1–20.

Rosch, E. (1975). Cognitive representations of semantic categories. *Journal of Experimental Psychology, 104,* 192–233.

Rosch, E., Mervis, C., Gray, W., Johnson, D., and Boyes-Braem, P. (1976). Basic objects in natural categories. *Cognitive Psychology, 8,* 382–439.

Schwartz, S. (1979). Natural kind terms. *Cognition, 7,* 301–315.

Seligman, M. (1971). Phobias and preparedness. *Behavior Therapy, 2,* 307–320.

Simpson, G. (1961). *Principles of animal taxonomy.* New York: Columbia University Press.

Spelke, E. (1990). Principle of object perception. *Cognitive Science, 14,* 29–56.

Spelke, E., Breinlinger, K., Macomber, J., and Jacobson, K. (1992). Origins of knowledge. *Psychological Review, 99,* 605–632.

Sperber, D. and Wilson, D. (1986). *Relevance: Communication and cognition.* London: Blackwell.

Springer, K. and Keil, F. (1989). On the development of biologically specific beliefs: The case of inheritance. *Child Development, 60,* 637–648.

Stross, B. (1973). Acquisition of botanical terminology by Tzeltal children. In M. Edmonson (Ed.), *Meaning in Mayan languages* (pp. 107–141). The Hague: Mouton.

Taylor, P. (1979). Preliminary report on the ethnobiology of the Tobelorese of Halmahera, North Moluccas. *Majalah Ilmu-ilmu Sastra Indonesia, 8,* 215–229.

Tournefort, J. (1694). *Elémens de botanique.* Paris: Imprimerie Royale.

Turiel, E. (1983). *The development of social knowledge: morality and convention.* New York: Cambridge University Press.

Vosniadou, S. and Brewer, W. (1987). Theories of knowledge restructuring in development. *Review of Educational Research, 57,* 51–67.

Wallace, A. (1889). *Darwinism.* London: Macmillan.

Warburton, F. (1967). The purposes of classification. *Systematic Zoology, 16,* 241–245.

Warrington, E. and McCarthy, R. (1987). Categories of knowledge: Further fractionations and an attempted integration. *Brain, 110,* 1273–1296.

Wellman, H. and Gelman, S. (1992). Cognitive development: Foundational theories of core domains. *Annual Review of Psychology, 43,* 337–375.

Zubin, D. and Köpcke, K.-M. (1986). Gender and folk taxonomy. In C. Craig (Ed.), *Noun classes and categorization* (pp. 139–180). Amsterdam: John Benjamins.

29

Cognitive and Cultural Factors in the Acquisition of Intuitive Biology

GIYOO HATANO
KAYOKO INAGAKI

It is generally agreed that children possess theories about a few important aspects of the world, and that one such theory is about biological phenomena (Wellman and Gelman, 1992). In fact, a few observant early educators have reported instances revealing that young children's knowledge about biological phenomena enables them to make sense of what they observe about animals and plants and also to solve daily problems involving them. For example, Motoyoshi (1979) reports that a five-year-old girl summarized her accumulated experience with raising flowers by a superb analogy: "Flowers are like people. If flowers eat nothing [are not watered], they will fall down of hunger. If they eat too much [are watered too often], they will be taken ill." It demonstrates that young children's personifying biology can serve as the basis for understanding botanical phenomena and thus constitute what Keil (1992) calls a mode of construal. Motoyoshi (1979) also reports an anecdotal but impressive example of problem solving based on biological causal attribution for an animal's unusual physical reaction: Five-year-olds in a day-care center inferred that when they observed unusual excretion of a rabbit that they were taking care of every day, it might be suffering from diarrhea, as might a person. After a group discussion, they came up with the idea of making the rabbit take some medicine for its diarrhea.

However, whether young children have acquired an autonomous domain of biology has been an issue of debate in recent years. On the one hand, Carey (1985) claimed that children younger than 10 years of age make predictions and explanations for biological phenomena based on intuitive psychology (i.e., intentional causality). According to her, young children lack the mind–body distinction; more specifically, they do not recognize that bodily functions are independent of intention or that biological processes that produce growth or death are autonomous. On the other hand, a number of recent studies have suggested that children possess autonomous biology at much earlier ages than Carey claimed. Some developmentalists (e.g., Hatano and Inagaki, 1987) have asserted that the differentiation between psychology and biology occurs, if it does, much earlier than Carey (1985) assumed. Others have proposed that biological phenomena are conceptualized differently from other phenomena from the beginning (e.g., Keil, 1992).

It should be noted, however, that there are more conceptual agreements than disagreements among major investigators of young children's understanding of biological phenomena. All of them agree that young children possess "theories" (or cognitive entities equivalent to them) about biological phenomena, more specifically, concerning internal processes involved in the individual survival and reproduction of animals and plants, and their external behaviors and properties relevant to these processes. Here the term "theory" means a coherent body of knowledge that involves causal explanatory understanding. In other words, it is assumed that young children's body of knowledge about biological phenomena involves something more than a collection of facts and/or procedures to obtain desired results (Kuhn, 1989). It is obvious that this conceptualization is a distinct departure from the Piagetian position, which assumed young children to be preoperational and thus incapable of offering more or less plausible explanations in any domain. At the same time, however, none of the investigators have ever claimed that young children have acquired the modern science of biology. As Carey aptly put it, they are "totally ignorant of the physiological mechanisms involved" (1985, p. 45). They know that input (e.g., eating too much) is related to output (becoming fat), but they know nothing about what mediates them at physiological and/or biochemical levels. The debatable issue is whether they possess naive biology, a children's version of endogenous biology similar to ethnobiology or folk biology, which is separated from psychology.

In this chapter we will discuss (1) the nature of the naive theory of "biology" that young children have before schooling, (2) commonalities of and differences in children's biology in technologically advanced societies, and (3) how this naive biology interacts with school biology to result in intuitive biology that ordinary adults in modern society have. (We distinguish the naive biology that young children have from the intuitive biology that lay adults have because the latter is more or less influenced by teaching-learning of biology at school, even though lay adults may forget most of the knowledge that they were taught.) We will emphasize, based on recent research findings, that young children, before being taught in school, possess a fairly well-developed body of biological knowledge that enables them to make reasonable predictions and explanations regarding biological phenomena. Their body of biological knowledge has some core components shared across cultures, but other components may have been instantiated differently in different cultures. School biology or scientific biology can be learned by elaborating and extending naive biology rather than rejecting or replacing it.

Personifying and Vitalistic Biology

We are convinced that the body of knowledge that young children possess about biological phenomena has at least three components, which we believe constitute naive biology (Inagaki, 1993b). The first element is knowledge enabling one to specify objects to which biology is applicable; in other words, knowledge about the living-nonliving distinction, and also about the mind-body distinction. The second is a mode of inference that can produce consistent and reasonable predictions for attributes or behaviors of biological kinds. The third is a nonintentional causal explanatory framework for behaviors needed for individual survival and bodily processes.

Knowledge Needed to Specify Targets of Biology

Living-Nonliving Distinction   An increasing number of recent studies, most of them dealing with the distinction between animals and nonliving things or artifacts, have revealed that even preschool children can distinguish animals and nonliving things in terms of the ability to make self-initiated movements (e.g., Bullock, 1985; Massey and Gelman, 1988), possession of specific, primarily observable, properties (Gelman, Spelke, and Meck, 1983), or natural transformations over time (Rosengren, Gelman, Kalish, and McCormick, 1991). Let us look at an example from these studies.

Massey and Gelman (1988), using unfamiliar animate entities as target objects, found that preschool children can distinguish animals and inanimate objects in terms of whether they have a capacity for self-initiated movements or not. That is, three- and four-year-olds were shown photographs of unfamiliar objects, including mammals, nonmammalian animals, statues with familiar animal-like forms and parts, wheeled vehicles, and multipart rigid objects, and asked whether each of these objects could go up and down a hill by itself. About 85 percent of the first yes-no answers of these children were correct, indicating that they answered animals could go up and down a hill by themselves, while inanimate objects, even if they looked like animals, could not. This result was corroborated by analyses of children's individual patterns of responses; a great majority of them showed a pattern of responses that was best described by the rule, or its variant, that all animals can move by themselves and that all of the inanimate objects require an external agent in order to move. Analyses of explanations that the children gave spontaneously or in request for justifications of their yes-no responses suggested that these children tended to change their explanations depending upon the type of the object. When talking about animals, children often focused on parts that enable the target to move, such as, "It can move because it has feet," or referred to some general feature of the target's appearance, such as, "It's an animal because it has a face." For inanimate objects, such as wheeled vehicles or rigid objects, they also referred to parts enabling movement, such as, "It can roll down on its wheels," or to an agent needed to move the object, saying, "It needs a push and then it goes," or "You have to carry it down."

Based on these results, Gelman (1990) proposed a hypothesis that from an early age young children possess skeletal principles focusing on a "causal mechanism" enabling objects to move. More specifically, children possess the innards principle, which directs attention inside those natural kinds that move on their own, and the external-agent principle, which is applied to objects that do not move on their own. It is these principles that enable children to rapidly acquire knowledge about the animate-inanimate distinction. Gelman claims that the experimental evidence obtained by her and her associates supported this hypothesis.

Only a small number of studies have dealt with the distinction between living kinds, including both animals and plants, and nonliving things. Though studies asking whether animals, plants, and nonliving things were alive reported that young children have difficulty attributing the life status to both animals and plants but not to nonliving things (e.g., Piaget, 1929; Richards and Siegler, 1986), the term, "alive," for young children might not map that for adults, because it is ambiguous in a sense that it is used in varied ways (including metaphorical usages) in everyday life.

In more recent studies, researchers, using more specific indicators than the life status, examined whether young children can recognize both animals and plants as distinct from nonliving things. They indicated that they can do so in some respects. For example, Inagaki (1993a) found that children before age six distinguish plants and animals from nonliving things in terms of growth (i.e., changes in size over time) in a study done as an extension of Rosengren, Gelman, Kalish, and McCormick (1991), which investigated children's differentiation between animals and artifacts in terms of growth. Here children from ages four to six were presented with a picture of a flower bud (or a new artifact or a young animal) as the standard stimulus picture, and then asked to choose which of two other pictures would represent the same plant (or artifact or animal) a few hours later and several months/years later. Figure 29.1 shows an example of the standard and choice cards for each of plants, artifacts, and animals. Results indicated that the children showed "invariance" patterns (i.e., no change in size both a few hours later and several months/years later for all the items) for artifacts but "growth" patterns (i.e., increase in size either/both a few hours later or/and several months/years later) for plants and animals. It was also suggested that children characterize both animals and plants as "growers," which sometimes led them to predict that plants will grow more rapidly than they do in reality.

Hatano et al. (1993) indicated that five- and six-year-olds in Israel, Japan, and the United States attributed such properties as "grow" or "die (or wither)" to animals and plants, but not to inanimate things. Stavy and Wax (1989) found that though most Israeli children below 11 did not attribute to plants the properties of breathing, eating, and reproduction, they attributed a property of growth to them correctly. Backscheider, Shatz, and Gelman (1993) reported that four-year-olds recognize that when damaged, both animals and plants can regrow, whereas artifacts can be mended only by human intervention. Springer and Keil (1991) indicated that preschoolers differentiated plants (and animals) from artifacts in terms of causal mechanisms involved in color transmission; they preferred natural biological mechanisms in color transmission for plants and animals, whereas for artifacts they chose nonbiological mechanical explanations as plausible.

That young children treat nonliving things differently from animals and plants is not sufficient for claiming that they have an integrated category of living things. We need proof that they are aware of the commonalities between animals and

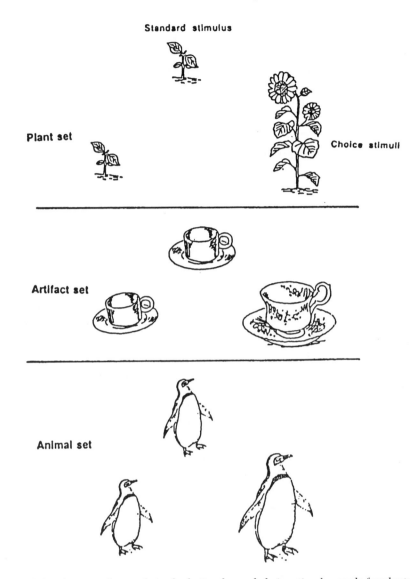

Figure 29.1   *An example set of standard stimulus and choice stimulus cards for plants, artifacts, and animals.*

plants. Hatano and Inagaki (1994a) asked five- and six-year-olds whether a few examples of plants or those of inanimate things would show phenomena similar to those we observe for animals. They found that a great majority of the children recognized commonalities between animals and plants in terms of feeding and growth in size over time, and thus distinguished them from inanimate things. Moreover, many of them justified their responses by mapping food for animals to water for plants, such as "A tulip or a pine tree dies if we do not water it" (for feeding); "If we give water, it will become bigger and bigger" (for growth in size).

In addition, about half of the children recognized the similarity between animals and plants regarding growth in number by reproduction, and a substantial number of them justified their responses by referring to the process of plants' increasing by producing seeds as being similar to animals' increasing by having babies or laying eggs. Based on these and other related studies, we can conclude that children have acquired the living-nonliving distinction by age six.

Mind-Body Distinction   Can young children distinguish between the body and the mind? Though studies dealing with this issue are small in number, the available data show that they can. That is, young children distinguish functions of the body from those of the mind—in other words, biological phenomena from social or psychological ones, both of which are observed among a subset of animate things.

Springer and Keil (1989) reported that children aged four to seven consider those features leading to biologically functional consequences for animals to be inherited, while features such as those leading to social or psychological consequences to be not inherited. Here children listened to descriptions about abnormal features that animal parents had, and then were asked whether the baby would be born with those features. The result indicated that the children considered characteristics leading to biologically functional consequences (e.g., a white stomach inside so they could eat a lot and stay strong) as inheritable, and those leading to social or psychological consequences (e.g., a white stomach inside that made them feel angry a lot) as noninheritable. Springer (1992) also revealed that even preschool children distinguish the biological relationship (parentage) from the social relationship (friendship) in attributing biological properties. In his study children were told that a target animal had a property and then asked to attribute the property to either of two other animals—i.e., a target animal's baby or an animal from a different family but a target animal's best friend. The results showed that the children attributed biological properties to dissimilar-looking related animals more often than similar-looking unrelated ones.

As Carey (1985) aptly pointed out, parentage is also a social relationship. Hence Solomon, Johnson, Zaitchik, and Carey (1993) examined whether children aged four to seven distinguished biological parentage from adoptive parentage in attributing biological/psychological properties. A close examination of their data revealed that children as young as six years of age associated a child with his or her biological parent on biological properties but with his or her adoptive parent on psychological properties. In addition, they indicated that these children understood birth as part of a process selectively mediating the acquisition of biological properties. Hirschfeld (1994) suggested that young children do not consider all the properties of a person to be equally determined by birth, and that skin color of the race is easy to be grasped as determined by birth. In fact, Hirschfeld (1995) found that preschoolers expected skin color to be inherited from a child's biological parents even when the child was switched with another at birth in the hospital.

Siegal (1988) reported that children aged four to eight recognize that illness is caused not by moral but by medical factors; they have substantial knowledge of contagion and contamination as causes of illness. Inagaki and Hatano (1987) revealed that five- and six-year-olds recognize that the growth of living things is beyond their intentional control. For example, a baby rabbit grows not because its owner wants it to but because it takes food. These findings all suggest that young children recognize the autonomous nature of biological processes.

A more systematic study on the mind-body distinction was reported by Inagaki and Hatano (1993, experiment 1). By using a variety of questions, they showed that even four- and five-year-olds have already recognized not only the differential modifiability among characteristics that are unmodifiable by any means (e.g., gender), that are bodily and modifiable by exercise or diet (e.g., running speed), and that are mental and modifiable by will or monitoring (e.g., forgetfulness), but also the independence of activities of bodily organs (e.g., heartbeat) from a person's intention. Another important piece of evidence for this distinction is young children's use of nonintentional (or vitalistic) causality for bodily phenomena but not for social-psychological ones; this point is discussed later in this chapter.

Personification as a Means to Make Educated Guesses About Living Things

When children do not have enough knowledge about a target animate object, they can make an educated guess by using personification or the person analogy in a constrained way. Young children are so familiar with humans that they can use their knowledge about humans as a source for analogically attributing properties to less familiar animate objects or predicting the reactions of such objects to novel situations, but they do not use knowledge about humans indiscriminately. In other words, they can use personification or the person analogy in an adaptive way in that they generate answers without committing many overpersonifying errors. How is it possible for young children who have not acquired an articulated taxonomy of properties (e.g., all-living-things properties, animal properties, etc.) to do so? They seem to be helped by two constraints when they transfer knowledge about humans to other animate objects.

The first is the differential application or similarity constraint, which requires the target object to be more or less similar to a human in order for the person analogy to be applied to it. As Vosniadou (1989) asserts, children tend to apply an analogy on the basis of salient similarity between the target and the source, though the "depth" of this perceived similarity varies with the richness and structuredness of the knowledge base children have. Generally, the closer the target object is biologically to a human being, the more often children recognize its similarity and thus apply the person analogy. In fact, some studies have found that young children attribute human characteristics to targets in proportion to the extent that they are perceived to be similar to people (Carey, 1985; Inagaki and Sugiyama, 1988).

The second constraint is the factual check or feasibility constraint that Inagaki and Hatano (1987) proposed. This requires that the predicted behavior of the target object through the person analogy be feasible, and that, if it is not, the prediction be rejected. They claimed that this constraint works after the person analogy is attempted—that is, one examines whether the analogical inference is tenable on the basis of factual knowledge about the target object. Even young children often know specific facts about "observable attributes" of an animate object—e.g., whether or not it has a mouth, walks, speaks to humans (e.g., Gelman, Spelke, and Meck, 1983; Inagaki and Hatano, 1987). Thus they may use this knowledge to check the plausibility of predictions reached by the person analogy, even though the knowledge is not powerful enough to generate predictions in itself. Inagaki and Hatano (1987, 1991) provided evidence supporting this idea of the feasibility constraint in personification.

In one of their studies, Inagaki and Hatano (1991) asked a group of six-year-olds to predict a grasshopper's or a tulip's reactions to three types of novel situations: (1) similar situations, in which a human and the target object would behave similarly, and thus the person analogy generated predictions plausible to them in light of their specific knowledge; (2) contradictory situations, where the target object and a human would react differently and predictions based on the person analogy contradict children's specific knowledge about the target; and (3) compatible situations, where the object and a human being would in fact react differently, but predictions obtained through the person analogy do not seem implausible to them. Example questions for each situation were as follows.

Similar situation: "We usually feed a grasshopper once or twice a day when we raise it at home. What will happen with it if we feed it 10 times a day?" [In the case of a tulip, the word *water* was used instead of *feed*.]

Contradictory situation: "Suppose a woman buys a grasshopper. On her way home she drops in at a store with this caged grasshopper. After shopping she is about to leave the store without the grasshopper. What will the grasshopper do?"

Compatible situation: "Does a grasshopper feel something if the person who has been taking care of it daily dies? [If the subject's answer is "Yes"] How does it feel?"

Results indicated that for the similar situations many of the children generated reasonable predictions with some explanations by using person analogies, whereas they did not give personified predictions for the contradictory situations. As expected, they produced unreasonable predictions for the compatible situations, where they were unable to check the plausibility of products of person analogies because of the lack of adequate knowledge (e.g., about the relation between the brain and feeling).

What follows are example responses of two children for the grasshopper questions and for the tulip questions, respectively:

M.K. (*6 years, 3 months*): For the "too-much-eating" question of the similar situation, "The grasshopper will be dizzy and die, 'cause the grasshopper, though it is an insect, is like a person [in this point]"; for the "left-behind" question of the contradictory situation, "The grasshopper will be picked up by someone, 'cause it cannot open the cage." ["*If someone does not pick up the cage, what will the grasshopper do?*"] "The grasshopper will just stay there." ["*Why doesn't the grasshopper do anything? Why does it just stay there?*"] "It cannot [go out of the cage and] walk, unlike a person"; for the caretaker's death question of the compatible situation, "The grasshopper will feel unhappy."

Y.S. (*6 years, 0 months*): For the too-much-eating question of the similar situation, "The tulip will go bad. [*Why?*] If we water the tulip too much, it cannot drink the water so much, so it will wither"; for the left-behind question of the contradictory situation, "The tulip doesn't speak. . . . Someone will bring the [potted] tulip to the police office, as a lost thing. ["*If there is no one who does such a thing, what will the tulip do? Is there anything the tulip can do?*"] "The tulip cannot move, because it has no feet"; for the caretaker's death question of the compatible situation, "The tulip will surely be sad. It cannot say 'sad,' but it will feel so inside."

These examples illustrate well how these children applied knowledge about humans differentially according to the types of situations. Generally speaking, children generate reasonable predictions, using person analogies in a constrained way, and the person analogy may be misleading only where they lack (biological) knowledge to check analogy-based predictions.

Young children's frequent use of personification is not limited to biological inference, but it is observed in other behavioral domains. However, it is a very useful tool in biological inference, because humans are a species of advanced animals, and they have a body and reveal biological phenomena like other animals.

Nonintentional Causality

The experimental evidence presented so far enables us to conclude that young children have a coherently organized body of knowledge applicable to living things. This body of knowledge can be called a theory only when a causal explanatory framework is included in it. This concerns the third component of their biological knowledge. Here the type of causality, intentional or nonintentional, determines the nature of a theory. Carey (1985) claimed that, as mentioned above, children before age ten base their explanations of biological phenomena on an intentional causality, because they are ignorant of the physiological mechanisms involved. On the contrary, we claim that young children, before schooling, can apply a nonintentional causality in explaining biological phenomena, and thus they have a form of biology that is differentiated from psychology.

Young children cannot give articulated mechanical explanations when asked to explain biological phenomena (e.g., bodily processes mediating input-output relations) in an open-ended interview (e.g., Gellert, 1962); sometimes they try to explain them using the language of person-intentional causality (Carey, 1985). These findings apparently support the claim that young children do not yet have biology as an autonomous domain. It seems inevitable to accept this claim so long as we assume only two types of causalities: intentional causality versus mechanical causality, as represented by Carey (1985). However, we propose an intermediate form of causality between these two. Children who are reluctant to rely on intentional causality for biological phenomena but who are not as yet able to use mechanical causality would often use this intermediate form of causality, which might be called "vitalistic causality."

Intentional causality means that a person's intention causes the target phenomenon, whereas mechanical causality means that physiological mechanisms cause the target phenomenon. For instance, a specific bodily system enables a person, irrespective of his or her intention, to exchange substances with its environment or to carry them to and from bodily parts. In contrast, vitalistic causality indicates that the target phenomenon is caused by activity of an internal organ, which has, like a living thing, "agency" (i.e., a tendency to initiate and sustain behaviors). The activity is often described as a transmission or exchange of the "vital force," which can be conceptualized as unspecified substance, energy, or information. Vitalistic causality is clearly different from person-intentional causality in the sense that the organ's activities inducing the phenomenon are independent of the intention of the person who possesses the organ.

In Inagaki and Hatano (1990) some children, ranging in age from five through eight, gave explanations referring to something like vital force as a mediator when given novel questions about bodily processes. For example, one child, asked what the halt of blood circulation would cause, said, "If blood does not come to the hands, they will die, because the blood does not carry energies to them." Another child offered this explanation: "We wouldn't be able to move our hands, because energies fade away if blood does not come there." However, as the number of these children was small, another experiment was done to ask children to choose a plausible explanation out of the presented ones.

Inagaki and Hatano (1993, experiment 2) predicted that even if young children could not apply mechanical causality, and if they could not generate vitalistic causal explanations for themselves, they would prefer vitalistic explanations to intentional ones for bodily processes when asked to choose one from among several possibilities. They asked six-year-old, eight-year-old, and college-age subjects to choose one explanation from a possible three for each of six bodily phenomena, such as blood circulation and respiration. The three explanations represented intentional, vitalistic, and mechanical causality, respectively. An example question on respiration with three alternative explanations was as follows: Why do we take in air? (1) Because we want to feel good [intentional]; (2) Because our chest takes in vital power from the air [vitalistic]; (3) Because the lungs take in oxygen and change it into useless carbon dioxide [mechanical].

Results indicated that the six-year-olds chose vitalistic explanations as most plausible most often; they chose them 54 percent of the time. With increasing age, the subjects came to choose mechanical explanations most often. It should be noted that the six-year-olds applied nonintentional (vitalistic plus mechanical) causalities 75 percent of the time, though they were more apt to adopt intentional causality than the eight-year-olds or the adults.

This vitalistic causality is probably derived from a general mechanism of personification. The subject who has no means for observing the opaque inside or details of the target object often tries to understand it in a global fashion, by assuming it or its parts to be humanlike (Ohmori, 1985). Hence, young children try to understand the workings of internal bodily organs by regarding them as humanlike (but noncommunicative) agents, and by assigning to their activities global life-sustaining characters, which results in vitalistic causality for bodily processes. We can see a similar mode of explanation in the endogenous or traditional sciences of Japan before the Meiji restoration (and at the beginning of its rapid modernization), which had evolved with medicine and agriculture as its core (Hatano and Inagaki, 1987).

Young children seem to rely on vitalistic causality only for biological phenomena. They seldom attribute social-psychological behavior, which is optional and not needed for survival, to the agency of a bodily organ or part, as revealed by Inagaki and Hatano (1993, experiments 3 and 3a). The following is an example question for such behavior used in the study.

"When a pretty girl entered the room, Taro came near her. Why did he do so?" Eighty percent of the 6-year-olds chose "Because Taro wanted to become a friend of hers" [intentional explanation], whereas only 20 percent opted for "Because Taro's heart urged him to go near her" [vitalistic]. For biological phenomenon questions, which were almost the same as those used in experiment 2 of Inagaki and Hatano (1993) except for excluding the mechanical causal explanation, they tended to choose vitalistic explanations rather than intentional ones.

Two theoretical issues then emerge. First, does the use of vitalistic causality by young children falsify Carey's claim? It does not do so necessarily. It is possible that children, especially younger ones, find organ-intentional vitalistic explanations appealing for biological phenomena. If this is the case, we must conclude that young children's biology is still "psychological" in the sense that it involves intentional states, though the domain is differentiated from psychology. However, our recent study revealed that when asked to choose between two types of vitalistic explanations—i.e., the organ-intentional and the organ-agential—not only six-year-olds but also five-year-olds preferred the latter as plausible (Hatano and Inagaki, 1994c). The possibility that young children's biology is "psychological" is low, though we do not know yet about the biology of four-year-olds and younger children.

Second, what is the relationship between the vitalistic explanation for biological phenomena and the teleological-functional explanation for biological properties, such as "Plants are green because it helps there be more plants" (Keil, 1992)? Both are certainly between the intentional and the mechanical; both seem to afford valid perspectives of the biological world. One interpretation is that they are essentially the same idea with different emphases—the teleological is concerned more with the why or the cause, whereas the vitalistic is concerned more with the how or the process. Another interpretation is that because the vitalistic explanation refers to activity of the responsible organ or bodily part (implicitly for sustaining life), it is closer to mechanical causality than is the teleological one, which refers only to the necessity. Anyway, it will be intriguing to examine these characterizations of young children's "biological" explanations in concrete experimental studies.

Young Children Possess a Naive Theory of Biology

From the above findings we can conclude that children as young as six years of age possess three essential components of biology: (1) the living-nonliving and the mind-body distinctions, (2) a mode of inference enabling them to produce consistent and reasonable predictions for animate objects, and (3) a nonintentional causal explanatory framework. These components correspond respectively to the three features that Wellman (1990) lists in characterizing framework theories: (1) ontological distinctions, (2) coherence, and (3) a causal-explanatory framework. We would like to emphasize that, contrary to Carey (1985), children have acquired a form of biology before schooling. This naive biology is personifying and vitalistic in nature, but it is differentiated from psychology.

Although we have stressed the individual survival and growth aspect of the life of animals and plants as the basis for children's understanding of biology, this does not mean that we ignore the reproduction aspect. Preserving species or one's own genes is probably the supreme goal of animate entities, and even young children have an intuition that offspring resemble parents (Solomon et al., 1993; Springer, 1992). However, whether they readily understand the biological nature of inheritance is debatable (Springer, 1992; Springer and Keil, 1989; Hirschfeld, 1994; Solomon et al., 1993). Because children do not engage in the enterprise of reproduction whereas they do in that of taking nutrition, it is conceivable that early biology is established around the latter. They would regard living things as those that are similar to humans in the sense that they take vital force from food and/or water to maintain vigor, with its surplus inducing growth. This triangular structural relationship of *food and/or water, active and lively* ("becomes active by taking in vital power from food"), *grow* ("vital power surplus induces growth") will be applied readily to animals. It may also be applied to plants, partly because children lack understanding of photosynthesis. We assume that this relationship constitutes "the core" of young children's understanding of the biological kinds or naive biology.

Commonalities of and Differences in Naive Biology

As already mentioned, the experimental data reviewed so far strongly suggest that children as young as six years of age have acquired a form of biology. This early acquisition of biology is not surprising from the perspective of human evolution, because it has been essential for our species to have some knowledge about animals and plants as potential foods (Wellman and Gelman, 1992) and also knowledge about our bodily functions and health (Hatano, 1989; Inagaki and Hatano, 1993). How early children acquire an autonomous domain of biology is still an open question, however, because no studies have ever examined whether very young subjects too possess a form of biology. Whether naive biology gradually emerges out of naive psychology (Carey, 1985) or is a distinct theory or mode of construal from the start (Keil, 1992) is also still debatable. Before discussing how universal children's naive biology is, across cultures, the major issue of this section, let us try to answer these two questions, because they are closely related to the issue.

Our conjecture about the "how early" question is that naive biology is acquired a little later than physics or psychology. More specifically, we assume that naive biology is gradually constructed, based on innate constraints, through daily experience in early years. Infants seldom need biological knowledge, since they do not need to take care of their health or try to find food themselves. Moreover, autonomous biology has to deal with entities that have agency (i.e., that initiate and maintain activity without external forces) but can hardly communicate with us, and thus has to apply a form of causality that is neither intentional nor mechanical in nature. Autonomous biology also presupposes the construction of an integrated category of living things including animals and plants, which appear so different. Though there is some evidence that even infants can distinguish objects having a capacity for self-initiated movement from those not having it (e.g., Golinkoff, Harding, Carlson, and Sexton, 1984), this cannot directly serve as the basis for the living-nonliving distinction.

As for the differentiation question, we take an eclectic view. We assume that there are innate constraints unique to the domain of biology, which lead to the construction of a distinct theory from the beginning. However, its construction can be affected by acquired knowledge including knowledge concerning how mind works, that is psychology, which has been established earlier. It is at least possible that very young children, whose biological knowledge is limited, are tempted to interpret biological phenomena by borrowing psychological knowledge.

Now let us discuss the issue of cultural universality of naive biology. As alluded to above in the answers to the two questions, we take the view of construction under multiple constraints. More specifically, we assume that, like other knowledge systems, naive biology is constructed under a variety of constraints, both by internal, cognitive constraints (innate tendencies and acquired prior knowledge; see Gelman, 1990; Keil, 1981) and by external, sociocultural constraints (culture as a set of artifacts and other persons; see Hatano and Miyake, 1991). Because of those constraints, which eliminate a large number of logically possible hypotheses and interpretations in advance, children can reach a reasonable choice readily and quickly in most cases. Needless to say, the same constraints may have negative effects, because they make it extremely hard for some correct hypotheses to even come to mind.

Are cognitive and sociocultural constraints treated equally in children's attempts to satisfy them, when they try to interpret biological phenomena and construct naive biology? We do not think so. We assume that cognitive constraints, especially early ones, are skeletal (Gelman, 1990) but strong, whereas sociocultural ones are weak but specified. As a result, naive biology in a variety of cultures share some basic, cognitive features but at the same time are instantiated differently according to those cultures.

It should be noted that our perspective on the issue of cultural universals in terms of constraints is considerably different from Carey and Spelke (1994). They seem to believe that all forms of naive biology before conceptual change occurs are more or less alike, because they are all enriched versions of innate principles. We assume, in contrast, that innate principles are too skeletal to be called naive biology and thus have to be instantiated by a variety of sociocultural constraints. We believe that even the initial form of naive biology may differ across cultures.

Cognitive Bases of and Universals in Naive Biology

Considering naive biology's early acquisition, as reviewed in the preceding section, it is very likely that innate or early cognitive constraints play a critical role in its construction. They serve to eliminate many competing alternatives, so that even young children can promptly derive a number of propositions that form a body of biological knowledge.

That innate constraints serve as the bases for acquiring naive biology has strongly been suggested also by the universality of folk biology, an adults' version of endogenous biology. As proposed by Atran (1990), it may be possible to find the "common sense" or core beliefs shared by all forms of folk biology and even by scientific biology. Although the exact nature of such core beliefs is debatable, the taxonomy of animate entities or a set of the ontological distinctions is certainly included among them, because all folk-biological classifications reported so far correspond very closely to the scientific one (e.g., Boster, 1991).

Likewise, much of the research inspired by Piaget—e.g., studies examining children's attribution of life status and consciousness to a variety of objects—has shown parallels in the biological understanding (or naive biology) of children in different cultures. The distinctions between animals and terrestrial inanimate objects are particularly strong. The frequent use of personification and reliance on vitalistic causality, important components of naive biology, are also expected to be more or less universal, though they have been documented only in a few countries.

Our speculation about how young children acquire the vitalistic causal framework is as follows. Children notice through somatosensation that several "events," uncontrolled by their intention, are going on inside the body. Since children cannot see the inside of the body, they will try to achieve "global understanding" through the general mechanism of personification—i.e., by personifying an organ or bodily part. Considering that young children use analogies in a selective, constrained way (Inagaki and Hatano, 1987, 1991; Vosniadou, 1989), it is plausible that they apply the person analogy to bodily organs in that way, too. More specifically, they attribute agency and some related human properties but not others (e.g., the ability to communicate) to these organs. They also through personification later generalize this global understanding of the human body to other living things.

A set of specific innate or very early cognitive constraints is probably another important factor in the acquisition of naive biology. It is likely that even very young children have tendencies to attribute a specific physical reaction to a specific class of events—for example, that diarrhea is caused by eating something poisonous. These tendencies enhance not only their rejection of intentional causality for bodily phenomena but also their construction of more specific beliefs about bodily processes.

To sum up, we are willing to admit that, because of the above general mechanism of personification and the resultant vitalistic causality, which "fit nicely with biology" (Keil, 1992, p. 105), and specific cognitive constraints, there must be some core elements in naive biology that are shared among individuals within and between cultures, as suggested by Atran (1990).

Cultural Variations in Naive Biology

However, we would like to emphasize that the significance of cognitive constraints does not mean that children's activity-based experiences in the culture surrounding them do not contribute to the acquisition of naive biology. Some such experiences are also universal in human ways of living, but others may vary and thus produce differently instantiated versions of naive biology. For example, if children are actively engaged in raising animals, it will be possible for them to acquire a rich body of knowledge about them, and therefore to use that body of knowledge, as well as their knowledge about humans, as a source for analogical predictions and explanations for other biological kinds. As asserted above, to choose knowledge about a highly familiar animal as the source for making analogical inferences for biological kinds is probably based on innate constraints and is universal, but what a highly familiar animal is may be directly influenced by culture.

Activity-based Experiences   Our studies have in fact revealed that such an activity may produce a slightly different version of naive biology from the standard one. Inagaki (1990a) compared the biological knowledge of kindergartners who had actively engaged in raising goldfish for an extended period at home with that of children of the same age who had never raised any animal. Although the two groups did not differ in factual knowledge about typical animals in general, the goldfish-raisers had much richer procedural, factual, and conceptual knowledge about goldfish. More interestingly, the goldfish-raisers used the knowledge about goldfish as a source for analogies in predicting reactions of an unfamiliar "aquatic" animal (i.e., a frog), one that they had never raised, and produced reasonable predictions with some explanations for it. For example, one of the goldfish-raisers answered when asked whether we could keep a baby frog at the same size forever, "No, we can't, because a frog will grow bigger as goldfish grew bigger. My goldfish were small before, but now they are big." It might be added that the goldfish-raisers tended to use person analogies as well as goldfish analogies for a frog. In other words, the goldfish-raisers could use two sources for making analogical predictions.

Moreover, in another study (Kondo and Inagaki, 1991; see also Hatano and Inagaki, 1992), another group of goldfish-raising children tended to enlarge their previously possessed narrow conception of animals. As shown in Figure 29.2, the goldfish-raisers attributed animal properties that are shared by humans (e.g., having a heart, excreting) not only to goldfish but also to a majority of animals phylogenetically between humans and goldfish at a higher rate than the corresponding nonraisers. This suggests that the experience of raising goldfish modifies young children's preferred mode of biological inferences.

Cultural and Linguistic Variables   That the biological understanding observed in different cultures is not identical strongly suggests that larger cultural contexts of

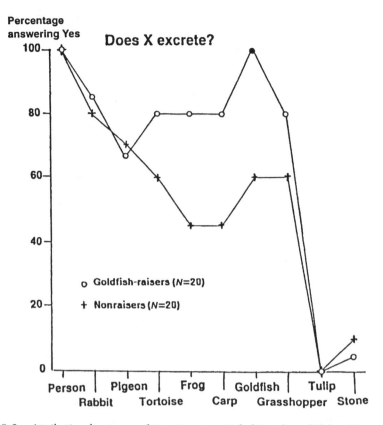

Figure 29.2 *Attributional patterns of excretion to varied objects by goldfish-raising and non-raising children.*

children's life also influence the construction of naive biology. The most striking of the differences thus far reported concerns ideas about plants among children in Israel. Stavy and Wax (1989) showed that about half of a sample of 6- to 12-year-olds, when asked to judge the life status of animals, plants, and nonliving things, classified plants either as nonliving things or as falling within a third category, things that are neither living nor nonliving. Beliefs about inanimate objects may also differ between cultures. Whereas recent studies conducted in North America indicate that young children seldom attribute life or other living-thing properties to any terrestrial inanimate objects (e.g., Dolgin and Behrend, 1984; Richards and Siegler, 1984), Inagaki and Sugiyama (1988) reported that some Japanese preschoolers extended mental properties even to inanimate objects without movement or function, such as stones.

Hatano, Siegler, Richards, Inagaki, Stavy, and Wax (1993) tried to differentiate between universal and culturally specific aspects of children's conceptions of life and understanding of attributes of living things, by comparing kindergartners, second and fourth graders from Israel, Japan, and the United States. The children were asked whether two instances each of four object types (people, other animals, plants, and inanimate objects) possessed each of 16 attributes that included life status (being alive), unobservable animal attributes (e.g., has a heart), sensory attributes (e.g., feels pain), and attributes true of all living things (e.g., grows bigger).

The results illustrate both similarities and differences across cultures in children's biological understanding. Children in all cultures knew that people, other animals, plants, and inanimate objects were different types of entities with different properties, and they were extremely accurate regarding humans, somewhat less accurate regarding other animals and inanimate objects, and least accurate regarding plants. At the same time, as predicted from cultural analyses, Israeli children were considerably more likely not to attribute to plants life status and other properties that are shared by all living things, whereas Japanese children, whose overall accuracy was comparable to the Israeli, were considerably more likely to attribute to inanimate objects properties that are unique to living things.

These differences are especially interesting because they suggest that children's naive biology is influenced by beliefs within the culture where they grow up. Consider why Japanese children might be more likely than children in the United States or Israel to view plants or inanimate objects as alive and having attributes of living things. Japanese culture includes a belief that plants are much like human beings. This attitude is represented by the Buddhist idea that even a tree or blade of grass has a mind. In Japanese folk psychology, even inanimate objects are sometimes considered to have minds. For example, it is at least not a silly idea for Japanese to assign life or divinity not only to plants but also to inanimate objects, especially big or old ones. In addition, linguistic and orthographic factors seem to influence Japanese children's attributional judgments. The *kanji* (Chinese character) representing life has a prototypal meaning of "fresh" or "perishable" as well as "alive." Therefore this *kanji* can be applied to cake, wine, sauce, and other perishable goods.

Similar features of culture and language may account for Israeli children being less apt than American or Japanese children to attribute to plants life status and properties of living things. Stavy and Wax (1989) suggested that within the Israeli culture, plants are regarded as very different from humans and other animals in their life status. This cultural attitude parallels that of a biblical passage (Genesis 1.30), well known to Israeli students, indicating that plants were created as food for living things including animals, birds, and insects. Adding to, or perhaps reflecting, their cultural beliefs, the Hebrew word for "animal" is very close to that for "living" and "alive." In contrast the word for "plant" has no obvious relation to such terms (Stavy and Wax, 1989).

How culture influences the development of biological understanding has yet to be studied. Culture may provide children with opportunities to engage in activities that lead them to construct some particular biological understanding, as in the case of children raising goldfish, as mentioned above, but this is not the only path through which the cultural influence is exerted. Parents, schools, and even mass media may serve to transmit cultural beliefs through dialogical interaction with young children. For example, Japanese parents may communicate the attitude through their actions toward plants and divine inanimate objects, though they do not usually tell their children this explicitly. We shall now examine mother-child interactions regarding biological kinds versus artifacts both in natural and experimental situations. For example, what does a mother say when a child breaks a flower? How different is it from when the child breaks a toy?

How Naive Biology and School Biology Interact

This final section will focus on how young children's naive biology changes as they grow older, and what role schooling in general or the teaching and learning of scientific biology in school plays therein. Let us start with the differences between young children's biological knowledge and the intuitive biology of ordinary adults in technologically advanced societies having the modern science of biology. In other words, we begin with the issue of what needs to be incorporated and/or modified for young children's naive biology to become the lay adult's intuitive biology.

We emphasized the strengths of young children's naive biology in the first section. What weaknesses does it have? Its weaknesses are obvious even when compared with intuitive biology in lay adults. Let us list some major ones: (1) limited factual knowledge, (2) lack of inferences based on complex, hierarchically organized biological categories, (3) lack of mechanical causality, and (4) lack of some conceptual devices (e.g., "evolution," "photosynthesis").

The use of inferences based on complex, hierarchically organized biological categories and of mechanical causality requires a theory change or conceptual change (i.e., fundamental restructuring of knowledge), whereas the accumulation of more and more factual knowledge can be achieved by enrichment only. Whether the acquisition of basic conceptual devices in scientific or school biology is accompanied by a theory change is not beyond dispute, but incorporating them meaningfully into the existing body of knowledge, we believe, can usually be achieved only with its restructuring. Let us discuss these changes in turn.

Naive Biology as Prior Knowledge for Learning About Animals and Plants

Young children's factual knowledge about the biological kinds is necessarily limited. However, this is not a serious weakness, because they can learn promptly those facts concerning animals and plants, as far as they are plausible within their naive biological framework. In a recent experiment examining how promptly kindergartners remember such facts, we presented a group of six-year-olds either a connected list or a random one, and asked them to remember sentences in it. Each sentence consisted of a moderately familiar animal as the subject, its behavior, and an outcome. In the connected list, the behavior and the outcome were causally connected in naive biology, in the sense that the cause induces the outcome in humans (e.g., "A wolf ate rotten meat and had diarrhea"). In the random list, causes and outcomes were randomly paired (e.g., "An alligator gave milk to its young and cured a wound promptly"). We found that the children could recall sentences in the connected list much better, even when sentences were false for those animals, as in the above example—eating rotten meat causes no ill health for a wolf.

Naive biology also serves as the basis for meaningfully learning procedures for taking care of animals and plants as well as themselves in everyday life. In other words, children could readily enrich their procedural knowledge about living things, especially about complex animals. Global understanding of internal bodily functions is enough for such purposes. Inagaki and Kasetani (1994) investigated five- and six-year-olds' comprehension and learning of the procedures needed to raise a squirrel. Although their study was aimed at examining whether inducing the person analogy would enhance learning, and they in fact found some effects of referring to humans, they also found that children could learn the procedures to a considerable degree even without such references, probably because those procedures (e.g., the necessity of giving a variety of food to a squirrel) are more or less applicable to humans.

Evolution Toward Purely Biological Biology   As children grow older, their personifying and vitalistic biology gradually changes toward truly "nonpsychological" (if not scientific) biology by eliminating weaknesses (2) and (3) mentioned above— namely, toward a biology that relies on category-based inferences and prefers mechanical causal explanations and rejects intentional ones. We assume that this change (or the fundamental restructuring of knowledge) is almost universal, at least among children growing up in highly technological societies, and that it can occur, unlike the acquisition of basic conceptual devices, without systematic instruction in biology, though schooling certainly has some general facilitative effects on it.

Let us present a few relevant empirical studies. Johnson, Mervis, and Boster (1992) found that, whereas ten-year-olds and adults possess a category of primates and include a human in it, seven-year-olds regard a human as very different even from a monkey. Carey (1985) also reported similar results, using the induction paradigm; when four-year-olds were taught some novel properties on people, they attributed them to other animals to a much greater degree than when they were taught on dogs. In contrast, ten-year-olds and adults who were taught on dogs were hardly distinguishable in attributional patterns from those taught on people. Rather, projections from dogs were slightly greater than from people. These results indicate that the status of humans changes from that of a prototype to what is not more prototypical than dogs.

Inagaki and Sugiyama (1988) examined how young children's human-centered or "similarity-based" inference would change as they grew older. They gave attribution questions, such as "Does X have a property Y?", to children aged four to ten and college students. Results indicated that there was a progression from the four-year-olds' predominant reliance on similarity-based attribution (attributing human properties in proportion to perceived similarity between target objects and humans) to adults' predominant reliance on category-based attribution (attributing properties by relying on the higher-order category membership of the targets and category-attribute associations).

This shift from similarity-based to category-based inferences is induced, we assume, not only by an increased amount of knowledge but also by the development of metacognitive beliefs evaluating more highly the usefulness of higher-order categories (Inagaki, 1989). Children realize that higher-order categories are more dependable than the similarities to people for predicting unfamiliar animals' behaviors, attributes, habitats, and so on. This realization facilitates the use of such categories in any situation in which a biological inference is required. Hatano and Inagaki (1991a) provided data to confirm this idea, using a task designed to assess children's metacognitive beliefs about the dependability of category-based versus similarity-based inference as well as a set of attribution questions.

As children grow older and accumulate more educational experience, a developmental change in causality for internal bodily functions also occurs. In contrast to young children's vitalistic, and sometimes even intentional, explanations, older children reject intentional explanations for biological phenomena and are inclined to use mechanical causality exclusively. In experiment 2 of Inagaki and Hatano's (1993) study, the difference between six-year-olds and eight-year-olds was larger than the difference between eight-year-olds and adults in terms of preference for mechanical explanations and avoidance of intentional ones.

These results suggest that young children's biology is qualitatively different from the biology that older children and adults have, and that, in accordance with Carey's (1985) claim, there occurs a conceptual change in biological understanding between ages four and ten. However, contrary to her claim, this change is characterized not as the differentiation of biology from psychology but as a qualitative change within the autonomous domain of biology, because children as young as six years of age already possess a form of biology.

Naive Biological Inference as a Default Strategy for Adults   Is the intuitive biology of adults no longer personifying at all? Does intuitive biology no longer rely on vitalistic causality? The answers to these questions are not affirmative. The fact that there exists a shift from similarity-based to category-based inferences does not mean that older children and adults never rely on the similarity to people in their attributions. Inagaki and Sugiyama (1988) reported that a substantial number of adults as well as older children still rely on similarity to people in attributing mental properties to varied animate entities. Morita, Inagaki, and Hatano (1988), using reaction time measures, revealed that college students use the similarity to people to some extent not only for mental properties but also for anatomical/physiological ones in a situation in which they have to respond very quickly and thus are not able to use the category membership of target objects and category-property relationships. These results strongly suggest that personification or the person analogy may be used even by adults as a fallback strategy.

The fact that college students preferred much more strongly mechanical causality to the vitalistic one (Inagaki and Hatano, 1993, experiment 2) does not mean that they never rely on the latter in any situation. One of the college students in

Inagaki and Hatano (1993) consistently chose vitalistic explanations, and answered at the interview after the experiment, "We usually choose those including 'oxygen' or 'the heart works like a pump' because we have learned in school to do so. However, I chose others because they were most convincing and comprehensible to me." This suggests that vitalistic biology continues to work as a basis of understanding and to be used in situations where people do not think they are required to answer based on so-called scientific biology.

Incorporating Scientific Biological Concepts The last type of weakness or needed change listed above—that is, coming to view the biological world with scientific conceptual tools—may occur as a result of an understanding of the scientific biology taught at school. In order to be able to understand and reason "scientifically" in biology, students need to know basic biological concepts and principles as major conceptual devices. For example, if students do not know the phenomenon of photosynthesis, they will not be able to understand the basic difference between animals and plants (i.e., that plants can produce nutriment themselves), and thus may accept the false analogy of mapping water for plants to food for animals. We assume that, unlike the conceptual change in inference and causality just described above, this change is very hard to achieve especially without educational intervention, and thus occurs only among a limited portion of older children or adolescents.

The teaching of school biology must include what goes beyond naive biology or even what contradicts it. How might we organize such teaching? Let us look at two examples, evolution and photosynthesis, from recent studies.

The (Darwinian) idea of evolution must be difficult for children to grasp. It has been fully accepted even among biologists only in the last two centuries. However, because naive biology assumes that living things, but not nonliving things, are able to adjust themselves to their ecological niche or ways of life, children are ready to accept any biological kind's gradual adaptive changes over generations, and thus to form a version of the Lamarckian idea of evolution.

The subject of photosynthesis is more difficult, because it has to be acquired against the intuitive grasp of the commonality among all living things that naive biology indicates. We would like to suggest, based on children's naive biological knowledge, two strategies for overcoming the difficulty. First, it could be effective to falsify the incorrect analogy between food to animals and water to plants, by drawing children's attention to the fact that animals also take in water. Second, the phenomenon of photosynthesis might be treated as a representative of vitalistically interpreted physiological processes, and such processes might be explained by using another analogy—for example, processing materials with proper means like baking bread from flour using heat (Yuzawa, 1988).

As children learn these and other scientific conceptions in school biology, their ways of understanding the biological world may in fact change. In other words, it is not only that school biology is learned meaningfully by being assimilated into existing knowledge of naive biology. It is also, as claimed by Vygotsky (1978), that it reorganizes naive biology by adding, say, physiological mechanisms and the evolutional perspective, so that the reorganized body of knowledge can effectively be used as the basis for answering a wider variety of biological questions.

Educational Implications

Since Carey (1985), young children's naive biology has been an exciting topic for research in conceptual development. As more and more ambitious researchers have joined to study it, not only has a richer database been built and finer conceptualizations offered about this specific domain, but also, through attempts to answer such conceptual questions as naive biology's structure, function, ontogenesis, change, and universality, a better understanding of conceptual development in general has been achieved (Hatano and Inagaki, 1994b). Young children's naive biology will probably be a popular topic for the next several years, and research questions about it can be better answered and/or rephrased. These topics will include, among others, (1) the time when the uniquely biological causal framework appears, (2) the integration of nativistic and cultural accounts of the acquisition of and change in naive biology, and (3) the interaction of naive knowledge with scientific knowledge in this domain.

This growing body of research on naive and intuitive biology has significant implications for education, especially for the teaching-learning of biology. This is because, as pointed out by Olson and Torrance, many pedagogical practices of teachers are premised on assumptions about the mind, knowledge and consciousness of the learner (this volume, chap. 1) and vice versa—our understanding of how children's mind works and grows can direct, or even specify, contents and methods of teaching. In this chapter, by reviewing studies on children's naive biology, we have concluded that (1) young children possess an autonomous domain of naive biology that produces reasonable predictions and explanations; (2) children's biological knowledge, though it may share some core components, is instantiated differently in different cultures; and (3) children's naive biology serves as the basis for learning school biology and is transformed by it. Let us discuss very briefly the educational implications of each conclusion.

The first conclusion concerns the learner's initial state of knowledge before instruction. Detailed descriptions of the initial state must be very helpful for designing an effective course of instruction, because the instruction aims at changing the learner's knowledge from initial state to goal state (Glaser and Bassok, 1989). Our conclusion acknowledging children's naive biology as an autonomous domain implies that starting instruction of biology at kindergarten or lower elementary grades is possible and can be effective. This implication is clearly distinct from that of Carey (1985) and others, who assume that young children have no form of biology, because, according to the latter, biology is taught as a totally new discipline in school or its teaching is postponed until the fifth grade or so.

The second conclusion indicates that there can be diverse routes in the development of biological understanding, and it encourages educators to build a curriculum for biology instruction by taking students' cultural perspectives into account. It also gives support to the idea of ethnographic translation of instructional materials and procedures (Serpell and Hatano, in press), in general as well as in biology, rejecting the idea of importing educational programs from other cultures as they are.

The third and final conclusion is a bit tentative at present but strongly suggests that educators activate students' informal biological knowledge and relate formal biology instruction to it as much as possible. It also implies that naive biology that is personifying and vitalistic in nature can provide students with a conceptual framework for learning school biology meaningfully. Future studies regarding interactions between naive and school biology will, we hope, specify how naive biology should be elaborated by formal instruction toward "scientific" biology, as well as how it should be relied on to help students understand school biology better (Inagaki, 1994).

References

Atran, S. (1990). *Cognitive foundations of natural history: Towards an anthropology of science.* Cambridge, England: Cambridge University Press.

Backscheider, A. G., Shatz, M., and Gelman, S. A. (1993). Preschoolers' ability to distinguish living kinds as a function of regrowth. *Child Development, 64,* 1242–1257.

Boster, J. S. (1991). The information economy model applied to biological similarity judgment. In L. B. Resnick, J. M. Levine, and S. D. Teasley (Eds.), *Perspectives on socially shared cognition* (pp. 203–225). Washington: American Psychological Association.

Bullock, M. (1985) Animism in childhood thinking: A new look at an old question. *Developmental Psychology, 21,* 217–225.

Carey, S. (1985). *Conceptual change in childhood.* Cambridge: MIT Press.

Carey, S. and Spelke, E. (1994). Domain-specific knowledge and conceptual change. In L. A. Hirschfeld and S. A. Gelman (Eds.), *Mapping the mind: Domain specificity in cognition and culture* (pp. 169–200). Cambridge, England: Cambridge University Press.

Dolgin, K. G. and Behrend, D. A. (1984). Children's knowledge about animates and inanimates. *Child Development, 55,* 1646–1650.

Gellert, E. (1962). Children's conceptions of the content and functions of the human body. *Genetic Psychology Monographs, 65,* 291–411.

Gelman, R. (1990). First principles organize attention to and learning about relevant data: Number and the animate–inanimate distinction as examples. *Cognitive Science, 14,* 79–106.

Gelman, R., Spelke, E., and Meck, E. (1983). What preschoolers know about animate and inanimate objects. In D. Rogers and J. A. Sloboda (Eds.), *The acquisition of symbolic skills* (pp. 297–326). New York: Plenum.

Glaser, R. and Bassok, M. (1989). Learning theory and the study of instruction. *Annual Review of Psychology, 40,* 631–666.

Golinkoff, R. M., Harding, C. G., Carlson, V., and Sexton, M. E. (1984). The infant's perception of causal events: The distinction between animate and inanimate objects. In L. P. Lipsitt and C. Rovee-Collier (Eds.), *Advances in infancy research* (vol. 3, pp. 145–165). Norwood, NJ: Ablex.

Hatano, G. (1989). Language is not the only universal knowledge system: A view from "everyday cognition." *Dokkyo Studies in Data Processing and Computer Science, 7,* 69–76.

Hatano, G. and Inagaki, K. (1987). Everyday biology and school biology: How do they interact? *The Quarterly Newsletter of the Laboratory of Comparative Human Cognition, 9,* 120–128.

Hatano, G. and Inagaki, K. (1991a). *Learning to trust higher-order categories in biology instruction.* Paper presented at the meeting of the American Educational Research Association, Chicago.

Hatano, G. and Inagaki, K. (1991b). *Young children's causal reasoning through spontaneous personification* [in Japanese]. Paper presented at the 33rd annual meeting of the Japanese Association of Educational Psychology, Nagano.

Hatano, G. and Inagaki, K. (1992). Desituating cognition through the construction of conceptual knowledge. In P. Light and G. Butterworth (Eds.), *Context and cognition: Ways of learning and knowing* (pp. 115–133). London: Harvester/Wheatsheaf.

Hatano, G. and Inagaki, K. (1994a). *Recognizing commonalities between animals and plants.* Paper to be presented at the meeting of the American Educational Research Association, New Orleans.

Hatano, G. and Inagaki, K. (1994b). Young children's naive theory of biology. *Cognition, 50,* 171–188.

Hatano, G. and Inagaki, K. (1994c). *Bodily organ's "intention" in vitalistic causal explanations* [in Japanese]. Paper presented at the 36th annual meeting of the Japanese Association of Educational Psychology, Kyoto.

Hatano, G. and Miyake, N. (1991). Commentaries: What does a cultural approach offer to research on learning? *Learning and Instruction, 1,* 273–281.

Hatano, G., Siegler, R. S., Richards, D. D., Inagaki, K., Stavy, R., and Wax, N. (1993). The development of biological knowledge: A multi-national study. *Cognitive Development, 8,* 47–62.

Hirschfeld, L. A. (1994). Is the acquisition of social categories based on domain-specific competence or on knowledge transfer? In L. A. Hirschfeld and S. A. Gelman (Eds.), *Mapping the mind: Domain specificity in cognition and culture* (pp. 201–233). Cambridge, England: Cambridge University Press.

Hirschfeld, L. A. (1995). Do children have a theory of race? *Cognition, 54,* 209–252.

Inagaki, K. (1989). Developmental shift in biological inference processes: From similarity-based to category-based attribution. *Human Development, 32,* 79–87.

Inagaki, K. (1990a). The effects of raising animals on children's biological knowledge. *British Journal of Developmental Psychology, 8,* 119–129.

Inagaki, K. (1990b). Young children's use of knowledge in everyday biology. *British Journal of Developmental Psychology, 8,* 281–288.

Inagaki, K. (1993a). *Young children's differentiation of plants from nonliving things in terms of growth.* Paper presented at the biennial meeting of Society for Research in Child Development, New Orleans.

Inagaki, K. (1993b). *The nature of young children's naive biology.* Paper presented at the symposium, "Children's naive theories of the world," at the 12th meeting of the International Society for the Study of Behavioral Development, Recife, Brazil.

Inagaki, K. (1994). *Personifying and vitalistic biology: Its nature and instructional implications.* Paper presented at the 13th meeting of the International Society for the Study of Behavioral Development, Amsterdam.

Inagaki, K. and Hatano, G. (1987). Young children's spontaneous personification as analogy. *Child Development, 58,* 1013–1020.

Inagaki, K. and Hatano, G. (1990). *Development of explanations for bodily functions* [in Japanese]. Paper presented at the 32nd annual meeting of the Japanese Association of Educational Psychology, Osaka.

Inagaki, K. and Hatano, G. (1991). Constrained person analogy in young children's biological inference. *Cognitive Development, 6,* 219–231.

Inagaki, K. and Hatano, G. (1993). Young children's understanding of the mind–body distinction. *Child Development, 64,* 1534–1549.

Inagaki, K. and Hatano, G. (1994). *Effects of biological contexts on children's induction of human properties* [in Japanese]. Paper presented at the 36th annual meeting of the Japanese Association of Educational Psychology, Kyoto.

Inagaki, K. and Kasetani, M. (1994). *Effects of inducing person analogies on young children's understanding of procedures for raising animals.* Paper presented at the 12th meeting of the International Society for the Study of Behavioral Development, Amsterdam.

Inagaki, K. and Sugiyama, K. (1988). Attributing human characteristics: Developmental changes in over- and underattribution. *Cognitive Development, 3,* 55–70.

Inagaki, K. and Suzuki, Y. (1991). *The understanding of the mind–body distinction in children aged 3 to 5 years* [in Japanese]. Paper presented at the 33rd annual meeting of the Japanese Association of Educational Psychology, Nagano.

Johnson, K. E., Mervis, C. B., and Boster, J. S. (1992). Developmental changes within the structure of the mammal domain. *Developmental Psychology, 28,* 74–83.

Keil, F. C. (1981). Constraints on knowledge and cognitive development. *Psychological Review, 88,* 197–227.

Keil, F. C. (1992). The origins of an autonomous biology. In M. R. Gunnar and M. Maratsos (Eds.), *Modularity and constraints in language and cognition; The Minnesota Symposia on Child Psychology* (Vol. 25, pp. 103–137). Hillsdale, NJ: Lawrence Erlbaum.

Kondo, H. and Inagaki, K. (1991). *Effects of raising goldfish on the grasp of common characteristics of animals* [in Japanese]. Paper presented at the 44th meeting of the Japanese Association of Early Childhood Education and Care, Kobe.

Kuhn, D. (1989). Children and adults as intuitive scientists. *Psychological Review, 96,* 674–689.

Kyokuchi Method in Science Education. (1974). Unit on animals' bodily structures and their ways of living [in Japanese]. Unpublished manuscript.

Massey, C. M. and Gelman, R. (1988). Preschooler's ability to decide whether a photographed unfamiliar object can move itself. *Developmental Psychology, 24,* 307–317.

Morita, E., Inagaki, K., and Hatano, G. (1988). *The development of biological inferences: Analyses of RTs in children's attribution of human properties* [in Japanese]. Paper presented at the 30th annual meeting of the Japanese Association of Educational Psychology, Naruto.

Motoyoshi, M. (1979). *Essays on education for day care children: Emphasizing daily life activities* [in Japanese]. Tokyo: Froebel-kan.

Ohmori, S. (1985). *The structure of knowledge and science* [in Japanese]. Tokyo: Nihon Hoso Shuppan Kyokai.

Piaget, J. (1929). *The child's conception of the world.* London: Routledge and Kegan Paul.

Richards, D. D. and Siegler, R. S. (1984). The effects of task requirements on children's life judgments. *Child Development, 55,* 1687–1696.

Richards, D. D. and Siegler, R. S. (1986). Children's understandings of the attributes of life. *Journal of Experimental Child Psychology, 42,* 1–22.

Rosengren, K. S., Gelman, S. A., Kalish, C. W., and McCormick, M. (1991). As time goes by: Children's early understanding of growth. *Child Development, 62,* 1302–1320.

Serpell, R. and Hatano, G. (in press). Education, schooling and literacy in a cross-cultural perspective. In J. W. Berry, P. R. Dasen, and T. S. Saraswathi (Eds.), *Handbook of cross-cultural psychology: Vol. 2. Basic processes and developmental psychology*. Boston: Allyn and Bacon.

Siegal, M. (1988). Children's knowledge of contagion and contamination as causes of illness. *Child Development, 59*, 1353–1359.

Solomon, G., Johnson, S., Zaitchik, D., and Carey, S. (1993). *Like father, like son: Young children's understanding of how and why offspring resemble their parents*. Paper presented at the Meeting of the Society for Research in Child Development, New Orleans.

Springer, K. (1992). Children's awareness of the biological implications of kinship. *Child Development, 63*, 950–959.

Springer, K. and Keil, F. C. (1989). On the development of biologically specific beliefs: The case of inheritance. *Child Development, 60*, 637–648.

Springer, K. and Keil, F. C. (1991). Early differentiation of causal mechanisms appropriate to biological and nonbiological kinds. *Child Development, 62*, 767–781.

Stavy, R. and Wax, N. (1989). Children's conceptions of plants as living things. *Human Development, 32*, 88–94.

Vera, A. H. and Keil, F. C. (1988). *The development of inductions about biological kinds: The nature of the conceptual base*. Paper presented at the 29th meeting of the Psychonomic Society, Chicago.

Vosniadou, S. (1989). Analogical reasoning as a mechanism in knowledge acquisition: A developmental perspective. In S. Vosniadou and A. Ortony (Eds.), *Similarity and analogical reasoning* (pp. 413–469). Cambridge, England: Cambridge University Press.

Vygotsky, L. S. (1978). *Mind in society*: The development of higher psychological processes. In M. Cole, V. John-Steiner, S. Scribner, and E. Souberman (Eds.). Cambridge: Harvard University Press.

Wellman, H. M. (1990). *The child's theory of mind*. Cambridge: MIT Press.

Wellman, H. M. and Gelman, S. A. (1992). Cognitive development: Foundational theories of core domains. *Annual Review of Psychology, 43*, 337–375.

Yuzawa, M. (1988). Understanding the meaning of the situation of a problem and a reasoning schema [in Japanese with an English summary]. *Japanese Journal of Educational Psychology, 36*, 297–306.

30

What Do "Just Plain Folk" Know About Physics?

ANDREA A. DISESSA

Introduction

Humans have a lot of interchange with the physical world. They lift heavy and light containers; push or roll objects across slippery or rough surfaces; move, twist, and spin themselves; bump into walls; toss and catch balls. In addition to "interchange," just plain folk manifest a certain degree of competence at all this. Most of us run into walls only occasionally and rarely miss-guess the weight of objects so much that we accidentally toss a surprisingly light one into the air while trying to lift it.

Thus there is a prima facie case that people have some knowledge of physics—of mechanics, to be more specific. The central question of this chapter is what connection, if any, does folk physics have with the physics that is taught in school, with physicist physics? The answer to this question is marvelously complex, and probably surprising. It is also state of the art because our views of this relation have undergone two revolutions in the last 15 years. Indeed, the view expressed here is far from unanimously espoused by those considering the question today.

A First Look

In order to get some purchase and perspective on this problem, let us consider some a priori possibilities.

1. *"Folk physics" has essentially no relation to school physics.* It seems entirely possible that people are merely physically competent; they do not have anything that can be reasonably called knowledge of physics. Instead, their competence is inarticulate—they cannot talk about it. It is "bottled up" in motor reflexes and the like and just cannot interact, either productively or destructively, with learning physics in school.

There is both scientific and commonsense plausibility to this view. Scientifically, for example, Jerry Fodor is famous for his notion of modular competencies that are so hidden from our inspection and introspection, so disconnected from other mental faculties that, apart from being able to exhibit those competencies, we might as well not have them. Language competence, according to Fodor (1983), is of this form. We all speak grammatically,[1] yet those rules are so inaccessible that, it seems, we must learn grammar in school from scratch.

From a commonsense point of view, we all know how hard it is to describe things we can do intuitively, without thinking. Culturally, as well, people are taught that physics is esoteric and difficult. In the United States we would not even think of teaching it until late high school. Students and adults whom I invite to think about some physics problems usually protest that they do not know anything about the subject, even if they have taken a course![2]

Until about 15 years ago, psychologists of learning and educators would likely have said the following: People have no knowledge of physics that is relevant to scientific physics. They need to be taught from scratch.

2. *"Folk physics" is in some substantial ways like scientific physics.* To elaborate on this possibility, we need to begin making some theoretical distinctions. Be forewarned that the short discussion below is simplified in various ways from what it would take to provide a state-of-the-art presentation. In addition, this chapter will focus on things like concepts and theories about which there continue to be serious scientific disagreements. Nonetheless, these simplified models are a good place to start.

Let us consider separately the form and content of folk physics. Answer 1, above, is really agnostic about content. It says, instead, that the form of our physical competence is so different from the words and ideas of real physics that contact is impossible. Presuming such a difference in form, we have no immediate reason to suspect a divergence in content. In whatever form it exists, intuitive physical knowledge (competence) would seem likely to be at least compatible with how physicists say the world works. Indeed, since intuitive and scientific world views (by this presumption) come in incompatible forms, it may be "only academic" whether or not they are actually compatible. It might not even be sensible to try to determine this.

Now, however, let us suppose just plain folk have some forms of physical knowledge in common with scientists. This is really what answer 2 means. Let us consider concepts, beliefs, and theories, three fairly prominent forms of ideas for physicists. These three forms of knowledge are roughly hierarchical. We really need to have some concepts before it is reasonable for us to have any beliefs. Think of concepts as a collection of terms in which we can say things. We might have the concepts of force, cause, and motion. With any given set of terms, many things can be said. We might say "force always causes motion," or "force never causes motion." Now some of these we may believe, and some we may not. Beliefs are a new layer on top of concepts that selects what we believe to be true from all the things we can conceive.

Theories are yet another layer. Theories are (probably) a complex but connected fabric of concepts and beliefs, not just any old collection of them. Theories are focused, about a particular slice of reality. While phenomena of light and mechanics are almost always conjoined in our experience, physicists have different theories to explain these. Similarly it seems exceedingly likely that folk physics, the fabric of concepts and beliefs we may have about the physical world, divides into multiple theories—if, indeed, it is theoretical. Theories also have primary concepts and secondary concepts that are derived from those. They have primary principles and derived principles. We do not have to decide exactly what a theory is to see that it is probably not sensible to call any collection of ideas a theory. The key distinguishing factor is probably some kind and degree of integration and connectedness —ideas that interconnect systematically and that are all about the same set of phenomena.

Even this simple taxonomy of forms—concepts, beliefs, and theories—leaves a lot of room for different possibilities for relations between folk and scientific physics. In this sketch, the foundation is concepts. A lot rides on the question of whether there is sufficient overlap between folk and scientific concepts even to start a comparison. Probably the majority of contemporary researchers in this area think the central action is here. In fact, the term "conceptual change" may be the most-used term to describe what learners go through in learning school physics. This presumes both folk and scientists have concepts, and we need to understand how concepts change to see their world views in proper relation.

It is possible, if not widely believed, that physicists and physics-naive individuals have enough conceptual overlap so that the key difference is at the level of beliefs. Everyone, after all, knows something about position, speed, and weight (physicists use the term mass), and force is a familiar word, if not exactly in a physicist's sense. Perhaps ordinary people believe these are related in a different way than physicists do.

What about theories? Do ordinary people have anything like theories of the physical world? It seems the most plausible a priori position is "no." Theories are things that belong to formal science. Geniuses like Newton, Maxwell, or Einstein build them.

But it turns out that there are good and long-standing reasons to keep this possibility alive. The most compelling is that concepts never seem to come in isolation. We always find families of ideas that reinforce and help interpret each other. Thus it is families of ideas and concepts that get overturned in conceptual change, not one concept at a time. These families may not be theoretical, but they must have interesting and important family relationships among their pieces. Whether we call them theories or not may be a semantic question.

Let me situate these considerations more carefully in a historical perspective. Toward the end of the 1970s and into the 1980s, a raft of empirical studies appeared that demolished possibility 1, that there might be no relation between folk and scientific physics. Known collectively as "misconceptions studies" (or, by some, as "the disaster studies") this work established the following:

a. In many or most cases, students do have uninstructed expectations and explanations to offer about many simple physical situations. Their "knowledge of the physical world" is not mute.
b. Their answers to a set of fairly simple, qualitative questions are not random or

simply mistakes. Instead, they seem conceptually based, if on a nonscientific set of concepts. Although a fair diversity of responses can be found, there are strong tendencies toward a few, most common answers.

c. These answers are surprisingly robust, extending relatively unchanged from before instruction at least through high school and introductory college physics. This is the "disaster" aspect of the work. Instruction does not seem to help much. (See Atran, this volume, chap. 28, for a similar conclusion about folk biology.)

One of the classic examples of a persistent "misconception" is how to describe a simple toss of an object vertically into the air. A typical folk physics explanation is that the hand imparts a force to the object, which drives the object up into the air against gravity. The hand force gradually dies away, eventually balancing gravity at the peak of the toss. Then gravity "overcomes" the force, and the object falls back down. In contrast a more scientific analysis denies that there is any force imparted by the hand to drive the object upward. The object merely starts with a certain speed or momentum, which would, in the absence of forces, keep it moving forever. But in this case, the force of gravity acts constantly to change the object's speed. At first it reduces the object's speed, eventually to zero. Then it continues the same process of changing speed toward the downward direction, which results in the object speeding up in downward fall.

A related example is that most people describe the pushing of an object across a table at a constant speed as an imbalance. The hand is pushing harder than the object (or friction) is resisting. Physicists see this as a balance of forces—friction and hand force—which leaves the existing momentum of the object unchanged.

Another especially nice example relates to the question of why an object rests without moving on a table, despite the fact that gravity is pulling it downward. A physicist says the table is exerting an equal upward force, canceling gravity. The canonical folk physics explanation is that the table just blocks the object's motion and that it is nonsensical to believe a passive thing like a table could be exerting a force.

These were exciting and frightening discoveries that propelled us from possibility 1 to possibility 2. Intuitive physics exists, it seems conceptual and articulate, and it opposes scientific physics. It looked like a key stumbling block to instruction had been discovered, although it was a formidable block that conventional instruction failed to remove.

Beneath this level of broad agreement, different researchers took somewhat different positions. The first position is perhaps the most commonsensical (which is not to say it is without sophisticated motivation as well). When we meet people in everyday life who say different things than we do, we tend to assign these differences to the level of beliefs. We have a democratic urge to believe people have mostly the same basic categories. They just differ in their beliefs about which of the many possibilities we can all conceive are true. If, as is the case in physics instruction, we have good reason to take some beliefs (folk physics) as misguided, we may proceed rationally to lay out both sets of beliefs and argue systematically that one is correct and the other is wrong. Instructionally, "draw out naive beliefs, confront them with scientific ones and arguments for them, and convince students to abandon old beliefs for scientific ones" was a dominant theme.

Other researchers were more worried about the conceptual level. They doubted students had the same conceptual foundations, so arguing to change beliefs without first changing concepts seemed dubious. Indeed, the long and complex process of reconstructing or building new concepts might completely obviate the need for "belief changing" tactics. By the time students can understand physicists' conceptual structure, their beliefs might simply change as an unproblematic matter of course.

Ideas about "naive theories" were also split. Some researchers and educators were convinced by the empirical data that students had relatively coherent, uniform and systematic theories. Others were more cautious in announcing particular naive theories, but on theoretical grounds looked for systematicity and fully expected some version of global coherence would emerge. Still others disbelieved, or at least were agnostic about naive theories.

Because of its importance to later discussion, I mention one naive theory that Michael McCloskey and others have proposed, which he described as surprisingly articulate and systematic (McCloskey, 1983). It is a version of a theory discussed by philosophers in the middle ages. The "impetus theory" has it that a kind of internal force is imparted to an object when thrown or otherwise violently propelled. That impetus drives the object's continued motion but gradually dies away spontaneously or because of the influence of other forces. This is essentially the naive explanation of the toss given earlier except that, instead of being merely an explanation of a particular event, it is claimed to be a theory that covers a broad range of situations.

To sum up, possibility 2 is that folk physics substantially shares knowledge forms with scientists' concepts, beliefs, or theories. Given this presumption, it seems inevitable that the discovery of students' uninstructed but articulate commentary on the physical world would be couched in negative terms as far as the content of these ideas is concerned—hence their description as *mis*conceptions, "naive" theories or beliefs. It would have been shocking beyond comprehension if we discovered people spontaneously develop the same physics, both form *and* content, as held by physicists.

A New View

It is time for a transition from historical and a priori analysis to a more principled view of folk physics. After its initial blossoming, the "misconceptions" and "naive theories" approach to folk physics sputtered in the following ways.

1. No one could make the "naive theory" idea stick in any detail. Students and physics-naive individuals, on closer look, just did not seem consistent and systematic enough in their views. Explanations varied too much from person to

person and context to context. In addition, proposed naive theories just did not seem to cover enough ground. The impetus theory is, at best, about tosses and similar phenomena. It does not explain how people think about objects on tables, or balance scales, or orbits. . . . Nothing having the scale of coverage of Newton's Laws appeared to exist. Of the three levels—theories, beliefs, concepts—theories faded fastest and most convincingly from consideration.

2. Beliefs did not have appreciably more success. A reasonable accounting of naive physics as a list of beliefs did not emerge. Moreover, the "articulate and counter with rational argument" strategy did not meet with resounding success. Instead and in contrast, various strategies that built on productive intuitive ideas showed promise. For example, Brown and Clement (1989) used contexts in which people had correct intuitions to bridge into contexts where they did not.

3. The concepts level of analysis did not fare so badly, but still it had only limited success in building a solid account of folk physics. No convincing decomposition into a basic set of concepts emerged.

My conviction is that the fundamental limitation in what has been said so far is a theoretical lack. We cannot rely on nearly commonsense knowledge terms like concept and belief to account for folk physics and its properties in relation to scientific physics. Instead, we need to be theoretically innovative and more precise. In the same way that quantum mechanics had to invent wave functions and particle waves to progress beyond "matter," so "concepts, beliefs, and theories" need to be abandoned or substantially transformed to do the necessary work. What follows is a short version of my best current account of folk physics.

The Evolution of Complex Knowledge Systems

Four general principles define this approach to understanding knowledge, and folk physics in particular.

1. *Diversity*: There are many different mental forms, modes, levels and contexts of knowledge that need to be taken into account. In particular, most accounts of knowledge skew toward "big" and formal types of knowledge, like facts, concepts, and methods. In contrast, I believe the most pressing need is to understand more subtle, "smaller" knowledge elements. "Impressions" seem vague and not very knowledge-like. Yet impressions and subtle judgments may constitute a critical core of folk physics.

2. *Complexity*: Any individual's knowledge state, as a backdrop for change, is extremely complex. In order to understand change (or lack of change), say, from folk to scientific physics, we need to engage this complexity. Complexity implies that we may need to know a lot about particular individuals to understand properties of their understanding. But even if there is a uniformity across individuals, the complexity of knowledge systems implies there is a lot to know.

3. *Systems level of analysis*: Although the forms of analysis I prefer to use rely heavily on element-by-element analysis, I believe many important properties of

an individual's knowledge are system properties. For example, I believe the apparent robustness of folk physics ideas is a systems matter. Consideration of systems and interactions of subsystems is critical.

4. *Knowledge level analysis*: Some analyses of cognition rely on an articulation of general "cognitive machinery" (typically, work related to artificial intelligence). In contrast, this analysis focuses primarily on "the architecture of knowledge," postponing in some measure a more mechanistic stance.

My expositional strategy will be to provide a short, but I hope telling, list of "new" knowledge forms along with comments on their properties and on the knowledge subsystems of which they are a part. In particular, each form has: (1) characteristic properties and behaviors in its use; (2) specific relations with other exemplars of its type and with other knowledge subsystems; (3) characteristic patterns of development—both in individual-element and systemic properties—in transformations like that from folk to scientific knowledge of physics.

P-prims

By far the most important knowledge type in understanding folk physics is the "phenomenological primitive," or "p-prim" for short. P-prims are intended to account for most of the observed properties of folk physics. The key move here is that p-prims are subconceptual; they are much smaller and more fluid pieces of knowledge than concepts or beliefs. I am slipping in a new and different layer beneath concepts, beliefs, and theories.

Humans have hundreds if not thousands of p-prims that they recognize more or less easily in situations and behaviors in the world. The "p" (phenomenological) in p-prim is intended to indicate this connection to the rich, experienced phenomenological reality, which makes the world and happenings in it familiar and comprehensible. Specifically, p-prims account for our feelings of naturalness or unnaturalness, for judgments of plausibility and explanatory sufficiency. The "primitive" part of p-prim indicates that they typically constitute explanatorily primitive descriptions of events; if a p-prim applies, nothing more needs inquiry— "that's the way things are." Heavy things need harder pushes to move. Things are drawn into vacuums. There is nothing much to say in response to "why?"

Use of p-prims tends to be fluid and data driven. Frequently, we may shift from one p-prim to another with nothing more than a shift of attention, or a minor change in the situation considered. In situations where multiple p-prims conflict, it is unusual that we have specific knowledge to resolve the conflict. As a system, p-prims are diverse and loosely coupled. There is no strict hierarchy, no global levels of importance, nor any logical chain from primary to derived p-prims. Some p-prims, of course, are more important than others, and knowing the more central ones tells us a lot about folk physics. Similarly there are family resemblances and relations among p-prims. But still, the complexities and diversity of the experienced world dominates the possibility of a simple, concise description of the pool of p-prims.

Developmentally, p-prims are likely to originate in relatively simple abstractions of familiar events, abstractions that come to serve more explanatory roles as they are found to underlie a broader range of situations. Learning, of course, sometimes means developing new p-prims. But more often it means a shifting in level of importance, in the context in which a p-prim is felt applicable, and in the typical-use connections with other p-prims and with other types of knowledge entirely. Reorganization and refinement are much better starting metaphors than replacement when considering the transition from folk to scientific physics.

P-prims are problematically related to language. People do not know they have p-prims the way they know they use various words. P-prims are hard to express in language since their natural "language" is one of visual or kinesthetic pattern. Even if we can say or explain a p-prim, getting it hooked up to the feelings of confidence and appropriateness that are the essence of p-prims' function is difficult to imagine through purely linguistic means. For all these reasons, and others besides, one-shot learning at the p-prim level is unlikely. A person's p-prims shift and change gradually through experience. Let's consider some examples:

1. *Ohm's p-prim*: A central and important p-prim that I call Ohm's p-prim is recognized in situations where there are three interconnected loci of attention. First there must be an energizing force or impetus. People may prototypically supply such an impetus, but so may machines and even inanimate objects. Second, there is a "result," typically some form of motion or action. Finally, there is some resisting or interfering effect between impetus and result. The natural patterns of behavior that are expected when Ohm's p-prim applies are that increased impetus produces increased result, increased resistance produces decreased result, and so on. Ohm's p-prim applies to all sorts of situations, from pushing harder or less hard against heavier or lighter ("weight resists motion") objects, to "working harder" in school to get better grades, and to convincing someone by wearing down his or her resistance or by "increased force" of argument.

2. *Force as mover*: In our everyday experience, things happen as we continue to make them happen. We push a chair across the rug; it moves in the direction we push it and only so long as we continue to push. Force as mover is a directed (vector) form of Ohm's p-prim that prescribes that the motion of an object follows the directed effort making it move.

3. *Balance and equilibrium*: Humans have a rich and deeply felt phenomenology of balance and equilibrium. Something "in balance" will be maintained perpetually in that state. Things that are perturbed or "out of balance," return naturally to equilibrium. A particular version of balance that I call dynamic balance is the state where two competing influences (forces) exactly cancel each other, resulting in no effect.

4. *Overcoming*: If one of the influences in a dynamic balance increases or the other diminishes, the stronger influence "overcomes" the other and "gets its way." People are familiar with a particular pattern of actions associated with changing strength of influence: A situation comes into dynamic balance from

dominance of one influence (and hence also of its effect) and emerges with dominance of the other.

5. *Dying away*: Lack of motion or activity is the natural state of inanimate objects. Any induced action or motion naturally fades, unless the agent of induction continues (as in force as mover). A struck bell's sound dies away.

6. *Blocking and guiding*: Motion can be blocked or stopped by solid, stable objects. Unlike a physicist's explanation that requires a counteracting force (e.g., countering gravity in the case of a book on a table), blocking is primitively explanatory to ordinary folks. Similarly, trains are guided along tracks, or objects moving in a tube follow the tube's course without any need for deeper explanation.

Readers may already see how these p-prims can account for naive conceptions such as those listed earlier. I will present one case in detail shortly.

Mental Models

Mental models are frequently instructed compound knowledge forms that, unlike p-prims, can be the basis for extended and articulate arguments in the course of developing or displaying explanations or in problem solving. Mental models rely on elaborate and well-developed descriptive components, which prototypically reflect the human ability to describe and reason about spatial configurations. In addition, there is a focused notion of basic causal events within a mental model, which perhaps we can understand as the selection of a few relevant p-prims. Logic and hypothetical reasoning are engaged easily in using a mental model, and we may check our reasoning in an explicit way, which is very atypical, if it is possible at all, with p-prims alone.

Instructed models of computer execution are excellent examples of mental models. One imagines a basic repertoire of places (e.g., variables) and actions (e.g., moving or clearing symbols) that can be chained into elaborate and checkable predictions and explanations. Similarly, instruction in electrical circuits relies on topological (geometric) descriptions of elements and connections, along with primitive behavioral or causal models of the components. Some particular systems involving mental models may be too complex to allow full analysis easily. But individuals who understand the mental model will still feel they understand the device "in principle."

A particular mental model seems to be of critical importance in learning Newtonian mechanics. I describe this as a moment-by-moment accountable model of motion. Basically, we may describe any object's motion by considering it a succession of instants, at each of which only a specific few entities interact to determine what happens next. Without going into detail, at each moment all we need to know is where an object is, what velocity it has, and what forces act on it. Velocity tells us where the object goes next, and force tells us how velocity changes from one instant to the next.

This moment-by-moment accountable model is notable for its sparsity. Only a very few elements are involved, and each one and their relations are easy, in principle, to see and check. P-prim analyses, in general, cannot be accountable in this way. Even if people knew they had knowledge elements like Ohm's p-prim, they would not know how to check details of its application. In addition, folk and p-prim analyses in particular are frequently synoptic, describing the beginnings and ends of fairly complex causal chains, without any need to do a moment-by-moment, local causal analysis. We may say, "The earthquake caused the books to fall," without a micro analysis of geometric lines of propagation of vibration or any account of how the shaking actually caused the books to move off the shelf.

Narratives

Given the backdrop of misconceptions research, it may be surprising that some parts of mechanics are easy to learn. But easy accomplishments are as telling as difficulties about the nature of folk physics and its relation to scientific physics. For example, the discovery of Ohm's p-prim was a consequence of considering why Ohm's law of electrical circuits seems so simple to most learners.

Narratives are a particular class of easy accomplishments that we find among physics students. These are basically stories of familiar events over which an explanatory physics story is cast. A classic example of this is the energy story in a toss. "The energy in a tossed object starts out entirely kinetic (energy of motion) and gradually shifts into potential energy (energy in elevation) until at the peak of the toss, kinetic energy is zero and all the energy is potential. After that, energy is converted from potential to kinetic in the fall." Virtually no one taking physics fails to learn this story easily and thoroughly.

A not-quite-so-familiar narrative is that of terminal velocity. A dropped object falls faster and faster because gravity acts on it. But as it increases in speed, friction drag (an upward push) also increases until it balances gravity, at which point the object ceases gaining speed.

Narratives are probably easy to learn both because the events depicted are literally familiar or easy to remember, and because the overlaid "physics story" involves little interpretation beyond naive ideas. For example, conservation is a powerful intuitive principle, and energy in motion is easy to "see" in the toss. Terminal velocity is a simple p-primish story of "coming into balance."

Nominal Facts

Students, and also people who have not been instructed in physics, frequently know a few "basic facts" of physics. "Gravity acts equally on everything," is a version of Galileo's story that heavy and light objects fall at the same rate, neglecting air friction. Other such facts are "Everything is relative," and "For every action there is an equal and opposite reaction." Nominal facts frequently have simple, memorable formulations as sentences and sometimes have a surface (p-prim) plausibility.

Developmentally, perhaps the most notable thing about nominal facts is how little effect they have on learning. The problem is that the terms in them frequently have so little meaning for students that the meaning and implications of the facts are haphazard consequences of the situation in which students try to use them.

Committed Facts

Once in a great while, students (and possibly others) build an articulate commitment to a principle of their own formulation. An example is, "It takes unbalanced forces to move something." A critical difference between these and nominal facts is that the person involved has espoused the fact as a result of a sometimes extended and memorable consideration of the fact, what it means, what the alternatives are, and why those are implausible. Committed facts are perhaps the closest thing to "naive theories" that I believe exist. But even these do not have the range and rich substructure that typify scientific theories. Furthermore, they are rare and probably provoked more frequently by instruction than they are spontaneous.

To sum up, these five categories of knowledge—p-prims, mental models, narratives, committed facts, and nominal facts—are conjectured to be a first cut of a richer, more theoretically accountable and empirically tractable view of the diverse pieces that constitute a knowledge system such as folk physics. Of these, p-prims are by far the most important for understanding folk physics. It would not be a bad approximation to say folk physics is the rather large, diverse and mildly organized collection of fairly simple phenomenological ideas, which are p-prims. On the other hand, spontaneous mental models, narratives, and nominal and committed facts exist, if relatively rarely (and dependent on the p-prim substrate). And during instruction, we are almost guaranteed to see these other knowledge structures develop and change in interaction with p-prims.

J: Knowledge Forms in Action

In this section I present segments of a case study of a student whom I call J. This research was part of a larger study of the "local dynamics of conceptual change."[3]

J was a female university freshman whom I interviewed for about seven hours, an hour at a time, with interviews separated usually by a week while she was taking introductory physics. J had taken high school physics, a course she liked and felt was well taught. She did not appear to be either unusually adept at physics, or to have particular problems. She was perhaps a bit more willing than some to talk for an extended period of time about her ideas about physics. But in most respects she provided interviews that were comparable to many others I have conducted through the years even if her interviews were sometimes unusually dense in intuitive ideas.

I present excerpts from analyses of J's protocols for the following reasons:

1. These will illustrate most of the knowledge forms, and even many of the specific examples listed above, in a real context.

2. Protocols generally are more convincing than abstracted argument that these forms are actually informative of intuitive thinking.
3. While much too limited to be convincing by themselves, these protocols and analysis provide data in support of the general claims made here.
4. The protocols are rich enough to provide grist for readers' own analyses, and raise important issues beyond the short sketch of theory provided above.

Near the beginning of the interview sequence, J was asked to describe the toss of a ball into the air. Her first description was quite professional. She used scientific terms in an account that is difficult to fault (except perhaps for expositional form). In particular, note that she twice emphasized that, after the ball leaves your hand, there is no longer any force from the hand in play. "The only force on that is gravity." Note also clear reference to the energy narrative. Emphasis has been added to mark especially relevant sequences.

J: Not including your hand, like if you just let it go up and come down, *the only force on that is gravity.* And so it starts off with the most speed when it leaves your hand, and the higher it goes, it slows down to the point where it stops. And then comes back down. And so, but *the whole time, the only force on that is the force of gravity,* except the force of your hand when you catch it. And, um, it...when it starts off it has its highest speed, which is all kinetic energy, and when it stops, it has all potential energy—no kinetic energy. And then it comes back down, and it speeds up again.

After about 30 seconds of small talk, I asked J a seemingly innocuous question: What happens at the peak of the toss? Rather than produce a straightforward answer, J proceeded to reformulate her description of the toss. The reformulation is not instantaneous, but rather follows a few detours through abandoned and rejected hypotheses. Strikingly, she winds up with an "impetus theory" account of the toss. "Your hand imparts a force that at first overcomes gravity, but gradually dies away. At the peak, there's a balance of forces, which is broken as the internal force fades further and gravity takes over." Segments are numbered for later reference.

J: (1) Um, well air resistance, when you throw the ball up, the air...It's not against air because air is going every way, but (2) the air force gets stronger and stronger to the point where when it stops. (3) The *gravity pulling down and the force pulling up are equal,* so it's like in equilibrium for a second, so it's not going anywhere. (4) And then gravity pulls it back down. (5) But *when you throw it, you're giving it a force upward, (6) but the force can only last so long* against air and against gravity—(7) actually probably more against gravity than against air. (8) But so *you give this initial force, and it's going up just fine,* slower and slower because gravity is pulling on it and pulling on it. And it gets to the point to the top, and then it's not getting any more energy to go up. You're not giving any more forces, so the only force it has on it is gravity and it comes right back down.

Shortly after this segment, J produced a clean reiteration of an impetus account.

From a p-prim view, this is a classic occurrence. A shift of attention (to the peak of the toss) brings a shift in analysis, in this case, from a standard scientific analysis to a folk physics, p-prim–based analysis. Furthermore, it is clear J is not applying an impetus theory so much as deriving it from more primitive pieces that she gradually puts together. Indeed, other data make it clear that she has not assembled a stable conceptualization that she will systematically apply in a broad range of circumstances. Instead, her "misconception" ("impetus theory") is a construction that is mostly particular to this situation.

I first provide an idealized view of this construction in order to highlight the p-prim pieces. Then I will provide some additional analysis of aspects of the construction more idiosyncratic to J.

Asking what happens at the peak of the toss was a deliberate and strong move.[4] Since p-prim physics is so dense and strong with respect to balancing and equilibrium phenomena, I intended to provoke these considerations. The peak is a stable, no-motion point, and likely explained by a balance. Even more, the switching of directions with a balance between may be an example of the extremely familiar overcoming scenario, where one influence loses dominance over another. Gravity evidently can serve as one influence, but another is needed. A successful candidate for the other influence is some force or energy communicated by the hand in the toss. Finally, why does that "force" (the term sounds too good not to use in a physics context) lose its dominance over gravity? Some sort of interference or wearing down would explain this. But in the absence of a clear interference, the dying away p-prim suffices. Thus p-prim pieces effectively generate an answer that appears to be an application of the impetus theory but, in fact, is a situation-specific p-prim-based answer to a particular question.

In J's case, she takes the balancing and overcoming bait at the peak of the toss. But then she needs another force or influence. In segment 1, she tries out air resistance to fill the slot. (The comment about "air is going every way" implicates an idiosyncratic model of hers that I will not explain here.) Indeed, air perhaps cues the "terminal velocity" narrative, "air resistance gets stronger and stronger leading to a balance" (segment 2), which seems to fit what's needed here. In segment 3, J seems to be restarting her analysis from the critical balancing point. She needs an upward influence to balance then succumb to gravity (segment 4). Finally, in segment 5, she "invents" the force communicated by the hand, and proceeds to analyze its fading (not the strengthening imported from "terminal velocity"). In segment 7, the interference of air and gravity are implicated in "dying away," which she fairly quickly corrects, withdrawing air finally and entirely from playing a major role in the situation. In her final recounting (segment 8), she seems to emphasize that the imparted force dies completely away, leaving gravity alone to cause the ball to come back down.

The story of J's explanations of a toss as they played out over further interviews is as wonderful and (possibly) surprising as its beginning. In this chapter, I have space only to sketch what happens and pull out two brief segments that relate directly to the main aims here.

In ensuing interviews, I brought J back again and again to the toss and related situations to explore how she thought about them. Strikingly, J continued to use both her intuitive analysis and her more scientific, single force explanation, depending on circumstances. This was true despite gentle and sometimes stronger intervention aimed at helping her see the problematic nature of her impetus explanation and at helping her solidify and make more precise her scientific explanation.

It is tempting to describe J's impetus explanation as a model of a toss, even if it is implausible to describe it as a theory. But according to the definition of model provided earlier, I claim J had no general model of motion, nor even a model of a toss. This is, in fact, one of the expected shortcomings of folk physics compared to scientific physics; for the most part, there are no models of central mechanics phenomena. I argue here that J does not have a moment-by-moment accountable model, rather than the more general claim that she has no mental model of any sort.

In the following two segments, which occurred in different interviews, I try to point out a central inconsistency in J's impetus explanation. At the peak of the toss, she claims that the force imparted by the hand balances the force of gravity, but she also says the imparted force reaches zero, fully died away, at that point. To a physicist, this is a clear contradiction. A moment-by-moment accountable model implies you must provide an accounting of what values relevant physical quantities (notably force and velocity) have at each instant and why they have those values. In the following segment, J seems at first to follow the logic. She says initially that at the point of expiration of the imparted force, the ball would already have to have started its fall. I try to capitalize on her realization, but in her second contribution below she argues that the time between peak balance and dying out is too short to be worth worrying about. She will not accept accountability at the peak instant.

A: If it's gone [the imparted force] though, how can it balance?
J: Well, at that second that it balances, which isn't very long, is when it's like it's on its last, you know, it's slowly, slowly dying out, and that one second is the one time when it's equal. So it's not gone at that second it's, obviously. Or it else, if it would be, if it was gone that second, then it would have been falling earlier, and it would have been gone a little bit lower. But at that one, when it's at its peak, it's right before it's going to be gone.
A: OK. That's right before, so it's gone some time after it starts the downward. . .
J: Well, when it stopped is when they're equal. But obviously it dies at that exact point for the gravity to pull it back down. So I guess you can say that at that point it goes away. But when it was completely stationary, it was still there enough to have it not fall. But, it's such a short amount of time, you know, it's not like it goes up and hangs out there for a while and then, oh, it dies out and comes back down. It goes up and it comes right back down. So it's like a really short amount of time. Just dies out.

In the following segment, J follows another tactic. She tries to maintain that even if you cannot say that the imparted force and gravity are equal in magnitude (because the imparted force is zero), you can say that they cancel. Despite acknowledging the argument that a died-out force cannot balance and also seeing that I am trying to tell her something is wrong with her analysis, she reverts to maintaining that canceling exists, evading accountability to say what entities cancel.

J: . . .At the top, the force is equal to zero because it's stopped. But, I guess you can't say they're equal to each other, I guess you have to say that they cancel each other out.
A: Which two forces cancel each other?
J: I'm obviously wrong. [Laughs.] About something.
A: I'm just trying to get all the details.
J: When it's at the top it only has one force on it. Downward. And—
A: So, what's canceling out?
J: I guess nothing's canceling out. . . . I still think forces are canceling out, but I don't know which ones they are. [Laughs.]

J continued to use both explanations, the physicist's account and the "impetus" account, after this discussion. Nearing the end of the series of interviews, I took J into a tutorial sequence based on some computer materials aimed at having her fill in all the details of the physicist's one-force model. J learned from the tutorial and during it only wavered slightly at one point toward her impetus explanation. But alas, directly after the tutorial, I asked her one more time to describe the toss. Her initial explanation was flawless scientific analysis. Prompted to remove energy from her analysis and talk only in terms of forces, she fell directly back into the imparted force explanation.

A: Describe one more time what happens.
J: Okay. You give the ball an initial velocity, and that comes from the force from your hand. And then, it travels with that momentum, and, once you let it go, it has no outside forces. *The only force it has on it is one force downward which is equal to mg*, the mass of the ball times gravity. And, so, it goes up and as it goes up, its kinetic energy decreases because it's not getting any energy from any outside forces. Until it gets to the point where velocity is zero for a split second. And that's where it has all potential energy and no kinetic energy because it doesn't have any more. And then, it comes back down. It starts off slow and then picks up speed because of the force downward. And then you catch it again.
A: Okay. So, um, could you describe that just in terms of forces.
J: Okay, starting from when it leaves your hand. *Initially, it has force up and a force down. The force up is the force that you gave it.* And force down is mg. And the force down stays the same all the time because. . .*The force up is what changes.* Because, it starts off big and then, as it goes up it gets smaller and smaller and smaller. So, it's just like *the forces are adding, like vectors.* And, so, *at the top, when it has no velocity, is the point where the vectors are the same for a second.* And then, this force stays zero, and this force overcomes it and then comes back down.

A: What vectors are the same at the top?

J: The up one and the down one.

A: The down one is what?

J: Mg. [Gravity.] And *the up one is the external force that you gave it with your hand.*

I have so far illustrated p-prims in J's invention of her impetus explanation. We saw repeated use of the energy narrative in the toss despite the fact that she was consistently prompted to use forces rather than energy in her explanation. Plausibly, we saw the involvement of the terminal velocity narrative as the basis for J's invoking air in a coming-to-equilibrium situation (the toss). And I argued that J did not have any mental model of motion generally, or of the toss in particular, at least by physicist standards of model. I need finally to illustrate nominal and committed facts, at least briefly.

J exhibited a common nominal fact and typical associated limitation in its influence on subsequent conceptual development. She consistently claimed that gravity acts equally on all objects, heavy or light. In contrast, the formula she used for gravitational force was $F = mg$, where m is the mass of the object in question. She never acknowledged any inconsistency between her equal influence claim, and the correct formula she used for gravitational force. Indeed, attempts at provoking the realization failed: After one pronouncement that the gravitational force on heavy and light objects is the same, I put heavy and light objects in her hands and asked her what she felt. She admitted the heavy one pushed down more but claimed that one cannot feel gravitational force! To a physicist, one *can* feel the gravitational forces, the different mg's of light and heavy objects. The story is too complex for details here, but J's nominal facts simply did not connect well enough to her own experience or to other physical knowledge to either self-correct or produce changes in the other things she knew.

Finally, J developed a committed fact that has an astonishing outcome. In one interview I asked J to consider the situation of pushing a book across a tabletop. I asked her to compare the force of her hand on the book to the countering force of friction exerted on the book by the table. J's initial intuitions were a little mixed. At first she tried "equal and opposite" but was troubled by the feeling that unless the force of friction was "overcome," there could be no motion. At one point, I "helped" by reminding her that Newton's famous $F = ma$ formula requires that, if there are unbalanced forces (leaving a net, nonzero force) there has to be an acceleration. J saw the conflict with her unbalanced forces account of the constant motion (no acceleration) in pushing on a book. After a long chain of consideration, J concluded that she really did believe you needed unbalanced forces to produce motion, and that $F = ma$ simply did not always apply to the real world. It was just a case where "those darn equations aren't applicable to every single thing; they're not always true. You can't live by them." J never recanted the claim that unbalanced forces are needed for motion. It did not seem to trouble her beyond this interview that the central, defining equation of Newtonian mechanics is "not always true," nor that it is not true, in particular, in the simple and almost paradigmatic case of pushing a book across a table.

In preparation for the next section, on educational implications, it is worthwhile reviewing what is evident in and suggested by J's case. First, it should be clear that many times, if not always, the answers students give us to questions are fairly complex constructions based on a rich underlying cognitive ecology. J's impetus explanation emerged in a process, which we were lucky enough to catch, that exposed pieces of her construction of it. As simple an observation as this may seem, it has important ramifications for both researchers and educators. The literature on intuitive physics is unfortunately full of lists of students' answers that are labeled as "misconceptions" with little or no analysis of the underlying reasons for the answers. An adequate account of conceptual development needs to dig deeper than this. Educationally, it is also tempting but misguided to teach to these apparent "misconceptions," treating symptoms rather than causes.

The second lesson we can learn from J is that the hidden world of folk physics is, itself, rich and complex. If my account is correct, we cannot expect to find "the folk theory of physics" or any other compact formulation underlying students' ideas. Indeed, p-prims—which I propose are the elemental pieces of intuitive physics—are unfamiliar knowledge types. They are not facts, concepts, theories, or beliefs, and their properties in development and application need attention beyond commonsense assumptions. In addition, there are many and diverse particular p-prims. We need a subconceptual psychology in the way we needed quantum mechanics as a subatomic physics.

The third point to make is that J clearly maintained multiple explanatory frameworks. Her intuitive account of the toss stood side by side with appropriate scientific accounts. Clearly, there is no exclusion principle that means science must displace other ways of understanding. The traditional method of focusing instruction only on scientific concepts may fail to displace other ways of thinking.

On the other hand, the failure of my attempts to get J to accept the contradiction of saying both that the force imparted by the hand in the toss is zero at the apex, and also that it cancels gravity at that point, suggests limits in the strategy of simply adding arguments against folk ideas to traditional instruction of scientific ideas. The "logic" by which we seek to undermine intuitive conceptions may not be at all apparent to students. In this case, J did not seem to think moment-by-moment accounts of motion are particularly definitive. She refused accountability of her own explanations (to name and justify the balancing forces at the peak of the toss) to the standards that would cause a physicist to reject them as inadequate. Not only conclusions but also patterns of reasoning and standards of judgment must be learned.

Educational Strategies

Education is a complex social practice, and creating social and material structures that aid learning is an equally complex matter of design. It follows (if it needs argument) that there is no one correct way to teach. Scientific accounts of knowledge and learning provide powerful descriptions and constraints that must be observed. But an excellent learning environment is a melding of many short- and long-term goals, a complex negotiation of many overlapping contexts, so that I feel it is quite unreasonable to expect the outlines of practice to follow directly from science. This ought to be familiar. Science provides many resources to the designers of airplanes, but never a particular design.

In this section I summarize implications of the existence and character of folk physics in four heuristic principles for educational design. Then I describe in a bit more detail one particular strategy that follows all four heuristics and has been successfully implemented in a number of instances.

1. *Count on extended, cumulative learning to achieve deep conceptual change.* J's persistent use of an intuitive explanation of a toss, despite extended discussions, argument, and even focused instruction, is emblematic of the difficulty facing teachers in reaching the results we hope for. Researchers of misconceptions have extensive documentation of similar difficulties. Moreover, the theoretical frame through which I interpreted J's protocols provides support for the idea that we must recalibrate our expectations. P-prims are many and diverse and they do not have verbal "handles" that would make them easy to evoke and consider. Deep change must be distributed and systematic. One-shot learning makes little sense at this level. Curricularly, "less is more" should rule, at least if we want students to experience any substantial shift from folk to "real" physics.[5]

2. *Engage experiential knowledge.* J's case makes clear that accumulated experiential knowledge (p-prims) provides alternative paths for students' developing knowledge, not just a pool of static "conceptual beliefs." J *constructed* her impetus analysis of the toss and decided, on reflection, that "it takes unbalanced forces to move objects" is a better principle than $F = ma$ in many circumstances. These are moves she might not have made under other circumstances. What I have not been able to demonstrate sufficiently here is how often and how effectively naive p-prims can be used as part of learning conventional physics, although the easy accomplishments of energy and terminal velocity narratives are suggestive.[6]

Traditional instructional strategies have no stance whatever toward folk physics, which means folk physics' most positive aspects are not capitalized on, and its negative influences are not negotiated either. A global stance—on the one hand wallowing in p-prim soup without seeking to build sharper, more systematic and accountable (by new standards) descriptions and explanations or, on the other hand, systematically attacking folk conceptions as misconceptions—is unlikely to be maximally helpful. Instead we need multiple appropriately fine-grained strategies. There is no a priori reason to favor engaging naive knowledge through appropriately designed discussion (some of which may mimic my interviews with J) or through more directly experiential encounters with physical or computer materials. Indeed, in some of my own work, discussions about physical situations mediated by computer simulations and formalisms have proved productive (diSessa, 1995).

3. *Focus on explanation and description.* Conventional instruction concentrates on problem solving to the near exclusion of exercising descriptive and explanatory skills. Taking a close look at how students think reinforces the importance of

learning to explain and describe. Indeed, misconceptions and other research (e.g., Larkin, McDermott, Simon, and Simon, 1980) show how misleading problem-solving capability can be as a measure of conceptual change. J's protocols and much other work suggest there are two levels of learning to explain. Of course, students should come to give more physicist-like explanations. But a parallel and perhaps deeper accomplishment is to help students adopt an evaluative stance toward explanations that is more accountable to physicists' aesthetics. J refused such accountability in her description of the peak of a toss as balanced.

4. *Seek to learn more about students' cognitive ecology and develop strategies to suit.* Heuristic 2, engage experiential knowledge, leaves plenty of room for both theoretical and empirical development to aid us in instructional contexts. The complex knowledge systems approach implies that details are extensive and important.

J's behavior in most respects appears unexceptional, even expectable against the theoretical background presented here. Yet it is safe to say most physics instructors would be surprised if not shocked by her performance. In my experience, physics teachers complain that the subjects in such interviews are unusual, that the interviewing technique is faulty, or that the problems posed are unusually hard or tricky. Whether or not teachers need well-developed theory and instructional design by researchers, I strongly believe that a lot could be gained if teachers were familiar with these learning phenomena, sought to have their classrooms serve, in part, as laboratories to tune up their own perceptions of them, and developed their own repertoire of strategies to deal with them.

Benchmark Lessons

I conclude this chapter with a brief description of benchmark lessons, which are a genre of full-class, teacher instigated and scaffolded discussions developed mainly by Jim Minstrell. This sort of lesson illustrates all of the heuristic principles listed above in a coherent and well-developed instructional practice. Consult diSessa and Minstrell (in press) for an extensive discussion.

Benchmark lessons are typically introductory lessons aimed at getting central issues and conceptions (intuitive and otherwise) on the table. The selection of topic is critical. It needs to evoke a rich set of perspectives about a situation that, eventually, may become a cornerstone accomplishment of reconceptualization. Discussing whether or not a table exerts an upward force to counter gravity and how to describe a toss may be excellent targets.

Benchmarks are designed to be memorable, as the term suggests. Students are expected to reflect on them as landmarks in conceptual development. An instructor expects to refer back to benchmarks on many occasions.

Students carry the main burden of benchmark discussion. For this and other reasons, the subject of discussions needs to evoke multiple positions on the central issue. Luckily, the richness of p-prim physics means this is not unusual. One of the teacher's many roles is to ensure that diversity gets organized into a number of alternatives that illustrate principled approaches to the problem rather than, for example, a more chaotic dispute.

Another critical role of the instructor is to prompt for reasoning and, in general, to highlight principles and reasoning rather than conclusions and answers. To emphasize this, while experiments or demonstrations may be part of benchmarks, the point of these (just as the point of the whole discussion) is almost never expected to be universal agreement and clarity. Benchmarks are the beginning of a long process. Prompting for reasoning and justification targets both content-level knowledge—concepts and principles—and also standards for argumentation.

Ownership is a critical feature of benchmark lessons. The teacher guides and in some measure organizes. Yet students supply almost all proposals, arguments, and judgments. The teacher may make suggestions. But these are almost always neutrally posed, without the weight of authority behind them, and they are as likely to be "devil's advocate" rather than "nudging in the 'right' direction." In contrast to other popularized strategies like cognitive apprenticeship (Collins, Brown, and Newman, 1989) and reciprocal teaching (Brown and Palincsar, 1989) the instructor makes no extensive display of expertise to emulate and does not explicitly coach students through sticky issues or through expert procedures. Neither teacher nor textbook defines the terms (e.g., technical physics terms) for discussion.

Benchmarks are cumulative constructions for a teacher. They make use of much experience in hearing what students have to say, of knowing what may be expected and what needs to be prompted, and of learning how students may respond to particular tactics and rephrasings of student-proposed issues.

In summary, benchmark lessons are intended to instigate conceptual development productively and to help lay the groundwork for an extended learning process (heuristic 1). They make use of the richness in students' naive ideas, which are the central focus and driving force behind the discussion (heuristic 2). They are intended to highlight explanation and processes of reasoned and rational consideration (heuristic 3). And finally, benchmarks capitalize in one particular way on teachers' cumulative expertise of anticipating and making productive use of students' ideas (heuristic 4) while not undermining the spontaneity and diversity that is the hallmark of letting student conceptions into the arena of discussion.

Conclusion

In this chapter I have argued two fundamental points: First, intuitive "folk physics" is a reality. It imposes important constraints—but also provides numerous positive opportunities—with which instruction in physics must deal to be effective. Second, the "flora and fauna" of the cognitive ecology of folk physics is complex. It requires a subconceptual psychology with innovative categories, like p-prims, extending or replacing commonsense terms like concept, belief, or theory. Such a "complex knowledge systems" approach to learning does not straightforwardly prescribe instructional techniques that are bound to be successful. Instead, it supplies new suggestions on how to think about instruction as well as critical phenomena (such as J's invention of the impetus explanation of a toss, her extended maintenance of it simultaneously with more scientific explanations, and her refusal to accept physical standards of accountability in her explanations) that can serve as landmarks to guide design. One also hopes that the complex knowledge systems view will supply further riches if pursued as a progressing research program.

Acknowledgment

This work was supported by a grant from the Spencer Foundation, for which I am grateful. The opinions expressed are those of the author and do not necessarily reflect those of the Foundation.

Notes

1. Speaking "ungrammatically" generally means speaking with a different, unsanctioned grammar.
2. To anticipate later discussion, almost everyone with whom I talk winds up spending hours discussing physics. And most even find it interesting.
3. David Hammer and Bruce Sherin are the other contributors to this study.
4. In diSessa (1988) I conjectured essentially the "derivation" of the impetus theory that J exhibits on the basis of the p-prim pieces I had already discovered, starting with balance, conflict, and overcoming as extremely salient in this situation.
5. There is growing evidence that students' understanding of the nature of their own physical knowledge and the required transformation to it is a critical feature in successful learning. Thus experiencing this change may be an important bootstrapping step toward broader accomplishment.
6. See also diSessa (1993) and Smith, diSessa, and Roschelle (1993) for an accounting of many productive roles for p-prims.

References

Brown, A. L. and Palincsar, A. S. (1989). Guided, cooperative learning and individual knowledge acquisition. In L. B. Resnick (Ed.), *Knowing, learning and instruction: Essays in honor of Robert Glaser* (pp. 393–451). Hillsdale, NJ: Lawrence Erlbaum.

Brown, D. E. and Clement, J. (1989). Overcoming misconceptions via analogical reasoning: Abstract transfer versus explanatory model construction. *Instructional Science, 18,* 237–261.

Collins, A., Brown, J. S., and Newman, S. E. (1989). Cognitive apprenticeship: Teaching the crafts of reading, writing, and mathematics. In L. B. Resnick (Ed.), *Knowing, learning and instruction: Essays in honor of Robert Glaser* (pp. 453–494). Hillsdale, NJ: Lawrence Erlbaum.

diSessa, A. A. (1988). Knowledge in pieces. In G. Forman and P. Pufall (Eds.), *Constructivism in the computer age* (pp. 49–70). Hillsdale, NJ: Lawrence Erlbaum.

diSessa, A. A. (1993). Toward an epistemology of physics. *Cognition and Instruction, 10* (2–3), 105–225.

diSessa, A. A. (1995). Designing Newton's laws: Patterns of social and representational feedback in a learning task. In R.-J. Beun, M. Baker, and M. Reiner (Eds.), *Dialogue and interaction* (pp. 105–122). Berlin: Springer-Verlag.

diSessa, A. A. and Minstrell, J. (in press). Cultivating conceptual change with benchmark lessons. In J. G. Greeno and S. Goldman (Ed.), *Thinking practices*. Hillsdale, NJ: Lawrence Erlbaum.

Fodor, J. A. (1983). *Modularity of mind: An essay on faculty psychology*. Cambridge: MIT Press.

Larkin, J., McDermott, J., Simon, D., and Simon, H. A. (1980). Expert and novice performance in solving physics problems. *Science, 208,* 1135–1142.

McCloskey, M. (1983). Naive theories of motion. In D. Gentner and A. Stevens (Eds.), *Mental models* (pp. 299–324). Hillsdale, NJ: Lawrence Erlbaum.

Smith, J. P., diSessa, A. A., and Roschelle, J. (1993). Misconceptions reconceived: A constructivist analysis of knowledge in transition. *Journal of the Learning Sciences, 3*(2), 115–163.

31

Agreeing to Disagree: Developing Sociable Mathematical Discourse

MAGDALENE LAMPERT
PEGGY RITTENHOUSE
CAROL CRUMBAUGH

All students have beliefs about what to do in school in order to learn. These beliefs—their "folk learning theories"—are an expression of what our culture believes about school knowledge and how it is acquired. As Jerome Bruner (1990) has noted:

> All cultures have as one of their most powerful constitutive instruments a folk psychology, a set of more or less connected, more or less normative descriptions about how human beings "tick," what our own and other minds are like, what one can expect situated action to be like, what are possible modes of life, how one commits oneself to them, and so on. We learn our culture's folk psychology early, learn it as we learn to use the very language we acquire and to conduct the interpersonal transactions required in communal life. (p. 35)

The beliefs that make up our folk psychology of learning are not necessarily explicit, but they shape norms of interaction in school settings. One component of students' folk learning theories is a set of beliefs about what the subject under study is and how knowledge of it might be acquired. Elsewhere, Lampert has written about how common assumptions about the nature of mathematical knowledge and its acquisition conflict with theories of practice in the discipline of mathematics (Lampert, 1990, 1992; Putnam, Lampert, and Peterson, 1990). This conflict is problematic for educational reformers who wish to bring classroom practice closer to what people who invent and use mathematics do.

In this chapter, we examine another potentially problematic aspect of student's folk learning theories: the potential conflict between the kind of discourse that scholars and reformers believe will foster learning in school and common beliefs about disagreeing in public. Although we agree with others in the field that certain cultural norms privilege some students and disenfranchise others in the performance of traditional school tasks (see Heath, 1983), we propose that this dichotomy does not apply as directly to the performance of the kinds of school tasks that students are being asked to perform in "reformed" classrooms. In particular, the dichotomy between home norms and school norms seems inadequate as we try to understand students' disagreeing with peers about ideas. We assume that school classrooms draw on diverse communities and have multicultural populations; classrooms are places where people who come from different family backgrounds work and learn together. In connecting communication and discourse practices with understanding and knowing, scholars and reformers are advocating the creation of norms of public debate about ideas in school lessons that may have no readily recognizable counterparts in most of the home cultures from which the school population is drawn. The differences between folk theories of public disagreement and theories of teaching and learning that hinge on classroom discussion and debate have significant implications for how we think about what teachers need to do to teach mathematics and what students need in order to talk mathematics—or any other subject—in school.

Mathematical Talk in One Classroom

We begin with a story told by Lampert about a disagreement that occurred in a whole class discussion[1] in her fifth-grade mathematics class.[2] Such disagreements were common in her classroom, and in fact, she designed the problems that students were to work on so that discrepancies would be likely to arise in both strategies and solutions. In whole class discussion, she monitored the presentation of discrepant perspectives on problems and their solutions. She also attempted to provide students with some ideas about what kind of language might be appropriate for their arguments with peers. We present this case of student disagreement about a mathematical idea to provide an image of the kind of teaching and learning practices that scholars and reformers currently advocate. The role in social and mathematical discourse that Lampert assumes as the teacher requires the establishment of a different set of "sociomathematical norms" (Cobb, Wood, and Yackel, 1993).

Here Lampert describes a part of the lesson:[3]

On April 6, 1990, the class had been working in groups of four on an exercise in which they were given several sets of ordered pairs and their task was to find the relationship between the pairs in each set (Willoughby, Bereiter, Hilton, and Rubenstein, 1990). During this introductory lesson on functions, I made the transition from small group work to large group discussion by calling the class's attention to one of the exercises that a number of students had said was the "hardest" on that page. "Number six" was a cluster of ordered pairs which many students had been discussing with their groups, and there had been considerable controversy about how to state the "rule" for getting from the numbers in the first column to their corresponding "outputs" in the second column. I asked the class how one might characterize the relationship between the number in the first column and its corresponding value in the second column (see Figure 31.1). Ellie was the first to speak.

ELLIE: Um, well, there were a whole bunch of—a whole bunch of rules you could use, use, um, divided by two—And you could do, um, minus one-half.

I responded to Ellie's second assertion with a question: "And eight minus a half is?" To which she answered: "Four."

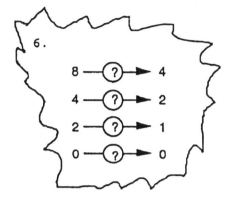

Figure 31.1

At this point a gasp arose from the class and several other students made bids to enter the conversation. I had solicited from Ellie a confirmation of her interpretation of "minus a half" and several of her classmates were surprised by what she said.

As the teacher in this situation, what I thought I needed to do first was to protect Ellie's right to practice mathematics in this fifth-grade classroom by monitoring the discourse so that she would have the opportunity to explain her thinking and justify her assertion. This kind of teaching move would make it possible for Ellie and the others to do a particular kind of learning move: trying to express their thinking in language or symbols, trying to understand what other people were thinking, and coming to some agreement on a usable definition for the operation "minus a half." So, before calling on any of the students who were eager to argue with Ellie, I set the terms of the conversation: You can express an idea that is different from Ellie's, but you also need to make an attempt to take her position seriously. Many of Ellie's classmates believed that she had asserted that eight minus a half is four. Most of the following discussion centered around the counter assertion that eight minus a half is seven and a half.

To set the terms of discussion, I asked for more ideas from the class and justified my move to get different ideas out on the table while also asking those who might disagree to treat Ellie's assertion with respect:

> You think that would be four? What does somebody else think? I, I started raising a question because a number of people have a different idea about that. So let's hear what your different ideas are and see if you can take Ellie's position into consideration and try to let her know what your position is. Enoyat?

Several students raised their hands and I chose Enoyat to speak first.

My reasons for structuring the discourse in this way were both mathematical and social. According to stated norms of the mathematical community, the people who invent and use mathematics, the legitimacy of an assertion is not judged without considering the assumptions and the reasoning that are supplied to justify the assertion. In the course of trying to explicate the assertion that "eight minus one half is four" or the counterassertion that "eight minus one half is seven and one-half," the students and I together became clearer about the assumptions and definitions that underlie Ellie's assertion. Ellie's assertion that the rule could be either "divide by two" or "minus one half" might be thought of as the result of a mathematical intuition. She "saw" both relationships in the set of ordered pairs that had been given in the exercise, but she was struggling to find a way to talk about what she saw. Based on the kinds of computations I had seen her do on other occasions, I did not think that the problem was that Ellie could not correctly perform the subtraction of one half from eight. Rather I proceeded as if the students were struggling with a big new mathematical idea: that a number could be both a *quantity* and an *operator on quantities*. (In this case, for example, "one-half" could mean either the quantity "one half of one whole" or the operation "take one half of".) This idea is fundamental to knowing how to interpret and to use rational numbers and confusion about this idea often gets in the way of students being able to work successfully with fractions. Even more significant perhaps is that this work occurs on the boundary between arithmetic and algebra. I used these exercises to engage students in thinking about the idea of a variable and how two variables are related. Ellie was struggling with finding a way to respond to her classmates that expressed her understanding of the relational nature of functions while many of them were focused on making a mathematical statement that would fit the constraints of one particular set of ordered pairs in the exercise.

On the social front, what I thought the students needed to learn was how to disagree respectfully, how to express the evidence for their disagreement, and how to revise their own thinking while saving face among their peers. In order to accomplish the goal of equitable participation, I could not let Ellie "go it alone"—some of her classmates would take pride in shooting down her idea, and then she would not again venture to participate for some time. I also knew that a few of the students would need special encouragement to enter the conversation, and that they might do little more than restate arguments that had already been made.

Mathematically, I expected that the students' talk would be a sort of "first draft" attempt to speak about the complex distinction between numbers as operators and numbers as quantities.[4] I sparingly tried to help them edit their talk as I asked for further clarification and justification. One after another, students expressed ideas about the meaning of one half and experimented with how to talk about it in relation to the other numbers.

As the following transcript excerpt shows, the students expressed not only disagreement, but conditions under which they might agree. I called on Enoyat first after Ellie's assertion because I knew that he would be gentle in his response, even if he disagreed.

ENOYAT: Well, see, I agree with Ellie because you can have eight minus one half and that's the same as eight divided by two or eight minus four.
LAMPERT: Eight divided by two is four, eight minus four is four? Okay, so Enoyat thinks he can do all of those things to eight and get four. Okay? Charlotte?
CHARLOTTE: Um, I think eight minus one half is seven and a half because—
LAMPERT: Why?
CHARLOTTE: Um, one half's a fraction and it's half of one whole and so when you subtract you aren't even subtracting one whole number so you can't get even a smaller number that's more than one whole. But I see what Ellie's doing, she's taking half the number she started with and getting the answer.
LAMPERT: So, you would say one half of eight? Is that what you mean?
CHARLOTTE: Yeah, one half of eight equals four.
LAMPERT: How do you know that?
CHARLOTTE: Because, um, eight and one half is um, eight and half of eight is four, so if you have two groups of four you would, is eight.

At this point, I decided to check in with Ellie:

LAMPERT: Ellie, what do you think?

ELLIE: Um, I still think, I mean, one half, it would be eight minus one half, they would probably say oh, eight minus one half equals four. Um.

LAMPERT: Who would say that?

ELLIE: I don't know. Well, well if if I saw something like that, like if we were having something and the answer was missing.

LAMPERT: Um. . .hm.

ELLIE: Um, and it was eight minus one half I would probably say four.

I wondered if more talk would help clarify the alternatives:

LAMPERT: What do other people think? Sam?

SAM: Um, I agree with Charlotte and um I don't agree with Ellie. Because um, like one half is not even one, so if, so when Ellie said that people that people would like, um a really good mathematician would probably, like, would probably write seven and a half, not four because they would have to know what the one half was meaning, half of a number to um, to understand it.

LAMPERT: You know when Charlotte was talking she said that she thought one half meant half of a whole. And it sounds like that's the way you are interpreting it. But Ellie might be interpreting one half to mean something else. Lev, what do you think?

LEV: I think um, I would agree with Ellie if she had said eight minus one half of eight because half of eight would be four because four plus four would be eight.

LAMPERT: So, in your case, you're saying one half, if Ellie meant one half was half of eight wholes, then it would work. Okay, Tyrone?

TYRONE: I agree with Charlotte and Sam and I disagree with Ellie and like I think Ellie meant like because four is half of eight, like one half would be a half, but, and I agree with Lev when he said if she meant one half uh equals, wait, eight, equals half of eight and I agree with Sam and uh Charlotte because, um if, if, uh, four is not, uh eight equals half of four is not right because it's seven and a half because half of like, eight is the whole and um, one number away from that is seven and plus a half would be seven and half.

LAMPERT: Uh huh. So um, that reminds me of some of the discussion that we were having yesterday, which is that if you, if you use addition, it helps you to understand what it means to take away something on the other side. Okay? Let's hear from Shahroukh.

SHAHROUKH: I would agree with Ellie if she had added something else to her explanation, if she said one half of the amount that you have to divide by two.

LAMPERT: Okay. You guys are on to something really important about fractions, which is that a fraction is a fraction of something. And we have to have some kind of agreement here if it's a fraction of eight or if it's a fraction of a whole. Let's, let's just hear from a couple more people Ellie, and then I'll come back and hear from you, okay? Er uh Darota?

DAROTA: Well, I think, um, I disagree with Ellie because if she means that one half of the whole you would get seven and then if you add that half on again you would get seven and a half.

LAMPERT: Okay. Well, that's quite similar to what Tyrone was saying that addition is a way of helping me think about the meaning of subtraction. But again, both you and Tyrone are assuming that one half means one half of one. Okay? Anthony.

ANTHONY: [Inaudible]. . .if you are assuming it is one half of the original number it would be different than if it is half of a whole. So it depends on what your point of view is.

LAMPERT: Right. And that, that would be very important to clarify. Okay.

My "Okay." was meant to bring some closure to the discussion, and I turned again to Ellie:

ELLIE: Um, well, I agree with Shahroukh and, um, when Charlotte said um, she thought that um, it should be one half of eight, um, instead of just plain one half, I don't agree with her because not all of them are eight. Not all of the problems are eight.

LAMPERT: Okay. Let's um, one of the things that is kind of a convention in mathematics is that when we just talk about numbers and we don't associate them with any objects or groups of objects, that this symbol means half of one whole. So if, if you were gonna communicate with the rest of the world who uses mathematics, they would take this [pointing to the expression "$8-^1/_2$" on the chalkboard] to mean eight wholes minus one half of a whole. Okay? Ellie?

ELLIE: Um, well, I—I think that eight if, you had, all you—all these numbers are that are going into the um.

LAMPERT: Function machine.

ELLIE: Um on number six, they're all, they can all be divided into halves and um four minus um well two is one half of four.

LAMPERT: Okay, so the number that comes out is one half of the number that went in. Okay. And in this case is that true?

ELLIE: Um.

LAMPERT: Is one one-half of two? Is zero one half of zero?

ELLIE: Um, yes.

LAMPERT: So, what do you think about that? We could write this in words, you know, we don't have to use these equations, but it's more efficient. You, you feel that—

ELLIE: One half is—

LAMPERT: If, if you said that the number that comes out is half the number that goes in, it would be easier for you to understand?

ELLIE: That's what I meant, but I just couldn't put it in there, but that's what was in my mind.

LAMPERT: Okay. But I think you raised a lot of interesting questions by your idea of taking away a half.

In this class, students are engaged in doing mathematics with one another and with their teacher. They are learning about mathematical forms of discourse by inventing ways to talk about quantitative relationships, making conjectures about patterns in relationships among numbers, justifying those conjectures with logic and mathematical evidence, and considering the reasonableness of the assertions made by others who seem to disagree. Working on the question of what makes an assertion true or acceptable for use is central to both the pedagogy and the mathematics in this class. As they try to figure out how "one-half" can mean something other than the quantity half of one whole, this teacher and her students are participating in a fifth-grade version of mathematical argument—a conversation whose purpose is to determine the mathematical legitimacy of a chain of reasoning and the appropriateness of applying that reasoning to a problem situation. They are also intentionally engaged in what we have come to call "the social construction of knowledge."[5]

But it is not only mathematical content knowledge that is being constructed here. And the students are not the only participants in this constructive activity. As teacher and students work together, they are inventing new forms of activity and interaction for learning mathematics in school. In order to be judged as successful learners of mathematics in this classroom, the students need to demonstrate that they are reasoning collaboratively toward their conclusions rather than accepting answers on the authority of the teacher or a textbook or a student who they have identified as "smart in math." The students' learning involves accepting the goal of "making sense" as a legitimate purpose for classroom work. In order for the teacher to judge herself successful at getting students to change their mathematical thinking, such a change must be effected through reasoned argument by teachers or other students rather than by simple exercise of authority.

Schooling Mathematical Intentions

Many of the students in Lampert's class in 1989–90 came from more traditional fourth-grade classrooms, where their experience of teacher-student interaction during mathematics lessons was quite different.[6] In the traditional mathematics classroom, the result of Ellie's answer of "four" to the teacher's question: "Eight minus a half is?" would likely be for students and teacher to judge Ellie to be wrong. Students might even be heard to mutter, "That's a dumb answer!" or to give nonverbal signals that they did not consider Ellie to be very bright. The teacher might be more polite, but equally straightforward in her judgment that Ellie was deficient. The teacher's job would be to explain to Ellie why she is wrong or to use some other means to get her to answer "Seven and one-half" the next time she is asked what eight minus a half is. Students and teacher would be likely to judge the students who were anxious to speak in reaction to Ellie's error as "smarter at math" than Ellie, and they might imagine that learning would occur if Ellie would listen to someone the teacher would call on to give the "right" answer. But they might also feel sorry for Ellie, imagining that this would be an embarrassing moment for her.[7] In most cases, there would be nothing like a discussion and no expectation on the part of students that they should know how to "agree" or "disagree" with Ellie and how to convince others their position makes sense.

In most school mathematics lessons, teacher and students make one assertion after another about what is true or false, right or wrong. In conventional teaching, what makes an assertion true or right is the authority of the teacher or the textbook or a "smart" student. In contrast, in the classroom we have just looked in on, all students are called upon to justify the correctness of their own assertions with mathematical evidence. They are asked to explain discrepancies between how they think about something and how someone else might think about it by examining their assumptions and defining their terms of discourse.

The teacher of the class in which this discussion took place engages students in such mathematical conversation in order to teach them what it means to do mathematics.[8] By posing interpretable problems and encouraging disagreement, the teacher sets the stage for students to clarify their thinking and relate thought to communication. Teaching and learning activities during lessons are related to the practice of doing mathematics by the teacher and her students raising questions about how one another's mathematical assertions are justified. In the process of justifying what makes sense to themselves and their peers, students struggle with constructing a mathematical language and a set of relationships among its terms that is internally consistent.

The teaching in this discussion reflects current trends toward thinking about learning and knowing as *social* as well as individual activities, both in the disciplines and in school classrooms. Acquiring knowledge is not thought to be a private interaction between knower and subject matter or a one-to-one interaction between teacher and individual student, but it is understood as a broadly social practice engaged in with peers and more knowledgeable others. These epistemological trends are reflected in the set of new "standards" for teaching mathematics established recently by the National Council of Teachers of Mathematics (NCTM). For example, in a section on "students' role in discourse," the *Professional Standards for Teaching Mathematics* say:

The teacher of mathematics should promote classroom discourse in which students:

- listen to, respond to, and question the teacher and one another;
- use a variety of tools to reason, make connections, solve problems, and communicate;
- initiate problems and questions;
- make conjectures and present solutions;
- explore examples and counterexamples to investigate a conjecture;
- try to convince themselves and one another of the validity of particular representations, solutions, conjectures, and answers;
- rely on mathematical evidence and argument to determine validity.

(National Council of Teachers of Mathematics, 1991, p. 45)

As with reform documents in other disciplines, this set of new standards puts a strong emphasis on changing the nature of classroom discourse to include talk in the spirit of disciplinary work. It is expected that students will consider and challenge one another's assertions, and even challenge the teacher, and presumably by using mathematical evidence, convince others of the reasonability of their claims. The *Teaching Standards* are premised on the assumption that the nature of classroom discourse is a significant influence on what students learn about mathematics. "Major shifts" in the environment of mathematics classrooms are advocated so that schools can "move from current practice to mathematics teaching for the empowerment of students."

We need to shift—

- toward classrooms as mathematical communities—away from classrooms as simply a collection of individuals;

- toward logic and mathematical evidence as verification—away from the teacher as the sole authority for right answers;
- toward mathematical reasoning—away from merely memorizing procedures;
- toward conjecturing, inventing, and problem solving—away from an emphasis on mechanistic answer-finding;
- toward connecting mathematics, its ideas, and its applications—away from treating mathematics as a body of isolated concepts and procedures.

(NCTM, 1991, p. 3)

"Reasoning" here is something that is fundamentally linked to communication: Making conjectures means putting out tentative ideas for consideration by oneself and others. What it means for something to be true is to be determined in social exchanges where mathematical evidence is used to verify an assertion. The social nature of learning is emphasized in the view that classrooms should be "mathematical communities" rather than collections of individual learners. Such communities would establish norms and patterns of discourse, not only for how to talk but for what counts as evidence and therefore as knowledge. This view of knowledge production is grounded in the discourse ideals of the discipline, and it is consonant with contemporary psychological theories about the role of discourse and disagreement in individual knowledge growth (Strike and Posner, 1985; Wiser and Carey, 1983; Hatano and Inagaki, 1991).

By using the word "promote" to describe the pedagogical activity of the teacher who seeks to have such things happen in the classroom, NCTM sidesteps the question of what exactly teachers need to teach and students need to learn for this kind of talk to be seen as an appropriate mode of public interaction between schoolchildren and their teacher (Ball, 1991). At the same time, NCTM emphasizes that it is setting standards for mathematics teaching and learning that are to apply to "every child":

Goals such as learning to make conjectures, to argue about mathematics using mathematical evidence, to formulate and solve problems—even perplexing ones—and to make sense of mathematical ideas are not just for some group thought to be "bright" or "mathematically able." Every student can—and should—learn to reason and solve problems, to make connections across a rich web of topics and experiences, and to communicate mathematical ideas. (NCTM, 1991, p. 21)

Our experience with school and university teaching and with communication among researchers suggests that this kind of discourse does not come easily, either to school learners or more advanced scholars. In the rest of this chapter, we will examine this problem.

Folk Theories about Appropriate Forms of Public Debate

How might we think about the cultural milieu into which we have dropped educational ideals like the NCTM *Teaching Standards*? How are we to understand what students bring with them from outside of school in the way of knowledge about how to disagree about ideas, how to argue with peers? "Arguing" is an activity most people engage in privately and publicly inside and outside of school. Even in sociable conversation, it is likely that participants will disagree. Although we come from different cultural backgrounds, we learn how to respond to such disagreements in ways that accomplish multiple goals, including preserving relationships with people who make assertions that we believe to be unreasonable. If maintaining such relationships contributes to other social and personal goals, we find ways to avoid or to ameliorate disagreement. We learn when it is acceptable to simply ignore an assertion with which we disagree, and when we can assert physical or political power to force agreement. From experience, we acquire a model of what it means to disagree in public and how to do it successfully.[9]

In *Roget's Thesaurus* we find that in its social sense, *reasoning* can be used synonymously with words like *commenting, discussing,* and *inquiring*. In arcane usage, one might use the phrase *torture a question* as a synonym for reasoning. More commonly, *reasoning* is also thought to be synonymous with *agitating, quarreling,* and *wrangling*. Somewhere in the middle between these extremes are more socially neutral synonyms for reasoning like *arguing* and *disagreeing*.

In the academic world, arguing about ideas is supposed to be our stock-in-trade, although in fact we rarely engage in doing it face to face. We believe that knowledge in a field grows from challenges to existing ideas and revisions of inadequate theories. In our ideal academic scenario, the quest for knowledge begins with conjecturing, and ideas get refined as conjectures get revised. Ideally, we avoid quarreling or agitating those with whom we have differences by following acceptable canons of academic discourse, such as reviewing manuscripts "blindly" and writing in the third person (Swales, 1990).

In the world of schoolchildren, arguing and disagreeing are closer to agitation and quarreling—not something you would do to a friend, or even to someone you knew you were going to have to work with every day for the rest of the week or month or year (Isaacs, 1971). Schoolchildren certainly modify their disagreement behaviors when they enter the classroom from the playground or the lunchroom, but when left to their own devices, they are not likely to carry on what we would recognize as an academic argument when someone says something in public that they believe is wrong. Children do not readily separate the quality of ideas from the person expressing those ideas in judging the veracity of assertions (Olson and Astington, 1993). It is also plausible that they would not naturally distinguish between norms for disagreeing about who should have the first turn on the swing and norms for disagreeing about who has expressed the most adequate formulation of a mathematical relationship.

What Some Fifth Graders Have to Say about Mathematical Disagreements in School

In the same way that we study how children think about number or spatial relations to help us figure out how to teach them arithmetic or geometry, it seems appropriate to try to examine their ways of understanding intellectual debate to help us think about how they might learn to engage in productive social encounters in school. One way to begin to study school learners' folk learning theories would be to look at both what they say about disagreement and what they do about it at a point in the school year when the teacher would not yet have had much influence on their ways of interacting and when the teacher is not present to moderate their activity (Spradley, 1972; Holland and Quinn, 1987). Data that have been collected in Lampert's classroom offer us these opportunities. First, there was a discussion in the classroom about the subject of "disagreement" that occurred a few days after the lesson we looked at above. Ellie, the girl with whom many students disagreed about the meaning of "eight minus a half," had a lot to say in that discussion about disagreement, and we will look particularly at her views. There were also several occasions at the beginning of the year when students worked in small groups to develop solutions to problems without much intervention from the teacher. After we look at what students had to say about disagreement, we will look in on a discussion that occurred early in the year among four other students in the class. In this discussion, the students disagreed about how to work on a problem relating time, speed, and distance. One of the central figures in the debate was Sam, a boy who had joined the class just the week before and was trying to figure out how to get his peers to see the problem his way.

A few days after the discussion of "eight minus a half" reported above, a colleague visited Lampert's classroom who was interested in the pedagogy of Socratic dialogue and how it might work in an elementary mathematics classroom. Lampert asked the students in her class to spend a few minutes at the beginning of math period telling the visitor about their discussions in math, and what they thought about having discussions in math: "What you like about them, what you don't like about them, what you think you learn from them." These students had been participating in whole class discussions about mathematical disagreements since early October, and it was now April. This was the first time they had publicly talked about their experience. Their "discussion of discussions" went on for the whole class hour.

The first student who spoke said, simply, "I don't like discussions when you are wrong." Lampert asked how that made him feel, but before he could answer, another student jumped in and said, "I think it's a way of trying to experience different people's point of views and what other people think, how they solve problems and things." The third student to speak said, "I don't like discussion because, because you have to give, you always have to give your reasoning and sometimes you just think of a problem and you don't think of why you said that." And another student disagreed: "I disagree with Karim because if you want to like give reasonings and if you are just thinking the problem, and you solve the problem for other people, they wouldn't know how they got the answer, and if you tell them how you got the answer they might not want to do the work."

Two of these students seem to be equating reasoning with conventional ideas about academic argument, expressing dispositions that are consonant with what we currently think is good learning practice in schools: find out how other people think about something, and do not be satisfied only with an answer if the answer has not been justified. The other two are somewhat less disposed toward the activity of discussing mathematics, one because he doesn't like to be wrong in public and the other because he is not always prepared to articulate why he thinks what he thinks. After this somewhat balanced exchange of opinions, the students' responses took a turn toward expressing almost entirely negative feelings about participating in mathematical discussions. Here we focus primarily on Ellie's contributions because of the role she played in the disagreement about how to interpret "eight minus a half."[10]

The first time Ellie spoke, she expressed a dislike for disagreement in the form of being the object of someone else's reasoned argument:

ELLIE: Um, I don't like reasoning because whenever you have a wrong answer people try so hard to prove you're wrong.

Her friend Saundra agreed with her and said that being in that position made Saundra feel embarrassed, even mortified:

SAUNDRA: Yeah, I agree with Ellie because you know it can get sort of embarrassing at times, because like everybody else, like you say something and everybody will raise their hand and want to say something different or they all disagree with you. And it makes you sort of feel like you want to crawl into a hole and die.

Ellie then commented on the persistence of those who might disagree, and echoed Saundra's social discomfort with being involved in this kind of exchange:

ELLIE: Um, when, when you do realize that you have the answer wrong they still want to prove it to you that it's wrong. Then um, like if you're going, like you have one lesson and you're wrong, and then the next lesson people are still raising their hands to prove that it is wrong. And saying, "Oh yeah this, and I think this because," um and you want to just crawl under your desk.

But Ellie had an intellectual concern as well. She was worried about her own capacity to hold on to her thinking in the face of disagreement:

ELLIE: Um, sometimes I don't like discussions because when you're trying to prove something it just turns into something else and you don't get to say what you think.

After she said this, several students in the class muttered agreement.

Later in the discussion, Ellie commented on still another aspect of classroom discourse that made her uncomfortable: the ownership of ideas. In a setting where collaboration was valued and rewarded by the teacher, both in math class and in other classes as well, the issue of individual productivity and recognition was clearly on students' minds. Ellie referred to a situation in which several students might work together to come up with the "answer" but only one gets to say what they think in the whole class discussion. What she says here suggests that there are consequences to such actions that go beyond feeling bad—if one "takes" someone else's answer, one risks being temporarily ostracized, perhaps by someone who had previously been counted as an ally.

ELLIE: Um, I um, I agree with Shahroukh and I sort of don't because if you were the only person that had their hand raised, of a couple people it's fun to have an answer that's right, but if everybody is raising their hand and um, you're called on, you feel really bad, if, if um, somebody really wanted that, to um, give that answer. And sometimes people say, "Oh, you took my answer," and they don't talk to you for a while.

As the discussion went on Ellie returned to her concern about the fact that she did not always get to say what she thought when she disagreed with someone, referring to an occasion when she had to leave a class discussion to go to an appointment. Again she reminds us that there are public consequences (teasing) beyond personal discomfort when students do not agree:

ELLIE: Well, um, when you were doing the fractions, then we did all those percents on that board back there and the eights and we tried to see what the differences were, before that we were working on something and everybody disagreed with me, and I didn't get to say what I thought.
LAMPERT: And um, say more about that. Why is that a problem?
ELLIE: Um, because you don't have a chance to tell them what you think and they and if their answer is wrong and maybe if you tell them your reasoning and why you think and maybe they'll think that um, maybe they won't tease you anymore.

She elaborates as she talks about disagreements in small group, rather than whole class discussions, claiming that teasing is a way for students to save face in a disagreement, so that when they find out they are wrong, "they don't feel bad":

ELLIE: Um, there is one other thing that I really don't like about small group. One is that like if you're right, and one person thinks that you're wrong, it turns out that you're right and then um, when they find out that they're wrong, they make fun of you. And they um, so they don't feel bad, if they didn't, that they weren't right.

After Ellie spoke about not liking discussion in small groups, she was countered by another student, Sam. What Sam likes about small group discussions compared with whole class discussions is that there are fewer people involved with whom one might have to engage in the repair of a relationship when the lesson is over:

SAM: Um, I like small discussions, small group discussions because like when Ellie said that the um, whole class discussion will prove you wrong, like [in small group] the most you can get is usually about five people trying to prove you wrong. Because other people, um, the rest of the class is all in their groups, some people well it all depends on who, how many people are absent or not and like the most is usually five.

These utterances indicate that what one does in mathematics class has both social and personal repercussions. How you handle a disagreement, even whether you participates in disagreements at all, can affect how you feel about yourself and how others feel about you and treat you. We might imagine, after listening to such comments, that a synonym these fifth graders would choose for "discussion" is "torture." The torture is milder, Sam reminds us, if fewer people are involved in doing it. We do not interpret his comments, or Ellie's, to suggest that these fifth graders are overtly mean to one another, either in small group or large group discussion. Rather it seems to be the case that these students experience "people trying to prove you are wrong" as a personal assault, even in situations where the teacher insists that assertions be justified with mathematical evidence.

What Some Fifth Graders *Do* about Mathematical Disagreements in School

We now turn to a study of student disagreement in a setting where students were not supervised by the teacher, yet had been asked to work with a small group to figure out a mathematics problem. (See Blunk, 1995.) This exchange was one of several that were videotaped in an attempt to collect a large sample of data about student interactions during "small group time." When we looked at a selection of these tapes, this one stood out because all four of the students in the group seemed to be actively engaged over a considerable period of time although there was no teacher intervention during the time they were on camera. We also chose to analyze this conversation because it was possible to hear most of the conversation among these four students even though the rest of the class was similarly engaged in argument.

It is early November in Lampert's fifth-grade mathematics class. Each day when the class comes into the room after recess, the problems to be discussed on that day are written on the blackboard (see Figure 31.2).[11]

In this lesson as in most every lesson during the year, about half of the one-hour class is spent in students working alone or with peers on the problems of the day. They talk and write in individual notebooks where they are expected to do "experiments" like drawing, figuring, and diagramming information, to make a conjecture about the solution to the problem, and to write their reasoning about why they think their solutions make sense. It is not required that the students reach a consensus in their small groups, but they are expected to understand the perspectives of others. The second part of class is a whole class discussion, like the one we looked at above, in which the teacher both participates in the mathematical conversation to model appropriate modes of discourse and speaks directly about how students are expected to interact with one another and use mathematical

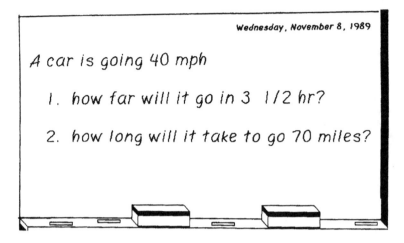

Figure 31.2

evidence to support their assertions. The teacher chooses the focus of the large group discussion based on her observations of students' work in the first part of the hour. During both parts of the lessons, students are expected to make and defend conjectures. They are expected to listen to, respond to, and question the teacher and one another. All assertions are open to investigation, and a frequently heard teacher response to any assertion is, "Why do you think that?"

Lampert provides some perspectives on how the problems she poses to her class might lead to discrepancies in students' thinking and disagreements about solutions. We include her reflections on the mathematics she expected students would be engaged in as students worked on these problems to provide a context for examining the nature of the students' disagreement:

When these problems were posed, my class had been investigating time-speed-distance relationships for about two weeks. I had not given them a set of rules to follow to solve these kinds of problems, and they had not had any formal instruction about the concepts of rate and ratio. The mathematical work in which I intended the students to be engaged was not simply finding the answer to the time-speed-distance questions. If that had been my goal, I would have taught them a formula and given them the opportunity to practice using it. Instead, I encouraged them to reason about how changes in one of the variables (time) would affect the other (distance) given a constant rate of speed. Before this particular day, they had worked on problems similar to number one, above, where the speed is given and the problem is to find out how far vehicle will travel at that constant rate in a given time. At first, I assigned problems where the speed was given in miles per hour and the time was given in hours. As they worked on these problems, their reasoning involved something like: if the speed is 40 m.p.h. that means it goes 40 miles in one hour. They calculated the distance in journeys of more than one hour using successive addition or multiplication. Students talked about these relationships and drew diagrams to illustrate them.

Then I gave them problems like problem 1 above, where the time was not a simple multiple of one hour, but included portions of an hour. In these problems, I expected that

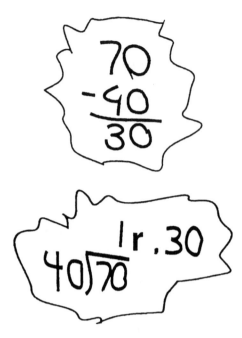

Figure 31.3

three operations would be needed to find the distance: first they would need to find how far a vehicle would go in three hours given that they knew about how far it would go in one hour; then they would have to find out how far it would go in half an hour given that they knew about how far it would go in one hour; and then they would need to add those two distances together. On the day of the discussion we look at here, I decided for the first time to give the class a problem where they knew the distance and they had to reason about the effect that it would have on the *time* the journey would take at a constant rate of speed.

So, what you know (in problem 2 above) is that the car goes 40 miles in one hour. And what you need to figure out is: How long will it take to go 70 miles? Using their by now familiar heuristic (i.e., that 40 m.p.h. means the car goes 40 miles in one hour), I expected that they might reason that it would take at least an hour for this journey, and that after an hour there would still be 30 *miles* left to go.

In terms of arithmetic operations, they could represent this as either taking 40 miles away from 70 miles and having 30 miles left, or dividing 70 miles by 40 miles per hour and having 30 left. But in either case they would face the question: Thirty what? How is that remainder of "30" to be related to the given information that the car goes 40 miles per hour? Based on what I had seen of their approaches to other problems, I expected to see students' first step in doing this problem look something like one or the other of the computations shown here (see Figure 31.3). Having done this computation, the students face a problem of mathematical interpretation: How does the difference of "30" in the subtraction or the "r. 30" in the division relate to the time-speed-distance relationship in the task they are working on? What does the remainder mean when you take 40 away from 70 and have 30 "left over." What is it that is left over? Would it be 30 minutes? Or 30 miles? Or is 30 a number on which another operation needs to be performed? That is the problem I expected them to struggle with on this day.

The relationship among 30, 40, 70, and 1 in this problem is not a simple one: The "1" in the quotient refers to one *hour*. The 30 in the "r. 30" is 30 *miles* and what is important here is that 30 miles is three-fourths of 40 miles. The next step is to figure out how to use that information to find how much more *time* the journey will take. Proportional reasoning is required to find the solution: because 30 miles is three-fourths of 40 miles, it will take *three-fourths of an hour* to complete the rest of the journey. After the proportional reasoning, another computation is required if one wants to express the time in minutes: how many minutes in three-quarters of an hour? And finally, one needs to remember that the car has already gone an hour before these extra 30 miles were under consideration. So, an hour for the first 40 miles, three-quarters of an hour for the next 30 miles, 1 hour and 45 minutes all together for the journey.

The tasks they were assigned on November 8 were deliberately designed to take me and my students on an interesting and worthwhile mathematical journey. I anticipated that there would be several ways in which discrepancies might arise in how students would think about this problem, especially in how they thought about the "30" that would be left. I was attempting to push their thinking, not only by giving distance and asking for time, but by giving a distance that involved their grappling with fractions of an hour in ways they had not done before.

As I introduced the task for the day, I sought from the students their interpretations of the difference between the two parts on this problem:

LAMPERT: Okay, this problem has two parts. It has one condition. The condition is: A car is going 40 miles per hour. And that condition applies to both problem 1 and problem 2. Problem 1 is: How far will it go in three and one-half hours? And problem 2 is: How long will it take to go 70 miles? Before you start, can you see the difference between problem 1 and problem 2? Raise your hand if you can see the difference.

After some discussion of the relationships among time, speed, and distance and the units in which each of these quantities might be measured, the class did not reach closure on the question of what units the solutions to each of these problems would be expressed in. I set the students to working on the problems with the hope that this would become clearer as they experimented with drawings and calculations and discussed their work with their small groups:

LAMPERT: Okay, I'd like everybody to work on this problem, and after you work on it, then we'll try and decide whether it should be miles per hour for the answer, miles for the answer, or hours for the answer. We need a number to go here and I want you to think about what all this means, and figure it out. And I want to see in your notebooks, I want to see the problem, I want to see experiments, and I want you to write your reasoning.

I was being deliberately unclear. I expected that as students talked with one another in their groups of four, they would grapple with the meaning of the numbers in this problem and how they should be related to one another. I also expected students to flounder as they explored what it would be like to try to get their mathematical ideas across, but I wanted to establish "talking with peers" as a norm for coming up with sensible interpretations and solutions. I also thought about such occasions as an opportunity to learn about students' capacities for communication about mathematics and to deliberate on what and how to teach them.

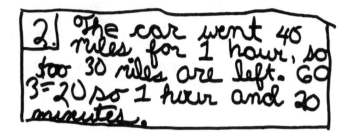

Figure 31.4

Having heard the teacher's perspective on the purposes of this lesson, we now look in on a group of students whose independent work on problem 2 (above) can be seen on videotape.

In the back of the room, during small group work time, four students are talking loudly and gesturing toward one another and their notebooks. The tone is contentious with intermittent attempts at reconciliation. They are working on the second part of the problem: How long will it take a car going 40 miles per hour to go 70 miles? First we see Sam and Enoyat, the two boys in the group, talking to one another. As Enoyat tries to figure out what to put in his notebook, he wants to know why Sam and Connie disagree, and he draws Connie into the conversation. There is some talk about the problem of figuring out the time, but they are distracted from their disagreement on this by the question of whether the "answer" is miles or minutes, and the disagreement here seems to be based on a misreading of what Connie has written in her notebook. In this exchange, Sam and Connie try to change one another's minds while also trying to convince another member of the group that their own approach is correct.

What Sam has written in his notebook under the heading "reasoning" is shown in Figure 31.4. This is the only clue we have to his reasoning besides what he says in the discussion while this group is on camera.

SAM: Sixty divided by 3 is gonna be 20 minutes. So it's 1 hour and 20 minutes, right? One hour and 20 minutes, not 120 minutes.

ENOYAT: One hour and 20 minutes?

SAM: Yes. One hour is going to be the 40 miles, there's 30 miles left. Sixty divided by 3 is 20. So 1 hour and 20 minutes. Do you understand?

ENOYAT: Now I do. Why doesn't, why doesn't she agree? [Pointing to Connie across the table.]

SAM: I don't know, she says, um, she thinks the answer is 1 hour and 40 minutes.

CONNIE: No, I *know* what it is. I think the answer is 1 hour and 40 minutes.

SAM: Well, you didn't figure that out though, you just guessed. You said it had to be over my number.

Connie's notebook is shown in Figure 31.5. Connie has accounted for 40 plus 20 (or altogether 60) of the miles using proportional reasoning. She has 10 miles left

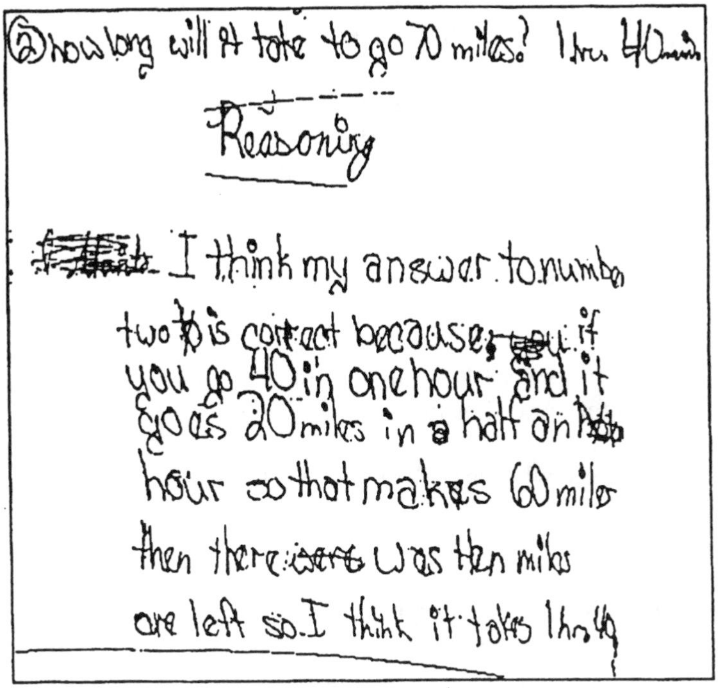

Figure 31.5

to account for, and it seems that what she does is add 10 minutes on to the time to account for the extra 10 miles.

ENOYAT: [Referring to both problems 1 and 2.] How can they both be 140 minutes?

SAM: No, no, one is talking about miles, one is talking about minutes.

ENOYAT: So, it can't be miles, it has to be minutes. It has to be. . .

CONNIE: I know! One hour and 40 minutes, not miles.

SAM: [Tapping aggressively on Connie's notebook.] You put miles.

CONNIE: [Pointing to her own writing.] M-I-N-period.

Connie seems to be in sort of a defend-my-answer mode, as she makes several attempts to explain her reasoning, her assumptions, even her penmanship. Sam's intonation, countenance, and notebook tapping, indicate that he is criticizing Connie. He seems to be trying to reduce her credibility with the others in the group, especially when he accuses Connie of "guessing" rather than "figuring it out." Sam's attempt to get Enoyat to "understand" involves repeating the calculations he did; he does not explain why he divided 60 by 3, or why the result of this calculation is 20 *minutes*. Connie's strong statement of her solution is not accompanied by an explanation of why she is so sure she is correct, either. Instead she exerts rhetorical power, emphasizing that she "knows" rather than "thinks" she is right, possibly believing that this will have a stronger effect on convincing her peers to agree.

After his disagreement with Connie about the time the journey takes is established, Sam turns to Catherine and tells her what he thinks. Catherine seems to be following his assertions when they are interrupted by Connie who offers a reasoned challenge to Sam's conclusion.

SAM: Okay, Catherine, have you heard what she told you, what she thought it was?

CATHERINE: Yes.

SAM: Now I think it's 1 hour and 20 minutes, okay? Cause the car is going 40, right? And that takes 1 hour.

CATHERINE: Uh-huh.

SAM: So there's, what is it, 30 miles left. Right?

CONNIE: Yeah.

SAM: Sixty divided by 3 is 20, right?

CATHERINE: Yeah.

SAM: So, 1 hour and 20 minutes.

Connie has been listening to this exchange, even assenting to the first part of Sam's reasoning about his solution. But when Sam states his conclusion, she strongly objects again, and tries to reason with Sam:

CONNIE: But NOOOOO! That's not right. How come it only goes 20 miles in half an hour and you're trying to get 30 so—

SAM: It doesn't go 20 miles, yes it does.

Marking her disagreement with a resounding "But NOOOOO!" Connie starts to ask an open-ended question, which points out the flaw in Sam's assumptions, and in his method and subsequent solution. Connie uses a technique familiar to mathematicians in her argument with Sam: She assumes that Sam's conclusion is true, and then reasons backward to show that his conclusion implies an assumption that is contradictory to the situation described in the problem. If the car goes 40 miles in 1 hour, and the length of the journey is 70 miles, it still has 30 miles to go after the first hour. Connie goes along with Sam's solution procedure up to this point.

But when Sam repeats the calculation he did—"Sixty divided by 3 is 20, right?"— Catherine agrees, and Sam goes on to conclude, "So 1 hour and 20 minutes." Here Connie strongly disagrees and draws attention to the weakness in Sam's thinking, which he starts to acknowledge. He listens to Connie explain that after 1 hour there are 30 miles left to travel, so if the car is going 40 miles per hour, it must take longer than 20 minutes to go that distance. Therefore, Connie reasons, the answer must be more than Sam's often-repeated "1 hour and 20 minutes." Perhaps because he is beginning to see her point of view, he wavers in his disagreement, saying, "It doesn't go 20 miles, yes it does."

If this discussion were going along as the teacher might have liked, what might happen at this point is that Connie would invoke stronger kinds of evidence to prove to Sam and to the group that it has to take more than 20 minutes for the car to go 30 miles. What happens instead is that reasoning and social negotiation become intermingled. In a mélange of social and mathematical moves, the students struggle to figure out how to both maintain their relationships and do what the teacher has asked.

As the discussion continues, all four students are struggling with the meaning of the "30" that is left over when 70 is divided by 40. They do some proportional reasoning, following Connie's lead, but it does not seem to result in any sort of mathematical resolution. Even Connie retracts her earlier certainty.

CONNIE: So, it should be more, cause you gotta try and get 30, 30 more.
CATHERINE: You gotta get 75.
CONNIE: It's gotta go 70 miles. You got 30 left.
SAM: You go 30.
CONNIE: Then in half an hour it would go 20 miles.
ENOYAT: Half an hour it would go 30.
CATHERINE: Huh?
ENOYAT: It's a half an hour.
SAM: No, it wouldn't. It would go 20 miles.
ENOYAT: Oh, okay. I thought you said half an hour is 20 minutes. I said no.
CONNIE: I don't know.

In this somewhat confusing exchange, Connie first says, "It's gotta go 70 miles. You got 30 left." This suggests that what she thinks is left is 30 *miles*. Sam takes the "30" that Connie asserts is left and explicitly turns it into miles saying, "You *go* 30." But then Connie says, "Then in half an hour it would go 20 miles." Here, the "30" refers to minutes, it is "half an *hour*." Enoyat seems to be trying to combine both of these ideas, maintaining some sort of agreement with both Connie and Sam when he says "Half an hour it would go 30." At this point, it seems like what the students are doing is grappling with the problem that the teacher intended them to grapple with, trying to figure out the meaning of the "30" that is left over.

But this struggle gets left behind as the teacher moves the class from small group to large group discussion. We see Sam, in the next transcript excerpt, returning to his original position, saying he's "putting 1 hour 20." Connie immediately reasserts her stance and says she'll "put 1 hour 40." Here the students say what they are writing in their notebooks. Mathematically, the disagreement is not resolved. But socially, Enoyat comes up with a solution that may be an attempt to resolve the discomfort he feels in choosing between Connie and Sam:

SAM: I'm just putting 1 hour 20.
CONNIE: I'll put 1 hour 40.
ENOYAT: What am I supposed to do, average you guys and write it down?
CONNIE: No, you write what you think.
SAM: Write 1 hour 30. I don't care. You write what you think the answer would be. Like, you either, you could either do it one of our ways or you could do it your way.
CONNIE: I'm going to try this.
ENOYAT: I like both of your ways.
CONNIE: I'll try it like this.
ENOYAT: I'll just average both of you guys out.

When Enoyat says, "I like both of your ways," he seems to be making a statement that has little to do with mathematical reasoning. Instead of arguing, he reminds Connie and Sam that he does not want to choose between them; he wants them to agree. In the next part of the conversation, Sam seems to be reminding everyone that they are supposed to have "experiments" in their notebooks—or perhaps he is using *his* experiments as a justification for what he is writing down as an answer. Connie has returned to her earlier conviction. Enoyat is still looking back and forth between Connie and Sam, and Catherine plays a comforting role by reassuring Connie that her handwriting is readable.

SAM: [Pointing to his notebook.] Experiments.
CONNIE: Yeah. Yeah, but I still think this is the answer.
ENOYAT: A car is going 40 miles per hour. How long will it take to go 70 miles? One hundred—[to Connie] what are you, what, what are you writing 1 hour and 40 minutes? [To Sam] 'Cause she wrote 140 minutes.
CONNIE: Look. ONE hour period dot, I mean 1 hour point 40 minutes.
ENOYAT: I thought that was a 1 and that was a 4 and a 0.
CONNIE: Nobody can ready my writing. I write too sloppy.
CATHERINE: No you don't.
             [Catherine is defending Connie's handwriting.]
STUDENT: One hundred and thirty.
STUDENT: One hundred and forty.
ENOYAT: Let me write my reasoning down first, okay?

What Enoyat has written in his notebook for "number two" is indeed an average of Connie and Sam's answers, but he also adds a mathematical justification which was not part of the conversation at all. For him, reasoning in this situation is a private matter, done after listening to the views of his peers. He says he thinks the answer is 1 hour and 30 minutes because "30 minutes" are "left over." His notebook entry is shown in Figure 31.6.

What Catherine winds up with in her notebook (see Figure 31.7) is an answer to problem 2 that is the same as Connie's. She has written no "reasoning" to explain why she thinks that answer is correct.

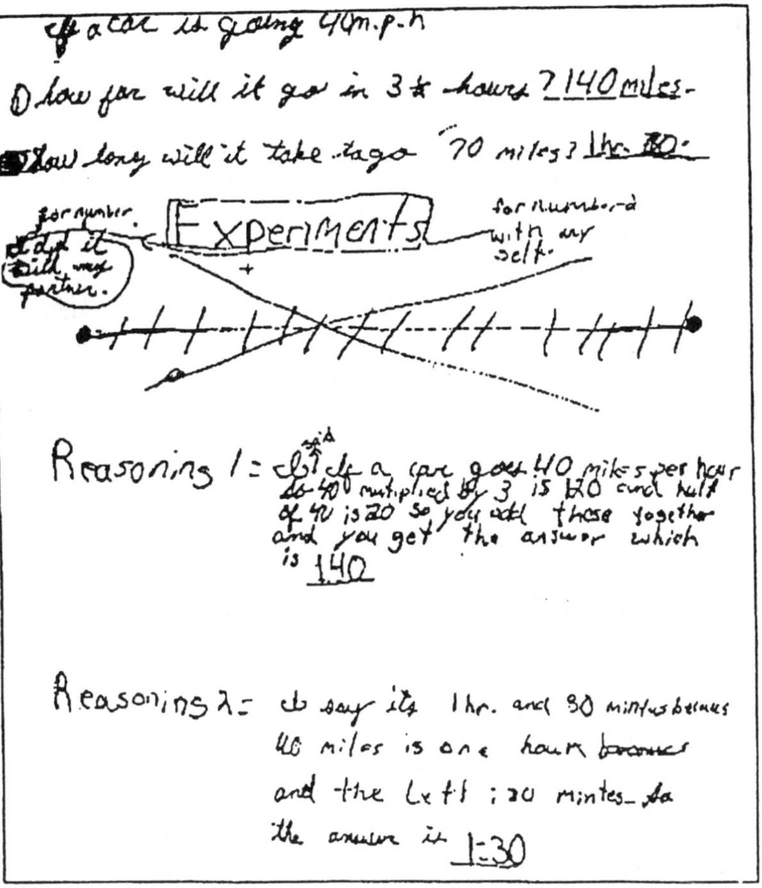

Figure 31.6

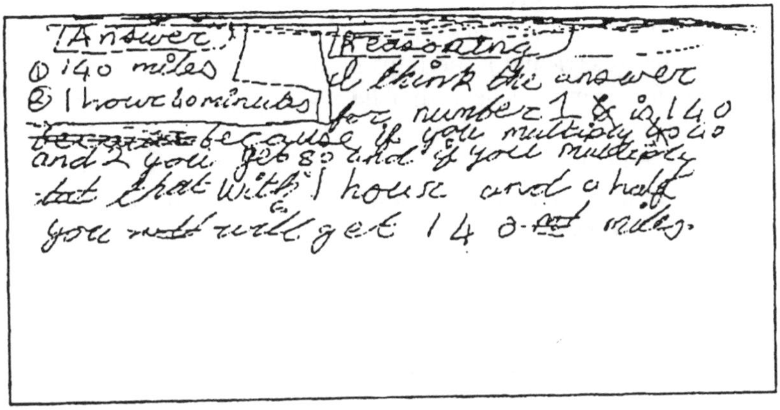

Figure 31.7

Reaching Agreement about Disagreement

In this discussion of a mathematics problem, Connie, Sam, Enoyat, and Catherine present evidence about their "theory in action" of what it means to disagree. How do they think they are supposed to act in a classroom when their answers to a math problem are different? As the teacher had hoped, the problem provoked some cognitive conflict, potentially productive of increased understanding—both about what computations are relevant and about how to label the answer. But the students experience discomfort and they believe it is important to smooth it over rather than quarreling. In this classroom where students have been told that "thinking" is valued, the conflict gets smoothed over by everyone "writing what they think." Their joint activity is not just an expression of what they bring to this conversation by way of beliefs about how to disagree—they are shaping those beliefs dynamically as they interact (Mead, 1964; Blumer, 1977; Davidson, 1986).

Connie, Sam, Enoyat, and Catherine are from different cultural backgrounds: African-American urban, white suburban, Muslim African urban, and Christian African rural. But they have all been attending an American school in a small city for several years. In addition to whatever they have learned about disagreement from their families, they have learned cultural routines for going to school, including learning what to do when they get a different answer to a math problem than their peers. We assume that they have refined their models of how to interact in such circumstances on the basis of what kinds of behaviors are functional for achieving a complex set of goals, including pleasing the teacher and maintaining friendships, or at least for avoiding getting teased or ostracized on the playground.

There is little evidence that anyone but Connie believes that what they are supposed to be doing as they "argue" mathematics is convincing the others, using mathematical evidence that an answer makes sense. Sam does try to convince others that he is right and Connie is wrong. His repetition of his calculations with increasing volume and gestural force might be interpreted as an expression of the belief that if the others would just listen to what he *did* they would change their minds, perhaps because *he* did it, perhaps because the computation is done correctly. He does not seem to believe that he needs to justify the need to do that particular calculation—it seems obvious to him, and presumably should be obvious to the others. Enoyat and Catherine act as if they believe that the most important thing to do in a mathematical argument is to maintain congeniality, letting everyone hang on to his or her idea, in the end, unchallenged. Although Sam's actions initially suggest that he believes that this conversation is supposed to be about convincing his peers to agree with him, in the end, his mathematical intention also gets confounded with a social one as he seems satisfied with everyone "writing what you think the answer would be."

The theory of how to manage a discrepancy in solutions and strategies here seems to be that any way is as good as any other way if someone "thinks" it. As it is played out in this exchange, the fifth graders' folk learning psychology seems to be relativistic. It seems important that everyone be able to "save face" and for Sam at least, this cannot be accomplished by letting himself be convinced that a peer's approach to the problem is more reasonable.

These students are interactionally defining the meaning of public argument among diverse peers as they argue in the classroom. They act in ways that take into account the actions of others, and because they have shared the culture of going to school, they can coordinate their actions and organize their responses on well-grounded assumptions about what the actions of others mean in this context. On the one hand, these students act as if it is appropriate to listen to others and try to communicate their understandings to them. (Whether they do this to learn or because they were directed to do so by their teacher is not clear.) On the other hand, they seem to feel that disagreement is hard and uncomfortable and that they have a responsibility not to make it too difficult on one another. They fail to resolve their disagreement in a way that draws on mathematical evidence and reasoning. At the end of the time allotted, Connie does not seem to have convinced anyone to think about the problem in a way that is true to the given conditions. But these students have solved another problem: They have invented moves for interaction that could be judged successful if the goal is for everyone in the group to feel socially comfortable at the point where the class turns from small group to large group work.

What happened in this conversation could be interpreted as an expression of competing conceptions of public disagreement. But, the practices of these students as they come to know mathematics collaboratively are not the ones that psychologists imagine should be in place if teachers embrace their theories about how learning happens; neither are they the practices celebrated in much of the mathematics reform literature. As in situations where learners are observed accommodating their prior beliefs to a new scientific theory to explain an observed physical phenomenon,[12] what we have seen here are temporary advances toward instantiations of the "new" theory of public argument put forth by the teacher and retreats to the more familiar norms that students bring with them in order to understand what they are supposed to do when someone has a different answer.

How Do We Interpret What These Fifth Graders Say and Do?

From the perspective of a teacher or an educational reformer who believes that mathematical discussion has the potential to produce understanding, there are several ways of interpreting what happened in this group and complementary ways of thinking about how to teach students to focus on the task of convincing others of the mathematical sense of their assertions. We might see these events as a characteristic of the children's stage of social development, imagining that older children or adults, less focused on finding an identity among their peers, would be more rationally assertive and persistent. In this case, we would simply need to be patient and wait until they "grow out of" their self-consciousness about disagreement. Or we might imagine that these fifth graders were ignorant of effective methods of group interaction, or that they had not been paying attention when lessons about how to develop consensus were taught, or that they simply need more practice. In this case we would want to reinforce the use of standard rules and roles, making clear to the students what counts as evidence and what sorts of challenges are allowed among peers. A third way to think about this case, and the one we will argue for here, is that these students were reflecting and reinventing cultural beliefs about how people are supposed to interact in public, protecting both their personal and political interests in a way that also enabled them to incorporate something of the practice of mathematical reasoning. What these students did *socially* made sense to them as a solution to the problem of the discrepancies in their answers to the problems. Their behavior could very well be described as functional, particularly in light of the kinds of interpretations of public disagreement illustrated by Ellie's comments above.

And their behavior is not atypical. Lynn Michel Brown and Carol Gilligan (1993) document several cases, drawn from a population of students in a good private school, of girls who as young children naturally seem to disagree and challenge one another or adults but starting around the age of nine or ten learn to value "being nice" and "studying the textbooks" over expressing their ideas because they want to avoid being negatively judged by their peers. As these girls link argument with losing relationships, they become better at figuring out how others think and at the same time they decide that accepting and pleasing others is safer than disagreeing. One girl refers to this development as "forgetting her mind" and focusing instead on "what's being shoved into her brain" (Brown and Gilligan, 1993, pp. 93, 138).

Catherine and Connie, Enoyat and Sam were in a classroom where they were expected to interact with one another and use mathematical evidence to support their assertions. Left to their own devices, what they did instead was to try to achieve agreement by repeating their positions, and by gathering social and political support (except for Connie). When these strategies failed to produce agreement, they agreed to disagree. The students' talk and actions suggest that, like the students studied by Brown and Gilligan, they believed it was at least as important to maintain relationships as it was to argue mathematics. The comments in the "discussion of discussions" by Ellie and other members of the class suggest that they are struggling with the social discomforts involved in figuring out the ways that others think and see. They do not entirely resist participation in discussions where disagreement occurs and is encouraged, like the discussion of "eight minus a half," but they do not wholeheartedly embrace this approach to learning mathematics, either.

Is this problem with maintaining social relations while talking about discrepancies in ideas only a problem for students at the upper elementary level? Is there any evidence that the problem "goes away" as people become more secure with their social positions? There are no formal studies of adult "folk theories" of public disagreement, but we can look at two sources for some hints about what their practice suggests such theories might say. Since we have written here about mathematical disagreement, we will look first at analyses of mathematical practice for evidence about what practitioners believe about debate and disagreement. Then we will look at what experience we might have as adults in this culture of discussing ideas with diverse groups of people in which disagreement and argument are expected, in or out of academia.

Although reform efforts like those reflected in the NCTM *Teaching Standards* are designed to bring classroom practice closer to practice in the discipline of mathematics, as we look at what adults in academic circumstances actually do, we recognize that what is being expressed in the *Standards* are the ideals of practice rather than reality (Lampert, 1992). In commentaries about mathematicians who try to grapple with disagreements, references to name-calling and social shaming are not unusual. In *Proofs and Refutations*, for example, in which Imre Lakatos portrays an interaction among mathematicians (including himself) arguing about a geometrical theorem, one way to manage the pain of disagreement is called "the Stoic theory of error": anyone who makes a mathematical mistake is considered by the others in the conversation to have a "sick mind" (Lakatos, 1976, p. 32). Further on in the discussion, Lakatos suggests to his fellow mathematicians that the person who was initially labeled by his peers as a "sick mind" instead might be thought of as an ally in the search for mathematical truth because his error turns into an insight. Here, he is expressing the sort of ideal that seems to be expressed in our thinking about what should happen in classrooms—students should expose their own and one another's mistakes and learn from discussing these mistakes about both the content and the discourse of mathematics. But in the discussion that Lakatos recounts, one of the participants responds to his idealism in a way that is reminiscent of what the fifth graders said about discussions with their peers: "Alpha" exclaims that "Opponents are less *embarrassing* than allies" (Lakatos, 1976, p. 33), suggesting that if one makes an error, the feeling of discomfort is not alleviated by knowing that someone else has made the same error. In their sociological analysis of mathematical rhetoric, Philip Davis and Reuben Hersch (1986, pp. 65–73) describe similar social norms governing actual disagreements among mathematicians. They list various methods that mathematicians are well known for using to convince their peers to agree, such as "proof by intimidation," "proof by eminent authority," and "proof by exhaustion (of the participants)."

The difficulties that arise from mixing social interaction with the refinement of ideas are characteristic of work outside of mathematics as well. Although we hold the ideal view that knowledge grows by revision and modification, it is risky to be the one whose idea gets revised or modified, even by oneself.[13] Considering all assertions to be tentative and open to reasoned challenge from one's peers—an approach to study that Peter Elbow (1986) calls "the doubting game" and Georg Polya (1968) calls "the inductive attitude"—seems to go hand in hand with damaged egos and feelings that one is being treated in a "mean" way. If it did not,

Polya would not have found it necessary to speak of intellectual *courage* and *wise restraint* as the virtues required to be a good scientist. These are moral commitments that govern the way we regard others and their ideas (Scheffler, 1960; Peters, 1959). These mores are not based on the rules of logic. They do not replace the rules of logic, but they make it possible for human beings to disagree with less pain than they might otherwise experience.

And what of public disagreement about ideas outside of the academic workplace? We have all been in situations as children and adults where "might makes right" or something comes to be the accepted truth because no one has the courage to disagree or because the process of challenging ideas in a community is tedious and often even boring. We also know of situations where everyone agrees to play by the rules to avoid confrontation or embarrassment even when the rules are meaningless. How many people have ever participated in a discussion in which they have listened to, responded to, and questioned the teacher or one another? Or tried to convince themselves and others of the validity of their representations, solutions, conjectures, or answers? Or relied on mathematical evidence and argument to determine validity? Although we imagine that these practices should happen with some frequency in academic research, they are not ordinary practices for working out public disagreements. They are not the activities that most people think of when they imagine trying to learn something.

Experience of academic argument as an amicable mode of interaction in our culture is rare. More likely, in the nonacademic community, adults and children justify their solutions to problems by reference to answer books or reference books or newspapers or television. It is considered appropriate to call upon authorities like teachers or parents or bosses to sanction the validity of our approaches to problems. Many people believe that "memory" or "natural genius" account for being able to get the right answer in a math problem (Schoenfeld, 1985; Stigler and Baranes, 1988; Dweck, 1983), and so by implication, there is nothing to discuss when someone gets the wrong answer. Since the rise of scientific problem solving at the beginning of this century, there has been an increasing tendency to believe that professional "experts" are responsible for coming up with solutions to social as well as physical problems, and the rest of us simply need to be kept informed of their results.

Both inside and outside of academic settings, people also have beliefs about appropriate ways to interact in public settings that are likely to bear on the choices they make about what they will do with one another to learn, in or out of school. "Arguing" is thought to be something that people do when they are being impolite, not getting along, or losing self control (Belenky, Clinchy, Goldberger, and Tarule, 1986). Disagreement, especially disagreement with a person in authority, is thought to be aggressive and even antisocial behavior. As a people, Americans are more disposed toward isolation than toward the reasoned determination of public consensus (Bellah, Madsen, Sullivan, Swidler, and Tipton, 1985). We do not have many cultural mores that support the conjunction of disagreement and civil social encounters. In the talk of adults outside of academic settings, there are few places where we can regularly witness debate among the kind of diverse populations found in many school classrooms. This form of talk has become popular on television and radio talk shows, and we sometimes see political figures engaged in debates. However, recent experience suggests that these interactions involve more name-calling and defamation of character than inquiry and reasoning.[14]

It is not surprising then, that students in a classroom, left to their own devices, would not choose to argue mathematics with their classmates without also giving some attention to smoothing over the social discomforts, even if this interferes with good reasoning. The school classroom is a place where friends are made and lost, where identity is developed, where pride and shame and caring and hurting happen to kids. What they learn from social interaction cannot be described simply in terms of the mathematics covered by hashing out logical conflicts between various approaches to a problem. Mustering evidence to prove that an assertion is right or wrong is not a decontextualized learning activity. In the classroom, mathematical argument is done with and to the same people one plays with, eats lunch with, lives next door to, or has a crush on.

In a recent study of the problems that arise for children when they are asked to evaluate one another's writing, Tim Lensmire (1994) observes:

Children bring to the classroom, playground and cafeteria experiences, individual and collective histories in and out of school, that contribute to their evaluation of each other as friends and audiences. As teachers of any particular group of children, we have limited control over important aspects of peer relations. I am certainly not saying that we can do nothing to influence or enhance these relationships. Only that, at any given moment, children are working out their relations with each other, and they are doing it from their pasts, behind our backs, and outside the room, as well as within the situations we have greater access to and upon which we exert greater influence. (pp. 73–74)

Like Lensmire, we are "certainly not saying that we can do nothing to influence or enhance" the kinds of relationships that students can develop with one another in school. What we do argue is that bringing about the kind of social climate in schools that supports academic argument requires a major shift in cultural norms. Simply providing rules for the standardization of interactions in "math groups" will probably not be enough to reduce the students' discomfort and make change possible. If students are to "listen to, respond to, and question the teacher and one another. . . . make conjectures and present solutions,. . .[and] try to convince themselves and one another of the validity of particular representations, solutions, conjectures, and answers" (NCTM, 1991), some way must be found to minimize the personal and social risks that does not interfere with serious argument.

Talking about communication in conjunction with understanding is a radical idea. Understanding used to be thought of as a function of individual minds, and teaching and learning as transactions between the teacher and individual learners, even when there are 30 of them in the room at one time. But school people are beginning to take into account the social construction of knowledge, the relations between thought and language, and the importance of collaboration to real problem solving. Our research suggests that the teacher is an important partner in the knowledge-building collaboration that occurs in classrooms. Without the teacher's intervention, the disagreement about the meaning of "eight minus a half" (described in the first part of this paper), for example, would likely have been very different. The teacher's knowledge of the fundamental mathematical structures behind the linguistic expressions that students were constructing in this discussion enabled her to focus the disagreement in ways that required the clarification of important conceptual differences (see also Hoyles and Noss, 1992).

But the teacher's role goes beyond the connection of students' work with big ideas in the discipline. Our analysis of how students "agree to disagree" when left to construct their own social interaction suggests that teacher intervention is also significant on the social front. Because common cultural beliefs about public argument run counter to the ideals of academic discourse, and those "folk theories" about how to learn in school are shared by students, the teacher must take on the task of modeling a different set of social norms and offering students safe mechanisms for expressing their thinking when it is different from that of their peers. Discourse-oriented reforms are not a simple matter of mandating different kinds of classroom structures like small-group problem solving or the discussion of discrepant ideas among peers. These reforms require not only a fundamental reconstruction of students' beliefs about what knowledge is and how it is acquired but also a re-forming of how everyone in the classroom thinks about what is appropriate in the way we talk with our friends and our enemies about ideas.

Acknowledgments

This chapter is based on a paper presented in 1994 at the annual meeting of the American Educational Research Association, in New Orleans. The authors wish to acknowledge the thoughtful comments of Peri Weingrad, Mary Catherine O'Connor, Susan Florio-Ruane, and David Cohen on earlier drafts of this chapter. We would also like to acknowledge the Spencer Foundation for funding the data analysis and the National Science Foundation for funding the data collection on which this chapter is based. The data presented, the statements made, and the views expressed are solely the responsibility of the authors.

Notes

1. In this paper, we use the terms "discussion" and "conversation" interchangeably to refer to the talk among students and teacher in Lampert's classroom. We do not intend to be making here a technical claim about the nature of this discourse.

2. During the 1989–90 school year, a research team collected extensive data to conduct an in-depth study of a year of teaching and learning practice in Lampert's fifth-grade mathematics classroom. They recorded daily classroom interactions on both video- and audiotape, kept field notes on all lessons, maintained daily logs of student work, interviewed students, and collected Lampert's thoughts about the lessons by having her keep a daily journal of plans and reflections and interviewing her on a regular basis. A portion of the data collected were used in the study reported in this chapter.

3. We are indebted to Nan Jackson for the close analysis she has done of this lesson segment and its relation to other occurrences in Lampert's class during the 1989–90 school year.

4. Douglas Barnes (1976) calls this "exploratory talk" and analyzes the difference between this kind of classroom discourse and the more "finished" talk that is conventionally employed in answers to teachers' questions.

5. We recognize that this is a problematic concept and we are not claiming to define "the social construction of knowledge" by our use of this term here. See Driver, Asko, Leach, and Scott (1994) and Cobb (1994) for a discussion of the multiple ways in which this term might be interpreted.

6. Although we do not have the space to report on this aspect of our research in detail, our claims here are substantiated by the analysis of interview data with the students collected before, during, and a year after their participation in Lampert's class.

7. See Stodolsky (1988) for a characterization of norms of interaction in American mathematics classes at the upper elementary level. For a contrast between this conventional set of American classroom norms and those found in Japan, see Stigler and Baranes' (1988) description of what happens to student "errors" in elementary-level mathematics classes.

8. It is not assumed that these students are becoming mathematicians. Rather they are being taught where mathematics fits in the lexicon of ways of knowing (Lampert, 1990). See also Kitcher (1984) for a discussion of the relationship between mathematical activity, mathematical language, and mathematical knowledge.

9. It is not assumed here that American culture is monolithic. Based on recognized differences in our own ethnic backgrounds, we are aware of the fact that families and communities range broadly in how they handle disagreement. What is at issue here is how people from different ethnic backgrounds behave when they disagree in the presence of others of similarly diverse backgrounds.

10. A paper in progress analyzes the entire "Discussion of Discussions" as well as interviews with Lampert's students after they have spent a year in more traditional sixth-grade classrooms.

11. Calling these "problems" does not mean to suggest that they were the mathematical problems that engaged students during their work together. They might more appropriately be called "tasks" or "questions." What we write here uses the everyday language of the classroom in which they were called "Problems of the Day." See Lampert (1990) for an analysis of the pedagogical difference between such "problems" and the mathematics that engages students as they work on them.

12. See for example diSessa's (1982, 1983) work on students learning Newtonian physics. We are indebted to Mary Catherine O'Connor for pointing out this analogy.

13. See Peter Elbow's essay on literary composition entitled "Closing my eyes as I speak: An argument for ignoring audience" and Pamela Richards' autobiographical reflections on writing for social scientists in Becker (1986). Richards says: "For me, sitting

762 *Magdalene Lampert et al.*

down to write is risky because it means I have to open myself up to scrutiny. . . . Every piece of work can be used as evidence about what kind of sociologist (and person) you are. . .I cannot face the possibility of people thinking I'm stupid" (pp. 113–114).

14. This seemed to be particularly the case in the November 1994 elections in the United States when many congressional members, senators, and governors were up for election.

References

Ball, D. (1991). "What's all this talk about discourse?" *Arithmetic Teacher, 39* (3), 44–48.

Barnes, D. (1976). *From communication to curriculum.* Harmondsworth, England: Penguin Books.

Belenky, M. F., Clinchy, B. M., Goldberger, N. R., and Tarule, J. M. (1986). *Women's ways of knowing: The development of self, voice, and mind.* New York: Basic Books.

Bellah, R. N., Madsen, R., Sullivan, W. M., Swidler, A., and Tipton, S. M. (1985). *Habits of the heart: Individualism and commitment in American life.* New York: Harper and Row.

Blumer, H. (1977). Sociological implications of the thought of George Herbert Mead. In B. R. Cosin, J. R. Dale, G. M. Esland, D. Mackinnon, and D. F. Swift (Eds.), *School and society: A sociological reader* (pp. 11–17). London: Routledge and Kegan Paul.

Blunk, M. (1995). "Communication in and about small group learning." Research report, Mathematics and Teaching through Hypermedia Project. Ann Arbor: University of Michigan.

Brown, J. M. and Gilligan, C. (1993). *Meeting at the crossroads.* Cambridge: Harvard University Press.

Bruner, J. (1990). *Acts of meaning.* Cambridge: Harvard University Press.

Cobb, P. (1994). Where is the mind? Constructivist and sociocultural perspectives on mathematical development. *Educational Researcher, 23* (7), 13–20.

Cobb, P., Wood, T., and Yackel, E. (1993). Discourse, mathematical thinking, and classroom practice. In N. Minick, E. Forman, and A. Stone (Eds.), *Education and mind: Institutional, social, and developmental processes* (pp. 91–119). New York: Oxford University Press.

Davidson, D. (1986). A nice derangement of epitaphs. In E. LePore (Ed.), *Truth and interpretation* (pp. 433–446). New York: Basil Blackwell.

Davis, P. and Hersch, R. (1986). *Descartes dream: The world according to mathematics.* Orlando: Harcourt, Brace, Jovanovich.

diSessa, A. A. (1982). Unlearning Aristotelian physics: A study of knowledge-based learning. *Cognitive Science, 6,* 37–75.

diSessa, A. A. (1983). Phenomenology and the evolution of intuitions. In D. Gentner and A. L. Stevens (Eds.), *Mental models* (pp. 15–33). Hillsdale, NJ: Lawrence Erlbaum.

Driver, R., Asko, H., Leach, J., and Scott, P. (1994). Constructing scientific knowledge in the classroom, *Educational Researcher, 23* (7), 5–12.

Dweck, C. S. and Bempechat, J. (1983). Children's theories of intelligence: Consequences for learning. In S. G. Paris, G. M. Olson, and H. W. Stevenson (Eds.), *Learning and motivation in the classroom* (pp. 239–256). Hillsdale, NJ: Lawrence Erlbaum.

Elbow, P. (1986). *Embracing contraries: Explorations in teaching and leaning.* New York: Oxford University Press.

Hatano, G. and Inagaki, K. (1991). Sharing cognition through collective comprehension activity. In L. B. Resnick, J. M. Levine, and S. D. Teasley (Eds.), *Perspectives on socially shared cognition* (pp. 331–348). Washington: American Psychological Association.

Heath, S. B. (1983). *Ways with words: Language life and work in communities and classrooms.* New York: Cambridge University Press.

Holland, D. and Quinn, N. (1987). *Cultural models in language and thought.* Cambridge: Cambridge University Press.

Hoyle, C. and Noss, R. (1992). *Learning mathematics and Logo.* Cambridge: MIT Press.

Isaacs, S. (1971). *The children we teach: Seven to eleven years.* New York: Schocken.

Kitcher, P. (1984). *The nature of mathematical knowledge.* Oxford, England: Oxford University Press.

Lakatos, I. (1976). *Proof and refutations: The logic of mathematical discovery.* J. Worrall and E. Zahar (Eds.). Cambridge, England: Cambridge University Press.

Lampert, M. (1990). When the problem is not the question and the solution is not the answer: Mathematical knowing and teaching. *American Educational Research Journal, 27* (1), 29–64.

Lampert, M. (1992). Practices and problems in teaching authentic mathematics in school. In F. Oser, A. Dick, and J.-L. Patry (Eds.), *Effective and responsible teaching: The new synthesis* (pp. 295–314). New York: Jossey-Bass.

Lensmire, T. (1994). *When children write: Critical re-visions of the writing workshop.* New York: Teachers College Press.

Mead, G. H. (1964). *On social psychology: Selected Papers.* Chicago: University of Chicago Press.

National Council of Teachers of Mathematics. (1991). *Professional standards for teaching mathematics.* Reston, VA: National Council of Teachers of Mathematics.

Olson, D. R. and Astington, J. W. (1993). Thinking about thinking: Learning how to take statements and hold beliefs. *Educational Psychologist, 28* (1), 7–23.

Peters, R. (1959). *Authority, responsibility, and education.* London: Allen and Unwin.

Polya, G. (1968). *Induction and analogy in mathematics.* Princeton: Princeton University Press.

Putnam, R., Lampert, M., and Peterson, P. (1990). Alternative perspectives on knowing mathematics in elementary schools. In C. Cazden (Ed.), *Review of research in education* (Vol. 16, pp. 57–150). Washington: American Educational Research Association.

Richards, P. (1986). Risk. In H. S. Becker (Ed.), *Writing for social scientists: How to start and finish your thesis, book, or article* (pp. 108–120). Chicago: University of Chicago Press.

Scheffler, I. (1960). *The language of education.* Springfield, IL: Thomas.

Schoenfeld, A. H. (1985). *Mathematical problem solving.* Orlando, FL: Academic Press.

Spradley, J. P. (1972). *Culture and cognition: Rules, maps, and plans.* New York: Chandler.

Stigler, J. and Baranes, R. (1988). Culture and mathematics learning. In C. Cazden (Ed.), *Review of research in education* (Vol. 15, pp. 253–306). Washington: American Educational Research Association.

Stodolsky, S. (1988). *The subject matters: Classroom activity in math and social studies.* Chicago: University of Chicago Press.

Strike, K. and Posner, G. (1985). A conceptual change view of knowing and learning. In L. West and A. L. Pines (Eds.), *Cognitive structure and conceptual change* (pp. 211–232). Orlando, FL: Academic Press.

Swales, J. (1990). *Genre analysis: English in academic and research settings.* Cambridge, England: Cambridge University Press.

Willoughby, S., Bereiter, C., Hilton, P., and Rubenstein, J. H. (1990). *Real math: Level five.* LaSalle, IL: Open Court.

Wiser, M. and Carey, S. (1983). "When heat and temperature were one." In D. Gentner and A. L. Stevens (Eds.), *Mental models* (pp. 267–298). Hillsdale, NJ: Lawrence Erlbaum.

32

Conceptualizing the Growth of Historical Understanding

PETER SEIXAS

It seems to me obvious that we have a connection to the historical past, as ordinary persons, prior to and independently. . .of the investigative frameworks of professional historians. (Carr, 1986, pp. 2–3)

The educational research community has paid substantial attention to the problems of the development of understanding in mathematics and science. The paucity of comparable work in history is remarkable. David Lowenthal (1985, p. xxvi) calls it "astounding" that on a topic of almost universal concern, "how people in general see, value, or understand [the past]," there has been so little research. Within the educational research community, Downey and Levstik noted as recently as 1991 "a disturbing lack of attention to what children do know and to how they came to learn what they know [about history]." While there are hopeful signs of new interest in the field, investigations of historical thinking and learning still lag far behind those in science and math (Leinhardt, Beck, and Stainton, 1994; Carretero and Voss, 1994; Wineburg, 1994, in press). Why is this so?

The answer may well lie somewhere in the tangled but much-traveled paths of "the structures of the disciplines" (Lee, 1983; Shemilt, 1983; Wilson, 1988, pp. 214–253; Hirst, 1965; Bruner, 1960).[1] The structure of a discipline, roughly speaking, constitutes a way of knowing the world. Such a structure not only provides the foundations for academic scholarship in a field but also helps to define the parameters of prior or pretheoretical (in David Carr's terminology) understandings in the same areas (Gardner, 1991; Carr, 1986). But I use the term "structure" with reserve, and what I propose as a "structure" of history is perhaps no more than a set of closely related core issues that must be confronted in order to foster growth in historical knowledge.[2] Without addressing these core issues, we could not begin to think historically, nor could we become more expert. Conversely, the way we address them shapes our historical thinking. To return to our earlier question, then, is there something that distinguishes the structure of history from the structures of mathematics and the sciences in a way that fundamentally affects the educational research efforts and accomplishments in these respective fields?[3]

VanSledright and Brophy (1992, p. 841) see a different relationship to "experience" in scientific and mathematical thinking. Their formulation is flawed, but it may help to explain why researchers have been slow to explore prior understanding in history.

[Children] lack an experiential knowledge base. . .from which to draw information for developing historical constructions and understandings. They learn about the physical world, about plants and animals, and about numbers and quantitative relationships through direct, experiential contact with manipulable aspects of their environment. By contrast, most aspects of historical understanding lack this experiential base. . . .

VanSledright and Brophy's stark contrast between the raw experience (of natural phenomena) and the constructed interpretation (of historical phenomena) is misleading. On the one hand, we should not minimize the degree to which language and cultural legacies shape people's experiences of the natural world, even at a very young age. The forms of their interrogation, the kinds of answers they expect and accept, are never simply the results of "direct" culturally unmediated experience (Driver et al., 1994). On the other hand, people (young and old, novice and expert) do directly encounter two distinct forms of stimuli that generate historical questions and hypothetical answers (again, like scientific questions, culturally mediated in profound ways).

First, we encounter everywhere *traces* of the human past in artifacts and relics, documents, the built environment, landscapes, or, on a more complex level, institutions and languages. In fact, our culture is suffused with the raw materials of historical understanding. As David Lowenthal (1985, p. 185) puts it, "The past surrounds and saturates us; every scene, every statement, every action retains residual content from earlier times. All present awareness is grounded on past perceptions and acts. . . . Centuries of tradition underlie every instant of perception and creation, pervading not only artifacts and culture but the very cells of our bodies."

Second, we experience *accounts* of the human past, in innumerable presentations of the past that we confront outside of formal history-learning through family stories and the media, including television news, film, historical fiction, historical references in advertising, and popular commemoration. Some accounts are so fragmentary that they might better be called "references" to the past. Nevertheless, such cultural references implicitly convey a fuller account. Roger Simon (1993) noted within 18 months of the Columbian quincentenary, for example, the production and marketing of books, films, TV and radio programs, theater performances, and rap songs as well as buttons, decorative and declarative fabrics, calendars, puzzles, and games.

All of the problems addressed by historical thinkers (novice or expert) are rooted, ultimately, either in these pervasive historical traces or in historical accounts. Questions that arise from the traces include: Is this what I think it is? How did this come to be? What was it like before? Is it the first of its kind? Questions suggested by accounts of the past include: Who constructed this account and why? What does it mean for us? What other accounts are there of the same events/lives/ phenomena? How and why are they different? Which should we believe?[4]

But if, in one sense, "the past is everywhere," as Lowenthal (1985, p. xv) asserts, in another sense the past is also irretrievably gone (and Lowenthal explores this too). So what we confront is never the past itself but presentations of the past, both traces that inevitably undergo change over time, and accounts or interpretations of the past addressed to us in the present. Coherently organizing all of this material so that we can understand our own situation in time is a task for each (individually) and all (collectively) of us. How might we go about theorizing the discipline-specific structures of historical understanding that enable us to do this?

Carr (1986, p. 167) argues persuasively that we must organize experience as narrative, that experience without a narrative organization is incoherent to us as humans.

The communal event of the present, in which *we* participate as subjects of experience or action, gets its sense from the background of comparable events to which it belongs. *We* participate in them (enjoy or suffer, act in common, and understand what we are doing) to the extent that we place the event in this context. And our placing it there is a function of the overall story *we* tell, and if necessary retell, to each other about ourselves and what we are doing.

Organizing our collective experience of the past—i.e., the traces and presentations of the past that we encounter in the present—in such a way that they provide a meaningful context for our present experience, is thus the central task of historical understanding. (On narrative as the essential mode for sense-making in time, see Bruner, 1986; Holt, 1990; Levstik and Pappas, 1992; Levstik, 1986, 1992; Mink, 1987; White, 1978.)

The core of this chapter is an exploration of the issues we face as we do this, issues that together constitute the structure of historical understanding. It would be highly ironic, however, if an essay on the elements that help us to build historical meaning in our own time did not also take into account the specificities of our own historical moment. Who should be conscious of the historicity of that moment, if not the author and readers of this essay? Thus I do not attempt to write a transhistorical analysis of the structures of historical understanding. While the structure of the discipline of history as a key to pedagogy has been under active discussion for two or three decades, and related discussions go back to the beginnings of historical scholarship, the current exploration takes place at a particular moment of rapid social, cultural, and economic change. If the entire modern era is one in which "all that is solid melts into air," the past two decades are even more destabilized (Berman, 1982). As the world political-economic order undergoes fundamental restructuring, what Harvey (1989) has called space-time compression has an impact on every aspect of our culture. Answers to the questions that arise from a concern with change through time cannot help but be affected by accelerated change through time. A related aspect of the contemporary moment, which has a direct and substantial impact on the structures of historical understanding, is the heightened awareness of cultural diversity. If history is largely the construction of a story of the origins, analogues, and antecedents of "us," our contemporary community, then who defines "us," and how it is defined are of great importance (Hollinger, 1993; Appleby, 1992; Tyrrell, 1991; McGerr, 1991). Both the accelerated pace of change and the destabilized, contingent boundaries of our communities contribute to loosening our canons, shaking the certainties of an earlier age (Gates, 1992). In our own era, these difficulties are superimposed upon the perennial problem of the past: the distance between ourselves in the present and all that has gone before. All this is to say that the structures of historical understanding are not only developmental but also cultural and historical.

Recent academic historiography has been shaped by the same cultural conditions that provide the seedbed for contemporary, naive or novice historical thinking (Seixas, 1993a). For that reason, I conjecture, it provides insights into naive historical thinking in our own time, which might be more difficult to uncover with other tools. In the remainder of this essay therefore, I make use of recent historiography to define the issues faced by all historical thinkers. Where relevant research on historical cognition exists, I introduce it as well.

Elements in the Structure of the Discipline of History

Significance

"History," as George Herbert Mead put it, is always an "interpretation of the present" (quoted in Trachtenberg, 1989, xxiii). If our interest in the past is to contextualize the present, then the *significance* of historical events (or people, or dates) is ultimately tied to their relationship to the present. What makes any particular event significant is the richness and complexity of its connections to other events and processes, and ultimately to ourselves. The concern with historical significance links the historian and naive thinker, and distinguishes them both from the antiquarian and the chronicler.

Peter Rogers (1987, p. 6) discusses the process of historical meaning-making as differentiating "between the various members of a mass of crude facts and of showing their significance in relation to some theme or development" (see Lomas, 1990, pp. 41–46; Polkinghorne, 1988). Neither the naive historical thinker nor the historian, in fact, does confront "a mass of crude facts." (Perhaps only the readers of school textbooks face this grim challenge.) But otherwise, in confronting the various fragmentary traces and accounts, a sorting and sifting and drawing-of-relationships (ending ultimately with ourselves) must take place in building an understanding.

In order to examine the paradoxes and problems involved in this process, we turn to an exemplary case from recent historical scholarship. In *A Midwife's Tale: The Diary of Martha Ballard*, Laurel Thatcher Ulrich (1990) mines Martha Ballard's account of her own life to shed light on social patterns and gender definitions in a small Maine town in the eighteenth century. While previous historians dismissed Ballard's diary as trivial and insignificant, Ulrich makes it meaningful by constructing a web of interpretation that relates it to contemporary concerns. Women's work, women's lives, once marginalized, now become the locus of significance, in part because women in the late twentieth century have redefined the "we" to whom historical accounts must relate.

But here is the paradox that Ulrich negotiates so artfully. While good history studiously avoids decontextualizing the past (i.e., anachronistically interpreting the past in the terms of the present), it must demonstrate the importance of the past for the present. Aware of this tension, Ulrich (1990, p. 34) writes of "the complexity and subjectivity of historical reconstruction" and of "the affinity and the distance between history and source." She calls what she does, "open[ing] out Martha's book for the twentieth-century reader."

The connections between historical events and issues of concern in our own time may take the form of a narrative chain, whereby the past is shown to be causally related through a series of events to our present circumstances (Carr, 1986), or through analogy with issues in our own time (Rogers, 1987). But at least two kinds of problems may differentiate the way naive thinkers assign significance to historical events from the way Laurel Thatcher Ulrich and other historians do so. First, naive thinkers simply lack the breadth of information that historians have, so that their choices of what is more or less significant are severely constrained. While historians immerse themselves in traces and accounts of the past (in archives, documents, and their colleagues' writings), students encounter and recognize traces and representations of the past only sporadically (Kunen, Tang, and Ducey, 1991; Frisch, 1990; Sleeper, 1973). As one student responded when asked why she felt that "wars" were the most significant events in history, "that's probably the only thing anybody knows about" (Seixas, 1993d). Second, they may be much more likely than historians to decontextualize the past in the search for meanings for the present. In so doing, they may either miss the significance for their own lives of historical actions and decisions that are inexplicable in their own frame of reference, or they may draw unwarranted "lessons" from the past, by ignoring the historical *mentalité*, the culture in which the historical actors were embedded. Each of these challenges for naive historical thinkers risks a failure to negotiate the tensions between past and present, Ulrich's (1990, p. 34) "affinity and distance" between history and source.

Epistemology and Evidence

In constructing historical knowledge, another cognitive task involves separating warranted belief from that which is not. How should we handle traces in such a way that we can learn about the past? What accounts of the past should we believe? On what grounds? With what reservations?

Again, if either historians or naive thinkers worked with "masses of crude facts" the problem would be radically different from what it is. Historical epistemology would simply involve testing individual claims of fact against the documentary and artifactual evidence. What makes things complex is that historians begin their thinking not in discrete "facts," but in the accounts of other historians, in historical records, and in traces of the past, just as naive thinkers generally ground their historical thinking in the accounts and traces of the past available in the broader culture. So the first questions in historical thinking are more apt to be formulated as, "What are the problems with these accounts?" and "Shall I take them as is, or do they need revision?" (Levstik and Pappas, 1992, p. 378). And at a more sophisticated level, how does my knowledge of the situation and perspectives of the author(s) of the account or record lead me to revision, to new interpretations, to new meanings buried in the old stories (and thus new stories)?" As Peter Novick (1988) has shown, the claim that one historian's revision of another rests simply on the accumulation of more "evidence" to support a new interpretation has become increasingly difficult in recent years.

Denis Shemilt (1987) devised a four-stage hierarchy for analyzing adolescents' ideas about historical evidence. At the lowest level, there is no questioning about the authenticity or reliability of the source, and no question of "using" evidence other than as information. Students at that stage are unable to revise or to discount historical interpretations. They accept what is written. The range of students' use of evidence progresses through questioning the reliability and authenticity of sources (still failing to *use* a source in the revision of an account it provides), then through understanding evidence as a basis for inference about the past, to understanding the historicity of all sources and accounts (that is, the necessity of revising and discounting all accounts) at the highest stage.[5]

A second basis for historical epistemology—other than traces—lies in expert historical authorities. All of us rely selectively on the knowledge of experts (Haskell, 1984), but young people's choices of which authorities to believe may be more or less warranted. They may rely uncritically on those whom they take to be experts, express general skepticism, or be able to articulate criteria for distinguishing reliable from unreliable authorities. Wineburg (1991) found high school students highly likely to trust historical texts written in an authoritative voice, i.e., a simple narrative, even when the account was inconsistent with primary sources given to the students in the same session. Seixas (1993b) similarly found 16-year-olds generally viewing a popular historical film as if it were a window on the past. When challenged, they resorted to a range of grounds for their belief in the reliability of the filmic depiction including (1) the film's conformity to their understanding of human nature; (2) the familiarity of the depiction of the historical characters; (3) the film's compatibility with school history accounts; (4) the fact that it was a recent film; (5) the technical sophistication of the film; and (6) the emotional impact of the film. Some of these are better grounds for belief than others; all deserve investigation as components of these students' historical epistemology.

As Epstein (1994b) has shown, students' social location is an important factor in their responses to the problem of historical authority. While Epstein compared African-American and white students, she implicitly raised questions about the impact of gender, race, ethnicity, and class. Epistemological beliefs (implicit or explicit) provide the basis for historical knowledge. Without such a basis, young people have no reason to believe anything in particular about the past. They generally do have beliefs; investigation into the grounds for those beliefs, as well as the variation in those beliefs, is a worthwhile, but largely unexplored, inquiry (see Shemilt, 1980).

Continuity and Change

The concepts of continuity and change are so fundamental to historical understanding, that the Organization of American Historians identified treatment of "continuity and change" as the fundamental criterion for selecting articles for its expanded journal (Thelen, 1992). Continuity and change are relational. In order to identify historical change, we have to set a phenomenon against an unchanging, or continuous, backdrop. For instance, if we want to study change over time in modes of transportation, we posit a continuous category, "transportation," which is, for the moment, ahistorically conceived. Without such a transhistorical category, it becomes difficult or impossible to understand change within the category. Conversely, the concept of continuity of any phenomenon over time depends upon a backdrop of change elsewhere or in other phenomena. Thus we might speak of the continuity of a political constitution enduring periods of social and economic disruption. We might even look back on a period in which society, economy, and politics were, in a traditional society, apparently relatively unchanging, but only from a time after which there had been a development we regard as fundamental change. If everything were static, then "continuity" would make no more sense than "change."

The interaction between the concepts of change and continuity raises a host of problems for consideration in respect to naive historical thinking. A naive thinker, even when considering profound change in one aspect of social, political, or economic life, may assume much more continuity in other aspects of life than is warranted. For instance, a student looking at the technological development of photography (an example of what the British call "development studies"; see Shemilt, 1980; Lomas, 1990, p. 23) may fail to consider related changes in the purposes of photography, in the availability of photographs and camera equipment, in various people's modes of "reading" photographs, and so on (Douglas, 1992; Trachtenberg, 1989). Highlighting any example of change in the foreground may inadvertently contribute to a set of ahistorical assumptions about the background to the change. Yet the more that is brought into the changing foreground, the more complex the picture becomes.

This pedagogical problem is a recapitulation of the historiographic problem of the past 20 years, as historians have increasingly turned their attention to previously unexamined aspects of human life. The resulting work has historicized, for example, gender, childhood, death, the body, desire, leisure, work, and (most problematically) knowledge itself (e.g., Scott, 1988; Laqueur, 1990; Aries, 1962; Wilson, 1990; Novick, 1988). Acknowledgment of the historicity of knowledge, of course, implies the historicization of history writing. This scholarly development is the analogue to the student's subjecting further aspects of human life to historical scrutiny. Up to a certain point, the picture becomes more richly complex. After that point, the question of what continuous ground provides the foundation for the observation of change becomes pressing (Seixas, 1993c). We return to the image of all that is solid melting into air.

People's own experience with historical change is relevant to their conceptualizing change and continuity. Age is clearly a significant factor in such experience.

Leaving aside any differences in cognitive development, a 60-year-old in twentieth-century North America has simply lived through more historical change than has a ten-year-old, and is likely to have more direct experience with how fundamentally things can change. But age is not the only factor in contributing to such historical experience. One's historical location is also significant. A person who lives through a war or a coup d'état, who experiences the ramifications of a technological innovation, who immigrates to a new country or who sees the impact of demographic change on a neighborhood has a different experience of historical change from one who lives in traditional stability. How much more likely is it that adult or child would be sensitive to the nuances of fundamental historical change, if he or she had lived through a period during which a social order was destabilized?

What is the impact on young people, then, of a pace of historical change demanding that meaning must "be discovered and defined from within the maelstrom of change, a maelstrom that affects the terms of discussion as well as whatever it is that is being discussed" (Harvey, 1989, p. 11). They may experience social and cultural instability much more pervasively than did, for instance, even many of their teachers (or researchers investigating their cognitive processes). Contrary to the suggestion offered in the last paragraph, it may be that younger people growing up in an era of uncertainty and instability have a more profound experience of rapid change than their elders, that they *assume* deep, pervasive, and destabilizing change, rather than assuming continuity and stability (Elder, Modell, and Parke, 1993; Giroux, 1994). Representations of time, which shift with the broader cultural currents, are presently undergoing a critical period of challenge (Kammen, 1992; Gutman, 1987; Cruikshank, 1991; Samuel and Thompson, 1990; Ermarth, 1992; Jameson, 1991). Seen in this way, the historiographic challenge of the past two decades is just one aspect of an epistemological challenge felt in different ways throughout the culture, as historians and nonhistorians as well cope with locating themselves in time in a period of upheaval (Entrikin, 1991).

Progress and Decline

One of the most fundamental ways we organize the past in relation to the present is in terms of the concepts of progress and decline. Though it is often unarticulated by historians, textbook writers, or laypeople, a sense of progress or decline underlies most accounts of the past. Until the recent impact of narrative theory upon historians, there was little critical attention to the role it played in shaping the meaning of historical knowledge (White, 1978). Cronon (1992) raises a host of questions about historical interpretation by juxtaposing accounts of Great Plains history as progress and as decline. He demonstrates how the same historical phenomenon acquires very different meanings in relation to the present and is left somewhat perplexed as to how to deal with contending accounts (see Novick, 1988). The "evidence" is necessary, but not apparently sufficient to be sure that we have the story "right."[6]

Historical revisionism on the occasion of the Columbian quincentenary is a clear example of how popular thought about the past is organized into progress or decline, or complex combinations of the two (Simon, 1993; Maxwell, 1993). School textbooks have typically told a whig history, conveying an underlying message of the growth of democracy, knowledge, and enlightenment through time. Pointing in a different direction is what Kammen (1989) called the "heritage phenomenon," an attempt to appeal to a nostalgic vision of some lost, better days. Samuel (1990) explains the mass interest in British history in similar terms. The widely held concept of "declinism" may well signal a fundamental shift in popular conceptions of progress and decline (Heilbroner, 1993).

Open-ended questioning can probe young people's sense of progress and decline, providing an opportunity for students to express the sense of the past that they have integrated into their own conceptual structures. Recently in a discussion about historical progress and decline, I asked an eleventh-grade student whether she thought life for most people was getting harder or easier as we approached the end of the twentieth century:

STUDENT: Oh definitely easier.

INTERVIEWER: ...What makes you say that?

STUDENT: Well...I refer back to when I watched "The Little House on the Prairie" shows, how the girls, say, they be around 10, they have to do all the farming and they have to get their eggs and make their own bread and butter and that and now we just go to the store, we buy it, we have instant food and it's a lot less time-consuming it seems. But on the other way it has declined in that there's more crime and all that, but I don't really look at it, that's not my major focus.

INTERVIEWER: Is there any other kind of evidence that you could bring up?

STUDENT: Oh, just two days ago my mom was complaining—the income tax and she says oh I don't imagine how we survived ten years ago without calculators; she was just saying how hard it was and that she can't imagine doing it now without some of these calculators.

This student had assembled her sense of historical progress, as expressed here, from a combination of television watching (Little House on the Prairie), daily experience (instant food), news reportage ("more crime...but I don't really look at it"), and comments from her mother (the use of calculators). My question was phrased in terms of life being "harder or easier" but other values (security, health, democracy) might be substituted and compared (see Szacka, cited in Lowenthal, 1985, p. 36). Comparison of an internalized, believed account of the past, with perceptions of the present, along these lines is likely one of our most compelling uses of the past, both for individuals and for the culture as a whole. Such accounts might provide the starting point for historical inquiry.

The Confrontation with Difference: Empathy and Moral Judgment

Investigating what life was like in the past involves asking the questions, how was it different and how was it better or worse than today? (see above). People in the past not only lived in different circumstances (in terms of, e.g., technology, shelter, and political institutions), but also experienced and interpreted the world through different belief systems. When naive thinkers confront the differences of the past, however, they may mistakenly assume that people living in different circumstances nevertheless thought in ways essentially similar to themselves. Here is a failure to realize what they do not know about the past. Two aspects of our intellectual relationship with peoples different from ourselves are empathy and moral judgment.

Of empathy, Peter J. Lee (1983, pp. 34–35) says, "There can be few notions so commonly employed in talking about what children need to be able to do in history, and so little examined." Upon examination, the notion becomes very problematic. Some have considered empathy as an affective exercise, in which students feel the human commonality between themselves and historical figures. As it is put in the California *History-Social Science Framework* (California State Board of Education, 1987, pp. 12–13),

The study of history involves the imaginative reconstruction of the past. . . . Historical empathy is much like entering into the world of a drama, suspending one's knowledge of "the ending" in order to gain a sense of another era and living with the hopes and fears of the people of the time.

This formulation of historical empathy specifies no safeguards against thoroughly ahistorical "imaginative reconstructions" based on insufficient evidence from traces of the past. Imagining oneself in very different circumstances—in just this way— provides the core of Jenkins' (1991, pp. 42–43) comic attack on empathetic understanding in the classroom,

Think here of those imaginative leaps we might well have been asked to make so that we could pretend to be a fox, a snowflake, an angry king; such appeals were (and are) to make pupils feel involved and engaged. . .where all pupils bring their equally valid/valued opinions to school, then opportunities for their expression must be encouraged: what do they think of the past, what is history for them, what is their explanation—let them try and put themselves into the mind-set of (their) medieval prince.

The examples are ridiculous precisely because students have no data to support their imaginative leaps, and in the absence of any data, any assertion of what anyone feels is equally plausible.

Lee (1983) provides a more substantial conception of historical empathy as "an achievement, not as a special power, or as an activity." In his account, we understand historical agents through a study of evidence (i.e., traces of the past) and empathy is the product of that study. Ashby and Lee (1987) use the concept of historical empathy to examine students' understandings of the differences between their own age and that of the historical subject. In their definition of levels of historical empathy, the more students can follow the sometimes radically different thinking of someone from an earlier age, the higher level they have achieved. Downey (1994) pursued this problem in an investigation of fifth-grade students' ability to adopt the perspectives of historical actors. He found the students "at the threshold of perspective taking," but concluded that "most of them could not step across." He suggests that a rich base of information about "the fundamental structures and processes of everyday life" is necessary for successful historical empathy. Moreover, he advises that "teaching for historical thinking probably should focus more on the differences than on the continuities between past and present" (Downey 1994, p. 18).

Keith Jenkins' (1991) challenge to historical empathy (a term he dismisses altogether), rests on the argument that, as we reconstruct the world of the past, we inevitably do so from within our own frame of reference. Without our own frame of reference, we have no frame of reference at all. "Given that there is no presuppositionless interpretation of the past, and given that interpretations of the past are constructed in the present, the possibility of the historian being able to slough off his [sic] present to reach somebody else's past on their terms looks remote" (Jenkins, 1991, p. 40; cf. Jenkins and Brickley, 1989; Harlan, 1989).

In the face of the impossibility of a perfect, "presuppositionless" knowledge of the past (if such a phrase even makes sense), Jenkins appears to give up on historical knowledge altogether, on the part of children and everyone else. But there are various levels of understanding: History teachers correctly see an error when their students ahistorically assume that their own frameworks of assumptions, meanings, purposes, and values were also present in historical people who lived in different circumstances. Thus Ashby and Lee discuss students who interpreted fasting and drinking holy water before the Saxon practice of the ordeal as "a foolish practical mistake." "That sort of thing," said one of their subjects, "we wouldn't be doing nowadays 'cos we're not that stupid nowadays" (Ashby and Lee, 1987, p. 70). Even if the quest for perfect understanding of historical people "on their own terms" may be epistemologically naive, there still remain more or less sophisticated understandings. Historians strive to provide interpretations that more fully comprehend a foreign climate of opinion, and thus to understand otherwise inexplicable actions and statements. In Jenkins' all-or-nothing account, naive and sophisticated historical readings of documentary traces become indistinguishable.

The presentism of Ashby and Lee's student takes a different form among teachers, filmmakers, and historical novelists. These architects of historical accounts may attempt to make their characters "come alive" for their contemporary audiences by writing onto them familiar behaviors, motivations, assumptions, and conventions from their own culture. The resulting anachronisms are pervasive in the popular media. Thus after watching Native Americans discuss how to handle the white intruder in the overwhelmingly popular and successful *Dances with Wolves*, one student said revealingly, "You get a sense that these are real people and they're trying to deal with a real problem, as opposed to just a 'bunch of Indians'." What made the film so "real" for him? "I could see very easily a bunch of white people talking about almost exactly the same thing." The power of the film comes, then, from rendering the natives of 1863 familiar, like "white people" today (Seixas, 1993b). This student responded "empathetically" to the historical account that presented the "other" as fundamentally like himself. After all, we "understand" someone's actions if we believe that, facing similar circumstances, we would do the same. The paradox of empathy, then, is that it involves an effort to confront difference which, at every turn, tempts us to impose our own frameworks of meaning on others. The challenge is, again, one of negotiating between "affinity and distance," understanding human commonality without mistaking the contingent cultural constructions of our own time as transhistorical. In the epistemological confusion of the current moment, the task is particularly difficult.

Moral judgments in history pose similar kinds of problems. We make judgments by understanding historical actors as agents who faced decisions, sometimes individually, sometimes collectively, which had ethical consequences. Moral judgments require empathetic understanding—that is, an understanding of the differences between our moral universe, or ideological surround, and theirs, lest they be anachronistic impositions of our own standards upon the past. That having been said, we want to (and generally do) avoid a relativistic historicism that abjures historical judgments because the past is such a "foreign country." We deal with this exactly as we did with the problem of historical empathy: Our ability to make moral judgments in history requires that we entertain the notion of a historically transcendent human commonality, a recognition of our humanity in the person of historical actors, at the same time that we open every door to the possibility that those actors differ from us in ways so profound that we perpetually risk misunderstanding them.

Kieran Egan (1990, p. 232) uses the paradox of affinity and distance in his prescriptions for history teaching, without, however, acknowledging the potentially contradictory approaches to the past. On the one hand, he says:

We do not just learn about, say Alexander the Great or Florence Nightingale and then admire their courage and energy. Rather, we recognize them as a reflection of our own developing courage and energy.

Here, the struggles of characters of the past become those of students. But on the other hand, he says, "This is also the time for the more exotic features of history. . .We want to consider the alienness [of the Greeks]. We will explore their curious rites and rituals." Egan, and perhaps all of us, are caught somewhere between the alternatives of affinity as identity (a decontextualized past), and distance as "curious" and strange (an incomprehensible past).

Historical Agency

Historical agency is one aspect of the problem of historical causation. The concept of agency, however, focuses the historian on relationships of power. Who makes historical change and how (Mahoney and Yngvesson, 1992)? Central to the historiography of the past 30 years has been the project of bringing previously marginalized peoples into the purview of the discipline, not as victims or textbook "sidebars," but as active participants. Historians and activists-as-historians have sought a way to understand the historical agency of relatively powerless groups, as they operated within the constraints of their social and historical positions. E. P. Thompson's (1963) seminal *The Making of the English Working Class* generated a school of new working-class history, arguing that, in important ways, the working class "made itself." But the notion of active agency rooted in a culture of resistance, as a source of explanation of historical change did not go unchallenged (Anderson, 1980; Calhoun, 1982; Fink et al., 1988). Analogous debates arose among feminist historians (e.g., Cott, 1977; Scott, 1988; Gordon, 1988), historians of the African-American experience (e.g., Gutman, 1976; Genovese, 1974) and others (e.g., Goodwyn, 1976).

To what extent do young people have such a democratic sense of historical causation? How do they view their own relationship to social change? Do accounts of the past in which significance is located only among elites have an impact upon their own potentially active role? The most virulent arguments about history curriculum have involved assertions about the psychological impact of national consensus history on marginalized groups. Proponents of women's, ethnic, and working-class history claim, plausibly, that their histories would offer students a chance to see themselves as active forces for historical change; opponents may, of course, fear exactly that (Coulter, 1989; Schlesinger, 1992). How young people in a variety of social and historical situations understand their own life activity as a part of historical change is, then, an important, but heretofore unstudied question.

Toward a New Pedagogy of History

History is the discipline through which we organize the residua (traces and accounts) of the past into a form meaningful to us in the present. Neither simply a "mass of facts," nor a set of fictions, history is a form of knowledge rooted in a set of problematic issues that I have attempted to define in this paper. Young people encounter these issues prior to their first formal experiences of history education, and develop ideas about the past through their partial resolution. Given the current conceptual and empirical research base, it is too early to tell whether such resolutions can be arrayed along a continuum of sophistication, or whether they constitute a set of discrete stages or levels. Researchers are now in a position, however, to ask these questions and others: To what extent does historical thinking undergo development as children get older? Can explicit instruction in the problems of historical knowledge speed that development? What accounts for differences in sophistication in students' historical thinking (cf. Shemilt, 1980; Kuhn, Amsel, and O'Loughlin, 1988)?

In the meantime, much formal history education begins as if students had no prior ideas about the past, nor prior experience of working with the issues that help to define the meaning of the past. Moreover, it proceeds too frequently on the implicit assumption that students learning more historical facts means understanding more history. The identification of a structure of historical understanding, constituted through a series of issues whose resolution remains problematic even for professional historians, provides the basis for a different kind of historical pedagogy. A curriculum based on these issues might promote students' ability to develop meaningful, critical historical understanding on the basis of the traces and accounts presented in formal schooling, as well as those they encounter in the broader popular culture. Identification and definition of the issues are thus first steps not only in plotting a research agenda for historical thinking, but also more immediately in developing effective strategies for improving history education.

Peter Lee (1983, p. 44) urged the creation of classroom opportunities to expose young people's "misconceptions" in history. What I have discussed in this paper are not "misconceptions," then, but issues, complex tangles that are virtually unavoidable in thinking about our place in time. Historians, no less than novice thinkers about the past, must confront them in dealing with the distances between past and present. Both start from traces and accounts in the present to draw more or less integrated, more or less warranted conclusions about what has happened and what it means.

Without temporal bearings, we cannot make sense of our lives. In gaining these bearings, we assign significance, assess traces and accounts, conceptualize change, judge progress and decline, and employ empathy, moral judgment, and ideas of human agency. These intellectual processes are, as I have attempted to demonstrate, epistemological minefields through which there is no one simple, well-beaten path. And however difficult the dangers may be for professional historians, the most naive historical thinkers also confront them at every turn. Today the explosives are perhaps closer to the surface than ever. Our job as researchers into historical understanding is to dust them off and expose them, for each other, for teachers, and for students, without getting injured in the process.

Notes

1. Of course, the difference may inhere in institutional or historical factors, rather than in differences in the nature of these forms of knowledge, but investigation of such differences would constitute a different subject than the one I wish to address here.
2. Rejecting lists of substantive historical concepts, as well as catalogs of historical "skills," Peter Lee explores what he calls "structural second order concepts," including evidence, cause, empathy, change, and time as "the usual choices" (Lee, 1983, p. 25). Lomas (1990), in a similar list, includes significance but omits empathy.
3. Prior historical understanding is a problematic term in that it implicitly asks the question, prior to what? Nevertheless, I use it throughout this chapter because it links this exploration to work on prior understandings or prior knowledge in other disciplines. I also use the term "naive" to connote nonexperts in the field, though I realize there is some risk in this term. Other candidates are Carr's (1986) "pretheoretical" history, which he has explicated fully, but whose meaning without full explication is not immediately apparent, and "intuitive understanding" (Gardner, 1991) which seems somewhat more appropriate for science and math than history.
4. Kuhn, Amsel, and O'Loughlin (1988) identify *theories* and *evidence* at the core of scientific thinking, and their research program aims to provide a developmental framework for the relations between the two as scientific thinking develops. *Accounts* and *traces* in historical thinking may correspond to theories and evidence in scientific thinking. Traces

provide the evidence with which the historical thinker assembles an account (theory) of what happened, while our selection and reading of traces (evidence) are informed by the accounts (theories) that we bring to the question. There may be differences, however, in the degree to which a narrative structure is fundamental to historical accounts and less so to scientific theories. Furthermore, while Kuhn, Amsel, and O'Loughlin refer to "correct theories," the notion that historians are working toward a "correct" account is highly problematic.

5. Recent work by Terrie Epstein (1994a) and Marcy Singer Gabella (1995) offers promising insights on the arts as historical evidence. The use of evidence has been built into the National History Curriculum of the United Kingdom (National Curriculum History Working Group, 1990). Booth (1993, see also 1987) has criticized the National Curriculum's use of stages, arguing that, separated from specific content, such stages are meaningless as generic measures of students' historical abilities.

6. Historians' new interest in the problem of decline is evident in the program of the Eighteenth International Congress of Historical Sciences (1995), one of whose themes is "Decline as an Historical Concept."

References

Anderson, P. (1980). *Arguments within English Marxism*. London: Verso.

Appleby, J. (1992). Recovering America's historic diversity: Beyond exceptionalism. *Journal of American History, 79* (2), 419–431.

Aries, P. (1962). *Centuries of childhood: A social history of family life*. New York: Random House.

Ashby, R. and Lee, P. J. (1987). Children's concepts of empathy and understanding in history. In C. Portal (Ed.), *The history curriculum for teachers* (pp. 62–99). London: Falmer.

Berman, M. (1982). *All that is solid melts into air: The experience of modernity*. New York: Simon and Schuster.

Booth, M. (1987). Ages and concepts: A critique of the Piagetian approach to history teaching. In C. Portal (Ed.), *The history curriculum for teachers* (pp. 22–38). London: Falmer.

Booth, M. (1993). Students' historical thinking and the national history curriculum in England. *Theory and Research in Social Education, 21* (2), 105–127.

Bruner, J. (1960). *The process of education*. Cambridge: Harvard University Press.

Bruner, J. (1986). *Actual minds, possible worlds*. Cambridge: Harvard University Press.

Calhoun, C. (1982). *The question of class struggle*. Chicago: University of Chicago Press.

California State Board of Education. (1987). *History-social science framework*. Sacramento: Author.

Carr, D. (1986). *Time, narrative and history*. Bloomington: Indiana University Press.

Carretero, M. and Voss, J. F. (Eds.). (1994). *Cognitive and instructional processes in history and the social sciences*. Hillsdale, NJ: Lawrence Erlbaum.

Cott, N. (1977). *The bonds of womanhood: Woman's sphere in New England, 1780–1835*. New Haven: Yale University Press.

Coulter, R. (1989). To know themselves: The transformative possibilities of history for young women's lives. *History and Social Science Teacher, 25* (1), 25–28.

Cronon, W. (1992). A place for stories: Nature, history, and narrative. *Journal of American History, 78* (4), 1347–1376.

Cruikshank, J. (1991). *Reading voices*. Vancouver: Douglas and McIntyre.

Douglas, S. (1992). Notes toward a history of media audiences. *Radical History Review, 54,* 127–138.

Downey, M. T. (1994). Historical thinking and perspective taking in a fifth-grade classroom. Paper presented at the meeting of the National Council for Social Studies, Phoenix.

Downey, M. T. and Levstik, L. S. (1991). Teaching and learning history. In J. P. Shaver (Ed.), *Handbook of research on social studies teaching and learning* (pp. 400–410). New York: Macmillan.

Driver, R., Asoko, H., Leach, J., Mortimer, E., and Scott, P. (1994). Constructing scientific knowledge in the classroom. *Educational Researcher, 23* (7), 5–12.

Egan, K. (1989). Layers of historical understanding. *Theory and Research in Social Education, 17* (4), 280–294.

Egan, K. (1990). *Romantic understanding: The development of rationality and imagination, ages 8–15*. London: Routledge.

Eighteenth International Congress of Historical Sciences. (1995). *Registration Circular*. Montreal: Author.

Elder, G. H., Modell, J., and Parke, R. D. (Eds.). (1993). *Children in time and place: Developmental and historical insights*. Cambridge, England: Cambridge University Press.

Entrikin, J. N. (1991). *The betweenness of place: Towards a geography of modernity*. Baltimore: Johns Hopkins University Press.

Epstein, T. (1994a). The arts of history: An analysis of secondary school students' interpretations of the arts in historical contexts. *Journal of Curriculum and Supervision, 9* (2), 174–194.

Epstein, T. (1994b, April). *"Makes no difference if you're Black or White"? African-American and European-American working-class high school students' beliefs about historical significance and historical authority*. Paper presented at the American Educational Research Association, New Orleans.

Ermarth, E. D. (1992). *Sequel to history: Postmodernism and the crisis of representational time*. Princeton: Princeton University Press.

Fink, L., Lears, J., Diggins, J. P., Lipsitz, G., Buhle, M. J., and Buhle, P. (1988). A round table: Labor, historical pessimism, and hegemony. *Journal of American History, 75* (1), 115–161.

Frisch, M. (1990). American history and the structures of collective memory: A modest exercise in empirical iconography. In M. Frisch (Ed.), *A shared authority: Essays on the craft and meaning of oral and public history* (pp. 29–54). Albany: State University of New York Press.

Gabella, M. S. (1995). The art(s) of historical sense: An inquiry into form and understanding. *Journal of Curriculum Studies, 27* (2), 139–163.

Gardner, H. (1991). *The unschooled mind: How children think and how schools should teach*. New York: Basic Books.

Gates, H. L. (1992) *Loose canons: Notes on the culture wars*. New York: Oxford University Press.

Genovese, E. (1974). *Roll, Jordon, roll: The world the slaves made*. New York: Pantheon.

Giroux, H. (1994). Doing cultural studies: Youth and the challenge of pedagogy. *Harvard Educational Review, 64* (3), 278–308.

Goodwyn, L. (1976). *Democratic promise: The populist moment in America*. New York: Oxford University Press.

Gordon, L. (1988). *Heroes of their own lives: The politics and history of family violence*. New York: Viking.

Gutman, H. G. (1976). *The black family in slavery and freedom: 1750–1925*. New York: Pantheon.

Gutman, H. G. (1987). Historical consciousness in contemporary America. In H. G. Gutman (Ed.), *Power and culture: Essays on the American working class* (pp. 395–412). New York: Pantheon.

Harlan, D. (1989). Intellectual history and the return of the prodigal. *American Historical Review, 94* (3), 581–609.

Harvey, D. (1989). *The condition of postmodernity*. Cambridge: Blackwell.

Haskell, T. (Ed.). (1984). *The authority of experts: Studies in history and theory*. Bloomington: Indiana University Press.

Heilbroner, R. (1993, February 14). The worst is yet to come. *New York Times Book Review*, pp. 1, 25.

Hirst, P. H. (1965). Liberal education and the nature of knowledge. In D. Archambault (Ed.), *Philosophical analysis and education* (pp. 113–138). London: Routledge and Kegan Paul.

Hollinger, D. (1993). How wide the circle of the "we"? American intellectuals and the problem of the ethnos since World War II. *American Historical Review, 98* (2), 317–337.

Holt, T. (1990). *Thinking historically: Narrative, imagination, and understanding*. New York: College Entrance Examination Board.

Jameson, F. T. (1991). *Postmodernism, or, the cultural logic of late capitalism*. Durham: Duke University Press.

Jenkins, K. (1991). *Rethinking history*. London: Routledge.

Jenkins, K. and Brickley, P. (1989). Reflections on the empathy debate. *Teaching History*, 55, 18–23.

Kammen, M. (1989). History is our heritage. In P. Gagnon (Ed.), *Historical literacy* (pp. 138–156). New York: Macmillan.

Kammen, M. (1992). *Mystic chords of memory: The transformation of tradition in American culture*. New York: Knopf.

Kuhn, D., Amsel, E., and O'Loughlin, M. (1988). *The development of scientific thinking skills*. San Diego: Academic Press.

Kunen, S., Tang, W., and Ducey, S. J. (1991). Sex and age differences in adolescents' value judgments of historically important events: Theory, stereotypes and data. *Adolescence, 26* (101), 159–182.

Laqueur, T. (1990). *Making sex: Body and gender from the Greeks to Freud*. Cambridge: Harvard University Press.

Lee, P. J. (1983). History teaching and the philosophy of history. *History and Theory, 22* (4), 19–49.

Leinhardt, G., Beck, I. L., and Stainton C. (Eds.). (1994). *Teaching and learning history*. Hillsdale, NJ: Lawrence Erlbaum.

Levstik, L. S. (1986). The relationship between historical response and narrative in a sixth-grade classroom. *Theory and Research in Social Education, 14* (1), 1–15.

Levstik, L. S. (1989). Historical narrative and the young reader. *Theory into Practice, 28* (2), 114–119.

Levstik, L. S. (1992). Narrative and students' historical understanding. Paper presented at the annual meeting of the American Educational Research Association, San Francisco.

Levstik, L. S. and Pappas, C. C. (1992). New directions for studying historical understanding. *Theory and Research in Social Education, 20*(4), 369–385.

Lomas, T. (1990). *Teaching and assessing historical understanding*. London: The Historical Association.

Lowenthal, D. (1985). *The past is a foreign country*. New York: Cambridge University Press.

Mahoney, M. and Yngvesson, B. (1992). The construction of subjectivity and the paradox of resistance: Reintegrating feminist anthropology and psychology. *Signs, 18* (11), 45–72.

Maxwell, K. (1993). Adios Columbus! *New York Review of Books, 40* (3), 38–45.

McGerr, M. (1991). The price of the "new transnational history." *American Historical Review, 96* (4), 1056–1067.

Mink, L. (1987). *Historical understanding*. B. Fay, E. O. Golob, and R. T. Vann (Eds.). Ithaca: Cornell University Press.

National Curriculum History Working Group. (1990). *Final Report*. London: Department of Education and Science and the Welsh Office.

Novick, P. (1988). *That noble dream: "Objectivity" and the American historical profession*. New York: Cambridge University Press.

Polkinghorne, D. E. (1988). *Narrative knowing and the human sciences*. Albany: State University of New York Press.

Rogers, P. (1987). The past as a frame of reference. In C. Portal (Ed.), *The history curriculum for teachers* (pp. 3–21). London: Falmer.

Samuel, R. (1990). The return of history. *London Review of Books, 12* (11), 9–12.

Samuel, R. and Thompson, P. (1990). (Eds.), *The myths we live by*. London: Routledge.

Schlesinger, A., Jr. (1992). *The disuniting of America*. New York: Norton.

Scott, J. (1988). *Gender and the politics of history*. New York: Columbia University Press.

Seixas, P. (1993a). Parallel crises: History and the social studies curriculum in the USA. *Journal of Curriculum Studies, 25* (3), 235–250.

Seixas, P. (1993b). Popular film and young people's understanding of the history of native–white relations. *The History Teacher, 26* (3), 351–370.

Seixas, P. (1993c). The community of inquiry as a basis for knowledge and learning: The case of history. *American Educational Research Journal, 30* (2), 305–324.

Seixas, P. (1993d). Historical understanding among adolescents in a multicultural setting. *Curriculum Inquiry, 23* (3), 301–327.

Shemilt, D. (1980). *History 13–16 evaluation study*. Edinburgh: Holmes McDougall.

Shemilt, D. (1983). The devil's locomotive. *History and Theory, 22* (4), 1–18.

Shemilt, D. (1987). Adolescent ideas about evidence and methodology in history. In C. Portal (Ed.), *The history curriculum for teachers* (pp. 62–99). London: Falmer.

Simon, R. (1993). Forms of insurgency in the production of popular memories: The Columbus quincentenary and the pedagogy of counter-commemoration. *Cultural Studies, 7* (1), 73–88.

Sleeper, M. (1973). The uses of history in adolescence. *Youth and Society, 4*, 259–274.

Thelen, D. (1992). Of audiences, borderlands, and comparisons: Toward the internationalization of American history. *Journal of American History, 79* (2), 432–462.

Thompson, E. P. (1963). *The making of the English working class*. New York: Random House.

Trachtenberg, A. (1989). *Reading American photographs: Images as history*. New York: Hill and Wang.

Tyrrell, I. (1991). American exceptionalism in an age of international history. *American Historical Review, 96* (4), 1031–1055.

Ulrich, L. T. (1990). *A midwife's tale: The diary of Martha Ballard*. New York: Knopf.

VanSledright, B. and Brophy, J. (1992). Storytelling, imagination, and fanciful elaboration in children's historical reconstructions. *American Educational Research Journal, 29* (4), 837–859.

White, H. (1978). *Tropics of discourse*. Baltimore: Johns Hopkins University Press.

Wilson, D. J. (1990). *Science, community, and the transformation of American philosophy, 1860–1930.* Chicago: University of Chicago Press.

Wilson, S. (1988). *Understanding historical understanding: Subject matter knowledge and the teaching of history.* Doctoral dissertation, Stanford University.

Wineburg, S. S. (1991). On the reading of historical texts: Notes on the breach between school and academy. *American Educational Research Journal, 28* (3), 495–519.

Wineburg, S. S. (Ed.). (1994). The teaching and learning of history. *Educational Psychologist, 29* (2).

Wineburg, S. S. (in press). The psychology of learning and teaching history. In D. C. Berliner and R. Calfee (Eds.). *The Handbook of Educational Psychology.* New York: Macmillan.

Author Index

(italics denote reference listing)

Abdi, H. *642*
Abelson, R. P. 633, *645*
Aboitz, F. 121, *140*
Abramson, L. Y. *273*
Achenbach, T. M. 261, 263, *271*
Ackerman, P. *142*
Acredolo, L. 43, 52
Adams, C. 135, *137*
Adams, M. J. 123, *137*
Adams-Curtis, L. E. 279, *298*
Adanson, M. 658, *679*
Adler, T. F. 354, *366*
Ahern, G. 342, *344*
Ahlberg, A. 551, 559, 560, *562*
Aiello, R. 37, *51, 52*, 53, 55
Alba, J. W. 131, *138*
Alexander, J. M. 597, 601, 607, *618*
Alexandersson, M. 589, *590*
Allen, L. 588, *590*
Allington, R. 213, *223*
Altwerger, B. 175, 197, *199*
Amaya-Williams, M. 80, *96*
Ames, L. B. 108, 109, *114*
Amsel, E. 777, 778, 779, *781*
Anastasi, A. 126, *137*, 471, *478*
Andersen, E. 177, *198*
Anderson, C. W. 502, *513*
Anderson, J. R. 77, *95*, *298, 299*, 509, *511*
Anderson, P. 777, *779*
Anderson, R. C. 259, *271*, *644*
Andrews, R. 239, *255*
Antinucci, F. 293, *301*
Applebee, A. N. 118, *137*, 520, *532*
Appleby, J. 768, *779*
Aram, D. 135, *137*
Aries, P. 771, *779*
Aristotle 630, 647, 657, 660, 672, 677
Arkes, H. R. 131, *137*
Armstrong. M. 521, 522, *532*
Arnaudin, M. W. 622, *644*
Arnheim, R. 30, *52*
Aronowitz, S. 132, *137*
Ashby, R. 774, 775, *779*
Asoko, H. 761, *763*, *780*
Asplund Carlsson, M. 554, *563*, 584, *592*
Astilla, E. 553, *564*
Astington, J. W. 4, 13, 20, 22, 25, 78, 79, *95*, 153, 158, 160, *169, 171*, 370, 384, *387*, 486, *511*, 593, 599–602, 610, 614, *615, 616, 617*, 629, *642*, 647, *679*, 740, *763*
Atran, S. 622, 637, *642*, 647, 651, 652, 654, 656, 658–661, 671, 678, *679, 680, 681*, 696, 697, *705*, 712

Austin, J. L. 595, 596, *615*
Avis, J. 647, *679*

Backett, K. C. 348, *364*
Backscheider, A. G. 686, *705*
Baddeley, A. D. 124, 135, *137, 140*
Baillargeon, R. 625, 628, *642*, 647, *679*
Baker, C. 193, *198*
Baker-Sennett, J. 390, 410, *414*
Bakhtin, M. M. *255*, 354, 355, 429, *431, 438, 458*
Baldwin, J. M. 78, *95*
Ball, D. 739, *762*
Ballard, M. 768
Bamberger, J. 38, 39, 40, 41, *52*
Banet, B. 609, *617*
Baranes, R. 506, *513*, 758, 761, *763*
Barclay, C. R. 601, *616*
Bard, K. A. 284, *298, 299, 300*, 385
Barlett, D. 136, *137*
Barnes, D. 761, *762*
Barnes, J. A. 364, *364*
Barnes, W. 187, *200*
Barnett, S. A. 277, 291, *298*, 305, *321*
Baron, J. 125, 131, 132, *137*
Barron, R. 124, *137*
Barsalou, L. W. 621, *642*
Bartlett, H. 673, 678, *679, 680*
Bartlett, L. 401, 408, 411, *412, 413, 414*
Bartlett, R. C. 634, *642*
Bartsch, K. 596, 599, *615*
Baruch, D. 110, *114*
Barzun, J. 496, *511*
Basso, A. 37, *52*
Bassok, M. 704, *705*
Bates, E. 34, *52*, 309, *321*
Bauer, P. 158, *169*
Baumrind, D. 601, *615*
Beals, D. 178, *199*
Beatty, B. 2, 103, 104, 105, 109, 111, *114*
Beaty, E. 554, *563*
Beck, I. L. 765, *781*
Becker, H. S. 761, *763*
Beech, J. 124, 127, *137*
Beeghly, M. 472, *479*, 596, 598, *615*
Beeghly-Smith, M. 596, *615*
Beer, R. D. 509, *511*
Behrend, D. A. 698, *705*
Beilin, H. 79, *95*, 171
Belenky, M. F. 758, *762*
Bell, N. 406, *413*
Bellah, R. N. 758, *762*
Ben-Dror, I. 124, *137*
Benjamin, W. 63, *74*

Bennett, K. P. 391, *412*
Bentin, S. 123, *137*
Bereiter, C. 4, 13, 20, *25, 26*, 77, 88, 90, 92, *95, 98*,
    99, 157, *169*, 469, 470, 477, *481*, 488, 489, 503,
    507, 511, *511, 513*, 608, *615*, 636, *642*, 732, *764*
Berlin, B. 651, 652, 653, 678, *680, 682*
Berliner, D. C. 265, *272*
Berman, M. 767, *779*
Bernhard, J. G. 381, *385*
Bernstein, M. 129, *145*
Berry, D. C. 630, *642*
Bettelheim, B. *532*
Bever, T. 43, *52*
Bidell, T. 153, *170*
Biemiller, A. 602, *617*
Bierwisch, M. 595, *615*
Biggs, J. B. 86, *95*, 552, 553, *562*
Bigler, K. 597, 607, *618*
Birdzell, L. E. 94, *98*
Birnbaum, R. 127, *137*
Bishop, D. 135, *137*
Blackburn, I. 122, *141*
Blanton, W. 176, *200*
Bless, H. 269, *273*
Block, N. J. 129, *137*
Bloom, A. 125, *138*
Blount, B. G. 350, *364*
Bluestein, N. 43, *52*
Blum-Kulka, S. 178, *198*
Blumer, C. 131, *137*
Blumer, H. 754, *762*
Blunk, M. 744, *762*
Boccia, M. L. 294, *298*
Boden, M. A. 434, *458*
Bodis-Wolliner, I. *479*
Boesch, C. 289, 290, *298*, 374, 375, *385*
Boesch, H. 289, *298*
Boix-Mansilla, V. 41, *53*
Booth, J. R. 601, *615*
Booth, M. 779, *779*
Booth, S. A. 4, 11, 544, *562*, 565, 568, 583, 588
Bos, C. S. 117, *142, 146*
Boster, J. S. 648, 655, *680*, 696, 701, *705, 707*
Botheroyd, P. F. 445, *458*
Bourdieu, P. 255, 347, 349, 354–356, *364*, 370,
    372, *385*
Bower, G. 149, 152, 161, *170*, 534, *562*
Bowerman, M. 196, *198*
Bowers, P. 127, *138*
Bowes, J. A. 348, *365*
Bowey, J. A. 123, *138*
Bowlby, J. 267, *271*
Bowles, S. 132, *138*
Boyd, R. 638, *642*
Boysen, S. T. 289, *298, 299, 300*
Brademas, J. 84, *95*
Bradley, L. 91, *95*, 123, *138*
Bradshaw, P. 400, *412*
Brady, S. 127, *143*
Braine, M. D. S. 164, *169*
Bredekamp, S. 157, *169*
Breinlinger, K. 625, *645, 682*
Brenner, H. G. 133, *141*
Brentano, F. 328, *344*
Bretherton, I. 596, 598, 599, *615*
Brett, C. *26*
Brewer, W. F. 622, 632, *643, 645*, 676, *682*

Briggs, L. J. 76, *96*
Broadbent, D. 630, *643*
Bronfenbrenner, U. 126, *138*, 471, *478*
Broniarczyk, S. 131, *138*
Brookhuis, K. 126, *142*
Brooks-Gunn, J. *478*
Brophy, J. 765, 766, *782*
Brophy, J. E. 259, 262, *272*, 608, *615*
Brown, A. L. 15, 20, *25, 26*, 81, 91, *95*, 396, *412*,
    437, *459*, 566, 569, *590*, 609, *616, 642*, 728, *729*
Brown, D. E. 714, *729*
Brown, G. D. A. 124, *138*
Brown, J. L. 304, *321*
Brown, J. R. 597, *616*
Brown, J. S. 81, *95*, 430, *431, 432*, 509, *511*, 609,
    616, 728, *729*
Brown, L. M. 756, *762*
Brown, R. 164, *169*, 316, *321*
Bruck, M. 118, 123, 124, *137, 138*
Bruner, J. S. 1, 2, 6, 8, 11, 13, 16, 19, *26*, 28, 32, 34,
    35, *52*, 80, 81, 86, 87, *95, 99*, 101, 153, 159, 164,
    165, 166, *169*, 175, *198*, 214, 220, 255, 339, *344*,
    373, 375, *385*, 417, 419, 422, 427, *431*, 434, 435,
    441, 457, *458*, 461, 464, *478*, 485, 486, 510, *511*,
    568, 588, *590, 762, 779*
Bruns, G. L. 530, *532*
Bryant, P. 91, *95*, 123, 124, *140*
Bryant, P. E. 123, 124, *138*
Bryson, M. 477, *481*
Bullock, M. 685, *705*
Bulmer, R. 678, *680*
Burk, C. 105, *114*
Burk, F. 105, 111, *114*
Burtis, P. J. *26*
Burton, R. B. 430, *431*
Burton, R. R. 509, *511*

Cahan, E. D. 396, *412*
Cain, M. T. 123, *138*
Caldwell, G. 110
Calhoun, C. 777, *779*
Calkins, L. 174, 197, *198*
Call, J. 384, *385*
Callahan, R. E. 391, 392, *412*, 521, *532*
Camp, L. 178, 195, *199*
Campione, J. C. 15, 20, *26*, 81, *95*, 396, *412*, 609,
    616, 642
Campos, J. J. 294, *298*
Capitani, E. 37, *52*
Carey, S. 31, *52, 53*, 78, 79, *95*, 154, 159, 161, 162,
    169, 170, 171, 300, 601, *618*, 621, 622, *642*, 645,
    647, 658, *680*, 683, 684, 688, 689, 691,
    693–695, 701, 702, 704, *705, 708*, 739, *764*
Carlson, V. 695, *705*
Caro, T. M. 286, 287, 291, *298*, 374, *385*
Carpenter, P. A. 126, *138*
Carpenter, T. P. 89, *95*
Carr, D. 765, 767, 769, 778, *779*
Carretero, M. 765, *779*
Carrier, J. G. 136, *138*
Carroll, J. B. 487, *511*
Caruso, D. 608, *617*
Case, R. 2, 4, 79, 91, 93, *95, 96, 97*, 271, *271*, 472,
    478, 478, 490, 506, 507, *512*, 607, 609, *616, 617*
Cashmore, J. 346, 355, 359, 362, *364, 365*
Cassirer, E. 33, *52*
Catts, H. W. 135, *138, 141*

Cazden, C. 354, 355, *364*
Cazden, C. B. 91, *96*, 215, 220, *223*, 316, *321*
Ceci, S. J. 117, 118, 125, 126, 129, 133, *138*, *144*, 471, 476, *478*, *479*
Chaiken, S. 258, *272*
Chandler, J. 187, *200*
Chandler, M. J. 601, 602, *616*
Chang, G. L. M. 389, 396, *414*
Change, F. 474, *479*
Chapman, J. P. 621, 624, *642*
Chapman, L. J. 621, 624, *642*
Chard, S. 566, *591*
Charness, N. 31, *53*
Chase, W. 77, *98*
Chavajay, P. 369, 371, *387*
Chen, C. 264, *273*
Cheney, D. L. 12, *26*, 286, 288, 293, 296, *298*, *299*
Cheng, K. 43, *52*
Chevalier-Skolnikoff, S. 280, *298*
Chi, M. T. H. 77, 79, *96*, 625, *643*
Childs, C. P. 373, 379, *385*
Chinn, C. A. 632, *643*
Chomsky, C. 601, *616*
Chomsky, N. 154, 158, *169*, 172, 173, 174, *198*, 418, *431*
Christensen, C. 131, *137*
Churchland, P. 418, *431*
Churchland, P. S. 486, *511*
Cicchetti, D. 472, *479*
Clancy, P. 176, *198*
Clandinin, J. 607, *616*
Clark Brown, P. 608, *618*
Clay, M. M. 3, 203, 205, 210, 218, *223*, 467, 567, *590*
Cleeremans, A. 623, *643*
Clinchy, B. M. 759, *762*
Clinchy, E. 102, *114*
Clokey-Till, M. 408, *413*
Clore, G. L. 269, *271*
Cobb, P. 89, 90, *99*, 507, *513*, 732, 761, *762*
Coe, R. 520, *532*
Cohen, L. J. 131, *138*
Cohn, D. 445, *458*
Cole, K. N. 117, 135, 136, *139*
Cole, M. 34, *54*, *55*, 81, 87, 91, *96*, 369, *385*, 389, 396, *413*, 418, *432*, 464, *479*, *481*, *533*, *708*
Cole, S. R. 418, *432*
Coles, G. S. 117, 126, 133, 136, *139*
Coley, J. 654, 655, 658, 661, 677, *680*, *681*
Collier, G. 32, *52*, 319, *322*
Collins, A. 87, 93, 94, *96*, *97*, 609, *616*, 728, 729
Collins, W. A. 362, *364*
Collis, K. 86, *95*
Comenius, J. A. 149, 166, *169*
Comer, J. P. 47, *52*, 112, 113, *114*, 264, 265, 267, *272*
Connelly, M. 607, *616*
Conners, C. K. 261, *271*
Conners, F. 118, 121, 122, *142*
Connolly A. 521, *532*
Conrad, F. G. 509, *511*, 597, *618*
Conway, B. 129, *145*
Cook, M. 280, 284, 285, 294, *299*
Cooney, T. 99, *513*
Corbett, A. T. 509, *511*
Corcos, E. 118, *147*
Cosmides, L. 267, *273*, 647, *680*

Cott, N. 777, *779*
Coulter, R. 777, *779*
Coupe, P. 44, *55*
Crago, M. 196, *198*
Crain, S. 127, *143*
Cramer, B. 123, *145*
Crane, L. L. 472, 476, 477, *480*
Cremin, L. A. 106, *114*, 397, *412*
Critchley, M. 118, *139*
Cronbach, L. J. 126, *139*
Cronon, W. 772, *779*
Crossland, J. 123, *138*
Cruikshank, J. 772, *780*
Cryns, T. 408, *413*
Csikszentmihalyi, M. 32, *52*, 268, *272*
Cuban, L. 101, 106, 113, *114*, 391, *412*
Cubberley, E. P. 392
Cuddon, J. A. 438, *458*
Cullen, J. 567, *590*
Cunningham, A. E. 123, 133, *145*
Cunningham, V. 529, *532*
Custance, D. M. 284, 286, *298*
Custodio, R. 123, *142*
Cynader, M. 471, 474, 478, *479*

D'Andrade, R. 597, *616*, 648, *680*
D'Andrade, R. G. 347, *365*, 415, *432*
d'Azevedo, W. L. 435, *458*
Dahlgren, G. 579, *590*
Dahlgren, L. O. 544, *562*
Dale, P. S. 117, 135, *139*
Dall'Alba, G. 553, 554, *563*
Damon, W. 384, *387*, 582, *590*
Danto, A. C. 60, *74*
Darling-Hammond, L. 113, *114*
Darwin, C. 265, *272*, 651, *680*
Dasser, V. 311, *321*
Davidson, B. 123, *142*
Davidson, D. 131, *139*, 681, 754, *763*
Davidson, J. E. 129, *139*
Davidson, L. 38, 39, 40, 41, *52*
Davies, B. 358, 359, 363, *365*
Davis, M. 608, *619*
Davis, P. 757, *762*
Davison, M. L. 133, *141*
Davydov, V. V. 426, *432*
Dawes, R. M. 131, *139*
Day, B. 155, 157, *169*
De Renzi, E. 127, *141*
De Temple, J. 178, *199*
Deering, P. D. 397, *412*
DeFries, J. 121, 122, *142*, *143*
DeFries, J. C. 120, 121, *139*
Delpit, L. 177, 195, *199*
Deming, A. H. 70, *74*
Dennett, D. 131, *139*
Dennett, D. C. 435, *458*
Denton, S. M. 601, *616*
Descartes, R. 58, 77, *96*, 647, *680*
Detterman, D. 126, *139*
Detterman, D. K. 97, 125, *140*, *145*, *480*
Deutsch, D. 37, *52*
Deutsch, M. 90, *96*
deVilliers, J. G. 600, *616*
DeVries, R. 94, *97*, *169*
Dewey, J. 1, 2, 6, 13, 18, 19, *26*, 28–30, 50, 51, *52*, 56–73, *74*, 100, 101, 105–108, 112, *114*, 150,

Dewey, J. *contd.*
  151, 160, 166–168, *170*, 395, 396, *412*, 417,
  464, *479*, 515, *532*
Diamond, J. 673, 678, *680*
Diaz, R. M. 80, *96*
Dickinson, D. 178, 187, 189, 197, *200*
Dickinson, D. K. 437, *459*
Dienes, Z. 630, *642*
Dionnet, S. 581, *590*
DiSessa, A. A. 4, 162, 676, *680*, 727, 729, *730*, 761,
  762
Dix, T. H. 361, *365*
Doehring, D. G. 118, 133, *139*
Dolgin, K. G. 698, *705*
Donald, M. 463, 465, *479*, 522, 531, *532*
Donaldson, M. 1, 3, *6*, 23, *26*, 329, 333, *344*
Donnellan, K. 652, *680*
Dornbusch, S. M. 136, *145*
Dorner, W. W. 131, *147*
Dorr-Bremme, D. 177, *199*
Dougherty, J. 654, *680*
Douglas, S. 771, *780*
Doverborg, E. 570, 580, 581, *590*
Dowling, W. 38, *53*
Downey, M. T. 765, 774, 775, *780*
Downs, R. 43, 44, *54*
Doyle, W. 501, *512*
Draper, P. 315, *321*
Driver, R. 581, *590*, 761, 762, 766, *780*
Drucker, P. F. 94, *96*, 492, *512*
Ducey, S. J. 769, *781*
Duckworth, E. *432*
Duguid, P. 81, *95*
Dunbar, R. 463, *479*
Duncker, K. 269, *272*
Dunn, J. 267, *272*, 596, 599, *616*
Dupré, J. 638, *643*, 676, *680*
Duranti, A. *200*, 435, *458*
Durkheim, E. 419
Durkin, D. 152, *170*
Durkin, D. 152, *170*
Dweck, C. S. 267, *272*, 759, *763*
Dworkin, G. 129, *137*
Dwyer, P. 678, *680*
Dyer, F. 43, *53*
Dyson, A. 175, 198, *199*
Dyson, X. 440, *458*

Eagly, A. H. 258, *272*
Eccles, J. C. 504, *512*
Eccles, J. S. 346, *365*, 389, *412*
Eckert, P. 354, *365*
Eco, U. 35, *53*
Edelsky, C. 175, 197, *199*
Edwards, A. C. 106, 107, *115*
Egan, K. 4, 14, *26*, *53*, *199*, *532*, 776, *780*
Eggan, D. 380, *386*
Eisenberg, L. 118, *139*
Elbow, P. 757, 761, *762*
Elder, G. H. 772, *780*
Elias, N. 421, 422, 427, 428, *432*
Eliopulos, D. 121, *143*
Elkind, D. 565, 569, *590*
Ellis, N. 124, 125, *139*
Ellis, N. C. 124, *137*
Elster, C. 177, *199*
Enerstvedt, R. T. 572, *591*
Engelmann, S. 90, *95*, 157, *169*, 608, *615*

England, P. 353, *365*
Ennis, R. H. 131, *139*
Entrikin, J. N. 772, *780*
Entwistle, N. 20, *26*, 552, *562*, *563*
Epstein, T. 770, 779, *780*
Erdoes, R. 381, *386*
Ericsson, K. A. 31, *53*, 259, *272*
Eriks-Brophy, A. 196, *198*
Erikson, E. H. 28, 29, *53*, *101*
Ermarth, E. D. 772, *780*
Evans, B. 129, *139*
Evans, E. D. 567, *591*, 608–610, *616*
Evans, J. B. T. 131, *139*
Ewer, R. F. 304, 305, *321*
Eysenck, H. J. 471, *479*

Fabricius, W. F. 597, 601, 607, *616*, *618*
Fairbanks, L. 287, *298*
Farkas, G. 353, *365*
Farris, H. 131, *139*
Faux, D. 123, *144*
Feeman, D. J. 133, *145*
Fegley, S. 136, *145*
Feistner, A. T. C. 288, *300*
Felch, L. 630, *644*
Feldman, C. 611, *616*
Feldman, C. F. 3, 19, *26*, 436, 439–441, 447, 448,
  450, 451, 453, 454, 457, 458, *459*
Feldman, D. 31, 33, 37, *53*
Feldman, H. 195, *199*
Felton, R. H. 123–125, *139*
Feltovich, P. J. 625, *643*
Fennema, E. 89, *95*
Ferreiro, E. 223, *255*
Feuerstein, R. 80, *96*
Feyerabend, P. 86, *96*
Fieberg, E. L. 622, *644*
Fink, L. 777, *780*
Fiorito, G. 285, *298*
Firth, J. R. 236
Firth, R. 380, *386*
Fischer, K. W. 153, *170*
Fischhoff, B. 131, *139*
Flapan, V. 346, *367*
Flavell, J. 569, *591*
Flavell, J. H. 85, *96*, 400, 599, *616*, *642*
Fletcher, J. M. 120, 124, 127, *139*, *144*
Flores, B. 175, 197, *199*
Fodor, J. 35, *53*, 154, 158, 161, *170*
Fodor, J. A. 434, *459*, 489, *512*, *730*
Foltz, G. 123, *142*
Fondacaro, R. 363, *366*
Foreman, E. A. 370, *386*
Forness, S. 117, *140*
Fortes, M. 378–381, *386*
Fortin, D. 37, *54*
Foucault, M. 347, 356, 357, *365*
Fouts, D. H. 12, *26*
Fouts, R. S. 12, *26*
Fowler, A. 120, *139*, 438, *459*
Fragaszy, D. M. 3, 11, 12, *27*, 279, 282, *298*, 299,
  300
Frake, C. O. 81, *96*
Francis, D. J. 120, *139*
Frankenberger, W. 118, 120, *140*
Fredman, G. 123, 124, *140*, *146*
Freebody, P. 193, *198*

Freud, S. 53, *101*
Frisch, M. 769, *780*
Frith, U. 123, *140*
Fromberg, D. 608, *616*
Fronzaglio, K. 118, 120, *140*
Frye, D. 602, *617*
Frye, N. 438, *459*
Fulker, D. 121, 122, *139, 142*
Furrow, D. 600, *617*

Gabella, M. S. 779, *780*
Gage, N. 84, *96*
Gage, N. L. 265, *272*
Gagne, R. M. 76, *96*
Galaburda, A. 121, *140*
Galaburda, A. M. 121, *140, 145*
Galanter, E. 76, *98*
Galbraith, J. K. 94, *96*
Galdikas, B. M. F. 286, *300*
Galef, B. G. 278, 282, 287, 303, *299, 321*
Galef, B. J., Jr. 303, *321*
Gallas, K. 175, 198, *199*
Gallaway, C. 176, *199, 200*
Gallimore, R. 389, 396, 408, 409, *414*
Gallistel, C. 43, 53, *54*
Gallistel, C. R. 163, *170*
Galton, F. 471, *479*
Gamble, C. 464, *481*
Garcia, J. 287, *299*
Gardner, H. 1, 2, 6, 13, 17, *26*, 31–35, 37, 38, 41,
   42, 45, 47, 49, 50, *53*, 76, 81, 94, *96*, 113, 129,
   140, 384, *386*, 472, 476, 477, *479*, 532, 602, *616*,
   765, *780*
Garnham, A. 123, *142*
Garvey, C. 348, *365*
Gates, H. L. 768, 778, *780*
Gathercole, S. E. 135, *140*
Gaudia, G. 90, *96*
Gauvain, M. 369, *386*
Gearhart, M. 596, *616*
Gee, J. 195, *199*
Geertz, C. 32, *53*, 435, *459*
Gellert, E. 691, *705*
Gelman, R. 31, 52, *53*, 163, *169, 170*, 171, *300*,
   642, 643, 645, 685, 690, 695, *705, 707*
Gelman, S. A. 27, 158, 159, 162, *169, 170, 172*,
   311, *321*, 432, 619, 621, 622, 625, *642–645*,
   647, 648, 655, 658, *679–682*, 683, 685, 686,
   694, *705–708*
Genishi, C. 175, 198, *199*
Genovese, E. 777, *780*
Gentner, D. 497, *512*, 730, *762, 764*
Gentry, J. R. 206, *224*
Gergen, K. J. 435, *459*
Geschwind, N. 121, *140*
Gesell, A. 108, 109, 110, *114*, 152, 156, 210, 608,
   616
Ghent, P. 636, *643*
Giaconia, R. M. 389, *412*
Gibson, E. J. 625, *643*
Gibson, K. R. G. 298, *300, 387*
Gilger, J. 120, 121, *142, 143*
Gillham, B. 1, *6*
Gilligan, C. 756, *762*
Gilmore, M. 651, *680*
Ginsburg, H. 90, *96*
Gintis, H. 132, *138*

Giroux, H. 772, *780*
Giroux, H. A. 132, *137*
Gittleman, R. 204, *224*
Gladwin, T. 17, *26*, 380, *386*
Glaser, E. M. 131, *147*
Glaser, R. 76, 95, 96, 97, 474, 480, 512, 625, 643,
   704, *705*
Gleitman, H. 43, 54, *170*
Gleitman, L. R. 158, *170*
Glick, J. 356, *365*
Glucksberg, S. 604, *617*
Glymour, C. 473, *479*
Gold, B. A. 395, *413*
Goldberger, N. R. 758, *762*
Goldman, A. I. 130, *140*
Goldsmith, D. 390, 410, *414*
Golinkoff, R. M. 695, *705*
Gombrich, E. H. 44, *53*, 504. *512*
Gomez, M. 607, *616*
Göncü, A. 12, *26*, 396, 397, *414*
Gonzalez, J. 121, *141*
Good, T. 608, *615*
Good, T. L. 259, 262, *272*
Goodall, J. 12, *26*, 283, 290, *299*, 305, *321*, 374,
   386
Goodman, I. 187, *200*
Goodman, K. 174, 175, *199*
Goodman, N. 33, 35, 44, *53*, 454, *459*
Goodman, Y. 174, *199*
Goodman Turkanis, C. 402, 411, *412, 413, 414*
Goodnow, J. J. 3, 11, 345, 346, 347, 348, 353–356,
   359–362, 364, *365, 414*, 428, *432*
Goodwyn, L. 777, *780*
Gopnik, A. 159, *170*, 297, *299*, 594, 599, *616, 617*,
   621, 625, 627, *643, 647, 679*
Gordon, L. 777, *780*
Goswami, U. 123, 124, *140*
Gougis, R. A. 264, *272*
Gould, J. 43, *53*
Gould, S. J. 129, *140*, 155, *170*, 474, *479*, 515, 516,
   532
Gow, L. 498, 553, *562*
Graham, P. 50, *53*, 123, *146*
Grant, J. 109, *114*
Graubard, A. 395, *413*
Graves, D. 197, *199*
Graves, D. H. 81, *97*
Graves, K. 124, *142*
Green, B. F. 471, 473, *479*
Green, T. F. 57, 58, *74*
Greenberg, M. T. 600, *617*
Greenberger, E. 136, *140*
Greene, M. 2, 389, 391, *413*
Greenfield, P. M. 34, 52, 373, 379, *385, 386*
Greeno, J. G. 81, 87, 89, 93, *97, 98*, 730
Greenough, W. T. 474, *479, 481*
Greenwood, J. D. 134, *140*
Gregg, M. 43, 44, 45, *53*
Greider, W. 136, *140*
Griffin, P. 389, 396, *413*
Griffin, S. A. 79, 91, *97*, 506, 507, *512*
Griffin, T. 195, *199*
Grossen, M. 355, *367*
Grusec, J. E. 361, 362, *365*
Gunnar, M. 31, 52, *53, 367*
Gurwitsch, A. 539, *562*
Gustavsson, E. 582, *591*

Gutman, H. G. 772, 777, *780*, *781*

Habermas, J. 347
Hacking, I. 21, 23, *26*, 111, *114*
Haertel, E. H. 86, *97*
Haertel, G. D. 610, *619*
Hagtvet-Eriksen, B. 580, *591*
Haith, M. 121, *143*
Halász, L. 554, *563*
Hall, G. S. 100, 101, 103–105, 108, 109, 111, *114*, 116, 152, 515, *532*
Hall, N. 135, *137*, 174, *199*
Hall, W. S. 596, 598, 601, *615*, *616*, *617*
Halliday, M. A. K. 236, *255*
Hallpike, C. R. 515, 519, *532*
Hammill, D. 119, *140*
Hammill, D. D. 132, *140*
Hammond, K. 131, *137*
Hanlon, C. 164, *169*, 316, *321*
Hansen, V. R. 203, *224*
Harding, C. G. 695, *705*
Harding, L. 124, 127, *137*
Harkness, A. R. 131, *137*
Harkness, S. 369, *387*
Harlan, D. 775, *781*
Harper, J. 118, 120, *140*
Harré, R. 632, *643*
Harrington, S. 392
Harris, A. J. 127, 133, *140*
Harris, L. 43, *54*
Harris, M. 315, *321*
Harris, P. 647, *679*
Harris, P. L. 13, 20, *25*, 79, 95, 153, 158, 160, *169*, 486, *511*, 593, *615*, 635, *643*
Harris, W. T. 395
Harvey, D. 767, 772, *781*
Harvey, D. O. 93, *97*
Harwood, D. 38, *53*
Haskell, T. 770, *781*
Haste, H. 588, *590*
Hatano, G. 674, *680*, 683, 686–690, 692–698, 702–705, *706*, *707*, 739, *762*
Hauser, M. D. 286, 287, 291, *298*, 374, *385*
Haviland, J. M. 258, *272*
Hayek, F. A. 520, 521, *532*
Hayes, J. R. 77, *97*, *169*, *321*
Hayes, N. A. 630, *643*
Hays, T. 653, *681*
Hearst, E. 292, *299*
Heath, S. B. 32, 34, *54*, 731, *763*
Heaven, R. K. 127, *144*
Hedges, L. V. 389, *412*
Heller, J. I. 89, *98*
Heltne, P. 372, *387*
Hembree, R. 270, *272*
Hemphill, L. 3, 178, 187, 195, *199*, *200*
Henley, N. 665, *681*
Herdt, G. H. 365, *366*, 381, *386*, *387*, *432*
Hersch, R. 458, *762*
Hessler, G. L. 127, 128, *140*
Hewes, D. 43, *54*
Hewitt, J. 503, 511, *513*
Hewitt, J. P. 348, *366*
Heyes, C. M. 278, 279, *299*
Hickling, A. 648, *681*
Hicks, D. 195, *199*
Hidi, S. 269, *272*

Higgins, E. T. 363, *366*
Hikami, K. 287, *299*
Hilgard, E. 149, 152, 161, *170*
Hilgrad, E. R. 534, *562*
Hill, P. S. 104, 105, 111, *114*
Hilliard, A. 129, *140*
Hilton, P. 732, *764*
Hinton, G. E. 76, 77, 88, *97*, *98*
Hirsch, E. D. 63, 64, *74*
Hirsch, E. D., Jr. 501, *512*
Hirschfeld, L. A. 311, *321*, *432*, *619*, 621, 642, 643, *644*, 645, 647, *679*, 681, 688, 694, *705*, *706*
Hirsh-Pasek, K. 124, *146*
Hirst, P. H. 765, *781*
Hjelmslev, L. 236
Hodgson, V. 544, *562*
Hoffman, M. L. 362, *366*
Hogbin, H. I. 380, *386*
Hohmann, M. 609, *617*
Hoien, T. 121, *141*
Holahan, J. M. 120, *144*
Holdaway, D. 174, 175, *199*
Holland, D. 357, *366*, 415, *432*, 616, 741, *763*
Holligan, C. 123, 124, *141*
Hollinger, D. 768, *781*
Holt, L. K. 124, *142*
Holt, T. 767, *781*
Holton, G. 51, *54*
Homer, B. 600, 601, *615*, *617*
Hoover, W. 124, *146*
Horn, M. 102, 109, *115*
Hough, W. 651, *681*
Hounsell, D. 20, *26*, 544, *562*, *563*, *564*
Howard, A. 379, *386*
Hoyles, C. 760, *763*
Hudson, J. 195, *199*
Hudson, W. H. 528, *532*
Hughes, M. 177, 189, 197, *201*
Hull, C. 75, *97*
Hull, D. 675, *681*
Hume, D. 75, *97*, 647, *681*
Humphreys, L. G. 126, *141*
Hundeide, K. 567, *591*
Hunn, E. 652, 653, 655, *681*
Hunt, E. 471, *479*
Hunt, J. McV. 471, *479*
Husserl, E. 536
Hymes, D. 236
Hynd, G. S. 121, *141*, *143*
Hyon, S. 195, *199*

Inagaki, K. 674, *680*, 683, 684, 686–690, 692–694, 696, 697, 698, 701–705, *706*, *707*, 739, *762*
Ingold, T. *298*, *300*, *322*, 370, *386*
Ingram, T. 122, *141*
Inhelder, B. 639, *643*
Isaac, G. L. 314, *321*
Isaacs, S. 740, *763*
Isen, A. M. 269, *272*
Iser, W. 60, *74*
Itani, J. 303, *321*

Jackson, B. 354, *366*
Jacobs, J. E. 345, *365*
Jacobs, M. 673, *681*
Jacobson, K. 625, 645, *682*
James, W. 71, 100, 102, 103, 105, *115*, 150, 151, *170*

Jameson, F. T. 772, *781*
Jay, E. 132, *143*
Jelinek, A. J. 313, 315, *321*
Jenkins, J. M. 260, 261, *272*, 474, *480*, 602, *615*
Jenkins, K. 774, 775, *781*
Jeyifous, S. 649, *681*
Johansson, B. 557, *562*
Johansson, J.-E. 566, *591*
John-Steiner, V. *432*, *481*, 533, *708*
Johnson, C. N. 600, *617*, *619*
Johnson, D. 458, *682*
Johnson, D. J. 120, *141*
Johnson, K. 553, *562*
Johnson, K. E. 701, *707*
Johnson, M. 486, 496, *512*
Johnson, S. 688, *708*
Johnson-Laird, P. N. 268, *273*, 497, *512*, 595, *617*
Johnston, M. 408, *413*
Johnston, P. H. 220, *224*
Johnston, R. S. 123, 124, *141*
Jorm, A. 120, 125, *141*, *143*
Jouventin, P. 287, *299*
Just, M. A. 126, *138*

Kaczala, C. M. 354, *366*
Kafka, F. 445, 447
Kagan, D. 607, *617*
Kagan, J. 31, *54*
Kagan, S. L. 590
Kahneman, D. 131, *141*
Kaiser, M. K. 622, 630, *643*
Kalantzis, M. 255
Kalish, C. W. 685, 686, *707*
Kalmar, D. A. 3, 441, 457, *458*, *459*
Kamhi, A. 135, *141*
Kamhi, A. G. 135, *141*
Kamii, C. 94, 97
Kammen, M. 772, 773, *781*
Kant, I. 77, 78, 97, 647, *681*
Kao, S. F. 131, *147*
Kaplan, B. 34, *55*, 415, *432*
Karmiloff-Smith, A. 34, *54*, 153, *170*, 196, *199*, 634, 635, 636, *643*
Karplus, R. 94, 97
Kasetani, M. 701, *707*
Katz, L. 120, *137*, *139*, 566, *591*
Kaufmann, W. 79, 97, *532*
Kavale, K. 117, *140*
Kavale, K. A. 120, *141*
Kavanagh, J. F. 119, 129, 132, 133, *141*
Kavanau, J. L. 319, *321*
Kawamura, S. 303, *321*
Kay, C. 595, 598, *617*
Kaye, K. 383, *386*
Keane, M. T. J. 272
Keating, D. P. 3, 94, 97, 461–463, 465–478, *479*, *480*
Keeble, S. 295, *299*, 311, *322*
Keefer, C. 200
Keenan, T. 476, *480*
Keil, F. 4, 53, 154, 162, *170*, 311, *321*, 621, 622, 624, 629, 633, 637, 638, *644*, 647–649, 658, *681*, *682*, 683, 684, 686, 688, 693–696, *707*, *708*
Kekule, A. 628, *644*
Keller, G. 445
Kelly, K. 473, *479*
Kelly, M. 516, *533*

Kember, D. 553, *562*
Kesby, J. 678, *681*
Kessen, W. 37, *54*, 108, *115*, 344, 516
Ketron, J. 129, *145*
Kett, J. F. 350, *366*
Kiecolt-Glaser, J. K. 474, *480*
Kimberling, W. J. 121, *144*
King, P. M. 133, *141*
Kipman, D. 79, 99
Kirkpatrick, J. 383, *386*
Kirson, D. 121, *143*
Kitchener, K. S. 133, *141*
Kitcher, P. 130, *141*, 761, *763*
Klahr, D. 163, *170*, 511
Klerfelt, A. 582, 584, 589, *591*, *592*
Kliebard, H. M. 100, 103, 106, 113, *115*, 394, 395, 396, *413*
Kliegl, R. 123, *142*
Klug, F. 270, *272*
Knight, R. 346, 355, *365*
Kochanska, G. 346, 347, 358, 360, *366*
Koehler, W. 285, *299*, 308, *321*
Koelling, R. A. 287, *299*
Koffka, K. 454, *459*
Kohlberg, L. 28, 30, *54*, *169*
Köhler, W. 285, *289*, 308, *321*
Kohn, A. 395, *413*
Kondo, H. 697, *707*
Konner, M. 378, 380, *386*
Konner, M. J. 315, 316, *322*
Kopcke, K.-M. 654, *682*
Korat, O. 206, *224*
Kotovsky, L. 625, *642*
Krauss, R. M. 604, *617*
Kremer, K. E. 162, *170*
Kress, G. R. 3, 4, 231, 234, *255*
Kripke, S. 675, *681*
Krist, H. 622, *644*
Kristeva, J. 354, *366*
Kritchevsky, M. *54*, 55
Kruger, A. 593, 610, *619*
Kruger, A. C. 3, 12, 13, 24, *27*, *300*, 370–372, 383–385, *387*, 463, *481*
Kruk, R. 118, *147*
Krumhansl, C. 38, *54*
Kuczynski, L. 346, 347, 358, 359, 360, 361, *366*
Kuhn, D. 131, *141*, 412, 503, *512*, 684, *707*, 777–779, *781*
Kuhn, T. S. 19, 22, *26*, 85, 86, 97, 527, *532*
Kummer, H. 305, *322*
Kunda, Z. 131, *141*
Kunen, S. 769, *781*
Kyllonen, P. C. 601, *616*

Labuda, M. 121, *139*
Lacasa, P. 399, 410, *414*
Lagemann, E. C. 6, 51, 101, *115*
Lai, C. 131, *137*
Lakatos, I. 86, 97, 757, *763*
Lakoff, G. 255, 486, 489, 496, *512*
Lalonde, C. E. 602, *617*
Lamarck, J.-B. 658, *681*
Lame Deer, J. 381, *386*
Lamon, M. 92, *98*, 513
Lampert, M. 4, 15, 81, 89, 97, 505, 507, 508, 731, 732, 734–737, 741, 744, 745, 747, 757, 760, 761, *763*

Lamphere, L. 397, *413*
Lancy, D. F. 501, *512*
Landau, B. 43, 54, 158, *170*
Langer, J. 94, *97*
Langer, S. 33, *54*
Laqueur, T. 771, *781*
Large, B. 124, 125, *139*
Larkin, J. H. 77, *97*, 727, *730*
Larner, M. 609, *618*
Larsen, P. J. 121, *141*
Larsen, S. 119, *140*
Latour, B. 17, *26*, 439, *459*
Laurillard, D. 544, *562*
Lave, J. 81, *97*, 129, *143*, 369, 373, 379, *386*, 389, 390, 399, 411, *413*, 464, 476, *480*, 481, 506, *512*, *513*
Layton, J. R. 154, *169*, *171*
Layton, R. 156, 167, *171*
LeCompte, M. D. 391, *412*
Leach, E. 519, *532*
Leach, J. 761, *762*, *780*
Lee, P. J. 765, 774, 775, 778, *779*, *781*
Lee, S.-Y. 259, 262, 267, *273*
Leekam, S. R. 599, 600, *617*, *618*, *619*
Leigh, J. 119, *140*
Leinhardt, G. 765, *781*
Leinhardt, M. 43–45, *53*
Lendon, R. 358, *367*
Lenneberg, E. 154, *170*
Lensmire, T. 759, *763*
Leonard, R. 359, 360, *366*
Leont'ev, A. 175, *200*
Lerner, J. 117, *141*
Leroi-Gourhan, A. 315, *322*
Leslie, A. 628, *644*, 647, *681*
Leslie, A. M. 165, *170*, 295, *299*, 308, 311, *322*
Lesser, R. 133, *141*
Levin, H. 202, 217, *224*
Levin, I. 206, *224*
LeVine, R. 196, *200*, *366*
LeVine, S. 196, *200*
Levine, J. 37, *54*
Levine, J. M. 129, *143*, 474, *480*
Levstik, L. S. 765, 767, 770, *780*, *781*
Lewin, K. 218, *224*, 436, *459*
Lewis, M. 258, *272*
Lewis, M. D. 476, *480*
Leyhausen, P. 304, *322*
Liben, L. 43, 44, *54*
Liberman, I. 120, *139*
Lieven, E. 176, *200*
Light, P. 602, *617*
Liker, J. K. 133, *138*
Limongelli, L. 283, 285, 289, 295, 296, *299*, *300*
Lin, A. C. 284, *299*
Lindfors, J. W. 218, *224*
Lindgren, S. D. 127, *141*
Linnaeus, C. 658, 673, 674, 678, *681*
List, J. A. 471, 472, 476, *480*
Lloyd, G. E. R. 525, 526, *532*, 647, *681*
Locke, J. 29, 46, *681*
Logie, R. H. 124, *137*, *272*
Lomas, T. 768, 771, 778, *781*
Lombard, A. D. 157, *170*
Lopez, A. 661, 668, 677, *681*
Lotman, Yu. M. 424–426, 428, 429, *432*
Lowenthal, D. 765–767, 773, *781*

Lubeck, S. 111, *115*
Lubomudrov, C. 408, *413*
Luchins, A. S. 634, *644*
Lundberg, I. 121, *141*
Lutz, C. 381, *386*
Lybeck, L. 581, *591*
Lynch, E. 654, 677, *680*
Lyon, G. R. 117, 125, 128, *142*
Lyotard, J.-F. 530, *532*

Macaruso, P. 127, *143*
MacIntyre, A. 526, *532*
MacLean, D. J. 472, 475–477, *480*
Maclean, M. 123, *138*
Maclean, R. 120, *141*, *143*
MacLeod, C. 270, *273*
Macomber, J. 625, *645*, *682*
Madsen, R. 758, *762*
Maher, A. 389, 396, *414*
Maher, C. 79, *98*
Mahoney, M. 776, *781*
Mair, L. P. 381, *386*
Mallory, B. L. 111, *115*
Mandler, J. 34, *54*, 158, *169*
Mandler, J. M. *644*, 648, *681*
Manis, F. R. 123, 124, *142*
Maratsos, M. 31, *52*, *53*
Maratsos, M. P. 600, *617*, *707*
Margolis, H. 489, *512*
Margules, J. 43, *54*
Markman, E. M. 622, 625, *642*, *643*
Marks, I. 666, *681*
Marris, P. 400, *413*
Marsden, D. 354, *366*
Marshall. R. 121, *141*
Martin, L. L. *272*, *273*
Martin, W. B. W. 358, 363, *366*
Martini, M. 383, *386*
Marton, F. 4, 11, 20, *26*, 536, 544, 547, 553, 554, 556–560, *562–564*, 565, 568, 583, 588, *591*
Marvin, R. S. 600, *617*
Maslow, A. 101
Mason, A. 122, *141*
Massey, C. M. 685, *707*
Mathews, A. 270, 272, *273*
Matthews, D. J. 476, *480*
Matthews, R. 120, *141*, *143*
Matusov, E. 369, 373, *387*, 390, 398, 400, 403, 406, *412*, *413*, *414*
Matz, M. 430, *432*
Maughan, B. 261, 265, *273*
Maurice, D. 581, *591*
Maxwell, K. 773, *782*
Mayer, J. D. 294, *300*
Mayhew, K. C. 106, 107, *115*
Maynard-Smith, J. 314, *322*
Mayr, E. 314, *322*, 646, *681*
McCabe, A. 198, *199*, *200*
McCann, C. D. 363, *366*
McCarthey, S. 197, *200*
McCarthy, R. 678, *682*
McClelland, J. 35, *54*
McClelland, J. L. 76, 77, *97*, *98*, 489, *513*
McCloskey, M. 622, 630, *643*, *644*, 713, *730*
McCormick, M. 685, 686, *707*
McDermott, J. 727, *730*
McDermott, R. P. 391, *413*

McFarland, H. 37, 54
McGee, R. 122, 143, 144
McGerr, M. 768, 782
McGill Franzen, A. 126, 142
McGrew, W. 372, 386, 387
McKeough, A. 479, 602, 617
McLaughlin, T. 176, 200
McLoughlin, V. 123, 146
McLuhan, M. 486
McNaughton, S. 214, 224
McNew, S. 596, 615
McNutt, G. 119, 140
McRobbie, C. 392, 413
Mead, G. H. 28, 54, 71, 417–419, 432, 754, 763, 768
Mead, M. 353, 366, 378, 381, 386
Meck, E. 643, 685, 690, 705
Medin, D. 167, 170
Medin, D. L. 622, 644
Medin, M. 654, 658, 661, 676, 677, 680, 681, 682
Mehan, J. 352, 355, 358, 363, 366
Meichenbaum, D. 98, 602, 617
Meisels, S. 156, 157, 171
Meltzoff, A. 297, 299, 594, 617
Meltzoff, A. N. 158, 171
Menna, R. 477, 480
Merkel, I. 507, 513
Merleau-Ponty, M. 65, 74
Merriman, W. E. 471, 472, 476, 480
Mervis, C. B. 682, 701, 707
Metalsky, G. L. 266, 273
Meunchow, S. 157, 172
Michaels, S. 178, 197, 200
Miles, M. B. 395, 413
Millar, R. 557, 558, 559, 564
Miller, F. 476, 477, 480
Miller, G. A. 76, 98, 153, 165, 171, 595, 617
Millman, J. 131, 139
Mills, P. E. 117, 135, 139
Minami, M. 198, 200
Mineka, S. 280, 284, 285, 294, 299
Minick, N. 364, 394, 413, 762
Mink, L. 765, 782
Minstrell, J. 727, 730
Mintzes, J. J. 622, 644
Miscione, J. L. 600, 617
Mistry, J. 12, 26
Mistry, J. J. 396, 397, 414
Miyake, N. 695, 706
Modell, J. 772, 780
Moll, L. M. 80, 98
Montangero, J. 581, 590, 591
Moore, B. R. 285, 299
Moore, C. 601, 602, 617
Moore, J. L. 81, 97
Moore, M. 297, 299
Moore, M. K. 158, 171
Moorman, G. 176, 200
More, H. 527, 532
Morita, E. 702, 707
Morphett, M. V. 152, 156, 171
Morris, R. 135, 137
Morrison, F. J. 118, 123, 142
Morrison, S. R. 472, 480
Morrison, T. 58, 62, 74
Mortimore, P. 261, 262, 270, 273
Moser, J. M. 89, 95

Mosier, C. 12, 26, 395–397, 413, 414
Motoyoshi, M. 684, 707
Muenchow, S. 111, 116
Mulder, G. 126, 142
Mulder, L. 126, 142
Munkur, B. 666, 681
Murphy, G. L. 621, 642, 644, 658, 682
Murphy, J. 26, 300
Murray, B. 123, 124, 144
Mustard, J. F. 94, 97, 461–463, 465, 480

Nagel, T. 21, 26, 434, 459
Nagell, K. 286, 299
Nagle, A. 556, 563
Nagy, W. E. 598, 617
Nathan, R. G. 124, 145
Neal, C. J. 80, 96
Neale, D. C. 502, 513
Needham, A. 625, 642
Neisser, U. 129, 142, 387, 621, 644
Nelson, K. 175, 200, 458, 633, 644
Nemirovsky, R. 33, 53, 430, 432
Nesdale, A. R. 124, 146
Neuman, D. 580, 581, 585, 591
New, R. S. 111, 115
Newell, A. 35, 54, 76, 98, 486
Newman, D. 389, 396, 413
Newman, J. 174, 200
Newman, S. E. 609, 616, 728, 729
Newport, E. 154, 171
Nicholson, T. 206, 224
Nietzsche, F. 529, 532
Nisbett, R. E. 131, 141, 142, 509, 512, 631, 644
Nishida, T. 281, 299, 305
Noddings, N. 79, 98
Norman, D. 639, 644
Norris, C. 531, 533
Norton-Griffiths, M. N. 304, 322
Noss, R. 760, 763
Novak, J. D. 498, 512
Novak, M. A. 300, 308, 322
Novey, E. 121, 143
Novick, P. 770, 771, 772, 782
Noyes, C. R. 597, 607, 618
Nozick, R. 130, 142
Nye, C. 120, 141

O'Brien, R. G. 600, 617
O'Loughlin, M. 777, 778, 779, 781
O'Reilly, A. W. 621, 643
Oakes, J. 132, 142
Oakes, P. 608, 617
Oakhill, J. 123, 142
Oakley, A. 353, 366
Oates, R. E. 205, 223
Oatley, K. 3, 14, 260, 267, 268, 272, 273, 343, 344, 474, 480
Ochs, E. 176, 178, 196, 198, 200, 301, 366, 378, 387, 435, 459
Ochs, E. E. 350, 351, 352, 366
Odegaard, H. 121, 141
Offord, D. R. 260, 273, 478
Ogden, C. K. 54, 519, 533
Ogilvie, M. 477, 481
Ohlsson, S. 507, 512
Ohmori, S. 692, 707
Okamoto, Y. 79, 95, 96

Olson, D. R.　2, 13, 16, 20, *25, 26,* 30, 34, 51, *54,* 79, 81, 94, *95, 98,* 113, 153, 158–160, *169, 171,* 244, 255, 344, *344,* 372, 384, *387,* 420, 424, *432, 458,* 464, *480,* 486, 510, *511,* 522, 526, *533,* 593, 594, 601, 603, 605, 610, 611, *615,* 631, 642, *644,* 704, 740, *763*
Olson, R.　123, *142*
Olson, R. K.　118, 120–124, 127, *142, 143*
Olsson, L. E.　579, *590*
Olver, R. R.　34, *52*
Omanson, S. F.　505, *512*
Ong, W.　255, 526
Ortony, A.　*432,* 598, *618, 645, 708*
Overton, W.　79, 94, *98, 458*
Owen, D.　129, *142*

Paisner, M.　133, *141*
Palincsar, A. S.　437, *459,* 728, *729*
Pappas, C.　198, *200*
Pappas, C. C.　767, 770, *781*
Parke, R. D.　412, 772, *780*
Parker, C. A.　133, *141*
Parks, K. A.　308, *322*
Parsons, J. E.　354, *366*
Pascual-Leone, J.　477, *481*
Passeron, J.-C.　355, *364*
Patrick, K.　561, *563*
Pauls, D.　121, *143*
Pea, R.　87, *98*
Pea, R. D.　20, *26*
Pearson, D.　213, *224*
Peindich, K.　37, *54*
Peirce, C. S.　252, *255*
Pelletier, J.　4, 13, 158, 607, 609–611, *618*
Pennington, B. F.　120–123, *142, 143, 144*
Penrose, R.　434, *459*
Penuel, W.　3
Pepper, S. C.　51, *54,* 94, *98*
Perfetti, C. A.　123, 127, *137, 142, 143*
Perkins, D. N.　49, 126, 129, 132, *143, 147*
Perner, J.　20, *26, 171,* 308, *322, 323,* 599, 600, 603, *618, 619,* 629, *645*
Perret-Clermont, A.-N.　355, *366, 367*
Perrone, V.　49
Peters, R.　758, *763*
Peterson, P.　731, *763*
Phelps, E.　384, *387*
Philips, D.　516, *533*
Piaget, J.　2, 19, 28–32, 50, 51, *54,* 78–80, 85, 86, 88, 90, 94, *98,* 101, 153, 154, 219, 285, *300,* 325, 326, 338, *344,* 346, 356, *366,* 400, 415, 418–422, 425, 426, 427, 428, 431, *432,* 436, 486, 514, 515, 520, 634, 637, 639, *643, 644,* 686, 697, *707*
Piatelli-Palmerini, M.　153, *171*
Piechowski, M.　38, *54*
Pinker, S.　158, *171*
Plomin, R.　471, 474, 478, *480*
Pogrow, S.　217, *224*
Polkinghorne, D. E.　768, *782*
Pollatsek, A.　124, *137*
Polson, D.　405, *413*
Polya, G.　757, 758, *763*
Popper, K. R.　21–23, *26,* 493, 494, 499–501, 504–507, 510, 511, *512*
Porter, M. E.　94, *98*
Posey, D.　678, *682*

Posner, G.　739, *763*
Povinelli, D. J.　291, 295, 296, *300,* 308, *322*
Powys, A.　127, *144*
Pramling, I.　534, 550, 554–556, 560, *563* 566–571, 577, 578, 581, 582, 584, 588, 589, *590, 591, 592*
Premack, A. J.　303, *322, 642, 644*
Premack, D.　291, 296, *300,* 303, 308, 309, 311, 316, 319, *321, 322, 642, 644*
Pressley, M.　86, *98, 617*
Pribram, K. H.　76, *98*
Price, E. C.　288, *300*
Pritchard, J. B.　342, *344*
Proffitt, D. R.　622, 630, *643*
Prosser, M.　557–559, 561, *564*
Prusky, G.　471, *479*
Puleo, V.　608, *618*
Purcell-Gates, V.　177, *200*
Putnam, H.　434, *459,* 675, *682*
Putnam, R.　731, *763*
Pylyshyn, Z. W.　486, *512*

Quay, H. C.　261, *271*
Quine, W. V. O.　625, *645*
Quinn, N.　357, *366,* 371, 372, *387,* 415, *432, 616,* 741, *763*

Rabinow, P.　93, *98*
Rack, J.　118, 121, 122, 123, *142, 143*
Rack, J. P.　123, 124, *143*
Radzikhovskii, L. A.　426, *432*
Ramsden, P.　552, 559, *562, 564*
Range, D. C.　155, *169, 171*
Rashotte, C. A.　123, *146*
Rasinski, T.　174, *201*
Ratner, H.　12, 13, 24, *27,* 593, *619*
Ratner, H. H.　370–372, 383, 385, *387,* 463, *481*
Raum, O.　381, *387*
Raven, P.　657, *680, 682*
Ravitch, D.　113, *115*
Reber, A.　630, *645*
Reddy, M. J.　423, 425, *432*
Reed, J. C.　127, *143*
Rees, E.　77, *96*
Reese, E.　507, *512*
Reeve, R.　569, *590*
Regmi, M.　553, *564*
Renderer, B.　441, 457, *458*
Reskin, L.　125, *138*
Resnick, D. P.　213, *224*
Resnick, L.　31, *54,* 87, 93, *97, 199, 365, 366*
Resnick, L. B.　131, *142, 143,* 213, *224,* 474, 476, *480,* 505, *512, 616,* 705, 729, *763*
Revlin, R.　131, *139*
Reynolds, C. R.　118, 120, *140, 143*
Richards, B.　176, *199, 200*
Richards, D. D.　686, 698, *706, 707*
Richards, I. A.　38, *54*
Richards, P.　761, *763*
Richards, R. J.　516, *533*
Richman, L. C.　127, *141*
Richmond, G.　508, *512*
Riley, M. S.　89, *98*
Rips, L. J.　597, *618,* 621, *645,* 651, 665, 668, *682*
Ristau, C. A.　154, *171*
Rittenhouse, M.　4, 15, 89, 505, 507
Robenhagen, O.　203, *224*

Robinson, E. J. 363, *366*
Robinson, H. 608, *618*
Rock, I. 44, *54*
Rodman, H. 361, *367*
Rogers, P. 768, 769, *782*
Roget, P. M. 595, 597, *618*, 740
Rogoff, B. 3, 11, 12, *26*, 32, *54*, 80, 81, *98*, 129,
    143, 165, *171*, 292, *300*, 367, 369, 370, 373, 379,
    387, 389, 390, 395–398, 400, 403, 406,
    410–412, *412*, *413*, *414*, 420, *432*, 464, 476,
    481, 490, *513*, 568, *592*
Rohlen, T. P. 94, *98*, 491, *513*
Romberg, B. 445, *459*
Romer, P. M. 493, *513*
Rorty, R. 93, *98*, 530, 531, *533*
Rosaldo, M. Z. 435, 438, *459*
Rosch, E. 653–655, 668, *682*
Roschelle, J. 729, *730*
Rosen, G. 121, *140*
Rosenberg, M. 465, *481*
Rosenberg, N. 94, *98*
Rosengren, K. S. 685, 686, *707*
Ross, D. 97, 103, *115*, *479*, *480*
Ross, G. 81, *99*
Ross, L. 131, *142*, 631, *644*
Roth, K. J. 502, *513*
Roubinek, D. L. 155, *169*, *171*
Rourke, B. P. 120, *139*
Rousseau, J. J. 46, 64, 150, 151, 155, 164, *171*, 608,
    618
Rubenstein, J. 88, *99*
Rubenstein, J. H. 732, *764*
Rubinstein-Reich, L. 568, *592*
Ruddell, R. 175, 176, *200*
Rumelhart, D. E. 35, *54*, 76, 77, *97*, *98*, 489, *513*
Rumsey, S. 44, *55*
Russel, T. 581, *592*
Russon, A. E. 286, *300*, 385
Rutter, M. 118–120, 122, 133, *143*, 259, 260–262,
    271, *273*
Ryan, E. B. 118, 123, 124, *144*
Ryan, S. M. 123, *138*
Ryle, G. 16, *26*, 58, 59, 64, 71, *74*

Säljö, R. 539–541, 543, 544, 546, 547, 553, 556,
    557, *563*, *564*, 591
Salmon, W. C. 632, 638, *645*
Salovey, P. 294, *300*
Salzman, P. C. 357, *367*
Samuels, M. L. 595, 598, *617*
Sansom, B. 435, *459*
Samuel, R. 772, 773, *782*
Sapir, E. 236
Saracho, O. N. *592*, 608, *619*
Sartre, J.-P. 341, *344*
Saussure, F. de 236, *256*
Savage-Rumbaugh, E. S. 12, *26*, 290, *300*, 384, *387*
Saville, K. 521, *532*
Scanlon, D. 123, *146*
Scarborough, H. S. 135, *143*
Scardamalia, M. 4, 13, 20, 25, *26*, 77, 92, 95, *98*,
    469, 477, *481*, 488, 503, 507, 511, *511*, *513*, 636,
    642
Scarpati, S. 124, *137*
Schaeffer, R. W. 319, *322*
Schank, C. C. 633, *645*
Schatschneider, C. 120, 135, *146*

Scheffler, I. 128, *143*, 758, *763*
Scheines, R. 473, *479*
Schenk, S. M. 547, *564*
Schieffelin, B. B. 176, *198*, *200*, 352, *366*, *367*, 383,
    387
Schlesinger, A., Jr. 777, *782*
Schlossman, S. L. 109, *115*
Schmit, C. 346, *367*
Schoenfeld, A. H. 758, *763*
Schoenfeld, D. 12, *26*
Scholnick, E. K. 598, *618*
Schubauer-Leonie, M. L. 355, *367*
Schuler, M. 476, *480*
Schutz, A. 71, *74*
Schwanenflugel, P. J. 597, 601, 607, 616, *618*
Schwartz, B. 626, *645*
Schwartz, S. 608, *618*, 675, *682*
Schwarz, N. 269, *273*
Schweinhart, L. 566, *592*, 609, *618*
Scott, J. 771, 777, *782*
Scott, P. 761, *762*, *780*
Scotto, P. 285, *298*
Scribner, S. 34, *54*, 55, *432*, 464, *479*, *481*, 488,
    513, *533*, 708
Scripp, L. 38, 40, 41, *52*
Scriven, M. 215, *224*
Seagrim, G. 358, *367*
Searle, J. R. 434, *459*, 596, 597, *618*
Seeley, L. 516, *533*
Segal, J. 126, 129, *147*
Seixas, P. 4, 21, 768–771, 775, *782*
Seligman, M. 668, *682*
Semrud-Clikeman, M. 121, *141*, *143*
Senf, G. F. 117, 133, *143*
Senge, P. M. 465, *481*
Sepkoski, J. 675, *681*
Sergent, J. 37, *55*
Serpell, R. 705, *707*
Sevcik, R. A. *26*, *300*
Sexton, M. E. 695, *705*
Seyfarth, R. M. 12, *16*, 286, 288, 293, 296, *298*, 299
Shafrir, U. 477, *481*
Shankweiler, D. 120, 127, *139*, *143*
Shannon, P. 174, *200*
Shapira, E. C. 358, *367*
Shapiro, L. 195, *199*
Shapiro, M. S. 105, *115*
Sharan, S. 607, *619*
Share, D. 120, *141*
Share, D. L. 123, 124, *143*
Shatz, M. 596, 598, *618*, 686, *705*
Shaw, C. 471, *479*
Shaw, J. C. 76, *98*
Shaw, R. 489, *513*
Shaywitz, B. A. 120, *139*, *144*
Shaywitz, S. E. 120, *139*, *144*
Shell, P. 126, *138*
Shemilt, D. 765, 770, 771, 777, *782*
Shepard, L. 118, 119, *144*, 155, 156, 157, *169*, *171*
Shephard, L. 206, 208–213, 215, *224*
Sherin, B. 729
Sherman, G. 121, *140*
Shilony, T. 25, *27*, 429, *432*, 597, 607, *619*, 622,
    645
Shrager, J. 77, *98*
Shweder, R. A. 365, *366*, 369, 371, *387*, *432*, 435,
    459

Siefert, K. 609, *618*
Siegal, M. 688, *708*
Siegel, A. 103, *115*
Siegel, L. S. 118, 120, 123–125, 127, 131, 133, *144, 145*
Siegler, R. S. 77, 79, 91, *97, 98,* 506, 507, *512,* 686, 698, *706, 707*
Sigg, H. 295, *300*
Silber, S. 596, *618*
Silberman, C. E. 391, 395, 396, 400, *414*
Silberstein, C. 4
Silva, P. A. 122, 125, *144*
Silverstein, S. 554, *564,* 583, *592*
Simmons, B. 156, 167, *171*
Simon, D. 727, *730*
Simon, H. A. 76, 77, *98,* 267, *273,* 727, *730*
Simon, R. 766, 773, *782*
Simpson, G. 646, *682*
Singer, E. 566, *592*
Sipay. E. R. 127, 133, *140*
Sizer, T. 47, *55,* 112, 113
Skinner, B. F. 75, *98,* 152
Sleeper, M. 769, *782*
Sloboda, J. 38, *51, 52, 53, 55*
Sloboda, J. A. 53, *643, 705*
Slovic, P. 131, *141*
Smetana, J. G. 347, 356, 359, *365, 367*
Smid, H. 126, *142*
Smith, C. 622, *645*
Smith, D. R. 81, *97*
Smith, E. 502, *513,* 677, 661, *681, 682*
Smith, F. 176, *200,* 566, *592*
Smith, G. 127, *144*
Smith, J. P. 729, *730*
Smith, M. A. 261, *272*
Smith, M. L. 155, 156, *171*
Smith, R. *200,* 435, *459*
Smith, S. A. 121, *143*
Smith, S. D. 121, *143, 144*
Smith Lea, N. 26
Smolensky, P. 35, *55*
Smythies, J. R. 532
Snow, C. 3, 176, 178, 187, 188, 197, *198, 200,* 437, *459*
Snowling, M. 123, *138, 140, 144*
Snowling, M. J. 123, *143*
Sodian, B. 601, *618*
Solomon, G. 688, 694, *708*
Souberman, E. *432, 481, 533, 708*
Spacks, P. M. 527, *533*
Spearman, C. 94, *99*
Spelke, E. 43, *54,* 78, 79, *99,* 153, 154, 158, 159, 161, *169, 171,* 295, *300,* 625, 628, *645,* 647, 648, *682,* 686, 690, *695, 705*
Spencer, H. 516, *533*
Sperber, D. *645, 647, 679*
Spindler, E. 87, *99*
Spindler, G. 87, *99*
Spirtes, P. 473, *479*
Spitzer, S. 441, *458*
Spodek, B. 567, *591, 592,* 608, 609, *616, 618, 619*
Spradley, J. P. 741, *763*
Springer, K. 648, *682,* 686, 688, 694, *708*
Staeheli, F. S. 581, *591*
Stahl, S. A. 124, *144*
Stainton, C. 765, *781*

Stallman, A. 213, *224*
Stanley, G. 127, *144*
Stanovich, K. E. 3, 118, 120, 122–128, 130, 131, 133, *144, 145, 224,* 259, *273,* 468
Stanovich, P. 3, 468
Starkey, P. 79, *99*
Stavy, R. 686, 698, 699, *706, 708*
Steele, J. 136, *137*
Steffy, R. 127, *138*
Steinberg, L. 136, *140, 145*
Steinmetz, H. 121, *145*
Stepans, J. 581, *592*
Stern, D. 164, *171*
Sternberg, R. J. *97,* 125, 126, 129, *139, 140, 141, 145,* 471, 477, *481*
Stevens, A. 44, *55, 730*
Stevens, A. L. 497, *512,* 762, *764*
Stevenson, H. W. 259, 262, 263, 264, 267, *273, 274,* 466, *481, 762*
Stevenson, J. 121–124, *140, 145, 146*
Stich, S. 130, 131, *146,* 435, *459*
Stich, S. P. 148, *171,* 485, *513*
Stigler, J. W. 466, *481,* 506, *513,* 758, 761, *763*
Stiles-Davis, J. 43, *54, 55*
Stipek, D. J. 389, *414*
Stock, B. 19, *27*
Stodolsky, S. 355, *367,* 761, *763*
Stokes, R. 348, *366*
Stolba, A. 295, *300*
Stone, A. 440, *458, 762*
Strauss, C. 371, 372, *387*
Strauss, S. 25, *27,* 429, *432,* 597, 607, *619,* 623, *645*
Strickland, C. 103, *115*
Strike, K. 739, *763*
Stringer, C. 464, *481*
Strizich, M. 440, *458*
Stross, B. 649, 653, *682*
Stuebing, K. 120, *139*
Suboski, M. D. 280, 285, *300*
Sugiyama, K. 689, 698, 701, 702, *707*
Sullivan, W. M. 758, *762*
Sulzby, E. *171,* 195, *199*
Suomi, S. J. 471, 474, 478, *481*
Super, C. M. 369, 379, *387*
Svensson, L. 544, 557, *562, 564*
Swales, J. 740, *763*
Swallow, J. 43, *55*
Swanwick, K. 38, *55*
Swidler, A. 758, *762*
Sydow, K. 174, *200*
Szeszulski, P. A. 123, 124, *142*

Tabachnick, B. 607, *616*
Tager-Flusberg, H. *299,* 595, 596, 598, *617, 619*
Tang, W. 769, *781*
Tarule, J. M. 758, *762*
Tate, E. 127, *138*
Taylor, C. *200,* 435, *459*
Taylor, H. G. 120, 135, *146*
Taylor, P. 564, 649, *682*
Teale, W. 174, 175, *200*
Teasley, S. 130, *143*
Teasley, S. D. 474, *480, 705, 763*
Teberosky, A. 223, *255*
Terman, L. M. 94, *99*
Terman, L. S. 471, *481*

Tesser, A. 272, 273
Tharp, R. G. 389, 396, 408, 414
Thelen, D. 771, 782
Thom, D. 108–110, 115
Thompson, E. P. 776, 782
Thompson, L. 471, 474, 480
Thompson, P. 772, 782
Thomson, M. 127, 138, 146
Thorndike, E. L. 75, 99, 100–102, 105, 107, 112, 113, 149, 152
Thorndike, R. L. 126, 146
Tillman, J. 38, 55
Tinbergen, N. 314, 322
Tipton, S. M. 758, 762
Tishman, S. 132, 143
Tizard, B. 177, 189, 197, 201
Tizard, J. 260, 273
Tobin, K. 392, 413
Tobin, W. 113, 115
Tochinsky-Landsmann, L. 206, 224, 679
Tomasello, M. 3, 12, 13, 16, 24, 27, 284, 286, 299, 300, 370–372, 383–385, 385, 387, 463, 481, 593, 602, 605, 609, 610, 619
Tooby, J. 267, 273, 647, 680
Torff, B. 2, 17, 38, 55
Torgesen, J. K. 123, 125, 127, 143, 146, 147
Torney-Purta, J. 552, 564
Torrance, N. 526, 533, 704
Toulmin, S. 435, 436, 459, 460
Tournefort, J. 658, 682
Trachtenberg, A. 768, 771, 782
Treiman, R. 123, 124, 138, 143, 145, 146
Trevarthen, C. 383, 387
Trigwell, K. 561, 564
Trowbridge, J. E. 622, 644
Trudgill, P. 240, 256
Truss, T. J. 119, 129, 132, 133, 141
Tschirgi, J. E. 131, 146
Tse, L. K. 553, 554, 563
Tullberg, A. 560, 564
Tunmer, W. E. 124, 146
Turiel, E. 647, 682
Turner, A. 474, 481
Turner, V. 15, 27
Turvey, M. T. 489, 513
Tversky, A. 131, 141
Tversky, B. 44, 55
Twain, M. 58, 62, 74
Tyack, D. B. 102, 113, 115
Tyler, F. T. 148, 149, 152, 163, 166, 171
Tyler, R. 521, 533
Tyrrell, I. 768, 782

Ulbaek, I. 311, 321
Ulichny, P. 197, 201
Ulrich, L. T. 768, 769, 782
Uttal, D. H. 264, 273

Vacca, J. L. 80, 99
Vacca, R. T. 80, 99, 174, 201
Valsiner, J. 214, 224, 350, 356, 367
Van Huizen, F. 471, 479
Van Orden, G. 121, 143
van Rossum, E. J. 547, 564
VanSledright, B. 765, 766, 782
Vaughn, S. 117, 142, 146
Veinstein, R. 567, 592

Vellutino, F. 118, 123, 127, 146
Vendler, Z. 596, 597, 619
Verdonik, F. 346, 356, 367
Vernant, J.-P. 526, 533
Vernon, P. A. 126, 146, 480
Vinovskis, M. 111, 113, 115
Visalberghi, E. 3, 11, 12, 27, 279, 282, 283, 285, 295, 298, 299, 300
Viscott, D. 37, 55
Vlastos, G. 530, 533
Voloshinov, V. N. 256
Volterra, V. 293, 301
Von Frisch, K. 154, 172
Vosniadou, S. 622, 645, 676, 682, 689, 696, 708
Voss, J. 126, 129, 147
Voss, J. F. 765, 779
Vygotsky, L. S. 2, 28, 32, 34, 55, 80, 81, 86, 99, 256, 265, 274, 369, 370, 383, 387, 415–418, 420, 422, 425–429, 431, 432, 433, 464, 481, 514, 516, 517, 533, 568, 592, 703, 708

Waal, F. de 290, 307, 372, 387
Wagner, M. 125, 138
Wagner, R. K. 123, 126, 129, 145, 146, 147
Waites, B. 129, 139
Walberg, H. J. 610, 619
Walkerdine, V. 177, 201, 345, 367
Wallace, A. 646, 682
Wallace, J. G. 163, 170
Wandersee, J. H. 622, 644
Wanner, E. 158, 170, 198
Warburton, F. 651, 682
Warren, A. 445, 460
Warrington, E. 678, 682
Washburn, A. 630, 644
Washburn, D. A. 295, 301
Washburn, S. L. 314, 322
Washburne, C. 152, 156, 171
Wasserman, E. A. 131, 147
Wassermann, S. 132, 147
Watkins, D. 553, 554, 563, 564
Watson, F. L. 124, 138
Watson, G. 124, 131, 147
Watson, J. 109, 115
Watson, J. S. 75, 99
Watson, R. 3
Watson-Gegeo, K. 197, 201
Watt, D. 581, 592
Watts, I. 527, 533
Wax, N. 686, 698, 699, 706, 708
Weaver, C. 174, 201
Webb, J. 503, 511, 513
Weichbold, V. 296, 301
Weikart, D. P. 157, 172, 566, 567, 589, 592, 609, 617, 618
Weiner, B. 265, 266, 274
Weinstock, J. 346, 367
Wellek, R. 445, 460
Wellman, H. M. 20, 27, 78, 99, 158–160, 162, 170, 172, 308, 322, 596, 599, 600, 615, 617, 618, 619, 621, 622, 625, 627, 629, 643, 645, 647, 680, 682, 683, 694, 708
Wells, C. G. 175, 201, 389, 396, 414
Welsh, P. 38, 40, 52
Wen, Q. F. 553, 554, 556, 562, 564
Wenger, E. 81, 97, 369, 386, 389, 390, 399, 411, 413, 506, 512

Werner, H. 28, 34, 55, 415, *433*
Wertsch, J. V. 3, 175, *200, 201*, 354, 355, *367*, *414*,
    417, 428, *432, 433, 458*, 439, 440, *459*, 514, 516,
    533, 611, *616*
West, C. 66, *74*
West, L. H. T. *562, 763*
Wheatley, B. P. 281, *301*
Wheatley, G. *99*, 507, *513*
Wheelock, L. 104, *115*
Whelan, G. 544, 547–549, 556, *564*
White, C. 3, 11, 165, 412, 490
White, H. 767, 772, *782*
White, J. 44, *55*
White, S. H. 101–103, 106, 113, *115, 116*
Whitehead, A. N. 18, 48, *55*, 344
Whiten, A. 295, *298, 301, 322*, 617, *643*
Whitfield, E. 156, 167, *171*
Whitmore, K. 260, *273*
Wijers, A. 126, *142*
Wiley, D. E. 86, *97*
Wilkening, F. 622, *644*
Williams, S. 122, *143, 144*
Williams-Graneld, P. 589, *592*
Willinsky, J. 174, *201*
Willis, P. 240, *256*, 355, *367*
Willoughby, S. 732, *764*
Willowby, S. 88, *99*
Willows, D. M. 118, *147*
Wilson, D. J. 771, *782*
Wilson, E. O. 303, *322*
Wilson, S. 765, *782*
Wilson, T. 509, *512*
Wimmer, H. 296, *301*, 308, *323*, 599, 600, 603,
    618, 619

Wineburg, S. S. 765, 770, *783*
Winner, E. 38, 45, *55*, 600, *619*
Wise, B. 118, 121, *142*
Wiser, M. 79, *99*, 622, *645, 764*
Witelson, S. 43, *55*
Witkin, H. 31, *55*
Wolf, D. 178, 195, *199*
Wolf, D. P. 34, *53*
Wood, D. 609, *619*
Wood, F. R. 123–125, *139*
Wood, P. K. 133, *141*
Wood, T. 81, *99*, *513*, 732, *762*
Woodruff, G. 291, *300*, 308, 316, *322*
Woodworth, R. S. 488, *513*
Woolgar, S. 17, *26*, 439, *459*
Woolley, H. T. 108, *116*
Wrangham, R. *299*, 305, 372, *386, 387*
Wundt, W. 10, *27*, 105

Yaakobi, D. 607, *619*
Yackel, E. 89, *99*, 507, *513*, 732, *762*
Yerkes, R. M. 305, *323*
Yngvesson, B. 776, *781*
Yuill, N. 600, *619*
Yule, W. 120, 122, *143*
Yuzawa, M. 703, *708*

Zaitchik, D. 601, *618*, 688, *708*
Zenderland, L. 103, *116*
Zigler, E. 111, *116*, 157, *172*, 591
Zinchenko, V. P. 417, *433*
Zolman, J. E. 124, *145*
Zubin, D. 654, *682*

Subject Index

abilities 4, 5, 9–13, 24, 39, 118, 127–128, 131,
  152–155, 176–177, 203, 211, 263, 373, 383,
  603
  cognitive 16–19, 160, 164, 166–168, 241, 257
  intellectual 80–81, 206, 209
  language 196
  learning 217
  mathematical 89
  mental 8, 17–18, 29, 155, 471, 477, 487, 510
  musical 37, 38
  primate 291, 293, 296
  reading and writing 174 *see also* reading ability
  spatial 42–46
Accelerated Schools 217
acceleration 153, 202, 724
  technological/social 464, 767–768
achievement 12, 16, 22, 37, 38, 42–46, 49, 50, 112,
  117–120, 127–128, 132–136, 148, 158, 204,
  207, 209, 248, 257–259, 262–264, 284, 291,
  302, 314, 336, 345, 380, 393–397, 466, 489,
  552–553
activities, endeavors
  academic 263, 490, 496–506, 551, 567, 571,
    588, 601–609
  cognitive 20, 328–329, 476–478, 486, 602
  enculturating 259, 283, 369–370, 372–382
  musical 41
  literacy 175, 198, 202, 208–222
  teaching 13, 104, 106–107, 399–406, 738
  scientific 80, 699
  shared 373, 396, 397, 398, 403–404, 408, 411,
    474
  sociocultural 388, 390, 396, 397, 411
aesthetic, aesthetics, esthetics 45, 46, 57–60, 63, 72,
  246, 303, 317, 319, 320, 727
affect 241, 257–265, 296
African-Americans 91, 754, 770, 777
agency as a concept 32, 162, 233, 670, 692,
  695–696, 776–778
Age of Innocence 28–51
anger 258, 266, 268
anthropomorphism 36, 296, 297
anxiety 73, 102, 257, 258, 261, 268, 270
apprenticeship 16, 34, 39–48, 81, 149, 150, 165,
  192, 379–381, 464, 609, 637, 728
archival 23
Aristotle 9, 17, 436, 438, 517, 525, 557, 630, 647,
  657, 660, 672, 677
arithmetic skills 119
art (as experience) 56–73
Arts PROPEL 41
ascription (non-human) 12
assessment and diagnosis 41, 208–209, 411, 598

assessment, educational 84, 467
attendance 261, 262, 265
attention deficit 199
attitude 64, 67, 69, 151, 157, 165, 257–264, 271,
  341–342, 371–373, 404, 699, 700, 757
attribution theory 265–267
authority, historical 19, 24, 244–245, 268, 500,
  525, 608, 728, 737–739, 770
awareness, tacit 539

basics 88, 353, 395, 466–467, 488
belief
  attribution of 321
  systems 653, 660, 665
beliefs 3–5, 9–25, 48–49, 79, 89, 131, 166–168,
  257, 268, 310–311
  about learning 126, 148, 155, 263, 376–380,
    382, 553, 731, 755, 760
  about the mind 153, 158, 160, 370, 486–487,
    599–614, 622
  shared 4, 25, 630
  tacit 613
  about teaching 50, 210, 217, 382
  understanding of 13, 167, 606, 614
  about the world 316, 334, 353, 494, 503, 529,
    530, 537, 594–597, 622, 628–631, 668, 674,
    696–699, 710–715, 726, 769, 771

causality 30, 79, 204, 235, 295–297, 624, 658, 674,
  683, 689, 691–693, 716–717, 776–777
child-centered education 19, 29, 151, 608, 610
children's theories
  as frameworks 159
  naive 159, 162, 621–641 *see also* theories, naive
  of mind *see* theories of mind
  teaching 11, 353, 355, 602–606
cognitive deficits 125
cognitive revolution 10, 76, 77, 131, 434, 487
cognitive skills 41, 122, 135–136, 154, 384
cognitive stage 2, 28, 78, 83, 90, 153–156, 177,
  206, 267, 325–330, 337, 425–426, 514–516
collaborative learning 20, 93, 372, 373, 464, 469,
  478, 602, 605, 614 *see also* learning
communication, models of 3, 422–424, 430
communicative purpose, shared 197
community of learners 3, 91–92, 388–411, 609
competencies, reading and writing 175, 178, 188,
  191–195, 204–222
conceptual change 78, 160, 557–558, 621, 636,
  695, 700–703, 711, 719, 726, 727
connectionism 487, 489, 490
constructive learner 207, 215, 216

continuity as a concept 68, 173, 295, 629, 638, 771–772
cultural differences 119, 133, 207, 262–263, 303–304, 345, 646, 650–659, 666–678, 683–684, 695–699, 704, 732, 740, 755, 767
cultural learning 79–80, 369–385
culture
  archival function 22, 36, 310
  effects of schooling on 3
  enculturation 3, 11, 15, 34, 35–39, 64, 71, 228–229, 233, 248, 257–260, 369–370, 515–532, 561, 766
  and folk biology 4, 646–678, 683–705
  and folk physics 710
  and folk psychology 10, 12, 148–149, 731
  growth of 3, 16
  and historical understanding 768–770, 778
  of home 264–265, 732
  intentional instruction 370–382
  of learning 497
  literate 193, 226, 228–229, 238, 438
  oral/literate 231,238, 438–456
  and pedagogy 2, 22–25, 34–46, 69, 79–81, 91, 103–106, 164–165, 176, 196, 198, 233, 313–314, 324, 337–341, 347–364, 370–385, 485–511, 515–532, 553–556, 588–589, 593, 609, 667, 731–732, 739, 757–761
  of primates 281–293, 302–321
  of schooling 10, 262, 264–265, 398, 455, 485–511, 755–756
  traditional 16, 302, 637, 646–678
  transformation of 302–303, 463–464
  transmission of 3, 5, 10, 16, 32, 36–46, 279, 302–303, 310, 371–376, 463–478
  understanding of 16
  Western 30, 231, 326–327, 674, 678
curriculum 41, 45, 80, 87–94, 100, 102, 106–113, 151–168, 177, 203–211, 216, 347, 394–396, 399, 401–408, 456, 506, 515, 527, 559, 577–589, 608, 641, 777–778

decentering 338–339
decline
  of empiricism 85
  historical concept of 772–779
deficit model 212
demonstration 12–24, 41, 376, 379, 501, 593, 728
desire 4, 12–16, 66–69, 158–160, 307, 486, 530, 596–598, 629, 647
designed learning 377, 379, 610
development, modal theory of 328–343
  advents 328–329
developmental model 100, 470, 478
Dewey, J. 1, 2, 13, 18, 19, 28–30, 50, 56–73, 100–101, 105–113, 151–152, 160, 166–168, 395–396, 417, 464, 515
dialectic, dialectical 19, 82, 428–429, 527
diagnostic and statistical manual of mental disorders (III–R) 119
discipline structure 767–767
discourse
  collaborative 4, 182, 221, 397, 409, 475, 593–4, 731–761
  context effects 19, 197
  factual 20, 525
  frames 438–440, 457
  hypothetical 20, 525

interpretive 23, 409
  personal experience narrative 178, 195
  mathematical 731–762
diversity
  cultural 1, 3, 12, 69, 112, 209, 767
  in development 467– 478, 573, 728
  experience 56, 69, 326, 364, 461
  linguistic 202, 203, 209
  in literacy learning 202–222
  principle of 669–677
domain-specific cognition 30, 79, 154, 129, 158–159, 477, 646–655, 676
drama 15, 438, 569, 774
dyslexia 118–135, 629
dysrationalia 130–134

ecology 669
educational outcomes 204
educational practice 2–3, 13–15, 25, 37, 46–47, 84, 87, 120, 125, 151–156, 167, 202, 208, 330, 384, 392, 465–471, 491, 610, 622–623
educational reform 1, 12, 13, 47, 100–113, 498, 731, 755
effort 263–267, 314, 361, 395, 551, 716
emotion 29, 68, 100, 150–151, 257–271, 280, 294–297, 324–343, 381–382, 474–477, 525, 528, 596–599
emotional disorder 258, 119
empathy 296, 297, 773–778
empiricism 29, 75–94
enculturation 257–259, 264, 369, 372, 438, 561
Enlightenment 342, 527–530
environment
  acting on the 28, 83, 310, 312, 337, 627
  adaptation to 131
  adult reference to 383
  affordances 371
  assumptions 34
  deprivation 119, 212
  diversity 29, 72, 90–91, 119, 133, 212, 463, 468, 476, 655–678
  dysfunctional 136
  emotion and interpretation of 268–269, 518
  environmentalism 29
  and experience 62, 65, 78, 159, 766
  heredity and 5, 212, 471, 473
  intuitive theories about 631
  learning 395, 400–401, 410, 470, 506–510, 566, 726, 738
  learning from the 28, 62, 83, 278, 282, 373, 495, 639, 648–654
  literate 174–176, 195
  and pedagogy 49, 57, 76–77, 104, 478, 566
  relation of organism to 66–67, 154, 156, 158, 267, 418–419, 427, 472–474, 490, 499, 515, 608–609, 692
  school 195, 262, 270
  semiotic 237–238
epidemiology 121, 260
epistemology 19–21, 77, 79–94, 244, 419, 421, 501, 515–517, 529–532, 600, 677, 769–772, 775, 778
ethos 262–264
evidence, documentary and artifactual 22, 101, 131, 470, 503, 596, 599, 601, 739, 754–762, 771–779
exclusionary criteria 118–119, 133

expected learning 376, 610
experience
    adult perspective on 3, 324–343
    of learning 556–561
    as object of research 536–549
    nature of 56–73, 89, 136, 418
    shared 72, 188
expert, expertise 16–25, 31, 36, 39–44, 77, 214,
    259–260, 279–282, 289, 340, 346–352, 356,
    379, 401, 409, 456, 465–469, 476–478, 485,
    625–629, 636–640, 728, 765–766, 770
externalist theories 5, 27

facilitation 176, 374, 407
false belief
  in humans 20, 598–606
  in non-humans 12
falsification strategies 131
fear 268, 270, 284, 294, 525, 665, 669
female, male–female 238, 289–290, 345, 347, 354
feminist 777
folk theories
    biology 646–678
    pedagogy 9–25, 37, 148, 607–613
    physics 709–729
    psychology 9–25, 37, 148, 155, 345, 461, 485–
        491, 494–497, 507, 510, 537, 647, 699, 731
frame, objective 455
frame of reference, shared 79
framework, shared 25

genetic psychology 103
genre 3, 178, 191–198, 218, 231–233, 249, 250,
    434–457
    autobiography 341, 437, 442–457
    as cognitive models 438
    fiction 191–195, 437–457
    folktale 448, 454, 517–519
    spy story 441
    travelogue 441
genreless discourse 439–440
goal setting
    by children 91, 404, 406
    by teachers 393
goals
    adult-centered/child-centered 361
    and dysrationalia 130
    educational 16, 42, 47, 49, 57, 83, 177, 197, 205,
        268, 339–341, 405, 726, 734, 740
    and emotions 258, 267, 268
    expert modeling 339–340
    and intentions 9
    of the learner 9, 10, 14, 16, 40–41, 49, 186, 476,
        497, 501, 557, 738–740, 755
    pedagogical 149, 194, 257, 307, 405, 495, 640
    personal 361, 740, 754, 756
    shared teacher/learner 10, 257, 338, 384, 569
    societal 132, 421, 470
    of the teacher 9, 23, 188–190, 193–195, 384,
        403, 558, 570, 589, 609, 612, 614, 747
grade retention 210–211
guided discovery 79–83, 502
guided learning 377–378, 610
guilt 266

habitus 229, 370–373
habit training 101, 108–112

happiness 266, 268–270
Hall, G. S. 100–112, 152, 515
Hegel 79
Hegelianism 103, 105
heredity 8, 212, 473
heroic stage 4, 518, 524–526
high-order skills 213
historical film 770
historicity 768–771
historiography 768–776
history
    cultural 516–532
    pedagogy of 767, 777
    understanding of 514, 765–779

identity *see* self-concept
ignorance 3, 12, 58, 288
    acceptable 345–364
imitation 3, 12–13, 16, 24, 158, 304, 311, 320, 594,
    603–605, 614
    in monkeys 277–297
implicit knowledge 631
individual difference 31, 38, 94, 125, 131, 152, 202,
    211, 214, 217, 219, 260, 310, 312, 470, 472,
    475, 602
instructed learning 3, 370–372, 383
intelligence, general 476
intention 3–5, 9–10, 14, 20, 61–62, 67, 148, 153,
    158, 232, 268, 278, 282, 286, 293, 319–320,
    376, 382–383, 446, 535, 567, 641, 683, 692,
    754
intentional instruction 374, 378, 381–382
intentional learning 160, 161, 477
intentional state 5, 20, 25, 371–372, 693
intentional theories 160–163, 168
intentionality 10, 65, 79, 160, 164, 328, 497, 531,
    598
interest, research on 64–65, 269–270
interpretive cognition 3, 434–457
intersubjectivity 5, 18–25, 383
intervention
    programs 130, 135, 149, 155, 157–158,
        264–269, 556–558, 589, 611
    Reading Recovery 202–203, 208, 212, 222
IQ 118, 125–134, 136, 206, 212, 263, 602
ironic stage 4, 515, 529–531
irony 528, 530, 600

James, W. 72, 100, 102–105, 150–151, 526

knowledge
    accumulated 5, 16, 22, 47, 57, 85, 254, 514–517,
        522, 530, 700, 726
    biological 4, 50, 66, 151, 160, 162, 503, 516,
        629, 646–678, 683–705
    building 469–470, 477, 491, 500–511, 614
    construction 214, 502, 508, 632, 695, 698, 721,
        737, 760, 761
    historical 765–779
    objective *see* objective knowledge
    shared 5, 10, 15, 19, 20, 25, 188, 611, 684, 696
    intersubjective 594
    propositional 16, 17–18, 594, 610
    systematic 19
    tacit 11
    theoretical 621–641, 658

language of mind 594–598, 602–607
LD (Learning Disabled) 117–119, 129, 209, 468
learning
    collaborative 221, 373–374, 388, 397, 406–408,
        464, 469, 470, 478, 503, 602, 604–605, 614,
        737, 755
    deficit 37, 90, 120–136, 467–468
    didactic 75, 292
    disability 117–136, 176, 209, 469, 472
    to learn 571
    shared responsibility for 409
    theory 9, 153, 157, 161, 213, 509, 608, 731,
        741
    within-mode 123–125, 135
Learning Society 3, 461–478
literacy 3, 30, 64, 91, 128, 135, 173–198, 202–222,
    225–254, 336, 342, 409, 437, 440, 464, 471,
    501, 514, 522–530
living kinds 647–649, 656, 668, 670, 699
love 267, 325, 332, 337
low achievement 119, 204, 209–210

Marx, Marxist, Marxism 416, 422, 526
mathematical knowledge 14, 257, 329, 354, 410,
    505, 508, 731, 761
mathematics 3, 33, 70, 77, 91, 151, 269, 345, 354,
    516, 676, 765
    education 87–90, 163, 263, 267, 271, 353, 355,
        430, 439, 501–510, 559, 580, 731–762
maturationist view 103, 152, 154–158, 166,
    607–614
meaning
    in art 33, 57–62, 66–73
    communicating 175
    conceptions 14, 597
    construction 29, 207, 212, 213, 214, 425, 430,
        453, 530, 579, 768
    contextual 38, 767
    in discourse 438
    and emotion 266, 270
    historical 765–769
    of learning, 572
    -making 34, 35, 56, 65, 266, 434–436, 441, 768
    narrative 187–188, 213, 446, 454, 518, 770
    negotiated 87, 89, 213, 214, 358–360
    personal 494, 559
    social 279
    textual 206, 225–230, 234, 244, 245, 424,
        537–540, 544–549, 554, 584
    word 196, 205, 425, 595, 600, 675, 734
mediated action 417, 514
mental models 267–268, 434, 439–440, 453–454,
    497–499, 536, 622, 717–724
mental states 12, 20, 158, 308, 351–352, 453, 494,
    510, 594–600, 626, 628
metacognition, metacognitive 4, 5, 20, 160, 213,
    219, 220, 464, 476, 568–588, 600–604,
    611–613, 676, 702
metarepresentational 160–161, 166
mind
    of children 10, 149–150, 453–454
    children's assumptions about teachers' 11
    children's theories of 13, 160, 165, 383, 598–601
    connectionist 489–490
    cultural beliefs about 10, 13
    development of 324–343, 518–532
    habits of 3, 64, 461–478, 646–677

language and 71, 231, 418, 420–430, 453–454,
    518–532
language of 4, 593–598, 602–606
mind/body dualism 56, 58, 435, 683, 685, 694
modular 37
Other Minds 10, 18, 153, 158, 257, 294,
    351–352
psychological assumptions 2, 10, 35–48, 58–68,
    75, 78, 82–83, 103, 159, 160, 268, 307,
    324–343, 515–518, 635, 646–647
effects on teaching and learning 16–25, 167,
    205–208, 346, 384–385, 494–509, 537–561,
    641, 704, 726–729, 731–760, 765–778
teacher assumptions 2, 4, 11, 12–13, 607–614
theory of 12, 15, 158, 160, 166, 295, 308–310,
    316, 351, 486–490, 593–614, 629
understanding of 5, 10, 12, 14, 35–48, 58–68,
    104, 148, 150–153, 160–166, 205, 208, 271,
    461–478, 486–490, 731
World 2 493–494
mind/body dualism 56, 58, 688–693
misconceptions 31–32, 38, 40–44, 46, 49, 476,
    621–622, 641, 711–713, 718, 725–727, 778
model constructing 18, 65, 76, 394, 498
modes of thought 424, 436
mood 38, 258, 269–270, 455
moral judgment 496–497, 773–776, 778
multiple weakness 31, 207
musical skills 37
mythic stage 4, 515, 517, 518–522, 531

naive realism 13, 494
narrative, experience as 67, 176, 178–198, 718, 767
    see also genre
natural history 646, 657, 673
natural kinds 625, 637, 675
negation 292–293
negotiation *see* meaning, negotiated
novice (expert) 16, 77, 164, 346, 351, 356–358,
    409, 625–626, 636, 766
novice teachers 607

objective comparisons, explanations, observations 63,
    85, 286
objective knowledge 18, 21–25, 56, 65, 492–493,
    593–594
objective reality 655
objective understanding 611
objectives
    of curricula 76, 193, 608
    of inquiry 364
    learning 75, 501–502, 506
    of pedagogy 487, 491, 501
oral language 173–198, 229, 514
organization in writing, sequential to hierarchical 3,
    231–233, 244
other minds 10, 12, 18, 19, 257, 594, 731

participation theory 388–411
pedagogic disposition 11, 12, 291, 309
pedagogy
    anthropology of 315–317
    didactic 18–19, 102, 166, 295, 389, 593–594
    models of 2, 3, 16–25, 157, 388–411
    soft 150
phenomenography 536–537, 539, 568
phenomenology 4, 65, 71, 476, 537, 539, 715–719

physics 3, 4, 78, 86, 150, 158, 160–162, 503, 509, 557, 561, 629–631, 635, 639, 647, 674, 694, 709–729
Piaget, Jean 2, 19, 28–33, 50–51, 78–85, 101, 153, 219, 285, 325–326, 355, 400, 415, 431, 436, 486, 634, 636, 639, 684, 686, 696
Piagetian stages 324, 329, 514
pity 266
placement policies 208
potential 4, 29, 127–128, 134, 136, 162, 211, 237, 244, 245, 250, 334, 395, 534
    developmental 78
    inductive, inferential 654, 671
    intellectual 126
    neurobiological 35
predispositions 11, 159
    biological 36, 42
    cognitive 152, 159
    for individual interests 269
    for language 236
prejudice 69, 150, 264
preliteracy 240, 519, 622
prescribed sequence of instruction 212, 216
prescription 207
    for teaching 776
prescriptive curriculum 207
prescriptive model 213
prescriptive programs 204
prescriptive teaching 216, 355
prescriptive writing 197
prior understanding 9, 766, 778
problem solving 17, 20, 67, 76, 85, 90, 212, 214, 219–222, 353, 360, 402, 406, 503, 544, 580, 683, 717, 726, 739, 759, 760
procedural knowledge 16, 17, 603, 508, 701
Project Head Start 90, 157
progress, concept of 219, 773
progressive movement 2, 40, 47, 48
progressive traditions 28–51
progressivism 1, 2, 47, 51
    model 609
pseudowords 123–124
psychiatric disorder 260–261
punishment 261–263, 270, 293, 305, 405, 543, 545

Rationalism 77–78
rationality 130–134, 267, 343, 427, 529, 530
recapitulation theory 515
readiness 3, 11, 148–168, 211, 598
    theories of 5
reading
    ability 118, 121, 175, 602
    comprehension 133, 269, 437
    instruction 151, 174, 176, 178, 202–222, 558
    learning by 539–543
    maps 42, 44
    music 37
    performance 135
    purposes of 195, 522, 538, 544–546
    as sign use 226, 237–238, 247–248, 250–253
    skills 120, 602
    techniques (Dewey) 107
    understanding of 578–584
reading disabled 122, 135 *see also* learning disability
    discrepant vs. non-discrepant 120
Reading Recovery 202–222
reductionism, reductionist 204, 213, 418, 422, 429

reification of learning disabilities 117
representation
    domain-specific 648–649, 738
    of language 123
    mental 34–48, 153, 158, 160, 165–167, 214, 306–307, 383–384, 537, 599–605, 629, 633, 635
    systems of 623–625
    of writing 28, 225–254
response repertoire 204, 208, 212, 217, 267–268
romantic stage 4, 515, 522–525, 526–527, 531

safety 268, 270, 293
scaffolding 50, 81, 190, 346, 376–379, 382, 609
Sartre, J. P. 341
Saussure, F. de 236
schooling
    effectiveness of 84, 111, 197, 261–262, 360
    effects of 4, 80, 257, 259–260, 471, 476, 497
    home 202
    nature of 2–3, 149, 237, 354, 608
    and theoretical knowledge 622–642
    transition to 164–165, 226, 230, 566, 684
    and transmission of knowledge 80, 496–498, 504–510, 666, 701, 738–739, 777
    universal schooling 341
self-concept 64, 209, 337, 383
semiotic 34, 225–254, 420
sequence of acquisition 206
signs
    diagnostic 209
    in nature 574
    making of 225–254
    systems 419, 514, 517
situated cognition 490, 494, 495, 506, 639
social attribution 295, 296
social melioristic approach 100
social perspective 5
social semiotic approach 225, 226–252
social skills 119, 129, 132, 312, 491
society
    democratic 29, 30, 50
    industrialized 30
    influences of 32, 229, 419–431, 486
    knowledge-based 492, 496, 505
    "learning society" 3, 461–478
    obligations 51, 113 149–150
    technological 622, 684
    traditional 17, 378–382, 771
    understanding of 582–587
    values of 231, 252, 271, 335, 341, 355, 357
    Western 36–37, 264–265, 271, 357, 486
socio-cultural/historical theory 79–83, 86, 89, 91, 416, 428, 485, 609 *see also* cultural learning
spatial cognition
    biological origins 43
    development 36, 42–46
    misconceptions 128
special education 118, 202–212, 466–468, 471
standards 32
stream of consciousness 61, 539
streaming 353–354
subjectivity 60, 229, 236–240, 244, 252, 769
symbol systems 30, 33–41, 46, 48, 50, 51, 383

tabula rasa 18, 317
teacher-learner 5, 9, 12, 87–92, 95, 202–222, 233,

teacher-learner *contd.*
    246, 266, 269, 338, 346, 384, 527–532,
    565–589
  negotiation 358–361, 372, 374
  strategies of teachers 190, 193, 241, 640
  teacher models 4, 189
  teacher theories 11, 155
  teacher's theory of children's minds 607–615
  transmission of knowledge 486–507
  understandings, shared 614
teaching-learning 5, 10, 11, 14–25, 59–72, 148,
    165–167, 286–287, 335, 363, 388–411,
    464–467
  active teaching 289
  differentiated 203–222
  models of teaching 3, 40, 49, 89, 92, 101,
    102–113, 163, 174, 388–411, 429
  non-humans 277–297, 302
  of biology 684, 700, 703–704
  of history 773, 775, 778
  of mathematics 731–762
  of physics 725–729
  principles for teaching 559–561
theory, theories
  construction 627, 658
  constructive 77–79, 485, 502, 609
  internalist 5, 25
  of learning 8, 75–76, 396 *see also* learning theory
  of mind 12, 13, 15, 17, 20, 148, 158, 160,
    165–166, 295, 308, 316, 351, 486–487,
    494–502, 510, 593–615, 629
  naive 621–641, 684, 693–703, 709–729
    see also children's theories
  Piagetian 78, 80, 83, 90, 94, 153, 157, 162, 166,
    346, 355, 415, 431, 515, 520
  and practice 1, 3, 9, 112, 152, 167–168, 206, 376

  scientific 4, 86, 165, 429, 627–628, 666–668, 755
  "theory" 78
  Vygotskian 81, 233, 356, 486, 609
tracking 209–211
traits 2, 56, 559, 631, 651
transmission
  of habitus 373
  of information 303–304, 320–321, 394,
    422–425, 429
  of knowledge 40, 84, 388, 394, 463, 486
  theory of learning 390–393, 396
  view of education 30
  univocal 422–428
tyranny of the average 202, 205–206

understanding historical and developmental stages
  ironic 529–531
  mythic 518–522
  philosophic 525–529
  romantic 522–525

value(s)
  cultural 373, 379–382
  development 3, 33, 341
  and judgments (Dewey) 72–73
  judgments in IQ scores 128–134
  social 70, 345–347, 353–354, 360, 363, 421
  -sensing modes 332–337, 340, 342, 343
vitalism 674–675

Watson, John B. 75, 109
whole child 156
whole language 64, 174, 176, 178, 192, 196, 197
word recognition 123–125, 135
world, subjective and objective 537–538
World 3 494–498